Simplified Overview of an Integrated Audit

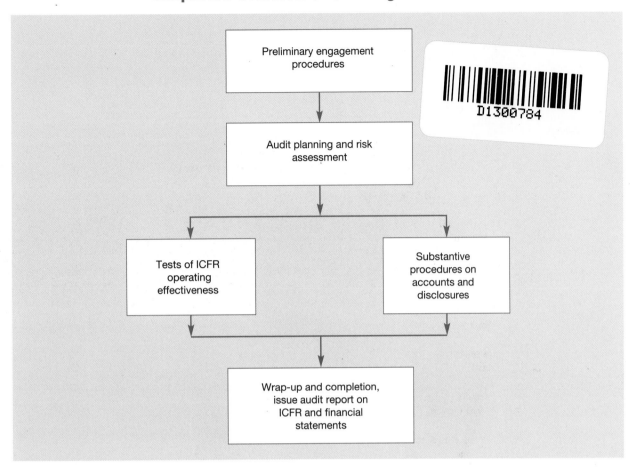

PCAOB Auditing Standards

Auditing Standard No. 1: References in Auditors' Reports to the Standards of the Public Company Accounting Oversight Board

Auditing Standard No. 2: 1An Audit of Internal Control Over Financial Reporting Performed in Conjunction With an Audit of Financial Statements (superseded)

Auditing Standard No. 3: Audit Documentation

Auditing Standard No. 4: Reporting on Whether a Previously Reported Material Weakness Continues to Exist

Auditing Standard No. 5: An Audit of Internal Control Over Financial Reporting That Is Integrated with An Audit of Financial Statements

Auditing Standard No. 6: Evaluating Consistency of Financial Statements

Auditing Standard No. 7: Engagement Quality Review

PCAOB Rules Related to the Auditing Standards

Rule 3100: Compliance with Auditing and Related Professional Practice Standards

Rule 3101: Certain Terms Used in Auditing and Related Professional Practice Standards

Rules 3501, 3502, 3520 to 3524, and 3526: Ethics and Independence Rules and Related Information

Rule 3525: Audit Committee Pre-Approval of Non-Audit Services Related to Internal Control Over Financial Reporting

AUDITING AND ASSURANCE SERVICES
Understanding the Integrated Audit

KAREN L. HOOKS

Florida Atlantic University

WILEY
John Wiley & Sons, Inc.

Associate Publisher	*Christopher DeJohn*
Project Editor	*Ed Brislin*
Senior Marketing Manager	*Julia Flohr*
Assistant Marketing Manager	*Diane Mars*
Marketing Assistant	*Laura Finley*
Senior Production Editor	*William A. Murray*
Editorial Assistant	*Kara Taylor*
Senior Designer	*Kevin Murphy*
Cover Design	*Wendy Lai*
Cover Image	*Scott Stulberg/©Corbis*
Cover Inset Images	*iStockphoto*
Senior Photo Editor	*Elle Wagner*
Interior Photos	*iStockphoto*

This book was set in 10/12 Minion by Preparé, Inc. and printed and bound by R.R. Donnelley.

This book is printed on acid free paper. ∞

ISBN: 978-0-471-72634-0

Printed in the United States of America

10 9 8 7 6 5 4 3 2

Brief Contents

To Steve

Contents

PART II
THE AUDIT ENVIRONMENT

PART IV
ADDITIONAL TRANSACTION CYCLES AND OTHER TOPICS   625

About the Author

Dr. Karen L. Hooks is a Professor of Accounting at Florida Atlantic University. Professor Hooks received her PhD from Georgia State University and her undergraduate accounting degree from the University of South Florida. A Florida CPA since 1976, Dr. Hooks worked as an auditor for Touche Ross & Co. prior to her start in academia. She was the first female professional hired in the Tampa office of Touche Ross & Co. She has been on the faculty at FAU since 1996 where she served as School of Accounting Director from 1998 to 2000. She began her academic career on the faculty of the University of South Florida. While at USF she served as Accounting PhD Program Coordinator and received the College of Business Research Award. Dr. Hooks was also a Visiting Professor at Arizona State University and the University of Miami. She held the position of Price Waterhouse and PricewaterhouseCoopers Practice Issues Research Professor at both USF and FAU. Dr. Hooks worked for the Canadian Institute of Chartered Accountants as a research manager for the Commission to Study the Public's Expectations of Audits. She is currently an Associate Editor for *Issues in Accounting Education*. She received the Florida Institute of CPAs Outstanding Educator Award, the American Women's Society of CPAs Outstanding Educator Award, and the American Women's Society of CPAs Literary Award. She is a member of the American Accounting Association where she has served as an officer on the Executive Committee and in positions with various sections. She is a member of the AICPA where her positions have included Chair of the Women and Family Issues Executive Committee and member of the Nominating Committee.

Dr. Hooks's research areas include accounting education, the public accounting workplace environment, human resources issues, ethics, sociology of professions, and standard setting and regulation. Dr. Hooks has published more than 40 articles in various journals including: *Accounting Organizations and Society, Auditing: A Journal of Practice and Theory, Behavioral Research in Accounting, The CPA Journal, Critical Perspectives on Accounting, Issues in Accounting Education, Accounting Horizons,* and the *Journal of Accountancy*.

Dr. Hooks has been teaching auditing on an almost continuous basis at the undergraduate and master's levels since 1979.

Preface

TO THE INSTRUCTOR

The audit process has changed significantly in recent years due to the influences of major frauds, the Sarbanes-Oxley Act (SOX), SEC responses to SOX, and standards and activities of the Public Company Accounting Oversight Board (PCAOB). Recognizing the influence of these dynamics on audit activities, this textbook relies on two important communication strategies. This text initiates its presentation with an **integrated audit of financial statements and internal control over financial reporting (ICFR)**. It uses a public company integrated audit as its primary teaching platform. This approach provides an effective means to *also* facilitate an understanding of a **non-public company financial statement audit**. Additionally, to accomplish the top down, risk-based approach used for both PCAOB integrated and AICPA financial statement audits, today's auditors need to understand their audit clients' businesses when planning and conducting audits. Consequently, information on various selected industries is used in this text to provide students with a real-world understanding of risks and audit activities as they are tailored for the needs of an audit engagement.

The breadth of information that auditing students are now expected to understand and retain is staggering. Auditing standards are promulgated by various standard setters including the PCAOB, AICPA, IAASB, U.S. Government Accountability Office, and other regulators. The various standards focus on different types of entities—publicly traded entities, privately owned entities, governments and not for profits. The International Standards on Auditing are available for use in an international setting even as the AICPA and IAASB move toward aligning their respective sets of auditing standards.

This overwhelming breadth of information virtually requires some means of streamlining the content for students to be able to sufficiently absorb it in an academic setting. Two conditions drive the efficiencies that can be attained by learning auditing using the PCAOB integrated audit of a publicly traded company as the primary platform. First, SOX requires that public companies be audited via a single engagement that produces two opinions, one on the financial statements and one on ICFR. Thus, the integration of planning, risk assessment, wrap up activities and reporting is mandatory in auditing practice, and thus mandatory knowledge for students. Second, in its recent standards the AICPA has clearly established that even if an auditor does not rely on ICFR in a financial statement audit, an understanding and assessment of ICFR is required to identify the major risks of an audit client's activities. Consequently, learning everything required in an integrated audit as the baseline, then identifying the specific activities and outputs not required when a company is not publicly traded is efficient. Put simply, there are situations in an audit of a nonpublic company, and less frequently in an audit of a public company which cause an auditor to forego testing the operating effectiveness of ICFR. Also, in the audit of a nonpublic company, the auditor does not issue an opinion on the effectiveness of ICFR. Using these simple stipulations, students can learn an integrated audit and easily transfer the knowledge to the financial statement audit of a nonpublic company. The reverse transfer of knowledge—from a nonpublic to a public company audit—is far less transparent, because of the integration required by SOX, the SEC, and the PCAOB in planning, risk assessment, wrap up and reporting. These *integrated* phases are not simply "add-ons" to a financial statement audit.

Understanding ICFR to assess an audit client's risks and controls is now required. However, ICFR is not "one-size-fits-all" across industries. With the exception of cost accounting for inventory production, almost all industries have some transactions representing all common business cycles or processes. Even though this is true, the importance of different business activities and the related controls varies widely. An example used in this text is the difference between the cash receipts in the form of currency in the retail and health care industries. Since the frequency of transactions involving currency is greater in many retail establishments, the physical and documentary control of currency is likely to be more important. This impacts both the company's ICFR and the audit. In contrast, billing is a function likely to be of greater importance in a hospital and is a greater concern for both management and the auditor. As with the example of currency, this text uses selected industries to highlight the relationships of business activities, transactions, risks and controls, particularly as these relationships impact material financial statement accounts. Using examples from real industries brings auditor judgment to life, even in the classroom.

FUNDAMENTALS OF THIS TEXTBOOK

Audits of Public and Non-Public Companies

This textbook uses the audit of a public company as its basic platform and consequently teaches an **integrated audit**. An integrated audit, using PCAOB standards is the most comprehensive type of audit engagement. If students know the biggest picture, they can easily adapt to what is *not* required when auditing only the **financial statements of a non-public company**. Teaching how to audit using a public company integrated audit as the starting point is the approach used **throughout the book**—not just in specific chapters.

The approach used in this textbook also provides the opportunity for professors whose students begin their **careers primarily in sectors other than public accounting**, to emphasize management responsibilities and activities that are driven by SOX, SEC certifications and the ICFR audit. When ICFR is discussed, it is presented in the context of company controls and tests of controls that are important to both management and the auditor. The distinction is made that both management and the external auditor will need to use tests of controls while only the external auditor performs and reports on substantive procedures. This also provides the opportunity for discussion of **internal auditors** as the individuals within a public company who likely have significant involvement with SOX-related activities. Given the "trickle down" effect of the SOX ICFR standards **to not-for-profits** and some privately-held companies, an understanding of an integrated audit is important throughout an expanding number of business sectors.

Industry Examples

An important feature of this textbook is the use of examples from various industries. Students understand audit risk and procedures more clearly when presented in the context of real, specific industries. Different companies and different industries have different risks. To help students get a "case-like" understanding of auditing, this textbook applies discussions of audit risk and procedures to real world industry facts. As early as Chapter 5, industries are discussed as the context in which the concept of risk must be considered. A different industry is also used in each of the chapters on business processes.

Chapter 5   Retail, Hospitality, Banking, and Other Industries
Chapter 5, Appendix A describes various industries, including business goals, important processes and risks. Industries covered include manufacturing, retailing, health care, banking, services, real estate development and construction, and hospitality.

Chapter 10   Health Care and Retailing Industries

This chapter, focusing on revenue and related processes and accounts, uses the health care and retailing industries as a teaching platform. These industries provide the opportunity to learn the audit of sales and billing, credit activities, receivables and cash collections, as well as sales for cash.

Chapter 12   Automotive Industry

This acquisitions and cash disbursements chapter highlights the automotive industry and is intended to display to students that what they *think* they know about an industry, because of what they have seen in everyday life, may not be comprehensive. The automotive industry works well as a platform for this chapter because it contains manufacturing, wholesale and retail distribution, and service components.

Chapter 13   Services Industries

Public accounting firms are discussed in this chapter on human resources, providing students with a look at the business side of public accounting while discussing the audit of human resources in service industries. Additionally, outside service providers and impacts on the audits of the service provider's clients are highlighted.

Chapter 14   Land Development and Home Building

This inventory chapter uses audits of the land development and home building industry as its platform. Using this industry provides the opportunity to communicate to students the importance of understanding different approaches to accounting for revenue, inventory, cost accounting and the related complex accounting standards to be able to audit effectively.

Chapter 15   Multiple Industries

This chapter addresses financing activities and uses examples from a variety of industries to teach the differences risk and capital structure have on the audit of these functions and accounts.

Developed After Sarbanes-Oxley and Cutting-Edge Coverage

All chapters of this textbook were developed and written after the passage of the Sarbanes-Oxley Act of 2002. The fundamental source materials for this textbook include PCAOB and AICPA auditing standards, SEC rules and guidance, and COSO publications. This textbook is current through and including:

- **PCAOB Auditing Standards No. 1-7**
- **AICPA Statements on Auditing Standards through SAS 117**
- **AICPA Statements on Standards for Accounting and Review Services through SSARS 19**

Updated content is continually posted to the *Auditing and Assurance Services* Web site, *www.wiley.com/college/hooks*.

Meaningful Content in Business Process Chapters

In addition to applying auditing concepts to various industries, the chapters on business processes convey in-depth audit knowledge related to the processes. As a result, there is substance included in these chapters that provides *a reason to include* as many of the cycle chapters as desired. If a course has limited time, it can be effective to rely on the summaries of different audit procedures provided in early chapters and through Chapter 9. Alternatively, with more time, a course can include the pages in the business process chapters that discuss the audit procedures in greater depth. As an example, the confirmation process is discussed in more summary form in early chapters, in greater depth in Chapter 10 relating to sales and collections processes, and is also presented more briefly in conjunction with the audit of accounts payable and cash disbursements in Chapter 12. The in-depth coverage of audit processes can be seen in the Table of Contents, but examples are as follows:

Chapter 10: external confirmations, bank confirmations, analysis of aged accounts receivable

Chapter 12: external confirmations, account analysis, search for unrecorded liabilities

Chapter 13: client's use of an outside service provider and auditor SAS 70 report use

Chapter 14: inventory observation, audit procedures for estimates, auditing valuation issues, auditing the accounting for variable interest entities

Chapter 15: auditing valuation, using the work of specialists, auditing other comprehensive income, auditing the consolidations process, audit issues for related parties

KEY FEATURES

Ethics

Ethical consideration is integral to the study of auditing. The importance of ethics is stressed with the placement of ethics topics in Chapter 3, *Auditors' Role in Society*, early in the textbook. Even with its early placement to emphasize the importance of ethics, Chapter 3 is structured so that it can be included at any point desired within a course curriculum. Ethical discussions are integrated throughout the textbook and ethics items are integrated in the end-of-chapter material throughout the chapters. They are highlighted with an ethics icon in the margin.

Auditing in Action

Items of interest, including applications of auditing concepts, are included as feature boxes throughout the chapters and chapter appendices. Many Auditing in Action features illustrate application of an auditing concept in a real world or fictional scenario. Descriptions of current events, references to applicable articles, and current standards are included. Coupled with the industry focus, the Auditing in Action features boost student comprehension.

Audit Plan and Procedure Linkages

As audit procedures are presented in the text, they are shown in the context of management's assertions, the purpose of controls, company controls, tests of controls, and when applicable, related substantive audit procedures. In the real world, and based on the approach called for by PCAOB AS 5, auditors identify important accounts and processes, examine risks and controls for the accounts and processes, and perform procedures to test controls and account balances. Whenever possible, these activities are integrated to increase audit efficiency. The presentations highlight that all activities up through tests of controls are performed both by management as it attests to ICFR effectiveness and the auditor while forming an opinion on ICFR. This information is of value to accountants regardless of their ultimate career path.

EXHIBIT 12-3

Examples of Tests of
Controls for Purchase
Transactions

If a company control (CC) is significant, both management and the auditor perform tests of controls (TofC). Management uses tests of controls to support its management report. The auditor uses tests of controls for the audit of ICFR and to confirm the planned reliance on controls in the financial statement audit. Related management assertions are displayed under the purpose of the controls. For ease of explanation, authorization and cutoff are used in addition to the five PCAOB management assertions.

Purpose of Controls	Company Control and Tests of Controls
To ensure that purchases and expenditures are consistent with company policies **(authorization)**	
	CC: *Purchase and expenditure transactions are authorized before they are executed, as evidenced by properly created and approved supporting documents*
	TofC: Examine a sample of document packages for inclusion of supporting documents appropriate for the specific transaction such as approved purchase requisitions and purchase orders
To ensure that purchase and expenditure transactions are approved by someone with appropriate authority before they are executed	

Review Questions

Brief but comprehensive questions are integrated at the end of topic discussions throughout all chapters of the textbook. Students can utilize these questions to stop and assess whether they have a complete understanding of the topic before they move further. Classroom use indicates that these are extremely useful to students in establishing their initial understanding and as comprehensive study tools.

REVIEW QUESTIONS

D.1 Why is management and Board of Directors integrity important to an audit firm?

D.2 Why might an auditor be concerned if all of the company's management authority is centered in one or two individuals?

D.3 What is the auditor's concern regarding a company that lacks a competent management team?

D.4 What is financial statement restatement? Why does the auditor investigate whether a company has restated its financial statements when addressing client acceptance?

D.5 In what way would management misrepresenting a company's performance in public speeches be a problem to an auditor?

International Coverage

International issues are discussed **throughout the textbook** when applicable. To help students grapple with the numerous auditing standards the focus is on the AICPA SAS and PCAOB AS, with discussion of the ongoing alignment of AICPA SAS and IAASB ISA. As reflected in current auditors' report content, the discussion acknowledges potential applicability of both international and US GAAP standards of reporting.

Risks of International Trade

Political, religious and economic instability
Local labor market conditions
Foreign tariffs and other trade barriers
Foreign government regulations
Effects of income and withholding taxes
Governmental expropriation
Differences in business practices

Toyota's 3/31/06 fiscal year-end information provides an example of the impact of operating in global markets in the following excerpt from a note to the financial statements:

> In September 2000, The European Union approved a directive that requires member states to promulgate regulation…: (i) manufacturers shall bear all or a significant part of the costs for taking back end-of-life vehicles put on the market after July 1, 2002 and dismantling and recycling those vehicles. … In addition, under this directive member states must take measures to ensure that car manufacturers … establish adequate used vehicle collection and treatment facilities and to ensure that hazardous materials and recyclable parts are removed from vehicles prior to shredding. This directive impacts Toyota's vehicles sold in the European Union and Toyota expects to introduce vehicles that are in compliance with … measures taken … pursuant to the directive.

Comprehensive End-of-Chapter Material

Much of the end-of-chapter material was developed by the textbook author and classroom tested over the past few years. To allow coverage of PCAOB materials as well as AICPA knowledge, many of the multiple-choice questions and problems were adapted from **professional examinations (AICPA, CIA, etc.)** End-of-chapter items include multiple-choice questions, discussion questions, problems, and activity assignments which direct students to research real-world content or apply relevant content on Web sites such as *www.pcaob.com*, *www.COSO.org*, or *www.sec.gov*.

Professional Simulations

Professional simulations adapted from the Wiley CPA Exam review are available on the textbook Web site at *www.wiley.com/college/hooks*. The simulations address multiple auditing topics, improve concept mastery, and prepare students for exams.

ACL Problems

Problems using ACL software are on the textbook Web site at *www.wiley.com/college/hooks*. The ACL problems address topics in select chapters of the textbook.

ORGANIZATION

Structured for Various Courses

Organization of the textbook is in four parts.

Part I: Introduction
These two chapters introduce students to the topic of auditing and provide an overview to the phases of an audit engagement. Chapter 2 provides students with a first introduction to numerous fundamental concepts.

Part II: The Audit Environment
Chapters 3 and 4 are paired to communicate to students the value auditors contribute to society and the personal, organizational, and cultural responsibilities that accompany auditors' positions. Chapter 3 discusses ethical responsibilities and professional standards. Chapter 4 discusses legal impacts on auditing and the auditing profession.

Part III: Executing an Integrated Audit
Chapters 5 through 11 move chronologically through the activities of an integrated audit. The chapters begin with client acceptance and continuance in Chapter 5 and proceed to risk assessment, introducing the top down approach to an integrated audit in Chapter 6. Chapter 7 describes the process of understanding a client's system in order to assess design effectiveness of ICFR and complete the integrated audit plan. Chapter 8 introduces concepts of sampling and presents tests of controls that contribute to the ICFR audit opinion and confirm the reliance on controls for the financial statement substantive tests. Chapter 9 covers substantive procedures for the financial statement audit including tests of details of balances and analytical procedures. Chapter 10 provides a review of concepts presented earlier and applies them to the revenue-related processes and accounts. Chapter 11 addresses both the ICFR and financial statement opinions through wrap-up procedures and presents audit reports.

Part IV: Additional Transaction Cycles and Other Topics
This module presents material that often is often covered only selectively in a one semester audit course. Chapters 12 through 15 address auditing additional business processes of acquisition and disbursement, human resources, inventory, and investments, debt and capital. Chapter 16 briefly describes a variety of other services provided by those who also perform independent audits.

The book segments are intended to appeal to a variety of course structures. Throughout, information that is typically covered in other accounting classes, for example systems and financial reporting, is often briefly reviewed to provide students with a baseline for understanding the immediate auditing topic.

Some recommended reading structures include the following:

- For a **one-semester** course, the choice may be to include Chapters 1 through 11, with only selected materials out of 12 through 15.
- A **two-semester** course can cover Chapters 1-16, including all chapter appendices and Chapter 16, *Topics Beyond the Integrated Audit.*
- If many students in a class are likely to go into **accounting or management positions rather than entering auditing**, the approach may be to focus less on Chapters 9 and 11 which address financial statement audit procedures and the report of the integrated audit, and more on Chapter 10 and 12 through 15 addressing audits of business processes.

Appendices for Flexibilty

Appendices are used throughout the book to provide an easy way for instructors to include or omit in-depth coverage of specific topics as time and preferences allow. For example, students may have covered IT controls extensively in another course, and require at most a quick review. In contrast, if students have not covered IT controls, the instructor will likely want to spend more time with Chapter 7 Appendix A on IT general controls and Chapter 8 Appendix A, on IT application controls. An overview of industry descriptions is provided in an appendix to Chapter 5. This appendix will be particularly helpful for students with limited real world business experience and for courses that do not include Chapters 12 through 15. In addition to its value for potential auditors, Chapter 6, Appendix A, *Using the Work of Others* may be of particular importance when students expect to go into a corporate environment and need to understand potential management tools available for issuing reports on ICFR effectiveness. Information on performing a SAS 70 engagement is included in Chapter 13, Appendix A. Chapter 13 on human resources includes the use of a SAS 70 report so the adjacent presentation of performing a SAS 70 engagement permits the professor to easily link the two topics if desired. The statistical analysis of internal control and account balance audit samples is included in appendices, based on awareness that while professors may choose to omit coverage in class, it is a topic covered in the CPA exam. Chapter 7, Appendix B on the COSO *Enterprise Risk Management* framework, and Appendix C on ICFR in smaller public companies are separate modules that may fit effectively into courses depending on student and professor interests.

Supplements

Solutions Manual
Written by the textbook author or adapted from professional examinations, the solutions manual contains solutions to all of the end-of-chapter material, including ACL exercises and professional simulations. The classroom-tested solutions were heavily reviewed to ensure accuracy.

PowerPoint
Drafted by the textbook author, the classroom-tested PowerPoint slides are designed to enhance lectures and discussions. Available for each chapter of the textbook, the comprehensive slides are also a useful tool for studying and note taking.

Instructor's Manual
The instructor manual includes detailed chapter reviews and sample syllabi with recommended homework assignments that will assist in organizing the course and preparing lectures.

Test Bank
The comprehensive test bank is comprised of all question types needed to assess student mastery of the material covered. Many of the classroom-tested questions were adapted from questions written by the textbook author or from professional examinations.

Computerized Test Bank
The user-friendly computerized test bank allows you to generate exams from all of the questions in the test bank. The software enables you to update existing problem statements, scramble the order of multiple-choice answers within a question, and more.

Textbook Web Site
All instructor components are available on the textbook Web site. There, students and instructors will also find a PowerPoint presentation detailing the key differences between PCAOB-audit and AICPA-based audits, ACL exercises, professional simulations, web quizzing, and other helpful resources.

Acknowledgments

I gratefully acknowledge and thank Professor Michelle Bertolini, University of Hartford, for her co-authorship of Chapter 4, Legal Environment Affecting Audits, and Professor Randall Rentfro, Nova Southeastern University, for his co-authorship of Chapter 16, Topics Beyond the Integrated Audit.

I also want to thank Professor Denise Dickins, East Carolina University, for her early work on the industry descriptions that eventually became Chapter 5, Appendix A.

I greatly appreciate the constructive ideas and feedback all instructors have given me while this textbook was developed. I especially would like to thank the following instructors who provided helpful comments: Jack Armitage, University of Nebraska-Omaha; LuAnn Bean, Florida Institute of Technology; Jane Baird, Minnesota State University-Mankato; Jeffrey R. Cohen, Boston College; John Coulter, Western New England College; Denise Dickens, East Carolina University; Bill Dilla, Iowa State University; Todd DeZoort, University of Alabama; Kathryn Epps, Kennesaw State University; Steve Fabian, Hudson County Community College; Chris Fenn, Georgia State University; Patricia Fedje, Minot State University; Thomas Fetzner, Cazenovia College; Diana Franz, University of Toledo; Mark Gleason, Metropolitan State University; Donald Kent, State University of New York-Brockport; Venkat Iyer, University of North Carolina-Greensboro; Claire Latham, Washington State University; Roger Martin, University of Virginia; Heidi H. Meier, Cleveland State University; Barbara Muller, Arizona State University; Srinivasan Ragothaman, University of South Dakota; Marianne Rexer, Wilkes University; Angela Sandberg, Jacksonville State University; Pamela Roush, University of Central Florida; Rex Schildhouse, San Diego Community College; Lydia Schleifer, Clemson University; Jay R. Semmel, Florida Atlantic University; James Specht, Concordia College; Abe Qastin, Lakeland College; John Trussel, Pennsylvania State University-Harrisburg; Andrea Weickgenannt, Xavier University; T. Sterling Wetzel, Oklahoma State University; Jana Wilhelm, Kentucky State University.

I would also like to thank the following instructors who helped ensure the accuracy of all textbook and solutions manual content as well as develop some of the end-of-chapter material, Auditing in Action boxes, and supplements: LuAnn Bean, Florida Institute of Technology; Mark Gleason, Metropolitan State University; Patricia Fedje, Minot State University; Barbara Muller, Arizona State University; Marianne Rexer, Wilkes University; Rex Schildhouse, San Diego Community College; Andrea Weickgenannt, Xavier University.

The professional support and commitment provided by Wiley's editorial, marketing, and production team were invaluable. I extend my sincere thanks to Chris DeJohn, Associate Publisher; Julia Flohr, Senior Marketing Manager; Bill Murray, Senior Production Editor; Ed Brislin, Project Editor; Kara Taylor, Editorial Assistant; Laura Finley, Marketing Assistant, and many others. My thanks to Jay O'Callaghan of Wiley for his help and encouragement at the beginning of this project.

I am grateful to my students who have used this textbook and inspired me throughout the development process. Particular thanks go to Grant Nelson, Jeremy Hurwitch, and Johnny Carson. I am encouraged when I hear my students who have graduated thank me for my textbook. They tell me that the textbook made it easy to understand their purpose and tasks after they started working and helped them successfully pass the most recent CPA exams.

Finally, my greatest thanks go to my husband, daughters, and close friends who encouraged me to accept the challenge of writing this book and supported me through the process. None of us had any idea what was to come. I can't imagine anyone writing an auditing textbook without a spouse who is an audit partner.

INTRODUCTION

CHAPTER 1

An Introduction to Auditing

LEARNING OBJECTIVES FOR THIS CHAPTER

1. Recognize an integrated audit report and a financial statement audit report.

2. Describe the overall purposes and value of an audit, and identify the differences among an integrated audit, an audit of internal control over financial reporting, and a financial statement audit.

3. Define and contrast the responsibilities and expectations of different parties affected by an audit.

4. Learn the roles and interaction of the governing and standard-setting bodies and other entities that affect auditing.

5. Understand the link between independent auditors and accountants who provide other professional services.

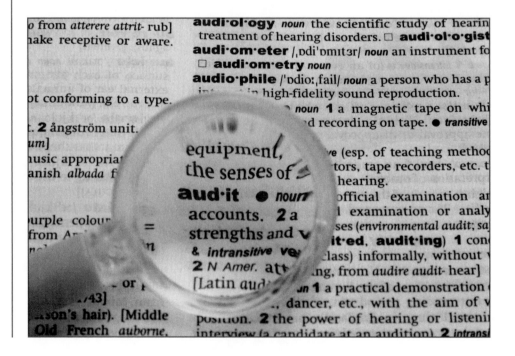

Chapter 1 Resources

American Accounting Association, *A Statement of Basic Auditing Concepts*

AU 110, AICPA, PCAOB, *Responsibilities and Functions of the Independent Auditor*

AU 326, AICPA, *Audit Evidence*

AU 326, PCAOB, *Evidential Matter*

AU 508, AICPA, PCOAB, *Reports on Audited Financial Statements*

Committee of Sponsoring Organizations of the Treadway Commission *Internal Control Framework*

FASB Concepts Statement No. 6, *Elements of Financial Statements*

PCAOB AS 5, *An Audit of Internal Control Over Financial Reporting That Is Integrated with an Audit of Financial Statements*

PCAOB AS 7, *Engagement Quality Review*

Securities Act of 1933

Securities Exchange Act of 1934

Sarbanes-Oxley Act of 2002

SEC 33–7919 *Revision of the Commission's Auditor Independence Requirements*

INTRODUCTION

An audit has a simple purpose: to provide assurance that financial statements are reliable. When an auditor issues a report that accompanies the financial statements, financial statement users have greater confidence in their decisions to rely on the financial information. This book helps you learn about the services provided by auditors, how auditors perform those services, and the reports they issue.

FINANCIAL STATEMENTS, INTERNAL CONTROL, AND INTEGRATED AUDITS [LO 1]

The term **audit** is sometimes used in everyday language to mean that someone checks that a representation is correct. For example, perhaps your university requires a "degree" or "graduation" audit. When applying to graduate from college, you state that you have fulfilled all degree requirements. Your university then checks your academic records to be sure that you have actually completed all of the requirements. In the accounting world, the term *audit* has a more specific meaning.

Historically, the term *audit* has been used in an accounting context to refer to a **financial statement audit**. A financial statement audit is a process through which an *auditor* examines supporting information and evaluates whether the financial statements represent the underlying economic events that the company has experienced. For companies that are traded on U.S. stock exchanges, the word "audit" currently refers to an **integrated audit**.

AUDITING IN ACTION

What Is an Audit?

You check your university's School of Accounting Web page regularly for announcements. Sometimes a new class is being offered or the time a class is scheduled is changed. Last week an "international" accounting class was announced for next summer, including travel to South America. That got your interest! But today's announcement includes a job posting. A public accounting firm is signing up students for job interviews. There are positions in both audit and tax. You have an idea of what a tax job involves, but you aren't so sure about an audit job. What is an audit, anyway? And, what does an auditor do? Eventually, you are going to be looking for a job, and you know that auditing is one of the fields your professors often mention.

EXHIBIT 1-1

An Integrated Audit

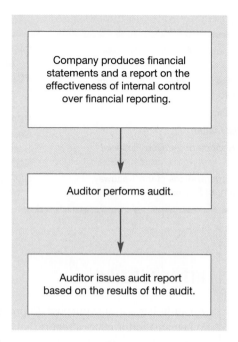

An integrated audit includes both an audit of the financial statements and an **audit of internal control over financial reporting (ICFR)**. This second component, the audit of ICFR, examines whether the company's internal controls are effective and, as a result, whether the controls enable the company to produce fair and reliable financial statements. Exhibit 1-1 is an overview diagram of an integrated audit.

AUDITING IN ACTION

Description of an Integrated Audit

An integrated audit is a process. The tangible result of this process is an audit report, which is the written document produced by the auditor stating an audit opinion about internal control over financial reporting (ICFR) and the financial statements. If, at the completion of the audit, the auditor concludes that ICFR is effective and the financial statements are a fair representation of the company's economic experiences and situation, the audit report is an unqualified or "clean" report.

The end product of an integrated audit is actually the auditor's conclusions about whether or not the ICFR is effective and the financial statements are fair. Being able to come to this conclusion is the ultimate purpose of all the planning and procedures that an auditor performs. However, the tangible result that other people can see is the report issued by the auditor. This **audit report** communicates to users of financial statements that an audit has been performed, and the auditor's opinion. The audit report is **unqualified** or **clean** if ICFR is effective and the financial statements are a fair representation of the company's economic experiences and situation. Audit reports are addressed in Chapter 11. Although they will likely seem foreign to you at this stage of your studies, you should read the audit report examples presented in this chapter.

This book centers on the process of performing an integrated audit and the outcomes of that process. The chapters address the purpose of an audit, the role that audits and auditors play in society, and the audit process. The audit process progresses from client acceptance and continuance (Chapter 5), through planning (Chapter 6), internal control over financial reporting (Chapters 7 and 8), **audit procedures** applied to financial statement audits (Chapter 9), and the wrap-up of an audit and reporting process (Chapter 11). Chapters 10 and 12 through 15 address how an audit is conducted for various cycles of a company's activities and for different types of companies. Chapter 16 introduces other services, beyond audits, offered by public accounting firms.

This text uses the terms *company* or *business* interchangeably to refer to a variety of entities, including for-profit and not-for-profit organizations. If a company has to register with the **Securities and Exchange Commission (SEC)** and undergo an integrated audit, it is referred to as a public company. Otherwise it is called a nonpublic company. Be aware that some companies that must register with the SEC are not traded on an active market.

Studying this book prepares you with a conceptual understanding of auditing. However, no amount of classroom training can teach you to perform an audit. An audit is a collab-

AUDITING IN ACTION

An Unqualified Audit Report for a Public Company

Report of Independent Registered Public Accounting Firm

To the Board of Directors and Shareholders
Mimimi Corporation

We have audited the accompanying consolidated balance sheets of Mimimi Corporation and its subsidiaries as of May 31, 2010 and 2009, and the related consolidated statements of income, stockholders' equity and comprehensive income, and cash flows for each of the years in the three-year period ended May 31, 2010. We also have audited Mimimi Corporation's internal control over financial reporting as of May 31, 2010 based on criteria established in *Internal Control—Integrated Framework* issued by the Committee of Sponsoring Organizations of the Treadway Commission (COSO). Mimimi Corporation's management is responsible for these consolidated financial statements, for maintaining effective internal control over financial reporting, and for its assessment of the effectiveness of internal control over financial reporting, included in the accompanying "Management's Annual Report on Internal Control Over Financial Reporting." Our responsibility is to express an opinion on these financial statements and an opinion on the company's internal control over financial reporting based on our audits.

We conducted our audits in accordance with the standards of the Public Company Accounting Oversight Board (United States). Those standards require that we plan and perform the audits to obtain reasonable assurance about whether the financial statements are free of material misstatement and whether effective internal control over financial reporting was maintained in all material respects. Our audits of the financial statements included examining, on a test basis, evidence supporting the amounts and disclosures in the financial statements, assessing the accounting principles used and significant estimates made by management, and evaluating the overall financial statement presentation. Our audit of internal control over financial reporting included obtaining an understanding of internal control over financial reporting, assessing the risk that a material weakness exists, and testing and evaluating the design and operating effectiveness of internal control based on the assessed risk. Our audits also included performing such other procedures as we considered necessary in the circumstances. We believe that our audits provide a reasonable basis for our opinions.

A company's internal control over financial reporting is a process designed to provide reasonable assurance regarding the reliability of financial reporting and the preparation of financial statements for external purposes in accordance with generally accepted accounting principles. A company's internal control over financial reporting includes those policies and procedures that (1) pertain to the maintenance of records that, in reasonable detail, accurately and fairly reflect the transactions and dispositions of the assets of the company; (2) provide reasonable assurance that transactions are recorded as necessary to permit preparation of financial statements in accordance with generally accepted accounting principles, and that receipts

(continued)

and expenditures of the company are being made only in accordance with authorizations of management and directors of the company; and (3) provide reasonable assurance regarding prevention or timely detection of unauthorized acquisition, use, or disposition of the company's assets that could have a material effect on the financial statements.

Because of its inherent limitations, internal control over financial reporting may not prevent or detect misstatements. Also, projections of any evaluation of effectiveness to future periods are subject to the risk that controls may become inadequate because of changes in conditions, or that the degree of compliance with the policies or procedures may deteriorate.

In our opinion, the consolidated financial statements referred to above present fairly, in all material respects, the financial position of Mimimi Corporation and its subsidiaries as of May 31, 2010 and 2009, and the results of their operations and their cash flows for each of the years in the three-year period ended May 31, 2010 in conformity with accounting principles generally accepted in the United States of America. Also in our opinion, the Company maintained, in all material respects, effective internal control over financial reporting as of May 31, 2010, based on criteria established in *Internal control—Integrated Framework* issued by the Committee of Sponsoring Organizations of the Treadway Commission (COSO).

Dikkens and McLand, LLP
Watercolor, Florida
July 27, 2010

(*Source*: Adapted from AS 5.87.[1])

AUDITING IN ACTION

An Unqualified Financial Statement Audit Report for a Nonpublic Company

Independent Auditor's Report

We have audited the accompanying balance sheets of Mimimi Corporation as of May 31, 2010 and 2009, and the related statements of income, retained earnings, and cash flows for the years then ended. These financial statements are the responsibility of the Company's management. Our responsibility is to express an opinion on these financial statements based on our audits.

We conducted our audits in accordance with auditing standards generally accepted in the United States of America. Those standards require that we plan and perform the audit to obtain reasonable assurance about whether the financial statements are free of material misstatement. An audit includes examining, on a test basis, evidence supporting the amounts and disclosures in the financial statements. An audit also includes assessing the accounting principles used and significant estimates made by management, as well as evaluating the overall financial statement presentation. We believe that our audits provide a reasonable basis for our opinion.

In our opinion, the financial statements referred to above present fairly, in all material respects, the financial position of Mimimi Corporation as of May 31, 2010 and 2009, and the results of its operations and its cash flows for the years then ended in conformity with accounting principles generally accepted in the United States of America.

Dikkens and McLand, LLP
July 27, 2010

(*Source*: Adapted from AICPA AU 508.08.[2])

---

[1] AS is the reference for Auditing Standards of the Public Company Accounting Oversight Board (PCAOB).
[2] AU is the reference for auditing standards that have been codified by the American Institute of Certified Public Accountants. AU is also used by the PCAOB to reference its Interim Auditing Standards that were adopted at its inception. When the two standards setters use different reference numbers, or only one set of standards is applicable to the text material, this is indicated by inclusion of PCAOB or AICPA before the abbreviation AU.

orative process performed by a team of professionals with different levels of knowledge and experience. Studying auditing in an academic environment prepares you to understand and perform tasks assigned to you as a member of an audit engagement team. The work setting is where you truly learn auditing.

AUDITING IN ACTION

The Audit Engagement Team

Steve is an audit partner with a Big Four firm. After two months of work, proposing and negotiating with a potential audit client, he learns his firm has been selected as the new auditor of a major restaurant chain. In anticipation of this assignment, Steve has been planning who should be on the **audit engagement team**. Although he is the engagement partner with primary responsibility for the complete engagement, a partner with expertise in tax and another partner with information technology (IT) expertise will also work on the audit. In addition, one other partner will conduct the **engagement quality review (EQR)** of the entire audit. Several "managers" and "seniors" with restaurant experience will be assigned to work on the audit. Steve meets with the managers and seniors as he plans the rest of the staffing because he knows that half of the "associates" assigned to the engagement are likely to be new hires and that this will be their first or second audit engagement. He stresses to the seniors—who are the immediate supervisors of the associates—how important it will be to actively supervise and review the work of the inexperienced associates since they will need significant guidance on how to perform their assigned tasks.

REVIEW QUESTIONS

A1. What is an audit? A financial statement audit? An audit of internal control over financial reporting (ICFR)? An integrated audit?

A2. What is the purpose of an audit?

A3. What types of companies must have an integrated audit?

A4. What is a clean or an unqualified audit opinion?

DEFINITION OF AN AUDIT [LO 2]

Auditing is a distinct area of study. Knowledge of accounting is fundamental to auditing because accounting information is the *target* of audit activities. However, auditing processes are not an intuitive extension of accounting knowledge. Studying auditing teaches you how to perform the processes through which you check the quality of a company's ICFR and financial reporting. But even if you learn the auditing processes, you must know accounting and what constitutes good ICFR to effectively apply your auditing knowledge. A formal definition of auditing, published by the American Accounting Association's Committee on Basic Auditing Concepts is shown in Exhibit 1-2.

EXHIBIT 1-2

A Definition of Auditing

Auditing is a *systematic process* of *objectively* obtaining and evaluating *evidence* regarding **assertions** about *economic actions and events* to ascertain the degree of correspondence between those assertions and *established criteria* and *communicating* the results to interested users[3] (emphasis added).

---

[3] American Accounting Association, Committee on Basic Auditing Concepts, *A Statement of Basic Auditing Concepts* (Sarasota, FL: American Accounting Association, 1973).

Although the audit process has evolved since this definition was first crafted, the fundamental purpose and activities remain consistent. The definition states that auditing is a *systematic process*. This means that an audit has a plan of action and specific steps to achieve an outcome. As we progress through the discussion of auditing, you will likely be surprised at the amount of planning that occurs before other auditing procedures begin. Each audit is designed based on information about the client's industry, business activities, structure, and organization. Based on that information, the audit is designed to do all that the auditor believes is necessary to evaluate the company's ICFR and financial statements. The audit plan is followed carefully and, as the definition states, systematically. After the steps of the plan are completed, the auditor forms conclusions about the effectiveness of the company's ICFR and the fairness of the financial statements. The auditor then issues an audit report based on those conclusions.

Referring again to the definition of auditing in Exhibit 1-2, we see that the audit process involves obtaining and evaluating **evidence** regarding management's financial statement assertions about *economic actions and events*. The Financial Accounting Standards Board (FASB) *Concepts Statement 6, Elements of Financial Statements* describes economic events and actions as those occurrences that affect a company's assets, liabilities, and equity. Based on the FASB's definitions, assets are the result of economic events that increase the current or future value of the company. Liabilities are the results of economic events or actions that require a company to use its assets in the future. When management drafts the company's financial statements, it is "asserting" that various economic events took place affecting the company and that the financial statements are a communication of those economic events and results. In other words, management's assertions about economic events and actions that affected the company are communicated through the financial statements (AS 5.28).

The audit process focuses on *objectively* obtaining and evaluating *evidence* about management's assertions. Auditors must be *objective* as they perform audit processes. This means that they may not be biased either favorably or unfavorably toward the company and management's assertions. Auditors select evidence that relates to management's assertions. Evidence is discussed extensively throughout this text, but for now you should understand that the documents and records that a company uses in its day-to-day business activities provide audit evidence (AU 326). A company's underlying financial records such as the general ledger and various journals constitute evidence. Documents in either electronic or paper form, such as checks, invoices, and contracts are audit evidence. The auditors collect some forms of evidence specifically for purposes of the audit. Other evidence is not even in document form. Evidence can be what the auditor observes, such as the procedures clients follow as they execute business transactions. Evidence can also be what the auditor hears in conversations with client personnel and others.

Once the evidence is collected, the auditor's task is to evaluate whether the evidence and management's assertions correspond, based on *established criteria*. For financial statements, the established criteria are the accounting standards followed. In the last paragraph of the audit reports shown earlier, they are referred to as accounting principles generally accepted in the United States of America. In the future the criteria may be international accounting standards. Auditors must conclude whether the evidence supports the statements that management has made in the financial statements about the economic actions and events. The auditor assesses whether they actually occurred as presented. Auditors determine whether the financial statements present the economic actions and events in accordance with the accounting standards used. If management has presented the actual economic events and situation according to the accounting standards, then there is a high degree of correspondence between the underlying evidence and the resulting financial statements. The auditor's job is to determine whether this high degree of correspondence exists.

In audits of ICFR, auditors assess whether the evidence supports management's assertion about the effectiveness of ICFR. To do this, the auditor again uses established criteria, but this time uses the criteria as a standard or benchmark against which ICFR is compared. One example of established internal control standards is the set provided in the **Committee**

of Sponsoring Organizations of the Treadway Commission (**COSO**) **Internal Control (IC) Framework**. You may have learned about COSO in previous accounting classes. COSO has produced a number of important publications that can be found on its Web site: *www.coso.org.* Auditors evaluate whether a high degree of correspondence exists between the evidence about ICFR and what an effective system of ICFR *should* be according to the COSO IC Framework criteria. If the evidence indicates effective controls, then there is a high degree of correspondence between the evidence and a management assertion that ICFR is effective.

Auditors consider internal controls when they audit nonpublic companies. However, their activities have a different purpose. When auditing a nonpublic company, auditors consider internal control to identify areas of concern or risk. Also, if the company's internal controls are strong, they can affect the auditor's plan for the financial statement audit. When an auditor gathers evidence about a company's internal control system and determines that it is effective and functions well, that information is a part of the auditor's evidence for the financial statement audit.

Although accounting and auditing are different, in order to be a good auditor you must first be a good accountant. Auditors must determine whether ICFR is effective and whether economic actions and events are presented in the financial statements according to the accounting standards. To do this, auditors must understand accounting standards and the controls required to produce proper accounting information. Auditors determine what information must be captured about an economic event and how it should be presented in the financial statements. Much of this book and your auditing course will focus on how to audit. Keep in mind that even if you know the steps to collect, document, and evaluate audit evidence, you must be a good accountant to be a good auditor. You must be able to determine what is important about the business activities and transactions and the appropriate accounting for the underlying events. Otherwise, you will not be able to audit management's assertions as presented in the reports and financial statements.

The last component of the definition of the audit process is *communicating* results to users. Management of a public company prepares:

1. a report on the effectiveness of ICFR, and
2. the financial statements.

Auditors do not write the internal control report. Neither do they control the content or form of the financial statements. Auditors only prepare the audit report. This report is the vehicle that auditors use to communicate the findings of the audit process. Management may choose to change its report on ICFR and the financial statements based on the auditor's evaluation. Management is especially likely to revise its ICFR report or the financial statements if the auditor concludes that there is a problem.

Be aware, however, that even though management's decision to revise its ICFR report or the financial statements may be *influenced* by the auditor's evaluation and conclusion, such a change is management's choice. Management has ownership of the report on ICFR effectiveness and the financial statements just as the auditor has ownership of the audit report. The various forms of the audit report and what is communicated by each variation are discussed in Chapter 11.

AUDITING INTERNAL CONTROL OVER FINANCIAL REPORTING [LO 2]

Even though it was published in 1973, the audit definition presented in Exhibit 1-2 is still accurate and relevant as it relates to the audit of the *financial statements*. However, the **Sarbanes-Oxley Act** of 2002 (**SOX**) requires that an audit of ICFR accompany the financial statement audit of a public company. This engagement to audit both ICFR and the financial statements is called an integrated audit. Remember that the financial statements report management's assertions about the economic actions and events of the company. Management's assertions regarding ICFR are presented in reports the company is required to file with the SEC. These reports state that management is responsible for establishing and maintaining ICFR, and provide a conclusion on the effectiveness of ICFR design and operations. The auditor reports on management's conclusion regarding the effectiveness of ICFR by issuing an independent opinion on ICFR effectiveness.

The components of the formal definition of auditing can also be applied to the audit of ICFR. When auditing ICFR,

1. The auditor is objective.
2. The auditor plans the audit to systematically obtain and examine evidence underlying management's conclusion regarding the design and operating effectiveness of ICFR.
3. The auditor determines whether management's conclusions regarding ICFR correspond closely with the supporting evidence.
4. The auditor reports an audit opinion.

Financial statements can be prepared based on various accepted criteria, such as United States generally accepted accounting principles (GAAP), International Financial Reporting Standards (IFRS) or an **Other Comprehensive Basis of Accounting (OCBOA)**. A statement on the basis of accounting used is included in the audit report. Similarly, the set of established criteria that management uses to assess the design and function of ICFR is identified in the audit report. As noted earlier, one of these accepted sets of criteria is the COSO IC Framework.

Later chapters discuss more about management assertions and audit procedures. For now, it is important to understand that an integrated audit consists of a financial statement audit and an audit of ICFR. The financial statement audit has been in existence and universally understood for a long time. The ICFR audit of public companies is newer, required by SOX, and governed by standards of the **Public Company Accounting Oversight Board (PCAOB)**.[4] When auditing either ICFR or the financial statements, audit activities look for a correspondence between the audit evidence and management's communications.

REVIEW QUESTIONS

B1. Why is auditing described as a systematic process?

B2. What are assertions? For purposes of an audit, who makes assertions?

B3. What is audit evidence?

B4. How are auditing and accounting different? Why do you have to be a good accountant to be a good auditor?

B5. Who is responsible for the report on internal control over financial reporting? Who is responsible for the financial statements? The audit report? How might these documents change as a result of the audit?

B6. What is the Sarbanes-Oxley Act?

B7. What is the COSO Internal Control Framework (COSO IC Framework), and why is it important?

B8. What is management's assertion that is assessed in a financial statement audit? In an audit of internal control over financial reporting (ICFR)?

B9. What entity issues the standards governing the integrated audit of a public company?

---

[4] An examination of ICFR is also available for nonpublic companies and other entities under attestation standards of the American Institute of Certified Public Accountants (AICPA). Attest engagements of the AICPA are discussed in Chapter 16.

PURPOSE AND VALUE OF AN AUDIT [LO 2]

The overall goal of an integrated audit is to provide the users of financial statements with assurance that the financial statements are reliable. Is this difficult to accomplish? Perhaps all that is necessary is to have laws in place that require companies to have effective internal control systems. Then the legal system can penalize anyone who creates incorrect, improper, or misleading financial statements. Actually, many laws are in place permitting prosecutors to penalize those who prepare and publish fraudulent financial statements. However, the difficulty with penalizing wrongdoers is that it happens after the problem occurs. Punishment for wrongdoing provides no assurance *in advance* to users that they can rely on the financial statements. The SEC presents the need for user confidence as follows:

> The SEC requires the filing of audited financial statements in order to obviate the fear of loss from reliance on inaccurate information, thereby encouraging public investment in the Nation's industries. It is therefore not enough that the financial statements be accurate; the public must also perceive them as being accurate.
> (SEC Final Rule, Revision of the Commission's Auditor Independence Requirements, 33-7919.htm)

The SEC suggests that one of the important motivators for requiring public companies to be audited is the need for orderly, functioning **capital markets**. In the introduction to its first standard on auditing ICFR, AS 2 (which has since been superseded by AS 5), the PCAOB stated:

> "The integrity of financial reporting represents the foundation upon which this country's public markets are built."
> (PCAOB Release No. 2004–001, March 9, 2004, p. 5)

If the investing public perceives audited financial statements to be more reliable than nonaudited financial statements, then audits make a significant contribution by increasing investor confidence. Investors who have confidence in the information are more likely to participate in the capital markets either through personal investing or savings and retirement programs. This participation in the capital markets is an important driver of successful U.S. and global economies. In addition, when the risk of incorrect financial information is decreased, so is the cost of capital to companies.

Several factors motivate the need for audits. First, as emphasized in the previous statements by the SEC and PCAOB, capital markets need to be both efficient and effective. Moreover, various parties use financial statements, and their interests are not always aligned. In other words, the different parties do not necessarily receive the same value from financial statements. The audit elevates the probability that everyone's needs are met with the same financial reports. For example, potential purchasers of a company's stock may be most interested in financial statements disclosing all risks as completely as possible. Management may want the financial statement disclosures to include any information that will promote the highest market price of the company's stock. In this case, an audit provides value to both parties by adding assurance that (1) all disclosures required by accounting standards are included, and (2) any information that might positively influence stock price is justified in accordance with accounting standards.

In addition to helping prospective **shareholders**, audits also directly benefit companies and current **stockholders**. Companies and their business transactions are complex. Owners who are not involved in the business are unlikely to have sufficient information or expertise to independently evaluate the inner workings of the company. An audit provides assurance that the complexities are appropriately presented based on accounting standards. Finally, the company receives specific value from an audit when a knowledgeable independent audit takes a "fresh look" at the company's accounting system and controls. Exhibit 1-3 highlights the different parties who receive benefit from an audit.

EXHIBIT 1-3

Beneficiaries of Audits

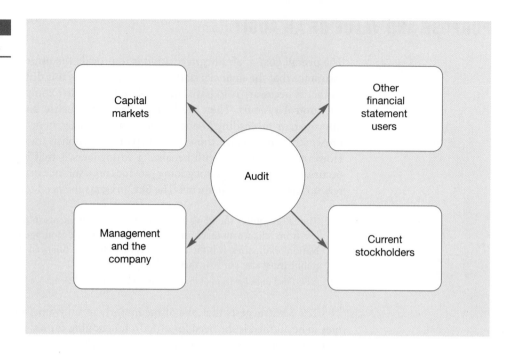

Misstated Financial Statements

Financial statement audits would not be needed if businesses consistently produced financial statements that correspond to the underlying economic events and are in accordance with accounting standards. But without audits, there is no assurance that the financial statements are not misstated or misleading. Some believe that audits contribute value by motivating businesses to be sure that their financial statements are fair and in accordance with accounting standards. In other words, audits can be proactive and preventive as well as serving to identify erroneous or misleading financial statements. If businesses know they will be audited and any errors or improprieties will be discovered, management is motivated to make sure the financial statements are proper before they are ever released to users.

This observation still skirts the question of why any businesses would ever prepare improper financial statements. The easiest explanation is that improper presentation of financial statements is sometimes unintentional. Much accounting is now a computer-based activity, and having an effective internal control system helps prevent unintentional errors. But even if the computer system processes data correctly, input **errors** are still possible. In addition, drafting financial statements requires a lot of human judgment. Accountants who prepare the financial statements must understand the company's economic events as well as the accounting standards that apply to those events. Many accounting standards and their application are complex. A lack of understanding of the accounting standards, or of skill in applying them, can lead to errors in the financial statements. Furthermore, even if they know what to do, people sometimes make mistakes.

Beyond improper financial statements caused by errors, history shows us that management or other insiders sometimes intentionally create misleading financial statements. The motivations for misrepresenting a company in its financial statements are numerous and diverse. The primary, important fact for the auditor and investing public is that the motivations do exist and fraudulent financial statements are sometimes crafted to deceive the unsuspecting user. Audits are needed to discover misstatements in financial statements whether they result from errors or fraud.

REVIEW QUESTIONS

C1. How does an audit benefit the capital markets? How does it benefit the company being audited?

C2. How might audits prevent as well as detect misstated financial statements? Why is this of value to the capital markets?

C3. What is the difference between a financial statement error and financial statement fraud?

Different Benefits to Different Parties [LO 3]

Another way to view the need for audits is to consider the perspectives of the various parties who have an interest in the quality of financial reporting. In any business environment, at least three major constituencies are interested in the fairness of the financial statements: shareholders, management, and the Board of Directors. The **audit committee**, which is a subset of the **Board of Directors**, is responsible for oversight of the audit function. Thus, among the directors, the audit committee has a heightened concern for financial statement quality.

Existing and potential shareholders all want audited financial statements because the audit provides assurance about what management has reported as the company's performance and financial position. Shareholders and potential shareholders use this financial information to make investment decisions. Even though the financial statements are not the only source of information, they are extremely important and often validate the legitimacy and credibility of other information available to the stock markets. Audits are valuable to shareholders and potential shareholders because they instill confidence that the information being used for investment decisions is reliable.

Management needs the audit for several reasons. An integrated audit report that does not indicate problems enhances management's credibility with shareholders and others. In addition, the audit is required by the SEC for access to the U.S. stock exchanges. It is also often required by creditors such as banks and lending institutions. Management benefits from the audit because it enables access to these various sources of capital at the best available cost. Management may also have a personal interest because an audit enhances the reliability of the company's performance indicators on which management is often evaluated. For example, an audit may be required before **performance-based compensation** and bonuses are awarded. Performance-based compensation might be, for example, compensation that is calculated based on the company's growth or earnings per share. Finally, the audit may provide feedback that helps management improve operational and financial efficiencies.

The *Board of Directors* is elected by the shareholders and is given responsibility for protecting shareholder interests. One way that the Board of Directors fulfills this responsibility is by hiring management to run the company. Management is charged with leading so that the company will achieve its goals. However, the directors must also safeguard shareholder interests by overseeing management's activities. Management is accountable to the Board of Directors for the company's performance. The Board of Directors relies heavily on the audit to fulfill its responsibilities to oversee the company.

Shareholders, management, and the Board of Directors all benefit from the ICFR and financial statement audits. However, each group has different views of its value. The audit produces increased assurance regarding the fairness of the financial presentation, and each constituency perceives the value of this assurance differently. Exhibit 1-4 shows that even though the audit committee and management have the most direct relationship with the auditor, all constituencies are linked together.

EXHIBIT 1-4

Relationships of Those
Who Benefit from the
Audit

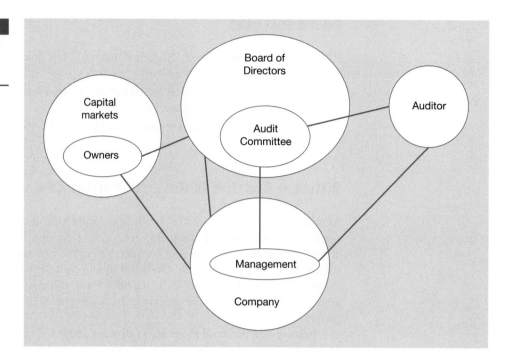

Remote Owners and Complex Transactions

A small business with a single owner and only a few, fairly simple business activities has straightforward accounting transactions and financial statements. The owner typically has the ability to understand all of the transactions without much accounting expertise. The owner is aware of all the activities in which the business engages and the economic impact of those activities. Consequently, the owner can personally manage and evaluate his or her investment.

In contrast, shareholders are the owners of large, multinational corporations with numerous lines of business. Shareholders are remote from the business and less likely to be able to understand and evaluate all of its activities. Individual shareholders may not understand all of the complexities of a large corporation's financial statement presentation. Even if shareholders are diligent and have the knowledge to read and understand the financial statements, they are not close enough to the business to be aware of all of the company's day-to-day activities. Furthermore, they would not likely want to spend the time to evaluate whether each transaction is properly recorded and disclosed. Fortunately, auditors can provide assurance regarding the effectiveness of ICFR and the appropriateness of the financial statements, producing a report that all shareholders can use.

Enron is a widely known example of a business that engaged in complex transactions that its owners were unable to effectively evaluate. The collapse of Enron motivated passage of SOX in 2002 and the downfall of Arthur Andersen, one of the world's largest public accounting firms. Enron traded in energy futures and used complex off-balance sheet transactions to maximize the appearance of its financial performance. We now know that in addition to reflecting very complex transactions, the financial statements also misrepresented the company's situation. When problems with Enron first surfaced and investigations began, observers noted that it would take years to research and unravel Enron's complex transactions. Clearly the shareholders, many of whom were company employees, did not understand the company's financial statements. Even Enron's auditor, Arthur Andersen, did not appropriately evaluate and report on the financial statements.

Fortunately, the Enron situation is the exception rather than the common occurrence. The majority of audits fulfill their responsibility. Audit reports provide owners who are remote from a company's day-to-day business activities with assurance regarding the propriety of the company's financial reports.

Internal Operations and Management

When considering the value of an audit to the company being audited, it is difficult to separate the company from either management or the investors. Several company benefits have already been described as benefits to management. These include access to capital markets, enabling the company to raise capital, and lower costs of capital. The company also benefits by having its stocks and bonds actively traded.

Another benefit from the audit is improvement to internal operations. During an integrated audit, the auditor examines and tests the functioning of numerous company controls and processes. While doing this, the auditor often becomes aware of ways that the company can improve and recommends them to management.

The suggested improvements may be ways the company can enhance efficiency and can apply to financial and accounting activities and operations. For example, the auditor might advise the company on streamlining a data entry process. Other recommendations may involve ways to increase the effectiveness of the company's activities. For example, effectively managing inventory records may mean that less inventory needs to be kept on hand, in turn freeing up money to earn investment income. Sometimes people say that companies only hire auditors because they are required to do so by regulators and creditors. Although the requirement to have an audit is certainly one motivation, businesses may find that an audit pays for itself as a result of the operating improvements and cost savings suggested by the **audit team**.

Benefits that accrue to the company from having an audit also benefit shareholders, management, and the Board of Directors. For example, an audit provides greater assurance that information produced by the company's information system is reliable. This assurance of reliability is a benefit to management because it enhances management's ability to run the company. At the same time, having good information helps the Board of Directors fulfill its oversight responsibility.

REVIEW QUESTIONS

D1. Why do shareholders value audited financial statements?

D2. Why do the Board of Directors and audit committee value an integrated audit?

D3. What benefits can management derive from a company having an integrated audit?

D4. Why is a shareholder usually a remote owner? Why does the fact that shareholders are remote owners cause them to benefit from an audit?

D5. What do the complex transactions that occur in many businesses today have to do with the value of an audit?

D6. How can a company benefit from an audit in terms of its operations and performance?

SERVICES PROVIDED BY AUDITORS

Companies being audited are often referred to as **audit clients**. The **public accounting firms** that perform audits are sometimes called *audit firms*. Public accounting firms are also called **external** or **independent auditors**. Sometimes, however, they are called CPA firms or professional services firms because of the other types of services they also provide. Public accounting firms can be large or small, and their organizations can be structured in various ways. What they all have in common is the professional knowledge and expertise to perform audits and provide other services their clients need. Their knowledge base extends beyond auditing and includes accounting, industry expertise, tax, and information technology (IT). Public accounting firms typically approach and structure engagement services using teams, with team members fulfilling responsibilities appropriate for their level of knowledge and experience. Public accounting firms are discussed in more detail in the Appendix to this chapter.

Among the different types of **auditing standards**, those governing the financial statement audit have existed for the longest period of time. However, guidance for various types of special engagements has also existed for many years. As businesses became more complex, companies asked for different types of services from their auditors. With each new service, the standard setters wrote guidance to perform and regulate the services.

STANDARD SETTERS AND GOVERNING AUTHORITIES [LO 4]

In the United States, various governing bodies regulate accountants and set the standards they must follow as they perform different types of engagements. Exhibit 1-5 portrays different governing bodies and their authority. The federal government is the ultimate authority for interstate commerce. It sets up the laws that control public companies and their auditors. The Securities Act of 1933 and Securities Exchange Act of 1934 (discussed in Chapter 4) set in motion the establishment of the Securities and Exchange Commission (SEC). The Securities Exchange Act of 1934 authorized the SEC to set up the regulations that now govern our capital markets.

Almost 70 years later, in 2002 Congress enacted the Sarbanes-Oxley Act (SOX), which resulted in the SEC structuring the Public Company Accounting Oversight Board (PCAOB). Prior to the existence of the PCAOB, the SEC delegated responsibility for setting auditing standards to the **American Institute of Certified Public Accountants (AICPA)**.

The AICPA still sets standards that govern the audits of nonpublic companies and nonaudit engagements in the United States. It also designs and administers the **CPA examination** that states rely on to confer CPA certificates. State laws control the licensing of certified public accountants and thus govern which CPAs can do business in each state. The SEC, PCAOB, and AICPA all have **independence standards** that auditors must follow. Other accounting organizations also have codes of ethics or conduct that members are expected to follow.

The global nature of today's business is increasing the importance of international standard setters such as the International Accounting Standards Board (IASB), which sets the

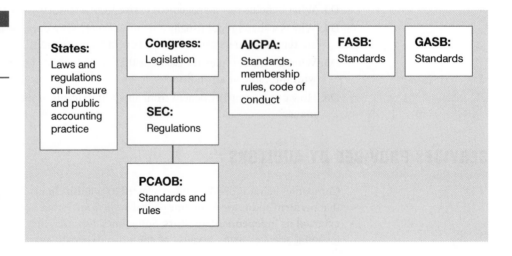

EXHIBIT 1-5

U.S. Governing
Authorities and
Standard Setters

International Financial Reporting Standards (IFRS). International Standards on Auditing (ISA) also exist, promulgated by the **International Auditing and Assurance Standards Board (IAASB)**, which is a part of the International Federation of Accountants (IFAC). The AICPA Auditing Standards Board (ASB) and the IAASB are making efforts to align their respective auditing standards. To date, the international auditing guidance has had little impact on the process of auditing U.S. companies that register with the SEC. The PCAOB has stated long-term plans to reduce the need for auditors to follow multiple sets of auditing standards by coordinating the structure of its standards with those produced by other audit standard setters such as the IAASB. For now, the content of the PCAOB's auditing standards continue to include the guidance and requirements deemed necessary for audits of companies traded on U.S. exchanges.

AUDITING IN ACTION

Interaction of Authorities Influencing the Auditing Process

Regulators and standard setters are involved in the audit process. Many of these entities are linked, and their responsibility and authority often overlap.

The SEC and PCAOB. The Securities and Exchange Commission (SEC) is a government agency that regulates publicly traded companies by its authority over the companies' SEC reports, stock exchanges, and the Public Company Accounting Oversight Board (PCAOB). The SEC sets accounting and reporting standards. It also oversees and approves the standards set by PCAOB and the stock exchanges. The PCAOB is a not-for-profit entity with the charge of standard setting and oversight of both the audits of public companies and the firms that perform the audits. Yet the SEC is also in an oversight role. The SEC must authorize all PCAOB standards before they become effective. It can reject the filings or suspend the stock market trading of a company based on its auditor or audit results.

FASB and GASB. The Financial Accounting Standards Board (FASB) and Government Accounting Standards Bóard (GASB) are not-for-profit entities that set accounting standards for entities in the United States in private and government sectors, respectively. The FASB performs its duties under the oversight of the SEC simply because the SEC has delegated to it the responsibility for setting accounting standards. The SEC can overrule accounting standards decisions made by the FASB. The GASB has authority based on legal requirements for entities to report using its standards.

AICPA. The American Institute of Certified Public Accountants (AICPA) is a not-for-profit entity that influences the governance of audits. The AICPA contributes to GAAP accounting standards and sets auditing standards for nonpublic companies. The AICPA works closely with the International Auditing and Assurance Standards Board (IAASB) that sets international auditing standards. It is also responsible for writing and administering the CPA exam. Successful performance on the CPA exam is one of the requirements for state licensing and to be able to audit financial statements. Therefore, this aspect of AICPA activities is also linked to the SEC and state authority.

State and federal government. The ultimate regulators involved in the audit process are state governments and the United States Congress. State governments issue CPA licenses and govern the work of accounting professionals working within their states. Even though all states have adopted the AICPA-administered CPA exam, each individual state decides what is required for an individual to be licensed and to work within its borders. State laws that affect and control CPAs go beyond licensing. They include various rules that govern entities and individuals, such as quality control for CPA firms and continuing education for individuals. The United States Congress is the author of the laws that created the SEC and authorize its power. The Sarbanes-Oxley Act is the most recent extensive example of the authority that Congress wields over the day-to-day business of audit clients, auditors, and the audit process.

Federal-Level Authority

Federal legislation and the SEC govern reports issued by public companies as well as independent audit activities. These reports include 10Ks and 10Qs. 10Ks are reports that companies file annually with the SEC. They contain management reports on ICFR, financial statements, and auditor reports. The 10Q reports are quarterly filings that contain management reports and quarterly financial statements. Quarterly financial statements are "reviewed," not audited. The review of a public company's quarterly reports involves less investigation than an audit and provides less assurance about the fairness of the financial statements. Reviews of public company quarterly financial statements are discussed in Chapter 16.

In addition to being responsive to regulations and other guidance communicated by the SEC, auditors are also guided by the Auditing Standards of the PCAOB in their involvement with 10K and 10Q reports. However, these Auditing Standards of the PCAOB are ultimately under SEC authority because the SEC must approve PCAOB standards before they become effective. Auditors also perform various tasks when companies issue securities and offer them for sale to the public. This involvement is also governed by the SEC.

PCAOB Authority

When the PCAOB first came into existence, it adopted the Statements on Auditing Standards (SAS) of the AICPA as its interim standards. Thus, at the inception of the PCAOB, the auditing standards affecting public and nonpublic company audits were identical. Since then, the PCAOB has drafted auditing standards that for public company audits have superseded the earlier AICPA-authored standards. Meanwhile, the AICPA has also drafted new standards, superseding those that existed at the inception of the PCAOB. Although the SAS apply to the audits of nonpublic companies, many of them align closely with the PCAOB's standards. As stated previously, the SAS also often align with the ISA of the IAASB.

New standards are continually being adopted by both the PCAOB and AICPA. This results in two sets of auditing standards that are "moving targets" for the audits of public and nonpublic companies. The Auditing Standards (AS) that the PCAOB had adopted as this book went to print are shown in Exhibit 1-6. Even though the PCAOB continues to authorize new standards, many of the Statements on Auditing Standards that were in existence at the time the PCAOB was formed have not been revised by the AICPA. These standards, labeled Interim Standards on the PCAOB Web site, are still used by the PCAOB. Therefore, those particular standards apply to both public and nonpublic company audits.

EXHIBIT 1-6

PCAOB Auditing Standards

Auditing Standard No. 1: References in Auditors' Reports to the Standards of the Public Company Accounting Oversight Board
Auditing Standard No. 2: An Audit of Internal Control Over Financial Reporting Performed in Conjunction With an Audit of Financial Statements (superseded)
Auditing Standard No. 3: Audit Documentation
Auditing Standard No. 4: Reporting on Whether a Previously Reported Material Weakness Continues to Exist
Auditing Standard No. 5: An Audit of Internal Control Over Financial Reporting That Is Integrated with An Audit of Financial Statements
Auditing Standard No. 6: Evaluating Consistency of Financial Statements
Auditing Standard No. 7: Engagement Quality Review

The PCAOB's primary guidance is in the form of Rules of the Board and the Auditing Standards. In contrast, in addition to the Statements on Auditing Standards, the AICPA has many sets of standards that cover other types of engagements and services. Some of these services are discussed in Chapter 16. Many of them are provided by accountants who also perform audits. However, based on SOX, SEC, and PCAOB rules, especially rules governing independence, auditors may not provide most of these services to a public company if they also perform the company's audit. Independence rules and their impact on the services that auditors provide to their audit clients are discussed in Chapter 3.

AUDITING IN ACTION

Other AICPA Standards

Code of Professional Conduct:
Applies to all AICPA members.

Statements on Standards for Attestation Engagements (SSAE):
Apply to engagements in which the auditor issues a report on subject matter or an assertion about subject matter that is the responsibility of another party.

Statements on Standards for Accounting and Review Services (SSAR):
Apply to engagements in connection with financial information or financial statements of a nonpublic company when the engagement provides less assurance than an audit or provides no assurance.

Statements on Quality Control Standards (QC):
Apply to firms' systems of quality control for accounting and auditing practice. Firms that are enrolled in an AICPA practice monitoring program must adhere to the standards.

Statements on Standards for Tax Service (SSTS):
Ethical standards that apply to tax practice, reflecting responsibilities to taxpayers, the public, the government, and the profession.

Statements on Standards for Valuation Services (SSV):
Apply to engagements that culminate in a valuation report.

Statements on Standards for Consulting Services (SSCS):
Apply to work performed solely to assist the client; generally, when the work is for the use and benefit of the client.

(*Source*: AICPA Web site.)

INTERNAL AUDITORS [LO 5]

This book focuses primarily on certified public accountants who perform integrated audits. However, a wide variety of services fall under the heading of auditing. Many companies have employees called **internal auditors**, who perform financial audit activities similar to those of the external auditor. In the ideal situation these internal auditors report to the audit committee. Internal auditors can participate in other types of activities, also.

Any company traded on the New York Stock Exchange must have an internal audit function. An external auditor evaluates whether a public company is of the size and complexity that it needs an internal audit function. If so—and the company either does not have one or has one that functions poorly—then the company has an internal control problem.

Internal auditors and their activities are very important to companies and have become even more important since the SOX legislation was passed. Internal auditors often assist in fulfilling the SOX requirement that management conclude and report on the effectiveness of ICFR.

OTHER AUDIT SERVICES

Accountants working as company employees may perform work called *operational auditing*. Rather than focusing on the appropriateness of recorded financial information, **operational auditors** assess and evaluate the functioning of the company. Primarily efficiency and effectiveness auditors, these professionals examine both financial and other operations.

The internal financial and operational auditor for the federal government is the **U.S. Government Accountability Office (GAO)**. This agency performs financial audits of government units. In addition, the GAO reports to Congress on topics as widespread as the efficiency of contractors working for the government to the effectiveness of programs on which federal funds are spent.

Another audit function that has actually been around for a long time, but is currently receiving a lot of media attention, is **forensic auditing**, which is sometimes called **forensic accounting**. In a general sense, a forensic audit engagement refers to the situation when an auditor is hired to look for specific and detailed information, usually in the records of a company. For example, operational auditors who look for errors or **fraud** in the payment of bills may be called forensic auditors.

The term *forensic accounting* is also used to apply to engagements that may be called litigation support. In disputes that are likely to go to court, auditors can be invaluable in producing evidence on transactions such as unapproved payments, hidden assets, or business valuations. Audits looking specifically for details of fraud are often called forensic audits, although they can also be called "fraud audits."

ACCOUNTANTS WHO ARE NOT AUDITORS

At this point you may believe that only accountants who follow an auditing career path need knowledge of auditing. But this perception is wrong. Knowledge about auditing is useful to accountants in varied roles and job positions.

Knowledge of the audit process is valuable to all accounting employees. Even if you work for a company that is the audit *client*, understanding the audit process gives you a perspective of the auditors' procedures and goals. In turn, you are more efficient and effective in providing the audit team with the information it needs. If you are an accountant in a management position, understanding the audit process helps you communicate with the auditors, not only during the audit engagement, but also when you are presented with their findings.

The requirement for audits of ICFR has introduced audit concepts into numerous operating functions of public companies. Effective ICFR requires that policies and procedures be in place and followed. Employees in nonaccounting roles may find themselves with documentation and reporting requirements related to internal control. Consequently, employees at most levels, even in nonaccounting roles, now have at least a basic awareness of control activities and know that controls are evaluated by auditors. As an accountant with audit knowledge, you are automatically ahead of most other employees.

If you, as the accountant, understand the audit process, you can be a valuable asset in supporting company policies, procedures, and documentation that contribute to effective internal controls. You may be the one who designs the controls or explains their importance to other employees. Regardless of your corporate position, audit knowledge will help you perform and manage more effectively.

The emphasis on ICFR in public companies has also had a "trickle-down" effect on entities that are not required to have an ICFR audit. Many not-for-profit and privately owned companies now place more emphasis on internal controls than in the past. Boards of various types of entities are often calling for internal control accountability. Understandably, management looks to the entity's accounting staff for help in meeting Board expectations.

REVIEW QUESTIONS

E1. Why is knowledge of auditing valuable to an accountant who is not working as an auditor?

E2. In terms of their impact on auditing standards and audits, what is the relationship of the SEC and the PCAOB? The SEC and the AICPA? The SEC and FASB? Congress and the SEC? State governments and the AICPA?

E3. What are Auditing Standards (AS)? Statements on Auditing Standards (SAS)? Which entity issues each? How are they related? To what kinds of audits does each apply?

E4. What standards does the AICPA produce in addition to auditing standards?

E5. What types of activities are performed by an internal auditor? An operational auditor? A forensic auditor?

CONCLUSION

Audits of public companies are integrated audits addressing both ICFR and the financial statements. Auditors play a vital role in the orderly functioning of capital markets by increasing confidence in the financial statements released into the public domain. Audits help a company's Board of Directors in its oversight role by increasing the reliability of the financial statements. This reliability also provides a benefit to the current stockholders. The credibility an audit adds to financial statements benefits management through impacts on external users. The audit may contribute to more effective management of corporate operations.

Various governing bodies set standards and provide guidance to auditors. Most of this guidance applies to auditors working for public accounting firms. However, accountants can also perform audit activities while working as company employees. Auditing can impact many areas of a business, and knowledge of auditing is useful to accountants regardless of their career activities.

KEY TERMS

American Institute of Certified Public Accountants (AICPA). The national professional organization of CPAs.

Assertions. Representations or declarations made by the individual or entity responsible for their validity. In an audit situation, assertions are made by management.

Audit. A professional service provided by CPAs resulting in an opinion on the fairness of the financial statements and the effectiveness of internal control over financial reporting.

Audit client. The entity that is the target of the audit activities; the entity for which the audit is conducted.

Audit committee. A committee (or equivalent body) established by and among the Board of Directors for the purposes of overseeing the accounting and financial reporting processes and audits of the financial statements; directly responsible for the hiring, compensation, and oversight of the external auditor.

Audit of internal control over financial reporting (ICFR). An examination, integrated with an audit of the financial statements, in which an auditor assesses and reports on management's assertion about the effectiveness of a company's internal control over financial reporting (see *internal control over financial reporting*).

Audit procedures. Activities carried out in conducting an audit; includes collecting and evaluating audit evidence.

Audit report. Issued by an auditor at the completion of an audit; for an integrated audit the auditor reports an opinion about the fairness of the financial statements and the effectiveness of ICFR. When the audit is of a non-public company the report is issued upon completion of a financial statement audit.

Auditing standards. Guidance and requirements of the Public Company Accounting Oversight Board (PCAOB) for audits of SEC registrants (Auditing Standards), and the American Institute of Certified Public Accountants (AICPA) for nonpublic companies (Statements on Auditing Standards).

Audit team. The group of professionals who work together to perform the audit; usually includes individuals at progressive levels of experience and rank within the public accounting firm.

Board of Directors. The individuals elected by shareholders and charged with governance and oversight of a company on behalf of the shareholders.

Capital markets. Trading markets for equity and debt financial instruments, and commodities; the public sources of funds for a business.

Clean audit report. See *Unqualified audit report.*

Committee of Sponsoring Organizations (COSO). Committee of Sponsoring Organizations of the Treadway Commission; composed of the AICPA, American Accounting Association, Institute of Internal Auditors, Institute of Management Accountants, and Financial Executives Institute.

COSO Internal Control Framework. Guidelines that define internal control, describe its components, and provide criteria against which managements, Boards of Directors, and auditors can assess internal controls.

CPA examination (Uniform CPA examination). Professional entry examination for accountants that is authored and administered under the authority of the AICPA.

Engagement quality review (EQR). Activity through which a partner not involved with an audit evaluates significant judgments and conclusions made on the engagement.

Enron. The large energy company that filed for bankruptcy in late 2001, triggering a response by Congress culminating in the Sarbanes-Oxley Act; as a result of related court actions (which were later overturned) one of the (then) Big Five public accounting firms, Andersen, went out of business.

Error. In an audit context, an unintentional misstatement or omission in the financial statements.

Evidence. Any information used by the auditor for audit procedures to come to an audit conclusion.

External, independent auditors. Certified public accountants working for professional firms that perform audits.

Financial statement audit. An examination of financial statements by a CPA, performed according to standards of the PCAOB (or for a nonpublic company, the AICPA) to report whether the financial statements follow generally accepted accounting principles (GAAP) or some other acceptable basis of accounting.

Forensic auditing, forensic accounting. A function in which an accountant examines records for fraud, business valuation, legal disputes, and so on.

Fraud. Intentional misstatement of financial statements, or theft of assets. Management is usually responsible for intentional misstatement of financial statements, whereas either employees or management can commit theft.

General Accountability Office (GAO). U.S. federal agency that functions as an internal financial and operational auditor; reports and is responsible to Congress.

ICFR. See *Internal control over financial reporting.*

International Auditing and Assurance Standards Board (IAASB). An independent organization that sets audit, review, and other standards for the purposes of supporting high-quality services and uniformity of services across countries.

Independence standards. Requirements of various organizations such as the AICPA and SEC indicating activities and relationships that a CPA must avoid when it performs audits.

Integrated audit. An engagement by a CPA involving the examination of internal control over financial reporting and the financial statements of an SEC registrant, resulting in an audit report.

Internal auditors. Auditors who are employed by a company; may perform a variety of activities including financial audits, efficiency and effectiveness audits, forensic audits, and special projects.

Internal control over financial reporting (ICFR). The processes and procedures in a company intended to provide reasonable assurance about the reliability of financial reporting and the preparation of financial statements for external purposes.

Operational auditors. Professionals who perform engagements related to efficiency and effectiveness.

Other Comprehensive Basis of Accounting (OCBOA). Accounting records and financial statements prepared in accordance with an accepted method that differs from GAAP such as a cash or tax basis of accounting.

Performance-based compensation. Compensation for employment that is based on performance of the company (often applies to top management), or personal performance.

Public accounting firm. An entity sometimes also called an audit or professional services firm or an external or independent auditor that employs CPAs; provides services to clients often including audit, review, tax, and consulting engagements.

Public Company Accounting Oversight Board (PCAOB). The board established to oversee the audit of public companies and the firms that provide those audits; established in 2002 subsequent to the Sarbanes-Oxley Act.

Sarbanes-Oxley Act (SOX). The Corporate and Auditing Accountability, Responsibility, and Transparency Act of 2002. Federal legislation that created new standards for corporate governance, auditors of public companies, and lawyers, as well as authorizing the creation of the Public Company Accounting Oversight Board (PCAOB).

Securities and Exchange Commission (SEC). The government agency established by Congress in 1934 to enforce the securities laws included in the 1933 and 1934 Securities Acts.

Shareholders. Stockholders; those who own an equity interest in a corporation.

Unqualified audit report. The report a CPA issues when all auditing conditions have been met; the auditor concludes that the report does not need to be modified for reasons relating to either ICFR or the fairness of the financial statements.

MULTIPLE CHOICE

1-1 **[LO 2]** An integrated audit is

(a) required for all companies.

(b) required by the IAASB.

(c) composed of a financial statement audit and an audit of internal control over financial reporting.

(d) conducted according to audit standards of the AICPA.

1-2 **[LO 2]** Evidence

(a) is composed of various items including underlying records of accounts and documents.

(b) must be in written form.

(c) includes records created by the auditor to document the audit activities.

(d) includes only corroborating information obtained from outside the audit client.

1-3 **[LO 4]** The PCAOB

(a) is a not-for-profit entity.

(b) shares its responsibility for standard setting with the AICPA.

(c) creates audit standards that CPA firms must use in all audits.

(d) is independent of SEC oversight.

1-4 **[LO 2]** Shareholders of large multinational companies need audits

(a) to be comfortable that management makes good decisions.

(b) because state laws require them.

(c) to have assurance regarding the fairness of financial statements.

(d) because all multinational companies are required by international law to be audited.

1-5 **[LO 2]** An audit of internal control over financial reporting (ICFR)

(a) addresses the same management assertion as a financial statement audit.

(b) is integrated with a financial statement audit.

(c) does not result in a audit opinion; the financial statement audit produces the opinion.

(d) is required for all companies.

1-6 **[LO 2]** An integrated audit

(a) is a systematic process.

(b) is not a systematic process because that definition only applies to a financial statement audit.

(c) uses only GAAP as the established criteria for assessing management's assertions.

(d) uses only the COSO Internal Control Framework as the established criteria for assessing management's assertions.

1-7 **[LO 2]** Economic events and actions

(a) are only important when studying the FASB conceptual framework.

(b) affect accounting but not auditing.

(c) are represented in fairly presented financial statements.

(d) do not impact either accounting or auditing.

1-8 **[LO 2]** When performing an audit, the auditor is objective, meaning

[Ethics]

(a) the auditor is highly skeptical of all the documents examined.

(b) the auditor tries to remain suspicious because of the possibility that documents are forged.

(c) the auditor evaluates underlying documents to be sure that management has used a conservative accounting approach.

(d) the auditor is not biased when evaluating evidence supporting management's assertions.

1-9 **[LO 2]** Auditing and accounting

(a) are highly related, so if you know one you do not need to know the other as well.

(b) are highly related, because to be a good accountant you have to be a good auditor.

(c) are highly related, because to be a good auditor you have to be a good accountant.

(d) overlap because accountants and auditors perform similar job functions.

1-10 **[LO 3]** The auditor

(a) can require management to change the financial statements.

(b) can require management to change the report on ICFR.

(c) can change the accounting information included in the SEC filings.

(d) can respond to the financial statements and management's reports by changing the audit report.

1-11 **[LO 4]** The COSO Internal Control Framework

   (a) is a set of criteria that the auditor can use to assess whether internal controls over financial reporting (ICFR) are effective.

   (b) is a set of criteria used by management, so the auditor does not use it to assess whether internal controls over financial reporting (ICFR) are effective.

   (c) is a set of criteria that governs the auditor's procedures in performing the internal control over financial reporting (ICFR) audit of a public company.

   (d) is the source of the requirement that management's report on internal control over financial reporting (ICFR) be audited.

1-12 **[LO 2]** Audits are of value because

   (a) when financial statements are audited, they are accurate.

   (b) when financial statements are audited, investors have more confidence in their fairness and reliability.

   (c) the IRS accepts them and the company will not have to pay additional taxes.

   (d) the PCAOB requires them.

1-13 **[LO 2]** Misstated financial statements

   (a) result from errors.

   (b) do not result from fraud because when they do they are called fraudulent financial statements.

   (c) are always the result of theft.

   (d) should be detected by audits whether they result from error or fraud.

1-14 **[LO 3]** The audit committee

   (a) elects the Board of Directors.

   (b) consists of members of the audit team and management.

   (c) is a subset of the board of directors.

   (d) is the body that governs the company and provides oversight on behalf of shareholders.

1-15 **[LO 2]** Audits are performed

   (a) because they are required and contribute value.

   (b) only because they are required.

   (c) only when they can improve the operating effectiveness of a company.

   (d) because management always wants to have them.

1-16 **[LO 3]** Which of the following statements is true?

   (a) Enron was a large energy company that went bankrupt.

   (b) Enron participated in complex off-balance sheet transactions.

   (c) Shareholders did not have an appropriate understanding of Enron's transactions.

   (d) All of the above are true.

1-17 **[LO 4]** Auditors of public companies

   (a) must follow AICPA attest standards when performing integrated audits.

   (b) must follow PCAOB Auditing Standards when performing integrated audits.

   (c) must follow IAASB standards when performing integrated audits if the company is a multinational corporation.

   (d) must adhere to the state laws governing public companies in all states where the company is located.

1-18 **[LO 4]** The SEC and the PCAOB

   (a) have equal authority.

   (b) both have the authority to issue accounting standards.

   (c) both have authority over the standards that affect integrated audits.

   (d) both have authority over the U.S. stock markets.

1-19 **[LO 4]** The PCAOB

   (a) uses all the AICPA Statements on Auditing Standards as the basis for its AS standards for integrated audits.

   (b) adopted the AICPA Statements on Auditing Standards on an interim basis and has replaced some of them with its Auditing Standards.

   (c) adopted the AICPA Statements on Auditing Standards on an interim basis and has now replaced all of them by issuing its own Auditing Standards.

   (d) has adopted the AICPA Code of Conduct and requires auditors to adhere to it.

1-20 **[LO 5]** Accountants who are employees of corporations

   (Ethics)

   (a) can have job descriptions that include audit functions.

   (b) cannot perform audit functions because they are not independent.

   (c) must follow the AICPA Code of Conduct if they perform independent audits and issue reports.

   (d) can perform operational and fraud audit tasks but not financial audit tasks.

DISCUSSION QUESTIONS

1-21 [LO 2] Why do you have to be a good accountant in order to be a good auditor?

1-22 [LO 3] Auditors cannot change the financial statements. Explain the influence the auditor has on management's decisions regarding financial statement presentation. Also, explain your perception of the possible tension created by any power struggle inherent in the management–auditor relationship. How do you think auditors should respond when management wants the company's financial statements to be presented in a certain way but the auditor disagrees?

Ethics

1-23 [LO 2] How do the capital markets and economy benefit as a result of all publicly-traded companies having an independent audit?

1-24 [LO 2] How do audits serve a "preventive" purpose?

1-25 [LO 3] Shareholders, management, and the Board of Directors/audit committee all benefit from an audit but are said to have different perspectives. If each group were solely responsible for the decision, would these three categories of constituents prefer to have the same set of economic events reported differently? For example, would one group benefit from more aggressive reporting, another from more conservative reporting, and so on? How might these different preferences impact reporting?"

Ethics

1-26 [LO 3] Why does having audited financial statements bring down a company's cost of capital?

PROBLEMS

1-27 [LO 2] Michael is a new employee in the financial reporting department of Goldberg Corporation, a midsize publicly-held corporation with annual revenues of $75 million. As Goldberg Corporation prepared for its annual audit, his manager came to him to complain about the auditors. Their audit fees were so high, yet every year they never found all of the mistakes made by the staff in Goldberg Corporation. One year, he explained, they even missed a $5,000 fraud.

Required:

(a) How can Michael use the objectives of an audit to help his manager understand the value that the company receives from an audit?

(b) How can Michael explain that missing a $5,000 fraud in a company with revenues of $75 million does not indicate that the auditors performed an ineffective audit?

1-28 [LO 2] Javier is an experienced, second-year staff accountant at a midsized CPA firm who has only worked on audits of large, private companies. His firm recently won a proposal for the year-end audit of a small, publicly-traded company. Javier's evaluations have indicated that he is a hard worker and value-added team player. The audit partner tells the human resources scheduler to assign Javier to the audit team of the new public company engagement. Javier finds out that his first task is to work on the audit of the internal controls over financial reporting (ICFR). Javier is excited because he knows that gaining experience on a public client is a good opportunity. However, he has only performed financial statement audits and is apprehensive about his lack of experience.

Required:

How can Javier apply the components of the formal definition of auditing to the audit of ICFR?

1-29 [LO 2] Jessica is an audit partner of an international accounting firm with experience auditing in the hospitality industry. Jessica recently won an engagement of a large, publicly-traded hotel chain. In planning the upcoming year's audit, she schedules one manager, three seniors, and six staff members, all of whom have experience in the hotel industry.

Required:

(a) Does Jessica have sufficient staff to complete the audit in accordance with PCAOB standards? Explain.

(b) Can Jessica schedule other experts on the audit?

(c) Will any other partners likely help Jessica work on the engagement?

1-30   **[LO 1, 2]** R&R is a public corporation that, as of December 31, 2009, is subject to a year-end integrated audit by its independent auditing firm, Young & Young. An excerpt of Young & Young's audit opinion states:

> In our opinion, the consolidated financial statements present fairly, in all material respects, the financial position of R&R and its subsidiaries as of December 31, 2009, and the results of their operations and their cash flows for the fiscal year ended December 31, 2009 in conformity with U.S. GAAP. Also in our opinion, R&R maintained, in all material respects, effective internal control over financial reporting as of December 31, 2009, based on criteria established in Internal control—Integrated Framework issued by the Committee of Sponsoring Organizations of the Treadway Commission (COSO).

Required:

(a) What kind of opinion did Young & Young give R&R for its 2009 year-end financial statements?

(b) Under which set of financial reporting standards does R&R report? Which set of auditing standards does Young & Young use in its audit of R&R?

(c) Under which financial reporting standards might R&R report if it were a corporation based in Germany?

1-31   **[LO 3]** Over the course of Young & Young's audit of SQL Group, a publicly traded company, Young & Young concluded that SQL's financial statements presented fairly according to U.S. GAAP, but its internal controls over financial reporting were not effective as of the audit date. Management's initial evaluation was that the ICFR is effective. This is the first time anything like this has happened to management and they are not sure what to do.

Required:

(a) Who is responsible for ensuring that SQL's internal controls over financial reporting are effective?

(b) Can SQL's management do anything to alter Young & Young's opinion concerning the effectiveness of its internal controls over financial reporting? How should Young & Young respond to any such pressures?

(c) Can Young & Young *require* management to change its report on ICFR effectiveness?

1-32   **[LO 5]** Jason is a senior accounting major at State University who is entering his last semester. He needs one more accounting class to fulfill his requirements and notices an opening in the undergraduate auditing class. As Jason's father is the chairman of the board for a public company in the area, Jason's goal is to graduate and work in the corporation's financial reporting department. Jason does not think that an auditing class will provide future value for his career objectives.

Required:

(a) Is Jason's perspective correct concerning the value-added nature of an auditing class?

(b) List the ways Jason can derive value from the class even if he does not plan to enter the audit profession.

1-33   **[LO 4, 5]** AH Family is a large private corporation in its fortieth year of operation. When Patricia, the founder's daughter, recently became AH Family's CEO, she formulated an aggressive multinational expansion plan that will add locations in Europe and Asia. To accomplish this goal, Patricia and the Board of Directors realized its need to raise $100 million in new capital. In order to raise such high levels of new capital, AH Family will have to go public. Currently, AH Family employs a local CPA firm to conduct yearly audits of the financial statements for its creditors.

Required:

(a) Identify the types of audits AH Family will have to undergo if management chooses to take the company public.

(b) Identify the governing and standard-setting bodies that will affect AH Family if it chooses to become a public company.

(c) Is it possible that new costs will result if the company goes public? Explain.

1-34   **[LO 4]** Your professor has asked you to complete a research paper concerning the link between the auditing profession and financial reporting standard setters and regulators.

Required:

For each independent situation, determine which regulating or standard-setting body you should research:

(a) The entity that sets accounting standards for the government sector.

(b) The entity that decides what is required to become a licensed CPA and conduct work as a CPA.

(c) The entity that sets standards for audits of publicly traded companies.

(d) The entity that sets financial reporting standards in the U.S.

(e) The entity that prepares and administers the Uniform CPA Exam.

(f) The entity that has ultimate authority over public company reports as well as accounting and reporting standards.

1-35   **[LO 2]** Meagan is a graduate student in the accounting program at your school. While she has excelled in her auditing, managerial and cost accounting, and AIS classes, she has not performed as well in her required financial accounting classes but has still maintained a high overall GPA. Meagan wishes to pursue a career in auditing because she has done well in auditing classes, and she wishes to avoid a career in financial accounting because she has not done well in those classes.

Required:

(a) Explain why Meagan's reasoning is flawed.

(b) Will Meagan be able to excel in her career without a strong base in financial accounting? Explain.

(c) Will her strong performance in her managerial and cost accounting classes and AIS class help her in her auditing career?

1-36   **[LO 2]** Barton and Sons, Inc., is a small, privately-held corporation that operates two retail stores in western Kentucky. Jorge Barton and his two sons own all of the company's stock and manage the store operations. The family takes pride in the corporation's success in terms of growing sales and lack of borrowing. The company is currently considering expansion into other regions of Kentucky and Indiana. Such expansion would likely require long-term borrowing and surrendering certain management responsibilities to non-family member employees. However, the family does not wish to sell stock in the company.

Required:

(a) Discuss the factors that would make it beneficial for a company like Barton and Sons to have an external audit.

(b) Discuss the factors that would make it beneficial for a company like Barton and Sons to implement an internal audit function.

1-37   **[LO 3]** You are a newly hired associate auditor for Praxo & Hanks, CPAs, a professional services firm that provides financial audits, integrated audits, and tax work for a variety of private and public company clients in the mid-Atlantic region of the U.S. Your first week with the firm was spent in a training program for audit staff, which was led by two of the firm's audit managers. The first day of the training program focused on understanding the responsibilities of auditors and the nature and objectives of the services provided to audit clients. Answer the following based on what you should have learned in the first day of training.

Required:

(a) Distinguish between the assertions made by management in presenting financial statements and reporting on ICFR, and the statements made within an auditor's report.

(b) How do management's assertions relate to audit evidence?

ACTIVITY ASSIGNMENTS

1-38   Go to the SEC Web site (*www.sec.gov*). Under "About the SEC" select "Laws and Regulations" Select the Sarbanes-Oxley Act of 2002. Find the full text of the law. Review the following sections: 103, 201, 202, 203, 204, 206, 301, 302, 404, and 407. As you read, prepare a list of questions regarding items you do not understand and bring them to class for discussion.

1-39   Select a publicly traded company of your choice. Find the most recent annual filing with the SEC (10K), or quarterly report filing (10Q) by going to either the SEC Web site or the company's Web site. Find management's report on ICFR (as required under Section 404 of the Sarbanes-Oxley Act.) Print out the management report. What are the primary points stated by management in the report?

1-40   Go to the PCAOB Web site (*www.pcaobus.org*). Find Auditing Standard No. 5, "An Audit of Internal Control Over Financial Reporting that is Integrated with an Audit of Financial Statements." Go to Appendix B and read paragraphs B1–B9. Summarize the content of these paragraphs about integrating a financial statement and internal control audit.

1-41   **[LO 6]** Go to the COSO Web site (*www.COSO.org*). Find the Internal Control Integrated Framework. What other publications are posted on the COSO Web site?

1-42   Go to the PCAOB Web site (*www.pcaobus.org*). Explain the PCAOB mission and its rulemaking process.

1-43   On the AICPA Web site (*www.aicpa.org*), find "Students and CPA Candidates." What is included under "The CPA Exam"?

APPENDIX A: WORKING IN A CPA FIRM

Services Provided by CPA Firms

This book is about auditing, and its primary focus is on the activities involved in performing an integrated audit. Public accounting firms, also often called CPA, audit, or professional services firms, provide many services in addition to audits. Some firms provide a wide variety of services. Others choose to offer fewer types of services because of the size of the firm and qualifications of its professional staff. For example, firms that do not have a full range of services may choose not to audit publicly traded companies or may refrain from audit work generally, focusing instead on tax or personal financial planning services.

Audit services are a very specific type of work with the objective of providing an opinion on the effectiveness of internal control over financial reporting (ICFR) and the fairness of the financial statements. CPAs perform reviews of interim financial reports that are filed with the SEC. They may perform reviews using a different set of AICPA standards, Statements on Standards for Accounting and Review Services (SSARs) for financial statements of nonpublic companies. A review provides less assurance than an audit, but is still directed toward adding credibility to the financial information.

Attest services are engagements in which a public accounting firm provides a report regarding the appropriateness of someone's representation or assertion. For example, a WebTrust engagement is a particular type of attest engagement developed and named by the AICPA. In a WebTrust engagement, the CPA addresses management's representation that a company's Web site contains controls needed for consumer confidence. CPAs can perform attest engagements for various assertions and representations.

Another example of an attest engagement is one required in 2009 by the federal government associated with loans authorized under the Term Asset-Backed Securities Loan Facility (TALF). Before the Federal Reserve makes loans associated with asset-backed securities, an attest report from a public accounting firm registered with the PCAOB is required. The attest report establishes that the collateral used to back the TALF loan meets the requirements of the program.

Even broader than an attest engagement is an assurance engagement. An assurance service is one that adds value to information by increasing the information's credibility or changing its presentation. The AICPA has developed and "branded" a category of services called "ElderCare" that often involves assurance engagements. For example, an ElderCare assurance engagement might involve verifying the quality of services being provided to an aging parent by an assisted living facility. The CPA providing this ElderCare service is increasing the credibility of the information presented by the assisted living facility regarding the quality of care.

Public accounting firms also provide services that fall completely outside the umbrella of assurance service. These nonassurance services, such as tax work, accounting and bookkeeping, and business advising or management consulting may be more familiar to you than some of the nonaudit attest and assurance services. Tax work may involve research and planning, or services involved with tax forms, sometimes referred to as compliance work.

Some public accounting firms provide accounting and bookkeeping services for nonpublic clients, actually maintaining the company's records. With the current popularity and affordability of easy-to-use computer packages for bookkeeping, this work now more often involves the higher-level work related to adjustments, analyses, and preparation of financial statements and reports.

Business advisory services and consulting services are the terms used for a very wide assortment of activities that may include helping a client prepare to purchase another company (also known as due diligence, transaction support, and merger and acquisitions work), or install a complex information technology system. The public accounting firm may be the source of assistance for many client needs. Exhibit A1-1 diagrams the relationship of the various services.

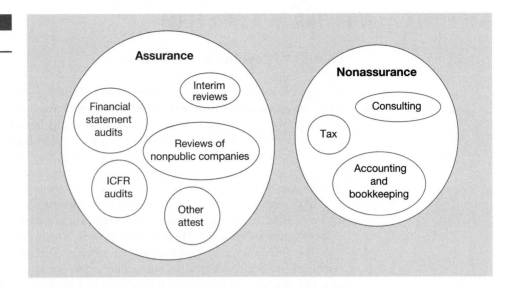

Common Firm Structures

Public accounting firms provide services to their clients. Their clients rely on the firms to use professional expertise in providing these services. This reliance and trust is an important part of the contract. To support the effectiveness of their relationships with clients, public accounting firms are organized and legally formed in specific ways that are authorized by government entities. These authorized firm structures are intended to protect clients in the event a public accounting firm damages a client or the public interest. Public accounting firms are set up so that the professionals who own them are personally responsible to their clients for performing competently, with possible financial damage to professionals if they behave in an irresponsible manner. Usually state laws have jurisdiction over the form of organization that public accounting firms may use.

When a CPA is the only owner of his or her firm, the organization of the firm may be a sole proprietorship or professional corporation. A professional corporation may also be set up with more than one owner. The owner may have employees who work under his or her supervision. Laws vary from state to state, but professional corporations typically must carry a specified amount of insurance or be capitalized at a certain level so that clients and other parties are protected.

CPA organizations also use various partnership and partnership-type structures. Although a general partnership is usually a permitted structure for a CPA firm, it is less likely to be used because the owners in a general partnership are subject to unlimited liability.

Two other common forms of organization that states often permit for public accounting firms are limited liability companies and limited liability partnerships. Though structured like general partnerships and subject to similar tax laws, as the name suggests, limited liability companies provide some protection to owners from personal liability as a result of company actions.

Both general partnerships and limited liability partnerships have one or more partners who own the firm. In a general partnership the personal liability of each partner extends to the debts and obligations of the entire partnership. However, in a limited liability partnership, partners are not personally responsible for liabilities that result from the professional behavior of their partners. They are personally responsible only for liabilities resulting from their own professional behavior and that of those they supervise.

Firm Size

Firms are often categorized by size: number and geographical dispersion of offices, number of partners and employees, and amount of service revenues. The largest firms are called the Big Four. This category name has evolved through the years as a result of mergers and the close of Andersen (as a result of Enron) from the Big Eight to the Big Six to the Big Five and finally the Big Four. The four largest firms are: Deloitte (*www.deloitte.com*), Ernst & Young (*www.ey.com*), KPMG (*www.kpmg.com*), and PricewaterhouseCoopers (*www.pwc.com*). These firms have many offices in the U.S. and affiliated firms throughout the world. They are called international firms.

The next tier of firms is labeled national firms. Firms included in this category, for example, Grant Thornton and BDO Seidman, have many offices throughout the U.S. Many of the firms in this tier are affiliated through networks with other firms that have offices in other countries. Therefore, the term *international networks* is sometimes used to identify firms in this tier.

The smallest firms are usually categorized as either regional and large local firms, or small local firms. The vast majority of public accounting firms are small local firms; many are sole practitioners. Firms in these two categories are typically one-office firms, although regional and large local firms may have more than one office. The range of services they provide is varied.

Hierarchy within the Firm

One way to view the hierarchy within public accounting firms is to classify people as owners; accounting and other professional staff; and support, administrative, or clerical staff. With the exception of professionals who provide ancillary services in areas such as marketing and human resource services, this grouping includes most people who work within public accounting firms. But this type of classification does not give much information on what people in different positions do with their time. Because the internal organization of CPA firms can be very complex, and different firms are structured very differently, the following explanation is limited to the audit function.

The Big Four have fairly consistent internal structures, but smaller firms are not uniform in the titles they use for different ranks or in the job responsibilities of professionals at each rank. Four general levels exist within the Big Four: partners, managers, in-charge accountants, and staff accountants. These may be further divided depending on a person's level of experience within each rank. For example, a person might first be called a manager and then be promoted to senior manager. In-charge accountants are often called "seniors," meaning senior accountants. Some of the owners in the Big Four are not CPAs because their areas of expertise are outside of accounting, for example, computer technology. These owners are sometimes called principals rather than partners, or non-CPA owners due to laws requiring partners to be CPAs.

Across smaller firms, human resources titles vary. The owners may be called partners, and all other professional accountants may be called staff. In contrast, many smaller firms use titles that are similar to those used in the Big Four.

An increasingly common title is "nonequity partner" or "salaried partner," used to refer to someone in a long-term position with partner-like professional responsibilities whose compensation structure does not involve participation in partnership earnings. The job descriptions of nonequity partners may exclude practice development (bringing in new clients) or may limit the hours the individual is required to work or the number of clients for which he or she is responsible.

Individuals who join a firm immediately after college, with either an undergraduate or a master's degree, begin as staff accountants. Their responsibilities include carrying out many of the tests and specific procedures called for in an audit. Depending on the size of the engagement, one or many staff accountants may be assigned to an audit.

An in-charge or senior accountant manages the day-to-day activities of the audit. Seniors are involved in engagement planning, supervision, and reviewing the work of staff accountants. They typically oversee one engagement at a time, although this depends on the size of the engagements. Those at the manager ranks often oversee more than one engagement simultaneously. Managers are significantly involved in planning. They supervise senior accountants and review audit work. Managers are also involved in administrative tasks such as billing the client and collecting fees.

Partners have ultimate responsibility for the success of the audit. Partners participate in planning, supervising, and managing the engagement as well as reviewing the work performed by those at lower ranks. Partners have responsibility for interacting with the client's upper management. As the ultimate authority over the audit, the engagement partner interacts with the client audit committee and client management during all stages of the audit, beginning with the client investigation and proposal process and continuing throughout the final communications and issuance of the audit report. Partners' interaction with potential clients prior to and during the proposal process may be referred to as practice development.

The hierarchical structure used in public accounting firms is designed to provide opportunities for learning, with increased responsibility becoming available as an individual professional's experience and skills develop. The structure allows for supervision and review at all stages, thus providing both a learning environment and quality control over the work performed.

The CPA Vision Project was a special project of the AICPA intended to ensure that the CPA profession remains flexible in its dynamic business environment. The concepts expressed by the Vision Project articulate the goals and objectives of practicing certified public accountants.

Review Questions

F1. What is the difference between an audit, a review, and other types of attest engagements?

F2. What is an assurance engagement?

F3. What are examples of nonassurance and consulting services?

F4. What different organizational structures can be used by CPA firms, and how are they different?

F5. Why are CPA firms not structured as typical corporations?

F6. What are the different tiers or categories of firm sizes into which CPA firms are grouped, and what are the characteristics of each tier?

F7. What are the different ranks of individual professionals within a CPA firm, and what responsibilities are assigned to each rank?

F8. In a CPA firm, the work of each person is reviewed by his or her supervisor. What is the purpose of having the work of each person reviewed by a professional with more experience?

F9. How does the CPA Vision Project intend to enhance value to the CPA profession?

ACTIVITY ASSIGNMENT

1-1.   Go to the Web site of one of the Big Four public accounting firms (Deloitte, Ernst & Young, KPMG, PricewaterhouseCoopers). How do these firms market themselves on their Web sites? What types of services and industry expertise are highlighted?

AUDITING IN ACTION

AICPA CPA Vision Project

CPA Vision Core Values

1. **Continuing Education and Life-Long Learning**—CPAs highly value continuing education beyond certification and believe it is important to continuously acquire new skills and knowledge.
2. **Competence**—CPAs are able to perform high quality work in a capable, efficient, and appropriate manner.
3. **Integrity**—CPAs conduct themselves with honesty and professional ethics.
4. **Attuned to Broad Business Issues**—CPAs are in tune with the overall realities of the business environment.
5. **Objectivity**—CPAs are able to deal with information free of distortions, personal bias or conflicts of interest.

Core Services

1. **Assurance and Information Integrity**—Provide a variety of services that improve and assure the quality of information, or its context, for business decision-making.
2. **Technology Services**—Services that leverage technology to improve objectives and decision-making including business application processes, system integrity, knowledge management, system security, and integration of new business processes and practices.
3. **Management Consulting and Performance Management**—Provide advice and insight on the financial and non-financial performance of an organization's operational and strategic processes through broad business knowledge and judgment.
4. **Financial Planning**—Provide a variety of services to organizations and individuals that interpret and add value by utilizing a wide range of financial information. These include everything from tax planning and financial statement analysis to structuring investment portfolios and complex financial transactions.
5. **International Services**—Provide services to support and facilitate commerce in the global market.

Core Competencies

1. **Communications and Leadership Skills**—Able to give and exchange information within meaningful context and with appropriate delivery and interpersonal skills. Able to influence, inspire, and motivate others to achieve results.
2. **Strategic and Critical Thinking Skills**—Able to link data, knowledge, and insight together to provide quality advice for strategic decision-making.
3. **Focus on the Customer, Client and Market**—Able to anticipate and meet the changing needs of clients, employers, customers, and markets better than competitors.
4. **Interpretation of Converging Information**—Able to interpret and provide a broader context using financial and non-financial information.
5. **Technologically Adept**—Able to utilize and leverage technology in ways that add value to clients, customers, and employers.

(http://www.cpavision.org/final_report/page08.htm)

CHAPTER 2

Overview of an Integrated Audit

1. Understand the legal and regulatory requirements for integrated audits.
2. Identify the basic requirements for an audit to be possible.
3. Recognize the basic stages of an audit.
4. Explain the meaning of fundamental terms related to auditing.
5. Describe the activities that comprise the general stages of an integrated audit.
6. Learn the basic differences between the audit of a public and a nonpublic company.
7. Explain the generally accepted auditing standards.

Chapter 2 Resources

AU 110, AICPA, PCAOB, *Responsibilities and Functions of the Independent Auditor*

AU 120, AICPA, *Defining Professional Requirements in Statements on Auditing Standards*

AU 150, AICPA, PCAOB, *Generally Accepted Auditing Standards*

AU 230, AICPA, PCAOB, *Due Professional Care in the Performance of Work*

AU 310, PCAOB, *Appointment of the Independent Auditor*

AU 311, AICPA, PCAOB, *Planning and Supervision*

AU 312, AICPA, PCAOB, *Audit Risk and Materiality in Conducting an Audit*

AU 314, AICPA, *Understanding the Entity and Its Environment and Assessing the Risks of Material Misstatement*

AU 316, AICPA, PCAOB, *Consideration of Fraud in a Financial Statement Audit*

AU 318, AICPA, *Performing Audit Procedures in Response to Assessed Risks and Evaluating the Audit Evidence Obtained*

AU 319, PCAOB, *Consideration of Internal Control in a Financial Statement Audit*

AU 326, AICPA, *Audit Evidence*

AU 326, PCAOB, *Evidential Matter*

AU 329, AICPA, PCAOB, *Analytical Procedures*

AU 333, AICPA, PCAOB, *Management Representations*

AU 339, AICPA, *Audit Documentation*

AU 350, AICPA, PCAOB, *Audit Sampling*

AU 380, AICPA, *The Auditor's Communication with Those Charged with Governance*

AU 380, PCAOB, *Communication with Audit Committees*

AU 508, AICPA, PCAOB, *Reports on Audited Financial Statements*

FASB Concepts Statement No. 2, *Qualitative Characteristics of Accounting Information*

PCAOB AS 3, *Audit Documentation*

PCAOB AS 5, *An Audit of Internal Control Over Financial Reporting That Is Integrated with an Audit of Financial Statements*

PCAOB Rule 3100, *Compliance with Auditing and Related Professional Pactice Standards*

PCAOB Rule 3101, *Certain Terms Used in Auditing and Related Professional Practice Standards*

PCAOB Rule 3526, *Communication with Audit Committees Concerning Independence*

Sarbanes-Oxley Act of 2002

SEC Staff Accounting Bulletin 99, *Materiality*

INTRODUCTION

What does it mean when we use the term *audit*? The definition can be very simple. An audit is a process used to determine whether a company's report on **internal control over financial reporting (ICFR)** and financial statements are reasonable representations of actual events and circumstances. The purpose of this chapter is to provide a "big picture" of an integrated audit. Topics introduced in this chapter are developed in greater detail later in this book.

The chapter begins with a discussion of integrated audits of public companies and distinguishes a public company audit from a financial statement audit of a nonpublic company. The environment and conditions necessary for an audit to be performed are discussed next, along with an overview of the stages of an audit. Then the chapter presents fundamental concepts that are important to understanding the process of auditing. A deeper look at the stages of an audit, including differences between audits of public and nonpublic companies is then presented. The chapter ends with a discussion of the 10 generally accepted auditing standards that are the underpinning for the more specific standards of the PCAOB and AICPA.

INTEGRATED AUDITS [LO 1]

This book focuses on audits of entities that must register with the Securities and Exchange Commission (SEC). Most of these entities are publicly traded companies. The term *publicly traded company* or *public company* is used to refer to any SEC registrant. Companies that are not publicly traded are also discussed and are called nonpublic companies.

The SEC is the regulatory agency that governs securities markets in the United States. As a result, the SEC has regulatory authority over public companies. Public companies file various reports with the SEC. Included in the required filings are audited financial statements and audited management reports on ICFR. The audit reports are also included in a company's SEC filings.

The term used to refer to an audit engagement examining both a company's financial statements and ICFR is an *integrated audit*. The auditor must perform an audit of the financial statements in order to audit ICFR. The audit must be an integrated audit because the Sarbanes-Oxley Act of 2002(SOX) requires that the two audits be a part of the same engagement.

The Public Company Accounting Oversight Board (PCAOB) has jurisdiction over firms that perform audits of U.S. public companies. As a part of this jurisdiction, the PCAOB is also responsible for setting the standards that auditors follow while performing audits of public companies. Audits of nonpublic U.S. companies are performed according to standards issued by the American Institute of Certified Public Accountants (AICPA). Firms that perform audits of both public and nonpublic companies follow the set of auditing standards that applies to each particular engagement.

SOX requires management of a public company to report on whether it believes the company's ICFR is effective. SOX also requires that management's report be audited. The SEC is charged with implementing and enforcing the requirements of SOX. The SEC and PCAOB have determined that an opinion on ICFR satisfies the SOX requirement of an audit of management's ICFR report. Therefore, the auditor of a public company issues an opinion directly addressing the effectiveness of ICFR. The auditor does not specifically issue an opinion on management's ICFR report. However, if the auditor disagrees with management's assessment of ICFR, this is disclosed in the audit report.

Companies that are not SEC registrants may choose to have their financial statements audited even though they are not required to report to the SEC. With the exception of certain financial services companies that are subject to regulatory requirements, nonpublic companies do not have to prepare reports on their ICFR.

The integrated audit of a publicly traded company is used as the basis for this book because it includes the audit of ICFR. When performing an audit of a nonpublic company, an auditor can omit the inapplicable steps and modify aspects of the broader PCAOB audit approach to perform only a financial statement audit.

AUDITING IN ACTION

Integrated Audits

SEC registrants are required to file audited financial statements and management reports on internal control over financial reporting.

Integrated audits are a single engagement examining both the financial statements and ICFR.

SOX requires that financial statements and internal control over financial reporting are examined through a single audit engagement.

The Public Company Accounting Oversight Board issues audit standards followed for audits of public companies.

The American Institute of Certified Public Accountants issues audit standards followed for audits of nonpublic companies.

By issuing an opinion on the effectiveness of internal control over financial reporting, an auditor satisfies the Sarbanes-Oxley Act requirement of an audit opinion on management's ICFR report.

If an auditor disagrees with management's assessment of the effectiveness of internal control over financial reporting, the auditor states this in the audit report.

Nonpublic companies often choose to have financial statement audits.

Except for when required by a regulatory agency, nonpublic companies do not typically have audits of internal control over financial reporting.

REVIEW QUESTIONS

A.1 What is the term for an engagement to audit both the financial statements and ICFR?

A.2 What entity sets standards for audits of U.S. public companies? Nonpublic companies?

A.3 What is the difference between audits performed under PCAOB and AICPA standards?

PRELIMINARY REQUIREMENTS FOR AN AUDIT [LO 2]

An integrated audit consists of examining (1) the effectiveness of internal control over financial reporting (ICFR) and (2) the fairness of the financial statements. Certain conditions must exist for an integrated audit to be possible. The first requirement is that benchmarks must exist against which ICFR can be compared for effectiveness, and the financial statements can be compared for fairness.

In the case of ICFR, a framework of internal control standards is used for comparison to assess the effectiveness of the company's ICFR. The Committee of Sponsoring Organizations of the Treadway Commission (COSO) Internal Control (IC) Framework is an example of an acceptable and a commonly used set of ICFR standards. In the case of financial statements, the content is typically compared to what is commonly called generally accepted accounting principles (GAAP). In a PCAOB audit report, accounting standards are referred to as accounting principles generally accepted in the United States of America. Financial statements can also be prepared using another basis of accounting, such as the International Financial Reporting Standards (IFRS). The financial statements are assessed against the standards on which they are based.

The auditor also needs guidelines on the manner in which the comparison and assessment is performed. These guidelines are called *audit or auditing standards*. Standards promulgated by the PCAOB for audits of U.S. publicly traded companies and by the AICPA for audits of nonpublic companies, provide guidance on how to perform an audit. The International Auditing and Assurance Standards Board (IAASB) also sets auditing standards. The AICPA and IAASB are currently committed to producing convergent sets of auditing standards.

Two other basic underlying requirements must be satisfied for ICFR and financial statement audits to be possible. First, the entity must have records that are sufficient for the auditor to gather evidence that can support conclusions. Second, the auditor must have reasonable confidence in management's integrity. If serious concerns exist about **management's integrity**, the auditor may conclude that the risk of **management misrepresentation** prevents the possibility of a successful audit.[1]

REVIEW QUESTIONS

B.1 What is the set of standards for internal control most frequently used in the U.S.?

B.2 What is the set of standards against which U.S.financial statements are usually analyzed in an audit?

B.3 What are the client prerequisites in order for an audit to be performed?

---

[1]A reference to AU indicates a paragraph number in the set of codified Statements on Auditing Standards (SAS) produced by the AICPA. The AICPA integrates all of the SASs together for easy reference. The AICPA audit standard codification for "non-issuers" is found on the AICPA Web site at www.aicpa.org. The PCAOB uses the same AU referencing system for its Interim Standards on auditing.

OVERVIEW OF AN INTEGRATED AUDIT [LO 3]

An integrated audit begins with preliminary engagement procedures and progresses to planning and risk assessment. Tests of ICFR operating effectiveness and substantive procedures of the financial statements follow. The audit is completed with-wrap up procedures and reporting.

Preliminary Engagement Procedures

An audit begins with preliminary engagement procedures including: (1) the process of client acceptance or continuance, (2) establishing an understanding about the terms of the engagement with the **client**, and (3) confirming the auditor's independence. Client acceptance is obviously the first step for a potential client. If the audit firm performed the audit in previous years, then it must decide whether to continue to audit the client.

Either situation requires an active decision process regarding whether to perform the audit for the company in the upcoming year. A number of client acceptance and continuance issues are considered. They address whether the auditor wants the company as its client, is willing to perform the engagement, and can do a good job performing the service. These topics are discussed in more detail in Chapter 5. If the audit firm and client company agree to terms of the engagement, the auditor completes the preliminary engagement procedures, including confirming the firm's independence. In a first-year audit engagement of a public company, the auditor is required to communicate about independence prior to accepting the engagement (PCAOB Rule 3526).

Planning and Risk Assessment

Next, the auditor performs activities labeled audit planning and risk assessment. In nonauditing environments, planning is typically viewed as a discrete task performed before the start of an activity. In auditing, the term *planning* is an umbrella term used for a number of processes that begin during client acceptance and continuance activities. Planning continues throughout the audit as new information causes the audit team to revisit and revise the audit plan. If new information suggests a need to reconsider the audit plan, the process becomes iterative. The auditor loops back to reconsider early decisions and make changes as needed.

In auditing guidance, the initial audit planning process is linked with risk assessment. This connection exists because as information is accumulated about the client, the auditor evaluates the information and makes decisions about the necessary audit procedures. The auditor plans procedures targeted at the "risks" of the client—risks such as important accounts, characteristics, and weaknesses, including the risk of fraud. Risks differ among companies. Client industry, size, information technology (IT) complexity, business activities, and transactions are characteristics that impact risk. Identifying, understanding and assessing risk is a major part of auditing. Once the auditor understands and assesses the important characteristics and risks of the company, the next step is designing the preliminary audit plan. The phrase audit strategy is also used to describe early risk assessment and planning. Conclusions about risk and the appropriate audit plan are often revised or updated as audit steps uncover new information.

The auditor gains the earliest information for risk assessment from the client acceptance and continuance decision process. Early in the engagement the auditor also performs specific steps to learn about the company's accounting information system. The auditor's primary focus when performing steps to understand the company is the accounting information system and particularly ICFR. The auditor may also extend the scope of activities used to understand the company to various parts of the comprehensive management information system.

AUDITING IN ACTION

Definitions of Information Systems

Management information system: The entire set of processes and procedures that management uses to collect and analyze information that is used for managing the business.

Accounting information system: A subset of the management information system that deals with processes and information that relate to accounting information and reports.

When an audit client is a public company, the auditor also performs engagements called reviews of the **interim**—usually quarterly—**reports** that are filed with the SEC. Interim financial statements are filed with the SEC using Form 10Q. Interim financial statement review engagements are an additional source of information that helps the auditor understand the client's information system.

In evaluating and reporting on the effectiveness of ICFR, management may produce and use documentation for its assessment process. Management's documentation can help the auditor understand the system and assess risk. The definition of ICFR communicates the links among a company's ICFR, its information system, and risks to fair financial reporting. ICFR is discussed extensively in various chapters throughout this book.

Definition of Internal Control over Financial Reporting:

Internal control over financial reporting is a process designed by, or under the supervision of, the company's principal executive and principal financial officers, or persons performing similar functions, and effected by the company's board of directors, management, and other personnel. The purpose is to provide reasonable assurance regarding the reliability of financial reporting and the preparation of financial statements for external purposes in accordance with GAAP and includes those policies and procedures that

1. Pertain to the maintenance of records that, in reasonable detail, accurately and fairly reflect the transactions and dispositions of the company's assets.
2. Provide reasonable assurance that transactions are recorded as necessary to permit preparation of financial statements in accordance with generally accepted accounting principles, and that receipts and expenditures of the company are being made only in accordance with authorizations of management and directors of the company; and
3. Provide reasonable assurance regarding prevention or timely detection of unauthorized acquisition, use, or disposition of the company's assets that could have a material effect on the financial statements.

Note: The auditor's procedures as part of either the audit of internal control over financial reporting or the audit of the financial statements are not part of a company's internal control over financial reporting.

(AS5.A5)

Once the auditor understands the system, the next step is to assess the design effectiveness of ICFR. To assess ICFR design effectiveness the auditor (1) considers the controls built into the system and (2) decides whether those controls are appropriate for the risks that are important to the company's business. This assessment of design effectiveness does not indicate whether those controls are operating as intended. It simply considers whether appropriate and sufficient ICFR is a part of the design of the accounting information system.

If the ICFR is not well designed, then there is more risk that the financial statements will be based on inaccurate information or will inappropriately represent the company's activities and financial position. Whether internal control is effectively designed impacts planning for the rest of the audit. For example, the auditor will not plan to test the function of controls that are not designed effectively. However, to compensate for risks when controls are not effective, the auditor plans to more thoroughly test amounts shown in the financial statements that may be affected by the lack of controls.

Planning for the financial statement audit requires the audit firm to consider the risk that the financial statements are materially misstated. A number of evaluations and analyses go into this risk assessment. Some of the information is obtained by the auditor during the client acceptance process. Other information is obtained during preliminary audit planning, direct risk assessment, understanding the system, and assessing ICFR design effectiveness. Information that can affect the audit plan is also obtained as a result of later testing.

Tests of ICFR Operating Effectiveness and Substantive Procedures

After risk assessment and audit planning, the audit proceeds to evidence-gathering steps called tests of controls and substantive audit procedures. An important part of the integrated audit is testing whether ICFR are operating as intended. At this point in the audit, the auditor has already assessed **design effectiveness**. Therefore, testing ICFR operating effectiveness is the next step that permits the auditor to come to a preliminary conclusion on overall ICFR effectiveness.

During the design effectiveness evaluation stage, the auditor might conclude that the ICFR are not effectively designed. If this happens, the auditor does not test the controls to see whether they function properly. Testing poorly designed controls is a waste of audit effort. Even if the auditor were to conclude that the controls operate well, poorly designed controls cannot help the company produce good financial information. The alternative outcome is that the auditor concludes that ICFR design is effective. During the controls testing stage, the auditor may also conclude that the controls operate effectively. This chain of events permits a preliminary overall conclusion that ICFR is effective.

The preliminary decision about ICFR effectiveness that results from controls testing is not final. The auditor also considers any relevant information obtained during the financial statement audit before coming to a final conclusion on the effectiveness of controls.

Procedures of the financial statement audit include activities called **substantive procedures** which examine the accounts and disclosures. During substantive procedures the audit firm may uncover evidence suggesting that the original audit plan is not based on an appropriate assessment of the risks; in other words, risks are higher than expected. Just as with ICFR procedures, if this occurs, the audit process becomes iterative. Risks are reassessed, the audit plan is revised, and new procedures are carried out. Depending on the findings, the auditor may decide that ICFR tests, as well as substantive procedures, need to be revamped.

After performing and evaluating controls tests and substantive procedures, the auditor tentatively concludes on the appropriate audit opinions.

Wrap-Up, Completion, and Reporting

Numerous final steps are required to complete the integrated audit. These include collecting overall information from management and the company's lawyers. The auditor is required to make specific communications to management and the audit committee of the Board of Directors.

At the completion of the final steps, the auditor issues a report. Several options exist regarding the format of the report. Opinions are issued on the effectiveness of ICFR and on the fairness of the financial statements. Exhibit 2-1 presents an overview diagram of an integrated audit.

EXHIBIT 2-1

Simplified Overview of
an Integrated Audit

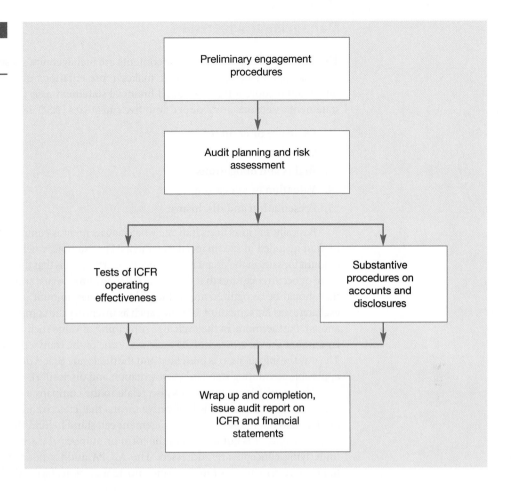

EXHIBIT 2-1

Simplified Overview of
an Integrated Audit

REVIEW QUESTIONS

C.1 What are preliminary engagement procedures?

C.2 What is the client acceptance and continuance process?

C.3 What is ICFR?

C.4 In general, how does the auditor obtain information about the client company for planning and risk assessment?

C.5 Why are audit planning and risk assessment considered together, early in the audit?

C.6 What does it mean when we say that an auditor assesses the design effectiveness of the system?

C.7 Why does audit planning continue throughout the audit? Give an example of why the auditor might revise planning after testing the operating effectiveness of a company's controls.

C.8 What audit results cause a preliminary conclusion that internal control over financial reporting is effective?

C.9 What are substantive audit procedures?

C.10 What are the final steps of an integrated audit?

FUNDAMENTAL CONCEPTS [LO 4]

Understanding the audit steps in greater detail requires knowledge of certain fundamental concepts related to audits. This section provides a brief introduction to these concepts.

Management Assertions

The financial statements and their contents are management's responsibility. By presenting financial statements, management makes representations about the financial statement information content that are called financial statement *assertions*. Management's financial statement assertions are grouped into five categories (AS 5.28):

1. **Existence or occurrence**
2. **Completeness**
3. **Rights and obligations**
4. **Valuation or allocation**
5. **Presentation and disclosure**

Basically, the assertions indicate what management is communicating through the information included in the financial statements. For example, when management shows a dollar amount for sales in the financial statements, an assertion is that those sales really occurred (existence or occurrence) and that they occurred in the time period when they are reported. All sales that should be recognized are included in the dollar amount presented (completeness). The exchange was for something of value, such as inventory the company owned (rights and obligations). Furthermore, in the exchange something of value such as cash was received. The dollar amount shown represents the exchange value of the transactions (valuation or allocation). The way the information is presented and the disclosure that is provided are in accordance with applicable accounting standards (presentation and disclosure).

The management assertions also relate to the company's internal controls. A management conclusion that ICFR is effective means that effective internal controls are designed, in place and operating so that management can stand behind the financial statement assertions. An auditor is not limited to the form or number of assertions used as long as the five underlying concepts are addressed. The AICPA audit guidance groups the management financial statement communications into 13 assertions (see Exhibit 2-2).

AUDITING IN ACTION

Management Assertions

Mike, Charles, and Ellen have had a lot of classes together but are in different auditing classes this term. Nevertheless, they decide to study together since they are using the same book. Charles is having a difficult time understanding his professor's discussion of the concept of management assertions and how auditors address them while performing an audit. Trying to explain it to Charles, Mike asks him, "If you are management and are responsible for the financial statements, what are you telling the financial statement reader by putting an amount on the 'Long Term Debt' line in the balance sheet." Mike responds, "I don't know; … that you owe the money?" Ellen agrees, but wonders if that is really the important assertion. "Wouldn't it be more important that the amount on the 'Long Term Debt' line shows ALL of the company's long term debt? That there hasn't been anything left out?"

At that point it all falls into place for Charles. "That's what my professor meant in class when she said that all of the assertions might not apply to every item in the financial statements and that some of them are more important for certain accounts than for others. For long term debt, even though management is stating that the company owes the liability—the existence assertion, the person using the financial statements is probably going to be at least as concerned that all the debt is included in the dollar amount—the completeness assertion. And since long -term debt is shown at net present value, it's important that a reasonable interest rate is used. So, the valuation assertion is involved, too. Plus, remember all the disclosure requirements that we learned when we studied debt last term? … and the rules about whether debt is presented as short or long term? So, the presentation and disclosure assertion is one that the auditor probably has to check out, too."

Audit Evidence

The independent auditor's goal is to obtain evidence that provides a reasonable basis for forming an opinion regarding the appropriateness of management's financial statement assertions and conclusions on the effectiveness of ICFR. **Audit evidence** can take the form of accounting data such as the general and subsidiary ledgers. Evidence can also be information that corroborates the accounting data such as invoices, contracts, and records of electronic funds transfers.

Corroborating information can be produced internally by the company or can come from third parties. Evidence can be the routine output of business activities, like invoices and contracts, or it can be produced specifically for the audit. An example of evidence produced specifically for the audit is that auditors often request outside parties to provide written confirmation of transactions and amounts included in a company's books and records. Evidence can be in paper or electronic form, or can even be provided orally. Direct personal knowledge obtained by the auditor through activities of inquiry and observation also provides evidence that corroborates accounting data.

Auditors' Use of Management Assertions

The auditor may reorganize and restate the PCAOB's five management assertions, as long as the important concepts are included. The AICPA states 13 management assertions to describe the same concepts that the PCAOB presents using 5. The AICPA structure includes one category of assertions for transactions activities, another about year-end account balances, and a third category on presentation and disclosure. Therefore, the AICPA's language provides another way to view the link between assertions, risk, audit procedures, and evidence.

The audit's purpose is to collect evidence to conclude as to whether managements' assertions are fair. Thus, the audit procedures have to address the risks that management assertions are not justified because the financial statements are in some way materially misstated. Exhibit 2-2 presents the AICPA's 13 management assertions.

AUDITING IN ACTION

Management Assertions Linked to Audit Evidence

Management assertions $\Rightarrow$ Risk of material misstatements $\Rightarrow$ Audit procedures $\Rightarrow$ Audit evidence

The AICPA assertions can be collapsed into the five PCAOB assertions. As a reminder, the PCAOB assertions are:

Existence or occurrence

Completeness

Rights and obligations

Valuation or allocation

Presentation and disclosure

Consider the following association between the PCAOB's 5 management assertions and the AICPA's 13 assertions shown in Exhibit 2-2. If transactions really occurred in the accounting period in which they are shown (existence or occurrence) and all transactions are recorded (completeness), then proper cutoff is achieved. Cutoff is an assertion

EXHIBIT 2-2

AICPA Management
Assertions

Classes of Transactions and Events for the Period under Audit
Occurrence. Transactions and events that have been recorded have occurred and pertain to the entity.
Completeness. All transactions and events that should have been recorded have been recorded.
Accuracy. Amounts and other data relating to recorded transactions and events have been recorded appropriately.
Cutoff. Transactions and events have been recorded in the correct accounting period.
Classification. Transactions and events have been recorded in the proper accounts.

Assertions about Account Balances at the Period End
Existence. Assets, liabilities, and equity interests exist.
Rights and obligations. The entity holds or controls the rights to assets, and liabilities are the obligations of the entity.
Completeness. All assets, liabilities, and equity interests that should have been recorded have been recorded.
Valuation and allocation. Assets, liabilities, and equity interests are included in the financial statements at appropriate amounts, and any resulting valuation or allocation adjustments are appropriately recorded.

Assertions about Presentation and Disclosure
Occurrence and rights and obligations. Disclosed events and transactions have occurred and pertain to the entity.
Completeness. All disclosures that should have been included in the financial statements have been included.
Classification and understandability. Financial information is appropriately presented and described and disclosures are clearly expressed.
Accuracy and valuation. Financial and other information are disclosed fairly and at appropriate amounts.
(AICPA AU 326.15)

used by the AICPA but not the PCAOB. If what is recorded actually occurred, then the recorded amount must be accurate. Accuracy is also used by the AICPA but not the PCAOB. If presentation and disclosure is proper, then classification—used by the AICPA—must also be correct. In addition, for presentation and disclosure to be appropriate, the disclosure must be understandable. Understandability is also specified by the AICPA but not the PCAOB.

In this book the 5 PCAOB management assertions are used but are sometimes augmented with the terms *authorization* and *cutoff* to simplify the explanations of audit procedures. Authorization means that a transaction that occurred was properly conducted by the entity because it was authorized or approved. Cutoff means that a transaction occurred or asset or liability existed, was recorded, and is presented and disclosed in the correct accounting period.

More Audit Concepts and Their Relationships

The auditor identifies specific **management assertions** that are relevant to an account or class of transactions. Then, the auditor assesses the expected levels of *risk* that the assertions are not appropriate. Based on the expected risk, the auditor decides on the **audit procedures.**

Assume an auditor is planning procedures for accounts receivable. Management's assertion about the existence of accounts receivable can be investigated by asking debtors if they agree that they owe the debts to the audit client and what amounts they owe. The auditor collects this **evidence** through a process called confirmation. The **confirmation process** consists of contacting the debtors, usually in writing, and asking them if they agree that they have payables to the company for the amounts specified. These confirmations collected by the auditor provide high-quality evidence on the existence of the receivables. However, this procedure provides limited evidence about the management assertion on valuation of the receivables. Just because a debtor acknowledges a debt does not mean that the debtor also intends and is able to pay it. The auditor uses other procedures to gather evidence on the value of the receivables.

The auditor collects evidence that pertains to management assertions, but is not able to examine support for every transaction or balance. Consequently, the auditor often selects a **sample** of all the transactions and performs audit procedures on that subset of the population. This approach is acceptable as long as the auditor exercises what is called **due professional care** in performing the work.

If an auditor lives up to all the audit guidance and standards while performing an audit, he or she is behaving with due professional care. An important part of behaving with due professional care is having an inquisitive and a skeptical frame of mind—also called **professional skepticism**. Using due professional care does not mean that the auditor has obtained **absolute assurance** that management's assertions are justified. Due professional care is linked to an expectation that the auditor has gained **reasonable assurance** about the financial statement management assertions.

Reasonable assurance is a high level of assurance. However, even if the auditor conducts the audit with due professional care, the auditor is not absolutely sure that management's assertions are justified. One detractor from absolute certainty regarding the auditor's conclusions is **professional judgment**.

Auditing involves many professional judgments, and auditors sometimes make **judgment errors**. Making judgment errors is different from behaving in a **negligent** manner. The auditor can exercise due professional care and still make judgment errors. Being negligent is what moves behavior to the realm of lacking due professional care. Even if something is later discovered to be wrong with the ICFR or financial statements that the auditor did not find during the audit, this does not necessarily mean that the auditor did not behave with due professional care or obtain reasonable assurance.

The exercise of due professional care allows the auditor to obtain reasonable assurance that the financial statements are **free of material misstatements**, whether the misstatements are caused by **error** or **fraud**. Also, due professional care allows the auditor to obtain reasonable assurance that there are no **material weaknesses** in ICFR. The specific definition of a material weakness in ICFR is discussed and used extensively in a number of later chapters. For now, assume that a material weakness in ICFR is an important indicator that the accounting information system may not always produce reliable financial information.

For several reasons, absolute assurance is not attainable. First, the nature of audit evidence may not allow for certain conclusions. For example, many financial statement numbers are based on estimates, and no evidence can identify the most accurate number. The second reason absolute assurance cannot be attained is that auditors often examine a sample rather than all of a company's transactions. The third reason is that those who commit fraud go to great lengths to conceal their actions. Consequently, auditors cannot have absolute assurance of finding fraud. Finally, regarding the choice and collection of evidence, auditors works within **economic limits**. In other words, although the auditor cannot omit collecting evidence that is vital, it is common to consider the *benefits and costs* of different approaches to gain evidence in an integrated audit. This **cost-benefit** trade-off is the reason that auditors often rely on samples.

An auditor is seldom convinced beyond all doubt about the appropriateness of management's assertions because evidence is typically only **persuasive** rather than **convincing**. Even if it is only persuasive, an auditor can conclude that the evidence is **sufficient** to be a basis for the audit opinion. The term *sufficient*, as used here, has the same general meaning it has in common use: as much as is needed. That is, sufficiency refers to the quantity of evidence needed.

To come to an opinion on management's assertions, the auditor must obtain evidence that provides both sufficient and appropriate support. As used in auditing, **appropriate** refers to the quality of audit evidence. In order to be appropriate, evidence must be both **reliable** and **relevant**. As the quality of evidence increases, the quantity of evidence needed to be sufficient may decrease.

The source of evidence impacts its reliability. Evidence from a source *outside the company* being audited is more reliable than evidence produced *internally*. Evidence obtained by the auditor through *direct personal knowledge* is more reliable than information learned secondhand. Also, internally generated evidence has higher reliability if the company producing the information has *good controls* in the accounting information system that creates and processes the information. *Original documents*, whether in paper or electronic form, are usually considered more reliable than photocopies and faxes. *Documentary evidence* is viewed as more reliable than *oral evidence*. For evidence to be relevant, it must relate to the audit conclusion being made. The auditor must determine what evidence is sufficient and appropriate based on professional judgment.

AUDITING IN ACTION

Important Concepts of Evidence

Sufficient ⟶ Refers to the quantity of evidence

Appropriate ⟶ Refers to the quality of evidence

Reliable and Relevant ⟶ Characteristics required for evidence to be competent

Reliability ⟶ Trustworthy source and manner of collection

Relevant ⟶ Relates to the audit issue being addressed

Materiality is defined in FASB Statement of Financial Accounting Concepts No. 2, Qualitative Characteristics of Accounting Information, as:

> The magnitude of an omission or misstatement of accounting information that, in the light of surrounding circumstances, makes it probable that the judgment of a reasonable person relying on the information would have been changed or influenced by the omission or misstatement. (CON 2-6)

The auditing standards flesh out the idea of materiality, although the description is still fairly abstract and theoretical.

> The concept of materiality recognizes that some matters, either individually or in the aggregate, are important for fair presentation of financial statements in conformity with generally accepted accounting principles. (AU 312.03)

The ICFR audit guidance adds no specificity, instead relying on the definitions already in place.

> …the auditor should use the same materiality considerations he or she would use in planning the audit of the company's annual financial statements. (AS 5. 20)

The PCAOB adds materiality concepts in instructing auditors on how to evaluate the importance of ICFR problems. When deciding if an ICFR problem is important, the auditor considers

> …the level of detail and degree of assurance that would satisfy prudent officials in the conduct of their own affairs. (AS 5. 70)

The lack of specificity in these descriptions of materiality is intentional. Accounting, auditing, and regulatory guidance all stresses that materiality decisions can only be made based on the judgment of the involved party who has all the information.

Materiality decisions are based on both quantitative and qualitative considerations. The FASB Concepts reference for materiality mentions magnitude. The magnitude reference means that the dollar amount of a misstatement impacts whether it is material. Larger misstatements are more likely to be important to a decision maker. In contrast, an example of qualitative materiality is a fraud carried out by management. The SEC's Staff Accounting Bulletin (SAB) No. 99 provides additional discussion of the concept of materiality, stressing quantitative and qualitative characteristics.

Materiality is a critical consideration in an auditor's work. If a misstatement exists within the financial statements, but it is immaterial, then the auditor can conclude that the financial statements are fair. If the problem is material, then the financial statements are not fair. Similarly, if ICFR problems exist but do not reach the threshold of material weakness, then ICFR is effective. If a problem with ICFR is a material weakness, then ICFR is not effective.

The representation in the auditor's standard report from a financial statement audit refers to financial statements being a **fair presentation**, in all material respects, in conformity with accounting principles generally accepted in the United States of America. The audit report statement indicates the auditor's belief that the financial statements taken as a whole are not materially misstated (AS 5.87). For the ICFR audit, the auditor's standard

AUDITING IN ACTION

Excerpts from SEC Staff Accounting Bulletin No. 99 on Materiality, August 12, 1999

The omission or misstatement of an item in a financial report is material if, in the light of surrounding circumstances, the magnitude of the item is such that it is probable that the judgment of a reasonable person relying upon the report would have been changed or influenced by the inclusion or correction of the item.

This formulation in the accounting literature is in substance identical to the formulation used by the courts in interpreting the federal securities laws. The Supreme Court has held that a fact is material if there is – a substantial likelihood that the... fact would have been viewed by the reasonable investor as having significantly altered the "total mix" of information made available.

Under the governing principles, an assessment of materiality requires that one views the facts in the context of the "surrounding circumstances," as the accounting literature puts it, or the "total mix" of information, in the words of the Supreme Court. In the context of a misstatement of a financial statement item, while the "total mix" includes the size in numerical or percentage terms of the misstatement, it also includes the factual context in which the user of financial statements would view the financial statement item. The shorthand in the accounting and auditing literature for this analysis is that financial management and the auditor must consider both "quantitative" and "qualitative" factors in assessing an item's materiality. Court decisions, Commission rules and enforcement actions, and accounting and auditing literature have all considered "qualitative" factors in various contexts....

The predominant view is that materiality judgments can properly be made only by those who have all the facts. The Board's present position is that no general standards of materiality could be formulated to take into account all the considerations that enter into an experienced human judgment.

[M]agnitude by itself, without regard to the nature of the item and the circumstances in which the judgment has to be made, will not generally be a sufficient basis for a materiality judgment....

(continued)

> Among the considerations that may well render material a quantitatively small misstatement of a financial statement item are –
> - whether the misstatement arises from an item capable of precise measurement or whether it arises from an estimate and, if so, the degree of imprecision inherent in the estimate
> - whether the misstatement masks a change in earnings or other trends
> - whether the misstatement hides a failure to meet analysts' consensus expectations for the enterprise
> - whether the misstatement changes a loss into income or vice versa
> - whether the misstatement concerns a segment or other portion of the registrant's business that has been identified as playing a significant role in the registrant's operations or profitability
> - whether the misstatement affects the registrant's compliance with regulatory requirements
> - whether the misstatement affects the registrant's compliance with loan covenants or other contractual requirements
> - whether the misstatement has the effect of increasing management's compensation – for example, by satisfying requirements for the award of bonuses or other forms of incentive compensation
> - whether the misstatement involves concealment of an unlawful transaction.
>
> This is not an exhaustive list of the circumstances that may affect the materiality of a quantitatively small misstatement....
>
> For the reasons noted above, the staff believes that a registrant and the auditors of its financial statements should not assume that even small intentional misstatements in financial statements, for example those pursuant to actions to "manage" earnings, are immaterial. While the intent of management does not render a misstatement material, it may provide significant evidence of materiality. The evidence may be particularly compelling where management has intentionally misstated items in the financial statements to "manage" reported earnings....

report also considers materiality, as it states a conclusion that the audit client maintained, in all material respects, effective internal control over financial reporting. (Recall that an example of an audit report is shown in Chapter 1.)

Audit risk for the integrated audit is the risk that the auditor may unknowingly fail to appropriately modify his or her opinion on financial statements that are materially misstated or on ICFR that is not effective. In other words, the auditor may conclude and report that financial statements are fairly presented when they are not. The auditor may also conclude and report that ICFR is effective when it is not. This audit risk of an incorrect opinion exists because the evidence collected permits reasonable, but not absolute, confidence in the conclusion.

REVIEW QUESTIONS

D.1 What is the relationship between management's financial statement assertions and audit evidence?

D.2 What is the relationship between due professional care and negligence?

D.3 Do auditors need to find immaterial financial statement misstatements?

D.4 What is sufficient competent evidence? What is the trade-off between sufficient and appropriate?

D.5 What is the difference between convincing and persuasive evidence?

D.6 How does the source of evidence affect its reliability?

D.7 When is evidence relevant?

D.8 What is audit risk?

PRELIMINARY ENGAGEMENT PROCEDURES [LO 5]

Audit firms often compete with one another to become the new auditor of a company. This occurs during what is called a **proposal** process. However, even before the proposal process, after a company announces that it is looking for a new auditor, potential new auditors must decide whether they want to propose on the engagement. This raises the question of why an audit firm might not always want whatever new work it can get. There are many reasons why it might not make sense for an auditor to propose on an engagement.

First, the audit firm must examine whether it wants the company as a client. Does the company have a good reputation? Based on everything the auditor knows, does it appear that management has a reputation for high integrity? Is the audit firm comfortable having its name associated with the business of the potential client? Are there obvious financial viability issues that cause the auditor to be concerned?

A potential client run by a CEO who served time in prison for financial fraud might be a client that an auditor wants to avoid. A company currently having serious financial difficulties might also be a potential client to reject. Sometimes a client is not willing to pay as much for the audit service as the audit firm thinks is appropriate.

The point is that not all potential clients may be good clients for a particular audit firm. Hypothetically, if there are no restrictions on the audit fee, every company can probably locate at least one auditor that is a good fit. Still, not every company and every auditor can be a good fit for each other, even with unrestricted audit fees.

If the audit firm is satisfied that the client will be a good addition to its client portfolio, the next step is to determine whether the firm can effectively perform the audit. This judgment includes issues such as whether the firm has expertise in the client's industry, and whether it has enough available personnel to assign to the audit during the time period when the work must be done. Sometimes a company is so large that an audit firm cannot sufficiently staff the audit. Or a company is in an industry that has very complex transactions and the audit firm does not have enough industry expertise to properly perform the audit. If the answers to questions about being able to perform the audit are positive, the auditor researches the client to try to verify that the information it has about the client is correct.

Even when the audit firm is not aware of anything negative about the client and understands the nature of the potential client's business and industry, that information is not enough. Whenever a public accounting firm audits a client, it accepts some level of engagement risk. This is the risk that being associated with the client will not be good for the accounting firm.

The public accounting firm conducts procedures to confirm its understanding of the client's situation to ensure that the risk of performing the engagement is within the range it is willing to accept. The audit firm conducts comprehensive discussions with the company about its organization and functioning. The audit firm also accesses other publicly available information about the company, as well as talking to the company's lawyers, bankers, and prior auditors. Media searches and other investigations may be performed. Sometimes auditors hire outside agencies to investigate a potential client.

When the audit firm is satisfied that the client is one that it wants, the emphasis shifts. Now, the audit firm tries to present a proposal that will cause the potential client to select it over other firms. Even though this part of the audit is referred to as client acceptance and continuance, the decision obviously does not lie entirely within the control of the audit firm. The audit firm "proposes" on the audit engagement. The proposal describes information such as who will be on the audit team, what experts the audit firm has available, and the financial payment the firm requires for the audit. After the company has heard from all the audit firms proposing to do its audit, it makes a decision. Exhibit 2-3 shows the important decisions leading up to the proposal.

The audit firm hired by the client begins its initial work. A contract, called an **engagement letter**, is drafted and signed. For an initial audit engagement of a public company, prior to executing the engagement letter the audit firm must communicate, in writing, with the client's audit committee about independence. The audit firm confirms its independence from the client and discusses any issues that might raise questions about independence. Requirements regarding auditor independence are discussed in Chapter 3.

EXHIBIT 2-3

Overview of Client Acceptance and Continuance

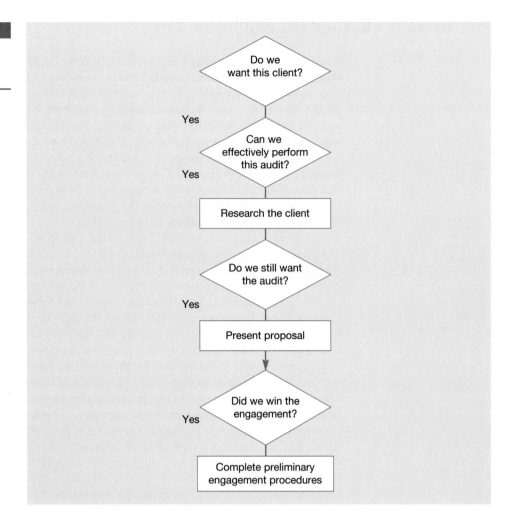

After these preliminary engagement procedures are complete, the audit firm plans who will work on or "staff" the engagement and the timing of the work. If the client is an SEC registrant, this planning must extend to work on the interim or quarterly financial information and any other SEC filings. Exhibit 2-4 summarizes preliminary engagement procedures.

EXHIBIT 2-4

Preliminary Engagement Procedures

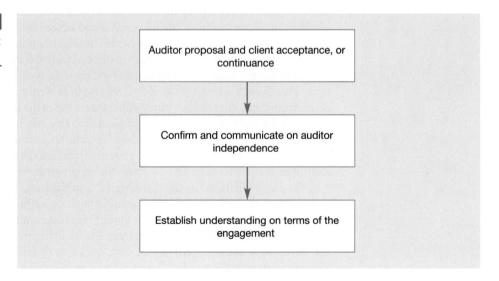

REVIEW QUESTIONS

E.1 What might influence an audit firm's decision about whether it wants a company as a client?

E.2 What considerations help the audit firm decide whether it can effectively perform an audit?

E.3 What is engagement risk? How does the auditor reduce this risk during the client acceptance process?

E.4 What are other preliminary engagement procedures beyond client acceptance and continuance?

AUDIT PLANNING AND RISK ASSESSMENT

Preliminary Audit Strategy

The planning and risk assessment process begins with initial decisions about staffing and timing, consideration of what amount or type of misstatement would make the company's financial statements materially wrong, and the beginnings of the overall audit plan. Then the auditor works to obtain an understanding of the client's business, activities, transactions, financial statement accounts, and information system. The auditor considers the "big picture" controls of the company, called **entity-level controls**. Before the auditor can progress with planning the audit, he or she must consider whether the company has ICFR that are well designed to deal with its risks.

As a part of understanding the financial statements to plan the audit, the auditor performs activities that are called **analytical procedures**. These procedures evaluate the company's financial information based on expected outcomes and relationships. For example, the auditor can compare the company to other businesses in the industry and to historical trends. The auditor also evaluates the possibility of fraud occurring in the client's business.

The auditing planning and risk assessment steps need to be performed even if the audit firm has audited the client in prior years. However, the steps are easier on a continuing engagement. The auditor can focus steps to update previous knowledge about the company with information about any changes the client has experienced.

Understanding the Company

The audit firm has three early sources of information on the company. First is any information obtained during client acceptance and continuance. Client acceptance includes obtaining a preliminary understanding of the client's business, its environment, and enough information about the client to propose on the engagement. This information provides a starting place. Information from prior years' audits is important in the continuance decision, and the continuance evaluation process refreshes the auditor's understanding of the company.

The second early source of information about a public company is work performed on the quarterly information filed with the SEC. This review work, though different and not as extensive as an audit, adds to the audit firm's understanding of the client's accounting information system. Review engagements are discussed in Chapter 16.

The potential third source of information that contributes to the auditor's understanding of the company is any of the client's own ICFR-related documentation. All public companies must include in their SEC filings a report by management regarding the effectiveness of ICFR. Management is required to have sufficient documentation to support its ICFR conclusion. To support its reporting process, management may construct or use documentation about the company's information system, ICFR, and tests performed. Although the extent of management documentation varies, the documentation can help the auditor understand the company's transactions and accounting information system. The audit firm uses various audit procedures to confirm that its understanding of the client system is correct.

Assessing Risk

After the auditor obtains an understanding of the client system, the next step is to begin assessing that information. The auditor asks company management about fraud risk and fraud controls, and considers the risk of fraud during a brainstorming session of the audit team. The auditor evaluates the company's financial statements and management's assertions. Using professional judgment, the auditor evaluates the importance of management's assertions to various components of the financial statements. The auditor accomplishes this evaluation after linking the financial statement accounts and internal controls to the important assertions. The important controls and assertions about financial statement accounts are tested in future stages of the audit.

Understanding and assessing entity-level controls is very important. An entity-level control is, for example, whether management requires employees to follow company procedures and enforces the requirement. Entity-level controls that are in place may reduce the overall risk that material financial statement misstatement will occur. Early consideration of entity-level controls is part of what the PCAOB calls a "top-down" audit approach.

AUDITING IN ACTION

Entity-Level Controls

Mike, Charles, and Ellen are having another study session. This time Mike is having a problem because he doesn't understand the concept of entity-level controls. Ellen did a group project on entity-level controls in her accounting information systems class, so she tries to explain. "Think about them as policies or rules that are enforced throughout the whole company. For example, a company that hires a lot of temporary labor would probably need to have a strict policy that before any of the departments can hire anyone the human resources department has to check out the potential employee's social security number to be sure the company doesn't violate any labor laws. Or a company that keeps a lot of customer financial information might have absolute protocols on encrypting the information no matter where in the company it is stored or used so the data won't get hacked and the company won't get sued."

Mike responds, "Ok, I understand that, but I thought these entity-level controls were supposed to be related to the financial statements." "Well, entity-level controls are related to internal controls over financial reporting—you know, ICFR. But those two examples I just gave you could be a source of huge contingent liabilities if they were not enforced. So, they affect the financial statements. You want another example? How about the controls over how the computer system pulls in information from all parts of the company and creates the financial statements at the end of the accounting period? And the company's rules about how adjusting journal entries get drafted and approved? Those would have to extend to the whole company. Even whether the company has a code of ethics that it enforces is an entity-level control that the auditor would look for."

The auditor assesses the design effectiveness of the specific ICFR that are linked to the important management assertions of the accounts and transactions. The audit question is, "Are the appropriate controls in place so that, if they are functioning properly, the system can be relied upon to produce reliable financial statements?" If the design of important controls is determined to be deficient, the auditor communicates this information to management as early as possible. Early identification increases the likelihood that management can resolve the problems by correcting the controls. Ideally, identification of design flaws occurs early enough during the year for management to correct any design problems before testing of ICFR operating effectiveness begins. The process through which management corrects internal control problems is often called **remediation**. If important controls are determined to have been designed effectively, controls tests indicate whether they operate effectively.

Audit Planning

After evaluating design effectiveness, the auditor likely has enough information to finalize the initial audit plan. With regard to the ICFR audit, this means the auditor can make an initial judgment of (1) which controls are important, (2) to what level those controls need to be functioning in order for them to be relied upon, and (3) how they should be tested. The auditor also utilizes the information collected up to this point to plan procedures on the financial statement account balances and disclosures.

An important audit activity throughout these processes is preparing documentation. Audit documentation must ultimately show the link of assertions to the results of audit procedures and support for the audit report. The auditor documents the procedures that are to be performed during an audit into the audit plan. At this point, the audit plan is more specific than what was begun at the time the engagement was started in the client acceptance phase. The audit plan document is sufficiently detailed to provide a guide to those members of the audit team who will actually perform the audit procedures.

The documentation process that was started in the preliminary engagement steps continues throughout the audit. By the time the audit is completed, documentation supports the auditor's conclusions regarding management assertions about the fairness of the financial statements and the effectiveness of ICFR. Exhibit 2-5 shows the steps in risk assessment and initial audit planning.

EXHIBIT 2-5

Audit Planning and Risk Assessment

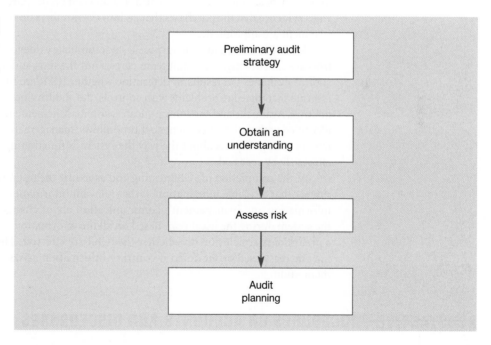

REVIEW QUESTIONS

F.1 How do planning and risk assessment procedures change in subsequent years after the auditor has already audited the client the first time?

F.2 What sources of information about the client company are available early in planning and risk assessment?

F.3 What procedure does the auditor use to assess the risk of fraud early in the audit?

F.4 What are entity-level controls? Why are they important?

F.5 What is remediation of internal control problems?

F.6 What is included in audit documentation? What is an audit plan document?

TESTS OF ICFR OPERATING EFFECTIVENESS

Audit tests are used to determine how well the important ICFR are functioning—in other words, to test the **operating effectiveness** of ICFR. These evidence-gathering procedures are called *tests of controls* and *dual purpose tests*. A test of a control is a test to determine whether a control is functioning as it is designed. A dual purpose test also collects information useful to the financial statement audit.

Assume a company has a control that states that its receiving clerks are only supposed to accept delivery of goods for which there is an approved purchase order. The auditor selects a sample of receiving reports and examines each one to see whether it is supported by the approved purchase order. If a receiving report is found for which there is no approved purchase order, this indicates that the control failed. The problem this failure indicates is that the company could be receiving and paying for goods that it does not really want or that are not authorized by management.

A dual purpose test takes this audit procedure further and examines information that can also be useful in the financial statement audit. The additional evidence collected with dual purpose tests informs the auditor about the appropriateness of dollar amounts recorded and disclosures. In the above test of receiving reports and purchase orders, the auditor also looks at the dollar amount on the purchase and related invoice, and uses that information for the financial statement audit. The dollar amount on the purchase order and invoice provides evidence that the purchases that go into the numbers on the balance sheet and income statement are appropriate.

Tests of controls and dual purpose tests accumulate evidence that indicates whether controls are functioning. The audit team carries out the tests and documents the results. The auditor evaluates the results to determine whether ICFR are functioning. If the outcomes indicate that there are problems with controls, the auditor does more testing to confirm the findings. Again, the auditor communicates with management, just as it did if problems were identified with design effectiveness. If time allows, management may change its control system, or change aspects about the way the system is functioning so that the ICFR function effectively by year end.

At the completion of ICFR testing and assessing the test results, the auditor also considers other available information. Other relevant information includes interim financial information and management's communication about changes that have been made to the system during the fiscal year. Based on all the information available, the auditor makes a preliminary conclusion on whether the ICFR are effective. This preliminary conclusion may be reassessed or modified if contrary information arises during the financial statement audit.

SUBSTANTIVE PROCEDURES ON ACCOUNTS AND DISCLOSURES

Sometime during the testing of ICFR operating effectiveness, the auditor begins substantive tests and procedures on the financial statement accounts and disclosures. For example dual purpose tests that collect evidence on ICFR operating effectiveness and account balances begin during early testing. Remember that results from the ICFR audit activities can cause the plan for the financial statement audit to be modified even before it starts, or after work begins.

The degree of ICFR operating effectiveness affects the type and amount of evidence-gathering procedures conducted during the financial statement audit. Analysis of ICFR design or testing for operating effectiveness may reveal problems with ICFR that are not or cannot be corrected by management. When this happens, the auditor does not have confidence that the financial statements are appropriate. As a result, the auditor does more substantive testing to determine whether the financial statement amounts and disclosures are fair.

The purpose of the audit of the financial statements is to express an opinion regarding whether the financial statements present fairly, in all material respects, the financial position and results of operations and cash flows for the years covered by the audit. The auditor is able to express an opinion on the financial statements after collecting and evaluating evidence on account balances and disclosures. The question the auditor seeks to answer is, "Does the evidence support the assertions management is making when it presents the company's financial statements?"

Many of the substantive procedures applied to the financial statements fall into the category called *tests of details of balances*. During these tests the auditor collects documentary evidence that supports the amounts in the client's records. Comparing documents and recorded amounts in tests of details of balances is commonly referred to as *vouching*. Ultimately, tests of details result in the auditor tying the amounts in the client's general ledger to those in the financial statements and evaluating the financial statement disclosures.

Analytical procedures, described earlier in the discussion of planning, can also be used to obtain evidence on accounts. When used for this purpose they are called **substantive analytical procedures**.

The substantive evidence-gathering procedures performed on accounts and disclosures that are decided on during the planning stage are partly driven by the characteristics of the transactions, account balances, related controls, and management assertions. For example, **inherent risk** is the term used to describe the risk that a financial statement amount is likely to be incorrect. Inherent risk is related to the nature of the account and the assertion.

Inventory has a low inherent risk related to existence. The auditor can see whether inventory exists. Similarly, the auditor can look at a purchase order and cancelled check to see that the company paid for the inventory. In contrast, inventory has a higher inherent risk related to valuation. The auditor cannot tell by looking at inventory, or by investigating the amount a company paid for inventory, whether its value has deteriorated lower than the recorded cost. Accounts payable have a lower inherent risk related to the assertion that they are an obligation of the company because the company is not likely to list a debt it does not owe. The greater inherent risk for accounts payable relates to the assertion of completeness. Omitting an account payable either intentionally or unintentionally is more likely than including a debt that does not exist.

Control risk is basically the risk that a misstatement is not prevented or that a misstatement that has occurred is not discovered by the ICFR. As stated earlier, if controls are poorly designed or do not operate well, there is a greater risk that a financial statement misstatement will occur. However, even if a control is well designed, control risk can be high if the control does not function as designed. When considered together, inherent risk and control risk are called the **risk of material misstatement**.

In documenting the audit plan, the auditor identifies needed audit procedures based on information or assumptions about inherent and control risks. The evidence-gathering procedures are designed to limit the probability that a material misstatement that exists will remain undetected by the audit. This possibility that a misstatement will be missed when audit steps are performed is called **detection risk**.

Detection risk is the risk that audit steps will miss (fail to detect) a misstatement that has occurred (inherent risk) and has slipped by the internal controls (control risk). The types of substantive audit procedures performed, the time of year at which they are performed, and the number of procedures are all related to the characteristics of the accounts and transactions, as well as the associated risks. The auditor considers inherent risk and control risk and decides the level of acceptable detection risk. Audit procedures are planned so that detection risk is not higher than the level determined to produce reasonable assurance about the auditor's conclusion. Generally, if the risk that material misstatement will occur is high, the auditor can accept only a very low risk that the audit procedures will fail to detect any misstatements.

One other characteristic of accounts and disclosures that affects the substantive procedures performed is materiality. As stated in the previous section that discusses planning, the auditor considers materiality in deciding on the audit plan. The auditor may decide that he or she needs to catch misstatements that are smaller. Another way to state this is that the materiality threshold is low on a particular account. When this happens, more extensive substantive procedures are performed in that phase of the audit. This is logical because you would expect it to take more audit work to detect small misstatements than to detect large misstatements.

The audit team completes the substantive procedures and assesses the results. Audit work papers document both the procedures and the conclusions about the findings. If the results indicate problems with the information in the financial statements, then the process becomes iterative. The auditor (1) reconsiders the available information, (2) reassesses risk, and (3) performs additional audit procedures. The additional audit procedures either confirm that the information in the financial statements is wrong, or indicate that the auditor's initial conclusions were wrong.

If the information in the financial statements is wrong or inappropriate, management corrects the financial statements. Problems with accounts identified during the financial statement audit may also require additional ICFR work, either by management or the auditor, or both. The auditor may need to reconsider the tentative conclusions made about the effectiveness of ICFR. Exhibit 2-6 recaps tests of operating effectiveness of ICFR. Exhibit 2-7 presents substantive procedures.

EXHIBIT 2-6

Tests of ICFR Operating Effectiveness

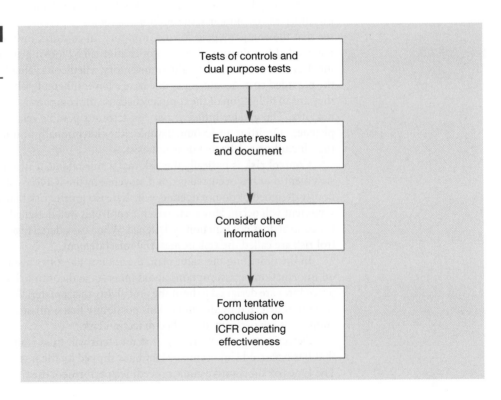

EXHIBIT 2-7

Substantive Procedures on Accounts and Disclosures

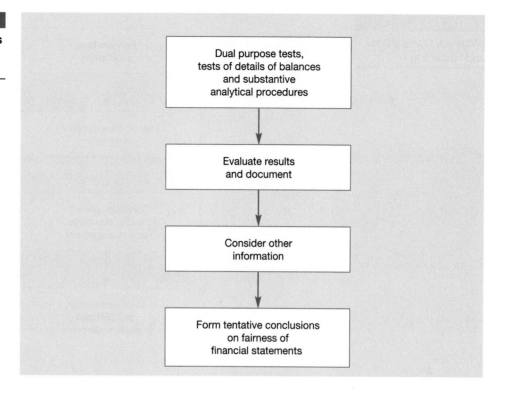

REVIEW QUESTIONS

G.1 What is a test of controls?

G.2 How does an auditor perform an analytical procedure? What might be an example?

G.3 How are tests of details of balances different from tests of controls and dual purpose tests? How are tests of details of balances related to evidence?

G.4 What is detection risk, and how does the definition relate to inherent risk and control risk?

WRAP-UP, COMPLETION, AND REPORTING

Additional audit steps are required to complete the audit. Wrap-up steps include communicating with the client's attorney and receiving assurance from the client that it has provided the auditor with honest information. Final review steps are also performed. When these steps are finished, the auditor should be able to determine whether ICFR is effective and whether the financial statements fairly present the company's financial position, results of operations, and cash flows. Based on these conclusions, the auditor decides on the appropriate audit opinions to issue.

The last audit steps prior to issuing the report involve various communications with the audit committee and management. Certain communications requirements have been in place for some time, such as on problems with internal control. Other communications respond to new requirements imposed by SOX, such as on the accounting treatments used by management. The auditor must also discuss his or her firm's independence with the audit committee. As stated earlier, independence is confirmed and communicated prior to accepting a first year-engagement of a public company. The specific time when it must occur on recurring audits is not designated. The auditor then issues the integrated audit report on ICFR and the financial statements. Exhibit 2-8 diagrams the audit wrap-up, completion, and audit reporting.

Wrap-up, Completion, and Reporting

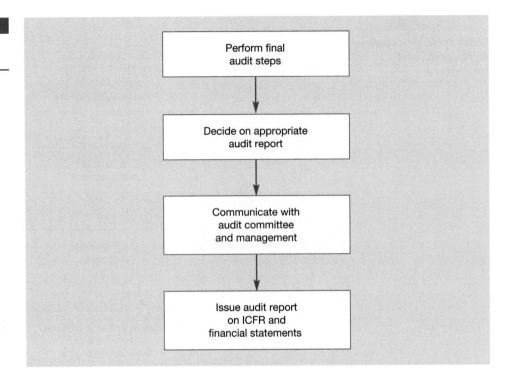

NONPUBLIC COMPANY AUDITS [LO 6]

Performing an audit of financial statements for a nonpublic company involves many of the same steps and procedures as an audit performed according to PCAOB standards. The fundamental difference is that an integrated audit according to PCAOB standards results in an opinion on both ICFR and the financial statements, whereas an audit based on AICPA standards reports an opinion only on the financial statements.

An audit according to AICPA auditing standards involves the steps related to client acceptance and continuance presented earlier. The audit firm decides whether it wants to be associated with the client and can effectively provide the services the client needs. A nonpublic company does not have the same publicly available information as a public company. Therefore, the auditor may have to use different sources of information. After the audit firm is engaged by the client to perform the audit, it goes through similar steps of understanding the client's business, understanding risks of the client's industry, and making an initial assessment of the company's fraud and other risks.

The auditor's purpose diverges from that of a public-company audit when the audit progresses to the step of understanding and assessing ICFR. In an audit of a nonpublic client, the auditor must go through the process of *understanding* the client's internal controls, similarly to the process carried out in a public-company audit. The auditor is required to identify the company's significant risks, whether or not those risks are addressed by ICFR. If ICFR does not mitigate the company's significant risks, the auditor pays even more specific attention to the significant risks during the substantive procedures of performing the financial statement audit (AICPA AU 314.110).

For a nonpublic company financial statement audit, the auditor assesses the internal control effectiveness solely for the purpose of planning and conducting the financial statement audit. This means that the auditor does not always test the operating effectiveness of ICFR of a nonpublic company. Because the auditor does not issue an opinion on ICFR, the purpose of assessing internal control is to determine whether or to what extent internal controls can be relied on in reaching a conclusion about the fairness of the financial statements. The auditor does not usually test the operating effectiveness of controls unless it is expected to be cost-beneficial by reducing the substantive procedures that need to be performed.

An exception to this cost-benefit rule is for companies, particularly those that rely heavily on complex IT, whose financial statements' fairness relies on ICFR. For this subset of companies, testing ICFR is mandatory to concluding on the financial statements. For these companies it is not an issue of relying on ICFR and reducing substantive procedures accordingly. In these situations the auditor simply cannot conduct enough substantive testing to have reasonable assurance that the financial statements are not materially misstated without also knowing that ICFR is effective.

If design of ICFR is assessed to be effective, and—based on testing—the functioning of the control system is also assessed to be effective, then the auditor may choose to rely on the controls in the financial statement audit. When relying on ICFR, the auditor usually adjusts the nature and timing or reduces the extent of substantive procedures. In this situation the change in substantive procedures is justified because of the lower level of control risk. The auditor receives some assurance on the financial statements from the effective functioning of the controls and some assurance from the substantive procedures. The auditor performs less substantive work because some of the audit assurance comes from the ICFR tests. When this is the audit plan, the ICFR tests and substantive procedures align closely with the audit of a public company.

For some clients, the auditor may choose to not rely on the ICFR. Consequently, the audit opinion is based primarily on tests of details of balances and substantive analytical procedures. This happens in several situations.

The first situation is when the controls are not designed effectively. The auditor does not test them for operating effectiveness because even if they operate effectively, they do not enhance the reliability and quality of the financial information. Recall that this situation can also exist for a public company audit.

The second situation is when the controls are designed effectively, but upon testing them, the auditor finds they do not operate as intended. Again, the auditor cannot rely on the controls to produce reliable and high-quality financial information. This set of circumstances can also exist for a public company audit.

The third situation is when the auditor of a nonpublic company determines that even if the controls are well designed and operate as intended, substantive procedures will not be significantly reduced. In this situation, testing the operating effectiveness is not cost-beneficial to the financial statement audit. This situation sometimes occurs on audits of public companies as well. In auditing a public company, the auditor may determine that it is not efficient to perform all or parts of the financial statement audit based on relying on ICFR. When this happens, the auditor examines ICFR only at fiscal year end to issue an opinion on the effectiveness of ICFR. The audit of information related to the rest of the year for the financial statement audit is conducted using substantive procedures.

When the auditor does not rely on ICFR to produce appropriate financial information, more audit time and effort is spent on substantive activities than when the auditor relies on ICFR. An important caveat is that even if an auditor does not rely on the functioning of the internal control system, the system must still be at least adequate to produce the information required for an audit to be possible. Also, as mentioned earlier, the auditor must still do enough ICFR-related work to identify the company's significant risks.

The foregoing concepts can be summarized as follows: Even for the financial statement audit of a nonpublic company, an auditor needs to understand the company, the business, and its internal control. Evaluating controls adds to the auditor's knowledge of significant risks to fair financial statement presentation. This knowledge in turn helps the auditor tailor the substantive audit procedures to collect and evaluate the needed amount of evidence regarding areas vulnerable to financial statement misstatement. For some companies, the

EXHIBIT 2-9

Overview of a Nonpublic
Company Audit

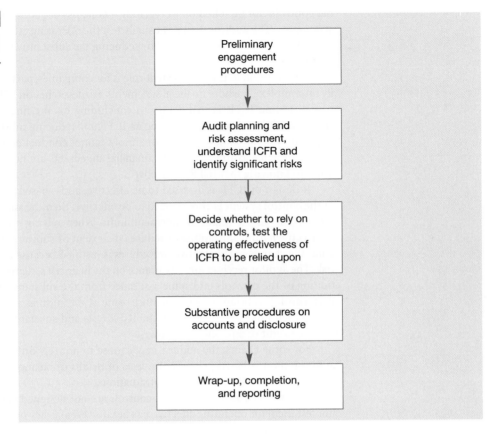

auditor may need to rely on ICFR to be able to complete the financial statement audit. In contrast, controls may be poorly designed or operate ineffectively, and consequently, be of no value to the financial statement audit. Regardless of control effectiveness, an auditor may choose to rely mainly on tests of details of balances and substantive analytical procedures because relying on controls will not increase the efficiency of the audit.

Other procedures in an audit performed according to AICPA auditing standards follow the same general path as a PCAOB integrated audit. Both require the same professional judgment on planning, risk, fraud assessment, and evidence. Both use the same procedures and testing approaches. The PCAOB has different standards related to documentation, and its reports use different wording. In addition, as mentioned earlier, the AICPA audit report covers only the fairness of the financial statements. Exhibit 2-9 presents an overview diagram of a nonpublic company financial statement audit. Although not shown in the diagram, an audit of a nonpublic company also involves continual reassessment and revision of the audit plan as needed, based on new information.

REVIEW QUESTIONS

H.1 What entity creates the auditing standards that are followed in the audit of a nonpublic company?

H.2 What is the fundamental difference in the audit purpose and reports for a public and nonpublic company?

H.3 Why might the auditor of a nonpublic company choose to omit testing of internal controls?

AUDITING IN ACTION

Standard Nonpublic Company Financial Statement Audit Report

Independent Auditor's Report

We have audited the accompanying balance sheets of X Company as of December 31, 20X2 and 20X1, and the related statements of income, retained earnings, and cash flows for the years then ended. These financial statements are the responsibility of the Company's management. Our responsibility is to express an opinion on these financial statements based on our audits.

We conducted our audits in accordance with auditing standards generally accepted in the United States of America. Those standards require that we plan and perform the audit to obtain reasonable assurance about whether the financial statements are free of material misstatement. An audit includes examining, on a test basis, evidence supporting the amounts and disclosures in the financial statements. An audit also includes assessing the accounting principles used and significant estimates made by management, as well as evaluating the overall financial statement presentation. We believe that our audits provide a reasonable basis for our opinion.

In our opinion, the financial statements referred to above present fairly, in all material respects, the financial position of X Company as of [at] December 31, 20X2 and 20X1, and the results of its operations and its cash flows for the years then ended in conformity with accounting principles generally accepted in the United States of America.

[*Signature*]

[*Date*]

(AICPA AU 508.08)

AUDITING STANDARDS [LO 7]

The audit processes discussed in this chapter are supported by a variety of standards set by the PCAOB and for nonpublic companies by the AICPA. Detailed standards of the PCAOB are called Auditing Standards (AS) and are numbered sequentially based on when they were released. To date, seven PCAOB Auditing Standards have been released, although the second one which addressed ICFR audits was superseded by the fifth one on the same topic. The PCAOB standards can be accessed on its Web site, *www.pcaobus.org*. Auditing standards released by the AICPA are called Statements on Auditing Standards (SAS) and are also numbered sequentially based on their release date. A codification of the SAS is also available, and references in this format are labeled as AU sections.

After the PCAOB was formed as a result of SOX, it adopted all of the AICPA auditing standards. The PCAOB modifies or supersedes the AICPA auditing standards on an ongoing basis as a result of the development of **PCAOB Auditing Standards**. To find the auditing standards that were originally authored by the AICPA and were adopted (and may have since been modified) by the PCAOB, select Interim Standards on the PCAOB Web site. AICPA **Statements on Auditing Standards** are found on the AICAP Web site at *www.aicpa.org*.

Collectively, the AS and SAS provide fairly specific guidance on audit procedures. However, they are all based on 10 underlying standards, called **generally accepted auditing standards (GAAS)**. The 10 GAAS for financial statement audits are grouped into three sections called general, field work, and reporting standards. AS 5, *An Audit of Internal Control Over Financial Reporting That Is Integrated with an Audit of Financial Statements*, states that it provides the field work and reporting standards for the ICFR audit of an integrated audit:

> The general standards are applicable to an audit of internal control over financial reporting. Those standards require technical training and proficiency as an auditor, independence, and the exercise of due professional care, including professional skepticism. This standard establishes the fieldwork and reporting standards applicable to an audit of internal control over financial reporting. (AS5.4)

The 10 GAAS[2] are:

General Standards

1. The audit is to be performed by a person or persons having adequate technical training and proficiency as an auditor.
2. In all matters relating to the assignment, an independence in mental attitude is to be maintained by the auditor or auditors.
3. Due professional care is to be exercised in the performance of the audit and the preparation of the report.

Standards of Field Work

1. The work is to be adequately planned and assistants, if any, are to be properly supervised.
2. A sufficient understanding of internal control is to be obtained to plan the audit and to determine the nature, timing, and extent of tests to be performed.
3. Sufficient appropriate evidential matter is to be obtained through inspection, observation, inquiries, and confirmations to afford a reasonable basis for an opinion regarding the financial statements under audit.

Standards of Reporting

1. The report shall state whether the financial statements are presented in accordance with generally accepted accounting principles (GAAP).
2. The report shall identify those circumstances in which such principles have not been consistently observed in the current period in relation to the preceding period.
3. Informative disclosures in the financial statements are to be regarded as reasonably adequate unless otherwise stated in the report.
4. The report shall contain either an expression of opinion regarding the financial statements, taken as a whole, or an assertion to the effect that an opinion cannot be expressed. When an overall opinion cannot be expressed, the reasons therefore should be stated. In all cases where an auditor's name is associated with financial statements, the report should contain a clear-cut indication of the character of the auditor's work, if any, and the degree of responsibility the auditor is taking. (PCAOB AU 150.02)

Both the PCAOB and AICPA provide instructions on the interpretation of certain words that are used in the auditing standards. Exhibit 2-10 displays the instructions as they are provided in PCAOB Rule 3101. The terms "must," "shall," and "is required" indicate that the audit procedure is mandatory. This is described as an "unconditional responsibility" of the auditor. The term "should" indicates a "presumptively mandatory" responsibility. The auditor must carry out an action that is presumptively mandatory unless other actions are followed that accomplish the same objectives. The auditor is responsible for documenting how any alternative actions satisfy the objectives of the standard for any presumptively mandatory responsibilities.

Under the PCAOB rule the terms "may," "might," and "could" indicate when the auditor has a responsibility to consider the action. The rule states that these words establish that an auditor needs to pay attention to and understand an item, but specific action is not required. Use of the term "should consider" means that the auditor has a presumptive responsibility to consider the action but not to carry it out.

AICPA AU 120 uses slightly different language to describe mandatory and presumptively mandatory responsibilities, but the meaning is the same. In the AICPA standard the terms "may," "might," and "could" are associated with what is called explanatory language, but the meaning is similar to that stated by the PCAOB.

---

[2]The AICPA amended the GAAS, and these amendments have not been made by the PCAOB. The amendments do not change the substance of the standards. They update the language and wording. The amended AICPA GAAS are presented in Appendix A to this chapter.

EXHIBIT 2-10

Explanation of Terms
Used in the Standards

(1) **Unconditional Responsibility:** The words "must," "shall," and "is required" indicate unconditional responsibilities. The auditor must fulfill responsibilities of this type in all cases in which the circumstances exist to which the requirement applies. Failure to discharge an unconditional responsibility is a violation of the relevant standard and Rule 3100.

(2) **Presumptively Mandatory Responsibility:** The word "should" indicates responsibilities that are presumptively mandatory. The auditor must comply with requirements of this type specified in the Board's standards unless the auditor demonstrates that alternative actions he or she followed in the circumstances were sufficient to achieve the objectives of the standard. Failure to discharge a presumptively mandatory responsibility is a violation of the relevant standard and Rule 3100 unless the auditor demonstrates that, in the circumstances, compliance with the specified responsibility was not necessary to achieve the objectives of the standard.

 ...In the rare circumstances in which the auditor believes the objectives of the standard can be met by alternative means, the auditor, as part of documenting the planning and performance of the work, must document the information that demonstrates that the objectives were achieved.

(3) **Responsibility to Consider:** The words "may," "might," "could," and other terms and phrases describe actions and procedures that auditors have a responsibility to consider. Matters described in this fashion require the auditor's attention and understanding. How and whether the auditor implements these matters in the audit will depend on the exercise of professional judgment in the circumstances consistent with the objectives of the standard....If a Board standard provides that the auditor "should consider" an action or procedure, consideration of the action or procedure is presumptively mandatory, while the action or procedure is not. (PCAOB Rule 3101)

General Standards

Training and Proficiency   The first general standard refers to an individual being appropriately qualified as an auditor in a general sense, as well as being appropriately knowledgeable for a specific audit engagement. Graduating with a university accounting degree and meeting any state licensing standards typically are considered the minimum requirements. Meeting state licensing requirements is not required to work on an audit engagement under a licensed auditor, but is required of the individual taking ultimate responsibility for the engagement. Auditors also participate in continuing education to stay current on professional information. The auditor ultimately responsible for any engagement must also have sufficient experience as an auditor and appropriate expertise in the client industry.

This standard also relates to the first field work standard indicating that the responsible auditor must supervise those working on the engagement who may not personally have sufficient knowledge and experience. Working under an experienced auditor who has an appropriate level of proficiency for the engagement may mean that the assistant needs less specific knowledge and experience than he or she would need if working alone.

Independence   The second general standard states that an auditor is to have "an independence in mental attitude" in all matters relating to the engagement. Since one of the primary purposes of an audit is to increase user confidence in the financial statements, this independence of thought is critical. Basically, the auditor should not be biased in any way—either positive or negative—or have any preconceived expectations regarding the outcome of the audit.

Although the independence standard refers to an independence in mental attitude, this is not a construct that can be evaluated or enforced. Therefore, numerous rules are in place defining behavior that is consistent with an appearance of independence. These enforceable rules of independence are covered in detail in Chapter 3.

Due Professional Care   The third general standard states that an audit is to be planned and performed with due professional care. Due professional care should be used in preparing the audit report. This concept was discussed earlier in the chapter as being the opposite of behaving in a negligent manner. Auditors should not only follow the guidance in the professional standards, but should be alert and diligent in performing their duties.

Standards of Field Work

Planning and Supervision   The first standard of field work states that the work should be adequately planned. Some of the auditors working on most engagements are considered assistants to the auditor responsible for the audit. For example, staff auditors at all levels are ultimately responsible to the partner in charge of the engagement. The work of those auditors who are assistants to the responsible auditor should be properly supervised.

The standards of field work refer to the work that is done "in the field" or at the site of the client's business. However, significant planning may be done before going to the client site and is also covered by the standard. The field work standards apply to all activities of a particular audit engagement apart from reporting.

In an audit team environment, each person's work is reviewed and approved by a person at a higher level. This not only provides required supervision, but also contributes to the training called for by the first general standard.

For an ICFR audit, AS 5 provides guidance related to planning and supervision, and specifically states: "The auditor should properly plan the audit of internal control over financial reporting and properly supervise any assistants" (AS 5.9).

Understanding   The second standard of field work refers to the auditor's need to understand the client and evaluate internal control in order to appropriately consider the interaction between the functioning of internal control and the fairness of the financial statements. The language requires a broad understanding of the entity, its environment and internal control as a basis for designing an audit of financial statements. This is very consistent with the risk assessment that is linked to audit planning. The ICFR audit guidance in AS 5 also requires a broad understanding of the company, its environment, and ICFR.

Evidence   The third standard of field work requires the auditor to obtain enough evidence that is of high enough quality on which to base the audit opinion. As was discussed earlier in this chapter, sufficient basically means that the auditor has gathered enough information, while appropriate and competent refer to the quality of the evidence gathered. AS 5 discusses sufficient evidence as part of describing how the audit should be integrated and presents the objectives of tests of controls as:

> To obtain sufficient evidence to support the auditor's opinion on internal control over financial reporting as of year-end, and to obtain sufficient evidence to support the auditor's control risk assessment for purposes of the audit of financial statements. (AS 5.7)

Reporting Standards

The first reporting standard requires the auditor to state whether the financial statements are presented in accordance with GAAP or another basis of accounting. Although U.S. GAAP is the basis of accounting most often used in the preparation of U.S. financial statements, other standards such as IFRS or industry-specified standards are sometimes used as the basis of presentation. When this is the case, the alternative presentation basis is stated. The second reporting standard requires that if there are any changes in the accounting principles used in the years covered by the report, those changes be identified and disclosed. The third standard of reporting takes a silent approach to dealing with disclosures. This standard states that the auditor does not have to mention the disclosures unless they are not reasonably adequate.

The last standard of reporting states that the auditor must express an opinion or clearly decline from giving one. If no opinion is given, the auditor is said to "disclaim" an opinion, and he or she must explain why this is happening. This standard also addresses when an auditor is "associated" with the financial statements. An auditor is "associated" when he or she has performed any work related to financial statements; as a result, the accompanying audit report must state what the work was. The auditor's report must clearly state whether the report is providing audit assurance, some other level of assurance, or no assurance at all.

With regard to reporting on an audit of ICFR, AS 5 states the following:

> The auditor should form an opinion on the effectiveness of internal control over financial reporting by evaluating evidence obtained from all sources, including the auditor's testing of controls, misstatements detected during the financial statement audit and any identified control deficiencies. (AS 5.71)

> The auditor may form an opinion on the effectiveness of internal control over financial reporting only when there have been no restrictions on the scope of the auditor's work. A scope limitation requires the auditor to disclaim an opinion or withdraw from the engagement. (AS 5.74)

AS 5 then goes on to specify the content of the auditor's report, manner of presentation, and reason for which the auditor should change the standard report.

REVIEW QUESTIONS

I.1 What are the generally accepted auditing standards, and what do they mean?

I.2 What is the source of the field work and reporting standards for an audit of ICFR?

CONCLUSION

An integrated audit is a professional engagement to report on the fairness of a company's financial statements and the effectiveness of its ICFR. The activities of an audit generally proceed from contracting with the client to planning and risk assessment, testing and other procedures, then forming an opinion and reporting. These activities are discussed in detail in later chapters. Many of the activities of an integrated audit are described with terms that have a particular meaning in the auditing context, and are explained in the professional standards. Although there is a lot of detail in the guidance provided to auditors, the underpinning for those procedures is the GAAS, consisting of general, field work, and reporting standards.

KEY TERMS

Absolute assurance. A level of certainty that is never attained on an audit.

Accounting information system. Generally refers to the portion of the management information system that collects data and produces information and reports relevant to the internal accounting needs of the company as well as to external financial reporting.

AICPA Statements on Auditing Standards (SAS). Guidance and rules of the AICPA Auditing Standards Board on conducting audits and issuing reports; since the creation of the PCAOB, SAS modified by the PCAOB apply only to audits of nonpublic companies.

Analytical procedures. Tests addressing comparisons and relationships, including, current year, prior year, budgets, nonfinancial data, and industry information. Intended to highlight the reasonableness of account balances and other data.

Appropriate. Evidence must be both sufficient and competent in order to be persuasive to an auditor. Competent evidence must be both reliable and relevant; pertinent to the goal of the specific audit procedure.

Audit evidence. See Evidence.

Audit procedures. A general term that refers to any audit activities other than acceptance and continuance, planning and reporting.

Audit plan. Document containing the specific audit procedures to be performed during the course of the audit.

Audit risk. The risk that the auditor will fail to appropriately modify the audit opinion when it should be modified due to problems with internal control over financial reporting or materially misstated financial statements.

Client. An entity for which a CPA performs an audit.

Completeness. A management assertion that the financial statement account presentation includes all of the transactions and amounts that should be included for the period covered.

Confirmation process. The process used by an auditor to gain independent verification of information; may be oral but is usually in writing.

Control risk. The risk that a material misstatement that could occur in an account will not be prevented or detected on a timely basis by internal control.

Convincing. Not attained on an audit; evidence is persuasive rather than convincing.

Cost-benefit. A trade-off evaluation for the cost of collecting evidence and the value the evidence presents to the audit; appropriately considered only when the audit goals can be attained in a less costly manner.

Design effectiveness. Exists when controls functioning as intended cause internal control objectives to be achieved. Controls must be appropriate for the goals, and the system must include all of the controls needed to accomplish the objectives.

Detection risk. The risk that the auditors' procedures will lead them to conclude that an internal control or a financial statement assertion is not materially incorrect when it is.

Due professional care. All aspects of the audit are to be conducted with due professional care. Indicates the auditor should be diligent, alert, and careful. Behaving in accordance with due professional care eliminates negligence but is no guarantee against professional judgment errors. Is linked to the concept of having obtained reasonable assurance about management's assertions.

Economic limits. One of the constraints that causes an audit to reach only the level of reasonable assurance.

Engagement letter. A written document summarizing the contract between the auditor and client.

Entity-level controls. Controls that are implemented throughout an entire business.

Error. In an audit sense, refers to a financial statement misstatement other than fraud; the audit report refers to financial statements being free of material misstatements whether they result from either error or fraud.

Evidence. All the information used by the auditor in arriving at the conclusions on which the audit opinion is based.

Existence or occurrence. Management assertion that assets and liabilities exist and that transactions represented in the financial statement presentation occurred.

Fair presentation. Generally, this term means that financial statements are presented fairly because they follow the requirement of GAAP. However, theoretically, departures from GAAP may be justified and appropriate if following GAAP prevents a fair presentation.

Fraud. Intentional misstatement of financial statements, or theft of assets. Management is usually responsible for intentional misstatement of financial statements, whereas either employees or management can commit theft.

Generally Accepted Auditing Standards (GAAS). Ten standards, divided into general, field work, and reporting standards, adopted by the AICPA and PCAOB guiding financial statement audit work. The general standards also apply to ICFR audits, whereas AS 5 provides the field work and reporting standards for ICFR audits.

Inherent risk. The risk of material misstatement of a financial statement assertion, assuming there were no related controls.

Interim reports. Financial statements and reports that cover less than a year; usually refers to a quarterly report.

Internal controls over financial reporting. Controls that address the objective of reliable financial reporting.

Judgment errors. Human errors in judgment made during decision processes; in an auditing context, refers to errors made in professional decisions.

Management assertions. The communications that management makes by preparing financial statements; PCAOB uses 5 management assertions, and the AICPA uses 13 management assertions.

Management information system. The information system, including any computer and IT aspects, that provides information to the company. The accounting information system is a subset of the management information system.

Management integrity. Refers to the attitudes toward ethics and honesty held by management.

Management misrepresentation. Material misstatement of financial statements by management, with the intent to mislead financial statement users.

Material financial statement misstatement. A misstatement in financial statements, either from error or fraud that meets the definition of being material.

Material weakness. Refers to a problem with ICFR that is serious enough to be important; reflects the possibility that the financial statements could have a material misstatement.

Materiality. Refers to the magnitude of an omission or misstatement of accounting information that, in the light of surrounding circumstances, makes it probable that the judgment of a reasonable person relying on the information would have been changed or influenced by the omission or misstatement; based on both qualitative and quantitative considerations.

Negligence. From a legal standpoint, the violation of a duty to exercise a degree of care that an ordinarily prudent person would exercise in a similar situation. In an audit sense, negligence is behaving with a lack of due professional care.

Operating effectiveness. Refers to whether internal controls over financial reporting function as they are designed to.

PCAOB Auditing Standards (AS). Standards written and issued by the PCAOB for public company audits.

Persuasive. Indicates the degree that the auditor is convinced the evidence supports the audit opinion; the auditor is typically persuaded rather than convinced.

Presentation and disclosure. Management assertion that components of the financial statements are properly presented, described, and disclosed.

Professional judgment. Human judgment made during decision processes; in an auditing context refers to professional decisions.

Professional skepticism. Having an objective attitude and a questioning mind while considering audit issues and audit evidence.

Proposal. The CPA firm's presentation to the potential client detailing its plan to perform the audit engagement and the estimated costs.

Reasonable assurance. A term referring to a high, but not absolute, level of assurance that the auditor obtains about management assertions.

Relevant. A quality of audit evidence. In order for evidence to be appropriate, it must be relevant. Relevant means that the evidence relates to the audit objective.

Reliable. A quality of audit evidence. In order for evidence to be relevant, it must be reliable. Evidence is more valid if it comes from a reliable source. Considerations for assessing reliability include whether the evidence comes from an outside objective party, was generated under conditions of strong internal control, and was the result of direct personal knowledge of the auditor.

Remediation. The process whereby a company corrects problems with its internal control.

Rights and obligations. A management assertion that assets and liabilities shown in the financial statements are real rights and obligations of the entity.

Risk of material misstatement. Inherent risk and control risk considered together; the risk that a misstatement in an account results because it is not prevented or detected by internal controls.

Sample. When the auditor bases an audit conclusion on a segment of the population of transactions or balances being analyzed.

Substantive procedures. Audit procedures that affect the financial statement audit.

Sufficient. Audit evidence that provides enough support for a conclusion.

Valuation or allocation. A management assertion that the amounts shown in the financial statements represent the proper value or allocated amount based on GAAP.

MULTIPLE CHOICE

2-1 **[LO 4]** When an auditor performs procedures to determine that a company has shown all of its liabilities on its year-end financial statements, the related management assertion is

(a) existence or occurrence.

(b) completeness.

(c) rights and obligations.

(d) presentation and disclosure.

2-2 **[LO 4]** For the accounts receivable account, consider management's assertion about "valuation." The audit objective for this assertion would be

(a) to determine that all accounts receivable are posted.

(b) to determine that the dollar amount posted is correct.

(c) to determine that the allowance for doubtful accounts is fair.

(d) all of the above.

2-3   **[LO 4]** In order for evidence to be sufficient it must be

(a) persuasive.

(b) convincing.

(c) competent.

(d) from an outside third party.

2-4   **[LO 4]** Evidence that is

(a) valid will usually be competent.

(b) relevant will usually be sufficient.

(c) sufficient is relevant.

(d) competent will usually be sufficient.

2-5   **[LO 4]** A change in the financial statement that causes a reasonable person to change a decision is

(a) persuasive.

(b) valid.

(c) material.

(d) negligent.

2-6   **[LO 4]** The risk that an auditor may unknowingly fail to modify his or her opinion on financial statements that are materially misstated is

(a) detection risk.

(b) opinion risk.

(c) inherent risk.

(d) audit risk.

2-7   **[LO 3]** An engagement letter

(a) is the client's copy of the audit plan.

(b) is drafted and agreed upon at the beginning of the audit.

(c) is received by the auditor indicating the company wishes to receive proposals for an audit engagement.

(d) informs the client's attorneys about the change in auditors.

2-8   **[LO 5]** When the auditor considers whether a company's controls are capable of preventing errors, the auditor is

(a) performing tests of controls.

(b) documenting the system.

(c) assessing design effectiveness.

(d) performing dual purpose tests.

2-9   **[LO 5]** Analytical procedures are

(a) used during the planning stage of the audit.

(b) used throughout the audit of the financial statements.

(c) designed to consider relationships.

(d) all of the above.

2-10   **[LO 1, 6]** A non-PCAOB audit

(a) is performed on a nonpublic company.

(b) is acceptable to the SEC.

(c) ignores internal controls.

(d) none of the above.

2-11   **[LO 7]** All of the 10 generally accepted auditing standards apply to

(a) a financial statement audit.

(b) an ICFR audit.

(c) a nonpublic company audit only.

(d) all parts of an integrated audit.

2-12   **[LO 5]** The PCAOB top-down approach to an integrated audit

(a) ignores entity-level controls.

(b) relies entirely on entity-level controls.

(c) considers entity-level controls because they may reduce risk.

(d) was created for nonpublic company audits.

2-13   **[LO 5]** Audit planning

(a) occurs at the beginning of the engagement only.

(b) is revisited throughout the audit as more information is obtained.

(c) is conducted separately for the financial statement and ICFR audits.

(d) must be completely documented before the audit begins.

2-14   **[LO 4]** The definition of materiality can include all of the following except

(a) amounts that will not make a difference.

(b) prudent officials.

(c) reasonable persons.

(d) individual or aggregated matters.

2-15   **[LO 4]** Reasonable assurance means

(a) absolute assurance.

(b) a low level of assurance.

(c) a high level of assurance.

(d) cannot be determined.

2-16   **[LO 3, 5]** Tests of controls

(a) can be combined with substantive procedures.

(b) apply only to the financial statement audit.

(c) are only important to a public company audit.

(d) include analytical procedures.

2-17   **[LO 5]** Management and the auditor

(a) do not communicate until the engagement is finished to prevent bias.

(b) must have an adversarial relationship during the audit.

(c) both provide reports on ICFR.

(d) are both members of the audit committee.

2-18 **[LO 5]** Design effectiveness of ICFR

(a) is evaluated to determine which controls to test for operating effectiveness.

(b) is not important as long as operating effectiveness is tested.

(c) never has to be considered in a nonpublic company audit.

(d) is tested after substantive procedures are completed.

2-19 **[LO 5, 6]** An auditor's report at the completion of an engagement

(a) uses the same language for an integrated audit and a financial statement audit of a nonpublic company.

(b) includes a reference to the audit standards used for the audit.

(c) provides a guarantee about the absence of errors and fraud.

(d) must be issued as soon as the substantive testing is completed.

2-20 **[LO 3, 5]** Client acceptance and continuance procedures

(a) are performed only before the first time an auditor works on a client's engagement.

(b) address the financial statements of a potential client.

(c) may inform the auditor about engagement risk of a client.

(d) all of the above.

DISCUSSION QUESTIONS

2-21 **[LO 3, 4]** What is the value of auditors going through a formal process of linking management assertions to audit procedures to collect evidence? How does this process improve the audit?

2-22 **[LO 1]** Why does the auditor have to issue two opinions, one on internal control and one on the financial statements?

2-23 **[LO 1, 3]** Why does the auditor begin planning the financial statement audit phase before the tests of operating effectiveness of ICFR? Why not after the internal control audit is completed?

2-24 **[LO 4]** Explain why auditors need to consider both existence or occurrence, and completeness when auditing an account balance? In terms of the transactions posted, how much "audit comfort" does investigating these two assertions provide?

 2-25 **[LO 4]** Is it possible that an auditor can make a professional judgment error and still be behaving with due professional care? Explain.

2-26 **[LO 4]** Statistics indicates concern for both alpha and beta errors. In audit terms, this might be described as being concerned about the risk of concluding that the financial statements are misrepresented when they are actually fair, AND the risk of saying that the financial statements are fair when they are not. However, audit risk is defined as the risk of issuing an unqualified audit report when the financial statements are misstated or ICFR is not effective. Why doesn't audit risk include the opposite error as well?

2-27 **[LO 5]** Why would the auditor want to inform management of problems with internal control as early as possible, so that remediation can be performed as early as possible?

2-28 **[LO 5]** Why are analytical procedures a required step in audit planning?

2-29 **[LO 4]** The following terms are important in an integrated audit. Explain what they mean in the context of an audit and how/why they are related.

- Materiality
- Reasonable assurance
- Detection risk
- Audit risk

PROBLEMS

2-30   **[LO 7]** List the 10 GAAS from the PCAOB standards and the 10 AICPA standards in two columns.

(a) Identify differences between comparable standards in the two sets.

(b) Highlight any differences that you think indicate a difference in meaning.

(c) Add a third column as shown below and list the field work and reporting concepts from AS 5 that are the parallel for an ICFR audit to the standards for financial statement audits. Identify any significant differences in the words or meaning.

PCAOB	AICPA	AS 5

2-31   **[LO 6]** You are the auditor for a nonpublic company, "A Golden Rule Carpentry." The company has a 12/31 fiscal year end. During your audit, you did not identify any material misstatements in the financial statements.

Required:

(a) Draft the appropriate audit report for the financial statement audit of "A Golden Rule Carpentry."

(b) What assurances are provided in the audit report when the auditor states that the financial statements "present fairly . . . in conformity with accounting principles generally accepted in the United States of America"?

(c) How does the audit report refer to materiality, and how does it relate to your response to (b)?

(d) How do you think the auditor should respond upon finding a misstatement that he or she believes is material, and the client disagrees? In other words, client management believes the misstatement is not material?

[Ethics]

2-32   **[LO 4]** For each of the following accounts, list the five management assertions from most to least important for that account. State the reason justifying your order. Cash is completed as an example.

(a) Cash (in home currency)

1. Existence
2. Rights
3. Presentation and disclosure
4. Completeness
5. Valuation

If cash does not exist, then none of the other assertions matter. However, even if cash is found to exist, it has to be owned by the company claiming it. Various disclosures can be required for cash, for example, if it is committed as a compensating balance. Completeness is not a big audit risk because it is unlikely that management would not report cash or that any amount omitted is material. Cash is reported at face value, so valuation is not an issue for cash unless it is in a foreign currency.

(b) Long term debt

(c) Officer salary expense paid through stock options

(d) Sales revenue

(e) Accounts receivable

(f) Property, plant and equipment

2-33   **[LO 1, 6]** Identify each of the following items as being associated with

(a) an AICPA financial statement audit.

(b) a PCAOB integrated audit.

(c) both sets of audit standards.

_____ AS 5

_____ "must" means a mandatory responsibility

_____ operating effectiveness of ICFR must be tested

_____ significant risks must be identified even if ICFR is not tested

_____ 10 generally accepted auditing standards

_____ competent evidence

_____ appropriate evidence

_____ sufficient evidence

2-34   **[LO 4]** Match the following terms and descriptions.

(a) Making a judgment error does not necessarily indicate this as long as the auditor uses due professional care

(b) Presentation and disclosure

(c) Having an objective viewpoint and a questioning mind

(d) Would make a difference in the judgment of a decision maker

(e) ICFR effectiveness

(f) Competent

(g) ICFR across the entire organization

_____ management assertion

_____ appropriate

_____ design and operating

_____ negligence

_____ material

_____ entity level

_____ professional skepticism

2-35   **[LO 4]** Order the following pieces of evidence based on their reliability from most to least reliable.

(a) A memo prepared internally and sent from the audit client CFO to the audit client CEO

(b) An oral communication with the same information as in (a) spoken to the auditor by the accounts receivable clerk

(c) A confirmation about debt owed to the audit client provided in writing directly to the auditor from the outside third party

(d) A copy of an invoice prepared inside the company, sent to a customer, and then returned by the customer with a check as a remittance advice

Without reordering the pieces of evidence, state whether the following would increase or decrease reliability, and why.

(a) The memo was sent to the CEO, audit committee chair, and the company's principal outside bank.

(b) The oral communication was received from the CFO rather than the accounts receivable clerk.

(c) The confirmation process was handled by the client rather than the auditor, and the response was forwarded to the auditor after it was received at the client's place of business.

(d) The client company has poor internal control, and the outside customer revised the invoice and paid a different amount from what was originally billed.

2-36 **[LO 5]** Given the following stages of an audit, identify in which stage the following audit activities occur.

Audit Stages

(1) Preliminary engagement activities

(2) Planning and risk assessment

(3) ICFR controls testing

(4) Substantive procedures

(5) Completion, wrap-up, and reporting

Audit Activities

(a) Vouching whether the amount at which a transaction is recorded agrees to the underlying document

(b) Identifying who should work on the audit engagement

(c) Determining whether the audit firm is independent of an audit client

(d) Communicating with the client's outside attorney

(e) Checking to see whether the cashier's office reconciles the bank account properly once a month

(f) Coming to a final decision on whether the ICFR is effective

(g) Determining the complexity of the different kinds of transactions that are handled at each of a company's places of doing businesses

2-37 **[LO 7]** Traber Electronics is a small privately owned retailer of electronic equipment and household appliances. Traber Electronics is required to provide audited financial statements as part of a due diligence investigation in consideration of a potential acquisition of Traber by a public company. In the interest of time, Traber appointed the audit firm of Makins & Howell, CPAs, without a formal proposal process. Makins & Howell immediately accepted the audit engagement in early October and agreed to the November 1 deadline for the auditor's report.

Katie Kammins, CPA, was recently promoted to in-charge auditor for Makins & Howell and was assigned to the Traber audit along with Joel Misten, the firm's university intern. Prior to her assignment to the Traber audit, all of Katie's audit experience was in the health-care industry. Because most of Katie's health-care clients had June 30 year ends, Katie was available in October to work on the Traber engagement.

Katie and Joel got right to work. Katie informed Joel that there was no time to test controls, so she instructed him as to the proper procedures for proving the mathematical accuracy of the accounting journals and ledgers and tying the totals to the financial statements. No footnotes or other supplemental disclosures accompanied the financial statements, and there were no prior-year financial statements to be used as a basis of comparison, which helped expedite the audit process.

While Joel was busy with the mathematical tie-ins, Katie analyzed the company's sales and inventories because these were the most significant revenue and asset accounts. For sales, Katie reviewed the monthly sales reports and learned that several large contracts had been accounted for on the percentage of completion method. Although she wasn't sure about the propriety of the profits recognized, Katie held a series of discussions with Traber's controller, who assured Katie that the profits had been recorded in accordance with generally accepted accounting principles.

For inventories, Katie observed the items in the retail store, noting the reasonableness of their descriptions and saleable condition. She was not present when Traber Electronics conducted its annual physical count of the inventory. She did not examine the inventory at the company's warehouse because it represented less than half of the value of the asset account.

One week before the deadline, Makins & Howell provided its standard audit report, which included an unqualified opinion on Traber's financial statements.

Required:

Refer to each of the 10 GAAS and indicate how the actions of Makins & Howell or its employees resulted in violations of these standards.

2-38 **[LO 5]** Arin Pate, CPA, is scheduled to work on the integrated audits of two client companies in the coming month: Jacoh Industries and Morton Baxx, Ltd. Arin was assigned to both of these audit engagements in the prior year. As she works on the preliminary audit planning phase, Arin notes the following facts and features pertaining to each of these client companies:

Jacoh Industries is a manufacturer of medical imaging equipment. Although Jacoh's equipment is distributed worldwide, the company operates at a single location. The equipment is promoted through sales teams, and sales are accepted through an online ordering system. There is a significant investment in inventories, and internal control in this area is strong. In fact, Arin's firm has never had any significant audit differences or disagreements with the client. Within the past year, however, a new competitor has entered the market, and Jacoh is experiencing a decline in sales volume. Although the company's income statement still shows a slight profit, cash flow challenges are now prevalent. Jacoh, however, has not suffered as much as several other competitors, who are reporting losses for the first time.

Morton Baxx publishes a monthly fashion magazine. Subscription revenues and many of the advertising revenues are deferred. Most subscriptions are sold on an annual basis, but advertising contracts range from one month to one year. Publishing costs are typically recorded in the period that they are incurred. Morton Baxx's internal controls have been effective in the past.

Required:

In order to minimize audit risks on each of these audit engagements, what audit areas should Arin emphasize?

2-39 **[LO 3, 5]** The beginning of an auditing class is often frustrating for students because they feel there are so many things that they do not thoroughly understand. One of the challenges is that so many parts of an audit are either concurrent or iterative.

Required:

Reference the overview diagram of an integrated audit in Exhibit 2-1 and identify the aspects that are difficult to place in a strict chronological sequence.

(a) List the audit activities that may be iterative.

(b) Match and list the parts that are conducted concurrently.

Activity 1: Activity 2:

2-40   Find the most current 10K (SEC annual report) and 10Q (SEC quarterly report) for Starbucks, either through the company Web site or the SEC Web site. Find the auditor's report for the annual financial statements and the auditor's review report for the quarterly financial statements (if there is one). Match the language to the PCAOB sample report.

2-41   Go to the PCAOB Web site (*www.pcaobus.org*). What do the Auditing Standards issued by the PCAOB as of the current date cover? Are there any standards that are currently proposed but not yet final?

2-42   Go to the Web site of one of the Big Four public accounting firms (Deloitte, Ernst & Young, KPMG, and PricewaterhouseCoopers). How do these firms market themselves on their Web sites? What type of service and industry expertise are highlighted? What do the Web sites present about the work environment and values of the firm? Is there discussion of a firm Code of Conduct or Values?

Ethics

2-43   Go to the Web site of an international company and review its financial statements, including its auditor's report.

(a) What auditing standards are applied by the company's auditors?

(b) Which Big Four audit firm is primarily associated with the company's audits?

(c) How does the company's auditor's report compare with the one presented in this chapter?

2-44   Go to the Web site for international auditing standards: *www.ifac.org/iaasb/*. Look for any standards and rules on that Web site that seem to parallel those of the AICPA and PCAOB. Describe what you see as similarities and differences.

Ethics

APPENDIX A: AICPA GENERALLY ACCEPTED AUDITING STANDARDS (AU 150.02)

General Standards

1. The auditor must have adequate technical training and proficiency to perform the audit.
2. The auditor must maintain independence in mental attitude in all matters relating to the audit.
3. The auditor must exercise due professional care in the performance of the audit and the preparation of the report.

Standards of Field Work

1. The auditor must adequately plan the work and must properly supervise any assistants.
2. The auditor must obtain a sufficient understanding of the entity and its environment, including its internal control, to assess the risk of material misstatement of the financial statements whether due to error or fraud, and to design the nature, timing, and extent of further audit procedures.
3. The auditor must obtain sufficient appropriate audit evidence by performing audit procedures to afford a reasonable basis for an opinion regarding the financial statements under audit.

Standards of Reporting

1. The auditor must state in the auditor's report whether the financial statements are presented in accordance with generally accepted accounting principles (GAAP).

2. The auditor must identify in the auditor's report those circumstances in which such principles have not been consistently observed in the current period in relation to the preceding period.

3. When the auditor determines that informative disclosures are not reasonably adequate, the auditor must so state in the auditor's report.

4. The auditor must either express an opinion regarding the financial statements, taken as a whole, or state that an opinion cannot be expressed, in the auditor's report. When the auditor cannot express an overall opinion, the auditor should state the reasons therefore in the auditor's report. In all cases where an auditor's name is associated with financial statements, the auditor should clearly indicate the character of the auditor's work, if any, and the degree of responsibility the auditor is taking, in the auditor's report.

THE AUDIT ENVIRONMENT

CHAPTER **3**

The Auditor's Role in Society

1. Describe the contribution that audit services make to society and relationships among auditors, audit clients, and the public.
2. Explain the different inputs to and influences on personal ethics and morals.
3. Understand the role and contributions of professionals in society.
4. Recognize the potential for ethical considerations and outcomes in decisions and the decision-making models applicable to ethical decisions.
5. Become familiar with external regulation and professional standards governing the accounting profession's conduct and quality control.

Chapter 3 Resources

AICPA, *Code of Professional Conduct*
AICPA QC 10, *A Firm's System of Quality Control*
AU 161, AICPA, PCAOB, *The Relationship of Generally Accepted Auditing Standards to Quality Control Standards*
AU 220, AICPA, PCAOB, *Independence*

PCAOB, Rules of the Board
Sarbanes-Oxley Act of 2002
SEC Rule 33-7919, *Revision of the Commission's Auditor Independence Requirements*

INTRODUCTION

Auditors play a special role in today's society. Their primary responsibility is to protect the public interest. Auditors are fundamental to the public trust required for our capital markets to function. The reports issued by auditors enhance the reliability of the financial information on which investors and others rely.

Auditors have a complex relationship with their constituents. Although the public is the ultimate benefactor of auditor services, other entities interact with auditors more directly. The company contracts with and pays the auditor for services. Regulators and stock exchanges require companies to purchase audit services. Auditors' interactions with the public are quite distant. Yet, for the most part, the public trusts and relies on auditors and their work.

The public's belief that auditors are professionals who behave with honesty and integrity engenders society's trust. Society trusts auditors to conduct themselves and perform their work in a manner that protects the public interest. Society's reliance on auditors makes it imperative that auditors deserve the trust extended to them. Consequently, it is important for accountants to understand influences on personal ethical behavior and the relationship between auditors and society. Although auditors benefit from the support they receive as members of a profession, each individual remains personally responsible for behaving morally and ethically.

SOCIETY'S RELIANCE ON AUDITORS [LO 1]

Who is the real beneficiary of audit services? The auditor's ultimate responsibility is to protect the public interest. An auditor is directly hired and paid by the client company, and interacts closely with the company while performing the audit. However, the auditor's professional charge is to issue appropriate opinions on the fairness of the company's financial statements and the effectiveness of its internal control over financial reporting (ICFR).

An audit firm's responsibility is to communicate to the public, or other users, its opinion on whether the corporation's financial statements fairly present the company's underlying economic events and circumstances, and whether ICFR is effective. The public, via the capital markets and a functioning economy, benefits from the work of the auditor.

Why does the public trust auditors in this important and challenging role? Auditors have knowledge that those untrained in accounting and auditing lack. The public needs auditors to use their knowledge in a competent and responsible fashion for the capital markets to function as efficiently and effectively as possible. The trust placed in auditors as independent professionals committed to their public interest responsibility is based on historical performance. Although audit failures and scandals have occurred periodically, the vast majority of audits have produced results supporting dissemination of reliable financial information. As a result, auditors and CPAs in general are held in high esteem by the public.

Fundamentally, an auditor performs a service, an integrated audit, and announces a conclusion on which others rely. Society needs to rely on what auditors do and on the conclusions they reach. This does not mean that auditors are expected to perform their services without ever making judgment errors. However, society needs to be able to trust that auditors will behave morally and ethically. Society needs to trust that auditors perform their services to the best of their technical ability. This reliance on auditors demands that accounting students understand the critical importance of committing to ethical behavior.

Auditors' Clients and Other Constituents

The service and payment relationships among auditors, companies undergoing audits, and the ultimate constituents of audit services are unusual and complicated. Payment for audit services differs from that for most other professional services benefiting the public interest. In fact, it may be unique.

Occupations classified as professions are made up of the experts on a specific body of knowledge. Professionals use their expertise in performing their work. Those who perform audit services fit the definition of professionals. Doctors and lawyers are also classified as professionals. Doctors and lawyers can be compared to auditors to exemplify the unusual nature of auditors' service contracts.

Doctors and private practice defense attorneys have fairly straightforward client relationships. A client hires a doctor or a defense lawyer to perform a service, and the client pays for the service. These professionals are client advocates. In a doctor–patient relationship, a doctor may have bad news for a patient, such as of an incurable disease. It is then the doctor's job to use his or her best efforts to help the patient achieve the best outcome. The same service–payment relationship holds true for a private defense attorney. Similarly, a CPA performing tax research or consulting for a client has a direct service and payment relationship with the client.

In contrast, consider a lawyer who works as a prosecutor. A prosecuting attorney has the responsibility of representing the public's interest in court. The prosecutor works for the government and is paid from public funds. Auditors' payment contracts are even more indirect than those of a prosecuting attorney. Although an auditor's responsibility is to audit a company as a means of protecting the public interest, the company being audited hires the auditor and pays the fee.

In a corporate environment, shareholders who own the company elect the Board of Directors. Shareholders delegate to the Board of Directors the responsibility to oversee shareholder interests. In turn, the Board of Directors hires management and empowers management to carry out the corporation's objectives and activities.

The Board of Directors typically has several committees. Directors participate as members of the various committees. One of the committees of the Board of Directors is the audit committee. In publicly traded companies, best practice is for the selection and hiring of the audit firm to be voted on and confirmed (also called "ratified") by the shareholders. However, the Sarbanes-Oxley Act (SOX) requires that the audit committee (1) select and hire the auditor, (2) oversee the auditor's compensation, and (3) interact with the auditor as needed regarding issues of the audit.

The shareholder group, as the company's owners, is actually the client. Even so, the auditor interacts to a great extent with management, to a lesser extent with the audit committee, and almost never with shareholders. This limited auditor interaction with the actual owners of the company highlights the complexity of the auditor's service contract.

An audit firm typically refers to the company it is auditing as its "client." The client company pays the audit firm. The work product, an integrated audit of the client company, results in a public document available to a broad, unspecified user group. The audit report does not have to convey opinions on ICFR and the financial statements that the client requests or prefers. In fact, the auditor is prohibited from helping the client or even holding a bias in favor of the client. Nor can the auditor have a bias against the client. The auditor is paid for behaving with professional competence and integrity and producing an objective report.

This audit employment contract requires auditors to perform their work with a mindset of independence from their client. Auditors must maintain a commitment to their public interest responsibility even though their financial contract is with the company under audit. Personal, professional, and regulatory influences all support auditors in achieving these goals and monitoring their performance.

REVIEW QUESTIONS

A.1 How is a doctor's professional relationship with a client different from an auditor's?

A.2 Who elects the Board of Directors?

A.3 Who hires management?

A.4 Under SOX, who selects and hires the auditor?

A.5 With whom does the auditor interact most—shareholders, the Board of Directors, or management?

A.6 In performing its work, to whom does the audit firm owe "ultimate responsibility"?

INFLUENCES ON BEHAVIOR [LO 2]

Using the assumption that auditors are expected to behave in a moral and an ethical manner, we come to the next question: What is moral and ethical behavior? No one has ever provided a universally accepted answer to this question.

What Is Right?

Many influences affect personal perceptions of right and wrong. These personal perceptions cause one person to label a particular action as good, while others label the same action as bad. Easy examples of differences in perceptions of good and bad are the divergent opinions in the U.S. on topics such as war, the federal deficit, taxes, abortion, and even availability of information on the Internet.

Family background, community ties, geographical location, faith or religious beliefs, and national legal and political systems all affect ethical and moral judgments. The extent and speed of information dissemination and the global economy provide huge amounts of information to process. Given our vast knowledge base and the diversity about which people are now aware, diversity in moral judgments is inevitable.

The field of philosophy provides sources for ethical or moral behavior analysis. Philosophy teaches that the correct answer to a question depends on the philosophical framework used, as well as the way the philosophy is applied. A thorough analysis of various philosophers' views is beyond the scope of this chapter. However, the following examples present some applications of different positions that have been set forth over time as the way to arrive at the "right" answer. The proper philosophical decision structures are always arguable.

Right is whatever creates the greatest good

The United States uses a progressive income tax rate. Wealthier people pay their income taxes based on a higher rate than poorer people because they can afford to pay more. Thus, poorer people receive more government services than they otherwise would, and wealthier people help to pay for it. This "spreads the wealth," puts more people above a minimum "quality of life," and thus creates the greatest good for the most people.

The argument against using the greatest good standard for making this decision is that wealthy people have the right to use their assets as they choose. The same arguments apply to both sides of a discussion on a legally mandated minimum wage, and universal health care.

Right is whatever is fundamentally "right" regardless of the consequences

Attitudes about the environment portray divergent conclusions about following a moral imperative in making decisions. Those who believe protecting the environment is a moral imperative believe that economic damage resulting from environmental protection must be accepted. Protecting the environment is simply the right thing to do, regardless of the cost.

Those who do not believe it is appropriate to make decisions based on a belief in what is fundamentally "right" propose that consequences are important. Applying the opposite position to the issue of the environment suggests that consequences to the environment and the economy must be balanced.

Conflicting conclusions can be made not only regarding which philosophical approach is best, but also from applying a single approach. Two people using the same philosophical standard can come to different conclusions. The following examples explore different applications of a greatest good philosophy.

Assume that one person believes that from a "greatest good" perspective it is right to have a progressive income tax rate. This person believes that a progressive tax keeps the most people out of poverty. Another person, who also believes in the "greatest good," believes that a progressive income tax is detrimental. The second person believes a progressive income tax rate discourages high earners from working hard and results in a less productive economy that negatively affects everyone.

Proponents of a universal health-care policy believe it creates the greatest good because everyone gets at least a minimum level of health care. Basic health care for everyone is most important, even if it causes delays or rationing of services. Detractors from universal health care believe that the greatest good results from letting the free market control health care. Free market competition creates new health-care delivery models encouraging innovation and bringing down costs in the long term, thus making affordable health care available to the most people and creating the greatest good.

The second philosophical framework presented is described as a categorical imperative.[1] Assume that two people believe in making moral decisions based on what is fundamentally right. These two people may still disagree about environmental protection: One person believes it is always fundamentally right to protect the environment for future generations. The other person believes it is fundamentally right to protect the economic welfare of those people alive today, even if their business activities might damage the environment. Some other widely adopted philosophical structures follow.

Right is whatever preserves the life of even one person

Numerous value systems exist supporting this philosophical position. Most Western religions support the protection of individual life. Ayn Rand, in her philosophy of objectivism, elevates the value of life, but also extols an ethic of self-interest.

Although the original movies are dated, the Star Trek culture continues in our society, as evidenced by the newest 2009 movie. In *Star Trek III: The Search for Spock* (1984) all the crew risked their lives to save Spock. Although Spock died, when his body was ejected into space, it landed on the Genesis planet and there was a chance he would come back to life. His friends believed that it was morally right for all of them to break the law to recover his body if his life could possibly be saved.

War, which is typically justified using a "greatest good" philosophy, is an obvious contrast to the concept of "saving a single life." In war, individual life is sacrificed for the lives of others.

---

[1]Immanuel Kant is credited with this basis for decisions.

Right is the decision made by a single ruler with ultimate authority

Using this philosophical view of a leader with ultimate authority, one can view as right the decisions of religious leaders such as the Pope and the Dalai Lama because of a belief in their absolute authority. Ancient belief in the inherited authority of royal blood lines is an example of this moral framework.

The view of shared authority that exists currently in many countries indicates the opposing view.

Right is the decision made by the group of people affected

This philosophy is the underlying belief for democratic forms of government. The election system of the United States follows this philosophy.

The opposing belief is that certain individuals or groups legitimately exercise decision-making power over others. As an example, the lack of input into British decisions affecting colonies in the New World, though perceived as appropriate by British royalty, was a major spark causing the American Revolution.

Right is whatever the law requires

This belief structure supports obeying the law even while believing it is wrong. For example, in the United States a person is charged with obeying the law even if he or she disagrees with that law and is trying to change it. Public disobedience, even in support of a widely popular cause, may be viewed as wrong under this value structure.

In contrast, public disobedience from the time of the Revolutionary War through the Vietnam War up to the present is a factual and often respected part of the U.S. landscape.

University business courses usually do not spend much time discussing different philosophical positions. Perhaps this is because the different philosophical perspectives that are available to analyze what is "right" are complex and require intensive study. Regardless of the reason for limited formal study in business curriculums, every student should reflect on the influences that have shaped his or her personal value structure. Family, community, faith or religion, national culture, laws and courts, as well as personal experiences, all influence the value structures used in every decision.

AUDITING IN ACTION

What Should the Health Clinic Do?

A not-for-profit health clinic that serves uninsured, low-income individuals is provided the opportunity to receive the largest donation in its history from a local business owner. Such a large donation will provide many benefits to the clinic and its patients—more doctors and nurses, new medical equipment, and even a new building that will be named after the donor. The dilemma is that the donor's business, though not illegal, is a little disreputable. (Again, definitions are a problem because what is seen as disreputable by one person may not seem so to another. Pick a business you believe to be legal but disreputable: legal gambling, adult businesses, poor quality rental housing, questionable insurance policies for the poor and elderly, etc.).

Both the clinic staff and its Board of Directors debate whether they want to be associated with a clinic named after an individual associated with this type of business. Some simply think it is wrong for a not-for-profit entity to affiliate itself in this way. Others object from the practical position that it will scare away other major donors. Still others feel very strongly that the clinic should accept the donation. Turning down the donation because of a possible taint on the health clinic's reputation means that many patients will not receive services that will be available if the donation is accepted.

What do you believe the health clinic should do? Accept the donation? Or turn it down?

Moral Development

One theory of individual decisions and ethics is called **moral development.** This theory suggests that the criteria a person uses to make decisions depends on his or her level of moral development.

Levels of moral development are descriptive. In other words, one level of moral development is not necessarily better or worse than another. Individuals are theorized to move in one direction through three levels of moral development. Not everyone moves through all the levels. The theory proposes that movement is *only* in one direction. Although some may believe it is better to be at a higher level of moral development, this is a personal judgment. The levels simply describe the way a person makes decisions. What follows is a brief summary of moral development theory. Extensive discussions of the theory can be found in other sources.

Individuals at the **pre-conventional level** of moral development make decisions in a self-centered way. At a pre-conventional level, the individual makes decisions based on personal consequences. Will I be punished if I am caught? How bad will the punishment be? If I break a rule and do not get caught, how much better will my life be? An example of pre-conventional analysis is someone asking, "Will I be caught if I cheat on an exam or on my income taxes?" The person analyzes whether the possible benefit is worth taking the risk. The pre-conventional level is classified as the earliest level of moral development. Young children begin with this decision framework and later add considerations characteristic of the conventional level.

Individuals at the **conventional level** of moral development consider impacts beyond those that affect them personally. Often they use societal norms such as rules and laws to decide what is right. Conventional-level analysis views following laws as behaving in a moral manner. Someone at the conventional level pays income taxes because the law requires it. Concern for what other people think is important. Someone at the conventional level may also pay taxes because of concern about what friends and family think.

Individuals at the **post-conventional level** engage in abstract analysis of what is right and wrong, often using philosophical positions. The analysis includes questions such as: "Will anyone be hurt as an outcome of my decision? Should I do this because it is a good thing to do, even though it is against the law?" Or, even more complex, "Should I not do this even though the law says I can?"

Assume an owner decides to lay off employees in a business setting. From a post-conventional perspective the decision may be agonizing. The decision maker knows that individuals will be hurt, even though the action keeps the company viable. Another post-conventional level decision is made by a volunteer who illegally runs a program feeding homeless people in an unlicensed location because that is the best place to reach the hungry people. The decision is an example of doing something good, even though it is against the law.

AUDITING IN ACTION

Levels of Moral Development

Pre-conventional: The individual decides what is right or wrong based on consequences.
Conventional: The individual is concerned about the expectations of significant others and relies on rules and laws to determine what is right or wrong.
Post conventional: The individual decides what is right or wrong using universal ethical principles such as the common good and justice.

(*Source*: J. Jones, D. W. Massey, and L. Thorne. "Auditors' Ethical Reasoning: Insights from Past Research and Implications for the Future." *Journal of Accounting Literature* 22 (2003): 46.)

Ethical Orientation

Another approach to describing personal ethical and moral decisions is through the **ethical orientation** of the decision maker. Different ethical orientations exist across cultures. Two orientations often discussed in the United States are an **ethic of rights** and an **ethic of care**. Rights orientation has been the predominant structure used in U.S. businesses. It reflects our legal and governance standards of individual rights. Ethics of care discussions originated as an alternative viewpoint in the feminist literature in the 1980s. This orientation has since migrated to a mainstream role, probably as a result of the emphasis on teams in the workplace. An ethics of care perspective also reflects the team loyalty emphasis of the military and various competitive sports.

An ethic of rights suggests that the decision maker focuses on individuals as separate entities. Connections are either hierarchical or contractual. The focus is on accruing benefits due to the individual. The goal is protecting whatever the individual has a "right" to receive. Individual strength, autonomy, and self-sufficiency are important. Although advancing personal rights is valued, so is respecting the rights of other individuals. This ethical structure fits well with the United States business emphasis on legal rights, competition, and personal advancement.

An ethic of care holds relationships paramount. Relationships are the natural order of the interdependence of individuals. Based on an ethic of care, decisions are made to strengthen relationships and meet the needs of others. The ethic of care provides a useful structure to describe and analyze moral decisions when the emphasis is on teams. For example, when using an ethic of care framework, personal sacrifice to achieve a team goal or help a co-worker is the right thing.

AUDITING IN ACTION

Ethical Orientation[2]

Ethic of rights

1. Individuals as separate
2. Relationships as hierarchical or contractual
3. Independence as strength
4. Importance of autonomy and self-sufficiency
5. Importance of rights of others

Ethic of care

1. Individuals as interdependent
2. Relationships of attention and response
3. Care as strength
4. Importance of interdependence and interpersonal connections
5. Importance of needs of others

---

[2]Sara Reiter, "The Ethics of Care and New Paradigms for Accounting Practice," *Accounting, Auditing & Accountability Journal*, 10, No. 3 (1997): 299–324. [From Code (1988); Gilligan (1987, 1988), as follows].

Code, L. (1988). "Credibility: A Double Standard?" In Code, L., Mullett, S., and Overall, C. (Eds.), *Feminist Perspectives: Philosophical Essays on Method and Morals*. Toronto: University of Toronto Press, pp. 64–88.

Gilligan, C. (1987). "Moral Orientation and Moral Development." In Kittay, E. F. and Meyers, D. T. (Eds.), *Women and Moral Theory*. Totowa, NJ: Rowman & Littlefield Publishers, pp. 19–33.

Gilligan, C. (1988). "Remapping the Moral Domain: New Images of Self in Relationship." In Gilligan, C., Ward, J. V., and Taylor, J. M. (Eds.), *Mapping the Moral Domain*. Center for the Study of Gender, Education and Human Development, Cambridge, MA: Harvard University Press, pp. 3–19.

REVIEW QUESTIONS

B.1 What are some of the influences on individual judgment regarding what is "good" or "bad"?

B.2 What are the three levels of moral development?

B.3 Compare and contrast an ethic of rights and an ethic of care.

AUDITING AS A PROFESSION [LO 3]

A **profession** is a professional or an occupational group of individuals with a collective identity. Originally, professionals were revered by others in society because they possessed valued knowledge. Consequently, religious clerics, doctors, and lawyers are identified as the earliest professionals. Historically, professionals were described as those providing a service to the rest of society because of altruistic motivations. As it has become openly acknowledged that professionals must support themselves through their work, more complete and realistic descriptions of professionals have developed. Even though professionals are expected to behave in the best interests of society, they are paid for their contributions.

A professional group always has a clearly specified body of knowledge about which it is known to have expertise. For auditors, this body of knowledge is financial statement accounting and auditing, as well as business activities and internal control. Professional groups have standards for entry and continued membership in the profession. Professions exercise some degree of **self-regulation**, although currently in the United States the government also regulates all professions to some degree.

Community of Peers

One hallmark of a profession is that its members make up a community. The collective group that makes up the profession exercises some degree of control over individual members. The control can span the range from informal influence of peer expectations to formal self-regulation through rules and requirements. Consistent with the concept of self-regulation, many regulations for the accounting and auditing profession are self-imposed. The main professional body representing certified public accountants in the United States is the American Institute of Certified Public Accountants (AICPA).

Any person who wishes to become a member of the AICPA must meet entry standards. Once the person becomes a member, the AICPA requires adherence to its **Code of Professional Conduct**, varying amounts of continuing professional education, and **quality control reviews**. The AICPA writes and publishes quality control standards used in quality control review processes. The AICPA, through its Board of Examiners, is responsible for developing, administering, and overseeing the CPA examination. Although individual state governments issue licenses to certified public accountants, all states in the United States delegate the entrance examination tasks to the AICPA. The AICPA is responsible for producing auditing standards for audits of companies that are not under the SEC's jurisdiction. When performing audits of public companies, regulation over auditors is no longer exercised by a community of peers, but shifts to government-imposed controls.

Entry and Membership

A profession typically controls standards for entry into the professional group. The CPA designation is the AICPA's professional entry-level threshold for full membership. Holding a CPA designation is a visible sign of achieving the status of professional accountant or auditor. The AICPA's control over the CPA designation is an example of entry and membership standards established and applied by a profession.

Before anyone can take the CPA examination, he or she must complete the college education standards required by the state's Board of Professional Regulation (or comparable regulatory agency). These statewide educational standards are usually developed using input from professional accounting groups such as the AICPA and local CPAs. Currently, most states require 150 semester hours to be certified, but many states permit applicants to sit for the exam after completing 120 semester hours. Once an individual has met the requirements to take the exam, he or she must achieve a specified level of performance to pass the exam.

Many state jurisdictions also require individuals to have work experience before they can become certified or licensed. Finally, all CPAs are required to participate in continuing education as a requirement to keep their CPA certificates currently valid. All of these standards are expected to contribute to high-quality performance by CPAs. They are also examples of ways that accounting and auditing professionals control entry and continued membership in the profession.

External Regulation

Professions are all granted some level of self-regulation. Many, including accountants and auditors, also answer to regulatory and government bodies. In the case of the medical profession, laws require doctors to have insurance, treat patients who are in serious need and unable to pay for services, and maintain special documentation for medicines that are experimental or addictive. Accountants also experience external regulation—by state governments, the SEC, and PCAOB.

States issue the occupational licenses under which CPAs legally practice. The SEC regulates the contents of companies' financial reports it receives, as well as many of the standards auditors must follow for those companies. The PCAOB, a not-for-profit entity that answers to the SEC, sets standards that must be followed for audits of public companies. Furthermore, any audit firm that audits a publicly traded company must register and file reports with the PCAOB, and submit to PCAOB inspections.

Individual Characteristics

Another way to understand the nature of a profession is to consider the characteristics or traits of the individual members. Common descriptions of individual professionals, including auditors, are that they possess technical expertise; behave with integrity; and believe their work is valuable and important, and makes a contribution. Professionals with integrity are objective and do their best work regardless of self-interest. Traditionally, all these characteristics have been used to describe auditors.

Social Contracts

Professionals are also described through their **social contracts**. What professionals contract to give society is a commitment to serve the public good through their work, thus enabling society's trust. Professionals commit to maintaining standards of excellence and policing their own ranks through self-governance. In return for this commitment, professionals receive prestige, the right to some level of self-governance, and economic reward for their service. An invaluable benefit that a profession often receives is a monopoly right to provide a service. For example, licensed doctors are the only people who can legally practice medicine. The parallel in the case of auditors is the monopoly rights to perform audits. An audit can only be performed by a licensed CPA meeting all state, regulatory, and professional standards.

AUDITING IN ACTION

Auditor's Contract with Society

Commitments the Auditor Makes	What the Auditor Receives from Society
To serve the public good	Prestige and economic reward
To maintain standards of excellence	Right to (some) self-governance
Internal policing of the profession	Monopoly rights to provide audits

REVIEW QUESTIONS

C.1 What are the characteristics of a profession?

C.2 What personal characteristics are usually associated with a person who is called a professional?

C.3 Describe the view of auditors as professionals who have a contract with society.

ETHICAL DECISION MAKING [LO 4]

Individuals make decisions on a daily basis, often without considering the process. When a choice presents itself, people use whatever information is available and make the decision. Embedded in this seemingly simple process are many steps, sources of information, and cognitive or mental shortcuts.

Decisions with ethical or moral components or consequences follow a similar sequence of events. For the following discussion, the terms *moral* and *ethical* are used interchangeably. The **ethical decision framework**, used for making decisions with ethical impacts, highlights the inputs to and consequences of the decision. The framework presented in Exhibit 3-1 captures the components commonly recognized as important to an ethical decision process.

EXHIBIT 3-1

Decision Structure for Ethical Decisions

1. Determine the facts of the situation; who, what, where, when, and how.
2. Identify the ethical issues and people involved. Who are the stakeholders?

   Stakeholders are those who have an interest in or who may be affected by the outcome. Stakeholders may include shareholders, creditors, management, employees, and the community, among others.
3. Identify the values related to the situation: honesty, loyalty, compassion, integrity, etc. Values sometimes conflict. For example, in order to behave with honesty and integrity, an individual may have to sacrifice loyalty.
4. Identify alternative courses of action that are available.
5. Evaluate the various courses of action, and match each with the relevant values. For example, one course of action may result in honest behavior, while another course of action may emphasize loyal behavior.
6. Consider the consequences of viable courses of action remaining.
7. Make the decision; take indicated action.

(*Source*: From Harold Q. Langenderfer and Joanne W. Rockness, "Integrating Ethics into the Accounting Curriculum: Issues, Problems, and Solutions," *Issues in Accounting Education* (Spring 1989).
Same substance as: AAA Advisory Committee on Professionalism and *Ethics, Ethics in the Accounting Curriculum, Cases and Readings,* 1990.)

The first step in making an ethical decision is obtaining information and understanding the facts. The second step is identifying the stakeholders and ethical issues. The group of stakeholders can be very broad. It includes those directly affected by a decision and can even extend to those who simply care about the result. For example, when a case is decided in court, the people directly affected by the outcome are stakeholders. However, in addition, other people who expect to litigate a similar situation at some point in the future are stakeholders as well. The precedent set by the first case may affect the outcome of any case they later bring to trial.

Identifying the ethical issues involved may be difficult. Widely different perceptions exist regarding what is morally or ethically important. The broadest definition of a moral or an ethical issue is a decision that has an impact on others. This definition encompasses nearly every decision made in a business or personal setting. Those who support such a broad definition believe it is appropriate to view every decision as likely having a moral or an ethical impact.

A consideration required for ethical decision making is recognizing that the decision has an ethical impact. If the decision maker is not aware of the ethical impact, he or she may utilize a decision framework that is not appropriate for ethical issues. Whether a person recognizes that something is an ethical decision depends on the **moral intensity** of the issues involved.

Exhibit 3-2 presents recognition of moral issues as it fits within an ethical decision process. A situation must have moral intensity for the decision maker in order for that person to recognize the decision as having ethical components.

The moral intensity criteria that cause a decision maker to realize that a situation has moral components are as follows.

1. The consequences are very large or significant.
2. There is great social agreement (or disagreement) about the issue.
3. The consequences are very likely to happen, and to happen soon, and may affect people or environments close to the decision maker.
4. Consequences will have a broad or widespread impact, rather than affecting only a concentrated location or group of people.

If these moral intensity criteria are not experienced at a level high enough to be important to the decision maker, it is less likely that he or she will use an ethical framework

---

EXHIBIT 3-2

Decision Process for Moral Issues

1. Environment produces issues with moral components.
2. Decision maker recognizes the moral issue or moral components.

   Moral intensity affects whether the decision maker recognizes the moral components:
   a. Magnitude of the consequences
   b. Social consensus
   c. Probability of effect
   d. Temporal immediacy
   e. Proximity
   f. Concentration of effect

3. Decision maker goes through a decision process to make a judgment regarding the issue, and selects and carries out a behavior.

(*Source*: Adapted from Karen L. Hooks and Thomas Tyson. "Gender Diversity Driven Changes in the Public Accounting Workplace." *Research on Accounting Ethics* (1995) 267–289; and T. M. Jones. "Ethical Decision Making by Individuals in Organizations: An Issue-Contingent Model." *Academy of Management Review* 16, No. 2 (1991): 379.)

in making the decision. The decision maker will instead use an economic or some other decision framework.

Consider a CEO and CFO team contemplating a major accounting fraud. If they analyze the consequences, the moral intensity they perceive may affect the decision. For example, if the company goes bankrupt from the fraud, the financial loss to the company stockholders will likely be a large dollar amount and all of society will disapprove. If the company does not go bankrupt, whether the company will be damaged enough to hurt shareholders is uncertain. The possibility that shareholders will not be damaged might be sufficient justification for the fraudsters. As a result, they can make their decision without an ethical decision framework. Similarly, the villains might perceive that if damage occurs it will be so far in the future that the people who will be hurt are not even involved with the company right now. The damage will only hurt a limited group of future shareholders. Again, this conclusion might be used to ignore moral issues related to the decision.

Alternatively, if the CEO and CFO factor in a prison sentence as punishment for the fraud, the decision process changes. They may decide that the magnitude of the consequences is too great. This conclusion results because everyone thinks going to jail is bad. The fraudsters feel the proximity issue because the possibility of jail is happening to them. Under this analysis it is more difficult to justify the fraud based on a low probability of getting caught. The CEO and CFO understand that their decision has moral implications.

Refer back to the decision structure presented in Exhibit 3-1. After the stakeholders and ethical issues are identified, the next step is to consider what values affect the decision. These values often conflict. For example, honesty and integrity may conflict with loyalty. A person whom someone knows and is close to, and would like to be loyal to, may have done something wrong. The problem arises if the observer believes the wrongdoing should be reported to superiors or a legal authority. Another example is that of a manager who has to sacrifice compassion to employees by laying them off. The decision may be necessary for the manager to perform his or her job with integrity and conscientiously protect shareholder net worth.

Another part of the decision process is identifying the available courses of action and evaluating them. To return to the preceding examples, the person with knowledge of wrongdoing could choose to report or not report the wrongdoer. The manager could choose to retain or lay off the unneeded employees. After evaluating the courses of action, the remaining steps are to consider the consequences of the various choices, make the decision, and take action.

Going through this deliberate process of considering ethical issues, stakeholders, values, options, and consequences does not ensure a moral or an ethical outcome. Moral decisions are not guaranteed. Further, people often have differing perceptions of what outcome is ethical. The benefit of the process is ensuring that the decision maker recognizes any moral components of the decision that he or she believes are important. As long as any moral components that exist are recognized, then the decision maker can consider them in the decision process.

MORAL DILEMMAS

Moral dilemmas present a special kind of ethical decision. An easy way to think of a moral dilemma is to consider a decision for which the decision maker believes there is no clear-cut right or wrong answer. A moral dilemma may involve selecting from multiple positive options but often is viewed as choosing the "lesser of two evils."

Imagine a supervisor who has to choose which of two very good employees to promote. Both employees are excellent at their jobs, and both need the salary increase that comes along with the promotion. This situation presents a moral dilemma. To make the dilemma more difficult, add the discriminating factor that one employee is better technically at the job, but the supervisor likes and works better with the other one. What is the "right" answer?

AUDITING IN ACTION

Moral Dilemmas in the Movies

Gone in 60 Seconds (2000) tells the story of a group of friends who were also car thieves. The leader of the group, played by Nicholas Cage, stopped stealing cars and left town after a promise to his mother, who was concerned that the leader's younger brother would follow him into his "career path." This was quite a sacrifice because he left behind not only his friends, but also his highly talented and beautiful girlfriend played by Angelina Jolie. Unfortunately, the younger brother became a car thief anyway.

When the younger brother fails to deliver an order of special cars, the "bad guy" buyer gives him the ultimatum that if he doesn't deliver the cars he will be killed. The older brother returns to town, reunites his car theft ring, and makes the delivery owed by his younger brother. At the climax of the movie, the lead car thief saves the life of the police officer who is trying to capture him. The police officer has the choice of arresting the car thief or letting him go. The officer recognizes the situation as a moral dilemma. What tips the balance is not only that the thief saved the police officer's life rather than running away, but he also returned to stealing cars for the right reason—love of his brother. The police officer lets him go.

Moral dilemmas abound in the business world, and auditing is no exception. Audit budgets and timekeeping present an example of a dilemma with which a staff auditor might be confronted early on in his or her career. Auditors keep track of the time spent on various sections of an audit. This provides information when billing the client and as a baseline for planning the work in future years. An audit engagement budget is based on initial estimates of the time various parts of the audit are expected to take.

Consider the scenario of an entry-level staff auditor. The audit partner makes it extremely clear that he or she wants careful and accurate time records kept for various parts of the engagement. The partner needs good information for proposing a fee to the client for next year's audit. However, the senior auditor in charge of the engagement, the staff auditor's immediate supervisor, is up for promotion this year. The message from the senior auditor is that no corners are to be cut and all the work is to be done. In addition, however, timekeeping records are to be managed so that *no* areas on the job go over budget. The senior thinks this will help the chances of promotion—and, by the way, the staff auditor agrees that it may make a difference.

By "following the rules," this is a straightforward and simple situation. The proper response is to record the time, After all, the partner's instructions are clear, and it is very important for planning the engagement next year. However, what if the organization's culture is such that on *all* engagements throughout the office run by a senior auditor who is up for promotion, time is not recorded if it makes the job go "over budget"? Also, what if the staff auditor really likes the senior, thinks he or she is very good, and wants to do everything possible to support the promotion? Maybe the senior is in competition with someone else for the promotion, and all the staff on the other senior's jobs are following the "don't go over budget" rule. Finally, consider that the staff auditor also has some "self-interest" at stake because the senior—not the partner—writes the staff auditor's performance evaluation. This situation creates an ethical dilemma. Many approaches are possible. The best start is likely for the staff auditor to talk to the senior and explain the conflict.

The important message from this discussion is that moral dilemmas are real. In the academic setting, students often believe that it will always be easy to choose the "high road"; in the real world many decisions are not easy. Sometimes it is even hard to determine which decision *is* the high road. That lack of clear direction creates a moral dilemma. Important considerations are the situation, people, and consequences. Ultimately, personal values guide the decision.

Now is the time for introspection rather than when working and confronting one's first job-related ethical dilemma. Individuals benefit from taking the time to understand the different approaches that can be used in a decision with ethical components and consequences.

Take the time now to consider your own personal views. You will then be much better prepared to make challenging decisions when you confront them in the workplace.

REVIEW QUESTIONS

D.1 What are the steps in a decision model that is to be used for making decisions that have ethical components and outcomes?

D.2 What is moral intensity?

D.3 Does using an ethical decision framework guarantee a moral decision outcome? Would the moral decision outcome be the same for everyone?

D.4 What is a moral dilemma?

EXTERNAL REGULATION [LO 5]

Many professional organizations, standard-setting bodies, regulatory organizations, and government actions influence and control auditor behavior. Some of the authority that affects auditors originates from the PCAOB, **AICPA Auditing Standards Board**, AICPA Code of Professional Conduct, SOX, state law, and federal regulatory agencies.

AUDITING IN ACTION

Sources and Statements of Authority over Auditors

PCAOB: The Board [PCAOB] shall, by rule, establish, including to the extent it determines appropriate through adoption of standards proposed by one or more professional groups of accountants… and amend or otherwise modify or alter, such auditing and related attestation standards, such quality control standards, and such ethics standards *to be used by registered public accounting firms in the preparation and issuance of audit reports*, as required by this Act or the rules of the Commission [SEC], or as may be necessary or appropriate in the public interest or for the protection of investors. [Sarbanes-Oxley Act, Sec. 103(a)(1)]

AICPA Auditing Standards Board: In 2004, after the formation of the PCAOB, "… the ASB was reconstituted and its jurisdiction amended by AICPA Council to *recognize the ASB as a body with the authority to promulgate auditing, attestation, and quality control standards relating to the preparation and issuance of audit and attestation reports for* **non-issuers**." (AICPA Auditing, Attestation and Quality Control Standards Setting Activities Operating Policies; p. 18)

AICPA Code of Professional Conduct, Rules 201 and 202: *A member who performs auditing and other professional services must comply with standards promulgated by bodies designated by AICPA Council.* (e.g., ASB, PCAOB)

Sarbanes-Oxley, Section 209, Considerations by Appropriate State Regulatory Authorities: In *supervising nonregistered public accounting firms and their associated persons, appropriate State regulatory authorities should make an independent determination of the proper standards applicable*, particularly taking into consideration the size and nature of the business of the accounting firms they supervise and the size and nature of the business of the clients of those firms. The standards applied by the Board [PCAOB] under this Act should not be presumed to be applicable for purposes of this section for small and medium sized nonregistered public accounting firms.

AICPA Statement on Independence Rules: In performing an attest engagement, *a member should consult the rules* of his or her *state board of accountancy*, his or her *state CPA society*, the *U.S. Securities and Exchange Commission* (SEC) if the member's report will be filed with the SEC, the *U.S. Department of Labor* (DOL) if the member's report will be filed with the DOL, … the *Government Accountability Office* (GAO) if law, regulation, agreement, policy or contract requires the member's report to be filed under GAO regulations, and any organization that issues or enforces standards of independence that would apply to the member's engagement. Such organizations may have independence requirements or rulings that differ from (e.g., may be more restrictive than) those of the AICPA. [AICPA Code of Professional Conduct Section 101(.01)]

The authoritative standards for auditors are sometimes directed at individual professionals and sometimes at the firms in which they work. Individual auditors act both as separate individuals and as part of an audit firm. In each of these roles, professional behavior is influenced and regulated by a variety of factors. As already discussed, personal values are shaped by culture, religion, and family. Decision processes reflect moral development and ethical orientation. While individual auditors are performing their roles as firm members, these personal influences continue to have an impact. However, additional influence results from firm culture, professional organizations, regulatory agencies, and governments.

Regulation of professional behavior includes governance by the profession and the various states. The state **Board of Professional Regulation** (or similar regulatory body) bestows upon an individual recognition as a certified public accountant and a license to practice as a public accountant within that state. After that, the CPA auditor's professional behavior is guided and circumscribed by the standards of that state regulatory body. This includes any state code of ethics and continuing professional education requirements. The individual may choose to join the AICPA, the **Institute of Internal Auditors (IIA)**, the **Institute of Management Accountants (IMA)**, or any of a group of accounting and auditing organizations. All of these membership organizations have rules and standards to which members must adhere, including codes of ethics or conduct. Often the state standards and professional organization standards are similar.

Since primary membership in these voluntary organizations is for individuals, it is important to recognize that the rules of these organizations may also impact the firms for which members work. For example, for an individual to be an AICPA member the firm for which he or she works must be structured using an accepted form of organization and name. Another example is that firms for which AICPA members work must undergo some type of **quality control or peer review** in order for the firm's employees to be permitted membership. If the firms are not in compliance with the rules, then partners and employees may not be members of the AICPA.

In contrast to the voluntary membership organizations, the PCAOB and the SEC exercise direct control over firms. Firms must register, file reports with, and be inspected by the PCAOB in order to audit publicly traded companies and have their audit reports accepted by the SEC. The SEC has the ability to discipline firms in a variety of ways if the firms are found culpable of wrongdoing. The SEC also works with the United States Justice Department when the nature of wrongdoing extends into the realm of criminal misconduct.

In addition to government, regulatory, and professional organization controls, laws and legal sanctions administered through the court systems influence and control auditor behavior. Major legal issues and cases are discussed in Chapter 4.

The U.S. court system addresses both tort and criminal cases involving auditors. Tort cases occur when one party is trying to receive compensation for various types of damage that it believes was the fault of another party. Criminal cases are brought by government attorneys to determine whether criminal wrongdoing has occurred and the appropriateness of possible punishment.

Even though legal authority may influence and control auditor behavior, it is not as effective as other tools simply because it comes into play after wrongdoing or failure has occurred. Remember that the public must trust auditors as competent professionals with integrity, whose primary responsibility is to protect the public interest. Guiding, influencing, and controlling the professional behavior of auditors and their firms to prevent failure and wrongdoing is a much better system than relying on the courts to deal with compensation, punishment, and other issues after a problem occurs.

AICPA CODE OF PROFESSIONAL CONDUCT

The AICPA is the primary national professional organization of CPAs. Many other organizations targeted and focused on accountants and auditors exist, both at national and regional or local levels. Designating the AICPA as the primary CPA organization does not lessen the value of the other organizations. The AICPA is simply the oldest, largest, and broadest in scope. Many of the other membership organizations service more specialized interests such as the focus of the **Institute of Internal Auditors (IIA)** on internal auditing. Some organizations provide for the interests of accountants and auditors working in a particular industry. Many of these organizations, including the AICPA, have a Code of Ethics or Code of Conduct for their members.

The **AICPA Code of Professional Conduct** provides guidance for CPAs in their professional behavior. Adherence to the Code is required only if an individual wishes to have and retain AICPA membership. However, all states also have some form of an ethics or a conduct code for CPAs that is largely similar to the AICPA Code.

The AICPA Code has been revised over time, but its overall structure has remained stable. The Code is made up of **Principles of Professional Conduct, Rules of Conduct, Interpretations of the Rules of Conduct**, and **Rulings** by the Professional Ethics Executive Committee.

The Principles of the Code are set as ideal standards. All CPAs should aspire to these goals. The Principles are not written as standards against which behavior can be compared, so they are not enforceable.

Rules of the Code are enforceable because they are more specific and written in language that indicates behavior that is acceptable and unacceptable, and against which behavior can be compared. Some of the Rules apply to all members of the AICPA, for example, Rule 102 referring to behaving with integrity and objectivity. Other rules apply only to AICPA members who are working for a public accounting firm, in "public practice." Rule 101 on independence and Rule 301 on confidential client information are examples of Rules that apply only to members in public practice.

Reading the Rules makes it clear that some *should* apply only to members in public practice because of the differences between their jobs and the jobs of CPAs not in public practice. A CPA who is performing an audit of a client needs to be independent of that client in order for users of the audit report to feel comfortable relying on the objectivity of the audit opinion. Yet, when an accountant is working within a company, as an employee reporting to management or an internal auditor reporting to the audit committee, the circumstances are different. That individual could not be—and further would have no benefit from being—independent of the company.

Interpretations and Rulings of the Code result from issues that arise when working CPAs use the Code. When members frequently question a particular issue about the understanding or application of a Rule, the AICPA Division of Ethics may provide an Interpretation to explain the issue. Rulings, the next level in the AICPA Code, are very specific and are provided as responses regarding the application of Rules to actual situations encountered by members. If a member does not follow an Interpretation or Ruling, he or she may have to justify the departure.

AUDITING IN ACTION

Organization of the AICPA Code of Professional Conduct

Principles of Professional Conduct
    conceptual, ideal standards
    not enforceable

Rules of Conduct
    threshold for minimum acceptable behavior
    stated in behavior-related language
    enforceable

Interpretations of the Rules of Conduct
    response when there are frequent questions about a rule
    departures must be justified in any disciplinary hearing

Rulings by the Professional Ethics Executive Committee
    rulings on individual cases; responses to specific factual circumstances
    justification for departures may be requested in any disciplinary hearing

REVIEW QUESTIONS

E.1 List organizations and entities that exercise authority over auditors.

E.2 What is the relationship between the AICPA Code of Conduct and the codes of the various states?

E.3 What are the four levels in the structure of the AICPA Code of Conduct?

E.4 Which level of the AICPA Code is intended to be the ideal standard of conduct? The enforceable guide of conduct?

E.5 Do all rules of the Code of Conduct apply to all members of the AICPA?

E.6 Why are Interpretations of the AICPA Code written?

The AICPA Code, as well as publications by other entities such as the SEC and PCAOB, use terms in ways that have a very precise meaning. For example, terms in the AICPA Code such as *attest engagement team, client,* and *close relative* are important because they may indicate who is affected by a particular Rule and in what way. The definitions help to answer questions such as:

Does a "firm" consist of both local and national components, as long as it is the same entity? (Yes.)

Is the "specialist" that is brought in to confirm the authenticity of the diamonds in the inventory of a jewelry store considered a member of the engagement team? (No.)

What is the difference in the meaning of an "immediate family" member—who "steps into the shoes" of the auditor when considering the Rules—and a "close relative" who is considered separate from the auditor.

As you study the Code, use the definitions of terms in Exhibit 3-3 to clarify your understanding.

EXHIBIT 3-3

Important Terms Used in the Code of Professional Conduct

Attest engagement. An attest engagement is an engagement that requires independence as defined in AICPA Professional Standards.

Attest engagement team. The attest engagement team consists of individuals participating in the attest engagement, including those who perform concurring and second partner reviews. The attest engagement team includes all employees and contractors retained by the firm who participate in the attest engagement, irrespective of their functional classification (for example, audit, tax, or management consulting services). The attest engagement team excludes specialists as discussed in SAS No. 73, *Using the Work of a Specialist*, and individuals who perform only routine clerical functions such as word processing and photocopying.

Client. A client is any person or entity, other than the member's employer, that engages a member or a member's firm to perform professional services or a person or entity with respect to which professional services are performed. For purposes of this paragraph, the term "employer" does not include—

a. Entities engaged in the practice of public accounting; or

b. Federal, state, and local governments or component units thereof provided the member performing professional services with respect to those entities—

i. Is directly elected by voters of the government or component unit thereof with respect to which professional services are performed; or

ii. Is an individual who is (1) appointed by a legislative body and (2) subject to removal by a legislative body; or

iii. Is appointed by someone other than the legislative body, so long as the appointment is confirmed by the legislative body and removal is subject to oversight or approval by the legislative body.

Close relative. A close relative is a parent, sibling, or nondependent child.

(continued)

Council. The Council of the American Institute of Certified Public Accountants.

Covered member. A covered member is—

a. An individual on the attest engagement team;

b. An individual in a position to influence the audit engagement;

c. A partner or manager who provides nonattest services to the client beginning once he or she provides ten hours of nonattest services to the client within any fiscal year and ending on the later of the date

   i. the firm signs the report on the financial statements for the fiscal year during which those services were provided or

   ii. he or she no longer expects to provide ten or more hours of nonattest services to the attest client on a recurring basis;

d. A partner in the office in which the lead attest engagement partner primarily practices in connection with the attest engagement;

e. The firm, including the firm's employee benefit plans; or

f. An entity whose operating, financial, or accounting policies can be controlled (as defined by generally accepted accounting principles for consolidations purposes) by any of the individuals or entities described in (a) through (e) or by two or more such individuals or entities if they act together.

Financial Institution. A financial institution is considered to be an entity that, as part of its normal business operations, makes loans or extends credit to the general public. In addition, for automobile leases… an entity would be considered a financial institution if it leases automobiles to the general public.

Financial Statements. A presentation of financial data, including accompanying notes if any, intended to communicate an entity's economic resources and/or obligations at a point in time or the changes therein for a period of time, in accordance with generally accepted accounting principles or a comprehensive basis of accounting other than generally accepted accounting principles….

Firm. A firm is a form of organization permitted by law or regulation whose characteristics conform to resolutions of the Council of the American Institute of Certified Public Accountants that is engaged in the practice of public accounting. Except for purposes of applying Rule 101: Independence, the firm includes the individual partners thereof.

Holding out. In general, any action initiated by a member that informs others of his or her status as a CPA or AICPA-accredited specialist constitutes holding out as a CPA. This would include, for example, any oral or written representation to another regarding CPA status, use of the CPA designation on business cards or letterhead, the display of a certificate evidencing a member's CPA designation, or listing as a CPA in local telephone directories.

Immediate family. Immediate family is a spouse, spousal equivalent, or dependent (whether or not related).

Individual in a position to influence the attest engagement. An individual in a position to influence the attest engagement is one who

a. Evaluates the performance or recommends the compensation of the attest engagement partner;

b. Directly supervises or manages the attest engagement partner, including all successively senior levels above that individual through the firm's chief executive;

c. Consults with the attest engagement team regarding technical or industry-related issues specific to the attest engagement; or

d. Participates in or oversees, at all successively senior levels, quality control activities including internal monitoring, with respect to the specific attest engagement.

Institute. The American Institute of Certified Public Accountants.

Interpretations of rules of condut. Pronouncements issued by division of professional ethics … concerning… the rules of conduct.

Joint closely held investment. A joint closely held investment is an investment in an entity or property by the member and the client (or the client's office or directors, or any owner who has the ability to exercise significant influence over the client) that enables them to control (as defined by generally accepted accounting principles for consolidation purposes) the entity or property.

Key position. A key position is a position in which an individual:

a. Has a primary responsibility for significant accounting functions that support material components of the financial statements;

b. Has primary responsibility for the preparation of the financial statements; or

c. Has the ability to exercise influence over the contents of the financial statements, including when the individual is a member of the board of directors or similar governing body, chief executive officer, president, chief financial officer, chief operating officer, general counsel, chief accounting officer, controller, director of internal audit, director of financial reporting, treasurer, or any equivalent position.

For purposes of attest engagements not involving a client's financial statement, a key position is one in which an individual is primarily responsible for, or able to influence, the subject matter of the attest engagement, as described above.

Loan. A loan is a financial transaction, the characteristics of which generally include, but are not limited to, an agreement that provides for repayment terms and a rate of interest. A loan includes, but is not limited to, a guarantee of a loan, a letter of credit, a line of credit, or a loan commitment.

Manager. A manager is a professional employee of the firm who has either of the following responsibilities:

a. Continuing responsibility for the overall planning and supervision of engagements for specified clients.

b. Authority to determine that an engagement is complete subject to final partner approval if required.

Member. A member, associate member, or international associate of the American Institute of Certified Public Accountants.

Normal Lending Procedures, Terms, and Requirements. "Normal lending procedures, terms, and requirements" relating to a covered member's loan from a financial institution are defined as lending procedures, terms, and requirements that are reasonably comparable with those relating to loans of similar character committed to other borrowers during the period in which the loan to the covered member is committed. Accordingly, in making such comparison and in evaluating whether a loan was made under "normal lending procedures, terms, and requirements," the covered member should consider all the circumstances under which the loan was granted, including

1. The amount of the loan in relation to the value of the collateral pledged as security and the credit standing of the covered member.

2. Repayment terms.

3. Interest rate, including "points."

4. Closing costs.

5. General availability of such loans to the public.

Related prohibitions that may be more restrictive are prescribed by certain state and federal agencies having regulatory authority over such financial institutions. Broker-dealers, for example, are subject to regulation by the Securities and Exchange Commission.

Office. An office is a reasonably distinct subgroup within a firm, whether constituted by formal organization or informal practice, where personnel who make up the subgroup generally serve the same group of clients or work on the same categories of matters. Substance should govern the office classification. For example, the expected regular personnel interactions and assigned reporting channels of an individual may well be more important than an individual's physical location.

Partner. A partner is a proprietor, shareholder, equity or non-equity partner or any individual who assumes the risks and benefits of firm ownership or who is otherwise held by the firm to be the equivalent of any of the aforementioned.

(continued)

Period of the professional engagement. The period of the professional engagement begins when a member either signs an initial engagement letter or other agreement to perform attest services or begins to perform an attest engagement for a client, whichever is earlier. The period lasts for the entire duration of the professional relationship (which could cover many periods) and ends with the formal or informal notification, either by the member or the client, of the termination of the professional relationship or by the issuance of a report whichever is later. Accordingly, the period does not end with the issuance of a report and recommence with the beginning of the following year's attest engagement.

Practice of public accounting. The practice of public accounting consists of the performance for a client, by a member or a member's firm, while holding out as CPA(s), of the professional services of accounting, tax, personal financial planning, litigation support services, and those professional services for which standards are promulgated by bodies designated by Council. Such standards include Financial Accounting Standards Board (FASB) *Accounting Standards Codification* (ASC), Statements of Auditing Standards, Statements on Standards for Accounting and Review Services, Statements on Standards for Consulting Services, Statements of Governmental Accounting Standards, International Financial Reporting Standards and International Accounting Standards, Statements on Standards for Attestation Engagements and Statements on Standards for Valuation Services.

However, a member or a member's firm, while holding out as CPA(s), is not considered to be in the practice of public accounting if the member or the member's firm does not perform for any client, any of the professional services described in the preceding paragraph.

Professional services. Professional services include all services performed by a member while holding out as a CPA.

Significant influence. The term significant influence is as defined in FASB ASC 323-10-15.

(*Source:* Code of Professional Conduct Section 92.)

REVIEW QUESTIONS

F.1   What is the difference between immediate family and close relative?

F.2   What is the difference between being in a key position and being in a position to influence an engagement?

F.3   How can the definition of covered member apply to both an individual and a firm?

F.4   Why is the phrase "holding out" important?

Principles of Professional Conduct

The AICPA Code Principles of Professional Conduct convey ideals consistent with the auditor's mission of protecting the public interest. The second principle specifically refers to serving the public interest. Others state that CPAs should use due care in their work, exhibiting their best skills and competence. They should exercise their best judgment using both professional and ethical standards. CPAs should behave with integrity and objectivity and not have conflicts of interest. Those in public practice should be independent of their clients. Furthermore, they should follow professional guidance in deciding what work they should and should not do—the "scope and nature" of services to be provided.

These Principles can be displayed and discussed as a list of discrete concepts, but they are more meaningful when considered in relation to each other. For example, in order to make their best judgments, CPAs must be knowledgeable in both technical matters and concepts of integrity and ethics. In order to perform with due care, they must make their best judgments. In order to protect the public interest, they must not only have knowledge that permits them to exercise due care, they must use their best judgments, behave with integrity and objectivity, have an independent mind-set, and follow professional guidance.

The concept of independence is critical to auditors performing their work objectively and protecting the public interest. Independence is given significant attention in the AICPA Code Rules. In the Principles, the concepts of **independence in fact** and **independence in appearance** are introduced. *Independence in fact* means that the auditor does his or her work objectively without having any bias or predetermined preference regarding the audit conclusions.

The difficulty with the *independence in fact* standard of behavior is that no one can be sure of what an auditor is thinking. If the public and other users of the audit report could be sure that the auditor was *independent in fact,* that certainty would be sufficient for users to feel confident in relying on the auditor's objective conclusions. However, since they cannot see what is going on in an auditor's thoughts, users must rely on external and visible indicators of an auditor's independence.

The need for visible indicators consistent with an objective state of mind is the reason for the independence rule that is part of the AICPA Code. The rule presents a logical correlation of actions and thought. When an auditor adheres to practices that outsiders find consistent with independent and objective thought processes, there is a likelihood that the auditor is actually *independent in fact*. Important external indicators of independence are a lack of financial or managerial interest in an audit client. *Independence in fact* is the goal. Independence is the objective state of mind that all auditors should have. Since it is impossible to be certain that an auditor is *independent in fact,* the Code also sets the standard for *independence in appearance*. The AICPA Principles of Professional Conduct are shown in Exhibit 3-4.

Rules of Conduct

The AICPA Code Rules of Conduct are the enforceable guidance against which behavior can be compared. The Rules serve as guidance to CPAs regarding minimum levels of behavior as they strive to attain the ideal goals expressed in the Principles. The rules are structured in a manner parallel to the Principles. The official language of the AICPA Rules of Conduct is shown in Exhibit 3-5. The meaning of the rules is explained in the following section. Whether the rules apply depends on whether the CPA works in public practice or as an employee. Even for CPAs working in public practice, whether (and how) the rules apply depends on the type of professional service being provided to the client.

EXHIBIT 3-4

AICPA Principles of Professional Conduct

Responsibilities: In carrying out their responsibilities as professionals, members should exercise sensitive professional and moral judgments in all their activities.

The Public Interest: Members should accept the obligation to act in a way that will serve the public interest, honor the public trust, and demonstrate commitment to professionalism.

Integrity: To maintain and broaden public confidence, members should perform all professional responsibilities with the highest sense of integrity.

Objectivity and Independence: A member should maintain objectivity and be free of conflicts of interest in discharging professional responsibilities. A member in public practice should be independent in fact and appearance when providing auditing and other attestation services.

Due Care: A member should observe the profession's technical and ethical standards, strive continually to improve competence and the quality of services, and discharge professional responsibility to the best of the member's ability.

Scope and Nature of Services: A member in public practice should observe the Principles of the Code of Professional Conduct in determining the scope and nature of services to be provided.

(http://aicpa.org/about/code/sec50.htm)

EXHIBIT 3-5

AICPA Rules of Conduct

Rule 101 Independence

A member in public practice shall be independent in the performance of professional services as required by standards promulgated by bodies designated by Council.

Rule 102 Integrity and Objectivity

In the performance of any professional service, a member shall maintain objectivity and integrity, shall be free of conflicts of interest, and shall not knowingly misrepresent facts or subordinate his or her judgment to others.

Rule 201 General Standards

A member shall comply with the following standards and with any interpretations thereof by bodies designated by Council.

A. Professional Competence. Undertake only those professional services that the member or the member's firm can reasonably expect to be completed with professional competence.

B. Due Professional Care. Exercise due professional care in the performance of professional services.

C. Planning and Supervision. Adequately plan and supervise the performance of professional service.

D. Sufficient Relevant Data. Obtain sufficient relevant data to afford a reasonable basis for conclusions or recommendations in relation to any professional services performed.

Rule 202 Compliance with Standards

A member who performs auditing, review, compilation, management consulting, tax, or other professional services shall comply with standards promulgated by bodies designated by Council.

Rule 203 Accounting Principles

A member shall not (1) express an opinion or state affirmatively that the financial statements or other financial data of an entity are presented in conformity with generally accepted accounting principles or (2) state that he or she is not aware of any material modifications that should be made to such statements or data in order for them to be in conformity with generally accepted accounting principles, if such statements or data contain any departure from an accounting principle promulgated by bodies designated by Council to establish such principles that has a material effect on the statements or data taken as a whole. If, however, the statements or data contain such a departure and the member can demonstrate that due to unusual circumstances the financial statements or data would otherwise have been misleading, the member can comply with the rule by describing the departure, its approximate effects, if practicable, and the reasons why compliance with the principle would result in a misleading statement.

Rule 301 Confidential Client Information

A member in public practice shall not disclose any confidential client information without the specific consent of the client.
This rule shall not be construed

(1) to relieve a member of his or her professional obligations under Rules 202 and 203,

(2) to affect in any way the member's obligation to comply with a validly issued and enforceable subpoena or summons, or to prohibit a member's compliance with applicable laws and government regulations,

(3) to prohibit review of a member's professional practice under AICPA or state CPA society or Board of Accountancy authorization, or

(4) to preclude a member from initiating a complaint with, or responding to any inquiry made by, the professional ethics division or trial board of the Institute or a duly constituted investigative or disciplinary body of a state CPA society or Board of Accountancy.

Members of any of the bodies identified in (4) above and members involved with professional practice reviews identified in (3) above shall not use to their own advantage or disclose any member's confidential client information that comes to their attention in carrying out those activities. This prohibition shall not restrict members' exchange of information in connection with the investigative or disciplinary proceedings described in (4) above or the professional practice reviews described in (3) above.

THE AUDITOR'S ROLE IN SOCIETY

Rule 302 Contingent fees

A member in public practice shall not

(1) Perform for a contingent fee any professional services for, or receive such a fee from a client for whom the member or the member's firm performs,

    (a) an audit or review of a financial statement; or

    (b) a compilation of a financial statement when the member expects, or reasonably might expect, that a third party will use the financial statement and the member's compilation report does not disclose a lack of independence; or

    (c) an examination of prospective financial information, or

(2) Prepare an original or amended tax return or claim for a tax refund for a contingent fee for any client.

The prohibition in (1) applies during the period in which the member or the member's firm is engaged to perform any of the services listed above and the period covered by any historical financial statements involved in any such listed services.

Except as stated in the next sentence, a contingent fee is a fee established for the performance of any service pursuant to an arrangement in which no fee will be charged unless a specified finding or result is attained, or in which the amount of the fee is otherwise dependent upon the finding or result of such service. Solely for purposes of this rule, fees are not regarded as being contingent if fixed by courts or other public authorities, or, in tax matters, if determined based on the results of judicial proceedings or the findings of governmental agencies.

A member's fees may vary depending, for example, on the complexity of services rendered.

Rule 501 Acts Discreditable

A member shall not commit an act discreditable to the profession.

Rule 502 Advertising and Other Forms of Solicitation

A member in public practice shall not seek to obtain clients by advertising or other forms of solicitation in a manner that is false, misleading, or deceptive. Solicitation by the use of coercion, over-reaching, or harassing conduct is prohibited.

Rule 503 Commissions and Referral Fees

A. Prohibited commissions

    A member in public practice shall not for a commission recommend or refer to a client any product or service, or for a commission recommend or refer any product or service to be supplied by a client, or receive a commission, when the member or the member's firms also performs for that client

    (a) an audit or review of a financial statement; or

    (b) a compilation of a financial statement when the member expects, or reasonably might expect, that a third party will use the financial statement and the member's compilation report does not disclose a lack of independence; or

    (c) an examination of prospective financial information

B. Disclosure of permitted commissions

    A member in public practice who is not prohibited by this rule from performing services for or receiving a commission and who is paid or expects to be paid a commission shall disclose that fact to any person or entity to whom the member recommends or refers a product or service to which the commission relates.

C. Referral fees

    Any member who accepts a referral fee for recommending or referring any service of a CPA to any person or entity or who pays a referral fee to obtain a client shall disclose such acceptance or payment to the client.

Rule 505 Form of Organization and Name

A member may practice public accounting only in a form of organization permitted by law or regulation whose characteristics conform to resolutions of Council.

(continued)

A member shall not practice public accounting under a firm name that is misleading. Names of one or more past owners may be included in the firm name of a successor organization.

A firm may not designate itself as "Members of the American Institute of Certified Public Accountants" unless all of its CPA owners are members of the Institute.

(AICPA, Code of Professional Conduct, Sections 100 through 500)

Rule 101, Independence, is similar to the Principle but states that AICPA standards must be followed. Independence is discussed in greater detail in the next section.

Rule 102, Integrity and Objectivity, is also similar to the Principles but adds that it is wrong to present information incorrectly when the CPA knows it is wrong, and that it is wrong to subordinate judgment to others. This simply means that a CPA should not let someone else make a decision that is his or her responsibility.

Rule 201, titled General Standards, provides more information about what it means to perform work using technical competence and due professional care. The guidance of Rule 201 extends to both the individual and the firm, stating that the member or the member's firm must have the skills and knowledge to perform the engagement. Further, "due professional care" is required including the planning and supervision of the work as well as obtaining sufficient support in the form of evidence or data to support the auditor's conclusion. Due professional care means performing services with competence and a questioning attitude. Due professional care is discussed again in Chapter 4 relating to legal concepts.

Rule 202, Compliance with Standards, basically states that the CPA must look to any professional standards that are available in performing his or her work.

Rule 203, Accounting Principles, states that the financial statements must be in conformity with GAAP in order for the auditor to state that in the audit report. The auditor cannot say that there are not any material modifications that should be made to make the financial statements in conformity with GAAP unless that is actually the case. There is an exception for the situation in which complying with GAAP would make the financial statements misleading, but the company that prepares the financial statements must explain the circumstances and justify why GAAP would make the financial statements misleading. This exception does not exist when performing an audit of financial statements for a public company under PCAOB standards. GAAP can be U.S. accounting standards, or (for companies that qualify) international standards, or other bases of accounting produced by standard setting bodies whose authority is recognized by the AICPA.

Rule 301, Confidential Client Information, states that a CPA cannot disclose client information learned during the course of an engagement without the client's consent. The exceptions to this rule are (1) when it is necessary related to reporting on a financial statement that is in violation of GAAP, (2) to comply with a subpoena or review of work by the AICPA, a state or professional board, or (3) to initiate a complaint with a professional or state body regarding another CPA's work. The logic behind the exceptions regarding subpoenas, reviews, and complaints is that those who will be receiving the information that would otherwise be confidential are bound by confidentiality rules related to the roles in which they are performing the oversight or disciplinary work.

Rule 302, Contingent Fees, for the most part prohibits any fee arrangement in which the amount the CPA is paid depends on the outcome of the work. For example, a CPA who performs an audit cannot contract to receive a certain fee if an unqualified opinion is issued and a different fee if the CPA concludes that only an adverse opinion is appropriate. This prohibition is logical because the prospect of receiving different fees for different audit outcomes would damage the auditor's ability to be independent and impartial about the audit outcome. A CPA performing tax work cannot contract for a fee that is contingent on the amount of tax liability that is determined. Fees are not considered contingent if they are

THE AUDITOR'S ROLE IN SOCIETY **103**

fixed by "courts or other public authorities" and depend on judicial or governmental agency proceeding outcomes. An example of this situation is when a bankruptcy judge sets the fee a CPA is paid based on the events of the bankruptcy proceedings.

Rules 501 and **502** deal with general behavior. The rule on discreditable acts basically bars illegal behavior such as employment discrimination and harassment and not paying taxes owed. The advertising rule prohibits trying to obtain business through dishonest or inappropriately forceful means.

Rule 503, Commissions and Referral Fees, states that if a CPA performs an audit or a review of financial statements, or examines prospective financial information, he or she cannot receive a commission from the client for referring the client to someone. (The details differ somewhat for compilation services.)[3] For example, if a CPA audits a home video installation provider, he or she cannot recommend the company to clients and receive a payment from the home video company for the referrals. In addition, when performing those services (audit, review, or prospective financial information examination) for a client, the CPA cannot receive a commission for recommending to the client a vendor or service provider. An example is when a CPA audits a company and, at the conclusion of the audit the company decides that it needs to buy computer equipment and services. The CPA cannot recommend a computer vendor to the audit client and receive a commission from the vendor. If the CPA is not providing an audit, a review, or an examination of prospective financial information, commissions are not prohibited, but the CPA must disclose that he or she may receive a commission for the recommendation or referral. Any fees paid or received by the CPA must be disclosed to the client.

Rule 505, Form of Organization and Name, deals with constraints on the organizations for which AICPA members may work. An AICPA member can practice public accounting only while working for a firm that is organized according to the rules of the AICPA. Typically, sole proprietorships and various types of partnerships are accepted under AICPA rules. (These were discussed in Chapter 1, Appendix A.) Also, the name used by an employing firm may not be misleading. For example, a name that indicates a partnership when there is only one owner would be considered misleading. A firm name that includes former owners who have either died or left the firm is not considered misleading. A firm can only label itself as "Members of the American Institute of Certified Public Accountants" if all the CPA owners are members of the AICPA.

REVIEW QUESTIONS

G.1 What does Rule 102 mean in stating that a CPA should not subordinate judgment?

G.2 What does Rule 201 mean when it calls for "due professional care"?

G.3 Under Rule 203, is it ever acceptable for financial statements to NOT conform to GAAP?

G.4 What are the exceptions to Rule 301 that permit a CPA to disclose confidential client information without the client's permission?

G.5 What is a contingent fee? How do fees fixed by courts or other public authorities fit into Rule 302?

G.6 Can a CPA ever receive a commission or referral fee?

G.7 Summarize Rule 505 regarding the form of organization under which a CPA can practice, and the limitations on names for such an organization.

---

[3] These different types of services are discussed in Chapter 16. In brief, a review is a CPA-provided service on financial statements that provides less assurance than an audit. An examination of prospective financial information provides the same level of assurance as an audit, but the target of the auditor's activities is a forecast or projection rather than traditional financial statements. A compilation describes a service in which a CPA uses client-prepared information to draft financial statements.

PCAOB RULES OF THE BOARD

The PCAOB is the not-for-profit entity structured by the SEC in response to SOX to oversee the auditors and audits of public companies. The goal of the PCAOB is to protect investors and the public interest by ensuring that registered public accounting firms are conducting fair and independent audits.

The PCAOB has authority to prose and adopt rules and standards. It submits its rules and standards to the SEC for approval. The PCAOB's adoptions do not take effect unless approved by the SEC.

The PCAOB's standards direct professional practice. Rules are more overarching in that they state the requirement to follow PCAOB standards. Rules also address topics beyond those covered by the standards, such as registering with the PCAOB and inspection of firms. Currently, the PCAOB rules that have been approved by the SEC are separated into seven sections. Exhibit 3-6 outlines the rules of the PCAOB.

EXHIBIT 3-6

PCAOB Rules of the Board

Section 1—General Provisions
- Rule 1001 – Definitions of Terms Employed in Rules
- Rule 1002 – Time Computation

Section 2—Registration and Reporting
- Rule 2100 – Registration Requirements for Public Accounting
- Rule 2101 – Application for Registration
- Rule 2102 – Date of Receipt
- Rule 2103 – Registration Fees
- Rule 2104 – Signatures
- Rule 2105 – Conflicting Non-U.S. Laws
- Rule 2106 – Action on Applications for Registration
- Rule 2107 – Withdrawal from Registration
- Rule 2200 – Annual Report
- Rule 2201 – Time for Filing of Annual Report
- Rule 2202 – Annual Fee
- Rule 2203 – Special Reports
- Rule 2204 – Signatures
- Rule 2205 – Amendments
- Rule 2206 – Date of Filing
- Rule 2207 – Assertions of Conflicts with Non-U.S. Laws
- Rule 2300 – Public Availability of Information Submitted to the Board; Confidential Treatment Requests

Section 3—Professional Standards
- Rule 3100 – Compliance with Auditing and Related Professional Practice Standards
- Rule 3101 – Certain Terms Used in Auditing and Related Professional Practice Standards
- Rule 3200T – Interim Auditing Standards
- Rule 3300T – Interim Attestation Standards
- Rule 3400T – Interim Quality Control Standards
- Rule 3500T – Interim Ethics Standards
- Rule 3501 – Definitions of Terms Employed in Section 3, Part 5 of the Rules
- Rule 3502 – Responsibility Not to Knowingly or Recklessly Contribute to Violations
- Rule 3520 – Auditor Independence
- Rule 3521 – Contingent Fees
- Rule 3522 – Tax Transactions

- Rule 3523 – Tax Services for Persons in Financial Reporting Oversight Roles
- Rule 3524 – Audit Committee Pre-approval of Certain Tax Services
- Rule 3525 – Audit Committee Pre-approval of Non-audit Tax Services Related to Internal Control Over Financial Reporting
- Rule 3526 – Communication with Audit Committee Concerning Independence
- Rule 3600T – Interim Independence Standards
- Rule 3700 – Advisory Groups

Section 4—Inspections

- Rule 4000 – General
- Rule 4001 – Regular Inspections
- Rule 4002 – Special Inspections
- Rule 4003 – Frequency of Inspections
- Rule 4004 – Procedure Regarding Possible Violations
- Rule 4007 – Procedures Concerning Draft Inspection Reports
- Rule 4008 – Procedures Concerning Final Inspection Reports
- Rule 4009 – Firm Response to Quality Control Defects
- Rule 4010 – Board Public Reports
- Rule 4011 – Statement by Foreign Registered Public Accounting Firms
- Rule 4012 – Inspections of Foreign Registered Public Accounting Firms

Section 5—Investigations and Adjudications

- Rule 5000 – General
- Rule 5100 – Informal Inquiries
- Rule 5101 – Commencement and Closure of Investigations
- Rule 5102 – Testimony of Registered Public Accounting Firms and Associated Persons in Investigations
- Rule 5103 – Demand for Production of Audit Workpapers and Other Documents from Registered Public Accounting Firms and Associated Persons
- Rule 5104 – Examination of Books and Records in Aid of Investigations
- Rule 5105 – Requests for Testimony or Production of Documents from Persons Not Associated with Registered Public Accounting Firms
- Rule 5106 – Assertion of Claim of Privilege
- Rule 5107 – Uniform Definitions in Demands and Requests for Information
- Rule 5108 – Confidentiality of Investigatory Records
- Rule 5109 – Rights of Witnesses in Inquiries and Investigations
- Rule 5110 – Noncooperation with an Investigation
- Rule 5111 – Requests for Issuance of Commission Subpoenas in Aid of an Investigation
- Rule 5112 – Coordination and Referral of Investigations
- Rule 5113 – Reliance on the Investigations of Non-U.S. Authorities
- Rule 5200 – Commencement of Disciplinary Proceedings
- Rule 5201 – Notification of Commencement of Disciplinary Proceedings
- Rule 5202 – Record of Disciplinary Proceedings
- Rule 5203 – Public and Private Hearings
- Rule 5204 – Determinations in Disciplinary Proceedings
- Rule 5205 – Settlement of Disciplinary Proceedings Without a Determination After Hearing
- Rule 5206 – Automatic Stay of Final Disciplinary Actions
- Rule 5300 – Sanctions
- Rule 5301 – Effect of Sanctions
- Rule 5302 – Applications for Relief From, or Modification of, Revocations and Bars
- Rule 5303 – Use of Money Penalties
- Rule 5304 – Summary Suspension for Failure to Pay Money Penalties

(continued)

- Rule 5400 – Hearings
- Rule 5401 – Appearance and Practice Before the Board
- Rule 5402 – Hearing Officer Disqualification and Withdrawal
- Rule 5403 – Ex Parte Communications
- Rule 5404 – Service of Papers by Parties
- Rule 5405 – Filing of Papers With the Board: Procedure
- Rule 5406 – Filing of Papers: Form
- Rule 5407 – Filing of Papers: Signature Requirement and Effect
- Rule 5408 – Motions
- Rule 5409 – Default and Motions to Set Aside Default
- Rule 5410 – Additional Time For Service by Mail
- Rule 5411 – Modifications of Time, Postponements and Adjournments
- Rule 5420 – Stay Requests
- Rule 5421 – Answer to Allegations
- Rule 5422 – Availability of Documents For Inspection and Copying
- Rule 5423 – Production of Witness Statements
- Rule 5424 – Accounting Board Demands and Commission Subpoenas
- Rule 5425 – Depositions to Preserve Testimony for Hearing
- Rule 5426 – Prior Sworn Statements of Witnesses in Lieu of Live Testimony
- Rule 5427 – Motion for Summary Disposition
- Rule 5440 – Record of Hearings
- Rule 5441 – Evidence: Admissibility
- Rule 5442 – Evidence: Objections and Offers of Proof
- Rule 5443 – Evidence: Presentation Under Oath or Affirmation
- Rule 5444 – Evidence: Presentation, Rebuttal and Cross-examination
- Rule 5445 – Post-hearing Briefs and Other Submissions
- Rule 5460 – Board Review of Determinations of Hearing Officers
- Rule 5461 – Interlocutory Review
- Rule 5462 – Briefs Filed with the Board
- Rule 5463 – Oral Argument Before the Board
- Rule 5464 – Additional Evidence
- Rule 5465 – Record Before the Board
- Rule 5466 – Reconsideration
- Rule 5467 – Receipt of Petitions for Commission or Judicial Review
- Rule 5468 – Appeal of Actions Made Pursuant to Delegated Authority
- Rule 5469 – Board Consideration of Actions Made Pursuant to Delegated Authority
- Rule 5500 – Commencement of Hearing on Disapproval of a Registration Application
- Rule 5501 – Procedures for a Hearing on Disapproval of a Registration Application

Section 6—International

- Rule 6001 – Assisting Non-U.S. Authorities in Inspections

- Rule 6002 – Assisting Non-U.S. Authorities in Investigations

Section 7—Funding

- Rule 7100 – Accounting Support Fee
- Rule 7101 – Allocation of Accounting Support Fee
- Rule 7102 – Assessment of Accounting Support Fee
- Rule 7103 – Collection of Accounting Support Fee
- Rule 7104 – Service as Designated Collection Agent

(http://www.pcaobus.org/Rules/Rules_of_the_Board/All.pdf)

AUDITOR INDEPENDENCE

Auditors provide a vital service by protecting the public interest. They enable the functioning of the capital markets by conducting audits and reporting opinions on the ICFR and financial statements. It is universally agreed that the value of the service and audit report depends on the credibility of the auditor.

Auditor credibility is not *sufficient* for the audit report to have value, but it is *necessary*. The audit report has value only if the users of the report believe that the auditor performed the audit to the best of his or her technical ability and issued a report that was appropriate for the results found. In order for the public and other users to believe in the audit report, the auditor must have no personal preference and must not benefit from the particular findings of the audit. The auditor must be just as willing to issue an audit report indicating negative findings as he or she is to issue an unqualified report. If the auditor were to have a preference, then the public and others could not rely on the auditor to issue the most appropriate report. This means that the auditor must be "independent."

The requirement that the auditor be independent of the client is so important that it is one of the fundamental and primary concepts in both the AICPA Code of Professional Conduct and generally accepted auditing standards. Independence from audit clients is required by the SEC as well.

AUDITING IN ACTION

Independence in the Generally Accepted Auditing Standards

Auditors... should not only be independent in fact; they should also avoid situations that may lead outsiders to doubt their independence. (AU 220.03)

The auditor must maintain independence in mental attitude in all matters relating to the audit. (AICPA AU 220.01)

The SEC recognizes the importance of auditor independence as a fundamental underlying component to ensure audit value. The SEC describes auditors as "gatekeepers." This means that the SEC relies on auditors to identify financial statements that do not fairly represent the company that issues them. In order to perform this role as gatekeepers, auditors must have no preference or vested interest in the outcome of the audit. The auditor must be just as willing to state that ICFR is not effective as effective and just as willing to identify the financial statements as problematic as to report that they are fair.

AUDITING IN ACTION

Importance of Auditor Independence Requirements—Gatekeepers to the Securities Markets

The federal securities laws require... that financial information filed... be certified or audited by "independent" public accountants. To a significant extent, this makes independent auditors the "gatekeepers" to the public securities markets. This statutory framework gives auditors both a valuable economic franchise and an important public trust. Within this statutory framework, the independence requirement is vital to our securities markets.

(SEC Rule 33-7919)

Even the **corporate governance structure** that directs management as it carries out the Board of Directors' objectives depends on auditor independence. The audit committee of the Board of Directors is responsible for hiring and interacting with the external auditor. The audit committee then relies on the external auditor as it fulfills its oversight responsibilities. For the audit committee to benefit from the external auditor's work, the auditor should be objective, even-handed, nonpreferential, and independent.

AUDITING IN ACTION

Audit Committee Reliance on Independent Auditors

If the audit committee is to effectively accomplish its task of overseeing the financial reporting process, it must rely, in part, on the work, guidance and judgment of the outside auditor. Integral to this reliance is the requirement that the outside auditors perform their service without being affected by economic or other interests that would call into question their objectivity and accordingly, the reliability of their attestation.

(*Source: Report and Recommendations of the Blue Ribbon Committee on Improving the Effectiveness of Corporate Audit Committees*, 1999, p. 44.)

Widespread consensus supports the proposition that an audit report has value only when the auditor is independent. Does this also mean that everyone agrees on the definition of independence? Generally, most people agree that independence, as used in an auditing context, means that the auditor has an objective state of mind regarding the audit activities and outcomes, and is not biased with any personal preference. Again, this refers to the state of mind known as *independence in fact*. However, unless the users of audit reports can suddenly become mind readers, there is no way to know the state of an auditor's mind.

External indicators are used to infer an auditor's state of mind. Outsiders look at external markers to suggest whether an auditor is *independent in fact*. Though not foolproof, *independence in appearance* is the best indicator available that an auditor is independent in fact. The SEC provides the following discussion of independence in fact versus appearance.

Except where an auditor accepts a payment to look the other way, is found to have participated in a fraudulent scheme, or admits to being biased, we cannot know with absolute certainty whether an auditor's mind is, or at the time of the audit was, "objective." It is even harder to measure the impact that a particular financial arrangement with the audit client had on the auditor's state of mind. Similarly, it is difficult to tie a questionable state of mind to a wrong judgment, a failure to notice something important, a failure to seek important evidential matter, a failure to challenge a management assertion, or a failure to consider the quality—not just the acceptability—of a company's financial reporting.

(SEC Rule 33-7919)

Much of the rules and literature related to auditor independence creates standards regarding what an auditor may and may not do and still maintain independence in appearance. The ultimate hope is that if an auditor avoids those situations that would make him or her *appear* to be lacking in independence, then situations will be avoided that would impair independence *in fact* as well. The AICPA also presents a conceptual framework that can be used for analyzing independence matters. (ET 100.01)

AUDITING IN ACTION

Conceptual Framework for AICPA Independence Standards

ET 100.01… a member's relationship with a client is evaluated to determine whether it poses an unacceptable risk to the member's independence. Risk is unacceptable if the relationship would compromise (or would be perceived as compromising by an informed third party having knowledge of all relevant information) the member's professional judgment when rendering an attest service to the client.

The SEC sets forth the concept of a "reasonable investor." This concept is a benchmark to use in assessing independence in appearance. Would a reasonable investor who knows all the facts of the auditor's relationships and involvements with the client company believe that the auditor was able to be objective and impartial? The reasonable investor concept links to the SEC's general standard of auditor independence:

> Independence generally is understood to refer to a mental state of objectivity and lack of bias.
>> Direct evidence of the auditor's mental state would be independence in fact.
>> Generally, mental states can be assessed only through observation of external facts.
>> Thus, an auditor is not independent if a reasonable investor with knowledge of all relevant facts and circumstances would conclude that the auditor is not capable of exercising objective and impartial judgment.

(SEC Rule 33-7919)

SEC General Standard of Auditor Independence:

Does the relationship or the provision of a service:

> Create a mutual or conflicting interest with the audit client?
> Place the accounting firm in the position of auditing its own work?
> Result in the accounting firm acting as management or an employee of the audit client?
> Place the accounting firm in a position of being an advocate for the audit client?

The next step to understanding auditor independence is learning the situations that the profession and regulators have decided interfere with the appearance of independence. AICPA Code Interpretation 101-1, shown in Exhibit 3-7, deals with explanations regarding independence impairment.

EXHIBIT 3-7

AICPA Interpretation 101 of Rule 101, Independence

Independence shall be considered to be impaired if:

A. During the period of the professional engagement a covered member
1. Had or was committed to acquire any direct or material indirect financial interest in the client.
2. Was a trustee of any trust or executor or administrator of any estate if such trust or estate had or was committed to acquire any direct or material indirect financial interest in the client.
3. Had a joint closely held investment that was material to the covered member.
4. Except as specifically permitted in interpretation 101-5, had any loan to or from the client, any officer or director of the client, or any individual owning 10 percent or more of the client's outstanding equity securities or other ownership interests.

(continued)

B. During the period of the professional engagement, a partner or professional employee of the firm , his or her immediate family, or any group of such persons acting together owned more than 5 percent of a client's outstanding equity securities or other ownership interests.

C. During the period covered by the financial statements or during the period of the professional engagement, a firm, or partner or professional employee of the firm was simultaneously associated with the client as a(n)

   1. Director, officer, or employee, or in any capacity equivalent to that of a member of management;

   2. Promoter, underwriter, or voting trustee; or

   3. Trustee for any pension or profit-sharing trust of the client.

Application of the Independence Rules to Covered Members Formerly Employed by a Client or Otherwise Associated with a Client

An individual who was formerly (i) employed by a client or (ii) associated with a client as a(n) officer, director, promoter, underwriter, voting trustee, or trustee for a pension or profit-sharing trust of the client would impair his or her firm's independence if the individual

1. Participated on the attest engagement team or was an individual in a position to influence the attest engagement for the client when the attest engagement covers any period that includes his or her former employment or association with that client; or

2. Was otherwise a covered member with respect to the client unless the individual first dissociates from the client by—

   (a) Terminating any relationships with the client described in interpretation 101-1.C;

   (b) Disposing of any direct or material indirect financial interest in the client;

   (c) Collecting or repaying any loans to or from the client, except for loans specifically permitted or grandfathered under interpretation 101-5;

   (d) Ceasing to participate in all employee benefit plans sponsored by the client, unless the client is legally required to allow the individual to participate in the plan (for example, COBRA) and the individual pays 100 percent of the cost of participation on a current basis; and

   (e) Liquidating or transferring all vested benefits in the client's defined benefit plans, defined contribution plans, deferred compensation plans, and other similar arrangements at the earliest date permitted under the plan. However, liquidation or transfer is not required if a penalty significant to the benefits is imposed upon liquidation or transfer.

Application of the Independence Rules to a Covered Member's Immediate Family

Except as stated in the following paragraph, **a covered member's immediate family is subject to rule 101, and its interpretations and rulings.**

The exceptions are that **independence would not be considered to be impaired** solely as a result of the following:

1. An individual in a covered member's immediate family was employed by the client in a position other than a key position.

2. In connection with his or her employment, an individual in the immediate family of one of the following covered members participated in a retirement, savings, compensation, or similar plan that is a client, is sponsored by a client, or that invests in a client (provided such plan is normally offered to all employees in similar positions):

   a. A partner or manager who provides ten or more hours of non-attest services to the client; or

   b. Any partner in the office in which the lead attest engagement partner primarily practices in connection with the attest engagement.

For purposes of determining materiality under rule 101 the financial interests of the covered member and his or her immediate family should be aggregated.

Application of the Independence Rules to Close Relatives
Independence would be considered to be impaired if—

1. An individual participating on the attest engagement team has a close relative who had
   a. A key position with the client, or
   b. A financial interest in the client that
      (i) Was material to the close relative and of which the individual has knowledge; or
      (ii) Enabled the close relative to exercise significant influence over the client.

2. An individual in a position to influence the attest engagement or any partner in the office in which the lead attest engagement partner primarily practices in connection with the attest engagement has a close relative who had
   a. A key position with the client; or
   b. A financial interest in the client that
      (i) Was material to the close relative and of which the individual or partner has knowledge; and
      (ii) Enabled the close relative to exercise significant influence over the client.

Grandfathered Employment Relationships
Employment relationships of a covered member's immediate family and close relatives with an existing attest client that impair independence under this interpretation and that existed as of November 2001, **will not be deemed to impair independence** provided such relationships were permitted under preexisting requirements of rule 101, and its interpretations and rulings.

Other Considerations
It is impossible to enumerate all circumstances in which the appearance of independence might be questioned. In the absence of an independence interpretation or ruling under rule 101 that addresses a particular circumstance, a member should evaluate whether that circumstance would lead a reasonable person aware of all the relevant facts to conclude that there is an unacceptable threat to the member's and the firm's independence. When making that evaluation, members should refer to the risk-based approach described in the Conceptual Framework for AICPA Independence Standards. If the threats to independence are not at an acceptable level, safeguards should be applied to eliminate the threats or reduce them to an acceptable level. In cases where threats to independence are not at an acceptable level, thereby requiring the application of safeguards, the threats identified and the safeguards applied to eliminate the threats or reduce them to an acceptable level should be documented.

(http://www.aicpa.org/about/code/et_101.html#et_101interpretations)

As Exhibit 3-7 displays, Interpretation 101 is long and uses language that has been specifically defined in the AICPA Code of Professional Conduct. Now is a good time to review definitions presented in Exhibit 3-3 of a *covered member*, *immediate family*, and *close relative*. In addition, recall from Exhibit 3-3 that a *direct financial interest* means that the auditor is the one attributed with whatever the financial interest may be, whether it results from personal ownership or ownership by an immediate family member. An *indirect financial interest* means that there is another party—for example, another company—between the auditor and the financial interest in the company being audited.

Materiality has the same meaning as it does in other accounting contexts. An item is considered material if it would change a decision maker's judgment. In most cases materiality questions regarding auditor independence address whether the dollar magnitude of an *indirect financial interest* is large enough to affect the decisions or behavior of the auditor. In other words, is the indirect financial interest material to the auditor? A summary of important concepts of Interpretation 101 follows.

A covered member (i.e., the auditor) **will not be independent from the client if he or she:**

Has (or is going to get) a direct financial interest in a client

Has (or is going to get) a material indirect financial interest in a client

Is a trustee or administrator of an estate or trust that has (or is going to get) a direct or material indirect financial interest in a client

Has a joint investment with a client

Has a loan to or from a client, an officer of a client, or any individual owning more than 10 percent of a client (… there are some exceptions)

Was formally employed by the client in a position to influence the audit or acted as an officer, director, promoter, underwriter, or trustee of a pension or profit-sharing trust of the client

A covered member (i.e., the auditor) **will not be independent from the client if his or her immediate family:**

Has a direct financial interest in a client

Has a material indirect financial interest in a client

Is an employee of the client in a key position

A covered member (i.e., the auditor) **will not be independent from the client if his or her close relatives:**

Have a key position with a client

Have a material financial interest in a client that is known to the covered member

Have a financial interest in a client that allows the relative to have significant influence over the activities of a client

Are in a position to influence the audit

A partner or professional employee will not be independent from the client if he or she is:

A director, officer, employee, promoter, underwriter, voting trustee, or trustee of a pension or profit-sharing trust of the client

REVIEW QUESTIONS

H.1 What is the difference between independence in fact and independence in appearance?

H.2 Why do auditors need to be independent?

H.3 In what situations of financial interest is materiality important?

H.4 Do most of the independence rules address independence in fact or in appearance?

INDEPENDENCE REQUIREMENTS OF SOX AND THE SEC

SOX and the SEC also address auditor independence. Section 206 of SOX states that if an auditor worked on a company's audit engagement and goes to work for the client, it can impact the audit firm's independence. If the person leaving the audit firm goes to work for the client as CEO, CFO, chief accounting officer, controller, or any equivalent position, the audit firm will not be independent with respect to the client for one year.

While the SEC's general standard of independence is simple and straightforward, the SEC's independence *rules* are extensive and differ somewhat in details from those of the

AUDITING IN ACTION

Sarbanes-Oxley Act, Section 206, Conflicts of Interest

It shall be unlawful for a registered public accounting firm to perform for an issuer any audit service required by this title, if a chief executive officer, controller, chief financial officer, chief accounting officer, or any person serving in an equivalent position for the issuer, was employed by that registered independent public accounting firm and participated in any capacity in the audit of the issuer during the 1-year period preceding the date of the initiation of the audit.

(*Source*: Section 10A of the Securities Exchange Act of 1934 amended by Sarbanes-Oxley, Section 206.)

AICPA. In 2001 the SEC changed the rules defining the group of people in an audit firm to whom the independence rules apply. The independence rules apply to:

> All partners and staff who work directly on the audit engagement
>
> Managers and partners who provide 10 hours or more of nonaudit services to the audit client
>
> Partners in the audit chain of command
>
> Partners who are located in the same office as the lead partner on the audit engagement

The shift in the rules as a result of focusing on who is included in the pool of individuals who must be independent of an audit client was made so that the rules would better fit with the current business environment of technology and dual career families.

AUDITING IN ACTION

SEC Personal Independence Rules

The principal feature of the 2001 rule is a new definition of who has to be independent of an audit client:

> Partners and staff who provide audit services to the client
>
> Managers and partners who provide 10 or more hours of nonaudit services to the client
>
> Persons in the audit "chain of command"
>
> Partners resident in the same office as the lead audit partner

AUDITING IN ACTION

SEC Rule Change

[T]here have been significant demographic changes, changes in the accounting profession, and changes in the business environment that have affected accounting firms. Among other things, there has been an increase in dual-career families and an ever-increasing mobility among professionals. Accounting firms have expanded internationally. Most SEC registrants now have their financial statements audited by firms that have offices and professionals stationed in hundreds of cities around the globe, and many of those offices and professionals have no connection to, or influence over a company's audit.

… under the [former] rules, the spouse of a partner at an accounting firm could not hold certain positions at an audit client or stock in an audit client, even through an employee stock compensation or 401(k) plan, even if the partner had no connection to the audit. In light of the trends noted above, including the growth of dual-career families, we sought to address this and similar situations.

… final rules… among other things, reduce the pool of people within audit firms whose independence is required for an independent audit of a company and shrink the circle of family members whose employment by an audit client impairs an accountant's independence.

… [the former] rules are broader than necessary to protect investors and our securities markets

(SEC Rule 33-7919.)

SERVICES THAT IMPAIR FIRM INDEPENDENCE

A firm is not independent of a company if the firm provides certain **prohibited services** to that company. Recall that a CPA cannot conduct an audit if he or she is not independent of the client. Exhibit 3-8 identifies public accounting firm services that damage independence for public company audits.

EXHIBIT 3-8

Non-Attest Services that
Impair Independence
for Audits of Companies
under the Jurisdiction
of the SEC

An accountant is not independent if the accountant provides the following non-audit services to an audit client:

Bookkeeping or other services related to the accounting records or financial statements of the audit client.
Any service unless it is reasonable to conclude that the results of these services will not be subject to audit procedures during an audit of the audit client's financial statements, including:

1. Maintaining or preparing the audit client's accounting records;
2. Preparing the audit client's financial statements or
3. Preparing or originating source data underlying the audit client's financial statements.

Financial information systems design and implementation.
Any service unless it is reasonable to conclude that the results of these services will not be subject to audit procedures during an audit of the audit client's financial statements including:

1. Directly or indirectly operating, or supervising the operation of, the audit client's information system or managing the audit client's local area network; or
2. Designing or implementing a hardware or software system that aggregates source data underlying the financial statements or generates information that is significant to the audit client's financial statements or other financial information systems taken as a whole.

Appraisal or valuation services, fairness opinions, or contribution-in-kind reports.
Any appraisal service, valuation service, or any service involving a fairness opinion or contribution-in-kind report for an audit client, unless it is reasonable to conclude that the results of these services will not be subject to audit procedures during an audit of the audit client's financial statements.

Actuarial services.
Any actuarially-oriented advisory service involving the determination of amounts recorded in the financial statements and related accounts for the audit client other than assisting a client in understanding the methods, models, assumptions, and inputs used in computing an amount, unless it is reasonable to conclude that the results of these services will not be subject to audit procedures during an audit of the audit client's financial statements.

Internal audit outsourcing services.
Any internal audit service that has been outsourced by the audit client that relates to the audit client's internal accounting controls, financial systems, or financial statements, for an audit client unless it is reasonable to conclude that the results of these services will not be subject to audit procedures during an audit of the audit client's financial statements.

Management functions.
Acting, temporarily or permanently, as a director, officer, or employee of an audit client, or performing any decision-making, supervisory, or ongoing monitoring function for the audit client.

Human resources.

1. Searching for or seeking out prospective candidates for managerial, executive, or director positions;
2. Engaging in psychological testing, or other formal testing or evaluation programs;
3. Undertaking reference checks for prospective candidates for an executive or director position
4. Acting as a negotiator on the audit client's behalf, such as determining position, status or title, compensation, fringe benefits, or other conditions of employment; or
5. Recommending, or advising the audit client to hire a specific candidate for a specific job (except that an accounting firm may, upon request by the audit client, interview candidates and advise the audit client on the candidate's competence for financial accounting, administrative, or control positions).

Broker-dealer, investment adviser, or investment banking services.
Acting as a broker-dealer (registered or unregistered), promoter, or underwriter, on behalf of an audit client, making investment decisions on behalf of the audit client or otherwise having discretionary authority over an audit client's investments, executing a transaction to buy or sell an audit client's investment, or having custody of assets of the audit client, such as taking temporary possession of securities purchased by the audit client.

Legal services.
Providing any service to an audit client that, under circumstances in which the service is provided, could be provided only by someone licensed, admitted, or otherwise qualified to practice law in the jurisdiction in which the service is provided.

Expert services unrelated to the audit.
Providing an expert opinion or other expert service for an audit client, or an audit client's legal representative, for the purpose of advocating an audit client's interests in litigation or in a regulatory or administrative proceeding or investigation. (An accountant is permitted to provide factual accounts, including in testimony, of work performed or explain the positions taken or conclusions reached during the performance of any service provided by the accountant for the audit client.)

Sarbanes-Oxley, Section 201, also disallows any other service determined by regulation to be impermissible.
(*Source*: Sarbanes-Oxley Act, Section 201: Amendment to Section 10A of the Securities Exchange Act)

The services described in Exhibit 3-8 are fairly easy to categorize as:

1. having the potential to put the audit firm in a position of auditing its own work,
2. causing the audit firm to make or advise client decisions that are the responsibility of client management, and
3. requiring the audit firm to be an advocate for the client.

Auditing the Firm's Own Work
Bookkeeping
Actuarial services
Internal audit outsourcing
Systems design and implementation
Appraisal, valuation, etc., services

Making Management Decisions
Management functions
Broker services
Human resources

Being an Advocate
Broker-dealer services
Expert services
Legal services

The services listed in the preceding table and in Exhibit 3-8 are those that absolutely may not be provided to a public company by the same firm that performs its integrated audit. Certain tax services are also prohibited by PCAOB rules. Audit firms are allowed to provide these services to nonaudit clients. However, providing the services removes the firm's independence with respect to the company receiving the services. Therefore, firms may not perform these "prohibited services" *and* the integrated audit for the same public company.

Other nonaudit work that an audit firm provides for a public client (services that are not prohibited) must be approved in advance by the client's audit committee. The SEC also requires that fees paid by the client to the audit firm be disclosed in the proxy that goes to shareholders. On the proxy, the fees paid by the client company to the auditor are grouped into categories. Audit-related fees are a separate category.

An underlying issue related to prohibited services, approval of nonaudit services by the audit committee, and disclosure of fees paid to the auditor deals with economic influence. Much has been written about the possibility that auditors who provide both audit and nonaudit services to the same client may lose their independence. The stated concern is economic considerations.

Do auditors lose their independence to keep nonaudit services that command very high fees? Until rule changes prohibited some services such as design and implementation of IT systems, many auditors received a large proportion of fees from audit clients for nonaudit services. The rule change was motivated by the concern that auditors could be influenced to try to please the client management in their audit conclusions and audit report. Prohibiting more nonauditing types of services, requiring audit committees to approve any nonaudit services in advance, and making sure shareholders are well informed as to the amount of fees the auditors receive for nonaudit services are all steps designed to prevent inappropriate influence as a result of economic pressure.

REVIEW QUESTIONS

I.1 What does Section 206 of SOX say about the independence of an audit firm when a member of the audit team goes to work for a client?

I.2 What is the emphasis of the most recent revision of the SEC rules regarding independence?

I.3 What services does the SEC prohibit for a CPA that also performs a company's audit? How can these services be grouped consistently with the SEC's personal independence rules?

I.4 What services that are provided by a company's auditor must be approved by the audit committee of a public company?

I.5 What information related to CPA firms fees appears on a public company's proxy statement?

PUBLIC ACCOUNTING FIRMS AND QUALITY CONTROL

Individual auditors, the standards to which they must conform, and the quality of work expected from them are the focal points of much of the ethics and professional standards. Several rules, discussed earlier, affect firms. Basically, the rules state that a firm's partners and owners can only work for firms that follow the standards. However, an entire set of **AICPA Quality Control Standards** is focused directly on the CPA firms that provide audit services. The AICPA Elements of a System of Quality Control that are the heart of the quality control standards specify a variety of areas for which firms are expected to have policies and procedures.

For example, firms must have policies and procedures in place that help them ensure that all employees and partners adhere to independence requirements. Policies should exist to provide "reasonable assurance" that the firm hires qualified people and that they have the technical skills and experience levels sufficient to perform the jobs to which they are assigned. Other elements deal with acceptance and continuance of clients and engagement performance. Finally, the last element of quality control calls for a monitoring system so that the firm can check on whether the policies and procedures in place are functioning.

SOX also addresses the issue of quality control standards for firms by requiring the PCAOB to establish standards for the public accounting firms that come under the PCAOB's jurisdiction. The quality control areas specified by SOX are similar to those covered by the AICPA Elements of a System of Quality Control.

AUDITING IN ACTION

AICPA Elements of a System of Quality Control

Leadership responsibilities for quality within the firm (the "tone at the top")
Relevant ethical requirements
Acceptance and continuance of client relationships and specific engagements
Human resources
Engagement performance
Monitoring

(AICPA QC 10.14)

AUDITING IN ACTION

PCAOB Quality Control Standards Required by SOX

The [PCAOB] shall include in the quality control standards that it adopts with respect to the issuance of audit reports, requirements for every registered public accounting firm relating to—

1. monitoring of professional ethics and independence from issuers on behalf of which the firm issues audit reports;
2. consultation within such firm on accounting and auditing questions;
3. supervision of audit work;
4. hiring, professional development, and advancement of personnel;
5. the acceptance and continuation of engagements;
6. internal inspection; and
7. such other requirements as the PCAOB may prescribe

[Sarbanes-Oxley Act, Section 103 (a)(2)B]

The purpose of quality control standards for firms is at least twofold: (1) to provide guidance for firms regarding policies needed for well-functioning practices; and (2) to provide standards against which firms can be compared in a monitoring or an inspection process. Any firm that provides audit, attest, review, ot compilation services is required to undergo a practice monitoting review. The **AICPA Peer Review Board** is the umbrella entity within the AICPA that administers practice monitoring for individuals and firms. The AICPA Peer Review Program (PRP) produces standards for performing and reporting on peer reviews. Public accounting firms that must undergo practice monitoring reviews but do not audit public companies can satisfy their practice monitoring requirements with a PRP review. The AICPA National Peer Review Committee (National PRC) PRP provides practice monitoring reviews for firms who are registered with the PCAOB. Firms that are registered with the PCAOB because they provide audit services for public companies also undergo inspection by the PCAOB.

PCAOB Oversight of Firms

The PCAOB has several mechanisms through which it monitors the management and performance of audit firms. First, audit firms that want to audit companies under the SEC's jurisdiction must register with the PCAOB. SOX, Section 102, requires that any reports prepared by a public accounting firm to be submitted to the SEC come from a firm registered with the PCAOB. The registration process requires communication of a considerable amount of firm information to the PCAOB. In addition, the CPA firm must consent, or

EXHIBIT 3-9

Public Accounting Firm
Registration with the
PCAOB

It shall be **unlawful for any person that is not a registered public accounting firm** to prepare or issue, or to participate in the preparation or issuance of, any audit report with respect to any issuer. [Sarbanes-Oxley Act, Section 102(a)]

Consents. Each application for registration under this subsection shall include

(A) a consent executed by the public accounting firm to cooperation in and compliance with any request for testimony or the production of documents made by the Board (PCAOB) in the furtherance of its authority and responsibilities under this title (and an agreement to secure and enforce similar consents from each of the associated persons of the public accounting firm as a condition of their continued employment by or other association with such firm); and

(B) a statement that such firm understands and agrees that cooperation and compliance, as described in the consent required by subparagraph (A), and the securing and enforcement of such consents from its associated persons in accordance with the rules of the Board, shall be a condition to continuing effectiveness of the registration of the firm with the Board.

[Sarbanes-Oxley Act, Section 102 (b)(3)]

agree, to cooperate with the PCAOB, particularly in any inspections or investigations. Exhibit 3-9 lists the SOX requirement for registration and cooperation. In 2009 the PCAOB began requiring CPA firms to also file annual and special reports. The reports are required by SOX Section 102 (d).

SOX, Section 104, requires the PCAOB to inspect public accounting firms that provide audits to companies that report to the SEC. The PCAOB inspections are required every year or every three years, depending on how many publicly traded companies the firm audits. These inspections cover the quality control system of the audit firm, the inspection of selected audits and interim financial statement review engagements, and testing as deemed necessary. Written reports of the PCAOB inspections are provided to the SEC, state authorities, and the inspected public accounting firm, and at least a part of the report is released to the public. Exhibit 3-10 presents the SOX requirement for inspections.

REVIEW QUESTIONS

J.1 What are Quality Control Standards? What authoritative sources require quality control standards?

J.2 Identify the elements of quality control.

J.3 What are practice monitoring programs?

J.4 Explain the PCAOB registration and practice inspection requirements.

CONCLUSION

From a student's perspective, the rules and regulations that apply to individual accountants and firms regarding ethical conduct and quality control can seem overwhelming. While it is important to know and understand the rules, it is equally important to understand the purpose of the rules. Auditors play a vital role in society and the U.S. economy because they are trusted to behave in a professional and ethical manner. The standards not only provide enforceable rules, but also serve as a guide to accountants about the performance and behavior they must exhibit to continue to deserve and earn the public's trust. The function auditors fulfill in society is protecting the public interest. Ethics, moral and professional behavior, and a commitment to quality control help auditors fulfill that role.

EXHIBIT 3-10

PCAOB Inspections of Registered Public Accounting Firms

The Board (PCAOB) shall conduct a continuing program of inspections to assess the degree of compliance of each registered public accounting firm and associated persons of that firm with this Act, the rules of the Board, the rules of the Commission (SEC), or professional standards, in connection with performance of audits, issuance of audit reports, and related matters involving issuers.

Inspections required by this section shall be conducted annually with respect to each registered public accounting firm that regularly provides audit reports for more than 100 issuers; and not less frequently than once every three years with respect to each registered public accounting firm that regularly provides audit reports for 100 or fewer issuers. The Board shall, in each inspection…

(1) identify any act or practice or omission to act by the registered public accounting firm, or by any associated person thereof, revealed by such inspection that may be in violation of this Act, the rules of the Board, the rules of the Commission, the firm's own quality control policies, or professional standards;

(2) report any such act, practice, or omission, if appropriate to the Commission and each appropriate State regulatory authority; and

(3) begin a formal investigation or take disciplinary action, if appropriate, with respect to any such violation in accordance with this Act and the rules of the Board.

In conducting an inspection of a registered public accounting firm under this section, the Board shall—

(1) inspect and review selected audit and review engagements of the firm (which may include audit engagements that are the subject of ongoing litigation or other controversy between the firm and one or more third parties), performed at various offices and by various associated persons of the firm, as selected by the Board;

(2) evaluate the sufficiency of the quality control system of the firm, and the manner of the documentation and communication of that system by the firm; and

(3) perform such other testing of the audit, supervisory, and quality control procedures of the firm as are necessary or appropriate in light of the purpose of the inspection and the responsibilities of the Board.

The rules of the Board shall provide a procedure for the review of and response to a draft inspection report by the registered public accounting firm under inspection. A written report of the findings of the Board for each inspection…shall be—

(1) transmitted, in appropriate detail to the Commission and each appropriate State regulatory authority, accompanied by any letter or comments by the Board or the inspector, and any letter of response from the registered public accounting firm; and

(2) made available in appropriate detail to the public (subject to issues of confidentiality), except that no portions of the inspection report that deal with criticisms of or potential defects in the quality control systems of the firm under inspection shall be made public if those criticisms or defects are addressed by the firm, to the satisfaction of the Board, not later than 12 months after the date of the inspection report.

[Sarbanes-Oxley Act, Section 104 (a)-(g)]

KEY TERMS

AICPA Auditing Standards Board. Writes and issues Statements on Auditing standards.

AICPA Code of Professional Conduct. Provides guidance for CPAs in their professional behavior.

AICPA Peer Review Board. Entity within the AICPA that provides practice monitoring for individuals and firms.

AICPA Quality Control Standards. A set of standards specifying elements of quality control about which CPA firms are expected to have policies and procedures.

Board of Professional Regulation. The state regulatory (or similar) agency that issues individuals their CPA certificates for that state and regulates the licensing of CPAs.

Conventional level. Level of moral development at which individuals consider impacts beyond those that affect them personally when making decisions.

Corporate governance. The process of setting and enforcing the policies and procedures of a corporation; includes many actions of the Board of Directors and management.

Ethic of care. An ethical orientation that focuses on relationships and the interdependence of individuals.

Ethic of rights. An ethical orientation that focuses on accruing benefits due to the individual and protecting that individual's rights.

Ethical decision framework. The sequence of steps used by a decision maker when making a decision recognized to have ethical components.

Ethical orientation. The focus of the decision maker when making ethical decisions.

Independence in appearance. A phrase meaning that the auditor behaves in a manner causing him or her to appear independent to others. Relates to a rule of the AICPA Code of Professional Conduct, indicating that financial, management, and family interests impair an auditor's ability to be independent with respect to an audit client.

Independence in fact. An auditor's state of mind, with no bias toward or against a client or issues related to an audit engagement.

Institute of Internal Auditors (IIA). A professional organization focusing on the needs and interests of internal auditors.

Institute of Management Accountants (IMA). A professional organization focusing on the needs and interest of management accountants.

Interpretations of the Rules of Conduct. Guidelines issued by the AICPA relating to the Rules of Conduct.

Moral development. A theory that people use different criteria to make decisions, based on their personal level of moral development.

Moral dilemma. A special case of ethical decision in which, even after applying an ethical decision framework and one's own values there is no clearcut answer.

Moral intensity. Describes specific variables and the level at which they cause an individual to recognize that a situation or decision has moral and ethical components.

Nonissuers. Nonpublic companies; companies that are not required to file audited financial statements with the SEC.

Post-conventional level. Level of moral development at which individuals make decisions based on abstract analysis of what is right and wrong, taking philosophical issues into consideration.

Pre-conventional level. Level of moral development at which individuals make decisions in a self-centered way.

Principles of Professional Conduct. The ideal behavior standards included in the AICPA Code of Professional Conduct.

Profession. An occupational group with known expertise for a clearly specified body of knowledge that controls standards of entry and membership for the group and has some degree of control over its self-discipline and regulation.

Prohibited services. Activities that when performed by a CPA make that CPA lack independence regarding an audit. Certain prohibited services are specified by the SEC, but all fall into categories of auditing one's own work, making management decisions, and being an advocate for the client.

Quality control/peer review. A review conducted by another CPA firm or a team of CPAs that evaluates the quality control policies and procedures of a CPA firm.

Rules of Conduct. The enforceable standards included in the AICPA Code of Professional Conduct.

Rulings. Pronouncements of the AICPA that explain the application of Rules and Interpretations of the Code of Professional Conduct. Rulings relate to specific factual situations for which AICPA members have requested guidance.

Self-regulation. The self-discipline and self-policing of a profession.

Social contract. A profession's contract with society through which professionals commit to serving the public good through their work, maintaining standards of excellence and policing their own ranks, in return for economic reward and some degree of prestige and self-governance.

MULTIPLE CHOICE

3-1 **[LO 5]** A CPA who performs audits

    (a) probably only has to adhere to a Code of Conduct if he or she is a member of the AICPA.

    (b) will likely have to adhere to the Code of Conduct in the state where he or she is licensed.

    (c) will only have to follow the state's Code of Conduct if he or she is not a member of the AICPA.

    (d) has to follow the PCAOB's Code of Conduct if he or she performs public company audits.

3-2 **[LO 2]** The ethical orientation known as ethic of care

(a) is applicable to the team setting used in public accounting firms.

(b) originated in the health-care professions.

(c) applies only to feminist literature.

(d) cannot be applied to U.S. businesses because of the rights orientation of the court system.

3-3 **[LO 2]** Moral development theory

(a) proposes that those at the highest level of moral development are right.

(b) describes the differences between adults and children.

(c) is useful in deciding what decision should be made.

(d) describes the conventional level as a belief that obeying the law and acting out of concern for what others think is behaving in a moral manner.

3-4 **[LO 5]** Independence in fact is

(a) indicated by independence in appearance.

(b) easy to determine.

(c) the ideal standard for auditors.

(d) achieved by following the rules of the Code of Conduct.

3-5 **[LO 3]** Using the assumption that auditors are professionals who have a contract with society,

(a) auditors receive prestige and economic reward for their commitment to behave as professionals and protect the public interest.

(b) auditors contract with the government on the amount they are paid for audits.

(c) auditors require complete self-governance.

(d) none of the above.

3-6 **[LO 3]** CPAs constitute a profession because

(a) there are standards for entry and membership.

(b) although CPAs share their governance with other organizations, there is some self-discipline and self-regulation.

(c) CPAs recognize and acknowledge a commitment to the public interest.

(d) all of the above.

3-7 **[LO 5]** State governance over CPAs

(a) is superseded by the Sarbanes-Oxley Act because SOX is federal legislation.

(b) has ultimate control over the ability of an individual to be licensed as a CPA.

(c) has control over the companies that a licensed CPA audits.

(d) is limited because the AICPA controls the Uniform CPA Examination.

3-8 **[LO 5]** AICPA membership

(a) is usually avoided by CPAs because of the additional constraints it places on behavior.

(b) is not required of individuals as long as the firm the individuals work for becomes a member of the AICPA.

(c) is voluntary.

(d) is available to individuals regardless of the characteristics of the firms for which they work.

3-9 **[LO 1]** Using the court system as a primary control for the behavior of auditors

(a) is effective because auditors are threatened with the possibility of going to jail.

(b) is not effective because auditors are rarely found guilty of criminal behavior.

(c) is not effective because auditors win on appeal.

(d) is not effective at promoting public confidence because it occurs only after a problem has been discovered.

3-10 **[LO 4]** Using a moral decision-making model is valuable because

(a) it helps decision makers to make the decision most often perceived as ethical by the audit client.

(b) it helps decision makers to make the decision most often perceived as ethical by the regulators.

(c) it helps decision makers recognize the moral components in a decision they are making.

(d) it helps decision makers "tune out" the moral intensity of the decision so they can choose the most ethical option.

3-11 **[LO 5]** The AICPA Code of Conduct

(a) applies to all members.

(b) applies uniformly to all CPAs regardless of their AICPA membership or their employer.

(c) affects all members uniformly regardless of their employer or job description.

(d) does not affect some AICPA members because of their employer or job description.

3-12 **[LO 5]** Rulings and Interpretations of the AICPA Code of Conduct

(a) are intended as ideal principles for all members.

(b) are the primary enforceable guidelines published for the Code of Conduct.

(c) do not have to be considered by AICPA members because they apply to specific situations.

(d) require justification if a member departs from them.

3-13 **[LO 5]** Rule 102 of the AICPA Code of Conduct discusses integrity and objectivity, and includes a prohibition on subordinating judgment to others. This simply means that

(a) the CPA makes judgments without seeking input from more experienced auditors.

(b) the CPA must make all the audit decisions based on whatever professional judgment he or she thinks is best without consulting others.

(c) the CPA should not let others make a decision that is his or her responsibility.

(d) the CPA should not attach weight to the input of subordinates who do not yet have their CPA license.

3-14 **[LO 5]** A CPA should be concerned about violating AICPA Rule 301 on Confidential Client Information

(a) when disclosing information gained about the client during the audit without the client's permission and when none of the exceptions to disclosure are met.

(b) when disclosing information gained about the client during the audit, even with the client's permission.

(c) even though the disclosure is in connection with a peer review.

(d) even though the disclosure is in response to a court order such as a subpoena.

3-15 **[LO 5]** The AICPA rule on contingent fees

(a) prohibits auditor fees that may be different from the estimated amount if the engagement is more complex or takes longer than expected.

(b) prohibits audit fees that change based on out-of-pocket expenses incurred by the audit firm.

(c) prohibits audit fees that are dependent on the outcomes of court decisions.

(d) prohibits audit fees that vary based on the type of audit opinion issued.

3-16 **[LO 5]** The SEC general standard of auditor independence

(a) includes guidance on specific services that are prohibited.

(b) includes guidance that the audit firm cannot perform services that would result in it performing management tasks or auditing its own work.

(c) includes guidance on how the audit firm can perform management services without damaging independence as long as it does not actually become a part of the management team.

(d) includes guidance on the situations of mutual interest between the auditor and audit client that do not impair the auditor's independence.

3-17 **[LO 5]** Based on AICPA guidance, an auditor's independence is impaired by

(a) owning any of an audit client's stock.

(b) owning a material amount of the stock of the parent company of an audit client.

(c) his or her spouse owning any of an audit client's stock.

(d) all of the above.

3-18 **[LO 5]** For the audit of a public company an audit firm's independence is impaired if

(a) the partner in charge of the engagement leaves the CPA firm and takes a job with the audit client in the position of head of sales within 12 months of completing the audit engagement.

(b) the firm's consulting department assists the audit client by providing information on possible reference sites where the audit client can research data to use as it negotiates job description, compensation, and fringe benefits with a candidate for an executive position.

(c) a partner involved with the engagement leaves the CPA firm and takes a job with the audit client in the position of CEO within six months of when the firm started the audit engagement.

(d) the partner in charge of the engagement leaves the CPA firm and takes a job with the audit client in the position of CEO 18 months after the firm completed the last audit engagement.

3-19 **[LO 5]** Quality control standards

(a) only exist for audit firms that are under the jurisdiction of the PCAOB.

(b) only exist for audit firms whose partners are all members of the AICPA.

(c) are only used for purposes of peer review practice monitoring by the AICPA.

(d) are required by the Sarbanes-Oxley Act.

3-20 **[LO 5]** The SEC

(a) will not accept the filings of a company if the audit is performed by a firm that is not registered with the PCAOB.

THE AUDITOR'S ROLE IN SOCIETY 123

123

(b) is the original source of the requirement that audit firms register with and are inspected by the PCAOB in order to audit public companies.

(c) waives the requirement that audit firms agree to cooperate with PCAOB investigations when

the audit firms have in-house attorneys to advise them of when it is necessary.

(d) performs the inspections of CPA firms that audit public companies as required by the Sarbanes-Oxley Act.

DISCUSSION QUESTIONS

3-21 **[LO 1, 5]** Do you trink it is necessary to prohibit all of the services on the "prohibited services" list in order to protect the public interest? Are there any on the list that you would permit, and why?

3-22 **[LO 1, 5]** Should tax services be a "prohibited service" for a firm that is conducting an audit? Consider whether performing more services for a client may increase the audit firm's knowledge of the client. Also consider whether additional services may make the audit firm more economically dependent on the client.

3-23 **[LO 2]** Can you choose the philosophical position discussed in this chapter with which your views are closest? Which one is furthest from your views?

3-24 **[LO 1, 3, 5]** Some people have said that auditing is no longer self-regulated because of the SOX mandated registration and inspection process of the PCAOB, and because the PCAOB now sets auditing standards. Does this loss of some of its self-regulation diminish the profession, or does it just increase public confidence? Why?

3-25 **[LO 4]** What moral dilemma have you experienced? (Whether to cheat on a test does not count ... too easy!)

3-26 **[LO 2]** Explain the theory of moral development, including the three levels identified by the theory. When auditors are performing their jobs, which level applies to their behavior? Would it be a problem if this were not the case?

3-27 **[LO 3]** Explain the difference in the compensation contracts of doctors and their patients and auditors and their clients, and the significance this difference has for auditor independence.

3-28 **[LO 1, 3]** Assume the auditor has a contract with society. What are the components of that contract? In other words, what does the auditor commit to give, and what does the auditor receive?

3-29 **[LO 5]** What do we mean when we use the phrases "independence in fact" and "independence in appearance"? Why does the auditing profession use both phrases? How do both relate to ideal behavior and the rules that govern auditors.

PROBLEMS

3-30 **[LO 5]** For the following situations indicate whether a rule of the AICPA Code of Conduct applies; if yes, state which rule, whether the rule has been violated, and why or why not.

(a) Walker, CPA, is purchasing a home and received a large mortgage, under normal lending procedures, with a bank that became an audit client after the mortgage was set up; the mortgage amount is material to him.

(b) Logan, CPA, accepted as an audit client a modeling agency that signs up and places models primarily using Internet interactions. Logan has never audited a modeling agency before.

(c) Letchworth and Miller, a local CPA firm, advertised that its audits will always save clients money because the increased efficiencies resulting from audit recommendations will be more than the audit fee.

(d) The firm of Masser & Masser disclosed confidential client information during the course of its inspection by the PCAOB.

(e) Jiggs, CPA, always sets audit fees that are contingent on the number of hours it takes to perform the audit.

(f) Srygley, CPA, pays an attorney, Bill Suttle, a "finder's fee" if Suttle refers a company to him that becomes an audit client.

(g) Cutter and Gaspar, CPA, are having some cash shortages because they recently remodeled their offices. Consequently, they issued an unqualified financial statement audit opinion as a result of an integrated audit, even though they concluded that some of the accounting treatments were not GAAP. They were concerned that if they issued anything other than an unqualified opinion they would lose the client.

(h) A local CPA firm is named "Best Buy Audits."

3-31   **[LO 2, 4]** Reread the Auditing in Action titled "What Should the Health Clinic Do?" dealing with the clinic's moral dilemma as to whether to accept a large donation from a donor of questionable reputation.

Required:

(a) Respond to the dilemma explaining what you would do if it was your decision to make.

(b) Justify or explain why you believe your decision is the right one. The decision has many potential ramifications, and you should identify as many of them as you can in justifying or explaining your decision.

(c) Identify the underlying ethical philosophy that guided your decision.

3-32   **[LO 2, 5]** For the following topics list arguments both in support of and against the topic, basing your arguments on any of the philosophical positions provided in the text. You may use the same or different underpinning philosophies for the different positions.

(a) Restrictions prohibiting an auditor from providing auditing and IT installation services to the same company.

(b) Restrictions on what auditors may name their firms.

(c) Having PCAOB inspections rather than just AICPA peer reviews for companies that audit public companies.

3-33   **[LO 5]** Respond to the following:

(a) Chris Armas, CPA, is a partner responsible for the audit engagement of Mario Manufacturing. Chris has a dependent daughter who is employed by Mario Manufacturing as a machine operator—a nonfinancial and nonaudit-sensitive position.
Is this a violation of the AICPA Code of Conduct? Explain.

(b) Paul Brent, CPA, is a partner in the CPA firm that audits Keystone, Inc., a closely held corporation. Brent's sister is the chief financial officer of Keystone, Inc. The CPA firm has only one office, so Paul Brent and the partner responsible for the audit work in close contact on a regular basis.
Is this a violation of the AICPA Code of Conduct? Explain.

(c) The accounting firm of Jenne & Jenne, CPAs, is negotiating a fee with a new audit client. They agree the client will pay $75,000 if Jenne & Jenne issues a clean unqualified opinion, and $50,000 if any type of opinion other than a clean opinion is issued.
Is this a violation of the AICPA Code of Conduct? Explain.

(d) Don O'Kroy, CPA, is a member of the engagement team that performs the audit of Torok Corporation. Don's 5-year-old daughter, Precious, received 10 shares of Torok Corporation's common stock for her fifth birthday. The stock was a gift from Precious's grandmother—Don's wife's mother.

Is this a violation of the AICPA Code of Conduct? Explain.

3-34 **[LO 5]** The following are paired lists of terms that have specific meaning within the AICPA Code of Conduct. For each, explain how the pair of terms interacts or contrasts regarding their impact on auditor independence:

(a) Direct financial interest: immediate family

(b) Material: indirect financial interest

(c) Covered member: immediate family

(d) Covered member: close relative

(e) Covered member: key position

3-35 **[LO 5]** Jacoby & Ricks, CPAs, is responding to a request for proposal from Z-Berr Industries, a privately held company located near Milwaukee. Z-Berr is a rapidly growing company engaged in the manufacture and distribution of bicycle wheels and tires. The company recently expanded its product offerings into the areas of motor scooters and other small vehicles used for sports and recreation.

Because of its recent growth, Z-Berr is in need of a great deal of assistance in improving its financial reporting systems. It indicates that it needs assistance with some nonaudit services, including its income tax planning and tax return preparation, computer systems upgrade and the hiring and training of a systems administrator, and implementation of an internal audit function, including the hiring and training of internal audit staff. In addition, the company has requested an integrated audit, as it suspects that an initial public offering is on the horizon.

Required:

(a) Assuming that Jacoby & Ricks desires to bid on Z-Berr's audit engagement, which of the additional nonaudit services can the firm include in its proposal? Explain.

(b) How would your answer to part (a) change if Z-Berr was already a public company?

3-36 **[LO 5]** Perrie Brenigen, CPA, is an in-charge accountant for the firm of Duben & Associates. During her four years with Duben & Associates, Brenigen has served on the audit teams for several health-care clients. Brenigen recently received an employment offer from one of her audit clients, Health Initiative Partners (HIP). Brenigen is being recruited to work as an associate in HIP's new financial planning department, where her responsibilities would include evaluating investment options and capital expenditure alternatives, assistance with departmental budgeting, and tax planning.

Required:

(a) If HIP is a public company, will Brenigen be able to accept the position without impairing the independence of Duben & Associates? Explain.

(b) If Brenigen accepts the new position with HIP, what changes will occur with regard to her obligations under the AICPA Code of Professional Conduct?

3-37 **[LO 2]** Ellison Courtley is a staff accountant for Bronson, Burkes & Hunt, CPAs. During his second year on the audit staff, Ellison becomes quite frustrated with the number of overtime hours required for his job. He dislikes the firm's policy of rewarding additional vacation time in lieu of overtime pay. Ellison also believes that he is underpaid. One of his roommates works for another CPA firm and earns a salary that is nearly 10% higher than what Ellison is paid by Bronson, Burkes & Hunt.

Ellison developed a plan for taking matters into his own hands and "leveling the playing field" with respect to his compensation. He is maximizing his payout under the firm's policy of reimbursing job-related expenses. By inflating the mileage on client-related travel, duplicating receipts for parking, and borrowing receipts from his roommates for so-called overtime meals, Ellison has been able to increase his take-home pay by about 8%.

Ellison shared his strategy with Shannen Folkes, who works as the staff accountant on some of the same audit engagements with Ellison. Shannen has experienced some of the same frustrations as Ellison with regard to her paycheck, and she knows first-hand that Ellison is a hard worker who is deserving of increased compensation. Yet, Shannen is reluctant to alter her expense report for fear of getting caught. When she expresses her concern to Ellison, he criticizes her for not being a team player. He tries to convince her that there is less chance of getting caught if all of the engagement team members' expense reports are within a similar range. Besides, Ellison argues that even this elevated level of expense reimbursement does not make up for the firm's substandard pay structure.

Required:

(a) Which ethical orientation is Ellison demonstrating? Which level of moral development is exemplified by Ellison's behavior? Explain.

(b) Assume that Shannen is reflecting on Ellison's behavior. In addition to the risk of getting caught, she considers the impact to the firm if all of its associates implemented a similar plan. She also thought about the inequity to those who strictly followed the firm's policies. As a result of these considerations, if Shannen decided to report Ellison's unethical actions to one of the firm's partners, which level of moral development would she be demonstrating? Explain.

(c) According to the "greatest good" philosophy, do you think Shannen could be justified in joining Ellison in this method of maximizing expense reimbursements? Present arguments for opposing perspectives under this philosophy.

3-38 **[LO 5]** The situations that follow pertain to Rule 101 of the AICPA Code of Professional Conduct as it relates to family relationships. Indicate whether each situation violates the Code and which provisions apply.

(a) A staff accountant's mother retired from her position as controller for an audit client. Upon retirement, she was awarded shares of stock, which increased her ownership share to 5%, Her stock ownership is material to her net worth. The staff accountant participates as a member of this client company's audit team.

(b) A CPA manager is a member of the audit team of Hudson Motorworks, Inc. A cousin of the CPA's wife is Hudson's vice president and sales director. This cousin also owns a very small proportion (less than 1%) of the shares of the company's stock.

(c) A CPA manager has a sister who holds a 50% ownership interest in the CPA's audit client. This investment is material to the sister's net worth.

(d) A partner was formerly a shareholder in a company, but upon receiving a request for proposal for the company's current-year audit engagement, the partner transferred all shares of stock to her dependent daughter.

(e) A CPA participates in the audit of a vacation resort complex. The CPA's parents own a timeshare in this resort complex, which is material to their net worth.

(f) A partner's dependent parent has a minor (less than 5%) ownership interest in an audit client of the partner's firm. The audit is conducted by other CPAs in the partner's office, but the partner does not participate in this audit engagement.

(g) A CPA manager is married to the CEO of an audit client. The CPA is also a shareholder of this audit client company. The audit is performed by CPAs in the firm's southside office. The CPA manager works in the firm's northside office and therefore is unable to exercise any influence over the audit engagement.

3-39 **[LO 5]** Each of the scenarios that follow portrays a possible violation of the AICPA Code of Professional Conduct. Complete the table by checking Yes for any violations of the Code or No if the scenario does not represent a violation.

Scenario	Yes	No
(a) While performing the audit of a retail company, a CPA identified internal control weaknesses and immediately reported them to the company's audit committee. Corrections were made to the system before the fiscal year end, resulting in cost savings to the client company. As a gesture of appreciation, the client company rewarded the CPA with a discount card for use on merchandise sold in the company's retail store.		
(b) While performing the audit of a manufacturing company, a CPA determined that going-concern disclosures were warranted. However, the client has requested a delay in the audit completion, as it argues that its financial condition will improve when it obtains financing. It expects to have a decision on its loan application next week. The application has been filed with a financial institution that is also an audit client of this CPA. The CPA, being aware of the questionable financial status of the manufacturing company, warns the financial institution client of the related risks of extending credit to this company.		
(c) A CPA provided extensive management advisory services to her private company audit client, including consultations on possible diversification plans and monitoring of internal controls.		
(d) A CPA provided extensive management advisory services to his private company audit client, including design and implementation of a financial software system and screening/interviewing candidates for the newly-created position of chief information officer.		
(e) A CPA Partner developed a friendship with an audit client's CFO. The CPA and CFO purchased a boat together. The boat is material to the personal net worth of both the CPA and the CFO.		
(f) A CPA is requested by her public company audit client to perform additional nonaudit services. These services included reviewing contract negotiation documents and providing recommendations on approval of denial of the contract.		
(g) A CPA provided audit services for a private company. Due to difficulties with cash flow, the client company issued shares of stock to the CPA in payment of its audit fees. The CPA disposed of the stock before commencing the subsequent year audit engagement. The investment income earned for the period of holding the stock is not material to the CPA's personal net worth.		

3-40 **[LO 5]** Birk Dorren is a partner with the firm Shelby, Dorren & Ruppe, CPAs. Birk serves as the audit partner on the financial statement audit engagement for Pundley Fasteners, Inc., a nonpublic company.

    One week after issuing an unqualified opinion on the fairness of Pundley's financial statements, Birk learned that the company was in violation of its loan covenants. Such violation is grounds for the financier to demand immediate payment of the loan, which would likely force the company into bankruptcy. This situation was not disclosed in the financial statements or accompanying footnotes.

    Birk approached the client about the situation and suggested that the company's stockholders be notified that the financial statements and audit report could no longer be relied upon due to the misstatements resulting from the omitted information pertaining to the loan covenant violation. Birk indicated that revised financial statements could be available within two weeks, given the company's cooperation.

Pundley's management refused to comply with Birk's request, claiming that the financial statements were, in fact, materially correct. Furthermore, Pundley threatened to file a grievance against Shelby, Dorren & Ruppe if the stockholders are notified of the situation, claiming that the firm would be violating an auditor–client principle of privileged communication if it were to divulge such confidential information.

Required:

(a) What are the requirements of the AICPA Code of Professional Conduct with regard to confidential client information? Is Birk in violation of the Code?

(b) What do you think Dorren should do in this case?

3-41   **[LO 5]** John Thomas is a certified public accountant. He is the audit partner responsible for auditing the financial statements of Core Technology's U.S. operations for the fiscal year ended December 31, 2010. During all times relevant to this case, Thomas was a partner with Weiss and Associates, LLP. Core Technology, based in Frankfurt, Germany, is an international advertising and media services conglomerate with offices throughout the world. Kuhn and Dieter is of Core Technology's Frankfurt-based auditing firm and issues joint reports with Weiss and Associates, LLP. During the relevant period, Core Technology was a foreign private issuer whose American Depository Receipts were registered with the Securities and Exchange Commission and were listed on the NYSE.

Between October 2010 and May 2011, Thomas engaged in employment discussions with his audit client Core Technology to become the chief accounting officer of the U.S. subsidiary, responsible for the financial reporting of Core Technology's U.S. operations. During this period, he signed confirmations required by Weiss and Associates, LLP, attesting that he had complied with the auditor independence rules. On March 4, 2011, Thomas informed the managing director of Core that he wanted to complete the year-end audit work before informing his supervisors. In early May 2011, Thomas learned that Core would be sending him an employment contract, so he asked the joint auditing firms Weiss in the United States and Kuhn in Germany to be removed from the Core audit on May 10. He accepted the Core offer on May 11. In a May 28 quality control review regarding his employment at Weiss, Thomas's memorandum stated that Core had first approached him about possible employment in early May 2011 and that he promptly stopped working on the Core audit at that time. Kuhn and Dieter filed its Form 20-F for its fiscal year ended December 31, 2010, issued jointly with Weiss and Associates, LLP. The audit report included in the Form 20-F states that the firm of Kuhn and Dieter was independent and had conducted its audit in accordance with PCAOB standards.

Required:

Based on this scenario, what are the violations with respect to the auditing environment, and what possible sanctions do you anticipate upon discovery by the SEC?

3-42   **[LO 5]** Joseph Newport, CPA, is the engagement partner for the audit of Yonker Plumbing Supplies, Inc. He works for the firm Harrison and Ford, LLP. The Harrison and Ford standard audit plan for this type of engagement includes procedures for testing revenue. Suggested revenue procedures include basic audit steps such as sales cutoff testing and the investigation of revenue transactions with related parties. Newport's audit team has identified several risks for Yonker Plumbing Supplies, including Yonker's small and inexperienced accounting staff, the pressures on Yonker to meet budget expectations, and the potential for Yonker's management to manipulate information and improperly recognize revenue.

Newport tells his team that billable hours will reach the maximum for this client at the end of the week. Consequently, Newport instructs that the basic analytical procedures do not need to be performed. Newport urges that it is time to move on to the Martin, Inc. audit. An unqualified audit report for 2010 is issued for Yonker, backed by workpapers indicating that most of Harrison's standard audit plan was initialed as "not considered necessary," or initialed as "done" without any supporting documentation.

Required:
Based on the scenario, describe which two key AICPA Rules of Conduct have been violated and explain why.

ACTIVITY ASSIGNMENTS

3-43   On the AICPA Web site (*www.aicpa.org*) find Professional Resources and click on the Peer Review tab. What does the summary say is the purpose of the AICPA's practice monitoring programs?

3-44   On the AICPA Web site, under Professional Resources, find the Code of Professional Conduct. How is the Code organized on the Web site?

3-45   Go to the PCAOB Web site (*www.pcaobus.org*). Find the inspection section. Find the most recent inspection reports posted. Read and briefly summarize one of the inspection reports.

3-46   On the AICPA Web site, select Professional Resources, then Professional Ethics/Code of Conduct, and click on Professional Ethics. Click on Resources and Tools. Find the Plain English Guide to Independence. What is the purpose of this document? Does it explain differences between the AICPA, PCAOB, and SEC independence standards?

3-47   Go to the Web site of the Institute of Internal Auditors (*www.theiia.org*). Find the IIA code of ethics. Briefly compare the IIA code to the AICPA Code.

3-48   Go to the Web site for your state's Department of Professional Regulation or Board of Accountancy. Find the CPA exam information. What are the criteria to sit for the CPA exam in your state?

3-49   Rent the movie *John Q* starring Denzel Washington. The movie's plot deals with a child who needs a heart transplant. The child's family does not have insurance and cannot afford the surgery. Focus on the hospital and hospital administrator and look for an ethical dilemma from her perspective. Her first advice is for the family to go home and enjoy the time they have left, since they can't afford the surgery. Her later decision, in the midst of a media fury, is that the hospital is going to donate the surgery. Analyze her decisions based on the benefit to one child and one family, and describe her fiduciary responsibilities and the benefit to the shareholders of the hospital. Do you believe she changed the basis of making her decision as a result of events? In other words, do you think she moved from making the decision for the benefit of stockholders to making it for the benefit of the family and child?

CHAPTER 4

Legal Environment Affecting Audits

LEARNING OBJECTIVES FOR THIS CHAPTER

1. Learn the meaning of legal standing and the characteristics of various legal standing classifications of plaintiffs.
2. Describe the processes that occur in a legal action resulting in a trial.
3. Understand the different causes of action typically used in cases against auditors, along with likely defenses and damages.
4. Recognize various statutory laws that may affect auditors in civil and criminal actions.

Chapter 4 Resources

AICPA, *Code of Professional Conduct*

AU 230, AICPA, PCAOB, *Due Professional Care in the Performance of Work*

AU 316, AICPA, PCAOB, *Consideration of Fraud in a Financial Statement Audit*

AU 317, AICPA, PCAOB, *Illegal Acts by Clients*

AU 380, AICPA, *The Auditor's Communication with Those Charged with Governance*

AU 380, PCAOB, *Communication with Audit Committees*

Foreign Corrupt Practices Act of 1977

Private Securities Litigation Reform Act of 1995

PCAOB AS 5, *An Audit of Internal Control Over Financial Reporting That is Integrated with an Audit of Financial Statements*

Racketeer Influenced and Corrupt Organization Act

Sarbanes-Oxley Act of 2002

Securities Act of 1933

Securities Exchange Act of 1934

Securities Litigation Uniform Standards Act of 1998

SEC Rules of Practice

Title 18 U.S.C. § 1512, Obstruction of Justice

INTRODUCTION

The legal system plays an important role in supporting the quality of work provided by auditors. It provides the final judgments regarding accountability for behavior in our society. Legal actions may result in outcomes with appropriate negative consequences for an auditor who does not fulfill his or her professional responsibilities. A by-product of providing opportunities for justice is that our legal system also allows lawsuits to be directed at innocent individuals, including auditors who perform their work with due professional care.

Using due professional care is the best way an auditor can avoid a guilty verdict in court and liability for damages. But the auditor's use of due professional care will not necessarily prevent a damaged party from initiating a lawsuit against the auditor. The possibility is real that an auditor may be sued and will have to present a defense in court. Auditors need to consider these risks when they accept or continue client relationships and perform audit engagements.

Auditors need to understand the legal impacts affecting the environment in which they work. Specifically, they need to know who can sue them, events involved in a legal action, allegations typically made in lawsuits against auditors, and defenses that auditors use in court. Particular types of lawsuits are brought in certain courts. Therefore, it is helpful to understand the structure of the court systems.

AUDITORS AND RISK [LO 1]

Auditors need to understand the legal environment in which they do business because it affects the risk of their activities. All auditors experience **audit risk**, which is the possibility that they issue opinions that internal control over financial reporting (ICFR) is effective and the financial statements are fair when that is not true. An **audit failure** occurs when an auditor issues an inappropriate audit report. No one actually knows how many audit failures occur because there is no way to track those that occur and remain undiscovered. Most often audit failures are revealed when the client company experiences business problems. For example, audit failures are exposed when a fraud is discovered or when the company defaults on debt or goes bankrupt.

Some aspects of audit risk cannot be influenced by the auditor. The activities and structure of the audit client and the quality of its ICFR are under the control of management and the Board of Directors. In contrast, the type and quantity of audit activities also affect audit risk. The auditor has complete control over the choice and use of audit procedures. Therefore, the auditor can design the audit to keep audit risk at an acceptable level.

The degree of audit risk an auditor is willing to accept on any specific audit engagement is influenced by the **business risk** the audit engagement presents to the audit firm. If an audit failure occurs and the client company experiences business problems, the audit failure is more likely to be exposed. Discovery and exposure of an audit failure subsequently creates business problems for the audit firm. Many of these business problems are monetary. The audit firm is not likely to collect the fee for the audit. Also, the audit firm experiences damage to its reputation as the audit failure becomes known. The audit firm may lose clients as a result of the damaged reputation, resulting in more monetary losses. The audit firm may also experience legal problems including litigation and any resulting negative consequences. Thus, audit risk, including the potential for legal action, creates business risk for an auditor.

WHO CAN SUE THE AUDITOR?

The issue of **standing** determines whether a court permits a **plaintiff** to bring a legal **cause of action** against an auditor. Four different descriptions of standing apply to the relationship between the auditor and plaintiff:

1. Privity
2. Near privity
3. Foreseen third parties
4. Foreseeable third parties

A cause of action is the reason used to initiate a legal action. Causes of action that are important when learning about auditor liability are as follows:

Negligence

Fraud

Breach of contract

Statutory violations

The closer the relationship between the plaintiff and the auditor, the less severe the auditor's wrongdoing needs to be for a legal claim to result in a decision against the auditor. For example, only those in the closest relationships to an auditor will likely be granted standing for **negligence**. This means that only those defined as in "privity" are allowed to initiate a legal action and have any chance of a successful lawsuit based on a claim that the auditor was "merely" negligent. In contrast, an auditor may have committed **fraud** rather than negligence. For fraud charges, parties who do not have a direct relationship with the auditor can initiate a cause of action. If the allegation is fraud, parties who are distant are more likely to be awarded compensation for the damages they have experienced. The meaning of these different terms related to standing and cause of action are explained in the following sections.

Privity

Black's Law Dictionary defines **privity** as "[t]he connection or relationship between two parties, each having a legally recognized interest in the same subject matter."[1]

The first important case involving accountants and privity is *Ultramares Corporation v. George A. Touche et al.*, 255 NY 170 (1931). The case is so well known that it is often referred to simply as **Ultramares**. The precedent set by *Ultramares* is that a person or entity has to have privity with an auditor to be able to collect damages if the auditor is found

---

[1]*Black's Law Dictionary*, 8th Edition, Eagan, MN: West, 2004.

culpable of no greater wrongdoing than negligence. Negligence is the absence of due professional care. Using due professional care means that an individual performs his or her work with an expected level of competence and technical knowledge. Although not a term with real legal meaning, *ordinary negligence* is sometimes used to refer to negligence to distinguish it from **gross negligence**. The difference between the two is that gross negligence is more severe and represents complete disregard for the negative results of one's actions. The *Ultramares* outcome was so important that it continues to guide legal decisions more than 70 years later.

The *Ultramares* case deals with whether a third-party plaintiff has standing to sue for damages based on the actions of the auditor using an allegation of ordinary negligence. As a reminder, standing means that a party has met the court's requirements to initiate a particular legal cause of action. In *Ultramares,* the public accounting firm of Touche, Niven & Co. had performed an audit of Fred Stern & Co. Fred Stern & Co. factored receivables to and received loans from Ultramares Corporation. Fred Stern & Co. went bankrupt, and Ultramares Corporation suffered damages (monetary losses) because it was unable to collect all that was due from Fred Stern & Co. on the loans. Ultramares Corporation sued the auditors under the legal theory of negligence.

The Honorable Judge Benjamin Cardozo was Chief Justice of the New York Court of Appeals that ruled on the *Ultramares* case. In what has since become a famous ruling, he stated that even if there was negligence on the part of the auditor, the plaintiff, Ultramares Corporation, did not have standing to sue the auditor for ordinary negligence under the jurisprudence of that time.[2]

In disallowing that a case of negligence could be brought against an auditor by a third party lacking privity, the Honorable Judge Cardozo stated:

> If a liability for negligence exists, a thoughtless slip or blunder, the failure to detect a theft or forgery beneath the cover of deceptive entries, may expose an accountant to a liability in an indeterminate amount for an indeterminate time to an indeterminate class. The hazards of business on these terms are so extreme as to enkindle doubt whether a flaw may not exist in the implications of a duty that exposes to these circumstances. [255 N.Y. 170, 174 N.E. 441, 1931]

Judge Cardozo believed that if there was not a determinable class of potential plaintiffs, an auditor might be subject to unlimited liability, for an unlimited amount of time to unknown individuals. The *Ultramares* decision held that privity, which can be thought of as a direct connection between the plaintiff and defendant, was required for a negligence case. But the court also anticipated certain types of cases for which strict privity would not be required, such as in cases of fraud. (See footnote 2.)

Near Privity

In *Credit Alliance Corp. v. Arthur Andersen,* 101 A.D.2d. 231 (1984), the court established another precedent that is often considered in cases involving auditors. In this case, the court laid out a three-part test in applying the privity concept that was established under *Ultramares.* The *Credit Alliance* case dealt with a situation in which the plaintiff (Credit Alliance Corp.)

---

[2]The legal decision also expanded on the concept of privity and discussed circumstances in which, (1) fraud occurred and (2) the damaged party relied on the financial statements and experienced actual damage. The decision stated that if the plaintiff could prove that both of these conditions were met, then a third party could obtain relief through the theory of constructive fraud. Proving fraud required proving that the financial statements misrepresented a material fact and that the misrepresentation was made either knowingly or without adequate knowledge to have an opinion. While fraud requires the intent to do wrong, "misrepresenting…a material fact…without adequate knowledge" referred to the concept of constructive fraud.

claimed that it had standing to sue the auditor (Arthur Andersen) for ordinary negligence because the auditor knew the plaintiff was relying on financial statements it had audited. Credit Alliance Corp. was using a company's audited financial statements while making decisions about extending credit to the company.

The case's legal ruling stated that if the circumstances satisfy a three-part test the plaintiff may be found to be in **near privity** with the auditor. As a result of being in near privity, a plaintiff may have standing to sue when the wrongdoing is less severe than fraud. The three-part test looks first at whether the auditor understood that the financial statements were going to be used for a specific purpose. The second part of the test requires both that the auditor knew the third party and that the third party relied on the financial statements. The last part of the test is a requirement for some action by the auditor showing an understanding that the third party was going to rely on the financial statements. Credit Alliance Corp. was able to establish that the auditor knew about its reliance on the audited financial statements by proving that it had communicated with Arthur Andersen about them.

The *Credit Alliance* case that originated the three-part test for near privity occurred in 1984. The three-part test was applied in 1992 in the case of *Security Pacific Business Credit, Inc. v. Peat Marwick Main & Co.*, 79 N.Y.2d. 695 (1992). The facts of the *Security Pacific* case established that one telephone call had taken place between the auditor and the third-party plaintiff. The court decided that a single telephone call between the auditor and the third party that was going to rely on the financial statements was insufficient to justify near privity under the three-part test. The single call did not satisfy the part of the test requiring action by the auditor indicating an understanding that the third party was going to rely on the financial statements. Consequently, in this case the plaintiff was not determined to be in near privity with the auditor.

During a typical audit, the auditor is not likely to have much contact with any third-party users of the audited financial statements. As a result, the near privity test actually provides a strict requirement for standing to sue for ordinary negligence in an audit situation. Establishing privity (or near privity) with the auditor is important because only those plaintiffs have standing to allege ordinary negligence as a cause of action. Consequently, only those with privity or near privity have any likelihood of collecting damages from a court finding of ordinary negligence on the part of the auditor.

Foreseen Third Parties

The **foreseen third-party** standard is based on the *Restatement of Torts, 2d. Section 552*. A majority of the states and the federal government follow the foreseen third-party standard when determining the standing of a potential plaintiff to sue an accountant.

Restatement of Torts, 2d. Section 552

(1) One who, in the course of his business, profession or employment, or in any other transaction in which he has a pecuniary interest, supplies false information for the guidance of others in their business transactions, is subject to liability for pecuniary loss caused to them by their justifiable reliance upon the information, if he fails to exercise reasonable care or competence in obtaining or communicating the information.

(2) Except as stated in Subsection (3) [below], the liability stated in Subsection (1) [above] is limited to loss suffered

   (a) by the person or one of a limited group of persons for whose benefit and guidance he intends to supply the information or knows that the recipient intends to supply it; and

   (b) through reliance upon it in a transaction that he intends the information to influence or knows that the recipient so intends or in a substantially similar transaction.

(3) The liability of one who is under a public duty to give the information extends to loss suffered by any of the class of persons for whose benefit the duty is created, in any of the transactions in which it is intended to protect them.

The legal language in Restatement Section 552 basically means that an auditor can be liable for damages if he or she is associated with false information in a set of financial statements because of a failure to use reasonable care or skill when performing an audit. The potential liability is for damages experienced by a person who could have been expected to rely on the information—such as a financial statement user. The auditor's liability is limited to the actual loss experienced by individuals or groups who could be foreseen to rely on the audited financial statements.

The legal standard expressed in Restatement Section 552 expands the group of potential plaintiffs against auditors to include foreseen users. Over time the courts have given a number of reasons for expanding the group to which the auditor has potential liability. Some of the reasons given for expanding the group of potential plaintiffs to include foreseen users are:

1. the increase in liability of other professions to non-privity plaintiffs,
2. a general concern for fairness to the innocent user of financial statements who is harmed by the negligent or fraudulent behavior of the auditor, and
3. the ability of the auditor to absorb the damages and spread the costs of litigation to multiple clients.

The justification that the auditor can absorb damages and spread costs to multiple clients places the auditor in a role similar to that of an insurance company. The logic is that the auditor knows that litigation risk exists and that sometimes costs of litigation will have to be paid. Consequently, the auditor can increase the fees for all audits to cover costs that are eventually bound to result from legal claims. Also, to the extent it is available, the auditor can purchase professional liability insurance to cover legal claims and judgments. As a result, theoretically, all of the auditor's clients will pay increased audit fees and share in covering the losses suffered by innocent financial statement users. The obvious flaw in this theory is an assumption that the auditor will be able to shift the costs and collect increased fees from all clients to cover the costs of legal actions and judgments.

Foreseeable Third Parties

The standard of **foreseeable third parties** allows for the largest number of potential plaintiffs against auditors. This legal theory of standing allows anyone who can be "reasonably foreseen" as a user of the financial statements the same right to initiate a legal action against the auditor as a financial statement user with privity. In the past, a number of courts have allowed what they considered reasonably foreseeable plaintiffs to initiate a cause of action against an accountant or auditor. Currently, the only jurisdictions that permit use of this standard are Mississippi and Wisconsin.[3]

Allowing **reasonably foreseeable third parties** standing to sue for ordinary negligence causes many concerns. As Judge Cardozo forewarned in the *Ultramares* case, the definition of reasonably foreseeable might be assumed to include everyone who has access to the audited financial statements. Since auditors typically carry at least some professional liability insurance, one risk in today's world of high insurance costs is that accountants might lower their insurance premiums simply by getting out of the business of performing audits. This cost-benefit decision mirrors what many medical doctors do by avoiding high-risk medical practices in certain geographic regions because of the costs of medical malpractice insurance. Society as a whole suffers when doctors are not available to perform certain medical

---

[3]Two case examples using the reasonably foreseen standard are *Rosenblum, Inc. v. Adler*, 93 N.J. 324 (1983) and *Citizens State Bank v. Timm, Schmidt & Co.*, 113 Wis. 2d. 376 (1983). In both cases, the court allowed unforeseen plaintiffs to sue for foreseeable injuries.

procedures. Similarly, society's financial and commercial structures will suffer if accountants decide to avoid performing audits. On a positive note, no state high court has yet to follow the reasonably foreseeable standard.[4]

In summary, the plaintiff's legal standing is influenced by two variables: the closeness of the connection between the potential plaintiff and the auditor; and the nature of wrongdoing alleged against the auditor. The number of potential plaintiffs grows as the standard moves from strict privity to that of a foreseeable third party.

AUDITING IN ACTION

Negligent Conduct, Accountants, and Nonclients

The theory nearest to one requiring a contract and the theory most protective for accountants is that accountants may be held liable in negligence to nonclients only in those cases in which the accountants were aware that the financial reports were to be used for a particular purpose, and there was conduct by the accountants linking them to the nonclient (*Credit Alliance Corp. v. Arthur Andersen & Co,* 1985).

A theory providing a measure of protection for accountants is that they may be held liable for negligence to third parties only if they intend to supply the information for the benefit of third parties in a specific transaction or type of transaction identified to the accountants (Restatement Second of Torts)[4].

The most expansive theory is that accountants may be held liable in negligence to all those whom the accountant should reasonably foresee as recipients of the financial statements for authorized business purposes (*H. Rosenblom, Inc. v. Adler,* 1983).

[Quoted from p. 422: David S. Ruder. 1994. "Accountants' Liability: Regulatory and Legal Issues." *Journal of Economics & Management Strategy* 2, Number 3 (Fall 1993): 419–426.]

REVIEW QUESTIONS

A.1 Why does audit risk create business risk for an auditor, and how does the legal environment of business affect the auditor's business risk?

A.2 What is meant by the term *standing* as it refers to a plaintiff, and why is standing important?

A.3 What are the various categories of standing of plaintiffs in actions against auditors? What characteristics cause a plaintiff to have each type of standing?

A.4 What important precedent did the *Ultramares* decision set?

A.5 What reasons have been given for expanding auditor liability for negligence to foreseen users?

EVENTS INVOLVED IN A LEGAL ACTION [LO 2]

Auditors may be tried for criminal wrongdoing, but the majority of cases against auditors are civil cases covered by tort law. Civil cases involve disputes between private individuals or entities. **Tort** law addresses situations in which a party suffers a loss and wants to collect damages. An important aspect of a civil case is the severity of the alleged wrongdoing. The

---

[4]Some courts have specifically rejected the reasonably foreseeable standard, as in, for example, the case of *Bily v. Arthur Young & Company,* 834 P.2d 745 (1992). In this case the California Supreme Court adopted the "intent to influence" test and rejected the foreseeability test for negligence. The intent to influence stated: "The representation must have been made with the intent to induce [the] plaintiff, or a particular class of persons to which [the] plaintiff belongs, to act in reliance upon the representation in a specific transaction."

severity of wrongdoing interacts with whether a specific plaintiff has standing and can sue for damages. The previous section discussed legal standing and described the classes of plaintiffs. This section first examines the concept of settling cases out of court. It then presents the components of a civil case and describes how the case proceeds by addressing the following topics:

1. The beginnings of a civil case against an auditor
2. Different motions and pleadings between the parties
3. Various steps that take place if the case goes to trial

Arbitration, Negotiations, and Settlements

Before or during a trial, the plaintiff and auditor may participate in arbitration or may voluntarily settle a case. **Arbitration** is a process in which negotiation occurs, directed by an independent party called an *arbitrator*. The negotiation involves an attempt to settle differences and agree on a financial arrangement acceptable to both parties before a case goes to or is concluded by a trial. Arbitration can be entered into voluntarily. Sometimes arbitration is required by a contract. A judge may require that the opposing parties participate in arbitration to try to come to an agreement on their differences. Auditors of public companies must take care regarding arbitration agreements because, depending on the specifications, arbitration required through terms of the engagement letter may impair the auditor's independence.

Regardless of whether it occurs from independent discussion between the parties or arbitration, many times disputes are settled. Claims against auditors can be settled before the case goes to trial or while the trial is taking place. An audit firm may choose to settle a case even when it believes it would prevail through a trial. The common-sense reason for settling a case is because the audit firm concludes it is less costly to settle and pay the negotiated amount than to pay the cost of going through the litigation. Another motivator for settling is that even if an auditor is not guilty, there is never a guarantee regarding the outcome of a trial. Also, trials can create media attention that casts a taint on the audit firm regardless of the legal outcome.

When a case is not settled and results in a civil legal action, the components of the legal action are the complaint, the answer, discovery, court proceedings, and final processes.

AUDITING IN ACTION

Deloitte Settles in Adelphia Case

News reports on December 9, 2006 indicated that Deloitte & Touche had agreed to pay $210 million to settle a lawsuit related to Adelphia Communications. The settlement, which included Deloitte & Touche and 38 banks, was for a total of $455 million. Adelphia Communications, a cable television company, filed for bankruptcy after an accounting fraud. John J. Rigas, who started the company, and his son were both criminally convicted. The lawsuit against Deloitte & Touche and the banks was brought by investors, related to monetary damages they suffered.

"Neither Deloitte & Touche nor the banks admitted wrongdoing.... A spokeswoman, Deborah Harrington, said that Deloitte & Touche felt 'it was in the best interests of the firm and its clients to settle this action rather than to continue to face the expense and uncertainty of protracted litigation.'"

(*Source*: From the newyorktimes.com, published December 9, 2006, "Deloitte and Banks to Pay $455 Million to Adelphia Investors.")

Step 1: The Complaint

The **complaint** is a document stating the facts as seen by the plaintiff. These include:

Proposed cause of action

Remedies being sought

Dollar amount of damages sought from the auditor

The plaintiff is required to assert sufficient factual issues to proceed in a case using one of the causes of action. As stated earlier, the primary causes of action are negligence, fraud, breach of contract, and statutory violations. In addition, the plaintiff provides any information legally required under the cause of action used as the basis for the complaint. Required information may be as straightforward as the name and legal address of the plaintiff and that the plaintiff hired the auditor. Some required information may be more complex. The plaintiff does not need to prove anything at this stage. The requirement is to present the information with a sufficient factual basis for the case to move forward.

Once the complaint is drafted, the plaintiff has the responsibility to "serve" the complaint on the defendant. Through the process of service, the defendant receives documents of the legal action. Service can be to the individual auditor. If the complaint is against the public accounting firm, service can be at the place of the business. A copy of the complaint is filed in either state or federal court.

Step 2: The Answer

The **answer** is the defendant's response to the various contentions presented in the complaint. In the answer, the defendant agrees with uncontested facts such as the name of the firm and address. The defendant normally answers "no" or "disagree" to contested facts or assertions. Within an answer, the defendant usually does not offer any additional facts. However, the defendant can offer affirmative defenses in the answer, such as lack of standing.

Step 3: Discovery

Discovery is the fact-finding portion of a case. Both parties seek to establish facts to support their positions. The plaintiff seeks to establish facts sufficient to prove the cause of action. The defendant seeks to establish facts showing that there is insufficient support for the cause of action or to establish the stated or intended defenses.

Two standard discovery techniques are reviewing documents and deposing individuals. Document review occurs after either party requests documents to establish facts. The second and more powerful technique is deposition. During a deposition the opposing attorney questions the plaintiff, defendant, or some third party with knowledge of the case while that person is under oath.

AUDITING IN ACTION

Objectives and Desired Outcomes of Depositions

Discovering facts sufficient to establish or defend against the allegations.

Establishing a defendant's testimony under oath.

Obtaining an admission of the alleged negligence or other cause of action.

Narrowing the contested factual aspects of the case; as a result of the deposition, both parties may "stipulate" or state that they agree about certain facts.

Establishing testimony that can be used to impeach or discredit a witness at a later point during the trial.

Step 4: Court Proceedings

The final step of a civil legal action is the trial. This step has more than one component. Typically, the defendant's attorney first seeks a **summary judgment** against the plaintiff. In seeking a summary judgment, the defense attorney proposes that the plaintiff has not established the necessary components of the cause of action. If the case has made it this far in the process, the summary judgment is usually denied and the case proceeds.

Next, both the plaintiff and the defendant present facts, question witnesses, cross-examine witnesses, and present expert testimony to try to support their respective positions. Once the presentation of testimony is complete, the judge "charges the jury." This means that the judge issues instructions to the jury explaining the law on which the case is based. If there is no jury, then the judge considers the facts and applicable law. Finally, the case is decided—either by the judge in a judge-only trial, or by a jury. The judge or jury "holds for," or decides in favor of, either the plaintiff or the defendant.

The procedural steps, such as charging the jury, can be critically important to the outcome of a case. Many people are aware that the public accounting firm, Arthur Andersen, was found guilty of obstruction of justice for actions related to its audit client, Enron. Fewer people are aware that on May 31, 2005 the Supreme Court of the United States unanimously overturned the conviction against Arthur Andersen due to flaws in the jury instructions. So, while Arthur Andersen may continue to be found guilty in the "court of public opinion," no legal or professional conclusions of wrongdoing by Arthur Andersen actually exist.

Step 5: After the Proceedings

If the decision is in favor of the plaintiff, a judgment is made *against* the defendant. The judge issues the judgment "into the record," and the defendant is now liable for damages. If the judgment is *for* the defendant, then the defendant won the case and is not liable for damages. The losing party in either situation has the right to appeal the ruling to the next higher court. If an appeal is granted, the parties file briefs with the appeals court. When a case is granted an appeal, the appellate judges decide the case. They either concur with or reverse the original decision or they remand the case back to the lower court for further fact finding or with instructions of actions for the lower court to pursue.

REVIEW QUESTIONS

B.1 What is arbitration?

B.2 Why might an auditor choose to settle a case rather than go through with a trial?

B.3 What are the steps in a legal action up to and including the trial? What happens during each step?

CAUSES OF ACTION, DEFENSES, AND POTENTIAL DAMAGES [LO 3]

The first requirement of any lawsuit is that the plaintiff have a cause of action. The cause of action is the legal theory the plaintiff uses to allege the wrongdoing of the defendant and support the request for damages. The second aspect of a lawsuit is the attempt by the plaintiff to prove that the defendant, who in this chapter is the auditor or CPA firm, is culpable of the legal theory of the cause of action. The third important component of a case is whether sufficient defenses exist against the plaintiff's assertions to prevent the defendant from being found liable. If a defendant is found liable, the last issue is damages.

In a criminal case, the plaintiff is the government. In criminal cases, the components of the suit are similar to those in civil cases, but requirements to prove that the accused party is guilty are stricter and the potential damages more severe. Time in prison is a possible outcome of severe criminal cases.

Within the business environment in which auditing takes place, the potential for a lawsuit against the client company, auditor, or public accounting firm always exists. Plaintiffs sue auditors and CPA firms based on **common law** and statute. Common law is judicially created law that results from a court either interpreting statutory law or creating a parallel common law principle. The three major common law causes of action used against auditors are negligence, fraud, and breach of contract. Statutory-based lawsuits against auditors are often based on the 1933 Securities and 1934 Secuirities Exchange Acts. In addition, various other **statutory laws** enable the government to assess civil penalties or charge an auditor with a criminal act.

Negligence and Gross Negligence

Cause of Action

Negligence is the most common cause of action against auditors. Gross negligence is a cause of action distinguished from negligence. Negligence is defined in the *Restatement of the Law, 2d, Torts, §282* as:

> conduct which falls below the standard established by law for the protection of others against unreasonable risk of harm.

Contained within this definition is the idea of standards established by law. In addition, based on the *Restatement of the Law, Second, Torts, §292*, an accountant is included in the following definition:

> One who undertakes to render services in the practice of a profession or trade [and] is required to exercise the skill and knowledge normally possessed by members of that profession or trade in good standing in similar communities.

Within the U.S. judicial system this standard in the area of negligence is considered the **reasonable man standard**, also known as the **prudent person standard**. This standard for the professional is best expressed in *Cooley on Torts*:

> Every man who offers his services to another and is employed assumes the duty of exercise in employment such skill, as he possesses with reasonable care and diligence. In all these employments where particular skill is prerequisite, if one offers his service, he is understood as holding himself out to the public as possessing the degree of skill commonly possessed by others in the same employment, and, if his pretensions are unfounded, he commits a species of fraud upon every man who employs him in reliance on his public profession. But no man, whether skilled or unskilled, undertakes that the task he assumes shall be performed successfully, and without fault or error. He undertakes for good faith and integrity, but not for infallibility, and he is liable to his employer for negligence, bad faith, or dishonesty, but not for losses consequent upon pure error of judgment.
> (D. Haggard, *Cooley on Torts* 472, 4th Edition, 1932, from AU 230.01)

The plaintiff must prove the following to sustain a legal action of negligence against the auditor:

1. The financial statements were materially misleading.
2. The auditor was negligent in the performance of the audit engagement:
   a. The auditors did not meet the professional standards of a "reasonable man" or "prudent person," or
   b. The auditors did not perform pursuant to their own (for example, PCAOB, AICPA) professional standards.

3. The plaintiff relied on the financial statements.

4. The auditor was known or was responsible to the plaintiff, that is, standing.

5. The plaintiff was damaged by relying on the financial statements.

If unsuccessful in establishing proof, the plaintiff will not prevail in the lawsuit.

The definition of gross negligence builds on negligence. Gross negligence means that not only is due care lacking, but the professional shows a reckless disregard for the duty owed to the person who was harmed. The same items listed in the previous paragraph related to negligence must be proven for gross negligence. However, rather than proving that the auditor did not perform to a reasonable man or prudent person standard the plaintiff needs to show more. The plaintiff must prove that the auditor recklessly performed the audit or a portion of the audit. In some states, there is no difference between negligence and gross negligence. In those states, actions meeting the "reckless disregard" definition likely constitute **constructive fraud**. The main motivation for a plaintiff to allege gross negligence rather than ordinary negligence is the ability of the judge or jury to award punitive damages in response to findings of gross negligence. In other words, if an auditor is found guilty of gross negligence, the plaintiff may receive not only the amount of his or her loss, but a payment for punitive damages also.

Defenses

Being sued does not mean that an auditor will be found guilty, culpable, or liable for damages. But the auditor must present an effective defense. In typical negligence cases, the main factor that courts and juries review is whether auditors acted in a manner equal to how a professional, reasonable man or prudent person would have acted in a similar situation. The *Second Restatement of Torts §299A* dealing with professional standards states:

> Unless he represents that he has greater or less skill or knowledge, one who undertakes to render services in the practice of a profession or trade is required to exercise the skill and knowledge normally possessed by members of that profession or trade in good standing in similar communities.

The important question is how this standard of skill and knowledge normally possessed by professionals affects an audit. What procedures should the auditor perform to meet the standard?

The most common defense to a negligence claim is that the auditor or firm acted in a professional manner. The defense states that the auditor or firm followed PCAOB or AICPA auditing standards. Another phrase often used to describe this level of professional behavior is acting with **due professional care**. When this defense is successful, the auditor shows that, even though a mistake or an omission was made, he or she followed the professional standards and behaved with due professional care. With this outcome the auditor is not held liable. However, if the auditor fails on another front that may not be specifically required by the professional standards, the auditor may be found negligent. Examples of other potential failures are not notifying the audit client's Board of Directors of events, or even failing to find a fraud that the jury or court believes a professional of standard knowledge would have uncovered.

Other Defenses

In addition to nonnegligent performance, an auditor may use other defenses in response to an allegation of negligence.

1. The auditor can argue that there was no duty of care in his or her relationship with the plaintiff.

    As was presented in the discussion on standing, the auditor only owes a "duty of care" to specific parties. If there is no duty of care because the plaintiff does not have standing, the auditor can typically request a summary judgment against the plaintiff and the case is dismissed.

2. Even if the auditor was actually negligent, the auditor can still argue that the plaintiff did not rely on the financial information in his or her decision-making process; thus the negligent act did not harm the plaintiff.

This is a more difficult fact pattern to prove when the audit is of a public company because of the widespread access to the financial statements that results from SEC offerings documents, and quarterly and annual SEC filings.

3. The auditor can argue that there was no causal connection between the negligent act and the damages suffered by the plaintiff. In order for the plaintiff to prevail, he or she must show a close causal connection between the auditor's negligent action and the damages being sought.

   An example for which this defense applies is an auditor not finishing an audit of the plaintiff on a timely basis and a bank refusing to close on the plaintiff's expected loan. However, if the reason for the bank's refusal was not the late audit but the weak financial condition of the plaintiff, the auditor's negligence is not the cause of the damage.

4. **Contributory negligence** is the last of the major defenses. The argument is that management of the corporation that was audited was partially responsible for the negligent act.

   This defense applies, for example, if the corporation hid liabilities or allowed some other accounting impropriety to occur. The main objective when using a contributory negligence defense is to divide the potential liability between the auditor and the company that was audited. The benefit of the contributory negligence defense is that the court, depending on the state, may allow a split in responsibility for payment of the damages.

AUDITING IN ACTION

Defenses Used against Claims of Negligence

1. Due professional care was used.
2. No duty of care existed.
3. The plaintiff did not rely on the financial information.
4. The negligent behavior did not cause the damages.
5. The plaintiff was culpable of contributory negligence.

Damages

Damages awarded for negligence depend on the losses of the plaintiff. Two basic forms of damages are **compensatory** and **punitive damages**. Compensatory damages are limited to the loss the plaintiff suffered because of the auditor's negligence. Compensatory damages equal the amount needed to put the plaintiff in the same position that would have existed had the lack of due professional care not occurred. Normally, in cases related to audits of public companies, compensatory damages equal the loss on the investment that resulted from the auditor's negligence. In other words, the plaintiff would be granted the difference between the amount paid or received for securities and what the amount would have been absent the auditor's negligent action.

A finding of gross negligence can result in punitive damages. Consequently, the outcomes of lawsuits alleging negligence and gross negligence can be very different. Punitive damages are awarded to a plaintiff if the jury or court believes the defendant auditor should be punished for negligent actions. Recall that gross negligence is related to the reckless disregard for some audit requirement. As a consequence, gross negligence may motivate a damage award that includes punishment.

Joint and severally (often called joint and several), and **separate and proportionate** are two distinct theories of liability that impact payment of damages for negligence. Joint and severally liability applies when there is more than one defendant and each defendant can be liable for the total amount of damages. For example, if there are two defendants and one goes bankrupt, the remaining defendant is liable for the entire judgment. In contrast, under the legal theory of separate and proportionate liability, each defendant is only liable for the percentage of the judgment allocated to that particular defendant. An example is that a $1 million award is given, and the judgment assesses 30% of the negligence upon defendant 1 and 70% upon defendant 2. Defendant 1 is only liable for $300,000 regardless of defendant 2's ability to pay.

Relevant Cases

Ultramares Corporation v. George A. Touche et al., 255 NY 170 (1931): *Ultramares,* discussed earlier in this chapter, is likely the most often cited case related to auditor negligence. In this case the auditor was found to have been negligent for issuing an unqualified opinion on financial statements that included an accounts receivable overstated by $700,000. The conclusion was that a nonnegligent audit performed with due professional care would have uncovered the misstatement. Even though the auditor was negligent, no damages were awarded to Ultramares Corporation because Ultramares lacked privity with the auditor.

Rusch Factors, Inc. v. Levin, 284 F. Supp 85 (1968): In this case, Levin was the audit client, and Rusch Factors obtained audited financial statements from Levin prior to extending a loan to Levin. The auditor issued an unqualified opinion, even though Levin was insolvent. The auditor was found guilty of negligence. The auditor was liable for damages to Rusch Factors because Rusch Factors was a foreseen third party.

REVIEW QUESTIONS

C.1 What are the differences between a civil and criminal case?

C.2 What is the reasonable man or prudent person standard?

C.3 What circumstances lead to a negligence cause of action against an auditor?

C.4 What defenses can be used?

C.5 For what would an auditor be liable as the result of a negligence finding?

C.6 How do your answers to 3, 4, and 5 change for a gross negligence cause of action?

C.7 What are the main legal theories of liability, and how do they differ?

Fraud

Cause of Action

Fraud is a frequent cause of action in cases against auditors. Fraud can be further broken down into three distinct but related areas:

1. Constructive fraud
2. Actual fraud
3. Fraud as defined in the Securities Act of 1933 and the Securities Exchange Act of 1934

Constructive fraud can be thought of as a form of severe negligence and is similar to behavior characterized by the term *gross negligence.* Both gross negligence and constructive fraud require a blatant or reckless disregard in performing the audit. When states do not have a separate gross negligence statute, they may have a constructive fraud statute. Damages for constructive fraud may be similar to those specified in other states for gross negligence.

The second legal theory of fraud used as a cause of action in civil cases is *actual fraud.* Actual fraud, for auditors and accountants, is defined as an intentional misstatement in or omission from the financial statements caused by the auditor. Since the client rather than the auditor prepares the financial statements, often the auditor is not the party charged with fraud. The auditor is typically charged with negligence for not catching a company's fraud that resulted in an omission or a misstatement of facts within the company's audited financial statements.

The named party who is the actual defendant in a fraud cause is important. When the fraud cause of action is *against the auditor*, the accusation is that the auditor or public accounting firm actually performed or participated in the fraud. The alternative situation is that the auditor failed to recognize or catch the fraudulently misstated financial statements. When the auditor fails to detect a fraud, the most likely cause of action is negligence and, at the extreme, gross negligence or constructive fraud.

In order for a plaintiff to prove constructive fraud he or she must prove the same items required in a gross negligence case. However, if a plaintiff seeks to prove actual fraud by the auditor, the plaintiff must prove the following,

1. The financial statements were materially misleading.
2. The auditor *knowingly* misrepresented or intentionally omitted items within the financial statements.
3. The plaintiff relied on the financial statements.
4. The auditor was responsible to the plaintiff, that is, standing.
5. The plaintiff was damaged by relying on the financial statements.

The final fraud type is defined within the 1933 and 1934 Securities Acts. The definition of this type of fraud is statutorily established. If a plaintiff successfully claims the auditor fraudulently misrepresented or omitted information, and this made the financial statements materially misleading, the auditor may be found liable under statutory law. An auditor found guilty of fraud under statutory law may have to pay civil damages and face regulatory and criminal penalties.

Defenses

The defense against a charge of fraud is that the defendant did not knowingly or intentionally perform the act or omit the information associated with the accusation. The main difference between an allegation of fraud and one of negligence is the charge that the defendant *knowingly* did something to cause the harm. If this accusation of "knowing" is overcome, the case is normally brought into the sphere of negligence. Then, the standard defenses against negligence can be used by the defendant.

Damages

The damages for fraud are similar to those awarded for gross negligence. The major difference is the greater likelihood that punitive damages will be awarded when the auditor is found guilty of fraud. For cases involving fraudulent financial statements, the plaintiff may not even have to prove that the auditor's behavior caused the damages in order to collect.

Relevant cases

State Street Trust Company v. Alwin C. Ernst, 278 N.Y. 104, 15 N.E. 2d 416 (1938): The main legal question in the *State Street Trust Company* case was whether an auditor can be held liable for damages when the auditor did not intentionally seek to perpetrate a fraud. In this case, the auditor failed to investigate an obvious issue that affected the balance sheet in a material way and did not appropriately address the consequences of the failure to investigate.

The basic facts of the case are that the auditor issued an unqualified opinion on a client's financial statements and later determined that the receivables were overstated. The auditor informed the client but did not inform State Street Trust Company even though the auditor knew that State Street had executed a loan to the audit client based on the audited financial statements. The court held that the auditor was liable for the damages experienced by State Street Trust Company, stating that the auditor displayed "reckless disregard" for the potential outcomes. This case set a precedent that if an auditor does not have sufficient knowledge to offer an opinion on the financial statements, this lack of knowledge can lead to an inference of constructive fraud.

Houbigant v. Deloitte & Touche LLP, 303 A.D.2d 92 (2003): This case highlights the interplay between privity and cause of action. In *Houbigant*, the plaintiff alleged that the auditor's behavior reflected negligence, fraud, and aiding and abetting in fraudulent activities. The fact pattern, as presented, was that the audited financial statements of Renaissance Cosmetics were misstated due to an overstatement of asset values and that Houbigant suffered losses. The fraud cause of action was based on an allegation that the auditor was aware of the misstatement. The lower court dismissed the case because Houbigant lacked privity. The lower court did not consider the fraud cause of action. It simply looked at the fact that Houbigant was not a client of Deloitte & Touche and then dismissed the case. This action was consistent with long-standing precedent established in the *Ultramares* case.

The *Houbigant* case is significant because a five-judge panel of the New York Appellate Division overturned the lower court's dismissal of the case after reviewing the evidence related to the *fraud* cause of action. This changed the direction from outcomes of previous cases that had seemed to indicate that fraud charges against accountants and auditors had to be accompanied by hard evidence at the time of the complaint. Based on its review, the Appellate Division found that the cause of action for fraud was valid and remanded the case back to the lower court. Even though the plaintiff did not have privity and therefore had no legal standing for a *negligence* cause of action, the lower court had to determine the validity of the allegation of *fraud* against the auditor.

Reisman v. KPMG Peat Marwick LLP, 57 Mass.App.Ct. 100, 787 N.E.2d. 1060 (2003): Along with *Houbigant*, this case is important regarding the issue of how much the courts may require a plaintiff to prove to permit a case alleging fraud to move forward rather than being dismissed. The *Reisman* case dealt with a fraud that was committed to induce shareholders to enter into a pooling of interests transaction to permit an outsider to acquire their interests in a corporation. In this case the plaintiff (the shareholders) was not required to show the reason for the fraud. The plaintiffs' only requirement was to show they were among the parties the auditors should have had reason to know would rely on the auditor's representations. This case set a precedent that when the cause of action is fraud, the plaintiff does not always need to prove reliance on the misstated financial information.

Breach of Contract

Cause of Action

Another common law civil action a plaintiff may use against an auditor is **breach of contract**. In the area of auditing, the breach of contract claim is valid only if the plaintiff had a contract with the auditor and the auditor did not comply with the requirements of the contract. In an audit context, the engagement letter is normally seen as the contract.

Multiple cases have been brought under a breach of contract cause of action in which plaintiffs have sued auditors as third-party beneficiaries of a contract. In this context the term **third-party beneficiary** refers to a plaintiff who is not a party to a contract with the auditor, but was affected by a financial outcome that was somehow linked to the audit.

For example, a transaction is planned among Companies A, B, and C. Company A requires that Company B produce audited financial statements prior to execution of the contract. The auditor begins the audit but withdraws because the company has insufficient books and records or because of problems with management integrity. Company C might try to sue the auditor for breach of contract, claiming losses suffered because the audit was not completed and therefore the transaction was not executed. Company C would not prevail because of lack of privity.

The courts have consistently ruled against third-party beneficiary plaintiffs in breach of contract lawsuits. To be able to sue, a party to a contract must:

1. Prove there was an actual breach of contract.
2. Have privity of contract.
3. Establish the damages caused by the breach.

Defenses

Two basic defenses are available to an auditor for a breach of contract cause of action.

1. The contract was not breached. If the auditor or the public accounting firm defendant can show that the contract was not actually violated, then the plaintiff does not have a valid cause of action.

   This might happen when the audit client failed to meet its obligations specified in the engagement letter, such as providing the auditor with access to records. In this situation, when the client violated the contract the auditor was released.

2. The plaintiff does not have privity of contract.

   This is the likely defense for a breach of contract cause of action by a third party. Privity typically exists when the individual is a party to the contract. A majority of the claims against auditors based on breach of contract are from supposed third-party beneficiaries. As stated above, the courts, for the most part, have not been willing to extend the opportunity to collect damages from an auditor for a breach of contract to plaintiffs who were only third-party beneficiaries rather than actual parties to the audit contract.

Damages

Typical damages in a breach of contract lawsuit are compensatory, thus compensating the plaintiff for actual damages incurred. Under contract law, there is also a remedy called specific performance that may be desired by a plaintiff. In the case of a breach of contract lawsuit related to an audit, a specific performance remedy is to require an auditor to finish the audit pursuant to the contract. An auditor most likely fails to finish an audit by withdrawing from an engagement. Auditors rarely withdraw from engagements unless the auditing standards call for it, such as when there are concerns about the integrity of client management or the auditor's independence.

To date, no cases have advised an auditor to complete a contract when professional standards required withdrawal from the engagement. **Engagement letters** are carefully crafted and typically list conditions that release the auditor from the commitment to complete the audit. So, even if a third party wants the audit completed, the contract between the auditor and audit client likely specifies the terms under which the audit is halted.

Relevant Case

National Medical Transp. Network v. Deloitte & Touche, 62 Cal. App. 4th 412 (1998): This case included many different causes of action (professional negligence, negligent interference), but the main point of the case was a breach of contract claim. The plaintiff brought a breach of contract claim against Deloitte & Touche when the audit firm withdrew from the engagement because of the professional standards of CPAs and auditors. The plaintiff claimed it was harmed by this breach of contract. The court held that when an auditor breaches (i.e., withdraws from an engagement) because of guidance in professional standards, the jury must be informed of the professional standards. The outcome of this case indicates that in a breach of contract claim, the auditor may seek to use the professional standards as a legal defense.

REVIEW QUESTIONS

D.1 What are the circumstances for a fraud cause of action against an auditor?

D.2 What defense is appropriate?

D.3 For what amount would an auditor be liable as the result of a fraud finding?

D.4 How do your answers for 1, 2, and 3 change for a constructive fraud cause of action?

D.5 Why might a breach of contract cause of action be brought against an auditor?

D.6 What defense is typically used?

D.7 What unique remedy may be requested in a breach of contract case?

AUDITING IN ACTION

Evolving Causes of Legal Action

Over time various other legal theories have been used in cases involving auditors. To date these theories have not had a major impact...

"Fraud on the market theory." This legal theory proposes that for an auditor to be liable for losses, the plaintiff need not have relied on misstated financial statements. The theory proposes that if the financial statements are relied on by others in the financial markets, then they affect the price that an investor pays for securities, and thus are a part of the cause of the plaintiff's loss.

"Product liability rule." As applied to auditors and financial statements, this legal theory proposes that auditors are responsible for the quality of their work products, similarly to the manufacturer of a consumer product.

"Deepening Insolvency." There is no consensus on whether this theory can be used as an independent cause of action or is just appropriate as an argument for damages. This theory proposes that auditors can play a role in extending the life of a company and allowing its debt load to increase if the company's financial statements are faulty and the auditor does not report it. The theory is based on the assertion that the company or its creditors may be damaged as a result of the company continuing in business after it begins a downward trajectory.

> When a case involving a new theory reaches the Supreme Court, the applicability of the theory may be decided. This was the situation on January 15, 2008 when the United States Supreme Court decided *StoneRidge Investment Partners v. Scientific-Atlanta* and ended the usefulness of "scheme liability."

"Scheme Liability." Scheme liability was advanced as a legal theory after Enron, in which individual shareholders' lawyers proposed that a company's business advisors and partners, including accountants, lawyers, and bankers, should be liable to shareholders for damages resulting from a company's fraud. Justice Anthony Kennedy wrote the majority opinion for the *StoneRidge* case. He stated that giving investors the power for this kind of claim made the entire marketplace vulnerable from a company's misdeeds. The Supreme Court ruling does not change or limit the SEC's ability to bring fraud cases against outside parties in either civil or criminal actions. The ruling only applies to cases brought by individual shareholders.

STATUTORY CIVIL LAW [LO 4]

The two main causes of civil action under statutory law are based on the Securities Act of 1933 and the Securities Exchange Act of 1934. Both Acts give a plaintiff the right to sue an auditor or a public accounting firm if there is a material misrepresentation or omission contained within audited financial statements or a registration statement.

Cause of Action, Securities Act of 1933

The Securities Act of 1933 deals with registration statements for issuance of securities to the public. **Registration statement** is the term used for a document that must be filed with the SEC providing information about the company and the new securities being offered. Section 11 of the 1933 Act defines the legal rights of third parties and auditors regarding the issuance of audited financial statements included in registration statements as follows:

1. Any third party that purchased securities described in a registration statement, which included audited financial statements and representations by the auditor, may sue the auditor for any material misrepresentation or omission contained within the financial statements.

2. The third party does not have the burden to prove that the financial statements were relied upon in the decision to purchase the securities or even that the auditors were negligent or committed fraud during the audit of the financial statements. The only requirement of the third party is to show there was in fact a material misrepresentation or omission in the financial statements.

Under Section 11(a), Congress enacted a safe harbor provision relating to forecasts. The safe harbor provision states that a plaintiff must show that an auditor did not act in good faith when the case involves reporting on forecasts. This Section is different from other parts of the 1933 Act because it places the burden of proof on the plaintiff when forecasts are a part of the legal action.

Typically, audited financial statements are completed well in advance of the issuance of a registration statement. As a result of this time lag, in addition to planning the audit of the financial statements, the auditor must also plan procedures to address the time frame between the issuance of the audit report and the issuance of the registration statement. The auditor is responsible for reviewing any transaction that might affect the registration that occurs between the issuance of the audit report and the registration filing date. Appropriate disclosures are required to avoid potential liability.

The Securities Act of 1933 gives the third-party plaintiff many avenues to pursue legal action against an auditor without the proof requirements that exist for common law negligence. Most important is that the plaintiff does not have to prove any wrongdoing on the auditor's part or reliance on the financial statements. Even so, there have been relatively few auditor liability cases based on the 1933 Act.

Defenses

Section 11 gives specific defenses to an auditor regarding legal actions taken under the Securities Act of 1933. Section 11(b) allows a due diligence defense. If an auditor can prove a reasonable audit examination was performed, then the auditor is not liable for the related damages. This particular defense is very similar to the negligence defense of the reasonable man/prudent person standard applicable to professionals under common law. In fact, Section 11(c) defines the term *reasonable* as how a prudent person would manage his or her own property. In addition, an auditor may use or rely on another professional's opinion in a registration statement. When this happens, the auditor is not required to perform any further investigations on that opinion and will not suffer liability for it as long as there are no reasonable grounds for disbelief. Other professionals on whom an auditor might rely are appraisers and attorneys.

A second defense outlined in Section 11(e) applies when there has actually been a lack of due diligence on the part of the auditor, but there is no causal connection between the lack of due diligence and the plaintiff's damages. To effectively use this defense, the auditor has to prove that the plaintiff was not injured by the misleading or negligently prepared registration statement. The auditor must show that something else caused the loss instead of his or her actions. For an *initial public offering* there is usually very little information available in the financial marketplace about the issuing company other than what is included in the registration statement. Consequently, it is difficult to prove that information other than the misstated financial statements or registration statement caused the investor's loss.

Relevant Cases

Escott v. Barchris Construction Corp., 283 F. Supp. 643 (D.C.N.Y., 1968): The *Barchris* case dealt with an auditor who did not perform any due diligence work, beyond asking the client some basic questions, between the issuance of the audited financial statements and the date of the registration statement. The court held that based on Section 11 of the Securities Act of 1933, auditors have a responsibility to update their understanding of the client and to adjust or disclose any material differences that arise between the audit report date and the registration statement filing date.

Bernstein v. Crazy Eddie, Inc., 702 F. Supp. 962 (E.D.N.Y. 1988): The legal questions in the *Crazy Eddie* case dealt with the auditor's knowledge or intent to commit fraud and whether the plaintiffs were required to prove fraud or gross negligence to proceed under Section 11. In this case, there were numerous indicators of financial statement fraud. The client, Crazy Eddie, overstated inventory and net income. The court held that under Section 11, the plaintiff did not need to prove either fraud or gross negligence. The plaintiff only needed to prove that the registration statement was materially misleading, by showing that there was a material misstatement contained therein, to bring a case against the auditors.

Cause of Action, Securities Exchange Act of 1934

Section 10b-5 of the Securities Exchange Act of 1934 is the most well-known section that can be used as a basis for legal action against auditors. Section 10b-5 targets fraud.

> **1934 Act, section 10b-5:**
>
> It shall be unlawful for any person directly or indirectly, by the use of any means or instrumentality of interstate commerce, or of the mails or of any facility of any national securities exchange
>
> **a.** [T]o employ any device, scheme, or artifice to defraud,
> **b.** [T]o make any untrue statement of material fact or omit to state a material fact necessary in order to make the statements made, in the light of the circumstances under which they were made, not misleading, or
> **c.** [T]o engage in any act, practice, or course of business which operates or would operate as a fraud or deceit upon any person in connection with the purchase or sale of any security.

The courts have expanded the application of Section 10b-5 to actions against not only dealers in securities, but also accountants, underwriters, and others associated with fraud. The Supreme Court case, *Ernst & Ernst v. Hochfelder*, 425 US 185 (1976), discussed later in the section on relevant cases, is an example of how the 1934 Act has been used to initiate cases against auditors.

Defenses

Scienter is a legal term which, when applied to cases against auditors, means that the auditor intended to deceive. In a formal legal sense, it describes the concept of knowingly and intentionally committing the wrongdoing. The defense available to the auditor for cases brought using the 1934 Act is simply to prove that intent to deceive did not exist. The *Ernst & Ernst v. Hochfelder* case established that the plaintiff must prove scienter in order to have a valid cause of action under the Securities Act of 1934. If the auditor is able to prove that he or she had no intent to deceive, the plaintiff can still allege that the auditor was negligent. However, negligence is not sufficient to bring a case under the 1934 Act. If an auditor's wrongdoing is not intentional, then a plaintiff needs to rely on a different statue or common law to sue.

Damages

The 1933 and 1934 Acts are the primary statutes that affect an auditor's risk related to third-party liability. The damages for both the Securities Act of 1933 and the Securities Exchange Act of 1934 are similar to those discussed earlier for findings of negligence. Both Acts allow for compensatory damages. Damages awarded should place the plaintiff into the same situation as would have existed before the loss. However, a judgment against an auditor under these Acts could be financially ruinous because of the potential magnitude of losses that shareholders of a large public company might experience.

Before 1995, the federal legal doctrine for liability on payment of a judgment was joint and severally liability. Recall that joint and severally liability means that each defendant is liable for the full amount of the judgment if another defendant is unable to pay. In 1995, Congress changed the vulnerability of audit firms when it passed the Private Securities Litigation Reform Act of 1995 (PSLRA). A major impact of the PSLRA is that the legal theory for liability was changed to proportionate liability.[5] Thus, in federal cases, a defendant is only liable for the *percent of damages assessed* based on the *percentage of fault* the jury assessed to the defendant.

Proportionate liability is important in cases involving auditors. After a business failure, the public accounting firm that performed the audit may be the only entity associated with the legal action with sufficient assets to pay the judgment owed to the damaged parties. Prior to the PSLRA, because of joint and severally liability, audit firms were vulnerable to very large liabilities from legal judgments. They were often the only entities with any funds that could be linked to, for example, a fraud leading to bankruptcy. The bankrupt company, management, and members of the Board of Directors might not have the net worth to pay their parts of the judgment, leaving the audit firm responsible for paying the full damages. The proportionate liability standard of the PSLRA protects auditors from having to pay all the damages awarded to injured third parties when the audit actions were not the main cause of the damage.

Relevant Cases

The following cases present liability issues under Section 10b-5 of the Securities Exchange Act of 1934. All the cases involve the requirement that the plaintiff must prove scienter. In these cases scienter means the auditor knowingly sought to deceive the plaintiff or anyone else the auditor should have reasonably foreseen as a potential user of the financial statements.

Ernst & Ernst v. Hochfelder, 425 US 185 (1976): The *Hochfelder* case dealt with a fraud perpetrated by Lestor Nay, the president of a small brokerage firm. Nay convinced some of the firm's investors to address and send checks directly to him that were made out with him as the payee (rather than being made out to the brokerage firm). Although he told the fraud victims he would direct it into high-yield investments, he stole the money. Nay was able to accomplish the fraud because he enforced a "mail rule" at the brokerage firm that prohibited employees from opening any mail that was addressed directly to him. The fraud was only discovered after Nay's suicide.

The victims of the fraud in the *Hochfelder* case sued the auditor under the Securities Exchange Act of 1934, Section 10b-5. The accusation was that an audit performed with due professional care would have included a sufficient examination of internal control to uncover the mail rule. Ultimately, the Supreme Court held that accountants could only be held liable under 10b-5 if they had "intent to deceive, manipulate or defraud." The general conclusion was that poor judgment in conducting an audit, even to the point of negligence, was not sufficient for a finding against the auditor under 10b-5. However, the Supreme Court's ruling left open the possibility that reckless behavior might be sufficient for a cause of action against an auditor under 10b-5 of the 1934 Act. This has since been the conclusion of some lower court decisions.

Herzfeld v. Laventhol, 378 F. Supp 112 (S.D.N.Y. 1974) *aff'd* 540 F.2d 27 (2d Cir. 1976): In the *Herzfeld* case the auditor issued a modified audit report indicating uncertainty regarding the collectability of receivables shown in an audit client's financial statement. The company went bankrupt, and a suit was brought by an investor who suffered loss. Even though the audit report was modified in accordance with professional audit guidance and indicated the uncertainty related to the receivables, the court allowed the plaintiff to recover losses. The court concluded that following professional standards was not necessarily enough to satisfy an auditor's public obligation. Although the case occurred in the same year as the *Hochfelder* case, the implication for auditors reflected the interpretation that existed *before* the Hochfelder finding.

Fischer v. Kletz, 266 F. Supp. 180 (D.C.N.Y. 1967): The older *Fischer v. Kletz* case dealt with an audit in which Peat, Marwick, Mitchell & Co. (the predecessor firm to KPMG) issued an unqualified audit report on annual financial statements and later learned that the financial statements were misstated. The audit firm eventually released the information that the

---

[5]A second change resulting from the PSLAR is an increase in pleading requirements to bring cases, discussed in Appendix A.

financial statements were misstated and did so consistently with the professional standards in effect at the time. There was a delay from the time the audit firm learned about the problem to when it released the information. The delay was acceptable under the professional standards. The auditor filed a motion to dismiss the case since auditing standards were not violated. The courts refused the auditor's motion to dismiss the case because the audit report was associated with financial statements that were misleading at the time they were released.

Both the *Herzfeld* and *Fischer* cases held the auditor accountable to a standard that was greater than what was considered due professional care based on the auditing standards. Because of when these cases were tried, neither was influenced by the *Hochfelder* case outcome that negligence was not sufficient for culpability under 10b-5.

The outcome of a post-*Hochfelder* case, *Nappier v. Price Waterhouse*, 227 F. Supp. 2d (D.N.J. 2002), produced a different outcome reflecting the Hochfelder decision that judgment errors or negligence are not sufficient for a finding under 10b-5. In Nappier the plaintiffs alleged that Price Waterhouse failed to appropriately react to warning signs that surfaced during the audit. The court ruling stated that "so-called 'red flags'…must be closer to 'smoking guns' than mere warning signs." The language supports the inference that while reckless behavior might sometimes be interpreted as constructive fraud, and thus sufficient to support a cause of action under the 1934 Act, poor judgment or negligence while conducting an audit is not.

REVIEW QUESTIONS

E.1 What types of claims are brought under the 1933 Act?

E.2 How does the burden of proof differ in a cause of action brought under the 1933 Act from one brought under a common law negligence claim?

E.3 What is the most well-known section of the 1934 Act relating to charges brought against accountants? For what type of behavior does an auditor have liability under this section of the 1934 Act?

GOVERNMENTAL CIVIL ACTIONS

In addition to actions brought under the 1933 and 1934 Securities Acts, the following can be used to bring or act upon **civil legal actions** against auditors:

> SEC Rules of Practice
>
> Racketeer Influenced and Corrupt Organization Act (RICO)
>
> Foreign Corrupt Practices Act of 1977 (FCPA)
>
> Sarbanes-Oxley Act of 2002 (SOX)

As this list suggests, the United States government has quite an arsenal available to impose civil penalties against auditors. In addition to these federal laws, states have laws that mirror or expand on the Securities Acts. States also have RICO-like statutes. Thus, auditors must be aware of not only the potential for third-party liability, but also governmental action at both the federal and state levels. Following is a short analysis and description of how the United States government has used the SEC Rules of Practice and other statutes to bring legal actions against auditors.

SEC Rules of Practice

The SEC can impose powerful sanctions and penalties through its Rules of Practice. Although not criminal convictions, these sanctions and penalties can put a public accounting firm or auditor out of business. For example, the SEC refused to accept audit reports issued by Arthur Andersen after the firm was convicted of felony obstruction of justice. Even though the guilty verdict was eventually overturned by the Supreme Court, by the time of the reversal all of Arthur Andersen's clients had hired other auditors. As a result of the SEC sanction based on its Rules of Practice, Arthur Andersen was effectively out of business. As with all SEC standards that affect auditors, the Rules of Practice apply only to those firms and auditors that perform audits for public companies.

The SEC can use Rule 2(e) to police auditors of public companies. Rule 2(e) states:

> The commission may deny, temporarily or permanently, the privilege of appearing or practicing before it in any way to any person who is found by the commission…
> 1. not to possess the requisite qualifications to represent others, or
> 2. to be lacking in character or integrity or to have engaged in unethical or improper conduct.

"Practicing before [the SEC]," the term used in Rule 2(e), includes all engagements to audit financial statements and ICFR that are reported in SEC filings under either the 1933 or 1934 Acts.

Racketeer Influenced and Corrupt Organization Act (RICO)

Congress enacted the Racketeer Influenced and Corrupt Organization Act (RICO) to combat the infiltration of organized crime into legitimate business operations. Even though many regard RICO as a criminal statute, it is also used as a basis for civil penalties. The largest of these penalties is treble damages. Treble damages means that the penalized entity must pay three times the amount of the actual assessed damages. Historically, auditors have been less likely to settle RICO civil cases for purposes of expediency if it means accepting the treble damages.

RICO is typically used for violations of the federal mail or wire fraud statutes. The basic description of a violation of the federal mail and wire statutes is when a defendant devises or intends to devise a plan to defraud. In this case, "to defraud" means using the United States Postal Service to obtain "money or property by false or fraudulent pretenses, representations or promises." The government can bring either a criminal or civil case against a defendant under RICO.

Relating to cases against auditors and the burden of proof, the Supreme Court, in *Reves v. Ernst & Young*, 507 U.S. 170 (1993), established an "operations and management test" that requires the plaintiff to prove the auditor participated in the operations and management of the company and the fraud. The Court stated that the plaintiff must prove the auditor actively participated in the fraudulent act. Mere performance of attestation services is insufficient participation for a finding against the auditor. The current independence rules in the post–Sarbanes-Oxley era greatly limit the consulting that auditors are allowed to provide for companies they audit. Based on limited auditor involvement with management consulting and given the burden of proof required, judgments against auditors under RICO are probably less likely than in the past.

Foreign Corrupt Practices Act of 1977

The Foreign Corrupt Practices Act (FCPA), passed by Congress in 1977, makes bribing foreign officials illegal. The FCPA also addresses records retention required under the Securities Exchange Act of 1934. Through the FCPA, Congress increased the bookkeeping and accounting records requirements of those corporations bound by the 1934 Act. The major change was that the FCPA requires companies to maintain reasonable records and have an adequate system of internal control. For records to be reasonable they must be both complete and accurate. The FCPA applies to the work of auditors since integrated audits report on internal controls. Theoretically, the main area of application is the auditor's assessment of the effectiveness of the client's internal control over financial reporting (ICFR). If the auditor concludes that ICFR is effective and it is proved otherwise, the auditor may be liable under the FCPA. To date, no cases have been brought against auditors using this legislation.

Sarbanes-Oxley Act of 2002, the Civil Statutes

The Sarbanes-Oxley Act of 2002 (SOX) is the most comprehensive legislation affecting public companies and their auditors since the 1933 and 1934 Securities Acts. The most important implications for possible civil penalties against auditors come from SOX Sections 104 and 105. The basis for potential liability is the government's ability to inspect audit firms and their work.

Under SOX Section 104(b), the Public Company Accounting Oversight Board (PCAOB) is required to inspect public accounting firms that audit public companies. If the PCAOB finds deficiencies during one of these inspections, it may choose to investigate further. Under Section 105(b), the PCAOB has the power to issue subpoenas, gather information, and depose witnesses. Anyone within or associated with an inspected public accounting firm is subject to the PCAOB's investigative authority.

SOX Section 105(c)(4) gives the PCAOB the authority to assess penalties against a public accounting firm or an individual auditor. Penalties may be assessed if the deficiencies identified during an inspection are not corrected or the investigation is hindered. As a penalty, the PCAOB can suspend or revoke an auditor's or firm's privilege of practicing before the SEC. In addition, SOX gives the PCAOB the authority to impose a monetary penalty of up to $750,000 for an individual and $15 million for a firm. The maximum monetary penalties are intended for "intentional or knowing" behavior and include reckless behavior. Repeated instances of negligent conduct are also subject to these harsh monetary penalties. In addition, an auditor's right to practice before the SEC can be suspended or revoked as a result of negligence.

Another source of potential auditor liability that is less widely discussed is bankruptcy proceedings. Bankruptcy law and federal Bankruptcy Court proceedings are complex and beyond the scope of this book. Bankruptcy Court actions can, however, have important impacts on auditor liability.

REVIEW QUESTIONS

F.1 How is SEC Rule 2(e) associated with Arthur Andersen going out of business?

F.2 What are treble damages under RICO?

F.3 What does the Foreign Corrupt Practices Act have to do with a public company's system of internal control?

F.4 What is the content of SOX Section 104(b)? 105(c)(4)?

CRIMINAL ACTIONS

The only entities that can bring charges for criminal causes of action are governments. **Criminal actions** are based on statutory law. The list of potential charges under various statutes is immense. The following statutes are most applicable to audits and criminal prosecutions:

1. Securities Acts of 1933 and 1934, for fraud
2. Title 18 U.S.C. §1512, for obstruction of justice
3. Sarbanes-Oxley Act of 2002

This list does not include the myriad state laws that allow state governments to press charges.

AUDITING IN ACTION

…and Then There Is Bankruptcy Court

In addition to legal actions initiated by injured third parties and the government, actions against auditors can also come from bankruptcy courts.

New Century Financial Corp. filed for bankruptcy in April 2007, but at one time was the second-largest subprime mortgage lender in the United States. In March 2008 a 581-page report authored by Michale J. Missal, an examiner appointed by the Bankruptcy Court, was unsealed. The report proposes New Century's collapse to be one of the early markers of the economic problems associated with the subprime mortgage and housing markets.

The essence of the accounting problems with New Century's financial statements is highlighted by misstatements in third quarter 2006, when New Century reported profit of $63.5 million and should have reported a loss. KPMG was the company's auditor and resigned on April 27, 2008. In Missal's report, he proposed that "the bankrupt estate may be able to sue KPMG for professional negligence."

(*Source:* Tiffany Kary. "New Century Bankruptcy Examiner Says KPMG Aided Fraud." *Bloomberg.com.* 3/26/08. *http://www.bloomberg.com/apps/new?pid=20601103&sid=aXebBO*, accessed 8/24/08.)

E. S. Bankest, a factoring company, failed in 2003 as a result of management fraud. The president, Hector Orlansky, and his brother, Eduardo Orlansky, who was chairman of the board, were both sentenced in 2008 to 20 years in prison. On August 13, 2008 after having been found negligent for not finding the fraud by a circuit court jury in Miami, BDO Seidman was ordered to pay $170 million in compensatory damages and $350 million in punitive damages. BDO Seidman was ordered to pay the damages to Banco Espirito Santo, a Portuguese bank that was a major investor in E. S. Bankest.

BDO Seidman began appealing the circuit court outcome. Meanwhile, the bankruptcy receiver for E. S. Bankest in the U.S. Bankruptcy Court for the Southern District of Florida has also filed suit against the public accounting firm. The bankruptcy receiver, Lewis B. Freeman, claimed "breach of fiduciary duty and deceptive and unfair practices," seeking $170 million in compensatory damages. Statements by BDO include the following.

> Given recent events, the continued pursuit of this case in the bankruptcy court and in the media would seem to indicate that the receiver and those whose interests he is supposed to protect have serious concerns that the state court verdict and the subsequent damages awarded against BDO will ever survive the appeal process.
>
> One has to wonder how many times must a plaintiff be paid.

(*Source*: Jim Freer. "E. S. Bankest Receiver Seeks $170M in Damages from BDO." *South Florida Business Journal*, September 7, 2007. *http://southflorida.bizjournals.com/southflorida/stories/2007/09/10/story6/html*.)

Securities Act of 1933 and Securities Exchange Act of 1934, Fraud

The Securities Acts are seldom used for criminal prosecutions, but are available to the government when an auditor commits a fraudulent act connected with a public offering of securities, or with a public company's financial statements or registration statement. Two important and relevant cases for the auditing profession are *United States v. Simon* and *United States v. Natelli*. In both of these cases the auditor knew certain frauds were being committed but did not disclose the information. Based on this, the government prosecuted the individual auditors under the criminal section of the Securities Exchange Act of 1934.

The penalties possible under the 1933 and 1934 Acts are described in Exhibit 4-1. As can be seen from the statutory language, the government has authority to seek a prison sentence when an individual is found guilty of criminal violations of these Acts. Recall from the previous section that civil monetary penalties may also be assessed based on the Securities Acts. The government can seek additional civil penalties or charge an individual auditor or public accounting firm with a crime even if another plaintiff seeks and receives civil reparations.

EXHIBIT 4-1	
1933 and 1934 Securities Acts	### Securities Act of 1933, Section 24

Securities Act of 1933, Section 24

Any person who willfully violates any of the provisions of this title, or the rules and regulations promulgated by the commission under authority thereof, or any person who willfully, in a registration statement filed under this title, makes any untrue statement of a material fact or omits to state any material fact required to be stated therein or necessary to make the statements therein not misleading, shall upon conviction be fined not more than $10,000 or imprisoned not more than five years, or both.

Securities Exchange Act of 1934, Section 32(a)

Any person who willfully violates any provision of this title, or any rule or regulation thereunder…or any person who willfully and knowingly makes, or causes to be made, any statement…which…was false or misleading with respect to any material fact, shall upon conviction be fined not more than $1,000,000, or imprisoned not more than ten years, or both…but no person shall be subjected to imprisonment under this section for the violation of any rule or regulation if he proves that he had no knowledge of such rule or regulation.

Relevant Cases

US v. Simon, 425 F.2d 796 (2d Cir. 1969): This case involved an audit by Lybrand, Ross Bros. & Montgomery, one of the predecessor firms of Coopers & Lybrand, which has since merged to become a part of PricewaterhouseCoopers. Harold Roth was the president of Continental Vending Machine Corporation. Roth owned 25% of both Continental Vending and Valley Commercial Corporation. He used these companies as a source of cash to finance his transactions in the stock market. Intercompany receivables and payables were managed to obscure the personal debt. Eventually, Valley Commercial Corporation was unable to pay its recorded debt to Continental Vending.

The facts of the fraud were not contested in the case against the auditors, but the appropriateness of the financial statement presentation and disclosure was challenged. The case against the audit partner, Carl Simon, along with a junior partner and senior associate, hinged on the adequacy of the disclosure in the notes of Continental Vending's financial statements, the extent of the auditors' knowledge, and the point at which they became aware of the fraud. The auditors were found guilty of conspiring to create misleading financial statements and were fined under Section 32(a) of the Securities Act of 1934. They did not receive jail time.

US v. Natelli, 527 F.2d 311 (2d Cir. 1975): The case of *US v. Natelli* was a landmark because the auditors were convicted and sentenced to time in prison. Anthony Natelli was a Peat, Marwick, Mitchell & Company (predecessor firm of KPMG) partner. He and audit supervisor Joseph Scansaroli were involved in the audit of National Student Marketing Corporation. The financial statements for fiscal year ended August 31, 1968 were misstated because the company reported as actual sales amounts that were really only commitments. A material amount of the commitments was known to be uncollectible and was written off in the next fiscal year but was still shown as income in the financial statements used in the September 30, 1969 proxy statement. The two auditors were convicted of willingly and knowingly making false and misleading statements in the proxy statements under the Securities Act of 1934. Both received fines in addition to prison sentences. Scansaroli's conviction was later reversed.

United States v. Weiner, 578 F.2d 757 (1978) and *ESM Government Securities v. Alexander Grant & Co.*, 820 F. 2d 352 (1987) are also important cases involving auditors and criminal prosecution. *United States v. Weiner* dealt with Equity Funding Corporation of America. Equity Funding sold insurance. To maintain the value of the company's stock, management directed that fraudulent sales of insurance policies and related receivables be recorded in the company's records. Eventually, the fraud evolved to a reinsurance scheme in which fraudulent policies were resold to other insurers. The scheme required a massive amount of fictitious document creation and recordkeeping to maintain appearances. In the *Weiner* case, the auditors were found guilty because the fraud was so extensive that they should have known about it. One public accounting firm partner and two managers received criminal convictions, and over $40 million of civil penalties were paid.

The *ESM* case involved a fraud perpetrated by ESM management that was voluntarily revealed to the Alexander Grant audit partner responsible for the engagement. Alexander Grant was the predecessor firm to Grant Thornton. The audit partner, Jose Gomez, chose to remain silent about the fraud, purportedly with the expectation that management would be able to reverse the problems if given time. In addition, the fraud had been going on for years, and Gomez did not want to admit and report to his firm that he had missed finding the fraud in prior audits. Because of his silence, which helped the fraud to continue, Gomez was charged with knowingly filing false and misleading auditing reports. In addition, he was charged with having received secret payments from ESM officers totaling $125,000. Gomez was sentenced to 12 years in prison.

Title 18 U.S.C. § 1512, Obstruction of Justice

In recent cases, the government has used the obstruction of justice statutes under Title 18 U.S.C. §1512 to bring charges. The language of the statute is presented in Exhibit 4-2. The most famous auditing-related case involving charges based on this statute is *US v. Arthur Andersen*, 374 Fl.3d 281 (5th Cir. 2004).

EXHIBIT 4-2

Title 18 U.S.C. § 1512

Tampering with a witness, victim or an informant…
(b) Whoever knowingly uses intimidation or physical force, threatens or corruptly persuades another person, or attempts to do so, or engages in misleading conduct toward another person, with intent to…
(2) causes or induces any person to…
(b) Alter, destroy, mutilate, or conceal an object with intent to impair the object's integrity or availability for use in an official proceeding.
Shall be fined under this title or imprisoned for not more than ten years, or both.

The obstruction of justice charges against Arthur Andersen were predicated upon actions by personnel in Houston and other offices. As directed by the partner in charge of the Enron engagement, Andersen employees shredded documents and destroyed electronic data related to the Enron audit. The document destruction was ordered immediately prior to an SEC investigation of Enron. The main issue in the court case was whether the destruction was a routine disposal of documents or an attempt to eliminate information before it became legal evidence.

The jury held for the government. Arthur Andersen was fined $500,000 and treated as a convicted felon. Since the firm as a whole was charged and found guilty, Arthur Andersen could not practice before the SEC after August 31, 2002. This essentially shut down Arthur Andersen as an accounting firm. The case was appealed to the U.S. Supreme

Court in *Arthur Andersen LLP v. US,* 544 U.S. 696 (2005). Although the Supreme Court reversed the Appeals Court ruling and remanded to the lower court for further proceedings, that outcome made no real difference since Arthur Andersen was already effectively out of the accounting and auditing business. Many people are surprised to learn that the legal entity, Arthur Andersen, continued in existence with a limited number of employees after it halted its auditing business.

Sarbanes-Oxley Act of 2002

The most recent major addition to government legislation available for criminal prosecution of auditors is the Sarbanes-Oxley Act (SOX). SOX increased penalties under the criminal statutes from 5 to 10 years if the prosecution is under either the 1933 or 1934 Securities Acts. In addition, SOX specifically prohibits the destruction of documents and increases the prison penalty for such actions to 20 years.

Finally, under SOX Section 303 it became a crime,

> for any officer or director of an issuer to take any action to fraudulently influence, coerce, manipulate, or mislead any auditor engaged in the performance of an audit for the purposes of rendering the financial statements materially misleading. (Section 303(a))

This part of the law helps to *protect* auditors because it gives the government the ability to prosecute officers and directors who try to deceive auditors regarding fraudulent financial statements.

JURISDICTION

Perhaps one of the most complex areas of the law is **jurisdiction**. Jurisdiction determines who has the right to sue, which court has the right to hear the case, and whether the court with the right to hear the case has the authority over the defendant to actually issue a judgment. These issues are called, respectively, standing, subject matter jurisdiction, and personal jurisdiction. Standing was discussed earlier in the chapter. Other issues of jurisdiction are introduced in Appendix A. These include a discussion of

1. United States federal and state court systems,
2. **stare decisis**, and
3. **pleading requirements** impacting subject matter jurisdiction.

REVIEW QUESTIONS

G.1 What are the possible penalties for intentional (willful) material misstatements of financial statements under the 1933 Act? The 1934 Act?

G.2 What type of charge was made against Arthur Andersen?

G.3 What aspect of SOX protects auditors, and how?

CONCLUSION

Auditors are often involved in legal actions resulting from either their own work or the business situations of their clients. These legal actions can be based on common or statutory law and can involve civil claims or criminal charges. Exhibit 4-3 presents the more important topics in this chapter and their relationships.

Criminal Action	Civil Action		
		Standing	**Cause of Action**
Fraud 1933, 1934 Securities Acts Obstruction of justice SOX State laws	Common law	Privity	Negligence Gross negligence Constructive Fraud Fraud Breach of contract
		Near privity	
		Foreseen third parties	
		Foreseen third parties	Fraud
		Third-party beneficiaries	Same as foreseeable third parties...may seek specific performance for breach of contract, but no successful precedent exists

	Statutory law
	    1933 Act
	    1934 Act
	        (Affected by PSLRA)
	    RICO
	    FCPA
	    SOX
			Mistated financial statements
			Fraud
			Gross negligence

The SEC can impose regulatory penalties and sanctions. Sanctions can be imposed by PCAOB.

EXHIBIT 4-3

Simplified Relationship among Laws, Standing, and Cause of Action

The standing of the plaintiff has an important impact on the duty of care owed by an auditor. A plaintiff determined to have privity has standing to claim damages as a result of auditor negligence. A plaintiff further distanced from the auditor may only be able to collect damages as a result of more serious wrongdoing on the part of the auditor. The most common causes of action against auditors are negligence, fraud, breach of contract, and violation of statutory laws.

The standing of a plaintiff initiating a legal action against an auditor may be one of privity or near privity, indicating a close relationship. A plaintiff may also be considered a foreseen or foreseeable third party. Although foreseen parties may be afforded the same standing as an entity with privity, foreseeable third parties are unlikely to be awarded damages from an auditor in most courts. Claims made by entities or individuals identifying themselves as third-party beneficiaries are typically made under a breach of contract cause of action and are rarely successful. Equally, plaintiffs have not been successful in claims for specific performance when auditors have withdrawn from engagements and, as a consequence, breached their contracts to follow auditing standards.

Beyond common law, statutory law is important to the legal environment affecting auditors. The Securities Act of 1933 and the Securities Exchange Act of 1934 both provide opportunities for individuals and businesses, as well as the government, to initiate legal action against auditors. Even though many avenues exist for plaintiffs to allege wrongdoing or make claims against an auditor, the auditor's best defense continues to be performing work following professional standards and with professional care.

Numerous other regulations and laws can be applied to auditors and their work. These include the SEC Rules of Practice, RICO, FCPA, and SOX. Auditors can also be required to make reparations subject to actions in Bankruptcy Courts. In addition, auditors can be subject to criminal charges under the 1933 and 1934 Securities Acts, obstruction of justice statutes in the criminal code, and SOX.

KEY TERMS

Answer. The step in a civil legal action in which the defendant responds to the plaintiff's complaint.

Arbitration. A process through which parties in dispute try to agree on an acceptable resolution to their differences, aided by a third party (the arbitrator).

Audit failure. When an undeserved unqualified audit report is issued.

Audit risk. The possibility that an auditor will issue an unqualified report on internal control over financial reporting and the financial statements when an unqualified report is not justified.

Breach of contract. When a binding agreement is not honored by one of the parties.

Business risk. Refers to possible damages an audit firm might suffer as a result of being associated with a particular client; can include monetary, reputation, and legal ramifications.

Cause of action. The legal theory used to initiate a legal action.

Civil actions. Legal processes carried out in court that address disputes between private individuals or entities.

Common law. The body of law that is developed as a result of court cases rather than statutes.

Compensatory damages. A judgment against a plaintiff that is intended to put the plaintiff back into the position that would have existed had the problem never occurred.

Complaint. The first step in a civil legal action in which the plaintiff initiates the process.

Constructive fraud. A fraud in which the offending party had no knowledge of or participation in the deception but exercised behavior that was so unconcerned or negligent that it enabled the fraud.

Contributory negligence. Theory of defense asserting that the defendant is not entirely responsible for the damages because the plaintiff also was a part of the cause.

Criminal actions. Legal processes involving government charges against an alleged offender for wrongdoing.

Discovery. The step in a legal action in which both sides collect information about the case; involves mainly document inspection and depositions.

Due professional care. Standard of behavior that is expected from a person with special technical expertise while providing services to others.

Engagement letter. The document used by auditors and their clients as the contract for an audit engagement; includes responsibilities of both the client and the auditor.

Foreseeable third party. A step beyond a foreseen third party; someone who might be expected to receive the outcome or products resulting from a contract.

Foreseen third party. Similar to a third party beneficiary; someone who is expected to receive the outcome or products resulting from a contract.

Fraud. Knowingly and intentionally deceiving others; in the case of financial statements, intentionally preparing financial statements with material misstatements or omissions.

Gross negligence. Behavior that is worse than negligence, with the offending party acting without any level of concern or care.

Joint and severally liability. Legal theory of damages that holds each defendant responsible for the full amount if other defendants cannot pay their share.

Jurisdiction. Legal concept dealing with who has the right to sue, which court has the right to hear a case, and whether the court with the right to hear the case has authority to issue a judgment over the defendant.

Near privity. Status of certain plaintiffs who do not actually have a contract with a plaintiff but are deemed close enough to be able to sue for negligence.

Negligence. Behaving with a lack of due professional care.

Plaintiff. The party stating a cause of action initiating a lawsuit.

Pleading requirement. The requirement that must be met for a plaintiff to bring a lawsuit.

Privity. The status of someone who is party to a contract that carries with it rights that flow from the agreement.

Punitive damages. A judgment against a defendant that is in excess of the damage suffered by the injured party; intended to punish the wrongdoer.

Reasonable man/prudent person standard. Standard according to which a person with technical expertise offering services to others will exercise a level of care that is expected from those possessing the technical expertise.

Reasonably foreseeable third party. See *Foreseeable third party*.

Registration statement. Document that is filed with the SEC associated with the issuance of securities to the public.

Separate and proportionate liability. Legal theory of damages that holds each defendant responsible for a share of the judgment that reflects that defendant's share of responsibility for the problem.

Standing. Indicates whether a particular plaintiff has the right to initiate a specific cause of action against another party.

Stare decisis. The requirement that a court follow legal precedent when the same issue or question comes before the court.

Statutory law. Laws that are created by a legislature or other governing authority.

Statutory violations. Actions that are contrary to statutes.

Summary judgment. Refers to the situation when a decision is made on a legal action (or a part of a legal action) without a full trial.

Third-party beneficiary. A person or entity claiming the right to receive the outcome or products resulting from a contract.

Tort. The body of law that enables recovering damages from the person responsible.

Ultramares. Landmark case addressing auditors and privity.

MULTIPLE CHOICE

4-1   [LO 3] Plunk-It, Co. hired Sume CPAs to perform its December 31, 2010 audit of ICFR and the financial statements. The accounts receivable balance in Plunk-It's financial statements was materially overstated, and a material weakness in ICFR permitted the misstatement. Sume CPAs did not identify the material weakness in ICFR or find the overstatement of accounts receivable. Sume CPAs issued an audit report with unqualified opinions for both ICFR and the financial statements. Plunk-It used the financial statements to borrow money and subsequently used the proceeds of the loan on a planned business expansion. The business expansion proved unsuccessful, and Plunk-It incurred a substantial loss, followed by defaulting on the loan. If Plunk-It sues Sume CPAs for negligence because both the ICFR and financial statement opinions were inappropriate, Sume CPAs' best defense is that

(a) Plunk-It misunderstood what an audit is.

(b) Plunk-It had no standing to sue because of lack of privity.

(c) Plunk-It had no standing to sue because the allegation was not for gross negligence or constructive fraud.

(d) Sume CPAs followed the PCAOB auditing standards in performing the audit.

4-2   [LO 3] The responsibility of a CPA when performing an audit is to

(a) correct any departures from GAAP in the client's financial statements.

(b) behave as a "reasonably prudent CPA" would in performing the audit.

(c) find fraud.

(d) be limited to avoiding gross negligence and constructive fraud.

4-3   [LO 3] Which of the following describes what a plaintiff must prove under the liability provisions of the Securities Act of 1933 to be awarded damages from a CPA who issued an unqualified opin-

ion on financial statements included in a registration statement?

(a) The financial statements audited by the CPA were materially misstated.

(b) The plaintiff relied on the CPA's unqualified opinion.

(c) a and b.

(d) neither a nor b.

4-4   [LO 4] Isle of Palmtrees, Inc. needed an audit for an initial offering of stocks to the public. Isle of Palmtrees, Inc. hired Hanna CPAs. Because an ICFR audit was not required yet, Hanna was only hired for a financial statement audit. Hanna CPAs was negligent and failed to identify material misstatements in the financial statements. Hanna CPAs issued an unqualified audit report. The financial statements and Hanna CPAs' unqualified opinion were included in Isle of Palmtrees' stock offering documents. Gustov obtained a copy of Isle of Palmtrees' prospectus and purchased shares of Isle of Palmtrees. Gustov did not read the prospectus and other offering documents containing the financial statements and audit report either before or after purchasing the stock. Eventually, the misstatements in the financial statements became known, and the value of the Isle of Palmtrees stock deteriorated. Which of the following would most likely be used in a successful lawsuit against Hanna CPAs?

(a) 1934 Act, 10b-5 and 1933 Act, Section 11

(b) Neither the 1933 Act nor the 1934 Act

(c) 1934 Act, 10b-5

(d) 1933 Act, Section 11

4-5   [LO 4] Which of the following will cause an auditor to be vulnerable to a criminal lawsuit under the Securities Acts?

(a) Intentionally helping the client's CEO and CFO to redraft the company's financial statements to include material fraudulent information

(b) As a result of negligence, failing to find a material fraudulent transaction included in the client's financial statements that are part of a registration statement

(c) Performing the audit in a manner that is later determined to lack due professional care

(d) Issuing an audit report with unqualified opinions on ICFR and the financial statements when the financial statements have departures from generally accepted accounting principles that are later judged to be material

4-6 **[LO 3]** Among the things that a plaintiff must prove for an auditor to be liable for damages under 10b-5 of the 1934 Securities Exchange Act is:

(a) The company had never issued publicly traded securities prior to the offering triggering the cause for the lawsuit.

(b) The financial statements were materially misstated.

(c) The company that issued the security triggering the cause for a lawsuit was registered with the SEC.

(d) The auditor's behavior in connection with the security was somehow negligent.

4-7 **[LO 1]** Based only on the original outcome of the *Ultramares* case, to which of the following parties will an accountant be liable for negligence?

(a) All third parties

(b) Foreseen third parties

(c) Parties in privity

(d) Foreseeable third parties

4-8 **[LO 3]** When a CPA is found guilty of being actively involved in a fraud, and as a part of the fraud issued a misleading and inappropriate unqualified opinion on a company's financial statements, to whom will the auditor probably be found liable under common law?

(a) Parties that the CPA knew were relying on the financial statements

(b) The client

(c) Anyone who suffered a loss as a result of the fraud

(d) Parties in privity

4-9 **[LO 1, 3]** Doll, CPA performed an integrated audit for Show Corp. and, though unintentionally, failed to follow PCAOB Auditing Standards. Doll, CPA issued unqualified opinions on ICFR and the financial statements that were not justified. Doll, CPA knew that Show Corp. was going to attempt to obtain bank financing and planned to use the audited financial statements and audit report in its negotiation processes with several banks. Show Corp. was successful in its negotiations and received a loan from Urban Bank. Unfortunately, Show Corp. experienced a severe business downturn and failed to repay the loan. Urban Bank sued Doll, CPA. Based on applying the Restatement of Torts extension to the *Ultramares* case decision, what is the most likely outcome if Urban Bank sues Doll, CPA.?

(a) Urban Bank will win because Doll knew that Show was presenting the financial statements and audit reports to banks that would rely on the financial statements.

(b) Doll, CPA will have no liability using a defense of contributory negligence by Urban Bank.

(c) Urban Bank will lose because Doll, CPA was "merely" negligent in performing the audit.

(d) Urban Bank will be unsuccessful because it is not in privity with Doll, CPA.

4-10 **[LO 3, 4]** If a CPA is sued using the 1934 Act, 10b-5, which of the following does a shareholder need to prove to prevail in the suit?

(a) Intentional misleading conduct intended to damage the shareholders (scienter) by the auditor

(b) Negligence by the auditor

(c) a and b

(d) neither a nor b

4-11 **[LO 3]** Assume a CPA conducts an audit in accordance with generally accepted auditing standards and issues an unqualified audit opinion on financial statements that contain misstatements that are immaterial both individually and on an aggregated basis. The CPA is sued under common law by one of the client's shareholders. Of the following defenses, which one should the CPA use?

(a) The stockholder contributed to the problem because of his or her own negligence.

(b) The problems in the financial statements did not make them materially misstated.

(c) The CPA did not financially benefit from the misstatement.

(d) The CPA did not commit fraud.

4-12 **[LO 4]** Old CPA is sued by Young Corp. using 10b-5. If Young Corp. prevails in the suit, it will be entitled to   .

(a) recover only the original public offering price.

(b) receive the amount of any loss caused by negligence.

(c) receive the amount of any loss caused by fraud.

(d) receive punitive damages.

4-13   **[LO 1, 3]** The three-part test for near privity established in the Credit Alliance case

(a) makes it relatively easy for third-party financial statement users to establish near privity with the auditor and therefore to sue for negligence.

(b) affects which third-party plaintffs can sue for fraud.

(c) makes it relatively difficult for third-party financial statement users to establish near privity because it is uncommon for them to have direct interaction with a company's auditor.

(d) affects the auditor's ability to defend against an allegation of fraud.

4-14   **[LO 1, 3]** Which of the following is not true based on the Restatement of Torts, Section 522, affecting the auditor's liability to foreseen third parties?

(a) The auditor can be liable for damages.

(b) Liability for damages may extend to financial statement users who could have been expected to rely on the audited financial information.

(c) The auditor may be successful by using a defense that establishes that reasonable care and skill were used in performing the audit.

(d) Liability for damages will extend to those who could have been expected to rely on the audited financial statements only when the auditor is found guilty of, at a minimum, gross negligence or constructive fraud.

4-15   **[LO 2]** An auditor will only enter into negotiation or arbitration related to a lawsuit if

(a) the auditor is guilty.

(b) the auditor is not guilty but is concerned that the plaintiff may prevail.

(c) the auditor believes it will cost less to settle a case than pursue defending against the allegations.

(d) All of the above may cause an auditor to agree to a settlement.

4-16   **[LO 3]** A company files for bankruptcy after it becomes known that the CFO stole millions of dollars and fraudulently manipulated the financial statements to cover the theft. The theft had been going on for years, and the auditor had consistently issued unqualified audit reports on the financial statements during the period of the fraud. In a fed-

eral court the CFO was found guilty of fraud, and the CEO and CFO were both found guilty of lesser charges. The damage settlement was assessed 80% against the CFO and 10% each against the CEO and audit firm. Even though the CFO has no assets to pay the damage award, the audit firm only has to pay 10%. This is an example of

(a) equitable damage liability theory.

(b) joint and severally liability theory.

(c) separate and proportionate liability theory.

(d) federal liability theory.

4-17   **[LO 2]** In the Arthur Andersen case, the Supreme Court did not uphold the finding of the lower court because

(a) of the jury instructions.

(b) Arthur Andersen conducted an audit that was in accordance with generally accepted auditing standards.

(c) while Arthur Andersen was guilt of negligence, it was not guilty of obstruction of justice.

(d) only the individuals within Arthur Andersen could be charged with obstruction of justice.

4-18   **[LO 4]** The SEC rules of practice

(a) can be used to bring a cause of action in court.

(b) can result in criminal convictions.

(c) can be used to bar an auditor or audit firm from practicing before the SEC.

(d) cannot be used to bar an auditor or audit firm from practicing before the SEC.

4-19   **[LO 2, 4]** The PCAOB

(a) must refer any complaints that will result in penalties against CPA firms to the SEC for action.

(b) is granted by SOX the power to issue subpoenas.

(c) is granted by SOX the power to instigate lawsuits in federal and all state courts.

(d) can suspend or revoke a firm's privilege of practicing before the SEC but cannot impose monetary penalties.

4-20   **[LO 3]** Being found guilty of criminal fraud

(a) requires the same level of proof as a civil fraud.

(b) results from an allegation made by a damaged party.

(c) will not result in jail time.

(d) results from a charge made by the government.

4-21   **[LO 1, 3]** Why are auditors not the parties typically charged with fraud in cases of fraudulent financial statements? What will cause civil allegations against an auditor to be constructive fraud and actual fraud? In what ways do the court processes and outcomes of a civil allegation of fraud differ from a criminal charge of fraud?

4-22   **[LO 3]** When an audit client's financial statements are found to be materially misstated due to fraud and the auditor fails to discover the misstatement, what are the various potential consequences for the auditor? What are the likely allegations and charges, and by whom? How does the capital structure of the audit client impact your answer?

4-23   **[LO 3, 4]** Is it important whether an auditor is charged under common law or statutory law, and why or why not? How do the laws differ? What are the reasons why a plaintiff might prefer to bring a case in state or federal court?

4-24   **[LO 3, 4]** What are all the possible allegations and charges that might be brought against an auditor for a single case?

4-25   **[LO 1]** The foreseeable third-party doctrine of standing has yet to be used as a viable requirement of standing in a case against auditors. Why may such a doctrine be catastrophic to auditors? Why may such a doctrine be catastrophic to society as a whole if all auditors believe their business risks outweigh their benefits.

4-26   **[LO 3]** Discuss how the theory of proportionate liability enacted by the Private Securities Litigation Reform Act of 1995 (PSLRA) can actually protect auditors. Compare proportionate liability with jointly and severally liability.

4-27   **[LO 4]** Discuss how Section 303 of the Sarbanes-Oxley Act of 2002 can actually serve to limit an auditor's liability. How else does the Act affect the legal environment of auditors. Do you think the provisions of SOX would have prevented recent corporate scandals like Enron?.

4-28   **[LO 3]** An important component of the U.S. legal system is the right to a trial by a jury of one's peers. Does a typical jury have the ability to understand complex accounting issues? Should fraud cases be decided by individuals with some threshold level of accounting knowledge? Discuss how these issues affect the risk burden of auditors.

4-29   **[LO 3]** Briefly explain why the severity of the wrongdoing alleged against the auditor and the closeness of the relationship between the plaintiff and auditor have an impact on the likelihood that the auditor will have to pay damages in a legal case.

4-30   **[LO 4]** If a plaintiff purchased securities and initiates a civil liability suit against a CPA, what must be proven under the 1933 and 1934 Securities Acts for the plaintiff to prevail? Place yes or no in the space provided for each of the following.

	Section 11 1933 Act	10b-5 1934 Act
1. material misstatement in the financial statements	_____	_____
2. a monetary loss occurred	_____	_____
3. lack of due diligence by the CPA	_____	_____
4. privity with the CPA	_____	_____
5. reliance on the financial statements	_____	_____
6. the CPA had scienter	_____	_____

4-31   **[LO 1, 2, 3, 4]** Fill in the blank with the answer. Each answer in the list may be used more than once or not at all.

a. Separate and proportionate

b. Racketeer Influenced and Corrupt Organization Act (RICO)

c. Foreign Corrupt Practices Act

d. Fraud

e. Negligence

f. Reasonable professional care

g. Gross negligence

h. Securities Act of 1933

i. Compensatory damages

j. Damages

k. Criminal victim compensation

l. Punitive damages

m. Hochfelder

n. *Ultramares*

o. Privity

p. Near privity

q. Standing

r. Deposition

s. Constructive fraud

t. Breach of contract

u. Joint and severally

v. Securities Exchange Act of 1934

_____1. A federal statute used for legal action related to the initial offering of securities to the public by a company.

_____2. Absence of the level of care that an auditor owes to another party that has privity with the auditor.

_____3. Prior to SOX, the first federal statute requiring companies to have a functioning internal control system.

_____4. The federal statute that does not require the plaintiff to prove that he or she relied on the financial statements to be able to obtain a judgment against the auditor.

_____5. A case that established that fraud on the part of the auditor is required for an injured party to collect damages under 10b-5 of the 1934 Act.

_____6. Cause of action which plaintiffs without privity have not been successful at using to obtain the remedy of specific performance.

_____7. A judgment for the return of the loss the plaintiff experienced.

_____8. Liability theory that is now used for federal civil cases against accountants and auditors based on the Private Securities Litigation Reform Act of 1995.

_____9. When a state law does not specify the concept of gross negligence, this is the legal concept that is likely used.

_____10. The motivation for a plaintiff to allege gross negligence.

_____11. Can result in treble damages.

_____12. Typically requires the auditor to commit fraud before there will be a finding and judgment against the auditor.

_____13. Often a part of the process of discovery.

_____14. Requires that the offending party's behavior must have been intentional (scienter).

4-32   **[LO 1, 3]** Jean and Cheramy, LLC, a firm of CPAs, has been the auditor of Moose Pix for five years. Moose Pix is a nonpublic corporation that coordinates wildlife sightseeing tours in the area around Jackson, Wyoming. Moose Pix is well known for leading amateur photographers into areas where they are likely to be able to photograph at least one moose.

Jean and Cheramy, LLC, completed the current year's audit and issued an unqualified audit report. Unbeknownst to Jean and Cheramy, LLC, the Moose Pix financial statements were materially misstated and showed sales and accounts receivable that were overstated. During the current year (in the time frame since last year's audit), Moose Pix's management had invested in several Florida condominiums. Moose Pix thought it had gotten a good price because the condominiums had already been marked down. But the condominiums continued to experience a loss in value as a result of ongoing changes in the real estate market. In addition, the rate of the mortgage Moose Pix negotiated had already "reset" to a higher rate. Unable to make the payments or resell the condos, Moose Pix lost the investment. Moose Pix management fraudulently manipulated the financial statements to hide the loss from the other shareholders. Shortly after the audit was completed, Moose Pix filed for bankruptcy.

During the audit, Jean and Cheramy, LLC, did not detect the fraudulent entries in the financial statements. The nonmanagement shareholders sued management for fraud and Jean and Cheramy, LLC, for negligence for not finding the fraud.

(a) What proofs are required of a plaintiff in a common law cause of action against an auditor for negligence? In other words, what must the plaintiff prove?

(b) Can the plaintiff establish the required proofs in this case? Explain.

4-33 **[LO 3]** Refer to the case facts presented in Problem 32.

(a) What defenses are available to an auditor when charged with negligence under common law?

(b) Which defense is the auditor most likely to use in this case? Explain.

4-34 **[LO 3]** Big Boi Co., a U.S. publicly traded company regulated by the SEC, and its auditor, Chappelle CPA, were recently found liable in a civil case pursuant to the Securities Exchange Act of 1934. The judgment entered against the codefendants totaled $10 million, proportionately liable 70% to 30%, respectively. Before the judgment, however, Big Boi entered bankruptcy proceedings and became insolvent.

In this case, how much is Chappelle CPA liable for? If they were found jointly and severally liable, what would be Chappelle CPA's liability?

4-35 **[LO 3]** Kaufman & Kaufman conducted an audit of Brady MVP Co., a publicly held corporation, in which it conducted its audit wholly in accordance with the professional requirements of the PCAOB. However, during the year in question, the management of Brady MVP Co. committed fraud, and the company's shares fell 75%. Shareholders for Brady MVP Co. brought suit against Kaufman and Kaufman for negligence, arguing that a reasonable person would have discovered the fraud if acting with due professional care.

In deliberations, the jury has come to the conclusion that they are more than 50% sure that Kaufman & Kaufman should have detected the fraud in the course of their audit work. However, they are not 100% sure that the firm is in fact negligent.

Since they conducted the audit in accordance with PCAOB standards, do you think the jury will find Kaufman & Kaufman negligent? Would your answer change if it were a criminal case?

4-36 **[LO 3]** Assume the same facts are present as in paragraph 1 of the Kaufman & Kaufman case presented in Problem 35. Instead of seeking negligence, however, plaintiffs are seeking a judgment for gross negligence.

What must the plaintiffs prove in addition to the requirements of ordinary negligence to pursue a successful case against Kaufman & Kaufman? Why would the plaintiffs seek gross negligence rather than ordinary negligence?

4-37 Mustian Properties, Inc. recently filed for bankruptcy because it is unable to make payments on several vacant properties in its condominium complexes near Las Vegas and Lake Tahoe.

Last year, Mustian borrowed $3 million from Field Centre Bank under the terms of a 36-month note payable. The loan application process required Mustian to present audited financial statements. The firm of Delan & Delan, CPAs, performed the audit and issued an unqualified opinion on Mustian's financial statements. The audit was performed under an expedited schedule, thus causing Delan & Delan to be negligent in documenting the results of their risk assessment and other evidence on which their opinion was based.

Field Centre Bank is now suing Delan & Delan, claiming that Mustian's financial statements contained material misstatements and that it relied on the firm's unqualified opinion on those financial statements in its decision to extend financing to Mustian. Delan & Delan expects to avoid liability based on the privity defense.

Required:

(a) Explain the privity defense.

(b) Does the privity defense apply to Delan & Delan in its defense against Field Centre Bank's lawsuit?

(c) Will Field Centre Bank be able to argue its case based on exceptions to the privity defense?

4-38 Paxon Laboratories filed an initial public offering of equity securities in order to raise capital to carry out its expansion plan. On September 30, 2009, it sold $50 million of its $2 par common stock in accordance with the registration statement requirements of the Securities Act of 1933, which stipulates that the filing include audited financial statements for the company's most recent three-year period. The audits were performed by Hawken & Miles, CPA, and unqualified audit opinions were issued for each of these three years. On the basis of audited financial statements and the unqualified audited opinion thereon, Dean Borgg made a substantial investment in Paxon's stock.

Less than a year following the initial public offering, the market price of Paxon's common stock fell over 40% upon the discovery of misstated financial information included in the audited financial statements accompanying the registration filing. Net assets and net income were both materially overstated. Hawken & Miles failed to discover these overstatements because it failed to exercise due professional care in the performance of its audit procedures.

Required:

(a) Will Dean Borgg be able to bring a civil action against Hawken & Miles under the Securities Act of 1933? Why or why not?

(b) Will Dean Borgg be able to bring a criminal action against Hawken & Miles under the Securities Act of 1933? Why or why not?

(c) What defense might Hawken & Miles choose to use?

(d) What damages may Hawken & Miles have to pay if it is found that the firm violated the Securities Act of 1933?

4-39 Bruer Sportswear, Inc. is a small privately owned distributor of men's athletic apparel located in Portland, Oregon. The company was founded by Drake Bruer, who serves as the company's president and chief executive officer. He is actively involved in the day-to-day operations of the business and has been instrumental in facilitating the company's merchandising success and recent growth. Drake recognizes, however, his lack of sophistication in the areas of accounting and financial matters. He relies on the financial expertise of his corporate treasurer and chief financial officer, Janet Kourier, and her staff, as well as the CPA firm of Duncan & Blavich LLP.

Early in 2009, Drake Bruer discovered a troubling note in the company's suggestion box. The note suggested wrongdoing within the company's accounting function, but provided no further information regarding the circumstances or perpetrator. The note was unsigned. Drake decided to turn the matter over to Duncan & Blavich and engage them to perform more detailed services; however, he avoided telling the firm about the note from the suggestion box. Since the note was anonymous, he wondered about its legitimacy. Therefore, he decided to wait and see if the work of Duncan & Blavich turned up anything suspicious.

Duncan & Blavich had been serving Bruer Sportswear since the company's inception. Since Janet Kourier was hired, the firm's services consisted of compilation work and tax return preparation. Now Drake decided that it was time for audited financial statements. Moreover, he thought that the company might make an initial public offering at some point in the future, so it seemed like a good time to begin audit work. This way the company would be ready with the necessary audited financial statements at the appropriate time. Both parties signed a standard audit engagement letter.

Duncan & Blavich performed a financial statement audit in accordance with generally accepted auditing standards for the year ended December 31, 2009. It issued an unqualified opinion on these financial statements.

In mid-2010, it was discovered that Janet Kourier had been stealing cash from the company's operating account through the company's purchasing and payroll functions. The transactions were cleverly concealed. Individually, the dollar amounts of these transactions were relatively small; yet they had occurred repeatedly over a two-year period to total over $500,000.

Bruer Sportswear is suing Duncan & Blavich for the amount of the embezzlement. Duncan & Blavich denies liability and is vigorously defending the propriety of its audit work.

Required:

(a) Will Bruer Sportswear prevail in its claim against its audit firm? Why or why not?

(b) Does the company or its president have any responsibility for the matter? Explain.

(c) Has Duncan & Blavich failed in its professional responsibilities by not communicating sufficiently with Bruer Sportswear on the lack of assurance provided by nonaudit services?

4-40 Aves Manufacturing Solutions is a public company that produces specialty automated manufacturing equipment used in the automotive industry. The company is pursuing both debt and equity financing in order to raise funds for planned plant expansion. The company's 2009 financial statements are being audited by Hester & Cham, CPAs. Hester & Cham is aware that the financial statements will be included in loan applications provided to lending institutions and in the prospectus for a stock offering.

Hester & Cham completed its audit and issued an unqualified opinion on March 24, 2010. The following additional information is available about the audit:

- The auditors failed to obtain sufficient evidence to support a series of sales transactions that occurred near the end of the year. As a result, Hester & Cham did not discover that the company's sales and inventory accounts were overstated by a material amount.

- Attorneys provided the auditors with documentation pertaining to a major lawsuit in which Aves Manufacturing Solutions is the defendant. The attorneys believed that the lawsuit was likely to result in a future material loss to Aves. Hester & Cham did not propose any financial statement adjustment for this item because the case was still pending at year end. The financial statements did not include either a recorded liability or any disclosure about the lawsuit.

In mid-2010, Aves obtained financing through the following means:

- Borrowed $1 million from Bourey Financial Services, Inc. under the terms of a 48-month note payable. Bourey relied on the financial statements and Hester & Chem's audit opinion as a basis for extending the loan.

- Raised nearly $9 million from the sale of common stock to investors.

Aves Manufacturing began experiencing financial difficulties late in 2010. Equipment orders had plummeted, yet substantial financial commitments had already been made for the plant expansion. The company was able to stay in business through 2010 due to the financing it had obtained. However, in early 2011, Aves was found liable in the lawsuit and was ordered to pay damages of $5 million. Aves was forced into bankruptcy, as it was unable to pay its loan obligations or its legal damages. Soon thereafter, Hester & Cham was sued by both Bourey Financial and the class of investors who purchased Aves's stock through the 2010 stock offering.

Required:

(a) Will Bourey Financial prevail in its case against Hester & Cham? Can its case be based on negligence or common law fraud, or both?

(b) Will the investors who purchased Aves's stock through the 2010 stock offering prevail against Hester & Cham based on Rule 10b-5 of the Securities Exchange Act of 1934? Explain.

ACTIVITY ASSIGNMENTS

4-41   Look up news articles on the Supreme Court decision reversing the Arthur Andersen verdict. Explain your reaction to the content and tone of the news report. Cite your source.

4-42   Trace the outcome of the BDO Seidman appeal in the E. S. Bankest case and the bankruptcy court action against BDO Seidman. What have been the financial impacts to date on BDO Seidman?

4-43   Do a search on New Century Financial Corp. What have been the most recent legal actions related to the company and its bankruptcy?

4-44   Rent the movie *The Firm*. At the conclusion, what evidence is used against the law firm, and what statute applies? What does this statute have in common with legal actions that can be brought against accountants?

4-45   Research the following cases. Determine the business situations and facts of the involved companies causing them to become involved in litigation. Was the legal action civil? Criminal? Who was charged? What were the outcomes? Were there any appeals? What were the outcomes of the appeals?

Enron	Cendant
Worldcom	Baptist Foundation of Arizona
Tyco	HealthSouth
Global Crossing	Phar Mor
Qwest	Xerox
Sunbeam	Vivendi
Waste Management	AIG
Parmalat	

APPENDIX A: UNITED STATES COURT SYSTEMS

The systems for both federal and state courts are structured in a similar manner. Exhibit A4-1 provides a visual depiction of federal and state court organization.

EXHIBIT A4-1

Federal and State Court Systems

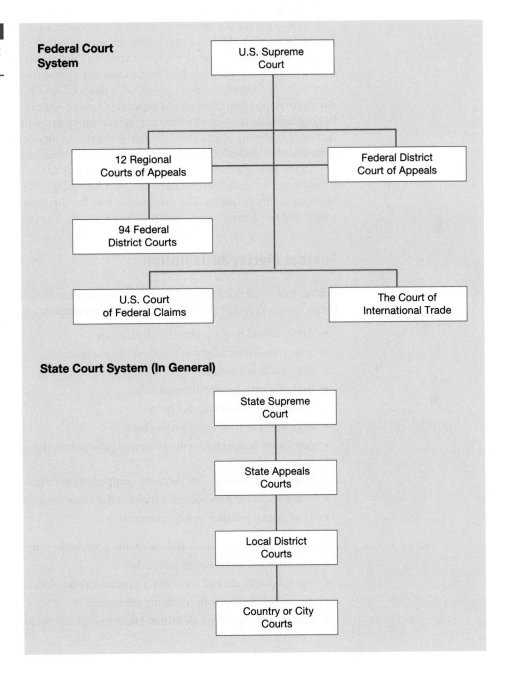

Federal Court System

- U.S. Supreme Court
- 12 Regional Courts of Appeals
- Federal District Court of Appeals
- 94 Federal District Courts
- U.S. Court of Federal Claims
- The Court of International Trade

State Court System (In General)

- State Supreme Court
- State Appeals Courts
- Local District Courts
- Country or City Courts

Stare Decisis

Black's Law Dictionary defines stare decisis as

> [t]he doctrine of precedent, under which it is necessary for a court to follow earlier judicial decisions when the same points arise again in litigation. (*Black's Law Dictionary*, 8th edition, 2004)

The definition seems to suggest that courts are bound by prior decisions of other courts. Although this is true in theory, there are many exceptions.

Within the federal system, a hierarchy establishes which precedent must be followed by which court. The United States Supreme Court is the law of the land. All federal and state courts must follow the law or interpretation of a law decided by the United States Supreme Court. Next in importance is the Federal District Court of Appeals, which has a strong influence on the 12 Courts of Appeals as well as the district courts. Within the 12 Courts of Appeals, any district court contained within a specific Court of Appeals jurisdiction—in other words, its geographical area—must follow the law and interpretations established within that jurisdiction. The district courts normally follow the precedent of other district courts within the same Court of Appeals district; however, there is no requirement to follow such precedent.

In the state systems, the hierarchy is very similar to the federal system. In addition to being bound by United States Supreme Court rulings, all state courts are bound by the State Supreme Court decisions. The same holds true for the Court of Appeals over the district courts and the district courts over the city or county courts.

Subject Matter Jurisdiction

Subject matter jurisdiction deals with which court can hear a particular issue. The typical breakdown is that state courts hear the following matters:

- Any criminal issues under state legislation
- State constitutional, statute, and regulation issues
- Any family law issues
- Real property, landlord/tenant issues
- Most private contractual disputes[6]
- Regulation of trades and professions
- Any issues dealing with entity internal governance, that is, corporate or partnership issues
- Most personal injury and workers' compensation claims
- A majority of the professional malpractice cases, for example, accountant liability
- Most estate, probate, or inheritance issues

Federal courts, on the other hand, normally address the following issues:
- Any criminal issues under federal law
- Federal constitutional, statutory, or regulatory legislation
- Any issues dealing with interstate commerce
- Cases involving public securities, takeovers, and associated regulations

---

[6]However, bankruptcy is a federal issue and is not handled by state courts.

- International trade and admiralty cases
- Patent, copyright, and intellectual property issues
- Any cases involving foreign governments or territories
- Bankruptcy issues
- Any disputes between the states

In some matters, either federal or state courts have subject matter jurisdiction involving the following:
- Any criminal issues that fall under both state and federal law
- Federal constitutional issues
- Certain civil rights claims
- Normally, class action cases

As can be seen from the proceding lists, accountants' malpractice appears to fall under state subject matter jurisdiction unless there is a federal statute in question. Certain federal statutes and Acts may require the plaintiff or state court to remove the case to a federal court.

Private Securities Litigation Reform Act of 1995 and the Securities Litigation Uniform Standards Act of 1998

Two federal Acts have significantly changed subject matter jurisdiction in auditor cases where federal statutes are used. The first Act, the Private Securities Litigation Reform Act of 1995 (PSLRA), changed the legal theory of payment liability related to judgments. This legislation was discussed in the chapter. But the PSLRA also changed the pleading requirements to bring cases before a federal court. The PSLRA increased the burden of the plaintiff. A plaintiff can no longer make a general claim of fraud and then use discovery to seek the information to substantiate the claim. This action was sometimes called a fishing expedition on the part of the plaintiff. The PSLRA requires the plaintiff to present the time, place, and contents of the false representation as well as the person who made the fraudulent representation.

In response to this change in the pleading requirements, lawyers began taking their cases to state courts and filing class action lawsuits under state laws instead of federal statutes. Congress sought to prevent this behavior by enacting the Securities Litigation Uniform Standards Act of 1998. This Act deals only with securities that are publicly traded. The Act requires any large class action suit to be filed in federal district court even if applying state-law. The Act gives the federal courts preemptive rights to pull certain state-level malpractice cases into the federal court system. The Class Action Fairness Act of 2005 strengthened this congressional action by expanding federal jurisdiction to cover most multistate class action lawsuits if the amount involved is at least $5 million. The purpose of the Securities Litigation Uniform Standards Act was to strengthen the Private Securities Litigation Reform Act of 1995 by forcing certain large cases into the federal system and thus enforce the stricter pleading requirements.

EXECUTING AN INTEGRATED AUDIT

CHAPTER 5

Client Acceptance and Continuance and Preliminary Engagement Procedures

1. Understand the purpose and role of client acceptance and continuance activities.
2. Recognize the professional standards relating to client acceptance and continuance.
3. Analyze various considerations in an auditor's client acceptance and continuance decisions.
4. Learn the important components of the understanding established between the audit firm and client regarding terms of the engagement that are documented in the engagement letter.

Chapter 5 Resources

AICPA, Code of Professional Conduct

AICPA, Quality Control Standards

AU 150, AICPA, PCAOB *Generally Accepted Auditing Standards*

AU 310, PCAOB, *Appointment of the Independent Auditor*

AU 311, AICPA, PCAOB, *Planning and Supervision*

AU 315, AICPA, PCAOB, *Communications Between Predecessor and Successor Auditors*

AU 316, AICPA, PCAOB, *Consideration of Fraud in a Financial Statement Audit*

AU 322, AICPA, PCAOB, *The Auditor's Consideration of the Internal Audit Function in the Audit of Financial Statements*

AU 324, AICPA, PCAOB, *Service Organizations*

AU 333, AICPA, PCAOB, *Management Representations*

AU 334, AICPA, PCAOB, *Related Parties*

AU 336, AICPA, PCAOB, *Using the Work of a Specialist*

AU 341, AICPA, PCAOB, *The Auditor's Consideration of an Entity's Ability to Continue as a Going Concern*

AU 350, AICPA, PCAOB, *Audit Sampling*

AU 543, AICPA, PCAOB, *Part of the Audit Performed by Other Independent Auditors*

AU 722, AICPA, PCAOB, *Interim Financial Information*

Committee of Sponsoring Organizations of the Treadway Commission, *Enterprise Risk Management–Integrated Framework*

Committee of Sponsoring Organizations of the Treadway Commission, *Internal Control–Integrated Framework*

PCAOB AS 5, *An Audit of Internal Control Over Financial Reporting That is Integrated with an Audit of Financial Statements*

PCAOB Rule 3526, *Communication with Audit Committees Concerning Independence*

Sarbanes-Oxley Act of 2002

INTRODUCTION

Client acceptance refers to an audit firm's decision to begin performing audit work for a company with which it has not been associated in the past. **Client continuance** refers to the decision to continue performing audit work for a company that is an ongoing client. Once an auditor decides to provide services to a new client, or continue to provide services to an ongoing client, preliminary engagement procedures begin. Client acceptance and continuance decision processes allow the auditor to learn about prospective and ongoing clients. Consequently, they enhance an auditor's ability to provide quality professional services and manage business risk.

Client acceptance and continuance processes are an important part of every audit. Both auditing and quality control standards provide guidance on client acceptance and continuance. Through client acceptance and continuance activities a public accounting firm can control its risks of being associated with clients by selecting those that fit well with its competencies and risk preferences. When a firm provides services only on engagements for which it is well qualified, with a clear understanding of the risks of being associated with the client, then the client acceptance and continuance procedures have been successful.

Client acceptance processes extend beyond consideration of whether an auditor wants a company as a client. They include the **proposal process**. During a proposal, an audit firm presents details to a potential client about its plans and the estimated cost of the audit engagement.

The process of deciding on and seeking a company as a new audit client is typically extensive. The decision about whether to continue performing work for a company that is already a client is usually less time consuming. Client continuance is just as critical as client acceptance, but is easier because the audit firm already knows a lot about the company. As a result of performing the audit in prior years, current information about the client is readily available.

After the acceptance and continuance activities, the audit team performs other preliminary engagement procedures and begins audit planning. Preliminary engagement procedures include establishing the terms of the engagement in a document called an **engagement letter**. The audit firm is also required to establish that it is independent of the company. Exhibits 5-1 and 5-2 are overview diagrams for client acceptance and continuance and preliminary engagement procedures. Information obtained during the client acceptance and continuance process impacts audit planning, which is the subject of Chapter 6.

EXHIBIT 5-1

Overview of Client Acceptance and Continuance

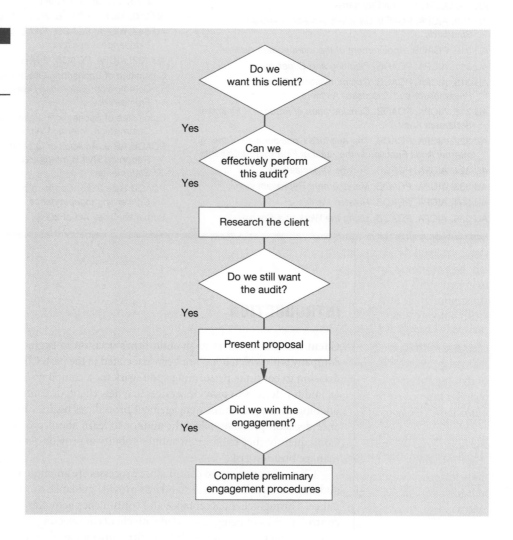

EXHIBIT 5-2

Steps before the Audit Begins

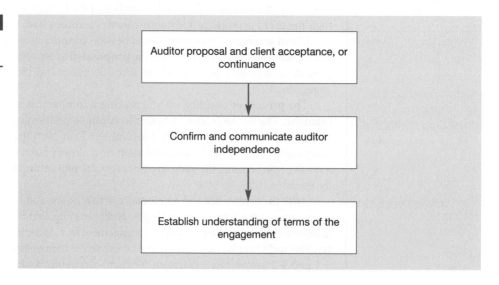

CLIENT ACCEPTANCE AND CONTINUANCE [LO 1]

Client acceptance and continuance decisions are important for several reasons. First, auditors should only perform audits that they can complete with **professional competence**. When performing an audit, the public accounting firm must have the knowledge, professional staff, and other resources necessary for the engagement.

Second, auditors want to associate themselves with clients that are law-abiding and reputable. Auditors work hard to establish their reputations. A good reputation is a valuable asset. Thus, audit firms do not want to accept clients that might signal to others that the firm does not have high standards.

Beyond the signal it sends, if an audit firm has doubts about a client's management's integrity, then it must also have doubts about its ability to perform an audit that results in a reliable opinion. The possibility that an auditor cannot perform an effective audit because of management dishonesty is part of what can be called the risk of client misconduct. The risk of auditor damage from client misconduct can be reduced by choosing clients carefully.

When an audit fails—in other words, when an auditor issues an unqualified audit report that is not justified—the consequences to the audit firm can be catastrophic. Damages can include lost business, litigation, and financial losses. The first step in minimizing the risk of audit failure is accepting the "right" clients—the particular clients that are right for the particular audit firm.

The **business risks** of the public accounting firm are tied to the clients it accepts. For example, when the *client's* business risk is high, the risk to the audit firm increases. The audit firm can be pulled into litigation against a client if the client suffers serious financial decline. The auditor's reputation can be tainted by association. A firm's business risk also includes its ability to make profits from the work it performs. Pursuing the "wrong" clients—those it does not understand well—can result in the auditor making an inappropriate bid on the engagement and an unprofitable audit.

A variety of risks are associated with audits. Later chapters explore how an auditor can reduce the risk of issuing an incorrect opinion on **ICFR** or financial statements as a result of performing an audit. This chapter focuses on risks that are controlled by effective client selection decisions.

GUIDANCE IN THE PROFESSIONAL LITERATURE AND STANDARDS [LO 2]

Guidance in the auditing standards addresses client acceptance and continuance decisions. The standards deal with auditor's qualifications, firm processes for considering potential clients, and guidance for engagement letters. Engagement letters are contractual agreements with clients establishing the terms of the engagement.

The first general standard of the 10 **generally accepted auditing standards (GAAS)** that were presented in Chapter 2 applies to client acceptance and continuance. It states that the audit is to be performed only by those having adequate technical training and proficiency as an auditor. Thus, an auditor should not accept and perform any audit engagement when he or she is not competent to do so. Other auditing standards on audit risk, internal control and fraud provide information that is useful in client acceptance and continuance decisions.

Auditor's **Quality Control (QC) Standards** also provide guidance that addresses client acceptance and continuance. (The QC Standards are discussed in Chapter 3.) Quality control includes processes for client acceptance and continuance. The audit firm should have policies and procedures for determining whether to accept or continue to perform an audit engagement. A firm's client acceptance and continuance policies should minimize the likelihood that the audit firm will be associated with a client whose management lacks integrity. The policies and procedures should help the firm determine whether it has the professional competence for the engagement and the risks associated with providing the services of the engagement.

Another major source of information is the Committee of Sponsoring Organizations (COSO) of the Treadway Commission. COSO's Internal Control (IC) Framework and Enterprise Risk Management (ERM) Framework address company characteristics and risks that an auditor considers. Although these framework documents are primarily targeted at assisting companies, they also provide significant important benchmarks against which an auditor can assess a potential client.

Throughout this chapter, excerpts are presented from AU 316, "Consideration of Fraud in a Financial Statement Audit," Appendix, *Examples of Fraud Risk Factors*. These examples come from the auditing standard addressing **fraud**. Nevertheless, they provide concrete examples of situations that an auditor would weigh seriously when deciding whether to accept or continue a company as an audit client. The fact patterns that warn an auditor with hints that fraud may be occurring can also inform the auditor's judgments on client acceptance and continuance. Short summaries of several representative legal cases are also provided.

REVIEW QUESTIONS

A.1 Distinguish between client acceptance and client continuance.

A.2 What guidance exists in the professional standards literature regarding client acceptance and continuance?

OPPORTUNITY FOR A NEW CLIENT (LO 3)

The opportunity to provide audit services to a new client typically begins with an informal communication directed at a partner or member of the public accounting firm. Someone from the company looking for an auditor calls the firm. In the case of a small company, or one that does not require a formal proposal, the entire process may be oral and informal. In other cases, after receiving the telephone call, the audit firm receives a **request for proposal (RFP)**.

When more than one audit firm is asked to propose on the engagement, an RFP serves as a vehicle through which the company communicates with all of the proposing firms. The RFP includes information about the company, engagement, and timeline for the proposal and decision process. The RFP describes the company's industry, business, size, location, capital structure, and regulatory reporting requirements. It provides details about the services the company wishes to purchase. In government and government-related entities, such as not-for-profit entities funded by grants, the RFP and proposal process may be very structured.

Part of the job responsibilities of public accounting firm partners—and to some extent, managers—is to bring new clients to the firm. As in other professions and occupations, in public accounting the term *rainmaking* is used to describe the process of selling services, bringing in new clients, and increasing professional services fees. Being a "rainmaker" is good. When a potential client is an acceptable addition to the firm's client portfolio, this reflects well on the partner who sells the work. Again, however, not all companies are considered appropriate or even acceptable potential clients.

After being contacted by a company that is searching for a new auditor, the auditor makes the first decision about whether to pursue the engagement. Factors considered are firm policies, as well as the auditor's perceptions and "street knowledge" about the client. For example, the audit firm considers the general reputation of the potential client, whatever is known about management's integrity, and whether the company is one with which the firm wishes to be associated.

An important reason a firm might decide against pursuing a company's audit work is simply that the engagement is inconsistent with the firm's business strategy. The potential engagement might be too big or too small. The company might be in an industry that the audit firm has decided to avoid.

The audit firm next considers what the potential client wants in terms of audit and **nonaudit services**. Does it appear that the firm is capable of meeting those needs? Although any initial conclusion on ability to provide the service will still need to be confirmed, if the firm believes it is not able to meet the company's service needs the process stops. The firm must have or be able to obtain sufficient knowledge and skills to perform the audit. The firm must also have sufficient human resources with appropriate amounts of experience and skills for the engagement tasks. The firm needs people available not only to perform the work, but also to provide necessary supervision and review.

Independence

Another early consideration is whether the public accounting firm is independent of the potential audit client. The audit firm evaluates independence concerns that would rule out the possibility of performing an audit for this client. As discussed in Chapter 3, audit independence can be impaired by various financial interests and business relationships with the company or its affiliates. Providing certain nonaudit services to a client also violates independence. The current business environment creates numerous challenges that can be encountered in maintaining independence. The largest firms now have comprehensive recordkeeping systems to assist in tracking client and personnel relationships and activities that may impair independence.

AUDITING IN ACTION

PricewaterhouseCoopers Independence Case

Price Waterhouse (PW) and Coopers & Lybrand (C&L) merged in July 1998. On January 14, 1999 the SEC censured PricewaterhouseCoopers for independence violations. The January 1999 censure resulted from the following independence violations that occurred between 1996 and 1998.

- Four occurrences when professionals owned securities of public company audit clients and they personally worked on the engagements
- 31 instances of partners or managers who owned securities of public companies that were firm clients, although the partners and managers did not work on the engagements
- 45 instances in which C&L's retirement plan owned securities of public company audit clients of C&L and PW; PW audit clients were a problem because the pension plan did not divest the PW audit clients before the PW-C&L merger

The violations and censure triggered improvements across the audit profession in the methods used by firms to maintain and enforce firm policies on independence, for example, the use of databases documenting firm clients, and the financial interests of all partners and employees. The databases are kept up-to-date with any changes and are used to monitor financial interests and business relationships for independence threats.

(http://www.sec.gov/news/press/pressarchive/1999/99-5.txt)

When a professional employee or partner has worked on the audit of a public company and then goes to work for that company in a major financial or management role, the firm lacks audit independence for one year. Section 206 of the Sarbanes-Oxley Act (SOX) states a requirement known as the one-year "cooling-off" period. A firm is not independent and therefore should not propose on a client engagement, if one of its employees or partners has recently taken a CEO, CFO, or similar position at the client.

Exhibit 5-3 summarizes considerations addressed by the audit firm in the early client acceptance stage.

AUDITING IN ACTION

Sarbanes-Oxley Act, Section 206 Conflicts of Interest One-Year Wait Period

It shall be unlawful for a registered public accounting firm to perform for an issuer any audit service required… if a chief executive officer, controller, chief financial officer, chief accounting officer, or any person serving in an equivalent position for the issuer, was employed by that registered independent public accounting firm and participated in any capacity in the audit of that issuer during the 1-year period preceding the date of the initiation of the audit.

(Section 10A of the Securities and Exchange Act of 1934 amended by Sarbanes-Oxley, Section 206)

REVIEW QUESTIONS

B.1 What is a request for proposal? Is a formal RFP always used? What information is included in an RFP?

B.2 What would cause a CPA firm to immediately rule out proposing on a company's audit, in terms of independence?

INVESTIGATING THE POTENTIAL CLIENT

Assume the auditor's initial conclusions are positive. No information has ruled out the company as a potential audit client. The audit firm is unaware of any problems that prevent the client acceptance process from moving forward. Now, the audit firm investigates the potential client. The initial conclusions must be strengthened based on information confirmed through objective investigation of facts.

Before accepting a company as a first-time client, the auditor gathers information from public sources, business resources, and the outgoing or prior auditor. In the auditing literature the outgoing or prior auditor is called the **predecessor auditor**. The auditor also holds discussions with the potential client's management and directors. The auditor may contract for special investigations such as background checks of individuals.

EXHIBIT 5-3

Early Deliberations about Engagement Opportunities

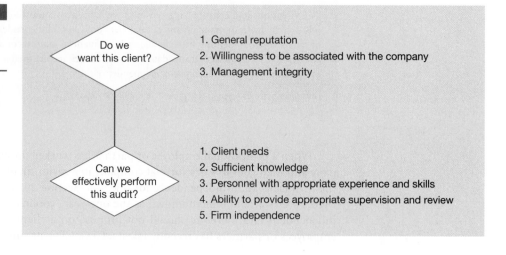

Published Financial Information

Much information about a potential client can be learned from its published financial information. **Annual reports**, financial statements, and other financial reports such as SEC filings indicate the size of the company's assets, revenue, and market capitalization. These provide preliminary indicators about the size of the audit job and expertise required. This information helps the firm begin to assess whether it has the human resources necessary to perform the potential client's audit.

Assuming the client is publicly traded or has announced an **initial public offering (IPO)**, the audit firm must consider the experience and skills needed to do the work. Does the firm have the appropriate professional personnel? The firm knows that more time is required to do an integrated audit of a public company, or one that is "going public." Utilizing at least some audit firm personnel with public filing experience is preferable.

Often companies change auditors prior to going public. A company may switch auditors before an IPO if its current auditor has limited public company audit experience. Companies pursuing IPOs often expect to benefit from the experience of an audit firm that has participated in many public offerings.

Audit firms with experience in providing audit services contiguous to public offerings pay close attention to the time and work required by the potential engagement. For example, sometimes audit procedures have to be applied to information from prior fiscal periods in order to produce the audit reports a company needs for its IPO. Since a number of years of audited financial information must be provided when a company goes public, auditing prior years is required if the company has not previously been audited.

Performance Information

Profit performance indicates to financial statement users the quality and potential of a business. Similarly, profit performance tells an auditor whether a potential client is a viable business. A potential client's publicly available financial information, including profit performance data, gives the audit firm clues as to the risk it may assume if it takes on the client. For example, if a company has financial or cash flow problems, this triggers questions about the company. Will it be able to fulfill its financial obligations? Does it have **going concern** problems? Is it at higher risk for being sued? Is it more likely to experience management fraud? The auditor also considers whether a financially troubled company will be able to pay its audit fees.

Caution Indicator: *Recurring negative cash flows from operations and an inability to generate cash flows from operations while reporting earnings and earnings growth.* [AU 316.85 A.2 (Incentives/Pressures) a]

The auditor evaluates any financial or cash flow problems the company is experiencing. In addition, the auditor investigates whether the company is in an industry that is experiencing difficulties across the United States or globally. Whenever a higher risk of business failure exists, the audit firm may have concerns about being included in investor lawsuits. Lawsuits against an auditor are more likely if the auditor is associated with a company that fails.

Caution Indicator: *Significant declines in customer demand and increasing business failures in either the industry or overall.* [AU 316.85 A.2 (Incentives/Pressures) a]

Financial performance information available from public documents assists the auditor in understanding a potential client company. For example, the Form **10K** that is filed with the SEC presents information on the business, risk factors, the market for the company's equity, management discussion and analysis, and market risk. These disclosures include a vast amount of information. A 10K includes:

- Sensitivity to changing economic conditions
- Likelihood of being affected by industry conditions
- Regulations affecting financial performance
- Potential lawsuits
- Vulnerability to global conditions such as trade agreements and exchange rates
- Domestic and global competition

In addition to reading the potential client's published information the auditor can observe or read transcripts of the company's earning calls. Another possible source of information is the trading activity of the company's securities, particularly if it is significant or unusual.

A potential client's business performance can also be assessed from financial information. Business performance is affected by business risk. Business risk is influenced both by components internal to the company and the external environment in which the company operates. The pressures on the business from external sources include factors such as regulation and competition. Many business risks are specific to the industry in which the company operates. The auditor investigates the potential client's industry and general economic environment for indications of how the business and financial performance may be affected.

> **Caution Indicator:** *High degree of market saturation, accompanied by declining margins.* [AU 316.85 A.2 (Incentives/Pressures) a]

> **Caution Indicator:** *New accounting, statutory or regulatory requirements.* [AU 316.85 A.2 (Incentives/Pressures) a]

Other information found in a company's 10K is useful to the auditor when making a client acceptance decision. Business performance information that is discussed in the 10K includes:

- Business activities
- Cash flows, and consequently sales, needed to satisfy fixed financial commitments
- Economies of scale available and achieved
- Ability to limit production if needed
- Ability to maintain sufficient inventory
- Historical instances of needing to reduce inventory
- Customer recognition of product differentiation from other suppliers in the industry
- Reputation for quality among customers

Accounting Practices and Disclosures

A company's publicly available financial disclosures describe the accounting principles it uses. If enough details are provided, the auditor can assess management's choices. To at least some extent, management's philosophy about accounting and corporate reporting can be inferred by analyzing its choice of accounting principles.

For example, assume that multiple accounting treatments are all considered GAAP. Management may choose an aggressive rather than a conservative accounting treatment for a given fact pattern. This reflects management's willingness to accept risk, as well as its attitude toward financial reporting. As a result of the management choice, an auditor can consider whether management's philosophy on accounting treatment and presentation may increase audit risk if the company is accepted as an audit client.

The importance of management's choice of accounting principles is highlighted by SOX Section 204. Section 204 requires the auditor to inform the audit committee about management's choices of accounting treatments. In addition to communicating about management's

AUDITING IN ACTION

Sunbeam, Aggressive Accounting

The legal case of Sunbeam Corporation addressed many accounting practices of this household appliances and outdoor products manufacturer. Sunbeam's management, the most well known of whom was Al Dunlap, also known as Chainsaw Al, adopted various aggressive accounting practices during the 1996–1998 period. One aggressive accounting practice used by Sunbeam is known as "channel stuffing," which refers to pulling revenue that would ordinarily occur in a future period into an earlier period. Sunbeam accomplished this through concessions to purchasers such as price discounts and other incentives to place their orders early. In many cases the sales were completed in later periods or not at all.

(*Source*: Daniel Kadlec, "Chainsaw Al Gets the Chop," *Time*, June 29, 1998, *http://www.time.com/time/magazine/article/0,9171,988628-1,00.html.*)

selection, the auditor must express a preference on the options. The auditor communicates to the audit committee whether management's choice is the treatment the auditor prefers.

Top management's excessive involvement in selecting accounting principles, making estimates, or determining accounting treatments can impact an auditor's decision to accept or continue with a client. If the company is already an established audit client, the auditor knows about management's behavior. With a potential client, it is unlikely that the auditor learns this information unless it is provided by the predecessor auditor.

Management's interest in and involvement with accounting outcomes and presentation can be excessive or inappropriate. When this occurs, it raises the question of whether management is trying to use accounting to present the company in a desirable way that is biased rather than in a fair way. This is sometimes called *earnings management*. The auditor considers whether management involvement in accounting decisions increases the risks of being associated with the company.

Caution Indicator: *Recurring attempts by management to justify marginal or inappropriate accounting on the basis of materiality.* [AU 316.85 A.2 (Attitudes/Rationalizations)]

Caution Indicator: *Nonfinancial management's excessive participation in or preoccupation with the selection of accounting principles or the determination of significant estimates.* [AU 316.85 A.2 (Attitudes/Rationalizations)]

Related party transactions are business transactions between individuals or entities that have some type of additional connection—often an ownership relationship—outside of the transaction. Related party transactions are always considered a source of additional audit risk and are addressed by audit procedures.

AUDITING IN ACTION

Enron, Related Parties

The business failure of Enron that led to its bankruptcy is complicated and involves numerous causes. One cause that is unquestioned is Enron's use of special-purpose entities (SPEs) to present a desirable financial picture to the public. SPEs used by Enron were separate legal entities that were related parties, supported by guarantees of Enron stock. When Enron stock lost value, these SPEs were subject to having to repay loans, beginning the domino effect associated with the Enron collapse. The related party SPEs used by Enron were very complicated and apparently not well disclosed by the company or understood by many investing in Enron stock.

The audit risk posed by related party transactions can affect whether an audit firm wants a company as its client. Accounting standards require financial disclosure on related party transactions. The extent of a potential client's related party transactions portrayed in the disclosure, along with the transparency with which the information is presented, influences an auditor's decision about client acceptance (AU 334).

> **Caution Indicator:** *Significant related party transactions not in the ordinary course of business or with related entities not audited or audited by another firm.* [AU 316.85 A.2 (Opportunities) a]

The existence of related parties and related party transactions will not necessarily cause an auditor to avoid a company. The auditor is, however, looking for confidence in management's willingness to allow related party transactions to be carefully scrutinized and completely and clearly disclosed.

REVIEW QUESTIONS

C.1 What performance indicators are found in a 10K?

C.2 Why would firms review a potential client's financial disclosures for information about management's choices on accounting principles?

C.3 What are related party transactions?

Management and Board of Directors Integrity

A critical consideration in the decision of whether to accept or continue a client is management and Board of Directors (BOD) integrity. Management integrity is discussed throughout various auditing standards and audit-related documents. The impact of management integrity is so pervasive that it is one of the auditor's most important considerations. Management and BOD integrity is discussed in the Sarbanes-Oxley Act, COSO ERM and IC Frameworks, PCAOB Auditing Standards, AICPA Statements on Auditing Standards, Quality Control standards, and various SEC publications.

Try to imagine how risky it would be to perform an audit of a company when the auditors have no idea whether people are being truthful and whether the documents and information they are inspecting are valid and legitimate. Yet, this scenario can occur if management does not want to be truthful and sets the example for employees to mislead auditors.

AUDITING IN ACTION

The Leslie Fay Companies, Management Integrity

The story of the Leslie Fay Companies is fascinating when considering the issue of management integrity and the impact of autocratic and domineering management. Leslie Fay was a dress company that became less successful, noticeably during the late 1980s when fashion for women became much more casual. The fraud that was ultimately discovered at the company was intended to cover up the company's failing profitability. The fraud involved manipulation of inventory and false period-end postings for sales and expenses. A domineering CFO was eventually identified as mastermind of the fraud. This CFO had a powerful impact on his employees who helped him perpetrate the fraud. He had so much personal power and influence that for several years after the fraud was discovered he was able to bully one of his senior accounting employees to take full responsibility for designing and carrying out the fraud. Other employees close to the situation questioned the fact pattern because it seemed inconsistent with the personality of the supposed fraudster. The individual who took responsibility did not benefit from the fraud in any way. During questioning by federal investigators, the employee finally identified the CFO as the mastermind of the fraud.

(*United States of America vs. Paul Polishan*, 2001 US Dist LEXIS 10662)

When researching management and directors, auditors look for obvious indicators of integrity problems such as investigations or actions by law enforcement and regulatory agencies. AS 5.69 states that fraud of any size by senior management is considered a strong indicator of a material weakness in ICFR. Media searches are a common way to look for all of this information. Adverse publicity and even anonymous tips can be informative.

> **Caution Indicator:** *Known history of violations of securities laws or other laws and regulations, or claim against the entity, its senior management, or board members alleging fraud or violations of laws and regulations.* [AU 316.85 A.2 (Attitudes/Rationalizations)]

AUDITING IN ACTION

Health Management, Inc., Anonymous Tips

Health Management was a pharmaceuticals distributor that engaged in an inventory fraud, inflating its 1995 year-end inventory to improve year-end income. The CFO of Health Management involved in the fraud had been hired away from BDO Seidman, where he had served as the senior audit manager on the Health Management engagement. After he left BDO Seidman, one of his former subordinates took over the role as audit manager of the engagement. One of the concerns regarding the fraud was that the friendly relationship between the new BDO Seidman manager and the Health Management CFO, her former boss, prevented the manager from having a sufficient amount of skepticism regarding the integrity of the financial transactions and the possibility of fraud. BDO Seidman even received an anonymous letter indicating that the relationship between people at Health Management and the audit firm was damaging the audit firm's independence. The audit partner discussed the letter with the audit team but unfortunately never specifically questioned any of the team members about their relationship with the CFO.

(*In re Health Management Inc.*, 96-CV-889, Eastern District of New York)

A company's code of conduct can signal the auditor about the entity's values and ethical standards. Section 406 of SOX requires companies to disclose whether they have a **code of ethics** that applies to senior management. If a company lacks such a code, it must disclose the reason for the omission. Companies often disclose their ethical philosophies and codes of conduct prominently in their public information, for example, on their Web sites. Auditors use all these sources to learn whatever possible about the integrity of management and the BOD.

> **Caution Indicator:** *Ineffective communication, implementation, support, or enforcement of the entity's values or ethical standards by management or the communication of inappropriate values or ethical standards.* [AU 316.85 A.2 (Attitudes/Rationalizations)]

Company Leadership

The COSO Enterprise Risk Management (ERM) framework highlights the need for competent company leadership. The BOD and management need to be capable of making appropriate decisions in setting objectives, identifying risks to achieving objectives, and responding to those risks. The COSO documents further state that management should pursue a "commitment to competence" throughout the organization as displayed by making sure that competent personnel are appropriately assigned and delegated responsibility. These statements suggest that for a company to be well run and able to effectively manage its risks, the management team and BOD must also be competent and appropriately skilled.

In considering whether to accept or continue a client, the auditor looks to the composition of the management team and BOD. The auditor assesses whether the individuals in management and director positions have the necessary attributes to make the company a desirable client. Some management competency considerations include the following:

- Composition of top management team
- Each individual's time with the company
- Industry experience
- Organizational structure
- Management compensation structure

Management philosophy and operating style are discussed extensively in the COSO reports. Although information on management behavior may be difficult for the auditor to obtain and understand in depth prior to accepting a new client, it is an important factor in client acceptance and continuance. Questions to consider include the following:

Is authority and power concentrated in one or a few individuals?

What is the structure, size, and composition of the management team?

Many cases of management fraud have shared the management characteristic of an autocratic and dictatorial style. Learning about the company's compensation arrangements for senior management can help the auditor understand whether motivation exists for certain management behaviors, such as aggressive or autocratic leadership.

Another issue to consider is the turnover rate of the company's executives, particularly those involved in accounting. Frequent turnover of individuals in positions of responsibility may indicate nothing more than a strong job market. However, in deciding whether to pursue a company as a new client, the auditor considers the possibility that top people find the environment unacceptable. Do they feel pressure from their superiors to make decisions or take actions with which they are not comfortable? If top employees choose not to be associated with a company, the auditor has to ask why.

> **Caution Indicator:** *Domination of management by a single person or small group (in a nonowner-managed business), without compensating controls.* [AU 316.85 A.2 (Opportunities) b]

> **Caution Indicator:** *High turnover of senior management, counsel, or board members.* [AU 316.85 (Opportunities) c]

Audit Committee and Board of Directors Involvement and Qualifications

SOX places much greater emphasis on **audit committees** and their responsibilities than has been typical in the past. The auditor considers the audit committee of a potential client as it investigates the company. (Audit committees are discussed in Appendix B to this chapter.)

AS 5.69 states that lack of sufficient involvement in the financial reporting function by the BOD and audit committee may suggest a **material weakness in ICFR**. The auditor considers the level of involvement of the company's BOD and audit committee. If they are not actively involved in the company's governance, the auditor evaluates whether there is greater risk in accepting the company as an audit client.

> **Caution Indicator:** *Ineffective board of directors or audit committee oversight over the financial reporting process and internal control.* [PCAOB AU 316.85 A.2 (Opportunities) b, AICPA uses similar language]

AUDITING IN ACTION

HealthSouth, Management Style

HealthSouth made its name as a provider of outpatient surgery, diagnostic, imaging, and rehabilitation health-care services. In 2003 the company and CEO Richard M. Scrushy were charged with accounting fraud that overstated earnings. The fraud dealt with intentional manipulation of corporate accounts to increase earnings so that the company would meet analysts' earnings expectations. Although eventually acquitted of criminal wrongdoing in 2005[1] Scrushy settled with the SEC in 2007 for $77.5 million plus $3.5 million in civil penalties.[2] Scrushy was accused of managing the company in such a way that it influenced employees to participate in the fraud. He placed extreme emphasis on meeting earnings expectations. The entire senior management team was relatively young and inexperienced, enabling Scrushy to manage the team through fear. He routinely held Monday morning meetings in which financial information was discussed, and these meetings were known among employees as "Monday morning beatings."[3] On June 18, 2009 an Alabama judge ordered Scrushy to pay $2.88 billion as a result of an additional fraud lawsuit by shareholders. At the time of the judge's order, Scrushy was already in prison for an unrelated bribery lawsuit.

AUDITING IN ACTION

Sarbanes-Oxley Audit Committee Definition

A committee (or equivalent body) established by and amongst the board of directors of an issuer for the purpose of overseeing the accounting and financial reporting processes of the issuer and audits of the financial statements of the issuer. [SOX Section (2)(3)(A)]

As a requirement for listing, the New York Stock Exchange requires a company to have an audit committee. The legislators who drafted SOX also place great importance on the audit committee. SOX addresses the quality of audit committees through the qualifications of a "financial expert." Exhibit 5-4 provides the SEC rules defining an audit committee financial expert.

If a public company's audit committee does not have at least one financial expert, this fact must be disclosed. Thus, information on the lack of any audit committee members with financial expertise is available to an auditor investigating a potential public company client. When a company lacks a financial expert on the audit committee, the auditor carefully investigates the BOD's regulatory and oversight skills and the competency of management.

The COSO ERM Framework includes BOD activities as an important factor in its "Internal Environment" component. Auditors can infer much about BOD capabilities from questions about the composition of the BOD. For example, what percentage of the BOD is somehow connected to the company through financial investments or transactions, or a management position? Directors who are not independent of the company's finances and management may make oversight decisions that differ from those of directors without ties.

Other questions may be:

What employment and educational backgrounds do the directors have?
Do they have the knowledge and experience needed to oversee the company's management?

---

[1]Dan Morse, Chad Terhune, and Ann Carrns. June 29, 2005. Clean Sweep—HealthSouth's Scrushy Is Acquitted. *The Wall Street Journal,* http://www.nacdl.org/public.nsf/whitecollar/wcnews005 http://www.bloomberg.com/apps/news?pid=20601103&sid=ak.i6Qzw0CQw&refer=us.

[2]Laurence Viele, Davidson May 11, 2007. "Scrushy's Sentencing Shows No Chief Executive Is Left Behind" Bloomberg.com, http://www.bloomberg.com/apps/newss?pid=206011038

[3]M. Jennings 2003. "The Critical Role of Ethics; Recent history has shown that when individual ethics are compromised, corporate ethics fail and financial disaster is not far behind." *Internal Auditor* 60, no. 6, 46.)

EXHIBIT 5-4

Qualifying
Characteristics of a
Financial Expert

SEC rules define an audit committee financial expert as a person with the following attributes:

- An understanding of generally accepted accounting principles and financial statements;
- The ability to assess the general application of such principles in connection with the accounting for estimates accruals and reserves;
- Experience preparing, auditing, analyzing or evaluating financial statements that present a breadth and level of complexity of accounting issues that are generally comparable to the breadth and complexity of issues that can reasonably be expected to be raised by the registrant's financial statements, or experience actively supervising one or more persons engaged in such activities;
- An understanding of internal controls and procedures for financial reporting;
- An understanding of the audit committee functions.

These attributes may have been acquired through:

- Education and experience as a principal financial officer, principal accounting officer, controller, public accountant or auditor or experience in one or more positions that involve the performance of similar functions;
- Experience actively supervising a principal financial officer, principal accounting officer, controller, public accountant, auditor or person performing similar functions;
- Experience overseeing or assessing the performance of companies or public accountants with respect to the preparation, auditing or evaluation of financial statements;
- Other relevant experience

(SEC release #3-8177A, 34-47235A, "Disclosure Required by Sections 406 and 407 of the Sarbanes-Oxley Act of 2002")

How much work is involved in being on the BOD?

Is the compensation structure for directors appropriate given the qualifications and what is expected of them?

If they are not appropriately compensated, directors may not put forth the effort needed to fulfill their responsibilities.

Various sources provide guidance concerning the characteristics needed for an effectively functioning Board of Directors. COSO discusses directors in both its ERM and IC Frameworks. Among the characteristics expected of individual directors are the skills, experience, and knowledge to understand the company and its actions. Commitment to fulfilling duties and responsibilities, including management oversight, is important. Directors should be effective in taking appropriate action—which can mean providing a different approach or perspective from that of management. A willingness to respond if they become aware of wrongdoing within the company is critical. Many of these desirable BOD characteristics involve providing a counterbalancing force to management authority.

Although an auditor can investigate the composition of a potential client's BOD and audit committee prior to accepting the engagement, learning how effectively these groups function is more difficult. Early information on the function of the audit committee and BOD can likely be obtained only through inquiry of BOD and audit committee members themselves, or from the predecessor auditor.

Potential Client Business Activities

In contemplating whether it wants a company as a part of its client portfolio, a public accounting firm investigates the business activities in which the company is involved. As with much of the other information discussed so far, the information for public companies is usually available from public documents. Large companies are often involved in many different types of business activities, frequently extending beyond those for which the company is well known. Auditors investigate a potential client's business activities for at least three reasons. They desire to:

1. determine whether the activities are within the audit firm's area of industry and audit expertise.
2. confirm that the company's activities are compatible with the firm's preferences for its client portfolio.
3. assess whether the company's activities are too risky for the firm to be willing to be associated with the company.

Financial Statement Restatements

An important signal to an audit firm is recent restatement of a potential client's financial statements. The auditor wants to know why the financial statements were restated. If the company is publicly traded, this information is easily obtained through the financial reports. **Financial statement restatements** can also be found by researching press and media releases.

Financial statement restatement is a major event because it corrects an error in previously issued financial statements. Restatement also occurs because more information or evidence about a transaction becomes available to management after financial statements have been released.[4]

AS 5.69 indicates that restatement of previously issued financial statements to correct a misstatement or an error is a strong indicator of a material weakness in ICFR. If a potential client has recently restated its financial statements, the auditor seriously considers why the financial statements have been restated. The auditor questions whether it indicates anything negative about management integrity or competence.

Public Information Releases by Management

Auditors consider how management presents the company to outsiders. Press releases and even events like trade show speeches can indicate whether management's public statements represent the company in an appropriate light. CEOs may sometimes engage in "puffing" when they talk about their company's future. However, misleading outsiders by presenting an unrealistically positive picture raises questions of integrity.

> **Caution Indicator:** *Profitability or trend level expectations of investment analysts, institutional investors, significant creditors or other external parties... including expectations created by management in, for example, overly optimistic press releases or annual report messages.* [AU 316.85 A.2 (Incentives/Pressure) b]

REVIEW QUESTIONS

D.1 Why is management and Board of Directors integrity important to an audit firm?

D.2 Why might an auditor be concerned if all of the company's management authority is centered in one or two individuals?

D.3 What is the auditor's concern regarding a company that lacks a competent management team?

D.4 What is financial statement restatement? Why does the auditor investigate whether a company has restated its financial statements when addressing client acceptance?

D.5 In what way would management misrepresenting a company's performance in public speeches be a problem to an auditor?

---

[4]FABS ASC 250-10-05-2 calls for retrospective application when an accounting standard is changed. Typically, when a new accounting standard is introduced, it includes transition rules. "[R]etrospective application [is] the application of a different accounting principle to prior financial statements as if the principle had always been used or as the adjustment of previously issued financial statements to reflect a change in reporting entity (SFAS 154, Summary).

Organizational Structure

Information about a company's **organizational structure** can answer several questions for an auditor. Assume the auditor examines financial disclosures and performs Internet searches on a potential client's organizational structure and ownership. The auditor may find that the information is easy to obtain and understand. This suggests that management is not using the organizational structure to withhold information or keep secrets. Although business reasons may motivate a potential client to obscure its ownership and organizational structure, limited information is a red flag to an auditor indicating the need for further investigation.

> **Caution Indicator:** *Difficulty in determining the organization or individuals that have controlling interests in the entity.* [AU 316.85 A.2 (Opportunities) c]

Organizational structure is a part of a company's ICFR. No particular organizational structure is necessarily better than another. The critical factor is that the structure used is appropriate for the company. The degree of centralization or decentralization and delegation of authority must be accompanied by the appropriate amount of oversight and accountability. The selected structure should fit the business needs and management style.

Information on a potential public company client's organizational structure is likely available through publicly available documents such as the annual report and SEC filings. More information can be obtained through discussion and interviews. Determining how appropriate the organizational structure is for the business requires judgment on the part of the audit firm.

> **Caution Indicator:** *Overly complex organizational structure involving unusual legal entities or managerial lines of authority.* [AU 316.85 A.2 (Opportunities) c]

Financial Difficulty and Going Concern

Evaluating whether a business has the resources to continue as a viable entity for the next year is referred to as assessing whether the business is a going concern. The auditor indicates in the audit report if uncertainty exists about whether the company has the resources, cash, or borrowing capability to meet its obligations for the upcoming year. Accepting a potential client that has going concern issues is not unusual. Even so, the auditor wants to know that this possibility exists as early as possible.

> **Caution Indicator:** *Operating losses making the threat of bankruptcy, foreclosure, or hostile takeover imminent.* [AU 316.85 A.2 (Incentives/Pressures) a]

> **Caution Indicator:** *Marginal ability to meet exchange listing requirements or debt repayment or other debt covenant requirements.* [AU 316.85 A.2 (Incentives/Pressures) b]

> **Caution Indicator:** *Perceived or real adverse effects of reporting poor financial results on significant pending transactions, such as business combinations or contract awards.* [AU 316.85 A.2 (Incentives/Pressures) b]

Cash flow problems, difficulty in coming up with funds to pay back debt, and credit limitations all indicate problems that impact going concern questions. Knowing in advance that a company has problems and that a going concern assessment is expected to be a critical part of an audit helps the auditor evaluate a potential client. The information is useful for estimating the work that will be involved in completing the audit. It also provides information about the risk of being associated with the company and its financial statements. The auditor cannot determine a company's going concern risks with certainty prior to accepting the engagement. However, careful scrutiny of publicly available financial information provides significant information. A potential client's going concern and financing issues can be assessed by considering the company's financing sources, cost of capital, cash flows, and committed schedule of debt payments.

Multiple Business Locations

The number of locations in which a potential client does business is an important topic that may be revealed through publicly available information. Does the business have multiple locations? Where are those sites located? This information helps the auditor assess the resources needed to complete an engagement. For example, an auditor may decide that a company's international or very distant business locations prohibit the possibility of accepting it as a client.

Sometimes concerns about integrity and legality may be inferred from considering locations where a potential client does business. As an extreme example, assume a business has many legitimate U.S. cash transactions. However, the company also has a banking relationship, with no apparent business purpose, in a country with significant drug trafficking. This fact pattern raises questions regarding whether the company is involved in illegal activities, such as money laundering. Clearly, such considerations are important to auditors when pursuing new client relationships.

> **Caution Indicator:** *Significant operations located or conducted across international borders in jurisdictions where differing business environments and cultures exists.* [AU 316.85 A.2 (Opportunities) a]

> **Caution Indicator:** *Significant bank accounts or subsidiary or branch operations in tax haven jurisdictions for which there appears to be no clear business justification.* [AU 316.85 A.2 (Opportunities) a]

Client Accounting Function

In considering whether a company is a desirable potential client, the auditor considers whether the company has (1) an accounting system with effective controls, (2) sufficient accounting personnel to get the work done, (3) a budgeting process, and (4) an appropriate **internal audit** function. Another area of interest is the complexity of the IT system.

> **Caution Indicator:** *Inadequate monitoring of controls, including automated controls and controls over interim financial reporting.* [AU 316.85 A.2 (Opportunities) d]

> **Caution Indicator:** *High turnover rates or employment of ineffective accounting, internal audit or information technology staff.* [AU 316.85 A.2 (Opportunities) d]

> **Caution Indicator:** *Ineffective accounting and information systems.* [AU 316.85 A.2 (Opportunities) d]

> **Caution Indicator:** *Inadequate internal control over assets that may increase the susceptibility of misappropriation of those assets.* [AU 316.85 A.3 (Opportunities) b]

This information helps the audit firm estimate the amount of work that is involved, audit firm personnel needed, and how long it will take to complete the audit.

Management's Use of Information

Management's use of accounting and other information and its oversight of day-to-day business activities provide valuable information to an auditor. For example, it is a positive indicator if management has the information necessary to run the business and a good system of monitoring the company's activities. Delegation of responsibility and authority differ based on organizational structure. Therefore, no two companies are exactly the same in terms of management and decision-making processes. Even so, the auditor can assess whether all those with authority have the information they need to appropriately manage their areas of responsibility. Interviews with the potential client may provide the auditor with some information on management's use of information. However, it may be that this aspect of management performance can only be effectively assessed on continuing engagements.

REVIEW QUESTIONS

E.1 What are the concerns regarding an obscure or a very complex organizational structure?

E.2 What does "going concern" mean?

E.3 What happens to the audit report if there is a question about the client's ability to continue as a going concern?

E.4 What impact does multiple geographical business locations have on the client acceptance decision?

E.5 Would the auditor have questions about a potential client having an operating location or bank account in another country when there is no readily apparent business purpose for the foreign location?

E.6 Why is complexity of a potential client's IT system important to the proposing auditor?

SOURCES OF INFORMATION

Auditors want to collect a lot of information about potential clients. The obvious question is, "Where do auditors get their information?" As just discussed, a major source of information available to the auditor is published or publicly available documents. The audit firm reviews this information both before and after conducting interviews with the client. Public information is accessed on the company's Web site, in its prior-year financial statements and auditors reports, earnings calls, and reports filed with the SEC. Other sources of information are the predecessor auditor, resources within the business community, media reports, published data, and special investigations.

Publicly Available Information

Documentary sources about a potential client provide the auditor with a wealth of information, touching on many of the areas the auditor investigates. The company Web site usually provides information about business activities, financial information, geographic areas in which the company operates, and the company's history. Financial statements and audit reports disclose financial performance, accounting policies and the prior auditor's opinion. SEC reports, particularly Form **8K**, provide information on events that may be of interest such as ownership and management changes, acquisitions and dispositions, and auditor changes. **Management discussion and analysis** included in SEC filings provides trend information. Also, the company's annual report, including the **letter to shareholders**, provides the auditor with an understanding of the perspective the company tries to convey to its shareholders and other outside constituents. Proxy statements include disclosures about fees paid to the public accounting firm for both audit and nonaudit work, and other required disclosures regarding the audit committee.

Interviewing the Potential Client

Another initial source of information, and one of the most important, is the company. When an audit firm begins to investigate a business, prior to proposing on the work, the auditor typically talks to management. Interviews extend to various company personnel, including members of the Board of Directors and audit committee. Many topics that are also investigated through publicly available information can be investigated through these discussions.

By speaking with individuals inside the company, the auditor gets a sense of:

Management's philosophy and integrity
Makeup of the Board of Directors and audit committee
Business activities, financial structure, and performance
Organizational structure
Accounting function performance

Company management can also describe the business stressors, risks, and outside pressures on the company. These interviews can confirm information already communicated to the audit firm regarding the professional services the company needs, why it needs the services, and why it is changing audit firms.

Communication with the Predecessor Auditor

Auditing standards (AU 315) require that an incoming auditor communicate with the predecessor auditor. This auditing standard applies specifically to the client acceptance and continuance process.

In practice, the timing of this communication is somewhat flexible. It may occur before the new auditor proposes on the engagement or after the client has selected the new auditor. Timing of the communication depends to some degree on the information needs of the new auditor. The number of audit firms proposing on the engagement also affects the timing of the communication. One practical scenario is for the proposing auditor to contact the predecessor auditor with preliminary questions before proposing on the engagement. The successor auditor then follows up with a request for more information after being selected to conduct the audit.

The auditing standard requires the predecessor auditor to obtain permission from the client prior to providing any information to the auditor making the inquiry. A refusal by the client to grant this permission is regarded as a red flag. Refusing indicates that a problem may exist that the client does not want the outgoing auditor to discuss.

Assuming the client gives permission, the outgoing auditor responds to the inquiry. The professional standards require the predecessor auditor to provide some type of response to the communication request. That response may be as limited as: "unable to respond." This is most typical in the case of a lawsuit or some other dispute involving the client and prior auditor. The prior auditor can also respond to some of the inquiries, but provide a limited response. When this occurs, the prior auditor must indicate that the response is limited.

The communication between predecessor and successor auditors may be limited or extensive. At a minimum, the successor auditor asks questions about management integrity and reasons for the change in audit firms. Other possible questions address management's openness and cooperation with the auditor, and Board of Directors and audit committee availability and involvement. Successor auditors inquire about disputes with management and problems encountered on the audit, such as fraud or illegal acts. Finally, the successor auditor may ask to review or copy the predecessor's **work papers**. Not only does this provide valuable information to the new auditor in planning the engagement, it may highlight potential problem areas.

REVIEW QUESTIONS

F.1 What are the auditor's sources of information about a potential client?

F.2 What is an 8K? Annual report? Management discussion and analysis?

F.3 Why does an incoming auditor communicate with the predecessor auditor? What information does the proposing or incoming (successor) auditor request?

F.4 Does the predecessor have to respond to the successor auditor? Why might the prior auditor not be willing or able to communicate fully with the successor auditor? Is this okay, according to professional standards?

Business Resources

The business community is another source of information for an auditor investigating a potential client. The auditor may ask the potential client for permission to speak to lawyers and bankers with whom the company does business. Again, refusal to let these professionals speak openly with the auditor indicates the possibility that information exists that the company wants to withhold from the auditor. Even though a lawyer's discussion may be limited by **client-attorney privilege**, the conversation can provide the auditor with important background information. Another source of information may be customers of the potential client. Customers are likely to be a practical and useful source only if the company has a limited number.

Media and Data Searches; Other Investigations

Finally, an audit firm considering proposing on the engagement of a new client conducts electronic media and data searches. The searches are similar to what a student performs in the library researching a topic for class. The audit firm either performs the search or hires a company that specializes in providing search services.

Media and data searches produce instances when the potential client has been discussed in the print media. These print references provide the auditor with information ranging from financial performance to market positioning. Even legal proceedings of high-ranking management within the company or the BOD can be surfaced through media searches.

Sometimes audit firms also hire investigative agencies to research clients. These investigations often extend to background checks of significant personnel such as top management and directors. Extensive investigations may be a part of an audit firm's routine procedures, or they may occur only when other investigations have produced information that requires follow-up. Exhibit 5-5 summarizes sources that may be used and information obtained when researching a potential audit client.

EXHIBIT 5-5

Researching the Potential Client

Sources	Information
Published financial information	Size of assets
Annual reports	Size of revenue
Financial statements	Market capitalization
SEC filings	Industry
Earnings calls transcripts	Type of business
Press releases	Business activities
Published economy and industry information	Financial statement restatements
Searches of media and other records	Public offerings planned
Web sites	Sources of capital
Prior auditor	Financial performance
Management	Going concern questions
Board of Directors and audit committee	Management team
members	Audit committee financial expert
Special investigations and background checks	Customer demand for the industry
	Business failures in the industry
	Accounting principles used
	Related party transactions
	Law enforcement and regulatory actions
	Ethical philosophies
	Code of ethics
	Composition of BOD and audit committee
	Functions of BOD
	Organizational structure and ownership
	Locations of the business
	Structure, composition, and quality of the accounting function

FIRM RESOURCES AND EXPERTISE

Information obtained by the auditor in the process of investigating a potential client also helps the firm decide whether it has the ability to successfully perform and complete the audit engagement. Before proposing to perform the audit of a potential client, the firm must have confidence in its ability to do the work.

If a potential client company is very large, or has multiple geographic locations, the audit firm may decide it does not have sufficient personnel for the engagement. If the client is planning an IPO and the auditor has limited or no experience with that type of engagement, the firm may decide not to pursue the engagement. Also, if the potential client is in an industry that is highly regulated or for which significant industry expertise is required—or even has a very complex IT system—the audit firm may determine that it does not have the professional expertise for the engagement. Appendix A to this chapter introduces various industries and begins to explain issues related to industry risk. Understanding industry risk helps to clarify why auditors need industry expertise for many audit engagements. Beyond these considerations, firms also consider the staffing requirements for the engagement and the human resources it has available during the time the engagement must be completed.

AUDITING IN ACTION

Lincoln Savings and Loan Association

The collapse of Lincoln Savings and Loan in 1989 is most often associated in the public memory with Charles Keating. The failure of Lincoln Savings and Loan eventually led to congressional hearings into the fraud, and to the prosecution and conviction of Keating. Another part of the Lincoln Savings and Loan story is about industry complexity and the expertise that is often needed to audit transactions and companies in highly complex and regulated industries. The most complicated part of the Lincoln Savings and Loan collapse was not related to savings and loan regulation, but rather to its purchases and sales of real estate. Lincoln engaged in highly complex real estate transactions with related parties that permitted Lincoln's profits to be inappropriately inflated. Kenneth Leventhal & Company (since merged with Ernst & Young), a public accounting firm that was widely recognized for its knowledge of the real estate industry, testified before Congress about the difficulty in accounting properly for complex real estate transactions. Furthermore, Leventhal indicated that the improper accounting for Lincoln's real estate deals represented form over substance.

ECONOMIC CONSIDERATIONS

Chapter 3 discussed the responsibilities of auditors to protect the public interest. However, audit firms are still for-profit businesses. Therefore, audit firms consider whether a potential client is the most profitable way to utilize the firm's human resources. The information accumulated thus far gives the audit firm some idea of the work involved in the audit. The auditor considers any special risk areas identified, as well as any areas that require unusual amounts of audit effort and time. Based on this information about expected hours required, the audit firm estimates what it expects to charge the client for the audit. Exhibit 5-6 summarizes the questions an auditor considers after researching a potential audit client.

PROPOSING ON THE ENGAGEMENT

At this point, the audit firm is in a position to make its final decision about whether to propose on the engagement. Final considerations include whether other firms are also

EXHIBIT 5-6

Do We Still Want the Audit?

Do we have the required knowledge about the company's industry?

Do we have sufficient human resources to do the work?

Do we have personnel with adequate experience and skills to provide the services the client needs?

Is the company's financial situation adequate?

Is the company's industry and area of business expanding? Stable? In decline?

Does the company have important vulnerabilities? (such as the economy, industry litigation, global conditions, competition, high commitments for expenses or debt, inventory requirements, going-concern questions)

Is management aggressive in its accounting presentation?

Does management seem to be risk seeking?

Do any members of management or the Board of Directors have a known history of violating laws or regulations?

Does the company have a code of ethics, particularly one for management?

Is the management team appropriately skilled, experienced, and competent?

What is the predominant management style?

Does the audit committee appear involved and effective?

What are the composition, qualification, and experience levels of the Board of Directors?

Have the company's recent financial statements been restated, and if yes, why?

Is information about the company's organizational structure and ownership easy to obtain?

Is the organizational structure appropriate for the business?

Do the company's various locations make sense from a "business purpose" perspective?

Are the locations consistent with our desire and ability to do the audit?

Is there anything about the client's accounting function that suggests high audit risk?

proposing on the engagement, and the timing and format of the proposal process. The audit firm considers all the accumulated information in deciding whether to continue with the proposal process.

An audit proposal may be formal or informal, oral, or both oral and documentary. The proposal is basically a presentation to the potential client, confirming the services the audit firm will provide, identifying audit team leadership, communicating the firm's expertise and benefits it can provide to the client, and establishing the fee for performing the engagement.

Some specific additional information that might affect the engagement is verified by the audit firm before it proposes on the engagement. For example, the audit firm may be required to also audit prior years that have not been audited, such as for an IPO. Or the auditor may have to re-audit years that have been audited by another firm. In these situations, the engagement requires more labor and the fee will be higher. Sometimes another auditor is to be involved in part of the audit. This affects the amount of work to be performed by the proposing firm.

If a company **outsources** some of its accounting function to an outside service provider, the audit of that function may be handled in several ways. The audit firm may need to audit aspects of the service provider company, or it may rely heavily on a report issued by the service provider's auditor. These options are discussed in Chapter 13. How outsourced services are audited affects the amount of audit work required, and thus the audit firm's proposal.

AFTER THE SELECTION [LO 4]

Assume an audit firm proposes to perform an audit engagement and the client company selects the audit firm. The audit firm then moves from client acceptance to other preliminary engagement procedures. The remaining preliminary engagement procedures are to establish an understanding with the client about the terms of the engagement and confirm the audit firm's independence.

Terms of the Engagement and Engagement Letter

The auditor and client must establish an understanding about a number of items regarding the audit engagement. The understanding must be documented in the workpapers, and it is preferred that the understanding be established through a written communication between the auditor and client. Public client auditors must establish the understanding through a written engagement letter signed by the client. Items about which the auditor and client establish an understanding and therefore include in the engagement letter follow (PCAOB AU 310.06).

- The objective of an integrated audit is the expression of an opinion on both management's assessment of ICFR and on the financial statements.
- Management is responsible for the entity's financial statements.
- Management is responsible for establishing and maintaining effective ICFR. If, in an integrated audit of financial statements and ICFR, the auditor concludes that he or she cannot express an opinion on ICFR because there has been a limitation on the scope of the audit, he or she should communicate, in writing, to management and the audit committee that the audit of ICFR cannot be satisfactorily completed.
- Management is responsible for identifying and ensuring that the entity complies with the laws and regulations applicable to its activities.
- Management is responsible for making all financial records and related information available to the auditor.
- At the conclusion of the engagement, management will provide the auditor with a letter that confirms certain representations made during the audit.

The last item in the preceding list above refers to what is called a **management representation letter,** which is an item of audit evidence the auditing standards require the auditor to obtain. The management representation letter is signed by management and indicates that management has been honest with the auditor and has provided valid information to the auditor. The management representation letter is discussed in Chapter 11. PCAOB AU 310.06 continues:

- The auditor is responsible for conducting the audit in accordance with the standards of the Public Company Accounting Oversight Board. Those standards require that the auditor obtain *reasonable assurance* about whether the financial statements are free of *material misstatement*, whether caused by error or fraud, and whether management's assessment of the effectiveness of the company's ICFR is fairly stated in all material respects. Accordingly, there is some risk that a material misstatement of the financial statements or a material weakness in ICFR would remain undetected. Although not absolute assurance, reasonable assurance is nevertheless, a high level of assurance. Also, an integrated audit is not designed to detect error or fraud that is immaterial to the financial statements or deficiencies in ICFR that, individually or in combination, are less severe than a material weakness. If, for any reason, the auditor is unable to complete the audit or is unable to form or has not formed an opinion, he or she may decline to express an opinion or decline to issue a report as a result of the engagement.

This segment of the engagement letter includes many of the fundamental concepts presented in Chapter 2. PCAOB Auditing Standards is the set of standards that the auditor is obligated to follow in conducting an integrated audit. Audits only provide reasonable assurance, and not a guarantee. Finally, the auditor must either express an opinion as a result of the audit or decline to provide an opinion, which is known as **disclaiming an opinion**.

- An audit includes planning and performing the audit to obtain reasonable assurance about reporting:
  Planning and performing the audit to obtain reasonable assurance about whether the company maintained, in all material respects, effective ICFR as of the date specified in management's assessment. The auditor is also responsible for obtaining an understanding of internal control sufficient to plan the financial statement audit and to determine the nature, timing, and extent of audit procedures to be performed. The auditor is also responsible for communicating in writing:

> To the audit committee—all significant deficiencies and material weaknesses identified during the audit.
>
> To management—all internal control deficiencies identified during the audit and not previously communicated in writing by the auditor or by others, including internal auditors or others inside or outside the company.
>
> To the board of directors—any conclusion that the audit committee's oversight of the company's external financial reporting and internal control over financial reporting is ineffective.

- Management is responsible for adjusting the financial statements to correct material misstatements and for affirming to the auditor in the representation letter that the effects of any uncorrected misstatements aggregated by the auditor during the current engagement and pertaining to the latest period presented are immaterial, both individually and in the aggregate, to the financial statements taken as a whole.

For an integrated audit the engagement letter explains what constitutes an audit, specifically addressing the audit of internal control over financial reporting. The communications required of an auditor are presented, along with more of management's responsibilities. Other matters that may be included in an engagement letter are (AU 310.07):

- Conduct of the engagement, for example, timing and client assistance regarding the preparation of schedules and availability of documents
- Involvement of specialists or internal auditors, if applicable
- Involvement of a predecessor auditor
- Fees and billing
- Any limitation of or other arrangements regarding the liability of the auditor or the client, such as indemnification to the auditor for liability arising from knowing misrepresentations to the auditor by management (Regulators, including the SEC, may restrict or prohibit such liability limitation arrangements)
- Conditions under which access to the auditor's working papers may be granted to others
- Additional services to be provided relating to regulatory requirements
- Other services to be provided in connection with the engagement

Similar information regarding the engagement letter for nonpublic companies is found in the AICPA codification at AU 311.09-.10.[5] Engagement letters are lengthy because they must include all the items set forth for inclusion by the auditing standards.

AUDITING IN ACTION

Sample Engagement Letter for Audits of Public Companies

Date

Dear Members of the Audit Committee:

This letter is to confirm our understanding of the terms of our engagement as independent accountants of Smith Inc. (the "Company").

Services and related report

We will perform an integrated audit of the consolidated financial statements of the Company at December 31, 2010 and for the year then ending and of the Company's internal control over financial reporting as of December 31, 2010. Upon completion of our work, we will provide the Company with our report on the audit work referred to above. If, for any reasons caused

---

[5]For nonpublic company audits the engagement letter may include information on limitations of liability for the auditor or client; however, these types of arrangements are not acceptable to the PCAOB for audits of public companies.

by or relating to the affairs or management of the Company, we are unable to complete our integrated audit, we may decline to issue a report as a result of this engagement.

In conjunction with the annual financial statement audit, we will perform reviews of the Company's unaudited consolidated quarterly financial information for each of the first three quarters in the year ending December 31, 2010, before the Form 10-Q is filed. These reviews will be conducted in accordance with the standards established by the Public Company Accounting Oversight Board (the "PCAOB") and are substantially less in scope than an audit. Accordingly, a review may not reveal material modifications necessary to make the quarterly financial information conform with generally accepted accounting principles. We will communicate to the audit committee and management any matters that come to our attention as a result of the review that we believe may require material modifications to the quarterly financial information to make it conform with accounting principles generally accepted in the United States of America. If, for any reasons caused by or relating to the affairs or management of the Company, we are unable to complete our review, we will notify the audit committee and management.

Our responsibilities and limitations

The objective of a financial statement audit is the expression of an opinion on the financial statements. We will be responsible for performing the audit in accordance with the standards established by the PCAOB. Those standards require that we plan and perform the audit to obtain reasonable assurance about whether the financial statements are free of material misstatement. The audit will include examining, on a test basis, evidence supporting the amounts and disclosures in the financial statements, assessing the accounting principles used and significant estimates made by management, and evaluating the overall financial statement presentation. We will consider the Company's internal control over financial reporting in determining the nature, timing and extent of auditing procedures necessary for expressing our opinion on the financial statements.

The objective of an audit of internal control over financial reporting is the expression of an opinion on the effectiveness of the Company's internal control over financial reporting. We will be responsible for performing the audit in accordance with the standards established by the PCAOB. Those standards require that we plan and perform the audit to obtain reasonable assurance about whether effective internal control over financial reporting was maintained in all material respects. The audit will include obtaining an understanding of internal control over financial reporting, assessing the risk that a material weakness exists, testing and evaluating the design and operating effectiveness of internal control over financial reporting based on the assessed risk, and performing such other procedures as we consider necessary in the circumstances.

Each of the following circumstances is an indicator of a material weakness:

- Identification of fraud, whether or not material, on the part of senior management;
- Restatement of previously issued financial statements to reflect the correction of a material misstatement;
- Identification by the auditor of a material misstatement of financial statements in the current period in circumstances that indicate that the misstatement would not have been detected by the company's internal control over financial reporting; and
- Ineffective oversight of the company's external financial reporting and internal control over financial reporting by the company's audit committee.

Under the standards established by the PCAOB, the existence of one or more material weaknesses will require us to issue an adverse opinion regarding the effectiveness of the Company's internal control over financial reporting.

All significant deficiencies and material weaknesses relating to internal control over financial reporting identified while performing our work will be communicated in writing to management and the audit committee. All deficiencies in internal control over financial reporting (i.e., those deficiencies in internal control over financial reporting that are of a lesser magnitude than significant deficiencies) identified while performing our work will be communicated in writing to management of the Company, and the Audit Committee will be informed when such a communication has been made. We will communicate in writing to the Board of Directors of

(continued)

the Company if we conclude that the oversight of the Company's external financial reporting and internal control over financial reporting by the Company's audit committee is ineffective.

Because of its inherent limitations, internal control over financial reporting may not prevent or detect misstatements. Also, projections of any evaluation of effectiveness of internal control over financial reporting from December 31, 2010, the date of our audit of the Company's internal control over financial reporting, to future periods are subject to the risk that controls may become inadequate because of changes in conditions, or that the degree of compliance with the policies or procedures may deteriorate.

We will design our audits to obtain reasonable, but not absolute, assurance of detecting errors or fraud that would have a material effect on the financial statements as well as other illegal acts having a direct and material effect on financial statement amounts, and of identifying material weaknesses in internal control over financial reporting. Our audits will not include a detailed audit of transactions, such as would be necessary to identify errors or fraud that did not cause a material misstatement of the financial statements or procedures designed to identify deficiencies in internal control over financial reporting that, individually or in combination, are less severe than a material weakness. There are inherent limitations in the auditing process. Audits are based on tests of the data underlying the financial statements, which involve judgments regarding the areas to be tested and the nature, timing, extent and results of the tests to be performed. Audits are, therefore, subject to the limitation that material errors or fraud or other illegal acts having a direct and material financial statement impact, if they exist, may not be detected. Because of the characteristics of fraud, an audit designed and executed in accordance with the standards established by the PCAOB may not detect a material misstatement due to fraud. Characteristics of fraud include

i. concealment through collusion among management, employees, or third parties;
ii. withheld, misrepresented, or falsified documentation; and
iii. the ability of management to override or instruct others to override what otherwise appears to be effective controls.

While effective internal control over financial reporting reduces the likelihood that errors, fraud or other illegal acts will occur and remain undetected, it does not eliminate that possibility. For these reasons we cannot ensure that errors, fraud or other illegal acts, if present, will be detected. We will communicate to the audit committee and management of the Company, as appropriate, any such matters identified during our audit.

We also are responsible for determining that the audit committee is informed about certain other matters related to the conduct of our audits, including

i. any disagreements with management about matters that could be significant to the Company's financial statements or our report thereon;
ii. any serious difficulties encountered in performing the audit;
iii. information relating to our independence with respect to the Company;
iv. other matters related to the Company's financial statements including its significant accounting policies and practices, including critical accounting policies and alternative treatments within accounting principles generally accepted in the United States; and
v. all significant deficiencies and material weaknesses identified during the audit, as previously mentioned.

Lastly, we are responsible for ensuring that the audit committee receives copies of certain written communications between us and management, including management representation letters and written communications on accounting, auditing, internal control or operational matters.

The financial statement audit and the audit of the Company's internal control over financial reporting will not be planned or conducted in contemplation of reliance by any specific third party or with respect to any specific transaction. Therefore, items of possible interest to a third party will not be specifically addressed and matters may exist that would be assessed differently by a third party, possibly in connection with a specific transaction.

Management's responsibilities

The Company's management is responsible for the financial statements and information referred to above including establishing and maintaining adequate internal control over financial reporting. In this regard, management is responsible for establishing policies and procedures that pertain to the maintenance of accounting records, the authorization of receipts and disbursements, the safeguarding of assets, the proper recording of transactions in the accounting records, and for reporting financial information in conformity with accounting principles generally accepted in the United States of America. Management also is responsible for the design and implementation of programs and controls to prevent and detect fraud, and for informing us

i. about all known or suspected fraud affecting the entity involving
   a. management,
   b. employees who have significant roles in internal control over financial reporting, and
   c. others where the fraud could have a material effect on the financial statements; and
ii. of its knowledge of any allegations of fraud or suspected fraud affecting the entity received in communications from employees, former employees, analysts, regulators, short sellers, or others.

Management is responsible for

i. adjusting the financial statements to correct material misstatements and for affirming to us that the effects of any uncorrected misstatements aggregated by us during the current engagement and pertaining to the year under audit are immaterial, both individually and in the aggregate, to the financial statements taken as a whole; and
ii. notifying us of all deficiencies in the design or operation of internal control over financial reporting identified as part of management's assessment, including separately disclosing to us all such deficiencies that it believes to be significant deficiencies or material weaknesses in internal control over financial reporting.

Management also is responsible for identifying and ensuring that the Company complies with the laws and regulations applicable to its activities. Management of the Company is also responsible for

i. accepting responsibility for the effectiveness of the Company's internal control over financial reporting;
ii. evaluating the effectiveness of the Company's internal control over financial reporting using suitable control criteria;
iii. supporting its evaluation with sufficient evidential matter, including documentation, and
iv. presenting a written assessment of the effectiveness of the Company's internal control over financial reporting as of the end of the Company's most recent fiscal year.

As part of management's responsibility for the financial statements and the effectiveness of internal control over financial reporting, management is responsible for making available to us, on a timely basis, all of the Company's original accounting records and related information and company personnel to whom we may direct inquiries. The absence of sufficient documented evidence to support management's assessment of the operating effectiveness of internal control over financial reporting is an internal control deficiency that could result in a limitation on the scope of the audit.

As required by the standards of the PCAOB, we will make specific inquiries of management and others about the representations embodied in the financial statements and the internal control over financial reporting. Standards of the PCAOB also require that we obtain written representation regarding the financial statements and the internal control over financial reporting from certain members of management. The results of our tests, the responses to our inquiries and the written representation comprise the evidential matter we intend to rely upon in forming our opinion on the financial statements and the effectiveness of the Company's internal control over financial reporting. The results of our analytical procedures, responses to our

(continued)

inquiries and written representations obtained comprise the basis for our review on the unaudited quarterly financial information.

To assist us in planning our audits, the Company will authorize its previous auditors, to allow us to review their working papers and to respond fully to our inquiries.

Document retention

The Company agrees to maintain documentation sufficient to support its assessment of internal control over financial reporting as of December 31, 2010 for a period of seven years from the date of our audit report.

Other documents

Standards established by the PCAOB require that we read any annual report that contains our audit report. The purpose of this procedure is to consider whether other information in the annual report, including the manner of its presentation, is materially inconsistent with information appearing in the financial statements or management's assessment of the effectiveness of the Company's internal control over financial reporting. We assume no obligation to perform procedures to corroborate such other information as part of our audit.

With regard to filings with the SEC's Electronic Data Gathering, Analysis, and Retrieval ("EDGAR") system, before filing any document in electronic format with the SEC with which we are associated, management of the Company will advise us of the proposed filing. We will provide the Company with a manually signed copy of our report(s) and consent(s) which will authorize the use of our name for electronic transmission by the Company.

Timing and fees

Completion of our work is subject to, among other things,

1. appropriate cooperation from the Company's personnel, including timely preparation of necessary schedules;
2. timely responses to our inquiries; and
3. timely communication of all significant accounting, financial, and internal control over financial reporting matters.

When and if for any reason the Company is unable to provide such schedules, information and assistance, the fee will be mutually revised to reflect additional services, if any, required of us to complete our work

Our fees are based on the time required by the individuals assigned to the engagement. We estimate our fees for this integrated audit engagement will range from $_____ to $_____. This fee estimate assumes that we incur ___ to ___ hours in performing our integrated audit, based on an assumed mix of staff. We will update you on significant changes in our fee estimate as the audit progresses. If actual hours incurred exceed this range or the mix of staff necessary to perform the work varies significantly, we will notify you as soon as possible. If actual hours incurred are less than this range, we will adjust our fee accordingly.

We also will bill the Company for our out-of-pocket expenses.

Any additional services that may be requested and we agree to provide will be the subject of separate arrangements.

Very truly yours,
Andrea Bingham Courtney, LLP

Confirming Independence

Quality control procedures help an audit firm determine its independence from potential clients. Quality Control Standards and procedures are discussed in Chapter 3. As was mentioned at the outset of this chapter, for practical reasons, an auditor determines that no independence problems exist before beginning the proposal and client acceptance process.

PCAOB Rule 3526 requires an audit firm to communicate its independence in writing before accepting an audit engagement of a public company for the first time. For ongoing engagements, the rule requires that the auditor communicate independence to the audit committee at least once a year. A final step in preliminary engagement procedures for ongoing clients is for the audit firm to confirm its audit independence.

REVIEW QUESTIONS

G.1 What is a media or data search?

G.2 What are some reasons an audit firm might decide to refrain from proposing on an engagement?

G.3 What is an engagement letter, and what are its contents?

CONCLUSION

Client acceptance and continuance procedures are an important part of an audit firm's activities. Effective client acceptance and continuance procedures permit an audit firm to select clients to which it can provide high-quality services as well as manage the firm's business risks. Client acceptance and continuance procedures are so important that they are an integral part of an audit firm's quality control. After completing client acceptance and continuance procedures, establishing an understanding with the client on terms of the engagement, and confirming independence, the audit firm is ready to begin risk assessment and planning.

KEY TERMS

8K. Form filed with the SEC reporting on current events.

10K. Form filed with the SEC annually, which includes management's report on internal control over financial reporting and the financial statements, along with the audit report(s).

Annual report. Document prepared by a company that presents various kinds of information about the entity, including a letter to shareholders, financial reports, and the audit report.

Audit committee. A committee (or equivalent body) established by and among the Board of Directors for the purposes of overseeing the accounting and financial reporting processes and audits of the financial statements. Has direct responsibility for the hiring, retention, compensation, and oversight of the external auditor.

Business risk. The risks of a company associated with failure in achieving its objectives.

Client acceptance. The process leading to a CPA firm's decision about whether to accept a company as a new client.

Client-attorney privilege. The right of a client and attorney to keep information they discuss confidential.

Client continuance. The process leading to a CPA firm's decision about whether to continue performing work for a company that is already a client.

Corporate code of ethics. Refers to a code of ethics adopted by a company as a part of its corporate governance.

Disclaim an opinion. An audit firm issues a report stating that it does not express an opinion on the financial statements or system of internal control over financial reporting. The report includes the reason for the disclaimer and any reservations the auditor has regarding the financial statements and internal controls.

Engagement letter. A written document summarizing the contract between the auditor and client.

Financial statement restatement. Occurs when financial statements that have been released into the public domain are replaced with a new version that reflects correction of an error or the availability of new information or evidence.

Fraud. Intentional misstatement of financial statements, or theft of assets. Management is usually responsible for intentional misstatement of financial statements, while either employees or management can commit theft.

GAAS. The 10 generally accepted auditing standards that are the basis for the auditing standards of the PCAOB and AICPA. (Discussed in Chapter 2.)

Going concern. Term used to apply to the situation in which there is significant uncertainty about an entity's ability to continue in business for the next year.

ICFR. Internal control over financial reporting.

Initial public offering (IPO). Occurs when a company offers equity securities on the public markets for the first time. Requires a registration statement, which is a document including audited financial statements that must be filed with the SEC.

Internal audit. A function performed by corporate employees; activities may include financial statement audits, efficiency and effectiveness audits, forensic audits, and special projects.

Internal control over financial reporting (ICFR). Controls that relate to the preparation of reliable published financial statements, including interim and condensed financial statements and selected financial data derived from those statements, such as earnings releases, that are reported publicly.

Letter to shareholders. Communication to shareholders included in the annual report, usually signed by the company president.

Management discussion and analysis. Disclosure required in reports filed with the SEC including risk information and trend analysis.

Management philosophy and operating style. Part of the control environment; related to issues such as business risks accepted, communication style and attitudes, and actions toward financial reporting.

Management representation letter. A letter from the client, signed by upper management, to the auditor, documenting client assertions to the auditor in areas related to the financial statements, completeness of information, recognition, measurement, disclosure, subsequent events, and internal control.

Material misstatement. A misstatement in the financial statements from error or fraud that is judged to be important enough to be material.

Material weakness in ICFR. A deficiency, or a combination of deficiencies, in ICFR causing a greater than remote chance that a material misstatement of the company's annual or interim financial statements will not be prevented or detected on a timely basis. (See also *Reasonable possibility*.)

Nonaudit services. General term used for all services performed by a CPA that are not audits.

Organizational structure. The layout of an entity, including division of authority, responsibility, and duties. A centralized organization structure is "tall," indicating numerous layers of management, while a decentralized organization structure is "flat," indicating limited layers of management with delegation of authority and responsibility to lower layers of the entity.

Outsource. Contracting with and using an outside service organization to perform a service rather than having the function handled in-house.

Predecessor auditor. A CPA firm that formerly audited a specific company.

Professional competence. Having the skill and knowledge to perform an engagement with due professional care.

Proposal process. The process through which a CPA firm presents to the potential client details about its plan to perform the audit engagement and the estimated costs.

Quality Control Standards. Professional guidance regarding the procedures of a public accounting firm.

Reasonable assurance. A high, but not absolute, level of assurance provided by an audit.

Related party transactions. Transactions in which one party has the ability to influence the decisions, management, or operating policies of the other party. Related parties may be an affiliated company or any entity with which a client deals.

Request for proposal (RFP). A document issued and distributed by a company requesting submissions by firms, in this situation by auditors, regarding details and terms under which they would perform the engagement.

Working papers, work papers. Records that document the evidence gathered by auditors and show their audit work, procedures, and conclusions. Though referred to as working "papers," these are typically created and maintained in electronic format.

MULTIPLE CHOICE

5-1   **[LO 2]** Professional standards related to client acceptance are legally required by

(a) AICPA.

(b) PCAOB.

(c) SOX.

(d) all of the above.

5-2   **[LO 1]** An RFP

(a) is required for a client to change auditors.

(b) contains information about the proposal process and engagement.

(c) is only used by publicly traded companies.

(d) is issued by the auditor.

5-3 **[LO 3]** Independence issues that would stop an audit firm from proposing on a potential client

(a) can only be determined at the end of the client investigation process.

(b) may result from financial and business interest in the potential company.

(c) are not affected by the Sarbanes-Oxley Act.

(d) are only binding for clients who are SEC registrants.

5-4 **[LO 3]** When financial statements are "restated," it may result from

(a) retrospective application.

(b) discovery of an error in past financial statements.

(c) an adjustment of previously issued financial statements to reflect a change in reporting entity.

(d) all of the above.

5-5 **[LO 3]** Which of the following is least important to the auditor when investigating a potential new audit client?

(a) Whether the audit committee has a financial expert

(b) Level of the CEO's charitable giving in the community

(c) Existence of a company code of ethics

(d) Extensive amounts of regulatory oversight in the company's industry

5-6 **[LO 3]** Although they may all be informative regarding risk, which of the following may be of concern for a large, international audit firm considering accepting a company as a new client?

(a) Management authority is concentrated in one or two people, even though the client company is very large.

(b) The potential client has multinational operations with many operating locations.

(c) The potential client has either a highly centralized or highly decentralized organizational structure.

(d) There is a history of (successful) products that have very quick technological obsolescence.

5-7 **[LO 1]** Auditors review the financial information of potential clients to

(a) look for information about related parties.

(b) assess management philosophy regarding employee overtime.

(c) determine the competence of the audit committee.

(d) all of the above.

5-8 **[LO 3]** An auditor issues a going-concern opinion when

(a) the client company is in the process of liquidation.

(b) the auditor feels an obligation to warn financial statement users about the company's tight cash flow.

(c) there is uncertainty about whether the company will have or be able to obtain sufficient resources to meet its obligations in the upcoming year.

(d) there is not enough information available to be able to issue an unqualified report.

5-9 **[LO 3]** Auditors obtain information about potential clients from all of the following except

(a) shareholders.

(b) prior auditors.

(c) published documents.

(d) business contacts.

5-10 **[LO 4]** An engagement letter

(a) must be in a particular format and include information on fees.

(b) must be signed by the CEO and head of the audit committee.

(c) documents the understanding of the engagement between the auditor and client.

(d) is only created prior to beginning work in the first year of auditing a new client.

5-11 **[LO 3]** Which of the following would the auditor not consider as an indicator of the need for further investigation of a potential new client?

(a) One of the directors, though not a member of the audit committee, was recently convicted of tax evasion.

(b) The company is highly decentralized; top management delegates a significant amount of decision-making authority and spends most of its management time on oversight of those decision makers.

(c) The industry is experiencing a significant downturn, and a number of similar companies have filed for bankruptcy.

(d) The company has an audit committee, although none of the members qualifies as a financial expert.

5-12 **[LO 3]** Which of the following may be difficult information for an auditor to obtain prior to accepting a public company as a client?

(a) The amount and quality of information available to the people within the company who have decision-making responsibility.

(b) The existence of business locations that may have uncertain or questionable business purposes.

(c) A going-concern uncertainty that has been in existence for several years.

(d) That management habitually provides inappropriately optimistic commentary about the company to outsiders.

5-13 **[LO 3]** Financial statement restatements

(a) are an important consideration for an auditor investigating a potential client.

(b) may be needed to correct an error.

(c) may be an indicator of the possibility of a material weaknesses in ICFR.

(d) all of the above.

5-14 **[LO 1]** An auditor investigates a potential client's business activities

(a) because public companies keep many of their business activities secret.

(b) to confirm that the company's business activities are compatible with what the audit firm wants in its client portfolio.

(c) because companies that are involved in several different industries are not required to disclose all of the industry information.

(d) none of the above.

5-15 **[LO 2]** Professional guidance useful to the client acceptance and continuance process is found in

(a) Quality Control Standards and Auditing Standards on fraud.

(b) COSO Enterprise Risk Management and Internal Control frameworks.

(c) Auditing Standards on risk and Auditing Standards on ICFR.

(d) All of the above.

5-16 **[LO 3]** Inquiry of the predecessor auditor.

(a) is not helpful because the predecessor does not have to respond.

(b) is helpful even if the predecessor responds with a statement indicating that no information or only a limited response can be made.

(c) is useful because the predecessor auditor is not limited in communicating any confidential client information since the individual

requesting the information is also a CPA and therefore is subject to confidentiality rules.

(d) is a standardized procedure that must be performed at a specific stage of the client acceptance process.

5-17 **[LO 4]** An engagement letter

(a) includes a copy of the management representation letter.

(b) for an audit can only address the audit and cannot include terms for any other services; a separate engagement letter must be drafted for other services.

(c) specifies that the auditor has responsibility for the accuracy of the company's financial statements and effectiveness of internal control.

(d) distinguishes those responsibilities that are management's and those responsibilities that are the auditor's.

5-18 **[LO 3]** Which of the following would *not* cause the auditor concerns about management?

(a) Management stays fully informed about the financial performance of the company on a regular basis.

(b) Nonaccounting management is always involved and has significant influence in the choice of accounting principles and structuring the way transactions are recorded.

(c) A very large company has a small management group with most of the decision-making authority limited to one or two people.

(d) Management expresses a strong preference to provide as little disclosure about related parties as possible.

5-19 **[LO 2, 3]** Related party transactions

(a) tend to make auditors avoid companies as potential clients.

(b) must be disclosed.

(c) cannot be shown on the financial statements because they are assumed to be non-arms length.

(d) are very uncommon and create an unacceptable level of audit risk.

5-20 **[LO 3]** An audit firm's knowledge and experience

(a) do not limit the clients a firm can audit because the firm can always get sufficient knowledge from the auditing standards.

(b) are not addressed in the audit guidance as potential limiting factors affecting the acceptance of audit clients.

(c) are important because a firm must have SEC experience before accepting a public company as an audit client.

(d) must be considered by the audit firm in client acceptance decisions to determine whether the firm has the competence to provide the professional services requested.

DISCUSSION QUESTIONS

5-21 **[LO 1, 3]** What happens to client companies that are not desired as clients by the CPA firms that are very concerned about client reputation? These might be companies with known management integrity issues or fee disputes with prior auditors. Will these companies still be able to get audits? From whom? What do you think this means regarding protecting the public interest and integrity of the capital markets?

5-22 **[LO 3]** Why does a recent or upcoming IPO create more risk for the auditor? Which audit firms seem best positioned to accept the risk? Which audit firms likely have the greatest expertise with that type of client? What would be the ultimate outcome if the most qualified audit firms turn down companies with IPOs because they do not want the risk, and the companies must use audit firms with less experience and expertise? How does this scenario fit in with protecting the public interest?

5-23 **[LO 3]** Why would an auditor be concerned about a potential client with an overworked accounting staff? With a potential client that has had multiple turnover of people in top accounting positions?

5-24 **[LO 3]** What circumstances might motivate an audit firm to hire an investigative agency to research a potential client?

5-25 **[LO 4]** What is the purpose of an engagement letter? Is the engagement letter considered a binding contract between both parties? If a CPA firm works over the explicitly specified engagement hours provided for in the engagement letter, do you think the firm can bill the client and collect for those hours? What might impact the firm's ability to collect?

5-26 **[LO 4]** Assuming no independence issues, if you are a partner at a CPA firm and your firm is engaged to audit your best friend's company, should you take on the engagement on a verbal contract agreement? Why or why not? What influences your decision?

5-27 **[LO 1]** Your firm has been the auditor of a company for the last 15 years. In those 15 years, your firm has never identified any significant red flags regarding the company. By all methods of judging, your client is a dream client. Considering the professional relationship your firm has with the company, should you still undergo client acceptance/continuation procedures? Why or why not?

5-28 **[LO 1]** What is an RFP? Who issues an RFP? What information can the auditor expect to obtain from a company's RFP? Contrast the benefits and disadvantage of formal and informal proposal processes.

PROBLEMS

5-29 **[LO 3]** Global Technologies Corporation (GTC) is a large, international electronics company that is headquartered and traded in the United States. GTC was founded in 1976, went public in 1983, and has had no known accounting "issues" since it went public. GTC has diversified operations on five continents around the world in the electronics, research, energy, and communications industries. GTC recently issued an RFP for an audit.

Required:

Identify and list the important items a potential auditor should consider when deciding whether to propose on the GTC audit work.

5-30   **[LO 3]** S&W LLP is a midsize, national audit firm with 55 offices in 40 states around the United States. S&W is also a member of an international network of firms that share technologies and some services. S&W is known to specialize in the technology and health-care sectors, and audits primarily nonpublic and small publicly traded companies. Recently, S&W's leadership has decided that the best business direction for the firm is to pursue growth, develop a practice specializing in the financial services industry, and pursue larger publicly traded clients.

First International Bank is a large, multinational bank that operates in 40 countries on four continents. First International Bank is the fifth largest bank in the world and engages in many specialized services besides banking, such as complex derivative offerings, mortgage-backed securities offerings, and reinsurance.

Required:

(a) List the characteristics of S&W's current structure and future plans that make First International Bank a desired audit client.

(b) What characteristics of S&W make First International Bank an undesirable audit client for the firm?

5-31   **[LO 1]** Assume the role of a member of the Audit Committee of the Board of Directors of a midsize, publicly traded company that has decided to ask for auditor proposals for the upcoming year's integrated audit.

Required:

List the steps the company should take when solicitin proposals for next year's audit, including information that might be included in the RFP.

5-32   **[LO 3]** Instead of a role on the audit committee, assume the role of a partner in a public accounting firm that is considering whether or not to propose on a company that recently issues an RFP.

Required:

(a) List the steps the auditing firm should take when deciding whether or not to propose to a potential client company.

(b) List the important considerations of the firm concerning its staff, industry expertise, and potential engagement profitability.

(c) What should the auditor investigate about the company?

5-33   **[LO 3]** Grandslam Co. operates the largest sports and entertainment business in the United States. Grandslam recently became one of the largest U.S. nonpublic corporations, was named number two on the Best Place to Work list, and was recently listed on the Most Ethical Company list. Grandslam's accounting department has never had negative publicity, nor has the company ever restated financial statements for any reason. As Grandslam Co. is growing fast, it has issued an RFP because the audit committee feels it requires a larger audit firm to fulfill its professional services needs.

At first glance, Jim, the managing partner of a midsize public accounting firm, thinks that Grandslam would be a great opportunity to expand his firm's portfolio of clients into the sports and entertainment industry. Furthermore, its clean accounting record suggests that Grandslam would be a low-risk client for the firm. Upon putting together his firm's proposal, Jim realizes that to fill the audit's needs, his firm would need to fly in an array of specialists and resources from around the country. This would create a significant cost that Grandslam would likely view unfavorably. Furthermore, there have been recent rumors that Grandslam is considering an IPO.

Required:

(a) Although Grandslam appears to be a great opportunity and low-risk client, what are some issues that would make the company an unfavorable potential client for Jim's firm?

(b) Why are the potential costs of staffing the audit significant? What are the business risks to Jim's firm?

(c) Why is the potential IPO significant to Jim's decision on the proposal?

5-34 **[LO 3]** Adrianna is an up-and-coming audit partner who specializes in health-care audits at Sterling Cooper, LLP, a rapidly growing midsize public accounting firm.

Adrianna's compensation is based partially on her client work and partially on her ability to bring new audit clients to the firm. In fact, the senior partners in her firm admitted Adrianna as a partner largely because she is a "rainmaker" for the firm. The firm has even set ambitious sales goals for the coming year that she is expected to meet.

Although the firm has limited resources and can only staff one new engagement in Adrianna's office for the year, Adrianna has a good chance of winning each of three engagements that are currently out for bid. Each engagement comes with different revenue potential and risks for Sterling Cooper.

Company 1 is a privately owned health-care operator that is considered a low risk to the firm and will result in a projected $300,000 profit for the firm. Company 2 is a small, publicly traded company that operates in the health-care and pharmaceutical sectors, is considered a medium risk to the firm, and is projected to result in a $700,000 profit for the firm. Finally, Company 3 is an international media conglomerate, is assessed as a high-risk client to the firm, and is projected at a $1.4 million profit for the firm.

Required:

(a) Set up a table with side-by-side columns listing the positives and negatives of each client.

(b) Is there any additional information you would like to have in selecting the company that Sterling Cooper should choose as a new client? If so, list it.

(c) Using the information you have, and different possibilities for the information you feel you are lacking, explain under which conditions you would or would not select each company as a client.

(d) Explain the trade-off between profitability and risk that you considered in your answer to (c).

5-35 **[LO 2, 3]** Williams 400 Company, a publicly traded company, recently issued an RFP for quarterly reviews and the annual audit. The company is generally perceived to be a desirable client and is expected to be extremely profitable for whichever firm lands the engagement. Shapiro, LLP, a public accounting firm, wishes to propose for the Williams 400 Co. engagement.

Required:

(a) What potential sources can Shapiro, LLP, utilize to gather information about the Williams 400 Company?

(b) After researching the company, what should Shapiro, LLP, consider concerning the staffing needs of the audit?

(c) If Shapiro, LLP, determines that Williams 400 Company falls within a suitable level of risk, and expected engagement profitability, and that the firm has sufficient staff to perform the engagement, what are the next steps in the client proposal-acceptance process?

5-36 **[LO 1, 2, 3]** Ellis & Jarrick, CPAs, received an RFP from the audit committee of the Board of Directors of Lunar Mills, Inc., to perform an audit of the company's financial statements for the year ended December 31, 2009. In connection with its client acceptance procedures, Ellis & Jarrick requested permission to meet with Lunar Mills's former auditors, Percy & Brice, LLP. Management and the Board of Directors of Lunar Mills refused to authorize such a meeting, saying that it would be a waste of time.

They further explained that their relationship with Percy & Brice had deteriorated significantly as a result of disagreements pertaining to their separation. They noted that the company and the former CPA firm ultimately agreed to "go their separate ways." The company believed that its former auditors were harboring feelings of ill will and would provide derogatory information if called upon by Ellis & Jarrick.

Required:

(a) What information should be obtained by an auditor during its inquiry of a predecessor auditor prior to accepting an audit engagement?

(b) How does the communication between predecessor and successor auditor impact the successor auditor's risk assessment?

(c) What are the ethical implications of Lunar Mills's refusal to authorize the meeting between auditors? How should Ellis & Jarrick respond to this situation?

5-37   **[LO 3]** Custiss & Branch, CPAs, is considering whether to propose performing the audit of BF Hemings Enterprises. The company is a large manufacturer of plumbing materials and hardware whose products are sold worldwide. Hemings is headquartered in the United States, and all of its manufacturing and warehousing properties are located in the United States; yet, it has a considerable market share in Germany, Austria, and Switzerland. Recently, the company acquired an Austrian company that provides marketing and promotion services. Management of BF Hemings Enterprises claims that the acquisition will enable the company to handle its own global marketing and promotion activities, and will also help it establish a stronger European presence.

Kelsee McCloud is an in-charge auditor who has been assigned to conduct additional background investigation for Custiss & Branch. As a result of a media search and analytical procedures, Kelsee learned the following:

- BF Hemings's major supplier is a firm that is 50% owned by Brock Hemings, founder and majority shareholder of BF Hemings Enterprises.
- The company's profit margin exceeds the industry average despite declines in cash flows from operations and inventory turnover.

BF Hemings stated that Custiss & Branch was being invited to propose on the engagement because of its experience at both performing integrated audits for publicly traded businesses and assisting companies that issued IPOs. BF Hemings is anticipating an IPO within the coming year.

Required:

Based on this case scenario, list and explain significant risk factors that will affect Custiss & Branch's decision regarding whether to propose on the engagement.

5-38   **[LO 4]** Camer & Associates, CPAs, received an RPF from the audit committee of Haspur Company's board of directors. Haspur is a midsized public company that fired its prior auditors due to scheduling issues. Haspur explained that the prior auditors did not handle many public company clients and were too slow in responding to the company's requests. Haspur indicated that the company needs to have an integrated audit for the fiscal year ended September 30, 2010 as well as assistance with the company's income tax return preparations. Jarrett Camer, CPA, knew that Haspur had a favorable reputation in the business community, as the company had been featured in a recent news article. Moreover, the engagement was determined to be a good fit for Camer's firm in terms of its industry expertise and timing of the engagement. In addition, Camer verified his independence from Haspur as well as that of his associates. As a result, Camer requested permission to meet with Haspur's predecessor auditors, bankers, and attorneys for the purpose of making the standard audit inquiries regarding new audit engagements. Hasper's audit committee agreed and authorized these parties to cooperate with the requests of Camer & Associates through their inquiries and responses.

After meeting with these parties, Camer & Associates determined that Haspur was a desirable client. Camer prepared an audit engagement letter and mailed it to Haspur's audit committee. This letter set forth the terms of the engagement, using the standard language. Supplemental language was included in the letter regarding the agreement for income tax assistance, involvement of the predecessor auditors, and fees and billing arrangements.

Required:

(a) List the standard matters that would be included in an engagement letter for the Haspur Company engagement.

(b) What are the benefits derived from preparing an engagement letter?

5-39   **[LO 1, 3, 5]** Sun Element Enterprises (SEE) is a manufacturer and retailer of patio furniture and outdoor accessories that sells its products throughout the Atlanta metropolitan area. The company operates one manufacturing facility and four retail outlets. Management of SEE invited Cames & Littler, CPAs, to participate in the proposal process for the company's financial statement audit for the year ended December 31, 2010.

Management of SEE invited Cames & Littler, CPAs, to participate in the proposal process for the company's financial statement audit for the year ended December 31, 2010.

John Hartigy, CPA, is an audit manager for Cames & Littler who performed the preliminary evaluation of SEE's business. John gathered information during a visit to SEE's company headquarters, where he took a tour of the manufacturing facilities and administrative offices, observed company personnel performing their duties, held discussions with client personnel, and reviewed certain accounting records and financial statements. Significant findings are as follows:

- SEE's sales revenues for the prior year were $3.7 million, and an increase of 8% is projected for the current year. Net assets are $15 million.

- SEE recently acquired a nursery and landscaping business that services customers in its same geographic region.

- Computer systems were outdated, but the company plans to implement a new, customized automated system.

- Perpetual inventory records are not currently maintained due to limitations of the computer system.

- Management indicates that there is no need for an audit committee or internal audit function due to the small size of the company. There are only two full-time employees in the accounting department.

- Management indicates that the prior auditors, Elwey & Makk, LLP, were dismissed because the company was disappointed with their lack of expertise related to the selection and implementation of an automated accounting information system. Elwey & Makk were not yet available for consultation.

- Management was not willing to divulge specific details pertaining to the company's internal controls until its new auditors were named, but indicated that the systems were strong.

Required:

(a) What initial considerations apply to an auditor's decision regarding a new client proposal?

(b) What is the significance of obtaining preliminary information prior to accepting a new audit engagement?

(c) Consider each of John's findings and determine how they will affect the audit engagement and whether they present significant concerns that may influence the firm's decision to accept this new audit client.

(d) Specifically consider whether the auditor should have any concerns regarding management integrity with this company. How will any concerns about management integrity and the related risk be balanced against the potential for revenue?

ACTIVITY ASSIGNMENTS

5-40 Access the SEC Web site and perform a search of company filings for a company you like or one that is located in your hometown. Review 8K forms. What types of information do you see reported in 8K forms? Do you see any reports of changes in auditors?

5-41 Pick a publicly traded company that you wonder about regarding its "reputation" (perhaps, adult magazine publishers, liquor manufacturers, gun manufacturers). Read its business description to see whether your perception of the company's business activities is accurate. Find the auditor's report, noting the name of the auditor. Summarize the company's business activities and indicate whether your perception prior to researching the company was accurate. List the auditor.

Ethics

5-42 Select a publicly traded cruise line and access its Web site (e.g., Carnival, Princess, Royal Caribbean). Read the information on fixed assets and determine where the company's ships are constructed and in what country the ships are registered. Based on your reading, is there a legitimate business purpose for the site of the construction?

5-43 Select a public company you know. Look for its annual report. (*Hint*: Try to go through the company's Web site. Look for something like investor relations.) Make a general list of what is included in the annual report.

5-44 Go to the AICPA Web site and find the Statements on Auditing Standards. Access the section on appointment of the independent auditor. Briefly outline the guidance and edit it to update it for an Integrated Audit.

5-45 Search news sources and locate 2 or 3 situations where auditors have "fired" their clients. What what was the reason for the separation?

PROFESSIONAL SIMULATION

Go to the book's companion Web site at www.wiley.com/college/hooks to find a simulation similar to those on the computerized CPA exam.

APPENDIX A: INDUSTRY DESCRIPTIONS

Throughout the chapter, discussion on client acceptance and continuance refers to auditors having appropriate professional competence and expertise to perform an audit engagement. Some of this discussion also references sufficient knowledge of the industry.

At the outset of any individual's auditing career it is unlikely that he or she will have a high level of knowledge in any particular industry. The exception is when auditing is a second career and the individual has already worked in the noted industry. The few "new entrants" to the auditing profession who have significant industry expertise are typically highly sought after in the job market. However, over time, as a result of training, experience, and continuing education, most auditors develop significant knowledge about one or more particular industries. This increased industry knowledge permits the auditor to contribute to the audit engagement based on a greater understanding of the industry environment, transactions, risks, and appropriate audit procedures.

If industry expertise is so valuable in the auditing world, should it be included in auditing curriculums? People have different answers to this question. No doubt, industry knowledge makes a new accounting graduate more valuable to an audit firm. But with the breadth of possible industries from which to choose, how do professors select the industry to teach, or the student the industry to study? The possibilities are endless, and it is an impractical and impossible goal to expect any real industry expertise to be passed on in the auditing classroom. However, what is possible is exposing students to a few

EXHIBIT A5-1

Examples of Industry Categories

Aerospace	Lodging
Airlines	Marinas
Airports	Medical devices
Automotive	Metals
Banking	Mining
Biotechnology	Motion pictures
Broadcasting	Music
Bus companies	Oil and gas
Cable television	Pharmaceuticals
Cargo shipping	Port operators
Chemicals	Professional sports
Computers	Publishing
Construction	Railroads
Convention centers	Real estate
Cruise lines	Real estate developers, owners, and
Defense	operators
Education	Real estate investment trusts (REITS)
Electric power	Restaurants
Electronics	Semiconductor and related industries
Engineering	Software
Food and beverage	Spas
Forest and paper	Sports facilities
Gaming	Sports teams
Government contracting	Timeshare and interval ownership
Governmental units	Technology
Health care	Telecommunications
Hospitality	Telecommunications and networking
Hospitals	Trucking
Industrial manufacturing	Universities
Insurance	Utilities
Investment management	Water

industries by tying industries to discussions of audits of transaction cycles and audit procedures. The purpose of this appendix is to provide that exposure.

Although gaining industry expertise is not contrary to gaining general business knowledge, one person cannot be an expert in all types of businesses. To illustrate this point, Exhibit A5-1 provides a list of fairly specific, though certainly not comprehensive, industry categories.

A close examination of Exhibit A5-1 suggests that any one of the business areas listed likely has many characteristics that are time consuming to learn and understand. Even though that may be true, many of these businesses are grouped together in broader categories. These broader categories are sometimes called market sectors. A sample of various market sector categories gleaned from the Web sites of the Big Four accounting firms is presented in Exhibit A5-2.

Trying to place the specific industries shown in Exhibit A5-1 into the broader market sectors presented in Exhibit A5-2 indicates that there are numerous possible categorizations and potential overlaps. Indeed, the Web sites of each of the Big Four reflect slightly different groupings.

Another way to classify businesses is by a general description of their primary activities. A fairly classic approach is to divide businesses into those that are manufacturers, distributors, and service providers. Some accounting classes teach students to recognize these broad categories based on the inventory accounts on a company's balance sheet. If a company has raw materials, work-in-process, and finished goods inventory accounts, it is classified as a manufacturer. If it has only a finished goods inventory account, it is considered

EXHIBIT A5-2

Examples of Broadly Described Market Sectors

Banking	Manufacturing:
Capital markets	*Aerospace*
Communications	*Consumer products*
Construction	*Defense*
Consumer	*Industrial*
Business	*Metals*
Products	*Paper*
Retail	*Technology*
Service	Media
Energy	Natural resources
Entertainment	Not-for-profit
Financial services	Public sector services
Government contracting	Real estate
Government entities	Regulatory authorities
Health care	Retail distribution
Hospitality	Technology
Industrial products	Telecommunications
Infrastructure operators	Tourism
Insurance	Transportation and logistics
Leisure industries	Wholesale distribution
Life sciences	

a distributor—wholesaler or retailer. A company with no inventory accounts is a service provider, or perhaps just a holding company. Exhibit A5-3 displays an example of the simple categorization that can result from these functional groupings.

Functional groupings are used in the classroom because they are simple. However, in the current complex business environment, groupings based on functional categories do not correspond sufficiently to most companies' business activities. An example of the difficulties with functional categories is exemplified with hospitals. Based on everyday knowledge, most people would classify hospitals as service providers. Yet large hospitals have such significant inventories that inventory is shown as a separate financial line item.

To display the difficulties with both functional and market sector classification, Exhibit A5-4 presents a few selected industries and groups them by both functional category and market segment. Many overlaps exist in just the partial analysis presented in the exhibit. For example, the food and beverage industry consists of manufacturing activities, retail and wholesale distribution activities, and service activities. The food and beverage industry provides products and services to the consumer segment, the industrial or business segment, and the hospitality and entertainment segment. Although it is not reflected in Exhibit A5-4, given that some foods are now being manufactured using biotechnological developments and packaged using new high-tech procedures, it might even be appropriate to list the food and beverage industry in the technology column.

Even with all the difficulties of teaching industry information, examples of the relationship of industry characteristics, risks, and audit procedures can be explained. A major

EXHIBIT A5-3

Examples by Functional Categories

Manufacturing	Distribution	Service
Automotive	Retail:	Airlines
Construction	Consumer products	Cruise lines
Defense industries	Industrial products	Hospitals
Food Products	Wholesale:	Hotels
	Consumer products	Universities
	Industrial products	

EXHIBIT A5-4

Samples of Industry Classifications

	Consumer Segment	Industrial and Business to Business	Technology	Hospitality and Entertainment
Manufacturing	Food and beverage Medical devices Forest and paper Motion pictures Construction Automotive	Food and beverage Medical devices Forest and paper Motion pictures Construction Biotechnology Defense Automotive	Medical devices Cable television Biotechnology Defense Airlines	Motion pictures Construction Cable television
Distribution	Food and beverage Medical devices Forest and paper Motion pictures Health care Cruise lines	Food and beverage Medical devices Forest and paper Motion pictures Health care Biotechnology Defense Airlines	Medical devices Health care Cable television Biotechnology Defense	Food and beverage Motion pictures Cable television Cruise lines
Service	Banking Food and beverage Health care Cruise lines Cargo shipping Airlines	Banking Food and beverage Cargo shipping	Cable television	Food and beverage Cable television Cruise lines

consideration for auditors is the risks of the business being audited. Therefore, auditors must understand the client's industry and the risks that are important or peculiar to that specific industry. Later chapters describe audit processes for particular transaction cycles and related accounts. Although all of the transaction cycles are important in most businesses, certain transaction cycles are more important in some industries than in others.

For example, the revenue cycle with billing and collection activities is very important to health-care providers such as hospitals. Billing for medical services is a very complicated process due to all the services that are provided, and to insurers and third-party payers that are billed. If an invoice is not prepared correctly, the insurance company or other payer will likely refuse to pay until it receives a proper invoice. A hospital's lack of an effective billing and collection cycle causes serious financial problems—even if it has plenty of patients and provides good medical care. The hospital might also overstate revenue if it does not carefully track discounts for which it has contracted with patients' insurance companies. Thus, in Chapter 10, which addresses the revenue cycle and related accounts, the health-care industry is used to exemplify the issues.

One transaction type that is less important in a hospital is cash sales. In contrast , retail businesses such as department and discount stores have lots of sales for cash. Since cash collection at the point of sale is an important part of the revenue cycle, the consumer retail industry is also used as an example in Chapter 10.

As an introduction to industry characteristics and their importance to auditors, this appendix provides a simple description of several broadly defined industries sometimes called market sectors. The discussion focuses on business activities, important transactions and financial statement accounts, management financial statement assertions associated with those accounts and transactions, and related ICFR. The management assertion for presentation and disclosure is not emphasized. The emphasis here is on the description of the business rather than GAAP or SEC accounting and disclosure requirements.

Manufacturing

Manufacturing is the business of making products and selling them to wholesalers or retailers, for ultimate resale to the final purchaser or consumer. This definition of the term does not envision differences between manufacturers and assemblers. The finished goods of either a manufacturer or an assembler can be the raw materials of the next assembler in the chain of production.

The manufacturing industry's important transactions include the purchase of raw materials to be used to manufacture inventory, the production of finished goods from raw materials, and the sale of finished goods to wholesale or retail distributors. The production of finished goods from raw materials includes tracking in-process inventory, and the process of tracing, allocating, and applying raw materials, labor, and overhead to inventory costs. Risks in the manufacturing industry include (1) proper physical and documentary controls over inventory as it moves through the manufacturing process, and (2) proper accumulation of cost amounts that are aggregated as the recorded amount of the inventory.

The accounts used for purchase transactions are raw materials inventories and accounts payable. The important management assertions are existence or occurrence, completeness, and rights and obligations. In other words, did the purchase occur so that the inventory exists? Are accounts payable posted so that liabilities, as shown, are complete? Does the company have rights to the recorded inventory and obligations for the recorded accounts payable?

Transactions are recorded as a result of moving items out of raw materials. In addition, inventory production transactions are recorded to labor, overhead, and finished goods accounts. The primary management assertions for these activities and transactions are existence or occurrence, completeness, and valuation or allocation. When a transaction was posted, had the event occured and was the inventory moved from stores? Were all the movement transactions, properly posted so that the inventory shown as raw materials and work in process actually exists? Is labor and overhead properly posted to the inventory account so that complete costs have been captured? Was overhead properly calculated so that it is allocated properly to the appropriate inventory and expense accounts?

For the balance sheet inventory accounts, existence or occurrence is the assertion with which the auditor is most concerned because of the need to properly capture, record, and aggregate the cost of manufacturing inventory.

Sales of finished goods involve the finished goods, sales, accounts receivable, and cost of sales accounts. The management assertions related to these accounts are also existence or occurrence, completeness, and rights and obligations. Did the sales occur? Was the cost of sales account posted properly so that the amount shown is complete? Does the company have rights to the inventory still shown in the accounts? Manufacturing entities have few sales for cash, so the primary audit risks for sales are that sales actually occurred and the related receivables are properly valued.

Certain controls are necessary to support proper accounting for the activities and related transactions of a manufacturing business. The process of receiving materials that have been ordered occurs in a central location. When raw materials (and any other items) are received, they are logged in on some type of receiving report. In the current business environment, receiving reports are usually computer based and perhaps automated.

The log of receipts is reconciled to both the accounts payable process before the bill for the goods is paid, and to the inventory "stores" or warehouse records that document the raw materials that are on hand. This enables the business to be sure that raw materials that are received actually make it into the supply of inventory available to be used for production. It also establishes a control so that the company only pays for items it has actually received. In addition, the reconciliation between goods received and invoices that are recorded as accounts payable supports management's completeness assertion that all accounts payable are shown on the financial records.

Good accounting for the manufacturing process is based on, or integrated with, a cost accounting system. Depending on the needs of the business and the sophistication of the IT system, dollars associated with production costs may be accumulated during the production process. Alternatively, the production process may simply keep track of units, with dollars per unit being added on later.

Costs of production include direct materials, labor, and overhead. This means that the controls must document movement of raw materials from stores to the factory floor. Labor must be accounted for not only for payroll purposes, but also in a manner that permits the costs of labor to be added to work in process. Direct labor is tracked based on hours—or through the use of a standard costing system. Indirect labor and other aspects of overhead are estimated and applied using some sort of an allocation system. Thus, for overhead, the management assertion of valuation or allocation focuses on the allocation aspect.

For recorded transactions of work-in-process and finished inventory to be correct, all these systems and controls must be established and functioning. Physical control and records are also required. Documentation that controls physical movement supports the posting of transactions when upon completion goods are moved from the manufacturing floor to finished goods storage.

Finally, the billing function requires accountability between shipment and sales. Goods are physically removed from finished goods storage and shipped. The shipment is documented in the shipping department. The billing department verifies that bills are sent to all purchasers to whom goods are shipped.

Even when physical controls and accounting recordkeeping are in place to track and record all the transactions, a periodic physical count of inventory is needed. This means that people, often assisted with computer and technical devices, physically count the raw materials, work-in-process, and finished goods inventory. The results of the count are compared to the accounting records. This process permits updating the accounting records to reflect the actual inventory the company owns, since the records become inaccurate due to errors, unrecorded damage, and theft.

Retailing

Retailing is the business of selling finished goods to consumers. Sales can occur between a manufacturer and a wholesaler before the product is sold to a retailer, but retailing generally refers to the final sale to the ultimate consumer. Traditionally, this activity was conducted mainly in stores and through catalogues. Recently, retailing has experienced growth in sales transacted over the Internet through e-commerce. E-commerce retail sales are made by businesses that also have traditional store locations, as well as by businesses whose only presence is on the Internet.

The most important transactions for retail businesses are their purchases of inventories and sale of those inventories to customers, including cash collections. Some retailers offer credit sales using their own credit-granting function. More often retailers accept the credit cards of banks or other credit-granting companies like American Express. Sales made via these credit cards are effectively cash sales for the retailer.

When inventories are purchased for resale by a retail entity, the accounts involved are inventory and accounts payable. When inventories are presented on the financial statement, the most important management assertions are that the inventories exist, are owned by the company (rights and obligations), and are shown at an appropriate value. The valuation assertion is critical because inventory is shown at lower of cost or market. When inventory is shown at cost, management is asserting that the value has not permanently dropped below the price at which it was purchased. Regarding the accounts payable account, important management assertions are completeness—that all accounts payable are shown—and valuation—that they are shown at the proper amount.

When goods are sold, the accounts involved are sales, cash, inventories, and cost of sales. Except for the cash account, these are the same accounts important in the sales phase of the manufacturing industry. The important management assertion for sales is occurrence—that the sales actually occurred and that they occurred in the period in which they are recorded. Regarding the cash involved in the sales transaction, the management assertion is that the company actually has (existence) and owns (rights) the cash.

Inventories and costs of sales entail assertions similar to those in the sales phase for a manufacturing entity. The inventory that is shown in the accounts and financial statements exists. All inventory is shown at the proper value, and the amounts that have been removed from inventory and added to cost of sales are at appropriate amounts.

Many of the activities, transactions, accounts, and assertions of the retail industry are similar to the purchasing and sales phases of manufacturing. However, several characteristics of retail establishments require a different control emphasis to ensure effective business function and proper financial records.

First, many sales are for cash. Sales that are not for cash are usually transacted with checks, debit cards, and credit cards. Cash requires a heightened level of physical control at the point of sale and after. The control objective is to immediately document the sale and cash receipt, and lock up the cash. Fortunately, cash terminals perform both of these functions quite well. The control that cash terminals provide is augmented by the customer's desire for a receipt. Strict control procedures are also necessary for moving the cash from the secure terminal to the bank at day's end.

For those transactions that involve checks, debit cards, and credit cards, physical security is not as important. The focus is on proper recording, approval, and authorization procedures. Retail vendors typically contract with other agencies, such as the debit or credit card provider, and check approval companies to approve these transactions at the time of the sale. This transfers the risk of nonpayment by the customer to those entities. Carrying out the approval steps required by the approving agency is critical. If the retail establishment's employees do not follow the required approval procedures, the transfer of risk is invalidated and the retail establishment is vulnerable to uncollectible accounts. In addition to following proper procedures at the point of sale, credit card charges are reconciled on a timely basis to deposits to the retailer's bank account. The retailer needs to follow up and verify that the credit card issuer pays the correct amount of cash for the credit sales.

A second area of risk that retail establishments encounter to a greater extent than manufacturing entities is physical control of inventories and theft prevention. Manufacturing environments are at risk of theft mainly from insiders. While retail establishments share this risk of employee theft, they are also at risk of theft by customers.

Various physical security measures, many electronic and high tech, are now used by retail establishments to limit theft. Regardless, no method is perfect. The risk of shrinkage heightens the need for periodic physical inventory counts to establish the actual inventory on hand and enable correction of the documents and records.

From an audit perspective, the concern is that inventory shown on the balance sheet exists. A related concern is that the amount recorded for inventory reflects proper valuation since GAAP requires inventory to be presented at lower of cost or market. The audit addresses the risk that the value of inventory has dropped below cost and is not properly reflected in the financial statements.

Sale of retail goods over the Internet adds another layer to the complexity of the retail industry. Internet sales are not limited to retail business as many business-to-business transactions are now Internet based. Even so, it is in the retail industry that Internet sales to a broad and unknown population of customer have flourished. E-commerce sales add the need for more controls over information security and credit approval. Further, e-commerce requires heightened controls over filling orders, shipping, billing, and collection. The use of e-commerce eliminates some of the traditional customer-provided checks on procedures.

Most additional controls necessitated by e-commerce are provided by information technology (IT) and are part of a complex IT environment. For example, before a sale is completed, electronic checks on availability of inventory and credit must be carried out. Sometimes this involves interface with an external security system (for example, a commonly known one is PayPal). Data input checks on delivery location must be completed. These are simple examples of the many additional technology requirements retail establishments must meet when they function in an e-commerce environment.

Health Care

Health care, as the term is used here, is limited to those who deliver health-care services, whereas other definitions of health care extend to insurers or third-party payers. The definition used in this description, however, includes only those that are in the business of caring for patients. Hospitals make up a large part of the health-care delivery industry and can be for profit or not-for-profit. Hospitals range from regional or community centers to large research and teaching institutions and federal facilities. Other health-care providers include long-term care facilities—often nursing homes, continuing care retirement communities (CCRCs)—and doctors.

The primary activities of health-care providers involve servicing patients. This utilizes labor such as nursing services, inventories such as medicines and supplies, and services such as laboratory tests and operating room use. Proper billing is critical in a health-care provider setting. Therefore, recording the transactions that capture the process of providing services is important. In effect, services provided that have yet to be billed is the "work-in-process" of a health-care provider. When the patient care process is complete, so is the "production of inventory." At that time the service is billed.

In addition to transactions that capture services provided, payroll transactions are important in a health-care setting. Hiring and paying skilled health-care laborers is of great importance. Other significant activities and transactions are purchasing supplies, controlling supplies through appropriate inventory accounts, and paying liabilities.

Accounts involved in providing services, billing, and collecting in the health-care industry are unbilled services, accounts receivable, allowances for contractual discounts, and allowances for uncollectible accounts. "Unbilled services" is the account through which medical services that have been provided to patients are captured until billing is appropriate.

Management assertions related to these accounts are existence or occurrence, completeness, and rights and obligations. Have the services actually been provided (existence or occurrence)? Are all services included in the billings (completeness)? Are all accounts receivables shown (completeness)? Does the hospital really have the right to the accounts receivable (rights and obligations)?

From an auditor's perspective, the greater concern for accounts receivable is that they are not overstated. The auditor's concern contrasts with the hospital management's primary concern that the accounts receivable account captures and reflects all the amounts owed to the hospital by patients and third-party payers.

The allowance for contractual discounts account is a critical account for health-care providers. It reflects the reduction in sales price for services provided to patients covered by specific insurers and third-party payers. The insurers and third-party payers are those with whom the health-care provider has entered into contractual agreements. The composition of this account is usually very complex because a health-care provider typically does business with a large number of third-party payers with different contractual arrangements. In addition, many services provided have different agreed-upon fees.

Consequently, for the contractual discounts account, as well as the allowance for uncollectibles account, management's assertion of valuation is important.

In a hospital, the control processes for services begin with patient charts. Data on unbilled services are captured using patient charts. Therefore, patient charts provide the primary support for the management assertion that transactions occurred.

The patient chart is the data-capture document on which each patient's medical status and services received are recorded. Patient charts are continuously updated by various departments such as surgery, radiology, pharmacy, and laboratory for inventory and services provided to the patient. Departments reconcile their records to patient charges, including use of physical goods such as medicines, radiology supplies, and laboratory and operating room supplies.

Another control mechanism that is in place at the point when a patient is admitted is verification of the patient's payment status. This is typically accomplished through contact with the third-party payer. Verification of insurance coverage relates to the management assertion that the receivables are appropriately valued because collectibility is determined in advance of providing the service.

The payroll expense account is material for health-care providers, including hospitals. Typical payroll assertions are vital, such as that the transaction occurred and the amount shown is complete. However, hospitals sometimes also use payroll costs as a basis for the standard cost amount they bill patients for services such as an overnight stay on a particular hospital floor, or the use of an operating room for a given number of hours. Although there is no direct link of payroll costs to the development of these "loaded billing rates" for specific services, reliable documentation is important.

From a quality perspective, many hospital employees are certified professionals, and hospitals obtain and verify their certifications. Regulatory controls may govern this compliance process.

Finally, similar to other service industries, many employees are required to "clock in" to their shifts via either time clocks or computer terminals. These time records are reconciled before payroll expense is recorded and payment is disbursed. For any unpaid payroll at year end, this reconciliation process relates to the management assertions of existence, completeness, and obligation of the payroll payable.

Hospitals and other health-care providers deal with complex tracking, contracts, and regulations that often require complex IT systems. Not only do various departmental inputs need to be integrated and reconciled, but the billing system must be correct and current regarding the specifics of the many contractual arrangements. Finally, numerous laws and regulations affect health-care providers, ranging from the professional certifications to control over certain types of medicine, and beyond. The Health Insurance Portability and Accountability Act (HIPAA), for example, requires health-care providers not only to collect various aspects of information about their patients, but also to guarantee the privacy protection of that information. Accuracy of patient and health-care provider activity information also relates to patient safety. Beyond the obvious importance that quality control related to this information has for human life, it also has financial implications for liabilities.

Banking

Banking is described here in a very narrow sense and excludes many aspects of financial institutions and financial services. Banking is the business of taking deposits from customers and, using those resources to make loans, earning revenue on the difference between the interest that is paid to depositors and received from debtors. In another form of this basic transaction, the loans are often sold to investors. Banking also involves receiving fees from customers for various services.

The business activities involved are accepting customer deposits, and approving and making loans to customers. The accounts involved are:

Cash

Liability for customer deposits

Interest payable

Loans receivable

Interest receivable

Allowance for doubtful accounts

An obvious management assertion is that cash said to be on hand exists and the bank has rights to it. Other management assertions for these accounts are that the deposit and loan transactions occurred, receivables for loans are a right of the company—and through use of the allowance for doubtful accounts are valued properly, liabilities for deposits are an obligation of the company, and interest accounts are valued properly showing rights and obligations.

Banking is a highly regulated entity; thus compliance with all applicable laws and regulations is critical to the fair presentation of its financial reporting. This reporting includes collecting and verifying required information such as address and social security or other identifying number when an account is opened. Another requirement is keeping sufficient cash on hand to meet reserve requirements. An issue that is vital to the lending aspect of the banking practice, and ultimately related to its regulatory environment, is analyzing the sufficiency of collateral in the loan-granting process. Sufficiency of collateral relates to the probability of collection on the loan and ultimately the valuation management assertion.

The amount of collateral on a loan affects the loan's risk of collection. From a big picture perspective, the risk of a bank's loan portfolio is related to the adequacy of its capital to protect depositors. If a bank cannot collect on its loans, and does not have rights to sufficient collateral to make up for any loan loss, then the bank must have sufficient earnings and capital accounts to absorb the losses. Otherwise the bank is unable to meet its obligations to its depositors.

In the United States, under most circumstances, the FDIC insures depositors against losses when a bank cannot meet deposit obligations. Although a bank's capital is composed of the same items as most businesses—for example, owners' investment and retained earnings—the bank and the adequacy of its capital must meet standards of "safety and soundness." To assure they meet the safety and soundness threshold, banks are subject to review by various regulatory authorities, dependent to some degree on whether the bank has a state or federal charter. Furthermore, the FDIC has an interest in the "safety and soundness" of the bank's operations and the adequacy of its capital to protect depositors. This regulatory environment makes operations, loan approval, and proper valuation of the loan portfolio critical areas to be examined during the audit.

In general, bank loan approval processes and requirements depend on the amount of the loan. The process includes using a standard application and standardized loan criteria. Often a loan committee, independent of the loan officer working with the transaction, must approve the loan. The collections department is responsible for following up on late payments. An allowance for uncollectible accounts is established based on these follow-up activities, as well as banking regulation requirements. Generally, a high-ranking bank officer approves all write-offs of loans receivable.

Because of the daily updates and calculations required and the prevalence of ATM terminals and Internet banking, it may seem that the IT systems for banks must be very complex. Although highly effective IT security and reliable functioning of the bank's computer systems are imperative to the bank's operations, the processes may be simpler than systems in other industries such as manufacturing and health care.

The IT system calculates interest payable on customer deposits and posts amounts to customer accounts. Monthly statements are sent to customers to enable their independent verification of account activity. The IT system also calculates interest receivable on outstanding loans and posts these to loan accounts. As with deposit accounts, monthly statements are sent to customers to enable their verification of account activity.

Service

In the current economic environment, a large percentage of U.S. businesses are classified as service industries. For example, health care and banking are classified as service businesses. The service businesses discussion here covers those entities other than health care and financial services whose primary activities do not involve manufacturing or selling inventory. Examples are airlines and university education. CPA firms and law firms fall within the service industry. Hotels, restaurants, and entertainment venues are also sometimes classified within the service industry. However, in this appendix they are considered separately in the hospitality market sector.

Service entities do not sell inventories; they sell services. Revenue and human resources transactions are important. A difference between sales transactions in a service business, when compared to, for example, retail or health care is that the payment is often collected in advance of the service. Air tickets are paid for prior to a flight. University tuition must be paid at some point during the semester, after the drop date and before the semester is completed. Thus, revenues and unearned revenues, as well as cash, accounts receivable, and allowance for doubtful accounts are important accounts for service industries.

Revenue recognition relates to management's assertion that a sale occurred. A parallel management assertion, important for sales transactions in the service industry, is completeness of the unearned service revenue liability account.

The date at which revenue is recognized and the unearned revenue liability is reduced depends on the business and its policies. For example, universities recognize revenue at the date when students can no longer drop a course with a refund. Typically, revenue for an airline ticket could be recognized when the flight is taken. However, if the ticket is not used, appropriate revenue recognition depends on whether the ticket can be returned for a full or partial refund or whether credit can be issued to be used at a later date.

Instead of inventory, payroll is a major cost in service industries. Typical of all payroll systems, the accounts involved are payroll expense, cash, payroll payable, and any amounts for withholdings from employee earnings. Management assertions associated with these transactions and accounts are existence or occurrence, completeness, rights and obligations, valuation, and allocation. A complexity regarding personnel expense in the service industry is often tracing specific employees' labor contributions to the client jobs they perform. For example, in an accounting or law practice, a client may be billed based on hours of input by employees at different billing rates.

From an audit perspective, an important factor is that payroll expense is appropriately calculated and recorded, and either paid or shown as a liability. Proper billing based on the capture of labor efforts by client personnel is also important to the billing process. Capturing labor efforts and assigning them to the jobs receiving the hours is akin to capturing direct labor for the work-in-process cycle of a manufacturer. Rather than being classified as inventory, unbilled labor in a service entity can be compared to unbilled services in a health-care environment. The integration of personnel and payroll transactions with billing, if done via computer, requires a sophisticated IT system to handle the process.

As with other industries, if sales are paid for using a means other than cash, check, debit card, or credit card, a collection department or function follows up on outstanding balances on a regular basis. The valuation assertion is important for the accounts receivable account. In professional services firms such as accounting or law practices, collection efforts may be the responsibility of the professional team.

Real Estate Development and Construction

Real estate development and construction as used here refers to businesses that acquire land for development, including the construction of residential and commercial buildings. Thus, land in the real estate and construction industry is inventory rather than a fixed asset. The developer may sell parcels of the land to others, who will ultimately construct buildings and sell the buildings and underlying land. Alternatively, the initial purchaser of the land—the developer—may construct the buildings and sell them to the ultimate consumer. The developer also contributes to the project by constructing or providing community infrastructure such as roads, access to utilities, and common areas. Engaging in retail land sales to the end consumers is not part of the definition as it is used here.

Significant transactions include (1) acquisition of the land for development, (2) accounting for project development and any construction performed by the developer, and (3) sale of completed projects. Usually, these activities require loans for either the purchase of land, construction, or both. The accounts associated with the purchase and construction transactions include "land held for development," notes payable, and construction-in-progress, which is an inventory account.

Management assertions most important to these transactions are:

Purchases and building processes occurred.

The company has obligations for the notes payable.

Notes payable shown are complete and reflect all the debt.

Inventory accounts are complete.

The construction-in-process account reflects proper valuations and allocations.

The percent that construction accounts are recorded as being complete is typically based on information received from the construction site on each item of inventory under construction. Final amounts are the result of an estimation process. The auditor views management's valuation assertion as an important risk area.

Construction loans are taken out in increments called draws. Draws are initiated based on progress report information supplied from the construction sites, again based on estimates of completion. Draws are approved by a company officer with the authority to enter into debt agreements. In addition to completeness, the rights and obligations management assertion is important for construction loans.

The underlying economic activity associated with recording development and construction transactions is analyzed because these projects are long term and require significant estimates. For example, as mentioned earlier, recording the progress on specific construction is based on information conveyed from the job site. Infrastructure costs for roads and common areas usually need to be allocated (valuation and allocation assertion) and matched against revenue (existence or occurrence assertion) from the sale of parcels of land or completed buildings.

Revenue may be recognized using one of several accounting principles. The accounting principle selected must be appropriate for the nature of the sales contract. Often, revenue recognition needs to appropriately reflect the stage of the project's completion. GAAP specifies that the amount of revenue that can properly be recognized is always related to the certainty of the payment to be collected. Thus, risk is related to management's valuation, and rights and obligations assertions.

The accounts used to account for sales are fairly typical, including revenue, costs of sales and inventory. Depending on the financing associated with the sale, either cash or some type of receivable account is also used. The assertions for sales in this industry are those that are typical for sales transactions generally: existence, occurrence, completeness, rights, and valuation.

An overarching complication in the real estate and construction industry is that many of the agreements upon which estimates, allocations, and revenue recognition are based are contractual. A thorough understanding of the contracts is required before economic activity can be properly valued or allocated, and transactions recorded.

Hospitality

Hospitality is a market sector that is described in a variety of ways. Sometimes hospitality is grouped with real estate. Sometimes it is labeled hospitality and leisure. Yet another categorization is hospitality and entertainment. The description used in this appendix includes lodging—basically hotels, restaurants, and entertainment venues—such as cruise ships and theme parks. You may question including the cruise industry as an entertainment venue, but cruise ships are basically a combination of hotels, restaurants, bars, casinos, theater, movies, and so on. The grouping of lodging, restaurant, and entertainment venue industries under the label of hospitality was intentional because each of these industries represents a hybrid of other business categories.

Hotels provide temporary lodging and, therefore may be classified as a service industry. In common with service industries, hotels do not sell a product that the customer can take home. They charge for the service provided in advance (when the customer checks in), whether or not the customer stays the night.

Alternatively, from the hotel's perspective, although it does not have an inventory account on its balance sheet, it is in the business of selling a product. A hotel's business is to sell a product called a hotel room. On a given night, the hotel has an inventory of rooms, some of which are sold and some of which may remain unsold. At the end of the night the inventory of unused hotel rooms for that night has no value. For the management assertion regarding the occurrence of the sale of hotel rooms, the auditor can perform an analytical procedure based on the average number of rooms sold per night times the average price at which rooms are sold. This audit procedure is similar to one that might be performed for inventory reasonableness in a manufacturing or retail environment.

An added layer of industry complexity is that hotels are often composed of two businesses—the hotel property, meaning the land and building, and the hotel management association that runs the business. In auditing the hotel property, the primary asset is the land and building. Debt is associated with those assets.

The management company's revenue is an expense of the hotel property owner and is usually a commission and contingent fee arrangement. The hotel has revenue from the sale of the service of providing hotel rooms. Expenses include payments to the management company, payroll expenses, and various expenses related to running the hotel. Expenses range from paying the electricity bill to providing grounds maintenance. Hotel management companies may manage the restaurants in the hotel properties.

Restaurants are also hybrid industries in that they provide both a service and a product. Clearly, meals are the product, and preparing and delivering the meals is the service. Restaurants can take many organizational forms. They can be individual locations, or they may be franchises. Franchise arrangements vary significantly, and the details of the franchise contract affect the accounts of the business, management assertions, and necessary audit steps. The owner(s) may own or lease the land. Even if the restaurant owners do not own the land, they may have significant fixed asset investments in the property via leasehold improvements.

Beyond these possibilities, restaurants have fairly similar operations. Restaurants purchase food items and other supplies. They add labor and overhead to transform the food items into meals and ultimately sell the meals. Although this sounds a lot like a manufacturing process, restaurants generally do not consider meals to be "finished goods inventory." Some entities, for example McDonald's, have major raw materials tracking systems related to the production of their food items, but these are used for cost control and operating productivity analysis.

Sales are for meals, whereas costs of sales generally are food and supplies purchases. Some items, typically liquor and frozen foods, may be shown as inventory on the balance sheet, while other less expensive and perishable items may be expensed. Other expenses are payroll and those typically required for running a business. Management assertions, again, are typical: sales that are recorded actually occurred; any food items and supplies that are on hand and shown as inventory actually exist and are valued properly; cash exists and the company has rights to the cash; liabilities such as accounts payable are complete and shown at proper amounts.

Controls applicable to the restaurant industry include (1) controls over the inventory receiving process similar to those of a manufacturer or retailer, (2) cash and credit card controls at point of sale for a retailer, and (3) personnel and payroll controls of a service or retail business.

Entertainment venues combine a variety of business activities. For example, theme parks and cruise lines share the service industry characteristic of collecting fees for entry in advance. The timing of revenue recognition depends on the commitments that go along with the ticket purchase. If the theme park has to close for technical difficulties or bad weather, the ticket purchaser may be entitled to another day at the park. Cruise ships initially record a liability for unearned revenue when they receive payment for a cruise, and recognize the revenue at some point during or at the completion of the cruise. Both theme parks and cruise ships include at least two other types of businesses that generate revenue: restaurants and retail sales. In addition, cruise ships sell lodging for a specified period of days during the cruise. The accounts used, management assertions, and business controls are those required of the separate entities already discussed.

An additional component of entertainment venues, only briefly touched upon when referring to hotel properties, is property, plant and equipment or fixed assets, and related debt. Management assertions are that the assets are shown at proper amounts, the company has rights to them, and any allocation required such as depreciation is appropriate. Management assertions related to debt accounts such as notes payable and mortgages payable are that the obligations exist, all the obligations are shown (completeness), and any allocations such as effective interest calculations are proper.

Conclusion

Different types of businesses and industries have accounts and transactions that reflect the business activities. Differences in major financial statement accounts and transactions drive differences in the management assertions that are most important, resulting in different focuses of ICFR. Similarly, the auditor plans and performs audit procedures to focus on the important risks of the different industries related to the management financial statement assertions. This need to focus on differing risks is behind the need for auditors to possess significant industry knowledge.

REVIEW QUESTIONS

Identify the most important accounts, management assertions, and risks for each of the following industries:

H.1 manufacturing

H.2 retailing

H.3 health care

H.4 banking

H.5 service

H.6 real estate development and construction

H.7 hospitality

PROBLEM

5-46   Create a table, and for each industry discussed provide the following information:

(a) List the primary business activity.

(b) Identify the most significant risk about which the auditor is concerned.

(c) What accounts and related management assertions are related to the risk?

(d) What could happen to cause the account or disclosure to be materially misstated related to the assertions you identified?

(e) What control could management implement to prevent or detect the event that would cause the material misstatement?

APPENDIX B: AUDIT COMMITTEES AND CORPORATE GOVERNANCE

An audit committee is a subset of a company's Board of Directors. Members of the audit committee are also members of the Board. Although the audit committee is one of many Board committees, it is a very important one. The audit committee not only contributes to the governance of the company, but also helps meet the expectations of outsiders for strong corporate oversight. The responsibilities assumed by audit committees are significant. This was the case even before SOX, but audit committee responsibilities are even more important in the post-SOX era. Regulators and others rely on audit committees to monitor and help direct a company's system of corporate governance.

SOX, Section 205(58)(A) defines an audit committee as:

> a committee (or equivalent body) established by and amongst the board of directors of an issuer for the purpose of overseeing the accounting and financial reporting processes of the issuer and audits of the financial statements of the issuer.

In this definition, a company that has publicly traded equity or debt securities is called an issuer. SOX goes on to state that if the company does not have an audit committee, the entire Board of Directors serves as the audit committee. In AICPA auditing standards the phrase "those charged with governance" includes the Board of Directors and audit committee (AICPA AU 380).

Although a nonpublic company may not have a formal audit committee, all companies traded on the New York Stock Exchange have an audit committee as a prerequisite for listing. New York Stock Exchange requirements, Section 803 B(2) states the following:

a. Each issuer must have, and certify that it has and will continue to have, an audit committee of at least three members, each of whom:
  i. satisfies the independence standards specified…
  ii. must not have participated in the preparation of the financial statements of the issuer or any current subsidiary of the issuer at any time during the past three years; and
  iii. is able to read and understand fundamental financial statements, including a company's balance sheet, income statement, and cash flow statement. Additionally, each issuer must certify that it has, and will continue to have, at least one member of the audit committee who is financially sophisticated.

Exceptions exist that allow one member of the audit committee to lack independence under certain criteria and that permit audit committees of smaller companies to be made up of only two members.

The Value of Audit Committees

SOX introduced requirements that clearly increase the importance of audit committees to corporate governance. However, the value of audit committees was recognized much earlier. An important milestone in the history of audit committees was the *Blue Ribbon Committee on Improving the Effectiveness of Corporate Audit Committees.* The next Auditing in Action box provides excerpts from an SEC press release on September 28, 1998 announcing the Blue Ribbon panel. In February 1999 the Blue Ribbon panel released recommendations on the requirements and composition of audit committees and various audit committee-related communications.

AUDITING IN ACTION

Blue Ribbon Panel on Audit Committees

New York, NY, September 28, 1998—The Securities and Exchange Commission, the New York Stock Exchange and the National Association of Securities Dealers are pleased to announce that the NYSE and NASD will sponsor a "blue-ribbon" panel drawn from the various constituencies of the financial community to make recommendations on strengthening the role of audit committees in overseeing the corporate financial reporting process. This action was taken in response to recent concerns expressed by SEC Chairman Arthur Levitt about the adequacy of the oversight of the audit process by independent corporate directors.

The panel of eleven members ... will undertake an intensive study of the effectiveness of audit committees in discharging their oversight responsibilities and ... make concrete recommendations for improvement.

Chairman Arthur Levitt, who delivered a major address on the state of financial reporting on Monday at New York University, praised the actions of the NYSE and the NASD, saying, "The swiftness of their response indicates the type of financial community leadership we need to keep the American capital markets the deepest, most liquid in the world. I am confident that this group will produce tangible recommendations for improving audit committee oversight of the financial reporting process."

Since the time of the Blue Ribbon Panel, multiple requirements related to audit committees have been put in place. The New York Stock Exchange, SOX, SEC, PCAOB, and AICPA have all produced requirements. The requirements reflect a belief that audit committees are vital to the corporate governance that protects the public interest.

Audit committees provide a counterbalance to the powers held by management because they are specifically charged with understanding and oversight of the financial workings of the company. Furthermore, audit committees have specific responsibilities related to the auditor. The relationship and interactions between the audit committee and outside auditor strengthens each of them, permitting them to contribute to the company's honest financial governance and reporting.

Composition of Audit Committees

The New York Stock Exchange requires audit committees to have at least three members who must be independent. (As stated earlier, there are limited exceptions.) This differs from the requirements for Board of Directors membership, since directors are not required to be independent. SOX sets criteria for independence that have been implemented through SEC requirements (SEC Release Nos. 33-8220; 34-47654). The SEC requirements are also referenced by the New York Stock Exchange in its rules. The SOX independence requirements state that an audit committee member cannot be affiliated with the company or any of its subsidiaries. Furthermore, audit committee members cannot be compensated by the company for any activities except their participation on the Board of Directors, audit committee, and any other Board committees. The SEC rule reflects the substance of the SOX requirement.

Audit committees are also expected to have at least one member who is a financial expert. The SEC rule that became effective in March 2003 implements SOX and requires companies to disclose if they have at least one "audit committee financial expert" serving on the audit committee. The company must also disclose the name of the expert and state that the expert is independent of management. If a company does not have an audit committee member who qualifies as a financial expert, it must disclose this fact and explain why.

AUDITING IN ACTION

SEC Definition of Audit Committee Financial Expert

An audit committee financial expert [i]s a person who has the following attributes:

- An understanding of generally accepted accounting principles and financial statements;
- The ability to assess the general application of such principles in connection with the accounting for estimates, accruals and reserves;
- Experience preparing, auditing, analyzing or evaluating financial statements that present a breadth and level of complexity of accounting issues that are generally comparable to the breadth and complexity of issues that can reasonably be expected to be raised by the registrant's financial statements, or experience actively supervising one or more persons engaged in such activities;
- An understanding of internal controls and procedures for financial reporting; and
- An understanding of audit committee functions.

A person must have acquired such attributes through any one or more of the following:

1. Education and experience as a principal financial officer, principal accounting officer, controller, public accountant or auditor or experience in one or more positions that involve the performance of similar functions;
2. Experience actively supervising a principal financial officer, principal accounting officer, controller, public accountant, auditor or person performing similar functions;
3. Experience overseeing or assessing the performance of companies or public accountants with respect to the preparation, auditing or evaluation of financial statements; or
4. Other relevant experience.

(Item 401(h)(2) of Regulation S-K, Item 401(e)(2) of Regulation S-B, Item 16A(b) of Form 20-F, and paragraph (8)(b) of General Instruction B to Form 40-F)

Audit Committee Charter

The requirements for New York Stock Exchange listing go beyond simply requiring a company to have an audit committee of a certain size and with members of specific qualifications. Every listed company's audit committee is also required to have a formal, written charter. The charter describes the audit committee's responsibilities, including oversight of the accounting and reporting processes and interacting with the independent auditor.

Responsibilities of Audit Committees

Audit committees fulfill responsibilities defined by SOX and the stock exchanges. The stock exchange requirements are enforced through requirements for listed companies and, as with other listing requirements, mesh with the SEC's rules. Responsibilities of audit committees, as set forth by the New York Stock Exchange, include the following:

- Meet on a regular basis, usually at least quarterly.
- Receive and handle complaints related to accounting, ICFR, and auditing issues.

AUDITING IN ACTION

NYSE Requirements for Audit Committee Charters

NYSE Section 803 B. (1) Charter
Each issuer must certify that it has adopted a formal written audit committee charter and that the audit committee has reviewed and reassessed the adequacy of the formal written charter on an annual basis. The charter must specify the following:

a. the scope of the audit committee's responsibilities, and how it carries out those responsibilities, including structure, processes, and membership requirements;

b. the audit committee's responsibility for ensuring its receipt from the outside auditors of a formal written statement delineating all relationships between the auditor and the issuer … and the audit committee's responsibility for actively engaging in a dialogue with the auditor with respect to any disclosed relationships or services that may impact the objectivity and independence of the auditor and for taking, or recommending that the full board take appropriate action to oversee the independence of the outside auditor;

c. the audit committee's purpose of overseeing the accounting and financial reporting processes of the issuer and the audits of the financial statements of the issuer; and

d. the specific audit committee responsibilities and authority.

SOX Section 301 creates statutory responsibility for audit committees and their interaction with companies' independent auditors. Section 301 requires that the audit committee appoint the company's independent auditor, set the compensation that the company pays to the auditor, and oversee the work of the auditor. The oversight function includes resolving any disagreements that arise between auditors and management on financial report issues.

Part of the oversight responsibility of the audit committee extends to approving in advance all work the auditor performs for the company. The preapproval requirement exists for audit and nonaudit work. Approval for audit work is provided because the audit committee selects the auditor and authorizes the audit fee. Auditors can perform very limited nonaudit services for public companies and still remain independent. If there are any nonaudit services provided to the company by the auditor, they also must be preapproved by the audit committee.

In addition to hiring, compensating, and overseeing the company's independent auditor relationship, the audit committee has other responsibilities imposed by SOX. SOX Section 301(4) requires that the audit committee have procedures for receiving and handling complaints about accounting, internal control, and auditing matters. As stated above, these requirements for these responsibilities are in place through SEC and stock exchange rules. Besides having procedures for receiving any complaints regarding accounting, auditing, and internal control, the audit committee must be able to receive and deal with confidential and anonymous complaints submitted by employees. Many audit committees outsource this function

AUDITING IN ACTION

SOX Section 301—Public Company Audit Committees

(m)(2) Responsibilities Relating to Registered Public Accounting Firms

The audit committee of each issuer, in its capacity as a committee of the board of directors shall be directly responsible for the appointment, compensation, and oversight of the work of any registered public accounting firm employed by that issuer (including resolution of disagreements between management and the auditor regarding financial reporting) for the purpose of preparing or issuing an audit report or related work, and each such registered public accounting firm shall report directly to the audit committee.

to services that provide hot line telephone numbers for complaints. The audit committee responsibility goes beyond just receiving complaints and extends to responding to them.

Reports to Audit Committees

The audit committee is aided in fulfilling its responsibility of overseeing the financial reporting and audit function through numerous communications that others are required to submit. These required communications come from the company, the auditor, and even from attorneys. The SOX required communications are developed further by rules of the SEC and standards of the PCAOB. The AICPA requires auditors of nonpublic companies to communicate with audit committees or those responsible for governance. The communications of auditors are similar under PCAOB and AICPA standards, although PCAOB standards include communications related to the ICFR audit.

SOX Section 302(a)(5) requires companies to include reports in their SEC filings that are often called *302 certifications*. These reports include among other statements that:

> the signing officers have disclosed to the issuer's auditors and the audit committee of the board of directors…all significant deficiencies in the design or operation of internal controls which could adversely affect the issuer's ability to record, process, summarize and report financial data and have identified for the issuer's auditors any material weaknesses in internal controls, and any fraud whether or not material that involves management or other employees who have a significant role in the issuer's internal controls.

SOX Section 204 (k) requires the auditor to communicate to the audit committee:

1. all critical accounting policies and practices to be used;
2. all alternative treatments of financial information within generally accepted accounting principles that have been discussed with management officials of the issuer, ramifications of the use of such alternative disclosures and treatments, and the treatment preferred by the registered public accounting firm; and
3. other material written communications between the registered public accounting firm and the management of the issuer, such as any management letter or schedule of unadjusted differences.

In addition, the PCAOB rules on independence require the auditor to communicate with the audit committee about the firm's independence. The communication occurs before accepting a first-time engagement and annually on a recurring audit. These communications from the auditor help the audit committee fulfill its fiduciary oversight responsibilities.

Auditing standards also require communications by the auditor to the audit committee (PCAOB AU 380, AICPA AU 380, AS 5). These are a standard part of all audits and are discussed in Chapter 11. The communication includes significant findings from the audit and adjustments made to the financial statements. The auditor also tells the audit committee about any significant or unexpected problems experienced in completing the audit and any disagreements with management.

SOX Section 307 provides direction regarding required communications to audit committees from attorneys. If attorneys learn that the company may be involved with material violations of securities laws or breaches of fiduciary duty, they first report it to the company's chief legal counsel or chief executive officer. If the reporting attorney is unsatisfied with the response, a further report is made. The audit committee is listed as one potential recipient of the second report. The apparent reason behind the audit committee as a recipient is because the audit committee is composed of independent directors. Other possible recipients of the second communication can be other Board committees composed entirely of independent directors or the full Board of Directors.

Conclusion

Audit committees play a vital role in the oversight of public companies. The requirement that audit committees be independent, coupled with the expectation that they have at least one member meeting the qualifications of an audit committee financial expert, positions audit committees to be able to understand and objectively evaluate their companies' financial issues. The audit committee's responsibilities for involvement with the auditor and oversight of the company's audit provide the auditor with a direct line to a powerful and knowledgeable party outside of management. Access to the audit committee provides the auditor with the ability to verify that those responsible for the company really understand the company's accounting, controls, and financial situation.

PROBLEM

5-47. As a result of the Sarbanes-Oxley Act of 2002, much greater emphasis has been placed on audit committees and their responsibilities than was the case in the past. Public companies are required to have an audit committee as a subset of its Board of Directors. Thus, the presence of audit committees has become more widespread, and their roles have increased significantly. Accordingly, auditing firms for public companies have become more involved with their clients' audit committees.

Required:

(a) What is an audit committee?

(b) Why are audit committees formed, and what function do they serve?

(c) What are an auditor's responsibilities with regard to communicating with the client company's audit committee?

PROFESSIONAL SIMULATION

Go to the book's companion Web site at www.wiley.com/college/hooks to find a simulation similar to those on the computerized CPA exam.

CHAPTER **6**

Audit Planning and Risk Assessment

1. Learn the steps of the planning process for an integrated audit.
2. Become familiar with the components that impact the audit strategy and audit plan.
3. Understand the relationship of risk assessment, materiality, and planning.
4. Define the Fraud Triangle and recognize fraud risk factors.
5. Identify triggers for reevaluating the audit strategy and audit plan.
6. Summarize important information that is documented as part of audit planning.
7. Identify changes that can be made to audit approaches for higher risk areas.
8. Explain different types of audit activities and their purposes.

Chapter 6 Resources

AU 110, AICPA, PCAOB, Responsibilities and Functions of the Independent Auditor

AU 150, AICPA, PCAOB *Generally Accepted Auditing Standards*

AU 311, AICPA, PCAOB, *Planning and Supervision*

AU 312, AICPA, PCAOB, *Audit Risk and Materiality in Conducting an Audit*

AU 314, AICPA, *Understanding the Entity and Its Environment and Assessing the Risks of Material Misstatement*

AU 315, AICPA, PCAOB, *Communications between Predecessor and Successor Auditors*

AU 316, AICPA, PCAOB, *Consideration of Fraud in a Financial Statement Audit*

AU 317, AICPA, PCAOB, *Illegal Acts by Clients*

AU 318, AICPA, *Performing Audit Procedures in Response to Assessed Risks and Evaluating the Audit Evidence Obtained*

AU 319, PCAOB, *Consideration of Internal Control in a Financial Statement Audit*

AU 322, AICPA, PCAOB, *The Auditor's Consideration of the Internal Audit Function in an Audit of Financial Statements*

AU 324, AICPA, PCAOB, *Service Organizations*

AU 326, AICPA, *Audit Evidence*

AU 326, PCAOB, *Evidential Matter*

AU 329, AICPA, PCAOB, *Analytical Procedures*

AU 330, AICPA, PCAOB, *The Confirmation Process*

AU 334, AICPA, PCAOB, *Related Parties*

AU 336, AICPA, PCAOB, *Using the Work of a Specialist*

AU 341, AICPA, PCAOB, *The Auditor's Consideration of an Entity's Ability to Continue as a Going Concern*

AU 342, AICPA, PCAOB, *Auditing Accounting Estimates*

AU 350, AICPA, PCAOB, *Audit Sampling*

AU 543, AICPA, PCAOB, *Part of Audit Performed by Other Independent Auditors*

AU 722, PCAOB, *Interim Financial Information*

FASB Concepts Statement No. 2, *Qualitative Characteristics of Accounting Information*

Office of Management and Budget, Circular A-133, *Audits of States, Local Governments, and Nonprofit Organizations*

PCAOB AS 5, *An Audit of Internal Control Over Financial Reporting That Is Integrated with an Audit of Financial Statements*

Sarbanes-Oxley Act of 2002

United States Government Accountability Office, *Government Auditing Standards*

INTRODUCTION

An integrated audit is made up of an audit of internal control over financial reporting (ICFR) and an audit of the financial statements. ICFR and financial statement audits have different objectives, but are planned and carried out as one engagement. The planning process designs the audit work to meet the objectives of both audits and integrates the work as much as possible. AS 5.7 states that the auditor's procedures in an ICFR audit should be designed to obtain sufficient evidence to support the auditor's

1. opinion on internal control over financial reporting as of year end, and
2. control risk assessment for purposes of the audit of the financial statements.

The integrated audit planning process designs the ICFR audit procedures, substantive financial statement audit procedures, and "wrap-up" processes for the integrated audit. Collecting and analyzing information used for planning the audit begins during the process of deciding whether to accept a new audit client or continue to provide audit services to an existing client, which was covered in Chapter 5. More information is obtained as the terms of the engagement are agreed upon between the client and the auditor. This chapter discusses planning the audit and the risk assessment that is an integral part of planning. Exhibit 6-1 presents an overview of audit planning and risk assessment.

OVERVIEW OF THE PLANNING AND RISK ASSESSMENT PROCESS [LO 1]

This book presents audit planning as a series of discrete topics and activities. However, audit planning is actually a continuous process that occurs throughout the engagement. Planning

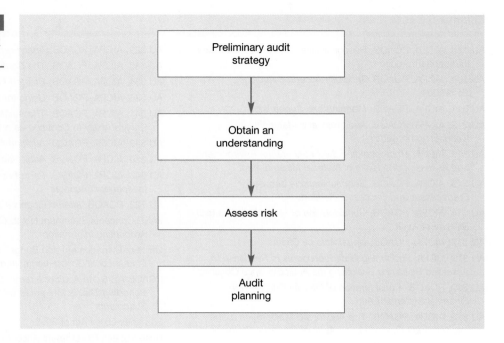

is revisited when new audit information indicates that the auditor may need to revise steps or change assumptions. Often the iterative process is needed because "disconfirming" information arises. Disconfirming information is anything that contradicts the auditor's prior understanding or assumptions. For instance, new information can indicate that risks are greater than the auditor thought they were when the original audit plan was drafted. Another example is that the audit plan might need to be revisited if an area of the company's activities turns out to be larger or more complex than originally expected.

Planning is not always a set of activities that are completely separated from each other or from other audit work. Aspects of client acceptance and continuance, developing the audit strategy, and designing the audit plan often are based on the same information and can take place concurrently. Once the auditor knows that an engagement is going to take place and needs to be planned, the work begins.

The first step in audit planning is developing the **audit strategy**. Generally, this includes identifying the **scope of the engagement** and establishing the timing of the work. Scoping the engagement means specifying the work that has to be performed and when it must be done. Scope of the engagement relates directly to the reports or other products contracted for in the engagement letter. The audit strategy also defines initial estimates of the risk and materiality levels for the engagement.

The next step is to identify and plan for the **audit resources** needed. In an audit context the resources needed are people. Planning the resources involves identifying the specific auditor skill levels and hours, and even the specific people needed on the engagement to complete the work.

An audit plan is the next planning output. The audit plan includes specific tasks to be accomplished by the audit team. The audit strategy lays out the "big picture," and the audit plan documents detailed information about audit procedures to be performed. The audit plan also provides guidance to each member of the audit team on what he or she is supposed to do.

Risk assessment is integrated throughout the planning process. Risk assessment points the auditor to the important areas of the client's operations and financial statements and identifies what may go wrong. Identifying important areas and potential problems enables the auditor to determine what needs to be accomplished during the audit. The audit strategy and audit plan lay out how to accomplish those audit objectives.

REVIEW QUESTIONS

A.1 What is the purpose of evidence collected during an ICFR audit?

A.2 When does the collection of information that is used for the planning process begin? When does it end?

A.3 What are some reasons why the original strategy and plan for an integrated audit may need to be modified?

A.4 What is involved in developing the audit strategy?

A.5 Why does the audit firm have to plan the audit resources needed for an audit engagement?

A.6 What is an audit plan?

A.7 What is accomplished by risk assessment during planning?

ESTABLISHING THE OVERALL AUDIT STRATEGY [LO 2]

As stated earlier, the audit strategy can be viewed as the "big picture" for the audit. Sometimes it is difficult for students to understand how the audit team can do any planning when they have not yet begun any substantial work on the client engagement. The answer to this puzzling concept is that the auditors working on the planning process have experience doing audits.

Even though the audit team may not know all the specific information about a particular client company, experienced auditors know the general framework of what has to be done on any audit. An auditor experienced in the client's industry also understands the activities and risks of businesses in the industry. This experience gives the auditor an understanding of the material financial statement accounts and important ICFR areas for those accounts. In addition, the auditor has actually gained quite a bit of client-specific information during the processes of accepting the client and executing the engagement letter. The audit team uses this knowledge base to begin planning, with an understanding and expectation that revisions may be needed as the audit progresses.

Scope of the Engagement

In establishing the overall audit strategy the auditor considers the scope of the engagement. Scope of the engagement describes how much and what type of work the auditor needs to do, and when and where the work is done. A related term that AS 5 uses is *scaling* the audit, which means to fit the audit work needed to the size, environment, and complexity of the company.

Another term that is often used in determining the scope of the engagement is **deliverables**. In this context, deliverables is a term referring to those products and services the audit firm has contracted (in the engagement letter) to provide to the client. For example, in conjunction with an engagement to perform an integrated audit of a public company, the auditor is engaged to perform reviews of quarterly financial statements that must be filed with the SEC. The timing of the work performed on the quarterly financial statements and the information obtained through that work may affect the work scheduled for the annual integrated audit. The services that can be provided without violating independence are quite limited. Even so, if the audit firm provides other services to the client, any impact these services may have on the audit engagement are also considered.

Accounting Presentation

The scope of the engagement is affected by the way the client's accounting information is presented. For example, historically, most public corporations have presented their financial statements in accordance with U.S. GAAP. As regulatory requirements change, however, the basis of accounting may change. The current move is toward international accounting standards.

State and local government entities present their financial information using standards set by the Government Accounting Standards Board (GASB). Units of the federal government use a different set of standards that is GAAP for the U.S. government. Clients in certain industries may have to provide information that is specifically required by the industry regulator. Sometimes **statutory audits** must be performed in conjunction with the integrated audit. An example of such an audit is one governed by the Office of Management and Budget (OMB) Circular A-133, *Audits of States, Local Governments, and Non-Profit Organizations*. All of these reporting characteristics and requirements affect the auditor's work and therefore must be considered during planning. Exhibit 6-2 presents an audit report for a not-for-profit organization. Government Auditing Standards and OMB Circular A-133 are referenced in the audit report.

EXHIBIT 6-2

An Audit Report of a Not-for-Profit Organization

REPORT OF INDEPENDENT CERTIFIED PUBLIC ACCOUNTANTS
Board of Directors
Important Not-for-profit Organization, Inc.
Anywhere, Any State

We have audited the accompanying statements of financial position of Important Not-for-profit Organization, Inc. (the INO), as of June 30, 2010 and 2009 and the related statements of activities, cash flows and functional expenses for the years then ended. These financial statements are the responsibility of the INO's management. Our responsibility is to express an opinion on theses financial statements based on our audits.

We conducted our audits in accordance with auditing standards generally accepted in the United States of America, and the standards applicable to financial audits contained in *Government Auditing Standards,* issued by the Comptroller General of the United States. Those standards require that we plan and perform the audit to obtain reasonable assurance about whether the financial statements are free of material misstatement. An audit includes examining, on a test basis, evidence supporting the amounts and disclosures in the financial statements. An audit also includes assessing the accounting principles used and the significant estimates made by management, as well as evaluating the overall financial statements presentation. We believe that our audits provide a reasonable basis for our opinion.

In our opinion, the financial statements referred to above present fairly, in all material aspects, the financial position of the INO as of June 30, 2010 and 2009, and the changes in its net assets and its cash flows for the years then ended in conformity with accounting principles generally accepted in the United States of America.

In accordance with *Government Auditing Standards,* we have also issued our report dated October 1, 2010 on our consideration of the INO's internal control over financial reporting and our tests of its compliance with certain provisions of laws, regulations, contracts and grants agreements. The purpose of that report is to describe the scope of our testing of internal control over financial reporting and compliance and the results of that testing, and not to provide an opinion on the internal control over financial reporting or on compliance. The report is an integral part of an audit performed in accordance with *Government Auditing Standards* and should be considered in assessing the results of our audit.

Our audits were performed for the purpose of forming an opinion on basic financial statements of the INO taken as a whole. The accompanying Schedule of Expenditures of Federal Awards and State Projects is presented for purposes of additional analysis as required by the U.S. Office of Management and Budget Circular A-133, *Audits of States, Local Governments, and Non-Profit Organizations,* and chapter 10.650, Rules of the Auditor General, and is not a required part of the basic financial statements. Such information has been subject to the auditing procedures applied in the audit of the basic financial statements and, in our opinion, is fairly stated, in all material respects, in relation to the basic financial statements taken as a whole.

Anyfirm, LLP
Anywhere, Anystate
October 1, 2010

Entity Structure

The structure of the entity affects the scope of the audit engagement. If the company is either a parent or subsidiary of another entity, this affects the auditor's scope of work. When the auditor does not audit both the parent and subsidiary, the engagement is affected by the audit work performed and reports provided by the auditors of the related entities. If a company has multiple locations, the auditor determines how much work is to be done related to the different locations. The scoping decisions related to multiple locations are affected by the materiality of the dollar amounts each location contributes to the financial statements. The activities and controls at each location also affect the scope of the audit. On some engagements other auditors are hired to perform work at distant locations. This affects the scope of the "primary" auditor's work because of a need to plan, supervise, and review the other auditor's work.

Information Technology

The pervasive use and importance of IT to the company's activities and ICFR also impact the scope of the engagement. The nature and extent of audit tests over the processing controls and final accounting balances are influenced by the client's IT. An auditor may be able to reduce other tests when the IT system has good **entity-level controls** and good controls over specific application programs.

Client Outsourcing

Various circumstances can impact the volume of work performed by an auditor. For example, if a company "**outsources**" any of its financial activities to a service provider, the auditor's plan differs from what it would be if all the financial activities were performed "in house." Outside service providers are discussed extensively in Chapter 13, which covers the audit of the human resources cycle.

An **outside service provider** is an entity with which a company (called the **user organization**) contracts to receive a service. Payroll processing is a service that is commonly outsourced, as are various IT activities. When a process is outsourced, the auditor must determine whether the outsourced service is important enough to be material to the audit client's ICFR. If it is material, the auditor determines how much audit work needs to be performed to obtain assurance that the service provider's ICFR is effective and its outputs can be relied on as inputs to the financial statements.

The user company's auditor may be able to rely on a report provided by an auditor of the service provider. Alternatively, the user company's auditor may have to perform various audit steps related to the service provider. Thus, use of a service provider and circumstances surrounding the service provider affect the scope of an audit engagement. Exhibit 6-3 presents the parties involved in audits when the client outsources services.

EXHIBIT 6-3

User Companies, Service Providers, and Auditors

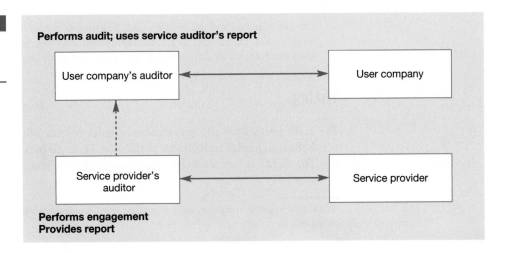

Work of Others

The volume of work, and consequently, scope of an audit engagement, is impacted by the auditor's ability to rely on and use the work performed by others. Individuals who perform work for an audit client can impact the scope of an external auditor's work. For instance, internal auditors perform a variety of financial and other audit procedures. Other individuals, either hired from the outside or employees of the company, evaluate and test ICFR to support management's effectiveness assessment. Sometimes the work of others can impact the tests the auditor needs to perform. The impact can be to decrease (or increase) the amount of testing the external auditor performs or to change the nature of the tests.

Changes to audit tests involve the **nature, timing, or extent** of the tests. Nature, timing, and extent of testing are discussed both in this chapter and throughout other chapters. *Nature* simply refers to the audit procedures used. *Timing* refers to whether the audit work is performed before the end of the fiscal year or after the client closes its books. *Extent* concerns the amount of audit tests or procedures performed.

In some situations employees of an audit client, such as internal auditors, can perform audit steps, and the external auditor can use that work as audit evidence. While this may reduce the scope of the audit team's work in performing the tests, it increases the audit resources that must be directed toward supervision and review of the work. The scope of the independent auditor's work is also affected by the availability of client personnel and data that contribute to evidence. If client personnel and data are readily available to the auditor, this can reduce the amount of work that the audit team performs, or at least make accomplishing the work more efficient.

First-Year and Continuing Audits

A first-year audit engagement requires more work than a recurring audit. The scope of a first-year engagement is greater. Information learned on prior engagements can affect the nature, timing, and extent of audit work. For example, if the prior year's audit found no material weaknesses in ICFR and no material misstatements in the financial statements, this information can help the auditor plan which areas should receive more or less audit coverage in the current year.

PCAOB standards require that internal controls that are necessary to prevent or detect material misstatements be tested in some way in the ICFR audit each year. But audit information obtained through prior-year audits can impact the scope of the current-year engagement and allow the auditor to alter the nature, timing, or extent of the tests.[1]

In a continuing audit engagement, the auditor already knows a lot about the client's business, organization, personnel, and accounting systems. In subsequent years, updating that knowledge requires less audit effort than learning it all during the first year of the engagement. Use of analytical procedures is required in the planning process and can be useful in providing information relating to the scope of the engagement. **Analytical procedures** are:

> evaluations of financial information made by a study of plausible relationships among both financial and nonfinancial data. Analytical procedures range from simple comparisons to the use of complex models involving many relationships and elements of data. (AU 329.02)

Timing

The audit strategy for any engagement includes consideration of the time frame within which the engagement activities are performed. Timing is part of the big picture audit strategy. The client has various events that create audit deadlines. Consequently, the audit firm

---

[1] In audits of nonpublic companies audited according to AICPA standards, each control does not have to be tested every year.

must consider the human resources it has available and ensure that those human resources are available at the required times. Two timing considerations for developing the big picture audit strategy are:

> Key dates for auditor communication with management, the **audit committee,** and the Board of Directors
> SEC deadlines for filing quarterly and annual financial reports

The auditor schedules tasks in time to meet the deadlines.

If the company has business units or related party entities for which other auditors perform audit work, expectations of reporting by the other auditors must be considered in the time plan. For example, when a company has a major investment in another company, the auditor of the investor may need the financial statements and audit report of the investee in order to finish the audit of the investor company. In addition, any requirements and deadlines beyond those of the SEC, such as other regulators, must be investigated and established. For example, financial institutions have deadlines for filing regulatory reports. The audit strategy establishes the overall timing of audit work based on these established key dates, including the parts of the work that are performed at different times throughout the year.

REVIEW QUESTIONS

B.1 How are auditors able to begin planning an audit engagement for a first-year audit when they have not yet spent any significant time working on the client?

B.2 What services that the auditor performs for an audit client may assist in scoping the audit engagement?

B.3 How does the client's industry, its basis of reporting, and regulatory reports required affect scoping the engagement?

B.4 How is the audit plan affected if the entity has a parent or subsidiary, or other entities that are related parties?

B.5 How can planning for the audit be affected by the work of the client's internal auditors? By whether the company outsources any of its processes?

B.6 What is important about analytical procedures and audit planning?

B.7 Does the work performed in audit planning change in the subsequent years of auditing the same client?

B.8 What are some events that must be considered when planning the audit from a timing perspective?

Materiality and Risk [LO 3]

The risk of material misstatement of the financial statements is a fundamental underpinning to audit planning. **Materiality** refers to a difference that would cause a decision maker to change his or her decision. Statement of Financial Accounting Concepts No. 2 defines materiality as:

> the magnitude of an omission or misstatement of accounting information that, in the light of surrounding circumstances, makes it probable that the judgment of a reasonable person relying on the information would have been changed or influenced by the omission or misstatement. (SFAC No. 2, p. 7)

This definition highlights the importance of the perception of the information user.

Auditors assess whether a misstatement of an amount or disclosure is material based on whether it would influence the economic decisions of users with certain qualifications. These qualifications are:

1. Having an appropriate knowledge of business and economic activities and accounting and a willingness to study the information in the financial statements with an appropriate diligence.

2. Understanding that financial statements are prepared and audited to levels of materiality.

3. Recognizing the uncertainties inherent in the measurement of amounts based on the use of estimates, judgment, and the consideration of future events.

4. Making appropriate economic decisions on the basis of information in the financial statements. (AICPA AU 312.06)

Materiality is not determined solely on the basis of quantitative factors but is influenced by qualitative characteristics as well. For example, fraud committed by management is always considered material. In addition, any uncertainties about transactions with related parties may be considered material because the supporting evidence might be less reliable as a result of the relationship.

AS 5 directs the auditor to use a "top down" approach that applies to materiality in both the financial statement and ICFR aspects of an integrated audit. First the auditor determines what is material at the financial statement level. Next, the auditor identifies the various accounts and disclosures that are significant to the financial statements. The auditor identifies the management assertions that are relevant for those **significant accounts and disclosures**. The auditor makes a professional judgment about the amount of a misstatement in that account or disclosure that would be material. The auditor's materiality judgments also consider the aggregation of materiality in all the significant accounts that could cause the financial statements to be materially misstated.

Based on all the knowledge accumulated about the company, the auditor determines risks in the business that might cause material misstatements in each financial statement account. A **significant risk** is a risk of material misstatement that is important enough to require special audit consideration. The risk of material misstatement of an account is linked to the relevant assertions. One approach to determining the risks is to consider "what could go wrong" to cause the material misstatement.

For both expressing an opinion on ICFR and determining reliance on controls in the financial statement audit, the auditor looks for controls that address the significant risks. Auditors structure the audit plan to test the design and functioning of the controls that address the risks of material misstatements. If the controls are ineffective to the extent that they might not keep the financial statements from being materially misstated, then a **material weakness** exists in ICFR.

For planning the **substantive procedures** of a financial statement audit, the auditor evaluates what would be a material misstatement for an account or disclosure assertion. Substantive audit procedures are then designed to identify any such material misstatements that have occurred, whether they result from error or fraud (AS 5.21-41, AICPA AU 312.07). Exhibit 6-4 summarizes materiality considerations in a top down approach to planning.

Auditors use professional judgment in setting the amount that is considered quantitatively material at the financial statement level. One factor that auditors may consider in setting financial statement materiality is a "rule of thumb" or **benchmark**. A rule of thumb might be a percentage of total revenue, gross profit, or profit before taxes for continuing operations. Auditors consider characteristics of the company such as size, nature of ownership, financing sources, and industry in considering benchmarks when setting financial statement-level materiality.

Financial statement materiality in a publicly owned entity in the retail industry might be based on a percentage of profit from continuing operations. In contrast, financial statement materiality for a not-for-profit entity might be some percentage of assets. A company in a highly regulated industry such as a bank or a brokerage firm might require a different benchmark. For instance, a stock brokerage company has minimum net capital requirements, and regardless of any other criteria used, a misstatement that caused the brokerage company

EXHIBIT 6-4

Top Down Approach

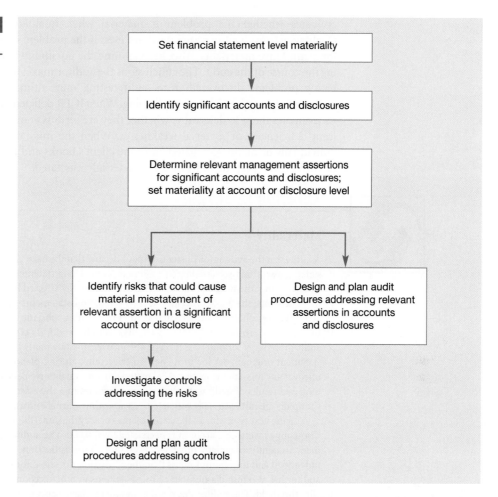

to miss its minimum net capital requirements might be judged material. Other qualitative characteristics, such as whether the misstatement would move the company from a profit to a loss might be layered on top of quantitative benchmark materiality considerations.

In addition to setting a materiality threshold at the financial statement level, the auditor must also determine a materiality level appropriate for each individual account balance or class of transactions. An auditor is willing to accept some dollar amount of misstatement in an account balance or class or transactions based on the judgment that it is not material. Similarly, the auditor is willing to accept some number (or percent) of errors in the application of a control applied to an account balance or class of transactions. Accepting some errors is based on the conclusion that the accepted rate of control failure will not allow a material misstatement in the account balance.

The auditor must set materiality for each significant account balance keeping in mind the aggregated impact of all the "less-than-material" misstatements that can occur in the financial statements. In other words, if every significant account is misstated up to, but not beyond, its materiality threshold, the resulting set of financial statements cannot be materially misstated. The materiality threshold for each account balance or class of transaction is called **tolerable misstatement** (AU 350.19, AICPA AU 312.34). The materiality threshold that relates to the number or percent of times an ICFR fails is called **tolerable rate of error**. For planning purposes, as long as the misstatement in an account balance is less than tolerable misstatement, the auditor does not expect the problem to be material. Similarly, if the extent of ICFR weakness is lower than the tolerable rate of error, the auditor does not expect the problem to cause a material misstatement.

The tolerable misstatement–tolerable rate of error guide is a planning concept that may also be useful for quantitative analysis evaluating audit findings. However, the auditor also evaluates whether the problem is material when qualitative factors are considered. Qualitative considerations are important even if the problem does not reach the threshold for quantitative materiality. Also, keep in mind the possibility that things may change during the course of the audit. The conclusions the auditor makes about materiality when evaluating problems discovered from audit testing may ultimately differ from what was considered to be material during planning. When ICFR deficiencies are identified, the auditor evaluates them to determine whether they are serious enough to be classified as significant deficiencies or material weaknesses. When the misstatements are material, either individually or on an aggregated basis, the client's books and financial statements need to be corrected to keep them from being materially misstated.

AUDITING IN ACTION

Materiality

Assume that the auditor for Buster Company decides that the balance sheet will be materially misstated if assets are overstated by $1 million or more. Understatements are considered separately. To ensure that the financial statements are not materially affected by the aggregation of smaller misstatements, the auditor decides to set tolerable misstatements for both the investment and accounts receivable accounts at $30,000. After performing substantive tests, the auditor concludes that there are errors of $10,000 in accounts receivable and $12,000 in investments. None of the audit procedures for other asset accounts uncover misstatements larger than the tolerable misstatement originally set for those particular accounts during planning. The audit tests did not uncover any misstatements that were material from a qualitative perspective. Based on the planning and results of audit tests, the auditor concludes that the asset account balances for Buster Company are not materially misstated. No adjusting journal entries are needed.

In the next year, with all the circumstances exactly the same, the auditor concludes that Buster Company's investment account is overstated by $50,000. The auditor concludes that the investment account is materially misstated. Even though this is the only materially misstated account indentified and the amount is less than the $1 million threshold for the financial statements, the auditor has also found a number of misstatements in other accounts that are below the materiality threshold. The auditor decides that in order to have reasonable assurance that the financial statements as a whole are not materially misstated the investment account needs to be corrected.

The auditor proposes that Buster Company makes an adjusting journal entry to the investment account for $50,000. If the Buster Company management makes the correcting journal entry, the auditor has reasonable assurance about the fairness of the financial statements and issues an unqualified financial statement audit opinion. Since the company prepared financial statements that include a material misstatement, the auditor concludes that ICFR has a material weakness. This conclusion is based on the definition of a material weakness that labels it as a control problem serious enough to cause a material misstatement. The auditor decides that since ICFR permitted a material misstatement, the control that let the misstatement slip through must be a problem.

During planning, the auditor defines the engagement's tolerable misstatement, tolerable rate of error, and qualitative materiality considerations. With these criteria in mind, the auditor is able to select which controls to test and to plan how to test them. The auditor is also able to plan how to test account balances and disclosures. The planning levels of materiality guide the auditor in deciding which risks will affect the nature, timing, and extent of the audit procedures conducted during the audit.

REVIEW QUESTIONS

C.1 What user characteristics do the auditing standards assume users have when judging what is material to a company's financial statements?

C.2 What are the risk assessment and planning steps that take the auditor from considering materiality at the financial statement level to designing the audit procedure to testing the operating effectiveness of an internal control?

C.3 What are the risk assessment and planning steps that take the auditor from considering materiality at the financial statement level to designing the substantive audit procedure intended to identify any material misstatements in the financial statements and disclosures?

C.4 What does it mean to use a benchmark to set financial statement materiality? What benchmarks are used? How might the benchmark differ based on the type of company being audited?

C.5 What is meant by the terms *tolerable misstatement* and *tolerable rate of error*? How do they relate to materiality?

Fraud Risk [LO 4]

Another important step in early planning is performing a preliminary assessment of fraud risk. Auditing standards specify that the audit team must discuss during planning "how and where" the financial statements might be misstated as a result of fraud. The standards also require the audit team to maintain professional skepticism while considering fraud risk—in other words, to maintain a questioning mind-set—and to consider fraud risk when evaluating audit evidence (AU 316.02). Fraud risk is a significant risk and considering the possibility of fraud is a necessary part of the planning stage:

> The auditor has a responsibility to plan and perform the audit to obtain reasonable assurance about whether the financial statements are free of material misstatement, whether caused by error or fraud. (AU 110.02)

The **Fraud Triangle** (AU 316.85) is proposed as an effective way to consider fraud risk in an audit client. The first component of the Fraud Triangle is *incentive* or *pressure*. The auditor must consider whether management and employees have the incentives and pressures to commit fraud. The second component is *opportunities*. Auditors consider whether the circumstances within the client company provide an opportunity for those who have the incentive to commit fraud. The final component of the triangle is *attitudes* or *rationalizations*. This consideration is whether a person committing fraud is able to personally justify or rationalize the fraud he or she has committed. Management might rationalize misstating financial statements to overstate profits by believing that it is "for the good of the company—all the shareholders and employees." An employee might try to justify petty theft by rationalizing that the company will never miss the item stolen, or that he or she is not paid enough and the theft helps to compensate for the low salary. Exhibit 6-5 presents the Fraud Triangle.

Although it begins at the planning stage, consideration of fraud risk is a pervasive component throughout the audit. The initial assessment is made during early audit planning. It is based on what the auditor already knows about the company and discussions with management and company personnel. As planning progresses, the auditor performs steps to understand the system of ICFR and test the effectiveness of ICFR design. Anti-fraud programs and entity-level controls are specifically investigated while the auditor learns about the ICFR system and assesses design. The **operating effectiveness of anti-fraud controls** is specifically tested during the control testing phase of the audit.

Audit procedures are more likely to miss material misstatements resulting from fraud than those due to error because fraudsters deliberately attempt to hide or disguise their wrongdoing. This makes the company's anti-fraud controls even more important. Anti-fraud controls include:

> controls over significant, unusual transactions, particularly those that result in late or unusual journal entries
> controls over journal entries and adjustments made in the period-end financial reporting process
> controls over related party transactions

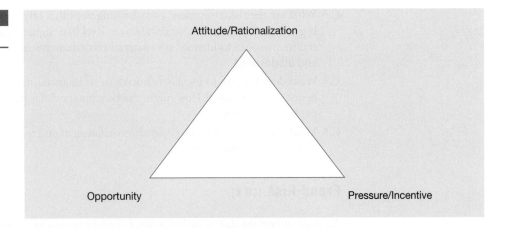

EXHIBIT 6-5

The Fraud Triangle

controls related to significant management estimates

controls that mitigate incentives for, and pressures on, management to falsify or inappropriately manage financial results (AS 5.14)

The Appendix of the audit standard on fraud, AU 316, provides indicators relating to fraud risk for fraudulent financial reporting. The standard also provides a list of indicators relating to fraud risk for misappropriation of assets. Misappropriation of assets refers to theft or unauthorized use. The audit standards use the Fraud Triangle as a framework for presenting risk circumstances. Many of the fraud risks and indicators were presented in Chapter 5, relating to client acceptance and continuance issues. The same indicators that help an auditor decide whether to accept a client for the first time can also help an auditor assess the likelihood that fraud has occurred. Exhibit 6-6 provides examples of fraudulent behaviors and the related controls that prevent or detect the particular fraud.

Another planning consideration similar to addressing fraud risk is the risk of illegal acts. The auditor focuses on the risk of illegal acts that can have a material impact on the financial statements (AU 317).

REVIEW QUESTIONS

D.1 Why is assessing the risk of fraud important for the planning stage? What do the audit standards require regarding fraud risk during planning?

D.2 What is the Fraud Triangle? What are its components? Why is it an effective way for the auditor to approach fraud?

D.3 What are client anti-fraud controls, and why are they important to the auditor?

Recent Significant Developments [LO 5]

Events can occur that change the conditions of the audit and affect the activities performed on an audit engagement. On a recurring audit engagement, recent significant developments are changes that have occurred since the last audit. For a new client, recent significant developments are changes that have occurred since the client was accepted. Significant developments are changes within the client and changes in the client's external environment.

Changes within the client that affect audit strategy include changes in the company's business activities, ownership, capital structure, and accounting information system. The auditor applies more audit effort to valuation and consolidation issues if an acquisition has occurred. Similarly, more audit effort is spent on financial statement presentation if the company has recently undergone a disposition, or plan for disposition or has discontinued operations. A change in capital structure or ownership means more audit effort in that area. A new or significantly modified accounting information system requires more audit effort to understand the new system and assess its design and operating effectiveness.

AUDITING IN ACTION

Fraudulent Financial Reporting Risk Factors

Incentives/Pressures

Financial stability or profitability is threatened by economic, industry, or entity operating conditions, such as

- High degree of competition or market saturation, accompanied by declining margins
- High vulnerability to rapid changes, such as changes in technology, product obsolescence, or interest rates
- Significant declines in customer demand and increasing business failures in either the industry or overall economy
- Operating losses making the threat of bankruptcy, foreclosure, or hostile takeover imminent
- Recurring negative cash flows from operations or an inability to generate cash flows from operations while reporting earnings and earnings growth
- Rapid growth or unusual profitability, especially compared to that of other companies in the same industry
- New accounting, statutory, or regulatory requirements

Excessive pressure exists for management to meet the requirements or expectations of third parties due to the following:

- Profitability or trend-level expectations of investment analysts, institutional investors, significant creditors, or other external parties…including expectations created by management in, for example, overly optimistic press releases or annual report messages
- Need to obtain additional debt or equity financing to stay competitive—including financing or major research and development or capital expenditures
- Marginal ability to meet exchange listing requirements or debt repayment or other debt covenant requirements
- Perceived or real adverse effects of reporting poor financial results on significant pending transactions, such as business combinations or contract awards

Information available indicates that the personal financial situation of management or the Board of Directors is threatened by the entity's financial performance arising from the following:

- Significant financial interests in the entity
- Significant portions of their compensation…being contingent upon achieving aggressive targets for stock price, operating results, financial position, or cash flow
- Personal guarantees of debts of the entity

There is excessive pressure on management or operating personnel to meet financial targets set up by the board of directors or management, including sales or profitability incentive goals.

Opportunities

The nature of the industry or the entity's operations provides opportunities to engage in fraudulent financial reporting that can arise from the following:

- Significant related party transactions not in the ordinary course of business or with related entities not audited or audited by another firm
- A strong financial presence or ability to dominate a certain industry sector that allows the entity to dictate terms or conditions to suppliers or customers that may result in inappropriate or non-arm's length transactions
- Assets, liabilities, revenues, or expenses based on significant estimates that involve subjective judgments or uncertainties that are difficult to corroborate
- Significant, unusual, or highly complex transactions, especially those close to period-end that pose difficult "substance over form" questions
- Significant operations located or conducted across international borders in jurisdictions where differing business environments and cultures exist

(continued)

- Significant bank accounts or subsidiary or branch operations in tax haven jurisdictions for which there appears to be no clear business justification

There is ineffective monitoring of management as a result of the following:

- Domination of management by a single person or small group (in a nonowner-managed business) without compensating controls
- Ineffective board of directors or audit committee oversight over the financial reporting process and internal control

There is complex or unstable organizational structure, as evidenced by the following:

- Difficulty in determining the organization or individuals that have controlling interest in the entity
- Overly complex organizational structure involving unusual legal entities or managerial lines of authority
- High turnover of senior management, counsel, or board members

Internal control components are deficient as a result of the following:

- Inadequate monitoring of controls, including automated controls and controls over interim financial reporting (where external reporting is required)
- High turnover rates or employment of ineffective accounting, internal audit, or information technology staff
- Ineffective accounting and information systems

Attitudes/Rationalizations

Ineffective communication, implementation, support, or enforcement of the entity's values or ethical standards by management or the communication of inappropriate values or ethical standards

Nonfinancial management's excessive participation in or preoccupation with the selection of accounting principles or the determination of significant estimates

Known history of violations of securities laws or other laws and regulations, or claims against the entity, its senior management, or board members alleging fraud or violations of laws and regulations

Excessive interest by management in maintaining or increasing the entity's stock price or earnings trend

A practice by management of committing to analysts, creditors, and other third parties to achieve aggressive or unrealistic forecasts

Management failing to correct known serious ICFR deficiencies on a timely basis

An interest by management in employing inappropriate means to minimize reported earnings for tax-motivated reasons

Recurring attempts by management to justify marginal or inappropriate accounting on the basis of materiality

The relationship between management and the current or predecessor auditor is strained, as exhibited by the following;

- Frequent disputes with the current or predecessor auditor on accounting, auditing or reporting matters
- Unreasonable demands on the auditor, such as unreasonable time constraints regarding the completion of the audit or the issuance of the auditor's report
- Formal or informal restrictions on the auditor that inappropriately limit access to people or information or the ability to communicate effectively with the board of directors or audit committee
- Domineering management behavior in dealing with the auditor, especially involving attempts to influence the scope of the auditor's work or the selection or continuance of personnel assigned to or consulted on the audit engagement

(Appendix, AU 316)

AUDITING IN ACTION

Misappropriation of Assets Risk Factors

Incentives/Pressures

Personal financial obligations may create pressure on management or employees with access to cash or other assets susceptible to theft to misappropriate those assets.

Adverse relationships between the entity and employees with access to cash or other assets susceptible to theft may motivate those employees to misappropriate those assets. For example, adverse relationships may be created by the following:

- Known or anticipated future employee layoffs
- Recent or anticipated changes to employee compensation or benefit plans
- Promotions, compensation, or other rewards inconsistent with expectations
- Fixed assets that are small in size, marketable, or lacking observable identification of ownership

Opportunities

Certain characteristics or circumstances may increase the susceptibility of assets to misappropriation. For example, opportunities to misappropriate assets increase when there are the following:

- Large amounts of cash on hand or processed
- Inventory items that are small in size of high value, or in high demand
- Easily convertible assets, such as bearer bonds, diamonds, or computer chips

Inadequate internal control over assets may increase the susceptibility of misappropriations of those assets. For example, misappropriation of assets may occur because there is the following:

- Inadequate segregation of duties or independent checks
- Inadequate management oversight of employees responsible for assets, for example, inadequate supervision or monitoring of remote locations
- Inadequate job applicant screening of employees with access to assets
- Inadequate recordkeeping with respect to assets
- Inadequate system of authorization and approval of transactions (for example, in purchasing)
- Inadequate physical safeguards over cash, investments, inventory, or fixed assets
- Lack of complete and timely reconciliations of assets
- Lack of timely and appropriate documentation of transactions, for example, credits for merchandise returns
- Lack of mandatory vacations for employees performing key control functions
- Inadequate management understanding of information technology, which enables information technology employees to perpetrate a misappropriation
- Inadequate access controls over automated records, including controls over and review of computer systems event logs.

Attitudes/Rationalizations

Disregard for the need for monitoring or reducing risks related to misappropriations of assets

Disregard for internal control over misappropriation of assets by overriding existing controls or by failing to correct known internal control deficiencies

Behavior indicating displeasure or dissatisfaction with the company or its treatment of the employee

Changes in behavior or lifestyle that may indicate assets have been misappropriated

(Appendix, AU 316 A.3)

EXHIBIT 6-6

Fraudulent Behaviors
and Related Controls

Fraud Scheme	Key Mitigating Controls
Improper revenue recognition	
Recording revenues from fictitious sales	All sales are supported by documentation
	Only employees with proper identification numbers can enter new sales into the accounting system
Asset overstatement/Liability understatement	
Inadequate reserves or failure to recognize bad debts	Policy is in place for calculating reserves and allowances
Improper capitalization of expenses	Capitalization policy exists at the entity level
	A review step is used to check that all invoices are properly coded
Schemes involving depreciation/ amortization	Capitalization policy exists at the entity level
	Depreciation expense is reviewed by a higher financial/accounting officer on periodic basis
	Review of quarter-to-quarter changes in depreciation expense is completed by authorized personnel
	Review of new additions is performed on a quarterly basis
Understating expenses or concealing liabilities	Search for unrecorded liabilities is performed quarterly
	Higher financial/accounting officer reviews quarterly accruals
	Review of budget to actual expense is performed quarterly
Fraudulent journal entries	All journal entries are approved and posted by authorized financial reporting personnel
	Top financial/accounting officer reviews all entries posted after period-end
Asset Misappropriation	
Disbursements	
Fraudulent disbursements to fictitious vendors	Checks produced only to vendors on approved vendors list
	New vendor setup is authorized and occurs outside of Accounts Payable department
	Taxpayer Identification Number (TIN) verified for new vendors before approval
Fraudulent disbursements for false credits, refunds, rebates, and bribes to legitimate vendors for which the employee receives a kickback	Purchase authorization responsibilities segregated from cash disbursement activity and approval
	New vendor setup separated from payment responsibilities
	Bidding policy in place for material contracts/purchases
	Code of Ethics
Fraudulent disbursements for overbidding schemes	Same person cannot authorize a transaction and approve material payments
	Bidding for material contracts/purchases required
Cash	
Fraudulent disbursements, theft of company checks and check tampering	Electronic disbursement authorization codes secured, checks stored in locked cabinets with limited access to keys

Fraudulent disbursements through expense report schemes	Accounts payable employees cannot post payments for themselves
	Supervisors approve all reimbursements to employees
	Large-item expenditures must be approved in advance
Personal purchases	Supervisors approve all reimbursement requests by employees
	Large-item expenditures must be approved in advance
Withdrawal of cash at bank by authorized signers	Monthly bank reconciliation process
	Daily cash review
Stealing/unauthorized use of petty cash	Written policies exist on proper use of petty cash
	Periodical audits of petty cash
	Internal audit department periodically reviews petty cash funds
Fraudulent electronic transfers of cash	Initial setup of recurring electronic funds transfers requires two approvals
	Electronic funds transfers to nonrecurring vendors require two approvals
	All nonrecurring electronic transfers over specified dollar amount require approval by top financial officer
Payroll	
Payroll fraud through fictitious employees	Additions and changes are approved by human resources; then request is sent by human resources to payroll
Payroll fraud through falsified hours	Electronic time reporting is used
Payroll fraud through payment to terminated employees	HR follow-up to verify that change requests sent to payroll are posted
Gifts/Favors	
Receipt of free or discounted goods and services from vendors/suppliers	Code of Ethics
	Gift policy
Financial Misconduct by a Member of Senior Management or the Board	
Use of corporate assets to commit unauthorized acts	Code of Ethics includes proper use of company assets
Insider trading	Officers and other senior executives must have stock trades preapproved
	Trading completed during open trading window
Conflicts of Interest	Conflicts of interest policy is included in the Code of Ethics
	Annual distribution of Code of Ethics to all employees
Background deception	Background checks for all employees

Developments in the client's external environment also affect audit strategy. These include industry conditions, industry regulations, economic changes, and changes in applicable accounting and auditing standards. If an industry has experienced a recent market downturn or increase in competition, the audit strategy focuses more on **going concern issues**.[2] Going concern questions may also arise if changes in the economy have negatively impacted the client. Alternatively, the economy may improve, and the client may increase its activities requiring more audit work because the company is doing better rather than worse.

---

[2]Reminder: A going concern question exists if there is substantial doubt that a company will be able to meet its financial obligations for the next 12 months through its ongoing routine business activities.

SOX and the resulting rules and standards of the SEC and PCAOB are examples of new developments in regulations, accounting standards, and auditing standards that affect audit strategy. Audit firms had to change their audit strategies to address internal control not only for the financial statement audit, but also for purposes of issuing an opinion on ICFR. Use of international accounting standards in the future may cause changes in audit strategies. Recent accounting standards on pensions, accounting for employee compensation, and the use of fair market value have significantly affected audit strategy. More audit time and effort are required in the early years of implementing these types of complicated accounting standards.

Sometimes recent developments trigger changes in the audit strategy that require additional audit team members. The audit may need individuals who have advanced knowledge and skills to audit the areas affected by the changes. When audit clients acquire complex IT systems this typically triggers the need for the engagement team to include auditors with advanced IT knowledge. Another example is the need to use a valuation specialist to address pensions, equity instruments and fair value of other accounts. Audit strategy has to adapt to incorporate the time and skill of human resources needed to address the audit's requirements based on any recent developments.

Sources of Information

The auditor obtains information about the client that helps with developing the audit strategy from the client acceptance and continuance process and setting the terms of the engagement. The auditor also gains information during other engagements conducted for the client company.

In an integrated audit, the audit firm must understand the client's ICFR and assess its **design effectiveness**. Understanding the client's system in order to understand ICFR and assess its design occurs early in the audit, typically when members of the audit team first spend time at the client location. Information obtained through this process:

1. helps the auditor develop the audit strategy,
2. informs the auditor about design effectiveness, and
3. provides important information for designing the audit plan.

Understanding the system guides the auditor in choosing which controls to test for operating effectiveness and how the tests may most efficiently and effectively be conducted. The process of understanding the client's ICFR system and assessing design effectiveness is the topic of Chapter 7.

Reviews of quarterly financial statements also provide the auditor with information. The auditor must review the quarterly financial statements filed with the SEC.[3] A review of a public company's quarterly financial statements is less extensive than an audit but still provides the auditor with information that is useful for planning the year-end integrated audit. Reviews provide the auditor with information including the company's ICFR system, changes to the system and to the business organization, and important transactions and customers. Similarly, if the company issues publicly traded stock or debt, the auditor's involvement with the **registration statement** provides information.[4] Auditing a parent company, or subsidiary, or another related party entity also provides additional information.

Planning Meeting and Planning Memorandum [LO 6]

At this stage of the audit, often concurrent with the beginning of on-location audit work, the audit team participates in a **planning meeting**. The people who participate in the planning meeting vary. The size of the audit and the different individuals who have a role in the audit activities can impact who attends.

The entire "core" audit engagement team may attend, from partners through entry-level staff. In addition, those who provide specialized knowledge or expertise, such as IT and other

---

[3]SEC quarterly review engagements are discussed in Chapter 16.
[4]Engagements related to public offerings are also discussed in Chapter 16.

specialists, tax professionals, and auditors with expertise in the application of new or complex accounting standards, may attend. Some planning meetings include only the core audit team plus partners and managers for the other contributing functional areas such as tax and IT.

Regardless of the specific composition of attendees, the purpose of the planning meeting is to establish an understanding among all the individuals who participate in the audit about the objectives of the engagement, risks—including fraud risk, and the general audit approach. This meeting may also be the time when the brainstorming session about fraud occurs (AU 316.14–18).

The auditing standards on planning and supervision indicate various topics that are likely discussed during a planning meeting:

> The auditor with final responsibility for the audit should communicate with members of the audit team regarding the susceptibility of the entity's financial statements to material misstatement due to error or fraud, with special emphasis on fraud. Such discussion helps all audit team members understand the entity and its environment, including its internal control, and how risks that the entity faces may affect the audit. (AICPA AU 311.29)

> … assistants should be informed of their responsibilities and the objectives of the audit procedures they are to perform. (AICPA AU 311.30, PCAOB AU 311.12)

> The auditor with final responsibility for the audit should direct assistants to bring to his or her attention accounting and auditing issues raised during the audit that the assistant believes are of significance to the financial statements or auditor's report so the auditor with final responsibility may assess their significance. Assistants also should be directed to bring to the attention of appropriate individuals in the firm difficulties encountered in performing the audit, such as missing documents or resistance from client personnel in providing access to information or in responding to inquiries. (AICPA AU 311.30)

The audit **planning memorandum (memo)** adds to the **audit documentation** started during the client acceptance and continuance process and includes the various issues discussed as a part of audit strategy. An outline of an audit planning memo for a public company engagement is presented in Exhibit 6-7. Some of the information shown in the audit planning memo outline will not be familiar to you yet. You will become familiar with everything in the planning memo as you study Chapters 7 through 11. The planning memo is presented in outline form because of its length and the amount of information included. As you review the outline, focus on the importance of this document as a milestone in planning the audit.

EXHIBIT 6-7

Outline of an Audit Planning Memo

Engagement objectives, deliverables, key dates
    Opinions on consolidated annual financial statements and effectiveness of ICFR to be included in the 10K
    Quarterly reviews
    Communication, in writing, to management of all control deficiencies noted
    Communication, in writing, to the audit committee and management of significant deficiencies and material weaknesses noted
Risk assessment from the top down
    Understand the business
        Market overview
        Activities
        Related parties
        Industry and entity regulation
        Financial performance
            Analytical procedures
            Going concern assessment
        Management's risk assessment

(continued)

Other audit risk considerations
    New and complex accounting matters
    Impact of past audits (e.g., history of errors)
    Fraud risk assessment
    Other considerations
        Independence
        Board and key committee activities (from minutes)
        Significant contracts
        Internal audit reports
Preliminary assessment of materiality
    Overall materiality (e.g., % of pretax income and resulting dollar amount)
    Planning materiality (will be less than overall materiality)
    De minimis (expressed as a % of overall materiality; the threshold below which audit findings representing differences are not proposed to the client for adjustment; all de minimis unadjusted auditing differences are documented in a workpaper that summarizes the unadjusted differences; all uncorrected errors that indicate fraud are posted to the workpaper summarizing unadjusted differences regardless of dollar amount)
    Materiality level for making balance sheet reclassifications, for example, 1% of total assets
Identified significant risks, including those from acceptance and continuance, fraud risk, and responses
    Significant risks: higher inherent risks that require special audit consideration because of the nature of the risk, potential magnitude of the misstatement or misstatements from the risk, probability of the risk occurring.
Scaling the audit—size and complexity
    Implementation of AS 5 guidance on smaller company audits and simpler or smaller components of larger company audits
Understanding the company's internal control and IT
    Entity-level controls
        Control environment, including the IT control environment
            Code of conduct
            Existence of company policies in areas needed
            Training
            Management review of organizational structure
            Audit committee charter, activities, interaction with internal audit
            Communication (including whistleblower process)
            Monitoring (including role of internal audit)
            Risk assessment (management process, BOD review)
            Anti-fraud programs as a part of ICFR
                Internal audit testing
                Controls against management override
            Human resources policies and procedures
            Management's role in ICFR
            Understanding of the IT environment:
                Services provided
                Location
                Significant applications
                ITGC testing methodology
                Complexity of operations, systems, and applications
                Recent changes
                Diversity of locations
                Variety of operating systems
                Outsourced service providers
                Spreadsheet and database controls

Period end financial reporting process
    Types of transactions
    Controls
        Segregation of duties
        Proper authorization
        Adequate supporting documentation
        Consolidation process
        Financial statement preparation and note drafting process
    Preliminary conclusions on entity-level controls, impact on audit of ICFR
Consideration of the company's use of information technology and related risks
Prior-year control deficiencies
Consideration of IT processing for ICFR and financial statement testing; identification of processes and cycles where reliance is planned on automated controls; whether ITGCs are expected to be effective; past benchmarking
Management's risk assessment processes
    Nature and rigor
    Competency and objectivity
    Changes in process
Planned use of the work of others during the audit
    Direct assistance of others
    Supervision, review, evaluation, and testing of others' work
Risk-based scoping to obtain sufficient competent (appropriate) evidence
Identifying significant accounts and relevant assertions
    Consider entity-level controls
    Judgments about multi-location considerations
    Selection of expected accounts, controls, and locations for testing
    Rationale for including or excluding specific accounts, controls, and locations
Summary of results and expected impact on audit plan
Summary of planned changes to prior-year audit approach for continuing clients
Communication and coordination
    Matters discussed with the audit committee/management
    Use of specialists
    Multi-location instructions
    Review schedule
    Key dates

REVIEW QUESTIONS

E.1 What are examples of "recent significant developments?" Why and in what ways would they affect the audit strategy?

E.2 As the auditor's association with a first-year audit client continues past the client acceptance process, what sources of information about the client become available to the auditor? What information may be received from these sources?

E.3 What would a first-year audit staff member learn from participating in the audit planning meeting of a client to which he or she has been assigned?

E.4 Why is the audit planning memo an important part of audit documentation?

AUDITING IN ACTION

Big Picture Considerations in Planning the Integrated Audit

Auditor knowledge about the company's activities, ICFR, and financial statements from client acceptance and continuance and other engagements performed

- Industry issues
  - Financial reporting practices
  - Economic conditions
  - Laws and regulations
  - Technological changes
- Company issues
  - Organization, including related parties
  - Operating characteristics, including complexity of operations
  - Capital structure
- Recent changes in the company
  - Operations
  - ICFR

- Preliminary Judgments
  - Quantitative materiality
  - Qualitative materiality
  - Risk
  - Effectiveness of ICFR
  - Material weaknesses of ICFR
- Known control deficiencies
- Known legal or regulatory concerns
- Evidence available for the audits

(Adapted from AS 5.9)

PLANNING THE AUDIT RESOURCES

Human resources are the primary resources used on an audit. Once the audit strategy is developed, the firm identifies the resources needed for the engagement. This audit planning step allows the audit firm to be sure it has partners and employees with both the skills and time available needed to perform a quality audit. Planning for the assignment and use of human resources is also necessary for the practical purpose of being able to run the public accounting firm's business. The audit firm must know what human resources the business needs to be able to hire enough people and deploy them so that the requirements of all the firm's engagements are met.

Assignments of the Audit Team

The need to plan for the assignments of individuals on the audit engagement team makes sense from a practical perspective and is required by the first field work standard. The first standard of field work states that the work must be planned and any assistants must be properly supervised. Supervision is broadly defined in the auditing standards and includes instructing members of the audit team and reviewing the work of team members. To accomplish instruction and review, the supervising auditor has to stay up-to-date on issues that come up as a result of the audit work and must manage differences of opinion among team members that arise as a result of audit findings.

The degree of instruction and management each individual member of the audit engagement team requires depends on that person's experience and expertise relative to the tasks to which he or she is assigned. Similarly, although everyone's work is reviewed, the nature of the review depends on the composition of the audit team and the tasks being reviewed. When the work of the client's internal auditors is considered to be part of audit evidence, the audit plan provides time for the internal auditor's work to be significantly supervised and reviewed.

A typical audit team's supervision and review structure is hierarchical, with each supervisor reviewing the work of those immediately subordinate. The standards allow for the "person with final responsibility for the audit," who is usually the engagement partner, to "delegate parts of the review responsibility to other assistants, in accordance with the firm's quality control system" (AICPA AU 311.31, paraphrase from PCAOB AU 311.02).

In planning the engagement, the audit firm should match jobs to individuals based on the difficulty and complexity of the job and the experience and expertise of the individual. When a team member is very experienced for the task to which he or she is assigned, the time budgeted for performing the task, review, or both may be adjusted accordingly. Alternatively, some tasks may not be performed significantly faster, even if the person doing the work is more experienced. For example, observing client personnel as they execute a control procedure takes the same amount of time regardless of who observes. If an audit area or procedure is new or complex relative to the person's experience and expertise, the audit plan should allow for more time for performance of the task, as well as more time for instruction and review.

Timing of Audit Work

Auditing procedures may be performed at various times during the fiscal year or may be performed after the end of the year. Some audit procedures may have to be performed by the auditor at the close of the last business day for the fiscal year. Whether certain procedures must be conducted exactly at fiscal year end depends on the type of company and the records and documents it produces. Use of electronic transactions and reliance on electronic verification of the times at which transactions occur can limit the auditor's need to be physically present to verify the state of a company's affairs at the end of the fiscal year. For example, if a company uses electronic banking, auditors may not need to be present to document the last manual check written during the year. Physically observing the last receipts and shipments of inventory on the last day of the fiscal year continues to be important for audits of companies with significant inventory activities.

Interim and Year End

The audit plan calls for audit procedures to be carried out at specific times based on expected efficiency and effectiveness. Procedures performed during the year being audited are performed at an "interim date" and are referred to as **interim procedures**. Sometimes it is more efficient to perform audit procedures during the year simply because the audit firm is very busy after the company's fiscal year end. Many companies have a December 31 fiscal year end. Consequently, the first few months in the calendar year are referred to as the auditor's "busy season."

Audit procedures conducted at an interim date can be very effective because they may uncover problems at an earlier date, allowing the auditor to inform management earlier than would have been possible with year-end tests.. The auditor can plan the year-end audit work so that more audit effort is directed toward the problem areas, if needed. If management takes steps to correct problems identified during interim audit work, the year-end audit plan is changed as appropriate. Sometimes audit procedures are performed at an interim date because the audit client does not retain the records that are needed as audit evidence through the time frame in which year-end audit work is performed. Similar to the possibility that the client may retain evidence for a limited time frame, some businesses change the format of evidence relatively quickly. For example, a business may scan paper documents and destroy the hard copies, retaining only electronic images. When this is the company's policy, the audit plan takes the timing into consideration when planning the audit.

In contrast, some audit work can only be performed after the fiscal year end. The audit plan must allow for the required timing. For example, the ICFR audit of the client's year-end financial reporting process must occur when financial reports are prepared, which is after the fiscal year end. In addition, "agreeing the financial statements to the accounting records" and "examining adjustments made during the course of preparing the financial statements" can only be done after the end of the fiscal year when the client has closed the accounting records for the year.

Even when an account balance can be examined before the end of the fiscal year, it is not necessarily best to do so. The auditor considers factors such as whether ICFR functions effectively and the risks of material misstatement to the specific account in deciding when to perform tests. If tests are performed at an interim date, audit evidence is still needed about the account balance between the interim testing date and the end of the fiscal year.

Roll Forward

When an audit team performs work at an interim date, it can only examine the performance of the controls and recorded transactions from the beginning of the year through the date of the interim work. The auditor must perform **roll forward audit procedures** to determine whether a control continued to perform the same way from the interim date through the end of the fiscal year. For the financial statement audit, roll forward procedures are also used to reconcile an account balance tested at the interim date with the year-end account balance.

The auditor relies on judgment to determine the type and extent of evidence required on operating effectiveness of a control during the roll forward period. This decision includes consideration of the importance of the control, how much evidence was obtained at the interim date, the length of time between interim testing and fiscal year end, and any changes that have occurred to ICFR between the interim testing date and the end of the fiscal year. These same issues affect judgments about roll-forward period substantive evidence about the account balances for the financial statement audit.

AUDITING IN ACTION

Roll Forward Testing

Shadow Company provides investigative services to individuals. Shadow Company's fiscal year end is December 31. The auditor performs tests during the month of October, as well as at and after the fiscal year end. At the interim testing date the auditor examines the bank reconciliations prepared each month by Shadow Company's accounting staff. The audit steps include recalculating the reconciliations for mathematically accuracy, tracing the amounts to the bank statement and accounting records, and inspecting whether the reconciliations were performed by an employee who had no access to cash or the cash records. The auditor performs the steps on the bank reconciliations for every month of the year through the end of September, and no failures or problems with the controls are found.

Upon returning to Shadow Company's offices after the fiscal year end, the first thing the auditor investigates is whether there have been any changes to the system since the interim date. Since no changes have occurred, the roll forward procedures for controls for the bank reconciliation process are less extensive because of the thorough tests performed at the interim date and results indicating strong ICFR.

The steps performed during testing after the fiscal year end are as follows

- Examine the documents for the existence of a bank reconciliation each month.
- Note the written evidence that the Shadow Company employee performed all of the steps required.
- Note the identification of the employee who performed the reconciliation as one with appropriate segregation of duties.
- Trace the amounts on the December reconciliation to the bank statements and general ledger.

High-Risk Areas [LO 7]

The audit identifies areas of the audit client's activities and financial statements that are at higher risk for material misstatement. The conclusion of high risk is based on the risk assessment procedures performed during audit planning. The audit strategy and audit plan direct more audit effort to these high-risk areas. For example, more experienced members of the audit team may be assigned to areas of high risk, and more tests may be planned for the related controls, account balances, and disclosures. In addition, the audit team may use specialists for high-risk areas.

A **specialist** is defined as "a person (or firm) possessing special skill or knowledge in a particular field other than accounting or auditing" (AU 336.01). A specialist may be employed by the client or the audit firm, or may be an outsider to both. Examples of specialists whose work might be used as audit evidence are actuaries, appraisers, engineers, environmental consultants, geologists, and lawyers. The auditor evaluates the qualifications and work of the specialist. If that evaluation is satisfactory, the auditor uses the findings of the specialist. If the auditor concludes that the findings of the specialist are unreasonable, the auditor must perform further audit work (AU 336.12).

AUDITING IN ACTION

Use of Professionals Possessing Specialized Skills

Are specialized skills needed on the engagement?

Are specialists to be involved with the audit in a role that effectively makes them a part of the engagement team? If yes, the lead auditor must be able to:

Communicate the objectives of the specialist's work.

Evaluate whether the specified audit procedures will meet the audit objectives.

Evaluate the results of the audit procedures and how they may affect further audit procedures. (AICPA AU 311.22)

Sometimes an audit team needs the work of a professional who is particularly knowledgeable about IT in order to effectively perform the audit. When this is the case, an auditor with advanced IT knowledge and skills is part of the audit team, even though he or she may not work on the engagement full time. An audit team member with IT skills is usually needed when the accounting information system is

Pervasive throughout the company and critical to its operations
New, recently changed, very complex, or uses emerging technology
Used by the company for its involvement in e-commerce

Significant IT skills may be necessary at the planning stage prior to performing any audit procedures to determine the scope of the engagement and identify risks. At the planning stage, an IT specialist may be involved in

1. asking the company's IT personnel how data are initiated, authorized, recorded, processed, and reported
2. asking the company's IT personnel how IT controls are designed
3. inspecting system documentation
4. observing operation of IT controls
5. planning tests of IT controls (AU 311.24)

The IT expert may also perform various audit tests once the audit procedures begin.

AUDITING IN ACTION

Need for and Use of an IT Expert

Considerations in deciding whether specialized IT skills are needed:

> Complexity of the accounting information system
>
> Complexity of the IT controls
>
> Effect and use of IT in conducting the company's business
>
> Recent changes made to the accounting information system
>
> New systems implemented
>
> Data that is used by multiple systems or processes
>
> Use of electronic commerce
>
> Use of emerging technologies
>
> Audit evidence that is available only in electronic form

Audit service contributions provided by a professional with specialized IT skills:

> Determining the effect of IT on the audit
>
> Understanding the IT controls
>
> Designing and performing tests of IT controls
>
> Designing and performing IT-related or IT-based substantive procedures

Engagement Budget

Initial audit planning tasks include preparing a preliminary time budget for the engagement. Audit firms use time budgets as a tool for planning engagements and evaluating staff, as well as for managing the firm. Budgets are typically detailed by areas of the audit, indicating the amount of anticipated time required of professionals at various levels for each area.

As the audit work is performed, the professionals working on the engagement track and report the time spent on each area. This reporting process allows the audit firm to compare its planned budget to actual outcomes. Budgeted to actual information is used for billing, evaluating staff performance' and bidding on future engagements.

REVIEW QUESTIONS

F.1   How is supervision defined in the auditing standards?

F.2   The supervision and review needed might vary based on the characteristics of the auditing professional and the task to which he or she is assigned. Why? How does that relationship or trade-off work?

F.3   Why might some audit procedures need to be performed exactly at the end of the fiscal year?

F.4   What are the reasons an auditor might plan to perform some procedures at an interim date and others during or after the client has closed its books after the fiscal year end?

F.5   Considering only the core members of the audit team, how might an area being labeled "high risk" affect the audit plan for staffing the area?

AUDITING IN ACTION

Simplified Engagement Budget and Time Record

Budgeted Hours by Area:	Associate	Senior Associate	Manager	Engagement Partner	Quality Review Partner
Planning & scoping	112	292	288	74	12
Entity-level controls	60	46	20		
Control & substantive audit evidence					
Revenues & receivables	296	147	8	4	
Purchases & payables	194	56	8	2	
Treasury	112	4	1	1	
Inventory	80	356	56	4	
FIN 46R	26	110	12	2	
Financial instruments & related derivatives	78	114	12	1	
Property & equipment	40	4	1		
Goodwill & intangibles	2	52	8	2	
Financing	132	98	4	2	
Payroll benefits, FAS 123R	100	74	4	1	
Income tax	2	260	88	22	
M&A		14	1		
Capital & equity	54	2	1		
Period-end financial reporting	332	118	12	2	
Other procedures					
Going concern	1				
Illegal acts, laws, & regulations	4				
Litigation, claims, & lawyers letters	16	20	8		
Risks, uncertainties, contingencies, & Commitments	6				
Testing the work of others	60	12	4		
Related party transactions	8	2			
Audit of ICFR, finalization process					
Update of scoping		12	4		
Summary of aggregate deficiencies		20	20	6	2
Financial statements, finalization process					
SEC services review			6		
Tie out/reading of financial statements	120	32	24		
Opinion		4	1	1	
Final analytical procedures	12	2	1		
Proxy	8	4	2	1	
Completion					
Subsequent events	12	2	1		
Management representations letter		4	1	1	
Other	40	96	64	20	
Meetings with client	20	60	100	50	
General partner, manager time			160	200	20
Audit committee meetings & preparation			60	32	
Quarterly reviews					
Planning	36	84	60	45	16
Analytical procedures	400	280	140	120	
Special issues			120	60	
Meetings	12	50	60	30	12
Financial statements	180	100	60	30	12

F.6 Why might specialists be needed on an audit engagement? What areas of knowledge and skills might be provided by specialists?

F.7 What client circumstances might cause the need for an IT specialist to be involved in an audit?

F.8 If an audit team needs an IT specialist to be involved in the audit, when might the IT specialist become involved? What tasks might the IT specialist perform at various stages of the audit?

AUDIT PLAN [LO 8]

The purpose of an integrated audit is to issue an audit report expressing opinions about the effectiveness of ICFR and fairness of financial statements. The auditor performs procedures to obtain **reasonable assurance** about the opinions expressed in the report. The audit steps that are performed need to reduce audit risk so that the auditor can have reasonable assurance that the report expresses the appropriate audit opinions. The auditor has to perform procedures to collect sufficient, appropriate evidence to persuade him or her that audit risk is acceptably low. The audit plan lays out the steps that are followed. After finishing the audit, the evidence gathered allows the auditor to issue an audit report expressing reasonable assurance.

Nature, Timing, and Extent

The knowledge necessary to understand the nature, timing, and extent of audit procedures includes management assertions, materiality, risk, and timing of different procedures. The audit plan documents the specific audit steps to be followed. The audit plan therefore describes the nature, or type of test; timing, or when the test is to be performed; and extent, or quantity of testing to be carried out. The nature of a test generally refers to whether the test is a test of controls or a substantive procedure and the type of activity involved in the audit procedure.

The controls that need to be tested for operating effectiveness can be selected after the auditor has identified significant accounts, relevant assertions, and likely sources of misstatement. In brief, if a significant account, type of transaction, or disclosure is susceptible to material misstatement, the auditor defines what causes that susceptibility. The auditor then looks for existence of controls in the client system that can prevent misstatements or detect misstatements that occur.

A control may exist that is effectively designed to prevent or detect the event that will cause the account on disclosure to be materially misstated. If so, the auditor selects that control and plans how to test its operating effectiveness. AS 5.41 states that auditors need to test the operating effectiveness of controls that are expected to sufficiently address the risk of misstatement to a relevant assertion. One control can address more than one risk. Alternatively, multiple controls can address a single risk (AS 5.39).

The substantive procedures of a financial statement audit have a straightforward purpose: the auditor plans tests to detect material misstatements that exist in the financial statements.

Audit evidence is obtained through **inspection, observation, inquiry, external confirmation, recalculation, reperformance** and **analytical procedures**. The type of procedure used depends largely on the evidence needed to evaluate management's assertion. For example, if the assertion is that cash in a bank account that is recorded in the client's records *exists* then the audit procedure may be that the auditor confirm the existence of the cash in the bank account with the bank. The audit procedure is different if the assertion about exis-

AUDITING IN ACTION

Selecting Controls and Accounts

In a retailing company, inventory has a large dollar account balance relative to other assets on the balance sheet. Therefore, inventory is a significant account for a company in the retail industry. A **relevant assertion** to the fair presentation of inventory on the balance sheet is that all of the inventory actually exists. A risk accompanying that assertion is theft of inventory by the public and employees. Various physical controls to prevent theft can be used—for example, electronic inventory tags on unsold merchandise with sensors at each store exit to detect sensors that were not removed at the point of sale.

These prevention devices are clearly important to the company in preventing theft. Even so, the most important control for the management assertion of inventory existence from the auditor's perspective is likely to be detection of errors in the inventory records. Detection and correction of inventory errors occurs when inventory items are compared to the records as the result of an inventory count and the records are adjusted to match the inventory that exists. A well-designed and executed physical count of inventory resulting in adjusting journal entries to write the inventory account balance down to what is counted is a detective control. It addresses the risk that inventory theft causes to the assertion of existence. The control addresses the risk that inventory that has actually been stolen is reported on the balance sheet.

A complete count of inventory once a year, analysis of the results, and subsequent adjustment of the accounting records are controls for detecting the results of theft that can cause inventory to be materially misstated. Therefore, if the inventory count and adjustment control exists, and appears well designed, the auditor will test whether the control operates effectively by testing the quality of the inventory count. The auditor also tests the inventory balance after the annual inventory count and adjustment process to determine whether the ending account balance is materially misstated.

tence is supposed to be supported by controls the client has over the cash records such as monthly bank reconciliations. For that situation, the audit program calls for an audit test to inspect the bank statement and bank reconciliation, and reperform the bank reconciliation calculations. The audit activities take whatever form is appropriate to gather evidence permitting the auditor to evaluate management's assertion.

Timing of audit procedures was discussed earlier, in a general sense, related to the planning required to make sure audit resources are available when they are needed. As was also discussed, the auditor must plan the timing of specific audit tests to be effective in providing sufficient audit evidence. The audit plan indicates when the activity is to be performed, for example, during interim or year-end work. For the ICFR audit, the audit opinion applies to the effectiveness of ICFR as of the date of management's ICFR report, which is at the fiscal year end. Therefore, tests have to provide evidence of the design and operating effectiveness at that date. AS 5.52 also stresses that testing ICFR over a longer period of time provides more evidence.

ICFR tests to provide evidence on whether the controls can be relied upon for the financial statement audit can be *performed* at any time the evidence is available, but must *test* the controls for the entire period of reliance. The audit activities providing evidence for the ICFR audit and financial statement audit may be performed at the same time. However, given that the audits have different objectives, the timing may also be different.

With regard to the extent of audit tests generally, as long as the tests are properly designed for the audit issue being evaluated, more testing provides more evidence. However, properly designed **sampling approaches** can provide sufficient evidence and permit the auditor to draw valid conclusions without examining all the transactions in an account balance.

Sampling approaches can limit the amount of detail testing performed and consequently reduce the audit resources that have to be expended. When sampling is used, the audit plan states what the sample size will be or how it is to be determined, as well as the population from which the sample is to be drawn.

Nature, timing, and extent of audit tests are discussed again as audit procedures are presented in Chapters 7 and 8 for the ICFR audit, and in Chapters 9 and 11 for the financial statement audit. Chapters 10, 12, 13, 14, and 15 present discussions of nature, timing, and extent of audit procedures when audits of the various business transaction cycles are presented.

Top Down Approach

In developing an audit plan consistent with a top down approach, the auditor relies on the identification of significant accounts and disclosures from earlier planning activities. Recall that the planning process identifies the assertions for the significant accounts and disclosures and develops conclusions about the threshold that makes a misstatement material. The auditor asks the question, "What is a material misstatement, and how would it happen?" Based on the answer, the auditor identifies a financial statement audit procedure that investigates the risk that this event has occurred. The nature, timing, and extent of the audit step are determined by whatever is needed to investigate the risk.

"How would the material misstatement happen?"

After answering this question, the auditor identifies the controls intended to prevent and detect the problem event. To identify the controls the auditor asks,

"What controls has management developed and implemented to deal with this potential misstatement?"

"Are the controls designed well?"

"What is a failure of these controls that would permit a material misstatement?"

The answers to these questions dictate the nature, timing, and extent of needed audit tests. The auditor designs **tests of controls** and includes them in the audit plan. ICFR audit procedures investigate the risks that a control failure has occurred. Exhibit 6-8 displays the links in top down audit planning.

Different Types of Audit Procedures

Audit evidence is an accumulation of activities, documents, and information that persuades the auditor to have reasonable assurance that management's assertions are appropriate. The evidence relevant to the management assertion the auditor is investigating impacts the audit procedures used. AS 5 identifies the following procedures that are used to test controls (AS 5.43, 5.45):

EXHIBIT 6-8

Top Down Audit Planning

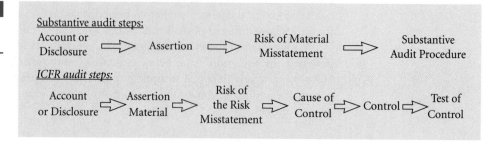

Substantive audit steps:
Account or Disclosure ⇒ Assertion ⇒ Risk of Material Misstatement ⇒ Substantive Audit Procedure

ICFR audit steps:
Account or Disclosure ⇒ Assertion Material ⇒ Risk of the Risk Misstatement ⇒ Cause of Control ⇒ Control ⇒ Test of Control

1. inquiries of appropriate personnel
2. inspection of relevant documentation
3. observation of the company's operations
4. reperformance of the application of the control

When inquiry, observation, and inspection are all used to trace a transaction as it is initiated, authorized, processed, and recorded, the process is called a **walkthrough**. This combination of audit procedures is used to accomplish the objectives of understanding the system and assessing design effectiveness. Walkthroughs are discussed again in Chapter 7.

A slightly different list of audit procedures also includes procedures appropriate for financial statement audits:

1. Inspection of records, documents, and tangible assets
2. Observation
3. Inquiry
4. External confirmation
5. Recalculation
6. Reperformance
7. Analytical procedures.

Auditor *inquiry* of client management and personnel is a source of audit evidence that occurs throughout the audit. Inquiry is a source of important information for client acceptance and continuance procedures. Not surprisingly, inquiry is an important information source as the auditor follows steps to understand ICFR. Inquiry continues to be important throughout the audit as the auditor obtains information about transactions, the results of audit tests, and financial statement disclosures.

The auditing standards use the term *inquiry* to cover a broad range of communications with various sources to obtain information. Even entry-level auditors are included in this process from very early in their careers. Audit programs instruct staff accountants to "interview the client" about a process or activity. Although it may sound more complex, this task is simply one of talking to client employees and asking questions to understand what goes on in the company.

Documentation is any type of paper, electronic file, or other media that records some item or process for which the auditor needs verification. The auditor can **inspect documentation**, such as reading a contract. The auditor can use documents for vouching or tracing. **Vouching** refers to looking at the underlying document supporting a number posted in the company's books and records. This provides support that the posted amount is valid because the transaction occurred or the asset or liability exists. **Tracing** refers to starting with a supporting document and making sure that the document is properly included or posted in the company's books and records, thus supporting the completeness assertion. The term *tracing* is sometimes used with a broader meaning to indicate following a transaction through various stages.

Observation goes a step further than inquiry because the auditor actually watches company personnel perform a business activity. Although observation provides the auditor with no assurance that the step is always performed the way he or she observes it, it lets the auditor verify his or her understanding of the way the business process is conducted. When trying to understand an aspect of the ICFR, the auditor might inquire of company personnel about how the step is performed, and then observe the step being performed. The auditor may even reperform the activity. If documentation is used to show that the control step was performed, the auditor can also inspect documentation.

Reperformance refers to the auditor personally going through steps that have already been performed by the client or the client's system. The auditor might reperform calculations used to arrive at the valuation of an asset, or reperform accounting processes such as footing (adding up a column of numbers). Reperformance provides the auditor with direct, personal knowledge about the process. *Recalculation* is a specific type of reperformance in which the auditor executes the same calculations previously carried out by the client.

When the auditor physically examines or looks at tangible assets the step is also called inspection. **Inspection** of tangible assets provides the auditor with direct, personal assurance that the item being examined exists.

External confirmation is an audit procedure used to verify the existence assertion and the rights or obligations assertion for certain assets or liabilities. The confirmation process occurs when the auditor receives verification from independent third parties. The confirmation document received from the outside party provides audit evidence. For example, an auditor can send a confirmation to a bank, asking whether the amount the company shows on its balance sheet is actually on deposit with the bank. The auditor can send confirmations to the debtors and creditors the company lists for its accounts receivable and payable, asking the outside party to confirm the existence and status of the account balance. Confirmations are discussed in detail in Chapter 10 and are also presented in later chapters when the assets and liabilities to which they apply are discussed.

Analytical procedures are performed throughout the audit to gain evidence regarding the best way to plan the audit, relationships among accounts, and evaluation of test results. Analytical procedures are a required part of audit planning. Analytical procedures address the relationships among both financial and nonfinancial data. For example, if a company has a long-term debt liability shown on the balance sheet, the auditor should be able to find and understand the portion of interest expense related to that debt based on the terms of the debt obligation. Since analytical procedures are used throughout the audit, they are discussed at various stages in future chapters.

The audit plan also documents the audit procedures that are conducted during the wrap up phase of the audit. These procedures include communicating with management and the audit committee, communicating with the client's attorney, and obtaining a management representation letter. These procedures are discussed in Chapter 11.

REVIEW QUESTIONS

G.1 What do the auditing standards mean when they refer to the nature, timing, and extent of audit tests? How does nature, timing, and extent relate to materiality, management's assertions and controls?

G.2 How does the auditor plan for the ICFR audit? For the financial statement audit? In other words, what linkages are important to develop and document as a part of drafting the audit plan?

G.3 What audit procedures are useful for a financial statement audit but not an ICFR audit, and why?

G.4 What are the wrap up steps of the audit that are included in the audit plan?

COMMUNICATION ON PLANNING

When initial planning is completed, the auditor is in a position to meet with management and the audit committee to provide an overview of the plan for the audit. The auditor does not communicate information at a level of detail that compromises the audit's purpose of providing an outside check on the company. However, the communication provides general information about the scope and timing of the audit.

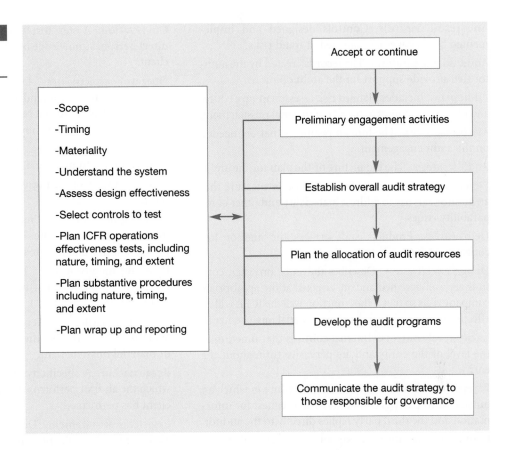

EXHIBIT 6-9

Planning and Risk Assessment

-Scope

-Timing

-Materiality

-Understand the system

-Assess design effectiveness

-Select controls to test

-Plan ICFR operations effectiveness tests, including nature, timing, and extent

-Plan substantive procedures including nature, timing, and extent

-Plan wrap up and reporting

Accept or continue

Preliminary engagement activities

Establish overall audit strategy

Plan the allocation of audit resources

Develop the audit programs

Communicate the audit strategy to those responsible for governance

CONCLUSION

Exhibit 6-9 displays a summary of risk and planning activities as they fit into the overall audit.

A major part of risk assessment and audit planning involves the steps the auditor performs to understand the company's system and assess the design effectiveness of ICFR. This audit process, along with similar steps that management performs to provide its own assessment of the company's ICFR in its report submitted to the SEC, are the topics covered in Chapter 7. When planning, including risk assessment, understanding and assessing the design of ICFR, and writing the audit plan document, is completed, the auditor moves on to testing the operating effectiveness of ICFR and audit procedures for the financial statement audit. The audit of operating effectiveness of ICFR is discussed in Chapter 8, and substantive procedures for the financial statement audit are the topic of Chapter 9.

KEY TERMS

Analytical procedures. Audit steps in which information is examined looking for the expected relationships; can be performed on financial and other quantitative information and information both internal and external to the company.

Audit committee. A committee (or equivalent body) established by and among the Board of Directors for the purposes of overseeing the accounting and financial processes, hiring the auditor and overseeing the integrated audit.

Anti-fraud controls. Controls designed and implemented by management targeted at fraud risks.

Audit documentation. The records created by the auditor that provide support for the audit opinions.

Audit plan. Includes planned risk assessment procedures and planned responses to the risk of material misstatement.

Audit resources. The human resources that are needed on the audit engagement.

Audit strategy. The big picture of the plan for the audit.

Benchmark. An account balance or other measure that an auditor can use to address materiality and other comparability issues.

Deliverables. Products and services the auditor has contracted to provide to the client.

Design effectiveness. Describes the situation when controls are well designed and are targeted at the appropriate company risks so that if they function well the ICFR will be effective in preventing or detecting material misstatements.

Entity-level controls. Internal controls that function at the level of the entity and are pervasive throughout the entity.

External confirmation. An audit procedure in which an outside third party is contacted with a request for information and the third party replies directly to the auditor.

Fraud Triangle. Incentive–opportunity–rationalization.

Going concern issues. Topic addressed by the auditor evaluating whether the company will be able to meet its obligations and have adequate cash flow for the fiscal year following the balance sheet date.

Inquiry. When the auditor asks client company personnel or others about a topic to gain audit evidence.

Inspection. The audit step of examining documents, usually to agree the amounts on the documents to posted amounts, but also for various control-related reasons; observing that tangible assets exist.

Interim procedures. Audit procedures conducted at a date prior to the client's fiscal year end.

Material weakness. A deficiency, or a combination of deficiencies, in ICFR, such that there is a reasonable possibility that a material misstatement of the company's annual or interim financial statements will not be prevented or detected on a timely basis.

Materiality. The quantitative magnitude or qualitative importance of an omission or misstatement that will likely affect the judgment of a reasonable person.

Nature, timing, extent. Terms used in the audit standards that describe the characteristics of audit procedures; refers to the type of audit procedure to be used, when it is to be used, and the amount of evidence to be collected.

Observation. A step through which the auditor gains direct personal knowledge of an action performed by the client.

Operating effectiveness. Describes the situation when controls function as intended; when a person executes that control (rather than it being automated), the individual has the appropriate knowledge and authority.

Outside service providers. An entity with which a company contracts to provide a service.

Outsourcing. Contacting with an outside entity for a service.

Planning meeting. Meeting of those on the audit team intended to communicate the audit strategy, division of responsibilities, and information about risks of the client.

Planning memorandum. Document prepared during the planning process that includes information on the audit strategy.

Reasonable assurance. At high, but not absolute, level of assurance about whether the financial statements are free of material misstatement.

Recalcuation. A specific type of reperformance during which the auditor performs the same calculation that the client has performed.

Registration statement. Document filed with the SEC associated with public offerings.

Relevant assertion. A financial statement assertion that if materially misstated, could cause the financial statements to be materially misstated; based on inherent risk without regard to the effect of controls.

Reperformance. Going through the same activities that have been carried out by client personnel.

Reviews of quarterly financial statements. Services provided to companies who file with the SEC; less than an audit.

Risk assessment. Integrated throughout the planning process; points the auditor to the important areas of the client's operations and financial statements to plan the audit.

Roll forward audit procedures. Audit procedures performed between the interim date and the fiscal year end to reconcile the account balances at the two dates and to determine whether ICFR continued to function in the same manner between the interim date and year end.

Sampling approaches. Refers to the various ways auditors can use sampling; sampling is used in auditing when it is reasonable and possible to form an audit conclusion after examining less than 100% of a population (such as looking at less than all sales transactions or less than all the individual subsidiary ledger accounts that make up the accounts receivable control account).

Scope of the engagement. The work that has to be performed on the audit so that the auditor can issue the reports or other products contracted for in the engagement letter.

Significant accounts or disclosures. Refers to an account or a disclosure that could contain a material misstatement that, individually or when aggregated with others, could have a material effect on the financial statements.

Significant risk. Risk of material financial statement misstatement that is important enough to require special audit consideration.

Specialist. An individual with skills beyond accounting and auditing needed for certain areas of the audit.

Statutory audits. Engagements required by law.

Substantive procedures. Audit procedures that address account balances and disclosures.

Tests of controls. Audit procedures that address controls.

Tolerable misstatement, tolerable rate of error. The level of account balance misstatement, or rate of ICFR failure, indicating the threshold beyond which a problem meets the standard of being material.

Tracing. The audit procedure that begins with the supporting document and examines the company's books and records to determine that the information is properly recorded.

User organization. An entity that contracts with a service provider for services.

Vouching. Inspecting the underlying document to agree the amount and other information on the document to the recorded information.

Walkthrough. Term for a combination of steps that follow a transaction from its inception through reporting; consists of inquiry, inspection, observation, and sometimes reperformance; useful for assessing design effectiveness.

MULTIPLE CHOICE

6-1 **[LO 2]** The audit strategy for an integrated audit
(a) lists the specific audit steps related to a financial statement assertion.
(b) is usually developed before the auditor will sign an engagement letter.
(c) documents the big picture issues of an audit.
(d) includes the plan for statistical evaluation of audit test results.

6-2 **[LO 2]** Information for developing the audit strategy comes from all the following sources except
(a) communication with the audit client's outside attorney.
(b) client acceptance and continuance procedures.
(c) auditor experience.
(d) client deadlines on deliverables documented in the engagement letter.

6-3 **[LO 2]** Scoping decisions
(a) provide direction to individual auditors in performing audit procedures.
(b) are affected by how many professional staff the audit firm has available.
(c) are affected by the audit fee.
(d) include consideration of multiple client locations.

6-4 **[LO 3]** Entity-level controls
(a) are not considered unless the auditor is going to test the operating effectiveness of a control.
(b) can affect the audit plan for tests of program controls.

(c) are only important within the context of IT.
(d) are assumed to exist and do not significantly affect the audit program.

6-5 **[LO 3]** For the ICFR audit of an integrated audit, outsourced operations
(a) are not a part of the audit client's accounting system and therefore are not considered in audit planning.
(b) are always considered a part of the audit client's accounting system and must be tested if the related financial statement accounts are material.
(c) may be material to the audit client's ICFR, and in that case operating effectiveness must be tested by the auditor of the company that purchases the outsourced services.
(d) may be material to the audit client's ICFR, and in that case audit evidence must be obtained and evaluated.

6-6 **[LO 8]** The nature, timing, and extent of audit procedures
(a) must be set during the initial audit planning process based only on information obtained during the current year.
(b) may be influenced by information obtained on prior-year audits of a recurring audit engagement once the information has been updated.
(c) are not revised during the audit once they have been planned.

(d) only refer to substantive procedures and are determined based on the results of tests of operating effectiveness.

6-7 **[LO 3]** For purposes of an integrated audit, materiality

(a) should consider whether the economic decision of any decision maker would be affected by the information.

(b) should consider whether the economic decision of any decision maker within the company being audited would be affected by the information.

(c) is assessed within the context of users with certain qualifications.

(d) is assessed within the context of investors who buy and sell publicly traded stocks.

6-8 **[LO 8]** During audit planning the auditor finds that gross profit is much greater in the current year than in prior years and decides to increase the audit emphasis on sales and inventories. The auditor most likely discovered the change in gross profit by

(a) preparing an audit program to test controls over inventory.

(b) analytical procedures.

(c) reviewing last year's audit program and working papers.

(d) inquiry of management on profit trends.

6-9 **[LO 3]** After the auditor has determined materiality at the financial statement level, he or she evaluates the amount of misstatement that would be material at the account balance level. The term for this threshold amount is

(a) tolerable misstatement.

(b) overall materiality.

(c) account misstatement.

(d) account materiality.

6-10 **[LO 3]** When evaluating the dollar amount of financial statement materiality, the auditor's judgment mainly addresses

(a) the dollar amount of the most important account balance.

(b) whether to use a percentage of total assets or net income as the benchmark.

(c) the cost of audit procedures related to using that level of materiality.

(d) the amount of misstatement that would influence an economic decision of a reasonable person with appropriate qualifications relying on the financial statements.

6-11 **[LO 3]** Which of the following is not part of risk assessment?

(a) Performing substantive procedures

(b) Brainstorming about fraud

(c) Understanding the client's system

(d) Evaluating design effectiveness of ICFR

6-12 **[LO 4]** Which of the following is the most serious indicator of higher risk?

(a) The company is experiencing a very substantial growth rate, although it is typical of its industry and the overall economy.

(b) Competition in the industry is increasing, and the company is experiencing unexpected obsolescence of its products.

(c) The company must provide warranties on its products because this is the norm for its industry.

(d) Growth in the overall economy is slowing.

6-13 **[LO 1,2]** Which of the following is not considered in scoping an audit engagement?

(a) The company is a subsidiary, and the parent is audited by another audit firm.

(b) The company does business in multiple locations.

(c) The general level of economic activity in the company's geographic environment.

(d) Services the company outsources.

6-14 **[LO 4]** Using the terms of the Fraud Triangle, if management places great importance on achieving the financial performance predicted by analysts and it seems that the predictions will not be achieved—for example, when net income or earnings per share is going to be lower than predicted by analysts, this is an example of

(a) opportunity for fraudulent financial reporting.

(b) incentive for misappropriation of assets.

(c) rationalization for fraudulent financial reporting.

(d) incentive for fraudulent financial reporting.

6-15 Which of the following is not true about significant, unusual, or highly complex transactions, especially those close to period-end?

(a) They should be addressed by the company's anti-fraud controls.

(b) Controls over them are tested by the auditor.

(c) They are expected as a part of the financial closing process and represent typical risk.

(d) If not appropriately controlled, they provide an opportunity for fraudulent financial reporting.

6-16 [LO 2] Obtaining an understanding of ICFR and assessing its design effectiveness contribute to the auditor accomplishing all of the following except

(a) selecting the controls to test.

(b) developing the audit strategy.

(c) determining whether ICFR is effective.

(d) It helps for all of the above.

6-17 [LO 1] The audit planning meeting

(a) provides an opportunity to instruct assistants on the need to communicate accounting and auditing matters they feel are significant to the financial statements to the auditor responsible for the audit engagement.

(b) must be attended by everyone who works on the engagement to provide an opportunity for them to be briefed by the in-charge accountant on fraud risks.

(c) provides an opportunity to communicate the audit strategy to the appropriate individuals in the client company.

(d) occurs before the audit firm makes a decision about client acceptance.

6-18 [LO 3] The amount of supervision required for a staff auditor

(a) is specified in the audit standards.

(b) will be consistent regardless of the individual's experience.

(c) will depend on the difficulty of the task and the skills and experience of the individual.

(d) depends on the amount of time the audit partner spends on the engagement since this task cannot be delegated to anyone other than the person ultimately responsible for the audit.

6-19 [LO 8] Which of the following audit procedures cannot be performed at an interim date?

(a) Understanding the client's system and assessing design effectiveness.

(b) Substantive tests of account balances.

(c) Tests of controls.

(d) Tests of the year-end closing process.

6-20 [LO 7] A specialist who assists on an audit

(a) must be employed by the audit firm.

(b) does not have to be an employee of the audit firm but cannot be an employee of the audit client.

(c) can be an employee of the audit firm, client, or neither.

(d) must have the specific credentials listed in auditing standards so that his or her conclusions can be relied upon in the audit.

6-21 [LO 8] A walkthrough

(a) is a discussion with the client on how a transaction is initiated, processed, and recorded.

(b) is an audit procedure in which the auditor inspects tangible assets.

(c) is a combination of inquiry, observation, inspection, and reperformance used for understanding the system and assessing design effectiveness.

(d) requires reperformance of all the client's steps for initiating, processing, and recording a transaction.

6-22 [LO 7] The auditor-in-charge of an engagement that requires the skills of an auditor particularly trained to deal with the impacts of IT

(a) cannot delegate to the IT auditor the task of communicating with the company's IT personnel.

(b) can perform the tasks personally as long as the IT auditor provides direction.

(c) must be sufficiently knowledgeable to work with the IT auditor.

(d) None of the above.

DISCUSSION QUESTIONS

6-23 [LO 3] Why do the audit standards address qualifications of the user of financial statements in the discussion of materiality?

 6-24 [LO 4] Why is fraud that is committed by management always considered material, even if the amount is not quantitatively material?

6-25 [LO 1] What is a top down approach to planning an audit? What are the steps? How does this approach link the financial statements to ultimate audit program steps? Why does AS 5 direct the auditor to use this approach in assessing materiality?

6-26   **[LO 3]** When a benchmark approach is used to set materiality at the financial statement level, why are different benchmarks used for different types of entities, or companies in different entities?

6-27   **[LO 5]** When a control is tested at an interim date, the following are things the auditor considers in deciding how much audit evidence must be obtained about the control during the roll forward period. How would each one affect the evidence needed and why?

(a) The importance of the control

(b) How much evidence was obtained at the interim date

(c) The length of time between interim testing and fiscal year end

(d) Any changes that have occurred to ICFR between the interim testing date and the end of the fiscal year

6-28   **[LO 3]** Explain why controls have to be tested for the entire fiscal year if they are to be relied on in the financial statement audit. Why do they only have to be tested related to their effectiveness at the fiscal year end for an ICFR audit?

6-29   **[LO 6]** Review the Outline of a Planning Memo presented in the chapter. List all of the items included in the planning memo that are still new to you. Use the index of the book to find the topics. Identify the stage of the audit where these topics fit.

PROBLEMS

6-30   **[LO 2]** Samantha is a senior manager at a national CPA firm. She has recently taken over the planning responsibilities on her firm's largest client, a midsize publicly traded company with multiple subsidiaries around North America. The client chose her firm primarily because of its cost efficiencies compared to those of larger firms. The client is publicly traded, so Samantha is planning an integrated audit as well as quarterly review work.

Required:

(a) How will each of the following concepts affect Samantha's audit planning?

(1) Nature

(2) Timing

(3) Extent

(b) Should Samantha consider the audit budget when planning the audit? Explain, particularly addressing pressures to limit any audit procedures to keep the budget within an expected range.

6-31   **[LO 1,3]** Stephanie is a senior auditor at Hart & Brand CPA firm. This is Hart & Brand's first year on a new public client, Bellezza Casa. Bellezza Casa is a home and garden specialty retailer that consists of 120 retail locations nationwide and has no subsidiary businesses. This year, Bellezza Casa books show gross profits of $1.2 million, net income of $720,000, and total assets of $4.5 million. Stephanie is assigned the task of determining materiality for Bellezza Casa's financial statements.

Required:

(a) In which stage of the audit should Stephanie determine overall financial statement materiality and planning materiality for the various accounts?

(b) If Stephanie is assigned the task of testing the accounts receivable account during the year-end audit, should she use the same level of materiality she formulated for financial statement materiality? If not, will materiality for accounts receivable be higher or lower? Explain.

6-32   **[LO 4]** You are the senior on an audit team for a large public company. This is your second year on the engagement, and you have established a good working relationship with some of the client's staff. Your firm has only been the independent auditor of this company for four years, and the company has a history of fraud prior to your firm's involvement.

At lunch with some staff from the client, you overhear that Danilo, the long-time assistant controller for the company's South America operations, has had problems paying his mortgage. He may even face foreclosure if he doesn't find an opportunity for some supplemental income. Furthermore, through the fraud brainstorming meeting conducted at the beginning of the fiscal year's audit, you learned that the South America division was thought to be responsible for the fraud in the past. Danilo and his department were even investigated by the internal audit department, but all prior investigations were inconclusive due to lack of evidence.

Upon reviewing the current year's ICFR testing performed by a staff accountant working on the engagement, you see that the test results indicate that ICFR are effective. The audit plan for the financial statement audit relies on the operating effectiveness of controls for the entire fiscal year. The ICFR controls testing gives no indication that the financial statement audit plan needs to be revised.

Required:

(a) What are the three elements of the Fraud Triangle?

(b) Are all of the elements necessary for Danilo to commit fraud present?

(c) What should you do upon learning of this situation?

(d) How do you feel about the possibility of increasing the level of investigation if it might end up in Danilo being exposed—even though you know the nature of his activities is not on a significant enough scale to have a material impact on the company's financial outcomes?

6-33   **[LO 1, 3]** Philly Communications is the largest provider of telephone and cable service in Pennsylvania. During its year-end audit, the manager at Dell & Wayne, Philly's independent audit firm, determined that the appropriate amount for materiality at the financial statement level to be used during planning for the current year's audit is $1 million. Derek, a staff auditor at Dell & Wayne, is assigned the task of performing substantive tests on Philly's asset accounts. The following table summarizes Derek's findings. All the misstatements are overstatements.

Account	Tolerable Misstatement	Actual Misstatement
Cash	115,000	95,000
Accounts Receivable	310,000	245,000
Investments	145,000	120,000
Inventory	120,000	80,000
Buildings	510,000	450,000
Prepaid Expenses	100,000	20,000

Required:

(a) When viewed independently of one another, do any of the actual misstatements in the individual asset accounts indicate a material misstatement that calls for an adjusting journal entry in Philly Communications' books?

(b) Should Derek recommend adjusting journal entries to Philly's management? If so, what journal entry might Derek propose?

(c) How does the concept of aggregate misstatement affect your answer?

6-34   **[LO 2, 3]** Fred is a partner at D&Y, an international professional services firm. Fred's primary client, Green Investments, is a publicly traded holding company with subsidiaries around the world. Most of Green Investments subsidiaries are audited by D&Y's worldwide affiliates. However, two of its subsidiaries are audited by local firms not affiliated with D&Y. One of these subsidiaries accounts for approximately 10% of Green's annual income, and the other accounts for only 0.3% of Green's annual income. This year, all of Green Investments subsidiaries received an unqualified audit opinion.

Required:

(a) List elements of audit planning impacted by Green Investments' structure of multiple subsidiaries.

(b) Identify how the ICFR audit changes because of multiple locations. Particularly consider the impact of the overseas operations.

(c) How is the audit plan affected by the two subsidiaries audited by other CPA firms? Address each subsidiary in your answer.

6-35   **[LO 5,7]** Assume the role of the audit manager on a publicly traded Internet auction company. The company is known as an industry innovator and has recently implemented a new IT system. Upon review of the company's operations, you also discover that the client has a heavy reliance on complex IT controls and has undergone a new "green" movement to enhance paperless operations.

Required:

(a) When preparing the plan for this year's audit, what are some special considerations you should include?

(b) What are indications of high-risk areas?

(c) What are some indicators that specialists may be necessary for the audit?

(d) According to AU 311, what are some planning activities a specialist may be involved in?

(e) Summarize the company's characteristics that require special attention in the audit plan.

6-36   **[LO 8]** As a manager at RHC, LLP, part of Charlie's tasks include drafting the audit plan for his audit clients, including determining the appropriate audit procedures to be performed over the course of the audit.

Required:

(a) List the procedures Charlie can utilize to complete the audit in accordance with AS 5.

(b) List the procedures Charlie can utilize to complete the audit in accordance with AU 326 and identify which are appropriate for the audit of financial statements and which are appropriate for the ICFR audit.

6-37   **[LO 1,3]** Classify each of the following based on whether they can be performed at an interim date (assuming appropriate procedures are performed during the roll forward period) or whether they must be performed at or after the fiscal year end. Briefly justify your answer. State why for each.

(a) Control tests of the client's year-end closing and financial reporting process

(b) Observations and tests of the client's count of physical inventory

(c) Substantive tests of accounts receivable amounts

(d) Audit of cash

(e) Design effectiveness evaluation of ICFR

(f) Operating effectiveness evaluation of ICFR

6-38   **[LO 1]** The following two paragraphs are used to present the auditor's opinions of XYZ company:

> In our opinion, the financial statements referred to present fairly, in all material aspects, the financial position of XYZ Company as of October 31, 2010 and 2011, and the changes in net assets and its cash flows for the years then ended in conformity with accounting principles generally accepted in the United States of America.
>
> Our audits were performed for the purpose of forming an opinion on the basic financial statements of XYZ Company taken as a whole. The accompanying Schedule of Expenditures of Federal Awards and State Projects is presented for purposes of additional analysis as required by the U.S. Office of Management and Budget Circular A-133, *Audits of States, Local Governments, and Non-Profit Organizations,* and chapter 10.650, Rules of the Auditor General, and is not a required part of the basic financial statements. The Schedule of Explicit and Discrete Disclosure for Able County and the Schedule of Revenue and Expenses are presented for purposes of additional analysis and are not a required part of the basic financial statements. Such information has been subjected to the auditing procedures applied in the audit of the basic financial statements and, in our opinion, is fairly stated, in all material respects, in relation to the basic financial statements taken as a whole.

(a) What do you know about XYZ Company based on the audit report?

(b) How are the deliverables in this audit engagement different from those of a "standard" integrated audit of a company that has to file with the SEC?

(c) Based on the information you can glean from the audit report paragraphs above, what would the auditor consider in planning the scope, timing, and resources for the audit engagement?

6-39   **[LO 6]** The first standard of field work of the generally accepted auditing standards states that audit work is to be adequately planned. Two tools that auditors use to document their planning activities are an audit planning memorandum and an audit plan or program.

Required:

(a) Describe an audit planning memorandum. What purpose does it serve on an audit engagement? List types of information that it includes.

(b) Describe an audit program. What purpose does it serve on an audit engagement? List types of information that it includes.

6-40   **[LO 8]** Refer to Auditing in Action: Roll Forward Procedures featuring Shadow Company. Assume that Shadow holds a significant amount of cash in an interest-bearing bank account and that the auditors performed substantive procedures to determine the fairness of the recorded amount of interest revenue through September 30. These procedures included recalculation of monthly interest earned based on balances and interest rates documented on the bank statements, and tracing the amounts to the accounting records.

List roll forward procedures that Shadow's auditors can perform at year-end regarding the interest revenue.

6-41   **[LO 8]** Several specific audit procedures are listed below. For each item, identify the type of procedure listed and which of the assertions is being addressed by the procedure.

(a) Examine a list of investment securities held by the client's trustee.

(b) For a sample of transactions posted to the client's accounts payable subsidiary ledger, examine supporting purchase orders and receiving reports agreeing amounts and information.

(c) Send a written request to the client's customer for verification of the amount owed to the client company.

(d) Examine the dealer's invoice for a new vehicle reported on the client's fixed assets subsidiary ledger.

(e) Ask the client's credit manager about the collectibility of certain customer account balances.

(f) Watch the client's process of conducting the physical inventory counts.

(g) Compute interest expense on notes payable.

(h) Verify the client's bank reconciliation by testing the proper inclusion of all reconciling items.

(i) Send a written request to the client's attorney for verification of legal matters.

(j) Compare key ratios for the current year with the same ratio results for the prior year.

(k) Trace the total of the client's accounts payable subsidiary ledger to the general ledger.

6-42 **[LO 8]** Several audit objectives are listed below. For each item, identify the related assertion and a specific audit procedure that can be applied to accomplish the objective.

(a) Establish whether recorded amounts due from customers are valid.

(b) Determine whether leases are properly recorded as capital or operating leases.

(c) Assess the adequate inclusion of related party transactions.

(d) Determine that year-end inventory quantities are actually on hand.

(e) Determine whether prices used in the client's billing program are authorized.

(f) Determine whether payroll is properly accrued at year end.

(g) Verify whether all cash collections are included in bank deposits.

(h) Determine whether the general ledger includes any unusual adjusting entries.

6-43 **[LO 8]** Auditors can use documentary evidence for vouching or tracing. Several audit objectives are listed below, each of which may apply inspection of documentary evidence to accomplish the objective. For each item, indicate whether the specific audit procedure that could be applied would involve (1) vouching or (2) tracing.

(a) Determine whether credits in the accounts payable subsidiary ledger represent actual purchase transactions.

(b) Determine whether debits in the accounts receivable subsidiary ledger represent actual sales of goods or services.

(c) Determine whether all transactions in the sales journal represent shipments of goods.

(d) Determine that all purchase invoices have been recorded in the proper vendor account in the accounts payable subsidiary ledger.

(e) Determine that all shipments of goods have been recorded as credits in the perpetual inventory records.

(f) Determine the propriety of the recorded amount of newly acquired machinery.

(g) Determine whether all cash collections are recorded in the cash receipts journal.

(h) Determine whether all recorded cash disbursement transactions are supported by an authorized purchase order.

6-44 Go to the AICPA Web site and access AU 311 on planning and supervision. The standard covers some aspects of client acceptance discussed in Chapter 5 as well as topics covered in this chapter. (Note that this SAS has been revised by the AICPA since the adoption of the interim standards by the PCAOB, and therefore applies to the audit of nonpublic companies.) Other SASs are listed in the following locations in the standard. What are the names of the other standards to which reference is made? Why do you think these other standards are related to the Planning and Supervision auditing standard?

(a) footnote 1

(b) 311.07

(c) footnote 7

(d) footnote 8

(e) 311.21

(f) 311.25

(g) 311.26

(h) footnote 9

(i) 311.31

6-45 Go to the PCAOB Web site and access AS 5. Read paragraphs 9 through 20 on planning. What guidance do you find in these paragraphs related to planning the audit for smaller or less complex companies?

6-46 Refer to Problem 6-38. Look up US OMB Circular A-133. What is it? What does this tell you about XYZ Company?

PROFESSIONAL SIMULATIONS

Go to the book's companion Web site at www.wiley.com/college/hooks to find simulations similar to those on the computerized CPA exam.

APPENDIX A: USING THE WORK OF OTHERS

Auditors obtain evidence to form their audit opinions. Evidence obtained through **direct personal knowledge** such as observation, reperformance, and inspection is most persuasive to the auditor. However, since the quality of audit evidence is never convincing, evaluating how much to rely on different forms of evidence is a major part of the professional judgment required for any audit. The work that others have conducted related to a company's ICFR and financial information can provide useful evidence to the auditor in performing an integrated audit. In addition, the individuals who perform this work may sometimes provide direct assistance to the independent auditor.

Internal Auditors and Others

AU 322, *Auditor's Consideration of Internal Audit Function in an Audit of Financial Statements*, provides the bulk of the guidance to independent auditors in considering the work of others on an audit. AU 322 was originally written to address only a financial statement audit. As a result, it addresses only the subject of **internal auditors** and lacks guidance on some more recent developments. One such development is when management has individuals other than internal auditors perform work on its assessment and report on ICFR for filing with the SEC. AS 5 states that AU 322 also applies when considering the work of internal auditors for the ICFR audit of an integrated audit. AS 5 also states that the concepts of AU 322 should be applied by external auditors when considering the work performed on ICFR by individuals other than internal auditors. Guidance on the work performed by others on ICFR applies to both expressing an opinion on ICFR and considering ICFR for assessing control risk for the financial statement audit.

> … the auditor may use the work performed by, or receive direct assistance from, internal auditors, company personnel (in addition to internal auditors), and third parties working under the direction of management or the audit committee that provides evidence about the effectiveness of internal control over financial reporting. (AS 5.17)

Relying on the work of others affects the auditor's decisions about the nature, timing, and extent of the work he or she would otherwise have performed. Using the work of others in an audit can be very efficient, limit redundancy of procedures, and help control the costs of the audit. Even so, the auditor is ultimately responsible for the integrated audit opinion, and the auditor's decision to use the work of others does not reduce that responsibility.

AUDITING IN ACTION

Impact of the Internal Auditor's Work

Assume that a company has four production facilities for its manufacturing processes. The company uses the same procedures and central IT processing for tracking and aggregating the costs of manufactured inventory at all four processing locations. During the year the company's internal audit staff visits each location several times on a surprise basis and performs tests of whether the standard procedures are being followed, and the costs of inventory are captured and recorded correctly. During the past year the internal audit staff visited each facility three times. Although no other problems were found, at manufacturing facility "C" the internal auditors repeatedly found errors in the cost records. Based on this finding, the independent auditor will likely decide to direct more audit effort to location "C" than to the other locations.

This is an example of the work of others causing the independent auditor to do more work; the reverse can be true as well. If the internal auditors had found no problems at any of the manufacturing locations, the independent auditor might have decided that less work was needed related to recording and aggregating inventory costs.

Responsibility Shared between Independent Auditors

In contrast to when the auditor uses the "work of others," there are times when the **principal auditor** *does* share responsibility for the audit opinion with another auditor. Sharing responsibility occurs when another independent auditor has done a significant portion of the work. Sometimes another independent auditor does so much work that the principal auditor does not think it is appropriate for his or her firm to claim the opinion related to the entire company as its own. This might occur, for example, when another auditor performs all the audit procedures for a subsidiary or branch of the company located in another country. If it is appropriate for auditor responsibility to be shared, the principal auditor refers to the other auditor in the audit report, explaining the division of work and responsibility (AS 5.C8, AU 543).

REVIEW QUESTIONS

H.1 What impact does the work of others have on decisions the auditor makes about work he or she must perform?

H.2 How does the work of others affect the auditor's responsibility for the audit opinions?

H.3 Who can perform work that may be of value to the independent auditor?

Deciding to Rely on the Work of Others

In deciding whether and to what extent to rely on the work of others on an integrated audit, the auditor must assess two important influences. The first consideration is the individual who performed the work, and the second is the object of the work that was performed. When considering the individual who performed the work, the auditor evaluates the competence and objectivity of the individual. When considering the subject matter or target of the work performed, the auditor evaluates:

- **Materiality** of the account balances or classes of transactions
- Risk associated with controls
- Subjectivity of the evaluations that are a part of the procedures

Competence and Objectivity

The auditor considers the **competence** and **objectivity** qualifications of other individuals performing work. The more objective and competent the person is, the more the auditor will consider using the work performed. Alternatively, if the auditor judges the other person to lack *either* competence or objectivity, the work performed will not be useful to the audit. The auditor must make this judgment about competence and objectivity of the person performing the work every year of the audit engagement. On a continuing audit engagement, the judgment made in the prior year cannot *automatically* be assumed to still be valid because circumstances may have changed. The auditor considers information from prior engagements along with information about any changes that have occurred since then. The auditor may decide there is a need to perform procedures to evaluate the competence and objectivity of others, even on a recurring engagement, if there have been changes since the prior engagement.

The auditor's opinion about the competence and objectivity of those performing the work is important for deciding not only whether the work performed may be useful, but also for assessing the amount of testing that must be performed on others' work before the auditor can feel comfortable using it.

Indicators of competence that the auditor looks for include:

- education level
- professional experience
- professional certification
- continuing education
- policies, programs, and procedures
- assignment of individuals to work areas
- supervision and review
- quality of documentation of the work
- quality of reports and recommendations
- evaluations of performance

(AU 322.09)

Objectivity refers to whether the person performing the work reports to an officer of sufficient status within the company to ensure broad coverage in the procedures performed and "adequate consideration of, and action on, the findings and recommendations" (AU 322.10). This means that the person performing the work must rank high enough within the organization to minimize the possibility that management decides what work should be done, evaluates the outcomes, and might be able to suppress undesirable results. Indicators that a person performing the work has an appropriate organizational position to be objective include having direct access and reporting regularly to the Board of Directors and audit committee. Also, if the BOD or audit committee oversees the hiring process, this supports the likelihood that the "appropriate" people are hired for the job and will not be fired simply for reporting an unpopular finding.

Objectivity is also tied to a person's loyalties. For example, the auditor will not judge a person to be objective if that person is testing controls or performing other work in departments that employ his or her family members. Likewise, objectivity is not likely for internal control or other work performed in departments where the tester recently worked or will be assigned in the near future.

REVIEW QUESTIONS

I.1 How do the competence and objectivity of others affect the auditor's use of their work?

I.2 What are indicators of the competence of others performing work that is used by the auditor?

I.3 What are indicators of the objectivity of others performing work that is used by the auditor?

I.4 How can management's control over a low-ranking person affect the value of that person's work to the auditor?

Effect on the Independent Auditor's Work

The controls and accounts on which the other person worked influences its potential impact. The work may affect the nature, timing, and extent of the independent auditor's work.

Nature of Controls

The auditor may find the work of others useful in obtaining an understanding of the accounting system. To decide whether and how to use the work of others related to auditing ICFR effectiveness, the auditor first assesses the nature of the controls involved. For example, the auditor carefully considers whether to use the work of others that applies to the **control environment**. The control environment, which is discussed in Chapter 7, is sometimes described as the "softer" aspects of a company's ICFR. The control environment includes:

- Integrity and ethical values
- Commitment to competence
- Board of Directors or audit committee participation
- Management's philosophy and operating style
- Organizational structure
- Assignment of authority and responsibility
- Human resources policies and procedures

The control environment has a pervasive impact on overall ICFR. So, if the auditor uses the work that others have performed on the control environment, that work affects the auditor's assessment of risk at the financialstatement level and the overall audit strategy.

Risk

In considering work at the account balance or class of transaction level, the auditor assesses the materiality of the related accounts and disclosures, associated risk of a material financial statement misstatement, and controls to address the risk. Whenever an account, disclosure, or control is associated with greater risk, the independent auditor performs more audit work personally.

For example, estimates are related to greater risk than other areas of the audit. If an internal auditor examines and recalculates management's estimates of the fair value of material assets, the auditor is not likely to rely solely on the work of the internal auditor. The independent auditor will also perform audit procedures on the estimates. In contrast, if the internal auditor recalculates each bank reconciliation performed by the treasurer's department, the independent auditor may decide to use that work rather than recalculating again. The independent auditor may limit audit work to testing the internal auditor's work and examining documentation that a sufficient number of recalculations were performed.

The work performed by others and the results may cause the auditor to change the nature, timing, and extent of audit procedures. The independent auditor can decide to perform more or less work, a different type of test than the one performed by others, or to test at a different time of year or different location from that already covered by others' work.

Judgment Required in the Audit Work

When more judgment is required to determine whether a misstatement is important or a control is performing effectively, the auditor performs more audit work and relies less on others. This occurs when the decisions are "subjective" rather than "objective." For example, an audit test may call for inspecting documents to see whether a control step is performed, such as having a required signature. Evidence examined in this step is quite objective. Determining whether or not the control is working is easy to accomplish. Either the signature is on the document or it is not.

In contrast, an audit step may require understanding the flow of a particular type of transaction through the accounting system and assessing whether controls intended to prevent material misstatement are designed effectively. This audit procedure requires significant judgment. In evaluating whether a control is designed effectively, the auditor typically asks company employees questions such as when control failures have occurred, what caused the failures, and what were the follow-up procedures. Deciding whether these responses indicate that the control is designed effectively is an important audit judgment. Controls over period-end financial reporting is another example of a process that requires more personal work by the auditor. The auditor does the work personally because problems with the period-end financial reporting process present significant risk of misstatement to the financial statements.

Estimates and Judgment Affecting the Account

Accounts that require the company to make important estimates or judgments demand more personal audit work. This is consistent with the conclusion presented earlier that estimates have higher risk. Significant estimates and judgments, and therefore more audit work, are required for revenue recognition, collectibility of receivables, and appropriate accounting for derivatives. If an account is susceptible to **management override**, the auditor relies less on the work of others and more on evidence that provides direct personal knowledge. The possibility of management override is increased when estimates and judgments are required, as well as in other situations.

Some accounts and assertions can have a low enough risk of material misstatement that work performed by others may be sufficient for the auditor. In these situations the auditor may decide that personally performing more tests is not required. Such a decision regarding the nature, timing, and extent of tests occurs only after the auditor has performed all the audit work needed as a basis for the decision.

AU 322.22 provides the following examples of assertions that may pose low enough risk to rely on the work of others completely:

Existence of cash
Existence of prepaid assets
Existence of fixed asset additions

In contrast, AS 322.21 also gives examples of areas that can have a high risk of material misstatement or require a high degree of judgment in evaluating the audit evidence. High risk or a need for significant judgment can motivate the auditor to perform more audit work in addition to whatever work is performed by others. Examples where more work will likely be performed are:

> Valuation of assets and liabilities involving significant accounting estimates
>
> Existence and disclosure of related party transactions, contingencies, uncertainties, and subsequent events

REVIEW QUESTIONS

J.1   In what way can work on the control environment performed by others affect the auditor's work?

J.2   Does materiality and risk of misstatement have a positive or an inverse relationship with the amount of work the auditor performs personally?

J.3   What do the subjectivity and judgment involved in a procedure have to do with the auditor's use of the work of others?

Evaluating and Testing the Effectiveness of Others' Work

When planning to rely on the work performed by others, in deciding the nature, timing, and extent of audit work the auditor has to evaluate the quality of the others' work. The amount of testing and evaluation that must be done by the independent auditor is a matter of audit judgment. This judgment is affected by how much the work of others will affect the auditor's decisions. In addition, the auditor considers judgments made earlier about (1) the competency and objectivity of the others doing the work, and (2) the nature of the accounts and controls that were the target of the work.

Procedures the independent auditor may use to test and evaluate the work of others include:

- Examining some of the controls, transactions, or balances that others examined
- Examining similar controls, transactions, or balances not actually examined by others
- Comparing the results of his or her own tests with the results of the work of others

Although AS 2 was superseded by AS 5, it includes language addressing tests of the work performed by others that describes the types of questions an auditor may want to address in examining the work performed by others.

> - Is the scope of the work appropriate for the objectives?
> - Are the audit work programs adequate?
> - Is the work adequately documented?
> - Is the work appropriately supervised and reviewed?
> - Is the supervision and review evident in the documentation?
> - Are the conclusions reached appropriate for the circumstances?
> - Are reports consistent with the results of the work?

(AS 2.125)

Direct Assistance to the Auditor

The independent auditor may request others to provide direct assistance on the audit. These other individuals might be internal auditors, company personnel in addition to internal auditors (related to ICFR), and third parties working under the direction of management or the audit committee (related to ICFR). In addition to assessing the competence and objectivity of these other individuals, as described earlier, the independent auditor must supervise, review, evaluate, and test the work performed by others. Finally, the auditor must inform others, providing direct assistance about the following:

- Responsibilities
- Objectives of the procedures they are to perform
- Matters such as accounting and auditing issues that may affect the nature, timing, and extent of audit procedures
- That all significant accounting and auditing issues identified should be brought to the auditor's attention

REVIEW QUESTIONS

K.1 What does the auditor consider in evaluating the work of others? What tests might the auditor perform?

K.2 What does the auditor have to do if others provide direct assistance on the audit?

Conclusion

The requirements of SOX that management evaluate and report on the effectiveness of its ICFR created increased work within companies. The individuals who perform the work may be internal auditors, other employees, or nonemployees hired by management for the specific project. When justified, based on the competency and objectivity of the individuals, internal auditors have traditionally had an impact on the work of external auditors. Now, internal auditors and others whose work is related to ICFR can impact the work of the independent auditor in performing an integrated audit.

As audits continue to evolve, the impact of others on the independent auditor's work also changes. Since the SOX mandate for integrated audits of public companies, internal auditors perform an increasingly important role in helping management fulfill its ICFR reporting responsibilities.

KEY TERMS

Competence of others. Refers to whether the other person performing work has appropriate levels of education, experience, certification, supervision, review, work assignments, and work performance.

Control environment. Aspects of a company's ICFR, including integrity and ethical values, commitment to competence, BOD and audit committee participation, management's philosophy and operating style, organizational structure, assignment of authority and responsibility, human resource policies, and procedures.

Direct personal knowledge. Refers to audit evidence that the auditor knows as a result of an action he or she actually performs, such as observation, reperformance, and inspection that does not require relying on someone else performing the action.

Internal auditors. Corporate employees whose normal duties may include financial statement audits, efficiency and effectiveness audits, forensic audits, and special projects.

Management override. When an effective internal control exists and typically functions, but a member of management exercises authority to prevent the control procedure from being carried out.

Materiality. Refers to the magnitude of an omission or a misstatement of accounting information that, in the light of surrounding circumstances, makes it probable that the judgment of a reasonable person relying on the information would have been changed or influenced by the omission or misstatement.

Objectivity of others. Refers to whether the other person performing work reports high enough in the entity to ensure that the tests performed include enough coverage and the tests results receive appropriate consideration and action.

Principal auditor. Distinguishes an audit with a single auditor from the situation when another auditor has done a significant portion of the audit work, and the "main" auditor refers to the work of the other auditor in the audit report with an explanation of the division of work and responsibility.

MULTIPLE CHOICE

6-47   In assessing the competence of other individuals performing work that might be used, the auditor considers

(a) whether management has confidence in the internal audit department's hiring processes.

(b) level of education and certification.

(c) the rank within the organization of the person performing the work.

(d) the nature of the controls being considered.

6-48   In assessing the objectivity of other individuals performing work that might be used, the auditor considers

Ethics

(a) the individual's education level.

(b) whether the company has a code of conduct.

(c) whether the person has direct access to the BOD and audit committee.

(d) The nature of the controls being considered.

6-49   When considering the work that has been performed by others,

(a) the auditor may decide to reduce the amount of audit work to be performed as long as the head of the audit department has appropriate credentials such as being certified as an internal auditor.

(b) the auditor may decide it is appropriate to modify the audit strategy.

(c) the auditor is likely to omit the audit work related to year-end financial reporting.

(d) the auditor may not be influenced in deciding the appropriate audit strategy.

6-50   An auditor is least likely to need more audit evidence than what is provided by other's work for which of the following:

(a) When the judgment of whether a control is working is objective and easy to determine

(b) When an account or disclosure that a control addresses involves material risk to the financial statements

(c) IT controls that affect all of the company's accounting systems

(d) Controls affecting accounts that require important estimates

DISCUSSION QUESTION

6-51   Access and read AICPA AU 322, "The Auditor's Consideration of the Internal Audit Function in an Audit of Financial Statements."

Do you believe that the auditor will be able to determine whether and how to utilize the work of the internal audit function in the financial statement audit as a result of considering the work of others for the ICFR audit? What does this mean in terms of efficiency for the ICFR and financial statement components of an integrated audit?

Understanding Internal Control over Financial Reporting and Auditing Design Effectiveness

1. Understand the value of effective internal control.
2. Learn the components and mechanisms of internal control.
3. Describe the internal control-related requirements imposed on management of public companies.
4. Analyze the relationship between management's assertions, ICFR, and activities of an integrated audit.
5. Explain the approach and steps an auditor uses to understand a company's ICFR and assess its design effectiveness.

Chapter 7 Resources

AU 312, AICPA, PCAOB, *Audit Risk and Materiality in Conducting an Audit*

AU 314, AICPA, *Understanding the Entity and Its Environment and Assessing the Risks of Material Misstatement*

AU 316, AICPA, PCAOB, *Consideration of Fraud in a Financial Statement Audit*

AU 318, AICPA, *Performing Audit Procedures in Response to Assessed Risks and Evaluating the Audit Evidence Obtained*

AU 319, PCAOB, *Consideration of Internal Control in a Financial Statement Audit*

AU 322, AICPA, PCAOB, *The Auditor's Consideration of the Internal Audit Function in an Audit of Financial Statements*

AU 324, AICPA, PCAOB, *Service Organizations*

AU 326, AICPA, *Audit Evidence*

AU 326, PCAOB, *Evidential Matter*

AU 342, AICPA, PCAOB, *Auditing Accounting Estimates*

Committee of Sponsoring Organizations of the Treadway Commission, *Enterprise Risk Management Framework*

Committee of Sponsoring Organizations of the Treadway Commission, *Guidance on Monitoring Internal Control Systems*

Committee of Sponsoring Organizations of the Treadway Commission, *Internal Control Framework*

Committee of Sponsoring Organizations of the Treadway Commission, *Internal Control over Financial Reporting— Guidance for Smaller Companies*

Foreign Corrupt Practices Act of 1977

New York Stock Exchange Rules

PCAOB AS 3, *Audit Documentation*

PCAOB AS 5, *An Audit of Internal Control over Financial Reporting That is Integrated with an Audit of Financial Statements*

PCAOB Release 2004-001, *An Audit of Internal Control over Financial Reporting Performed in Conjunction with an Audit of Financial Statements*

PCAOB Staff Views, *An Audit of Internal Control that is Integrated with an Audit of Financial Statements: Guidance for Auditors of Smaller Public Companies*

Sarbanes-Oxley Act of 2002

SEC 33-8238, *Management's Reports on Internal Control over Financial Reporting and Certification of Disclosure in Exchange Act Periodic Reports*

SEC 33-8810, SEC 34-55929, Interpretive Release, *Commission Guidance Regarding Management's Report on Internal Control over Financial Reporting Under Section 13(a) or 15(d) of the Securities Exchange Act of 1934*

INTRODUCTION

An integrated audit focuses on internal controls to (1) express an opinion on internal control over financial reporting (ICFR) effectiveness and (2) permit the auditor to make judgments about evidence needed for the financial statement audit. Assessing the quality of internal control was an important component of planning financial statement audits even before the Sarbanes-Oxley Act (SOX) required an audit opinion on ICFR of public companies. This chapter begins by introducing internal control and its contributions to reliable financial reporting, company operations, and financial statement audits. After that, it presents management responsibilities for evaluating and reporting on ICFR as required by SOX and the Securities and Exchange Commission (SEC). The discussion then proceeds to the auditor's processes of understanding a client's ICFR and assessing design effectiveness. Understanding ICFR and evaluating design effectiveness provides the information needed to design the audit plan for testing the operating effectiveness of ICFR and substantive procedures for the financial statement audit. The ICFR steps enable the auditor to complete the development of audit strategy and audit planning. Exhibit 7-1 presents the overview of audit planning and risk assessment.

INTERNAL CONTROL AND RELIABLE FINANCIAL REPORTING [LO 1]

Internal control is of interest to auditors, investors, management, and regulators. Effective internal policies and procedures help a company handle and report its business activities

EXHIBIT 7-1

Audit Planning and Risk
Assessment

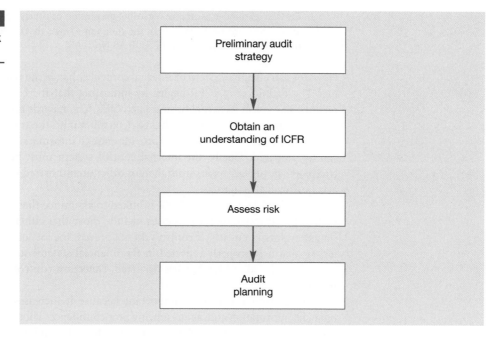

and financial transactions in the way an honest management group specifies. When this happens, there is a good chance that reliable financial reporting results from the information collected by the company. Reliable financial reporting is dependent on many conditions that have already been introduced in earlier chapters. Management must design the policies and procedures that make up internal control so that they are effective and operate as intended. Furthermore, management must have integrity and support the functioning of the system.

What Is ICFR?

Internal control over financial reporting (ICFR) is a "subset" of the company's entire internal control system. Likewise, the internal control system is a subset of the company's management information system (MIS). While the company needs its entire MIS to effectively run the business, the auditor focuses primarily on ICFR when auditing internal control and planning the financial statement audit. The definition of ICFR provided by the PCAOB in AS 5 indicates that it is a process for which individuals high in the company's organization are responsible:

> Internal control over financial reporting is a process designed by, or under the supervision of, the company's principal executive and principal financial officers, or persons performing similar functions, and effected by the company's board of directors, management, and other personnel, to provide reasonable assurance regarding the reliability of financial reporting and the preparation of financial statements for external purposes in accordance with GAAP and includes those policies and procedures that—

> 1. Pertain to the maintenance of records that, in reasonable detail, accurately and fairly reflect the transactions and dispositions of the assets of the company;

> 2. Provide reasonable assurance that transactions are recorded as necessary to permit preparation of financial statements in accordance with generally accepted accounting principles, and that receipts and expenditures of the company are being made only in accordance with authorizations of management and directors of the company; and

3. Provide reasonable assurance regarding prevention or timely detection of unauthorized acquisition, use, or disposition of the company's assets that could have a material effect on the financial statements. (PCAOB AS No. 5.A5)

How does an effective system of internal control enhance the reliability of financial reporting? The definition of ICFR begins by indicating that the company must produce good records that reflect its actual business activities. The records must be complete enough for someone analyzing them to be able to determine if all the transactions are legitimate for the business. The records must also provide enough information so that financial statements can be prepared. Finally, the internal control system must be structured to protect the company's important assets from theft or other unauthorized use, or at least to detect these acts quickly if they occur.

The ultimate purpose of ICFR is linked to assurance that financial statements are not materially misstated. ICFR processes include those that either prevent or detect financial statement misstatements. If controls do not *prevent* the loss of assets, ICFR must *detect* the loss so that it is properly reflected in the financial statements. This means that detection controls deal with a loss that has occurred. Detection controls make sure that the loss is recorded and adequately disclosed.

Good internal control is important because it increases the reliability of reported financial information and, as a result, investor confidence. Those companies that are publicly traded must file with the SEC and must include in their filings management's report on its assessment of ICFR's effectiveness. The requirement of a management ICFR report is directly linked to investor confidence. In discussing AS 2, the original PCAOB audit standard on ICFR audits that was later superseded by AS 5, the PCAOB provides a good explanation of this concept.

> In the simplest terms, investors can have much more confidence in the reliability of a corporate financial statement if corporate management demonstrates that it exercises adequate control over bookkeeping, the sufficiency of books and records for the preparation of accurate financial statements, adherence to rules about the use of company assets and the possibility of misappropriation of company assets. (PCAOB Release 2004-001, p. 3)

Strong internal control is good for those outside the company who rely on the company's external financial reporting. It is also important to the company's management and independent auditor.

MANAGEMENT'S MOTIVATION FOR GOOD INTERNAL CONTROL

Management is responsible for the effective design and operation of ICFR. This responsibility should motivate management to strive for an effective system. However, management's desire for effective internal control really results from what good controls can produce for the company. First, effective internal control enhances the reliability of financial reporting. Producing reliable financial information that external users can rely on permits those users to make decisions. A trickle-down effect from investor confidence is that reliable external financial reporting supports the external financial activities in which the company is involved such as borrowing funds and selling stock. This is good for management and the company.

Effective ICFR supports the efficiency and effectiveness of the company's operations. Managers and other internal users need reliable and timely financial information to make decisions while running the company's day-to-day operations. Without an effective internal control system, it is less likely that internal decision makers will have relevant and correct information when they need it. Good internal control can also provide operating benefits such as:

Identifying procedures that are not cost effective

Producing accounting information more efficiently

Improving the company's financial activities

Streamlining accounting and financial information systems

A final management benefit of effective internal control relates to the laws and regulations that businesses must follow. Effective internal control enables management to better lead the company in complying with those laws and regulations.

THE FINANCIAL STATEMENT AUDIT AND INTERNAL CONTROL OVER FINANCIAL REPORTING

The auditor of a company's financial statements issues a report that communicates the auditor's opinion on whether the financial statements provide a fair representation of the business, its financial activities and financial position. To accomplish this, the auditor must gather, examine, and conclude on **audit evidence**. Audit evidence provides information about the correspondence between what is shown in the financial statements and the affairs of the company being audited. If the company being audited has an effective system of ICFR, the auditor can make judgments about the quality and reliability of the evidence being examined. If the company's ICFR is not effective, the auditor has less confidence about relying on the evidence.

The auditor's concern regarding the client's ICFR extends beyond the quality of evidence to the actual financial reporting outputs of the accounting information system. When planning the audit, the auditor considers whether ICFR is expected to be effective in achieving the goal of producing financial information free of material misstatements. Since initial audit planning is an early step in deciding what types and how much evidence are needed for the financial statement audit, the auditor's expectation about the effectiveness of ICFR impacts the way the financial statement audit is planned.

DEFINITIONS OF INTERNAL CONTROL [LO 2]

Definitions of internal control have evolved over time. Early use of the term was primarily limited to those involved with financial statement audits. Internal control was understood in terms of the company's business processes. From the perspective of financial statement audits, traditional consideration of internal control effectiveness still applies. If one of the company's processes is not producing complete or appropriate financial information, then the auditor judges the internal control in that area to be inadequate. The auditor then changes the plan regarding the nature and amount of audit work that needs to be performed for the financial statement audit. Conversely, if internal controls are determined to be good, and a process is producing reliable and complete financial information, the auditor might choose to "rely on" the internal control system and reduce the planned substantive audit work on the financial statements (SEC 33-8238).

The **Foreign Corrupt Practices Act** (1977 as amended 1988, 1998) placed the concept of internal control into legislation and prompted the following definition, which was included in auditing standards promulgated by the American Institute of Certified Public Accountants (AICPA):

Internal accounting controls were to be sufficient to provide reasonable assurance that

1. transactions are executed in accordance with management's general or specific authorization.

2. transactions are recorded as necessary to permit preparation of financial statements, and to maintain accountability for assets.

3. access to assets is permitted only in accordance with management's general or specific authorization.

4. recorded accountability for assets is compared with the existing assets at reasonable intervals and appropriate action is taken with respect to any differences.

This definition provided a fairly narrow view of internal control, specific to financial reporting, and did not extend to operational efficiency and effectiveness.

In 1992, the **Committee of Sponsoring Organizations of the Treadway Commission (COSO)** published *Internal Control—An Integrated Framework* (IC Framework) with the definition of internal control currently used. The **COSO IC Framework** defines internal control as "a process, effected by an entity's board of directors, management and other personnel, designed to provide reasonable assurance regarding the achievement of objectives" in three categories (COSO IC Framework, Executive Summary, p. 1). Those categories are:

Reliability of financial reporting

Effectiveness and efficiency of operations

Compliance with laws and regulations

In 1994, COSO added to its internal control definition by including the **safeguarding of assets**. Safeguarding assets means that assets should only be acquired, used, and disposed of consistently with management's authorization. The COSO IC Framework stresses the following fundamental concepts of the definition:

Internal control is a process. It's a means to an end, not an end in itself.

Internal control is effected by people. Its not merely policy manuals and forms, but people at every level of an organization.

Internal control can be expected to provide only reasonable assurance, not absolute assurance, to an entity's management and board.

Internal control is geared to the achievement of objectives in one or more separate but overlapping categories. (COSO IC Framework, Chapter 1, p. 8)

REVIEW QUESTIONS

A.1 What does the definition of ICFR imply as requirements for ICFR to enhance reliable financial reporting?

A.2 What are management's motivations for effective internal control?

A.3 What are internal control benefits related to operations and management?

A.4 What effect does the auditor's assessment of ICFR have on the financial statement audit?

A.5 What is the COSO definition of internal control? How is it different from the definition of ICFR?

COMPONENTS OF INTERNAL CONTROL

The COSO IC Framework provides a structure of internal control components that are the foundation for the work of both management and the auditor regarding ICFR. The COSO IC Framework structure identifies internal control as being composed of

Control environment

Risk assessment

Control activities
Information and communication
Monitoring

Control Environment

> The control environment sets the tone of an organization, influencing the control consciousness of its people. It is the foundation for all other components of internal control, providing the discipline and structure.
>
> (COSO Internal Control Framework, Executive Summary, p. 4)

This definition of **control environment** is often referred to using the shorthand "tone at the top." Basically, an internal control system is effective only in an environment in which management supports the internal control system by behaving ethically and making business decisions that emphasize its importance. The COSO IC Framework also sets forth factors that are important to a successful control environment. These control environment influences are universally important, although they may differ among businesses depending on characteristics such as size and industry. Aspects of the control environment discussed in the following sections are:

Integrity and ethical values
Commitment to competence
Board of Directors or audit committee participation
Management's philosophy and operating style
Organizational structure
Assignment of authority and responsibility
Human resources policies

Integrity and Ethical Values

The "corporate culture" of an entity refers to the way people in any organization perceive acceptable behavior. Corporate culture defines the way members of the organization act. Thus, in a business, the values that management embraces and lives by, the standards it sets, the manner in which it communicates standards, and the reinforcement of the standards all affect the environment and corporate culture. An ethical culture is important because it influences the behavior of people at all levels within the organization. Moreover, businesses are increasingly supporting the notion that having strong ethical standards is profitable.

Commitment to Competence

The competence of employees affects a company's control environment because workers need knowledge, skills, and training to make appropriate judgments required by their job responsibilities. A commitment to competence requires two management steps. First, management needs to decide what skills are required to appropriately perform job responsibilities. Second, management must staff those jobs with individuals who have the needed skills. Trade-offs can be made in fulfilling these required steps, such as placing a less experienced person in a demanding job and providing that person with extra supervision. Regardless of how it is accomplished, a control environment cannot function effectively unless jobs are matched with people of sufficient competence. The PCAOB emphasizes the importance of a commitment to competence by stating that for ICFR to operate effectively it must function as intended and be implemented by a person with appropriate qualifications.

Board of Directors or Audit Committee Participation

The importance of the Board of Directors and **audit committee** participation in the corporate environment was recognized when the COSO IC Framework was written. Since then, other authoritative guidance continues to emphasize Board of Directors and audit committee impact. For example, AS 5.69 states that "Ineffective oversight of the company's external financial reporting and internal control over financial reporting by the company's audit committee" is an indicator of a material weakness in ICFR. A material weakness exists when there is a problem with ICFR that causes more than a remote chance that the financial statements will be materially misstated.

SOX requires that a company disclose if its audit committee does not have at least one financial expert. And the New York Stock Exchange, whose operations are governed by the SEC, requires companies to have an audit committee in order to be listed on the exchange (NYSE Euronext, Listed Company Manual, 303A.06). Thus, SOX, the SEC, and PCAOB stress the involvement of the Board of Directors and audit committee in company governance and the control environment.

Management's Philosophy and Operating Style

The way that management runs its business is called management's philosophy and operating style. Some people prefer to use a formal management style, for example, with written policies and rules, while others prefer a more casual or informal style. Neither approach is better than the other, although just as a result of size, large entities sometimes require greater formality. Management's philosophy also affects the company's willingness to accept risk. Appendix B of this chapter discusses enterprise risk management (ERM).

Management's attitude toward accounting and financial reporting is of great importance to both the financial statements and integrated audit. For example, management can be either aggressive or conservative in choosing among accounting principles. This aspect of management philosophy is sufficiently important that SOX Section 204 requires the auditor to report to the audit committee on management's selection of accounting principles. Management's approach to the development of accounting estimates is also a result of philosophy and operating style. For example, management may choose to be careful and conscientious when making accounting estimates, or it may have a less concerned attitude. Management may be conservative or aggressive in its estimation process.

Organizational Structure

The important aspect of organizational structure is that the one used is appropriate for the company and supports an effective control environment. Organizational structures vary widely. Some companies are centralized; others are decentralized. Some companies use single, direct lines of reporting, while others share authority in a system referred to as matrix management. Regardless of the structure, for the control environment to be effective the company must have clearly defined responsibility and authority, and lines for communication and reporting.

Assignment of Authority and Responsibility

Organization structure reflects management philosophy, company size, and industry. Management's assignment of authority and responsibility relates to organizational structure. Again, many ways exist to assign authority and responsibility. Some companies empower employees across the entire organizational hierarchy with decision-making authority. Others limit decision-making responsibility. The key to successful empowerment and an effective control environment is to

1. delegate only as much authority as is needed to achieve the organization's goals.
2. ensure that those making decisions understand that they will be accountable.
3. hold those who are responsible accountable for their actions.

Human Resources Policies

Commitment to competence and appropriate human resources policies and practices go hand in hand. Before appropriately knowledgeable and skilled people can be assigned responsibility, the right people must be hired. This requires appropriate standards for recruiting and hiring. In addition, training and evaluation policies leading to performance-driven placement and promotion help support the control environment.

REVIEW QUESTIONS

B.1 What are the COSO components of internal control?

B.2 What is "tone at the top"? "Corporate culture"?

B.3 Why do companies need competent workers for good internal control?

B.4 What aspects of management's philosophy and operating style may affect ICFR and financial reporting?

B.5 What is important to ICFR about organizational authority?

B.6 What is important to successful empowerment of employees and delegation of authority?

RISK ASSESSMENT

Risks are defined as anything that can keep an organization from achieving its objectives. It follows then that objectives must be set and threats to achieving those objectives must be identified before the risks can be assessed. **Risk assessment** is a critical activity for every business and is discussed from the perspective of the entire entity in Appendix B on ERM. Risks are also relevant to the entity's internal control. These risks deal with all three categories of objectives: operations, financial reporting, and compliance. Again, the auditor is primarily concerned with risks to ICFR.

Understanding the breadth of what financial reporting covers is important in considering risks to ICFR. The COSO IC Framework discusses financial reporting:

> Financial reporting objectives address the preparation of reliable published financial statements, including interim and condensed financial statements and selected financial data derived from such statements, such as earnings releases, reported publicly. Entities need to achieve financial reporting objectives to meet external obligations. Reliable financial statements are a prerequisite to obtaining investor or creditor capital, and may be critical to the award of certain contracts or to dealing with certain suppliers. Investors, creditors, customers and suppliers often rely on financial statements to assess management's performance and to compare it with peers and alternative investments.
>
> (Chapter 3, p. 2)

This quote from the COSO IC Framework indicates that the impacts of financial reporting are widespread and can affect operations and the overall success of the company. So, the auditor's focus on risk assessment related to ICFR is actually linked to all aspects of the entity's success.

Risks that must be identified and assessed can relate to **external** and **internal factors**. Risk can occur at the **entity level** or be related to specific activities of the business. **Activity-level risks** deal with those related to a company's business units or functions. Techniques to identify risks include qualitative and quantitative approaches to identifying higher-risk activities, periodic review of economic and industry factors, business planning conferences and meetings, forecasting, and strategic planning.

Risk assessment requires considering:

- Significance or degree of impact of the risk on the company
- Likelihood of the risk occurring or frequency with which it may occur
- Best ways to manage the risk

AUDITING IN ACTION

Entity Level, External and Internal Risk Factors

External Factors

Technological developments can affect the nature and timing of research and development, or lead to changes in procurement.

Changing customer needs or expectations can affect product development, production process, customer service, pricing, or warranties.

Competition can alter marketing or service activities.

New legislation and regulation can force changes in operating policies and strategies.

Natural catastrophes can lead to changes in operations or information systems and highlight the need for contingency planning.

Economic changes can have an impact on decisions related to financing, capital expenditures, and expansion.

Internal Factors

A disruption in information systems processing can adversely affect the entity's operations.

The quality of personnel hired and methods of training and motivation can influence the level of control consciousness within the entity.

A change in management responsibilities can affect the way certain controls are effected.

The nature of the entity's activities, and employee accessibility to assets, can contribute to misappropriation of resources.

An unassertive or ineffective board or audit committee can provide opportunities for indiscretions.

(COSO IC Framework, Chapter 3, p. 6)

Managing the risk entails simply deciding what action to take and moving forward with the action. Estimating the expected significance and likelihood may be a formal quantified process or a subjective one. Either approach requires assumptions that will affect the quality of the estimates. The risk assessment process ends at the determination of the preferred approach to managing the risk. Auditing standards state that certain conditions need particular attention in the risk assessment process. These are shown in Exhibit 7-2.

REVIEW QUESTIONS

C.1 What are risks? How are objectives and threats related to risk assessment?

C.2 About which aspect of a company's internal control is the auditor primarily concerned?

C.3 How are risks from external and internal factors different? Give examples.

C.4 What is involved in risk assessment and risk management?

Control Activities

"**Control activities** are policies and procedures that help ensure management directives are carried out" (COSO IC Framework, Chapter 4, p. 1). As the COSO IC Framework uses the terms, *policies* establish what should be accomplished in carrying out management's directives to address risk, and *procedures* are the activities that should be followed to carry out the policies. Although consideration of control activities has always had a role in the audit of financial statements, it is vital in the ICFR audit of an integrated audit. Management's decisions on risk have a fundamental impact on whether ICFR is effective.

EXHIBIT 7-2

Circumstances
Demanding Special Risk
Assessment Attention

Changed Operating Environment. A changed regulatory or economic environment can result in increased competitive pressures and significantly different risks. "Divestiture" in the telecommunications industry and deregulation of commission rates in the brokerage industry for example, thrust entities into a vastly changed competitive environment.

New Personnel. A senior executive new to an entity may not understand the entity's culture or may focus solely on performance to the exclusion of control-related activities. High turnover of personnel, in the absence of effective training and supervision, can result in breakdowns.

New or Revamped Information Systems. Effective controls can break down when new systems are developed, particularly when done under unusually tight time constraints—for example, to gain competitive advantage or to make tactical moves.

Rapid Growth. When operations expand significantly and quickly, existing systems may be strained to the point where controls break down; where processing shifts or clerical personnel are added, existing supervisors may be unable to maintain adequate control.

New Technology. When new technologies are incorporated into production processes or information systems, a high likelihood exists that internal controls will need to be modified. Just-in-time inventory manufacturing technologies, for instance, commonly require changes in cost systems and related controls to ensure reporting of meaningful information.

New Lines, Products, Activities. When an entity enters new business lines or engages in transactions with which it is unfamiliar, existing controls may not be adequate. Savings and loan organizations, for example, ventured into investment and lending arenas in which they had little or no previous experience, without focusing on how to control the risks involved.

Corporate Restructurings. Restructurings—resulting, for example, from a leveraged buyout, or from significant business declines or cost reduction programs—may be accompanied by staff reductions and inadequate supervision and segregation of duties. Or a job performing a key control function may be eliminated without a compensating control put in its place. A number of companies learned too late that they made rapid, large-scale cutbacks in personnel without adequate consideration of serious control implications.

Foreign Operations. The expansion or acquisition of foreign operations carries new and often unique risks that management should address. For instance, the control environment is likely to be driven by the culture and customs of local management. Also, business risks may result from factors unique to the local economy and regulatory environment. Or channels of communication and information systems may not be well established and available to all individuals.

(AU 314.77)

Management determines which risks are important, and which and how many controls are appropriate to respond to those risks. Control activities are grouped into the following areas: performance reviews, information processing, physical controls, and segregation of duties (PCAOB AU 319.41; AICPA AU 314.B15).

Performance reviews are activities used to monitor the success of a business. For example, performance reviews include comparing actual results to the budget or the prior-year results. Another performance review is evaluating financial and operating performance together. The combined evaluation permits corrective action if unexpected relationships exist between the two types of data. For example, lower than expected revenue from sales for the outflow of finished goods inventory can indicate a problem with sales, inventory, or cost of goods sold.

Control activities for information processing are those intended to check the accuracy, completeness, and authorization of transactions. The control activities are considered relating to all important transactions of the entity whether processed manually or using information technology. The following is a definition of information technology:

> Information technology (IT) encompasses automated means of originating, processing, storing, and communicating information, and includes recording devices, communication systems, computer systems (including hardware and software components and data), and other electronic devices. An entity's use of IT may be extensive; however, the auditor is primarily interested in the entity's use of IT to initiate, record, process, and report transactions or other financial data. (PCAOB AU 319.02, footnote 2; AICPA AU 314.15, footnote 4)

The description of information processing as a control activity includes considerations of both general controls and application controls. *General controls* are "controls over data center and network operations; system software acquisition and maintenance; access security; and application system acquisition, development and maintenance" (AICPA AU 314.94). IT general controls (ITGC) and the audit of ITGC are discussed in Appendix A of this chapter. *Application controls*, as used here, means the control activities needed for a specific IT processing application. Audit procedures for testing application controls are discussed in Chapter 8, Appendix A. Given the fairly universal use of IT-based accounting in the current business environment, the audit of IT controls is largely integrated with other control activities. In complex IT environments, the IT controls are given special consideration and may be audited by a team member with specialized IT knowledge.

Physical controls are control activities that safeguard the physical security of a company's assets. Physical controls include procedures such as locking up valuables and storing assets in secured buildings. They extend to limiting access to assets and records, and requiring appropriate authorization for access to IT programs and data files. When appropriate, such as in the case of an annual physical count of inventory, physical controls require comparing assets to their supporting documentation. This validates that the amount recorded is accurate or permits corrections needed as a result of shrinkage, waste, or other loss.

Segregation of duties is a fundamental ICFR activity. Segregation of duties refers to assigning to different people the responsibility for authorizing transactions, recording transactions, and maintaining custody of assets. The goal of segregation of duties is to prevent a single person from being able to steal or process unauthorized transactions and also cover up the transaction in the records and accounts.

Segregation of duties is not always effective because individuals can work together or collude. Through **collusion**, individuals can be successful in a theft or fraud that segregation of duties would have prevented. Also, in a small business environment there may be too few employees to accomplish segregation of duties. A compensating control for lack of segregation of duties in a small business environment is day-to-day involvement and oversight of financial and accounting tasks by an owner. Another situation in which segregation of duties is difficult to accomplish is an IT environment where much of the institutional and technical knowledge is held by a single individual. Similarly, an IT environment with a "super-user" who has the ability to authorize and input transactions, as well as troubleshoot IT data and program problems, makes segregation of duties difficult. The cumulative access and authority may give the "super-user" the ability to access assets and change the records.

Methods for auditing the design effectiveness of ICFR control activities are discussed later in this chapter. Auditing the operating effectiveness of ICFR control activities is discussed in Chapter 8.

REVIEW QUESTIONS

D.1 What does management have to decide before a company implements control activities?

D.2 What are performance reviews? How do they serve as a control activity?

D.3 What are control activities for information processing, and what purpose do they serve? How do general and application IT controls differ?

D.4 What activities fall into the category of physical controls?

D.5 What is segregation of duties? How is it useful? How can it be rendered ineffective?

D.6 Why can accomplishing good segregation of duties be difficult in some IT environments?

Information and Communication

Auditors focus on ICFR. However, the COSO IC Framework is clear in emphasizing the overlap and integrated uses of business information. Information that supports achieving the entity's objectives of efficiency and effectiveness of operations integrates with reliability of financial reporting and compliance with applicable laws and regulations. Information that a company relies upon is used for all three categories of objectives. Therefore, it is difficult to identify internal controls that apply only to information for financial reporting. Companies identify, capture, process, and report information that is used for both operating decisions and financial reports. Furthermore, the same information may be used to satisfy obligations to comply with laws and regulations.

We often think of business information as being limited to what is generated internally. The COSO IC Framework discusses external information that is also part of business information activities. For example, externally generated information that is identified, captured, and used might relate to

- Market or industry economics
- Goods and services needed for production
- Intelligence on customers or providers
- Legislative and regulatory developments affecting the company

The COSO IC Framework does not specify requirements related to information. Rather, it says that the information should have appropriate quality to meet the entity's needs. The COSO IC Framework indicates that the information system that identifies, captures, processes, and reports information crosses all three business objectives. Therefore, the information system should provide for the company's overall information needs. Information may be obtained formally or informally and as part of a routine or a specific, special effort.

AUDITING IN ACTION

COSO IC Framework on Quality of Information

The quality of system-generated information affects management's ability to make appropriate decisions in managing and controlling the entity's activities.... It is critical that reports contain enough appropriate data to support effective control. The quality of information includes ascertaining whether:

Content is appropriate — Is the needed information reported?
Information is timely — Is the needed information reported when required?
Information is current — Is reported information the latest available?
Information is accurate — Are the data correct?
Information is accessible — Can reported information be obtained easily by appropriate parties?

(COSO IC Framework Chapter 5, p. 3)

Communication overlaps with aspects of the control environment. The organizational structure has to coordinate with the communication and reporting channels. In addition, management philosophy and "tone at the top" must be clearly communicated. The communication channels should permit flow of information up and down the organization, as well as across functions and units. Internal control must be considered for communication to both external parties and those within the company. The COSO IC Framework discusses communication as a tool for control and as a means of enabling achievement of the business objectives. In contrast, the auditing standards emphasize the control aspects of communication as they relate to ICFR.

> [H]aving the right information, on time, at the right place is essential to effecting control…information systems must provide information to appropriate personnel so that they can carry out their operating, financial reporting and compliance responsibilities. But communication also must take place in a broader sense, dealing with expectations, responsibilities of individuals and groups and other important matters. (COSO IC Framework Chapter 5, p. 4)

Monitoring

Monitoring is the process that assesses, over time, the quality of the internal control system. Monitoring is performed both on an ongoing basis and in the form of **separate evaluations**. Individual managers' awareness of the functions they oversee provides monitoring of the control system. Managers will notice or question outcomes that seem inappropriate. Interactions with those outside the business also provide a monitoring function. For example, when vendors pay invoices sent to them by the company, they provide outside verification that the ICFR over the process generating the invoices is working. If the process were producing incorrect invoices, the vendors (at least, those with effective internal controls) would not pay them, indicating an internal control breakdown related to the process. Internal auditors also participate in the monitoring function through both routine activities and special evaluation projects.

In planning the monitoring function, management makes decisions on what information to use, monitor, and report. Furthermore, management determines to whom the report should be made. Monitoring can be performed as a special and separate activity. However, as **ongoing monitoring** is more effective, less separate monitoring will likely be required.

AUDITING IN ACTION

Ongoing Monitoring

Personnel, in carrying out their regular activities, obtain evidence as to whether the system of ICFR continues to function.

Communications from external parties corroborate internally generated information, or indicate problems.

Amounts recorded by the accounting system are periodically compared with physical assets.

The company responds to recommendations from the internal and external auditors on means to strengthen internal controls.

Training seminars, planning sessions, and other meetings provide feedback to management on whether controls operate effectively.

Personnel are periodically asked to state whether they understand and comply with the entity's code of conduct and regularly perform critical control activities.

Internal audit activities are effective.

(Adapted from COSO IC Framework, Chapter 6, p. 7)

In January 2009 COSO published more guidance titled *Guidance on Monitoring Internal Control Systems.* The information included in the guidance is intended to augment the COSO IC Framework and COSO's June 2006 report, *Internal Control over Financial Reporting—Guidance for Smaller Public Companies.* The COSO ICFR guidance for smaller companies is discussed in Appendix C to this chapter.

COSO's most recent guidance is based on the assumption that businesses want good ICFR because it is good for their businesses and because they have to make periodic reports on the effectiveness of ICFR. The COSO guidance suggests that effective monitoring is the easiest, most effective, and least costly way to maintain good ICFR. Monitoring permits management to keep ICFR effective by identifying problems quickly so they can be corrected on a timely basis. As a consequence, management has good information to run the company and prepare financial statements, as well as the ability to easily report on the effectiveness of ICFR.

The plan set forth in the COSO monitoring guidance is a common-sense, practical approach. Management establishes an expectation that monitoring is a normal state of affairs in the organization. Monitoring procedures are addressed in a formal fashion. Someone has responsibility for developing monitoring procedures, and employees have the responsibility of executing monitoring activities and making reports as a normal part of their jobs. Finally, when monitoring outcomes are reported, management assesses them and takes whatever action necessary to correct, maintain, or improve ICFR.

Other parts of the COSO monitoring guidance are steeped in the practices of auditing. For example, the focus is a risk-based approach, and key controls that reduce risks should be monitored. Not "just anyone" should perform monitoring. The individual's skills, abilities, knowledge, and experience, as well as freedom from bias about the particular monitoring target, all affect whether a person should perform monitoring. A consideration is that management must make a choice on what information (similar to evidence) should be observed in a monitoring process to get the most information. Finally, monitoring should be conducted in the most efficient (lowest cost) manner that will not reduce its effectiveness. The following is a list of monitoring procedures from the COSO monitoring guidance:

Periodic evaluation and testing of controls by internal audit

Continuous monitoring programs built into information systems

Analysis of, and appropriate follow-up on, operating reports or metrics that might identify anomalies indicative of a control failure

Supervisory reviews of controls, such as reconciliation reviews as a normal part of processing

Self-assessments by boards and management regarding the tone they set in the organization and the effectiveness of their oversight function

Audit committee inquiries of internal and external auditors

Quality assurance reviews of the internal audit department

(COSO, Internal Control—Integrated Framework: Guidance on Monitoring Internal Control Systems, January 2009, p. 3)

REVIEW QUESTIONS

E.1 What are the five questions COSO IC proposes as indicators of the quality of information?

E.2 What does AU 319 indicate as a necessary condition for communication? In what way is the COSO expectation broader?

E.3 How do managers monitor ICFR? How do those outside the business contribute to monitoring ICFR?

MANAGEMENT'S RESPONSIBILITIES FOR ICFR [LO 3]

Foreign Corrupt Practices Act

The Foreign Corrupt Practices Act of 1977 (FCPA) set up the first law about internal control responsibilities for management of public companies. The FCPA was passed in the wake of a scandal when it was discovered and reported that U.S. companies were bribing high officials of foreign governments. In addition to its antibribery provisions, the FCPA requires management of public companies to maintain a system of internal control. At the time the FCPA was enacted, the intent was to require controls that would prevent companies from being able to maintain off-the-books "slush funds" that could be used to pay bribes. Regardless of its primary intent, the FPCA made management accountable for ensuring that public companies have a system of internal control. Exhibit 7-3 provides excerpts from the FCPA related to management's internal control responsibilities, recognizable as similar to the AICPA definition of internal control presented earlier.

SOX

The Sarbanes-Oxley Act of 2002 also establishes management responsibility related to accounting. Section 302 of SOX, shown in Exhibit 7-4, requires the SEC to set rules requiring members of top management to certify that

> they have reviewed the annual or quarterly financial report being filed with the SEC,
>
> the financial report—to the best of the individual's knowledge—is fair and not misleading, and
>
> management is responsible for establishing and maintaining internal controls.

EXHIBIT 7-3

Foreign Corrupt Practices Act, Internal Control Provisions

Every issuer which has a class of securities registered and ... every issuer which is required to file reports ... shall

(A) make and keep books, records, and accounts, which, in reasonable detail, accurately and fairly reflect the transactions and dispositions of the assets of the issuer; and

(B) devise and maintain a system of internal accounting controls sufficient to provide reasonable assurances that—

   (i) transactions are executed in accordance with management's general or specific authorization;

   (ii) transactions are recorded as necessary

      (I) to permit preparation of financial statements in conformity with generally accepted accounting principles or any other criteria applicable to such statements, and

      (II) to maintain accountability for assets;

   (iii) access to assets is permitted only in accordance with management's general or specific authorization; and

   (iv) the recorded accountability for assets is compared with the existing assets at reasonable intervals and appropriate action is taken with respect to any differences.

(United States Code, Title 15, Chapter 2B, §78m (b)(2))

With regard to internal control, the members of top management certify that they have designed the internal controls so that officers of the company receive the information they need; evaluated the effectiveness of the company's internal controls within the last 90 days; and stated their conclusion in their report. Members of top management also certify that they have disclosed any significant deficiencies in internal control, fraud by management, and changes in internal control.

Section 404 of SOX also adds to management's responsibilities by directing the SEC to require that management include in its annual SEC filings a report on internal control. The

EXHIBIT 7-4

Sarbanes-Oxley Act of 2002, Section 302

CORPORATE RESPONSIBILITY FOR FINANCIAL REPORTS.

a. REGULATIONS REQUIRED—The Commission shall, by rule, require, for each company filing periodic reports under section 13(a) or 15(d) of the Securities Exchange Act of 1934 (15 U.S.C. 78m, 78o(d)), that the principal executive officer or officers and the principal financial officer or officers, or persons performing similar functions, certify in each annual or quarterly report filed or submitted under either such section of such Act that—

(1) the signing officer has reviewed the report;

(2) based on the officer's knowledge, the report does not contain any untrue statement of a material fact or omit to state a material fact necessary in order to make the statements made, in light of the circumstances under which such statements were made, not misleading;

(3) based on such officer's knowledge, the financial statements, and other financial information included in the report, fairly present in all material respects the financial condition and results of operations of the issuer as of, and for, the periods presented in the report;

(4) the signing officers—

(A) are responsible for establishing and maintaining internal controls;

(B) have designed such internal controls to ensure that material information relating to the issuer and its consolidated subsidiaries is made known to such officers by others within those entities, particularly during the period in which the periodic reports are being prepared;

(C) have evaluated the effectiveness of the issuer's internal controls as of a date within 90 days prior to the report; and

(D) have presented in the report their conclusions about the effectiveness of their internal controls based on their evaluation as of that date;

(5) the signing officers have disclosed to the issuer's auditors and the audit committee of the board of directors (or persons fulfilling the equivalent function)—

(A) all significant deficiencies in the design or operation of internal controls which could adversely affect the issuer's ability to record, process, summarize, and report financial data and have identified for the issuer's auditors any material weaknesses in internal controls; and

(B) any fraud, whether or not material, that involves management or other employees who have a significant role in the issuer's internal controls; and

(6) the signing officers have indicated in the report whether or not there were significant changes in internal controls or in other factors that could significantly affect internal controls subsequent to the date of their evaluation, including any corrective actions with regard to significant deficiencies and material weaknesses.

EXHIBIT 7-5

Sarbanes-Oxley Act of
2002, Section 404

MANAGEMENT ASSESSMENT OF INTERNAL CONTROLS

(a) RULES REQUIRED—The Commission shall prescribe rules requiring each annual report required by section 13(a) or 15(d) of the Securities Exchange Act of 1934 (15 U.S.C. 78m or 78o(d)) to contain an internal control report, which shall—

    (1) state the responsibility of management for establishing and maintaining an adequate internal control structure and procedures for financial reporting; and

    (2) contain an assessment, as of the end of the most recent fiscal year of the issuer, of the effectiveness of the internal control structure and procedures of the issuer for financial reporting.

(b) INTERNAL CONTROL EVALUATION AND REPORTING—With respect to the internal control assessment required by subsection (a), each registered public accounting firm that prepares or issues the audit report for the issuer shall attest to, and report on, the assessment made by the management of the issuer. An attestation made under this subsection shall be made in accordance with standards for attestation engagements issued or adopted by the Board. Any such attestation shall not be the subject of a separate engagement.

required report states that management is responsible for establishing and maintaining internal control and providing an assessment on the effectiveness of internal control as of the end of the fiscal year. Section 404 requires that the assessment of ICFR effectiveness be audited by an audit firm registered with the PCAOB. "Attestation" is the word used in the law for the required service, but has been interpreted to mean audit. The law has been implemented by the SEC and PCAOB. The SEC set rules for management's evaluation and report. The PCAOB's AS 5 set rules that were approved by the SEC for the audit of internal control.

The basis used for setting and evaluating internal control must be a **suitable framework**, which, so far, as used by U.S. companies has been the COSO IC Framework. However, other currently available frameworks are acceptable, and more may be developed and used in the future. AS 5 states that the auditor should use the same framework that management does for work on ICFR. Exhibit 7-5 presents Section 404 of SOX.

SEC Interpretive Guidance

In 2007 the SEC provided interpretive guidance to management for assessing and reporting on the effectiveness of ICFR required by SOX Section 404 (33-8810; 34-55929). The interpretive guidance is not established as a required approach that management must use in performing the evaluation. Rather, the SEC states that if the evaluation is performed based on the guidance, it will be acceptable. The lengthy interpretive release provides detailed guidance to management.

The SEC's guidance instructs management to assess whether the company's controls, including **entity-level** controls are appropriate to address risks of material financial statement misstatement. Like auditing guidance, the SEC's guidance includes considering **effectiveness of ICFR** that prevent misstatements or detect them in a timely manner. If the controls exist, management should test whether they operate sufficiently to prevent or detect a material financial statement misstatement. Thus, the SEC guidance addresses both **design effectiveness** and **operating effectiveness**.

The SEC guidance also states that management should consider risk in evaluating the amount and types of evidence needed to be able to come to a conclusion about operation of controls. This addresses the concept of operating effectiveness. The expectation is that those controls that are more important to preventing or detecting material misstatements will receive more attention.

Not surprisingly, the SEC interpretive guidance provides the grounding for the approach found in AS 5. Management may use a top down, risk-based approach. Such an approach is expected to identify risks that might result in material financial statement misstatements. Furthermore, a top down, risk-based approach focuses on the controls needed to address identified risks. If controls appropriately address the risks, indicating design effectiveness, management tests the controls to assess operating effectiveness. The SEC guidance focuses on cost effectiveness by stating that management only needs to test those controls that are important to material misstatements in the financial statements. Management can tailor the nature and extent of procedures used to evaluate whether the controls operate effectively for the company's unique circumstances.

Details of the specific **management documentation of ICFR** that must be drafted and evidence maintained are not provided. The SEC interpretive guidance states that management must maintain evidence to provide reasonable support for its assessment of ICFR effectiveness. Third parties, like the external auditor, can review the evidence and consider the work performed by management. If a single material weakness in ICFR is identified, management may not conclude that ICFR is effective.

AUDITING IN ACTION

An Example of a MANAGEMENT REPORT ON INTERNAL CONTROL OVER FINANCIAL REPORTING

TO THE SHAREHOLDERS OF RYDER SYSTEM, INC.:

Management of Ryder System, Inc., together with its consolidated subsidiaries (Ryder), is responsible for establishing and maintaining adequate internal control over financial reporting as defined in Rules 13a-15(f) and 15d-15(f) under the Securities Exchange Act of 1934. Ryder's internal control over financial reporting is designed to provide reasonable assurance regarding the reliability of financial reporting and the preparation of the consolidated financial statements for external purposes in accordance with accounting principles generally accepted in the United States of America.

Ryder's internal control over financial reporting includes those policies and procedures that (1) pertain to the maintenance of records that, in reasonable detail, accurately and fairly reflect the transactions and dispositions of the assets of Ryder; (2) provide reasonable assurance that transactions are recorded as necessary to permit preparation of financial statements in accordance with generally accepted accounting principles, and that our receipts and expenditures are being made only in accordance with authorizations of Ryder's management and directors; and (3) provide reasonable assurance regarding prevention or timely detection of unauthorized acquisition, use or disposition of Ryder's assets that could have a material effect on the consolidated financial statements.

Because of its inherent limitations, internal control over financial reporting may not prevent or detect misstatements. Also, projections of any evaluation of effectiveness to future periods are subject to the risk that controls may become inadequate because of changes in conditions, or that the degree of compliance with the policies or procedures may deteriorate.

Management assessed the effectiveness of Ryder's internal control over financial reporting as of December 31, 2008. In making this assessment, management used the criteria set forth by the Committee of Sponsoring Organizations of the Treadway Commission in "Internal Control—Integrated Framework." Based on our assessment and those criteria, management determined that Ryder maintained effective internal control over financial reporting as of December 31, 2008.

Ryder's independent registered certified public accounting firm has audited the effectiveness of Ryder's internal control over financial reporting.

(*Source:* Ryder System Inc 10K for 12/31/08 from SEC Web site.)

REVIEW QUESTIONS

F.1   What is the FCPA? What instigated its passage? What did it do?

F.2   What management responsibility is established by Section 302 of SOX?

F.3   What management responsibility is established by Section 404 of SOX? How is the independent auditor involved?

F.4   What is the purpose of the SEC's Interpretive Release on management's assessment and reporting on ICFR? Does it impose requirements for management reporting?

BACKGROUND TO AN AUDIT OF ICFR [LO 4]

The Sarbanes-Oxley Act Section 404 and related SEC and PCAOB standards control the professional environment for auditing ICFR. Remember that the objective of an integrated audit is to report on ICFR and the financial statements of a public company. A more specific description is that the auditor issues an opinion on ICFR and an opinion on the financial statements.

The auditor may express these two opinions in a single report or in a report on ICFR and a separate report on the financial statements. The auditor's opinion on the financial statements addresses the fairness of the financial statements. The auditor's opinion on ICFR addresses whether ICFR is effective. To satisfy the requirements of SOX, the SEC, and the PCAOB, both management and the auditor must assess the design and operations of ICFR. If the auditor disagrees with management's assessment, this is added to the audit report. Thus, although the auditor's report offers a single opinion on ICFR effectiveness, it also reflects on management's report on ICFR effectiveness.

The auditor *must* audit the financial statements in order to audit ICFR. Even though the audit of ICFR is a separate activity with its own objectives and requirements, an ICFR audit is part of an integrated audit. The financial statement audit and audit of ICFR are not separate audit engagements. The auditor is expected to utilize information and conclusions from one aspect of the audit in the rest of the integrated audit.

AS 5 specifically addresses the integration of the audits (AS5, B1-B9). The auditor should use conclusions made in the ICFR audit as input to the financial statement audit and vice versa. In addition, the auditor should use the information that is collected in one aspect of the integrated audit for testing other areas when appropriate. For example, when the auditor is gathering information to understand the design of ICFR, the same information or documents may be useful in assessing whether the ICFR is operating as designed. The same documents used as ICFR audit evidence may help the auditor determine whether accounts balances in the financial statements are presented fairly.

The approach to an integrated audit is to first identify what would make the financial statements materially misstated. Second, the auditor applies that judgment to the accounts, transactions, and disclosures that make up the financial statements. The assertions that management makes about accounts and disclosures are the focus of audit procedures. The auditor focuses on management's assertions in understanding the accounting system. The auditor identifies important controls that address significant risks associated with management's assertions about the accounts and disclosures. The auditor assesses whether the controls are designed effectively so that, if operating effectively, they can prevent or detect material misstatements resulting from the risks.

MANAGEMENT ASSERTIONS AND AUDIT PROCEDURES

In reporting financial information through financial statements, management asserts that the financial statements reflect the company's activities and financial position according to the basis of accounting used. These assertions, as presented by the PCAOB, are:

1. **Existence or occurrence**. Assets and liabilities exist. Transactions that are recorded actually occurred.
2. **Completeness.** All accounts and transactions that exist and have occurred are included in the presentation. The financial statements include everything that they should.
3. **Rights and obligations**. The presentation of assets represents what the company has rights to. The presentation of liabilities represents the company's obligations.
4. **Valuation or allocation**. Assets, liabilities, and equity on the balance sheet and revenues and expenses on the income statement are valued appropriately. Transactions and financial statement presentations, including necessary allocations among periods, are reflected in the proper accounting period.
5. **Presentation and disclosure**. Items and amounts shown in the financial statements follow the presentation and disclosure standards required by the basis of accounting used.

Management Assertions

Audit steps in an ICFR audit relate to management's financial statement assertions. ICFR design and operations are effective when they provide reasonable assurance that the financial reporting and financial statements that are produced by management are in accordance with accounting standards. It is possible that the financial statements are proper even if ICFR is not effective. But in contrast, if ICFR is effective, it provides additional support for the likelihood that the financial statements are fair.

The auditor uses management's assertions to plan the audit procedures conducted in an integrated audit. Planned audit procedures relate to management's report on ICFR and the various management assertions for the financial statements. The auditor carries out audit procedures, collecting evidence that gives the auditor a basis to conclude whether ICFR is effective and management's financial statement assertions are appropriate. In the ICFR phase of the integrated audit, the procedures relate to controls. The controls ultimately relate to the company producing financial statements that are not materially misstated.

The auditor tests management's assertions for classes of transactions and events that occurred during the year. Although final account balances are examined during the financial statement audit, evidence regarding management's financial statement assertions also results from ICFR audit procedures.

The AICPA's description of management's assertions is different from the PCAOB's list of five assertions. The AICPA's 13 assertions from AU 326.15 are as follows.

Assertions about classes of transactions and events for the period under audit:
    Occurrence
    Completeness
    Accuracy
    Cutoff
    Classification
Assertions about account balances at the period-end:
    Existence
    Rights and obligations
    Completeness
    Valuation and allocation
Assertions about presentation and disclosure:
    Occurrence and rights and obligations
    Completeness
    Classification and understandability
    Accuracy and valuation

In addition to assertions used by the PCAOB, the AICPA uses management assertions of accuracy, cutoff, and classification for classes of transactions and events. One way to think about the two sets of management assertions is to view the additional AICPA categories as subsets of the PCAOB management assertions. For example, a transaction posted at the wrong amount did not really occur as shown. Because the amount posted is not accurate, other management assertions are violated. A transaction posted in the wrong period because of poor cutoff did not occur in the period when it is shown. A transaction posted to the wrong account is misclassified. Therefore, the transaction as shown did not occur. The transaction that occurred is different from the one shown.

The AICPA's list of management assertions also includes understandability for presentation and disclosure. This is not a part of the PCAOB's assertion list but, again, fits well. The PCAOB's management assertion is that presentation and disclosure is consistent with requirements of the applicable accounting standards. The implied assumption is that to meet the standards' requirements the presentation and disclosures must be understandable. In a similar manner, the AICPA's ownership assertion is an expansion of the rights and obligations assertion. The discussion that follows includes the PCAOB management assertions and the additional ones presented by the AICPA standards.

REVIEW QUESTIONS

G.1 How many opinions does the independent auditor issue as a result of the annual engagement?

G.2 In what way does the auditor's report on ICFR relate to management's ICFR assessment?

G.3 Why does the ICFR audit address the financial statement assertions?

Existence or Occurrence

The *occurrence assertion* relates to the auditor's need to know that recorded transactions are real and actually occurred. The auditor plans audit procedures to gather evidence about this assertion. For example, to gain reasonable assurance that sales transactions actually occurred, the auditor looks for evidence that ICFR is designed so that fictitious sales cannot be entered into the system. Then, during the ICFR operations testing phase, the auditor tests those controls that prevent fictitious sales from being recorded to see that they function. An example is an ICFR requirement that a sale is only posted when all sales steps are completed and documented. Commonly required steps for which the auditor tests are (1) receiving a customer order, (2) approving the customer's credit and (3) shipping the goods.

Additional aspects of this same sales transaction relate to the existence of accounts receivable and inventory accounts. To test the management assertions of occurrence and existence related to year-end accounts receivable and inventory balances, the auditor can use various procedures. For example, the auditor can test that the computer program that aggregates sales transactions (1) functions properly and (2) has appropriate controls over reconciling the total amount of postings to the resulting account balances. The auditor tests the existence of inventory by examining whether the physical count of inventory corresponds to the inventory general ledger account balance at year end. The auditor tests the existence of accounts receivables balances by looking for payments to the company from the debtors. Another audit procedure for testing the existence of accounts receivable is asking the outside parties whether they agree that they owe money to the company and agree with the amount. This process is called external confirmation and is part of the financial statement audit procedures.

Completeness

A straightforward way to describe *completeness* is that it addresses whether everything that should be has been recorded and is included in the balances. The audit procedures investigate the accuracy of management's assertion that everything that should be is included. If the completeness assertion is violated, the financial statement results are misstated.

The audit procedures for completeness primarily address the risk of items being unrecorded or under-recorded. Omission or under-recording transactions can cause balances to be over- or understated.

As an example, to gain evidence on the proper design of controls targeting completeness, the auditor looks for ICFR processes that make sure all expenses for purchases during the year are recorded. This includes recording all amounts owed at the end of the year for purchases during the year, whether or not the bill has been received by year end. If the company has not received an invoice by the time it closes its books, it must estimate the amount.

To test the operating effectiveness of the controls over the recording of purchases and accounts payable, the auditor tests the purchase order system and the controls over year-end accruals. To test the completeness of the related accounts payable balances, during the financial statement audit the auditor traces payments made early in the next fiscal year. Payments early in the next fiscal year should be for purchases made in that year or recorded to accounts payable for the year under audit. If the cash payments in the next fiscal year are for purchases of the prior year that are not recorded as accounts payable on the balance sheet, then accounts payable is understated. These steps provide audit evidence that the controls established to assure completeness of the accounts payable balance are effective and that the account balance is complete. The auditor may also choose to verify with all the company's banks and financial institutions that there are no debt agreements that are not included in the financial statements.

Accuracy

The **accuracy assertion** deals with the correct arithmetic calculation of numbers that go into the financial statements. A simple accuracy example deals with the mathematically correct aggregation of transactions into balance totals that go forward to the financial statements. An example of a complex process for which accuracy is important is the calculation required for transactions involving foreign currencies. The computer program applications that calculate translation of foreign currency transactions are part of the ICFR. The auditor examines whether the design of accuracy controls is effective while examining design effectives of the overall IT environment. The auditor also tests particular programs to verify the accuracy of the calculations. If complex calculations, such as foreign currency transactions or derivatives, have a material impact on the financial statements, significant audit effort goes into investigating the accuracy of the financial statement amounts.

Cutoff

The **cutoff assertion** refers to the separation between fiscal years. Cutoff relates to the existence or occurrence and completeness assertions. A management assertion that balances are complete includes two parts. First, it includes an assertion that all transactions that occur before the end of the fiscal year are captured in the earlier year. Second, all transactions that occur after the end of the fiscal year are included in the later year.

Although cutoff may sound like a simple consideration, it can present challenges. For example, inventory on the balance sheet should include everything that the company owns as of the end of the day at the end of the fiscal year. Care must be given to exclude inventory items that have been sold but not yet shipped and to include items owned by the company but held in a different location. Cash accounts often have items "in transit" at the end of the fiscal year, such as deposits and outstanding checks or transfers. These should be recorded in the fiscal year in which the transaction occurred, not the year the transactions clear the bank. All companies have expenses they have incurred but for which they have not yet received bills at the end of the year. These expenses must be accrued and the liabilities shown at the end of the year.

To gain evidence supporting the management assertion of a proper cutoff, the auditor looks for controls designed as part of the system to verify the cutoff between fiscal years. The auditor tests the operation of the important controls, and also tests the financial statement balances. The purpose of the tests is to obtain evidence that provides reasonable assurance about the effectiveness of the ICFR and material fairness of the account balances related to the cutoff.

Classification

The **classification assertion** relates both to activities for the period under audit, and to presentation and disclosure. Proper classification simply refers to ensuring that transactions are posted to and balances shown in the correct accounts. Audit procedures testing classification use evidence indicating whether transactions are posted to the correct accounts.

A classic fraud scheme that was used at WorldCom shows how important misclassification can be. The simple fraud scheme is to classify expenses as long-term assets. When current-period expense transactions are classified as long-term assets, they are expensed over a long period of time as depreciation or amortization. This inappropriately elevates income in the immediate time period because the full amount of the expense is not recorded. The impact of the expenses on income is spread over a number of years.

Another example related to the importance of classification deals with short- and long-term debt. When long-term debt comes due, if the company has accomplished certain requirements related to refinancing the debt, the debt can continue to be shown as long term. Moving major balances of debt from long to short term can cause significant changes in various ratios and financial indicators. The auditor looks for evidence that supports the company's continued classification of debt as long term.

Ownership, Rights, Obligations

The **ownership assertion** relates to the *rights and obligations* of assets and liabilities shown in the financial statements. Audit procedures that provide evidence related to ownership show (1) that the company really has *rights* to the assets it says it owns and (2) that its liabilities are actual *obligations* of the company. For example, a company should not show inventory that it is selling on a consignment basis for another company as an asset. And a company should not show a debt of a member of management as a liability, when the debt is the personal obligation of the individual.

The ICFR procedures for ownership, rights, and obligations that the auditor looks for and tests depend on the characteristics of the company. A company that routinely consigns inventory to others, or sells inventory consigned by others, will have a set of significant control procedures for consignments. A company that is in a position to factor or sell accounts receivable—thus it no longer has rights to the asset—will have important controls over factoring receivables. The auditor looks for appropriate controls for the company's transactions, whatever those transactions are, to be part of the ICFR design. The auditor tests to see if those controls are operating properly. During the financial statement audit, the auditor tests to gather evidence regarding the fairness of the account balances.

Valuation, Allocation

The **valuation or allocation assertion** relates to amounts shown in the financial statements often resulting from management's estimates made during the period-end reporting process. Some valuation issues may be straightforward, such as estimating a reasonable allowance for doubtful accounts for accounts receivable, or the useful lives used for depreciating assets. Alternatively, many estimates and valuations that go into the preparation of the financial statements are complex. These require considerable audit effort before an auditor is persuaded that the amount is appropriate.

An example of difficult valuations can be found in the construction industry. Construction requires estimates of how close projects are to completion in order to determine appropriate revenue and inventory balances. Estimating the stage of inventory completion for most manufacturing companies is probably not as difficult as for long-term construction projects. However, the estimate can still be very important because it often involves a large dollar amount. Consequently, the estimates require significant audit effort. The company's industry and specific characteristics drive its valuation issues, appropriate controls, and the audit evidence that must be accumulated. As with other assertions, audit evidence must support a conclusion about the effective design and operation of the controls and fairness of the financial statement balances.

REVIEW QUESTIONS

H.1 What do the following assertions mean?

a. Occurrence	**d.** Accuracy	**g.** Ownership	**j.** Valuation
b. Existence	**e.** Cutoff	**h.** Rights	**k.** Allocation
c. Completeness	**f.** Classification	**i.** Obligations	

ICFR Tests and Time Period Covered

Management's assertions relate to the fairness of the financial statements. Management's report on ICFR refers to effectiveness at the end of the fiscal year. The time frame is different. For the auditor's report to conclude that ICFR is effective, it has to be effective only at fiscal year end. To meet this threshold, ICFR must be effective at and for a period of time prior to fiscal year end so that the auditor has confidence in that conclusion.

If the auditor knows that all or a part of ICFR was not effective throughout the entire financial period, this knowledge affects the financial statement audit procedures. Absent effective ICFR, the financial statement audit procedures must provide evidence on management's assertions and the financial statements without expecting ICFR to produce good information. The situation can occur when ICFR is ineffective at fiscal year end. It can also occur when ICFR was ineffective for the entire fiscal year or management changed the system part way through the year to correct a material weakness.

In contrast to an audit plan expecting *ineffective* ICFR, the auditor can expect that ICFR were *effective* throughout the financial reporting period, as well as at the fiscal year end. When this happens, the integrated audit plan reflects this expectation. If ICFR is expected to be effective, the auditor usually plans to rely on ICFR in the financial statement audit. The auditor plans the integrated audit to test whether ICFR was functioning effectively for the entire reporting period and *plans* the financial statements audit to rely on the effectiveness of ICFR. If the expectation is wrong and audit procedures reveal that ICFR is not effective, the financial statement audit plan is revised. An exception to this general audit approach is when it is more efficient to test a financial statement year-end account balance using only substantive procedures. Then, the auditor may decide *against* testing operating effectiveness of certain controls for the entire year, even if they are expected to be effective.

REVIEW QUESTIONS

I.1 To what time period does management's report on the effectiveness of ICFR relate?

I.2 Would the auditor be likely to test and attempt to rely on ICFR for the financial statement audit if ICFR changed during the year? Why?

I.3 Even if ICFR is expected to have been effective for the entire fiscal year, why might the auditor choose to NOT test effectiveness during the year?

AUDITOR'S UNDERSTANDING AND ASSESSMENT OF DESIGN EFFECTIVENESS OF ICFR [LO 5]

Obtaining an understanding of ICFR is a major part of the ICFR audit. The auditor must obtain the understanding, gather evidence to evaluate ICFR design, choose the controls that need to be tested for operating effectiveness, and test and evaluate ICFR operations. The steps to obtain an understanding of the client's system and ICFR and assess design effectiveness are largely performed together. The important components of obtaining an understanding are identifying:

1. Significant accounts and disclosures
2. Relevant assertions for those accounts and disclosures
3. Risks that may cause material misstatements
4. Controls designed to address those risks

In identifying risks and controls, the auditor may find that there are several classes of transactions that make up the important accounts. Moreover, certain important processes may affect the classes of transactions that make up the important accounts. The auditor uses many of the risk assessment and planning procedures to understand ICFR and assess design effectiveness. The auditor specifically addresses entity-level controls and fraud risk while gaining an understanding of the ICFR.

Evidence Related to ICFR

Procedures the auditor uses to gain an understanding of specific controls in ICFR are **inquiry, inspection, observation, reperformance,** and **tracing.** Tracing deals with selecting a document and looking for the posting of the document in the books and records. So, the term *tracing* is generally used to refer to a specific type of document inspection.

AUDITING IN ACTION

Audit Procedures to Understand Specific Controls

- Making inquiries of appropriate management, supervisory, and staff personnel
- Inspecting company documents
- Observing the application of specific controls
- Tracing transactions through the information system relevant to financial reporting

Walkthrough is the term for a set of audit procedures that are often performed together and used in an ICFR audit. "In performing a walkthrough, the auditor follows a transaction from origination through the company's processes, including information systems until it is reflected in the company's financial records, using the same documents and information technology that company personnel use" (AS 5.37). Even though it is called a tracing procedure, a walkthrough also includes inquiry and observation.

> In performing a walkthrough, at the points at which important process procedures occur, the auditor questions the company's personnel about their understanding of what is required by the company's prescribed procedures and controls. These probing questions combined with other walkthrough procedures, allow the auditor to gain a sufficient understanding of the process and to be able to identify important points at which a necessary control is missing or is not designed effectively. (AS 5.38)

Questions that an auditor may ask company personnel during the course of a walkthrough include the following:

- What do you do when you find an error?
- What are you looking for to determine if there is an error?
- What kinds of errors have you found?
- What happens as a result of finding errors?
- How are errors resolved?
- Have you ever been asked to override the process or controls? If so, what happened and why did it occur?

(AS 2, para. 81)

AS 5 stresses that walkthroughs are a very efficient way to understand ICFR and assess design effectiveness.

AUDITING IN ACTION

Fundamental Information from a Walkthrough

WHO	...performs the control? Or, if automated, what system?
WHAT	...is performs and why? What is the management assertion?
WHEN	...is the activity performed, including how often?
WHAT	...evidence is produced showing that the control occurred?
HOW	...are problems or exceptions investigated and resolved?

REVIEW QUESTIONS

J.1 What are the important steps of obtaining an understanding of the client's ICFR?

J.2 What are inquiry, inspection, observation, reperformance, and tracing?

J.3 What is a walkthrough?

J.4 What questions might be relevant for the auditor to ask company employees during a walkthrough?

Audit Documentation

Understanding the company's system and assessing design effectiveness are part of audit planning. In addition, assessing whether the ICFR design is effective is also part of forming an ICFR audit opinion. Therefore, the auditor prepares documentation of the assessment of ICFR design. Information and evidence collected during the client acceptance and continuance process and audit planning are included as the earliest part of **audit documentation**. By the time the auditor addresses design effectiveness, audit documentation is already well underway.

Audit documentation is the written record of the auditor's work. Audit documentation may be called **work papers** or working papers and can be in paper, electronic, or other media formats. Audit documentation must include the basis for the auditor's conclusions and support for the "auditor's representations." Documentation includes support for the auditor's stated position, whether that position is included in a written report, or a different communication form such as an oral report to management or the audit committee. In addition to presenting support for the auditor's conclusions, auditors prepare documentation to help them with planning, performing, and supervising the audit work. To concisely sum up the records created by audit work papers, they document:

- Planning and performance of the work
- Procedures performed
- Evidence obtained
- Conclusions reached (AS 3.2)

Audit documentation is so important that it is the subject of the third standard issued by the PCAOB. AS 3 stresses that audit documentation must be sufficient for various users to understand the audit activities and to provide evidence of the auditor's work. For example, audit documentation must:

- demonstrate that the engagement complied with the standards of the PCAOB,
- support the auditor's conclusions concerning every relevant financial statement assertion, and
- demonstrate that the underlying accounting records agreed or reconciled with the financial statements.

The AS 3 requirements are very rigorous and cover all aspects of the audit. To show that PCAOB standards have been followed and support the auditor's conclusions for *all* relevant financial statement assertions, audit documentation must be very complete. The documentation must show the nature, timing, extent, and results of the procedures performed. This means that the work papers must clearly show exactly what the audit procedures were, when they were performed, and the outcomes. The work papers must also show who did the work and on what date, as well as who reviewed the work and the date on which it was reviewed.

Exactly how extensive documentation must be to meet these standards is a matter of professional judgment. The auditor must decide what should be included in the work papers. A reviewer, PCAOB inspector, or any other appropriately knowledgeable and authorized person must be able to understand the work performed. The work papers require enough detail to show that audit standards were followed and that the audit conclusions reached are justified. In deciding what documentation should be prepared, the auditor considers:

- Nature of the auditing procedure
- Risk of material misstatement associated with the assertion
- Extent of judgment required in performing the work and evaluating results
- Significance of the evidence obtained to the assertion being tested
- Responsibility to document a conclusion not readily determinable from the documentation of the procedures performed or evidence obtained (AS 3.7)

Characteristics that drive a need for more documentation are:

- An audit task that is difficult to understand or interpret
- An audit task that requires a lot of judgment
- An audit task that is very important to the audit
- A management assertion that has a lot of risk

In contrast, a straightforward audit procedure for which conclusions are self-evident requires less documentation.

AS 3 requires auditors to include significant information that was considered during the audit even though it supports a different audit conclusion than the one finally reached. In other words, if

1. the auditor uncovered information suggesting a significant problem with an aspect of internal control or an account balance, and then,
2. upon further investigation decided that there was not really a problem, then
3. this contrary information must be included as a component of the audit documentation.

> **AS 3.8:** In addition to the documentation necessary to support the auditor's final conclusion, audit documentation must include information the auditor has identified relating to significant findings or issues that is inconsistent with or contradicts the auditor's final conclusions. The relevant records to be retained include, but are not limited to, procedures performed in response to the information, and records, documentation, consultations on, or resolutions of, differences in professional judgment among members of the engagement team or between the engagement team and others consulted.

Documentation of the ICFR and financial statement audits should include procedures performed and identification of the items inspected, as well as results. The audit documentation associated with steps to understand the system and evaluate its design likely includes

- A copy of ICFR-related documentation prepared by management
- Audit steps and outcomes including inquiry and observations
- Identification of items inspected

REVIEW QUESTIONS

K.1 What is audit documentation?

K.2 When completed, the set of audit work papers documents what information?

K.3 What does AS 3 state in terms of sufficiency required of audit documentation and evidence it must provide?

K.4 For each audit, what must audit documentation show about:

  (a) PCAOB standards?

  (b) Auditor conclusions?

  (c) The company's accounting records?

K.5 Describe how extensive audit documentation must be. What purposes must it be able to serve?

K.6 How are conflicting conclusions that are arrived at during the course of the audit handled in the audit documentation?

Documentation of the Company's ICFR

The SEC's Interpretive Release on management's report on ICFR (33-8810, 34-55929) discusses the documentation management prepares as part of its assessment of the effectiveness of ICFR. Management's documentation can vary depending on the company's characteristics. Management must have sufficient evidence to support its conclusions. As part of that evidence, the company may have documentation of the important processes or classes of transactions that link the transactions to accounts and management assertions. Whatever form it takes, management must produce sufficient documentation to show that its process and assessment of the effectiveness of ICFR is reasonable. Further, the documentation must provide some means of displaying the link between significant financial statement accounts, management assertions, and controls.

The auditor may use management's documentation of ICFR as one source for gaining an understanding of the system. Auditors are likely to use the company's documentation as a starting point, particularly if management develops documentation specifically for the purpose of its assessment of ICFR. Management can also elect to rely on the documents it uses in its day-to-day operations as evidence of its assessment. Information that may be included when management develops specific documentation of its ICFR assessment is:

- The design of controls over relevant assertions related to all significant accounts and disclosures in the financial statements
- Information about how significant transactions are initiated, authorized, recorded, processed, and reported
- Information about the flow of transactions to identify the points at which material misstatements due to error or fraud could occur
- Controls designed to prevent or detect fraud, including who performs the controls and the related segregation of duties
- Controls over the safeguarding of assets
- The results of management's testing and evaluation of ICFR

ICFR is documented using various techniques. The documentation methods used by management are those that auditors have also used historically. **Flowcharts** or **process models**, **narrative** descriptions, and job descriptions are all used to document ICFR. Samples of transaction documents and forms, procedures manuals, and organization charts may also be part of management's ICFR documentation. **Questionnaires** and checklists may also be used.

Management may combine these various methods of documentation. For example, for parts of the system that are judged to be of highest risk or materiality, management may use flow charts or systems diagrams, narratives, and sample documents. For parts of the system that are of limited risk and materiality, management may document the system only with narratives. Because management has probably not performed a complete assessment of risk and materiality the first time it begins to document ICFR, the process may be iterative. In other words, management may create preliminary documentation of a portion of the system and later develop more extensive documentation if materiality is judged to be different from what was originally expected.

Flowcharts are diagrams of the ICFR system. Most likely you have encountered flowcharting technique prior to this course. "Standard" flowcharts typically show an overall "system" (meaning the activities performed throughout some aspect of a business),

Partial Flowchart for Cash Receipts Process

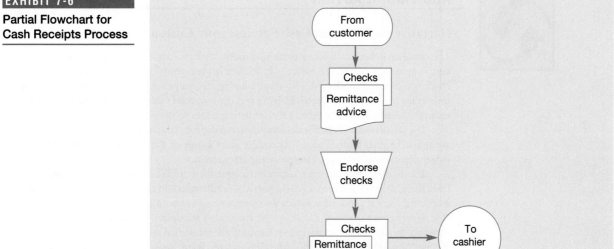

document flows, or the steps in a computer program. The flowcharts used to document an ICFR usually show activities and processes, including control steps and documents. The flowchart can show control steps actually programmed into specific computer programs. Flowcharts generally use standard symbols and are read from the top left to the bottom right. Many companies use computer flowcharting programs in documenting their ICFR. For more details on flowcharting you may refer to various information systems books. Exhibit 7-6 shows an example of flowcharting for a cash receipts process.

Narratives are basically memoranda (memos) or written descriptions of the business process, including descriptions of the documents and controls. Narratives are more likely to be used for simple processes or parts of the ICFR deemed to be of lower risk or with a nonmaterial impact on the financial statements. Documenting a complex system using a narrative format is difficult. Narratives or memos may be used to augment flowcharts for important segments of the system.

Questionnaires and checklists are lists of questions about the system that are structured with a "check-off" space for documenting whether a process or control exists in a system. These documents are useful for indicating whether controls and weaknesses exist. They do not provide a description of the flow of transactions or documents through processes of a company.

REVIEW QUESTIONS

L.1 How can management's documentation of its system and ICFR be useful to the auditor?

L.2 If management does not prepare specific documentation when it assesses the effectiveness of ICFR, what does it use for evidence?

L.3 What methods are often used for documenting an accounting system and ICFR? Under what conditions is each method most effective? Is any method required?

AUDITING IN ACTION

Narrative for System of Cash Receipts from Customer

The customer's check is received in the mail room. With two employees participating, the envelope is opened, a remittance advice is immediately prepared (if one is not included), and the check is restrictively endorsed. Two receipt listings are prepared. Checks are passed on to the cashier for processing. One receipt listing and the remittance advices are sent to the accounts receivable department. The second receipt listing is sent to the general ledger department.

The cashier receives the checks and prepares a deposit ticket. Checks received are deposited at the end of each business day. The cashier gives a copy of the deposit ticket to the general ledger department as support to record the transaction.

The accounts receivable department receives the remittance advices and receipts listing from the mail room and reconciles the totals of remittances and receipts. This process provides additional clerical check of accuracy and completeness of both records. The accounts receivable department then posts credits to the customer's subsidiary ledger account. Monthly the accounts receivable subsidiary ledger accounts are reconciled with control totals. Statements are mailed to customers monthly. The accounts receivable department keeps files of receipts listings and remittance advices.

The general ledger department receives the receipts listing document and deposit ticket copy. The receipts listing total is compared and reconciled to the deposit ticket. The transaction is then posted to the cash and accounts receivable control accounts. The receipts listing and deposit slips are filed. Monthly, the bank statement is reconciled with the general ledger cash account. Computer application controls routinely compare accounts receivable totals to the general ledger accounts receivable account balance and produce discrepancy reports when called for.

(*Source*: Based on *Auditing: An Assertion Approach*, Taylor & Glezen, p. 254.)

ENTITY-LEVEL CONTROLS

To audit design and operation of ICFR, the auditor has to link accounts and assertions to the related controls. The auditor must identify those accounts that are significant to the financial statements. Then the auditor determines what assertions are relevant to those accounts. Next, the auditor looks for risks that may cause the financial statement accounts to be materially misstated regarding the assertions. At that point the auditor can determine what company controls address the risks of material misstatement.

In addition to the accounts-assertions-controls approach, the auditor must also consider controls that have a pervasive effect on the ICFR. **Entity-level controls** are those that exist at the organization or company level, but have an impact on controls at the process, transaction, or application level. Some of these entity-level controls are called "softer" controls. The softer controls in the COSO IC Framework are tone at the top, assignment of authority and responsibility, and policies and procedures. Other entity-level controls are IT-related controls and monitoring. For example, general IT controls (ITGC) have a pervasive impact. ITGC include controls over program development, program changes, computer operations, and access to programs and data. These are entity-level controls because they all affect the company's processing of transactions. Appendix A of this chapter addresses ITGC in greater detail.

Entity-level controls are important because they impact other tests the auditor conducts to evaluate effectiveness of ICFR. Entity-level controls can be grouped into three categories:

1. Entity-level controls that have an important, but indirect effect on the likelihood that a misstatement will be detected or prevented on a timely basis. These controls might affect the other controls the auditor selects for testing and the nature, timing, and extent of procedures the auditor performs on other controls.

2. Entity-level controls that monitor the effectiveness of other controls. Such controls might be designed to identify possible breakdowns in lower-level controls, but not

at a level of precision that would, by themselves, sufficiently address the assessed risk that misstatements to a relevant assertion will be prevented or detected on a timely basis. These controls, when operating effectively, might allow the auditor to reduce the testing of other controls.

3. Entity-level controls that are designed to operate at a level of precision that would adequately prevent or detect on a timely basis misstatements to one or more relevant assertions. If an entity-level control sufficiently addresses the assessed risk of misstatement, the auditor need not test additional controls relating to that risk. (AS 5.23)

AUDITING IN ACTION

Example of Entity-Level Controls

Control related to the control environment
    Tone at the top
    Assignment of authority and responsibility
    Consistent policies and procedures
    Company-wide code of conduct
    Company-wide fraud prevention program

Controls over **management override**
The company's risk assessment process
Centralized processing and controls
Controls over shared service environments
Controls to monitor results of operations
Controls to monitor other controls

    Internal audit
    Audit committee
    Self assessment programs

Period-end financial reporting process
Policies that address significant business control and risk management practices
(AS 5.24)

Audit Committee and Those in Governance

The audit committee plays an important role in the entity-level controls and control environment of the company. Although internal control is the responsibility of management, the monitoring activities of an effective audit committee strengthen the control environment. The Board of Directors is responsible for evaluating the audit committee. However, the auditor assesses the functioning of the audit committee when evaluating pervasive, entity-level controls. If the company does not have an audit committee, the audit committee functions should be performed by the Board of Directors. By this point in the audit, the auditor has already considered effectiveness of audit committee function, especially during client acceptance and continuance. Auditor assessment of audit committee function includes issues such as:

Oversight of external financial reporting
Oversight of internal control over financial reporting
Independence of audit committee members from management
Clarity of responsibilities, as shown in the audit committee charter
Interaction with independent and internal auditors
Interaction with chief financial officer, chief accounting officer
Interaction with other key members of financial management

Questions asked of management and the auditor
Understanding of critical accounting policies
Understanding of accounting estimate judgments
Responsiveness to issues raised by the auditor (AS 2.57-58)

"Ineffective oversight of the company's external financial reporting and internal control over financial reporting by the company's audit committee" is one of the few conditions specified by AS 5 as being an indicator of a material weakness in ICFR (AS 5.69). If a company's ICFR has even one material weakness, it is not effective. Determining the seriousness of a deficiency in ICFR and whether a deficiency is a material weakness is discussed in Chapter 8.

Fraud Risk Assessment

A part of management's responsibility when it designs the internal control system is to include programs and controls that prevent, deter, and detect fraud. These are called anti-fraud controls. In addition to implementing specific anti-fraud controls, management and the audit committee should set a proper tone at the top so that the entity has an organizational culture that values honesty and ethical standards. An effective tone at the top, along with an ethical culture and effective controls aimed at preventing and detecting fraud, is expected to reduce the opportunities for fraud to occur.

The auditor has a responsibility to evaluate fraud risk in both the ICFR and financial statement audit. Controls identified and evaluated in the ICFR audit may contribute to a lower assessed risk of fraud for the financial statement audit. In contrast, the ICFR audit may show that controls intended to prevent and detect fraud are missing or ineffective.

The auditor considers the risk of fraud throughout the integrated audit. Potential fraud is an ongoing consideration in procedures in the ICFR audit. The auditor evaluates all controls that are specifically directed at the risk of potentially material fraud. Some controls apply to specific processes and financial statement accounts, while others are among the "softer" controls that affect the business environment. Controls the auditor should evaluate include those listed below. Many of these items should sound familiar as they were considered in the client acceptance and continuance process, and discussed in Chapter 6 related to the Fraud Triangle.

- Controls restraining misappropriation of company assets
- Risk assessment processes
- Codes of ethics or conduct provisions, especially those related to conflicts of interest, related party transactions, illegal acts, and the monitoring of the code by management and the audit committee or board
- Adequacy of the internal audit activity and whether the internal audit function reports directly to the audit committee, as well as the extent of the audit committee's involvement and interaction with internal audit
- Adequacy of the company's procedures for handling complaints and for accepting confidential submissions of concerns about questionable accounting or auditing matters

The last item in this list involves the company's procedures for handling complaints and receiving tips regarding accounting and auditing matters. This issue is also specifically addressed by SOX. SOX requires that companies have a system in place to receive and evaluate this type of information—often referred to as whistleblower information (SOX ß 1514A). The auditor has a responsibility to evaluate the effectiveness of processes for receiving and evaluating whistleblower information.

Chapter 6 introduced the Fraud Triangle of incentives, opportunities, and rationalization. The more the audit team learns about the company's ICFR, the better the team is at identifying opportunities for fraud that result from missing or ineffective controls. Audit procedures designed to understand and evaluate ICFR, as noted earlier, are inquiry, inspection, observation, tracing, and walkthroughs. Concurrently with helping the auditor understand and evaluate ICFR, these procedures provide fraud risk information.

Inquiry is a particularly important procedure. Auditors spend a lot of time making inquiries of management, the audit committee, internal auditors, and other employees of the company. As members of the audit team gather evidence from inquiry or other steps, communicating that evidence with everyone on the team is vital for proper consideration of fraud risk.

AUDITING IN ACTION

Inquiries about Fraud Risk

Inquiries of Management

- Whether management has knowledge of any fraud or suspected fraud affecting the entity
- Whether management is aware of allegations of fraud or suspected fraud affecting the entity
- Management's understanding about the risks of fraud in the entity
- Programs and controls the entity has established to mitigate specific fraud risks the entity has identified, or that otherwise help to prevent, deter, and detect fraud, and how management monitors those programs and controls.
- For an entity with multiple locations, (a) the nature and extent of monitoring of operating locations or business segments, and (b) whether there are particular operating locations or business segments for which a risk of fraud may be more likely to exist
- Whether and how management communicates to employees its views on business practices and ethical behavior
- Whether and how management has reported to the audit committee on how the entity's internal control serves to prevent, deter, or detect material misstatements due to fraud.

Inquiries of the Audit Committee

- The audit committee's views about the risks of fraud
- Whether the audit committee has knowledge of any fraud or suspected fraud affecting the entity

Inquiries of Internal Audit Personnel

- Views about the risk of fraud
- Whether they have performed any procedures to identify or detect fraud during the year
- Whether management has satisfactorily responded to any findings resulting from these procedures
- Whether they have knowledge of fraud or suspected fraud

(AU 316.20-24)

REVIEW QUESTIONS

M.1 What do entity-level controls impact?

M.2 What are the three categories of entity-level controls described in AS 5? Why is analyzing an entity-level control in this manner useful?

M.3 What is the impact of ineffective oversight by the audit committee?

M.4 What is "tone at the top," and how does it relate to fraud?

M.5 What does SOX require regarding whistleblower reports?

AUDITING IN ACTION

More Fraud Questions for Management and those in Governance

To understand any past frauds and management's commitment to fraud prevention, deterrence, and detection:

1. Do you have any knowledge of any fraud that could result in a material misstatement of the financial statements?
2. Do you have any knowledge of any other fraud, regardless of materiality?
3. Have you received any letters or communications from employees or outsiders alleging fraud?
4. What past frauds have been committed by employees or executives?
5. What incentives and pressures for fraud exist? How are the fraud risks managed?
6. How is fraud that has been identified investigated and remediated?

To understand management's fraud risk assessment and related controls:

1. What is your understanding about the entity's fraud risks?
2. Has management established any programs and controls to limit specific fraud risks? Has management established any programs to prevent, deter, and detect fraud?
3. How does management monitor the fraud-prevention and detection programs?
4. Are you aware of any requests made to withhold information from the auditors? To alter documents? To make fictitious journal entries?
5. Do you know of any unusual or suspicious activities related to adjusting journal entries?

To understand management's communication of its commitment relating to fraud prevention and detection:

1. What are management's communications on ethical business behavior?
2. Has management made reports to the audit committee on the entity's ICFR and its usefulness for fraud prevention and detection?
3. How does management monitor its behavior to ensure behavior is consistent with the anti-fraud message it communicates?

To understand management monitoring of various locations and business segments:

1. What procedures are used for monitoring the anti-fraud programs at the entity's multiple operating locations or lines of business?
2. Is there any location or segment that holds a great risk of fraud?
3. How are unusual or unexpected business results at other locations and lines of business identified and monitored?

Information Technology

Virtually all businesses requiring an audit have some degree of computerized information systems. The auditor must consider the impact of IT on the company and the integrated audit. The nature and extent of IT within the company affects the ICFR risks and therefore the controls needed to achieve ICFR objectives. The auditor considers this impact of IT in the approach to understanding ICFR, assessing ICFR design and testing and assessing ICFR functioning.

IT can have fundamental impacts on a company and its audit. For example, IT affects the initiation, recording, processing, and reporting of financial information. If a company

EXHIBIT 7-7

Benefits and Risks of IT
to Internal Control

Benefits

- Consistently applies predefined business rules and performs complex calculations in processing large volumes of transactions or data
- Enhances the timeliness, availability, and accuracy of information
- Facilitates the additional analysis of information
- Enhances the ability to monitor the performance of the entity's activities and its policies and procedures
- Reduces the risk that controls will be circumvented
- Permits implementing security controls in applications, databases, and operating systems

Risks

- Relying on systems or programs that inaccurately process data, that process the wrong (inaccurate) data or both
- Unauthorized access to data
- Unauthorized changes to data
- Unauthorized changes to systems or programs
- Failure to change systems or programs as intended
- Inappropriate manual intervention
- Potential loss of data

(PCAOB AU 319.18-19, AICPA AU 314.59-60)

is highly automated, all of these steps may be handled by a computer, based on preprogrammed authorizations and steps, with little human intervention.

Consider an e-commerce transaction, such as a sale over the Internet. Computer programs handle the initiation of the transaction based on the customer's input and the authorization of the transaction based on the customer's credit card information. IT processes also determine the availability of the product being sold. Technology carries out the processing and reporting of the financial records affected by the transaction. In this situation, the auditor knows the audit must be planned to thoroughly understand the IT aspects of the system and controls, and to test the IT controls. Even in a company that relies less on IT, the auditor will consider its impact. Exhibit 7-7 lists fundamental benefits of reliance on IT, as well as heightened risks that can occur from reliance.

Period-End Financial Reporting Process

The period-end financial reporting process must be considered on every ICFR audit. The period-end reporting process includes procedures to:

Enter transaction totals into the general ledger.

Select and apply accounting policies.

Initiate, authorize, record, and process journal entries into the general ledger.

Record recurring and nonrecurring adjustments to the annual and quarterly financial statements.

Prepare annual and quarterly financial statements and related disclosures. (AS 5.26)

AUDITING IN ACTION

Auditor Evaluation of the Period-End Financial Reporting Process

- Inputs, procedures performed, and outputs of the processes the company uses to produce its annual and quarterly financial statements
- The extent of IT involvement in each period-end financial reporting process element
- Who participates from management
- The locations involved in the period-end financial reporting process
- Types of adjusting and consolidating entries
- The nature and extent of the oversight of the process by management, the Board of Directors, and the audit committee

(AS 5.27)

These activities occur after the end of the year, creating an unusual sequence of audit work and reporting. For an annual integrated audit the auditor's work occurs after the "as of" date to which the opinion on ICFR applies.

REVIEW QUESTIONS

N.1 Describe why a company's IT processing is important to the design effectiveness of ICFR.

N.2 When are period-end reporting processes conducted? How does this relate to the date of management's report?

IDENTIFYING SIGNIFICANT ACCOUNTS, DISCLOSURES, AND RELEVANT ASSERTIONS

Auditing ICFR requires identifying:

> significant accounts and disclosures and their relevant assertions. Relevant assertions are those financial statement assertions that have a reasonable possibility of containing a misstatement that would cause the financial statements to be materially misstated. (AS 5.28)

Based on this definition, the auditor must determine what amount is material to the financial statements to be able to identify significant accounts. The auditor considers quantitative and qualitative characteristics that make accounts and disclosures significant. The ICFR audit focuses on controls for significant accounts. Therefore, the auditor has to understand what is material to the company to identify significant accounts and conduct the ICFR audit. The auditor's opinion about the effectiveness of ICFR is based on the controls that address risks of material financial statement misstatement.

Analyzing the Relevance of Assertions

When management places an account balance or disclosure on the financial statements, it "asserts" various things about that information: existence or occurrence, completeness, valuation or allocation, rights and obligations, and presentation and disclosure. While all of the assertions are important, they do not all have the same level of importance for each account on the financial statements. For example, the occurrence assertion relates to transactions that have taken place, while existence relates to assets the company owns or liabilities it owes. Completeness relates to all the balances presented on the financial statements. However, from the auditor's perspective the *risk of unrecorded liabilities* is greater

AUDITING IN ACTION

Qualitative Characteristics of Accounts and Disclosures

- Size and composition of the account
- Susceptibility of misstatement due to errors or fraud
- Volume of activity, complexity, and homogeneity of the individual transactions processed through the account or reflected in the disclosure
- Nature of the account or disclosure
- Accounting and reporting complexities associated with the account or disclosure
- Exposure to losses represented by the account
- Possibility of significant contingent liabilities arising from the activities represented by the account
- Existence of related party transactions in the account
- Changes from the prior period in account characteristics

(AS 5.29)

than the *risk of unrecorded assets.* Therefore, the auditor more extensively tests controls for completeness assertion on liability accounts than asset accounts.

The valuation assertion is critically important for certain financial statement items such as foreign currency and receivables that are presented at net realizable value. Allocation is very important for other items, such as fixed assets and natural resources. The rights assertion is important for assets, and the obligations assertion is important for liabilities. The assertion of appropriate presentation and disclosure is important for all items.

Once the auditor has identified significant accounts, he or she must then determine the financial statement assertions that are relevant to those accounts. AS 5.28 defines **relevant assertions** as "assertions that have a reasonable possibility of containing a misstatement that would cause the financial statements to be materially misstated." For each significant account the auditor goes through an analysis to decide which of the financial statement assertions are relevant. This gives the auditor the ability to determine the likely sources of misstatement related to the account.

For example, the existence and rights assertions, as well as presentation and disclosure, are relevant to the cash account. A cash account balance is fairly stated if it shows the amount that is actually in the bank and owned by the company and not pledged or otherwise committed, with proper disclosure. If the account balance shows more cash than actually exists, then the account is overstated. If the account balance includes cash that the company does not have rights to, because it is pledged or committed in some way, then the account is overstated. The auditor understands from this analysis that for cash, the risks are that the cash shown on the balance sheet does not exist or that the company does not have rights to it. This means that if cash is a significant account, the auditor knows that the ICFR design should include controls related to existence, rights, presentation and disclosure. The operation of those controls should be tested in the ICFR audit.

Classes of Transactions

In evaluating which assertions are relevant for significant accounts the auditor may identify major classes of transactions within the accounts. A significant account can be composed of one or more classes of transactions. For example, cash transactions, in-person credit transactions and online credit transactions can all be posted to the same sales account. But credit sales have different risks than cash sales, and the risks of in-person sales differ from those of online sales. In a retail company, inventory is only composed of finished goods.

Alternatively, a manufacturing company's inventory account is composed of raw materials, work-in-process, and finished goods accounts. Each aspect of the manufacturer's inventory is comprised of transactions that may need to be assessed separately. Different types of inventory are recorded as the result of different processes. The processes have different risks of material misstatement and different controls addressing those risks.

Different classes of transactions are the result of the company's business activities. First, the business activities occur. Second, they are recorded by the company's accounting system. Eventually they end up on the financial statements, shown in the significant accounts. The auditor assesses design effectiveness leading to the eventual audit decisions about which controls to test for operating effectiveness. To do this, the auditor has to understand the way the company's accounting system authorizes, records, and reports those transactions.

AS 2, the PCAOB's original standard for auditing ICFR, presents one useful tool for identifying and understanding the major classes of transactions. The approach is to group classes of transactions into categories called **routine transactions**, **non-routine transactions**, and **estimation transactions**. Each category is susceptible to misstatement from a different source, so grouping transactions into the categories helps auditors indentify the risks of misstatement.

> **Routine transactions** are recurring financial activities reflected in the accounting records in the normal course of business (for example, sales, purchases, cash receipts, cash disbursements, payroll).
>
> **Non-routine transactions** are activities that occur only periodically (for example, taking physical inventory, calculating depreciation expense, adjusting for foreign currencies). A distinguishing feature of non-routine transactions is that data involved are generally not part of the routine flow of transactions.
>
> **Estimating transactions** are activities that involve management judgments or assumptions in formulating account balances in the absence of a precise means of measurement (for example, determining the allowance for doubtful accounts, establishing warranty reserves, assessing assets for impairment). (AS 2.72)

The auditor can categorize major classes of transactions to consider management assertions. The financial statement assertion of existence or occurrence is relevant to many routine transactions such as sales, purchases, and paying employees. The completeness assertion is extremely relevant for non-routine transactions. Many non-routine transactions are recorded specifically to place appropriate revenues and expenses, along with any corresponding assets and liabilities, into the correct period. Many of the estimating transactions relate to valuation, so an emphasis is placed on the valuation assertion. If the auditor is trying to identify in what ways the assertions may be unsupported and the financial statements misstated, he or she may consider the transactions from the perspective of the three categories.

Likely Sources of Misstatement

Activities in a company's accounting information system account for a transaction from its inception through reporting. These activities are the important or significant processes affecting the transaction. They include whatever the company uses to initiate, authorize, record, process, and report transactions. Processes include tasks such as the following:

- Capturing input data
- Sorting and merging data
- Making calculations
- Updating transactions and master files

- Generating transactions
- Summarizing, displaying, and reporting data
- Correcting and reprocessing previously rejected transactions
- Correcting erroneous transactions with adjusting journal entries

Considering the processes that affect a transaction helps the auditor

- Understand the flow of transactions
- Determine at what point in each process a misstatement could arise
- Identify the controls management has implemented in the system that are intended to prevent each type of potential misstatement
- Identify any controls that are specifically intended to prevent or detect the unauthorized acquisition, use or disposal of assets that could cause a material financial statement misstatement. (AS 5.34)

If a company uses an outside service provider for a process, the auditor must consider how this fits into the overall ICFR.

AUDITING IN ACTION

Understanding Likely Sources of Misstatement

Understand the flow of transactions, including how transactions are initiated, authorized, recorded, processed, and reported.

Identify the points within the process at which a misstatement—including a misstatement due to fraud—related to each relevant financial statement assertion could arise.

Identify the controls that management has implemented to address these potential misstatements.

Identify the controls that management has implemented over the prevention or timely detection of unauthorized acquisition, use, or disposition of the company's assets.

(AS 2.74)

IT Related to Likely Sources of Misstatement

The benefits and risks of automated accounting processes using IT impact the auditor's procedures for understanding the flow of information, potential misstatements, and controls in the processes. An overview of this effect is summarized as follows.

> The use of IT affects the fundamental manner in which transactions are initiated, recorded, processed and reported.... An entity may have information systems that use automated procedures to initiate, record, process, and report transactions, in which case records in electronic format replaces such paper documents as purchase orders, invoices, shipping documents, and related accounting records. Controls in systems that use IT consist of a combination of automated controls (for example, controls embedded in computer programs) and manual controls. Further manual controls may be independent of IT, may use information produced by IT, or may be limited to monitoring the effective functioning of IT and of automated controls, and to handling exceptions. An entity's mix of manual and automated controls varies with the nature and complexity of the entity's use of IT. (PCAOB AU 319.17, AICPA AU 314.58)

For example, if a system relies heavily on IT, transactions are processed uniformly and embedded controls are not likely to be circumvented. However, consider the following:

If the program uniformly processes the data incorrectly or uses the wrong steps, then it will uniformly misstate the output.

If the program has been changed in an unauthorized way, then the system will uniformly process the data in an unauthorized manner.

If the data used by the program are incorrect, then the output will be uniformly incorrect. In an audit of a company using a highly automated IT environment, the auditor specifically considers the risks to accounts and assertions resulting from the automated processing. Then the auditor identifies the company's controls designed to address those IT risks. When identifying potential sources of misstatement and the controls designed to prevent or detect those misstatements, the auditor considers the nature of the accounting information system including the extent of IT complexity.

In some IT environments the audit will likely need the skills of an auditor who is particularly trained to deal with IT impacts. Typically, audit firms employ auditors who can contribute their specialized IT knowledge to the audits on which it is needed. As a reminder, factors that impact the need for specialized IT knowledge include:

- Complexity of the entity's systems and IT controls and the manner in which they are used in conducting the entity's business
- Significance of changes made to existing systems, or the implementation of new systems
- Extent to which data is shared among systems
- Extent of the entity's participation in electronic commerce
- Extent of the entity's use of emerging technologies
- Significance of audit evidence that is available only in electronic form

(PCAOB AU 319.31, AICPA 311.23)

REVIEW QUESTIONS

O.1 What is a significant account?

O.2 What is a relevant assertion?

O.3 Are all assertions relevant for all accounts? Why not?

O.4 What is quantitative materiality? Qualitative materiality?

O.5 Why should the auditor care about different classes of transactions for an account?

O.6 What is a likely source of misstatement, and why does the auditor care about likely sources of misstatement?

O.7 How do controls link to likely sources of misstatement?

O.8 How is IT important to likely sources of misstatement?

ASSESSING DESIGN EFFECTIVENESS AND CHOOSING THE CONTROLS TO TEST

The auditor's ICFR work involves identifying:

- Significant accounts and disclosures
- Assertions relevant to those accounts and disclosures
- Risks to those assertions
- Likely sources of the risks
- Controls implemented by management intended to address the risks

After performing steps of inquiry, inspection, observation, and tracing, the auditor understands the accounts, assertions, risks, and ICFR. The auditor also has gained enough knowledge and accumulated sufficient evidence to assess the design effectiveness of the system. Material misstatement resulting from fraud is a specific part of the risk assessment.

CONCLUSION

At this stage the auditor can select the controls to test. The auditor selects and then plans how to test the controls that are intended and effectively designed to prevent or detect material misstatements of significant accounts and disclosures. After selecting the controls to test and completing the initial planning, the auditor moves to the next phase of the audit which is testing the operating effectiveness of the ICFR system and fairness of financial statement accounts and disclosures.

KEY TERMS

Accuracy assertion. The numbers in the accounts and financial statements are accurate.

Activity-level risk factors. Sources of risk from either external or internal factors linked to specific activities of the business.

Audit committee. A committee (or equivalent body) established by and among the Board of Directors for the purposes of overseeing the accounting and financial reporting processes and audits of the financial statements.

Audit documentation. The written record of the auditor's work.

Audit evidence. The accumulation of activities, documents and information that persuades the auditor to have reasonable assurance that management's assertions are appropriate.

Classification assertion. Transactions are posted to the correct accounts and included in the correct financial statement items.

Collusion. When more than one person works together to circumvent internal controls and defraud a business.

Completeness assertion. Everything that should be is included in account balances and financial statement items.

Control activities. Policies and procedures that help ensure management directives are carried out, including performance reviews, information processing, physical controls, and segregation of duties.

Control environment. Sets the tone of an organization, influencing the control consciousness of its people.

Committee of Sponsoring Organizations of the Treadway Commission (COSO). Composed of the AICPA, American Accounting Association, Institute of Internal Auditors, Institute of Management Accountants, and Financial Executives Institute.

COSO Internal Control (IC) Framework. A document published in 1992 by the Committee of Sponsoring Organizations of the Treadway Commission, which includes a definition of internal control intended for widespread users and identifying components of internal control.

Cutoff assertion. Accounting records and financial statements reflect transactions in the period in which they occurred.

Design effectiveness. Exists when controls operating as intended cause internal control objectives to be achieved. Controls must be appropriate for the goals, and the system must include all of the controls needed to accomplish the objectives.

Effectiveness of ICFR. Refers to whether the ICFR are designed and operate so that they can be relied on to produce financial statements consistent with management's assertions at the end of the fiscal year.

Entity-level controls. Controls that exist at the organization or company level.

Entity-level controls, from the SEC Interpretive Release. Aspects of a system of internal control that have a pervasive effect on the entity's system of internal control, such as controls related to the control environment; controls over management override; the company's risk assessment process; centralized processing and controls, including shared service environments; controls to monitor results of operations; controls to monitor other controls, including activities of the internal audit function, the audit committee, and self-assessment programs; controls over the period-end financial reporting process; and policies that address significant business control and risk management practices.

Entity-level risk factors. Sources of risk from either external or internal factors linked to the overall company.

Estimation transactions. Activities that involve management judgments or assumptions in formulating account balances in the absence of a precise means of measurement.

Existence assertion. Assets and liabilities shown in the company's books and records and financial statements actually exist.

External risk factors. Sources of risk originating outside the company, such as technological developments, customer preferences, competition, legislation, regulation, natural disasters, and economic changes.

Flowcharts. Diagrams of the ICFR system (or parts of the system).

Foreign Corrupt Practices Act. Federal legislation that prohibits payments to foreign officials; prohibiting bribes intended to facilitate or secure business. Also requires companies to maintain a system of internal control providing reasonable assurance of management knowledge and authorization of transactions.

Information and communication. Relates to a company's process of identifying, capturing, and communicating information needed to enable people to carry out their responsibilities.

Inquiry. The auditor obtains audit evidence through verbal communication.

Inspection. The auditor looks at documents and tangible assets.

Internal control. A process put in place by an entity's management and Board of Directors to provide reasonable assurance regarding achievement of objectives in the areas of effectiveness and efficiency of operations, reliability of financial reporting, and compliance with applicable laws and regulations.

Internal control over financial reporting (ICFR). A process to provide reasonable assurance about the reliability of financial reporting and the preparation of financial statements for external reporting purposes.

Internal risk factors. Sources of risk originating inside the company such as problems with IT, personnel quality, changes in management, business activities, the Board of Directors, and audit committee oversight.

Management documentation of ICFR. May be used by management to support its assessment and report on the effectiveness of ICFR.

Management override. When an effective internal control exists and typically functions, but a member of management exercises authority to prevent the control procedure from being carried out.

Monitoring. Ongoing and period assessment internal control performance.

Narrative. Written description of a business process.

Non-routine transactions. Activities that occur only periodically; data involved are generally not part of the routine flow of transactions.

Observation. The auditor obtains audit evidence by watching an activity take place.

Occurrence assertion. Transactions that are recorded are real and actually took place.

Ongoing monitoring. The continuing assessment of internal control that is a part of regular business activities.

Operating effectiveness of ICFR. Refers to whether the control functions as designed and whether the person performing the control possesses the necessary authority and qualifications to perform the control effectively.

Ownership assertion. The company has rights to assets and obligations for liabilities shown in the accounts and financial statements.

Presentation and disclosure assertion. Information and appearance of items, amounts and description comply with the standards of the basis of accounting used.

Process models. See *Flowcharts*.

Questionnaires. Lists of questions about the system that are structured with a "check-off" space for documenting whether a process or control exists in a system.

Recalculation. A specific type of reperformance in which the auditor checks the numerical procedures of the client.

Relevant assertions. Have a meaningful bearing on whether the account is fairly stated.

Reperformance. The auditor obtains audit evidence by conducting steps performed by the client.

Rights and obligations assertion. The presentation of assets represents what the company has rights to; the presentation of liabilities represents the company's obligations.

Risk assessment. The identification and analysis of relevant risk to achievement of the objectives, forming a basis for determining how the risks should be managed. Follows the establishment of objectives.

Risks. Anything that can keep an organization from achieving its objectives.

Routine transactions. Recurring financial activities reflected in the accounting records in the normal course of business.

Safeguarding assets. Prevention or timely detection of unauthorized acquisition, use, or disposition of the company's assets that could have a material effect on the financial statements.

Separate evaluation monitoring. Specific activities and events performed to assess internal control performance.

Suitable control framework. The framework for use in developing and evaluating internal control; the SEC identified the COSO Internal Control Framework, "Guidance on Assessing Control," published by the Canadian Institute of Chartered Accountants, and "Internal Control: Guidance for Directors on the Combined Code," published by the Institute of Chartered Accountants in England and Wales as examples of suitable control frameworks.

Tracing. The audit procedure that involves inspecting documents of a particular transaction through all the processing steps.

Valuation or allocation assertion. Management's estimates are appropriate, particularly referring to the value of balance sheet amounts and allocation of transactions and balances among years and accounts.

Walkthrough. An audit step the auditor uses to trace a transaction through from beginning to end.

Work papers. Term for the auditor's records that result from the documentation activity that occurs during the audit process.

MULTIPLE CHOICE

7-1 **[LO 5]** Which audit procedure would an auditor most likely select to understand and assess the effectiveness of the design of ICFR?

(a) Analytical procedures

(b) Walkthrough

(c) Vouching a sample of transactions

(d) Reperformance of the application of the control

7-2 **[LO 3]** Which of the following is not a requirement for the auditor to issue an opinion on ICFR?

(a) The auditor must audit the financial statements.

(b) The auditor must conclude on management's assessment of ICFR.

(c) The auditor must rely on the effectiveness of ICFR for the financial statement audit.

(d) The auditor must assess the effectiveness of ICFR.

7-3 **[LO 5]** For the auditor to conclude that ICFR is functioning effectively as of the end of the fiscal year,

(a) the controls must be functioning effectively at the end of the fiscal year.

(b) the client's year-end ICFR activities must be tested before or at the end of the fiscal year and not after.

(c) The controls must be functioning effectively for a reasonable period of time after the fiscal year end.

(d) The controls may not have required remediation in the second half of the fiscal year.

7-4 **[LO 5]** Which of the following is true regarding management documentation of ICFR?

(a) Very complex aspects of the system must be documented using a combination of flowcharts, narratives, and sample documents.

(b) Checklists can provide information on the flow of information.

(c) The auditor prepares documentation supporting management's assessment of the effectiveness of ICFR.

(d) Documentation that shows the flow of transactions so that points of potential material financial statement misstatement can be identified and can be a part of management's evidence supporting its ICFR effectiveness assessment.

7-5 **[LO 4]** Which assertions are important when the auditor is testing transactions and events that occurred during the period being audited?

(a) Occurrence, completeness, accuracy, cutoff, and classification

(b) Occurrence, existence, rights and obligations, and completeness

(c) Completeness, accuracy, cutoff, valuation, and understandability

(d) Accuracy and valuation, occurrence, completeness, and cutoff

7-6 **[LO 5]** Which of the following audit procedures is least likely to provide helpful evidence for forming a conclusion in the ICFR audit?

(a) Inquiries of appropriate personnel

(b) Inspection of relevant documentation

(c) Inspection of tangible assets

(d) Observation of the company's operations

7-7 **[LO 5]** Audit documentation

(a) will not likely include a copy of management's ICFR documentation.

(b) does not need to include significant findings that contradict the auditor's final conclusion as long as the final conclusion is appropriately supported.

(c) must support the final numbers in the financial statements but does not need to link those numbers to the underlying accounting records.

(d) must show audit procedures and conclusions in enough detail for a knowledgeable person, such as a PCAOB inspector, to understand.

7-8 **[LO 5]** Which of the following questions will an auditor most likely ask a company employee during a walkthrough?

(a) How long have you worked for the company?

(b) What kinds of errors have you found?

(c) How many other people perform a function similar to yours?

(d) How quickly can you perform your control task?

7-9 **[LO 1]** What happens if the design evaluation phase of the ICFR audit shows that controls intended to prevent and detect fraud are missing or ineffective?

(a) The auditor will perform a fraud audit along with the financial statement audit.

(b) No opinion on ICFR can be issued.

(c) The auditor will change the nature, timing, and extent of procedures performed during the financial statement audit.

(d) The auditor will perform more tests on the operating effectiveness of the fraud controls.

7-10 **[LO 2]** Entity-level controls

(a) are not expected to function in the same way at all locations and business units.

(b) include general IT controls over program development and program changes.

(c) impact activities primarily in the corporate office.

(d) affect all general controls except those over shared services.

7-11 **[LO 2]** The audit committee

(a) is an important part of the control environment.

(b) is evaluated by the Board of Directors.

(c) if ineffective, is an ICFR deficiency.

(d) All of the above.

7-12 **[LO 4]** Which of the following assertions is least relevant to the cash account?

(a) Valuation

(b) Rights

(c) Existence

(d) Presentation and disclosure

7-13 **[LO 2]** Compliance with laws and regulations that are directly related to fairness of the financial statements

(a) is not related to the reliability of financial reporting.

(b) may be related to the reliability of financial reporting.

(c) must always be a target of audit procedures.

(d) b and c

7-14 **[LO 2]** Which of the following is most important to the control environment?

Ethics

(a) Tone at the top

(b) Internal risks

(c) Entity-level risks

(d) Internal communication

7-15 **[LO 2]** Monitoring

(a) cannot be performed by management because management is also being monitored.

(b) must always include ongoing monitoring and separate evaluations.

(c) will have less separate evaluations if ongoing monitoring is effective.

(d) is only necessary if other internal control components do not function well.

7-16 **[LO 2]** Which of the following is not a limitation of internal control?

(a) Collusion

(b) Management override

(c) Cost-benefit limitations

(d) Dishonest employees

7-17 **[LO 2]** Which of the following is an external risk factor?

(a) The nature of the entity's business transactions

(b) Changing customer preferences and requests

(c) The Board of Directors and audit committee

(d) Personnel hiring practices

7-18 **[LO 2]** High turnover of personnel may generate special risk assessment attention because

(a) extra catch-up training will be required to prevent unusual breakdowns.

(b) new employees and management may not understand the entity's culture.

(c) new employees or management may focus on performance and downplay internal control.

(d) All of the above.

7-19 **[LO 2]** Information processing controls

(a) can be appropriately delegated to IT personnel.

(b) consist of general controls and application controls.

(c) do not need to include general controls if application controls are sufficiently effective.

(d) include locked cabinets to prevent the theft of personal computers.

7-20 **[LO 2]** For information to be of high quality it must be

(a) available when required.

(b) easily available to everyone who wants it.

(c) updated to the most recent convenient time.

(d) able to be adjusted for any known errors.

7-21 **[LO 2]** COSO specifies that all information should be

(a) available at all levels of the organization.

(b) in written or electronic document form.

(c) appropriate to meet the entity's needs.

(d) always of the highest quality.

DISCUSSION QUESTIONS

7-22 **[LO 1, 4]** To which of the following accounts would the management assertion "valuation" be relevant, and why? For any accounts to which it would not be relevant, explain why.

Cash

Cash when foreign currency translation is involved

Gross amount of accounts receivable

Net amount of accounts receivable

7-23 **[LO 1, 2, 4]** For a company that sells retail goods to customers both online, and in stores located in shopping malls with payment made via cash and bank credit cards, which of the following are important classes of transactions? Why? For those that are not, why not?

Online sales

In-store sales

Purchase of raw materials

Purchase of finished goods merchandise

Lease expense

Payroll expense

Costs of goods manufactured

Purchase of fixed assets

7-24 **[LO 1, 2]** A company uses inventory tags that are electronically scanned into its accounting information system to track receipt, movement, and removal of items of inventory from the manufacturing floor. Prior to producing quarterly and annual financial statements, the company performs a physical count of inventory. The typical outcome of the physical count is that journal entries must be made after the count to correct the inventory accounts and records because some employee theft and unrecorded waste always occurs.

Does the occurrence of inventory loss that the company routinely records mean that a deficiency in ICFR exists? Why or why not?

7-25 **[LO 2]** How does the commitment to competence of the COSO IC Framework control environment relate to the quality control concept of assignment of staff to certain tasks on an audit engagement?

7-26 **[LO 2, 4]** Exhibit 7-2 discusses "Circumstances that Demand Special Risk Assessment attention." Pick four of the eight shown in the exhibit. Explain how these situations might ultimately result in financial statement misstatements.

7-27 **[LO 3]** Compare and contrast the internal control provisions required under the Foreign Corrupt Practices Act (1977) and the Sarbanes-Oxley Act (2002).

7-28 **[LO 5]** Explain the importance of a walkthrough, how one is performed, and list five relevant questions that the auditor might ask during a walkthrough. What types of responses to your questions might the auditor receive that would cause concern about the effectiveness of ICFR?

PROBLEMS

7-29 **[LO 1, 2, 5]** Stan is an auditor for Cartman & Kenny, CPA. He has recently been assigned to a new private client called Southpark Services, a provider of Web management services. Southpark has clients throughout the United States. The company manages the clients' Web sites, keeping them up to date, resolving problems, and doing any other programming or troubleshooting that their clients need.

The two Southpark owners are hands-on managers. They, along with three other employees, provide the Web site management services for their clients. Although they don't have access to their clients' books or bank accounts, they have the ability to alter the Web site, and any data that flows through the Web site before it goes to the company or the customer. Southpark has one office manager with an undergraduate accounting degree and one full-time bookkeeper.

In discussions with management, Stan learns that Southpark Services "doesn't bother" to maintain any processes specifically directed toward good internal controls. When Stan asked why, management replied, "internal control is too expensive for us, and since we are not a public company and Section 404 does not apply to us, we don't see any value internal control can offer our management."

Required:

(a) Develop a list of concerns that Southpark's clients might have based on management's attitude. Classify those concerns into two lists—concerns that affect the business and concerns that might affect their productive output, and thus the client's business operations. Some of the concerns you identify might end up on both lists.

(b) Suggest processes and controls that Southpark can implement to limit the risk of the items you listed in (a).

(c) How would Stan examine or test each of the processes and controls you list in (b)?

7-30 **[LO 2, 5]** Natasha is a staff-level auditor assigned to evaluate the ICFR for the XYZ Corporation audit. Natasha follows her firm's audit plan to assess ICFR. Step 1.3 of the audit plan says: "the auditor should evaluate the overall attitude and awareness of an entity's board of directors concerning the importance of internal control."

(a) With which component of internal control is Step 1.3 concerned?

(b) Draft specific audit steps that Natasha might find in her plan, in addition to the general direction.

(c) What would Natasha include in her work papers to document her work?

7-31 **[LO 1, 2, 4]** You have been assigned to work on your firm's largest client, DOMO Electronics, a publicly traded company with operations in North and South America, Europe, and Asia. In your process of evaluating ICFR, your audit plan instructs you to evaluate DOMO Electronics' Control Environment, a major component of COSO's IC *Framework*. In your evaluation you have found the following:

- DOMO Electronics has a written code of conduct that it requires all employees to understand and follow. It has never had any ethical conflicts reported and therefore does not have a formal mechanism for top management or the Board of Directors to receive confidential information from employees lower in the organizational hierarchy.

- All of DOMO's staff are required to complete a certain amount of continuing education credits every year. From what you can see, they seem to be well trained at their tasks, or at least they stay very busy.

- The Board of Directors and audit committee consist of several *financially savvy* individuals who take their jobs very seriously. Furthermore, all members of its audit committee are top managers in the company, so they are intimately familiar with the company's operations.

- Management stresses an ethical environment. In their weekly meetings each team reports its operating results, and the different teams quiz each other and respond with solutions and challenges. In the weekly meetings, management encourages the teams to act ethically while achieving their mandatory year-over-year, 40% revenue growth numbers.

- Due to high industry growth, DOMO has enhanced its market share largely by significant mergers and acquisitions. To keep up with its growth, DOMO is constantly upgrading its internal control system. Fortunately, the well-trained staff have been able to continue testing the new programs after they are put in place and to change programming problems as they crop up.

- The human resource department ensures that workers are assigned to work that they are capable of doing and ensures that every employee understands his or her responsibilities.

Required:

(a) What "red flags" do you see in the above description concerning DOMO's control environment?

(b) What accounts and financial statement management assertions might ultimately be affected if the red flags indicate problems?

(c) Develop an audit step you would use to follow up on the concern raised by each of the red flags.

7-32 **[LO 1, 3, 4]** Suppose you are a new auditor with a small audit firm on the audit of Juan Stuart's Daily News, a large private corporation with a significant minority stockholder that operates media outlets across the United States. The majority stockholder manages the day-to-day activities of the business. Because your audit firm is a new, small firm, it has yet to formulate its own guidance concerning the audit of ICFR. You remember hearing a lot about Section 404 of the Sarbanes-Oxley Act of 2002 concerning internal control audits.

Required:

(a) Does Section 404 of the Sarbanes-Oxley Act pertain to the audit of Juan Stuart's Daily News? Why or why not?

(b) Is there anything related to ICFR that you are concerned with as the financial statement auditor of Juan Stuart's Daily News?

(c) Who are the stakeholders related to Juan Stuart's Daily News? How do good financial statements benefit them? What ICFR issues would be of concern to the different stakeholders?

(d) Develop audit steps to test the ICFR issues of concern.

7-33 **[LO 2, 5]** Lois is evaluating the ICFR for Pawtucket Patriot Brewery. She is examining an activity that occurs periodically, specifically an inventory count. This is not an everyday operation of Pawtucket Patriot Brewery. But they don't have a good IT system to track inventory, and the only way the purchasing department knows what it needs to buy and the production manager knows how much and what to make is as the result of the physical count. The company makes and sells beer. Inventory consists of beer that has already been placed in bottles and is ready for distribution; beer in huge vats still being processed; and all the supplies that go into making beer—not only the beer ingredients, but also empty bottles and the supplies needed to bottle the beer.

Required:

(a) Classify this inventory observation activity using the AS 2 groupings of: routine, nonroutine, estimating.

(b) As Lois reads through the client's plan for the inventory count, what processes and procedures should she be looking for? Why? What are the assertions that are important to address for this account?

(c) What are one or more audit steps you think Lois should conduct while the client counts inventory?

7-34 **[LO 4, 5]** *[Adapted from Wiley CPA Review]* Suppose you are the auditor on the ICFR audit of Big Papi, Inc., a publicly traded company. Your senior has assigned you a significant list of steps to perform testing the operating effectiveness of ICFR. She tells you that before you can perform the list of audit procedures, you obtain an understanding of the entity's processes and controls. Based on the prior year's audit, she gives you a list of accounts that she believes you will find to be important, and the classes of transactions that fed into each of those important accounts—at least last year. As she walks off to go to another engagement, she reminds you that this year's ICFR audit must be very efficient and you should only test the assertions that you need to.

Required:

(a) How will you go about obtaining an understanding of the company's processes and controls? What will you do? What will you look at? Who will you talk to? How will each of the procedures help you?

(b) After you understand the system, what will you do?

(c) How will you decide which accounts and assertions to test for operating effectiveness?

(d) What will you put in your work papers up through the completion of analyzing design effectiveness?

7-35 **[LO 4]** *[Adapted from Wiley CPA Review]* Dana, an auditor for the audit firm C&C, recently finished up testing controls relating to management's assertion concerning the completeness of sales transactions. In her audit work papers, Dana included the following:

- "I inspected the entity's reports of prenumbered shipping documents that have not been recorded in the sales journal"

- "In the course of my testing, I have found 0 items that have been sold but have not recorded in the sales journal."

- "Since testing was performed without exception, I have determined that the controls to address the completeness of sales transactions are operating effectively."

Which essential elements of AS 3's documentation requirements did Dana omit from her documentation?

7-36 **[LO 2]** Separate and assign the following activities to employee A, B, and C to accomplish the best control. Explain why.

(a) Assemble supporting documents for cash disbursements.

(b) Maintain custody of the signature plates used for the computer processes when checks are produced.

(c) Authorize the update of the general ledger each month and review all accounts for unexpected balances.

(d) Cancel supporting documents for cash disbursements to prevent their reuse.

(e) Approve customers' applications for credit.

(f) Approve the write-off of accounts receivable determined to be uncollectible.

(g) Input the shipping and billing information resulting from sales and shipments.

7-37 **[LO 4, 5]** Joan Hacker, CPA, is the CFO of Smooth Ride, a publicly held boat trailer manufacturer. At the close of the second quarter of 2010, Joan received the physical count of raw materials inventory amounting to $2,695,872. At the same time, Joan's self-designed computer model for deriving inventory figures showed a raw materials inventory calculation of $3,374,024, which was $678,152 higher than the physical count calculation. Since Joan was rushed to prepare the financial statements, she used the computer model figure, resulting in a $181,000 net income and $0.03 per share earnings. She adjusted the inventory to equal the correct count for the end of the third quarter when she had more time. The result for Quarter 3 was a net loss of $253,000 and a loss of $0.04 per share.

Required:

What are the control ramifications of Joan's actions?

7-38 **[LO 2, 4]** Greg Norman is the auditor in charge of the Rogers Pharmaceutical Company audit. In assessing the internal controls for the company, Greg finds that the company bills customers and receives payments at three offices in three separate states using three different and incompatible software systems for tracking payments. Rogers's terms of sale varies with the customer and varies from 30 days to 90 days. Open invoices are aged based on when they were booked to the receivables, but cash, chargebacks, or rebates are aged based on when they were applied to the account. Thus, a credit could be posted to the customer's account when it was received, but the related invoice(s) remains open as a receivable and continues to age. Chargebacks are significant and linked to batch of product rather than invoice. Most similar companies have credit limits or credit checks but Rogers's does not because all wholesalers are board certified M.D.'s, like the company's founder.

- Rogers's total accounts receivable was $25,276,025.
- Rogers's total accounts receivable past due over 61 days was $17,434,500.
- Rogers's past top-five wholesalers had accounts receivable of $13,457,516.
- Rogers's top-five wholesale customers had $5,428,850 past due over 61 days.
- Rogers's allowance for doubtful accounts of $266,000 did not include any estimates for the top-five wholesale customers because it was management's belief at the time that the top-five wholesalers did not present a collection risk.

Required:

Based on these control issues and findings, explain some of the most likely sources of misstatement that exist.

7-39 **[LO 5]** Hammer Orthopedic Corporation periodically invests large sums in marketable equity securities. The investment policy is established by the investment committee of the Board of Directors, and the treasurer is responsible for carrying out the directives of the investment committee. All securities are stored in a bank safe-deposit box.

The following issues are included in the independent auditors' plan for auditing internal control with respect to the company's investments in marketable equity securities. To understand the design of the system, the audit procedure is to make the following inquiries of management:

1. Are all securities stored in a bank safe-deposit box?

2. Is investment policy established by the investment committee of the Board of Directors?

3. Is the treasurer solely responsible for carrying out the investment committee's directives?

Required:

In addition to these questions, what other questions should the auditor ask with respect to Hammer's marketable equity security investments?

7-40   **[LO 2]** Simmons Optics Company is a medical device manufacturing company in Florida. As such, it has a number of new products at various stages of development, with many swings notable in its Research and Development budget aimed at taking advantage of tax credits. With the downswing in the economy and change in the optics technology, a new competitor, Bright Eyes Instruments, Inc., is taking a larger percentage of the optical market. As a result, the CEO is pushing supervisors to reduce product development time from 24 months to 10 months, but without any new capital expenditures. The Board of Directors almost always agrees with the CEO's initiatives and has rubber-stamped this course of action.

The new CFO of the company has only been at his job for six months. He is a hands-off CFO and sees this position as a way to enjoy sunshine, golf, and the ocean. During his first six months he has realigned the reporting responsibilities of the company, so that the credit and collections department reports to the Sales Controller rather than the head of the treasury department. He also gave the Sales Controller increased authority to develop business by negotiating the terms of sales transactions and the authority to recognize revenue. The Sales Controller developed and negotiated a new type of agreement called Guaranteed Profit agreements that relieve Simmons's direct customers (primarily optometrists) of any obligation to pay for goods unless they were sold through to end users or patients. In these agreements, Simmons books the revenue when the goods go to the customers. The CFO is not aware of any reversals for unsold goods, but admits that the information system has had significant disruptions in processing during his tenure.

Required:

Identify the Entity Level—External and Internal Risk Factors in this scenario.

7-41   **[LO 2, 3, 4]** You are engaged to audit the financial statements of Sebastian Construction Company. The company specializes in the construction of medical clinics. Sebastian uses the percentage-of-completion method to account for all construction projects. As Sebastian completes a project, the building and property are sold to the clinic operator, who makes a 20% down payment and gives an installment note for the balance. Sebastian discounts the note with First State Bank and receives the proceeds minus the bank discount. Sebastian remains contingently liable for the discounted notes. With the economic downturn, 60% of the notes are now in default, and Sebastian has constructed virtually nothing within the last 10 months. When you arrive to discuss the upcoming audit, you notice that the parking lot, which was full last year, is nearly empty. The CFO assures you that the slowdown is merely temporary and that the company is starting to get in new contracts every day. In fact, the CFO brags that they have hired new crews to begin five new projects next week.

As you begin the audit, you notice the following:

1. Of the 250 requests for confirmations of accounts receivable that were mailed, only 30 were returned after two mailings.

2. A number of the general ledger transactions lacked documentary support.

3. The company's property and equipment ledgers for depreciation could not be reconciled to the general ledger.

4. The internal control report represented and signed by the CFO as "Excellent" showed a significant number of internal control compliance problems.

Required:

(a) Based on this information, discuss the circumstances demanding special risk assessment attention.

(b) What are the most important assertions for Sebastian Construction?

(c) Based on the Sarbanes-Oxley Act of 2002, what corporate responsibility for financial reports does the CFO appear to have violated?

7-42 **[LO 1, 2]** Think about the businesses and other entities with which you interact in your everyday life. Select a particular business that you know to complete the following.

Required:

(a) Identify an observable step of the way the entity does business that you believe is carried out for control purposes. Consider the following example, "If you do not get a receipt your purchase is free." This note, frequently seen by a sales terminal, adds the consumer as a control element to be sure the salesperson enters the transaction.

(b) Identify some aspect of the entity for which there should be a control and a control activity does not exist. (*Hint:* One way to find these controls that are lacking is to evaluate how a customer could get in free, or receive their product or service and "get away" without paying.)

7-43 **[LO 3]** Milton Baxter is the in-charge auditor for Apex Company, a long-time client of the Baxter CPA Group. The company has expanded into a new industry by acquiring equipment that will be used to manufacture several types of products. The CEO has indicated that as one of the conditions for providing financing for the new equipment, the bank must receive a copy of the annual financial statements. Another condition is that the total assets cannot fall below $300,000. The loan will be called for immediate repayment, if this happens.

Currently, the total assets are reported at $308,000 (including the new equipment but prior to making the adjustment for depreciation). The CEO of Apex has asked Baxter to examine the facts and provide audited financial statements that are acceptable to the bank. The depreciation method for the equipment has not been adopted yet. Equipment in other parts of the company uses the double-declining balance method. The cost of the new equipment is $60,000, and it is estimated to be worth $5,000 at the end of five years. Because the new products have not yet begun to catch on with consumers, the company produced just 5,000 units this year, and it is expected that a total of 40,000 units will be made over the five-year period.

Required:

Based on this information, calculate straight-line, double-declining balance, and unit of production depreciation for the new machine. Which depreciation method would allow Apex to stay within the bank's threshold? Is it ethical to recommend that method to the company prior to audit?

7-44 Go to the 10K report for Starbucks. Find the following: management's Section 404, 302, and 906 reports and the auditor's report. Compare the management reports to the examples provided in the text. Do you note any differences? Read the auditor's report. Is there a separate report providing the internal control opinions? Or are all the internal control and financial statement audit opinions provided in one report?

7-45 Go to the COSO Web site. Find the IC Framework and ERM Framework. What is the major difference between the two frameworks, in terms of their stated purposes? Compare the components of the two frameworks. (*Hint:* Appendix B to this chapter will help.)

7-46 Go to the SEC Web site and access the Sarbanes-Oxley Act, Section 906. What are the monetary and criminal penalties specified, and for what type of wrongdoing?

7-47 Go the SEC Web site. Access 33-8810; 34-55929. What title do you see? Read the first few pages. How does this relate to what is covered in this chapter?

7-48 Search for management reports that utilize internal control frameworks other than COSO (probably found in reports of companies in countries other than the United States).

7-49 Conduct a search in the business journals and print media regarding increased audit costs for companies as a result of the Sarbanes-Oxley Act. Look particularly for internal costs associated with management documenting and testing internal control.

APPENDIX A: SPECIFICS OF IT GENERAL CONTROLS

Introduction

IT general controls (**ITGC**) are critically important to the company and to the audit of ICFR. ITGC are the IT policies and procedures that apply throughout the entire company. Many are policies carried out by humans. Others are automated or programmed controls that affect the whole company. Importantly, ITGC are pervasive, and ICFR is not likely to be effective if either their design or operation is ineffective.

The effectiveness of **application controls** is linked to the effectiveness of ITGC. Again, application controls are programmed, and sometimes manual, controls that are specific to a single process or activity. Chapter 8, Appendix A, discusses application controls in the context of an audit. Application controls rarely can be relied on to function well when the ITGC environment is faulty. For example, an application control may depend on ITGC passwords to control access and ensure validity of data input. If the ITGC over access to the entire system are ineffective, then passwords for a particular application are less likely to be reliable. ITGC and application controls are not synonymous with entity-level and transaction-level controls. Furthermore, the terms are not interchangeable. Exhibit A7-1 provides examples illustrating different possibilities.

Problems with ITGC have serious negative implications for the financial statement audit. Virtually all companies carry out their business activities to some extent using IT. The input of data and resulting production of financial reports are usually IT-dependent activities. Therefore, weaknesses in ITGC can have far-reaching financial statement consequences.

The auditor assesses the effectiveness of both the design and functioning of ITGC. Although some stand-alone tests may be appropriate, the assessment of ITGC often results from audit procedures that provide evidence for various areas of the audit. Many of the audit steps designed to understand the system and evaluate its design also permit the auditor to collect evidence regarding the function of the ITGC. By the point at which the auditor completes walkthroughs (or comparable audit steps) for the important processes, enough

Relationship among Entity and Transaction Level and ITGC and Application Controls

Entity-Level Controls

Non-IT Controls
Example, Corporate Code of Conduct

IT General Controls
Example, Entity-wide use of identification and passwords to access the system

IT Application Controls
Example, Programmed checks for accurate transmission when data are moved among any and all locations throughout the company

Transaction-Level Controls

Non-IT Controls
Example, Supervisor review of supporting documents to approve transaction

IT General Controls
Example, Second layer of security passwords for certain types of transactions (such as adjusting entries) to limit users to specifically approved individuals

IT Application Controls
Example, programmed recalculation for accuracy when transactions are posted to data files

audit evidence may be available to assess the effectiveness of design and—sometimes operations—of ITGC. Some general controls, such as passwords mentioned above, may also be tested further during the tests of IT applications.

Approaches to Understanding ITGC

ITGC are grouped and classified in various ways. One way to approach ITGC is using the COSO categories of control environment, risk assessment, control activities, information and communication, and monitoring. However, ITGC are so pervasive that they cross all the COSO categories, and this approach produces a lot of redundancy. Therefore, using the COSO grouping scheme does not particularly clarify the discussion. More often ITGC are discussed within the specific context of the IT environment. An example of an ITGC organization scheme is presented in Exhibit A7-2.

EXHIBIT A7-2

Classification Scheme for ITGC

Security Controls
   Physical security
   Logical security
Information Controls
   Input controls
   Processing controls
   Database controls
   Output controls
Continuity Controls
   Data backup
   Hardware backup
   Disaster recovery controls
(Adapted from Hunton, Bryant, Bagranoff, 2004)

EXHIBIT A7-3

Extended List of IT General Controls

IT control environment
    Policy development and communication
    Segregation of duties
    Monitoring procedures
Software acquisition
Hardware acquisition
Network technology acquisition
Program development
Program changes
Computer operations
    Policies and procedures
    Batch processing and end user computing
    Backup management
    Data center controls
    Capacity planning and performance issue management
    Recovery procedures for operational failures
Access to programs and data
    Security policies and procedures
    Testing security measures
    Authorization decisions for access
    Monitoring security measures
    Application software access
    Operating system security
    Network security administration
    Data security
Software and interface controls
Contingency controls
    Backup procedures
    Service interruption, disaster, and recovery
Human resources
    Hiring policies
    Training
    Termination policies and controls
Physical facilities controls
    Protected environment
    Controlled climate
    Fire suppression and evacuation plans
    Inconspicuous facilities

The structure used for discussion in this appendix is presented in Exhibit A7-3. While this list is not necessarily comprehensive, it includes enough of the general controls issues to convey the importance and pervasiveness of ITGC and to suggest the amount of audit effort that goes into their evaluation.

IT Control Environment

Policies

The critical aspect of maintaining an effective IT control environment is developing needed policies and communicating them to everyone in the company. Some of the areas for which policies are needed are:

- Licensing agreements
- Passwords
- Use of company resources, Internet, and e-mail
- Physical control over portable resources

- Social engineering issues
- Control breakdowns
- Use of third-party providers

Licensing Agreements   Many of the policy needs are very straightforward and likely involve controls to which students have been exposed, even in the college environment. For example, companies that use licensed software should have policies (1) regarding the appropriate use of that software and (2) ensuring that the obligations involved in the **license agreement** are met. Students comply with these same types of license policies when they use university licensed programs for the purposes specified by the university's license agreement, for example, when they use computers in the university's computer lab.

Passwords   Companies that use passwords to limit access to the system need policies such as required complexity and security over the passwords. Generally, passwords should not be written down or shared, and no one should be required to tell his or her password to anyone, even the network administrator.

Use of Company Resources, Internet, and E-mail   Use of company IT resources has become a major target of policy, especially since the advent of widespread use of e-mail and the Internet. For example, employers are aware that at least sometimes personnel likely use the company's e-mail for "nonbusiness" purposes. Therefore, policies should define acceptable employee uses of the company e-mail system. Internet access policies should indicate the types of activities and sites that are prohibited (for example, ordering personal purchases, viewing pornography, etc.). Employers should communicate openly that employees should not consider messages conveyed via company e-mail to be private.

Physical Control over Portable Resources   Policies on the use of company IT resources may extend to whether employees may take portable equipment with them and the use of company assets for personal purposes. Employers generally would not want to provide use of the company's IT assets for an employee creating a start-up business or running another business on the side. Along these same lines, companies should have policies regarding the physical safekeeping of computer assets, such as laptop computers [and devices that double as telephones and e-mail or data transmitters (smartphones)] and sensitive data.

Social Engineering   **Social engineering** is a human behavior that instigates the need for various policies in the IT environment. Social engineering is the term used to describe the behavior of someone who intends to circumvent an IT environment's controls with the help of the current employees. Social engineering is used to describe, for example, the situation in which a person appeals to an employee or the help desk bemoaning a lost password and needing assistance in getting in to the system. Social engineering refers to the behavior of an outsider who walks into the IT environment and confidently goes about performing procedures without interacting with other employees—and is not stopped or questioned, even though the other employees do not recognize the newcomer.

The problems that come from social engineering do not result because the company does not have policies in place. Any company that has password and entry controls should be able to prevent the two examples of inappropriate access given above. Social engineering manipulates employees, causing them to overlook or circumvent controls that are in place, which they know should be followed. The ITGC should include policies that specifically address social engineering behaviors such as informing and warning employees of the risks associated with circumventing controls for any reasons.

Control Breakdowns   Regardless of the controls in place, breakdowns occur. Passwords are stolen or become insecure, and unauthorized access occurs. The IT control environment should have clear policies regarding what to do in these situations. The policies should include steps such as how to identify and report the incident, immediate steps to limit damage, and follow-up steps to correct the problem.

Third-party Service Providers   Finally, policies covering **third-party service providers** are a necessary part of the ITGC. Services that can be purchased from third-party providers are extensive. In addition to being IP and ASP providers, third-party service providers can process payroll, build and manage Web sites, handle IT and Internet operations, provide IT security, and assist with documenting and testing ICFR. Policies should address who makes the decisions regarding third-party providers and on what basis. Policy must specify what services may be purchased and the characteristics required of the service provider.

Segregation of Duties

In the IT world, the term *development* includes systems analysis, computer programming, database administration, and quality control. IT operations responsibilities include input, processing, output, and backup. The nature of these IT function makes **segregation of duties** challenging. The optimum situation is one in which personnel charged with development responsibilities do not participate in operations—and—those with primary responsibilities for operations duties are separated from development. Having those responsible for the company's IT security in a separate organizational unit is also preferred but is not as critical as separating development and operations. Many companies have too few employees to be able to have good segregation of duties between development and operations functions.

Monitoring

Monitoring is a fundamental aspect of internal controls over the IT function. Specific activities, for example purchasing hardware or software, or hiring IT personnel have oversight that is similar to other functions within the company. Supervisors authorize the transactions in advance and review outcomes.

Other activities use monitoring processes that are more specific to the IT environment. For example, logs are automatically created by the computer as a result of access, input, processing, and output activities. Logs also document when unauthorized access is attempted and when errors occur. These logs present valuable monitoring opportunities provided there is sufficient follow-up and investigation to the content of the logs. For the logs to be useful someone must read them and note deviations from controls or control breakdowns. When the logs highlight deviations and breakdowns, a person needs to follow up, investigate why the problem occurred, and ascertain that an adequate resolution is reached.

REVIEW QUESTIONS

P.1 Why are application controls not likely to be effective if general controls are not?

P.2 How does the auditor gather evidence on the effectiveness of ITGC?

P.3 What are some of the IT areas for which policies are needed?

P.4 How can social engineering cause the breakdown of good ITGC?

P.5 What duties of the IT function should be performed by different people, or located in separate departments? Why?

Software Acquisition

Controls related to software acquisition are needed by all companies with any IT activities. Virtually all companies acquire or purchase software at some point. This fact exists, even though some companies modify software after the purchase, and other companies develop certain software programs completely in-house. Appropriate controls address:

Plans for software acquisition

The fit of software acquisition and the particular software purchased into the overall company strategy

Compatibility of the software to be acquired with other software programs already in place

Cost and effectiveness for the company

Once the need for a software purchase is established, a purchase is authorized. Responsibility and accountability for acquisition decisions then rest with an authorized individual who decides on the vendor. One risk of uncontrolled software acquisition is that a disparate group of programs, perhaps overlapping, perhaps just nonuniform, are in place in different organizational units. After software is acquired, controls for its implementation and start-up are needed.

Hardware and Network Technology Acquisition

Just as with software acquisition, an authorized and responsible party is the decision maker for hardware acquisitions. The company should have policies and procedures in place that require appropriate approval before hardware is purchased. The approval process should consider the specified requirements and criteria. Hardware that is purchased needs to fit into the organization's overall strategy and be compatible with the hardware and software already in place. The decision on hardware acquisition includes capability issues and security.

Network technology includes both software and hardware, and the acquisition of network technology is subject to the same types of controls that are appropriate for software and hardware. Because risk of security breaches increases with remote access and external network interactions, controls addressing security are very important when network technology is acquired.

Program Development

Some companies choose to develop programs in-house rather than acquiring them from outside vendors. This process is not found in all companies, but when it occurs, requires significant controls. The first control that should be in place is the overall management of **development** and implementation activities. Project initiation typically follows a set of steps, uniform within the company, during which the project is requested, analyzed, and ultimately approved by a knowledgeable and authorized party. Specific controls cover the analysis and design phase to ensure that the program will accomplish its intended goals and be compatible with the rest of the system. Controls of the construction phase relate not only to the effectiveness of the process—making sure that the project does what it is supposed to do and is finished in the required time frame—but also limit work on the project to the appropriate personnel and verify that sufficient and accurate documentation is constructed.

Controls relating to testing and quality assurance are primarily to verify that the required steps in this stage are fulfilled and completed successfully. Data conversion, the decision to implement, and documentation and training are the final steps in the process. Data conversion controls deal with verifying data integrity and completeness before the program goes live. Documentation and training controls exist to verify that these last steps of the project are completed to support the effectiveness and security of operations.

Program Changes

Program change activities fall in between the acquisition of standard programs and the fully-in-house development of programs. While many companies may not have the in-house resources for program development, auditors will sometimes encounter situations where the client has customized or changed "off-the-shelf" software. Many of the controls appropriate for program changes are the same as those required when a program is completely developed. The process must be controlled and monitored, including construction, testing, and quality assurance. The request for changing a program, specifications of what the change should be, approval to make the change, and tracking the changes are the most important approval and monitoring controls. Changes made without a proper request and approval, that do not fit the company's needs, and that are not carefully tracked and documented can lead to major problems throughout the company. A critical control is that the program changes meet the desired threshold of testing and quality assurance before the modified program is introduced into the live environment.

Computer Operations

Policies and Procedures

Just as in other parts of IT, policies and procedures are the fundamental controls of computer **operations**. Policies should address the organizational structure within the operations function—who is supposed to do what—as well as who has access to programs, data, and output. Policies also cover correction of errors.

Batch Processing and End User Computing

Processing controls needed depends on whether the environment is completely end user computing or also has batch processing. Batch processing requires controls over the scheduling and processing functions. An end user computer environment needs controls that address authorized access. Access controls involve both keeping out those who should not be accessing files and programs, and limiting bona fide users to the areas for which they have authorized access.

Backup Management

Computer operations controls include the backup of data, including the level of sophistication needed for the backup process. This is discussed further with "Contingency Controls" but can range from the company owner taking home an electronic copy of the files each night to a sophisticated electronic backup and storage plan.

Data Center Controls

Controls that should be in place in the data center range from limiting the people who have physical access to the building to climate control, directives to physically lock up equipment, and stringent control over passwords.

Capacity Planning and Performance Issue Management

Some computer operations controls involve long-term management issues. Planning for capacity needs ensures that the business's processing can be performed effectively over time. A less well known concept of capacity planning is managing computing performance levels. This deals with managing the understanding between computer operations and end users regarding the level of service to be provided and received.

Managing computing performance levels is a strategy issue because differing service levels mandate different commitments of company resources. Controls are needed to be sure that computer operations receive the resources necessary to provide the level of computing performance management desires. Then, further controls are needed to monitor that the computer function provides the level of service consistent with the company's strategy and the resources it receives. The level of computer performance needed for effective ICFR is one of the inputs to management's decision about the company's standard for computer performance.

Recovery

Recovery is discussed extensively with **contingency controls**. However, it also applies to the more mundane occurrences of power outages and software failures. Controls should be in place to verify that the computer operations function has an appropriate recovery plan and that it is tested and updated as needed.

Access to Programs and Data

Controls over access to programs and data again start with *policy*. Passwords, privacy controls, and even biometrics can play a role. Basic passwords requirements include that passwords should not be written and should be complex enough to deter cracking. The company will set its own parameters, but passwords of seven or eight digits, with a mix of alpha and numeric characters, and upper- and lowercase letters are the types of criteria that might be part of password controls.

Another very important password policy deals with disclosure to others. An important control is a policy that says passwords should not be communicated over the telephone or by e-mail. Requesting passwords via these media, while posing as a diligent employee, is a common ruse of those employing social engineering. Privacy controls address protecting not only the company's information, but also the private information of others. A privacy policy should be established and in place and should be enforced. IT actions such as the management of cookies are also an important privacy control.

Management's involvement in program and data access controls is critical. First, management must decide, or authorize whoever is to decide about access. Once access decisions are made and security measures are in place, they should be tested and the measures should be monitored. Records of unauthorized access attempts in **logs**, and monitoring those logs, which were mentioned earlier in the appendix, are an important part of access controls. Access controls apply to application software, the operating system, and any networks that are part of the system.

Data security is a major goal of access controls. The accuracy, integrity, and confidentiality of data are affected by the methods of data collection and processing. For example, the controls necessary to ensure data security will differ based on the number and locations of points of data entry, whether the environment is one of batch processing or end user computing, and the degree to which the computing environment is centralized or decentralized. Data security also ensures the timeliness of data and that it is available as planned. Controls on data timeliness and availability extend beyond data capture and processing, and overlap with considerations of capacity and service level discussed earlier.

REVIEW QUESTIONS

Q.1 Why is it important for a company to have IT-performance-related controls over the acquisition of software, hardware and network technology?

Q.2 What controls are most important when a company develops or changes computer software?

Q.3 What areas of computer operations should company policies specifically address?

Q.4 How do access controls affect data security?

Q.5 Why are different data security methods needed for different methods of data collection and processing?

Software and Interface Controls

Software and interface controls that are part of ITGC can most easily be considered in the context of the threats and vulnerabilities against which they are intended to protect. **Denial**

of service attacks are assaults by outside parties intended to keep the system from being available to its intended users. Denial of service attacks are most familiar in their ability to shut down Web sites and e-commerce. A variety of controls assist in heading off denial of service attacks. **Firewalls** are an access control specifically directed at telecommunications entry. They combine hardware and software to permit access to authorized users, while, when successful, keeping out unauthorized users and program threats such as viruses.

Intrusion detection controls are another form of access control that alerts IT security when an unauthorized user has gained access. Control policies should require regular use of **patches**, which are additions to standard software written to cover known vulnerabilities in the program code. Most companies utilize virus protection programs and recognize the need to update these programs regularly.

Cookie detection and the appropriate security settings to manage them prevent inappropriate intrusion into the system by others. Companies should also manage cookies in terms of the cookies they send, as well as those they are vulnerable to receive.

Contingency Controls

Backup Procedures

Many of the ITGC included in this category have already been mentioned or alluded to in the other categories. First are the controls a company should have in place when control breakdowns occur. Notice that the phrase used is when (not if) control breakdowns occur because no system is sufficiently perfect to prevent them. Passwords may be communicated in an unauthorized fashion, unauthorized downloads may contain unexpected viruses, and unauthorized users may access the system. The company should have controls in place to respond when this occurs. Preparation for breakdowns should include plans for incident detection and the appropriate immediate reaction to limit damage. Detailed analysis of the control breakdown should follow, resulting in recovery procedures. Finally, follow-up monitoring should be instituted to limit repeat breakdowns.

Data backup procedures were mentioned in the section on computer operations, and that is the functional area in which responsibility for backups reside. Full backups involve backing up the entire system at regular intervals. In addition, incremental backups can be performed between full backups, capturing transactions since the last full backup. Using either of these methods, in the event of data loss the company re-creates its files since the last backup, either by re-inputting data or by using the backup transaction files. The backed-up data can be saved on a storage medium and physically removed from the company, called **physical vaulting**, or sent electronically to another computer for storage, called **electronic vaulting**. Whatever the method, good IT controls require a plan of backup and storage appropriate for the company's structure and business needs.

Service Interruption, Disaster, and Recovery

Service interruption refers to the situation in which the company is not able to process its computer operations. A service interruption may be brief and may derive from an easily identified source such as a power outage. In this case, a backup or alternate power source may be the answer. For longer term interruptions, or when a company cannot tolerate any interruptions, redundant computer processing systems may be worth the cost. In the case of true serious interruptions, such as the case of a natural disaster or sabotage, disaster and recovery plans are critical controls.

As is the case with other controls, disaster planning and recovery should be the responsibility of an identifiable, accountable party. A formal plan should exist, including recovery procedures such as offsite processing capacity. Company needs and costs play a major role in these plans and controls because the speed with which a recovery center can begin processing and the cost are related.

Human Resources

Hiring Policies

Controls over human resources are at least as important for IT as they are for other aspects of a company. For example, companies should implement hiring policies that cover recruiting, verifying information, and testing and interviewing potential IT employees before their hire. Verifying information about education, training, and past jobs is a critical step because it may reveal information relevant to the integrity of the potential employee. Testing and interviewing provide information regarding the individual's ability to perform the intended tasks, although they may also provide information about the person's honesty and integrity.

IT employees often have access to sensitive data and operations. This highlights the risk that those IT employees with great technical skill and knowledge of the computer system can figure out ways to circumvent controls. Therefore, any additional comfort that can be obtained regarding an IT employee's integrity is welcome. If any concerns are uncovered about a potential IT employee's honesty and integrity, they should be weighted heavily in hiring decisions.

Even when the best and most conscientious efforts are made in the hiring process, internal procedures can be implemented that may provide additional protection against wrongdoing by IT employees. For example, controls should be in place requiring cross training, job rotations, and mandatory vacations. Cross training prevents any employee from being so critical to operations that he or she cannot be replaced, and permits another person to actively observe the processes. Job rotations and mandatory vacations provide an opportunity for every job to be performed by another employee, increasing the probability that if wrongdoing is occurring it will be discovered during the employee's absence.

Training

Again although important for employees across the entire company, training is of heightened importance for IT personnel. Ongoing training keeps IT personnel up to date in their technical knowledge. Training may also be perceived by employees as another, though perhaps expected, form of compensation. Even though it keeps IT personnel marketable, training may also engender a sense of loyalty to the company.

Termination Policies and Controls

Termination policies for IT employees are necessary to limit the possibility that an unhappy or disgruntled person sabotages or damages the system or information. IT employees possess a level of knowledge and access that makes the risk of leaving them in place after their termination is planned simply too great. Regardless of whether the termination is instigated by the individual or the company, the policies should be followed.

Appropriate termination procedures for IT employees include immediately revoking computer access and physical access to the computer environment. Passwords and access codes should be changed. Completely preventing the employee access to the building may need to be a part of the physical control. Alternatively, removing the employee to another area of the business may be sufficient. Computer files on which the employee was working should go immediately under the control of the network administrator or IT manager.

Physical Facilities Controls

Many of the ITGC that relate to the physical IT facilities are common sense. The IT facility should be placed in a protected environment, for example, where there is limited risk of floods, hurricanes, tornadoes, and, if possible, earthquakes. Climate control over temperature and humidity are necessary for the equipment and data storage media. Fire suppression and fire evacuation plans, though necessary for all the physical plant of the company, are especially important to the physical IT facilities because of the sensitivity to heat and smoke. In the current age of terrorism, the need to house physical IT facilities in inconspicuous places is more widely recognized.

Given an expected level of protection and safety, other controls should apply to the IT physical facilities. Access should be limited, and only the people who need to be should be admitted. Beyond access to the overall IT facility, admission to network administration offices should be even more limited to prevent unauthorized access to data and information. Critical equipment such as routers, switches, and servers should be kept in secure places—such as closets—and locked up. Computer equipment should be physically secured by being turned off and locked. Finally, portable equipment such as laptops, should be physically secured, and no more confidential information than is absolutely necessary should be stored on them. Functions that automatically lock a device after two or three attempts of entry with an incorrect user ID or passcode can help prevent unauthorized access to sensitive or confidential information in the event a portable device is stolen or lost.

ITGC and the Integrated Audit

Even in a company that does not have an extensive or a highly sophisticated IT environment, many of the controls discussed here are needed. In performing the ICFR audit, the auditor directs much audit time and effort to evaluating the design, existence, and functioning of ITGC. As stated at the outset, in collecting audit evidence on the design of ITGC, the auditor may also gain evidence about function. For example, many of the controls over physical security of the IT facility can be verified by observation. Alternatively, verifying that proper authorization was received before computer programs were purchased will require specific testing of that control, probably through document inspection. ITGC are pervasive. The auditor must understand and evaluate ITGC because many of the more specific application controls that directly affect the fairness of account balances cannot function effectively in the absence of effectively designed and operating general controls.

REVIEW QUESTIONS

R.1 What are some of the threats software and interface controls are intended to protect against? Which controls protect against the different threats?

R.2 What different types of backup procedures can be performed, and when are the various procedures appropriate?

R.3 What are different sources of services interruptions, and what types of contingency plans are appropriate for each?

R.4 Why are human resources policies on hiring, training, and termination important ITGC?

R.5 What controls over the physical IT facility are considered ITGC?

KEY TERMS

Application controls. Controls built into specific applications or processes that are carried out by the computer.

Contingency controls. Controls in place to respond to breakdowns of general controls.

Denial of service attacks. Actions from outside parties intended to keep the system from being available to its intended users.

Development. Duties including systems analysis, computer programming, database administration, and quality control.

Electronic vaulting. When backed-up data is sent to another computer for storage.

Firewalls. An access control specifically directed at telecommunications entry.

ITGC. Deal with the IT environment and IT policies and procedures.

Intrusion detection controls. Alerts to IT security when an unauthorized user gains access.

License agreements. Agreements entered into by companies that license software specifying parameters on the software's use.

Logs. Computer-generated documentation covering (for example) access, input, processing, output, unauthorized access attempts, and errors.

Operations. Duties including input, processing, output, and backup.

Patches. Additions to standard software written to cover known vulnerabilities in program code.

Physical vaulting. When backed-up data is saved on a storage medium and physically removed from the company location.

Segregation of duties. Refers to having different employees perform tasks that, if performed by the same person, would permit breakdown or circumvention of internal controls.

Service interruption. When a company is not able to process its computer operations.

Social engineering. Describes manipulative behavior used to get an employee to help someone circumvent the controls in an IT environment.

Third-party service providers. Outside entities from which a company purchases services related to IT activities and functions.

MULTIPLE CHOICE

7-50 All of the following are related to employee use of company IT resources except

  (a) social engineering.

  (b) personal e-mail.

  (c) portable equipment.

  (d) physical safekeeping of equipment, data, and passwords.

7-51 Social engineering

  (a) can be prevented with effective programmed controls.

  (b) can be prevented with effective general controls.

  (c) is a problem that should be addressed by the human resources department.

  (d) occurs rarely.

7-52 The most important separation of duties in the IT control environment is

  (a) separating IT security and IT operations.

  (b) separating IT security and IT development activity.

  (c) separating IT development activities and IT operations.

  (d) separating systems analysis and database administration.

7-53 Network technology

  (a) includes both hardware and software.

  (b) increases the risk of security problems.

  (c) should be subject to approval prior to acquisition.

  (d) All of the above.

7-54 Effective ITGC require that companies have policies for all but which of the following:

  (a) Correction of errors that result from computer processing

  (b) Program development and program changes

  (c) The specific application processing controls built into various programs

  (d) Which services may be purchased from third-party service providers

7-55 In auditing ICFR, ITGC

  (a) are important primarily for companies with highly sophisticated IT systems.

  (b) will often require a significant amount of audit time and effort.

  (c) are not important as long as the design and operation of application controls is effective.

  (d) involve primarily hardware and software issues.

7-56 Which of the following is true?

  (a) The type of data backup and storage plan required depends on a company's structure and business needs.

  (b) To have effective ITGC, every type of company must be able to at least limit denial of service assaults.

  (c) Because everyone knows they are important, company policies regarding the use of patches are not an integral part of ITGC.

(d) Companies need appropriate data security controls only to ensure that they can maintain business operations as desired.

7-57 Which of the following HR policies is least critical to ITGC?

(a) Verifying information about applicants' education, training, and past jobs

(b) Cross training, job rotations, and mandatory vacations

(c) Termination policies that limit the possibility of sabotage by employees who are leaving the company

(d) Availability of a retirement plan to limit employee dissatisfaction

DISCUSSION QUESTIONS

7-58 Why is the auditor concerned about whether a company has controls over the development or changes it makes to computer software? What impact do these controls have over the auditor's conclusions for the ICFR audit? The financial statement audit?

7-59 What concerns does the auditor have over access controls and their impact on data security? What impact would a problem with access controls have on the auditor's conclusions in an ICFR audit of a company with an extensive IT system? Do you think management could assert that the financial statements are accurate and complete if access controls are insufficient? Why?

7-60 If all of a company's ITGC are effective except its contingency controls, would the auditor be able to conclude that the ICFR is effective? What if other controls are lacking but contingency controls are effective? How would the auditor modify plans for the financial statement audit if the conclusion in the ICFR audit is that many general controls are lacking but contingency controls are consistently effective?

7-61 If the head of the IT department and the CFO have complete access to all aspects of the IT system and the ability to input, change, and delete transactions, is this a weakness in ICFR? If so, how important is it? Would this situation have any impact on the audit procedures of the financial statement audit? Given the positions these individuals hold, how might their authority and activities be changed to enhance the control environment while still permitting them to do their jobs?

PROBLEM

7-62 AS 2, paragraph 11, defines preventive controls as having "the objective of preventing errors or fraud from occurring in the first place that could result in a misstatement of the financial statements." Detective controls "have the objective of detecting errors or fraud that have already occurred that could result in a misstatement of the financial statements."

Required:

Set up a work paper with two columns, one labeled preventive and the other labeled detective. Using the discussion of ITGC presented in Appendix A, classify the various controls discussed as preventive or detective controls. Are there any you placed in both columns because they serve both a preventive and detective function? Examine your controls and answer the following.

(a) Are there any preventive controls that you believe are less important if a related detective control is effective? What would the related detective control be? Explain how it would compensate.

(b) Are there any detective controls that you believe are less important if the related preventive controls are effective? What would the related preventive control be? Explain who it would compensate.

7-63 View or review the movie, *Catch Me If You Can* (Leonardo DiCaprio, Dreamworks, 2002). Investigate information on Frank Abagnale Jr., the individual whose early life is portrayed in the movie, including his current occupation.

(a) Explain how the main character in the movie used social engineering.

(b) Although the events of the movie occurred before much of today's information technology was developed, many of the processes used by the villain could be successfully used today. Give examples and explain why this is the case.

(c) Why are the knowledge and skills used by Frank Abagnale Jr. during his early life applicable to what he does now?

APPENDIX B: ENTERPRISE RISK MANAGEMENT, INTEGRATED FRAMEWORK

Introduction

In September 2004, the Committee of Sponsoring Organizations of the Treadway Commission (COSO) published a framework on Enterprise Risk Management (ERM). This framework does not replace the Internal Control (IC) Framework COSO released in 1992. It adds to the IC Framework information by addressing the environment within which controls function. As stated in the ERM Framework,

> Internal control is encompassed within and an integral part of enterprise risk management. Enterprise risk management is broader than internal control, expanding and elaborating on internal control to form a more robust conceptualization focusing more fully on risk. (Appendix C, p. 109)

Given that the ERM Framework encompasses the IC Framework, it is no surprise that many of the descriptions and guidance are similar and overlapping.

The COSO ERM Framework defines ERM as

> a process, effected by an entity's board of directors, management and other personnel, applied in a strategy setting and across the enterprise, designed to identify potential events that may affect the entity, and manage risk to be within its risk appetite, to provide reasonable assurance regarding the achievement of entity objectives. (p. 4)

The ERM Framework was developed with the intent of providing a logical and orderly way for management to identify, analyze, and manage all of a company's risks. These risks extend beyond the risks contemplated by the COSO IC Framework. Thus, the ERM Framework offers management something additional by providing guidance on managing all of a company's risks and uncertainties.

Objectives

The COSO ERM Framework guides management in considering risk and the company's goals, focusing on four categories of objectives:

1. Strategic objectives
2. Operations objectives
3. Reporting objectives
4. Compliance objectives

The operations and compliance objectives are titled the same in both the IC and ERM frameworks. The reporting objective title differs. In the COSO IC Framework the reporting objective is called financial reporting and addresses reliability of published financial statements. The ERM objective of reporting is much broader, addressing the reliability of all the reports the entity produces. From an ERM perspective, the objective is for reliable reporting, both financial and nonfinancial, and to internal users such as management, as well as external users such as regulators and stockholders.

The COSO ERM Framework includes an additional category of objectives, beyond the three in the IC Framework. The additional category is strategic objectives. Strategic objectives are described as "higher level," but can be thought of as those goals that relate to what the business is trying to accomplish. Strategic objectives should be tied to the company's mission. Operations, reporting, and compliance objectives should be created in order to help achieve the strategic objectives.

As with a good internal control system, a good ERM system does not guarantee that a company will be successful. Also, an ERM system suffers the same inherent limitations as internal control: human failure, unusual breakdowns, collusion, and management override. However, if an ERM system is functioning effectively, the Board of Directors and management should have confidence that the company's objectives are being achieved. This basically means that they have confidence that the actions the company takes to achieve business goals fit within the parameters of risk the company intends to accept.

Components

The ERM framework lists eight components, compared to five related to internal control. The five components in the COSO IC Framework are:

Control environment

Risk assessment

Control activities

Information and communication

Monitoring

The ERM Framework modifies control environment to become internal environment; adds objective setting, event identification, and risk response; and reutilizes risk assessment, control activities, information and communication, and monitoring. The components of the COSO ERM Framework are presented in Exhibit B7-1.

EXHIBIT B7-1

COSO ERM
Components of
Enterprise Risk
Management

Internal Environment—Management sets a philosophy regarding risks and establishes a risk appetite. The internal environment sets the basis for how risk and control are viewed and addressed by an entity's people. The core of any business is its people—their individual attributes, including integrity, ethical values, and competence—and the environment in which they operate.

Objective Setting—Objectives must exist before management can identify potential events affecting their achievement. Enterprise risk management ensures that management has in place a process to set objectives and that chosen objectives support and align with the entity's mission and are consistent with its risk appetite.

Event Identification—Potential events that might have an impact on the entity must be identified. Event identification involves identifying potential events from internal or external sources affecting achievement of objectives. It includes distinguishing between events that represent risks, those representing opportunities, and those that may be both. Opportunities are channeled back to management's strategy or objective-setting process.

Risk Assessment—Identified risks are analyzed in order to form a basis for determining how they should be managed. Risks are associated with objectives that may be affected. Risks are assessed on both an inherent and a residual basis, with the assessment considering both risk likelihood and impact.

Risk Response—Personnel identify and evaluate possible responses to risks, which include avoiding, accepting, reducing, and sharing risk. Management selects a set of actions to align risks with the entity's risk tolerances and risk appetite.

Control Activities—Policies and procedures are established and executed to help ensure the risk responses management selects are effectively carried out.

Information and Communication—Relevant information is identified, captured, and communicated in a form and timeframe that enable people to carry out their responsibilities. Information is needed at all levels of an entity for identifying, assessing, and responding to risk. Effective communication also occurs in a broader sense, flowing down, across, and up the entity. Personnel receive clear communications regarding their role and responsibilities.

Monitoring—The entirety of enterprise risk management is monitored, and modifications made as necessary. In this way, it can react dynamically, changing as conditions warrant. Monitoring is accomplished through ongoing management activities, separate evaluations of enterprise risk management, or a combination of the two.

(COSO Enterprise Risk Management—Integrated Framework, September 2004, p. 22)

Just as with the COSO IC Framework, all the objectives relate to all the components and can be applied across all levels of the company.

Internal Environment

The control environment in the COSO IC Framework refers to "tone at the top," integrity, ethical values, competence of people, management philosophy and operating style, authority and responsibility, development of people, and Board of Directors involvement. Again, the parallel component in the ERM context is broader and includes an awareness of risk. However, just as the control environment is the overarching influence for internal control, so is the internal environment the overarching influence for ERM. Many of the important aspects of the internal environment overlap those of the control environment.

AUDITING IN ACTION

Key Principles, Internal Environment

Risk Management Philosophy
Risk Appetite
Board of Directors
Integrity and Ethical Values
Commitment to Competence
Organizational Structure
Assignment of Authority and Responsibility
Human Resource Standards

(COSO ERM Framework, pp. 101–102)

Objective Setting

Objective setting is a component of the ERM framework that is not part of the IC Framework. The sequence or timing of objective setting is important. Objective setting occurs first and is followed by event identification, risk assessment, and risk response, in that order. In other words, first management sets objectives for the company. Then management identifies events that may affect the achievement of those objectives.

Events may positively affect the achievement of the objectives. In contrast, events can increase the risk that objectives will not be achieved. Management evaluates those events that are identified as risks to achieving objectives to assess how great a threat they are and how likely they are to occur. Finally, management decides what to do about the risks or how to respond. The sequential nature of these steps means that objectives must be set and be set as a first step.

In identifying objectives, management specifies those that are critical to company goals or strategies and those that are not as critical, and then selects the objectives to be pursued. In deciding how to pursue its objectives, management needs to determine its attitudes about risks—the level of risk desired and acceptable in the company's activities that are intended to achieve the objectives.

AUDITING IN ACTION

Key Principles, Objective Setting

Strategic Objectives
Related Objectives
Selected Objectives
Risk Appetite
Risk Tolerances

(COSO ERM Framework, pp. 102–103)

Event Identification

Event identification in the ERM Framework encompasses events that have the potential to be either positive or negative influences in achieving company objectives. Those events that are expected to be positive influences are actively considered in management's objective setting process. In other words, if an event is expected to have a positive impact, management considers it on the next round of setting objectives and performing strategic planning to maximize the likelihood of the positive impact.

Event identification goes beyond just knowing what the expected events are. Important aspects of event identification include how management identifies them, other things that may influence or impact the events, relationships or "interdependencies" among events, and the importance of recognizing the positive or negative direction of impact. Events that will have a positive impact can be viewed as opportunities, while others that are negative should be assessed as threats or risks.

AUDITING IN ACTION

Key Principles, Event Identification

Events
Influencing Factors
Event Identification Techniques
Interdependencies
Distinguishing Risks and Opportunities

(COSO ERM Framework, pp. 103–104)

AUDITING IN ACTION

External and Internal Sources of Risk

External Sources	Internal Sources
Economic	Infrastructure
Natural Environment	Personnel
Political	Process
Social	Technology
Technological	

(COSO ERM Framework, pp. 46–47)

Identification of events that represent risks is part of both the ERM and IC Frameworks. Both frameworks acknowledge that events that represent risks can arise from internal and external environments.

Risk Assessment

The ERM description of risk assessment includes specific management actions. Generally, risk assessment analyzes company objectives and events that may affect achievement of the objectives. Management assesses the potential impact of the events on achieving the objectives. This is not a one-time event but a continuous activity. Although management identifies expected events before the risk assessment process takes place, unexpected events are also considered.

In assessing risk, management first addresses inherent risk, which for ERM is defined as "the risk to an entity in the absence of any actions management might take to alter either the risk's likelihood or impact" (COSO ERM Framework, p. 49). Assessment of inherent risk includes likelihood and impact. This means management considers the probability that something will happen, as well as how great the effect will be if the event occurs. The combination of these two characteristics influences what management decides to do about the risk. If the likelihood that something will occur is small, management may not take any action. Alternatively, if it is very likely that an event having an important impact on the company's ability to achieve a major objective will occur, management will be very aggressive in managing the risk. The risk that remains after management implements its response is called residual risk. Management's goal is to choose a risk response that brings residual risk down to a level that is acceptable to the entity.

Management must decide what methods are to be used for assessing the likelihood and impact of risks. This requires choosing how to perform the assessment. Management also looks at relationships among the risk events. Recall that considering the relationships of events was also part of event identification.

Management uses whatever information is available to assess the likelihood and impact of an event. Management may consider past experiences of the company or forecasts by outside experts. Regardless of the information that is used, management can use both quantitative and qualitative methods to assess the risk. Quantitative techniques like statistical analyses may be used along with management exercising its judgment.

AUDITING IN ACTION

Key Principles, Risk Assessment

Inherent and Residual Risk
Estimating Likelihood and Impact
Assessment Techniques
Relationships between Events

(COSO ERM Framework, p. 104)

Risk Response

Risk response refers to management's decision regarding what to do about the risks it has assessed. The ERM framework provides four categories of risk response: avoidance, reduction, sharing, and acceptance. The explanations for these four response categories are straightforward.

If management assesses a risk and concludes that the likelihood and impact are so major that it cannot accept the risk at all, it avoids the risk completely. Management most likely terminates whatever activity is causing the risk. An example of risk avoidance is when banks and other lenders completely stopped providing credit to certain classes of customers in response to the economic downturn in 2008.

Risk reduction describes actions management takes to control known risks of its business. The lenders in the above example had other options beyond risk avoidance that could have reduced risk. Risk reduction might include performing credit checks on loan applicants to identify those the lender wishes to avoid. Many basic internal controls fall into the category of risk reduction. For example, physically securing cash at the point of sale reduces the risk of theft. Requiring supporting documentation before paying invoices and canceling the documentation when the funds are disbursed reduce the risk that invoices will be paid that are not legitimate obligations of the company or that bills will be paid twice.

Risk sharing occurs when a risk cannot be avoided or reduced enough to fall within the parameters that management is willing to accept. Purchasing insurance rather than "self -insuring" is a common example of risk sharing. An employer can provide only part of the cost of health insurance premiums as an employee benefit and can require employees to pay for part of the cost. In this situation, the employer is sharing the risk of rising healthcare costs with employees. The movement away from defined benefit pension plans to defined contribution plans is another example of employers sharing risks with employees. Hedging transactions represent actions taken by management to share the risk of future changes in the prices of various items (interest rates, inventory costs, foreign currency exchange rates, etc.) with willing investors.

Sometimes, even though a risk is very important, no practical way exists for management to engage in avoidance or risk sharing. An example of this is failure of a company's IT system. Failure of its IT system would be catastrophic to some businesses and is a risk that cannot be avoided because the company cannot avoid the use of IT. While management may be able to purchase business interruption service, the magnitude of damage from an IT failure may be greater than just business interruption. In this situation, management will share whatever risks it can through insurance and implement any risk reduction procedures available, which could include not only significant IT controls and but even a redundant system.

Finally, risk acceptance describes the situation when management concludes that risk falls within the range that it can tolerate. Management assesses both the likelihood of an event occurring and the magnitude of the impact of an event if it does occur. An easy-to-understand example is when management chooses the deductible level on an insurance policy. The dollar amount of the deductible is the amount of uninsured loss management is willing to accept. If the likelihood of an insurable event occurring is low, management probably can accept the risk of cash outflow from a higher deductible. For each risk event identified, management selects the response that best matches the company's risk tolerance.

An additional concept included in the ERM risk response discussion is the portfolio view of risk. A portfolio view of risk is one in which management first considers risk for each business unit and then aggregates the risk across the entire entity. For some risks, the effect could add up to more risk than the entity as a whole can accept. For example, an airline company with several different divisions might be very vulnerable to increased fuel costs in each of its divisions. So the risk of increased fuel costs may be a risk the company chooses to reduce. Alternatively, a company that has different business units with different products and delivery methods might have less fuel risks when the company is considered as a whole.

For example, if the company has a unit that provides free delivery of its products locally, via its own trucks, that unit would be vulnerable to the risk of fuel cost increases. However, if the company also has an online sales unit that shifts any increases in fuel costs to the customer by shipping via UPS at the customer's expense, the company does not have the risk for that business unit. When both business units are considered together, the overall risk of increased fuel expenses may be below the company's tolerable risk threshold, and management's risk response can be acceptance.

AUDITING IN ACTION

Key Principles, Risk Response

Evaluating Possible Responses
Selected Responses
Portfolio View

(COSO ERM Framework, pp. 104–105)

Control Activities

Both COSO's IC and ERM Frameworks include control activities. In short, control activities help the company make sure that management's intent and directives are carried out. From an ERM perspective, control activities are directed at enforcing management's risk response decisions. Management selects and puts into place control activities that are needed to be sure its risk response selections are carried out. The range of activities mirrors those described in the COSO IC Framework: approvals, authorizations, verifications, reconciliations, reviews of operating performance, security of assets, and segregation of duties. Each control activity is composed of a policy establishing what should be done and a procedure explaining how to do it.

Similar to other control descriptions, the ERM Framework classifies controls over information systems as general controls and applications controls. General controls are the policies and procedures that support effective operations of the IT environment. General controls are discussed in Chapter 7, Appendix A. Applications controls are an integral part of the software used to process a company's data. Accompanying manual controls can also be part of application controls. General controls help to support the function of application controls.

Information and Communication

The information and communication component is an extensive aspect of both the IC and ERM Frameworks. Both Frameworks emphasize that information must be identified, captured, and communicated. This must take place in a manner and time frame that permits people within the company to use the information to carry out their responsibilities. The information system infrastructure must properly capture, process, analyze, and report information for effective communication.

The ERM Framework elaborates on information sources being both internal and external. Both historical and current data are important. Historical data permits the company to compare past performance to plans and expectations, identify trends, and make plans. Present data is critical to ERM because it enables the company to determine whether it is within its risk tolerances. Information should include the right amount of detail, in the right time frame if it is to be most useful for the company. The ERM Framework stresses the risks of information overload, given the increasing ease of data collection in the current information technology environment.

The communication aspect of ERM includes many issues emphasized for internal control. Communication must flow freely in all directions within the company. Even though internal communications are usually effective when following the organizational chain of responsibility, additional mechanisms for reporting outside the typical, normal reporting channels are also needed.

Management must send a clear and convincing message of the importance of ERM and be receptive to communications that identify issues. This need to be receptive extends especially to ethics concerns. Company personnel have to believe that they will not be negatively impacted if they report suspected ethics violations. Management has to prove that it wants to receive communications. The most effective way to accomplish this is through positive treatment of employees who make reports. Two-way communication between management and the Board of Directors is an important aspect of the free flow of information.

Finally, the ERM framework focuses on communication with external parties. Communication with external parties consists not only of an outward flow of communication, such as to regulators and other stakeholders. External communications include the inflow of information that may assist with ERM. Examples are the information customers and suppliers can communicate regarding design and quality of products and services in response to changing market demands.

Monitoring

Monitoring is a critical component of both the IC and ERM Frameworks. The best way to determine whether the IC and ERM systems are functioning is through a monitoring process. Ongoing monitoring is stressed in the ERM Framework as the basic method for determining the effectiveness of the system, as it is performed during day-to-day activities of the business. Managers responsible for various functions conduct this monitoring.

Separate evaluations of ERM are also necessary, but how frequent and extensive they are depends on the effectiveness of ongoing monitoring. "Higher priority" risk areas are separately evaluated more frequently. The entire system will likely only be evaluated when there has been a major change, such as a change of policies or a major change in the information system. When ERM is functioning effectively, problems with risk management will surface and either be handled as an ongoing part of managing the business or reported upward for action by those at higher organizational levels.

AUDITING IN ACTION

Key Principles, Monitoring

Ongoing Monitoring Activities
Separate Evaluations
Reporting Deficiencies

(COSO ERM Framework, p. 107)

Roles and Responsibilities

Roles and responsibilities are discussed in the COSO IC Framework. However, they are a separate component of the ERM Framework. Both frameworks address the Board of Directors, management, internal auditors, and other personnel. The ERM Framework also specifically discusses the role of a risk officer and financial executives.

Although external parties are not part of the ERM, they are discussed because they may contribute to the company's goals or provide information used by the ERM. External auditors have a particular role in that they provide management with an objective view of the company. Financial statement audit processes may produce information useful to the ERM. Useful information includes audit procedure results, analytical information, deficiencies in risk management, and deficiencies in controls. This audit-produced information may result in recommendations to improve ERM.

Legislators and regulators also affect ERM. Established laws and rules set a floor below which ERM cannot function and still meet requirements. An example of the floor effect of laws and rules is that any company reporting to the SEC must be able to produce reliable information to include in SEC required reports.

Limitations of Enterprise Risk Management

The ERM Framework wraps up with a discussion of the limitations of ERM. Even effective enterprise risk management does not guarantee a company's success. Enterprise risk management suffers the same limitations as internal control: human judgment may be wrong, unusual breakdowns of the processes may occur, individuals or entities may work together or collude to circumvent the system, and management may override the system. In addition, just as with internal control, the mechanisms built into an ERM system will be subject to the trade-offs of cost and benefit.

In addition to the limitations that also affect internal control, others are specified in relation to enterprise risk management. First, risks are future oriented and therefore cannot be known with certainty. The ERM Framework addresses this issue by considering likelihood of occurrence, but still the future is unknown. Another limitation is that an effective ERM system will provide only reasonable assurance that management and the Board of Directors know of the risks and have the information and procedures to address them. Finally, the system cannot guarantee that the risks will be managed appropriately.

APPENDIX C: INTERNAL CONTROL OVER FINANCIAL REPORTING IN SMALLER PUBLIC COMPANIES

The Committee of Sponsoring Organizations of the Treadway Commission (COSO) originally released its *Internal Control—Integrated Framework* (IC Framework) in 1992. The purpose of releasing the IC Framework was to help organizations evaluate and improve their internal controls.

Ten years later, Congress enacted the Sarbanes-Oxley Act (SOX). SOX Section 404 contains a provision that requires management of all public companies to provide an assessment of the effectiveness of the company's internal controls over financial reporting (ICFR). SOX also mandates that management's assessment of ICFR must be audited. Both management's report and the auditor's opinion on ICFR must be included in the company's annual filings with the SEC. The SEC issued regulations for implementation of Section 404 of SOX.

Based on the SEC's regulations, when Section 404 first became effective in 2004 it was only applicable to companies that met the definition of "accelerated filers." The definition of accelerated filers captures primarily those companies whose market capitalization exceeds $75 million. The SEC staggered the date at which smaller public companies had to implement SOX Section 404 to begin significantly later than the deadline for accelerated filers.

Although some professional guidance existed for auditor involvement with internal control, the legislative mandate for the auditor-provided service was the first major project on the PCAOB's agenda. In response to the SOX requirement, in 2004 the PCAOB released Auditing Standard (AS) No. 2: *An Audit of Internal Control Over Financial Reporting*

Performed in Conjunction With an Audit of Financial Statements. AS 2 provided guidance to auditing firms performing integrated audits of public companies.

Implementing the SOX Section 404 requirement for management assessment and independent audit of ICFR under AS 2 was very costly for accelerated filers. Consequently, significant concern existed that when smaller companies, called non-accelerated filers, were required to comply the costs would be overwhelming. The SEC repeatedly deferred the date at which SOX Section 404 applied to smaller public companies to provide time to work out a cost-effective means for smaller companies to comply. In 2007 the SEC produced Commission Guidance Regarding Management's Report on Internal Control Over Financial Reporting Under Section 13(a) or 15(d) of the Securities Exchange Act of 1934 (Interpretive Release) (Release 33-8810).

Also in 2007, the PCAOB replaced AS 2 with AS No. 5: *An Audit of Internal Control Over Financial Statements Reporting That is Integrated with An Audit of Financial Statements.* In October of 2007 the PCAOB followed AS 5 with the publication of preliminary staff views, *An Audit of Internal Control that is Integrated with an Audit of Financial Statements: Guidance for Auditors of Smaller Public Companies.* The staff views were finalized in 2009.

COSO also produced guidance intended to help smaller companies deal with the SOX requirement to assess and report on its ICFR effectiveness. COSO led the wave of guidance by releasing *Internal Control over Financial Reporting—Guidance for Smaller Public Companies* in 2006. This was followed in 2009 with *Guidance on Monitoring Internal Control Systems.*

All of the ICFR-related guidance targeted at smaller public companies and their auditors focuses on a risk-based approach and scaling the ICFR activities to what is appropriate for the size and complexity of the company. The SEC's Interpretive Release directs management to use judgment and tailor the evidence gathered to the evidence needed based on risk. The monitoring that management already conducts to run the business is stressed as an effective means for assessment, especially for lower risk areas. The SEC Interpretive Release also promotes flexibility in management decisions regarding the documentation it produces to support its assessment of ICFR effectiveness.

Both in AS 5 and *Guidance for Auditors of Smaller Public Companies,* the PCAOB highlights the difference company size and complexity makes in an audit of ICFR. Smaller companies offer the opportunity to scale the ICFR audit. The characteristics that auditors often find in smaller entities are:

Fewer business lines

Less complex business processes

Less complex financial reporting systems

More centralized accounting functions

Extensive involvement by senior management

Fewer levels of management with wide spans of control

The PCAOB emphasizes that along with offering opportunities to scale the audit these differences can cause unique risks.

SEC Interpretive Release

The SEC's guidance to management of small companies does not change the fundamentals of what needs to be done to assess ICFR effectiveness. The guidance states that management must identify risks, determine whether controls are in place that address the risks, and evaluate the operating effectiveness of the controls. The differences focus on how the activities are accomplished. The discussion of identifying reporting risks includes the following illustration:

For example, to identify financial reporting risks in a larger business or a complex business process, management's methods and procedures may involve a variety of company personnel, including those with specialized knowledge. These individuals, collectively, may be necessary to have a sufficient understanding of GAAP, the underlying business transactions and the process activities, including the role of computer technology, that are required to initiate, authorize, record and process transactions. In contrast, in a small company that operates on a centralized basis with less complex business processes and with little change in the risks or processes, management's daily involvement with the business may provide it with adequate knowledge to appropriately identify financial reporting risks. (SEC Release 33-8810, pp. 13–14)

Many aspects of the guidance mirror what is expected for larger companies. The SEC emphasizes that management must consider the risk of fraud. The three different categories of entity-level controls are again highlighted as: (1) important but indirect, (2) monitoring, and (3) precise enough to prevent or detect material financial misstatements. Management is afforded flexibility and judgment in considering whether all aspects of ITGC are relevant to its financial reporting risks. Some of the ITGC may be relevant to a company's financial reporting risk, but it is not necessary to evaluate those that are not.

Documentation of controls and evidence collected can vary based on management's judgment of importance to financial reporting and risk. The guidance directs management to adjust these components to the individual circumstances. The following addresses the potential tailoring of evidence to ICFR risk and business circumstances:

As the ICFR risk increases, management will ordinarily adjust the nature of the evidence that is obtained. For example, management can increase the evidence from on-going monitoring activities by utilizing personnel who are more objective and/or increasing the extent of validation through periodic direct testing of the underlying controls. Management can also vary the evidence obtained by adjusting the period of time covered by direct testing. When ICFR risk is assessed as high, the evidence management obtains would ordinarily consist of direct testing or on-going monitoring activities performed by individuals who have a higher degree of objectivity. In situations where a company's on-going monitoring activities utilize personnel who are not adequately objective, the evidence obtained would normally be supplemented with direct testing by those who are independent from the operation of the control. In these situations, direct testing of controls corroborates evidence from on-going monitoring activities as well as evaluates the operation of the underlying controls and whether they continue to adequately address financial reporting risks. When ICFR risk is assessed as low, management may conclude that evidence from on-going monitoring is sufficient and that no direct testing is required. Further, management's evaluation would ordinarily consider evidence from a reasonable period of time during the year, including the fiscal year-end. (SEC Release 33-8810, p. 29)

In this quote, emphasis is placed on the appropriate role of on-going monitoring as a source of evidence about the effectiveness of ICFR. The timely release of COSO guidance on monitoring ICFR fits with the SEC's discussion of the importance of monitoring. In its discussion of monitoring, the SEC proposes that "management's daily interaction" with the entity's ICFR may be sufficient to evaluate the effective operation of the controls. If a company has centralized controls and few individuals involved in carrying out the processes, management may be able to evaluate the effectiveness of control operations just from daily interactions. If the company has multiple layers of management or operating segments, it is expected that daily interaction will not provide enough evidence. In these situations, management needs to perform direct testing or more formal on-going monitoring evaluations.

Smaller companies can document evidence supporting management's assessment of ICFR using a wide range of tools:

For example, in smaller companies, where management's daily interaction with its controls provides the basis for its assessment, management may have limited documentation created specifically for the evaluation of ICFR. However, in these instances, management should consider whether reasonable support for its assessment would include documentation of how its interaction provided it with sufficient evidence. This documentation might include memoranda, e-mails, and instructions or directions to and from management to company employees. (SEC Release 33-8810, p. 32)

As complexity, judgment, and risk associated with a control increase, management will likely need more evidence and documentation of the assessment.

PCAOB Guidance

In contrast to the SEC Interpretive Release which directs management, PCAOB AS 5 and *Guidance for Auditors of Smaller Public Companies* directs information to auditors. Characteristics likely to exist in smaller companies are important considerations in their ICFR audits.

- *Use of entity-level controls to achieve control objectives.* *In smaller, less complex companies, senior management often is involved in many day-to-day business activities and performs duties that are important to effective internal control over financial reporting. Consequently, the auditor's evaluation of entity-level controls can provide a substantial amount of evidence about the effectiveness of internal control over financial reporting.*
- *Risk of management override.* *The extensive involvement of senior management in day-to-day activities and fewer levels of management can provide additional opportunities for management to override controls or intentionally misstate the financial statements in smaller, less complex companies. In an integrated audit, the auditor should consider the risk of management override and company actions to address that risk in connection with assessing the risk of material misstatement due to fraud and evaluating entity-level controls.*
- *Implementation of segregation of duties and alternative controls.* *By their nature, smaller, less complex companies have fewer employees, which limits the opportunity to segregate incompatible duties. Smaller, less complex companies might use alternative approaches to achieve the objectives of segregation of duties, and the auditor should evaluate whether those alternative controls achieve the control objectives.*
- *Use of information technology (IT).* *A smaller, less complex company with less complex business processes and centralized accounting operations might have less complex information systems that make greater use of off-the-shelf packaged software without modification. In the areas in which off-the-shelf software is used, the auditor's testing of information technology controls might focus on the application controls built into the pre-packaged software that management relies on to achieve its control objectives and the testing of IT general controls might focus on those controls that are important to the effective operation of the selected application controls.*
- *Maintenance of financial reporting competencies.* *Smaller, less complex companies might address their needs for financial reporting competencies through means other than internal staffing, such as engaging outside professionals. The auditor may take into consideration the use of those third parties when assessing competencies of the company.*
- *Nature and extent of documentation.* *A smaller, less complex company typically needs less formal documentation to run the business, including maintaining effective internal control over financial reporting. The auditor may take that into account when selecting controls to test and planning tests of controls.*

(PCAOB *Guidance for Auditors of Smaller Public Companies*, pp. 7–8)

Entity-level Controls

As with all ICFR audits, auditors of smaller public companies consider entity-level controls. Differences in entity-level controls that may affect the ICFR audit of a small business result from management's greater involvement in the company's daily activities. More senior management involvement enhances the possibility of management override but helps compensate for lack of segregation of duties. Both management override and lack of segregation of duties are highlighted by the PCAOB.

AUDITING IN ACTION

Entity-Level Monitoring Controls, Payroll Processing

Scenario

A manufacturer of alternative fuel products and systems for the transportation market has union labor, supervisors, managers, and executives. All plants run two shifts six days a week, with each having approximately the same number of employees. The chief financial officer (CFO) has been with the company for 10 years and thoroughly understands its business processes, including the payroll process, and reviews weekly payroll summary reports prepared by the centralized accounting function. With the company's flat organizational design and smaller size, the CFO's background with the company and his understanding of the seasons, cycles, and workflows, and close familiarity with the budget and reporting processes, the CFO quickly identifies any sign of improprieties with payroll and their underlying cause—whether related to a particular project, overtime, hiring, layoffs, and so forth. The CFO investigates as needed to determine whether misstatements have occurred and whether any internal control has not operated effectively, and takes corrective action.

Based on the results of audit procedures relating to the control environment and controls over management override, the auditor observes that the CFO demonstrates integrity and a commitment to effective internal control over financial reporting.

Audit Approach

The auditor evaluates the effectiveness of the CFO's reviews, including the precision of those reviews. She inquires about the CFO's review process and obtains other evidence of the review. She notes that the CFO's threshold for investigating significant differences from expectations is adequate to detect misstatements that could cause the financial statements to be materially misstated. She selects some significant differences from expectations that were flagged by the CFO and determines that the CFO appropriately investigated the differences to determine whether the differences were caused by misstatements. Also, in considering evidence obtained throughout the audit, the auditor observes that the results of the financial statement audit procedures did not identify likely misstatements in payroll expense. The auditor decides that the reviews could detect misstatements related to payroll processing because the CFO's threshold for investigating significant differences from expectations is adequate. However, she determines that the control depends on reports produced by the company's IT system, so the CFO's review can be effective only if controls over the completeness and accuracy of those reports are effective. After performing the tests of the relevant computer controls, the auditor concludes that the review performed by the CFO, when coupled with relevant controls over the reports, meets the control objectives for the relevant aspects of payroll processing described above.

(Example 2-2 PCAOB *Guidance*, pp. 16–17)

Risk of Management Override

Fewer levels of management with wide spans of control that often exist in smaller companies provide opportunities for management to override ICFR. Important company controls that can help address this risk are:

> Maintaining integrity and ethical values
>
> Increased oversight by the audit committee
>
> Whistleblower program
>
> Monitoring controls over certain journal entries (PCAOB *Guidance*, p. 19)

In a small-business environment, the auditor directs specific audit procedures to the design and operating effectiveness of these controls. Inquiry of management regarding its ethical communications, coupled with follow-up interviews of employees, can address integrity and ethical values. The correspondence between management's intended communications and employees' understanding indicates the strength of the ethical environment. The auditor can attend audit committee meetings to better understand the level of management oversight the audit committee exercises. Whistleblower programs are tested by investigating the manner of response and follow-up to tips and information received. Monitoring controls over journal entries are tested as part of the ICFR audit. These controls include those that restrict access to the general ledger, require authorization for manual entries, and review journal entries for authorization.

Segregation of Duties

Regardless of the size of the company being audited, segregation of duties requires the same outcome:

> Segregation of duties refers to dividing incompatible functions among different people to reduce the risk that a potential material misstatement of the financial statements would occur without being prevented or detected. Assigning different people responsibility for authorizing transactions, recording transactions, reconciling information, and maintaining custody of assets reduces the opportunity for any one employee to conceal errors or perpetrate fraud in the normal course of his or her duties. (PCOAB Guidance, p. 24)

However, segregation of duties can be difficult to accomplish in a small-business setting, and management may accomplish the goals through other strategies:

> By their nature, smaller, less complex companies have fewer employees, which limit their opportunities to implement segregation of duties. Due to these personnel restrictions, smaller, less complex companies might approach the control objectives relevant to segregation of duties in a different manner from larger, more complex companies. Despite personnel limitations, some smaller, less complex companies might still divide incompatible functions by using the services of external parties. Other smaller, less complex companies might implement alternative controls intended to achieve the same objectives as segregations of duties for certain processes. (PCAOB Guidance, p. 24)

These other strategies to compensate for lack of segregation of duties include increased review and involvement by management. As mentioned earlier, increased management involvement has its own risk of management override, which is best mitigated by strong audit committee oversight.

IT Controls

In smaller, less complex businesses, auditors find different IT environments and risk than in larger companies. The IT environment characteristics common in smaller businesses are manual controls, packaged software, centralized computer systems, and end user computing. In addition, outsourcing can play a large IT role in smaller businesses.

AUDITING IN ACTION

Less Complex IT Environment Characteristics

Transaction processing. Data inputs can be readily compared or reconciled to system outputs. Management tends to rely primarily on manual controls over transaction processing.
Software. The company typically uses off-the-shelf packaged software without modification. The packaged software requires relatively little user configuration to implement.
Systems configurations and security administration. Computer systems tend to be centralized in a single location, and there are a limited number of interfaces between systems. Access to systems is typically managed by a limited number of personnel.
End user computing. The company is relatively more dependent on spreadsheets and other user-developed applications, which are used to initiate, authorize, record, process, and report the results of business operations, and, in many instances, perform straightforward calculations using relatively simple formulas.

(PCAOB *Guidance*, p. 27)

Auditing any IT environment involves a risk-based evaluation in which IT is considered concurrently with the accounts, disclosures, and assertions. In planning to audit risks in a less complex IT environment, the auditor specifically considers: (1) the reports produced by the IT system that are part of the control process, and (2) automated controls the company relies on. The reports generated are typically used to execute manual controls, for example, reviews of transaction and access logs, and verification of proper correction of errors. The auditor must test the completeness and accuracy of the reports as well as the manual processes involved. Automated controls in smaller businesses are typically built into off-the-shelf packaged software. When these controls are tested, the auditor also considers the important surrounding ITGC.

Financial Reporting Competencies

Auditors focus on the control risk that a small business may lack sufficient personnel with skills and competencies in financial reporting. Small businesses need the ability to identify financial reporting issues that are important to the company and ensure that transactions are properly accounted for and presented in the financial statements. On recurring engagements the auditor has a base level of knowledge about the company's financial reporting competence. Inquiry and observation are appropriate procedures to gather other audit evidence needed to assess this area of the business. If the business hires outside personnel to supplement its internal human resources, the auditor can consider the combined competence in assessing the control.

Documentation

An auditor needs to adapt the audit strategy when a company has informal documentation of ICFR, which is often the case in smaller companies. For example, a company may choose not to construct formal flowcharts and process diagrams, but instead relies on source documents and job descriptions. The auditor may use these items to guide a walkthrough to understand the system and assess design effectiveness.

A smaller, less complex company may not produce or retain documentation of controls. The auditor should gain an understanding of the evidence that is available early in the period under audit. Then, the auditor can either modify audit procedures, particularly timing, or explore with management ways to handle any gaps in evidence. A practical solution to a lack of formal documentation is often for the auditor to use the documents that the company uses to run its business. If the auditor cannot obtain enough evidence about operating effectiveness, he or she may be unable to come to an audit conclusion.

AUDITING IN ACTION

IT Dependent Controls

Scenario

A company has a small finance department. For the accounting processes that have a higher risk of misstatement, senior management performs a number of business process reviews and analyses to detect misstatements in transaction processing. The company has a small IT department that supports a packaged financial reporting system whose software code cannot be altered by the user. Since the company uses packaged software, and there have been no changes to the system or processes in the past year, the IT general controls relevant to the audit of the internal control over financial reporting are limited to certain access controls and certain computer operation controls related to identification and correction of processing errors. Management uses several system-generated reports in the business performance reviews, but these reports are embedded in the application and programmed by the vendor and cannot be altered.

Audit Approach

The auditor determines that senior management personnel performing the business process reviews and analyses are not involved with incompatible functions or duties that impair their ability to detect misstatements. Based on the auditor's knowledge of the financial reporting system and understanding of the transaction flows affecting the relevant assertions, the auditor selects for testing certain process reviews and analyses and certain controls over the completeness and accuracy of the information in the reports used in management's reviews. The tests of controls could include, for example—

- Evaluating management's review procedures including assessing whether those controls operate at an appropriate level of precision.
- Evaluating how the company assures itself regarding the completeness and accuracy of the information in the reports used by management in the reviews. Matters that might be relevant to this evaluation include how the company determines that—
    The data included in the report are accurate and complete. This evaluation might be accomplished through testing controls over the initiation, authorization, processing, and recording of the respective transactions that feed into the report.
    The relevant computer settings established by the software user are consistent with the objectives of management's review. For example, if management's review is based on items in an exception report, the reliability of the report depends on whether the settings for reporting exceptions are appropriate.

The auditor verifies that the code in the packaged software cannot be changed by the user. The auditor also evaluates the IT general controls that are important to the effective operation of the IT-dependent controls (such as the access controls and operations controls previously described).

(Example 5-1 PCAOB *Guidance*, pp. 30–31)

Planning and Testing Operating Effectiveness of Internal Control over Financial Reporting

1. Learn the relationships of a control, evidence available, and tests of the control, including IT impacts.
2. Recognize the importance of audit considerations such as fraud, illegal acts, related parties, multiple locations, and service providers in controls tests.
3. Learn how sampling is applied to controls tests and the risks associated with sampling.
4. Understand the audit risk model.
5. Learn what is included in audit documentation and why it is important.
6. Understand the important judgments involved in evaluating test results and the impact of the severity of ICFR deficiencies.
7. Discuss the practical application of control concepts to ICFR audits.
8. Apply the results of ICFR tests to financial statement audit plans.

Chapter 8 Resources

AU 230, AICPA, PCAOB, *Due Professional Care in the Performance of Work*

AU 312, AICPA, PCAOB, *Audit Risk and Materiality in Conducting an Audit*

AU 314, AICPA, *Understanding the Entity and Its Environment and Assessing the Risks of Material Misstatement*

AU 316, AICPA, PCAOB, *Consideration of Fraud in a Financial Statement Audit*

AU 317, AICPA, PCAOB, *Illegal Acts by Clients*

AU 318, AICPA, *Performing Audit Procedures in Response to Assessed Risks and Evaluating the Audit Evidence Obtained*

AU 319, PCAOB, *Consideration of Internal Control in a Financial Statement Audit*

AU 324, AICPA, PCAOB, *Service Organizations*

AU 326, AICPA, *Audit Evidence*

AU 326, PCAOB, *Evidential Matter*

AU 329, AICPA, PCAOB, *Analytical Procedures*

AU 334, AICPA, PCAOB, *Related Parties*

AU 339, AICPA, *Audit Documentation*

AU 350, AICPA, PCAOB, *Audit Sampling*

FASB ASC 450-20-20, Accounting for Contingencies

FASB ASC 850-10-20, Related Party Disclosures

PCAOB AS 3, *Audit Documentation*

PCAOB AS 5 *An Audit of Internal Control Over Financial Reporting That is Integrated with an Audit of Financial Statements*

PCAOB Release 2004-001 *An Audit of Internal Control Over Financial Reporting Performed in Conjunction with an Audit of Financial Statements*

INTRODUCTION

Auditors evaluate the design of internal control over financial reporting (ICFR) and then test the operating effectiveness of the important controls. Auditors test operations of controls to gain audit evidence regarding whether the ICFR operate as they have been designed and whether the individuals who are involved are competent and authorized to perform their tasks. When the auditor evaluates whether the design of ICFR is effective, the auditor can conclude only about the possibility of ICFR performing effectively. If the design is inadequate, ICFR cannot be effective. However, even if the design is effective, ICFR must operate as planned in order to be effective. The auditor evaluates the operating effectiveness of ICFR to express an opinion on ICFR and to confirm that the plans made for relying on ICFR effectiveness for the financial statement audit are appropriate.

Chapter 6 discussed overall audit planning and explained that selecting the controls to test for operating effectiveness can only occur after the auditor assesses design effectiveness. Understanding the client's system and assessing design effectiveness were covered in Chapter 7. This chapter addresses testing the operating effectiveness of ICFR. Exhibit 8-1 presents audit activities during tests of operating effectiveness.

SELECTING THE CONTROLS TO TEST [LO 1]

Through understanding the company's ICFR and testing and evaluating the design effectiveness of ICFR, the auditor has identified those controls that must operate as planned for ICFR to be effective. In planning the appropriate tests of operating effectiveness, the auditor considers:

- Points at which material misstatements from errors or fraud could occur, considering both financial statement misstatements and unauthorized acquisition, use, or disposition of the company's assets
- Nature of controls implemented by management to prevent or detect misstatements
- Significance of each control, such as whether the control achieves more than one control objective and whether more than one control is needed to achieve the objective
- Risks likely to affect whether the controls operate effectively

EXHIBIT 8-1
Tests of ICFR Operating
Effectiveness

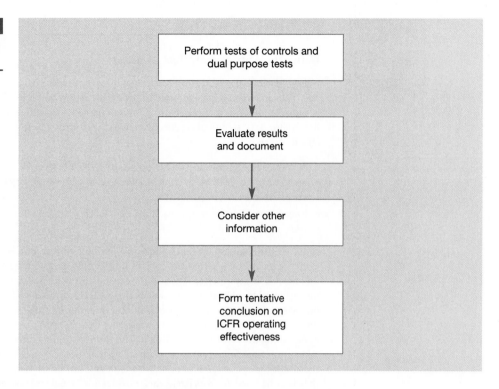

Locations and business units of the company and its use of service organizations also affect decisions on tests of operating effectiveness.

TESTING METHODS

Of the procedures for gathering evidence, the ones presented by AS 5 as useful in *testing controls* include **inquiry**, **inspection**, **observation**, and **reperformance**. Recall that **recalculation**, which can simply be viewed as a specific type of reperformance, may also be included in the list of audit procedures useful for testing ICFR.

The testing procedure used depends on the nature of the evidence available and the objective of the test. For example, *inquiry* of appropriate personnel is a means for the auditor to test whether employees understand how to properly perform control procedures. The auditor can also ask whether the control is performed regularly, what the outcomes are, and what the employee has done in the past when the control identified a problem. Although inquiry alone is not sufficient to support operating effectiveness of controls, it adds to or corroborates other test procedures (AS 5.50).

Inspection of relevant documentation is appropriate to test controls that require documentary evidence. For example, document inspection can ensure that documents are complete, or signatures or initials are noted on documents as required. Inspection can be used, for example, to test whether controls requiring credit checks and approvals prior to completing a sale function effectively. *Observation* is an audit procedure the auditor uses to test the way controls are performed. The auditor may observe employee activities to test whether the designated employee performs a specific procedure or whether a procedure is performed correctly. The clear drawback to observation is that it tests the performance of a control only at the time the observation occurs and conditions may change. *Reperformance* of the application of a control is an effective test when documentary evidence of the control exists. For instance, the auditor can recalculate numbers on a document to test whether the automated or manual control that verifies accuracy worked properly the first time.

AUDITING IN ACTION

Using the Appropriate Test Method

Nelson Marine Sales produces a report that lists recent sales invoices and gross margins of each sale. The sales manager is supposed to review the report and investigate invoices with unusually high or low gross margins. During the internal control testing phase of the integrated audit, the auditor tests the operating effectiveness of the control. The following test options are available to the auditor:

- Ask the sales manager whether he or she investigates high and low margin sales.
- Inspect reports or other documentation used in or generated by the sales manager during the review and investigation process.
- Evaluate whether appropriate actions were taken when called for on high and low margin sales.

Inquiry of the sales manager is a reasonable step but does not, by itself, provide sufficient evidence regarding whether the control is operating. Inspecting the reports and other documents is also appropriate. The auditor can look for evidence such as the initials of the sales manager and the date the review was performed. However, unless it is required that the sales manager initial the form, absence of initials does not indicate a problem. Furthermore, the presence of initials and a date simply indicates that the sales manager went through the steps of obtaining the form and initialing it. The auditor cannot conclude that a thorough review and appropriate follow-up was performed based on the evidence of initials on the form. If the auditor identifies transactions with high and low gross margins and evaluates whether they were handled appropriately, this provides additional corroboration that the control was operating effectively. Proper handling of transactions that are the object of the control indicates that the sales manager looked at the reports, performed a realistic inspection, and took appropriate actions.

(Adapted from AS 2, Appendix D)

The auditor performs the audit procedure that tests whether the control objective is achieved. A **control objective** is

> a specific target against which to evaluate the effectiveness of controls. A control objective…relates to a relevant assertion and states a criterion for evaluating whether the company's control procedures in a specific area provide reasonable assurance. (AS 5.A2)

For example, a control objective might specify that disbursements are made only for authorized purchases. The criterion for evaluation is that no disbursements are to be made unless the vendor is on the approved vendor list and the vendor's invoice is supported by an approved purchase order and receiving report. This control objective and evaluation criterion provides a target the auditor can use for comparison to evaluate the operating effectiveness of controls. The auditor can select disbursements and then examine and inspect the underlying documents. The purpose of the examination is to see that the disbursement is to an authorized vendor and that all the required documents are included in the support package. Exhibit 8-2 provides examples of assertions, objectives, and evaluation criteria for selected transactions.

CAATs

Computer-assisted audit techniques, frequently called CAATs, can be useful to the auditor in tests of control procedures as well as other audit activities. Auditors utilize computers for many of the procedures they perform on an audit and for preparing audit work papers. The

EXHIBIT 8-2

Examples of
Management
Assertions, Control
Objectives, and
Evaluation Criteria

Management Assertion	Control Objective	Criterion for Evaluation
Occurrence	Disbursements are made only for authorized purchases.	1. Disbursement is to a vendor on the approved vendor list
		2. Vendor's invoice is supported by an approved purchase order and receiving report.
Rights, Valuation	All sales transactions using credit cards follow credit card issuers' required procedures so that receivables are collectible from credit card issuers.	1. Credit cards are scanned at the point of sale, and an electronic approval is received before completing the sale.
		2. Credit cards are inspected by the cashier for customer signature.
		3. Customer signature is obtained on sales processing document.
Occurrence	Payroll disbursements are only made to current employees for labor actually provided.	1. The payroll master file is kept up to date to reflect new hires and separations
		2. Disbursements are to employees on the payroll master file.
		3. Disbursements are for amounts earned that are consistent with rates documented in personnel files and hours worked supported by time records or salaries supported by contracts.

basic requirements of audit documentation for the audit of a public company come from AS 3. The following list provides some general concepts describing the use of CAATS:

Work papers are usually constructed using computers and are kept in electronic form.

References for auditing and accounting standards are typically kept in electronic files and accessed via computer inquiry or search.

Audit teams communicate and work in groups using communication software.

Audit budget and time reports are maintained using audit software.

Auditors can use software to calculate appropriate sizes of samples. The software can aid in designing and selecting the sample.

Other audit software utilizes artificial intelligence and expert systems to assess risk and plan tests.

CAATs are used to perform various ICFR tests of an audit client's software applications, including reperforming procedures. For example, computer audit software can recalculate totals and verify the data integrity of an audit client's electronic files. Auditors may test whether a client software application is performing correctly by processing a file of test data and checking the results. Use of CAATs permits the auditor to examine an entire file for characteristics of interest rather than limiting the audit work to a sample of the population. Other computer-assisted audit procedures may be applied in complex computer environments. Appendix A to this chapter further discusses the use of audit software.

AUDITING IN ACTION

Audit Functions Assisted by Software Tools

Electronic work papers

Communications

Group interaction

Administrative tasks

   Time records

   Client Billing

Accounting and auditing standards reference files

Statistical sampling and related analysis

Data extraction

Recomputation

Test data analysis

Other data analysis

Statistical analysis and analytical procedures

REVIEW QUESTIONS

A.1 What is a control objective?

A.2 What procedures can be accomplished using automated audit software and CAATS?

A.3 How can the use of CAATS prevent an auditor from having to rely on sampling?

PLANNING THE TESTS

To plan the tests of the operating effectiveness of controls the auditor must:

- Define the potential error that results from failure of the control and the appropriate evidence related to the error.
- Identify when testing should be performed.
- Determine the extent of testing needed—how many different types of tests should be performed and how many items to test.

Define the Error and Identify Evidence Related to the Error

Direct documentary evidence does not exist for some controls. "Softer" internal controls identified by the Committee of Sponsoring Organizations of the Treadway Commission (COSO) Internal Control (IC) Framework, such as management's philosophy and operating style, will have little supporting documentary evidence. Audit evidence regarding management's philosophy and operating style might be inferred from documents such as the company's mission statement and code of conduct. For these types of soft controls, the appropriate tests are inquiry of appropriate personnel, corroborated by observing company activities and reading any related documents.

Identifying the control and the control's purpose, and defining what constitutes a failure in the control affect which audit evidence is relevant. Once the relevant evidence is identified, the auditor must consider whether that evidence is available.

Suppose that the controls the auditor needs to test are as follows:

Document packages supporting cash disbursements are reviewed by an authorized person.

Document packages signed by the authorized person indicate that the review has been completed and payment of the bill is approved.

Evidence can be examined for different criteria that indicate different levels of control effectiveness.

The following example suggests that different evidence for testing a cash disbursement transaction is appropriate based on how the control is defined.

- The auditor can inspect the "voucher package" (a term referring to the documents supporting the transaction) to verify that there is a signature on the document and that the signature is of someone who is authorized to provide the approval. Finding the signature indicates that the voucher package was handled and signed by the authorized party. The existence of the signature does not indicate that the person performed a substantive review of the voucher package before signing.

- The auditor can reperform the control review that is called for by the company. In this case the auditor checks to be sure that the prices are correct and that calculations such as extensions (price times quantity) and additions are correct. If the company uses an approved vendor list, the auditor traces the vendor name to the approved list. The auditor looks for all the documents that are supposed to be included in the package before the bill is paid. If the auditor does not find any errors and the voucher package has been signed by an authorized person, this indicates that the voucher is correct and that it was appropriate for the company to pay the bill. This reperformance step does not tell the auditor that the signer actually performed the required review. The signer *may* have performed the review and found the voucher package to be correct. Alternatively, the signer *may not* have performed a substantive review, but it did not cause any problems because the voucher was correct and the package complete.

- The auditor can reperform the control review and then talk to the signer to corroborate and extend the evidence. This inquiry step includes asking the reviewer questions such as:

    1. What procedures do you perform when inspecting and approving a voucher package for payment?
    2. Do you perform these procedures consistently on all voucher packages before signing them?
    3. What do you look for when you inspect a voucher package?
    4. How many errors in voucher packages have you found and over what time period?

- Although this inquiry is not sufficient on its own, and there is no guarantee that the employee will be truthful with the auditor, the answers to these questions can corroborate the inspection and reperformance steps.

- Finally, in addition to the inspection, reperformance, and inquiry steps, the auditor can obtain evidence about company-level monitoring controls. Obtaining this evidence may include investigating oversight of the person authorizing the voucher packages and inquiring about the quality of that person's performance.

(AS 2.97)

Plan the Timing and Extent of Testing

The auditor identifies the controls to be tested, defines the circumstances that indicate failure of the control, and identifies the sources of evidence available. Then he or she can determine whether the audit test will consist of inquiry, inspection, observation, reperformance, or some combination of these methods. Next the auditor decides the timing of the test—when it is to be performed—and the extent of testing. These decisions are affected by the risk related to the control. Risks associated with a control are:

1. the risk that a control might not be effective and
2. the risk that if a control is not effective a material weakness would result.

(AS 5.46)

Important questions that determine risk associated with a control include:

1. What misstatement is the control intended to prevent or detect?
2. What is the materiality of the potential misstatement?
3. How much risk does the account or activity have in the absence of any controls; in other words, what is the inherent risk?
4. Has the volume of transactions increased?
5. Has the nature of the activity or transactions to which the control relates changed?
6. Is there a history of errors in the account to which the control applies?
7. How frequently does the control operate?
8. When does the control operate?
9. Are entity-level controls, particularly monitoring controls, effective?
10. Does the control rely on the effectiveness of other controls? For example, do IT general controls have to be effective in order for the control to operate effectively?
11. What additional tests will be needed later in the financial reporting period if the control is tested at an interim date before the end of the fiscal year?
12. Who executes the control?
13. Is a high level of competence required of the person carrying out the control for it to be effective?
14. Have there been changes in the personnel who monitor or carry out the control?
15. Is the control automated or manual?
16. Is the control procedure complex?
17. How important are judgments to the effective operations of the control?

(AS 5.47)

Answers to all of these questions influence the nature, timing, and extent of audit procedures necessary to provide audit evidence that a control operates effectively.

TIMING OF TESTS

The frequency with which controls operate affects not only the time frame in which the operation of the control is tested, but also the sample size required. Some controls operate continuously. An example is controls over routine transactions like sales transactions. In contrast, some controls operate only on specific occasions. Among these are controls over the period-end financial reporting process or controls for the physical inventory count process.

The audit procedures for testing automated controls that operate continuously or frequently differ from those that are used for manual controls that operate with similar frequency. For example, automated controls in a computer environment that has not changed during the period being audited require testing of fewer items or occurrences of the control. Auditors may test as few as one transaction or operation of the control. Testing one transaction is known as benchmarking and is discussed in the next section.

Auditors limit the extent of tests of automated controls because the controls function in a consistent manner. Limited testing of automated controls can be appropriate if the controls are embedded in an environment of effective **IT general controls (ITGC)**. If the operating effectiveness of a control is tested early in the period, the auditor may decide to repeat testing close to the end of the period.

A manual control—one that requires human performance and judgment—that operates continuously or frequently needs more testing than an automated control that operates with similar frequency. Using audit software, the auditor may even be able to check an *entire* population—such as all of the transactions during the year. When this is the audit plan, the timing of the tests may be split or they may all occur after year end. A controls test conducted using audit software is for a specific characteristic such as mathematical accuracy. Whether the transaction is with an authorized party is another characteristic for which an entire data file or population is examined using audit software. For example, all payments by check may be audited to see that they are issued only to vendors on an approved vendor list. All sales on credit may be audited to determine whether they are all with approved customers.

Benchmarking

Benchmarking, a testing strategy for completely automated controls, relies on the assumption that **automated controls** are going to continue to function in a consistent manner unless something changes within the program or in the surrounding environment. This is one of the strengths of IT. Through benchmarking the auditor tests a computer application at a baseline point in time and establishes that it functions properly.

In the initial year, the auditor tests whether the program and its **application control** function correctly, and whether the entity's ITGC are effective. If so, then in subsequent audits the auditor can rely on the "benchmark" tests of application controls and limit testing to the ITGC. The ITGC tests are performed during each year's annual audit. ITGC include those controls that prevent application programs from being accessed or changed in an unauthorized way. If the audit collects sufficient appropriate evidence that programs are changed only when authorized, then when program changes are implemented the auditor retests the application controls. The retesting establishes a new baseline that can be relied on in future audits. The auditor must retest the application controls to establish a new baseline after a period of time, even when no changes occur. How often the auditor performs new benchmark testing in the absence of changes is determined by professional judgment (AS 5.28-33).

AUDITING IN ACTION

Benchmark Testing

Van CPAs has audited Smith & Co. for three years. During the past year, 2010, Smith & Co. completely revamped its computer system. The audit team decides this is a good time to implement benchmark testing on the audit. For the integrated audit of the fiscal year ending 2010, the audit team uses audit software to test the application programs, including controls. The tests produce no indications of control problems with the computer applications.

During the course of the audit the audit team also tests Smith & Co.'s general IT controls. Given their plan to rely on the benchmark tests of the application programs, the team pays special attention to the general controls for access and changes to application programs. The audit does not find any important deficiencies in IT general controls in the 2010 audit.

Smith & Co. does not need to update its computer system in the years 2011 and 2012. So, in these years the Van audit team begins its work on the IT system by testing general controls. In both years, the audit team finds general controls to be effective. Consequently, they choose to rely on the 2010 benchmark tests for audit evidence on the application programs.

During 2013 Smith & Co. decides to update its sales and billing application program to take advantage of the streamlined processes offered by the credit card vendors it accepts. Since it has been three years since the application programs were tested, and the sales and billing program has been changed, the audit team tests the operation of all the computer application programs during the 2013 integrated audit.

Benchmarking is only appropriate when

- both ITGC and application controls are effective.
- ITGC remain strong from year to year.
- the application programs do not change.

In appropriate situations benchmarking can be effective and very efficient. One example is when the audit client uses purchased software and the vendor has designed the program so that the source code cannot easily be modified or altered (AS 5.B32). Vendor-protected source code is vulnerable to alteration, but the risk is generally low because the vulnerability is limited to changes made by a sufficiently skilled programmer, who is allowed enough time and attempts to hack into the program.

Document Availability

Some controls can be tested at any time after their operation by inspection of documents—either paper or electronic—and reperformance of the control steps. But, the auditor needs to remain aware of the possibility that the electronic documentation may be retained in the company's records for a limited period of time. Even paper documents may be kept in their original form for only a limited time, after which they are scanned and retained electronically and the paper is destroyed.

When a company's documentary evidence is retained for limited periods of time or hard-copy records are changed into electronic format, the auditor considers this policy when developing the audit plan. In addition, the audit plan has to deal with the fact that some controls do not provide documentary evidence. Often these are the "soft" controls mentioned earlier. If a control does not produce documentary evidence, it must be tested while it is actually operating.

REVIEW QUESTIONS

B.1 How does the way a control failure is defined affect the audit evidence that is needed?

B.2 What affects the risks associated with a control?

B.3 What types of characteristics of transactions can be easily checked with CAATs?

B.4 What is benchmarking?

B.5 What impact does the client's retention policy for electronic and paper documentation have on the auditor's plan for testing ICFR?

Updating Interim Audit Work

When auditors perform control testing at an interim date, additional tests are usually needed closer to the end of the fiscal period. The period between the interim test date and fiscal year end is called the roll-forward period. Often auditors test controls early in the fiscal year and perhaps even at multiple points in time. Early testing gives the auditor additional evidence about the financial information that ultimately flows into the financial statements.

Auditors must test the operating effectiveness of ICFR at year end to issue an ICFR opinion. In addition, if the plan for financial statement audit evidence depends on the effectiveness of controls, the auditor must test the effectiveness of ICFR for the entire period being audited. The audit planning standards describe an audit plan that relies on the effectiveness of ICFR as one that sets "control risk at less than the maximum."

In other words, if the auditor assumes maximum control risk, he or she assumes the controls do not operate effectively. Consequently, the auditor will not plan to rely on the ICFR in the financial statement audit. In contrast, to conclude that control risk is *less* than the maximum, the auditor must test the function of the controls. To rely on ICFR in the financial statement audit, the auditor must test operating effectiveness of controls to determine whether the preliminary expectation about effective operation is valid.

Auditors may choose to test controls well before the "as of" or year-end date simply because they are less busy at those times. Then, the audit work that must be performed during busier times is limited to tests of the roll-forward period. Another advantage of testing controls early is that it is more likely to provide management the time to remediate (correct) any deficiencies that are discovered. This can impact the ICFR audit opinion if management is able to correct major problems before year end.

In determining what tests to perform during the roll forward period, the auditor considers which controls were tested earlier and the results of those tests. The auditor also considers how much evidence was collected earlier in the year, what length of time has passed since the tests were performed, and whether any changes were made to ICFR after the interim testing.

This last question is very important if deficiencies in ICFR were found at the interim date and management has taken steps to correct the deficiencies. The auditor needs to test the controls to obtain evidence about whether the deficiencies have actually been corrected. Even without changes to the system, the auditor needs to perform some roll-forward period tests to update the earlier ICFR conclusions and verify their continued relevance at the "as of" date to issue an audit opinion on ICFR.

The auditor may not need to test controls that were in place earlier in the year if they have been changed or were replaced later during the year under audit. For example, the auditor may not need to test the original controls if management decides to change the controls or remediate an ICFR deficiency before the auditor has performed any tests of the operation of that control. The auditor may decide to limit testing to the new controls that have been put in place.

Management, rather than the auditor, may identify the problem and initiate changes to the system. When this happens, for *purposes of the ICFR audit*, the auditor only tests the "new" controls. The auditor must judge whether the new controls are functioning effectively at the "as of" date at the fiscal year end. To do this, the auditor decides if the controls have been in place long enough and sufficient audit evidence has been obtained to reach that conclusion.

A change in controls during the year has additional implications for the financial statement audit. Even if ICFR is functioning effectively after the implementation of the new controls, the auditor must consider the impact of the earlier controls on producing fair financial statements for the entire period. If the controls in place early in the year were not effective and the auditor did not test them, more substantive evidence about the affected account balances is needed. During the financial statement audit, more evidence is collected for the part of the year when the auditor cannot rely on the controls.

EXTENT OF TESTS

The auditor must obtain sufficient evidence to form an opinion on the effectiveness of ICFR each year. This means that each audit must collect *persuasive* evidence about the effectiveness of *all* controls for relevant assertions for *all* significant accounts and disclosures *every year*. The auditor can rely on information learned about the company and its ICFR in prior-year audits and use that information to plan the nature, timing, and extent of tests needed in the current year. The auditor should vary the tests year to year to introduce unpredictability into the audit. The auditor might vary which tests are performed at the **interim testing date**, increase or decrease the number of tests performed for each control, and change the audit procedures performed.

The extent of testing needed to provide the auditor with evidence that a control is performing effectively depends on the nature of the control. For instance, **manual controls**—those relying on the company's personnel—generally require more testing than automated controls. The auditor needs to test many operations of a manual control and evaluate the results of the multiple tests. The auditor may test a sample of transactions each month for a control that relies on human performance, such as reviewing a voucher package or performing a manual reconciliation.

Alternatively, if an application control is automated and the ITGC are operating effectively, the auditor may only need to test a single transaction, or rely on the benchmarking approach, to determine that the control is functioning. ITGC, discussed in Appendix A to Chapter 7, provide assurance regarding authorization for program changes and access to programs and data. The auditor must have assurance that ITGC function effectively in order to rely on benchmarking or a "one-item" test approach to testing an application control.

Complexity, judgments involved, and competency required of the person executing the control affect the extent of tests needed. For example, the process of cross checking the number of items received in a shipment to an order document and the shipping document is straightforward and requires little judgment or technical skills. Consequently, from a complexity perspective such a control requires less extensive testing than a control over the decision to borrow from a line of credit. The decision to borrow from a line of credit is based on judgments regarding a company's current cash situation along with projections for its future cash needs. Such cash flow decisions require many judgments and specific skills to make those judgments. If these cash and borrowing decisions have the potential to be material to the financial statements, the auditor needs to test controls over line of credit decisions extensively.

A different consideration that affects the extent of testing is the frequency with which the control operates. Using the receiving example in the prior paragraph, when frequency of operation is also considered, the decision regarding the extent of testing required might change. The process of receiving goods, comparing the receipts to the order and shipping documents, and identifying exceptions is straightforward and not difficult. However, if it is a manual process it requires more testing. Also, the control operates frequently—every time a shipment is received. Given these specific conditions, controls over receiving need more extensive audit testing than an equally simple manual control that is executed, for example, only once a month.

The "extent of testing" decision is based on various issues. The auditor considers whether a control is manual or automated and the frequency with which it operates. The auditor also considers the importance of the control. For example, if the only important factor is that a control operates infrequently the extent of testing might be minimal. But if it is a very important control—such as a control over period-end financial reporting—the extent of testing needs to be greater even if it operates infrequently.

Period-End Reporting Process

The auditor will probably not test the controls over period-end financial reporting at the end of each month or each quarter. However, because the process is so important, when the operation of the controls is tested at year-end closing, the audit procedures will likely include extensive tests and in-depth evaluation. The controls that affect the period-end financial reporting process provide assurance regarding many financial statement assertions. Therefore, relatively more controls within the process will be tested. Exhibit 8-3 provides examples of entity-level controls over the period-end financial reporting process that a company may have and the auditor may test.

Other control risks affect the auditor's decisions about the extent of testing needed to obtain sufficient audit evidence. The auditor's assessment of the risks of **fraud** and illegal acts and the existence of transactions with related parties are important considerations.

EXHIBIT 8-3

Examples of Controls in the Period-End Financial Reporting Process

Process	Control
Input to financial reporting process	
	General controls over access, changes, and postings to the general ledger are maintained.
	General controls over access and changes to the chart of accounts are maintained.
	General controls over segregation of duties are maintained.
	General controls are maintained over postings of the general ledger to/from subsidiary ledgers and journals.
	General controls are maintained to investigate and appropriately manage any unauthorized postings.
	The company's accounting policies are kept current and consistent with current GAAP and other specifically applicable standards (international, SEC, etc.) as approved by high-level accounting and financial personnel and the audit committee.
	Interpretation of GAAP in company policies is correct as approved by high-level accounting and financial personnel and the audit committee.
	Transactions are posted only if they are in accordance with the company's accounting policies.
	Estimation methods are agreed to be appropriate by knowledgeable, authorized company personnel.
	Assumptions underlying estimates are appropriate; support for the assumptions is documented and agreed to by knowledgeable, authorized company personnel.
Authorization to input journal entries	
	Authorization to draft, approve, and input journal entries is reviewed for incompatible functions (segregation of duties concerns) by management on a regular basis.
	Access authorization for consistency with management decisions is confirmed after each management review.
Recording journal entries	
	The system rejects entries that do not balance, providing an error message to the person inputting the entry.
	Access controls reject attempts to input recurring and nonrecurring transactions, including journal entries and closing entries from users who are not specifically authorized to enter that type of transaction.
	System alerts are created when users attempt to input entries for which they are not authorized.
Development, approval, and input of nonrecurring journal entries	
	All nonrecurring journal entries are developed and input by personnel with a sufficient level of knowledge, who are authorized to do so.

(continued)

Before being entered, all nonrecurring journal entries are approved by an individual authorized to provide the approval and at a higher level in the organization.

Approval steps must include an examination of all supporting documents by the individual authorized to provide the approval, including an analysis of any dates involved.

After entry, the authorizing individual must follow up to be sure the entry was posted properly, including in the proper period.

Review of all posted nonrecurring journal entries is performed by management.

Closing process

All departments (or other organizational segments) submit closing entries for management's review using a standard format.

The company uses a standard set of recurring period-end closing entries that include all recurring accruals, depreciation/amortization, valuation, and cutoff entries.

Each item in the set of standard entries is compared to entries posted during the closing process, and discrepancies are noted, investigated, and corrected as necessary.

Activity in all relevant accounts is suspended (accounts are locked down) during the closing process by specific individuals authorized to begin and end the suspension of activity.

Drafting the financial statements

Balances from the general ledger are imported electronically into the software that prepares the financial statements.

Totals of the general ledger are compared to those received by the financial reporting package, with discrepancies investigated and corrected.

The financial reporting package is reviewed regularly for consistency with GAAP criteria and updated as needed.

IT-produced financial statements are reviewed, and amounts are recalculated manually by authorized personnel (to provide appropriate segregation of duties from those involved in the automated production).

Disclosure in financial statements

Authorized nonaccounting/finance personnel review and approve disclosures related to their technical/management areas.

Authorized accounting personnel review and approve disclosure for accuracy, based on supporting documentation as appropriate.

CFO (or equivalent) approves all disclosure prior to inclusion in financial statements.

Final management changes

All changes to financial statement balances and disclosure instigated and approved by top management are documented and approved by the CFO (or equivalent).

REVIEW QUESTIONS

C.1 What is the roll-forward period? What audit procedures occur related to the roll-forward period?

C.2 If the client changes the accounting information system during the year, what impact does this have on the auditor's tests of ICFR? Do controls have to be tested before and after the change? Why or why not? What impact might this have on the financial statement audit?

C.3 Why does a manual control require more tests of operating effectiveness than an automated control?

C.4 How does the complexity of a control and judgments required to apply it affect the extent of testing?

C.5 Why does the period-end reporting process require extensive controls testing?

FRAUD [LO 2]

The auditor's assessment of fraud risk begins with the client acceptance and continuance process and continues as the auditor gains an understanding of the system and assesses design of ICFR. In addition to looking for and testing specific controls intended to prevent fraud (anti-fraud controls), the audit team is continually aware of new information that may indicate fraud risk. The audit team should communicate and "brainstorm" about new information.

When planning the extent of tests of ICFR operating effectivess, the auditor includes specific tests of anti-fraud controls and plans other tests based on the expected risk of fraud. For example, auditors inquire of management and other company personnel about the likelihood of fraud. Auditors discuss their understanding of any fraud risk with members of the **audit committee**. The auditor inquires of the internal auditor about procedures intended to prevent or detect fraud. In addition, the auditor specifically considers fraud risk related to revenue recognition (AU 316.41). The auditor may conduct more tests or use larger sample sizes if there is a high risk of fraud (AU 316.52). A constant underlying consideration is that there is some threshold at which fraud risk is deemed too high for the auditor to be confident of producing a reliable audit opinion.

Consideration of fraud initially affects audit planning for tests of controls. However, fraud consideration is ongoing, and results of tests of operating effectiveness may also affect subsequent audit procedures. For example, results of tests of controls, including anti-fraud controls, may cause the auditor to perform additional tests or modify the plan for the financial statement audit.

ILLEGAL ACTS [LO 2]

Illegal acts are violations of laws and government regulations. Although fraud is illegal, in auditing literature the term **illegal acts** typically refers to behavior other than fraud. Auditors are not the final decision makers in determining whether an act is illegal. Whether an action violates a law is a legal judgment. Therefore, auditors focus on the *impact* of illegal acts on the financial statements.

Audit planning, including planning the extent of audit tests, focuses on the possibility of illegal acts that have a direct and material effect on the financial statements. Examples of illegal acts that may have a direct and material effect on the financial statements are tax laws that affect the amount of tax accruals and tax expense, and regulations that affect how much revenue can be recognized under government contracts (AU 317.05). Auditors consider the risk of *direct* and *material* illegal acts when deciding the extent of controls testing to be performed.

Other illegal acts do not have a direct effect on the financial statements but can have an indirect effect—typically, contingent liabilities that may exist because of the illegal act.

AUDITING IN ACTION

Examples of Control Test Results that May Affect Auditor Assessment of Fraud Risk

- Transactions that are not recorded in a complete or timely manner
- Transactions that are improperly recorded as to amount, accounting period, classification, or entity policy
- Unsupported or unauthorized balances or transactions
- Last-minute adjustments that significantly affect financial results
- Evidence of employees' access to systems and records inconsistent with that necessary to perform their authorized duties
- Tips or complaints to the auditor about alleged fraud
- Missing documents
- Documents that appear to have been altered
- Unavailability of original documents or electronic evidence
- Unexplained items on reconciliations
- Inconsistent, vague, or implausible explanations from management or employees
- Unusual and unexplained discrepancies among items of audit evidence
- Lack of evidence for program changes, etc. that are required by ITGC
- Missing electronic evidence
- Missing inventory or physical assets of significant magnitude

(AU 316.68)

Examples of indirect illegal acts are those related to securities trading, occupational safety and health, food and drug administration, environmental protection, equal employment, and price fixing or other antitrust violations.

In deciding on the extent of testing for ICFR operating effectiveness, the auditor does not actively consider these illegal acts that do not have a direct effect on the financial statements. However, if the auditor becomes aware of illegal acts that have an indirect effect on the financial statements, further audit testing is required. Just as with fraud, results of ICFR operations tests can provide evidence suggesting the possibility of illegal acts. This evidence might also be found during the financial statement audit.

AUDITING IN ACTION

Examples of Control Testing Evidence that May Affect Auditor Assessment of the Likelihood of Illegal Acts

- Unauthorized transactions, improperly recorded transactions, or transactions not recorded in a complete or timely manner in order to maintain accountability for assets
- Investigation by a governmental agency, an enforcement proceeding, or payment of unusual fines or penalties
- Violations of laws or regulations cited in reports of examinations by regulatory agencies that have been made available to the auditor
- Large payments for unspecified services to consultants, affiliates, or employees
- Sales commissions or agents' fees that appear excessive in relation to those normally paid by the client or to the services actually received
- Unusually large payments in cash, purchases of bank cashiers' checks in large amounts payable to bearer, transfers to numbered bank accounts, or similar transactions
- Unexplained payments made to government officials or employees
- Failure to file tax returns or pay government duties or similar fees that are common to the entity's industry or the nature of its business

(AU 317.09)

AUDITING IN ACTION

Indirect Illegal Act: Watering the Liquor

During interim testing of ICFR of a publicly traded bar and restaurant chain, the auditor identified checks written to pay fines because the bars and restaurants in several locations were diluting liquor supplies with water. While this illegal act was indirectly related to the financial statements, the auditor had to consider the potential impact on food and beverage sales if the violation became widely known. Further investigation, based on reading minutes of the Board of Directors meeting after the penalty payments were made, indicated that the Board cracked down on the managers of the locations where the problem was occurring and the problem was corrected. A review of checks written from that time to the current date showed that the company was not fined again.

RELATED PARTY TRANSACTIONS [LO 2]

Operating effectiveness of controls over related party transactions will likely be tested extensively. **Related party transactions** are transactions conducted with an entity or a person meeting the definition of a related party set forth in the FASB definition of related parties. Related parties include:

a. Affiliates of the entity

b. Entities for which investments in their equity securities would be required, absent the election of the fair value option under the Fair Value Option Subsection of Section 825–10–14, to be accounted for by the equality method by the investing entity

c. Trusts for the benefit of employees, such as pension and profit-sharing trusts that are managed by or under the trusteeship of management

d. Principal owners of the entity and members of their immediate families

e. Management of the entity and members of their immediate families

f. Other parties with which the entity may deal if one party controls or can significantly influence the management or operating policies of the other to an extent that one of the transacting parties might be prevented from fully pursuing its own separate interests transaction

g. Other parties that can significantly influence the management or operating polices of the transacting parties or that have an ownership interest in one of the transacting parties and can significantly influence the other to an extent that one or more of the transacting parties might be prevented from fully pursuing its own separate interest.

(FASB ASC 850–10–20)

Auditors are concerned with ICFR over related party transactions. Auditors consider the possibility that the transactions may not be "arms length." If a transaction is not arms length, then the dollar amounts recorded are not the real value of the exchange. Also, the audit addresses whether the financial statement disclosures meet the accounting standard requirements (AU 334). Auditors gather evidence regarding related parties and related party transactions during the financial statement audit. They pay particular attention during ICFR audit steps to identifying and testing the applicable controls.

REVIEW QUESTIONS

D.1 What kinds of illegal acts does the auditor address during testing?

D.2 What happens when the auditor becomes aware of possible illegal acts that have an indirect effect on the financial statements?

D.3 What are the audit concerns about related party transactions? How do these concerns affect the testing of operations of controls?

SAMPLING [LO 3]

Auditors use **sampling** in order to make audit procedures feasible. Basically, an auditor has the option of examining 100% of a company's financial evidence and records or looking at some subset of that information. Obtaining audit evidence based on a subset of the information often involves sampling. Thus, sampling is used on both the ICFR and financial statement phases of an integrated audit. Sampling is applying the audit procedure to less than 100% of a population. The targeted population may be all or a part of the items within an account balance or class of transactions (AU 350.01).

Sampling Risk

When the auditor does not examine or test all of the items in the targeted population of the account balance or class of transactions, **sampling risk** is introduced into the audit processes. Sampling risk is defined as the possibility that the sample does not represent the population from which it is selected (AU 350.10). In ICFR tests of **operating effectiveness**, sampling risk is the risk that rate of failure of controls in the sample of transactions the auditor examines is different from the rate of control failure for the rest of the transactions. The transactions included in the sample might have a larger or smaller rate of control violations than the rest of the transactions. Consequently, if the auditor uses the percent of control errors in the sample as an indicator of the percent of control errors in the entire population of transactions, he or she will come to the wrong conclusion about how well the control is operating.

If an auditor concludes that a control is not working well when it really is, the auditor *incorrectly concludes* that the control is *not functioning effectively*. This audit error is serious but generally does not jeopardize the outcome of the audit. When audit tests indicate that a control is not functioning effectively, the auditor conducts more testing. The additional procedures may confirm that the initial findings are correct, and the auditor may explore for the source of the problem. In contrast, when additional procedures are performed, the auditor may discover that the control is functioning and the initial conclusion was wrong because of **sampling error**. This is an efficiency problem for the audit because more tests are performed than need to be. However, the auditor will catch the error and ultimately come to the correct conclusion that the control is functioning effectively.

Sampling error with a different result can have more serious effects for the audit. If, based on tests of a sample, the auditor *concludes that controls are functioning effectively when they are not,* the auditor has no hint that sampling error has led to an incorrect audit conclusion. In this situation, the auditor has no reason to think there is a need for more testing. Consequently, the error can go undetected during the ICFR stage of the integrated audit. This represents the real risk to an ICFR audit of using samples: the risk of concluding that controls are functioning effectively when they are not.

The risk that the auditor *incorrectly* concludes that the control is *not effective* is called "the risk of assessing control risk too high," or incorrect rejection. Again, this occurs when the control is violated disproportionately more frequently in the sample than in the population. In other words, if the auditor could test the whole population (instead of just a sample), he or she would see that the control operates effectively. An incorrect rejection error is typically discovered through additional audit work. The biggest problem an incorrect rejection error presents is inefficiency because more audit work is performed than would have been necessary if a sample that was actually representative of the population had been used.

The sampling risk that the auditor *incorrectly* concludes that the control *is effective* is called "the risk of assessing control risk too low," or incorrect acceptance. An incorrect acceptance error can damage the audit's effectiveness. The control problem and audit error may still be caught – but if it is, it will be from other procedures of the integrated audit. Tests of details of balances and analytical procedures of the financial statement audit may reveal problems with the account balance. While investigating the account balance problems, the auditor may discover the control problem that was missed. When issuing an audit report on ICFR, or planning to rely on the operating effectiveness of a control during the financial statement audit, the auditor usually plans for a low risk of incorrect acceptance (AU 350.37).

The concepts of incorrect rejection and incorrect acceptance also apply to sampling in the financial statement audit and are presented again in Chapter 9. Exhibit 8-4 presents the concepts of incorrect acceptance and incorrect rejection for ICFR.

Planning the Sample

The auditor identifies the important characteristic that is to be tested when planning a sample. Important characteristics for financial statement audit samples include amounts, account classifications, and proper time period for reporting. The important control characteristic being tested in an audit of ICFR may be that a document exists, a document package is complete, certain steps have been performed, calculations have been verified and are accurate, an authorization is noted, or a transaction is posted correctly.

Based on the characteristic being tested the auditor identifies the physical population from which the sample will be selected, which is sometimes called the sampling frame. This physical population may be all the items in a computer file, a file of paper documents, or even the company's physical inventory. For some tests the sampling frame may be days of the fiscal year.

The auditor may decide that the population should be divided into subgroups before a sample is selected. For instance, if the auditor is testing whether voucher packages are complete and approved before they are paid, the population of transactions might be divided or **stratified** into two subgroups: the largest or most important transactions and all the rest.

The auditor of a manufacturing company might decide that the most important purchase and payment transactions are: (1) those for amounts over $100,000 and (2) those for items that are nonroutine and need to comply with engineering specifications. Those that deal with engineering specifications, would all require special review. Most likely, if the item purchased does not meet the engineering specifications, it cannot be used by the company, it has no value, and company policy is that the item should be rejected and not be paid for.

In this example the auditor separates the total population of purchase and payment transactions into three subgroups: transactions over $100,000; transactions for purchases with engineering specifications, and all other purchase and payment transactions. The auditor can then treat the three types of transactions differently in the testing process. For example, the auditor might examine 100% of the population of transactions over $100,000 for completeness of the voucher package and approval for payment. The auditor might examine 100% of the nonroutine purchases with engineering specifications for approval by an

---

EXHIBIT 8-4

Impact of Sampling Error on Audit Decisions

Auditor's Conclusion about the Control's Operation Based on the Sample		Actual Effectiveness of the Control's Operation in the Whole Population	
		Effective	*Not effective*
	Effective	correct audit decision	incorrect audit decision—incorrect acceptance, effectiveness problem
	Not effective	incorrect audit decision—incorrect rejection, efficiency problem	correct audit decision

AUDITING IN ACTION

Sampling Risk for Control Tests and Substantive Tests

Problem:	Applies to samples for:	What it means:
Assessing Control Risk Too Low	Tests of Controls	Sample indicates control operates effectively when it does not
Assessing Control Risk Too High	Tests of Controls	Sample indicates control does not operate effectively when it does
Incorrect Acceptance	Substantive tests of details	Sample indicates balance is not materially misstated when it is
Incorrect Rejection	Substantive tests of details	Sample indicates balance is materially misstated when it is not

authorized individual from the production department. Finally, the auditor might choose to sample the rest of the transactions and test them for a variety of characteristics such as completeness, accuracy, approval, posting to the proper account and in the proper time period, and payment of the liability. In addition, since information from this audit step is useful for the financial statement audit, the auditor may combine the controls and substantive testing processes, called dual purpose testing. To combine the tests, the auditor examines all three subgroups for accuracy of amount, proper posting and classification, and financial reporting in the proper time period. Knowing the important characteristics to be tested and the nature of the population is very important for designing an effective sample.

Approaches to Sampling

A "big picture" way to classify sampling methods is as either statistical or nonstatistical. Statistical sampling is based on the laws of probability and has the advantage of enabling the auditor to quantify the level of sampling risk associated with the sample (AU 350.46).

A statistical approach requires randomness in the selection process that can be accomplished with various selection methods. A sample may be randomly selected based on identifying document numbers produced by a **random number generator** computer program. A sample may be drawn using a systematic selection, meaning that a specified "skip interval" is used to identify the items included in the sample. When systematic selection is used, it needs random or multiple random starting points. Alternatively, a computer may generate random skip intervals to provide randomness to the sample selection method. Auditors use statistical sampling IT programs to assist them in determining the appropriate sample size and other sample selection specifics.

In contrast to statistical sampling, nonstatistical sampling does not utilize laws of probability. With nonstatistical sampling, the level of sampling risk cannot be quantified. If a nonstatistical approach is planned, the auditor may use the selection approaches already described (random selection, systematic selection) or simply select the items to be included in the sample and tests by picking out items in the population. This method was at one time called **judgment sampling** and is now referred to as **haphazard sampling** because there is no plan or justification for the items selected.

Nonsampling Risk

Both statistical and nonstatistical approaches to sampling carry with them certain risks. Sampling risk has already been mentioned as the risk that the sample is not representative of the population. All samples have sampling risk. All tests, whether applied to a sample or

100% of the population, also have **nonsampling risk**, or the risk of human error. Nonsampling risk includes:

- The risk that the auditor will use an audit procedure that is not appropriate for what the test is intended to accomplish
- The risk that the auditor may fail to detect a problem when applying an audit procedure
- The risk that the auditor may misinterpret an audit result

Nonsampling risk exists in all audit test procedures and cannot be quantified. However, quality control procedures such as training, proper supervision, and review are all intended to reduce and control nonsampling risk (AU 350.11).

Sampling and ICFR Testing

Attribute sampling is the term often used to describe the audit process when an auditor applies sampling methods to an ICFR sampling and testing procedure. The process is used to evaluate the frequency with which a characteristic, or "attribute" occurs in the underlying population based on a sample. In the case of ICFR testing, the attribute for which the auditor is looking is failure of the internal control. The question is, "Does the control fail to operate effectively in the population?" The control is not effective if it fails too frequently.

After the auditor identifies the control to test, defines the failure of the control, and determines the physical population from which to select the sample, he or she determines the sample size. Several decisions must be made in order to determine the size of the sample the auditor should use.

The first decision is how much risk the auditor is willing to accept of concluding that the internal control is operating effectively when it is not. Using the terms defined earlier, we note that this is the risk the auditor is willing to take of making an incorrect acceptance error.

The second decision involves determining the **tolerable deviation rate**. The tolerable rate of deviation is defined as the maximum deviation rate from a prescribed control that the auditor believes can occur in the sample and still permit a conclusion that the control is functioning effectively in the population (AU 350.31). In other words, what percent of the time can the control fail in the sample and the auditor still conclude that it is working effectively? The tolerable rate is based on the rate of deviation that the auditor believes is acceptable, with some added leeway built in to accommodate the fact that the decision is based on a sample.

The third decision deals with the likely rate of deviation in the population. Likely rate of deviation is also called the **expected population deviation rate**. The expected population deviation rate is the percentage of the time that the auditor *expects* the control to fail in the total population (AU 350.41). With these parameters the auditor can determine the required sample size.

The sample size can be calculated based on the principles of statistics. The calculation guides the auditor to use a sample of appropriate size so that he or she can measure and control sampling risk based on statistical analyses. Mathematical calculation of sample size is presented in Appendix B to this chapter. The auditor may also use judgment and non-numeric descriptors of risk to decide on an appropriate sample size.

The relationships between sample size and other characteristics for tests of controls are shown in Exhibit 8-5. These relationships are also reflected in statistical calculations of sample sizes. The auditor considers the direction of the relationships when sample size is based on judgment. For example, if based on professional judgment, the auditor is willing to accept a larger risk of making an incorrect acceptance error, the sample size needed to provide the auditor with sufficient evidence becomes smaller. If the auditor is willing to accept a larger tolerable rate of deviation, the sample size needed becomes smaller.

The logic for the inverse relationship between tolerable rate of deviation and sample size is that more audit evidence (i.e., a larger sample size) is needed to support an assertion

EXHIBIT 8-5

Factors Affecting
Sample Size

For controls testing		
As:		Sample Size:
Risk off assessing control risk too low	increases	decreases
	decreases	increases
Tolerable rate of deviation	increases	decreases
	decreases	increases
Likely rate of deviation in the population	increases	increases
	decreases	decreases
Population size	increases	increases

that the controls "rarely" fail than to support an assertion that controls fail "no more than quite frequently." The same logic applies to the expected population deviation rate, but the relationship is positive rather than inverse. If the expected rate of deviation in the population is larger—in other words, there is an expectation that the control may not work effectively—the auditor needs more evidence—and therefore a larger sample size—to support a conclusion that the control functions effectively. A larger sample is needed. Increases in the size of the population normally increase the sample size, but the impact is not important when the population is very large.

The auditor's next steps are to select the sample, perform the audit tests, identify the deviations (control failures), and analyze the meaning of the results. If the auditor calculates the sample size using principles of statistics and selects the sample using an approach that gives each item in the population an equal chance of being selected, the result may be analyzed statistically as presented in Appendix B.[1] The auditor may also move through these various steps without statistical determination of the sample size or statistical analysis of the results.

Regardless of the approach, the auditor basically uses the deviation rate in the sample as an estimate of the deviation rate in the population and allows for the likelihood that the sample does not exactly mirror the population's characteristics. The auditor concludes that the control is functioning effectively in the population if the sample's failure rate is no higher than the tolerable rate.

REVIEW QUESTIONS

E.1 What is sampling?

E.2 What is sampling risk?

E.3 What is the next step when an auditor concludes, based on a sample, that a control is not operating as designed?

E.4 Why is the risk that an auditor concludes a control is functioning when it is not more important to the audit than concluding that a control is not functioning when it is?

E.5 What does it mean to stratify a population, and why would the auditor do this?

E.6 What is the advantage of using statistical methods in sampling and evaluating the results of audit tests?

E.7 What are the sources of nonsampling risk? How are these controlled and reduced?

E.8 When using statistical methods, why does the auditor set or estimate the tolerable deviation rate and expected population deviation rate?

---

[1]To give each item in the population an equal opportunity of being selected, the selection method must be random, or at least incorporate random elements, such as systematic selection with a random start or random skip intervals.

AUDIT RISK MODEL [LO 4]

Auditors consider risk in developing audit strategy and in planning audit evidence gathering procedures. The approach used by auditors can be explained using a simple algebraic relationship that reflects the way auditors judge acceptable levels of risk based on what they know about their clients. Auditors do not have to use the algebraic relationship. It is shown here as a tool and to present the judgment process that goes into assessing risk and planning audit procedures. Overall **audit risk** is the risk that the auditor may unknowingly fail to appropriately modify the opinions on ICFR and the financial statements.

Other Risks

Audit risk, as the term is used in the auditing standards, is not the only risk the auditor accepts. For example, **engagement risk** is a term used for the overall risk to the auditor of being associated with a client. Engagement risk includes the possibility of financial loss or damage to the audit firm's reputation from a particular client. Addressing engagement risk is one of the important outcomes of client acceptance and continuance procedures discussed in Chapter 5.

As it is defined in the audit risk model, audit risk does not include the risk of incorrect rejection. Recall that incorrect rejection results in inefficiency. The inefficiency occurs because the auditor concludes that ICFR is ineffective or the financial statements are misstated and then, after doing more audit work, finds out that the conclusion was wrong. Additional audit procedures reveal that ICFR is effective and the financial statements are fair. Audit risk also does not incorporate engagement risk such as reputation damage, legal costs, the audit firm not making a profit on an engagement because the bid was too low or unexpected problems arising that require more audit work than was expected.

Audit Risk Model

Addressing audit risk while planning the ICFR and financial statement audits helps the auditor decide on the nature and timing of audit procedures, and extent of testing. The algebraic relationship is:

$$AR = RMM \times DR$$
$$\text{and}$$
$$AR = (IR \times CR) \times (TD \times AP)$$

AR stands for audit risk and is defined as uncertainty inherent in applying audit procedures. For a financial statement audit, it is the risk of issuing an inappropriate audit opinion when the financial statements are materially misstated. For an ICFR audit, it is reasonable to think of audit risk as the risk that the auditor will conclude ICFR is effective when it is not.

Overall, the definitions of the audit risk model are stated in terms of the financial statement audit. But they are important to the ICFR audit because problems with ICFR impact the risk evaluation for the financial statement audit.

RMM is the risk of material financial statement misstatement. This is the risk that an error or a fraud has caused a material misstatement; ICFR did not prevent a misstatement from occurring or detect it on a timely basis after it occurred. As the risk that there is a material misstatement in the financial statements gets larger, the auditor is willing to accept less risk of missing a misstatement while performing the audit. As shown in the equations, RMM is the outcome of IR × CR.

IR stands for **inherent risk** and means the susceptibility of an assertion to material misstatements, assuming no related internal controls (AICPA AU 312.21, PCAOB

AU 312.27). Another way to think about this is the vulnerability of a particular account or transaction type to error or fraud. For instance, transactions that require a lot of judgment or complex calculations, or that involve handling cash, are more vulnerable to misstatement than easily measured, straightforward transactions or those that are handled using bank documents.

CR stands for **control risk** and means the risk that the material misstatements that could occur in an assertion will not be prevented or detected by the internal controls (AICPA AU 312.21, PCAOB AU 312.27).

If controls are good, they can dramatically lower RMM no matter how high the IR. Clearly, CR is related to the ICFR audit. If the auditor concludes that ICFR is not effective, then CR is large.

DR stands for **detection risk**. Detection risk is the risk that the auditor will not detect a material misstatement related to an assertion. The higher the RMM, the less detection risk an auditor can accept. As shown in the equations, DR is a function of TD and AP (AICPA AU 312.26, PCAOB AU 312.27).

TD is the risk that a material misstatement will be missed by the auditor's **tests of details of balances**. A parallel concept in an ICFR audit is that by using controls tests, the auditor will not detect that a control does not operate effectively. A test of details of balances will miss a material misstatement for two reasons: nonsampling error or incorrect acceptance. Proper quality control, including planning, supervision, and review, reduces the risk of nonsampling error. Therefore, when a sample is used, TD is defined as the sampling risk of incorrect acceptance.

AP is the risk that a material misstatement is missed by the audit's analytical procedures.

Overall, for an audit of financial statements the model sets up audit risk as follows:

1. An error or fraud is about to cause a material misstatement in an account balance, and the ICFR does not prevent it; after the misstatement has occurred, ICFR does not detect it.
2. The auditor's tests of details of the account balance do not identify the material error.
3. The auditor's analytical procedures do not identify the material error.
4. As a result of the chain of events, the auditor issues an audit opinion that the financial statements are fair when they are materially misstated.

Since the algebraic relationship is used for planning, its purpose is to help the auditor think about the tests and procedures that need to be performed. Based on whatever the auditor estimates inherent risk and control risk to be, he or she plans audit procedures so that detection risk is low enough to bring audit risk for the assertion to an acceptable level. Notice that the definitions given above refer to material misstatements of *specific assertions*. This language means these risks are assessed to plan testing for individual accounts or classes of transactions.

Inherent Risk

Inherent risk and control risk exist independently of the audit and any of the auditor's actions. Inherent risk results from the nature of the account or class of transactions. For example, cash is risky from the perspective that it needs to be physically controlled and safeguarded because it is "fungible," meaning it all looks the same. Except for physical control, there is no way to definitively state that any particular dollar bill belongs to the company rather than to an employee or a customer. Another example is that transactions requiring skill and judgment for proper authorization, such as the decision of how much revenue to recognize on a long-term project, are inherently riskier than selling a product in a retail store at a predetermined and premarked price. Suspense accounts and related party transactions have more inherent risk. Accounts and transactions that are more susceptible to fraud have greater inherent risk. Separating major classes of transactions into routine, nonroutine, and estimation transactions, as discussed in Chapter 7, may assist the auditor in assessing inherent risk. Nothing in the audit plan or procedures can change the inherent risk associated with the nature of an account or class of transactions.

Control Risk

Like inherent risk, control risk exists independent of audit decisions. Control risk deals with the likelihood that any problems that occur with an account or class of transactions will not be prevented or detected by the company's ICFR. The effectiveness of the design and operation of ICFR are major components of control risk. All of the information the auditor has collected up to this point in the integrated audit may be useful in assessing the level of control risk. For example, management's method of assessing ICFR to make its report on effectiveness and ICFR design effectiveness may help the auditor estimate and set the level of control risk that is to be used in planning the substantive financial statement audit tests.

If, in the financial statement audit, the auditor plans to rely on the functioning of a control for the entire fiscal period—in other words, plans to set CR low—then the auditor considers this when testing controls for the ICFR audit. When planning to rely on controls in the financial statement audit, instead of testing for ICFR operating effectiveness just at management's reporting date the auditor tests operating effectiveness for the entire period. In addition, when the audit plan for the financial statement audit is based on an expectation that the ICFR system is effective for the entire period, and thus assumes a low CR, the auditor structures the control tests to accept a very low sampling risk for the entire period.

IT Considerations

An important risk consideration for the auditor when planning audit procedures is the impact of the IT system on risks. Distinguishing IT risks as inherent or control risks is difficult because an IT risk may have the characteristics of both. IT risks that are addressed by general as well as application controls include:

- Data confidentiality
- Data availability
- Data integrity
- Data timeliness
- Data accuracy
- IT infrastructure

Based on understanding the system and conclusions about ICFR design effectiveness, the auditor includes IT risks in planning tests of ICFR operating effectiveness and estimating inherent and control risks for the financial statement audit.

Using the Audit Risk Model for Planning

The algebraic relationship of the components that make up audit risk can make planning less complicated if the audit firm has guidelines regarding the level of audit risk it is willing to accept. Once the acceptable audit risk is set and inherent risk and control risk for the account or class of transactions are estimated, the auditor can calculate the detection risk that keeps audit risk at the acceptable level. The auditor considers the calculated detection risk while planning aspects of testing. Risk affects planning details such as number, timing, nature and extent of tests, as well as stratification of populations and sample sizes. Most importantly, understanding the use of audit risk in planning helps the auditor evaluate the different components of risk associated with the audit. This helps the auditor more effectively plan audit testing and the audit evidence that will be required.

The ultimate goal of considering audit risk in planning audit procedures and samples is to determine the acceptable level of detection risk, particularly the acceptable level of detection risk for tests of details of balances. Therefore the algebraic relationship of the components is sometimes expressed in the following form:

$$TD = AR/(IR \times CR) \times AP$$

The mathematical result of this calculation is the planned detection risk for tests of a particular account or class of transactions, expressed as a percentage. For example, if planned TD detection risk is calculated to be 10%, the auditor plans the audit tests to have not more than a 10% risk that a misstatement that is not prevented or detected by ICFR will be missed by audit tests of details. The parallel for a controls test is that the audit plan allows for no more than a 10% risk of concluding that the control is effective when it is not.

An alternative approach to calculating audit risk for planning is to classify the components into broad categories using descriptors of "low" and "high." Once the auditor makes conclusions about risk, those judgments are used when deciding on the sample size and evaluating test results. Exhibit 8-5 showed the relationships that exist between various population characteristics and sample size. Sample size is also related to the degree of assurance the auditor wants from the test. For example, if the auditor expects a low rate of control deviations in a population and wants to be able to rely significantly on the results of the test, a larger sample is needed.

When planning tests of the financial statement audit, if inherent risk of the account is high and the controls are not expected to be effective, the auditor needs a larger sample for substantive tests of details. The reasoning is that there is a greater likelihood that there will be a problem in the account balance and it will not be prevented or detected by ICFR. Therefore, the auditor wants to plan the financial statement audit tests to have a high likelihood of detecting any misstatements of the account balance. To keep detection risk low, the auditor may, for example, decide to test a large sample or 100% of the population, use multiple audit procedures or CAATs, and perform procedures at more times throughout the year or at more locations. The auditor may also incorporate substantive analytical procedures in the plan to lower total detection risk. If the expectation is that inherent risk and control risk are low, then the auditor may be willing to accept a higher level of detection risk for analytical procedures and tests of details of balances, and will plan the audit accordingly.

The impact of various characteristics is presented in Exhibit 8-6. The exhibit shows that for a given level of desired audit assurance, assuming the sample size does not change, the auditor will have to accept a higher tolerable rate of deviation if the expected population deviation rate is higher. Sampling and risks are discussed again in Chapter 9 related to the financial statement audit of the integrated audit.

REVIEW QUESTIONS

F.1 What components of risk are independent of the audit? Which components may be set by the auditor? What is the basis for setting them? Which components are estimated? Which component may be calculated based on the others?

F.2 Do the components of risk have to be set quantitatively?

EXHIBIT 8-6

Relationships of Audit Assurance and Characteristics

Expected Population Deviation Rate	Degree of Assurance Desired by the Sample's Audit Evidence	Tolerable Rate of Deviation
Low	High	5%
High	High	10%

F.3 Give examples of accounts and classes of transactions that have greater inherent risk for specific assertions. Why is their inherent risk greater?

F.4 After the auditor determines detection risk, what is it used for?

AUDIT DOCUMENTATION [LO 5]

Audit documentation is so important that it is the subject of the PCAOB's third auditing standard. Audit work papers provide support for the audit report. Auditors use work papers to conduct and supervise the audit (AICPA AU 339, PCAOB AS 3). All of the audit work performed using tests of controls is documented in the audit work papers. Details on how work papers are developed and used in practice explain their role in audit tests.

AUDITING IN ACTION

Audit Documentation for Samples

The identification of the items inspected may be satisfied by indicating the source from which the items were selected and the specific selection criteria, for example:

- *If the audit sample is selected from a population of documents, the documentation should include identifying characteristics (for example, the specific check numbers of the items included in the sample).*
- *If all items over a specific dollar amount are selected from a population of documents, the documentation need describe only the scope and the identification of the population (for example, all checks over $10,000 from the October disbursements journal).*
- *If a systematic sample is selected from a population of documents, the documentation need only provide an identification of the source of the documents and an indication of the starting point and the sampling interval (for example, a systematic sample of sales invoices was selected from sales journal for the period from October 1 to December 31, starting with invoice number 452 and selecting every 40th invoice). (AS 3.10)*

Permanent Files

Audit work papers are usually classified into two categories: **permanent files** and **current files**. Permanent files include information that is relevant to the company and its audit for recurring engagements. The permanent file typically includes the company's organizational chart, chart of accounts, accounting manual, corporate charter, important contracts, and documentation about stocks and bonds. Since work papers are typically kept in electronic format, when possible these documents are scanned for inclusion in the audit documentation. Alternatively, the auditor may keep hard copies. Other documents important to the specific company can also be included. The permanent file is reviewed and updated during each year's annual audit.

Current Files

The current files include all the information and audit evidence relating to the current integrated audit engagement. This likely includes:

1. The audit plan, including the planning memo
2. A copy of any of management's documentation of the company's system and ICFR

3. Work papers supporting procedures and conclusions of the audit of ICFR
4. Working trial balance with adjusting and reclassifying entries
5. Work papers supporting procedures and conclusions of the financial statement audit

The work papers supporting the ICFR and financial statement audits include information from important meetings such as those of the Board of Directors, audit committee, and other committees. Work papers document tests performed, results, and evaluation of the results. Memos on procedures and conclusions are part of the documentation supporting the audit conclusions. When the audit work is completed, the financial statements and audit report are added.

Organization, Indexing, and Cross Referencing

Audit work papers are now usually prepared in electronic format using audit software on the audit team's personal computers. Audit work papers have common characteristics such as a heading that identifies the audit activity and required information, notably

> who performed the work and when, and
>
> who reviewed the work and when

In addition, work papers are organized by **indexing** and **cross referencing**. Audit software assists in what would otherwise be the tedious construction of a set of work papers by providing the basic format and prepopulating information when possible.

Each audit firm has a method for organizing work papers. The firm's referencing system is used on all audits the firm conducts. Cross referencing means that work papers that relate to each other are marked so that the auditor or a reviewer can move in between work papers to examine the complete audit evidence. For example, documentation of a walkthrough intended primarily to understand the system and evaluate design effectiveness might also include cross references to any of the various controls that were tested for operational effectiveness during the walkthrough.

When using work papers prepared electronically, the software typically permits the user to "drill down" from general to prepared detailed work papers. The audit plan will usually be marked with the index references of the work paper that provides evidence of the completion of an audit procedure. This provides the audit team member performing the work with the opportunity to "sign off," indicating completion of the work and where the documentation can be found. References are also used by reviewers when they check to see that procedures specified in the audit program have been completed. Reviewers also sign off after reviewing audit evidence.

Tick Marks

Another characteristic common to work papers is the use of **tick marks**. The term *tick marks* refers to symbols used by the auditor performing the audit procedure to indicate what was done. A legend is provided explaining the meaning of each tick mark. As an example, an auditor might place the symbol next to each item in a list of transactions indicating that the control step was examined for each transaction and no errors or deviations from the control were found.

AUDITING IN ACTION

Example of Lead Schedules Tied to the Working Trial Balance

Audit Index: A-1
Prepared by: JC 1/18/2010
Reviewed by: JH 1/22/2010
Prepared by Client (PBC)

Cash Lead Schedule
FYE 12/31/2009

Acct#	Account Title	Audited Balance 1/1/09	T/M	Unaudited Balance 12/31/09	T/M	Adjusting Journal Entires	T/M	Final Audited Balance	T/M
11100	Patty Cash	15,000	PY	25,000	PY			25,000	TB
11200	Operating Account	80,000	PY	95,000	PY			95,000	TB

Working Trial Balance
12/31/2009

Audit Index TB-1

Ref	Account	Unaudited	AJE	Audited
A-1	Cash	240,000	(15,000)	225,000
B-1	Receivables	80,000	20,000	100,000
C-1	Investments	12,000	-	120,000
D-1	Inventory	45,000	(3,000)	42,000
E-1	Equipment	330,000	(10,000)	320,000
F-1	Buildings	1,200,000	90,000	1,290,000
G-1	Land	80,000	-	80,000

Detailed Work Paper: Bank Reconciliations
Audit Index A-1.2
Preparated by: JC 1/19/2010
Reviewed by: JH 1/24/2010

Account#	Description	Balanced per Books		Deposit in Transit	Outstanding Checks	Balance per Bank	Balance per Confirmat
11200	Operating	80,000	CLS	2,500	4,200	81,700	81,700 ✓
11300	Payroll	18,000	CLS	-	5,600	23,600	23,600 ✓
11400	Disbursement	6,000	CLS	1,200	800	5,600	5,600 ✓
11500	Saving	68,000	CLS	2,200	-	65,800	65,800 ✓

✓ Amount agreed to bank confirmations without exception.
CLS Amount agreed to cash lead schedule without exception.

AUDITING IN ACTION

Example of Work Paper Indexing and Tick Marks

Audit Index: A-2.1   **ACC Banking Corporation**
                                    Operating Account
                                    12/31/2010

Prepared by Client (PBC)
Reviewed by: JH (P&C LLP)

Balance per bank Statement				105,000	**A**
Add:	Deposit in Transit 12/29/10		14,000		**B**
	Daily Interest		2,000	16,000	**B**
				121,000	

Deduct: Outstanding Checks

Date	No	Payee			
12/19/10	154	Reynolds Supply	7,500	**V**	
12/21/10	162	Johnson Services	1,500	**X**	
12/21/10	167	Hooks Publishing	2,500	**V**	
12/24/10	189	Santa Services	880	**V**	
12/27/10	195	Rachlin LLP	8,570	**V**	
12/30/10	205	United Giving Foundation	5,000	26,000	
				95,000	**TB-1**

Balance per Book 12/31/09   **F**

Tickmark Legend

F Footed without exception
TB-1 Traced and Agreed to the Trial Balance in w/p **TB-1** of this year's audit index
A Traced and agreed w/o/e to the bank statement located inw/p **A-2.1.1**
B Traced and agreed to subsequent period bank statement (Jan 2011) in w/p **A-2.1.2**
V Vouched to paid checks cleared with subsequent bank statement (Jan 2011) in w/p **A-2.1.2**
X Per conversation with ACC Bank controller Stephan George, amount is in dispute with Johnson Services.

EVALUATING THE RESULTS [LO 6]

The testing and evaluation process for tests of ICFR operating effectiveness can be summarized as follows:

- Conduct the control test procedures (e.g., inquiry, inspection, observation, reperformance) that compare actual operations of ICFR to the control objective and evaluation criterion.
- Identify control errors or deviations from control procedures.
- Determine whether the deviation rate of each control is high enough to be a control deficiency.
- Consider both qualitative and quantitative factors related to the deficiency.
- Determine whether any deficiencies identified, either individually or in combination, meet the threshold of a significant deficiency or material weakness.

An auditor sometimes finds unexpected control errors or deviations from control procedures. When a higher percentage of problems with the control are found than was expected, the next step is to modify the audit plan and collect more evidence. As discussed earlier, audit tests may show an unexpected frequency of errors or control deviations because there actually is a significant problem or because of sampling error. To rule out the possibility of sampling error, the auditor extends testing. If additional audit procedures still indicate problems, then the audit conclusion is that an ICFR deficiency in operating effectiveness exists. An ICFR deficiency can result from the way a control is designed or from how it operates. An operating deficiency results from a well-designed control that does not function effectively.

> A *deficiency* in ICFR exists when the design or operation of a control does not allow management or employees in the normal course of performing their assigned functions, to prevent or detect material misstatements on a timely basis. (AS 5.A3)
>
> An *operating deficiency* exists when the control is effectively designed, but either the control does not operate as intended or the person carrying out the control procedure lacks the needed authority or competence. (AS 5.A3)

Severity of the Deficiency

When a deficiency exists, the auditor evaluates its severity. The important determination is whether the deficiency is serious enough to be either a significant deficiency or a material weakness. In assessing whether a deficiency is a significant deficiency or material weakness, the auditor uses the definitions and criteria presented in AS 5. Based on the definitions, the auditor concludes whether the deficiency or combination of deficiencies is likely to result in material misstatement of an account balance or disclosure.

AS 5 Definitions of Significant Deficiency, Material Weakness:

> A *significant deficiency* is a deficiency, or combination of deficiencies, in ICFR, that is less severe than a material weakness, yet important enough to merit attention by those responsible for oversight of the company's financial reporting. (AS 5.A11)
>
> A *material weakness* is a deficiency, or combination of deficiencies, in ICFR, such that there is a reasonable possibility that a material misstatement of the company's annual or interim financial statements will not be prevented or detected on a timely basis. (AS 5.A7)
>
> "*Reasonable possibility*" is either "reasonably possible" or "probable." (AS 5.A7 as used in Codification 450.20.20)
>
> If the auditor determines that a deficiency, or combination of deficiencies, might prevent *prudent officials in the conduct of their own affairs* from concluding that they have reasonable assurance that transactions are recorded in conformity with GAAP, then the auditor should treat the deficiency or combination of deficiencies as an indicator of *material weakness.* (AS 5.70)

Part of the auditor's assessment of the severity of the deficiency deals with qualitative issues. For example, fraud perpetrated by management, no matter how small the dollar amount, likely indicates a material weakness. Another major consideration is the magnitude of the potential misstatement. The auditor must consider not only the financial statement or total transaction dollar amounts involved, but also the volume of activity exposed to the deficiency in the current period or expected in future periods (AS 5.66). Furthermore, in assessing control deficiencies, the issue is not only whether a misstatement *has already occurred*, but also whether it *could have occurred*.

> The severity of a deficiency does not depend on whether a misstatement actually has occurred but rather on whether there is a reasonable possibility that the company's controls will fail to prevent or detect a misstatement. (AS 5.64)

Deficiencies include problems that have not yet caused, but could cause, misstatements. Assessing whether the type of control problem is a material weakness is a challenging concept and requires significant professional judgment. Consider the possibility that an ICFR deficiency has not caused a misstatement in an account balance in the current period. The auditor must also consider whether it could have in the current period or might do so in future periods. In addition, when evaluating the magnitude of a potential error, the auditor must remember that an overstatement error is limited to the amount posted to the records and financial statements, but an understatement error is virtually limitless.

Evaluating Deficiencies

When the audit team conducts tests of the operating effectiveness of controls, it may find exceptions or deviations from the controls. The first assessment required is about the effect the finding has on the nature and extent of additional tests of operating effectiveness. Again, additional testing addresses the possibility of sampling error—that the finding does not represent the population from which the sample was drawn.

The auditor also links the audit test result to a conclusion about the control's effectiveness. Evaluating the impact of the deficiency requires a judgment about whether the deficiency surpasses the threshold of a significant deficiency or material weakness. Even if the individual **control deficiency** is serious on a stand-alone basis, it may not be when other controls and processes are also considered.

A compensating control may exist for an ICFR deficiency, and therefore, the deficiency may not create a material financial statement misstatement if the compensating control is effective. After evaluating the effect of the deficiency, the auditor must decide what the results mean to the planning and conduct of the financial statement audit.

AUDITING IN ACTION

Compensating Controls

Suppose a company has a control step calling for the accounts payable clerk to match the items on a vendor's invoice to the items on the internal receiving report before processing the invoice for payment. However, the accounts payable clerk position has been staffed with temporary employees during most of the past fiscal year. The temporary employees have often failed to consistently perform the matching control process. This is a serious problem. The company treasurer is the authorizing party for cash disbursements. Aware of the problem with the temporary employees, he carefully reviews the supporting documents for disbursements. Any time the invoice items do not match the receiving report, he rejects the cash disbursement and sends it back to the accounts payable department for further investigation. In this situation, even though the control executed by the accounts payable clerk does not operate effectively, the compensating control provided by the treasurer's careful review mitigates the problem.

In making judgments and concluding on the impact of control exceptions, the auditor uses professional skepticism. Using **professional skepticism** in the assessment means the auditor has a questioning mind and makes critical assessments of the audit evidence. The fact that a company employee or particular procedure was not associated with control deficiencies in the past should not affect the auditor's assessment of current evidence. Conditions and people can change. Similarly, the auditor cannot rely on positive prior experience regarding management's integrity to downplay the possibility of fraud if current evidence raises concerns. Even though it has been superseded, AS 2 provides a good conceptual explanation:

> In exercising professional skepticism in gathering and evaluating evidence, the auditor must not be satisfied with less-than-persuasive evidence because of a belief that management is honest. (AS 2.106)

AS 5 provides general guidance but few specific guidelines for assessing the severity of deficiencies in ICFR. Again, AS 2 provides examples of deficiencies that auditors consider carefully:

1. Control deficiencies over the selection and application of accounting policies that are in conformity with GAAP
2. Deficiencies in anti-fraud programs and controls
3. Control deficiencies over nonroutine and nonsystematic transactions

4. Control deficiencies over the period-end financial reporting process

5. An ineffective internal audit function in a company that needs such a function for effective monitoring or risk assessment

6. An ineffective regulatory compliance function in a company that needs such a function to ensure compliance with laws and regulation

7. An ineffective control environment (AS 2.139-140)

AS 5.69 states that the following are indicators of material weaknesses in ICFR:

1. Identification of fraud, whether or not material on the part of senior management.

2. Restatement of previously issued financial statements to reflect the correction of a misstatement

3. Identification by the auditor of a material misstatement of financial statements in the current period in circumstances that indicate that the misstatement would have not been detected by the company's ICFR

4. Ineffective oversight of the company's external financial reporting and ICFR by the company's audit committee

REVIEW QUESTIONS

G.1 Why do audit work papers need to be indexed and cross referenced? Why do auditors need to use tick marks?

G.2 What are the next steps when audit tests indicate a problem with the operating effectiveness of a control? What are the criteria for evaluating the seriousness of a control deficiency?

G.3 What does it mean that the auditor must consider not only whether a material misstatement has already occurred from a control deficiency, but also whether a material misstatement could have occurred?

G.4 How much reliance can the auditor place on experience with people and conditions found in a company in prior-year audits?

ADDITIONAL DOCUMENTATION CONSIDERATIONS

AS 3 covers documentation requirements for integrated audits. AS 5 does not provide any additional specific guidance on documentation. However, the earlier ICFR audit standard, AS 2, provided examples that may be useful to auditing students in understanding the information that will likely be a part of the auditor's work paper documentation. Documentation will include information about the design effectiveness of the company's ICFR, audit procedures, use of the work of others, and findings.

AUDITING IN ACTION

ICFR Audit Documentation

- The understanding obtained about the company's system
- The evaluation of the design of each component of the company's ICFR
- Processes used to identify significant accounts and disclosures and major classes of transactions
- The determination of locations or business units at which to perform testing
- The identification of the points at which misstatements could occur
- The extent to which the auditor relied on work performed by others as well as the auditor's assessment of their competence and objectivity
- The evaluation of any deficiencies noted as a result of the auditor's testing
- Other findings that could result in a modification to the auditor's report (AS 2.159)

If the auditor finds ICFR deficiencies, he or she may conclude that there is more than a low risk of a problem occurring in the financial statements. When this happens, the audit report includes this conclusion, underlying reasoning, and any effects. Even if the deficiencies do not affect the ICFR audit opinion, they may instigate changes in the financial statement audit plan. For example, an auditor might assess more than a low risk of potential financial statement problems when a material weakness in ICFR existed *during* the fiscal period, even though it was corrected by the end of the period. This may also be the case when a control was replaced close to the end of the year and the auditor only tested the new control.

"BIG PICTURE" TOPICS AND OPERATING EFFECTIVENESS [LO 7]

Some of the control considerations discussed in Chapters 6 and 7 are important to the discussion of operating effectiveness.

Entity-Level Controls

In prior chapters, **entity-level controls** were described as controls that affect the way a company is run, and therefore the attitudes and standards of its people. Another way to describe this kind of control is as a pervasive control—one that affects many of the other more specific or transaction-oriented-application controls. ITGC are pervasive controls. Controls at the individual program or application level are less likely to function adequately if ITGC are not effective. When auditing the operating effectiveness of ICFR, testing entity-level and pervasive controls may or may not be sufficient to make a conclusion about operating effectiveness.

The auditor may conclude that effective operation of an entity-level control is ***necessary*** for ICFR to be effective. But usually the auditor needs to test more than just entity-level controls. Testing entity-level controls provides sufficient evidence for the auditor to conclude ICFR is effective only when the entity-level control falls into the category of greatest precision. AS 5 explains the precision of entity-level controls:

> Some entity-level controls might be designed to operate at a level of precision that would adequately prevent or detect on a timely basis misstatements to one or more relevant assertions. If an entity-level control sufficiently addresses the assessed risk of misstatement, the auditor need not test additional controls relating to that risk. (AS 5.23)

An example is a company doing business at multiple locations, and entity-level controls over data processing are uniform and strong over all locations. Evidence on the operating effectiveness of the entity-level data processing controls may be sufficient so that the auditor does not need to test at the multiple locations.

Soft Controls and Personnel Qualifications

For the ICFR report, the auditor tests controls to determine whether ICFR functions effectively as of year end. Various characteristics affect this conclusion. For example, "softer" internal control components mentioned by the COSO IC Framework, such as management's philosophy and operating style, require a different kind of testing than controls that produce documents as evidence. Soft controls may require testing methods such as talking to people or observing their behavior. Also, consideration of the competency of persons performing controls is important to assessing whether controls operate effectively. The auditor considers whether the person performing a control has the necessary authority and qualifications to perform the control effectively.

Preventive and Detective Controls

In planning ICFR testing, the auditor determines what controls to test. Part of this determination is considering the preventive and detective nature of controls. **Preventive controls** are those that keep a problem from occurring, while **detective controls** are those that find problems after the fact. Detective controls are intended to permit the company to identify on a timely basis and in the normal course of business any problems that occur.

From a company's perspective, it is often better to prevent problems than to detect them. For example, finding out that a sale on credit was made to an unapproved customer with a poor credit rating does not increase the likelihood of collecting from the customer. It does, however, permit the company to consider the event when estimating the allowance for doubtful accounts. From the auditor's perspective, detective controls can be just as useful as preventive controls. As long as a company at least catches a problem and properly accounts for it, the company's books and financial statements are not misstated. Most ICFR testing plans include both preventive and detective controls since the controls work together.

If a preventive control such as authorizing transactions functions poorly, any resulting problems may be quickly identified by an effective detective control such as a monthly reconciliation procedure of transactions processed. In other words, if an unauthorized transaction is processed because of the ineffective authorization control, the effective reconciliation procedure catches it. This type of compensating control can sometimes be all that is needed.

Suppose an employee manages to order something that his or her employing company does not need, and intends to divert the item for personal use. Even if the purchase order slips through the control system, as long as the company catches it before payment, the unauthorized purchase can be avoided. The company can either return the unauthorized purchase or require the employee to pay for it. Coincidentally, the company probably fires the employee.

The auditor may test either preventive or detective controls, or both. The auditor does not need to test *all* of the controls that make up ICFR. The auditor tests the operating effectiveness of only those controls that are important to achieve the control objectives. For example, the auditor does not have to test a control that duplicates another control that has already been successfully tested with good results. (An exception to this example is if control redundancy is the objective of the control such as with some computer actions.) The auditor's goal is not to test the operations of all of the company's controls—just those that have been identified as being important to the relevant assertions of significant accounts.

Materiality

Materiality of the affected financial statement accounts is an important concept when testing the operating effectiveness of controls. When planning, performing, and evaluating the operating effectiveness of ICFR, the auditor considers materiality for both the individual accounts and financial statements taken as a whole. The auditor considers the results of all the tests, both individually and in the aggregate, to determine whether ICFR is operating sufficiently and effectively to keep the financial statements from being materially misstated.

IMPACT OF MULTIPLE LOCATIONS AND BUSINESS UNITS

The different business units and locations that make up the company affect audit decisions about which controls to test. The auditor gains an understanding of the company structure through audit procedures for accepting or retaining the client. Using that and other available information, the auditor evaluates the relative financial significance of the different business units and locations to assess the possibility that a material financial statement misstatement could result from each one (AS 5.B10). Basically, the auditor identifies those locations or business units that are individually important or that are important when they are aggregated. "Important" in this context means that the individual location or combination of locations presents a reasonable possibility of causing the financial statements to be materially misstated.

The auditor may decide that testing entity-level control provides sufficient audit evidence about ICFR at the important locations. This may be the case when the design of entity-level controls is strong. An example is strong controls over central processing or shared services functions of the company. Shared services functions are activities such as data processing and "backroom operations" like accounts receivable, accounts payable, and payroll functions. Alternatively, the auditor may conclude that ICFR operating effectiveness of account- or transaction-level controls should be tested at the important locations and business units. In this situation, the auditor decides what controls need to be tested, and how, at the different locations and business units. The goal is to obtain sufficient appropriate audit evidence regarding whether the controls are operating effectively.

The easiest situation to audit is when the client has only a few locations or business units that have sufficient financial significance to pose a risk of causing material financial statement misstatement. In this situation, the auditor performs tests of operating effectiveness for controls affecting the relevant assertions related to significant accounts and disclosures at each one of these locations and business units.

A different and challenging audit situation is when the client has many locations and business units that are each individually capable of causing material misstatements of the financial statements. The ideal situation would be for the auditor to test the operating effectiveness of controls of *all* relevant assertions of *all* significant accounts at *all* financially significant locations and business units. However, this may not be feasible because of the costs. The auditor may be able to rely on the work of others or information obtained in prior-year audits to modify the nature, timing, and extent of tests and garner sufficient evidence in a cost-effective manner.

IMPACT OF OUTSOURCING

When planning the tests of the operation of controls, the auditor considers processes that are performed for the client by **service organizations** or third-party service providers. Service organizations are of concern to the auditor in an audit of ICFR when the service organization is judged to be a part of the client company's information system. A service organization's activities are considered to be part of the audit client's information system when they affect any of the following (**AU 324.03**):

- the classes of transactions in the entity's operations that are significant to the entity's financial statements
- the procedures, both automated and manual, by which the entity's transactions are initiated, recorded, processed, and reported from their occurrence to their inclusion in the financial statements
- the related accounting records, whether electronic or manual, supporting information, and specific accounts in the entity's financial statements involved in initiating, recording, processing and reporting the entity's transactions
- how the entity's information system captures other events and conditions that are significant to the financial statements
- the financial reporting process used to prepare the entity's financial statements, including significant accounting estimates and its disclosures.

Examples of service organizations are (**AU 324.03**):

- bank trust departments that invest and service assets for employee benefit plans and for others
- mortgage bankers that service mortgages for others
- application service providers that provide packaged software applications and a technology environment that enables customers to process financial and operational transactions.

The auditor may conclude that the client company's use of a service organization makes the service organization a part of the company's information system. When that happens, the auditor must consider how the activities of the service organization affect the evidence needed to support the auditor's opinion, and how to obtain the needed evidence. The auditor must gain an understanding of the functions provided to the company by the service organization. Then, the auditor must take steps to understand the controls that are in place both within the service organization and at the client company.

The service organization should have controls supporting the processes performed just as the company would if the activities were performed in-house. In addition, the user company (which is the audit client) should have controls surrounding its use of the service company. A simple example of these surrounding controls is control totals and hash totals to verify that all the authorized activities and transactions that the company submits to the service provider are processed and received back by the company.

If the service organization is determined to be "a part of" the client's system, the auditor first takes steps to understand the role of the service organization's operations and its interface with the company. Then the auditor gains an understanding of the service provider's and user organization's controls. If the auditor concludes that design of the controls is effective, the auditor must gain evidence regarding the effective operations of the controls.

Evidence on the operation of controls at a service organization can be obtained in several ways. The auditor may test the user organization's controls over the activities of the service organization. For instance, if the client company reperforms some of the service organization's steps or reconciles the data sent to the service organization with the reports received, the auditor may test these steps that have been performed by the client company. A second way to obtain evidence on the operating effectiveness of service organization controls is to actually perform tests at the service organization.

Service organizations are popular because they are efficient and cost effective for their clients. If a company uses a service organization to process payroll, the service organization may be able to do it less expensively than the company could do it in-house because of specialization and economies of scale. The use of service organizations for payroll processing is discussed in Chapter 13.

If all the service organization does is process payroll, and it performs that function for many user companies, the service organization's efficiencies should be significant. However, if the auditors of all the service organization's user companies decided to test the controls at the service organization, this would cause serious problems for the service organization. The activities at the service organization would be continually interrupted as auditors of the various user clients conducted tests. The solution to this problem is for the service organization to have a specific audit resulting in a report to be used as evidence by the auditors of all the users companies. This service organization audit engagement is discussed in the Appendix to Chapter 13, and an overview is provided here.

A service organization engagement may address the design of the controls or both the design and functioning of the controls. If the audit addresses the functioning of the controls by testing them, the report is referred to as a Type II report (or as a SAS 70 Type II report). The auditor of the user company may consider the information included in a Type II report as evidence regarding the effective operations of ICFR at the service organization. When deciding whether a Type II audit report provides sufficient evidence about the service organization the auditor considers:

- time period covered by the tests of controls
- relationship of the time period tested to the date of management's assessment of ICFR
- scope of the examination, applications covered, controls tested
- relationship of the controls tested at the service organization to the controls of the user company
- results of the tests of controls
- service auditor's opinion (AS 5.B21)

In addition, the auditor inquires about the reputation, competence, and independence of the service organization's auditor.

An auditor may conclude that additional evidence is needed about the effectiveness of the service organization's controls even if a Type II report has been issued. This is likely when a long period of time has elapsed between the date of the service auditor's report and the date management reports on its assessment of ICFR (AS 5.B24). The auditor may also judge that more evidence is needed if:

- Activities at the service organization are pervasive to or very important in their impact on the company
- The auditor's report of the service organization indicates there were problems with the service organization's controls
- The service organization has made changes to its system since the date of the auditor's report (AS 5.B25)

Additional evidence regarding the controls surrounding the functions performed by the service organization can be obtained by performing more tests at the user company, obtaining more information by contacting the service organization, and performing more audit tests of controls within the service organization.

ICFR EFFECTIVENESS AND THE FINANCIAL STATEMENT AUDIT [LO 8]

The financial statement audit provides a conclusion about the fairness of the financial statements. The nature of a complete set of financial statements requires that the auditor's opinion addresses both the results of activities for the entire fiscal period and the financial position at the fiscal year end. The ICFR audit results in an audit opinion about the effectiveness of ICFR. But management and the auditor form a conclusion about ICFR effectiveness only as of a particular date—the end of the fiscal year. In order to do this, they must decide that ICFR was functioning effectively for a reasonable period of time prior to that date, and perform tests of controls to support the conclusion. However, this process does not necessarily mean that ICFR was functioning effectively for the entire fiscal year. Neither the ICFR nor the financial statement aspects of an integrated audit report on the consistency of the quality with which ICFR functioned throughout the entire fiscal period.

If ICFR was effective throughout the entire year, or even a specified part of the year, the auditor can, in the financial statement audit, choose to rely on the controls for the period that they were effective. Reliance on the controls means the auditor may be able to change the nature, timing, and extent of substantive testing on the financial statements. To rely on controls and reduce the substantive audit work on the financial statements, the auditor must test the controls for design and operating effectiveness over the entire period of reliance. This requires more tests of control than is necessary for an ICFR audit. Thus, there is a trade-off. Substantive financial statement audit effort can only be reduced over the period for which controls are tested and found to be effective.

The auditor may conclude that, even if ICFR are effective for the entire period under audit, relying on ICFR will not significantly reduce the amount of substantive audit work that needs to be performed. In this situation, the auditor may elect to test the effectiveness of ICFR only enough to issue the opinion on effectiveness at the fiscal year end and use substantive audit procedures to test account balances and disclosures for the financial statement audit. The auditor can also use different approaches on different parts of the financial statement audit, choosing to rely on ICFR for some parts and to focus on substantive tests of account balances and disclosures for other parts.

REVIEW QUESTIONS

H.1 In what situation might an auditor need to test only entity-level controls to conclude on operating effectiveness?

H.2 Why doesn't the auditor need to test the operating effectiveness of all preventive and detective controls?

H.3 What makes a location or business unit important enough for the auditor to consider it in planning the ICFR audit tests?

H.4 What causes an auditor to need to consider outsourced services in an ICFR audit?

H.5 How can an auditor obtain evidence about the operating effectiveness of controls at an outsider service provider?

H.6 How does the result of the ICFR audit tests affect the financial statement audit?

CONCLUSION

Results of tests of operating effectiveness contribute to two aspects of audit evidence. When added to the auditor's conclusions about the effectiveness of the design of ICFR, conclusions about operating effectiveness shape the auditor's opinion about the overall effectiveness of ICFR. Conclusions about ICFR operating effectiveness also confirm or refute the auditor's risk assessment used to plan substantive audit tests for the financial statement audit.

KEY TERMS

Application controls. Controls built into specific applications or processes that are carried out by the computer.

Attribute sampling. The process whereby auditor applies sampling in a test of ICFR operating effectiveness.

Audit committee. A committee (or equivalent body) established by and among the Board of Directors for the purposes of overseeing the accounting and financial reporting processes and audits of the financial statements.

Audit risk. The risk that the auditor may unknowingly fail to appropriately modify an audit report; at the account balance or class of transactions level, the risk that the auditor will fail to detect a material misstatement or material weakness in ICFR.

Automated controls. Controls built into and operating as part of computer software or hardware.

Computer-assisted audit techniques (CAATs). Automated audit procedures, steps, and calculations performed by computer software.

Control deficiency. Condition that occurs when deviations from a control objective exist.

Control objective. The purpose that a control is intended to achieve expressed in a way that can be useful for comparing actual performance to the objective.

Control risk. The risk that material misstatements that could occur in an assertion will not be prevented or detected by ICFR.

Cross referencing. The labeling and organization system used for audit work papers that permits moving within the work papers to find related items.

Current files. Audit work papers containing the information and audit evidence relating to the current integrated audit engagement.

Detection risk. The risk that the auditor will not discover (detect through audit procedures) a material misstatement that exists in a management assertion.

Detective controls. Those controls that identify a problem after it has occurred; should identify problems in a timely fashion and as a result of normal company activities.

Engagement risk. The overall risk to the auditor of being associated with a client.

Entity-level controls. Controls that exist at the organization or company level but have an impact on controls at the process, transaction, or application level.

Expected population deviation rate. The percentage of the time that the auditor expects a control to fail.

Fraud. Intentional misstatement of financial statements, or theft of assets.

General IT controls. Controls that deal with the IT environment and IT policies and procedures.

Haphazard sampling. The auditor's selection of items to be included in the sample, with no plan or justification for the items selected.

Illegal acts. A violation of law by the audit client, although auditors are primarily concerned with those that have a direct and material effect on the financial statements.

Indexing. The labeling system used for audit work papers.

Inherent risk. The susceptibility of a management assertion for a particular account balance or class of transactions to material misstatement.

Inquiry. For ICFR, verbal questions by the auditor of company personnel to determine whether employees understand and are able to properly execute control procedures.

Inspection. Audit procedure in which documents are examined; for ICFR, addresses evidence that a control procedure has been carried out.

Interim date. Usually refers to a date significantly prior to the company's fiscal year end when the auditor chooses to test controls.

IT general controls. See *General IT controls.*

Judgment sampling. See *Haphazard sampling.*

Manual controls. Controls that require human performance and judgment.

Material weakness. Defined in AS 5 indicating an ICFR that is not effective and increases the likelihood of a material misstatement in the financial statements.

Nonsampling risk. The risk of errors related to audit procedures that come from sources other than sampling risk; risk of human error on the part of the auditor.

Observation. Audit procedure in which the auditor watches control processes being performed.

Operating effectiveness of ICFR. Refers to whether the control functions as it was designed to and whether the person performing the control possesses the necessary authority and qualifications to perform the control effectively.

Permanent files. Audit work papers with information likely to be relevant to a client's recurring audit engagements.

Preventive controls. Controls that keep a problem from occurring.

Professional skepticism. Refers to the auditor having a questioning mind and making objective assessments in all matters related to the audit.

Random number generator. A computer program that will provide a list of random numbers that the auditor can use for selecting items to include in a sample.

Recalculation. See *Reperformance.*

Related party transactions. A transaction with an entity or a person who meets the definition; may not be "arms length" and requires specific financial statement disclosure.

Reperformance. Audit procedure in which the auditor follows the same control steps previously carried out by employees; may include recalculation.

Sampling. When audit procedures are applied to less than 100% of the items in an account balance or class of transactions.

Sampling error. An incorrect conclusion that results because the sample does not represent the population from which it was selected. See *Sampling risk.*

Sampling risk. The possibility that the sample does not represent the population from which it was selected.

Service organization. Outside entities that are contracted to perform specific processes for a company, such as investment services or application processing.

Significant deficiency. As defined in AS 5, indicates when an ICFR is not effective, but reflects a problem that is not as serious as a material weakness; a problem that is serious enough to be a concern to those governing the entity.

Stratifying the population. Separating the total population into subgroups so that different audit procedures may be applied to the different subgroups.

Test of details of balances. Audit tests that address the fairness of financial statement account balances.

Tick marks. Identifying marks auditors use on work papers to indicate that an audit procedure has been performed and to highlight the result of the procedure.

Tolerable deviation rate. The maximum rate at which an internal control can fail to operate as intended and still permit a conclusion that the control operates effectively.

MULTIPLE CHOICE

8-1 **[LO 1]** Which of the following types of evidence provides the least assurance regarding the effective operations of ICFR?

(a) Confirmations of accounts receivable

(b) Computer logs documenting attempts at unauthorized access to the system

(c) Documents containing initials of the person authorizing the transaction being examined

(d) Oral responses to auditor inquiry during walkthroughs

8-2 **[LO 1]** Of the following control situations, for which one will the auditor need to test the greatest number of operations of the control?

(a) A continuously operating automated control in a computer environment that has not changed during the period being audited

(b) A control that requires extensive human performance and judgment that operates frequently

(c) A control that requires minimal human performance and judgment that operates frequently

(d) A control that requires extensive human performance and judgment that operates occasionally

8-3 **[LO 6]** Under which condition will the auditor likely perform additional tests of the operating effectiveness of controls near the end of the year to update interim tests?

(a) A control was found to be deficient when tested at the interim date, and management has since changed the system to remediate the problem.

(b) A control was tested early in the fiscal year.

(c) A control was tested midway through the year, but limited evidence was collected.

(d) All of the above.

8-4 **[LO 1]** What characteristic of automated controls makes it possible for the auditor to rely on a single test of the operating effectiveness of the control?

(a) Access controls prevent incorrect data from being input.

(b) Backup and data recovery procedures compensate for the possibility of lost information.

(c) If the application has not changed, automated processing causes transactions to be processed in a consistent fashion.

(d) Error logs will be consistently created.

8-5 **[LO 1]** The auditor will likely test the operating effectiveness of the controls in the period-end financial reporting process

(a) in an in-depth and extensive manner, as they relate to numerous financial statement assertions.

(b) moderately at the end of each month or quarter.

(c) on a selective basis, rather than testing many or most of the controls in the process.

(d) by testing one transaction for each control since the controls are automated.

8-6 **[LO 2]** The operating effectiveness of controls that are intended to prevent fraud is

(a) tested based on the initial plan drafted immediately after client acceptance.

(b) tested as a result of the information on fraud risk obtained from the internal audit staff.

(c) tested, and results are used as one source of information for the auditor's assessment of fraud risk.

(d) will not likely affect subsequent audit procedures that have already been planned.

8-7 **[LO 2]** Auditors consider illegal acts in testing operating effectiveness of ICFR because

(a) fraud is an illegal act.

(b) some illegal acts have a direct and material effect on the financial statements.

(c) the IRS requires the auditor to determine whether sufficient tax is reported and paid by the client.

(d) auditors are able to determine whether business activities are legal or illegal.

8-8 **[LO 2]** Which of the following is an illegal act that has a direct effect on the financial statements?

(a) Securities trading violations

(b) Environmental protection violations

(c) Antitrust violations

(d) Revenue recognition violations under government contracts

8-9 **[LO 3]** Sampling risk is

(a) the possibility that the items the auditor selects to examine do not represent the rest of the items in the population from which they are selected.

(b) the possibility that the auditor will not choose enough items to test.

(c) the possibility that the items the auditor selects to include in the sample will not be available for testing.

(d) the possibility that the auditor will perform the wrong test on the sample.

8-10 **[LO 3]** When an auditor selects a sample and, after testing the operating effectiveness of a control, concludes that the control doesn't function as designed, the next step is to

(a) look for compensating controls.

(b) extend the sample to confirm that the test results are accurate.

(c) discuss the test results with the client.

(d) redesign the testing to be done in the financial statement audit since the control cannot be relied on.

8-11 **[LO 3]** Which of the following statements is incorrect?

(a) Statistical sampling permits the auditor to quantify sampling risk.

(b) Statistical sampling is based on the laws of probability.

(c) A statistical sampling approach is required when the auditor examines less than 100 % of the population.

(d) A statistical approach to sampling requires an element of randomness in the selection process.

8-12 **[LO 4]** Inherent risk is greater for transactions involving

(a) related parties.

(b) routine sales made at standard prices.

(c) routine purchases of inventory from preapproved vendors.

(d) depreciation of fixed assets.

8-13 **[LO 4]** The purpose of considering risk in planning the nature, timing, and extent of audit tests is

(a) to set the auditor's acceptable level of financial statement level audit risk for a particular account or class of transactions.

(b) to determine the appropriate level of planned detection risk for tests of a particular account or class of transactions.

(c) to test the level of control risk set for a particular account or set of transactions.

(d) to guide the auditor in the appropriate audit opinion on ICFR.

8-14 **[LO 4]** If the auditor decides that the acceptable level of audit risk for a class of transactions is very low based on the potential for material misstatement of the financial statements, judges the inherent risk of the class of transactions to be high, and the control risk of the class of transactions to be moderate, the audit procedures will be planned to achieve what level of detection risk?

(a) Low

(b) Moderate

(c) High

(d) Cannot be determined from the information given

8-15 **[LO 5]** The current files of an integrated audit engagement would likely include

(a) copies of long-term debt agreements.

(b) copies of parts of management's documentation of ICFR that the auditor tested in the current-year audit.

(c) copies of long-term lease agreements.

(d) copies of stock compensation plans.

8-16 **[LO 6]** When the auditor identifies a material misstatement in the financial statements in the current period that would not have been identified by the company's ICFR,

(a) a material weakness in ICFR exists.

(b) the deficiency should be evaluated to determine whether it is a deficiency.

(c) the situation should be regarded as an indicator of a material weakness in ICFR.

(d) the auditor should reconsider whether the financial statement misstatement is actually material.

8-17 **[LO 8]** Which of the following statements is incorrect?

(a) An important limitation to the value of the ICFR audit conclusion regarding the effectiveness of ICFR is that it is as of the end of the fiscal year.

(b) The integrated audit opinions, when considered together, report on the consistent quality of ICFR effectiveness throughout the entire fiscal period.

(c) Even if ICFR problems that occurred during the year are corrected by year end, the system may not have produced accurate financial information throughout the entire fiscal year.

(d) The financial statement audit opinion does not report on the quality of the ICFR.

8-18 **[LO 7]** If an audit client uses a service organization to process its payroll,

(a) the auditor must test the design and effectiveness of ICFR at the service organization.

(b) the auditor will not test ICFR of the service organization as long as another auditor's report on the design of ICFR at the service organization is available.

(c) the auditor will not test ICFR of the service organization as long as another auditor's report on the design and effectiveness of ICFR at the service organization is available.

(d) the auditor may decide that additional evidence about the effectiveness of ICFR at the service organization is needed even though another auditor has reported that the design and operations of ICFR is effective at the service organization.

8-19 **[LO 5]** Which of the following reports the major components of an amount that ties to the working trial balance and is reported on the financial statements?

(a) Supporting schedule

(b) Lead schedule

(c) Client-prepared schedule

(d) Reconciling items schedule

8-20 **[LO 4]** Detection risk differs from inherent risk in which of the following ways?

(a) Detection risk is determined by the possibility of incorrectly applying audit procedures.

(b) Inherent risk may be assessed in either quantitative or qualitative terms.

(c) Detection risk cannot be changed at the auditor's discretion.

(d) Inherent risk exists independently of the audit.

DISCUSSION QUESTIONS

8-21 **[LO 6]** Assume that an auditor conducts an integrated audit in year one and issues a clean opinion on management's assessment of internal control, internal control effectiveness, and fairness of the financial statements. There is no change in the accounting information system. During the first quarter of year two, the auditor identifies a control deficiency that has not yet caused a material misstatement in the financial records or statements, but could cause a material misstatement. What does this mean regarding the appropriateness of the auditor's reports on ICFR in the prior year?

8-22 **[LO 7]** If a company owns many business locations (for example, many store locations), and in the aggregate they could cause material misstatements to the financial statements, the auditor would need to obtain sufficient audit evidence for all the locations to conclude on ICFR effectiveness. Assume the stores do not share a standard accounting system, and backroom operations and entity-level controls are not uniform across locations.

Is it possible that this situation could make the needed audit procedures cost prohibitive, so that the company could not get an audit? Discuss. How might the company need to modify its procedures?

8-23 **[LO 1]** Jessica Chatman is a staff auditor assigned the task of performing tests of internal controls for the JC Automotive Parts engagement. Before she begins testing, Jessica must first determine the timing of her tests. Because JC Automotive is a very small engagement, all controls are manual. In planning the tests, she identifies one control as a significantly recurring control over the revenue account that occurs once a week (52 times a year). For another area, she identifies a control that is over adjusting entries and occurs quarterly (four times a year).

In planning the timing of the tests of the internal controls over financial reporting, which should Jessica plan to test more frequently? Would your answer change if the controls over the revenue account were automatic controls that did not change over the reporting period? Explain.

8-24 **[LO 1]** Assume that you are assigned the task of testing internal controls over financial reporting for the Van Jacobs Corporation year 2010 audit. Van Jacobs Corporation has a December 31 fiscal year end. Due to poor controls that existed previously, Van Jacobs implemented a new internal control system that became operational on February 14, 2010 and did not change throughout the rest of the year.

How much testing would you need to perform on the previous system to issue the 2011 opinion on ICFR? Justify your answer.

8-25 **[LO 2]** While performing tests of controls for the cash-in-vault account ($50,000 total as of the balance sheet date) of P-Town Hotel, you realize that—contrary to the company's written controls description and your earlier walkthrough evidence—the front-desk manager has access via a vault key, can input transactions to the only set of records for the cash-in-vault, and even performs all the reconciliations between the cash in the vault and the records. Based on this newly discovered information, you decide to investigate further and discover that the front-desk manager has stolen cash and there is no money left in the vault. Because the P-Town Hotel has significant cash reserves, your materiality threshold for cash is $200,000.

Even though the fraud you've found is below your materiality threshold, do you need to take further steps? If so, what steps will you take? Does the fraud impact your audit opinion on ICFR effectiveness?

8-26 **[LO 3, 6]** C. Ronaldo is an auditor working on the ICFR audit for the Manchester Corporation. Interest expense is an account that could produce a material misstatement in the financial statements, so it is tested in the ICFR audit. After performing a walkthrough, the senior determines that the controls over interest expense are designed effectively. The audit plan for the ICFR audit includes testing an automated control for calculating interest expense transactions. In the audit planning stages, the senior sets the tolerable rate of error for this particular automated control at 2%. The audit plan directs C. Ronaldo to conduct his tests using a sample based on a nonstatistical approach. C. Ronaldo selects the sample and conducts the reperformance procedure the audit plan calls for to test the operating effectiveness of the control. He finds instances in 3% of his sample where the control did not operate as intended.

Does C. Ronaldo's testing indicate a deficiency in the control tested? If so, what is the next step? If C. Ronaldo's results are valid, do you think the deficiency is severe enough to be a significant deficiency or a material weakness? What impact does that have on the ICFR audit opinion? What impact do the findings have on the financial statement audit plan?

8-27 **[LO 5]** Gordon is a new staff auditor on the Fine Dining of London Co. engagement and is responsible for conducting some of the ICFR controls tests on the engagement. In the course of his audit work, Gordon finds instances where a control he is testing has numerous deviations from the prescribed procedures. Gordon discusses it with the senior and manager on the engagement. Based on evaluating the severity of the ICFR deficiency, they all conclude that there is only a very limited risk that the control deficiency will cause a material misstatement in the financial statements. Therefore, it is not considered a material weakness.

What is Gordon required to document in the work papers since the deficiency does not result in a material weakness? Will Gordon's test result cause the audit team to change its plans concerning the financial statement audit? If so, how?

8-28 **[LO 8]** Jaime, the senior auditor on the audit of the Boston Brewery Co., a public company, is responsible for initial planning of the integrated audit. She is responsible for the supervision and review of two staff accountants performing both controls tests and tests of details of balances. After the tests of controls are completed, she reviews the work of the staff accountants and concludes that no significant deficiencies or material weaknesses exist in ICFR. Based on this finding, she decides she can rely on the company's ICFR for the entire reporting period. This was not what she expected when she designed the initial audit plan.

How can Jaime's conclusion on internal controls affect the nature, timing, and extent of detail testing on the financial statement audit? Would your answer be different if the controls had changed halfway through the year and the audit team had determined that internal controls operated effectively only during the second half of the year?

PROBLEMS

8-29 **[LO 1]** Sea Duds is a retail clothing store specializing in resort clothing. The company purchases finished goods—apparel and accessories—and its other payments are for typical operating costs such as rent, utilities, and payroll. When bills are received and input to be paid, the software of the computer system requires certain information, such as the number from the chart of accounts and the company or person being paid. All of this information must match vendor names, employee information, and accounts that have been previously approved by management and input to a master file. If the information input for a check to be created does not match the preapproved information, the transaction is rejected and an exception report is printed. The clerk who entered the information investigates and resolves any exceptions identified. After the information is input, exceptions are resolved, and checks are printed the owner of the store reviews the supporting detail for each check and personally signs the check. The owner initials the supporting document package at the time of review. Any exception reports that were generated as a result of the input process also go to the owner with the checks and are reviewed to be sure the proper corrections were made. Once every two weeks the owner reviews a cash disbursement report for the period, and at least once each month a general ledger report, the bank statement, and a bank reconciliation are prepared by a different clerk than the one who inputs the bills for processing.

Required:

(a) Identify the controls present in this cash disbursements process and the errors they are designed to prevent or detect.

(b) What documentary evidence is available to the auditor?

(c) What audit procedures can the auditor use to test the operations of these controls?

8-30 **[LO 8]** Assume that management of a company with a December 31 fiscal year end began its assessment of ICFR early in the fiscal year. Based on its procedures, management concluded that deficiencies existed in ICFR and made major changes to the accounting information system that were completed by June 30. The auditor tested ICFR after the changes were made and concluded that ICFR was effective as of the fiscal year end.

Required:

(a) How does this situation affect the auditor's procedures for the financial statement audit?

(b) For the financial statement audit, can the auditor rely on internal controls for the second half of the fiscal year? The first half of the fiscal year? Why?

(c) How is the audit evidence for the financial statements for each half of the year affected?

8-31 **[LO 1]** You are a new auditor for B&O LLP, a large public accounting firm with many publicly traded audit clients. You have just been assigned to perform controls testing for the integrated audit on one of B&O's largest clients. One of the steps specified in your audit program is to test the review process over cash disbursements performed by the company's supervisor.

Required:

(a) Is inquiry the best way to test the control? If yes, why? If no, why not?

(b) Will inquiry provide sufficient audit evidence? Explain.

(c) Is inspection the best way to test the control? If yes, why? If no, why not?

(d) Is reperformance the best way to test the control? If yes, why? If no, why not?

(e) List the audit procedures you would perform to sufficiently test the control.

8-32 **[LO 2]** Jose is a senior auditor in charge of testing controls over financial reporting. The audit procedures require that Jose "maintain professional skepticism in assessing controls for fraud risk." In the course of his testing, Jose finds a transaction that occurred on January 5 at 11:30 P.M. that decreased the bad debts reserve account enough to increase earnings per share to $.20, which met analysts' predictions. Jose has a bad feeling about this transaction. For documentation purposes, he must articulate the red flags for fraud risk for this transaction.

Required:

(a) What are the red flags for fraud risk demonstrated by this transaction?

(b) For each red flag state (a) why it is important, in other words what it suggests to the auditor and (b) the follow-up procedure that Jose might use.

8-33 **[LO 3]** Kim is a senior auditor at the Wing CPA firm. She is in charge of formulating the audit plan for several key controls and accounts. Her manager has determined that if any of the accounts she is working on are misstated by $20,000 the misstatement is material. The account includes some unusual and significant transactions that have occurred during the year. Kim wants to utilize sampling for her testing.

Required:

(a) How can Kim stratify the transactions in the account to best utilize sampling?

(b) What is sampling risk? How might it affect the audit conclusions Kim makes based on the control tests?

(c) If Kim misses anything as a result of sampling, what audit procedures might uncover the error during the ICFR audit? During the financial statement audit?

8-34 **[LO 5]** Gloria is a newly hired inexperienced staff associate at a local accounting firm. She is given the task of performing a control test on the ICFR portion of the integrated audit for one of her firm's larger clients. Gloria conducts her test and finds no control deviations. She concludes that the control she tested is effective. Gloria marked the step complete in the audit program. When the senior on the engagement started the review, there were no work papers that documented Gloria's work.

Required:

(a) List the information Gloria should have included in her work paper documentation.

(b) Would any aspect of the procedure Gloria performed affect the permanent work paper file?

8-35 **[LO 1, 6]** Koburn and Carrie, CPAs, has determined that cash and accounts receivable are significant accounts to the audit of XYZ Company. XYZ outsources its cash receipts process to a bank. The bank deposits all cash receipts in XYZ's account and provides XYZ with detailed information about the source of the deposits. XYZ is able to download the detailed information directly into its IT system. Based on discussions with company personnel and review of company documentation, Koburn and Carrie learns that the company has the following procedures in place to account for cash received:

• XYZ receives a download of detail on cash receipts from the bank.

- The IT system uses the downloaded information to apply cash received to individual customer accounts.
- Any cash received that does not match or is not applied to a customer's account is listed on an exception report called the Unapplied Cash Exception Report.

The application of cash to a customer's account is a programmed application. The review and follow-up of unapplied cash from the exception report is a manual procedure. To determine whether misstatements in cash and accounts receivable are prevented or detected on a timely basis, the auditor decides to test the controls in the daily reconciliation of receipts to customer accounts. The auditor also plans to test control over reviewing and resolving unapplied cash in the Unapplied Cash Exception Report.

To test the programmed application controls for applying cash to a customer's account, Koburn and Carrie apply the following steps:

- Conducts interviews with company personnel about the software used to receive the download from the bank and process the transactions. Verifies with company personnel that the bank supplies the download software. The company uses accounting software acquired from a third-party supplier. The software consists of a number of modules. XYZ modifies the software only for upgrades provided by the supplier.

- Determines through further discussion with company personnel that the IT cash module operates the download of cash receipts information and posting of cash to the general ledger. The accounts receivable module posts the cash to individual customer accounts and produces the Unapplied Cash Exception Report, a standard report supplied with the package. The auditor agrees this information to the supplier's documentation.

- Identifies through discussions with company personnel and review of the supplier's documentation the names, file sizes, and locations of the program files that operate the cash receipts and accounts receivable function. The auditor then identifies the compilation dates of these programs and agrees them to the original installation date of the application.

- Identifies the objectives of the programs to be tested. The auditor wants to determine whether only appropriate cash items are posted to customers' accounts and matched to customer number, invoice number, amount, and so on, and that there is a listing of inappropriate cash items (that is, any of the above items not matching) on the exception report.

In addition, Koburn and Carrie evaluates and tests IT general controls, including program changes (for example, confirmation that no unauthorized changes are undertaken) and logical access (for example, data file access to the file downloaded from the banks and user access to the cash and accounts receivable modules) and concludes that they are operating effectively. The initial audit step to determine whether programmed controls were operating effectively was a walkthrough in the month of July. The computer controls operate in a systematic manner; therefore, Koburn and Carrie concluded that it was sufficient to perform a walkthrough for only one item. During the walkthrough, the auditor performed and documented the following items:

- Selected one customer and agreed the amount billed to the customer to the cash received by the service provider bank.
- Agreed the total of the bank report to the posting of cash receipts in the general ledger.
- Agreed the total of the cash receipt download from the bank to the supporting documentation.

- Selected one customer's remittance advice and agreed it to the amount posted to the customer's account in the accounts receivable subsidiary ledger.

(Adapted from AS 2, Example B1)

Required:

(a) Do the procedures performed by Koburn and Carrie provide sufficient evidence to conclude that the programmed controls functions effectively? Explain.

(b) What does each step accomplish?

(c) For the programmed controls, what would be a material weakness?

8-36 **[LO 1, 7]** Review the facts for the Koburn and Carrie, CPAs, audit of XYZ Company presented in Problem 35. To test the detective control of review and follow-up on the Daily Unapplied Cash Exception Report, Koburn and Carrie, CPAs:

(a) Makes inquiries of company personnel. To understand the procedures in place to ensure that all unapplied items are resolved, the time frame in which such resolution takes place, and whether unapplied items are handled properly within the system, the auditor discusses these matters with the employee responsible for reviewing and resolving the Daily Unapplied Cash Exception Reports. The auditor learns that when items appear on the Daily Unapplied Cash Exception Report, the employee must manually enter the correction into the system. The employee usually performs the resolution procedures the next business day. Items that typically appear on the Daily Unapplied Cash Exception Report relate to payments made by a customer without reference to an invoice or purchase order number or to underpayments of an invoice due to quantity or pricing discrepancies.

(b) Observes personnel performing the control steps. The auditor observes the employee reviewing and resolving a Daily Unapplied Cash Exception Report. The day selected contains four exceptions—three related to payments made by a customer without an invoice number and one related to an underpayment due to a pricing discrepancy. The auditor observes the employee resolving the exceptions as follows:

For the pricing discrepancy, the employee determines, through discussions with a salesperson, that the customer had been billed an incorrect price. A price break that the salesperson had granted to the customer was not reflected on the customer's invoice. The employee resolves the pricing discrepancy, determines which invoices were paid, and enters a correction into the system to properly apply cash to the customer's account, and reduce accounts receivable and sales accounts for the amount of the price break.

(c) Reperforms the control. Finally, the auditor selects 25 Daily Unapplied Cash Exception Reports from the period January to September. For the reports selected, the auditor reperforms the follow-up procedures that the employee performed. The auditor inspects the documents and sources of information used in the follow-up and determines that the transaction was properly corrected in the system. The auditor scans other Daily Unapplied Cash Exception Reports to determine that the control was performed throughout the period of intended reliance.

Because the tests of controls were performed at an interim date, the auditor has to determine whether there were any significant changes in the controls from the interim date to year end. Therefore, the auditor asks company personnel about the procedures in place at year end. The procedures had not changed from the interim period. The auditor observes that the controls are still in place by scanning Daily Unapplied Cash Exception Reports to determine the control was performed on a timely basis during the period from September to year end.

Based on the audit procedures, the auditor concludes that the employee was clearing exceptions in a timely manner and that the control was operating effectively as of year end. (Adapted from AS 2, Example B1)

Required:

List the detection controls related to the Daily Unapplied Cash Exception Reports.

8-37   **[LO 4]** Your audit firm uses the Audit Risk Model to plan detection risk and audit procedures for tests of details. The audit you are working on is a high-profile client. Therefore, for risk assessment and planning your firm uses an audit risk of 3% for this engagement's material accounts. In assessing the receivable accounts, you decide that an inherent risk of 80% is appropriate. Your history with the company indicates that its ICFR is good, and there have been no problems with ICFR for accounts receivable in the past. You set control risk at 25%. You plan to perform analytical procedures, but there have been changes in both the overall economy and the company's credit policies and price structure, so you don't think you can rely on trends to provide you with much assurance. You use an AP risk of 80%.

Required:

(a) Using the Audit Risk Model, what is your planned detection risk for tests of details for Accounts Receivable?

(b) What do the various risk estimates mean?

(c) What does this planned detection risk for Accounts Receivable test of details mean for your audit tests?

8-38   **[LO 7]** Sonia started working for Martin & Thomas, CPAs, in June, after her graduation from State University. She attended staff training school and was then assigned to the Young Industries audit. Her first assignment was to recalculate the inventory compilation, using audit test counts and audit unit prices for several hundred inventory items. The time budgeted for this task was six hours. She began the work at 12 noon and was not finished when the audit team left at 6 P.M. Since this was her first job and she didn't want to admit her shortcomings, Sonia took all necessary work papers and documentation home. She resumed working on the audit and also put her husband to work on the recalculation. They finished by 12 midnight. The next morning, she returned to work, put the completed documentation in the file, and recorded six hours as actual time spent. Her supervisor was pleased with her diligence to get the job done.

Required:

List at least three questions of ethics raised in this situation, one of which deals with future planning for next year's or similar audits.

8-39   **[LO 4]** Use the audit risk model as a framework to explain the following independent situations and to decide if the auditor's conclusion is appropriate.

(a) Jan Morris, CPA, is finishing an audit of Night Time Manufacturing and completed an extensive evaluation of internal controls. She thinks that control risk must be zero, since she has performed so many dual purpose tests. Is she justified in her belief?

(b) Upton Jordan, CPA, has participated in the audit of Bassetts, Inc. for five years—three years as a staff accountant and two years as a senior accountant. If this year's audit is the same as the rest, no accounting adjustments will be recommended. Is he justified in his belief that inherent risk is zero?

8-40   **[LO 1, 2]** You are auditing the Stanfish Hotel Corporation. At one of their facilities in San Francisco, you have been made aware of two senior purchasing employees who were recently fired for receiving several hundred thousand dollars in kickbacks from their meat and produce suppliers over a period of several years. Their "commission" amounted to 3% of the items purchased.

Required:

List preventive and detective internal controls that you recommend to prevent this situation from happening again?

8-41 **[LO 1, 2, 6, 8]** You are considering an audit engagement with a new, privately held entrepreneurial company (Moxy, Inc.) headed by Ryan Morris, a charming CEO. The company specializes in chemical lawn treatments. Ryan indicates that his business has really taken off, and he shows you last year's financial statements, which show a sales growth increase from $1,200,000 to $4,500,000 and gross profit growth from $575,000 to $2,800,000 in just one year. He has had to finance this growth with an $850,000 short-term promissory note, but would like to go public and attract investors. He also gives you the following limited information from his balance sheet:

	Year 1	Year 2
Assets		
Current assets:		
Cash	$ 30,100	$ 88,120
Accounts receivable	—	697,500
Other	77,320	942,000
Total current assets	$107,420	$1,727,620
Liabilities		
Current liabilities:		
Notes payable	$ —	$ 780,500
Taxes payable	—	29,000
Other	3,240	967,000
Total current liabilities	$3,240	$1,776,500

Required:

(a) Discuss why engagement risk, professional skepticism, and assessment of fraud risk are important in this scenario.

(b) Calculate the current ratios for year one and year two. What concerns do these calculations raise?

(c) Present at least three questions you would like to ask Ryan about the information provided, before making your decision about accepting the client.

8-42 **[LO 1]** Dottie Martin is the CEO of Martin Industries. She seeks your advice as to how to assign the functions among her three clerical employees in order to achieve the highest degree of internal control.

Below are the eight functions performed by these clerks:

- Maintains disbursement (payments) journal.
- Reconciles bank account.
- Prepares checks for signature.
- Opens mail and lists receipts.
- Deposits cash receipts.
- Maintains accounts receivable records.

- Determines when accounts receivable are uncollectible.
- Is responsible for the petty cash fund.

Required:

(a) Advise Dottie on how to distribute the various functions among Clerk #1, Clerk #2, and Clerk #3, assuming all functions require about the same amount of time.

(b) Explain at least three combinations of functions that would be unsatisfactory.

8-43 **[LO 1, 2]** At Genuine Products, Inc., the time cards of 550 employees are collected weekly by the plant foreman and delivered to the IS department. There, the cards are sorted and the hours worked are entered into the computer. These records are used to prepare individual payroll records, paychecks, and labor cost distribution records. The paychecks are compared with individual payroll records and signed by the treasurer, who returns them to the IS Department supervisor for distribution.

Required:

(a) Describe any weaknesses that exist.

(b) Indicate any frauds or material irregularities that might occur as a result of the weaknesses.

(c) List any recommendations for improvement of the process.

ACTIVITY ASSIGNMENTS

8-44 Go to the AICPA or PCAOB Web site and find AU 350 entitled "Audit Sampling." Find paragraph .07 where the discussion of Uncertainty and Audit Sampling begins. What are the sources of uncertainty described in this section of the auditing standard?

Read, beginning with paragraph .12 on Sampling Risk. With which types of sampling risks is the auditor concerned when performing substantive tests? Tests of controls?

8-45 Go to the AICPA or PCAOB Web site and find AU 316 entitled "Consideration of Fraud in a Financial Statement Audit."

Beginning with AU 316.05, how does the standard define *fraud*? What are the two types of financial statement fraud?

Beginning with AU 316.12, how does the standard present the auditor's responsibility related to detecting fraud?

Paragraph 14 discusses a brainstorming session regarding fraud in which all members of the audit team should participate. How does the guidance in paragraph 18 relate to the brainstorming session?

Based on what you have read, how might results of control tests impact the financial statement audit plan and procedures regarding fraud?

8-46 Go to the AICPA Web site. From the dropdown menu choose Professional Resources; Accounting and Auditing; Audit Committee Effectiveness Center. Find the article, "Fraud …Can Audit Committees Really Make a Difference?" Using any of the resources you find at this site, answer the following questions:

What should the audit committee know concerning how management can perpetrate fraud via internal control override? What actions should the audit committee take to address the risk of management override? What should the audit committee do once it discovers management override?

8-47 Perform an Internet search for "internal control failure" and find a story about one company that experienced an internal control failure. What was the impact of the failure on reported net income for the period? Did the company have to restate prior period earnings as a result of the failure? What was the announcement's effect on the company's stock price? Who, if anyone, was blamed for the failure?

APPENDIX A: TESTING IT APPLICATION CONTROLS AND COMPUTER-ASSISTED AUDIT SOFTWARE

Testing IT Controls

General IT controls (ITGC) deal with the IT environment and IT policies and procedures. Application controls deal with controls built into specific applications or processes that are carried out by computer programs. The auditor considers both ITGC and application controls, and evaluates them for design and operating effectiveness. The terminology **general controls** and **application controls** contrasts with the terms *entity-level* and *transaction-level* used by the PCAOB in other discussions. Most transaction-level controls in the IT system are application controls. In contrast, **entity-wide controls** may refer to application controls applied on a company-wide basis, as well as ITGC. For example, programmed controls that recheck the accuracy of automatic calculations are entity-wide controls if they apply to the entire company and all of its computer processes. They are also application controls within the various computer programs.

The auditor evaluates the design and operation of ITGC. The next step is to evaluate application controls. Specific circumstances exist for which the auditor does not test some of the application controls. One example is when application controls have changed late in the year. Another is when a company has many business units and locations that use uniform and central data processing. If the company has entity-wide controls including both general and application controls that are found to be effective, other specific application controls may not be tested at individual locations. If the auditor finds ITGC to be ineffective, significant audit judgment will go into deciding whether tests of application controls will be sufficient to provide assurance about the financial information being produced by the system.

While many control tests in an IT environment involve manual inquiry, inspection, observation, and reperformance, some tests are executed using the client's computer. A **test data approach**, **parallel simulation**, and **integrated test facility** are three well-known examples of automated controls tests. These are discussed in this appendix.

REVIEW QUESTIONS

I.1 How does the definition of general controls differ from that of entity-wide controls and applications controls? Explain the relationship of the three concepts.

I.2 Why might an auditor decide not to test certain application controls at specific business units or locations?

I.3 Why is it difficult for the function of application controls to be effective when the design or operation of general controls is not?

Test Data Approach

To use a test data audit procedure, the auditor prepares sample data that is then processed by the client's software application. The auditor knows the expected results for the test data and compares the actual results to the expected results. The test data procedure is used to test input and processing validation controls. So, in addition to using correct test data, the auditor inputs test data with a variety of errors to verify that the application controls properly handle the errors.

Common *input validation* controls that the auditor might test using test data include the following.

> **Access control and authorization.** Blocks or rejects any attempted access that is unauthorized.

Limit check. Sets an upper boundary for any data in a particular field. Data that are above the upper limit are flagged as a problem subject to error correction procedures.

Range check. Similar to a limit check, but sets both upper and lower boundaries for data entered into a specific field.

Validity check. Specifies the appropriate numbers and characters for a field. If a field should contain only numbers and an alpha character is entered, the validity check identifies the input error for correction.

Completeness check. Determines whether all the fields requiring data have data content. If a field should not have zeros or blanks, the completeness check specifies that there is an error when zeros or blanks are entered.

A test data audit procedure can also be applied to *processing controls*. The auditor can verify that **run-to-run control** totals are proper—meaning that data are not dropped or added from one computer step to the next. Limit or range checks can also be tested for effective application during processing. A limit or range check verifies that numbers produced as the result of a processing step (usually addition, subtraction, multiplication, or division steps) fall within an expected numeric range. The auditor can also use test data outcomes to verify that **error handling procedures** are followed and that access and error logs are created.

Parallel Simulation

To perform a parallel simulation procedure, the auditor reprocesses previously processed data using a program that accomplishes the same step as the client's original program. The results of the data processing performed via parallel simulation are then compared to the original output. Many parallel simulation reprocessing steps can now be performed using computer-assisted audit software (CAATs) without the need for a specialized program.

Integrated Test Facility

An integrated test facility gets its name from the fact that it is part of the client's system and tests the functioning of applications on a real-time basis as they are processing data. When an integrated test facility is used, dummy files exist in the system alongside real files. Test transactions are input and processed concurrently with real transactions and are posted to the dummy files during actual operations. The results posted to the dummy files are compared to expected results. The benefit of an integrated test facility is that it processes test data as part of regular operations. The risk is that test data and dummy files, if not properly controlled, could corrupt the company's real files. Great care must be taken to prevent contamination of the company's actual files.

REVIEW QUESTIONS

J.1   What types of input validation controls might an auditor test using test data? Explain what the input validation controls do.

J.2   What types of processing controls might an auditor test using test data? Explain what processing controls do.

J.3   What type of software is often used to perform parallel simulation, and why is this good?

J.4   What is the benefit of an integrated test facility? What is the risk to the client's records?

Using Computer-Assisted Audit Software to Facilitate Testing

Auditors now use computers and audit software as part of their daily work routine. Software is used for work paper preparation, time and billing recordkeeping, and group communication. Audit software is also employed to facilitate audit testing procedures. Historically, audit software was used mostly to test financial statement balances. With the increased emphasis on ICFR testing that is a part of an integrated audit, audit software is now also used to test the operating effectiveness of controls.

Some audit software is proprietary; being owned by a specific audit firm. However, various packages can be purchased and are widely used by many firms. **ACL**, short for Audit Command Language, is a popular and widely used audit software package. Audit software is typically menu driven and easy to learn to use. Regardless of the specific package, audit software has in common the ability to extract client data so that the auditor can examine and test it. The auditor may choose to extract the client's entire general ledger and transactions files. Then the auditor can perform various data selections and manipulations. The obvious advantage is the auditor's ability to examine all of the client's transactions rather than relying on a sample. The audit software also assists in the sample selection and evaluation process when sampling is the appropriate procedure.

Once client data are extracted from the client's records and copied for use by the audit software package, the auditor confirms the integrity of the new file. This is accomplished by counting and totaling the data in the audit work file and possibly using other verification procedures. Next, a basic but vital audit step is to perform tests that validate the quality of the client's financial books and records. This involves reperforming procedures such as counting records, totaling or "footing" account balances, verifying that the data are the proper alpha or numeric characters expected in the fields, and looking for duplications or gaps in the records. As was mentioned in the discussion of parallel simulation, transactions may be reprocessed to provide assurance that they are properly posted and classified.

Another important audit step performed by audit software is to examine the data for unusual transactions, errors, and unauthorized transactions. For instance, the audit program may screen for transactions that are input and processed after normal business hours. A transaction processed at midnight, when most personnel leave at 5:00 P.M. probably needs further inspection. The audit program can stratify transactions based on dollar amounts to segregate large transactions for further analysis. Transactions may be compared to authorization files, such as comparing the account numbers for sales on account to the authorized accounts receivable customer file, or the file of purchase transactions to the approved vendor list. Transactions with related parties can be identified by extracting all records with names of known related parties for further examination. Other high-risk transactions, such as important management estimates and nonrecurring adjusting entries, can be selected. After the transactions are chosen, the auditor examines them for compliance with whatever important control procedures are prescribed.

The audit procedures discussed earlier help the auditor identify deficiencies in ICFR. For example, if controls that authorize transactions or prevent unauthorized systems access have failed, these audit procedures can identify the failure. The procedures are also useful to the financial statement audit. Totaling or "footing" account balances provides assurance that the total number is properly added. Identifying transactions that are anomalies—large dollar amounts, processed at unusual times or with unapproved third parties— permits the auditor to continue the audit process beyond testing controls to investigating the validity and authorization of the transactions. This further investigation may reveal errors or fraud.

REVIEW QUESTIONS

K.1 For what nontesting purposes can audit software be used?

K.2 What is the advantage of extracting a client's complete general ledger and transactions files using audit software?

K.3 How does the auditor confirm the data integrity of the new audit work file that is created based on data extracted from the client's records?

K.4 What types of transactions will the auditor look for when scanning the client's files for unusual items?

Audit software can also manipulate client data to assess trends, analyze relationships among accounts, and perform ratio analysis. The analysis can use various methods, including calculating averages and standard deviations, and performing linear regression. Audit steps that use these manipulations and calculations are called **analytical procedures.**

Analytical procedures are required by audit standards as part of the planning process and are used throughout the audit. Auditors use analytical procedures to plan where they should spend their audit effort, identify unexpected financial statement results that may indicate the need for more audit work, assess the reasonableness of various financial statement numbers and in the wrap-up stage of the audit. Specific analytical procedures are discussed in later chapters related to the financial statement audit. The important point here is that audit software can assist the auditor in performing these and other investigative manipulations of the client's financial records.

Audit software can perform processes for specific audit steps. For example, many basic steps for confirmations can be completed using audit software. Confirmation was introduced in earlier chapters and will be discussed in greater detail as it is used in the financial statement audit. However, a quick summary of the process helps to explain how software can aid the auditor.

To confirm balances such as accounts receivable or accounts payable, the auditor selects a sample of accounts, and the client signs a request to the account holders asking them to respond directly to the auditor regarding the accuracy of account information such as balance and mailing address. In order to accomplish this process, the sample is selected, the letters or forms are prepared and printed, and a record must be kept of those accounts for which confirmations are sent. The auditor can use audit software to automate all of these processes rather than having to perform them manually, eliminating a lot of tedious labor and increasing the efficiency of the audit.

Finally, audit software can be used to perform specialized tasks. Audit software that utilizes **expert systems** can assist the auditor in audit planning, analyzing materiality, and performing risk analysis. Another example of a specialized task is programmed analysis for fraud detection using Benford's law. **Benford's law** states that individual digits in a group of random digits will occur with a predictable frequency. Software that applies Benford's law analyzes numeric data and identifies patterns of numbers that occur with a frequency inconsistent with Benford's law. The outcome of this type of program gives the auditor information regarding transactions that need further investigation.

REVIEW QUESTIONS

L.1 What are examples of analytical procedures that can be performed using audit software?

L.2 What steps of audit procedures associated with the confirmation process can be completed using audit software?

L.3 What audit steps can be assisted using expert systems audit software?

L.4 How can software utilizing Benford's law assist the auditor with procedures to detect fraud?

In summary, IT, computers, and software are an integral part of auditing. The client's IT system and outputs are the targets of audit procedures for both the ICFR and financial statement phases of an integrated audit. The use of computers and audit software is integral to planning, performing, and documenting audit work.

KEY TERMS

Access controls. Controls that block unauthorized access to the computer system.

ACL. An abbreviation for Audit Command Language, a widely used audit software package.

Analytical procedures. Audit procedures that examine relationships of financial and nonfinancial data used for planning, assessing trends, identifying unexpected financial statement amounts, assessing reasonableness of balances and audit wrap up.

Application controls. Controls built into programs executed by the computer.

Benford's law. A principle based on a mathematical process that analyzes numeric data to identify digits that occur with an unexpected frequency; used for identifying potentially fraudulent data.

Completeness check. Control that identifies or rejects inputs or processing that results in blanks or zeros in a field that should contain nonzero data.

Entity-wide controls. May refer to general or application controls but refers to those that are designed to be uniform throughout an entire entity.

Error handling procedures. Those steps specified by policies to be followed when an error has occurred related to IT input and processing.

Expert systems. In an audit context, computer programs designed to mimic the processing steps of an expert in making judgments about the planning needed, materiality, risk, and so on.

General controls. Controls that deal with the IT environment, policies, and procedures.

Integrated test facility. Files and programs that are part of the IT system's regular processing procedures that run test data simultaneously with real data.

Limit check. Control that identifies or rejects data submitted for processing that exceeds a specified upper limit.

Parallel simulation. An audit procedure that independently reprocesses a selection of the client's real data to determine whether the IT application produces correct results.

Range check. Control that identifies or rejects data submitted for processing that falls outside either an upper or lower specified limit.

Run-to-run controls. Control step to determine that no data are dropped or added between one processing step or batch run and the next.

Test data approach. Refers to the auditor testing the operating effectiveness of an application control by processing data specifically created for the test.

Validity check. Control that identifies or rejects data submitted for processing that is not consistent with what has been specified as appropriate for a given field.

MULTIPLE CHOICE

8-48 When using a test data approach,

(a) the set of test data must only include at least one example of all valid data conditions.

(b) the set of test data will include a variety of errors so that the manner in which the application handles the errors can be investigated.

(c) multiple transactions of each type of condition should be included in the set of test data.

(d) the auditor must copy the client's program and run the test using generalized audit software.

8-49 A parallel simulation

(a) uses test data.

(b) tests the functioning of applications by running test data while the applications are processing on a real-time basis.

(c) risks corrupting a company's real data files.

(d) uses real data that has been previously processed by the client's application program.

8-50 Audit software

(a) is typically used to prepare work papers and for administrative tasks associated with the audit.

(b) can extract all of the data in a client's general ledger and transaction files for data selection, testing, and manipulation.

(c) can be used to test the operating effectiveness of a client's application controls as well as the accuracy of processing financial statement account balances.

(d) All of the above

8-51 Detection of which of the following conditions is made much easier with the use of computer audit software?

(a) Transactions are input or processed at unusual times.

(b) Transactions are input for processing before manual review and approval have occurred.

(c) Transactions go unrecorded to cover up employee theft of cash sales.

(d) Individuals who are authorized to sign checks only up to a specified dollar amount sign checks for larger amounts.

ACTIVITY ASSIGNMENTS

8-52   Access AS 2, Example B1 from the PCAOB Web site.

(a) List programmed application controls included in this PCAOB example of cash and accounts receivable processes.

(b) What are the assertions related to cash and accounts receivable being tested in this example?

(c) What aspects of the programmed application control did the auditor test through inquiry (discussion)? How was the audit evidence that was obtained through audit inquiry supplemented?

8-53   Access the most recent 10K for Best Buy. Find Item 1A, "Risk Factors." Read through the risk factors explained and find those related to the management information system.

(a) Does Best Buy comment regarding risks related to order entry, order fulfillment, pricing, point-of-sale processes, and inventory replenishment processes?

(b) How do the application controls discussed in this chapter relate to these functions?

(c) Based on the company's disclosures, how might problems that could occur in Best Buy's applications controls affect the company's financial outcomes, and the auditor's concerns for the financial statement portion of the audit?

(d) Address questions (a), (b), and (c) for Best Buy's disclosures related to the integrity and security of the customer's information.

ACL

 An exercise requiring the use of ACL software is available on the Auditing and Assurances Web site at www.wiley.com/college/hooks.

APPENDIX B: STATISTICAL TECHNIQUES AND TESTS OF CONTROLS

Auditors are not required to apply statistical theory when selecting samples or analyzing the results of audit tests performed on samples. However, auditors often use statistical approaches because this permits them to quantify sampling error and enhances efficiency. Being efficient basically means that statistical techniques allow the auditor to use the smallest sample size that produces reliable results and limits sampling risk to the level set as acceptable. Greatest audit efficiency is achieved if the auditor does not examine any more documents than necessary to support the audit conclusion.

Statistics aid efficiency because the auditor needs to control sampling risk, and sampling risk and sample size are linked through laws of probability. Generally, a larger sample size is associated with less sampling risk, and a smaller sample size is associated with more sampling risk. The auditor wants to limit sampling risk to the level that is determined to be acceptable for the audit. At the same time, the auditor does not want to do any more audit work than is needed. Statistical techniques help the auditor achieve both of these goals.

When statistics are applied to sampling and tests of controls, the auditor first:

plans the audit procedures,
makes judgments about acceptable risk levels, and
estimates the expected population characteristics.

Using this information, the sample size that is needed for the audit test is calculated using statistical approaches. Next, the sample is selected, planned audit procedures are conducted, and any control problems found are documented in the work papers. If the auditor finds any deviations from the company's controls, he or she evaluates the reasons for the deviations. Statistical calculations are used to conclude whether, based on the sample findings, the population's estimated deviation rate exceeds the rate the auditor has determined to be acceptable. The auditor uses the statistical findings and audit judgment to form a final conclusion about the results of the audit procedures.

Specific steps and an example of how they can be applied to a control test for cash disbursements follow:

1. **Determine the objective of the audit procedure.** *The objective of the audit procedure for this cash disbursements example is to determine whether all the disbursements out of a particular checking account are approved by a responsible party acting within his or her authority and have proper supporting documentation.*

2. **Define the population to be sampled.** *In this example, the population is all the cash disbursements made from the company's general checking account.* **Define the physical representation or sampling frame** of the population from which the sample is to be selected. For cash disbursements approval, the sampling frame can be either the bank statements or cash disbursements journal. The cash disbursements journal is appropriate only if the auditor has performed tests that show that the journal has a complete record of all the cash disbursements transactions shown on the bank statement.

   For this example, assume that the auditor has performed tests supporting the integrity of the cash disbursements journal, so the cash disbursements journal is the sampling frame used for the audit procedure. Once the auditor knows the sampling frame to be used, he or she decides the best way to select the sample. For example, cash disbursement transactions typically have identifying transaction numbers. So, the auditor can obtain a list of random numbers and select the transactions with identifying numbers that correspond to the random numbers. The auditor gets the list of random numbers from a random number generator in the statistical sampling computer application used. Another option is systematic selection with random starting point(s) or a random skip interval. *In this example the auditor uses a list of random numbers and selects the cash disbursement transactions that have those numbers as their identifiers.*

3. **Specify the item that is to be selected,** called the sampling unit. *For the cash disbursements test, the sampling unit is a cash disbursement transaction.*

4. **Define the characteristic the auditor wants to examine,** called the attribute. Basically this requires specifying the control that is being tested and what is considered a deviation from the control. A control deviation can be defined as failing to perform a control step, performing a step inadequately, or failing to document that the process was performed. *For this example, the characteristic is a signature by the company treasurer on each cash disbursement supporting document package (either electronic or hard copy) and an approval signature authorizing execution of the electronic cash disbursement on the authorization form. If the approval signature is missing on either the document package or the electronic disbursement authorization form, the control was not followed. Similarly, if a document has a signature, but it is not the treasurer's signature, the control was not followed.*

5. **Design the test of the control.** What will the auditor do to determine whether the prescribed control has been followed? With all the information we already know, this is straightforward. *The auditor selects the sample of cash disbursement transactions, and retrieves the supporting documents and electronic transaction authorization form for each transaction. The auditor examines those documents for the signature of the treasurer.*

At this point the auditor knows how the sample will be selected, what documents will be examined, and what the audit procedure will involve.

6. **Determine the sample size**. The easiest way to determine the sample size for our example is to examine prepared tables. The table for our example is shown in Exhibit B8-1. When working on a real engagement, auditors use software with sampling applications that determine the required sample size.[2] To determine the necessary sample size, the auditor uses decisions and estimates about risk and population characteristics.

One required piece of information is the risk the auditor is willing to accept of concluding that a control is effective when it is not. This is called the "risk of assessing control risk too low" or in a more general language, the risk of incorrect acceptance. The auditor also uses the tolerable rate of deviation. The tolerable rate is the maximum rate of deviation from the prescribed control that the auditor is willing to accept without changing the ICFR audit conclusion about the operating effectiveness of the control.

The tolerable rate also impacts the financial statement audit. The financial statement audit plan for a particular account may be based on an assumption that controls for that account are effective. For the financial statement audit, the tolerable rate is the maximum rate of deviation from the prescribed control that the auditor is willing to accept without needing to change the substantive audit plan for the account If the deviation rate is too high the auditor changes the audit plan and performs more substantive tests on the account balance during the financial statement audit.

Finally, the auditor uses the likely or expected population deviation rate as a factor in determining sample size. This is the auditor's best estimate, prior to performing the test, of the rate that deviations from the control procedure occur in the population. It is an estimate, but it is based on any prior information the auditor has, including the assessment of design effectiveness and prior engagements with the client. If the auditor does not have enough information to make an estimate, for example, on a first-year audit engagement, a possible option is to examine a small sample of transactions specifically for the purpose of estimating population deviation rate.

For our cash disbursements example, assume that the risk of assessing control risk too low is set at 5%. The tolerable rate of deviation is 4%. The expected population deviation rate is 1%. Using these pieces of information, we find that the required sample size is 156. The table shown in Exhibit B8-1 is for determining a sample size with a 5% risk of assessing control risk too low. A different table (or computer calculation) would be used for a different risk level. The table also displays numbers in parentheses, next to the sample size. These indicate the maximum number of control deviations that can be found in a *sample* without causing an audit conclusion that the deviation rate in the population is higher than the tolerable rate.

7. **Perform the audit procedures and document the results. Evaluate why the deviations occurred.** AS 3 requires that the auditor document the procedure and results sufficiently so that a reviewer can identify the items that were examined, what was done, who performed the procedure, and the results. In documenting the results, the auditor clearly states whether the control procedure, was or was not followed. The auditor evaluates the deviations to determine whether they are the result of simple human error or of something more serious such as fraud.

In our example the auditor found two instances of deviation from the prescribed control. In the first the treasurer signed the electronic transaction authorization form but failed to sign the supporting document package for the transaction. When the auditor asked about the deviation, the treasurer reexamined the supporting document package. The package was complete, and everything in the package was correct.

---

[2]Many firms have their own proprietary software. Others use software that is available for anyone to purchase. Regardless of the source, this software is relatively easy to use.

EXHIBIT B8-1

AICPA Attribute Sample Size Table, 5% Sampling Risk

5% SAMPLING RISK (RISK OF ASSESSING CONTROL RISK TOO LOW)

Expected Population Deviation Rate	Tolerable Rate										
	2%	3%	4%	5%	6%	7%	8%	9%	10%	15%	20%
0.00%	149(0)	99(0)	74(0)	59(0)	49(0)	42(0)	36(0)	32(0)	29(0)	19(0)	14(0)
0.25	236(1)	157(1)	117(1)	93(1)	78(1)	66(1)	58(1)	51(1)	46(1)	30(1)	22(1)
0.50	*	157(1)	117(1)	93(1)	78(1)	66(1)	58(1)	51(1)	46(1)	30(1)	22(1)
0.75	*	208(2)	117(1)	93(1)	78(1)	66(1)	58(1)	51(1)	46(1)	30(1)	22(1)
1.00	*	*	156(2)	93(1)	78(1)	66(1)	58(1)	51(1)	46(1)	30(1)	22(1)
1.25	*	*	156(2)	124(2)	78(1)	66(1)	58(1)	51(1)	46(1)	30(1)	22(1)
1.50	*	*	192(3)	124(2)	103(2)	66(1)	58(1)	51(1)	46(1)	30(1)	22(1)
1.75	*	*	227(4)	153(3)	103(2)	88(2)	77(2)	51(1)	46(1)	30(1)	22(1)
2.00	*	*	*	181(4)	127(3)	88(2)	77(2)	68(2)	46(1)	30(1)	22(1)
2.25	*	*	*	208(5)	127(3)	88(2)	77(2)	68(2)	61(2)	30(1)	22(1)
2.50	*	*	*	*	150(4)	109(3)	77(2)	68(2)	61(2)	30(1)	22(1)
2.75	*	*	*	*	173(5)	109(3)	95(3)	68(2)	61(2)	30(1)	22(1)
3.00	*	*	*	*	195(6)	129(4)	95(3)	84(3)	61(2)	30(1)	22(1)
3.25	*	*	*	*	*	148(5)	112(4)	84(3)	61(2)	30(1)	22(1)
3.50	*	*	*	*	*	167(7)	112(5)	84(4)	76(3)	40(2)	22(1)
3.75	*	*	*	*	*	185(7)	129(5)	100(4)	76(3)	40(2)	22(1)
4.00	*	*	*	*	*	*	146(6)	100(4)	89(4)	40(2)	22(1)
5.00	*	*	*	*	*	*	*	158(8)	116(6)	40(2)	30(2)
6.00	*	*	*	*	*	*	*	*	179(11)	50(3)	30(2)
7.00	*	*	*	*	*	*	*	*	*	68(5)	37(3)

Source: AICPA, *Audit Guide, Audit Sampling* (New York, 2008).

Note: The number of expected misstatements appears in parentheses. These tables assume a large population.

* = Sample size is too large to be cost effective for most audit applications.

The treasurer offered that the missing signature was simply an oversight—a careless, human error.

In the second deviation, both documents were signed, but the signature was of the chief cashier in the treasurer's office. Further investigation revealed that the treasurer was out sick on the day of the second transaction. Also, the company's policies and procedures authorized the chief cashier to authorize cash disbursements up to $5,000 in that situation. The disbursement that the chief cashier approved was for $1,450.

8. **Calculate the rate of deviation found in the sample and the upper deviation rate.** The sample deviation rate, sometimes called the exception rate, is simply the number of control problems the auditor found divided by the total number of items in the sample. *For our example, the deviation is 2/156, or 1.3%. However, the auditor might make a different calculation based on the results of the audit procedure. The chief cashier was acting within the authority set forth in the company's policies by signing in the treasurer's absence for the disbursement of $1,450. Based on this, the auditor could decide that the signature was not a control deviation, and the sample deviation is then calculated as 1/156 or .6%.*

Sample Deviation Rate:

$$2/156 = .013$$

or

$$1/156 = .006$$

EXHIBIT B8-2

AICPA Tests of Controls
Results Evaluation
Table, 5% Risk of
Overreliance

Sample Size	Actual Number of Control Procedure Deviations Found										
	0	1	2	3	4	5	6	7	8	9	10
20	14.0	*	*	*	*	*	*	*	*	*	*
25	11.3	17.7	*	*	*	*	*	*	*	*	*
30	9.6	14.9	19.6	*	*	*	*	*	*	*	*
35	8.3	12.9	17.0	*	*	*	*	*	*	*	*
40	7.3	11.4	15.0	18.3	*	*	*	*	*	*	*
45	6.5	10.2	13.4	16.4	19.2	*	*	*	*	*	*
50	5.9	9.2	12.1	14.8	17.4	19.9	*	*	*	*	*
55	5.4	8.4	11.1	13.5	15.9	18.2	*	*	*	*	*
60	4.9	7.7	10.2	12.5	14.7	16.8	18.8	*	*	*	*
65	4.6	7.1	9.4	11.5	13.6	15.5	17.4	19.3	*	*	*
70	4.2	6.6	8.8	10.8	12.7	14.5	16.3	18.0	19.7	*	*
75	4.0	6.2	8.2	10.1	11.8	13.6	15.2	16.9	18.5	*	*
80	3.7	5.8	7.7	9.5	11.1	12.7	14.3	15.9	17.4	18.9	*
90	3.3	5.2	6.9	8.4	9.9	11.4	12.8	14.2	15.5	16.9	18.2
100	3.0	4.7	6.2	7.6	9.0	10.3	11.5	12.8	14.0	15.2	16.4
125	2.4	3.8	5.0	6.1	7.2	8.3	9.3	10.3	11.3	12.3	13.2
150	2.0	3.2	4.2	5.1	6.0	6.9	7.8	8.6	9.5	10.3	11.1
200	1.5	2.4	3.2	3.9	4.6	5.2	5.9	6.5	7.2	7.8	8.4
300	1.0	1.6	2.1	2.6	3.1	3.5	4.0	4.4	4.8	5.2	5.6
400	0.8	1.2	1.6	2.0	2.3	2.7	3.0	3.3	3.6	3.9	4.3
500	0.6	1.0	1.3	1.6	1.9	2.1	2.4	2.7	2.9	3.2	3.4

Source: AICPA, *Audit Guide, Audit Sampling* (New York, 2008).

Note: This table present upper limits (body of table) as percentages. This table assumes a large population.

*Over 20%

The auditor also calculates an upper deviation rate, which is an estimate of the possible rate of deviations in the *population* based on the audit step results *and* taking into consideration sampling risk. Since it also considers sampling risk, the audit conclusion incorporates the risk of incorrect acceptance, which was set at 5%. The auditor is able to conclude that there is no more than a 5% risk that the population deviation rate is higher than the calculated upper rate. Auditors use statistics software to calculate the upper deviation rate. For learning purposes we continue with our use of tables. We consult a table for a 5% risk of incorrect acceptance, shown in Exhibit B8-2.

In Exhibit B8-2, first find the column for 1 deviation, which is the number of deviations actually identified in the sample during the audit test. Move down the column to the rows closest to the actual sample size. You should notice that as the sample sizes get larger the computed upper deviation rates get smaller. This is logical since the table allows for sampling risk and sampling risk gets smaller as the sample size gets larger. For a sample size of 150, with one actual deviation found, the calculated upper deviation rate is 3.2%. *For a sample size of 150, with one actual deviation found, the calculated upper deviation rate is 3.2%. Our sample size was 156, which is larger than the sample of 150. This means that our calculated upper deviation rate is actually a little less than 3.2%. Note that the calculated upper deviation rate shown in the table for one actual deviation and a larger sample size of 200 is even smaller, at 2.4%. Even with a sample size of 150, the calculated upper deviation rate for our sample with one deviation is 3.2%, which is smaller than the tolerable deviation rate of 4%.*

If the auditor concludes that both transactions identified by the audit procedures are control deviations, the table does not provide enough information and a calculation is required. For the column representing 2 actual deviations, a sample of 150 produces a calculated upper deviation rate of 4.2%, which is larger than the tolerable deviation rate of 4%. In the same column, a sample of 200 produces a calculated upper deviation rate of 3.2. An interpolation calculation can be used to approximate the upper deviation rate using the tables, and produces a calculated upper deviation of approximately 4. Recall that Exhibit B8-1 that was used to determine the sample size indicated that 2 was the maximum number of deviations that could be found in a sample of 156 and not exceed the tolerable deviation rate of 4%. As stated earlier, when a statistical sampling application package is used, the exact upper deviation rate is calculated by the program.[3]

9. **Form final conclusions about the results. The auditor considers both the statistical outcome and any qualitative factors in concluding on the results of the audit procedure.** *In our example of cash disbursements, the auditor probably concludes that the control operates effectively. For the transaction in which the treasurer failed to sign the supporting documentation package, the form authorizing the electronic transaction was signed. As suggested in Step 7, the auditor probably talks to the treasurer to find out whether the deviation was an oversight in which the treasurer looked at the supporting documents and simply forgot to sign off. An explanation that would cause the auditor concern is if the treasurer states that he or she often reviews only the electronic transaction form without looking at the supporting documents. But this response from the treasurer would be surprising since only one problem was found in the sample.*

   Regarding the transaction authorized by the chief cashier, the auditor also follows up with a conversation. Questions the auditor asks include:

   How often is the treasurer absent?
   Is the chief cashier ever asked to authorize cash disbursement transactions that are for greater amounts than the company policy permits?
   If so, what happens?

   If the answers to these questions cause the auditor concern, further follow-up is needed. Otherwise the auditor concludes that the control operates as designed and is effective.

   The impact on the integrated audit of the conclusion that the control is effective is twofold. First, there is no indication from this test that a deficiency exists in ICFR that would impact the ICFR audit opinion. Second, if the auditor plans to rely on this control in performing the financial statement audit, this test provides no evidence that the auditor needs to reevaluate the audit plan.

---

[3]Linear interpolation producing a calculated upper deviation rate of approximately 4% is as follows:

$$CUDR = \left[\frac{(156 - 150)(3.2 - 4.2)}{200 - 150} \right] + 4.2 = 4.08$$

Substantive Procedures and the Financial Statement Audit

1. Recognize the audit associations of transaction cycles, account balances, management assertions, and audit steps.

2. Understand the reasons an audit opinion is limited to reasonable assurance.

3. Learn to draw conclusions from the results of audit tests of account balances.

4. Understand the audit documentation appropriate for substantive tests and procedures.

5. Become familiar with specific topics that are particularly important to financial statement audits, for example, estimation processes, going-concern considerations, and period-end cutoff.

6. Learn the substantive tests and procedures that are important for the various financial statement accounts.

Chapter 9 Resources

AU 230, AICPA, PCAOB, *Due Professional Care in the Performance of Work*

AU 312, AICPA, PCAOB, *Audit Risk and Materiality in Conducting an Audit*

AU 313, PCAOB, *Substantive Tests Prior to the Balance Sheet Date*

AU 314, AICPA, *Understanding the Entity and Its Environment and Assessing the Risks of Material Misstatement*

AU 316, AICPA, PCAOB, *Consideration of Fraud in a Financial Statement Audit*

AU 317, AICPA, PCAOB, *Illegal Acts by Clients*

AU 318, AICPA, *Performing Audit Procedures in Response to Assessed Risks and Evaluating the Audit Evidence Obtained*

AU 319, PCAOB, *Consideration of Internal Control in a Financial Statement Audit*

AU 326, AICPA, *Audit Evidence*

AU 326, PCAOB, *Evidential Matter*

AU 328, AICPA, PCAOB, *Auditing Fair Value Measurements and Disclosures*

AU 329, AICPA, PCAOB, *Analytical Procedures*

AU 330, AICPA, PCAOB, *The Confirmation Process*

AU 331, AICPA, PCAOB, *Inventories*

AU 332, AICPA, PCAOB, *Auditing Derivative Instruments, Hedging Activities, and Investments in Securities*

AU 334, AICPA, PCAOB, *Related Parties*

AU 339, AICPA, *Audit Documentation*

AU 341, AICPA, PCAOB, *The Auditor's Consideration of an Entity's Ability to Continue as a Going Concern*

AU 342, AICPA, PCAOB, *Auditing Accounting Estimates*

AU 350, AICPA, PCAOB, *Audit Sampling*

FASB ASC 820-10, *Fair Value Measurements and Disclosures*

FASB ASC 850-10, Related Party Disclosures

PCAOB AS 3, *Audit Documentation*

PCAOB AS 5, *An Audit of Internal Control Over Financial Reporting That is Integrated with an Audit of Financial Statements*

SEC Staff Accounting Bulletin 99, *Materiality*

SEC Staff Accounting Bulletin 108, *Considering the Effects of Prior Year Misstatements When Quantifying Misstatements in Current Year Financial Statements*

INTRODUCTION

This chapter presents an overview of the substantive tests and procedures that are used by auditors during the financial statement audit of an integrated audit. The audit activities you have learned up to this point are client acceptance and continuance, audit planning, and tests of controls. These activities include risk assessment, evaluating fraud possibilities, setting materiality thresholds for planning purposes, understanding the client's system, assessing the design effectiveness of internal control over financial reporting (ICFR), selecting controls to test, and testing and assessing the operating effectiveness of ICFR.

Many of the topics introduced earlier are also important for substantive audit procedures. Among these are:

Understanding the company's activities and accounting transactions

Audit planning

Fraud consideration

Supervision and review

IT impacts

Sampling and assessing test results

Audit documentation

The substantive procedures of the financial statement audit are different from what you have learned so far in that they specifically target account balances and disclosures. The purpose of substantive tests and procedures is to obtain audit evidence on any misstatements in the various accounts and disclosures that would prevent the auditor from concluding that the financial statements are free of material misstatement.

TRANSACTION CYCLES AND ACCOUNT BALANCES [LO 1]

Through client acceptance and planning activities, the auditor learns the client's business activities, important transactions and controls, management assertions that are important to the various financial statement accounts, and risks that might cause those management assertions to be incorrect. The auditor considers important accounts and the client processes from transaction initiation through financial statement reporting. Therefore, using **transaction cycles** is an effective way to organize audit work. Transaction cycles can be defined differently for different businesses and industries, but generally most businesses have a cycle dealing with

- Sales or sources of revenue and cash receipts
- Purchases or acquisitions and cash disbursements
- Human resources
- Production or inventory, which, when necessary includes cost accounting
- Activities that are financing related, such as investment, debt, and equity transactions

These transaction cycles comprise the activities of most businesses. They are used in the later chapters of this book to explain the integrated audit in greater detail. In discussing substantive procedures of the financial statement audit, this chapter assumes that you have a basic understanding of the various transaction cycles. This chapter also uses the organization of accounts as they are presented on financial statements to explain audit activities. Exhibit 9-1 presents the overview diagram of substantive procedures.

Organizing the Audit Tasks

The audit plan is part of the audit documentation that records planning and audit activities. The audit plan may be organized using transaction cycles or financial statement account balances. For example, when the auditor is testing controls over the sales cycle, he or she addresses how a sales transaction is initiated, processed and recorded, and how the payment

EXHIBIT 9-1

Substantive Procedures on Accounts and Disclosures

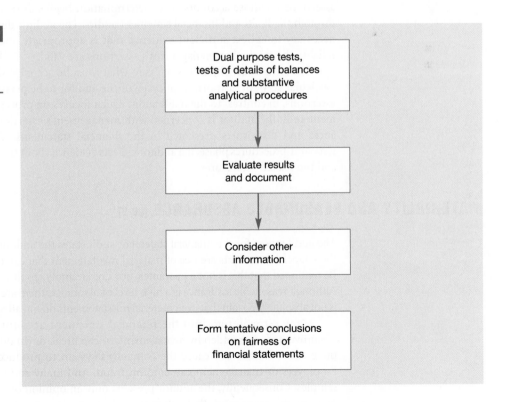

is collected. If the sale involves extending credit, this process also includes any approval and billing activities. Even though they are linked through transaction cycles, ultimately, the aggregation of all the transactions for all of the activities results in account balances shown on the financial statements.

The transaction cycles may guide the organization of the audit. But the *various accounts* that are important or material to the financial statements also impact the emphasis of audit activities and the way tasks are divided up among the audit team. The transaction cycle chapters (Chapters 10 and 12 through 15) explain the integrated audit based on a company's activities. The various financial statement accounts, their management assertions, risks to those assertions, and an overview of the audit steps applicable to the account balances and disclosures are introduced later in this chapter. This account-by-account overview should help you understand the steps as they are presented in later chapters related to the transaction cycles.

Management Assertions, Audit Objectives, and Evidence

This book's continuing theme is that an integrated audit investigates the fairness of management's assertions that are communicated through the financial statements. When management shows a "line item" description on the financial statements with a related account total, management is communicating that the amount is supported by transactions that really occurred, or assets and liabilities that really exist. Management is asserting that the amounts are correct, based on GAAP or whatever basis of accounting is used. Implied in the presentation is the proper historical cost or other valuation, such as fair value, if appropriate. The amount is presented in the correct period with proper recording of any necessary allocations to more than one accounting period. Management is also asserting that all the necessary disclosures are included and that the disclosures meet the requirements of applicable professional standards. The substantive procedures of the financial statement audit specifically and directly investigate whether these messages communicated by management are valid.

The auditor determines which accounts are significant and the relevant management assertions for those accounts. This determination begins during planning and continues through the ICFR and financial statement audits. The auditor decides what audit steps are necessary to collect sufficient evidence that is appropriate and thus both relevant and reliable about whether management's assertions are valid.

The term **audit objectives** refers to what must be accomplished during the audit of a particular account or transaction cycle for the auditor to be persuaded about management assertions. In contrast to the ICFR audit, which focuses on processes, in the financial statement audit the auditor is concerned with management's assertions about the account balances and disclosures presented in the financial statements. Thus, in the substantive-tests-and-procedures phase, the auditor collects evidence about the account balance amounts and the related disclosures.

MATERIALITY AND REASONABLE ASSURANCE [LO 2]

The audit report for the financial statement audit states the auditor's opinion about whether the financial statements are free of material misstatement that can occur from error or fraud. Be reminded that this is not a guarantee, nor does it imply absolute accuracy of the amounts. Although reasonable assurance is a high level of assurance, there are many reasons the auditor is not absolutely certain that even material misstatements do not affect the financial statements.

Many estimates go into the financial statement account balances. ICFR can be circumvented, overridden by management, or can break down due to human error. Any of these ICFR failures can cause the company's system to produce improper information. Employees or management can commit fraud. And many audit judgments are based on samples. Consequently, the auditor presents only an opinion of reasonable assurance. The opinion communicates that, although there may be misstatements in the financial statements, the auditor has accumulated persuasive evidence supporting the conclusion they are not of a nature or amount that is material.

Impacts of Sampling

Sampling was introduced in the discussion of ICFR and controls tests in Chapter 8. Sampling is also used for **tests of details of balances**. Tests of details of balances involve examining transactions to determine whether the underlying evidence corresponds with the amounts and other information that is in the company's records and reported in its financial statements. The existence of correspondence supports management's assertions. Tests of details of balances can be conducted using many of the audit procedures discussed earlier, for example, inspection, external confirmation, and reperformance.

The use of sampling is based on an underlying assumption that the auditor can examine evidence for less than 100% of all or part of an account balance and come to a conclusion about the population from which the sample was drawn. The accumulated experiences of auditors using sampling on innumerable audits support this assumption. However, when the auditor examines evidence from a sample of the transactions, assets, or liabilities that make up an account balance, possible sources of error must be considered.

Sampling Error

Errors in audit tests and procedures are either nonsampling or sampling errors. Nonsampling, human errors can happen for several reasons. First, the audit plan might be faulty. An audit plan that directs the auditor to use the wrong test or the wrong supporting document to examine an account balance causes the auditor to make unsupported conclusions. Another possibility is that an auditor might make a mistake in performing a test or interpreting a result. Auditors recognize that these types of nonsampling errors can occur. Quality control steps include supervision and review and are intended to increase the likelihood that nonsampling errors are prevented. If human errors occur, a high-quality review process should discover them during the audit.

Sampling error can also occur on an audit when the selected sample does not represent the population. Sampling error can cause the auditor to incorrectly conclude that an account balance is free of misstatement when it is actually materially misstated—incorrectly accepting the balance. Sampling error can also cause an auditor to conclude that an account balance is materially misstated when it is free of misstatement—incorrectly rejecting the balance. When the auditor is making decisions based on a sample, he or she is primarily concerned about concluding that the account balance is fair when it is not. This incorrect acceptance mistake impacts audit effectiveness because the auditor does not find the misstatement.

AUDITING IN ACTION

Impact of Sampling Error on Audit Decisions

		Account Balance	
		Fairly stated	Materially misstated
Auditor's Conclusion about the Account Balance	Fairly stated	Correct audit decision	Incorrect audit decision—incorrect acceptance, effectiveness problem
	Materially misstated	Incorrect audit decision—incorrect rejection, efficiency problem	Correct audit decision

AUDITING IN ACTION

Faulty Audit Conclusions Related to Sampling Risk

When the auditor uses a sample from a population that makes up an account balance, the sample may not be representative of the rest of the population.

Incorrect Rejection:
Audit Efficiency Problem

> Concluding
> that the
> account balance
> is materially
> misstated
> when it is not.

Incorrect Acceptance:
Audit Effectiveness Problem

> Concluding
> that the
> account balance
> is not materially
> misstated
> when it is.

The incorrect audit decision that the account balance is misstated when the amount is proper is an incorrect rejection error. This is not as important as an incorrect acceptance error. Incorrect rejection is an efficiency or "cost of the audit" problem. When evidence based on a sample indicates a problem, the auditor modifies the audit plan to investigate the problem. With an incorrect rejection error, additional audit work will almost certainly reveal that the problems identified are in a nonrepresentative sample and the account balance is proper. In contrast, if the auditor makes an incorrect acceptance error and concludes that an account balance is properly stated when it is actually materially misstated, the auditor has no "tip-off" of the problem. Since there is no indication of a problem, the auditor does not do additional work, and the incorrect acceptance error remains undetected.

Sampling error occurs when the sample the auditor uses to decide about the fairness of an account balance is not representative of the other transactions in the account balance. An example of examining invoices provides a simple way to see how sampling can cause the auditor to come to the wrong conclusion. Assume that the auditor examines a sample of payments for utilities and finds that several of the bills in the sample are recorded at less than the actual amount of the transaction. The auditor concludes that many of the bills are improperly recorded and the entire expense account balance is materially understated. This may occur because the auditor simply had the bad luck to pick a sample that included the only transactions in the account balance that were posted incorrectly. In this situation the auditor's preliminary conclusion about the account balance is that it is misstated. This is an example of incorrect rejection. As a follow-up procedure, the auditor performs more tests to investigate the extent of the problem. Very probably, during the follow-up procedures, the sampling error will be found.

Consider the reverse situation. What if many of the utilities payments are posted incorrectly, at amounts less than the actual transactions? However, this time all sample items selected by the auditor are posted at the proper amount. The auditor concludes that the utility expense account balance is proper when it is really understated. This is an example of sampling error causing incorrect acceptance.

Analytical Procedures

Just as quality control procedures can help the auditor detect human errors, **analytical procedures** can help auditors detect mistakes that result from sampling error. Continuing the example above, assume the auditor selects a sample of utility payment transactions, examines the supporting documents, and concludes that the account balance is fairly stated. But because the sample is not representative of the rest of the transactions, the auditor's conclusion is wrong.

The auditor also performs analytical procedures on the account, comparing the total amount in the utility expense account to the prior year's expense and the current year's budget. From this step a discrepancy is identified. If the account balance is materially understated, the balance in the current year's expense account will be less than both last year's account balance and the current year's budget. In this situation, because the analytical procedure produces conflicting evidence, the auditor performs more tests of details of balances that should result in the auditor finding the sampling error. This type of analytical procedure is usually called *fluctuation analysis*. Exhibit 9-2 shows an example of fluctuation analysis.

EXHIBIT 9-2

Analytical Procedures, Fluctuation Analysis

Income Statement	Current Year	Common Size	Prior Year	Common Size	Change $	Change %
Revenue	11,000,000	100%	10,500,000	100%	500,000	4.8%
Cost of Goods Sold	8,165,000	74%	8,035,000	77%	130,000	1.6%
Gross Margin	2,835,000	26%	2,465,000	23%	370,000	15.0%
Admin. Expenses	110,000	1%	112,000	1%	(2,000)	-1.8%
Selling Expenses	60,000	1%	58,000	1%	2,000	3.4%
Interest Expense	20,000	0%	30,000	0%	(10,000)	33.3%
Earnings Before Taxes	2,645,000	24%	2,265,000	22%	380,000	16.8%
Tax Expense (40%)	1,058,000	10%	906,000	9%	152,000	16.8%
Net Income	**1,587,000**	14%	**1,359,000**	13%	228,000	16.8%
Assets						
Cash	12,000,000	30%	10,500,000	28%	1,500,000	14.3%
Receivable (net)	8,000,000	20%	7,300,000	19%	700,000	9.6%
Inventory	1,600,000	4%	1,200,000	3%	400,000	33.3%
Prepaid Expenses	1,500,000	4%	1,000,000	3%	500,000	50.0%
PP&E (net)	17,500,000	43%	18,000,000	47%	(500,000)	-2.8%
Total Assets	40,600,000	100%	38,000,000	100%	2,600,000	6.8%
Liabilities and Equity						
Accounts Payable	1,013,000	2%	2,500,000	7%	(1,487,000)	59.5%
Long-Term Debt	14,000,000	34%	11,000,000	29%	3,000,000	27.3%
Capital Stock	4,000,000	10%	4,000,000	11%	-	0.0%
Paid in Capital	8,000,000	20%	8,000,000	21%	-	0.0%
Retained Earnings	13,587,000	33%	12,500,000	33%	1,087,000	8.7%
Total L + OE	40,600,000	100%	38,000,000	100%	2,600,000	6.8%

Audit Risk Model

The **audit risk model** presented in Chapter 8 can be used to explain the relationship of tests of details of balances and analytical procedures with audit risk and audit planning. The initial format of the audit risk model is:

$$AR = RMM \times DR$$
$$or$$
$$AR = (IR \times CR) \times DR$$

where AR is audit risk,
RMM is risk of material misstatement,
IR is inherent risk,
CR is control risk, and
DR is detection risk.

Overall audit risk is the risk of issuing a clean audit opinion when it is not justified. However, audit risk in this planning model is targeted at a more specific level and refers to the possibility of concluding that an account balance is fair when it is not. Risk of material misstatement is the likelihood that a material misstatement occurs in an account balance. The likelihood of a material misstatement in an account balance is a function of inherent risk and control risk.

Inherent risk is the risk that a relevant management assertion for an account balance is not appropriate—in other words, the likelihood that an account is misstated just because of the level of risk associated with that particular transaction or account. For example, the risk that management's *valuation* assertion is not justified is greater for an account that requires estimates and judgment for valuation than for an account whose value is reflected by the dollar amount of an exchange transaction with an outside party. Valuing obsolete inventory to determine the proper dollar value of the account has more inherent risk than counting cash.

Control risk is the risk that a company's ICFR is not sufficient to either prevent or detect a misstatement. In other words, control risk begins with the risk that the company's ICFR will not prevent a misstatement from occurring. The other aspect of control risk is the possibility that once a misstatement occurs, the ICFR will fail to detect it on a timely basis using the company's normal control procedures.

Finally, *detection risk* is the risk that (1) an account balance is materially misstated, (2) controls do not prevent or detect the misstatement, and (3) the auditor's procedures also miss the problem. The tools that the auditor uses to detect misstatements are tests of details of balances and analytical procedures. The auditor plans audit procedures to keep detection risk at an acceptably low level.

During audit planning, the audit risk model can be used to help the auditor analyze the various risks. When analytical procedures are included, the audit risk model is stated as:

$$AR = RMM \times DR$$
$$AR = (IR \times CR) \times (TD \times AP)$$

where TD is the detection risk of tests of details of balances and
AP is the detection risk of analytical procedures.

Again, this mathematical relationship describes the risk that an auditor will conclude that an account balance is properly stated when it is not.

In summary, the components of audit risk for an account balance are as follows.

1. The account balance is misstated because of the inherent nature of the account or transactions.
2. The company's control procedures do not prevent or detect the misstatement.
3. The auditor does not discover the misstatement through tests of details of balances.
4. The auditor performs analytical procedures and still misses the problem.

The impact of statistics on tests of details of balances is similar to what was discussed in Chapter 8 relating to controls tests. If statistical techniques are used to plan the sample size and evaluate the results, the probability that a sampling error occurs can be expressed quantitatively. In the audit risk model, the sampling error is expressed as TD, the detection risk of tests of details of balances. Said another way, TD is the risk that when the auditor is using a sample for tests of details of balances, he or she incorrectly accepts an account balance as fair when it is materially misstated because the sample used does not represent the population from which it was selected. For a statistically based quantitative evaluation of a sample to be reliable, the sample must be selected using a method that produces a random sample.

Sampling risk always exists, whether or not statistical techniques are used. Statistical techniques simply permit the risk of sampling error to be measured. By measuring the risk of sampling error, statistical techniques promote audit efficiency. The risk of sampling error is related to sample size. When the auditor measures the risk of sampling error, it is possible to use the smallest sample size possible while keeping risk at the acceptable level. Statistical techniques for tests of details of balances are discussed in Appendix A to this chapter.

REVIEW QUESTIONS

A.1 What is the difference between the target of controls tests and the target of substantive procedures?

A.2 What are tests of details of balances?

A.3 What types of human errors can occur in an audit, and how does the auditor reduce the likelihood that these human errors will go undetected?

A.4 What is sampling error?

A.5 How do tests of details of balances and analytical procedures interact in affecting detection risk?

PERFORMING SUBSTANTIVE TESTS AND PROCEDURES

Auditors perform substantive tests using tests of details of balances and **substantive analytical procedures**. Tests of details of balances can be applied to an entire population of transactions that make up an account balance. For example, 100% of transactions might be examined when the account balance is composed of very few transactions that can each be examined by the auditor in detail. For this situation the resolution at the end of the test of details of balances is usually straightforward: the company corrects any misstatements the auditor identifies in the company's records and financial statements.

Another possibility is for the auditor to select a sample from the population of transactions that make up an account balance. The auditor tests the sample of transactions for the important management assertions. If the auditor finds misstatements in the sample, he or she uses that information to estimate the misstatements in the total population. Then, the auditor proposes to the client that an adjusting entry should be posted to the company's records. The amount of the adjustment is determined using the auditor's test information and follow-up investigations made by the client.

The auditor can also stratify the population into different categories. This allows the auditor to use different procedures on the different categories. For example, the auditor may examine 100% of the transactions for one segment and test a sample of the population that makes up the other segment.

When dividing the population, auditors base stratification on important characteristics that may influence the risk of misstatement or ease of applying a particular audit approach. For example, the auditor can stratify the transactions based on dollar size or frequency of the company's transactions with particular customers. The auditor can then choose to examine 100% of the large dollar transactions and the accounts of all customers

AUDITING IN ACTION

Segmenting a Population for Tests of Details of Balances

Lam Optics and IT Equipment Corporation maintains and repairs computers and other equipment used by engineers for performing measurements and calculations. Lam has an operations center adjacent to Hometown Engineering Corporation. Second-Best Engineering is two blocks away. These two engineering companies are Lam's primary customers. Because of the nature and quality of its work, Lam has a total of 1,000 recurring customers over a multistate area. At the end of the fiscal year Lam's accounts receivable are $18 million, with 70% of that amount from Hometown and Second-Best.

The audit plan is to divide the population of accounts receivable into two segments. Segment one is made up of the accounts receivable from Hometown and Second-Best, and this segment of the population (the two customers' balances) is examined on a 100% basis. Using this approach, the audit team examines $12.6 million of the total balance of $18 million by examining only two customer accounts. Confirmations are sent to both customers, the responses reconciled if necessary, and supporting documents examined as appropriate. The auditor also monitors payments received by Lam in the next fiscal period to establish that payment is received.

The other segment of the population is examined using a sample. The remaining 30% of the accounts receivable balance of $5.4 million is owed by 223 of Lam's other 998 customers. The balances owed by the 223 customers all range between $20,000 and $30,000. The results of controls tests were good, and the auditor plans to perform other analytical procedures. The auditor decides not to use statistical analysis for this particular sample and selects a sample of 40 customer balances. The 40 selected accounts receivable are audited using confirmations, with reconciliation as needed, and follow-up in the next fiscal year for payments received.

with whom the company does business at least once a month. Transactions not fitting those criteria can be examined based on a sample.

A general description of the initial steps for a test of details of balances using a sample is as follows:

1. *Determine which account and assertion is being evaluated.* What is the audit objective that is to be accomplished with the procedure?
2. *Decide what audit procedure needs to be used to test the assertion.* Examining supporting documents, confirming with outsiders, and recalculating amounts are frequently used for substantive tests of details of balances.

For the test to be effective it must proceed in the proper direction. For example, if the auditor is evaluating the management assertion that all accounts receivable or inventory *exists,* the procedure is based on a sample selected from recorded accounts receivable or inventory subsidiary ledgers.

> For **existence** of *accounts receivable*, the auditor confirms that the debtor agrees that the recorded amount is owed to the audit client. The auditor selects the sample from the recorded accounts receivable subsidiary ledger and obtains evidence to support that the recorded accounts receivable exist. This procedure does not indicate whether the receivable will be collected, so valution is tested in other ways.

> For **existence** of *inventory*, the auditor inspects the physical inventory to see that the inventory items are real. The auditor selects the sample from the recorded detailed inventory ledger and examines the physical items to obtain evidence that the recorded inventory exists. This test does not accomplish all of the audit objectives for inventory. An inventory account balance has a number of other assertions that must also be tested, such as that the company has rights to the inventory and proper costing or valuation. Looking at the recorded inventory only establishes its existence.

If the assertion being tested is that recorded accounts payable are **complete,** the procedure is based on a sample selected from the company's vendor list.

For *completeness* of accounts payable, the sample selection is from the vendor list regardless of the amount of the payable shown in the company's records as owed to each vendor at year end. The concern for the completeness assertion is that some of the items that should have been recorded have been omitted. Selecting from the sample of recorded accounts payable gives the auditor evidence only about the items that *have* been recorded—not about whether any items *have not* been recorded.

The auditor may send a confirmation to each vendor and use any responses as evidence about whether the amount posted at year end is complete. The auditor includes in the confirmation process vendors for which the company's records show a zero balance at year end. If the confirmation response is that the company has a payable to the vendor that was more than the amount of the confirmation, this indicates that the company's year-end accounts payable are incomplete.

The auditor may also examine cash disbursements made to the vendors in the sample in the subsequent year. The purpose is to determine whether the cash disbursements are for recorded payables from the prior year or for expenses of the current year. A completeness assertion misstatement exists if the auditor finds a payment in the subsequent year that is for an account payable of the prior year that was not shown as a liability on the company's records at the fiscal year end.

3. *Decide on the sampling method.* The auditor determines whether to use a nonstatistical or a statistical approach. If a statistical sampling approach is used, the auditor decides among several methods and makes decisions appropriate for that method. These issues are discussed in Appendix A to the chapter.

4. *Decide on the sampling frame,* or physical population from which the sample is selected, and the sampling unit.

   The physical population has to be consistent with the audit procedure. In other words, the physical population has to allow the audit test to proceed in the direction specified. For example, a computer file of recorded transactions cannot be used for a test of whether all transactions are recorded.

   The physical population or sampling frame also has to be appropriate for the sampling method. If a statistical sampling method is used, the sample must be randomly selected and the sampling frame must allow for this.

   The sampling unit must be appropriate for the sampling frame.

   > If the auditor is selecting the accounts receivable balances of individual customers, then the sampling unit is a customer account balance. The appropriate sampling frame is the accounts receivable subsidiary ledger.

   > If the auditor is testing accounts receivables based on recorded invoices, then the sampling unit is the invoice number or amount of a sale on credit. For this test, the sampling frame has to include the detail postings to customers' accounts receivable records showing individual invoices, rather than just the subsidiary ledger balances.

5. *Determine the method to select the sample,* such as utilizing identifying numbers produced by a random number generator, systematic sampling with a random start, or haphazard sampling. Systematic sampling can also use multiple random starts or a random skip interval. Block sampling, which involves looking at a sample of contiguous items (for example, one week's worth of transactions or all invoices from #100 to #200) is sometimes used by auditors but rarely has the randomness necessary for the sample to be representative of the population.

   The selection method has to fit with the sampling method and sampling frame.

   > Assume a statistical sampling approach is used, the sampling frame is the accounts receivable subsidiary ledger and the sampling unit is customer accounts receivable balances. In this situation the auditor can use a random number generator to produce account numbers that can be used to select the sample.

In contrast, assume the test is of individual sales transactions on account. If the sampling frame is a drawer full of paper invoices for sales on account that are filed in chronological order based on date of sale, the auditor cannot use a random number approach applied based on customer account numbers. If the invoices are filed chronologically, the customer account numbers are not in order and the auditor cannot use them for selection. In this situation the auditor has to use a systematic sample with some element of randomness built in to the selection method.

6. *Determine the sample size needed.* Sample size can be determined by judgment when using a nonstatistical sampling method. For statistical sampling approaches, sample size is calculated based on the technique for the method used.

7. *Select the sample, perform the test, and identify discrepancies.* The discrepancies might be incorrect amounts, postings to incorrect accounts, postings in the wrong time period, or discrepancies of other details.

8. *Evaluate the sample results.*

Conclusions as a Result of Substantive Tests and Procedures: Evaluating Results. [LO 3]

If the auditor examines 100% of an account balance, evaluating the results is straightforward. Assuming that effective supervision and review prevents any nonsampling errors, as a result of examining all of the components of an account balance the auditor identifies all of the misstatements. The auditor may know right away, based on the quantitative and qualitative materiality thresholds set during planning, that the misstatements are material and need to be corrected.

Alternatively, the auditor may decide that on a "stand-alone" basis these misstatements are not material. In that situation the auditor documents the discrepancies as "unadjusted" differences in the audit work papers and evaluates their materiality again as more audit work is performed. Although these particular discrepancies are not material on their own, if other misstatements are identified, the total of all the misstatements may be material.

The auditor discusses identified discrepancies with management. It may be useful to the company to make the corrections even if they are not material to the financial statements. If a single discrepancy, or aggregated multiple discrepancies, cause the financial statements to be materially misstated, the auditor discusses with the client the need for an adjusting entry. The auditor likely proposes an adjusting journal entry he or she concludes will correct the financial statements so that they are not materially misstated. The client is responsible for the final decision and actually recording any adjusting journal entries. The auditor must obtain evidence and be satisfied that the client has corrected any material misstatements to be able to issue an unqualified opinion on the financial statements.

If a material misstatement is identified during the audit of account balances, the auditor needs to consider any implication this may have for the assessment of fraud risk and audit conclusions about the effectiveness of ICFR. The auditor may have formed a tentative conclusion that ICFR is effective. However, if the auditor finds a material misstatement that was not prevented or detected by ICFR, the finding is conflicting audit evidence regarding the tentative ICFR conclusion. The auditor evaluates the conflicting information and its impact on the ICFR audit opinion.

Finally, the auditor must consider all financial statements that are affected by a misstatement. For example, a misstatement that is not material to the income statement might cause the balance sheet to be materially misstated. Since both financial statements must be fairly stated, this misstatement triggers the need for an adjusting journal entry (SAB 108).

AUDITING IN ACTION

Immaterial Misstatements Become Material When Aggregated

During the audit of Stormline, Inc., audit steps identified some cash disbursements in February 2010 that were actually expenses incurred during December 2009. The expenses and an account payable for the transactions should have been recorded as of December 31, 2009. The invoices were sent very late by one vendor and were not received by Stormline until February 2010. The auditor judged that the amount was not material and that the payments were not for inventory, so the only accounts affected were operating expenses and accounts payable. The auditor also concluded that there was no attempt to manipulate the financial statements. These were simply invoices received so late from a vendor that the company did not pick them up as being expenses and payables of the prior year. The company recorded them as expenses and payables, and they were properly paid. However, the transactions were posted in February 2010. Discovery of the transactions and details were documented as unrecorded adjustments in the audit work papers. All other tests of accounts payable produced no discrepancies. The auditor carefully examined cash disbursements as the audit continued into March, but found no other vendor payments that resulted from late bills or that should have been shown as expenses and liabilities of 2009.

As the audit continued, more problems were identified when long-term debt was audited. Stormline had a 20-year loan that it was paying back. The terms of the loan required that one payment was due each year on January 1. Although Stormline properly made the payment that was due on January 1, 2010, it failed to show the payment that was due on January 1 as a current liability in its December 31, 2009 balance sheet. Instead, the liability was included in *long-term* debt.

The auditor had to reassess current liabilities after the most recent audit finding. The auditor determined that the combination of the unrecorded account payable identified earlier and the short-term debt shown as long term, when aggregated, caused current liabilities to be materially understated. The auditor presented the findings to the CFO of the company. The CFO corrected the errors, and the auditor was satisfied that currently liabilities were not materially misstated. The remaining issue for the auditor was to determine what controls in the ICFR system had failed related to these errors and whether that failure was a material weakness of ICFR.

When the auditor utilizes tests of details of balances of a sample rather than of all of the transactions or amounts that make up an account balance, he or she must estimate the proper or "true" account balance amount. The auditor does not actually know what the correct account balance is when only a sample is examined during the audit test. Steps to evaluate an account balance based on an audit test of a sample are summarized as follows:

1. *Determine the recorded amount of the sample.*
2. *Using evidence collected from the sample, investigate the misstatements.*
3. *Using the sample as a basis, estimate the "true" account balance.* In other words, determine what the recorded amount of the account *should be* based on the audit evidence.

The method used for making the projection depends on the nature of the account. A common technique is using a simple linear proportion to estimate the account balance misstatement. For example, if the sample is understated by 15% of its recorded dollar amount, then the account total is estimated to be understated by 15% of its recorded dollar amount.

Consider that the estimate of the population is based on a sample, so it is probably close to—but not exactly—the balance of the population. With a nonstatistical approach, the auditor makes a judgment about the quality of the estimate of the population. When using a statistical sampling plan, the auditor calculates a precision interval around the population estimate.

4. *Set a tolerable misstatement.* The tolerable misstatement reflects the quantitative threshold of misstatements in the recorded account balance that can be estimated based on the sample results without triggering the need for an adjusting entry to the account balance.

5. *Evaluate whether the account balance is materially misstated and requires an adjustment.* Misstatements are evaluated qualitatively as well as quantitatively. Discuss the findings with management, and either document the results in the work papers as an unadjusted difference (if not material) or follow through with the client on the adjustment needed for the financial statements to be fair.

6. *Consider the impact of the audit findings on other accounts, fraud risk, and ICFR.*

Discrepancies that the auditor finds during testing are called **known misstatements**. The company can easily correct those problems by posting adjusting entries. However, when examining a sample the auditor still asks, "Given that these are the misstatements that were found in the sample, what misstatements likely exist in the rest of the account that were not identified because they were not included in the sample?" Those additional, estimated misstatements are labeled **likely misstatements**. Because of likely misstatement, the auditor also asks, "In addition to correcting the known misstatements, does an additional entry need to be made to have reasonable assurance that the financial statements as a whole are not materially misstated?"

The auditor *estimates* the "true" account balance based on the results of auditing the sample and compares it to the recorded balance. However, the auditor recognizes that the estimate is based on a sample. So the real, "true" account balance is probably not exactly the amount estimated. Instead, the auditor expects the true amount to be close to the estimate that is projected based on the sample.

When considering the quantitative materiality of misstatements, auditors may use the concept of **tolerable misstatement**. This concept is similar to that of the tolerable rate of error presented in Chapter 8. During planning, the auditor sets a dollar amount that is a materiality threshold or "tolerable misstatement" for each account balance. This is one of the considerations when evaluating audit results. After the client makes any adjusting journal entries for known misstatements, the auditor evaluates whether the remaining likely misstatement exceeds the tolerable misstatement that was set during the planning process. To do so, the auditor evaluates whether the estimate of the true book value—and any "cushion" around the estimate the auditor establishes due to sampling—falls within the range of the recorded book value plus or minus the tolerable misstatement. When using a statistical sampling approach, the cushion around the population estimate is a calculated precision interval. Exhibit 9-3 presents this quantitative evaluation of results.

The auditor routinely revisits the decision of whether aggregated known and likely misstatements for which the client has not recorded adjustments are material. Reconsideration takes place whenever additional misstatements are found and in the final stages of the audit. An example of estimation of likely misstatement in the audit of a hotel's revenue account is now described.

The Fishtrackers' Inn requires a deposit equal to the price of one night's stay when a customer reserves a room in advance. The hotel takes credit card information over the phone or Internet and charges the card with the cost of one night at the time of the reservation. Customers may cancel their reservations up to 6:00 P.M. on the day before check-in. After the cancellation deadline, customers are not granted refunds if they cancel their reservations. At the time the reservation is made and the credit card deposit is received, Fishtrackers' posts the transaction as a deposit. For a two-night stay, at $150 per night, at the time of the reservation Fishtrackers' posts the following transaction (ignoring taxes):

Cash/Major credit card	150	
Unearned revenue/reservation deposit		150

If the customer has not canceled the reservation by 6:00 P.M. on the day before check-in, Fishtrackers' posts the following entry:

Unearned revenue/reservation deposit	150	
Revenue		150

The audit objective is to test whether all the transactions posted to the revenue account have actually been earned rather than being a deposit, which is a liability. The management assertion to be tested is that sales that have been posted have "occurred."

Fishtrackers' accepts reservations up to three months in advance and has a December 31 fiscal year end. So, to test for overstated revenue in the year-end balance, the auditor needs to test whether credits posted to revenue between October 1 and December 31 are for revenue actually earned.

The auditor is testing for the possible overstatement of revenue that would occur if a credit is posted to the wrong account. If any of the posted credits to revenue are for deposits on outstanding reservations (meaning that the deposit may still have to be returned to the customer if the reservation is canceled by the company's "6:00 P.M. the day before" deadline), they are not really revenue (at least not yet) and were posted to the wrong account.

During the time frame from October 1 through December 31, Fishtrackers' Inn charges $150 per night for each of its 300 rooms. The auditor plans the test and decides to rely on a sample. Fishtrackers' has posted credits to the revenue account of $3,312,000 for the 92 days between October 1 and December 31. The auditor selects transactions equal to $7,500 from the sales journal and examines the supporting documents. In the sample the auditor finds two transactions, equal to $150 each, which are actually deposits, that were incorrectly posted as revenue. In the sample, revenue is overstated and deposit liability is understated by $300. The auditor performs the following calculation:

$$(\$150 \times 2) / \$7,500 = 4\%$$

Based on this proportion of error in the sample, the auditor concludes that of the entire amount posted to revenue between October 1 and December 31, 4% is actually deposits

EXHIBIT 9-3

Quantitative Evaluation of Sample Results

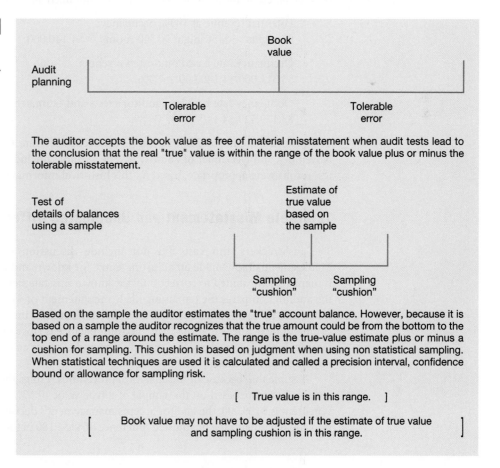

The auditor accepts the book value as free of material misstatement when audit tests lead to the conclusion that the real "true" value is within the range of the book value plus or minus the tolerable misstatement.

Based on the sample the auditor estimates the "true" account balance. However, because it is based on a sample the auditor recognizes that the true amount could be from the bottom to the top end of a range around the estimate. The range is the true-value estimate plus or minus a cushion for sampling. This cushion is based on judgment when using non statistical sampling. When statistical techniques are used it is calculated and called a precision interval, confidence bound or allowance for sampling risk.

[True value is in this range.   ]

[Book value may not have to be adjusted if the estimate of true value   ]
                        and sampling cushion is in this range.

(a liability) that have been incorrectly posted as revenue. To estimate the error in the revenue account, the auditor calculates 4% of the recorded revenue for the time period. Recall that credits posted to the revenue account between October 1 and December 31 equal $3,312,000. The calculation to estimate the overstatement in the revenue account and understatement in the deposit liability account is:

$$\$3,312,000 \times 0.04 = \$132,480$$

The auditor discusses the finding with the CFO, communicating that there is a known overstatement of revenue and understatement of deposit liability of $300, and a likely overstatement of revenue and understatement of deposit liability of $132,180. The CFO posts an adjusting entry to increase deposit liability and decrease revenue. After the CFO posts the correcting entry that reduces the September through December revenue account balance of $3,312,000 by $132,480, the corrected three month revenue account balance amount is $3,179,520.

Substantive Analytical Procedures

To provide additional support for the audit sample results, the auditor in the Fishtrackers' Inn case can also perform analytical procedures. For example, hotels measure their productivity in terms of their occupancy rate, which is the percentage of rooms sold during a specified time period. Fishtrackers' Inn caters to return customers who come for the nearby fishing opportunities at certain seasons of the year, and as a result, has a very stable occupancy rate on a year-to-year basis.

The following calculations show the occupancy rates for Fishtrackers' Inn that correlate with the posted revenue for the period from October 1 through December 31, and for revenue based on the auditor's sample results and likely misstatement calculation.

> Potential revenue at 100% occupancy:
> 92 nights $\times$ $150/night $\times$ 300 rooms = $4,140,000
>
> Occupancy rate based on posted revenue:
> $3,312,000/$4,140,000 = 80%
>
> Occupancy rate based on auditor's tests and estimated revenue:
> $3,179,520/$4,140,000 = 76.8%

The historical trend for Fishtrackers' is an occupancy rate for the months of October, November, and December of 76 to 77%. The auditor concludes that the audit sample and test results were appropriate, based on this historical information.

Tolerable Misstatement and Unadjusted Differences

The Fishtrackers' Inn case did not include discussion of tolerable misstatement. Management simply made an adjusting entry for known and likely misstatements. What if management wanted to correct only the known misstatement of $300? In that situation the auditor compares the remaining likely misstatement of $132,180 to the tolerable misstatement. Since this is a nonstatistical sample, the auditor must make a judgment on how confident he or she is that the "true" account balance is close to the estimate based on the sample. In the Fishtrackers' Inn example, the auditor uses analytical procedures that support the audit estimate.

Assume that because of the analytical procedures results, the auditor feels comfortable with the estimate based on the sample of a true value of $3,179,520. If the tolerable misstatement is $150,000, the auditor accepts management's decision to record a $300 correction and documents the unadjusted difference of $132,180 in the audit work papers. If there are no more likely or known misstatements to the revenue or current liabilities accounts found during the audit, the auditor's opinion on the fairness of the financial statements is not negatively affected by this test result. If more misstatements affecting revenue or current liabilities are found the auditor aggregates the likely misstatements, compares them to the tolerable misstatement, and revisits the need for an adjusting journal entry. Another possible outcome results at the Fishtrackers' Inn if the client decides to record an adjusting journal entry for only the known misstatement:

The auditor discusses the audit finding with the CFO, communicating that there is a known overstatement of revenue and an understatement of deposit liability of $300, and a likely overstatement of revenue and understatement of deposit liability of $132,180. The CFO's response is that there is no problem posting the $300. But to post the additional $132,180 the Fishtrackers' accounting staff will need to either post an entry for the full amount to the general ledger control accounts, or spend a lot of time investigating the current reservations to determine exactly which reservations deposits were posted incorrectly.

The CFO is not enthusiastic about posting an adjusting entry based on an estimate for this type of problem. The CFO thinks that the transactions were posted incorrectly while one of the regular accounting employees was out of work after a car accident and other staff from the hotel filled in. Since everything is back to normal now, and the mistakes will all reverse themselves within three months, the CFO does not want to spend a lot of staff time investigating the errors unless it is really necessary.

The auditor decides that the account balances are not materially misstated as long as no other problems are found. The CFO books the $300 adjusting journal entry, and the auditor records the $132,180 on the Summary of Unadjusted Differences work paper.

Exhibit 9-4 displays the quantitative analysis of the outcome at Fishtrackers' Inn if the client only books an adjusting entry for the known misstatement of $300.

EXHIBIT 9-4

Quantitative Evaluation of Fishtrackers' Inn Outcome

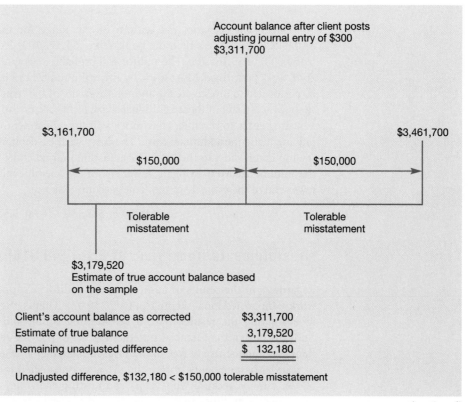

(continued)

The concept of a cushion around the estimate of the "true" account balance can also affect the Fishtrackers' Inn case. The revenue account might need more adjustment than the $300 adjusting entry for known misstatement:

Assume that the same conditions of the Fishtrackers' Inn case continue to exist, except that the auditor is less confident about the estimate of the "true" account balance based on the sample. The auditor believes that a cushion of $100,000 above and below the estimate is needed. This means that the auditor feels confident that the true account balance is between $3,079,520 and $3,279,520. What does this do to the auditor's conclusion? Remember that tolerable misstatement is $150,000.

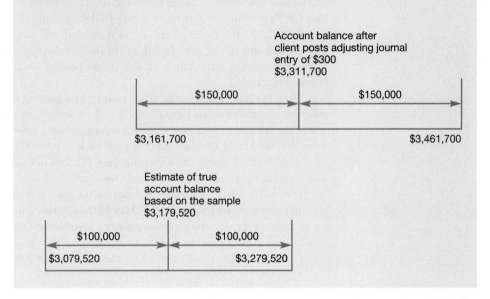

Under this scenario, the bottom of the range for the "true" account balance is $3,079,520. This is less than the book value ($3,311,700) less the tolerable misstatement ($150,000) of $3,161,700. The auditor will probably review all of the judgments made and audit work performed. More work, by either the auditor or Fishtrackers' Inn personnel, will be performed to investigate the auditor's estimate of the "true" account balance. If nothing changes as a result of these additional steps, Fishtrackers' Inn needs to make an additional adjusting entry to revenue. How much will the adjustment be? The amount depends on judgment and the additional work. The entry will be a debit to revenue. (As a consequence, the top graph slides to the left.) The adjusting journal entry will be for at least $82,180—the amount needed to bring the lower end of the tolerable misstatement range equal to the lower end of the estimate of the "true" account balance.

$$3,161,700 - $82,180 = $3,079,520$$

Misstatements from Fraud or Error (AU 316)

Regardless of the results of audit tests, the auditor is supposed to approach his or her work with professional skepticism (AU 230.07). That is, the auditor should be objective in evaluating the results, have a questioning mind, and make critical assessments. Auditors design the financial statement audit to provide reasonable assurance that the financial statements are free of material misstatements whether they result from errors or fraud. Misstatements from fraud are always expected to be harder to catch. Fraud is harder simply because whoever is committing the fraud is trying to deceive others, including the auditors, to keep them from discovering that the fraud has occurred. Fraud can be either misappropriation of assets (theft) or fraudulent financial reporting. When

AUDITING IN ACTION

Quantitative Evaluation of Audit Results

An accounts receivable balance has 2,500 individual accounts and a balance of $75,000. A sample of 100 accounts is selected. The recorded amount of the sample is 10% of the recorded amount of the population, $7,500. After performing the audit work, the auditor determines that the sample is misstated by $1,000. How should the auditor estimate the account balance?

1. $1,000 known misstatement/100 accounts = $10 per account
   $10 × 2500 = $25,000 estimate of misstatement in the account balance

2. $1,000 known misstatement/10% = $10,000 estimate of misstatement in the account balance

   (The 10% is used because the recorded, book value of the sample is 10% of the recorded, book value of the entire account.)

Which is right?

   If the misstatements the auditor found are constant across accounts, then Option 1 makes more sense. For example, all the accounts have misstatements ranging from $8 to $12, regardless of the account balance.

   If the misstatements the auditor found are proportionate to the account balance, then Option 2 makes more sense. For example, an account balance of $1,000 has a misstatement of $95, and an account balance of $500 has a misstatement of $55.

(Based on Taylor & Glezen, pp. 432–433.)

the auditor performs substantive tests, he or she considers to what degree the account is vulnerable to either misappropriation of assets or fraudulent financial reporting. This consideration of vulnerability to fraud, which is part of the professional skepticism mentioned earlier, is important throughout planning, performance, and evaluating the results of substantive procedures. The auditor analyzes the possibility of fraud in the Fishtrackers' Inn revenue overstatement:

   Going back to the Fishtrackers' Inn example, before discussing the revenue overstatement with the CFO the auditor considers the cause of the misstatement. Was it error or fraud? The auditor might consider whether the revenue recorded for any single day exceeded expected occupancy. For example, the auditor reviews the daily revenue reports for October, November, and December and looks for any daily revenue that exceeded 100% of potential occupancy revenue. If this threshold was ever passed, it might have been accomplished using a manually prepared journal entry. The auditor investigates any unusual transactions, such as daily revenue that exceeded expectations—especially if it exceeded the maximum possible before discussing the revenue overstatement with management. The auditor also likely reviews year-end journal entries for any unusual transactions before discussing the revenue overstatement with management.

REVIEW QUESTIONS

B.1 Why might an auditor divide an account balance into more than one segment before performing audit procedures?

B.2 What steps are followed when performing tests of details of balances and drawing conclusions using a sample?

B.3 What does the auditor do when misstatements are identified that are not material? Why would these nonmaterial misstatements be reevaluated?

B.4 How does the auditor form a conclusion about the fair presentation of an entire account balance based on the results of tests of details of balances performed on a sample?

AUDIT DOCUMENTATION [LO 4]

An audit process such as the audit of the Fishtrackers' Inn revenue account is documented in the audit work papers. Audit documentation has been discussed several times in earlier chapters. The authoritative standards describe what must be included in documentation by stating that a reviewer or an inspector must be able to identify what the auditor has done, evidence used by the auditor, the source of the evidence, audit conclusions, and that sufficient evidence was obtained to support the auditor's conclusions (AS 3.4). The standards do not specify exactly how the auditor's work papers must be organized, but auditors commonly use a working trial balance, lead schedules, and detailed work papers in their current files. Recall that the "current files" document only the current year's audit activities, while the "permanent file" contains documentation that may be useful to more than one year's audit.

AUDITING IN ACTION

Examples of Audit Documentation Content

Auditing procedures performed, including what was done and when
Preparer and reviewer identification, and date the work was performed
Items subjected to the audit procedure
Results of the audit activities
Significant findings or issues
Auditor conclusions on the significant matters
Evidence of agreement between the accounting records and the financial statements

Working Trial Balance, Lead Schedules, and Detailed Work Papers

Work paper current files are organized to support the auditor's ability to make judgments and conclusions about the audit evidence obtained. The fundamental starting place for the work paper organization is a working trial balance. A trial balance lists the client company's post-closing general ledger, providing both line item account titles and amounts. Generally, each line item on the trial balance is supported by a lead schedule work paper. **Lead schedule** is the term for the audit work paper that lists and specifies the components that make up the line item on the **working trial balance**. In addition, **detailed work papers** support the information on the lead schedule, providing information about the audit tests performed on each component of the trial balance line item and results of the tests.

Although audit documentation is still referred to as work papers, the documentation is usually in electronic form. The audit software used to draft work papers permits the user to drill down through the work papers. For example, the audit documentation software permits the auditor to start with the working trial balance, and by selecting a particular line item on the working trial balance, to link to the lead schedule providing details about the line item. The auditor can select an item on the lead schedule and follow its link to the detailed work paper that provides information such as the details of the sampling plan, items selected, tests performed, results of the tests, conclusions reached, and who performed and reviewed the work. The work papers at the working trial balance, lead schedule, and detailed work paper levels can also be referenced or linked to the audit plan. This allows a reviewer to move back and forth between the audit

EXHIBIT 9-5

Work Paper Examples

Prepared by Client (PBC)			
Audit File Ref.:	A-1		
Year-End 12.31.2010			
Testing Performed by: JH, on 1.14.10			
Fishtrackers Trial Balance			
Account	*Debits*	*Credits*	Lead Ref.
Cash	1,300,000		B-1
A/R	1,600,000		B-1
Inventory	120,000		C-1
PPE	6,600,000		D-1
A/P		(800,000)	F-1
Unearned Revenue		(240,000)	F-1
Long-term Notes		(3,800,000)	G-1
Common Stock		(1,200,000)	H-1
Retained Earnings		(420,000)	H-1
Revenue		(4,860,000)	I-1
Operating Expenses	1,100,000		J-1
Income Tax Expense	600,000		J-1
Totals	11,320,000	(11,320,000)	

Prepared by Client (PBC)				
Audit File Ref.:	I-1			
Year-End 12.31.2010				
Testing Performed by: JH, CwP on 1.14.10				
Revenue Lead Sheet				
Account	*Unadjusted Balance*	*AJEs*	*Adjusted Balance*	*Test Ref.*
Room Revenue	(3,312,000)	132,480	(3,179,520)	I-2A
F&B Revenue	(950,000)	-	(950,000)	I-2B
Telephone Revenue	(328,000)	-	(328,000)	I-3B
Equipment Rental Rev	(270,000)	-	(270,000)	I-3B
Totals	(4,860,000)	132,480	(4,727,520)	TB

Audit File Ref.:	I-2A				
Year-End 12.31.2010					
Testing Performed by: JH, on 1.14.10					
Room Revenue Cutoff Testing (Partial)					
Test No.	Reservation No.	Party Name	% Amount	Reservation Date	Properly Include/ Exluded
45	1209481	Jacobs	150	1/1/11	Properly Included
46	1219401	Chatman	150	1/1/11	Properly Included
47	1184901	Dunn	150	1/2/11	**Improperly Included**
48	1220540	Wing	150	1/1/11	Properly Included
49	1208950	Li	150	1/4/11	Properly Excluded
50	1214050	Ortiz	150	1/3/11	**Improperly Included**
			$7,500		

Known Error	
Error on #47	150
Error on #48	150
Total Known Error	300

Estimating Likely Error		
Total Known Error	300	
Divided by Sample Population	7,500	
= % Error	4%	
X Total Account Balance	(3,312,000)	I-1
= Likely Error (Overstatement)	(132,480)	AJE I-1

plan and the detailed work paper that documents the work done to accomplish a specific audit step of the audit plan.

In the example provided earlier of Fishtrackers' Inn, the auditor began with recorded revenue, selected a sample, performed tests, found results indicating a misstatement that needed to be corrected, and concluded that an adjusting entry was needed. The audit work papers for the Fishtrackers' Inn audit will include detailed work papers providing all of the information about the sample, items examined, and which items were incorrectly posted to revenue when they should have been posted to the deposit liability account. The audit lead schedule for revenue and the line item for revenue on the working trial balance will show the original post-closing general ledger amount for the revenue account, the adjusting journal entry posted by the client, and the final account balance. The auditor must trace the final account balances on the working trial balance to the financial statements. Exhibit 9-5 shows a working trial balance, lead schedule, and detailed work paper for the revenue overstatement audit test of Fishtrackers' Inn.[1]

---

[1]The work paper amounts in Exhibit 9-5 agree with the amounts in the Fishtrackers' Inn example so that you can trace the amounts. Note that the total annual room revenue would actually be more than the $3,312,000, which was recorded revenue for the last three months of the year.

IMPORTANT CONSIDERATIONS IN A FINANCIAL STATEMENT AUDIT [LO 5]

The following topics are introduced here and presented in later chapters as they apply to auditing the various transaction cycles. The transaction cycles chapters are Chapters 10 and 12 through 15. The sections that follow are intended as only an introduction. They should give you an idea of the issues that auditors consider during substantive procedures while performing financial statement audits. These topics may be important to the substantive procedures and audit evidence for any account on the financial statements.

Estimates (AU 342)

Management often uses estimates in determining amounts to be included in financial statements. Sometimes estimates are needed because an amount cannot be measured until something in the future happens. Often estimates are made because information about what has already happened cannot be gathered in a sufficiently timely or precise way to report a measured amount in the current financial statements. For example, the collectibility, and thus the value, of an account receivable cannot be known for certain until the cash is collected. The amount of a long-term productive asset's cost that should have been allocated to an accounting period cannot be measured until sufficient time has passed for the asset's value to have diminished. Fair value is defined as an exit value. But an exit value must be estimated unless a company disposes of an asset—unless there is an active market for the item, such as in the case of widely traded public securities.

Management is responsible for making accounting estimates and uses both accumulated past and current knowledge and assumptions. The auditor must understand management's method for making estimates. Based on his or her understanding, the auditor evaluates the reasonableness of management's estimation process and assumptions on which the estimations are based, as well as of the final outcomes. Based on these audit steps, the auditor concludes whether the estimates are appropriate so that the financial statements are not materially misstated.

Considering the estimation process and results is important during substantive audit procedures because many of the amounts presented in the financial statements are based on estimation. While performing substantive tests the auditor often has to evaluate the underlying assumptions and process management uses for making estimates.

AUDITING IN ACTION

Auditing Estimates

Understand management's method for making estimates and evaluate the reasonableness of the resulting estimates.

Consider the reasonableness of management's process and assumptions on which the estimations are based.

Consider the reasonableness of final outcomes.

Fair Value Measurements and Disclosures (AU 328)

While the historical cost amount of an exchange is the primary anchor for most recorded financial transactions, accounting standards require that certain items shown in the financial statements be recorded at fair value. Accounting standards also permit other items to be shown at fair value, although fair value presentation is not required. The auditor's responsibility is to understand the company's use of fair value and to audit

AUDITING IN ACTION

Examples of Estimates Used in Preparing Financial Statements

Collectibility of receivables
Useful lives and salvage value of assets
Expenses to be accrued
Revenue to be accrued
Percentage of completion
Interest rates for present values
Actuarial information
Future cash flow for fair value models

whether the application is proper. To do this, the auditor must have a strong knowledge of when fair value is required and permitted and how it is supposed to be measured or estimated. Depending on the characteristics of the client, the accounting knowledge required may extend to international standards or industry-specific standards. For public companies, the SEC may have additional standards as well.

The auditor must understand the company's process for determining the fair value of the items on its financial statements, including controls over the process and controls for determining or drafting the necessary disclosures. The auditor tests the results of the company's fair value measurement or estimation process. Testing provides the auditor with a means to evaluate whether the fair value measures and disclosures shown on the financial statements conform with GAAP or whatever basis of accounting is used.

Fair value processes are important for the substantive procedures phase of the audit process because many accounts can (or must) be expressed at fair value. The auditor must apply knowledge of fair value accounting standards in testing many financial statement account balances.

AUDITING IN ACTION

Auditing Fair Value

- Understand the company's use of fair value
- Understand the company's
  a. controls over the process
  b. method for determining or drafting necessary disclosures
- Test the results of the company's fair value measurement process

Illegal Acts (AU 317)

The auditor must consider illegal acts as they relate to the financial statements. However, this may be difficult because the auditor cannot unilaterally judge whether an act is illegal.

> The term illegal acts, for purposes of this section, refers to violations of laws or governmental regulations. Illegal acts by clients are acts attributable to the entity whose financial statements are under audit or acts by management or employees acting on behalf of the entity. Illegal acts by clients do not include personal misconduct by the entity's personnel unrelated to their business activities. (AU 317.02)

An auditor may recognize that some actions appear to be illegal. But the final determination of whether or not they are illegal has to come from a court of law.

The auditor is responsible for detecting and reporting material misstatements of the financial statements that result from illegal acts, in the same way that he or she is responsible for reporting material misstatements from error or fraud. The auditor is most likely to become aware of and recognize illegal acts that have a direct impact on the financial statements, such as violation of tax laws or financial reporting regulations.

The auditor is less likely to become aware of illegal acts by the client that have an *indirect* material effect on the financial statements. Still, the auditor should investigate specific information about possible illegal acts that comes to his or her attention. The auditor may inspect client documents as part of an audit step and during the inspection discover evidence that the client has paid fines assessed by a government agency because of a violation. As long as the fees are properly paid and posted, they do not cause a material financial statement misstatement. But the auditor must consider whether the illegal act may have an indirect impact on the fairness of the financial statements. For example, violation of workplace safety regulations might ultimately cause a company to lose business because of damage to its reputation among customers. The loss of business could mean that inventory is not marketable and should be written down. Or if the company does not correct the problem leading to the fine, the solution might have long-term implications for the company's viability.

> The auditor asks management about company policies intended to prevent illegal acts and obtains written representations from management concerning the absence of violations or possible violations of laws or regulations whose effects should be considered for disclosure in the financial statements or as a basis for recording a loss contingency. (AU 317.08)

If the auditor becomes aware of information that indicates the company committed an illegal act, the auditor performs additional steps. The steps are to obtain an understanding of the act that appears to be illegal, consult with legal counsel if appropriate, and consider the impact on the financial statements. The audit confirms that those responsible for the governance of the company are aware of the information. The auditor may choose to interact with the company's audit committee in its communications with those responsible for corporate governance. The auditor has to consider evidence about illegal acts when deciding which audit report to issue and whether to continue to serve as the company's auditor.

Illegal acts are important to the substantive procedures phase of the financial statement audit because the auditor tests account balances that may be directly affected by illegal acts, such as taxes. In addition, while performing substantive tests and procedures the auditor may become aware of illegal acts that have an indirect effect on the financial statements as a result of examining various types of audit evidence.

AUDITING IN ACTION

Illegal Acts

- The auditor is most likely to become aware of and recognize illegal acts that have a direct impact on the financial statements
  a. Violation of tax laws
  b. Violation of financial reporting regulations
- The auditor is less likely to become aware of illegal acts by the client that may have an indirect material effect on the financial statements.
- When the auditor becomes aware of information that indicates an illegal act was committed by the company:
  a. Perform addition steps to understand the act that appears to be illegal.
  b. Consult with legal counsel if appropriate.
  c. Consider the impact on the financial statements; be certain that those responsible for the governance of the company are aware of the information.
  d. Consider evidence about illegal acts when deciding what audit report should be issued.

Related Party Transactions (AU 334)

Related parties and transactions between related parties are covered by accounting standards, primarily FASB Codification 850-10. Transactions generally do not require different accounting treatment as long as they are at "arms lengths." However, specific disclosure is required. The auditor performs audit procedures directed toward identifying any related parties, finding transactions with related parties, and understanding the transactions with related parties. These steps allow the auditor to determine whether the disclosures about the related party transactions are in conformity with accounting standards. The auditor needs to obtain and evaluate sufficient and appropriate audit evidence to be persuaded that the financial statement disclosures are adequate.

Beyond adequacy of disclosure, related party transactions may have occurred at amounts or under terms that would not have been used with nonrelated parties. In other words, they are not "arms length." Unless it is a "routine" transaction (such as the sale or purchase of inventory at the same dollar amount used with other parties), there is often no practical way to determine whether a transaction would have been carried out with a nonrelated party in the same way and at the same amount that it was with the related party.

If the company includes disclosure in the financial statements asserting that a transaction with a related party was "arms length," the auditor evaluates whether the disclosure can be substantiated by management. If disclosure that a transaction was "arms length" cannot be substantiated by management, the auditor considers the impact this has on the audit report. Quantitative and qualitative materiality considerations affect the auditor's evaluation of related party transaction disclosures.

Related parties and related party transactions are important to the substantive procedures phase of the financial statement audit. In addition to direct inquiry of management, other audit procedures and evidence provide the auditor with information about the existence of related parties. The auditor examines evidence that explains transactions with related parties as a specific part of other substantive audit procedures.

AUDITING IN ACTION

Related Parties and Related Party Transactions

- Perform audit procedures directed toward identifying any related parties.
- Identify transactions with related parties.
- Understand the transactions with related parties.
- Obtain and evaluate sufficient and appropriate evidence to be persuaded that the financial statement disclosure is adequate.

Going Concern (AU 341)

The auditor has the responsibility to evaluate whether there is "substantial doubt" about an entity's ability to continue as a going concern for a year following the date of its financial statements. The term **going concern** is defined in the auditing standards by an explanation of conditions that violate the going concern assumption:

> Continuation of an entity as a going concern is assumed in financial reporting in the absence of significant information to the contrary. Ordinarily, information that significantly contradicts the going concern assumption relates to the entity's inability to continue to meet its obligations as they become due without substantial disposition of assets outside the ordinary course of business, restructuring of debt, externally forced revisions of its operations, or similar actions. (AU 341.01)

AUDITING IN ACTION

What You Need to Know about Related Parties

When I was preparing this section of the book, I asked an audit partner what students needed to know about auditing related party transactions. Admittedly, I asked the question during busy season when stress levels are high. In an "off-the-cuff" manner, the audit partner said, "Tell them that if they find out their client has material related party transactions the first thing they should do is throw up, and the second thing is to start working on it because of the risk."

Another professor told me that I really should not put that quote in this book because it is important to convey to you, the reader and future auditor, a constant attitude of professionalism. But the audit partner's reaction conveys the message that when a company engages in business transactions with related parties, it increases the auditor's risk concerns regarding proper presentation and disclosure of those transactions in the financial statements.

Auditors understand the importance of related party transactions and the audit risk associated with them. Internal controls can be circumvented by collusion and as a consequence can never give absolute assurance that fraud has not occurred. This same concept applies to related party transactions. Auditors can have assurance that a transaction has been recorded at the proper amount if the amount is the result of a recent arms-length market exchange. This assurance does not exist for transactions between related parties because there is no way to determine whether the transaction is arms length.

Basically, this explanation means that a company is a going concern if it can continue in business without taking drastic measures such as selling off productive assets or refinancing debt to be able to meet its day-to-day business obligations.

The auditor evaluates whether there is reasonable doubt about a company's ability to continue as a going concern for the year following the balance sheet date. The evaluation is based on information obtained during the audit process. Evidence obtained from analytical procedures, Board of Directors meeting minutes, communications with the client's attorneys, and external confirmations are useful to the auditor in evaluating a company's going concern status. Audit evidence related to long-term debt is also informative.

The auditor may conclude that there is a serious question, or substantial doubt, about a company's ability to continue as a going concern. The next step is to determine whether management has plans that may help reduce the risk. If management has plans intended to reduce the company's going concern risk, the auditor evaluates those plans to determine whether they can be effectively implemented. After all of these investigations, the auditor may conclude that there is substantial doubt about a company's ability to continue as a going concern for a year after the balance sheet date. The auditor then evaluates whether disclosure in the financial statements is adequate and the impact the going concern problem should have on the audit report.

An awareness of going concern is important to the substantive tests and procedures phase of the financial statement audit. Information that causes the auditor to have substantial doubt about a company's ability to continue as a going concern is generated as a part of audit evidence. If the auditor becomes aware of going concern questions, further audit investigation is performed.

Cutoff Issues and Substantive Procedures at Interim Dates

When the auditor conducts procedures to obtain substantive audit evidence prior to the end of the fiscal year, this is called *interim work*, or performing procedures at an *interim date*. Performing substantive procedures before the fiscal year end may be efficient for the auditor because it spreads the work throughout the year. When substantive procedures on account balances are performed before the year end, the auditor "updates" the informa-

AUDITING IN ACTION

Going Concern

- Information that significantly contradicts the going concern assumption deals with inability to meet obligations when due without disposing of assets, restructuring debt, revising operations, or other similar actions
- Evidence of whether there is reasonable doubt about a company's ability to continue as a going concern comes from
  a. Analytical procedures
  b. Board of Directors meeting minutes
  c. Communication with clients' attorneys
  d. Confirmations
  e. Long-term debt audit
- If substantial doubt about a company's ability to continue as a going concern exists:
  a. Determine whether management has plans that may help reduce the risk.
  b. Evaluate those plans to determine whether they can be effectively implemented.
- If after all of these investigations substantial doubt about a company's ability to continue as a going concern still exists:
  a. Evaluate whether disclosure in the financial statements is adequate.
  b. Evaluate the impact the going concern should have on the audit report.

tion to verify that the earlier audit evidence is still appropriate. For example, the auditor can observe the client's physical count of inventory which occurs several months before the end of the year. The auditor reconciles purchases and sales of inventory that occur after the physical count with year end balances. *Consideration of interim work is very important to substantive work at year end because the nature, timing, and extent of interim work, and conclusions reached, directly impacts the auditor's year-end efforts and emphasis.*

The auditor tests whether the client has an effective "cutoff" of its financial records at the end of its fiscal year. A good cutoff is integral to the auditor's conclusions about management's *existence or occurrence* and *completeness* assertions. If a transaction is recorded in the wrong accounting period due to poor cutoff, then both of these assertions will be improper. If a transaction occurs in year 1 but is recorded in year 2, then the financial information in year 1 is *incomplete* because the transaction was omitted. In addition, the financial information in year 2 is misstated because it includes information that did not *occur* during that year. Poor cutoff can have an even greater impact if a transaction impacts multiple accounts.

To accomplish an effective cutoff, management plans its accounting procedures to determine the period in which transactions occur and post them properly. Good cutoff requires control over transactions. Good outoff also requires controls over cash and other liquid assets at year end, and control over the receipt and shipment of inventory shortly before and after

AUDITING IN ACTION

Inventory and Cutoff

If inventory is reported as sold in year 1, then revenue is reported for the sale, along with a cash receipt or receivable. What if the part of the transaction that moves the cost of the inventory from the inventory-asset account to the cost-of-goods-sold expense account is not posted until year 2? Then, not only is year 1 incomplete and year 2 misstated, but matching is not achieved and the balance sheet and net income in year 1 are both overstated.

year end. In addition, the company must have procedures to properly capture and record data that are received in the subsequent fiscal year but apply to the activities of the year being audited. For example, the company inspects invoices received after the fiscal year end specifically to determine whether they are expenses of the prior or current year. As a result of the cutoff inspection, invoices for activities of the prior year can be properly posted as expenses and payables for the year being audited.

In addition to examining the company's cutoff procedures, the auditor checks the transactions that occurred and were posted shortly before and after the fiscal year end. This step allows the auditor to determine whether the company's cutoff was carried out effectively and transactions close to fiscal year end were posted in the proper period. *Various substantive audit procedures are used by the auditor for different accounts to determine whether the financial statements have any material misstatements from poor cutoff.*

REVIEW QUESTIONS

C.1 How do the working trial balance, lead schedules, and detailed work papers articulate?

C.2 What does an auditor have to know about management's estimation process? About the underlying assumptions management uses to make estimates?

C.3 To what extent is the auditor responsible for illegal acts that do not have a material, direct impact on the financial statements? Does the auditor's responsibility for material financial statement misstatements differ if they result from fraud, error, or illegal acts?

C.4 How do disclosures required by GAAP affect the auditor's responsibilities for related party and related party transaction information? Why is the auditor concerned if management makes disclosures indicating that nonroutine related party transactions are at arms length?

C.5 What is substantial doubt about going concern? For what period of time after the close of the fiscal year does the auditor need to assess going concern? From what sources does the auditor get information about going concern?

C.6 What management assertions are primarily affected by an improper cutoff?

AREAS ADDRESSED IN A FINANCIAL STATEMENT AUDIT [LO 6]

Substantive audit procedures are targeted at selected financial statement accounts for important assertions. The assertions that are the most important for different accounts vary. Generally, the most important assertions for assets are existence, rights, and valuation. Assertions of concern for liabilities are completeness and obligations. But this does not mean that completeness is inapplicable to assets. It means that completeness is not the highest audit risk.

The possibility that assets are omitted or understated on the financial statements is less important as an audit risk than the possibility that liabilities are omitted or understated. Considering conservatism, if presented with a choice, it is better to omit or understate assets than liabilities. Furthermore, from a fraud perspective, there is a greater risk that liabilities (rather than assets) will be intentionally omitted or understated.

For transactions aggregated in the income statement, the occurrence and completeness assertions are targets of audit activities. An assertion relevant to all financial statement components is proper and complete presentation and disclosure. However, from an audit risk perspective, accounts that require extensive and complex disclosures present a higher presentation and disclosure audit risk.

Cash

Auditing cash can require significant effort if an entity is large, has a complex cash management system, or has numerous cash accounts. Management assertions that are important to the cash account are existence, rights, cutoff, and disclosure. Notice that cash does not require estimation, nor are valuation issues involved unless the cash is held in different currencies requiring translation. Cash and "cash equivalents" are typically audited together.

Since the assertions of greatest concern are that the cash exists and is owned by the entity in the period in which it is reported, confirmation of year-end amounts with banks (and other custodians of cash equivalents) is an important substantive audit procedure. The auditor also focuses on reconciliations of the entity's cash records with documents, such as bank statements, produced by outside third parties. Disclosure for cash must indicate any limitations on the entity's ability to use the cash, such as restrictions imposed by a creditor or the Board of Directors. Exhibit 9-6 lists assertions and examples of substantive audit tests for cash.

EXHIBIT 9-6

Examples of Audit Steps for Cash

Assertion	Example of Substantive Test
1. Existence	1. Confirmation of bank balance and reconciliation to book balance.
2. Rights	2. Inquiry and review of board of director minutes and loan documents for evidence of pledging.
3. Completeness	3. Confirmations to all banks with which the client did business during the year whether the account is open or has been closed.
4. Valuation	4. Not applicable unless foreign currencies are involved.
5. Presentation	5. Inquiry and review of board of director minutes for evidence of compensating balances and escrow deposits

(*Source*: Adapted from Taylor & Glezen, p. 473.)

Receivables (AU 330)

If an entity's receivables are material, the major audit concerns are for management's assertions that the receivables actually exist, the company retains rights to the receivables, and the receivables are valued fairly. Confirming receivables with the debtor provides audit evidence about the existence of receivables. Confirmation produces less evidence about the valuation of receivables. Valuation depends on the likelihood that receivables will be collected.

External confirmations on receivables contain information from an outside third party, communicated directly to the auditor, indicating whether or not the debtor acknowledges the debt and its amount. Even though confirmations include an acknowledgment of the debt, the debtor may confirm that a debt exists and may still be unable or unwilling to pay it. Therefore, another audit step is evaluating the age of accounts receivable. Older balances are at greater risk of being uncollectible. Examining cash received in payment for accounts receivable in the accounting period subsequent to the balance sheet date also provides evidence on value. This step provides evidence that the receivable actually existed at the balance sheet date and was collectible—and therefore, properly valued.

An audit concern for receivables is whether the entity retains rights to them. Many entities factor receivables to accelerate the process of cash collection by either selling the receivables or using them as collateral for a loan. The proper accounting and disclosure for factored receivables depends on the nature of the factoring transaction.

AUDITING IN ACTION

Procedures for Bank Reconciliation

1. Foot the bank reconciliation and any supporting details.

2. Confirm the balance per bank directly with the bank by means of a standard bank confirmation.

3. Obtain a cutoff bank statement directly from the bank for the first 10 days after fiscal year end. A cutoff bank statement is a bank statement covering a portion of the month following the audit date used to test the validity of cash balances and reconciling items.

4. Trace the balance per bank in the reconciliation to the year-end bank statement and the beginning balance of the cutoff bank statement.

5. Trace the balance per books to the cash book.

6. Trace the dates and amounts of deposits in transit to the cutoff bank statement obtained directly from the bank.

7. For paper checks that cleared the bank within the period of the cutoff bank statement and are dated on or before the audit date, view the checks and perform the following steps. For electronic transfers and debits, perform all the steps that are applicable, using other documents such as authorizations, when appropriate.
   a. Trace to the outstanding checklist supporting the bank reconciliation to determine whether they are shown properly.
   b. Compare the signature with the list of authorized check-signers in the permanent audit file.
   c. Examine the endorsement to see that the check is endorsed by the payee and that there are no unusual second endorsements.
   d. Review payee for any that appear unusual such as checks payable to cash.
   e. Compare with cash book as to date, number, payee, and amount.

8. For paper checks that cleared within the cutoff bank statement period, dated after the audit date, examine the first bank endorsement to see that it does not precede the audit date.

9. For checks on the outstanding check list that did not clear with the cutoff bank statement, compare check number and amount with the cash book and investigate any that have been outstanding for an unusually long time.

10. Account for all check numbers issued during the month as having cleared with the year-end bank statement or as being on the outstanding checklist.

(*Source*: Adapted from Taylor & Glezen, pp. 474, 476.)

When an entity has material accounts receivable, the auditor directs specific substantive audit tests to investigate whether the entity retains rights to those assets. These audit procedures may be part of steps to understand the client's system and steps to confirm debt agreements with third parties. If the entity has factored receivables, the auditor evaluates whether the transactions were properly accounted for and disclosed in the financial statements. Exhibit 9-7 lists assertions and examples of substantive audit tests for receivables.

Inventory (AU 331)

The nature of a company's industry and business model determines the importance of inventory and the relevant management assertions. Consequently, the substantive audit procedures vary widely depending on the nature of the business. The management assertions of entities that purchase goods to resell them reflect physical security, documentary

EXHIBIT 9-7

Examples of Audit
Steps for Receivables

Assertion	Example of Substantive Test
1. Existence	1. Confirmation of account balance with customer
2. Rights	2. Inquiry and review of Board of Directors minutes and loan agreements for evidence of pledging
3. Completeness	3. Analytical procedures, particularly comparison of units shipped per sales records with units shipped per shipping records
4. Valuation	4. Inquiry of credit manager and review of aged accounts receivable trial balance and credit files
5. Presentation	5. Inquiry and review of Board of Directors minutes for evidence of related party transactions

(*Source*: Adapted from Taylor & Glezen, p. 482.)

AUDITING IN ACTION

Audit Procedures for Accounts Receivable

1. Total the accounts receivable listing (or subsidiary ledger) and agree with the general ledger.
2. Test the aging of accounts receivable.
3. Confirm customer account balances on a test basis.
4. Perform alternative procedures (examine invoice, shipping documents, and remittance advice) on customer balances selected for confirmation but for which no reply was received.
5. Test the adequacy of the allowance for doubtful accounts by
   a. review of credit files and discussion of the collectibility of all accounts over a specified threshold with the credit manager,
   b. review of subsequent collection of account balances, and
   c. comparison with the prior year of percentage of accounts receivable in each of the aging categories.

(*Source*: Adapted from Taylor & Glezen, p. 483.)

controls, and changes in the market value of inventory. This describes important aspects for a retail or wholesale merchandise distributor.

In contrast, a manufacturing entity purchases goods and then transforms the goods by adding labor and overhead in a production or an assembly process. For that entity management's assertions extend to whether the costs are captured and aggregated according to financial accounting standards, as well as the existence, completeness, rights, valuation, and presentation and disclosure assertions that apply to a distributor. The auditor performs substantive tests based on the nature of the business being audited. If an entity manufactures or assembles inventory, the auditor performs substantive tests on the account balances of all the components of inventory including raw materials, work-in-process, and finished goods.

Auditing standards require that in most cases auditors physically inspect inventory if it is material to the financial statements (AU 331.12). The purpose of the physical inspection is to evaluate the assertion that recorded inventory exists. Physical inspection can sometimes provide evidence that the value of inventory has deteriorated due to damage or obsolescence. The requirement to inspect inventory is usually fulfilled by observing and performing audit tests when the company performs a physical count of inventory.

Although **perpetual inventory** systems and advanced technology have expanded the options available, all businesses with inventory perform some form of physical counts. The count permits the company to reconcile its inventory records with the actual physical count of inventory on a periodic basis, and adjust the records to reflect the actual physical count. The auditor plans and performs substantive audit procedures to observe and test the client's count and adjustment of the records. This provides the auditor with evidence about the existence of recorded inventory. Exhibit 9-8 presents audit steps for inventory.

EXHIBIT 9-8

Examples of Audit Steps for Inventory

Assertion	Example of Substantive Test
1. Existence	1. Observation of physical inventory counts and reconciliation of test counts with perpetual inventory records
2. Rights	2. Inquiry and review of Board of Directors minutes and loan agreements for evidence of pledging
3. Completeness	3. Test receiving cutoff procedures
4. Valuation	4. Inspection of vendor invoices, payroll records, and overhead application worksheets
5. Presentation	5. Comparison of disclosures in financial statements with requirements of GAAP

(*Source*: Adapted from Taylor & Glezen, p. 510.)

Investments, Emphasis on Marketable Securities (AU 332)

Accounting for investments has become more complex as the securities markets have developed varied and sophisticated investment instruments. The increased availability of investments that businesses of all sizes can use to manage their **entity risks** means that the audit of investments typically requires more time and effort than it did in the past. This is true even for small businesses. Companies invest in securities as a means of productively using temporarily available cash. Businesses also commonly invest in financial instruments to hedge the risks of changes in (1) interest rates, (2) the cost of raw materials and energy, and (3) foreign currency exchange rates.

The audit objectives for investments include validating management assertions for existence and rights. Existence and rights assertions are tested by physical inspection of documents. Auditors also confirm existence and rights with outside parties who serve as custodians of investment documents. Investments may be easily converted to cash and cash may be used to purchase investments. Therefore, the auditor investigates the existence assertion for marketable securities simultaneously with substantive audit tests for cash and other cash equivalents.

Existence and rights are relatively easy to verify. Consequently, the valuation assertion and presentation and disclosure assertion receive the bulk of the substantive audit work for the investments account. Management's intent for the purpose of an investment asset may impact the proper accounting. Many investments must be shown at fair value, and others are shown at fair value as a result of management's choice.

Regardless of the applicable accounting method, the auditor performs procedures to understand and evaluate management's costing or valuation method, underlying assumptions, and outcomes of the process. The auditor must then agree the financial statement

AUDITING IN ACTION

Analytical Procedures for Inventory

1. Compare gross profit ratios in current and prior year.
2. Compare inventory turnover in current and prior year.
3. Compare inventory and cost of sales in current year with current-year budget and prior-year actual.
4. Compare standard and unit costs of major items of inventory in current and prior years.

(*Source*: Adapted from Taylor & Glezen, p. 511.)

presentation to the underlying records, supporting documents, and calculations. Disclosures required for investments are evaluated for compliance with the accounting standards and representational faithfulness of the details of the assets. Exhibit 9-9 lists audit steps for investments.

EXHIBIT 9-9

Examples of Audit Steps for Investment Securities

Assertion	Example of Substantive Test
1. Existence	1. Examine securities maintained in a safe deposit box. Confirm securities held by outside custodian.
2. Rights	2. Examine securities to determine if they are registered in the client's name with no indication of pledging.
3. Completeness	3. Analytical procedures: Match dividend and interest income with related investments.
4. Valuation	4. Review method of valuation for compliance with GAAP and test computation by reference to brokers' advices, market quotations, or audited financial statements of investees.
5. Presentation	5. Review classification of investments as long or short term and confirm management intentions in a representation letter.

(*Source*: Adapted from Taylor & Glezen, pp. 554–555.)

AUDITING IN ACTION

Audit Procedures for a Security Count

1. Obtain a list of the locations of all securities and the type and volume of securities at each place.
2. Perform a security count documenting the company name, certificate number, number of shares, par value, face value, interest rate, due date, and issue date (where applicable).
3. Test for apparent authenticity by examining the signatures of the trustee, registrar, transfer agent, and corporate officers.
4. Compare the results of the security count with the description of the investments in the accounting records.

(*Source*: Adapted from Taylor & Glezen, p. 556.)

Prepaid Assets

Prepaid assets, like accrued expenses, are sometimes combined with other accounts for financial statement presentation if they are not individually material. In addition to examining the supporting documents as evidence of existence and rights for prepaid assets or obligations for accrued expenses, the auditor's primary focus in substantive tests is allocation. For example, the cash disbursement that creates a prepaid asset is often allocated between expense in one period and an asset of the following period. The auditor recalculates the company's allocation and agrees amounts calculated to postings in the company's records.

Long-Term Productive Assets

Long-term productive assets are often labeled "Property" for land, "Plant" for buildings, and "Equipment." Leasehold Improvements are also included in this category. Property, Plant and Equipment is tested for existence and rights, and the auditor updates this information during each audit with information about newly acquired or recently disposed of assets. Physical examination of the assets and inspection of underlying documents are the main sources of substantive audit evidence. Determining that additions to fixed assets are properly capitalized is an audit step that can catch fraud. As in the WorldCom fraud, capitalizing cash disbursements that should be expensed defers the income statement effect and spreads it over future periods.

The auditor recalculates the allocation of the costs of the assets across accounting periods and reconciles the recalculated amounts with depreciation expense and accumulated depreciation. These audit steps support existence and rights of the net assets and occurrence of the expense. Other long-term assets that are depleted or amortized are audited in a similar manner. The auditor reads and evaluates financial statement disclosures to see that they correspond with the audit evidence and compliance with accounting standards.

Current Payables

Completeness is the management assertion targeted by substantive audit procedures for current payables. The primary audit risk is that they may be omitted or understated. Payables are generally tested through two mechanisms.

A substantive audit procedure addressing completeness of accounts payable is a review of cash disbursements made in the accounting period subsequent to the balance sheet date. Sometimes called the *search for unrecorded liabilities*, this audit step involves reviewing cash disbursements after the fiscal year end and determining whether they are expenses of the period being audited or expenses of the period when the cash was disbursed. For any cash disbursements that are expenses of the year under audit, the auditor should be able to trace the payment to a corresponding account payable posted on the company's year-end books.

Accounts payable may be confirmed with outside parties. When this audit step is performed, the auditor selects the sample from the list of vendors with whom the company does business, without regard for the amount posted to the payables account. To understand the lack of concern for the recorded amount, consider that if a company completely fails to record an amount payable to a vendor, the subsidiary ledger account balance is zero. An account receivable can only be overstated by the posted amount; in contrast, the amount by which an account payable can be understated is whatever amount is owed. Exhibit 9-10 lists assertions and examples of audit steps for accounts payable.

Long-Term Debt

Long-term debt accounts are composed of both routine and nonroutine transactions. Borrowing long-term debt is a nonroutine transaction that receives significant scrutiny from

EXHIBIT 9-10

Examples of Audit
Steps for Accounts
Payable

Assertion	Example of Substantive Test
1. Existence	1. Compare recorded accounts payable with vendor invoice and accompanying evidence of receipt of goods or service.
2. Obligations	2. Same as for existence.
3. Completeness	3. Send positive confirmation requests to vendors with whom the client has significant purchase transactions. Examine material invoices for the period after the balance sheet date up to the date that the auditor finishes work at the client location. Determine whether the item has been properly included as an expense and liability, or properly excluded.
4. Valuation	4. Not applicable.
5. Presentation	5. Inquiry and review of minutes of Board of Directors for indication of related party transactions.

(*Source:* Adapted from Taylor & Glezen, p. 524.)

management and others responsible for corporate governance. When the auditor examines new long-term debt, the substantive audit procedures consist of the following:

Review Board of Directors minutes for authorization.

Review the debt contract and terms to understand the transaction.

Trace the funds received into the cash account.

Evaluate whether the transaction is calculated and posted in compliance with accounting standards.

Routine transactions for long-term debt consist of periodic accruals and payments of interest and repayment of principle. The auditor tests debt either on an individual transaction basis or at the account level. The audit procedures include examining whether the cash disbursed is consistent with the contract terms, interest expense agrees to a calculated amount, and the amount of the debt principle is reduced as expected. The auditor also examines evidence of the cash disbursements.

Presentation and disclosure is an important assertion when auditing long-term debt. The auditor specifically addresses whether it is appropriate to exclude from short-term liabilities all debt that is shown as long term. This evaluation is especially important when debt is being refinanced and the auditor must evaluate whether the refinancing meets all the criteria to classify the debt as long term.

Another disclosure consideration is whether the company has violated any debt covenants, and if so, whether the violations need to be disclosed. Violation of debt covenants may be a disclosure issue only if the violation is at year end. Alternatively, in some situations, particularly for public companies, disclosure is required if there have been debt covenant violations at any time during the year. The need to audit the adequacy of long-term debt presentation and disclosure highlights one reason the auditor must read and understand the terms of debt agreements. Exhibit 9-11 shows audit procedures for long-term debt.

Owners' Equity

Just as with other financial statement accounts, the substantive procedures needed for owners' equity vary. Audit procedures differ based on the complexity of the company's structure and the volume of transactions that have taken place in the accounting periods being audited. If the entity has issued new stock or purchased treasury stock, these are

Assertion	Example of Substantive Test
1. Existence	1. Confirm balance due to creditor.
2. Obligations	2. Confirm obligation with creditor.
3. Completeness	3. Send confirmations to all financial institutions with which business was transacted during the period.
4. Valuation	4. Recalculate the computation of debt premium and discount.
5. Presentation	5. Recalculate current portion of long-term debt.

(*Source:* Adapted from Taylor & Glezen, pp. 559–560.)

AUDITING IN ACTION

Procedures to Test Borrowings, Repayments, and Accrued Interest

1. Examine all transactions in the account for the year.
2. Trace the proceeds from any borrowings to the cash receipts records, deposit slips, and bank statements.
3. Audit payments by examining canceled checks and canceled notes.
4. Trace the authorization of all significant borrowings and any repayments not made in accordance with the terms of the debt instrument to minutes of meetings of the Board of Directors.

(*Source*: Adapted from Taylor & Glezen, p. 560.)

nonroutine transactions. They are audited with many of the same techniques applied to nonroutine debt transactions. Just like nonroutine debt transactions, issuing and reacquiring stock is authorized, and the transactions are scrutinized at the company's highest levels of governance.

If equity instruments are issued to any employees as share-based compensation, these transactions are carefully examined by the auditor because of the complex valuation and accounting procedures required. If an entity has had a stock offering during the year, the auditor has likely been involved with the offering documents and is knowledgeable about the transactions.

Other substantive procedures for owners' equity include tracing net income from the income statement to the increase in retained earnings and reconciling the statement of owners' equity to the balance sheets. The auditor reconciles components of other comprehensive income (OCI) with the audit results of the related balance sheet accounts, and reconciles OCI and accumulated OCI among the financial statements. Just as with long-term debt, the auditor reviews presentation and disclosure for owners' equity for adequacy and compliance with accounting standards. Earnings per share is recalculated, and the earnings per share disclosure is examined for adequacy and compliance with accounting standards.

Revenue and Expenses

Tests of details of balances on revenue and expense accounts are often performed in combination with tests of controls and are called dual purpose tests. As transactions are selected and audited for the operating effectiveness of controls, the auditor also examines the supporting documents and recorded transactions for agreement of amounts and other details. When a company has a limited number of revenue or expense transactions, then directly examining supporting documents and recorded information and comparing them for agreement may provide sufficient audit evidence.

Often a company has many revenue and expense transactions of small dollar amounts that make up the account balances. Although the auditor will perform some tests of details of balances for the income statement accounts while conducting other audit work, these tests are not likely to provide sufficient evidence. Analytical procedures can be a major source of audit evidence for income statement accounts when they are used to reconcile the income statement details with changes in the balance sheets that have occurred during the period.

An example of other audit procedures on income statement accounts works well to explain this aspect of the audit. A chain of discount stores purchases and resells inventory; sales are the chain's primary revenue source. Cost of the inventory it sells is a major operating expense. The store chain incurs occupancy costs such as rent and utilities, as well as the costs of human resources. The auditor tests the amounts and other details of some of these transactions at the same time that controls are tested. When the auditor tests accounts receivable, some sales transactions are tested. When the auditor observes and audits the client's physical inventory count and tests ending inventory, some transactions affecting cost of goods sold are tested. While auditing personnel-related liabilities such as accrued payroll expense and accrued employee benefits expense (vacation, sick pay, etc.), the auditor tests some payroll transaction amounts. The auditor tests payroll expense from share-based compensation in conjunction with the related owners' equity accounts. Interest expense is examined when debt is audited. In addition, revenue is specifically evaluated for risk of fraud. None of these tests are likely sufficient to persuade the auditor about the fairness of the income statement accounts. However, multiple tests, considered along with analytical procedures, can be sufficient.

For the chain of discount stores, a variety of analytical procedures can be performed to augment the evidence obtained from direct testing of the income statement amounts. For example, the auditor expects to find a relationship between the terms specified in the lease agreement and lease expense. Lease expense may also be related to revenue if a percentage of sales is one of the criteria in the lease agreement. The auditor can evaluate gross margin (also called gross profit percentage) for recorded sales. Based on recorded purchases and sales, the auditor can calculate gross margin.

If gross margin is significantly larger or smaller that what is expected based on historical trends, or if it differs from the budget in an unexpected way, the auditor investigates why this difference occurred. If, for example, the gross margin percentage goes down, the auditor expects to find a reason explaining the decrease in the spread between the cost at which inventory was purchased and the price at which it was sold. An obvious reason, probably known before the audit step was performed, may be that the cost of inventory increased and the company was unable to increase prices to pass the cost increase through to customers.

Another example of predictable relationships that the auditor expects to find is among number of employees, average employee wages, and total salary expense. These examples show how analytical procedures add to direct tests of income statement balances and contribute to audit evidence.

SUMMARY OF SUBSTANTIVE TESTS AND PROCEDURES

Substantive audit tests and procedures vary based on the account being audited, the relevant management assertions of the account, and the resulting audit risk. The most appropriate audit test or procedure is selected based on the risks and audit objectives. In addition to direct examination of transactions and components of account balances, the auditor also employs analytical procedures to gather substantive evidence about account balances and disclosures.

Up to this point, analytical procedures have been discussed as a part of audit planning and the audit of specific account balances and disclosures. Analytical procedures are required during audit planning. And, as discussed, they are usually a necessary component for the auditor to have sufficient evidence on various financial statement accounts. Substantive analytical procedures also contribute to audit evidence when the auditor evaluates the financial statements taken as a whole. When used for this purpose, the auditor looks at big picture results rather than at year-end totals for individual accounts. These analytical procedures can alert the auditor to changes in trends, going concern doubts, and overall financial statement fairness. Analytical procedures are used in this manner in the wrap-up stage of the audit to support the overall audit conclusion and opinion to be issued. Use of analytical procedures in the wrap-up of the audit is discussed in Chapter 11.

AUDITING IN ACTION

Use of Analytical Procedures in Substantive Testing

If an analytical procedure is used as the principal substantive test of a significant financial statement assertion, the auditor documents:

a. The expectation, when it is not easily determined from the documentation of the work performed, and how the expectation was developed

b. Results from comparing the expectation to the amounts recorded in the company's books, or calculations based on those amounts

c. If significant unexpected differences are found, any other auditing procedures performed and the results of the additional procedures

(AU 329.22)

A final required substantive audit procedure is for the auditor to reconcile the company's general ledger to the financial statements. As part of this audit procedure, the auditor uses the work papers as a reference to verify that the company has recorded all the adjusting entries identified during the audit as necessary for the financial statements to be fair. When substantive tests and procedures are completed, the auditor moves on to the wrap up of the audit and issuance of the audit report. These topics are discussed in Chapter 11.

REVIEW QUESTION

D.1 List and briefly explain the typical audit steps for the following financial statement accounts: cash, receivables, inventory, investment securities, prepaid assets, property-plant-and-equipment, current payables, long-term debt, owners' equity, revenues, expenses.

CONCLUSION

The parts of the audit that you have now learned are client acceptance and continuance; planning—including understanding the client's system and assessing design effectiveness, setting planning materiality, and choosing the ICFR to test; conducting tests of controls and forming initial conclusions based on the results; and conducting substantive tests and procedures and forming initial conclusions based on the results. The initial conclusions based on the ICFR tests of controls are about the level of reliance that can be placed on the company's accounting system to produce reliable information during the year and the effectiveness of ICFR at the fiscal year end. The initial conclusions based on the substantive tests and procedures are about the fairness of the financial statements.

At this point, the remaining phase of an integrated audit consists of the wrap-up procedures and audit reports. These are explored and presented in Chapter 11. Chapter 10 gives an in-depth look at the audit of one of the transaction cycles to provide an example of audit procedures. Although each transaction cycle reports on different activities, the big picture audit steps followed for the various cycles follow a similar systematic process. By studying one transaction cycle in detail, you can understand the overall process used for all the transaction cycles.

KEY TERMS

Analytical procedures. Audit steps to assess the relationships that are expected to exist for financial and nonfinancial data, including exploring any unexpected findings.

Audit objective. Whatever is expected to be accomplished through an audit procedure.

Audit risk model. Planning model that expresses a mathematical relationship of audit risk, inherent risk, control risk, and detection risk.

Detailed work paper. An audit work paper that documents the audit tests and procedures, evidence, results, and conclusions for an item on the lead schedule.

Entity risks. Risks that are pervasive throughout the company, typically refering to elements of the control environment or processes used through the company.

External confirmation. The client sends a request to an outside party, asking the party to confirm the accuracy of specific information, in writing, by sending a response directly to the auditor.

Going concern. Term used to express the assumption that a company will continue in business for the next 12 months; an audit issue arises when there is substantial doubt about going concern.

Known misstatements. Misstatements in account balances and disclosures that are identified as a result of tests of details of balances.

Lead schedule. An audit work paper that identifies all the components of a line item on the working trial balance.

Likely misstatement. An estimation of the misstatement in an account balance or a disclosure calculated on the basis of results from auditing a sample.

Perpetual inventory. The balance in an inventory account is updated on a continual basis to reflect purchases and sales of inventory.

Sampling. For substantive tests in the financial statement audit, refers to examining evidence for less that 100% of target population or an account balance and using that evidence to develop an audit conclusion.

Sampling error. Making an incorrect conclusion because the sample used is not representative of the underlying population.

Sampling risk. The risk of selecting a sample that does not represent the population from which it is drawn.

Substantive procedures. Audit procedures that address the fairness of account balances and disclosures.

Tests of details of balances. Audit steps that examine transactions or components of account balances to assess the correspondence between supporting documents and recorded information.

Tolerable misstatement. A planning stage concept reflecting the estimate of the amount an account balance can be misstated and the account balance will still not be materially wrong; based on the misstatement expected to exist in the account and an allowance for sampling risk.

Transaction cycles. The group of business activities that relate to particular business objectives, such as sales and collections or purchases and payments.

Working trial balance. An audit work paper that lists all the line item account names and post-closing account balances on the client's general ledger.

MULTIPLE CHOICE

9-1 **[LO 3]** Which of the following is a benefit of using a statistical approach to sampling and making a conclusion about audit procedures?

(a) Statistical sampling permits the auditor to quantify sampling risk.

(b) Statistical sampling permits the auditor to quantify both sampling and nonsampling risk.

(c) Fraud is less likely to be missed when an auditor uses statistical sampling.

(d) Statistical sampling results in a correct sample size.

9-2 **[LO 3]** If an auditor relies on a sample and as a result concludes that the amount recorded in an account balance is appropriate when it is actually materially misstated, this reflects

(a) an efficiency problem with the audit.

(b) tolerable misstatement.

(c) an error in the preliminary judgment about materiality.

(d) an effectiveness problem with the audit.

9-3   **[LO 1]** Which of the following audit processes will the auditor have to wait until the end of the fiscal year, or after, to perform?

(a) Observing the inventory count

(b) Testing the operating effectiveness of the year-end closing and reporting process

(c) Inquiring of the client and identifying related parties

(d) Evaluating the possibility of illegal acts

9-4   **[LO 2]** An auditor is testing a company's expenses and cash disbursements. As a result of computer-assisted scanning, the auditor knows that most cash disbursements are small but that there have also been a few very large cash disbursements. Which of the following describes the approach the auditor is most likely to take when sampling cash disbursements?

(a) Design the sampling plan to continue increasing the sample size until all the large disbursements are included in the sample.

(b) Rely on a random sample to include a sufficient number of the large dollar transactions to be representative of the population.

(c) Increase the sample size over what would have been needed without the inclusion of the large cash disbursements.

(d) Stratify the population based on the dollar amount of the transactions, examining all of the larger disbursements and a sample of the smaller disbursements.

9-5   **[LO 1]** While examining the investments account of a client company, the auditor becomes aware of transactions involving derivatives. At this point, what does the auditor need to do?

(a) Require a specific representation from management indicating that management understands the degree of risk it is assuming through the derivative instruments.

(b) Understand the economic substance and nature of the transactions associated with the derivative instruments.

(c) Communicate with the audit committee to determine whether members of the audit committee understand the risk of the derivative investments.

(d) Confirm with the originator of the derivative instruments whether the investment should be accounted for using hedge accounting.

9-6   **[LO 5]** Regarding illegal acts, which of the following is not true?

(a) The auditor is more likely to become aware of illegal acts that have a direct impact on the financial statements.

(b) The auditor does not have to follow up on material illegal acts that he or she becomes aware of as long as they do not have a direct effect on the financial statements.

(c) Illegal acts are one of the topics that is covered in the management representations letter.

(d) All of the above are true.

9-7   **[LO 5]** Which of the following is not important to the auditor regarding related party transactions?

(a) Adequacy of disclosure of material related party transactions

(b) Material misstatement of any of the transactions because they are not arms length

(c) Identifying all the related parties so that the related party transactions and financial statement disclosure can be evaluated

(d) All of these are important to auditing related party transactions.

9-8   **[LO 6]** While auditing the fixed assets account, the auditor notes that a number of debits have been posted to the accumulated depreciation account. The auditor follows up by inquiring of management about the debits. Which of the following explanations from management would require only routine follow-up on the part of the auditor?

(a) The overhead variance related to inventory was adjusted at the end of the year.

(b) There was an error in the calculation of depreciation expense in the prior year, and therefore the expense was made larger in the current year.

(c) Numerous fixed assets were retired throughout the year.

(d) The estimated useful lives and salvage values of fixed assets were revised during the year.

9-9   **[LO 6]** In performing a test of details of balances, the auditor wants to test the existence assertion for the company's fleet of cars used by employees.

Which of the following most likely indicates the approach the auditor takes?

(a) Begin with the financial statements and trace to the underlying documents and fixed asset inventory records.

(b) Begin with the fixed asset inventory records and examine the cars.

(c) Begin with the cars and examine the fixed asset inventory records.

(d) Begin with the supporting documents from the time of purchase or lease and trace to the fixed asset inventory records.

9-10 [LO 6] An auditor compares this fiscal year's current ratio to last fiscal year's current ratio. This type of audit procedure is called a (an)

(a) test of details of balances.

(b) analytical procedure.

(c) test of controls.

(d) dual purpose test.

9-11 [LO 2] Nonstatistical or human error can cause an audit procedure to fail. For example, the auditor may perform the procedure incorrectly or reach the wrong conclusion as a result of examining documents. The likelihood of this type of error is reduced by

(a) increasing the sample size.

(b) supervision and review.

(c) multiple samples.

(d) performing the procedure before the fiscal year end.

9-12 [LO 1] If an auditor analyzes and examines the supporting documents for the larger dollar transactions that are posted to the repairs and maintenance account, the purpose of the audit procedure is most likely to

(a) determine that all of the large amounts that are supposed to be posted to repairs and maintenance have been recorded.

(b) trace whether cash disbursements for property maintenance have been recorded in the correct accounting period.

(c) investigate whether any amounts that should have been capitalized have been expensed.

(d) identify whether any amounts that should have been expensed have been capitalized.

9-13 [LO 5] Evidence contributing to substantial doubt about an entity's ability to continue as a going concern

(a) is collected during a specific phase close to the end of the audit.

(b) has to be considered in light of a company's five-year plan.

(c) is analyzed to determine what will be required for the company to meet its obligations for the 12 months after the audit report.

(d) None of the above.

9-14 [LO 5] Assume a company sells all of its merchandise to other businesses on credit and records revenue when inventory is turned over to a shipping company. In examining sales cutoff, the auditor

(a) only looks at whether the sales transaction is recorded in the proper period.

(b) considers whether the sales, receivables, and inventory components of the transactions are recorded in the proper period.

(c) will check the records to see whether anything left in the shipping area at fiscal year end should have been recorded as a sale.

(d) will confirm that customers intend to pay their accounts receivable for sales that were posted on the last day of the year.

9-15 [LO 5] Procedures for auditing amounts recorded at fair value

(a) may be limited to determining that the company has appropriately disclosed the items that are recorded at fair value and the method used to assign fair value.

(b) include understanding the company's process for determining fair value, assessing whether that process is in accordance with the accounting standards, and testing the results of the company's process for measuring fair value.

(c) must include a confirmation procedure with the source when measurement of the recorded fair value is based on publicly available information.

(d) b and c

9-16 [LO 6] When auditing cash,

(a) the auditor must determine that cash and cash equivalents are not combined in the financial statements.

(b) disclosure is only a major concern when the cash is composed of foreign and local currency.

(c) the auditor needs to address existence, rights, cutoff, and disclosure.

(d) All of the above.

9-17 [LO 6] The audit of accounts receivable

(a) will generally be completed using procedures that focus only on the receivables account.

(b) may include steps related to understanding the client's system.

(c) can often be limited to confirmation as long as the confirmation process asks about the customer's ability and willingness to pay, in addition to confirming the existence and amount.

(d) does not involve examining cash received in payment for receivables since those payments would be received in the following fiscal year, which is not the period being audited.

9-18 **[LO 6]** Which of the following is true about the audit of inventory?

(a) The auditing standards require that the auditor be involved in the physical count of inventory.

(b) The auditing standards require that some physical inspection of inventory by the auditor occur at the end of the client's fiscal year.

(c) The auditing standards require that the auditor physically inspect inventory to gain evidence about the existence assertion only if inventory is material to the financial statements.

(d) The auditing standard requiring that the auditor test the client's inventory count applies only to finished goods inventory since the primary concern about raw materials and work-in-process is the valuation assertion.

9-19 **[LO 6]** The audit of investments

(a) is very important on many audits because businesses may use investment vehicles to hedge various business risks as well as to make available funds productive.

(b) must be performed immediately after the audit of cash is completed since some investments can be quickly converted into cash.

(c) requires the auditor to physically inspect the specific investment documents to gain evidence that the client owns the recorded investments.

(d) always involves gaining an understanding of how the client applied fair value accounting to the assets.

9-20 **[LO 6]** The audit of liabilities shown in the financial statements as current

(a) typically includes confirming the largest current liabilities on the balance sheet.

(b) must include a confirmation procedure.

(c) often includes examining cash disbursements in the subsequent period to determine whether they were expenses of the current period or liabilities of the prior period and whether they were properly recorded.

(d) All of the above.

DISCUSSION QUESTIONS

9-21 **[LO 2]** Imagine that you are a new auditor scheduled on a year-end audit engagement. Your senior has instructed you to test the Accounts Receivable account. The account is large and contains many customer balances, so you have been instructed to use sampling techniques for your testing.

Required:

(a) Describe the audit risk model explaining the relationships of tests of details of balances detection risk and analytical procedures detection risk.

(b) What is the detection risk related to your task of auditing Accounts Receivable?

(c) Does the risk of incorrectly rejecting the Accounts Receivable balance affect your audit risk when using the audit risk model? What negative impact does incorrect rejection have on the audit?

9-22 **[LO 1, 5]** How does the auditor's approach and emphasis in auditing assets differ from auditing liabilities? Compare and contrast the objectives in the audit of current assets to those in the audit of current liabilities.

9-23 **[LO 5]** Discuss why assets are more likely to be overstated than understated. What effect does this have on the auditor's emphasis in the audit of assets? Are there any reasons why a company may want assets to be understated?

9-24 What audit step (or steps) would an auditor use to obtain evidence that recorded sales are for shipments actually made to nonfictitious customers? In other words—to determine that the sales really occurred? Explain how this audit procedure you describe accomplishes the intended objective.

9-25   A company's system includes the following control: The system requests a sales order number to be entered before a shipping document can be generated. If an invalid sales order number is entered, the system will not allow the user to proceed to generate the shipping document.

What is the purpose of this control, and to what management assertion(s) do(es) it apply?

9-26   [LO 3] Company A's balance sheet will be materially misstated if assets are overstated by $1 million or more. The auditor decides to set tolerable misstatement for the investment account at $30,000. After performing substantive tests, the auditor concludes that the investment account is overstated by $50,000. The auditor has also found a number of misstatements in other accounts, but they are all somewhat below the materiality threshold set for each of the accounts in which the misstatements are found. Assume the auditor has performed whatever additional steps necessary to be confident in the audit results found.

What does the auditor do next? What happens regarding the auditor's opinions on ICFR and the financial statements?

PROBLEMS

9-27   [LO 5] Salvadore is a staff auditor assigned to the year-end audit of Yachts R' Us, a manufacturer of high-end yachts based in Palm Beach, Florida. The senior assigned Salvadore to audit the allowance for doubtful accounts.

During his work, Salvadore notices that the allowance for doubtful accounts was roughly 1% of the Accounts Receivable balance, even though many large accounts were very old. He inquires of the CFO about the low percentages. The CFO indicates that there is no problem with slow payments because the company's policy is to refinance slow-paying companies. Generally, additional credit is not refused to a customer, regardless of the status of payments on an existing account. The client maintains that this policy makes possible a low allowance because few accounts have to be written off.

Required:

(a) Salvadore is concerned about the small size of the allowance account. What evidence can he gather to verify or alleviate his concerns?

(b) With accounts constantly being refinanced, what evidence can be gathered to provide reasonable assurance that the accounts are collectible?

(c) Assume that the client and Salvadore continue to disagree on the appropriate amount for the allowance for doubtful accounts. Given that the amount must be estimated, how much should Salvadore be influenced by the client's opinion?

9-28   [LO 2, 6] For many manufacturing and retail companies, the inventory account is a high-risk account because of its nature and size. Imagine that you are the audit partner responsible for signing off on a large retailer's financial statements. In the planning stages of the audit, the new senior on your job walks into your office to discuss the audit procedures involving inventory.

Required:

(a) What are the objectives in the audit of the inventory account?

(b) How will you advise your senior to use analytical procedures?

(c) How will you advise your senior concerning responsibilities for an effective observation of the client's physical inventory count?

(d) How will you advise your senior to test for obsolete, excess, or slow-moving items?

(e) For each audit process, what will your audit team need to document?

9-29   **[LO 4]** Ivan is an auditor on the Optical Illusions Corp audit. Upon examining the audit program, he sees that he was given the task of performing analytical procedures on several balance sheet accounts. Ivan's manager asked that he make sure that all of his documentation was in accordance with the proper auditing standards.

Required:

(a) Which auditing standards should Ivan examine pertaining to audit documentation if Optical Illusions is a public company? A nonpublic company?

(b) List content that his audit documentation should include.

(c) What should an outside third party examining Ivan's work be able to tell from the work papers?

9-30   **[LO 5, 6]** Listed below are several misstatements of inventory, accounts payable, and accrued liabilities accounts. Design a substantive audit procedure that provides reasonable assurance of detecting each misstatement.

1. A bonus earned by the president of the company has not been recorded.

2. Several accounts payable to vendors that the company has never purchased from before are omitted from the accounts payable listing.

3. When client employees counted the physical inventory, they included a number of items that were consigned to, but do not belong to, the company.

4. There is no disclosure in the financial statements that a large accounts payable is due to a related party.

5. Accrued payroll is understated.

6. One-third of the inventory of diamond jewelry is actually cubic zircona or white sapphires.

7. The client paid the same vendor invoice twice, although it is still shown as an account payable.

8. Client personnel informed the auditors that underground petroleum tanks contained an inventory of high-octane gasoline when they actually contained water.

9. The client failed to record warranty expenses incurred after year-end applicable to sales made before year-end.

10. Inventory in one corner of the warehouse is overlooked and not counted during the client's physical inventory count.

9-31   **[LO 4, 5]** You are a new staff auditor on Big Tuna Co. Your senior advises you that you are in charge of performing inquiry with management concerning long-term debt and should be ready with a list of questions for the interview. Prepare a list of at least five questions that you should ask management concerning the company's long-term debt.

9-32   **[LO 2]** You have been asked to perform substantive testing of the receivables account for Ocie's Manufacturing. You have been instructed to utilize sampling techniques. There are 3,000 customer accounts making up the balance. Of those 3,000 total accounts, 30 of them are for amounts over $20 million. Assume that you stratified the population and performed tests on the 30 large balances. You selected a sample of 30 from the remaining 2,970 balances, and found overstatements totaling $2 million.

Required:

(a) What is the known error of the portion of the account you sampled?

(b) Is there the possibility for any more misstatements? If so, how much?

(c) What might you discuss with Ocie's management about your findings?

9-33   **[LO 6]** Natasha is the senior auditor on the Propel Aviation audit. Propel Aviation is a wholesaler of plane and helicopter parts and electronics. The audit is in the planning stages, and Natasha must plan the audit procedures for all of the asset accounts. In order to plan the audit procedures, Natasha must first consider the relevant management assertions for each account. Then, she must determine which procedures will be most effective in testing the balances.

Required:

For each of the following items, list (1) the most important management assertions and (2) audit procedures to test the account:

(a) Cash

(b) Receivables

(c) Inventory

(d) Investments

(e) Prepaid assets

(f) Long-term productive assets

9-34   **[LO 6]** Johnny is the other senior auditor on the Propel Aviation audit. He must plan the audit procedures, but his responsibility is for the liability, revenue, and expense acounts instead of assets. Johnny must first consider the relevant management assertions for each account. Then, he must determine which procedures will be most effective in testing the balances.

Required:

For each of the following items, list (1) the most important management assertions and (2) the most effective procedures to test the account:

(a) Current payables

(b) Long-term debt

(c) Revenues and expenses

9-35   **[LO 5]** Gloria is a staff auditor on the Luxurious Hotels engagement. Luxurious Hotels is a subsidiary of Nantucket Resorts, a large hotel parent company that owns five international hotel chains (including Luxurious Hotels) and a mix of smaller bed and breakfast inns. Gloria is working on testing Accounts Receivables and Accounts Payables and has noticed that one step in the audit plan specifies that she should "test related party transactions and disclosures."

Required:

(a) What are the risks associated with related party transactions?

(b) How should Gloria audit related party transactions for Luxurious Hotels? List the audit procedures and the purpose of each step.

(c) How do related party transactions affect the overall risk for the audit engagement?

(d) How much flexibility on the client's part should Gloria be comfortable with regarding the amount of disclosure included in the financial statements?

9-36   **[LO 5]** You are the auditor of Take-Five Entertainment, an electronics company that focuses on the development and wholesale distribution of video games. At the year-end audit, you have been assigned the task of auditing Accounts Receivable, and consequently the Allowance for Bad Debts. Sales on account is a considerable part of Take-Five's wholesale business, so the Receivable and Allowance accounts are significant accounts. The economy has recently taken a downturn, so the accounts are considered to be higher risk than in the past.

Required:

(a) When testing the Accounts Receivable account, what management assertions do you focus on? What is the primary concern regarding the outstanding receivables?

(b) Design the audit procedures to test the receivables and allowance for doubtful accounts.

(c) List the steps you should take for auditing the underlying *estimates* for the Allowance account.

(d) List examples of other important estimates used in preparing financial statements.

9-37 **[LO 6]** Management assertions for the financial statements referenced in PCAOB Auditing Standards are:

Existence, occurrence

Completeness

Rights, obligations

Valuation, allocation

Presentation and disclosure

The purpose of tests of controls is to permit the auditor to assess whether properly designed controls operate effectively enough to prevent or detect material misstatements that would make these managements assertions wrong.

Required:

For each of the following audit procedures identify whether the procedure is:

(a) directed at a control or at an amount or disclosure, or both, and

(b) what assertion (or assertions) is (are) targeted.

Accounts, Classes of Transactions	Audit Procedure	Directed at:	Assertion:
All	Inquire who controls passwords for IT access.		
Sales, Receivables, Inventory	Examine document packages for items that have been shipped for inclusion of a customer order, credit approval, and shipping document. Make sure the documents are properly matched and complete, with all required signatures and trace amounts to the sales journal, accounts receivable subsidiary ledger, and inventory files.		
Payroll	For the Hourly Payroll Expense account, multiply the average number of workers times the average number of hours worked per year times the average hourly rate. Compare to the total posted annual amount.		
Cash	Inspect the client-prepared bank reconciliation for each month of the year, recalculate the amounts, examine the supporting bank statements, and trace the cash amount to the general ledger.		
Fixed assets	Obtain a list of fixed assets and physically look at the assets.		
Long-term debt	Read the contract related to each of the company's long-term borrowings and agree the terms of the contracts to the financial statements notes.		

Cash, Long-term debt	For each item of long-term debt that existed both at the beginning and end of the year, inspect the debt contracts and the company's analysis of the discounted debt amount and its analysis of violation of debt covenants and look for whether the details agree. Recalculate the amounts, and examine recorded entries and bank statements for cash disbursements for debt repayments. Using that information, determine whether the company has been in violation of any debt covenants during the year.		
Prepaid rent	Using the beginning financial statement amount, cash receipts and cash disbursements evidence, and the lease agreement, calculate year-end prepaid rent and agree that amount to what is shown in the general ledger.		
Inventory	At the end of the last day in the fiscal year, go to the client's shipping area and record the last shipment; trace the shipment into the client's records.		

9-38 **[LO 2, 6]** Assume that you are the audit manager for Techno Tech, Inc. in Houston, Texas, and that the in-charge senior has just presented you with the following list of unresolved issues from the audit work papers for the audit of the year ended October 31, 2010.

1. On October 31, 2010, the company accounts indicate that a large portfolio of marketable securities is held by a St. Louis brokerage firm. A confirmation request was mailed to the brokerage firm, but no reply has been received as of November 20, 2010.

2. A physical inventory count by the client was observed at the Houston facilities on October 31, 2010 (fiscal year end). Since Christmas is the company's big revenue season, Techno Tech merchandise is being held in Jacksonville, Florida, and Memphis, Tennessee, awaiting shipment to retailers during the Christmas season. Although confirmation requests were mailed immediately after the fiscal year end, no confirmation has been received from either warehouse as of November 18, 2010 confirming the existence and ownership of the inventory. These goods represent 9% of total finished goods.

Required:

(a) Identify the primary audit risks if the issues are not resolved satisfactorily.

(b) What audit procedure(s) would you recommend?

9-39 **[LO 4, 6]** In August 2010, John Smith, CPAs, released an audit report for a publicly traded company, Robertson Company, containing an unqualified opinion stating that his firm had performed an audit in accordance with PCAOB standards. Robertson Company included the audit report in its FY 2010 Form 10-K. The Robertson Company engagement accounts for 35% of all of John Smith, CPAs, income.

In October 2010, John Smith hires you as a staff auditor and new CPA. He indicates that he needs you to help "clean up" substantive comments about outlier revenue and audit procedures performed for Robertson Company in the August 2010 audit. You find that he had several unfinished analytical procedures concerning outlier revenue. (Outlier payments are a component of Medicare revenue. Outlier payments result from a provision in the law that allows the health-care provider to send a supplemental invoice when the costs of providing care significantly exceed the average or expected costs.)

When you raise the issue about the unfinished analytical procedures schedules, John ignores it and indicates that he has drafted a few modifications that he would like you to add to the work papers: (1) a statement in a memo that the Robertson audit was complete when the audit report was issued; and (2) information on the analytical procedures work paper indicating that Robertson's outlier revenue growth was sufficiently considered and it was determined that Robertson did not need to disclose that trend.

John assures you that everything was in order when completing the audit and that you won't need to include any information about the "cleanup work" made three months after the issuance of the audit report because it is not necessary. In fact, he assures you, this is done all the time when accounting firms like his are getting ready for a peer review.

You do more background work and notice that Robertson has had a recent loss of market capitalization of more than $3 billion and has been the focus of industry analysts' claims that Robertson's aggressive pricing strategy was driving earnings growth.

Required:

(a) What are the red flags for you as a new staff auditor?

(b) From an ethical standpoint, what should you do?

9-40 **[LO 1, 3, 6]** For each of the following substantive analytical procedures, list the possible misstatement it is intended to investigate. How would the result permit the auditor to identify the misstatement?

(a) Compare sales returns and allowances as a percentage of gross sales with previous years.

(b) Compare bad debt expense as a percentage of credit sales with previous years.

(c) Compare each "age" category on the accounts receivable aging schedule as a percentage of total accounts receivable with previous years.

ACTIVITY ASSIGNMENTS

9-41   Perform an Internet search to find information on the McKesson & Robbins case of 1939. How did the fraudsters successfully inflate reported assets and skim money for personal use? What did McKesson & Robbins's, external auditor agree not to do in the course of its audit procedures? What are some GAAS-mandated auditing steps surrounding inventory that would prevent such a fraud from being missed by the auditor's today?

9-42   Go to the FASB (*www.fasb.org*) and access codification 820-10 *Fair Value Measurements and Disclosure.* According to paragraph05-1, what is the definition of fair value? Read further and identify the three techniques that may be used to measure fair value. What are the three levels of inputs? Access AU 328 on the AICPA or PCAOB Web site. According to AU 328, how should an auditor obtain evidence about proper estimates of fair values?

9-43   Go to the PCAOB Web site (*www.pcaob.org*) and find the 2004 inspection of McGladrey & Pullen issued November 30, 2005. Read the inspection report, paying close attention to the firm's performance of analytical procedures. The firm used analytical procedures to test revenue and operating expense accounts. In what respect did the firm fail concerning the input data to the analytical procedures? In what respect did the firm fail in terms of documentation?

PROFESSIONAL SIMULATIONS

Go to the book's companion Web site at www.wiley.com/college/hooks to find simulations similar to those on the computerized CPA exam.

APPENDIX A: STATISTICAL TECHNIQUES AND TESTS OF DETAILS OF BALANCES

Auditors use both statistical and nonstatistical approaches for tests of details of balances. The use of statistical approaches, those that formally use **probability theory**, is not required. However, when the auditor chooses to use statistics, they can contribute to audit efficiency because of the relationship between risk of incorrect acceptance and sample size. The risk of incorrect acceptance is an important judgment for a test of details of balances. The auditor plans the test to limit the risk of incorrect acceptance to whatever has been set. Risk of incorrect acceptance is one of the parameters that drives the size of the sample needed. By measuring risk of incorrect acceptance using statistical techniques, the auditor is able to limit sample size to the smallest appropriate size.

Many of the mechanical steps in a statistical sampling audit procedure are now handled by computer software. This mitigates the major disadvantages of statistical sampling, which are the training and time required. However, even if computer software can perform the calculations, it is important for you to understand the underlying theory, why the calculation steps are performed, and what the results mean. This knowledge is required if you are to provide the inputs for the calculations and evaluate whether the computer-generated results are reasonable. Remember that one of the disadvantages of IT is that the software works consistently with whatever data are provided. If the input data are wrong, the output is wrong. Understanding the theory, relationships, and mechanics of statistical sampling enables you to meaningfully plan, execute, and review a statistical sample.

The steps set out in Chapter 9 for a test of details of balances using a sample are as follows.

1. Determine which account and assertion is being evaluated. What is the audit objective?
2. Decide what audit procedure needs to be used to test the assertion, including the direction of the test.
3. Decide on the sampling method—statistical or nonstatistical. If statistical, decide on which statistical approach and make decisions appropriate for the method.
4. Decide on the sampling frame and sampling unit.
5. Determine the method of sample selection. If statistical sampling is used, the method must produce a random sample.
6. Determine the sample size needed.
7. Select the sample, perform the test, and identify discrepancies.
8. Evaluate the sample results.
9. Consider the impact of the audit findings on other accounts, ICFR, and the need for any changes to the audit plan.

The following discussion focuses on explaining the theory, process, and steps. The discussion does not focus on documentation but assumes that the auditor prepares the appropriate documentation for all aspects of the sample, audit procedure, evaluation of results, and conclusion. This Appendix focuses only on the quantitative evaluation impacts in Step 8 and does not address Step 9. As was discussed in Chapter 9, audit procedure results are evaluated both qualitatively and quantitatively. The results are also evaluated for their impact on other aspects of the audit and the audit report.

Step 3 states that the auditor chooses either a statistical or nonstatistical approach. From that point on, the test is impacted by the approach used. Two statistical approaches are most common for tests of details of balances: **classical variables sampling** and **monetary unit sampling (MUS)** also called **dollar unit** or **probability proportional to size (PPS) sampling**. MUS is probably more frequently used in practice because it is easier and, if it can appropriately be used, generally requires a smaller sample. Classical variables sampling and MUS are discussed in this Appendix, and an example of each is provided.

Characteristic:	Causes required sample size to:
Tolerable misstatement is smaller	Increase
Expected misstatement in the population is larger	Increase
Standard deviation of items in the population is larger (mitigated by stratifying the population; no impact for PPS sampling)	Increase
Acceptable risk of incorrect acceptance is smaller	Increase
Needed level of reliability (complement of risk) is greater	Increase
Acceptable risk of incorrect rejection is smaller	Increase

Certain relationships are always expected between the sample size required and other characteristics of the account and the audit step. These relationships are considered as the auditor plans the test and sample. Exhibit A9-1 displays impacts on sample size.

REVIEW QUESTIONS

E.1 What is the major advantage of using a statistical approach to sampling, and why does this occur? What are disadvantages to choosing a statistical approach? What makes these disadvantages less of a problem?

E.2 What are the two most common statistical sampling methods used for tests of details of balances?

E.3 What characteristics cause sample size to change? For each item, is the change positively or inversely related to the change in sample size?

CLASSICAL VARIABLES SAMPLING

Classical variables sampling is an effective sampling approach that can be applied to audit procedures testing for either overstatements or understatements. Classical variables sampling is only an appropriate method when many of the items in the population have misstatements in the recorded book values. From the general list of steps for sampling presented above, the choice of classical variables sampling impacts Steps 3 through 8.

3. Decide on the sampling method—statistical or nonstatistical. If statistical, decide on which statistical approach and make decisions appropriate for the method.

To execute an audit procedure using classical variables sampling, the auditor must use information that is not required by all sampling approaches. The additional information is required to compute the sample size and analyze the result. To calculate sample size, denoted as n, for classical variables sampling the auditor needs to measure, estimate, or set the following:

N Population size
s Estimate of the population standard deviation
        Risk of incorrect acceptance
c Confidence coefficient
        Tolerable misstatement
A Population allowance for sampling error
        Expected amount of misstatement in the population

The population standard deviation is estimated using prior knowledge about the population or a pilot sample. This estimate is important because of the relationship between sample size and population standard deviation. If, during planning, the auditor estimates the population standard deviation lower than what is eventually calculated based on the sample, the sample size may have to be increased later. When this occurs, more items may have to be audited after the initial sample has been evaluated.

With everything else held constant, the amount of variability in the population is positively correlated with sample size. In other words, as the population standard deviation increases, sample size increases. For this reason, stratifying the sample can be an important step for classical variables sampling. If a wide dollar range exists in the items of the population, classical variables sampling will likely produce a sample size that is too large to be practical. The auditor can stratify the sample into more homogeneous groups. This brings down the calculated sample size. The auditor then performs procedures to accomplish the audit objective.

Risk of incorrect acceptance is set by the auditor. A firm may have guidelines on the risk of incorrect acceptance it deems to be appropriate. Generally, the auditor requires a lower risk of incorrect acceptance when the account balance or assertion is very susceptible to misstatement, ICFR is not effective or analytical procedures are not likely to be effective in detecting misstatements. With everything else held constant, a lower risk of incorrect acceptance causes a larger sample size.

Confidence level is the arithmetical complement of risk. In other words, if risk is 5%, the confidence level is 95%. **Confidence coefficients** are based on normal distributions and associated with various levels of risk and confidence. The technique currently in favor is to use the confidence coefficient related to incorrect acceptance only. (A confidence coefficient can also be determined that relates to the aggregated risk of incorrect acceptance and incorrect rejection.) Exhibit A9-2 shows risk of incorrect acceptance, confidence level, and confidence coefficient.

Tolerable misstatement is the amount of misstatement in dollars an auditor is willing to accept in an account balance and still conclude the account balance is fairly stated. Another way to describe tolerable misstatement is the potential misstatement in a particular account balance, which, when added to the misstatements in all the other accounts, will not cause the financial statements to be materially misstated.

The **population allowance for sampling error** is required to calculate sample size. Population allowance for sampling error is a function of tolerable misstatement and the estimated misstatement in the population. Tolerable misstatement less the estimated misstatement in the population equals the population allowance for sampling error. In other words, when the auditor sets tolerable misstatement, it is based on the **expected misstatement in the population** plus a component to compensate for the use of sampling. The population allowance for sampling error can be determined in several ways. The auditor can estimate it using tables or formulas and tolerable misstatement, risk of incorrect acceptance, and **risk of incorrect rejection**. Since all the components that go into the estimate or calculation are set based on the auditor's judgment, the population allowance for sampling error ultimately is based on auditor judgments.

As was discussed in Chapter 9, the auditor uses the sample to estimate the *true value* of the population. To use classical variables sampling, the auditor selects the approach to estimate the true value. Three common options are mean estimation, difference estimation, and ratio estimation.

EXHIBIT A9-2 Confidence Coefficients			
Risk of Incorrect Acceptance	**Confidence Level**	**Confidence Coefficient**	
5%	95%	1.96	
10%	90%	1.64	
20%	80%	1.28	
30%	70%	1.04	

Mean estimation assumes that the number of items in the population is known and that the total of the book value is arithmetically correct. Mean estimation does not require that the auditor know or use the recorded amounts of individual items in the population. To estimate the true value of the population based on a sample, the auditor computes the mean of the audited values of the sample items and multiplies this mean by the number of items in the population.

The **difference estimation** technique estimates the population value based on the differences between the recorded amounts and the audited amounts of the items in the sample. To estimate the true account value, the auditor finds the differences between recorded and audited values for sample items and calculates the average of the differences. This average difference is multiplied times the total items in the population. The product is added or subtracted from the account's recorded book value to arrive at the estimate of the true value. Difference estimation is the best choice when the misstatements are related to the number of items in the sample, rather than the dollar amount of the sample items.

Ratio estimation is used when the auditor wants to estimate the true population value based on the ratio of the recorded amounts and the audited amounts. The auditor calculates the ratio of the total audited value of the sample to the total book value of the sample, and multiplies the ratio by the account's total recorded book value. Ratio estimation is the best choice when the misstatements vary with the dollar amounts of the items.

The following example shows that the three methods approach the calculation differently but can all result in the same estimate. Alternatively, if the characteristics of the population and the nature of the errors are not uniform, the three methods can produce different results. Refer to Auditing in Action: Quantitative Evaluation of Audit Results in Chapter 9, which shows different account balance estimates using difference and ratio estimation techniques.

Book value of the account	$ 800,000
Book value of the items in the sample	$ 40,000
Sample's correct value as determined by the audit procedure	$ 41,000
Number of items in the account	2,000
Number of items in the sample	100

Mean per unit:	
Mean of the sample item's audited values:	$ 41,000/100 = $ 410
Estimated "true" account value:	$ 410 × 2,000 = $ 820,000

Difference:	
Mean of differences found in the sample:	$ 1,000/100 = $ 10
Estimated account difference:	$ 10 × 2,000 = $ 20,000
Estimated "true" account value:	$ 800,000 + $ 20,000 = $ 820,000

Ratio:	
Ratio of sample's audited to sample's book values:	$ 41,000/$ 40,000 = 1.025
Estimated "true" account value:	1.025 × 800,000 = $ 820,000

4. Decide on the sampling frame and sampling unit.

Classical variables sampling does not require a change of **sampling frame** and **sampling unit** from what is used in a nonstatistical sample. The sampling frame needs to represent the population and must be complete. The auditor performs tests to determine that the sampling frame reliably includes the entire population of items being sampled. For tests of details of balances, the sampling unit is typically a subsidiary ledger account balance, a transaction, or a document. The auditor considers the purpose and availability of the information in deciding on the sampling frame and sampling unit.

5. Determine the method of sample selection. If statistical sampling is used, the method must produce a random sample.

Generally, the sample selection methods described for tests of controls and nonstatistical tests of details of balances apply to classical variables sampling. The requirement is that the sampling method includes random elements so that the resulting sample is random. Random numbers or systematic sampling with random starting point(s) or random skip intervals satisfy the need for randomness.

6. Determine the sample size needed.

The sample size for classical variables sampling is calculated using the following formula:

$$n = \frac{c^2 \times s^2 \times N^2}{A^2}$$

n = sample size
c = confidence coefficient
s = estimated population standard deviation
N = population size
A = population allowance for sampling error

7. Select the sample, perform the test, and identify discrepancies.

The auditor's approach to performing the audit step using classical variables sampling does not differ from a nonstatistical approach. After identifying the discrepancies, the auditor analyzes them to determine what caused the misstatements. This may affect the auditor's conclusions regarding any impact on ICFR assessments and whether the fraud risk assessment needs to be addressed again.

8. Evaluate the sample results.

To evaluate the sample result the auditor first estimates the true population amount using the mean, difference, or ratio estimation method. The next step is to calculate the actual sampling error range (also called a **precision interval**, **confidence bound**, or **achieved allowance for sampling risk**) and an actual confidence level. Using the calculated precision interval, the auditor "builds" a range around the population estimate. The auditor evaluates the estimated true population value plus or minus the precision interval. Does any part of this interval fall outside the range of values bracketed by the recorded book value plus or minus the tolerable misstatement? If not, the auditor accepts the recorded book value. If any part of the interval falls outside the book value-tolerable misstatement range, the auditor takes steps to verify the test result and evaluate the need for an adjusting journal entry.

Precision is calculated using the following formula. All of the amounts are the same as those used to calculate sample size except that the **standard deviation** used is the *actual* standard deviation of the items in the sample rather than an *estimate* of standard deviation.

$$\text{precision interval} = \frac{c \times \text{actual } s \times N}{\sqrt{n}}$$

The actual confidence coefficient is also calculated. Again, only the standard deviation differs from what was used for calculating sample size. The actual standard deviation of the sample is used to calculate the actual confidence coefficient. Since the only item that differs from preliminary calculations is the standard deviation, the actual confidence coefficient changes significantly only if the auditor made a poor estimate of the standard deviation. Calculating the actual confidence coefficient permits the auditor to determine the actual risk of incorrect acceptance. If the actual standard deviation is larger than the estimated standard deviation used when calculating the sample size, then the actual risk of incorrect acceptance is larger than what was planned. The following formula is used to calculate the actual confidence coefficient.

$$\text{actual confidence coefficient} = \frac{\text{precision} \times \sqrt{n}}{\text{actual } s \times N}$$

Sampling without Replacement

Sampling can be conducted "with replacement" or "without replacement." In **sampling with replacement**, the assumption is that after an item is selected it is put back into the population and can be selected again. An item of audit evidence that has already been used contributes no new information to the auditor. Therefore, when sampling with replacement, the sample size calculation produces a sample size that allows for the possibility of selecting the same item twice. The sample size has to be large enough to allow for this possibility. The auditor typically samples without replacement, meaning that once an item is selected it cannot be available to be selected again. The **sampling without replacement** approach means that a smaller sample can be selected to accomplish the audit goal.[2]

Two changes are made to the initial classical variables sampling calculations when the auditor uses sampling without replacement. After the sample size is calculated, it is adjusted.

$$n \text{ without replacement} = \frac{n(\text{with replacement})}{1 + \dfrac{n(\text{with replacement})}{N}}$$

Similarly, after the precision interval is calculated, it is adjusted.

$$\text{Precision interval, without replacement} = \text{Precision interval, with replacement} \times \frac{\sqrt{N - n}}{N - 1}$$

(Again, for this calculation the standard deviation is the actual standard deviation of the sample.)

REVIEW QUESTIONS

F.1 Under what conditions is classical variables sampling an appropriate method?

F.2 How does the auditor estimate the population standard deviation? Why is a good estimate of population standard deviation important?

F.3 Why does the auditor usually have to stratify the population when using classical variables sampling?

F.4 What is a confidence level? A confidence coefficient? On what is a confidence coefficient based?

F.5 How are tolerable misstatement, population allowance for sampling error, and estimated misstatement in the population related to each other?

F.6 How are mean, difference, and ratio estimation used to estimate the true account balance? When is each method most appropriate?

F.7 What methods of sample selection are often used with classical variables sampling? Why?

---

[2]From a mathematics viewpoint, the sample size is smaller under sampling without replacement because every time an item is selected and is not placed back into the population the available items from which the sample is drawn decreases by one. As the population size gets smaller every time an item is sampled, the corresponding sample size decreases.

F.8   What are the steps followed to quantitatively evaluate the audit procedure results when classical variables sampling is used?

F.9   In calculating the precision interval and actual confidence coefficient, what input to the formula differs from what was used when the sample size was calculated? Why is it important if this number is different?

F.10 What is the difference between sampling with and sampling without replacement? Which do auditors usually use? Why? What items have to be adjusted when the auditor uses sampling without replacement?

AN EXAMPLE USING CLASSICAL VARIABLES SAMPLING[3]

Assume an audit objective of testing whether an accounts receivable balance is free of material misstatements. The auditor plans positive confirmations to confirm with the debtors that the accounts receivable balances are correct. The sampling frame is the accounts receivable subsidiary ledger, and the sampling unit is a single customer's account receivable balance. The auditor has performed tests and is satisfied that the receivable subsidiary ledger includes all the company's customers' accounts receivable. IT tests indicate that all the automated postings and mathematical processes function effectively. The auditor has already stratified the population and is confirming 100% of the large account balances. The book value of the remaining items to be sampled in the Accounts Receivable account is $ 677,309. The tolerable misstatement is $180,000. The auditor decides to use difference estimation to estimate the "true" value of the account.

The auditor calculates the sample size using the following information. (Although auditors usually sample without replacement, to simplify the example no adjustments for sampling without replacement are used here.)

$$n = \frac{c^2 \times s^2 \times N^2}{A^2} = \frac{(1.96^2)(\$5{,}953^2)(69^2)}{\$147{,}000^2} = 30$$

		Source:
risk of incorrect acceptance	5%	auditor sets this
c = confidence coefficient	1.96	from Exhibit A9-2
s = estimated population standard deviation	$5,953	auditor estimates this
N = population size	69	from company records
A = population allowance for sampling error	$147,000	estimated[4]

The auditor selects the sample. The book value of the sampled items is $294,480. The actual standard deviation of the sampled items is $5,900.

Under the auditor's supervision, the client prepares confirmations that the auditor sends to the customers. Confirmation responses are sent directly to the auditor's office. The auditor evaluates all confirmation responses received. If a response indicates a difference from the recorded amount, the auditor investigates the difference. Most of the reported differences are the result of transactions that occurred in the period between the end of the fiscal year and the time the customer received the confirmation. If the difference is resolved and the book balance is determined to be correct, the confirmation response is considered a reply with no difference. The auditor sends second requests to customers who do not reply and follows up with telephone calls, as needed. Eventually, the auditor receives

[3]Adapted from Taylor & Glezen, pp. 441–449.

[4]As indicated earlier, the population allowance for sampling error can be estimated based on auditor judgments of tolerable misstatement, risk of incorrect acceptance and risk of incorrect rejection; the amount is the result of auditor judgments. In this example, assume it is provided.

a response from all the customers to whom confirmations are sent. (Note that this may not be the case on a real audit, and the auditor may need to follow up with other procedures for nonresponses.)

After investigating all the confirmation responses, the auditor adds up the differences and divides the total by 30. The result is an average overstatement of $361 per item. The auditor estimates the population difference by multiplying this average overstatement difference by 69, with a result of $24,909. The auditor subtracts the estimate of the total difference from the recorded book value, resulting in an estimate of the true value of the account of $652,400.

$$\$361 \times 69 = \$24,909$$
$$\$677,309 - \$24,909 = \$652,400$$

The precision interval and actual confidence coefficient are calculated using the actual standard deviation of $5,900. Because the actual standard deviation is very close to the estimated standard deviation, the confidence coefficient (and, therefore, the risk of incorrect acceptance) is the same as what was originally set.

$$\text{Precision interval} = \frac{c \times \text{actual } s \times N}{\sqrt{n}} = \frac{1.96 \times \$5,900 \times 69}{\sqrt{30}} = \$145,685$$

$$\text{Actual confidence coefficient} = \frac{\text{precision} \times \sqrt{n}}{\text{actual } s \times N} = \frac{\$145,685 \times \sqrt{30}}{\$5,900 \times 69} = 1.96$$

The account book value is $677,309. The tolerable misstatement is $180,000. Thus, the range of book value, plus and minus tolerable error, is $497,309 to $857,309. As long as the estimated true population value plus or minus the precision interval is within this range, the auditor accepts the recorded book value as being free of material misstatement. The estimated true value ($652,400) plus or minus the precision interval ($145,685) is $506,715 to $798,085. This falls within the book value-tolerable misstatement range. Therefore, the auditor accepts the book value as being fairly stated. The auditor accepts a 5% risk that the true value of the population is smaller than $506,715 or larger than $798,085. Stated another way, the auditor has 95% confidence that the true account value is within that range. Exhibit A9-3 shows the results of the sample and auditor's analysis.

EXHIBIT A9-3

Results of the Sample and Audit Analysis

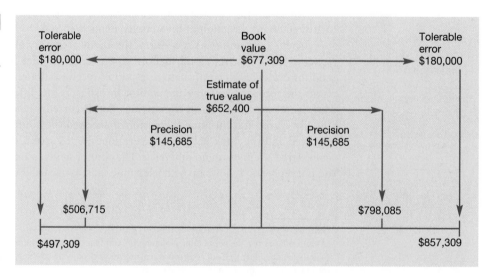

MONETARY UNIT SAMPLING

Monetary unit sampling (MUS), a sampling procedure used for tests of details of balances, is based on the theory used to test controls for attributes. **Attribute sampling** theory was discussed in Chapter 8, and the statistical approach was presented in Chapter 8, Appendix B. Attribute sampling addresses the question of whether a control fails no more often than a specified percentage of the time. Monetary unit sampling addresses the question of whether an account balance is misstated no more than a specified dollar amount.

Monetary unit sampling is also called dollar unit sampling because the sampling unit is a single dollar in the account balance. MUS uses **systematic selection**. The skip or **sampling interval** is calculated by dividing the account balance by the sample size. Then, the dollar corresponding to the next sampling interval is selected—throughout the population of dollars. If the skip interval equals 100, and the selection starts at the 10th dollar, then the 10th, 110th, 210th, 310th, and so on, dollars in the account balance are selected for the sample. The sampled item consists of the transaction or subsidiary ledger account balance that includes the selected dollar.

The method of selection used for MUS causes larger items in the account to have a greater probability of being included in the sample. Any item equal to or larger than the sampling interval is included. In the previous example of a sampling interval equal to 100, any transaction or account balance equal to or greater than $100 is included in the sample. This outcome automatically stratifies the population because it guarantees the selection of 100% of items that are at least the size of the interval. This automatic **stratification** makes MUS easier to use than classical variable sampling when the dollar values of items in the population have a large variability. Recall that classical variables sampling usually requires an extra step of stratifying the population to achieve a practical sample size when the population has a lot of variability.

Use of a single dollar as the sampling unit and systematic selection based on cumulative dollars makes MUS an effective method when the test is for overstatement of the account balance. MUS is especially appropriate when a small number of overstatements of large dollar amounts are expected. Since a larger item has a greater chance of being selected, MUS provides a greater chance of including overstated items in the sample and detecting the misstatement. The downside to the MUS selection scheme is that it is not appropriate for understatements, and zero and negative balance amounts will not be selected. Items in the population with zero or negative dollar values must be segregated, and a separate audit procedure used. Following the same logic, MUS does not provide a proportionate probability of selection if an item is overstated by more than its recorded value—if, for example, an item is recorded as $20,000 and its true value is −$5,000. This situation requires special treatment if MUS is used.

Following the same structure as was used for the classical variables sampling discussion, the general steps of a test of details of balances are used to explain MUS. Again, steps 3 through 8 are affected by the use of MUS.

3. Decide on the sampling method—statistical or nonstatistical. If statistical, decide on which statistical approach and make decisions appropriate for the method.

    When MUS is used, the auditor uses recorded book value and sets or estimates the following to calculate the sample size:

    Tolerable misstatement

    Risk of incorrect acceptance

    Number and dollar amounts of misstatements expected in the sample

    Recorded book value of the population

In addition, the auditor uses a **reliability factor** and an expansion factor based on the number of expected misstatements and risk of incorrect acceptance. Notice that this list is far less extensive than what was required to calculate sample size for classical variables sampling.

4. Decide on the sampling frame and sampling unit.

    MUS dictates the sampling frame and sampling unit that are used. As stated earlier, the sampling unit is a single dollar included in the population. Therefore, the sampling frame must be a detailed list of all the dollars that are recorded.

5. Determine the method of sample selection. If statistical sampling is used the method must produce a random sample.

    The selection method is systematic selection with a random starting point somewhere within the first sampling interval.

6. Determine the sample size needed.

    In MUS, the auditor calculates the sample size and sampling interval. The sample size, n, is calculated using the following formula:

$$n = \frac{\text{Population book value} \times \text{Reliability factor}}{\text{Tolerable misstatement} - (\text{Expected misstatement} \times \text{Expansion factor})}$$

The sampling interval is calculated as: Book value/n

The reliability factor and expansion factor are automatically available when a sampling software package is used to perform a MUS sample. Exhibit A9-4 presents the table of reliability factors and the table of expansion factors for number of overstatements and risk of incorrect acceptance. For calculating sample size the row for zero overstatement in the reliability factors table is always used.

7. Select the sample, perform the test, and identify discrepancies.

    Based on a calculated sampling interval of X, a random starting point is used between 0 and X. The starting dollar and every Xth dollar in the population are selected. The transaction or account balance in which the selected dollar is embedded is examined as part of the audit procedure. Any discrepancies are investigated, and differences are included in the evaluation steps. Just as with other sampling methods, the auditor evaluates the results for impacts on fraud risk assessment and other parts of the audit.

EXHIBIT A9-4

Monetary Unit Sampling Tables: Reliability Factors for Overstatement

Number of Overstatements	Risk of Incorrect Acceptance								
	5%	10%	15%	20%	25%	30%	35%	37%	50%
0	3.00	2.31	1.90	1.61	1.39	1.21	1.05	1.00	.70
1	4.75	3.89	3.38	3.00	2.70	2.44	2.22	2.14	1.68
2	6.30	5.33	4.72	4.28	3.93	3.62	3.35	3.25	2.68
3	7.76	6.69	6.02	5.52	5.11	4.77	4.46	4.34	3.68
4	9.16	8.00	7.27	6.73	6.28	5.90	5.55	5.43	4.68
5	10.52	9.28	8.50	7.91	7.43	7.01	6.64	6.49	5.68
6	11.85	10.54	9.71	9.08	8.56	8.12	7.72	7.56	6.67
7	13.15	11.78	10.90	10.24	9.69	9.21	8.79	8.63	7.67
8	14.44	13.00	12.08	11.38	10.81	10.31	9.85	9.68	8.67

Source: AICPA, *Audit Guide: Audit Sampling* (New York, 2008).

Expansion Factors for Expected Misstatement

	Risk of Incorrect Acceptance								
	1%	5%	10%	15%	20%	25%	30%	37%	50%
Factor	1.9	1.6	1.5	1.4	1.3	1.25	1.2	1.15	1.0

Source: AICPA, *Audit Guide: Audit Sampling* (New York, 2008).

8. Evaluate the sample results.

The auditor uses the sample results to make conclusions about the account balance. In MUS, discrepancies are used to estimate the overstatement in the account balance. All sampled transactions or account balances with discrepancies are evaluated.

If the transaction or account balance with a discrepancy is equal to or greater in size than the sampling interval, the amount of the discrepancy is treated as a **known misstatement**. If the transaction or balance is smaller than the sampling interval, the percent that the item is misstated is assumed to exist in the entire sampling interval and a **projected misstatement** for the sampling interval is calculated. In MUS terminology, the percent that the examined item is misstated is called a **tainting factor**. The tainting factor is used to project the misstatement in the transaction or account balance examined to the entire sampling interval. The known and projected misstatements are aggregated to determine the total likely overstatement in the account balance.

An allowance for sampling risk is calculated and added to the **likely misstatement** to derive an upper limit on overstatement. The upper limit is then compared to the tolerable misstatement.

The allowance for sampling risk includes a "basic" allowance and an allowance based on the misstatements found in the sample. The **basic allowance for sampling risk** is calculated as either tolerable misstatement or the sampling interval times the factor for risk of incorrect acceptance with 0 misstatements from the table in Exhibit A9-4.

The portion of the allowance related to misstatements is calculated using increments of projected misstatements. Projected misstatements from misstatements smaller than the sampling interval are listed from largest to smallest. The largest of these is multiplied by: (table factor for risk of incorrect acceptance and one misstatement) less (table factor for risk of incorrect acceptance and zero misstatements). The second largest is multiplied by (table factor for risk of incorrect acceptance and two misstatements) less (table factor for risk of incorrect acceptance and one misstatement). This process continues until all of the projected misstatements have been adjusted to include an allowance for sampling risk. The calculated amounts are added. The total likely misstatement (previously calculated) is subtracted from the total, leaving only the allowance for sampling risk related to the projected misstatements.

Total allowance for sampling risk is the basic allowance plus the allowance calculated based on projected misstatements. The **upper limit on misstatement** equals the total allowance for sampling risk plus the total likely overstatement. The calculations are presented in the MUS example presented next. (This is not the only set of instructions that can be used to derive the upper limit on overstatement. The algebraic nature of the calculations involved in determining the upper limit means that the result can be mathematically reached in several different ways.)

The upper limit on overstatement is compared to the tolerable misstatement. If tolerable misstatement is greater than the upper limit on overstatement, the audit procedure supports a conclusion that the recorded account balance does not need to be adjusted. The conclusion is that the account balance is not overstated by more than the tolerable misstatement, given the stated rate of incorrect acceptance. If the upper limit is greater than the tolerable misstatement, the conclusion is that the account balance is overstated.

MUS with Anticipated Misstatements

MUS is most appropriate when zero or few misstatements are expected in the sample. When misstatements are expected, the sample size increases. As a result, if many misstatements are expected, the MUS sample size may be too large to be practical. In the situation of expected misstatements, the auditor adjusts the tolerable misstatement downward using a calculation based on the dollar amount of the expected misstatement and the expansion factor that is based on the risk of incorrect acceptance shown in Exhibit A9-4. The smaller tolerable misstatement is then used to calculate the sample size with the standard formula. Using a smaller tolerable misstatement results in a larger sample size than would be calculated if no misstatements were expected.

REVIEW QUESTIONS

G.1 On what underlying sampling theory is MUS based?

G.2 Why is MUS also called monetary unit and dollar unit sampling?

G.3 Why is a sampling interval important for systematic selection? How is the sampling interval determined?

G.4 What does it mean that MUS automatically stratifies the population?

G.5 Why is MUS appropriate only for overstatements?

G.6 What must the auditor set or estimate before determining the reliability factor used to calculate the sample size for a MUS sample?

G.7 What must the sampling frame include for MUS that is not required for classical variables sampling?

G.8 What are the steps used to quantitatively evaluate the audit results of a MUS sample?

G.9 What happens when the auditor expects misstatements in a sample? Which calculation changes? How? Why?

AN EXAMPLE USING MONETARY UNIT SAMPLING[5]

For this example, assume an audit objective of testing whether an accounts receivable balance is overstated by more than the tolerable misstatement. The auditor plans positive confirmations to confirm with the debtors the amounts of the account receivable balances. The sampling frame is the accounts receivable subsidiary ledger, and the sampling unit is a single dollar. The auditor has performed tests and is satisfied that the accounts receivable subsidiary ledger includes all the company's customers' accounts receivable. IT tests indicate that all the automated postings and mathematical processes function effectively. The following information applies:

Tolerable misstatement:	$100,000
Risk of incorrect acceptance:	15%
Misstatement expected in the sample:	$0
Recorded book value of the account:	$1,579,000
Reliability factor:	1.90 (Exhibit A9-4)

Sample size and sampling interval are calculated as follows:

$$n = \frac{\text{Population book value} \times \text{Reliability factor}}{\text{Tolerable misstatement} - (\text{Expected misstatement} \times \text{Expansion factor})}$$

$$= \frac{\$1,579,000 \times 1.90}{\$100,000 - 0} = 30$$

$$\text{Sampling interval} = \frac{\text{Book value}}{n} = \frac{\$1,579,000}{30} = \$52,633$$

A random number generator is used to determine the starting point for sampling. The starting point is the 10,000th dollar, which meets the criteria of falling within the sampling interval.

The auditor selects the sample. The audit procedure is the same as what was used for the example of classical variables sampling: Under the auditor's supervision, the client prepares confirmations that the auditor sends to the customers. Confirmation responses are sent directly to the auditor's office. The auditor evaluates all confirmation responses received. If a response indicates a difference with the recorded amount, the auditor investigates the difference. Most of the reported differences are the result of transactions that occurred in

---

[5]Adapted from Taylor & Glezen, pp. 453–459.

the period between the end of the fiscal year and the time the customer received the confirmation. If the difference is resolved and the book balance is determined to be correct, the confirmation response is considered a reply with no difference. The auditor sends second requests to customers who do not reply and follows up with telephone calls, as needed. Eventually, the auditor receives a response from all the customers to whom confirmations are sent. (Note that this may not be the case on a real audit, and the auditor may need to follow up with other procedures for nonresponses.)

An excerpt of information from the sample and confirmation responses in the audit work papers follows. (The actual audit documentation would include all items in the sample.)

A. Sampling interval [$52,633]	Subsidiary ledger account number	B. Subsidiary ledger amount	C. Cumulative recorded balance	D. Recorded amount of item selected	E. Difference, % interval is tainted	F. Correct amount based on audit
$10,000	001	$10,200	$10,200	$10,200	0	$10,200
	002	9,040	19,240			
	003	40,760	60,000			
62,633	004	44,020	104,020	44,020	3,081 ^{H}7%	40,939
115,266	^{G}005	^{G}89,620	193,640	89,620	^{I}8,460	81,160
167,899	^{G}005	^{G}89,620	193,640	89,620	^{I}8,460	81,160
220,532	006	46,060	239,700	46,060	0	46,060
	007	21,060	260,760			
	008	4,020	264,780			
273,165	009	13,350	278,130	13,350	0	13,350
	010	32,400	310,530			
325,798	011	25,070	335,600	25,070	0	25,070
.	.	.	.			
.	.	.	.			
.	.	.	.			
694,229	042	26,520	645,460	26,520	6,360 ^{J}(24%)	20,160
.	.	.	.			
.	100	.	.			

Explanations

Column A. The numbers in the cells are derived by adding $52, 633 (the size of the sampling interval) to the dollar value of the prior sampling interval.

Column B. A listing of the items as they appear in the subsidiary ledger.

Column C. The running, cumulative account balance of items in the subsidiary ledger. Each cell amount is derived by adding the cell value in Column C to the cell value in the following row of Column B.

Column D. The amount shown in the accounts receivable subsidiary ledger for the customer account in which the selected dollar is embedded.

Column E. The difference between Columns D and F. A positive number indicates overstatement. A bracketed number indicates understatement.

G. This item spanned two sampling intervals and was selected twice.

H. Tainting percentage is calculated as: (44,020 − 40,939)/44,020 = 7%.

I. Tainting percentage is not applicable. This item is larger than the sampling interval, and the entire amount of the misstatement is a known error. Projection of the percentage of the misstatement to the sampling interval is not required.

J. Tainting percentage is calculated as: (26,520 − 20,160)/26,520 = 24%.

The sample is used to estimate the total overstatement in the account balance. For items smaller than the sampling interval, a tainting percentage is multiplied by the sampling interval of $52,633.

Account Number	Recorded Amount	Amount Based on Audit Step	Misstatement	Tainting	Projected Misstatement
004	$44,020	$40,939	$3,081	7%	$3,684
005	89,620	88,160	1,460	NA	1,460
042	26,520	20,160	6,360	24%	12,632
Total likely overstatement					$17,776

An allowance for sampling risk is calculated.

Basic allowance: $52,633 * 1.90 = 100,000 (rounded)

Allowance for sampling risk related to misstatements:

Projected misstatement, accounts smaller than sampling interval	*	Reliability factor increment		
$12,632	*	1.48	=	$18,695
$ 3,684	*	1.34	=	4,937
				$23.632

Less

Projected overstatement	$17,776
	$ 5,856

Reliability factor increments:

The factor for a 15% risk of incorrect acceptance for one misstatement (3.38) minus the factor for a 15% risk of incorrect acceptance for zero misstatements (1.90) equals 1.48.

The factor for a 15% risk of incorrect acceptance for two misstatements (4.72) minus the factor for a 15% risk of incorrect acceptance for one misstatement (3.38) equals 1.34.

Total allowance for sampling risk:

Basic	+	Related to misstatements		
$100,000		$5,856	=	$105,856

The upper limit on overstatement consists of total likely overstatement plus total allowance for sampling risk.

Total likely overstatement	+	Total allowance for sampling risk	=	Upper limit on overstatement
$17,776	+	$105,856	=	$123,632

The calculated upper limit on misstatement ($123,632) is greater than the tolerable misstatement ($110,000). Therefore, the auditor concludes that the Accounts Receivable account balance is misstated by more than the tolerable misstatement. If no misstatements had been found in the sample—as was expected when the sample was planned—the upper limit on misstatement would be equal to the basic allowance for sampling risk of $100,000. This is equal to the tolerable misstatement of $100,000. In this situation, the auditor accepts the hypothesis that the account balance is not overstated more than the amount of tolerable misstatement, with a risk of incorrect acceptance of 15%. Auditors often plan MUS samples assuming a minimal number of expected overstatements to be sure the sample size is large enough to analyze probability of overstatement if an unexpected misstatement occurs.

KEY TERMS

Achieved allowance for sampling risk. See *Precision interval.*

Attribute sampling. A method of sampling used to evaluate whether the percentage of time a control deviation occurs exceeds a tolerable rate.

Basic allowance for sampling risk. In a MUS, the allowance for sampling risk associated with zero misstatements.

Classical variables sampling. A method of sampling used for tests of details of balances to evaluate overstatements and understatements in account balances.

Confidence bound. See *Precision interval.*

Confidence coefficient. Based on normal distributions and associated with risk and confidence levels; in classical variables sampling, used for calculating sample size and evaluating the results of audit procedures performed on a sample.

Confidence level. The mathematical complement of risk; 1- risk.

Difference estimation. A method of estimating the "true" account balance based on the average of differences between recorded and audited values found in a sample.

Dollar unit sampling. Another name for monetary unit sampling.

Expected misstatement in the population. The auditor's estimate of the misstatement that actually exists in the population; affects sample size.

Known misstatement. The misstatements that are actually found in an account balance during the audit of a sample.

Likely misstatement. The aggregate of known and projected misstatement in an account balance.

Mean estimation. A method of estimating a "true" account balance in which the auditor computes the average of the audited values of items in a sample and multiplies that average by the number of items in the population.

Monetary unit sampling. An approach to statistical sampling for tests of details of balances that uses an individual dollar as the sampling unit.

Population allowance for sampling error. In classical variables sampling, refers to the component that, along with expected misstatement in the population, makes up tolerable error; required to calculate sample size.

Precision interval. A calculated amount that is added to or subtracted from the estimate of the "true" value of the account to produce a range within which the true value is expected to be.

Probability proportional to size (PPS) sampling. Another name for monetary unit sampling.

Probability theory. The mathematical foundation of statistics; relies on the law of large numbers and the central limit theorem.

Projected misstatement. The amount of misstatement that is not known, but, instead, is estimated based on the results of audit procedures applied to a sample; in MUS, the estimate of misstatement in a sampling interval based on the percent of error in the item audited.

Ratio estimation. A method of estimating the "true" account balance based on the ratio of the recorded and audited values of items in a sample.

Reliability factor. In a MUS sample, an input to sample size calculation that is based on the number of expected misstatements and risk of incorrect acceptance.

Risk of incorrect acceptance. The risk of concluding that an account balance is free of material misstatements when it is not.

Risk of incorrect rejection. The risk of concluding that an account balance is materially misstated when it is free of material misstatements.

Sampling frame. The physical source of a population from which a sample is selected.

Sampling interval. A skip interval used for systematic sampling; in MUS the sampling interval is the book value divided by the sample size.

Sampling unit. The item that is selected to include in a sample; a transaction, account balance, or invoice for nonstatistical and classical variables sampling; a single dollar for MUS.

Sampling with replacement. When an item is selected for a sample, it is placed back into the population and has an opportunity of being selected again.

Sampling without replacement. When an item is selected for a sample, it is not placed back into the population and, therefore, cannot be selected more than once.

Standard deviation. A measurement of the variability or dispersion in a population.

Stratification. The practice of separating a population into groups before sampling to reduce variability and produce groups that are more homogeneous; the purpose is to more effectively audit the subgroups and reduce sample size.

Systematic selection. A method of selecting samples that utilizes a skip interval; introduces elements of randomness through a random starting point or random skip intervals.

Tainting factor. In MUS, the percentage of misstatement in a sampled item; applies only to items smaller than the sampling interval; is used to project the misstatement to the sampling interval.

Upper limit on misstatement. In MUS, the sum of the total likely overstatement in the account balance plus the total allowance for sampling risk; compared to the tolerable misstatement to form an audit conclusion.

MULTIPLE CHOICE

9-44 When using classical variables sampling, which is correct regarding information needed to calculate sample size?

	Variability in the dollar amounts of inventory sampling units	Risk of incorrect acceptance
a.	yes	yes
b.	no	yes
c.	no	no
d.	yes	no

9-45 Based on an audit of a sample of inventory conducted using classical variables sampling, the auditor determines that the average audited value of items in the sample is $530. The auditor knows the total amount of the recorded inventory account balance but does not know the recorded amount of each item included in the sample. The inventory is composed of 20,000 items. Which method does the auditor use to estimate the "true" inventory account balance?

(a) MUS

(b) Difference

(c) Mean per unit

(d) Ratio

9-46 An auditor performed a test of details of balances of investments and concluded that the recorded account balance was materially misstated. The auditor followed up with more tests to investigate the problem and determined that the account balance was actually free of material misstatement.

This is an example of

(a) accessing control risk too low.

(b) incorrect acceptance.

(c) incorrect rejection.

(d) setting the confidence coefficient too high.

9-47 An auditor decides to use MUS to test accounts receivable. The sampling interval is $8,000. After selecting the sampling and conducting audit procedures, the auditor determines that one customer's accounts receivable balance is recorded as $4,000 at the end of the fiscal year, when it should have been $3,000. The misstatement occurred because the company failed to record a $1,000 payment received just before the end of the year. The projected misstatement is

(a) $1,000.

(b) $2,000.

(c) $3,000.

(d) $4,000.

9-48 Which of the following is correct regarding the impact of an increase in tolerable error and a decrease in risk of incorrect acceptance on sample size?

	Increase in tolerable error	Decrease in risk of incorrect acceptance
a.	Increase sample size	Increase sample size
b.	Increase sample size	Decrease sample size
c.	Decrease sample size	Increase sample size
d.	Decrease sample size	Decrease sample size

PROFESSIONAL SIMULATIONS

Go to the book's companion Web site at www.wiley.com/college/hooks to find simulations similar to those on the computerized CPA exam.

CHAPTER 10

Auditing Revenue Processes: Sales, Billing, and Collection in the Health-Care Provider and Retailing Industries

491

Chapter 10 Resources

AU 312, AICPA, PCAOB, *Audit Risk and Materiality in Conducting an Audit*

AU 314, AICPA, *Understanding the Entity and Its Environment and Assessing the Risks of Material Misstatement*

AU 316, AICPA, PCAOB, *Consideration of Fraud in a Financial Statement Audit*

AU 318, AICPA, *Performing Audit Procedures in Response to Assessed Risks and Evaluating the Audit Evidence Obtained*

AU 319, PCAOB, *Consideration of Internal Control in a Financial Statement Audit*

AU 326, AICPA, *Audit Evidence*

AU 326, PCAOB, *Evidential Matter*

AU 329, AICPA, PCAOB, *Analytical Procedures*

AU 330, AICPA, PCAOB, *The Confirmation Process*

AU 342, AICPA, PCAOB, *Auditing Accounting Estimates*

AU 350, AICPA, PCAOB, *Audit Sampling*

FASB ASC 605-15-25-1 *Sales of Product when Right of Return Exists*

FASB Concepts Statement No. 5 *Recognition and Measurement in Financial Statements of Business Enterprises*

FASB Concepts Statement No. 6 *Elements of Financial Statements*

PCAOB AS 3, *Audit Documentation*

PCAOB AS 5, *An Audit of Internal Control Over Financial Reporting That is Integrated with an Audit of Financial Statements*

PCAOB Release 2004-001, *An Audit of Internal Control Over Financial Reporting Performed in Conjunction with an Audit of Financial Statements*

Sarbanes-Oxley Act of 2002

SEC Staff Accounting Bulletin 101 *Revenue Recognition in Financial Statements*

INTRODUCTION

The sales and collections transactions cycle deals with business activities through which a company provides goods or services to a customer and receives payment. The cycle can also be defined in a broader way called a revenue cycle and include all revenues, such as investment income, in addition to operating revenues. This chapter begins with overviews of the health-care provider and retail industries, and then presents details of sales, billing, and collection processes that are found in most businesses. Next, the chapter discusses audit activities that apply to the revenue cycle. Finally, the chapter ends by discussing auditing the revenue cycle in the context of health-care provider and retail industries.

OVERVIEW [LO 1]

Virtually all businesses have a revenue and collection function that is fundamental to the primary productive activity of a company. As a result, the **revenue cycle** interacts with and depends on other cycles. A company must either purchase or manufacture the goods it sells, and it must have the human resources to produce goods and provide services. The customer may take possession of goods at the time of the sale, or the transaction may require a process to deliver the goods separate from the point of sale. The receipt of payment in the cycle may result from sales for cash at the point of sale or sales on credit. Sales on credit require a billing and collection function in addition to the activities that occur at the time of the sale. The process of granting credit and handling bad debt must be managed. All sellers of goods and services also have some policies and provisions that address and deal with sales returns and allowances. Typical transaction activities for sales, billing, and cash receipts are as follows.

Sales for cash and for accounts receivable

Cash receipts

Sales returns and allowances

Writing off uncollectible accounts receivable

Estimating bad debt expense

Accounts involved in the cycle are:

Cash	Sales
Accounts Receivable	Sales returns and allowances
Allowance for Uncollectible Accounts	Bad debt expense

Health-care providers and businesses involved in retail sales are used in this chapter to exemplify the revenue and collections transactions cycle because their activities include:

Sales of services
Sales of inventory that is shipped
Sales of inventory "carried out" by the purchaser at the time of sale
Sales settled via cash
Sales settled via electronic funds transfers
Sales paid for by the use of credit cards
Sales that are billed to individuals
Business-to-business credit sales "on account"

In addition to the revenue-producing aspect of the transactions, this chapter presents the processes used to handle and record any cash receipts that come into a business.

REVIEW QUESTIONS

A.1 What is the difference between a sales and collections cycle and a revenue cycle?

A.2 What types of transactions are included in the sales and collections cycle?

HEALTH-CARE PROVIDERS

Health-care providers sell a service. Recording the sale, collecting any payment due at the time the service is provided, and billing and collection are the important financial and accounting activities. Health-care providers also sell merchandise inventory, such as medicine, cosmetics, and other incidentals. The processes used for these sales are similar to those used by retailers. But the most important aspect of a health-care provider's business is selling a service. For that function no inventory is involved. When a patient is charged for a medical service, any medicines or other items used are treated as supplies and included in the overall charge for the service.

Health-care providers in the United States are often paid by **third-party payers** in addition to or instead of the patient who receives the service. When an individual has health insurance, the individual will likely have to pay a **co-payment** to the medical professional. A co-payment is a calculated portion of the fee. The insurance company then pays the rest. A third-party payer may be a government entity such as Medicare, Medicaid, or the Veterans Health Administration.[1]

Since much of a health-care provider's collections are paid by third-party payers, it is important for the seller (the health-care provider) to verify the patient's insurance coverage before providing services. Other types of businesses verify the creditworthiness of a potential customer before agreeing to grant credit. Similarly, health-care providers verify that patients have insurance covering the service to be provided before agreeing to bill the insurance company. Health-care providers verify insurance prior to giving care to decrease the risk of not being paid for the service. Many insurance companies have contracts with health-care providers that set the payment the health-care provider receives for specific services.

---

[1]The primary discussion presented here assumes a **fee-for-service contract** rather than a **capitation agreement**. Capitation agreements involve contracted payment amounts to health-care providers typically based on a set rate per patient.

AUDITING IN ACTION

DaVita, Inc., December 31, 2008 10K, Item 1A, Risk Factors

Approximately 35% of our dialysis and related lab services revenues for the year ended December 31, 2008 were generated from patients who have commercial payors as the primary payor. **The majority of these patients have insurance policies that pay us on terms and at rates that are generally significantly higher than Medicare rates. The payments we receive from commercial payors generate nearly all of our profit. We are experiencing a decrease in some of our commercial payment rates and it is possible that commercial payment rates could be materially lower in the future.** The downward pressure on commercial payment rates is a result of general conditions in the market, recent and future consolidations among commercial payors, increased focus on dialysis services and other factors....

Our revenue levels are sensitive to the percentage of our patients with higher-paying commercial insurance coverage. A patient's insurance coverage may change for a number of reasons, including as a result of changes in the patient's or a family member's employment status. Currently, for a patient covered by an employer group health plan, Medicare generally becomes the primary payor after 33 months, or earlier, if the patient's employer group health plan coverage terminates. When Medicare becomes the primary payor, the payment rate we receive for that patient shifts from the employer group health plan rate to the lower Medicare payment rate. In addition, our continued negotiations with commercial payors could result in a decrease in the number of patients under commercial plans. **If there is a significant reduction in the number of patients under higher-paying commercial plans relative to government-based programs that pay at lower rates, it would have a material adverse effect on our revenues, earnings and cash flows.**

The insurance contract also specifies the co-payment that the health-care provider collects from individual patients. The payment amounts agreed to between health-care providers and private and government insurers have an important impact on the health-care provider's income.

In addition to verifying insurance coverage and co-payment amount, proper billing is important to the health-care providers' revenue and collections cycle. Both private and government insurers typically have set amounts that they pay health-care providers for various services. The payment amount is based on the nature of the service, diagnosis, and negotiated payment contract.

For example, when a new patient sees a doctor for the first time, the doctor spends more time because he or she has never treated that patient before. The insurance company payment is greater when the doctor treats a new patient than an established patient with the same symptoms. Similarly, when a patient is diagnosed with a complicated medical problem that is difficult and time consuming to treat, the insurance company agrees to a larger payment than for a simple office visit. A doctor is paid more when a patient receives in-office surgery than a routine blood pressure check.

Accounting controls for billing are especially important because, under a fee-for-service plan, the insurance company typically pays the health-care provider based on a contract rate for a particular medical treatment or diagnosis. The health-care provider needs to bill accurately and on a timely basis. Suppose the health-care provider bills the insurance company for an established patient's in-office surgery using the code for a "new patient office visit." The insurance company will probably reject the bill and require the health-care provider to submit a corrected invoice. It takes time for the doctor's office to resubmit the invoice and the insurance company to process and pay it. During this period, the doctor does not have the cash that was earned as a result of providing the service to the patient. For a health-care service provider, it is very important that the billing process produces accurate invoices and meets all the documentary requirements of the third-party payer.

AUDITING IN ACTION

Billing Errors

Denise has been working on the ICFR portion of the integrated audit of an urgent care clinic that employs physicians. The clinic processes insurance billings and collections for its physicians. Denise's audit step is investigating how the system handles invoices that are rejected by insurance companies and returned to the clinic for reprocessing. Her senior told her that insurance companies often reject invoices because of errors in the codes for services provided—basically when the diagnosis number or code recorded by the physician is inconsistent with other information on the invoice or patient's records.

Denise talks with Bruce, the employee who handles the transactions that have identified errors. He explains that he doesn't get too many invoices kicked back from insurance companies for reprocessing. The clinic's computer program that creates the invoices has a large number of internal verification checks. The computer compares information on the patient's clinic record for consistency with the visit information and reasonableness of the diagnosis before the insurance invoice is produced and filed.

Denise asks whether many problems are identified during the billing process and what happens to those transactions. Bruce shows Denise a printout of patient billing transactions that were flagged and rejected by the billing program based on the automatic comparisons and screens of the diagnostic codes. He explains that he e-mails each physician about the problem billings and the doctor reviews the patient file and corrects the error. The transaction is then reprocessed using the billing program. When all the internal verification checks pass, the invoice is produced and filed with the insurance company.

Denise asks Bruce whether this is the most efficient way to handle the problem. She wonders because he said it usually takes a day or two after he e-mails the doctors before they make the corrections. Bruce responds that when a bill is actually sent to the insurer with an incorrect diagnostic code, it can take weeks of corresponding with the insurance company to identify the problem and resubmit a corrected invoice.

Accounting for the service transaction is relatively simple. Assume a patient with insurance requiring a co-payment comes to the doctor for an office visit. The doctor's charge for the visit is $100, and the required patient co-payment is $10. At the end of the visit the doctor records the revenue, account receivable, and cash received from the patient.

Cash	10	
Account Receivable	90	
Service Revenue		100

The doctor then bills the insurance company and receives payment for the services provided at the contracted rate. In this case, assume the doctor has contracted with the insurance company to accept $48 for the type of in-office service provided. The difference between the receivable from the insurance company of $90 and the contracted rate of $48 is recorded as a **contractual discount**, which is treated as a contra-revenue account.

Contractual Discount	42	
Cash	48	
Account Receivable		90

The process changes slightly if a service is provided over time and no cash collection or billing activity occurs until the service is complete. For example, a surgeon may provide preoperative tests and examinations days or weeks before a surgery is performed. Billing and cash receipt do not occur until after the surgery. In this situation, an "Unbilled Services" account is used to capture services that are provided before and during the surgery that have not yet been billed. The Unbilled Services account is most important at the end of the fiscal period so that proper revenue is recorded.

An alternative to a fee-for-service plan is a **capitation agreement**. An insurance company or a government program makes periodic payments based on the number of patients in the doctor's practice who are insured by that plan. Under this type of agreement, the payment is calculated on a capitation (number of patients) basis, regardless of the number and nature of treatments provided. The billing and collections processes under this type of plan are much simpler.

From Humana, Inc., Form 10K, year ended December 31, 2008:

> *[W]e contract with hospitals and physicians to accept financial risk for a defined set of HMO membership. In transferring this risk, we prepay these providers a monthly fixed-fee per member, known as a capitation (per capita) payment, to coordinate substantially all of the medical care for their capitated HMO membership, including some health benefit administrative functions and claims processing.*
>
> (Item 1, "Capitation" p. 12; *http://idea.sec.gov/Archives/edgar/data/49071/000119312509034123/d10k.htm*)

REVIEW QUESTIONS

B.1 What is a third-party payer? What are the most common entities that fall into the category of third-party payer?

B.2 What is a co-payment?

B.3 Why is it important for a health-care provider to verify the insurance of patients?

B.4 Why is proper billing especially important in the health-care provider setting?

B.5 What does it mean when a health-care provider has a fee-for-service contract with a third-party payer?

B.6 What transaction is captured by a Contractual Discount account? What type of account is a Contractual Discount account?

B.7 What transaction is captured by the Unbilled Services account?

B.8 What is the difference between a fee-for-service and a capitation agreement?

RETAILING

A retail entity's primary business activity is selling finished goods inventory to a customer for cash or on credit. In a traditional setting—in which customers actually enter a store to make a purchase—consumers pay for a purchase with cash, electronic or paper check, or through some type of credit arrangement, typically a credit card. Online sales between businesses are usually transacted using some form of preestablished credit. When a business sells to another business, for example, a wholesaler selling goods to a retailer, a "trade" credit account between the two businesses may be used. A possibility for any of these transactions is that payment may be made via electronic transfer using a debit card.

The simplest retail transaction is one for cash, in which the customer exchanges cash for goods at the point of sale. Selling on credit is one departure from the simplest transaction and requires some sort of credit approval for the specific transaction. If a credit card is used, the approval is usually requested and received electronically from the company that issued the card. Whether the transaction is approved depends on the amount of the transaction and the limits established by the credit card company.

A credit-*granting* process is also needed to determine the creditworthiness of the purchaser and the amount of credit the lender is willing to extend. This credit-granting process is performed before any sales transactions on credit are completed. A credit-granting process of some sort is used whenever credit is extended regardless of whether the credit is an open trade account between businesses or a credit card.

The sale of an item priced at $50, not considering any sales taxes, is recorded as:

Cash or Account Receivable   50

     Sales Revenue   50

Cash, checks received, and sales receipts resulting from transactions conducted using bank credit cards are deposited to the retailer's bank account like cash. Receipts from major credit cards (like Discover and American Express) are also deposited. In these cases the retailer has to wait, usually several days, before the funds become available. Retailers receive the proceeds of sales conducted using credit cards after they are reduced by a transaction fee taken by the sponsoring credit card company or bank.

In the same $50 sales transaction, if the customer uses a bank-sponsored credit card with a 3% fee, the outcome is:

Cash	48.50	
Transaction fee expense	1.50	
Sales Revenue		50.00

Exhibit 10-1 diagrams the flows in a credit card sale.

The process of selling goods to customers on credit differs when the seller is responsible for billing the customer and collecting the cash from the sale, as typically occurs with "trade" accounts between businesses. These sales are initially recorded with an entry to accounts receivable and sales. The accounts receivable subsidiary ledger documents the business to which the sale is made. The total posted to the accounts receivable subsidiary ledger is also posted to the general ledger. Recording this type of sale triggers a billing process through which an invoice is sent to the customer. When cash is received in response to the bill, it is posted to the cash receipts journal and accounts receivable subsidiary ledger. The totals posted to the cash receipts journal and accounts receivable subsidiary ledger are also posted to the general ledger.

Credit sales transactions are quite similar for entities as different as retailers and health-care providers when the sale is to the ultimate consumer. When retailers and health-care providers sell on credit, it is mainly through the use of credit cards, which does not require them to bill the customer or patient. Health-care providers usually collect co-payments from patients at the time of the service. Therefore, the primary billing they perform is to other "businesses"—private insurers and government third-party payers. Health-care providers do a limited amount of patient billing for uncollected co-payments and uninsured services. Sometimes they also bill patients for "deductibles," the amount an insurance plan requires patients to pay out-of-pocket each year before the plan begins paying.

EXHIBIT 10-1

Credit Card Sale

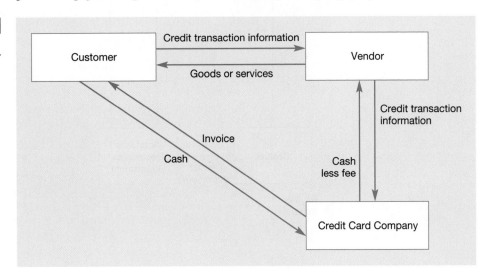

Retailers sell directly to end consumers and generally have few business customers whom they bill directly. Wholesale distributors have sales functions that are similar to retailers except that they do not collect sales taxes and their customer base is other businesses. Therefore, when wholesalers sell on credit, the transactions usually either utilize credit cards or the seller bills the business customer directly for the sale. In an e-commerce environment the billing and collection may be entirely electronic, but the steps are substantially unchanged.

Another activity that complicates sales transactions involves the shipment of goods to the customer rather than the customer taking the goods at the time of sale. The shipping process requires that the seller fill the order, typically removing the goods from storage or warehousing, before shipping. While credit sales requiring shipping may not seem like a major category of sales for traditional "brick-and-mortar" retail establishments, it is a very important category of sales for retailers who sell only or primarily online. Exhibit 10-2 diagrams the flows of a credit sale requiring shipment.

EXHIBIT 10-2

Sale on Trade Credit with Shipping

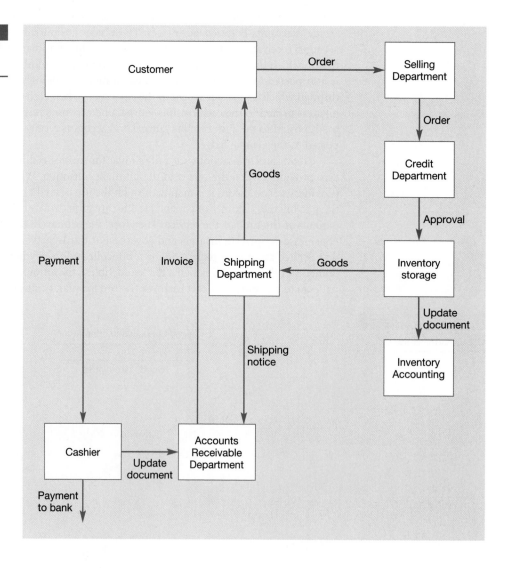

Amazon.com reports the following in Note 1 of its financial statements for the period ended December 31, 2008:

Fulfillment

Fulfillment costs represent those costs incurred in operating and staffing our fulfillment and customer service centers, including costs attributable to buying, receiving, inspecting, and warehousing inventories; picking, packaging, and preparing customer orders for shipment; payment processing and related transaction costs, including costs associated with our guarantee for certain seller transactions; and responding to inquiries from customers.

(*http://idea.sec.gov/Archives/edgar/data/1018724/000119312509014406/d10k.htm#tx74114_27*)

Retail sales businesses post sales activity to their inventory and cost of sales accounts as well as to revenue accounts. Using the previous sales example, assume that a perpetual method of posting inventory is used and that the sales price reflects a 100% markup. At the time the $50 sale occurs, the following transaction is posted for the cost of the inventory sold:

Cost of sales	25	
Inventory		25

Inventory is the topic of Chapter 14.

After inventory is sold to a customer, even though the sale is completed, there are usually circumstances for which the goods may be returned. The sales returns and allowances process deals with the return of inventory. To understand the process, begin again with a straightforward form of the transaction in which the customer returns undamaged inventory that can be resold. In this situation the process involves receiving the goods returned, documenting the transaction, refunding the customer's payment, and posting the transaction to the affected accounts as follows:

Sales returns and allowances	50	
Cash, Accounts receivable		50
Inventory	25	
Cost of sales		25

Departures from this simplest form of a return transaction include return of damaged goods or the return of only part of the goods that were purchased. Sometimes goods are defective, and an allowance is given to the purchaser even when the goods are not physically returned. This last situation is common when the return process is very costly, such as when an item is heavy and shipping costs are expensive.

REVIEW QUESTIONS

C.1 What is a trade credit account?

C.2 What is the difference between the business of a wholesale distributor and that of a retailer?

C.3 Why is the shipping function more important for an online retailer than for many traditional retailers?

BUSINESS PROCESSES, DOCUMENTS, AND INTERNAL CONTROLS

In the revenue cycle many important underlying concepts affect the way transactions are recorded and controlled. The first concept discussed here is **revenue recognition**.

AUDITING IN ACTION

Revenue Recognition and Fraud

- **Revenue recognition.** Because revenue recognition is dependent on the particular facts and circumstances, as well as accounting principles and practices that can vary by industry, the auditor ordinarily will develop auditing procedures based on the auditor's understanding of the entity and its environment, including the composition of revenues, specific attributes of the revenue transactions, and unique industry considerations. If there is an identified risk of material misstatement due to fraud that involves improper revenue recognition, the auditor also may want to consider:
  - Performing substantive analytical procedures relating to revenue using disaggregated data, for example, comparing revenue reported by month and by product line or business segment during the current reporting period with comparable prior periods. Computer-assisted audit techniques may be useful in identifying unusual or unexpected revenue relationships or transactions.
  - Confirming with customers certain relevant contract terms and the absence of side agreements, because the appropriate accounting often is influenced by such terms or agreements. For example, acceptance criteria, delivery and payment terms, the absence of future or continuing vendor obligations, the right to return the product, guaranteed resale amounts, and cancellation or refund provisions often are relevant in such circumstances.
  - Inquiring of the entity's sales and marketing personnel or in-house legal counsel regarding sales or shipments near the end of the period and their knowledge of any unusual terms or conditions associated with these transactions.
  - Being physically present at one or more locations at period end to observe goods being shipped or being readied for shipment (or returns awaiting processing) and performing other appropriate sales and inventory cutoff procedures.
  - For those situations for which revenue transactions are electronically initiated, processed, and recorded, testing controls to determine whether they provide assurance that recorded revenue transactions occurred and are properly recorded. (AU 316.54)

Revenue Recognition [LO 2]

Well-understood accounting guidelines describe when it is proper to recognize revenue. Revenue recognition is also important because decisions about whether and when to recognize revenue have played a major role in numerous accounting frauds. Auditors must specifically consider fraud risks related to revenue recognition and respond to any concerns identified. Managing the controls and processes for sales and bad debts is also important because of their impact on both the balance sheet and income statement.

Accounting terminology specifies that it is appropriate for a company to record (or recognize) revenue only when certain conditions exist. Revenue is defined in FASB Statement of Financial Accounting Concepts No. 6, *Elements of Financial Statements*, as

> inflows or other enhancements of assets of an entity or settlements of its liabilities (or a combination of both) from delivery or producing goods, rendering services, or other activities that constitute the entity's major or central operations. (SFAC 6.78)

The criteria for revenue recognition flow from this definition. According to FASB Statement of Financial Accounting Concepts No. 5, *Recognition and Measurement in Financial Statements of Business Enterprises* (SFAC 5.83), before revenue can be recognized, it must be both earned and realized. For a business to have earned the revenue, the earnings process must be substantially complete. For example, revenue has been earned and the earnings process completed when the goods have been delivered to or received by the customer, or the service to the customer has been provided. The realization process refers to an exchange taking place.

An exchange is not limited to goods or services for cash. Rather than cash, the purchaser may give a promise to pay, as happens in a sale on credit. However, if the exchange is for a promise of future payment, an arrangement must clearly exist. The arrangement must include a fixed price or one that can be determined based on the arrangement, and future collection must be reasonably certain. When these conditions are satisfied, revenue can be recognized.

The need to recognize and report revenue in the time period corresponding to the activity increases the difficulty of revenue recognition decisions. If revenue is simply recognized at the time cash changes hands, the appropriate timing of recognition is easy to determine. However, certain industries and types of transactions require analysis, judgment, and complex calculations to determine when revenue should be recognized, as well as the proper amount. For example, real estate development and sales, construction, long-term service contracts, and installment sales are not always certain regarding how much revenue should be recognized at specific times. The sale of condominium units in a tower building that is still under construction provides a good example of the difficulties with revenue recognition. Multiple criteria are described as necessary before revenue can be recognized:

> *In accordance with generally accepted accounting principles, we recognize revenues and profits from sales of tower residences during the course of construction. Revenue recognition commences and continues to be recorded when construction is beyond a preliminary stage, the buyer is committed to the extent of being unable to require a full refund of its deposit except for nondelivery of the residence, a substantial percentage of residences in a tower are under non-cancelable contracts, collection of the sales price is reasonably assured and costs can be reasonably estimated. Due to various circumstances, including buyer defaults and rescission claims, we may receive less cash than we expect.*

(WCI Communities, Inc., 10K, December 31, 2006)

Improper revenue recognition is a problem that has been seen many times in financial statements. For public companies the primary concern is that revenue may be overstated. Sometimes the misstatement is the result of an error, and sometimes it results from intentional actions by management of the company. In a privately owned company, the concern about improper revenue recognition also extends to understatement. For example, in an attempt to pay less income tax or not pay a minority investor the full fair share of profits, an owner-manager may intentionally not record cash sales. Auditors pay special attention to revenue recognition because of its vulnerability to error and fraud.

AUDITING IN ACTION

Revenue Recognition at Livent

One example of the vulnerability of revenue recognition to management fraud is seen in the case of "Livent," a company that produced live theater shows. In one case, Livent's contract with the theater owner permitted the theater to close down the show if ticket sales fell below a set threshold. To prevent this from happening, Livent's management entered into "side deals" with outsiders to buy tickets, fraudulently increasing revenue, thus keeping the show open. The outsiders were reimbursed for the tickets they purchased.

(Securities and Exchange Commission, *Accounting and Auditing Enforcement Release No. 1095*, May 19, 1999.)

REVIEW QUESTIONS

D.1 What must occur before revenue can be recognized?

D.2 Why is proper revenue recognition more difficult when an entity has long-term contracts?

D.3 What can cause revenue to be overstated?

AUDITING IN ACTION

Revenue Recognition at Sunbeam

Another example of management fraudulently recognizing revenue occurred at Sunbeam during the period from 1996 to 1998. In this case, management wanted to increase revenue with the expectation that the market price of stock would also increase. To accomplish this, Sunbeam took orders to be filled in the next year and recorded them as completed sales. In some cases the goods were delivered to the customers with the understanding that they could be returned. In other cases, the goods were not even delivered but were held in warehouses. This practice of accelerating sales that would normally have occurred in a future period is known as "channel stuffing." The following is a quote from a speech by Lynn Turner, then Chief Accountant of the SEC:

The Sunbeam Case

The recently issued Accounting and Auditing Enforcement Release No. 1393, In the Matter of Sunbeam Corporation, discusses two classic examples of improper accounting for inventories. In the first instance, we alleged that Sunbeam recorded an excessive restructuring reserve in one year that decreased the value of perfectly good inventory, and when that inventory was sold in the next year at regular prices, Sunbeam recognized inflated profit margins and thus overstated income. In the second instance, the Commission alleged that Sunbeam sold its spare parts inventory to a supplier at the end of the year, but improperly recognized income on the sale. The sale price had no practical relationship to any payment Sunbeam might obtain; by its terms, the contract would terminate in January 1998, absent agreement between the parties on the value of the inventory. Moreover, Sunbeam agreed to pay certain fees to its "customer" and guaranteed a 5% profit on the resale of the inventory. When the auditor reviewed the transaction it took exception, but then allowed recognition of the inflated income by passing its proposed audit adjustment as immaterial.

For those of you interested in further details, following are some of the more salient quotes from the Sunbeam order:

- In connection with its restructuring, Sunbeam planned to eliminate half of its household product lines. Its inventory of eliminated products was to be sold to liquidators at a substantial discount. In adjusting the capitalized variances associated with its inventory of household products at year-end 1996, however, Company management knowingly or recklessly failed to distinguish excess and obsolete inventory from "good" inventory from continuing product lines. As a result, Sunbeam understated the balance sheet value of its good household inventory at year-end 1996 by $2.1 million. This caused Sunbeam's 1996 loss to be overstated by $2.1 million, and improved Sunbeam's profitability by the same amount when household products were sold at inflated margins during the first quarter of 1997.

- Also, in the fourth quarter of 1997, Sunbeam recorded $11 million in revenue and almost $5 million in income from a "sale" of its spare parts inventory to a fulfillment house that did not comply with GAAP requirements. Its "customer" had previously satisfied the spare parts and warranty requests of Sunbeam customers on a fee basis. Sunbeam's auditors determined that the profit guarantee and indeterminate value of the contract rendered revenue recognition on this transaction improper. Sunbeam agreed to reserve $3 million against its putative profit margin on the transaction, but declined to eliminate the remaining income effect. Its auditors then passed the related proposed adjustment as immaterial.

- Sunbeam's auditors, in connection with their year-end 1997 audit, proposed additional adjustments to reverse $3.5 million related to inventory overvaluation and various other accounting errors. Management deemed these items, which added 5.4% to Sunbeam's earnings for the fourth quarter, immaterial, and declined to make the proposed adjustments. Given the demonstrated sensitivity of Sunbeam's stock price to even minor earnings shortfalls, these items were not in fact immaterial. See SAB 99. Moreover, they contributed to the cumulative effect of Sunbeam's numerous accounting improprieties, which in total were material, both to the quarter and the year.

("A Menu of Soup du Jour Topics," speech by Lynn Turner, May 31, 2001.
http://www.sec.gov/news/speech/spch498.htm)

AUDITING IN ACTION

Bill and Hold

When companies are pressured to meet or exceed analysts' expectations, auditors look for questionable overstatement schemes such as "bill and hold" sales transactions. In this type of deal, the customer agrees to buy goods by signing a contract, but the seller retains possession until shipment is requested.

U.S. GAAP permits a company to recognize revenues prior to delivery of a product if the bill and hold transaction has been structured properly. When proper, the practice of "bill and hold" is not fraudulent. However, the overselling of inventory can form the basis of securities fraud charges. As SEC litigation in 2000 against Digital Lightwave, Inc. indicates, these transactions can result in extensive fraud. For example, Digital's first bill and hold transaction represented approximately 28.4% of the company's total sales for the second quarter of 1997 and continued to escalate in order to exceed analysts' expectations.

Auditors carefully review any deviations from internal accounting policies or practices that might be evidenced by a lack of persuasive evidence that a sale exists or a lack of ownership risk transferred to the buyer. Persuasive evidence of a sale should include a proper or customary written contract initiated from the buyer. Cases of side letters, shipment of wrong product, and backdating of letters may be scrutinized by the SEC as evidence of fraudulent practices by the seller. Transfer of risk can be established through such evidence as a fixed delivery date that is consistent with the buyer's purpose, payment to the seller for separate warehousing services, nonrefundable upfront fees from the customer, segregation of goods from those used by the seller to fill other orders, and other documentation such as insurance coverage noting that the buyer has the risk of loss during the bill and hold phase.

Sales [LO 3]

The big picture issues of the revenue cycle are similar regardless of the type of industry. The issues apply to health-care suppliers, retail businesses, and businesses in all other industries with a sales function. One of the first concerns regarding the revenue cycle is that all recorded sales entries are the result of real transactions that meet the criteria for revenue recognition. If this is not true, then revenue will be overstated. Alternatively, it is important that no sales transactions go unrecorded. For a company to know that cash is appropriately collected or that proper billing occurs, all sales that occur must be properly recorded. If the sale is not recorded, the customer may never be billed, or the cash may be stolen by an employee and the business will never know. Recognizing and recording revenue appropriately and in the proper period is a major focus of controls in the revenue cycle.

Sales must be recorded and at the proper amounts. Revenue may be overstated, even though the sale is real, if the dollar amount shown for the sale is too high. On the other hand, the business is also concerned with ensuring that, for example, current price lists are used for pricing, recording, and billing sales transactions. If sales are billed at improperly low amounts, then cash collected is too low.

Accurate posting of accounts receivable subsidiary ledgers is important. If the accounts receivable subsidiary ledger is posted improperly, this means that either invoices were not correctly prepared or credit for cash received was given to the wrong customer. These types of errors are always to the disadvantage of the company. For example, if a customer is billed for the wrong amount, a complaint to the seller is far more likely when the amount is too high than when it is too low. If the billed amount is too low and the customer does not report the error, the foregone cash inflow may never be discovered or collected.

Similarly, the seller will hear from a customer when a cash payment the customer made is not posted to the customer's account balance. The seller is less likely to hear from the customer to whose account the cash payment is posted in error. In this case the error may be researched and corrected when the customer whose account was shorted reports the problem. Even though this type of problem may be caught and corrected, it is costly in terms of time spent researching the error and ill will with the customer whose payment was not properly posted. If the accounting information system does not guard against improper calculations and postings, many accounts can be affected.

REVIEW QUESTIONS

E.1 Why is it important that all sales transactions are recorded and that the amounts recorded are correct?

E.2 Under what circumstances is a customer most likely to complain to the seller regarding an error in a bill or statement? Why is this a problem since the seller will have the opportunity to correct the error?

Managing Bad Debts

As with any business that provides goods or services on credit, retail establishments and health-care providers must manage accounting for the portion of their accounts receivable that are ultimately uncollectible. Various methods are used for estimating and posting bad debt expense in the period of sale so that proper matching occurs. The transaction to record bad debt expense is posted as a debit to "Bad Debt Expense" and a credit to "Allowance for Uncollectible (or Doubtful) Accounts." Periodically, accounts receivable are evaluated to decide whether specific accounts are uncollectible. When a particular account is deemed uncollectible, it is written off and thereby removed from the accounts receivable subsidiary ledger and general ledger balance.

Documents and Processes

A customer may indicate the desire to make a purchase in various ways. In a health-care provider environment, the customer makes an appointment or "walks in" to the office. In a retail or wholesale environment the customer may also walk in to make the purchase. However, the customer may also place an order by calling the seller, faxing in an order, or placing an order over the Internet.

When a customer makes an appointment for service or places an order, the customer request is documented. In a service environment the request may be documented in an *appointment calendar*. In a sales environment a *customer order document* may be submitted by the purchaser to trigger the process of credit approval and completion of the sales transaction. The purchaser may manually submit to the vendor information about the desired transaction, or it may be captured by technology, as in the case of an Internet order. Some businesses use the term **customer order** to refer to any order document provided by the customer, and the seller may create a new document called a **sales order**.

The word "document," as it is used in this book, can refer to a record that is in either paper or electronic form. A paper document usually has multiple copies that are distributed to different departments. An electronic record can be accessed by various departments and individuals who are authorized and need access to the information. Application program controls should be designed to limit access and the ability to change information on the electronic record to those who are authorized. Paper documents should be prenumbered; electronic documents should be consecutively numbered.

If a customer order is for a credit sale, the seller approves the customer's credit and documents the approval before the transaction is processed. For consumers or business customers to whom the seller is granting credit for the first time, the seller should have a formal process of investigating the creditworthiness of the customer and extending credit. The result of this formal credit-granting process is documented using some type of **credit approval form**. The credit approval is entered into the customer's record in the information system. The customer's credit limit is also determined and documented as a result of this process.

AUDITING IN ACTION

Medical Sales Document

MILLER EYE ASSOCIATES, PA
1378 NE 83rd AVE
PHOENIX, AZ
Phone:
Tax ID

Kenneth A. Miller, OD
Lic #OPC6970
UPIN O6437
NPI 207533267
Medicare #H6349

Patient Name	ROBERT BENGO			Date of Service	02 / 09 / 10

OFFICE VISITS | | | | **PROCEDURES**

Proc	NP	EP	FEE	Proc	CPT	FEE
Comp Eye Exam	92004	92014	_____	Refraction	92015	_____
Int Eye Exam	92002	92012	_____	Vis Field Screen	92082	_____
Routine Eye Exam	S0620	S0621	_____	Vis Field Thresh	92083	_____
Office Visit Level 1	99201	99211	_____	Gonioscopy	92020	_____
Office Visit Level 2	99202	99212	_____	Ext. Opht. Init	92225	_____
Office Visit Level 3	99203	99213	_____	Ext. Opht. Sub	92226	_____
Office Visit Level 4	99204	99214	_____	Epilation	67820	_____
Office Visit Level 5	99205	99215	_____	Punctum Closure	68761	_____
				Punct D&I	68800	_____
CONTACT LENS				Conj FB Rem	65210	_____
Fitting	92310		_____	Cornea FB Rem	65222	_____
Supply Type: _Focus Dailies_			_104_	Rust Ring Rem	65435	_____
(2 B×S)				Fundus Photo Sc	92250-52	_____
				Fundus Photo	92250	_____

TOTAL FEES $ _104_

AMOUNT PAID $ _104_   cash check (amx) vi/mc dis debit

Balance Due $ _0_

DIAGNOSIS

ANT CHAMBER		CORNEA		LIDS			
Narrow Angles	365.02	Abrasion	918.10	Blepharitis	373.00	Ret Detach	361.00
Glaucoma Suspect	365.00	Burn	368.13	Chalazion	373.20	Ret Degen	362.60
Glaucoma, Open	365.11	Ulcer	370.00	Ectropion	374.10	Art/Vein Occt	362.30
Glaucoma, Closed	365.20	Dystrophy	371.50	Entropion	374.00	Scar	363.30
Uveitis	364.31	Edema	371.24	Hordeolum	373.11	Vit Degen	379.21
Ocular Hypertension	365.04	Erosion	372.42	Ptosis	374.30	**OPTIC NERVE**	
CONJUNCTIVA/SCLERA		Foreign Body	930.00	Trichiasis	374.50	Atrophy	377.10
Allergic Conjunctivitis	372.14	Keratitis	370.20	**RETINA/VITREOUS**		Neuritis	377.30
Infectious Conjunctivitis	372.03	Dry Eye Synd.	375.15	ICSC	362.41	Papilledema	377.00
Unspec. Conjunctivitis	372.30	Keratoconus	371.60	Mac Edema	362.83	**GENERAL**	
Episcleritis	379.00	Pigmentation	371.10	Drusen	362.57	Diabetes	250.50
Pterygium	372.40	**LENS**		Diab Ret	362.01	Migraine	346.80
Pinguecula	372.51	PXF	366.11	HTN Ret	362.11	**VISION**	
Subconj Hemo	372.72	Cataract NS	366.16	Lattice Degen	362.63	Myopia	(357.10)
MUSCLE		Cataract PSC	366.14	Mac Degen Dry	362.51	Hyperopia	357.00
Nystagmus	379.50	--------------	-------	Mac Degen Wet	362.52	Astigmatism	367.20
Paresis	378.55	--------------	-------	Ret Heme	362.81	Presbyopia	367.40
				Choroid Nevus	224.6		

In the case of a health-care provider, the parallel process is investigating whether the patient actually has the insurance coverage he or she claims to have. Documentation about the validity of the insurance coverage is then included in the *patient's file*. As mentioned earlier, when a customer pays using a credit card, the bank or company issuing the card is responsible for the initial investigation of the customer's creditworthiness and for setting the credit limit. The seller's responsibility is to follow the card issuer's procedures for completing individual sales transactions, usually by processing the credit card sales transaction electronically.

When a product is shipped to the purchaser, the seller's shipping department documents the shipment. The document is used to notify the billing department about the shipment. Upon receiving information about the shipment, the billing department initiates the process of billing the purchaser. If the product must be retrieved from storage or a warehouse before it can be shipped, a document is used to authorize the retrieval. This authorization is sometimes an approved copy of the customer order or sales order. Or it may be a separate document called a **pick ticket**. Documents associated with the shipping process may be called *shipping documents* or **bills of lading**.

Whatever its name, the shipping document includes information such as the shipping address and the contents of the shipment. If the shipping document is inside the package with an external bill of lading also used, the shipping document may simply be another copy of the *invoice*. If a shipping company such as UPS or FedEx is used, the external shipping document may not include information on the contents of the package. An exception to this may be for international shipments, when a customs requirement calls for more information on the external document.

Regardless of the specific form, documentary evidence shows that the shipping process occurred. This shipping documentation then initiates:

1. producing the customer invoice, and
2. posting the sales transaction.

If the transaction is paid for by credit card, the seller processes the sales transaction with the credit card issuer when the item is shipped. Again, the shipping document initiates the process.

An **unfilled order report** is an internal document listing customer orders that have received credit approval but have not been shipped. This report is monitored so that the seller can investigate any delays in filling customer orders. Orders are taken off the list after they are shipped and billed. This means that the *unfilled order report* can also be used as a quality control tool to verify that all shipments are billed. In other words, an item left on the unfilled order report for an extended period of time should be investigated to verify that it has not simply been shipped and the billing process overlooked.

The document used by a company when it bills a customer directly for a credit sale is called an *invoice*. The invoice specifies the item or service, quantity, sales price, and payment terms. Typically an invoice is created for each sales transaction. In addition to issuing an invoice, sellers may also send customers a *monthly statement* detailing all the transactions of the last month, including the customer's purchases and payments. In contrast, it is not unusual for health-care providers to send only monthly statements rather than invoices for specific visits. When the transaction is completed using a credit card, the seller is not involved in the billing process. Billing is handled by the issuer of the credit card.

At this point the earnings process is complete, and the seller appropriately records the sale transaction. In an automated environment, entry of the shipping activity or the sale transaction, or creation of the invoice, also initiates the updates of the *accounts receivable subsidiary ledger*, *sales journal*, or other sales reports and *general ledger*. The update may involve simultaneous or batch processing.

Cash received for sales comes in through several channels. Regardless of the mechanism, the receipt is documented and the accounting records are updated. Cash received directly from customers at the point of sale is locked in a cash drawer and documented on a *cash terminal record*. Typically, the customer receives a copy of the record as a *customer receipt*. When a credit card is used, the terminal record also documents the sale and provides a receipt for the customer.

When a payment is received through the mail, it is usually in the form of a check and is accompanied by a **remittance advice**. A remittance advice is a document that indicates the name and other identifying information of the payer, such as an account number and the amount of the payment. Often a paper remittance advice is a "tear-off" portion or copy of the invoice. When the invoice (or a portion of it) is also the remittance advice, it is sometimes called a turnaround document. The customer is instructed to return the invoice copy or "tear-off" portion with the payment.

AUDITING IN ACTION

Shipping Document and Invoice

8833217

SHIPPING DOCUMENT
SPLASH & SUNSHY WATER SPORTS
8814 ROBERTS AVE
FORT LAUDERDALE, FL 33301

SHIP TO:

GRANT MAGGIE
SWIM TALENTS
5745 BIMINI STREET
ISLE OF PALMS, SC 29451

Date: May 1, 2010
Order Number: 3654412
Shipper: Speedy Ship

Quantity	Description	Weight
300	Rimless swim goggles	32 pounds

Packed by: Received by:

N. George   T. McDonald

SPLASH & SUNSHY WATER SPORTS
8814 ROBERTS AVE
FORT LAUDERDALE, FL 33301

INVOICE

DATE: 5/1/10
INVOICE # 8833217

Bill To: SWIM TALENTS
ATTENTION: GRANT MAGGIE
5745 BIMINI STREET
ISLE OF PALMS, SC 29451

Ship To: SWIM TALENTS
5745 BIMINI STREET
ISLE OF PALMS, SC 29451

Comments or Special instructions:

SALESPERSON	P.O. NUMBER	SHIP DATE	SHIP VIA	F.O.B. POINT	TERMS
C. WALKER	663	5/1/10	SPEEDY SHIP	SHIP	Due on receipt

QUANTITY	DESCRIPTION	UNIT PRICE	AMOUNT
300	RIMLESS SWIM GOOGLES, NTYRSPEED, # 863	4.20	$ 1260.00

SUBTOTAL	$ 1260.00
TAX RATE	6%
SALES TAX	75.60
SHIPPING & HANDLING	25.00
TOTAL	$ 1360.60

Make all checks payable to: SPLASH & SUNSHY WATER SPORTS
If you have any questions concerning this invoice, contact Name, Phone Number, E-mail Address

THANK YOU FOR YOUR BUSINESS!

AUDITING IN ACTION

Monthly Statement, Remittance Advice

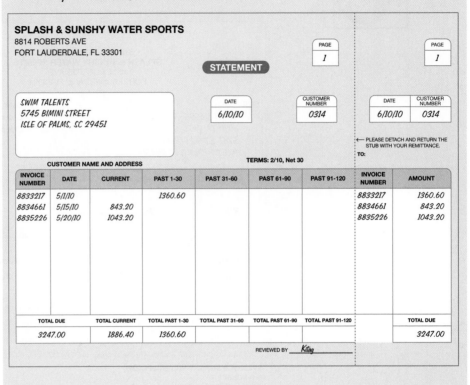

SPLASH & SUNSHY WATER SPORTS
8814 ROBERTS AVE
FORT LAUDERDALE, FL 33301

PAGE
1

PAGE
1

STATEMENT

SWIM TALENTS
5745 BIMINI STREET
ISLE OF PALMS, SC 29451

DATE	CUSTOMER NUMBER
6/10/10	0314

DATE	CUSTOMER NUMBER
6/10/10	0314

← PLEASE DETACH AND RETURN THE STUB WITH YOUR REMITTANCE.
TO:

CUSTOMER NAME AND ADDRESS   TERMS: 2/10, Net 30

INVOICE NUMBER	DATE	CURRENT	PAST 1-30	PAST 31-60	PAST 61-90	PAST 91-120	INVOICE NUMBER	AMOUNT
8833217	5/1/10		1360.60				8833217	1360.60
8834661	5/15/10	843.20					8834661	843.20
8835226	5/20/10	1043.20					8835226	1043.20
TOTAL DUE	**TOTAL CURRENT**	**TOTAL PAST 1-30**	**TOTAL PAST 31-60**	**TOTAL PAST 61-90**	**TOTAL PAST 91-120**			**TOTAL DUE**
3247.00	1886.40	1360.60						3247.00

REVIEWED BY _Kitag_

Bill Date: 12/23/2003
Please Pay by 01/17/2011
$ 010.30

Payment Coupon

Amount Enclosed

Account No. 8583-279

SPLASH & SUNSHY WATER SPORTS
8814 ROBERTS AVE
FORT LAUDERDALE, FL 3330

Send Payment to: ALWAYS ON SECURITY
633 CANAVAN WAY
PLANTATION FL 33337

Retain bottom portion for your records, detach and return stub with payment.

Service For:	Chateau Americans Inc. 3033 Vineyard Way Huntinoton, CA 95994	Your Account Number 8583 - 279	Rate Class Commercial	Billing Date 12/17/2010

Service Period:	11/10–12/15/10
Days:	29

Previous Balance	210.30
Payment	210.30
Balance Forward	–0–
Current Charges	210.30
Due Date: 1/17/2011	Total Due : 210.30

ALWAYS ON SECURITY, 633 CANAVAN WAY, PLANTATION, FL 33337

When the mail is opened and checks are received, a document called a **daily remittance list** is immediately prepared. This documents states the amounts of individual payments and from whom they are received.

Cash coming in to the business from all sources is deposited daily using a *deposit ticket*. The total of the cash terminal record and daily remittance list equals the amount that is deposited. This equals the amount of the deposit shown on the deposit ticket. Customers also use electronic banking, which results in payment received directly into the seller's bank account via electronic transfer. Various documents can accompany electronic transfer transactions. The documents associated with cash receipts are entered into the information system. This input triggers updates of the *cash receipts journal* or report, accounts receivable subsidiary ledger, and general ledger.

When a customer returns a purchase or the seller grants the customer credit for a defective item, a **credit memo** is prepared. A credit memo document indicates that the return has been received or the allowance has been approved. The document initiates either repaying the customer or crediting the customer's account receivable balance for the approved amount. The *sales returns and allowances journal* is updated based on the credit memo.

The activities involved in managing bad debts include estimating and recording the appropriate amount of bad debt expense and writing off those receivables believed to be uncollectible. The **aged accounts receivable trial balance** categorizes all of the balances in the accounts receivable subsidiary ledger based on how long the amount has been outstanding. For example, balances might be classified as current, 30–60 days old, 61–90 days old, and over 90 days old. This information is used to estimate the appropriate amount of bad debt expense. When an individual account is judged to be uncollectible, authorization for "writing off" the balance or removing it from the active accounts receivable balance is documented by a **write-off authorization**.

AUDITING IN ACTION

Aged Accounts Receivable Trial Balance

SPLASH & SUNSHY WATER SPORTS						
Customer	Total	Current	# of Days Past Due			
			30	60	90	Over 90
SWIM TALENTS	$3247.00	$1886.40	$1360.60			
Z & P SCUBA SUPPLIES	$300.00	$300.00				
ON THE BEACH	$450.00		$200.00	$250.00		
	$3997.00	$2186.40	$1560.60	$250.00		

The different business activities and documents used are listed in Exhibit 10-3.

EXHIBIT 10-3

Business Activities and
Related Documents

Business Activity	Related Documents
Receiving and processing customer orders	Customer sales order
	Sales order
	Unfilled order report
Granting credit, verifying insurance	Credit or other approval form
Shipping goods	Sales invoice
	Shipping document
	Bill of lading
Billing customers	Sales invoice
	Monthly statement
Recording sales transaction	Accounts receivable subsidiary ledger
	Sales journal
	General ledger
	Inventory files
Receiving and recording cash	Receipt for customer, cash terminal record
	Remittance advice
	Electronic transfer document
	Daily remittance list
	Deposit ticket
	Cash receipts journal or report
	General ledger
Receiving and processing sales returns and allowances	Credit memo
	Sales returns and allowances journal
	Inventory files
Managing receivables	Aged accounts receivable trial balance
Estimating bad debt	Write-off authorization
Writing off uncollectible receivables	

REVIEW QUESTIONS

F.1 At what point in a sales transaction should credit be approved by the seller? Why?

F.2 Who approves credit when a bank-issued credit card is used?

F.3 Explain the different formats and information of shipping documents. Why is a shipping document created?

F.4 What is the benefit of monitoring an unfilled order report?

F.5 How is an aged accounts receivable trial balance prepared, and what is it used for?

Potential Misstatements and Controls

Companies use documents to prepare records of sales and cash-related activities, assist in verifying that functions are completed, and trigger recording activities in the accounting records. Documentation also plays a major role in internal controls. Not all ICFR can be implemented or verified by documentation, but many are. Segregation of duties is also an important component of ICFR. The following discussion highlights controls for sales and collections.

The credit approval or insurance verification process must be completed and documented. Approval should always be *in advance* of providing the goods or services. A credit transaction is approved by the seller when the company itself extends the credit.

Authorization for the credit sale should come from a source that is independent of the person completing the sale. This segregation of duties prevents a salesperson from transacting a sale with someone who is unlikely to be able to repay the debt. Otherwise, a salesperson who is paid on a commission basis would be motivated to complete as many sales as possible regardless of customers' creditworthiness. Credit approval should be provided by an authorized person in the credit department. The approval might also be provided through technology if the criteria for approval are part of the company's automated information system.

Verification of prices and terms of the sale must also be performed prior to completing the transaction. For a point-of-sale transaction in which the customer takes the goods, verification may be accomplished by scanning a bar code or some other method of electronic entry when the transaction is recorded; otherwise, the seller should have some method of verification appropriate for the type of business. For example, input by a medical provider of a diagnostic code for a particular service can trigger an invoice with a preset billing amount.

AUDITING IN ACTION

Scannable Bar Code

Scanning a bar code and entering a diagnostic code are examples where the price charged for the good or service has been preset and therefore authorized in advance by management. When transaction details differ from the standard prices and terms, they should be specifically authorized before the sale is completed. For example, retail automobile sales often occur as the result of a price negotiation. When an automobile salesperson receives an offer for a car from a potential purchaser, the offer usually has to be approved by a supervisor or manager prior to completion of the sale.

Approved customer orders, sales orders, pick tickets, or similar documents authorize the release of goods from storage or warehousing. Accordingly, personnel responsible for warehousing should not release goods without receiving the approved authorization documents. As the inventory moves from storage to shipping, shipping personnel should verify that the goods they receive from warehousing match the information on the document. Warehousing personnel should receive a signature from shipping at the time of transfer, documenting that the shipping employee is accepting custody of the inventory. An unbroken chain of documentary evidence can limit theft of goods by employees.

Controls are needed to ensure that goods are shipped on a timely basis and bills are sent out for all goods that are shipped. For example, the customer order department, or another designated department, should remove orders from the unfilled order report when they are billed. If any customer order stays on the unfilled order report for an excessive period of time, it is investigated. If the order is actually unfilled, management can resolve the problem. If the order has been shipped but not billed, the problem will be identified and an invoice is produced. This type of control is called a **detective control**. It does not necessarily prevent a problem from occurring but permits company employees to detect problems in a timely manner during the course of their normal activities.

AUDITING IN ACTION

Medical Record

Doctor Name, Address, Phone:

TIM WOOD CHUCR, MD

101 MEDICAL LANE

NORTH BEND, MD 21201

Insurance Co., ID: *NEW Co., 08131957*

Service Date: *6/15/10*
Patient Name: *HALEY SMURF*
Address: *#113 34th ST, APT 216*
DOB: *8/28/87 BALTIMORE, MD 21216*
Group: *06674*

NEW PATIENTS	CPT	FEE		SCREENING DIAGNOSTICS	CPT	FEE		SCREENING LABORATORY	CPT	FEE
INITIAL PHYSICAL (5–11YRS)	99383			PSYCHOLOG. SCREENING	96101		X	COMP METABOLIC PANEL	80053	100
INITIAL PHYSICAL (12–17YRS)	99384		X	SPIROMETRY	94010	65	X	LIPID PANEL	80061	15
INITIAL PHYSICAL (18–39YRS)	99385		X	AUDIOGRAM-AIR ONLY	92552	35		Hs-CRP	86141	
INITIAL PHYSICAL (40–64YRS)	99386			AUDIOGRAM-AIR & BONE	92553			HOMOCYSTINE	83080	
INITIAL PHYSICAL (65+ YRS)	99387			TYMPANOGRAM	92557			FRUCTOSAMINE	82985	
							X	TSH	84443	65
			X	EKG WINTERP & REPORT	93000	75		FERRITIN LEVEL	82728	
				FITNESS SCREENING:			X	U/A W/MAICROSCOPY	87003	32
ESTABLISHED PATIENTS			X	DUKE ACTIVITY STATUS	99420	20	X	PSA TOTAL	84153	45
			X	NUTRITION EVALUATION	97802	20	X	VENIPUNCTURE	36415	20
ANNUAL PHYSICAL (5–11YRS)	99393		X	EPWORTH SLEEPINESS INDEX	99420	20	X	FECAL OCCULT	G0107	10
ANNUAL PHYSICAL (12–17YRS)	99394			CHEST X-RAY (SINGLE)	71010			IRON BINDING CAPACITY	83550	
ANNUAL PHYSICAL (18–39YRS)	99395		X	CHEST X-RAY (PA & LAT)	71020	100		SERUM. IRON BINDING	82040	
X ANNUAL PHYSICAL (40–64YRS)	99396	500		SEXUAL FUNCTION SCREEN	98420		X	URIC ACID	54550	30
ANNUAL PHYSICAL (65+ YRS)	99394			PAP SMEAR ADMIN	Q0091		X	CBC W/DIFFERENTIAL & COUNT	85025	50
OTHER ENCOUNTERS				BREAST/PELVIC EXAM	G0101			DIAGNOSIS CODES		
								HEALTH CHECKUP	V70.0	
EMAIL CONSULTATION	0074T							EXERCISE COUNSELING	V55.41	
								EXAMINE EYES/VISION	V72.0	
PHONE CONSULT, BRIEF	99371							EXAMINE EARS/HEARING	V72.1	
PHONE CONSULT, TEST								ROUTINE GYN EXAM	V72.31	
RESULTS/NEWPROBLEM	99372							ROUTINE CHEST X-RAY	V72.5	
X NEWCARE PLAN		255						ROUTINE LAB TEST	V72.5	
PHONE CONSULT. COMPLEX								SCREEN FOR UPID DISORDERS	V77.91	
LENGTHY	99373							SCREEN FOR DEPRESSION	V79.0	
								CARDIOVASCULAR SCREENING	V81.2	
RSIK FACTOR COUNSELING:								WELL. WOMAN SCREEN	V72.31	
APPROX. 15 MINUTES	99401									
APPROX. 30 MINUTES	99402									
APPROX. 45 MINUTES	99403									
APPROX. 60 MINUTES	99404									

Signature: *Tim Wood Chucr, MD*

Total Charges: _____

Payment Received _____ Cash _____ Check # _____

Credit Card _____

The invoice processing and billing function should be independent of the shipping function to provide adequate segregation of duties. Lack of segregation of duties for these functions can permit theft. For instance, if these functions were in the same department, an employee might be able to ship goods—perhaps to his or her home address, or a friend's home—and omit processing the invoice.

When cash is received, the goal is to create an immediate record of its receipt and place it in safekeeping. One way to accomplish this is to record cash received using a cash terminal with an internal record, lock the cash in the cash drawer, and provide the customer with a receipt of the transaction. Providing the customer with a receipt is not foolproof because customers do not always monitor their receipts. But it provides another person with the ability to verify that the proper amount was recorded.

When checks are received in the mail, they should immediately be restrictively endorsed and a daily remittance list should be prepared concurrently. The checks and daily remittance list received go to a cashier responsible for assembling and documenting the bank deposit. The remittance advices go to the accounts receivable department to update the cash receipts records, accounts receivable subsidiary ledger, and general ledger. Similarly, cash, checks, and credit card receipts from the cash terminal should go to the cashier for deposit to the bank, and the cash terminal record should be received by whoever is responsible for updating the general ledger.

Some businesses use a **lock box system** for checks received through the mail. In this system payments are sent directly to a company's bank. The bank records the checks received, deposits them in the business's account, and forwards the information to the business. The advantages of this type of system include fewer personnel requirements and quick deposit of checks. **Outsourcing** the cash receipts function can enhance segregation of duties in a company with a limited number of employees by moving cash handling completely out of the business.

Cash receipts should be deposited daily, and the accounting records should be updated on a timely basis. For some companies the update may be real time. For others it may be batch processing at the end of the day or later. Good segregation of duties requires separating the following activities:

1. Receiving the cash and making the deposit
2. Updating the accounts receivable records
3. Reconciling the initial cash records with the daily deposit ticket

The initial cash records are the cash terminal record and daily remittance list. If these duties are not segregated, an employee can steal the cash and either simply not record it or create false entries to hide the theft. Internal cash records should be reconciled with the bank statement on a timely basis. Finally, other potentially valuable resources such as blank checks, signature plates and online signatures, and authorization codes for e-commerce and online banking should be secured.

A classic fraud scheme related to cash receipts known as *lapping* is possible when poor segregation exists for duties of cash receipts and posting accounts receivable. An employee can "lap" by stealing cash and manipulating accounts receivable entries to conceal the theft. The top Auditing in Action box on page 514 provides an example of a lapping scheme.

Sales returns and allowances vary in their magnitude and may need differing levels of control and approval in different environments. In retail sales environments a credit memo is used. The credit memo is prepared, typically on an automated basis using a sales terminal, and then approved by someone with authority before cash is returned to the customer or a credit is recorded to the customer's account balance. Some retail environments have a separate returns department to handle return of goods. Others require authorization by a supervisor, who inspects the returned goods before signing the authorization.

Documented approvals of write-offs of accounts receivable should also be required before transactions are recorded. Write-offs are often authorized by the credit department manager or a designated employee.

All transactions in the **sales and collections cycle** should be recorded at the correct amounts, in the proper periods, and be classified properly when they are recorded. Policies for recording transactions, reconciling the various control totals, and comparing subsidiary ledgers and other reports to the general ledger are all part of the control process. As mentioned earlier, customer complaints and correspondence regarding transactions and account balances should be investigated.

AUDITING IN ACTION

Lapping: Accounts Receivables Fraud

Poor segregation of duties can permit an embezzlement scheme known as lapping. When an employee has access to cash receipts and the detailed entries to individual accounts receivable records, he or she can steal cash and conceal the shortage by delaying the recording of subsequent cash receipts. A simple example follows:

Date	Activity	Entry Recorded		
7/28	Erin pays $300 on account	None, Cash stolen		
7/29	Zeta pays $500 on account			
		Cash	500	
		Erin		300
		Zeta		200
7/30	Willis pays $200 on account			
	Moore pays $400 on account			
		Cash	600	
		Zeta		300
		Willis		200
		Moore		100

The next $300 that comes in will be posted to Moore's account. One way the employee might catch up to end the "past posting" is to receive a check, and instead of posting it to the proper record, post it to the lagged accounts. The employee then writes off the balance in the account for which the most recent payment was received. This will work only if the employee also has the authority to write off uncollectible accounts and the customer does not follow up. A write-off to end the scheme above would be:

7/31	Denzel pays $300 on account			
		Cash	300	
		Moore		300
		Allowance for Doubtful Accounts	300	
		Denzel		300

Zeta or Moore might alert the company to the fraud if they inquire why their payments were posted in two transactions instead of one.

AUDITING IN ACTION

Friends and Retail Store Controls

When Billy started working at an electronics store he learned as a part of his training that every time he input a return transaction a supervisor had to be called over to the terminal to approve the transaction. The supervisor had to see the returned merchandise before providing the approval. A friend of Billy's proposed a scheme: he would come into the store with some headphones he had purchased, have Billy process the return, but not take the headphones back. His friend figured that way his bill from the company would be reversed, and he could keep the headphones for free. Billy was trying to figure out how to tell his friend that the scheme wasn't going to happen … and trying to decide if he actually wanted this guy as his friend … when the store's internal control got him off the hook. When Billy processed his first return and the supervisor came over to approve it, he learned that the supervisor took the returned merchandise back to the storeroom so that everything returned during the day could be reconciled to the terminal records, added back to the inventory files and placed back out on the sales floor at the end of the day. It turned out that the internal control was smarter than Billy's friend.

REVIEW QUESTIONS

G.1 What are important characteristics of the credit approval process?

G.2 How does the customer fill a control function when a receipt is issued for cash sales?

G.3 What segregation of duties exists in a well-designed cash receipts process?

G.4 What are the advantages of a lock box system, including aspects of recording transactions?

G.5 What is lapping?

MANAGEMENT ASSERTIONS IN AN INTEGRATED AUDIT [LO 4]

Audit steps for the revenue cycle are anchored in the overall audit plan. The groundwork for understanding an integrated audit was developed in earlier chapters. Remember that an integrated audit sets out to express an opinion on the effectiveness of ICFR and fairness of the financial statements. Related to the internal control aspects of an integrated audit, management's report addresses the effectiveness of the ICFR. Therefore, management's report applies to the **design** and **operating effectiveness** of ICFR. In other words, is ICFR both designed well and operating effectively? **Management assertions** regarding the financial statement audit include the five assertions previously stated: existence or occurrence, completeness, rights and obligations, valuation and allocation, and presentation and disclosure.

Design Effectiveness

The first steps of an integrated audit are to understand the industry and contract with the client to do the audit. After that, the audit steps involve initial audit planning and risk assessment, which includes understanding the business activities of the client, understanding the ICFR system, and evaluating ICFR design effectiveness. Then, the auditor performs ICFR-operating effectiveness testing, followed by the rest of the financial statement audit.

Describing these steps in a chronological fashion is problematic. Auditors perform numerous steps concurrently. Auditors often loop back to modify their planning and conclusions, based on new information. Even so, there is an orderly, planned progression of what step occurs before the next one. By the time tests of the operating effectiveness of ICFR begin, the audit team understands the system, has assessed ICFR design effectiveness, and has planned the ICFR and financial statement audits. Walkthroughs are an important and effective procedure for understanding the system and auditing design effectiveness. AS 5 clearly states the goals of auditing design effectiveness, procedures that can be used, and activities included in a walkthrough.

Operating Effectiveness

The auditor evaluates ICFR to determine whether it operates effectively. Testing ICFR operating effectiveness also contributes to the auditor's evidence regarding the risk level assessed and used for financial statement audit planning. Tests of controls, and the controls-related portion of dual purpose tests, discussed later in this chapter, contribute to the audit evidence on operating effectiveness.

Financial Statement Assertions

The AICPA guidance defines 13 management assertions, and the PCAOB standards utilize five. Five management assertions (augmented sometimes by authorization and cutoff) are primarily used in the discussion and exhibits that follow. Recall that the number of assertions and the

AUDITING IN ACTION

Testing and Evaluating Design Effectiveness

AS 5.42. *The auditor should test the design effectiveness of controls by determining whether the company's controls, if they are operated as prescribed by persons possessing the necessary authority and competence to perform the control effectively, satisfy the company's control objectives and can effectively prevent or detect errors or fraud that could result in material misstatements in the financial statements.*

AS 5.43. *Procedures the auditor performs to test design effectiveness include a mix of inquiry of appropriate personnel, observation of the company's operations, and inspection of relevant documentation. Walkthroughs that include these procedures ordinarily are sufficient to evaluate design effectiveness.*

AS 5.37-38. *Walkthrough procedures usually include a combination of inquiry, observation, inspection of relevant documentation, and re-performance of controls. In performing a walkthrough, at the point at which important processing procedures occur, the auditor questions the company's personnel about their understanding of what is required by the company's prescribed procedures and controls.*

wording used to describe them are not mandated by auditing guidance. Auditing standards require that the auditor address all management assertions concepts. Auditors can gain audit evidence on the validity of management's financial statement assertions using tests of controls and substantive audit procedures. Exhibit 10-4 links management assertions to audit tests and procedures.

EXHIBIT 10-4

Financial Statement Assertions and Audit Evidence-Gathering Activities

Assertions	Tests and Procedures
Existence or occurrence: assets and liabilities exist, and transactions occurred	Document examination, external, confirmations, cutoff procedures
Completeness: everything that should be is recorded and included in the financial statements	Document examination, external confirmation, analytical procedures, cutoff procedures, bank reconciliations, cutoff bank statement, inter-bank transfer schedule
Rights and obligations: the company has rights to assets and obligations for liabilities shown in the financial statements	Document examination, external confirmations
Valuation or allocation: items shown in the financial statements are reported at appropriate amounts	Document examination, external confirmations, reperformance, inquiry, collectibility analysis
Presentation and disclosure: items are properly classified, described, and disclosed	Document examination, disclosure analysis

AUDIT TESTS AND PROCEDURES [LO 5]

Audit tests and procedures presented in this chapter for the sales, billing, and collections cycle describe how the auditor tests both ICFR and the account balances and disclosures affected. The controls tests and substantive procedures for the cycle are presented together. They are shown together because the audit team may use evidence obtained in one part of the audit to plan or develop conclusions in another part of the audit. Evidence gathered in one step may impact more than one area of the audit.

The procedures discussed in the following sections typically begin after the auditor has formed conclusions regarding the ICFR design effectiveness. The audit tests and procedures are combinations of the various audit activities presented in earlier chapters. They provide the auditor with evidence on whether controls are operating and account balances and disclosures are appropriate.

REVIEW QUESTIONS

H.1 Why is it not completely accurate to describe the steps of an audit in a chronological fashion?

H.2 Why does it make sense to address controls and substantive audit procedures together for an integrated audit?

TESTS OF CONTROLS

Tests of controls provide evidence about whether an ICFR is operating as designed and whether the control is being performed by someone with appropriate authority and qualifications. In an integrated audited, the auditor performs controls tests for two reasons. One is to reach conclusions for the ICFR audit. The other is to confirm the appropriateness of the risk level assessed during planning for the financial statement audit.

Management has responsibility for designing the controls and the effective operations of the ICFR. The auditor understands ICFR from initial planning steps, risk assessment, and auditing design effectiveness. If a control cannot achieve its objective because of poor design, the auditor will not test how well it operates. Even if the control operates as planned, it cannot be effective if it is not designed properly. Sometimes a control's design limits its effectiveness as a "stand-alone" control. However, the control may have effective design when combined with other controls. These types of controls may be referred to as complimentary or compensating controls. The auditor takes these issues into consideration when planning tests of controls.

Procedures that fall into the category of tests of controls are used by the company as well as the auditor. In order for management to report on the effectiveness of ICFR, it must implement and test its controls system. Although the auditor will not likely use exactly the same tests that management has used in its testing, both management and the auditor use tests of controls.

Some of the tests of controls performed by the auditor may be conducted simultaneously with earlier steps, such as walkthroughs. Walkthrough steps that provide information on control effectiveness are inquiry of company personnel, document inspection, and reperforming the control steps.

Some tests of controls are performed simultaneously with **tests of details of balances** that provide audit evidence on the amount and disclosure of the account balance. When a test addresses both a control function and the amount or disclosure, it is called a **dual purpose test**.

Some audit procedures, such as observing company employees and reperforming tasks, provide strong evidence regarding ICFR function. However, the steps only provide evidence about operating effectiveness at the point in time when they are conducted. An example of an inquiry step is asking a client employee why he or she is performing a particular activity. The response can provide the auditor with evidence about the employee's understanding and competence at performing the control, but again is limited to the specific situation encountered. Inquiry is used throughout the audit but is especially important in testing controls. The format of inquiry may range from oral and informal to written and formal. The following statement, from the first PCAOB standard on audits of ICFR, AS 2, explains the limitations of observations as audit evidence.

AS 2.93 For example, the auditor might observe the procedures for opening the mail and processing cash receipts to test the operating effectiveness of controls over cash receipts. Because an observation is pertinent only at the point in time at which it is made, the auditor should supplement the observation with inquiries of company personnel and inspection of documentation about the operation of such controls at other times.

Inquiry can provide new information that conflicts with what the auditor has already learned. Or the new information can be consistent with the auditor's prior knowledge and corroborate other audit evidence. Interpreting the response to an inquiry and determining its impact on the audit require judgment. Inquiry alone does not provide sufficient audit evidence for any conclusion. Additional audit evidence is needed. Further steps are planned, often based on the response to the inquiry. Additional steps that support inquiry evidence include inspecting documents used or produced during a control step. Similarly, auditing any actions that occurred or should have occurred as a result of the control step corroborates inquiry evidence.

Sometimes an aspect of ICFR, such as management's philosophy and operating style, has limited or no documentary evidence. If this is the case, the auditor's conclusion may have to be based largely on inquiry and observation. The auditor needs to integrate information obtained in this manner with conclusions made throughout the audit. Again, the first PCAOB auditing standard on the audit of ICFR, AS 2, provides a good background discussion of the role inquiry evidence can play in an audit.

AS2.95 Evaluating responses to inquiries is an integral part of the inquiry procedure. Examples of information that inquiries might provide include the skill and competency of those performing the control, the relative sensitivity of the control to prevent or detect errors or fraud, and the frequency with which the control operates to prevent or detect errors or fraud. Responses to inquiries might provide the auditor with information not previously possessed or with corroborative evidence. Alternatively, responses might provide information that differs significantly from other information the auditor obtains (for example, information regarding the possibility of management override of controls). In some cases, responses to inquiries provide a basis for the auditor to modify or perform additional procedures.

Tests of controls provide audit evidence for both the ICFR and financial statement components of an integrated audit. Therefore, careful planning of both the procedures to be used and their timing can increase audit efficiency. Tests of controls may be performed at an **interim date**. However, they must be updated or "rolled forward" for the auditor to express an opinion on effective function as of the date of management's report at the end of the fiscal year. Management may change the ICFR system during the year, for example, to eliminate control deficiencies or simply to improve effectiveness and efficiency. Unless the financial statement audit is going to rely on the superseded ICFR, the auditor does not need to perform tests of controls on the ICFR that have been replaced.

As stated earlier, some tests provide evidence on controls and on financial statement information. The auditor may choose to conduct those dual purpose tests at or close to the fiscal year end (rather than an interim date) to enhance the value of the audit evidence for the financial statement amounts and disclosures. If the auditor plans to rely on a control during the financial statement audit, the controls testing must cover the entire financial period involved. AS 5 describes the different objectives of controls tests for the financial statement and ICFR audits. The following relates to testing controls for purposes of the financial statement audit.

AS 5.B4 To express an opinion on the financial statements, the auditor ordinarily performs tests of controls and substantive procedures. The objective of the tests of controls the auditor performs for this purpose is to assess control risk. To assess control risk for specific financial statement assertions at less than the maximum, the auditor is required to obtain evidence that the relevant controls operated effectively during the entire period upon which the auditor plans to place reliance on those controls.

The different reasons for testing highlight the importance of good audit planning to maximize audit efficiency in an integrated audit. Steps that may be sufficient and appropriate for an ICFR audit may not provide enough evidence for the financial statement audit. For example, if the auditor tests ICFR only at the fiscal year end, this is sufficient to give an opinion on ICFR. Tests at fiscal year end are not enough if the auditor plans to rely on the control during the financial statement audit. The reverse is true as well. Substantive procedures on account balances and disclosures may be sufficient for coming to conclusions for the financial statement audit. However, they do not provide evidence addressing the audit questions of an ICFR audit. The auditor must keep in mind the evidence needed for both aspects of the integrated audit when planning and conducting tests of controls.

REVIEW QUESTIONS

I.1   What are the purposes of tests of controls for the ICFR and financial statement components of an integrated audit?

I.2   How does the auditor obtain an understanding of ICFR?

I.3   What is the effect of poor design of ICFR on the auditor's tests of ICFR operating effectiveness?

I.4   Who uses tests of controls?

I.5   What are the purposes of dual purpose tests?

I.6   Why is the evidence auditors can collect on controls that have no documents limited in what it tells the auditor?

I.7   How does the timing of different types of tests impact audit efficiency?

Tests of Controls for Sales

Sales activity controls are intended to ensure that transactions recorded as sales are bona fide sales. Either the cash was collected or invoices were sent so that the cash will be collected at a later time. Furthermore, the amounts recorded in the financial statements represent the correct dollar amount of sales. Tests of controls for sales address:

Credit approval

Billing evidence for all items shipped

Completeness of recorded sales

Actual occurrence and validity of any transactions recorded as sales

Tests of controls for proper recording of sales transactions address whether sales are posted to the correct account, in the correct period and for the correct amount. Exhibit 10-5 provides examples of tests of controls for the sales function. You should read and study this exhibit to understand the specific controls needed for sales transactions and how they are tested.

EXHIBIT 10-5

Examples of Tests of Controls for Sales

If a company control (CC) is significant, both management and the auditor perform tests of controls (TofC). Management uses tests of controls to support its management report. The auditor uses tests of controls for the audit of ICFR and to confirm the planned reliance on controls in the financial statement audit. Related management assertions are displayed under the purpose of the controls. For ease of explanation, authorization and cutoff are used in addition to the five PCAOB management assertions.

Purpose of Controls	Company Control and Tests of Controls
To ensure that credit is approved before a sale is executed and service is provided or goods are shipped **(authorization, existence or occurrence)**	**CC:** *Process for granting/approving credit and setting credit limit for new customers, or approving credit for each transaction for continuing customers is completed by authorized company employee and documented prior to completion of transaction* **TofC:** Select a sample of sales invoices and examine for evidence of credit approval, including authorization by appropriate individual, and date preceding service or shipment.
To ensure that goods are only shipped for real and appropriately documented sales **(existence or occurrence)**	**CC:** *The system requests a sales order number to be entered before a shipping document can be generated. If an invalid sales order number is entered the system will not allow the user to proceed to generate the shipping document* **TofC:** Observe personnel as they create shipping documents; attempt to create a shipping document without a sales order number and with an invalid sales order number
To ensure that all sales transactions are recorded, in other words, all shipments are recorded and the customer is billed **(completeness)**	**CC:** *Shipping documents are accounted for numerically and used to post sales transactions* **TofC:** Account for a continuous numerical sequence of shipping documents and examine evidence that the shipping transactions have been recorded by tracing to sales journal and accounts receivable subsidiary ledger
To ensure that sales that are recorded are actual sales to customers **(existence or occurrence)**	**CC:** *Customer order document is used to collect information prior to sale and initiate the transaction* **TofC:** Examine the customer order document for evidence of customer information

CC: *Bills to customers are based on documents which support that a sale has occurred*

TofC: Select a sample of sales invoices and examine supporting bill of lading and customer order.

CC: *Reconciliations verify that transactions are properly posted to company records*

TofC: Examine evidence of reconciliation of computer files for sales journal, accounts receivable subsidiary ledger and general ledger, and ledger of shipments if appropriate

(*Note*: This step is appropriate as a test of numerous controls but is only listed in this exhibit once)

To ensure that transactions shown as sales are properly classified

(existence or occurrence, presentation and disclosure)

CC: *Transactions are only recorded as sales when supported by appropriate records*

TofC: Select a sample of sales document packages (invoice and all supporting documents) and examine for consistency with sales policies and any other internal verification

To ensure that all recorded sales are for the amount of goods and/or services that were actually sold and shipped and that the transactions are correctly recorded and billed

(existence or occurrence, rights and obligations, valuation or allocation, presentation and disclosure)

CC: *When sales invoices are created, amounts are based on service provided or items included in shipments*

TofC: Select a sample of sales invoices and examine supporting documents for evidence of service provided or evidence that the items listed in the invoice are what was shipped

CC: *Sales invoice amounts are determined using approved price lists or other authorization*

TofC: Examine the approved price list or other supporting evidence for accuracy and proper authorization and agreement to the price used on the sales invoice

CC: *Customer invoices or statements are sent based on company records*

TofC: Observe whether customer statements (or invoices) are sent

CC: *Transactions are recorded to customer accounts receivable records based on supporting documentation*

(continued)

	TofC: Select a sample of document packages and trace to the accounts receivable subsidiary ledger agreeing specific transaction details and amounts
	TofC: Select a sample of transactions from the accounts receivable subsidiary ledger and examine supporting document packages agreeing specific transaction details and amounts
To ensure that sales transactions are recorded based on the correct dates **(cutoff)**	
	CC: *Sales are posted consistent with year-end cutoff procedures*
	TofC: Account for a continuous numerical sequence of shipping document that occur before and after year end, trace to sales journal and verify for posting in correct year; for service transactions, trace underlying documents such as project completion, work-in-process calculation or human resources records to sales journal to verify correct date of posting
To ensure that sales transactions are properly included in the accounts receivable subsidiary ledger and general ledger accounts **(completeness, presentation and disclosure)**	
	CC: *Accounts receivable subsidiary ledger and general ledger are reconciled*
	TofC: Examine evidence that the accounts receivable subsidiary ledger is reconciled to the general ledger

Tests of Controls for Sales Returns and Allowances

The primary control concerns for sales returns and allowances are the following:

Do all the sales returns and allowances transactions posted represent real transactions that actually occurred?

Have all sales returns and allowances events that occurred during the fiscal year been posted?

As discussed earlier in this chapter, sales returns and allowances transactions can occur in a variety of ways. The nature of the transaction affects the controls that are appropriate. Control over authorizing the transactions is important. Requiring authorization can prevent unintentional loss of assets that results from inappropriately refunding cash or posting a credit to a customer's account. For example, often a supervisor is supposed to approve a return before credit or cash was refunded. To test such a control, the auditor can select from the sales returns and allowances documents file and verify that a party who has authority to approve the transaction signed the document. The signature indicates that the authorizing person followed the procedures and saw the goods that were returned before the transaction was processed.

Proper financial statement reporting of sales returns and allowances requires that all transactions be included. This concern relates to the management assertion of completeness. If sales returns and allowances are not recorded, then net sales are overstated.

Consequently, accounting standards also require that an estimate of expected returns and allowances be recorded in the period of sale. Reporting these transactions in the correct period is also important to proper presentation—described using the term *cutoff*. Net sales can be improperly presented if the posting of sales returns and allowances are accelerated or delayed. Accelerating or delaying posting is a technique management might use to fraudulently manage earnings.

Analytical procedures comparing current-year amounts to prior year and budgeted amounts are appropriate audit steps for sales returns and allowances. Another common test is to calculate recorded sales returns and allowances as a percentage of sales, then compare the percentage to the historical or expected amount. To test whether transactions were recorded, items in a sample of sales returns and allowances documents are traced to the sales returns and allowances journal.

REVIEW QUESTIONS

J.1 What are the main audit concerns regarding sales returns and allowances?

J.2 What audit procedures are used for sales returns and allowances?

Tests of Controls for Cash Receipts

Controls over cash receipts focus on safeguarding cash and on cash-related documentation procedures. Tests of controls for cash receipts address how the company safeguards the cash both physically and with documentation. Safeguarding begins at the time the cash comes in and continues through the deposit in the bank. Controls cover processes through which the company updates its records for cash received, and reconciles its records with a reliable external record—typically a bank statement. Exhibit 10-6 provides examples of tests of controls for the cash receipts function. You should read and study this exhibit to understand the specific controls needed for cash receipts transactions and how they are tested.

EXHIBIT 10-6

Examples of Tests of Controls for Cash Receipts

Purpose of Controls	Company Controls and Tests of Controls
To ensure that all cash received by the company is deposited and recorded in the cash receipts journal and that amounts and details, including the date, are shown correctly **(existence or occurrence, completeness, valuation or allocation, presentation and disclosure, cutoff)**	
	CC: *Documentation of cash received is prepared immediately as appropriate for the company's operations (e.g., creation of cash terminal record, creation of daily cash receipts listing (prelists), creation of duplicate customer receipts)*
	TofC: Observe employee processes for immediately recording and securing cash and checks
	TofC: Scan documents and account for an unbroken sequence of daily receipt documents
	CC: *Checks are restrictively endorsed immediately upon receipt, and cash and checks are physically secured*

(continued)

TofC: Observe employee processes for restrictively endorsing checks and securing cash and checks immediately upon receipt

CC: *Cash receipts are recorded based on daily cash receipts records with controls appropriate for the manner of input, such as electronic aggregation and hash totals*

TofC: Trace items listed on a sample of daily cash receipts records to the cash receipts journal, agreeing amounts and details such as names and dates; verify documentary evidence of control activities when appropriate, such as existence of hash totals

CC: *Cash received each day is deposited daily, intact*

TofC: Trace amounts and details on a sample of daily cash receipts records to duplicate deposit slips or other deposit records

TofC: Observe unrecorded cash at a specific point in time and compare the amount to daily cash receipts records and bank deposit records

To ensure that when cash receipts are recorded they show cash that was actually received by the company, and deposited **(existence or occurrence, valuation or allocation)**

CC: *Entries of cash received and deposited are made only by authorized individuals, under the company's controls that have been established, such as at regular times and from regular input locations*

TofC: Use computer-assisted audit techniques to scan cash receipts journal for unusual transactions and amounts, including such details as inappropriate times, and unusual and unauthorized computer terminals

CC: *Entries of cash received are only posted based on legitimate information (and document sources) of cash deposited*

TofC: Trace posted entries for cash receipts from the cash receipts journal to bank statements

CC: *Bank reconciliations are prepared regularly by an authorized and independent employee and when appropriate a proof of cash is prepared*

TofC: Observe bank account reconciliation process, including authority and independence of the employee performing the work

TofC: Review bank reconciliations, and proofs of cash when appropriate, for preparation and completion by appropriate and authorized individual and for clerical accuracy

To ensure that transactions recorded as cash receipts are properly classified **(existence or occurrence, valuation or allocation)**

CC: *Transactions are only recorded as cash receipts when supported by appropriate records such as cash terminal records, daily cash receipts listings, duplicate customer receipts, and bank deposit records (e.g., receipts)*

TofC: Examine a selection of postings to the cash receipts journal and trace to daily cash receipts records for evidence of proper account classification

To ensure that cash receipts transactions are properly posted to the accounts receivable subsidiary ledger and general ledger **(completeness, presentation and disclosure)**

CC: *Cash receipts that were in payment for accounts receivable are reconciled with postings to the accounts receivable subsidiary ledger*

TofC: Examine evidence that posting to the cash receipts journal and subsidiary ledger are reconciled, are reconciled to the daily cash receipts records, and totals are reconciled to the general ledger; use computer-assisted audit techniques to recalculate as appropriate

SUBSTANTIVE PROCEDURES: DUAL PURPOSE TESTS, ANALYTICAL PROCEDURES, AND TESTS OF DETAILS OF BALANCES

Substantive procedures provide the auditor with evidence on financial statement amounts and disclosures. The three categories of substantive procedures are discussed in the remainder of the chapter: dual purpose tests, substantive analytical procedures, and tests of details of balances. The extent to which the auditor uses substantive procedures is affected by the auditor's assessment of risk and resulting reliance on ICFR. Substantive procedures of some type are performed for all relevant assertions on all significant accounts and disclosures.

For certain accounts and disclosures, the auditor may choose to perform more extensive **substantive tests** and procedures rather than rely on controls. The auditor might choose a substantive approach even after concluding that ICFR was functioning effectively as of management's report date. For example, suppose ICFR was not functioning effectively early in the year. Consequently, management made changes, and ICFR was functioning effectively at fiscal year end. In this situation the auditor could not rely on ICFR during the period of time before it was improved. For that time frame the auditor must rely on substantive procedures for audit evidence.

Another example is when an account can be efficiently audited using substantive procedures for the financial statement audit, so ICFR is tested only at the end of the fiscal year. AS 5.B7 states that substantive procedures must be performed for the financial statement audit. If performing tests of controls will not reduce the amount of substantive tests to be performed, the auditor will probably test controls only to the extent necessary to issue an ICFR opinion.

AS 5.B7. Regardless of the assessed level of control risk or the assessed risk of material misstatement in connection with the audit of the financial statements, the auditor should perform substantive procedures for all relevant assertions. Performing procedures to express an opinion on internal control over financial reporting does not diminish this requirement.

Results of controls tests in the audit of ICFR must be considered in the financial statement audit, just as the results of substantive tests must be considered in the audit of ICFR. These considerations across different areas of the audit apply particularly to risk evaluations, illegal acts, related parties, accounting estimates, selection of accounting principles, and potential financial statement misstatements. AS 5. B6 explains that ICFR results must be considered when planning substantive procedures.

AS 5.B6. If, during the audit of internal control over financial reporting, the auditor identifies a deficiency, he or she should determine the effect of the deficiency, if any, on the nature, timing, and extent of substantive procedures to be performed to reduce audit risk in the audit of the financial statements to an appropriately low level.

For example, an auditor applies the concept expressed in AS 5.B6 after finding problems in ICFR when testing operating effectiveness. Based on the ICFR results, a greater portion of the dollars recorded in the ending balance will be traced to supporting documents or confirmed with external parties. The auditor might look at more transactions in addition to examining support for a greater percentage of the dollars. The auditor might select two separate samples for testing or might use more than one testing technique, such as sending confirmations and examining supporting documents.

The financial statement audit findings affect the ICFR audit as well:

AS 5.B8. In an audit of internal control over financial reporting, the auditor should evaluate the effect of the findings of all substantive auditing procedures performed in the audit of financial statements on the effectiveness of internal control over financial reporting.

If the auditor finds problems when testing ICFR, then it will likely be no surprise if problems are identified during substantive testing. If this happens, substantive test results confirm the findings from the ICFR tests. However, the auditing guidance in AS 5.B8 is more meaningful in the reverse situation.

Suppose the operating effectiveness of ICFR has been tested and the results cause the auditor to think ICFR can be relied upon. Then, substantive tests reveal errors material to the financial statements. In this situation, the auditor reassesses the ICFR conclusions based on the evidence uncovered by the financial statement audit. The question is whether ICFR is reliable if it produces information containing misstatements that are material to the financial statements. The audit guidance does not dictate the answer to this question. However, the contrary substantive test results provide additional evidence to consider.

Dual Purpose Tests

When a single audit procedure contributes audit evidence about both controls and account balances, it is called a dual purpose test. Dual purpose tests increase audit efficiency because, if planned and executed properly, the same sample and set of client documents may be used to achieve more than one audit objective. For example, one client document can be examined to assess whether control procedures were followed and the transaction was properly posted.

To attain the greatest audit efficiency from dual purpose tests, the audit plan must carefully consider when various tests should be used. Assume that the audit plan for cash is designed so that inspection, inquiry, observation, and reperformance steps are all included at various times during the fiscal year. If the reperformance step for cash reconciliations is performed at year end, then along with providing evidence about controls it provides audit evidence about the year-end cash balance. If reperformance is conducted only once during the fiscal year, the most efficient timing is to have the reperformance of the cash reconciliation at year end. Dual purpose tests for assets and liabilities may be most efficient if conducted close to the fiscal year end. In contrast individual transactions affecting income statement accounts can be examined at any time during the year as a part of tests of controls and still provide evidence useful to the financial statement audit.

AU 350.44 emphasizes that in order to achieve the greatest audit efficiency from dual purpose tests, the same planning consideration applies to sample size as well as timing.

> **AU350.44** *In some circumstances the auditor may design a sample that will be used for dual purposes: testing the operating effectiveness of an identified control and testing whether the recorded monetary amount of transactions is correct. In general, an auditor planning to use a dual-purpose sample would have made a preliminary assessment that there is an acceptably low risk that the rate of deviations from the prescribed control in the population exceeds the tolerable rate. For example, an auditor designing a test of control over entries in the voucher register may plan a related substantive procedure at a risk level that anticipates a particular assessed level of control risk. The size of a sample designed for dual purposes should be the larger of the samples that would otherwise have been designed for the two separate purposes. In evaluating such tests, deviations from the prescribed control and monetary misstatements should be evaluated separately using the risk levels applicable for the respective purposes.*

Sometimes, dual purpose tests for sales may be the only detailed procedures the auditor performs that include examining the dollar amounts recorded for individual sales transactions and comparing them to the specific supporting documents. Exhibit 10-7 provides examples of dual purpose tests for the sales function.

EXHIBIT 10-7

Examples of Dual Purpose Tests for Sales Activities and Related Accounts

---

Note that these tests have two purposes: to test the operating effectiveness of a control; and to test the appropriateness of an amount or disclosure for the financial statements. The specific control for each of these following tests is not listed, but is implied in the purpose of the test. Management would not perform these tests for the substantive purpose but might perform them to test the operating effectiveness of ICFR. The auditor performs these tests with dual audit objectives to obtain audit evidence for the ICFR audit and the financial statement audit.

Purpose of Test:	Dual Purpose Tests
To obtain audit evidence that: Sales that are recorded represent shipments actually made to or services actually provided to customers **(existence or occurrence, rights and obligations, valuation or allocation)**	
	Select transactions that have been recorded from the sales journal; trace sales journal entries to supporting documents and records such as sales invoice, bill of lading, sales order, customer order; verify appropriateness of underlying documents and agree amounts
	Using computer-assisted audit techniques, scan sales journal and other journals and ledgers for unusual transactions and amounts; trace any that are identified to supporting documents
All sales transactions are recorded **(completeness)**	
	Trace a sample of shipping documents to the sales journal to be sure that each one is posted; agree amounts and other details of the sales transactions

(continued)

Recorded sales are for the amount of goods and/or services that were actually sold and shipped and that they are correctly billed and recorded
(existence or occurrence, completeness, rights and obligations, valuation or allocation, presentation and disclosure)

Trace entries in the sales journal to the supporting sales invoices; agree amounts; agree other transaction details on sales invoices to supporting documents such as shipping documents, sales orders, customer orders

Recompute price and other amounts on sales invoices, using authorized price lists or other approval documents

Transactions posted as sales are properly classified
(existence or occurrence, presentation and disclosure)

Trace a sample of transactions from the sales journal to the sales invoices and other supporting documents and examine for proper classification (that the transaction should be classified as a sale)

Sales transactions are recorded on the correct dates
(cutoff)

Select transactions from the sales journal and agree the date of posting to the sales date on the sales invoice and shipping document; agree amounts

Recorded sales transactions are included in the accounts receivable ledger and general ledger
(completeness, presentation and disclosure)

Select sales transactions from the sales journal and trace to the accounts receivable subsidiary ledger; agree amounts, dates, and invoice or other reference numbers; use computer-assisted audit techniques to check the clerical accuracy of the accounts receivable ledger and agree the total amount to the general ledger

Amounts shown in journals and ledgers are clerically accurate summations of transactions
(presentation and disclosure)

Use computer-assisted audit techniques to check the clerical accuracy of the sales journal and trace amounts to the general ledger

Exhibit 10-8 provides examples of dual purpose tests for the cash receipts function. You should read and study Exhibits 10-7 and 10-8 on dual purpose tests related to sales and cash receipts and compare them to both the tests of controls already presented and tests of details of balances discussed later in the chapter. A major difference you should be able to identify is that each dual purpose procedure includes collecting evidence about ICFR and the account balance. For purposes of audit efficiency, whenever possible, auditors will modify tests of controls to also collect account balance evidence. For cash receipts, gathering evidence useful for controls and account balances requires performing dual purpose tests close to year end.

EXHIBIT 10-8

Examples of Dual
Purpose Tests for Cash
Receipts Activities and
Related Accounts

Purpose of Test	Dual Purpose Tests
To obtain audit evidence that:	
Cash receipts that are recorded were actually received by the company **(existence or occurrence)**	
	Use computer-assisted audit techniques to scan the cash receipts journal for unusual transactions and amounts, including such details as inappropriate times, and unusual and unauthorized computer terminals; trace any that are identified to supporting documents
	Trace posted entries for cash receipts from the cash receipts journal to bank statements.
	Prepare a proof of cash
Cash received by the company was deposited and recorded in the receipts journal and that amounts and details are shown correctly **(completeness, valuation or allocation, presentation and disclosure)**	
	Trace items listed on a sample of daily cash receipts records to the cash receipts journal, agreeing amounts and details such as dates and names
	Trace amounts and details on a sample of daily cash receipts records to deposit records
Cash receipts transactions are properly classified and recorded in the period received **(presentation and disclosure, cutoff)**	
	Select transactions from the cash receipts journal and examine daily cash receipts records and deposit evidence (bank receipts, bank statements) for evidence that the transactions are properly classified as cash and that the cash was received in the period shown; agree amounts
	Select deposits on the bank statement immediately after the period end and trace to postings in the cash receipts journal to investigate whether any cash amounts from the subsequent period were improperly included in the period under audit
Postings of cash receipts are correctly made to the accounts receivable subsidiary ledger and general ledger **(presentation and disclosure)**	
	Select transactions from the cash receipts journal and trace to the accounts receivable subsidiary ledger agreeing specific account amounts, other account details and dates
	Select transactions from the accounts receivable subsidiary ledger and trace to the cash receipts journal agreeing amounts, other account details and dates
Amounts shown in journals and ledgers are clerically accurate summations of transactions **(presentation and disclosure)**	
	Use computer-assisted audit techniques to check the clerical accuracy of the cash receipts journal and trace amounts to the general ledger

REVIEW QUESTIONS

K.1 What are the three types of audit procedures that fall within the category of substantive tests?

K.2 Why would an auditor perform more substantive testing for one part of the fiscal year and less substantive testing for another part of the year?

K.3 When a sample is to be used for both the ICFR and financial statement components of an integrated audit, what must the auditor consider in determining the sample size?

Substantive Analytical Procedures [LO 5]

The term *analytical procedures* covers a wide variety of audit steps. Regardless of the specific step, the overall purpose of any analytical procedure is to collect audit evidence that is based on relationships among items. For example, looking at the aggregated amount of all sales transactions for the current year compared to the prior year tells the auditor whether the dollar amount of sales have increased or decreased. Noting this type of change, or lack thereof, has no real value in isolation. But the auditor can evaluate the result of an analytical procedure using other information and come to conclusions.

Consider an analytical procedure showing that the dollar amount of a company's sales increases by 10% from one year to the next. The auditor knows there was no change in the company's sales prices. An appropriate conclusion may be that 10% more inventory was sold in this year than last. The auditor can perform an analytical procedure on inventory to support the assessment that a greater volume was sold in the current year. In contrast, if the company had increased its sales price by 10% in the current year, then the appropriate conclusion may be that no change in the volume of inventory sold had occurred. The change in the sales amount resulted from the change in price. The auditor can perform an analytical procedure on inventory to explore the expectation that volume sold did not change.

Audit standards require analytical procedures as part of the audit planning process. The simple example in the prior paragraph explains why analytical procedures are specifically required in planning. If the 10% year over year sales increase occurred because more inventory was sold, then the auditor may need to spend more audit effort on the sales revenue and inventory-related accounts. If the sales increase resulted only from an increase in sales price per unit, then the audit of sales in the current year may take no more audit effort than in the prior year. However, even if the sales account does not need more time, the auditor may plan to spend more time and effort auditing the receivables balance because it may be larger than in the prior year. The auditing standards discuss the fundamental value of analytical procedures related to expected relationships.

> **AU 329.02** *Analytical procedures ... evaluations of financial information made by a study of plausible relationships among both financial and nonfinancial data. . . . A basic premise underlying the application of analytical procedures is that plausible relationships among data may reasonably be expected to exist and continue in the absence of known conditions to the contrary. Particular conditions that can cause variations in those relationships include, for example, specific unusual transactions or events, accounting changes, business changes, random fluctuations, or misstatements.*

In this chapter analytical procedures are discussed as they are used related to specific account balances or classes of transactions, such as sales, billing and collections. When used in that context, they are called substantive analytical procedures. A fundamental substantive audit procedure, sometimes called **fluctuation analysis**, compares a current account bal-

EXHIBIT 10-9

Fluctuation Analysis

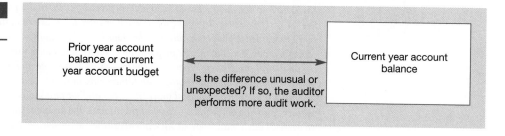

ance with that same account's balance in the prior year or with its budgeted amount. The auditor determines the difference in the two amounts and assesses whether the result was unexpected. In cases where there was an unusual or unexpected change in the account balance or activity, further audit work is appropriate. The audit process for this analytical procedure is shown in Exhibit 10-9.

Substantive analytical procedures can also provide audit evidence based on relationships among current-year account balances. For example, the auditor may investigate the relationships of the sales and inventory account balances, and of the credit sales and accounts receivable account balances. This is the type of analytical procedure presented in this chapter, specifically related to sales and cash receipts.

Auditors can obtain significant evidence about year-end balances in balance sheet accounts through procedures such as document examination, **external confirmations** (e.g., cash, receivables, and debt), and observing the client's physical count of inventory. In contrast, these procedures are not usually effective for an account like sales revenue in which there are often many transactions of small amounts spread throughout the year. For these types of accounts, the auditor relies heavily on tests of control and analytical procedures. Sometimes, if an income statement account has just a few transactions or the transactions are conducted with a limited number of outside parties, the auditor can obtain information from those parties, for example, about sales and purchase transactions.

As the auditor performs substantive tests of details on balance sheet accounts, the approach is usually to concurrently explore related income statement accounts based on relationships. For example, bad debt expense is related to accounts receivable and the allowance for uncollectible accounts. Cost of goods sold is related to inventory. Credit sales can be linked to accounts receivable. Interest expense relates to debt. Understanding the client's business and how various items are accounted for in its accounting system is mandatory to effectively use analytical procedures.

An important consideration when using substantive analytical procedures is the effectiveness of ICFR for the accounts being audited. If ICFR is not reliable, then the auditor should not expect to gain audit evidence from the relationships of amounts recorded in the accounts. The expectation that there are plausible relationships between the accounts stems from the expectation that the accounts represent the business activities. If ICFR is not effective, then the business activities may not be appropriately recorded and the relationships among the affected accounts will be changed. The possibility of **management override** as an ICFR weakness is important to substantive procedures because if management is able to override the controls then the accounts may be intentionally manipulated to portray a false relationship picture. These concerns over ICFR, the completeness and accuracy of the underlying information, and management override are discussed in AICPA AU 318, *Performing Audit Procedures in Response to Assessed Risks and Evaluating the Audit Evidence Obtained.*

AU 318.57. *In designing substantive analytical procedures, the auditor should consider such matters as . . . (t)he reliability of the data, whether internal or external, from which the expectation of recorded amounts or ratios is developed. . . . The auditor should consider testing the controls, if any, over the entity's preparation of information to be used by the auditor in applying analytical procedures. When such controls are effective, the auditor has greater confidence in the reliability of the information, and, therefore, in results of analytical procedures. When designing substantive analytical procedures, the auditor also should evaluate the risk of management override of controls. As part of this process, the auditor should evaluate whether such an override might have allowed adjustments outside of the normal period-end financial reporting process to have been made to the financial statements. Such adjustments might have resulted in artificial changes to the financial statement relationships being analyzed, causing the auditor to draw erroneous conclusions. For this reason, substantive analytical procedures alone are not well suited to detecting fraud.*

AU 318.14. *The auditor should obtain audit evidence about the accuracy and completeness of information produced by the entity's information system when that information is used in performing audit procedures. For example, if the auditor uses nonfinancial information or budget data produced by the entity's information system in performing audit procedures, such as substantive analytical procedures or tests of controls, the auditor should obtain audit evidence about the accuracy and completeness of such information.*

The auditor performs substantive analytical procedures to obtain audit evidence for the financial statement audit. In order to rely on analytical procedures the auditor must have tested ICFR. Typically, substantive analytical procedures alone do not provide sufficient evidence for the financial statement audit. For sales, the auditor relies largely on analytical procedures and audit procedures performed on related accounts such as inventory and cash. Examples of substantive analytical procedures for this cycle are presented in Exhibit 10-10.

EXHIBIT 10-10

Examples of Substantive Analytical Procedures for Sales, Cash Receipts, and Related Accounts

To identify possible over- or understatement of sales and account receivable

Compare gross margin percentage, by product line, with previous years

Compare sales, by product line, month-to-month over time

To identify possible over- or understatement of sales returns and allowances and accounts receivable

Compare sales returns and allowances as a percentage of gross sales, by product line, with previous years

To identify possible misstated accounts receivable and related income statement accounts

Compare large individual customer balances that are over a threshold amount with the same customers' balances in previous years

To identify possible uncollectible accounts receivable that have not been provided for

Compare bad debt expense as a percentage of gross sales with previous years

To identify possible over- or understatement of the allowance for uncollectible accounts, and bad debt expense; to identify possible fictitious accounts receivable

Compare number of days that accounts receivable are outstanding with previous years and related turnover of accounts receivable

Compare totals of various categories on the aged accounts receivable schedule as a percentage of accounts receivable with what existed in prior years

Compare the balance in the allowance for uncollectible accounts as a percentage of accounts receivable with the percentage that existed in prior years

Compare the accounts receivable written off in the current year as a percentage of accounts receivable with the percentage amount that was written of in prior years

REVIEW QUESTIONS

L.1 What account balances within the current year might be used for analytical procedures? How might balances between years be used for analytical procedures?

L.2 Why is effective ICFR required for reliable analytical procedures?

TESTS OF DETAILS OF BALANCES

Tests of details of balances are the last category of substantive procedures presented in this chapter. The purpose of tests of details of balances is to provide audit evidence regarding the appropriate statement of balances and disclosures in the financial statements. They are single-purpose tests in that they address only financial statement and not internal control assertions. While tests of details of balances can be specific to a single account amount or balance, they can also involve big picture procedures. Reviewing adjusting entries and agreeing the totals in the client records to the financial statements are tests of details of balances. Reconciling the accounting records and financial statements may often be efficiently performed using computer-assisted audit techniques.

The tests of details of balances discussion that follows begins by explaining external confirmations. The audit process of confirming information with outside parties is used in a variety of audit areas and is very important to the sales and collections cycle when auditing receivables. External confirmations are discussed again, when appropriate, for other transaction cycles and accounts in other chapters. The background to the confirmation process is presented here. The sales, billing, and collections cycle includes activities related to cash. Therefore, confirming bank accounts is presented along with the discussion of other confirmations. The client's activities for aging of accounts receivables are included earlier in this chapter, and the audit of the aging process is discussed after confirmations. Tests of details of cash in the bank are also discussed in this chapter even though cash activities involve all cycles except inventory.

External Confirmations [LO 6]

AU330.04 defines external confirmation as "the process of obtaining and evaluating direct communication from a third party in response to a request for information about a particular item affecting financial statement assertions." Confirming financial statement information provides relatively reliable audit evidence because the information comes from an independent party outside the entity. Furthermore, the communication goes directly from the third party to the auditor without the client having access during the process. AU 326 highlights evidence obtained directly by the auditor from independent outsiders as reliable.

> **AICPA AU 326.08.** *Audit evidence is more reliable when it is obtained from knowledgeable independent sources outside the entity.... Audit evidence obtained directly by the auditor... is more reliable than audit evidence obtained indirectly or by inference.*

The confirmation process involves the following:

1. Selecting the items to confirm
2. Designing the confirmation
3. Communicating directly with the third party from whom the confirmation information is requested
4. Receiving the response
5. Evaluating the information provided via the confirmation

Even though confirmations provide relatively high quality audit evidence, other related substantive audit procedures are usually performed as appropriate for the transactions and accounts being audited. Examples of tests that accompany confirmations are sales cutoff tests, examination of cash received for payment of receivables after the fiscal year end, inventory observations, and a search for unrecorded liabilities. The search for unrecorded liabilities is discussed in Chapter 11.

Confirmations can be in a "positive" or "negative" format. **Positive confirmations** request that the third party always respond. Usually, a positive confirmation requests that the third party agree or disagree with information provided on the confirmation, and may request the third party to provide information. Sometimes positive confirmations are in what is known as a "blank" form and simply ask the other party to provide information, such as an account balance. **Negative confirmations** ask the third party to respond to the confirmation only if there is a disagreement with the information provided. External confirmations can be prepared as a form or a letter. The confirmation includes a postage paid envelope or postcard preaddressed to the auditor's office, to enable the third party to easily comply with the confirmation request.

When positive confirmation responses are received, the auditor knows that the outside party at least went to the trouble to respond. However, even if the third party mailed the confirmation back without noting any problems with the information, the auditor cannot be sure that the information is accurate. It is always possible that the third party responded without examining the information. For this reason, additional substantive audit procedures are performed to augment confirmations.

A negative confirmation that is returned to the auditor disagreeing with the information on the confirmation also provides audit evidence. The auditor investigates the information provided and determines its impact on the account balance and audit conclusions. When a negative confirmation is not returned, it may be because the recipient agrees with the information, simply did not look at it, or chose to not respond. Therefore, nonresponses to negative confirmations provide no audit evidence.

Positive confirmations request that the outside party respond regardless of whether the information is correct. If third parties fail to respond to positive confirmations, the auditor follows up to try to get a response. Follow-up often includes a second and third request and may also include telephone calls. When the auditor does not receive a response to a positive confirmation, even after follow-up procedures are conducted, alternative audit procedures are performed to gain whatever audit evidence is available about the information that was included on the confirmation.

Blank positive confirmation forms (without any information about the accounts and balances included) ask the third party to fill in the information. Using blank positive confirmations virtually eliminates the risk that the respondent has just signed the form and sent it back without checking the accuracy of the information. However, these blank-form confirmations generally have a lower response rate because they take more effort on the part of the third party. Also, due to transactions that may have occurred between the time the confirmation was sent and when it was returned, the amounts filled in by the recipient may be different from what the auditor identified in the client's records. These discrepancies, which often indicate nothing but a timing difference, create audit inefficiency because they must be investigated and resolved.

Overall, the type of confirmation used depends on the amount of audit evidence needed and the expected success of using confirmations to obtain audit evidence. The quality of the audit evidence obtained from confirming information with third parties depends on more than the type of confirmation used. The nature of the information and the characteristics of the person responding are also important. Some types of information may be more difficult for the third party to provide. For example, a third party may be able to confirm the amount of a specific transaction, but not the total account balance. In the current environment of electronic access to account information, a third party knowledgeable about the account or transaction may be able to confirm the total balance, along with existence of an account or a loan, account number, and payment information.

The responsibilities of the various parties involved in the confirmation process are important, although they can also seem somewhat counterintuitive and may be tricky to understand.

- A confirmation request is a communication from the audit client to the outside third party, requesting that the third party respond as instructed directly to the auditor.

- The auditor identifies the third parties to whom confirmation requests are sent, even though they are communications from the audit client.

- The client may perform the clerical preparation of the confirmations, but the auditor supervises the process and physically mails the requests from a location that is away from the client's place of business.

- A return envelope is included that the third party uses to respond directly to the auditor at the auditor's office.

- The auditor controls the confirmation responses received and documents the responses in some sort of log. The auditor logs whether the third party agrees or disagrees with the confirmation information, and the nature of any disagreement. Disagreements are usually called exceptions.

- The auditor investigates any exceptions. The client may assist the auditor in investigating exceptions, but again, the auditor controls the process and decides about the appropriateness and adequacy of explanations.

The auditor usually performs alternative procedures such as examining other documents and subsequent cash flows for evidence that explanations are valid.

AU 330.33 lists the following considerations in evaluating confirmation results:

1. The reliability of the confirmations and alternative procedures
2. The nature of any exceptions, including the implications, both quantitative and qualitative, of those exceptions
3. The evidence provided by other procedures
4. Whether additional evidence is needed

Even direct communications to the auditor from apparently independent external third parties require some amount of skeptical assessment by the auditor. In 2003, during the audit of Parmalat, the auditor received forged information confirming a very large (but nonexistent) cash account. The Parmalat case highlights that the current sophistication of desktop publishing makes creating forged documents relatively easy.

AUDITING IN ACTION

Confirmations at Parmalat

In 2004 a major fraud was revealed at Parmalat, an Italian food producer with a name that is familiar worldwide. Various techniques were used by executives to pull money from the company for private use. One technique used to keep the fraud hidden involved creating a response to an auditor's confirmation request. The Bank of America letterhead was scanned and reproduced and used to create a fraudulent document verifying the existence of a deposit account holding over $4.98 billion.

Sverige, Chris. 1/6/04. "The Parmalat scandal: Europe's ten-billion euro black hole." Retrieved March 21, 2009, http://www.wsws.org/articles/2004/jan2004/parm-j06.shtml.

AUDITING IN ACTION

Confirming Information in Other Countries

A challenging situation for auditors of banks and other financial industry clients is when "off-shore" customers (those domiciled in a country outside the United States) are unwilling to respond to mailed confirmation documents because they believe their outgoing mailed is monitored by their home government. Auditors may receive faxed responses because the customers are unwilling to provide information about their business or finances in outgoing mail documents. In this situation, the auditor may choose to follow up with a telephone call on the fax response received. This is an example of a situation in which confirmations may not be the most effective way to collect audit evidence.

The auditor should try to obtain the most authoritative documentary evidence available. When the auditor receives a faxed response to a confirmation, follow-up is appropriate (AU 330.29). For example, the auditor should follow up with a telephone call and also consider asking the respondent to send back the original confirmation. When this is not possible, the auditor should conduct alternative procedures. Any oral confirmations should be received by the auditor with an appropriate level of skepticism and should be documented in the workpapers.

Accounts Receivables Confirmations

AU 330.34 states, "there is a presumption that the auditor will request the confirmation of accounts receivable." Confirmations of accounts receivable may provide the auditor with evidence that a receivable exists and that the amount shown as receivable is correct. The confirmation may even suggest that the receivable has value if there is an indication on the part of the third party of plans to pay the debt. However, a confirmation may provide evidence that the receivable exists in the amount shown even in the situation where the third party does not have the intention or the ability to pay off the debt. Thus, a confirmation may provide only limited audit evidence about the *value* of a receivable.

If the auditor decides against confirming accounts receivable, the decision must be justified. Possible reasons for deciding to not confirm accounts receivable are that the accounts receivable amounts are immaterial, using confirmations would not be effective to gain audit evidence, and other substantive tests alone would provide enough evidence for the audit objective.

In confirming accounts receivable, the auditor often stratifies the population of accounts receivable based on dollar amounts and varies the plan for different classifications. For example, all of the accounts receivable with a dollar amount balance over a specified threshold may be confirmed using positive confirmations. A sample of accounts with lower dollar balances may be confirmed using positive confirmations, and a larger sample of accounts at the lower dollar range may be confirmed using negative confirmations. The auditor may also use positive confirmations for all or a sample of accounts receivable of employees and related parties.

AUDITING IN ACTION

An Example of a Positive Accounts Receivable Confirmation

XYZ Company
4 Yawkey Way
Boston, MA

January 21, 20X9

Mr. Ted Williams
400 Club Incorporated
9 Hitters Way
Boston, MA 02215

Dear Mr. Williams:

Our auditors, Auditors & Co. LLP, are engaged in an audit of our financial statements. In connection with our audit, they desire to confirm the balance due us on your account as of December 31, 20X8, which was presented on our records as **$19,180**. (A-1)

Please state in the space below whether or not this is in agreement with your records at this date. If not, please furnish any information you may have which will assist the auditors in reconciling the difference. After signing and dating your reply, please mail it directly to Auditors & Co. LLP , 2004 Patriot Way, Boston, MA 02218. A stamped, addressed envelope is enclosed for your convenience.

It is very important that Auditors & Co. LLP receive your prompt reply. We sincerely appreciate your assistance.

Kind Regards,

Audrey Escobar

Audrey Escobar,
Controller

(A-1)
The above balance of $ 19,180 due XYZ Company agrees with our records at December 31, 20X8 with the following exceptions (if any):

_____

none
_____

Date: 1/26/20X9   Signed: *Miguel Chapman, Controller*

(note, the signature would have been manually signed)

AUDITING IN ACTION

An Example of a Negative Accounts Receivable Confirmation

XYZ Company
4 Yawkey Way
Boston, MA

January 21, 20X9

Mr. Ted Williams
400 Club Incorporated
9 Hitters Way
Boston, MA 02215

Dear Mr. Williams:

Our auditors, Auditors & Co. LLP, are engaged in an audit of our financial statements. In connection with our audit, they desire to confirm the balance due us on your account as of December 31, 20X8, which was presented on our records and is shown in the accompanying statement as **$19,180.**

Please examine the accompanying statement carefully. If it does NOT agree with your records, please report any differences directly to our auditors: Auditors & Co. LLP, 2004 Patriot Way, Boston, MA 02218. A stamped, addressed envelope is enclosed for your convenience.

Your prompt attention to this request is very important. We sincerely appreciate your assistance.

Kind Regards,

Audrey Escobar

Audrey Escobar,
Controller

REVIEW QUESTIONS

M.1 Why are confirmations considered more "reliable" audit evidence?

M.2 What other audit tests are used in conjunction with confirmation of accounts receivable?

M.3 What conclusions can the auditor make from a negative confirmation?

M.4 In what ways do client personnel participate in the confirmation process?

M.5 About which assertions(s) does a response to a positive account receivable confirmation provide audit evidence?

M.6 Why might the auditor choose to NOT confirm accounts receivable?

M.7 Explain the difference between positive and negative formats for confirmations and when each format is likely to be used.

Confirmations of Other Financial Statement Accounts

Confirmations are used to gather audit evidence for various account balances. For example, accounts and notes payables can be confirmed. For these liability accounts the greatest risks are that all accounts and notes payable may not be included, and that those presented may be shown at less than the correct amounts. The concern is for omission and understatement. Therefore, a major difference between confirming accounts receivable and accounts payable is the population from which the accounts to be confirmed are selected.

The specific accounts receivable that are confirmed are selected from the accounts receivable subsidiary ledger or trial balance. For accounts payable the client's vendor list is used as the sample frame from which to make the selection. The auditor does not select the accounts payable to confirm based on the amount of the account balance because an account balance shown as zero or a small dollar amount may be understated. Usually, the auditor intentionally includes in the confirmation sample vendors with which the client frequently does business but to which the client shows a zero liability at the fiscal year end.

Inventory that is held by others on **consignment** is also confirmed if the amount is material. Confirmation to the auditor by an outside third party about inventory it is holding and trying to sell on behalf of the audit client provides the auditor with information that the inventory exists. However, it usually does not provide much evidence on the value of the inventory.

In addition to the accounts mentioned here, when transactions are unusual or complex, the auditor may confirm the terms of the transactions with other parties. Sometimes when a company sells to one or a limited number of customers, or has a few very large sales transactions in addition to many small ones, the company's main sales customers may be asked to confirm major sales transactions. Confirmations are also discussed in the chapters addressing purchasing and cash disbursements, inventory, and financing.

REVIEW QUESTIONS

N.1 How is the population from which a sample is selected for confirmation of accounts payable different from that used for confirmation of accounts receivable?

N.2 What assertions do confirmation of inventory on consignment address?

Bank Confirmations

Confirmation forms are generally sent to all financial institutions with which an audit client has a banking relationship. As with other confirmations, the request comes from the company and the response is mailed directly to the auditor. The document frequently used for confirming bank accounts is called the "AICPA Standard Form to Confirm Account Balance Information with Financial Institutions." Since the document comes from a bank, it originates with an independent source. The form is intended to request that the financial institution substantiate information about specific accounts. The request is very clear that it does not solicit information about the existence or activity of accounts not listed on the form.

In some circumstances the auditor may choose to not confirm specific bank accounts. This might occur, for example, when a retail business has many locations with a bank account at each location for making deposits that are cleared to the company's central account on a daily basis. If sufficient controls exist over the cash deposits and central bank account, the auditor may decide to confirm only the main bank account. Whenever the auditor chooses to omit the step of confirming bank accounts, the justification and rationale for the decision are documented.

REVIEW QUESTIONS

O.1 Explain to what accounts the standard bank confirmation request applies.

O.2 Under what circumstance might an auditor decide not to confirm a bank account?

Aging of Accounts Receivable

Companies prepare an aged accounts receivable trial balance, sometimes called an accounts receivable aging schedule. An **aging schedule** assists in (1) managing collections and write-offs of accounts receivable, and (2) estimating bad debt expense and the appropriate balance

AUDITING IN ACTION

An Example of a Bank Confirmation

STANDARD FORM TO CONFIRM ACCOUNT
BALANCE INFORMATION WITH FINANCIAL INSTITUTIONS

> **ORIGINAL**
> To be mailed to accountant

SPLASH & SUNSHY WATER SPORTS
CUSTOMER NAME

Financial Institution's Name and Address
[   ]

[   ]

We have provided to our accountants the following information as of the close of business on *DECEMBER 31*, 20*10* regarding our deposit and loan balances. Please confirm the accuracy of the information, noting any exceptions to the information provided. If the balances have been left blank, please complete this form by furnishing the balance in the appropriate space below.* Although we do not request or expect you to conduct a comprehensive, detailed search of your records, if during the process of completing this confirmation additional information about other deposit and loan accounts we may have with you comes to your attention, please include such information below. Please use the enclosed envelope to return the form directly to our accountants.

1. At the close of business on the date listed above, our records indicated the following deposit balance(s):

ACCOUNT NAME	ACCOUNTS NO.	INTEREST RATE	BALANCE*
General Checking	*174 – 2412*	*NONE*	*$ 56,811.12*
Payroll Checking	*174 – 3833*	*NONE*	*$ 12,114.36*

2. We were directly liable to the financial institution for loans at the close of business on the date listed above as follows:

ACCOUNT NO./ DESCRIPTION	BALANCE*	DATE DUE	INTEREST RATE	DATE THROUGH WHICH INTEREST IS PAID	DESCRIPTION OF COLLATERAL
44-7822	*$26,846*	*10/1/11*	*10.14%*	*12/15/10*	*Vehicles & equipment*

Christine Walker
(Customer's Authorized Signature)

1/12/11
(Date)

The information presented above by the customer is in agreement with our records. Although we have not conducted comprehensive, detailed search of our records, no other deposit or loan accounts have come to our attention except as noted below.

Michael Farland
(Financial Institution Authorized Signature)

1/31/11
(Date)

Accounts Clerk
(Title)

EXCEPTIONS AND/OR COMMENTS

Please return this form directly to our accountants:

[*TUTTLE & OLIE*
III SWAMP LANE
[*CORAL SPRINGS, FL 33367*]

* Ordinarily, balances are intentionally left blank if they are not available at the time the form is prepared.

Approved 1990 by American Bankers Association, American Institute of Certified Public Accountants, and Bank Administration Institute. Additional forms available AICPA - Order Department, P.O. Box 1003, NY, NY 10108-1003

for the allowance for uncollectible (or doubtful) accounts. An aging schedule classifies accounts receivable based on how long they have been outstanding, separating those that are current from those that are 30, 60, 90, etc. days outstanding.

Because the aging schedule supports many calculations and decisions related to accounts receivable, bad debt expense, and the related allowance account, the auditor reviews the aging schedule, checks its clerical accuracy, and traces it to underlying records. The auditor also evaluates management's assumptions regarding collectibility of the different categories of receivables, particularly if there have been any major changes during the fiscal year in competitors, customer base, or the external economy.

Concurrently with the audit of accounts receivable, the auditor evaluates the assumptions underlying the determination of bad debt expense, reperforms any calculations, and traces the amount to the general ledger. The auditor is concerned with establishing that the amount of bad debt expense is appropriate and determined according to company policy.

REVIEW QUESTIONS

P.1 What audit procedure does the auditor use to examine the valuation of accounts receivable? Specifically, what steps does the auditor perform related to the aged accounts receivable trial balance?

Auditors use analytical procedures to test sales. In addition, tests of the relationship of sales to inventory, accounts receivable, and cash provide audit evidence. Exhibits 10-11 and 10-12 provide examples of tests of details of balances for sales and collections and for cash. You should read and study Exhibits 10-11 and 10-12 and consider what these audit procedures accomplish for the financial statement audit in contrast to what you have already learned about tests of controls.

EXHIBIT 10-11 Tests of Details of Balances Sales and Collections Cycle	**These steps combine to provide audit evidence about management assertions. The objectives of the audit are met when evidence is obtained enabling the auditor to form conclusions on the appropriateness of management's five financial statement assertions.**

Accounts receivables

    Review accounts receivable trial balance for large and unusual receivables

    Perform any remaining analytical procedures

    Review receivables listed on the aged accounts receivable trial balance for notes and related party receivables

    Inquire of management whether there are any related parties, notes, or long-term receivables included in the accounts receivable trial balance

    Review the minutes of the Board of Directors meetings and inquire of management to determine whether any receivables are pledged or factored

    Select accounts receivable from the accounts receivable trial balance and trace to the accounts receivable subsidiary ledger, agreeing the aging classification and account balance amount

    Recalculate the aged accounts receivable trial balance for clerical accuracy

    Trace total of the accounts receivable subsidiary ledger and aged accounts receivable trial balance to the general ledger

    Select accounts receivable accounts from the accounts receivable subsidiary ledger and trace to the aged accounts receivable trial balance

    Develop confirmation plan for accounts receivable and implement

    Confirm 100% of balances over dollar amount threshold

    Confirm 100% of balances of related parties

Allowance for uncollectible accounts

    Discuss with credit manager the likelihood of collecting older balances

    Examine cash receipts after fiscal year end on balances larger than threshold

    Evaluate whether receivables are collectible

    Evaluate whether allowance is adequate

    Trace bad expense calculated to general ledger

Examine cutoff

    Select sample of sales transactions from last days of fiscal year end from sales journal

    Select sample of sales transactions from first days of next year's sales journal

    Examine shipping documents for selected transactions; agree date of shipment and date the sale was recorded

    Select sample of recorded sales returns and allowances transactions immediately before and after the balance sheet date; verify that they were recorded in the correct period

(continued)

Identify and investigate
   Significant sales returns
   Significant sales and receivables in foreign currencies
   Significant scrap or bulk sales
   Related party sales and receivables
   Key item sales
   Intercompany sale and receivables
Review the financial statements for appropriate disclosures[2]

Cash [LO 7]

Tests of details of balances procedures for cash generally apply to cash on hand and cash in the bank. Cash balances relate to the revenue and expenditures cycles, as well as to the human resources and financing cycles. The auditor has to consider cash concurrently with other assets because cash can easily be converted into other highly liquid assets such as marketable securities and inventory. Cash and cash equivalents are easily interchangeable. Equally, the audit of cash must concurrently consider liabilities because liabilities can be incurred to produce cash. While cutoff of cash itself is important, so is the coordination of the cash cutoff with cutoff of other accounts. Overall, the auditor considers the following questions for cash:

Does the cash really exist?
Is all the cash that the company owns shown on the financial statements?
Does the company have rights to all the cash that is shown on the financial statements?
Is all appropriate disclosure provided?

The question of whether the company has rights to the cash shown on the financial statements refers to the possibility that the cash is committed for a specific purpose or that restrictions exist on its use. The management assertion regarding valuation does not require significant audit effort unless other factors are involved, such as situations where the cash is in a foreign currency and must be restated in U.S. dollars. Exhibit 10-12 presents tests of details of balances for cash.

EXHIBIT 10-12

Tests of Details of Balances, Cash in the Bank

Request, receive, and test bank confirmation
   Trace the amount confirmed by the bank to the amount on the client prepared bank reconciliation and investigate any discrepancies
   Trace all other information on the bank confirmation (information typically relates to loans) to appropriate audit work papers and investigate any discrepancies
   Review confirmation for any restrictions on the use of cash and compensating balances
Request, receive, and test cutoff bank statement
   Reconcile items on the cutoff bank statement with other client-prepared bank reconciliations, cash receipts journal, and cash disbursements journal

[2]For all accounts and cycles of the financial statement audit, the auditor will review the financial statements for appropriateness and sufficiency of disclosures. Disclosure requirements are often very lengthy and are not included in their entirety in the examples of audit procedures provided throughout this book.

Test client-prepared bank reconciliation

> Recompute for clerical accuracy
>
> *(The purpose of recomputing for clerical accuracy is to verify that the client is carefully preparing the bank reconciliations. The auditor checks to see that the client's recorded book balance is the same as the actual cash in the bank, except for deposits in transit, outstanding checks, and other reconciling items. If appropriate, the balance per books should be adjusted by the client to reflect any new information that comes from the bank statement reconciling items. In other words, the balance per books should be a corrected balance; the reconciliation should not simply be used to "prove" the balance.)*
>
> Trace reconciling items to underlying supporting documents
>
> Trace the book balance on the reconciliation to the general ledger
>
> Trace checks written and other disbursements initiated before the fiscal year end that cleared with the cutoff bank statement to the outstanding checklist of the prior bank reconciliation and to the cash disbursements journal, verifying that the date posted was before the fiscal year end
>
> *(If the dates are different, then the cash per books is incorrect. If the checks were written after the fiscal year end, then the liabilities on the balance sheet are understated.)*
>
> Investigate any checks written prior to year end that have not cleared the bank at the time of the cutoff bank statement; for example, discuss with the client and confirm whether they should be shown as accounts payable
>
> Trace any deposits in transit at year end to cutoff bank statement and client-prepared interbank transfer schedule if applicable
>
> Trace transfer of funds from branch bank (sweep) accounts to central account if appropriate, agreeing correct cutoff posting to both accounts
>
> Account for, agree, or investigate other reconciling items on the bank reconciliation and bank statement such as bank service charges, bank errors, bank corrections, and unrecorded transactions debited or credited directly by the bank

Prepare or recompute client-prepared (four-column) proof of cash if appropriate

Prepare or recompute client-prepared interbank transfer schedule if appropriate

> Trace all reconciling deposits in transit on banks statements to interbank transfer schedule (looking for omitted items on the interbank transfer schedule)
>
> Trace items on interbank transfer schedule to cash receipts and cash disbursement records, agreeing date recorded in both accounts
>
> Trace items on interbank transfer schedule to banks statements, agreeing date recorded on both statements
>
> Examine each interbank transfer for proper between-years reconciliation on bank reconciliation

Count cash on hand on the last day of the year and trace to posting in cash receipts journal, bank statement, and as a deposit-in-transit reconciling item on client-prepared bank reconciliation

Record last check number used on the last day of the year and trace to the cash disbursements journal, bank statement, and as an outstanding check reconciling item on client-prepared bank reconciliation

Examine minutes of Board of Directors and its committees

Examine loan agreements

Review financial statements for appropriate disclosures:

> Cash and cash equivalents specified as required
>
> Cash restricted to certain uses and compensating balances adequately disclosed
>
> Bank overdrafts without the right of offset against another account (for example, a savings account) shown as current liabilities

AUDITING SALES, BILLING, AND COLLECTIONS IN THE HEALTH-CARE PROVIDER INDUSTRY

Auditing the revenue and collections cycle in a health-care industry client begins by using patient records as a source of information. Patient records document the services performed. Standard service rates for procedures can be used in tests of controls over the revenues recorded and the billing process.

Accounts receivable is a relatively high-risk audit area for health-care industry clients because valuing receivables is a complex process. The amount of payments that is collected from a third-party payer is affected by the provider's contractual arrangement with that payer. A health-care provider receives payment from many third parties, and the contractual arrangement with each is different.

Recall that the contractual adjustment that reduces revenues is recorded at the time of billing or when payment is received. The auditor first needs to understand the contractual agreements, and then he or she can review and test the client's process of calculating and recording contractual adjustments. The next audit procedure is calculating an estimate of the contractual adjustment to corroborate management's calculation. Confirming receivables is another procedure that the auditor may choose to conduct. The auditor reviews correspondence and payments received from third-party payers subsequent to year end to validate the appropriateness of revenue recorded, the contractual adjustment to revenue, and accounts receivable.

Beyond proper calculation of these accounts, health-care providers must also manage bad debt. Any allowance for doubtful accounts should be separated between third-party payers and individuals. Based on client assumptions and processes, the auditor evaluates the appropriateness of the balance of the allowance for doubtful accounts and related bad debt expense.

For some health-care providers, estimates of revenue earned and anticipated collections from patients who have not yet been released from care or discharged at year end can be a material amount and, therefore, an important calculation. Various methods to estimate revenues and collections and allocate them to the appropriate fiscal years can be used. The methods should be reasonable and applied consistently.

Finally, auditors pay special attention to laws and regulations that apply to companies in the health-care industry. For example, the Health Insurance Portability and Accountability Act (HIPAA) sets regulations about electronic transaction formats and privacy regarding patient information. These regulations can have important impacts on controls needed in the health-care industry.

REVIEW QUESTIONS

Q.1 Why is the Contractual Discount account important to service revenue for a health-care provider? How does the auditor examine the contractual discount transactions and balances?

Q.2 What regulation is important for auditors' consideration when auditing clients in the health-care field, and why?

AUDITING SALES, BILLING, AND COLLECTIONS IN THE RETAIL INDUSTRY

Revenue recognition is generally not a difficult issue in the retail industry because completion of the transaction and payment are usually definite events. However, one area management and the auditor address carefully is the right of return on sales. In order to recognize revenue at the time of sale when the purchaser has a right of return, six criteria must be met (FASB ASC 605-15-25-1). Several of these criteria do not affect retailers who sell to the end consumer, but do affect those sellers whose customers resell the products. These criteria are as follows.

1. The price is fixed or determinable at the date of sale.
2. The buyer has paid (or has to pay) the seller, and this obligation is not contingent on any other events.
3. The seller does not have to do anything significant for the buyer to be able to resell the product.
4. The buyer's obligation to pay the seller would not change if the item were stolen, damaged, or destroyed.
5. The buyer and seller are entities with separate economic substance.
6. The future amount of returns can be reasonably estimated.

The last criterion, the ability to estimate future returns, is usually the most significant one for retailers. It can typically be met if the business has a historical track record upon which the estimate can be based. Information on historical patterns and any new factors should permit the company to estimate and the auditor to analyze expected returns.

Accounts receivable can also be an important area in the audit of a business that sells goods—a wholesaler or a retailer. The volume of accounts receivable may be high. Therefore, management may choose any of a variety of ways to convert them into cash, rather than waiting for them to be collected over the contracted time frame. Receivables may be sold outright or used as collateral for a financing arrangement. The auditor must understand both the transactions the company has entered into and the most recent accounting standards that govern the transaction. The transactions can be complex, including for example off-balance sheet financing, and affiliated financial companies. The appropriate accounting—including disclosures—for these topics is beyond the scope of this book. However, this presents a good example of why auditors must be skilled and knowledgeable accountants, as well as auditors, and must have appropriate knowledge of the industry. The auditor confirms any sales or financing transactions involving accounts receivable.

The auditor can both confirm and analyze those accounts receivables that the company holds at year end. Computer-assisted audit techniques can be a great resource to the auditor because of the high volume. Computer-assisted audit techniques include:

- Clerical testing of the accounts receivable files and resulting general ledger balances
- Identification of irregular and unusual accounts receivable, such as those that are over the credit limit, closed status, high balances, past due accounts, and employee accounts
- Analytical procedures, such as trend analysis of sales and account balances over time, and fluctuations in total sales, credit sales, and accounts receivable balances

Again, because of the likely high volume, the auditor uses computer-assisted audit techniques to analyze the collectibility of accounts receivable. Tests address whether credit was granted and a credit limit assigned to new customers, and whether credit was authorized for specific transactions on established customers. The aged accounts receivable trial balance is recalculated. Accounts that have been written off are identified to determine whether only approved write-offs are recorded. Analytical procedures conducted on accounts receivable include the following:

- Number of days credit sales in accounts receivable
- Turnover
- Aging
- Write-offs as a percentage of credit sales
- Recoveries of accounts written off
- Bad debt expense between comparative periods

Inventory is also important for the retail industry and is usually a material part of the assets on the balance sheet. In performing the overall audit, the auditor must understand the method the company uses for costing or valuing its inventory on the balance sheet. Various forms of the cost or retail method may be used. More important for the audit of the sales, billing, and collection cycle is the cutoff procedure used by the company. Cutoff procedures are followed for physical movement of goods and recording inventory purchases and sales immediately before and after the fiscal year end. For an effective year-end cutoff, the physical movement of goods must match the recording of sales and purchases. Auditing cutoff involves understanding the company's cutoff policies and procedures, and testing and evaluating the company's compliance with its policies.

REVIEW QUESTIONS

R.1 Why are sales returns and allowances activity and balance important when auditing retail entities?

R.2 How are computer-assisted audit techniques likely to be used when auditing accounts receivable of a retail entity?

R.3 What is required to accomplish an effective year-end cutoff for sales and inventory in a retail entity?

CONCLUSION

Revenue cycle processes are important for almost all businesses regardless of the industry. The health-care provider and retailing industries are useful examples to study because sales, billing, and collections are such a significant part of their activities. However, many of the business processes, documents, controls, and audit steps for the revenue cycle are similar across industries. An understanding of the overall model is critical for all auditors.

KEY TERMS

Aged accounts receivable trial balance. Categorizes all balances in the accounts receivable subsidiary ledger based on how long the amount has been outstanding.

Aging schedule. See aged accounts receivable trial balance.

Analytical procedures. Audit steps that gain evidence by investigating relationships among financial and nonfinancial data, typically using aggregated amounts.

Bill of lading. Term referring to a particular type of shipping document.

Capitation agreement. Agreement under which a health-care service provider is paid based on the number of patients covered under the contract rather than the number and nature of treatments provided.

Consignment. Refers to the situation when the entity actually selling inventory does not own it; the seller is providing the sales function on behalf of the owner.

Contractual discount. In the health-care provider industry, refers to the difference between the amount originally posted as receivable for a particular service and the contracted rate for that service with a specific third-party payer.

Co-payment. The part of the payment for health-care services paid for by the individual receiving the service usually at the time and place the service is received.

Credit approval form. Documents a seller's process and conclusion regarding extending credit to a customer.

Credit memo. Document indicating that a credit to a customer has been authorized, typically for a return or an allowance.

Customer order document. Records a customer's desire to purchase goods and triggers the process of credit approval (if needed) and execution of the sale.

Daily remittance list. Document created immediately upon opening mail, listing amounts of individual payments received and the source of the payment.

Design effectiveness of ICFR. Refers to whether ICFR, if it operates as designed, will be effective.

Detective control. Permits employees to find an error or problem in a timely manner during their normal job activities.

Dual purpose tests. Audit procedures that provide evidence on both the operation of a control and the appropriateness of a financial statement amount or disclosure.

External confirmations. Audit procedures in which agreement of outside parties to specific balance amounts, contracts, etc. is received by the auditor.

Fee-for-service contract. Arrangement under which the health-care provider is paid based on the service provided.

Fluctuation analysis. Term used for a substantive procedure comparing a current account balance with that same account's balance in the prior year or budget.

Interim date. Refers to audit procedures performed before the end of the fiscal year.

Lock box system. Payments are sent directly to a seller's bank (or the bank's post office box); receipts are collected and accounted for by the bank, the seller's bank account is updated for receipts and the bank informs the seller of the payment.

Management assertions. Management's messages communicated by financial statements: existence or occurrence, completeness, rights and obligations, valuation or allocation, presentation and disclosure.

Management override. Refers to the situation in which management can or does exercise authority causing internal controls to be ignored or performed incorrectly.

Negative confirmation. Requests a response from the third party only if there is disagreement with the information presented.

Outsourcing. When a company contracts with an outside entity to perform a specific accounting function.

Operating effectiveness of ICFR. Refers to whether ICFR operates as designed.

Pick ticket. A separate document that may be used to authorize the retrieval of goods from the warehouse or other storage function.

Positive confirmation. Requests a response from the third party regardless of agreement or disagreement with the information presented.

Remittance advice. Refers to a document enclosed with payment that provides information such as the name and account number of the payer.

Retail sales businesses. Entities that sell finished goods inventory to the final customer for cash or credit.

Revenue cycle. Broader than a sales and collections cycle; includes all revenue producing activities and related transactions.

Revenue recognition. The language "revenue is recognized" means that revenue is recorded; recognition is appropriate when the income is both earned (the earnings process is complete) and realized (an exchange has taken place).

Sales and collections cycle. The processes associated with providing goods or services and receiving the resulting payment.

Sales order document. Typically created by a selling firm to record a customer's desire to make a purchase, and used to initiate credit approval and the sales process.

Substantive tests. Audit procedures that investigate and provide evidence on the appropriateness of account balances and disclosures.

Tests of controls. Audit procedures that investigate and provide evidence on whether a control functions as described.

Tests of details of balances. Audit procedures that provide evidence on amounts and disclosures of specific accounts.

Third-party payer. As used in the health-care provider industry, refers to parties other than the individual who receives the services, such as insurers and government agencies that pay the provider.

Unfilled order report. Report used to track customer orders that have been received and for which credit has been approved that have not yet been filled and shipped.

Write-off authorization. Documents used to indicate approval for writing off a specific account receivable balance.

MULTIPLE CHOICE

10-1 **[LO3]** A company has a limited number of employees. When one person is absent due to illness, the cash receipts process has insufficient segregation of duties. The company vice president, who is both competent and otherwise independent of the cash receipts function, reconciles the cash accounts on a monthly basis. Which of the following controls is the type provided by the vice president's activity?
  (a) Management   (c) Compensating
  (b) Preventive   (d) Overriding

10-2 **[LO 4]** A retail entity sells its products in a traditional store environment and over the Internet via online transactions. How is this situation best described?
  (a) These two types of sales represent two major classes of transactions.
  (b) Management's financial statement assertions differ for the two types of sales.
  (c) Because of the different processes none of the same ICFR procedures will be effective for both types of transactions.

(d) Preventive controls must be stronger for the online sales transactions than the in-store sales transactions.

10-3 **[LO 3]** When sales employees receive a commission based on the dollar amount of their sales, they may try to increase sales volume by offering credit to customers who are poor credit risks. This ultimately increases bad debts. Which of the following controls will most likely minimize this problem?

(a) Shipping goods only when the proper sales documents are completed.

(b) Requiring that a competent employee independent of the sales function approve all credit before credit sales are completed.

(c) Matching sales prices to preapproved price lists before completing the sales transaction.

(d) Requiring approval by a competent employee independent of the sales function before accounts believed to be uncollectible are written off.

10-4 **[LO 7]** The evidence provided by a standard bank confirmation is limited because

(a) banks receive so many confirmation requests that their responses cannot be relied upon.

(b) time lags between the preparation of the confirmation and the auditor's receipt of the response often make the information outdated.

(c) clients often prevent their banks from responding to confirmation requests because banks charge for providing the service.

(d) banks respond only about the accounts listed on the form and other accounts may also exist.

10-5 **[LO 6]** For which assertion does a confirmation of an account receivable provide the most evidence?

(a) Existence

(b) Valuation

(c) Completeness

(d) Presentation and disclosure

10-6 **[LO 1]** In a retail environment, which of the following control procedures would an auditor test for operating effectiveness to gather evidence regarding the completeness assertion for cash received from cash sales?

(a) All cash from the cash registers is turned in to the central cashier and deposited at the end of each day.

(b) Employees use terminals with locked cash drawers to record each sale, produce a receipt that is provided to the customer at the end of

the sale, and safeguard the cash until it is turned in to the central cashier.

(c) Deposit tickets for cash that is deposited daily is reconciled to daily terminal records of cash sales.

(d) Refunds for sales returns are approved by authorized employees in a central returns department, and cash refunds are dispersed only by the central cashier.

10-7 **[LO 1]** The arrangement that takes place when a health-care provider receives payment based on the specific services is known as a

(a) capitation agreement.

(b) fee-for-service agreement.

(c) co-payment.

(d) private insurance agreement.

10-8 **[LO 1]** A health-care provider verifies the insurance coverage of a patient before providing services. This is parallel to a retail entity performing which of the following steps?

(a) Comparing the price for which an item is sold to a standard price list

(b) Confirming an account receivable

(c) Investigating the creditworthiness of a customer before executing a credit sales transaction

(d) Matching a vendor name to an approved vendor list

10-9 **[LO 2]** Which of the following transactions requires the most judgment for proper revenue recognition?

(a) Sale of a service contract that lasts one year

(b) Sale of a house in a planned community by the developer that will not be completely finished for five years

(c) Sale of retail goods on credit using a bank credit card

(d) Sale of health care provided by doctor under a capitation agreement

10-10 **[LO 4]** Which of the following statements is incorrect?

(a) Tests of controls are used by both management and the auditor.

(b) Tests of controls performed by the auditor impact both the ICFR and financial statement phases of an integrated audit.

(c) Tests of controls will not usually be performed if a control is poorly designed.

(d) Tests of controls involving reperformance of tasks that are not documented provide evidence on operating effectiveness throughout the entire period under audit.

10-11 [LO 5] Inquiry during the audit

(a) often provides sufficient audit evidence regarding the operating effectiveness of a control.

(b) may provide a large part of the audit evidence on control environment aspects of ICFR such as management's philosophy and operating style.

(c) usually replaces document inspection as a test of controls.

(d) can only be used to corroborate information the auditor has already obtained.

10-12 [LO 5] Dual purpose tests

(a) are useful only for determining whether transaction controls are operating effectively.

(b) provide the most audit evidence when they are performed early in the fiscal year.

(c) are useful only for determining whether transactions and account balances are accurate.

(d) may provide the greatest amount of useful audit evidence when performed close to the end of the fiscal year.

10-13 [LO 4] AS 5 emphasizes the importance of efficiency in an integrated audit by

(a) indicating that the planning and evaluation of results of audit procedures affect both the ICFR and financial statement audit.

(b) permitting reliance on ICFR rather than requiring substantive tests of relevant assertions when assessed risk of material financial statement misstatement is low.

(c) requiring the conclusion about ICFR effectiveness at the fiscal year end to dictate the auditor's reliance on ICFR for the financial statement audit.

(d) requiring different samples and sets of client documents be used for each audit objective.

10-14 [LO 5] Which of the following is not true about analytical procedures?

(a) Analytical procedures usually provide the auditor with evidence that is easy to interpret regardless of the client's business activities.

(b) Analytical procedures must be used during audit planning.

(c) Analytical procedures assist the auditor in planning by identifying areas that may require more audit effort.

(d) Analytical procedures depend on plausible relationships among financial and nonfinancial data.

10-15 [LO 5] Which of the following is a substantive audit procedure that provides evidence about the effectiveness of the client's year-end cutoff activities for sales?

(a) Confirming accounts receivable at year end with positive confirmations.

(b) Comparing sales returns and allowances as a percentage of gross sales, by product line, with previous years.

(c) Selecting a sample of sales transactions from the last day of the fiscal year's sales journal and examining the date of the related shipping document.

(d) Selecting a sample of sales invoices and examining for evidence of credit approval prior to the shipping date.

10-16 [LO 7] Which of the following tests is least likely to help determine whether controls are operating effectively, with respect to the recording and depositing of all cash received by the company?

(a) Observing employee processes for restrictively endorsing checks and securing cash and checks immediately upon receipt.

(b) Selecting a sample of daily cash receipts records and tracing the details to the related deposit records.

(c) Performing a surprise count of cash on hand during the day and comparing the amount to the daily cash receipts record that has been prepared.

(d) Tracing the amount of cash confirmed by the bank to the cash journal

10-17 [LO 5] Which of the following analytical procedures is primarily intended to provide audit evidence about over- or understatement of sales?

(a) Comparing number of days that accounts receivable are outstanding with previous years.

(b) Comparing gross margin percentage, by product line, with previous years.

(c) Comparing sales returns and allowances as a percentage of gross sales, by product line, with previous years.

(d) Comparing large individual customer balances that are over a threshold amount with the same customers' balances in previous years.

10-18 **[LO 1]** Accounts receivable requires significant audit effort in the health-care provider industry because

(a) patient records are used as a source of information about services performed.

(b) standard service rates for procedures are used to record revenues and create bills.

(c) contractual payment arrangements are usually complicated and are different for the various third-party payers.

(d) inappropriate calculation of the allowance for doubtful accounts for accounts receivable from individual patients is likely to cause the financial statements to be materially misstated.

10-19 **[LO 1]** The rights assertion as it relates to accounts receivable in the retail industry is an important audit area because

(a) retailers may choose to convert accounts receivable into cash using a variety of sales and financing transactions.

(b) retailers may have a large dollar amount of accounts receivable.

(c) estimating the collectibility of a retailer's accounts receivable is complex.

(d) retailers rarely have historical information that can be used to estimate the future amount of returns.

10-20 **[LO 6]** An auditor receives a response to a positive form account receivable confirmation indicating that the amount on the confirmation is too high. Which of the following actions should the auditor take first?

(a) Search for a clerical error

(b) Search for a payment received on account after the date of the confirmation

(c) Search for sales that occurred after the date of the confirmation

(d) Search for a payment stolen by the accounts receivable clerk

DISCUSSION QUESTIONS

10-21 **[LO 3, 4, 5]** Medco Hospital Buyers Group (MHBG) processes a significant number of intercompany transactions each month, mainly transferring cash between business units to meet the needs of operating cash flows. None of MHBG's intercompany transactions are material on an individual basis. The intercompany transactions only affect balance sheet accounts.

Company policy calls for intercompany accounts to be reconciled each month and for the balances between business units to be confirmed; however, the policy is not followed. The reconciliations are not performed regularly, and when they are performed, not in a timely manner.

Management reviews the financial reports of the various business units and follows up on any large amounts in the intercompany accounts. Management also reviews the operating expenses of each of the business units each month, using variances as an indicator of reasonableness. Management consistently investigates any large intercompany account balances and unusual or large variances that are identified in this monthly review. *(Adapted from AS 2, D1, Scenario A)*

Do you believe the lack of monthly intercompany account reconciliation and confirmation at MHBG is an ICFR deficiency? If you think it is, is it a significant deficiency or a material weakness, and why? *(AS 2, D1, Scenario B)*

10-22 **[LO 1, 5]** Scrubs Unlimited sells surgical scrub apparel and surgical drape materials to hospitals. Typically, an entire package is sold as an individual transaction. Therefore, individual transactions are often material to Scrubs Unlimited. The company has a standard sales contract, but it is often changed by the sales agent negotiating the sale. Consequently, gross margin often varies significantly on different transactions. Sales agents modify payment and delivery terms also, which can affect the appropriate timing and amount of revenue that should be recognized. Management does not approve modifications to sales contracts in advance, and the accounting function does not have a process in place to regularly review sales contracts to identify changes made by the sales staff. *(Adapted from AS 2, D2, Scenario B)*

The auditor believes that the lack of controls over modifying sales contracts and accounting for them constitutes a material weakness. Why?

10-23 **[LO 2]** FlexBandage, Inc., manufactures surgical wraps, which it distributes to hospitals and clinics around the country. FlexBandage uses primarily trade accounts when dealing with its customers and bases its accounts receivable valuation at year end on an aging schedule and prior history of overall collections.

(a) When should FlexBandage recognize revenue from its sales transactions?

(b) What are potential problems auditors need to consider for revenue recognition?

10-24 **[LO 3]** For each of the following situations decide whether proper controls have been implemented. If not, recommend any improvements that can be made.

(a) A catering company prices each job separately based on size, kind of food, and other variables. Currently, the event planner for each account prices the job, places all the necessary orders in advance, and collects payment at the time of the event.

(b) A department store has implemented an electronic system to process and authorize credit card transactions.

(c) A mail order company accepts both checks and credit cards as payment on sales. The checks received through the mail are collected and processed once a week when they are restrictively endorsed, and a remittance list is prepared.

(d) The same mail order company from part c does not release any inventory for shipping until employees have matched the inventory items to be shipped with an approved sales invoice.

(e) The accounting department at Carly Corporation reconciles its books to its bank statements every six months.

10-25 **[LO 1, 3, 4]** Sarah works in a clothing boutique whose return policy requires a manager to authorize any returns or exchanges. While auditing the boutique, you interview Sarah and learn that the weekend manager has given Sarah and several other employees the authorization code to process returns and exchanges so that the register does not get backed up when the store gets busy. As the auditor, would you continue to test this control during your audit? What recommendations would you make to improve this control?

10-26 **[LO 4]** For each of the following, determine which management assertion is addressed by the control. In addition, list a test that an auditor can perform to provide assurance that the control was effective.

(a) All sales orders are matched to shipping documents on a weekly basis to determine whether the orders are being filled in a timely manner and all items that are shipped are billed.

(b) The person who prepares the daily cash deposit is different from the person who reconciles the cash account with the deposit ticket.

(c) Any sale made for a price other than the specified selling price is approved by management.

10-27 **[LO 2, 4, 5]** Your client, Cars Unlimited, Inc., is currently the largest client for the local office of an the audit firm. Cars Unlimited, Inc. is a large car dealership that sells over 15,000 cars a year. You have been on this engagement for three years, but this is your first time as the senior associate. Over the past three years, you have developed a strong friendship with many of the car salesmen who work at the dealership.

During the audit planning process, the engagement manager identifies sales close to year end to be of high risk. The manager assigns you to perform the audit work for this high-risk area. As one step you used computer assisted techniques to compare VINs from the high-risk sales to VINs included in the year-end inventory count.

After comparing the VINs from the sales forms to the VINs included in the year-end inventory counts, you noticed that 10 vehicles that were reported as being sold at year end were still in the lot for the year-end inventory count. The total revenue for these 10 vehicle sales is not above the materiality threshold for the sales account.

After reviewing additional backup, you notice that the salesman was the same for all 10 vehicles. The salesman was Josh, one of the guys that you became friends with over the years. Before alerting anyone on your engagement team, you decide to talk to Josh about the situation and listen to his explanation. During the discussion with Josh, he tells you the following:

- He backdated the retail date for the vehicles to include them in his previous month's sales figure, without the knowledge of the dealership.
- His reason was so that he could reach the required sales figure and receive a bonus.
- He did it because his son was sick and he needed the money to provide his son with medical care. He ended the conversation by saying, "Please don't inform the company of this issue because I will lose my job and have to pay back the bonus that I don't have. My son is still very ill and I need this job to pay for the medical bills."

Identify the ethical issues in the above situation. How would you handle your dilemma?

PROBLEMS

10-28 [LO 5] For each of the following problems, provide an audit procedure that would have identified the problem.

(a) The allowance for doubtful accounts estimated by management is too small.

(b) Cash received in payment of an account receivable is deposited in the bank in the current period but is not posted to the accounts receivable record, trial balance, or general ledger until the subsequent period.

(c) For a month, sales are transacted using an outdated price list with amounts that are too low. The transactions are recorded accurately based on the price list used. Management is not aware the problem occurred.

(d) Cash for the exact amounts of sales are regularly pocketed by employees and not recorded on the sales terminal. Customers do not ask for receipts.

(e) Management records false sales close to year end and posts them as accounts receivable.

(f) Sales on account *for services* that take place in the first two days of the subsequent year are posted in the current year.

10-29 [LO 4, 5] You are responsible for performing substantive analytical procedures on services revenue for MDCosmetics, a company that employs and provides administrative services (billing, collections, supplies purchasing, etc.) for a group of plastic surgeons in the Orange County area of California. MDCosmetics is a public company, and this is the third year your audit firm has performed the audit. You have information on sales revenue, sales discounts (mostly for special promotions), cash, and accounts receivable. Others on your audit team have finished the audit of cash, accounts receivable, and payroll and have not found any major problems with either ICFR or accounts and disclosures. The results of the other audit work are available to you. You also have schedules related to operating room use time both in the doctor's private offices and at hospitals, as well as information on the number and pay grades of support staff who participated in the scheduled surgeries. Although your firm has conducted the audit previously, in prior years sales have been audited only as the result of the accounts receivable and cash collections audit.

Draft the analytical procedures that you would include in the audit program for sales.

10-30 **[LO 2, 5]** Your client, General Clinic is a small outpatient care clinic that provides a wide range of health-care services. Patients must provide the clinic with a valid form of identification and a current insurance card upon arrival. Before a patient receives services, the clinic must verify that the insurance is current and the individual is covered on the plan.

On New Year's Eve, an individual arrives at General Clinic with burns from a fireworks accident. Although the situation is not considered a medical emergency, the patient is uncomfortable enough that he does not want to fill out forms. He convinces the receptionist that he will fill out all the paperwork later and that he has valid insurance. The receptionist decides that the individual seems believable and processes the patient without checking the insurance but does receive a valid form of identification. After the patient receives medical services related to the fireworks accident, the receptionist asks him to complete all the necessary forms and provide a current insurance card. At that time, the individual informs the receptionist that he does not have his insurance card with him, but he will bring it to the hospital the next day. On January 2, the patient brings a copy of his current insurance card and the hospital verifies that the services he received are covered by his plan.

Use the criteria in FASB Statement of Financial Accounting Concepts No.5 and indicate when the client should recognize the revenue. Assume the company has a calendar year end. Explain your answer. In addition, what controls are in place, and how would you audit these controls?

10-31 **[LO 2, 5]** Nile.com is an online retailer of electronics, music, books, DVDs, and a variety of other consumer goods. All sales are made on the basis of FOB Destination Prepaid; the shipping costs are paid by the customer. During the last week of the year, Nile.com had a large year-end sale of all merchandise on the site. The company provided a guarantee that all orders would be shipped by the end of the year. During that week Nile.com had sales orders totaling $5.8 million, which was equal to 23% of total sales for the year before the sale. As the company promised, all the orders were shipped on December 31. At this time, all the money was collected, and no products for these orders were in the control of the company. The customers received their orders within five days of shipment.

Use the criteria in FASB Statement of Financial Accounting Concepts No.5 and indicate when and/or how the client should recognize the revenue. Assume the company has a calendar year end. Explain your answer. What controls are in place and how would you audit these controls?

10-32 **[LO 1, 3, 5]** You are on an engagement to provide an integrated audit on the financial statements of Carson's Orthopedic Shoes. This company is a small-size online retailer that sells custom shoes to the public. All orders are processed, packaged, and shipped by company employees at a small warehouse.

At the beginning of the audit engagement, the company provided your senior with the process diagram related to the shipping process. After reviewing the diagram, you have identified two "omissions" in the diagram. First, the diagram does not identify how the shipping department receives the signal to ship the product. Second, the diagram indicates that no invoice is included with the shipped shoes.

You are assigned by your senior to conduct inquiries of the shipping process. Prepare a list of questions that will provide you with an understanding of the controls that are in place. In addition, what documentation would you ask management for?

10-33 **[LO 4]** Understanding the management assertions related to a specific control is an important factor in preparing the tests of controls. Using the assertions provided below, select the management assertion(s) that relates to the purpose of the controls in the table. (A management assertion may be selected once, more than once, or not at all.)

Management Assertions

(a) Existence or occurrence

(b) Completeness

(c) Rights and obligations

(d) Valuation or allocation

(e) Presentation and disclosure

(f) Authorization

(g) Cutoff

Purpose of Control	Management Assertion
To ensure that credit is approved before a sale is executed and service is provided or goods are shipped	
To ensure that transactions shown as sales are properly classified	
To ensure that when cash receipts are recorded they show cash that was actually received by the company and deposited	
To ensure that cash receipts transactions are properly posted to the accounts receivable subsidiary ledger and general ledger	
To ensure that all cash received by the company is deposited and recorded in the cash receipts journal and that amounts and details, including the date, are shown correctly	
To ensure that sales transactions are recorded based on the correct dates	

10-34 **[LO 5]** Over the year, the Jackson Sports Supplies Company received multiple complaints from customers that their payments were incorrectly posted. While the total amount of payments received equaled the customers' total payments, the amounts were broken up in multiple entries at different dates. In addition, the company was experiencing cash flow problems at the end of the year. Management concluded that they had a problem in the billing and collection process. The Jackson Sports Supplies Company hired you to perform an examination of the billing and collection process to determine any deficiencies that exist in the process.

After studying the billing and collection process, you make the following conclusions:

1. A lack of segregation of duties exists in the accounts receivable department; only two bookkeepers perform all of the duties in the billing and collection process.

2. The receptionist is assigned to open the incoming mail but regularly just gives the mail to the bookkeepers unopened.

3. The main responsibilities of bookkeeper A are to:
   - receive payments that come in the mail
   - prepare a daily remittance list of all payments received
   - deposit receipts

4. The main responsibilities of bookkeeper B are to:
   - record receipts in the cash receipts journal
   - post payment's in individual customers' accounts and the general ledger accounts
5. In addition, you were told that bookkeeper A is regularly out of the office for business and personal reasons. On these days, bookkeeper B is responsible for performing bookkeeper A's duties.
6. Since there is a lack of segregation of duties and the company received complaints from customers of errors in their statements, you suspect that the bookkeeper may be performing an embezzlement scheme called lapping. Lapping occurs when the bookkeeper conceals the cash shortage by delaying the posting of cash remittances.

Required:
Describe why a lapping scheme is expected. List the audit procedures that you should perform to decide whether lapping exists in Jackson Sports Supply Company.

10-35 **[LO 4, 5]** Denice Williams, CPA, is the in-charge auditor for Midwest Health Solutions, Inc. She requested an aging analysis of accounts receivable as of 12/31/11, the company's year end. Following is the information she received.

Categories	Amount	Estimated Uncollectible
Current	$3,000,000	1%
1–30 days past due	2,000,000	2%
31–60 days past due	1,000,000	5%
61–90 days past due	500,000	10%
Over 90 days past due	1,750,000	25%

The controller for Midwest said that the same percentages have been used throughout his tenure with the organization (approximately 10 years). He also indicates that the current balance in the allowance for uncollectible accounts is $190,000, which is adequate in light of successful collection efforts for the 61–90 day and the over–90-day categories.

Required:
(a) Explain why it is important for the auditor to address the adequacy of the allowance for uncollectible accounts.
(b) What procedures should Denice apply to determine whether the allowance is adequate?
(c) Show an example of an analysis estimate that she might prepare, and discuss how you would use this to convince the controller that an adjustment is necessary.

10-36 **[LO 3]** You are the auditor for Johnson Products, a medical supply company. The company ships wholesale products to clinics and hospitals and some retail products to drug stores.
When flowcharting the revenue cycle, you discover the following information:
- All sales are made on open account via 1/10, net/30 credit terms, unless arrangements are okayed by credit manager approval. Credit terms were last evaluated 10 years ago.
- Inventory is maintained in real-time via computer.
- Official prices can be updated as needed by product managers or the sales vice president.
- Regional managers can override official prices.
- New customers require credit approval by the regional sales manager.
- Once a line of credit is established, a monthly credit report is generated to compare customer credit lines with outstanding balances to identify instances where credit has been exceeded. In those cases, a halt is placed on further sales.

Required:

What are the internal control weaknesses you identify? What problems could these cause, and what suggestions would you make to correct them?

10-37 **[LO 7]** Daniel Martin, CPA is the auditor for HMO Health Systems. He requests that the client's bank statement ending at the company's fiscal year end be sent directly to him at his CPA office. In tracing reconciling items to the fiscal year end bank statement, he lists the following:

1. A deposit in transit (dated 12/31/10) cleared the bank on 01/10/11.

2. Checks 1812, 1813, 1814, and 1815 recorded as of 12/31/10 did not clear the bank until 01/19/11, 01/20/11, 01/21/11, and 01/22/11, respectively.

3. An outstanding check payable to T. Simpson was endorsed by HMO's controller.

Required:

What possible errors or fraudulent activity is associated with each of these items? Explain whether any audit adjustments are necessary.

10-38 **[LO 5]** You are conducting an audit of the financial statements of Medical Complex Rentals, Inc. for the year ending March 31, 2010. You are assigned to examine the annual rent reconciliation (below) prepared by the controller of the company.

Medical Complex Rentals, Inc.
Rent Reconciliation
For the Year Ended March 31, 2010

Gross Office Rentals (Schedule 1)	$2,300,000 (a)
Less Vacancies (Schedule 2)	100,000 (b)
Net Office Rentals	$2,200,000
Less Unpaid Rents (Schedule 3)	25,000 (c)
Subtotal	$2,175,000
Add prepaid rent collected (Schedule 4)	15,000 (d)
Total cash collected	$2,190,000 (e)

Required:

The controller has provided you with Schedules 1–4 (not shown). You find that the internal controls can be relied upon and that the cash receipts for rentals are deposited in a special bank account. Based on this, what audit procedures would you use to substantiate each of the balances labeled (a through e)?

10-39 [LO 2] You are auditing Riverview Medical Center for its fiscal year ending December 31, 2010. During your tests of account balances you noted the following:

1. The November revenue journal indicates that patients were billed $150,000, and this amount was posted as a debit to accounts receivable and a credit to revenues. In fact, the footing of the journal shows that the correct amount of patient billings was $155,500.

2. You prepared a bank reconciliation at year end and found that an $8,000 check had been omitted from the list of outstanding checks. The check had been issued and recorded during October but had not yet cleared the bank.

Required:

Based on your brainstorming about possible frauds, what could these items indicate about an attempted concealment?

10-40 **[LO 1, 3, 4, 5]** You are auditing Seaside Hospital and Medical Complex. You complete a walkthrough with the help of Seaside's controller. The following comments relative to cash receipts are outlined in your memo describing Seaside's accounting procedures.

1. Cash receipts are sent directly to the accounts receivable clerk, with no processing by the mail department. The accounts receivable clerk keeps a cash receipts journal, prepares the bank deposit slip in duplicate, posts from the deposit slip to the subsidiary accounts receivable ledger, and mails the deposit to the bank within two days.

2. The controller validates the deposit slips directly (unopened) from the bank, also receives the monthly bank statements directly, and promptly reconciles the account.

3. At the end of the month the accounts receivable clerk notifies the general ledger clerk of the monthly totals of cash receipts for posting.

4. Each month, the general ledger clerk makes debit entries to record Cash from sources other than cash receipts from patients (i.e., borrowed funds).

Required:

List at least three problems indicated. For each, identify one audit procedure to investigate the problem, the reason for the audit procedure, and a recommendation that Seaside should implement. Use the following table to organize your answers.

Problem	Audit Procedure	Reason for the Procedure	Recommendation
1.			
2.			
3.			

ACTIVITY ASSIGNMENTS

10-41 Go to the Web site for *Mednax, Inc.* at *www.mednax.com.* Click through the menu tabs for investors, SEC filings, and 10K.

(a) Explain what *Mednax* does. Who works for *Mednax?*

(b) Explain its billing, collection, and reimbursement activities, as described by *Mednax.*

(c) Who are the third-party payers for *Mednax?*

(d) Read Item 1A, Risk Factors. Identify risks that you believe are directly related to ICFR. How could a material weakness in ICFR cause any of these risks to affect the financial statements?

(e) Search the 10K document for disclosures on revenue recognition and contractual allowances. How does the company determine what to record? What will the auditor need to investigate or test? Propose appropriate audit procedures.

10-42 Go to the Web site for *Best Buy* at *www.bestbuy.com.* Scroll to the bottom and select "For our Investors." Select SEC filings and the most recent 10K. Find Note 1 to the financial statements, "Summary of Significant Accounting Policies." For (a), (b), and (c) below, explain in your own words:

- The company's revenue recognition policies
- How the company determines what to record
- What the auditor will need to investigate or test
- Steps the auditor might use to perform the investigation of
    (a) Sales returns
    (b) Gift cards
    (c) Sales incentives

10-43 Access the SEC case of Serologicals Corporation, Inc. at *http://www.sec.gov/litigation/admin/34-45852.htm.*

Required:

(a) Briefly describe the way that Serologicals Corporation improperly recognized revenue with its largest clients.

(b) While the practice of bill and hold is not fraudulent, what are some of the criteria that Serologicals violated using this method?

(c) Search for a footnote from another company that lists its policy for bill and hold transactions that comply with GAAP and summarize its criteria (typically found under revenue recognition).

PROFESSIONAL SIMULATIONS

Go to the book's companion Web site at www.wiley.com/college/hooks to find simulations similar to those on the computerized CPA exam.

ACL

An exercise requiring the use of ACL software is available on the Auditing and Assurances Web site at www.wiley.com/college/hooks.

Completing the Integrated Audit and Reporting

1. Learn the various topics and steps addressed in the final phase of an integrated audit, including the integrated nature of the various procedures and their impacts on both the ICFR and financial statement audits.

2. Identify the circumstances in which unqualified and other audit reports are appropriate for ICFR and financial statement audits.

3. Recognize the content and language of audit reports, including the different forms used for different situations.

Chapter 11 Resources

AICPA ET 203, *Accounting Principles*

AU 316, AICPA, PCAOB, *Consideration of Fraud in a Financial Statement Audit*

AU 318, AICPA, *Performing Audit Procedures in Response to Assessed Risks and Evaluating the Audit Evidence Obtained*

AU 326, AICPA, *Audit Evidence*

AU 326, PCAOB, *Evidential Matter*

AU 329, AICPA, PCAOB, *Analytical Procedures*

AU 333, AICPA, PCAOB, *Management Representations*

AU 334, AICPA, PCAOB, *Related Parties*

AU 337, AICPA, PCAOB, *Inquiry of a Client's Lawyer Concerning Litigation, Claims and Assessments*

AU 339, AICPA, *Audit Documentation*

AU 341, AICPA, PCAOB, *The Auditor's Consideration of an Entity's Ability to Continue as a Going Concern*

AU 342, AICPA, PCAOB, *Auditing Accounting Estimates*

AU 380, AICPA, *The Auditor's Communication with Those Charged with Governance*

AU 380, PCAOB, *Communications with Audit Committees*

AU 390, AICPA, PCAOB, *Consideration of Omitted Procedures after the Report Date*

AU 410, AICPA, PCAOB, *Adherence to Generally Accepted Accounting Principles*

AU 411, AICPA, PCAOB, *The Meaning of Present Fairly in Conformity with Generally Accepted Accounting Principles*

AU 420, AICPA, *Consistency of Application of Generally Accepted Accounting Principles*

AU 431, AICPA, PCAOB, *Adequacy of Disclosure in Financial Statements*

AU 504, AICPA, PCAOB, *Association with Financial Statements*

AU 508, AICPA, PCAOB, *Reports on Audited Financial Statements*

AU 530, AICPA, PCAOB, *Dating of the Independent Auditor's Report*

AU 543, AICPA, PCAOB, *Part of the Audit Performed by Other Independent Auditors*

AU 550, AICPA, PCAOB, *Other Information in Documents Containing Audited Financial Statements*

AU 551, AICPA, PCAOB, *Reporting on Information Accompanying the Basic Financial Statements in Auditor-Submitted Documents*

AU 552, AICPA, PCAOB, *Reporting on Condensed Financial Statements and Selected Financial Data*

AU 560, AICPA, PCAOB, *Subsequent Events*

AU 561, AICPA, PCAOB, *Subsequent Discovery of Facts Existing at the Date of the Auditor's Report*

AU 623, AICPA, PCAOB, *Special Reports*

AU 722, AICPA, PCAOB, *Interim Financial Information*

FASB ASC 250–10, *Accounting Changes and Error Corrections*

FASB ASC 450–10, Contingencies

FASB ASC 850–10, Related Party Disclosures

FASB ASC 855–10, *Subsequent Events*

PCAOB AS 1, *References in Auditors' Reports to the Standards of the Public Company Accounting Oversight Board*

PCAOB AS 3, *Audit Documentation*

PCAOB AS 5, *An Audit of Internal Control Over Financial Reporting That is Integrated with an Audit of Financial Statements*

PCAOB AS 6, *Evaluating Consistency of Financial Statements*

PCAOB AS 7, *Engagement Quality Review*

Sarbanes-Oxley Act of 2002

SEC Staff Accounting Bulletin 99, *Materiality*

INTRODUCTION

The final steps of an integrated audit are procedures to complete the ICFR and financial statement audits and issue the audit opinions. At this stage the auditor considers findings from both the ICFR and financial statement audit activities. The findings from each audit must be considered in light of potential impact on the other audit. The final audit steps, such as required reviews and communications, address both the ICFR and financial statement audits together. Exhibit 11-1 is the audit overview of a complete integrated audit that was shown in Chapter 2. As a reminder, preliminary engagement procedures, and planning and risk assessment are integrated steps affecting both the ICFR and financial statement audits. Then, the auditor performs tests of the operating effectiveness of controls and substantive procedures. To whatever extent possible, evidence obtained from testing procedures is used for both the ICFR and financial statement audits. After the testing stage, the auditor addresses both ICFR and the financial statement audit in an integrated fashion to complete the audit.

The audit reporting process requires decisions leading to the appropriate audit opinions for the both the ICFR and financial statement audits. The reporting process may be straightforward when no additional language is needed. However, many circumstances require changes to the language of audit reports. This chapter presents considerations for selecting the proper report and examples of changes to standard reporting language.

EXHIBIT 11-1

Overview of an
Integrated Audit

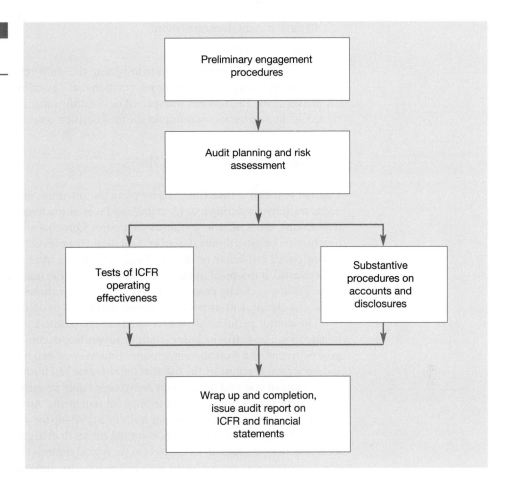

FINAL AUDIT PROCEDURES [LO 1]

The final audit procedures take place after the auditor has completed tests of controls, tests of details of balances, and substantive analytical procedures. At this stage the auditor has discussed with management any problems with ICFR that were identified before the fiscal year end. Management has implemented any improvements to ICFR that are both desired and possible. If material financial statement misstatements were identified during substantive tests and analytical procedures, the auditor has discussed these with management. Management has recorded any adjusting journal entries needed. Typically, at this stage the auditor has formed tentative conclusions regarding appropriate audit opinions for ICFR and the financial statements.

Wrap-up audit procedures include the following:

Audit of unusual year-end transactions

Audit of contingent liabilities and commitments

Inquiry of a client's lawyer

Obtaining management's written representations

Subsequent events review

Going concern evaluation

Consideration of other published information

Auditing other financial statements and financial statement disclosures

Communications

Final review

Review of audit documentation

Engagement quality review

Final audit steps are completed prior to issuing the audit report. These procedures may uncover unexpected information, or information that disconfirms audit evidence from earlier phases of the audit. When unexpected or disconfirming information arises, it is investigated by the auditor and may impact the final decision on the appropriate audit opinions.

Unusual Year-End Transactions

Unusual year-end transactions receive particular attention during final audit steps. Many audits use software during tests of controls and substantive tests to identify large and atypical transactions, and transactions with related parties. Consequently, many of these transactions have been investigated during the earlier audit steps. However, other large and nonroutine transactions posted just before or after the fiscal year may be identified. If so, they are examined and evaluated at this point in the audit. Any journal entries made outside the routine general ledger posting or closing processes are important. This includes consolidating entries, entries made after closing, and entries made during the process of drafting the financial statements.

The auditor performs steps to understand the business purposes of unusual year-end transactions. These steps include examining supporting documentation, speaking with company personnel, and recalculating amounts. Unusual year-end transactions receive significant auditor scrutiny because of the risk that they have no real business purpose. One possibility is that unusual year-end transactions are recorded only because management wants to alter the financial results presented in the financial statements. Another possibility is that what appears as an unusual transaction may really be a cover-up for wrongdoing such as illegal acts or fraud. Another source of risk is that journal entries drafted and posted outside the routine for transaction processes are not subject to the typical controls that the auditor has examined. This lack of normal control creates possibilities for error and other misstatement.

AUDITING IN ACTION

Baptist Foundation of Arizona

The story of the Baptist Foundation of Arizona (BFA) includes significant and unusual year-end transactions with outside entities. Baptist Foundation of Arizona originated as a not-for-profit entity with a religious purpose and religious exemptions. It entered into the real estate market at a time when the market was booming, purchasing real estate assets that later dropped in value. ALO and New Church Ventures, though not owned by Baptist Foundation of Arizona, were entities that fit the accounting definition of related parties as a result of overlapping directorships and common interests. Baptist Foundation of Arizona provided services to ALO and New Church Ventures since neither of these entities had any employees. Consequently, ALO and New Church Ventures both owed money to Baptist Foundation of Arizona for services received. The following diagram shows the relationships of the major entities involved.

To abide by its conditions of operations Baptist Foundation of Arizona had to remain self-supporting. Moreover, because it performed functions as a "passive trustee" for individual retirement accounts (IRAs), it had to meet minimum net worth requirements.

Overpriced and nonperforming real estate investments that were originally on the books of Baptist Foundation of Arizona should have been written down or written off. Instead, Baptist Foundation of Arizona sold them to ALO. As a result of these sales, many of the real estate investments that were collateral related to the IRA accounts held by Baptist Foundation of Arizona were owned by ALO.

New Church Ventures flowed cash into ALO by selling investment contracts and securities that were backed by mortgages on real estate that were on the books of ALO. Many of the New Church Ventures investment-contract customers were churchgoers who bought the investments from New Church Ventures because Baptist Foundation of Arizona encouraged the purchases.

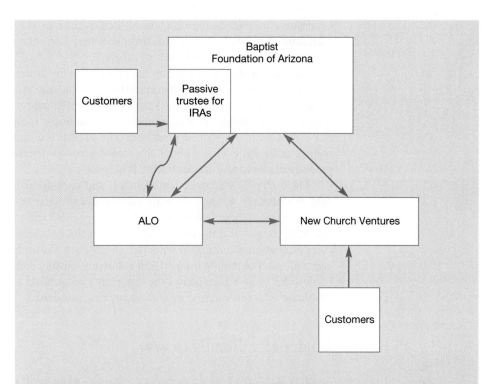

The investments and mortgage-backed securities to which these investment contracts were related were non-performing. They were the same overvalued securities ALO had previously purchased from Baptist Foundation of Arizona.

Using this basic Baptist Foundation of Arizona–ALO–New Church Ventures structure, various transactions, many occurring shortly before the fiscal year end, were used to perpetuate the appearance that Baptist Foundation of Arizona was a sound entity meeting all of its requirements. The year-end **related party transactions** that allowed BFA to avoid reporting a decrease in net assets for four consecutive years involved real estate sales, gifts, pledges, and charitable contributions.

The customers who bought the investment contracts from New Church Ventures and depositors who placed their individual retirement account funds with Baptist Foundation of Arizona were all misled. The related party relationship among Baptist Foundation of Arizona, ALO, and New Church Ventures accommodated non-arms-length year-end transactions that kept the fraudulent financial reporting of Baptist Foundation of Arizona appearing sound.

Contingent Liabilities and Commitments

A **contingent liability** is a payment or future use of assets for which a company *may* become obligated as a result of conditions existing at the current time. Sometimes whether the liability will exist is unknown, and typically, the amount of the ultimate liability is uncertain. For example, a company may have lost a court case resulting in a judgment. The judgment requires the company to pay a certain fee or penalty. But the company is appealing the court outcome. Not only is the ultimate amount that the company may have to pay uncertain, but whether the company will have to pay anything at all is unknown. The FASB Standard on accounting for contingencies defines the various probabilities of occurrence and the proper accounting for each type of contingency.

The auditor addresses contingent liabilities in final audit procedures. The procedures are intended to determine whether the auditor is aware of all contingent liabilities. Based on the audit evidence available, the auditor must judge whether the company has accounted for contingent liabilities according to the applicable accounting standards.

Common contingencies are litigation, such as used in the preceding example, income taxes, and warranty liabilities. Contingencies may also exist related to letters of credit or guaranties made for the liabilities of others.

Commitments are agreements a company has for future actions, such as to purchase inventory or execute leases. The commitment action and amount are specific and known. However, the action will occur in the future. Consequently, no transaction has yet been recorded. Even though no accounting entry is made, for most commitment situations the accounting standards require disclosure. The auditor is concerned about obtaining information and audit evidence about all commitments to determine whether they have been properly disclosed and accounted for, if necessary.

The auditor investigates commitments and contingent liabilities during the audit of debt. For example, when confirming information with banks, the auditor includes requests for information about letters of credit. The communication between the company's outside legal counsel and the auditor, discussed in the next section, requests information on commitments and contingent liabilities. In addition, the auditor makes inquiries of management. After obtaining information about any existing commitments or contingent liabilities, the auditor investigates the company's accounting and disclosures to determine whether they are in conformity with accounting standards.

Inquiry of a Client's Lawyer

Auditing standards provide guidance for **inquiry of an audit client's outside legal counsel** regarding "litigation, claims, and assessments" (AU 337). The purpose of the audit step is to determine whether all liabilities and contingent liabilities have been handled as required by accounting standards.

In the auditing standards, *litigation* refers to a legal action involving the audit client. **Claims** refers to possible obligations of the client that are being asserted by another party. **Assessments** are obligations of the client for which dollar amounts owed have already been set. The term **unasserted claim** refers to a situation in which another party may believe it can expect payment or compensation from the client. However, the claim is still "unasserted" because the other party has not yet taken any action.

A simple example of an unasserted claim is when a customer of a retail store slips while shopping and is injured because of some physical hazard left in the store aisle by an employee. If the customer is still at the hospital having the injury treated, the customer has not yet made a claim against the retail store. The customer has an unasserted claim against the store for the damages resulting from the accident.

The audit client is responsible for having a process in place for litigation, claims, and assessments. The process must be appropriate to identify, properly account for, and disclose these events. The auditor is responsible for obtaining audit evidence about

- The existence of litigation, claims, and assessments
- The period in which the causal event occurred
- The probability of an outcome resulting in a liability
- An estimate of the possible loss

The auditor obtains evidence on litigation, claims, and assessments by communicating with management and the company's outside attorney. Exhibit 11-2 lists typical audit procedures for litigation, claims, and assessments.

To obtain adequate audit evidence on litigation, claims, and assessments, the auditor must receive a letter from the client's outside legal counsel. The client company requests that the attorney provide the letter directly to the auditor. In its request the client company asks that the lawyer provide information, and the lawyer's response need only address those items that are material to the financial statements. Also, the lawyer need only respond on matters that he or she "has given substantive attention in the form of legal consultation or representation" (AU 337.12).

EXHIBIT 11-2

Audit Procedures
Addressing Litigation,
Claims and
Assessments

Ask and discuss with management its policies for identifying and accounting for litigation, claims, and assessments.

Obtain documentation from management listing all litigation, claims and assessments at year end and in the period of time since year end.

Obtain documentation from management regarding all matters referred to legal counsel.

Obtain written assurance from management that it has disclosed all matters as required by the accounting standards, including any unasserted claims that legal counsel has advised will probably be asserted.

Examine client correspondence with lawyers, invoices from lawyers and any other supporting documents that concern litigation, claims and assessments.

Read minutes of meetings of stockholders, directors, and other committees that have been held during and after the period being audited.

Read contracts, loan agreements, leases, correspondence from tax and other government authorities.

Obtain information on guarantees when confirming bank accounts.

Inspect other documents that may provide information on guarantees made by the client.

(AU 337.05–06)

If the client's outside legal counsel will not provide a response on litigation, claims, or assessments, or will not respond to all the matters in the inquiry, the lack of response causes a scope limitation in the audit. When a scope limitation exists, the auditor cannot issue an unqualified opinion.

Another possibility exists if the lawyer responds regarding the matters in the client's inquiry, but is not able to provide a conclusion on the *likelihood* of an unfavorable outcome on litigation, claims, or assessments. When this happens, the auditor considers whether the client's accounting and disclosure are appropriate. The auditor considers whether the matter is an uncertainty of such importance that it precludes the auditor from issuing an unqualified audit opinion. Exhibit 11-3 lists the contents of the inquiry letter sent to a client's lawyer.

EXHIBIT 11-3

Content of a Letter of
Inquiry to a Client's
Lawyer

1. Identification of the company, including subsidiaries, and the date of the audit
2. A list prepared by management, or a request by management that the lawyer prepare a list, that describes and evaluates pending or threatened litigation, claims and assessments (that the lawyer has been involved with on behalf of the company)

   For each item—

   a. A description of the nature of the matter, progress of the case and action the company intends to take

   b. An evaluation of the likelihood of an unfavorable outcome and an estimate, if one can be made, of the amount or range of potential loss

   c. An identification of any omission in the list (if prepared by management) of any pending or threatened litigation, claims and assessments, or a statement that management's list is complete
3. A list prepared by management that describes and evaluates unasserted claims and assessments that management considers to be probable of assertion, and that, if asserted would have at least a reasonable possibility of an unfavorable outcome (that the lawyer has been involved with on behalf of the company). A request that the lawyer comment on each item as to whether his or her views differ from those stated by management.
4. A statement that the client understands that in the course of providing legal services, the lawyer has the professional responsibility to discuss with the client when a matter is an unasserted claim that may require financial statement disclosure. A request that the lawyer confirm the accuracy of this statement.
5. A request that the lawyer specifically identify the nature and reason for any limitation on his or her response.

(*Source:* AU 337.09)

AUDITING IN ACTION

Sample Attorney's Letter

Closer Enterprises
8807 Roberts Road
Anytown, Anystate 90210

March 14, 20X0

To: Repeat Runner
    Smart and Smarter
    PO Box 1234
    Anytown, Anystate 90211

In connection with an audit of our financial statements at December 31, 20X9, and for the year then ended, management of Closer Enterprises has prepared and furnished to Michael and Michelle, CPAs, PO Box 5678, Anytown, Anystate, 90211, a description and evaluation of certain contingencies, including those set forth below involving matters with respect to which you have been engaged and to which you have devoted substantive attention on behalf of Closer Enterprises in the form of legal consultation or representation. These are regarded by the management of Closer Enterprises as material for this purpose. Your response should include matters that existed at December 31, 20X9, and during the period from that date to the date of your response.

Add a description of pending or threatened litigation.

Please furnish to our auditors such explanation, if any, that you consider necessary to supplement the foregoing information, including an explanation of those matters as to which your views may differ from those stated and an identification of the omission of any pending or threatened litigation, claims, and assessments or a statement that the list of such matters is complete.

Add a description of unasserted claims and assessments.

Please furnish to our auditors such explanation, if any, that you consider necessary to supplement the foregoing information, including an explanation of those matters as to which your views may differ from those stated.

We understand that whenever, in the course of performing legal services for us with respect to a matter recognized to involve an unasserted possible claim or assessment that may call for financial statement disclosure, if you have formed a professional conclusion that we should disclose or consider disclosure concerning such possible claim or assessment, as a matter of professional responsibility to us, you will so advise us and will consult with us concerning the question of such disclosure and the applicable requirements. Please specifically confirm to our auditors that our understanding is correct.

Please specifically identify the nature of and reasons for any limitation on your response.

Yours truly,

Brutus Lindsey

Chief Executive Officer, Closer Enterprises

(Adapted from AU 337A)

REVIEW QUESTIONS

A.1 What types of transactions and entries are considered unusual year-end entries? Why does the auditor pay particular attention to them?

A.2 What is a contingent liability? A commitment? A claim? An unasserted claim? What is the auditor's primary concern regarding commitments and contingencies?

A.3 Why does the auditor want a response from the client's attorney as part of audit evidence?

Management's Written Representations

The auditor must obtain written representations from management on items related to ICFR, the financial statements and the audit engagement. PCAOB AS 5, "An Audit of Internal Control Over Financial Reporting That is Integrated with An Audit of Financial Statements," provides specific guidance on management's representations for an ICFR audit. AU 333 provides parallel guidance for a financial statement audit.

The auditor relies on information provided by management for many conclusions made during the audit. The **management representations letter**, as the document is often called, is intended to establish that management understands the importance of its communications and emphasize the auditor's reliance on them. For an integrated audit, the client may include required written representations for both the ICFR and financial statement audits in one document.

AUDITING IN ACTION

Sample of Financial Statement Audit Written Representations

March 14, 20X0

To: Michael and Michelle, CPAs

We are providing this letter in connection with your audit of the balance sheet, income statement and statement of cash flows of Closer Enterprises as of December 31, 20X9 and for the year ended December 31, 20X9 for the purpose of expressing an opinion as to whether the consolidated financial statements present fairly, in all material respects, the financial position, results of operations, and cash flows of Closer Enterprises in conformity with accounting principles generally accepted in the United States of America. We confirm that we are responsible for the fair presentation in the consolidated financial statements of financial position, results of operations, and cash flows in conformity with generally accepted accounting principles.

Certain representations in this letter are described as being limited to matters that are material. Items are considered material, regardless of size, if they involve an omission or misstatement of accounting information that, in the light of surrounding circumstances, makes it probable that the judgment of a reasonable person relying on the information would be changed or influenced by the omission or misstatement.

We confirm, to the best of our knowledge and belief, March 14, 20X0, the following representations made to you during your audit.

1. The financial statements referred to above are fairly presented in conformity with accounting principles generally accepted in the United States of America.
2. We have made available to you all—
    a. Financial records and related data.
    b. Minutes of the meetings of stockholders, directors, and committees of directors, or summaries of actions of recent meetings for which minutes have not yet been prepared.
3. There have been no communications from regulatory agencies concerning noncompliance with or deficiencies in financial reporting practices.
4. There are no material transactions that have not been properly recorded in the accounting records underlying the financial statements.
5. We believe that the effects of the uncorrected financial statement misstatements summarized in the accompanying schedule are immaterial, both individually and in the aggregate, to the financial statements taken as a whole.
6. We acknowledge our responsibility for the design and implementation of programs and controls to prevent and detect fraud.
7. We have no knowledge of any fraud or suspected fraud affecting the entity involving—
    a. Management,
    b. Employees who have significant roles in internal control, or
    c. Others where the fraud could have a material effect on the financial statements.

(continued)

8. We have no knowledge of any allegations of fraud or suspected fraud affecting the entity received in communications from employees, former employees, analysts, regulators, short sellers, or others.

9. The company has no plans or intentions that may materially affect the carrying value or classification of assets and liabilities.

10. The following have been properly recorded or disclosed in the financial statements:

    a. Related-party transactions, including sales, purchases, loans, transfers, leasing arrangements, and guarantees, and amounts receivable from or payable to related parties.

    b. Guarantees, whether written or oral, under which the company is contingently liable.

    c. Significant estimates and material concentrations known to management that are required to be disclosed. [Significant estimates are estimates at the balance sheet date that could change materially within the next year. Concentrations refer to volumes of business, revenues, available sources of supply, or markets or geographic areas for which events could occur that would significantly disrupt normal finances within the next year.]

11. There are no—

    a. Violations or possible violations of laws or regulations whose effects should be considered for disclosure in the financial statements or as a basis for recording a loss contingency.

    b. Unasserted claims or assessments that our lawyer has advised us are probable of assertion and must be disclosed in accordance with accounting standards.

    c. Other liabilities or gain or loss contingencies that are required to be accrued or disclosed.

12. The company has satisfactory title to all owned assets, and there are no liens or encumbrances on such assets nor has any asset been pledged as collateral.

13. The company has complied with all aspects of contractual agreements that would have a material effect on the financial statements in the event of noncompliance.

To the best of our knowledge and belief, no events have occurred subsequent to the balance-sheet date and through the date of this letter that would require adjustment to or disclosure in the aforementioned financial statements.

[Brutus Lindsey, Chief Executive Officer, Closer Enterprises]

[Kandi Luke, Chief Financial Officer, Closer Enterprises]

A management representations letter is required and adds to the body of evidence on which the auditor relies. A management representations letter does not substitute for other evidence. Sometimes when limited other audit evidence is available for a particular item or activity, the auditor may ask management for written representations on that issue. If management's representations conflict with other evidence, the auditor investigates further. Since management integrity is a critical component of ICFR, any concerns that result from conflicts about management's representations may have a significant impact on the overall audit conclusions.

A **scope limitation** exists if the auditor is unable to obtain a written management representations letter for any reason, including a refusal on the part of management. As with other scope limitations, AS 5 states that if the auditor is not able to obtain written management representations for an integrated audit, the only options are to:

1. issue a report indicating that an opinion cannot be provided, or
2. withdraw from the engagement.

If the auditor is performing only a financial statement audit for a nonpublic company, lack of written management representations will typically cause the auditor to follow the same course of action as in an integrated audit. However, under certain circumstances the auditor may issue a financial statement audit report for a nonpublic company that still provides an opinion but is modified for the scope limitation.

AUDITING IN ACTION

Special Management Representations at Qwest

Qwest is a name that became familiar to the public along with Enron, WorldCom, and Global Crossing because of the drama associated with its corporate failure. Qwest started as a company focused on building a fiber-optic network across the United States. As a result of increasing competition it switched directions to become a communications services provider. Qwest violated numerous accounting principles that directed how it was supposed to report for sales and revenue of its fiber-optic line capacity. Qwest's auditor, Arthur Andersen, learned that the company had improperly applied accounting principles. Instead of obtaining objective evidence, the auditor relied on management representations that past problems had been fixed and correct accounting procedures were being used. Upon investigation, the SEC called this audit approach unreasonable reliance on management's representations (A.A.E.R. No. 2220, pp. 3–4).

Management addresses its written representations to the auditor and dates them as of the same date as the auditor's report. The date of the audit report is after the client's fiscal year end and coincides with completion of the audit. The audit report date signifies when the auditor has obtained enough knowledge for a final audit opinion. The written management representations are not dated as of the financial statement date because the auditor is also concerned about management's representations regarding events that occurred after the fiscal year end and while the audit was in process.

The chief executive officer (CEO) and chief financial officer (CFO), or the individuals in the company with positions equivalent to CEO and CFO, typically sign the management representations letter. Exhibit 11-4 lists the components of **management's written representations** for an ICFR audit specified in AS 5. Exhibit 11-5 lists the components of management's written representations for a financial statement audit provided in AU 333.

EXHIBIT 11-4

Management's Representations for an ICFR Audit

In an audit of internal control over financial reporting, the auditor should obtain written representations from management—

a. Acknowledging management's responsibility for establishing and maintaining effective internal control over financial reporting;

b. Stating that management has performed an evaluation and made an assessment of the effectiveness of the company's internal control over financial reporting and specifying the control criteria;

c. Stating that management did not use the auditor's procedures performed during the audits of internal control over financial reporting or the financial statements as part of the basis for management's assessment of the effectiveness of internal control over financial reporting;

d. Stating management's conclusion, as set forth in its assessment, about the effectiveness of the company's internal control over financial reporting based on the control criteria as of a specified date;

e. Stating that management has disclosed to the auditor all deficiencies in the design or operation of internal control over financial reporting identified as part of management's evaluation, including separately disclosing to the auditor all such deficiencies that it believes to be significant deficiencies or material weaknesses in internal control over financial reporting;

f. Describing any fraud resulting in a material misstatement to the company's financial statements and any other fraud that does not result in a material misstatement to the company's financial statements but involves senior management or management or other employees who have a significant role in the company's internal control over financial reporting;

g. Stating whether control deficiencies identified and communicated to the audit committee during previous engagements have been resolved, and specifically identifying any that have not; and

(continued)

h. Stating whether there were, subsequent to the date being reported on, any changes in internal control over financial reporting or other factors that might significantly affect internal control over financial reporting, including any corrective actions taken by management with regard to significant deficiencies and material weaknesses. (AS 5.75)

EXHIBIT 11-5

Management's Representations in a Financial Statement Audit

In connection with an audit of financial statements presented in accordance with generally accepted accounting principles, specific representations should relate to the following matters:

Financial Statements

a. Management's acknowledgment of its responsibility for the fair presentation in the financial statements of financial position, results of operations, and cash flows in conformity with generally accepted accounting principles.

b. Management's belief that the financial statements are fairly presented in conformity with generally accepted accounting principles.

Completeness of Information

c. Availability of all financial records and related data.

d. Completeness and availability of all minutes of meetings of stockholders, directors, and committees of directors.

e. Communications from regulatory agencies concerning noncompliance with or deficiencies in financial reporting practices.

f. Absence of unrecorded transactions.

Recognition, Measurement, and Disclosure

g. Management's belief that the effects of any uncorrected financial statement misstatements aggregated by the auditor during the current engagement and pertaining to the latest period presented are immaterial, both individually and in the aggregate, to the financial statements taken as a whole. (A summary of such items should be included in or attached to the letter.)

h. Management's acknowledgment of its responsibility for the design and implementation of programs and controls to prevent and detect fraud.

i. Knowledge of fraud or suspected fraud affecting the entity involving

1. management,

2. employees who have significant roles in internal control, or

3. others where the fraud could have a material effect on the financial statements.

j. Knowledge of any allegations of fraud or suspected fraud affecting the entity received in communications from employees, former employees, analysts, regulators, short sellers, or others.

k. Plans or intentions that may affect the carrying value or classification of assets or liabilities.

l. Information concerning related-party transactions and amounts receivable from or payable to related parties.

m. Guarantees, whether written or oral, under which the entity is contingently liable.

n. Significant estimates and material concentrations known to management that are required to be disclosed in accordance with the accounting standards.

o. Violations or possible violations of laws or regulations whose effects should be considered for disclosure in the financial statements or as a basis for recording a loss contingency.

p. Unasserted claims or assessments that the entity's lawyer has advised are probable of assertion and must be disclosed.

q. Other liabilities and gain or loss contingencies that are required to be accrued or disclosed.

> **r.** Satisfactory title to assets, liens or encumbrances on assets, and assets pledged as collateral.
>
> **s.** Compliance with aspects of contractual agreements that may affect the financial statements.
>
> *Subsequent Events*
>
> **t.** Information concerning subsequent events. (AU 333.06)

Subsequent Events Review

The auditor performs audit procedures during the period of time between the fiscal year end and the date of the audit report to obtain (1) newly available information on past events and conditions, and (2) information on events that occur during this time frame.[1] Some events that occur after the fiscal year end may still be important to the financial statements and audit report because of accounting and disclosure rules. In addition to events affecting the financial statements, changes in ICFR that occur after the end of the fiscal year may need to be disclosed by management and in the auditor's ICFR opinion. A *subsequent events review* describes the audit procedures directed to the post-fiscal-year-end information, changes, and events. Discovering information after year end that is relevant to the prior year's financial statements or changes in ICFR is learning of a **subsequent event**.

For the audit of the financial statements, subsequent events fall into two classifications. The first type of subsequent event refers to more information surfacing about an event that occurred during the fiscal year being audited on a condition that existed as of the balance sheet date. This is called a *recognized* or Type I subsequent event.

Consider the situation in which, at year end, a company knows that it will owe a monetary judgment as the outcome of litigation. However, at the balance sheet date the company does not know the amount that will be assessed and therefore must estimate the liability. Between the balance sheet date and the time the audit is completed, the judge handling the litigation makes a decision and the company finds out the exact amount owed. In this situation the "condition"—which in this case is the liability resulting from the legal judgment—existed at the balance sheet date, but the amount was unknown and had to be estimated. More information is now available before the audit is completed and the financial statements are released. Management uses the newly available information when preparing the financial statements. The auditor includes assessing that information as part of the audit.

The second type of subsequent event is one that occurs after the financial statement date but before the date of the audit report. This is called a *nonrecognized* or Type II subsequent event. Since the condition did not occur or exist during the period of the financial statements, the financial statements are not adjusted for the information. However, some events that occur between the financial statement date and the date the financial statements are issued (or, for a nonpublic company, available to be issued) are so important that they are disclosed in the financial statements. Examples of these types of subsequent events are:

1. Sale of a bond or capital stock issue
2. Purchase of a business
3. Settlement of litigation when the event giving rise to the claim took place subsequent to the balance sheet date
4. Loss of plant or inventories as a result of fire or flood
5. Losses on receivables resulting from conditions (such as a customer's major casualty) arising subsequent to the balance sheet date (AU 560.06)

---

[1] In addition, as a result of FASB codification 855-10, subsequent events refers to events or transactions that occur after the balance sheet date, but before the financial statements are issued for public companies. For nonpublic companies the term refers to events and transactions that occur after the balance sheet date but before the financial statements are *available* to be issued.

EXHIBIT 11-6

Financial Statement
Subsequent Events

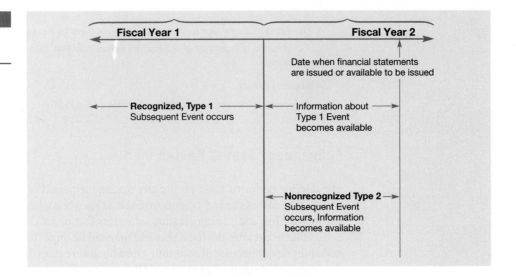

Sometimes the auditor highlights this type of subsequent event in the audit report. If management fails to include necessary disclosure about a nonrecognized, Type II subsequent event, the financial statements are not in compliance with generally accepted accounting principles. Exhibit 11-6 displays a timeline diagram for financial statement subsequent events.

Subsequent events are also important to an ICFR audit. Recall that management's assessment and the auditor's opinion on ICFR are as of the fiscal year end. The audit report is dated as of the date the audit is finished. The auditor may "obtain(s) knowledge about subsequent events that materially and adversely affect the effectiveness of the company's internal control over financial reporting" (AS 5.96) between management's assessment date (the fiscal year end) and the audit report date. If the condition existed as of the end of the fiscal year, the auditor considers that information and issues an adverse opinion on ICFR. Adverse opinions on ICFR are discussed later in this chapter. If the auditor obtains knowledge about subsequent events indicating ICFR is not effective, but the condition occurred after the end of the fiscal year, the auditor adds a paragraph to the audit report explaining the subsequent event. Exhibit 11-7 summarizes subsequent events and their consequences for both the financial statement and ICFR audits.

The subsequent events audit procedures are addressed in the guidance for both ICFR and financial statement audits. To obtain information about subsequent events that may affect ICFR, the auditor makes inquiries of management and obtains written management representations. The auditor reviews reports generated within the company during the time between the balance sheet date and the audit report date, such as those produced by the internal audit function. The auditor also reviews any reports of other auditors and regulatory agencies produced during the subsequent events period.

Audit procedures focused on financial statement subsequent events are conducted close to the end of the audit and include the steps listed in Exhibit 11-8. Reading the minutes of meetings of stockholders, directors, and other committees (Exhibit 11-8, Item g) is an audit procedure used for learning about subsequent events. This step is also a standard part of wrap-up audit procedures. It provides information on any of the company's activities or developments that are sufficiently important to be addressed by the stockholders, directors, or committees of the Board of Directors.

EXHIBIT 11-7

Subsequent Events

Before Fiscal Year End	During the Audit	Financial Statement Audit Impact
Event occurred or condition existed before the fiscal year end that should be reflected in the financial statements.	After fiscal year-end, information (or more information) is obtained about the event or condition.	**Recognized, Type 1:** Financial statements reflect the event. Any impact on the audit report is determined by the auditor.
	Material event occurs or condition exists after the fiscal year under audit but before the completion of the audit engagement. Condition or event will be reflected in the financial statements of the fiscal year end in which it occurs.	**Nonrecognized, Type 2:** Financial statements may require disclosure. Audit report may highlight the subsequent event.
At Fiscal Year End		**ICFR Audit Impact**
ICFR material weakness exists.	An event occurs after the fiscal year end but during the audit and information is obtained revealing that a material weakness existed at fiscal year end.	**Adverse audit opinion on ICFR**
	ICFR material weakness is determined to exist after the fiscal year end. (ICFR material weakness did NOT exist at fiscal year end.)	**Audit opinion includes a paragraph describing subsequent event**

New Information after the Date of the Audit Report

The auditing standards address two situations that occur after the date of the audit report. Recall that the term *subsequent events* refers to occurrences or information that become known before the financial statements are issued or available to be issued. Situations that occur after the release of the financial statements and audit report receive different treatment from subsequent events. After the financial statements and audit reports have already been released into the public domain, the actions available to the audit client and auditor are more limited than before the release date.

The first situation occurs when the auditor learns something after the audit report is released that might have changed the audit report had the auditor known of the information earlier. In this situation the auditor discusses the situation with management and tries to perform whatever procedures are needed to determine whether the audit report is invalid. If the audit report becomes invalid because of the new information, the auditor has to decide what other action may be appropriate.

The second situation occurs when, after the audit report is released, the auditor becomes aware that an audit step was omitted. Financial statement audit guidance states that when upon discovery of an **omitted audit procedure** the auditor considers the impact of the omission on the audit engagement and audit report (AU 390). The auditor does not have a responsibility to review the audit after the audit report has been issued. But he or she might become aware that an audit step was omitted as a result of a quality-related review or an inspection. The same general concept applies to an ICFR audit if an auditor realizes that either an audit step has been omitted or the audit documentation is not sufficient.

a. Read the latest available interim financial statements; compare them with the financial statements being reported on; make any other comparisons deemed appropriate.

b. Inquire of management whether the interim statements being examined and compared have been prepared on the same basis as that used for the statements under audit.

c. Inquire of management whether any substantial contingent liabilities or commitments existed at the balance sheet date or at the current date.

d. Inquire of management whether there was any significant change in the capital stock, long-term debt or working capital up to the current date.

e. Inquire of management about the current status of items that were accounted for in the financial statements based on tentative, preliminary or inconclusive data.

f. Inquire of management whether any unusual adjustments were made during the period from the balance-sheet date to the current date.

g. Read the minutes of meetings of stockholders, directors and appropriate committees; inquire about matters dealt with at meetings for which minutes are not available.

h. Inquire of the client's legal counsel concerning litigation, claims and assessment.

i. Obtain a letter of representations… as to whether any events have occurred subsequent to the date of the financial statements that would require adjustment or disclosure to the statements.

(AU 560.12)

If a long period of time has passed since the audit report date, the auditor may determine that no action needs to be taken regarding an omitted audit step. This typically occurs when there is no indication that the audit report would have changed because of the omitted step. In contrast, regardless of the time that has elapsed since the audit report was issued, the auditor may not be confident that the audit report is valid. When a procedure was omitted and the auditor knows that the audit report is still being relied upon, more work is appropriate. The auditor should attempt to apply the omitted procedures. Actions after that depend on whether the auditor is able to perform the omitted procedure and the results when it is performed.

In either the case of information discovered after the report release or discovery of an omitted audit step, the auditor may decide to perform additional audit procedures. The results of additional procedures may indicate that the audit report is still appropriate and thus no action is needed.

Alternatively, the auditor may decide that the audit report should no longer be relied upon. When the audit report should not be relied upon, the auditor's next steps are the same whether the improper audit report resulted from an omitted step or from unknown information that has now surfaced. The auditor informs the client. The client should take steps to make appropriate disclosures to those who may be relying on the financial statements and audit reports. If the auditor is not satisfied that the client has made appropriate disclosures, the auditor informs possible users and regulatory agencies (AU 561). The SEC requires an 8K filing for public companies in the event the financial statements and audit report are no longer to be relied upon. Filing an 8K is an effective means of quickly disseminating information about financial statements and an audit report that should no longer be relied upon.

The discussion in this chapter thus far indicates that the following audit procedures are important in the wrap-up phase of the audit:

Making inquiry of management

Obtaining information from the company's outside lawyer

Obtaining written representations from management

Reading the minutes of stockholder, director, and committee meetings

These steps provide the auditor with information about unusual transactions, commitments and contingencies, and subsequent events. They also play a significant role in the auditor's consideration of a company's going concern status.

Going Concern

The auditor must evaluate whether an audit client will continue as a **going concern** for a reasonable period of time. The audit standards define the time period as not longer than one year after the financial statement date. Although the audit may not initially include specific steps targeted at the entity's going concern status, the auditor is aware of the possibility of going concern issues, especially when performing the following:

> Confirmation procedures
> Audit of debt
> Reading minutes
> Performing analytical procedures
> Reviewing subsequent events
> Evaluating communications from the company's attorneys

Based on these and other steps, the auditor may determine that there is substantial doubt about an entity's ability to continue as a going concern. When this occurs, the auditor performs specific audit procedures to address going concern. First, the auditor considers any plans management has to deal with the going concern issue. After considering management's plans and the likelihood that they will be effectively implemented, the auditor may still conclude that there is substantial doubt about the entity's ability to continue as a going concern. In that case, the auditor assesses the adequacy of the disclosure in the financial statements and modifies the audit report.

If financial statement disclosure on the going concern problem is inadequate, the auditor concludes that a substantial doubt exists concerning the company's ability to continue as a going concern *and* that disclosure in the financial statements is inappropriate. In this situation the auditor modifies the audit report by adding explanatory language for the going concern doubt. This explanatory language is included in the later discussion in the chapter on audit reports. When the auditor concludes that the company's financial statements do not adequately disclose the extent of the substantial doubt about the entity's ability to continue as a going concern, the audit report is *also* modified for the inadequate disclosure. The effect of inadequate disclosure on the audit report is also discussed later in this chapter.

AUDITING IN ACTION

Financial Statement Disclosures Related to Going Concern

> Pertinent conditions and events causing substantial doubt about the entity's ability to continue as a going concern
> The possible effects of the conditions and events
> Management's evaluation of the conditions and events and factors that may offset or mitigate their significance
> Operations that may be discontinued
> Management's plans related to dealing with the going concern situation
> Information about assets and liabilities that may be affected by the going concern situation, including asset value and classification of assets and liabilities

AUDITING IN ACTION

General Motors Corporation, Form 10K, Notes to the Financial Statements, 12/31/08

Note 2. Basis of Presentation

Going Concern

The accompanying consolidated financial statements have been prepared assuming that we will continue as a going concern, which contemplates the realization of assets and the liquidation of liabilities in the normal course of business. We have incurred significant losses from 2005 through 2008, attributable to operations and to restructurings and other charges such as support for Delphi and past, present and future cost cutting measures. We have managed our liquidity during this time through a series of cost reduction initiatives, capital markets transactions and sales of assets. However, the global credit market crisis has had a dramatic effect on our industry … Our liquidity position, as well as our operating performance, were negatively affected by these economic and industry conditions and by other financial and business factors, many of which are beyond our control. These conditions have not improved through January 2009. … the lowest level for January since 1982. We do not believe it is likely that these adverse economic conditions, and their effect on the automotive industry, will improve significantly during 2009, notwithstanding the unprecedented intervention by governments in the United States and other countries in the global banking and financial systems.

Due to this sudden and rapid decline of our industry and sales, particularly in the three months ended December 31, 2008, we determined that, despite the far reaching actions to restructure our U.S. business, we would be unable to pay our obligations in the normal course of business in 2009 or service our debt in a timely fashion, which required the development of a new plan that depended on financial assistance from the U.S. Government. …

The following is a summary of significant cost reduction and restructuring actions contemplated by the Viability Plan:

U.S. Brands and Nameplates. …
Dealers. …
Labor Cost. …
Asset Sales. …

We are also currently engaged in negotiations with advisors to the unofficial committee of the unsecured bondholders to reduce our public unsecured debt by not less than two-thirds through an exchange of the bonds to equity or other appropriate means. …

In addition to the request for additional funding from the UST included in our Viability Plan, the success of our Viability Plan is conditioned on financial support from non-U.S. governments. …

Our ability to continue as a going concern is dependent on many events outside of our direct control. … Our significant recent operating losses and negative cash flows, negative working capital, stockholders' deficit and the uncertainty of UST approval of the Viability Plan, the UST funding of the Viability Plan and successful execution of our Viability Plan, among other factors, raise substantial doubt as to our ability to continue as a going concern. The accompanying consolidated financial statements do not include any adjustments that might result from the outcome of this uncertainty.

AUDITING IN ACTION

Going-Concern Disclosure The Bombay Company Inc. Form 10Q, For the Quarterly Period Ended May 5, 2007

Liquidity and Capital Resources

We have historically financed our operations through operating cash flow, proceeds of public offerings of common stock and asset sales, and on a seasonal basis, through working capital credit facilities. Over the recent past, we have made substantial investments of capital to address expiring leases and invest in technology and supply chain infrastructure. For the past three fiscal years, we have experienced cumulative operating losses and during Fiscal 2006 had negative net cash flows from operations. Operating losses continue through the first quarter of Fiscal 2007. All of these factors have reduced our cash balances and working capital from historical levels and increased the outstanding borrowings under our credit facility, *raising substantial doubt about the Company's ability to continue as a going concern.* (emphasis added)

As of May 5, 2007, the Company had $3.8 million in cash and cash equivalents, $36.6 million of working capital, $78.6 million in outstanding debt under our existing credit facility and $27.9 million of availability under the credit facility for additional borrowings or letters of credit. During Fiscal 2006, we undertook a number of measures to reduce expenses and improve liquidity, including reducing corporate headcount, commencing the exit of the dedicated BombayKIDS business, reducing advertising expenditures and entering into our new credit facility. Management has identified a series of additional activities that it believes will be critical to achieving the Company's long-term goals, including reducing inventory levels and returning to historical levels of inventory turnover, closing selected underperforming stores, and enhancing the merchandise assortment, allocation and presentation. The Company's plan contemplates incurring additional operating losses during Fiscal 2007.

During Fiscal 2006, the Board of Directors engaged William Blair & Company, an investment banking firm, to seek investment or other strategic alternatives. In April 2007, a confidential descriptive memorandum was distributed to potentially interested investors, and the Company is aggressively pursuing options. The process is progressing, and in May 2007, the Board of Directors received non-binding offers to purchase the Company. Such offers are subject to material conditions including substantial due diligence. While the Board is encouraged by these offers, there is no assurance that these offers will ultimately lead to a transaction.

In May 2007, the Company entered into an agreement for a new $10 million, secured term loan facility with a fund managed by GB Merchant Partners, LLC. The facility is coterminous with the Company's existing $125 million secured revolving credit facility with GE Commercial Finance. The new facility will provide incremental liquidity to fund working capital requirements and other corporate needs. See Note 7 to the Consolidated Financial Statements for additional information.

REVIEW QUESTIONS

B.1 What happens when management does not provide a representations letter? How does it affect the audit?

B.2 In general, what types of information are included in management's written representations?

B.3 What is the purpose of obtaining management's representations? What impact does the management representations letter have on other audit steps that need to be performed?

B.4 What are the two types of subsequent events that affect a financial statement audit? What subsequent events affect an ICFR audit? How does each of these impact the audit findings?

B.5 What is substantial doubt about going concern? How is the audit report modified when the auditor concludes there is substantial doubt about an entity's ability to continue as a going concern? When there is substantial doubt about going concern and financial statement disclosure is not adequate?

Other Published Information

Various audit steps may be appropriate if a company produces financial information other than or in addition to the basic financial statements. For example, sometimes companies choose to produce other financial or nonfinancial information and may request the auditor's evaluation of the information. Some companies are required to provide audited information in greater detail than is included in the typical financial statements because they receive funds from a federal grant. Sometimes companies present information in condensed form that is based on the audited financial statements. These situations require the auditor to consider whether PCAOB, SEC, AICPA, government, or some other set of standards apply.

A common situation for public companies is for a company to include the financial statements and audit report in a document that also includes other information, such as an annual report. When this occurs, the auditor reads the document containing the audited financial statements and audit report. As a result of the original SAS requiring this step, auditors still sometimes refer to the procedures as a SAS 8 review.

For practical purposes, the auditor reads and reviews the draft form of the client's complete document before it is finalized. This allows for the resolution of any auditor concerns. The client's finished document and the audited financial statements must be in at least a draft form before this step can be completed. Therefore, the step is performed during the wrap-up phase of the audit. The auditor looks for inconsistencies between the other information included in the document and the audited information (AU 550).

If the auditor identifies any information in the client-prepared document that is materially inconsistent with the audited information, further steps are needed. The auditor first investigates whether the inconsistency results from a problem with the audited financial statements or the other information included in the document. If the problem is with the audited financial statements, the auditor performs additional procedures directed toward investigating the problem. The auditor informs the company of the need to revise the financial statements.

If the material inconsistency reflects a problem with the other information, the auditor asks the client to revise the other information. If the client does not revise the other information, the auditor considers whether the audit report should include an explanatory paragraph regarding the inconsistency. The auditor may withhold the audit report or **withdraw** from the engagement.

Sometimes the auditor concludes that the other information includes an important statement that is factually incorrect. In other words, upon reading the document the auditor finds that it includes a material misstatement of fact, even though the misstatement does not appear as an inconsistency with the audited financial information. In this case the auditor discusses the issue with the client and may need to consult with legal counsel.

Based on SOX, managements of public companies are required to include in their SEC filings reports that are known as Section 302 certifications. As a reminder, Section 302 of SOX requires management to certify, by signing a report:

- that its interim and annual filings do not contain untrue information,
- that management is responsible for the company's ICFR,
- whether ICFR is effective, and
- that it has disclosed any important deficiencies in ICFR and frauds to the auditor.

AS 5 requires action from auditors when they believe there are problems with Section 302 certifications.

An auditor who concludes that management's report is not appropriate and needs to be changed reports this conclusion to management and the Board of Directors. If management and the Board of Directors do not take appropriate action, the auditor may need to modify the audit report. Guidance from AS 5 is as follows.

> If matters come to the auditor's attention as a result of the audit of internal control over financial reporting that lead him or her to believe that modifications to the disclosures about changes in internal control over financial reporting (addressing changes in internal control over financial reporting occurring during the fourth quarter) are necessary for the annual certifications to be accurate and to comply with the requirements of Section 302 of the Act and Securities Exchange Act, ... the auditor should follow the communication responsibilities as described in AU sec. 722 *Interim Financial Information,* for any interim period. However, if management and the audit committee do not respond appropriately, in addition... the auditor should modify his or her report on the audit of internal control over financial reporting to include an explanatory paragraph describing the reasons the auditor believes management's disclosures should be modified.
>
> (AS 5, C15)

Other Financial Statements and Financial Statement Disclosures

The auditor considers proper financial statement disclosure throughout the various audit procedures for both the ICFR and financial statement audits. At the wrap-up phase, the auditor performs an overall review of the client's financial statement disclosures to determine whether they are adequate. This disclosure review requires knowledge of the various accounts and activities of the client, as well as the disclosures required by accounting standards.

The auditor often uses a checklist to verify that all the disclosure requirements are met. A checklist also provides a mechanism for the auditor to document performance of the disclosure review. To audit disclosures, the auditor refers back to the work paper documentation resulting from earlier audit work, a procedure usually called tracing

The audit of disclosure accomplishes two goals. First, it evaluates the appropriateness of financial statement disclosures. Second, it establishes that the financial statement information is consistent with the audit evidence included in the work papers.

Similar to the tracing step between the financial statements and work papers when auditing financial statement disclosures, the auditor also traces back and forth when auditing the Statement of Cash Flows, Statement of Changes in Shareholder's Equity, and consolidation process. If a company prepares consolidated financial statements, the auditor traces information, examines documents prepared by the client, and recalculates amounts. Earlier audit steps examine the underlying information used by the audit client to consolidate the financial statements and prepare the Statement of Cash Flows and Statement of Changes in Stockholders' Equity. The goal of the audit step is to determine whether the financial statements are drafted properly, consistent with the information already audited and properly presented.

AUDITING IN ACTION

Auditing Financial Statement Disclosures

SAMPLE PARTIAL FINANCIAL STATEMENT DISCLOSURE CHECKLIST
SEC Registrants (Form 10-K)

Client :
Year End :
Statements Examined :

Cash and Cash Items:

	Yes	Workpaper Reference	N/A
1. Segregate cash or cash items that are legally restricted as to withdrawal or use. Cash restricted for use in acquisition or construction of a fixed asset may need to be presented as a noncurrent asset.			
2. Classify separately any legally restricted balances as current or noncurrent based on terms of borrowing arrangements and/or the classification of any related borrowings.			
3. Describe in a note the provisions of any restrictions. Restrictions may include:			
(a) Legally restricted compensating balances.			
(b) Contracts entered into with others.			
(c) Company statements of intention about particular deposits.			
4. Compensating balances:			
(a) If compensating balance arrangements do not legally restrict the use of cash, describe in a note these arrangements and the amounts involved, if determinable, for the most recent balance sheet.			
(b) Disclose compensating balances maintained to assure future credit availability (unused lines of credit), along with the amount and terms of the agreement.			
(c) Disclose compensating balances maintained for the benefit of affiliates, officers, directors, principal stockholders, or related parties.			
(d) Disclose deposits maintained by persons in (c) above on behalf of the entity.			
(e) For legally restricted compensating balances, disclose the agreed-upon collected balance at the bank before "float" adjustment relative to borrowings outstanding.			

	Yes	Workpaper Reference	N/A
(f) Disclose if the company was not in compilance with compensating balance requirements during the year, at balance sheet date, or to the opinion date, and possible or pending material sanctions for noncompliance under the compensating balance agreement.			
(g) Disclose arrangements which require compensating balances during the year which are materially greater than at year end.			
5. Disclose funds recently acquired subject to repayment on call immediately after the end of the period, usually on a short-term note payable.			
6. Segregate or disclose time deposits, including certificates of deposit.			
7. Cash overdrafts should be classified as a separate current liability (do not group with accounts payable).			
8. Netting of book overdrafts against positive cash book balances is not acceptable unless all of the following conditions are met:			
(a) Each of the two parties owes the other determinable amounts.			
(b) The reporting party has the right to set off the amount owed with the amount owed by the other party.			
(c) The reporting party intends to set off.			
(d) The right of set off is enforceable at law.			
9. Entities that lend to or finance the activities of others should disclose:			
Restrictions on the use or availability of certain cash balances, such as deposits with Federal Reserve Banks, Federal Home Loan Banks, or correspondent financial institutions to meet reserve requirements or deposits under formal compensating balance agreements.			
10. Reciprocal balances and related overdrafts— reciprocal balances (balances due from the same institution from which the financial institution accepts deposits) should be offset if they will be offset in the process of collection or payment. Overdrafts of such accounts should be reclassified as liabilities unless the financial institution has other accounts at the same financial institution against which such overdraft can be offset.			

AUDITING IN ACTION

Auditing the Statement of Cash Flows

STATEMENT OF CASH FLOWS WORKSHEET, FOR THE YEAR ENDED 12/31/XX

		Cash & Equiv.	Restricted Cash	Prepaid Insurance	Tenant A/R	Deferred Charges NET	PP & E Net	Note payable	A/P and Accruals	Partners' Capital	Balance
BALANCE	(PY) 31-Dec-xx										
BALANCE	(FS) 31-Dec-xx										
NET CHANGE-DR (CR)		0	0	0	0	0	0	0	0	0	0
CASH FLOW FROM OPERATING ACTIVITIES:											
NET INCOME	(FS) 0										
Depreciation & Amortization	0	0									
Bad Debt Expense	0	0									
Changes in operating assets & liabilities		0									
Restricted cash	0	0	0								
Prepaid insurance	0	0		0							
Tenant A/R and other	0	0									
A/P and accrued liabilities	0	0									
TOTAL ADJUSTMENTS	0	0	0	0	0	0	0	0	0	0	0
NET CASH PROVIDED (USED) BY OPER. ACT	0	0	0	0	0	0	0	0	0	0	0
CASH FLOW FROM INVESTING ACTIVITIES:	(RC)										
Additions to B & I	0	0									
Additions to deferred charges	0	0									
Capital Combinations	0	0									
NET CASH PROVIDED (USED) BY INVEST. ACT	0	0	0	0	0	0	0	0	0	0	0
CASH FLOW FROM FINANCING ACTIVITIES:	(RC)										
Contributions from Partners	0	0	0								
Distributions to Partners	0	0	0								
Repayment of debt	0	0	0								
		0	0								
		0	0								
NET CASH PROVIDED (USED) BY FIN. ACTIVITIES	0	0	0	0	0	0	0	0	0	0	0
NET CHANGE IN CASH	0	0	0	0	0	0	0	0	0	0	0
	0 (RC) 0	0	0	0	0	0	0	0	0	0

Noncash transactions
interest paid

PY - Amounts traced and agreed to prior-year financial statements
FS - Amounts traced and agreed to current-year financial statements
RC - Recalculated

REVIEW QUESTIONS

C.1 What audit procedures does the auditor perform when the audited financial statements and audit report are included in a document that contains other information? What is the auditor looking for?

C.2 What is the auditor's responsibility related to the client's SOX Section 302 certifications?

C.3 What steps are appropriate to audit other financial statements and financial statement disclosures?

Communications

Both PCAOB and AICPA standards require various communications from the auditor to those involved with governance of the audit client. PCAOB standards require certain communications to the Board of Directors, others to the audit committee, and still others to management. In a nonpublic company various individuals may fit the definition of being responsible for governance of the entity. Consequently, in a nonpublic company various parties may be the recipients of auditor communications. Information included in the required communications, such as the division of responsibilities between the auditor and management and the planned scope and timing of the audit, may be communicated through the engagement letter.

SOX, Section 204, specifically requires communications to audit committees. SOX requires the auditor to communicate to the audit committee:

The company's critical accounting policies and practices

Different acceptable accounting treatments for a company's transactions that the auditor has discussed with management—along with the auditor's preference in treatment

Other communications that the auditor has made to management

AUDITING IN ACTION

SOX Requirement for Communications with Audit Committees

SEC. 204. AUDITOR REPORTS TO AUDIT COMMITTEES.

Section 10A of the Securities Exchange Act of 1934 (15 U.S.C. 78j–1), as amended by this Act, is amended by adding at the end the following:

"(k) REPORTS TO AUDIT COMMITTEES.—Each registered public accounting firm that performs for any issuer any audit required by this title shall timely report to the audit committee of the issuer—

"(1) all critical accounting policies and practices to be used;

"(2) all alternative treatments of financial information within generally accepted accounting principles that have been discussed with management officials of the issuer, ramifications of the use of such alternative disclosures and treatments, and the treatment preferred by the registered public accounting firm; and

"(3) other material written communications between the registered public accounting firm and the management of the issuer, such as any management letter or schedule of unadjusted differences."

AS 5 also establishes communication requirements for auditors. If the auditor concludes that the audit committee provides ineffective oversight of the company's external financial reporting and ICFR, AS 5 requires the auditor to communicate this conclusion to the Board of Directors. AS 5 requires the auditor to communicate to the audit committee and management all material weaknesses in ICFR identified during the audit. This communication about material weaknesses must be in writing and must occur before the auditor issues the ICFR audit opinion.

In addition to information about material weaknesses, the auditor must inform the audit committee about all significant deficiencies. In addition, the auditor must inform management about *all* deficiencies—regardless of whether they reach the level of significant deficiencies or material weaknesses. The auditor also informs the audit committee that the communication to management has occurred. Required communications about ICFR deficiencies are summarized in Exhibit 11-9.

If the auditor identifies a material weakness during the ICFR audit and management's report of its assessment of ICFR does not include the material weakness, the auditor communicates this omission to the audit committee. Another possible situation is that an audit scope limitation occurs that prevents the auditor from performing all needed

ICFR Communications

	Ineffective Audit Committee Oversight	Other ICFR Material Weaknesses	ICFR Significant Deficiencies	ICFR Deficiencies
TO: Board of Directors		Audit committee Management	Audit committee Management	Management

(AS 5.78-81)

procedures to complete the ICFR audit. If this happens, the auditor informs the audit committee that the ICFR audit cannot be completed.

The audit standards that govern financial statement audits also require the auditor to communicate with the audit committee, or those charged with a company's governance. Exhibit 11-10 lists items that must be communicated. In addition to communicating the mandatory information, the auditor may also communicate with management about opportunities for improvement that were noted during the audit engagement. This communication, called a management letter, usually occurs in written form. A management letter may not be needed if all the problems, and therefore related opportunities for improvement, are included in the auditor's required communications on ICFR deficiencies.

Matters to Be Communicated to the Audit Committee

Auditor's responsibility for conducting the audit in accordance with PCAOB standards

Significant accounting policies, including critical accounting policies and alternative treatments within generally accepted accounting principles and the auditor's judgment about the quality of accounting principles

Management judgments and accounting estimates

Audit adjustments

Potential effect on the financial statements of any significant risks and exposures

Material uncertainties related to events and conditions, specifically going concern issues

Other information in documents containing audited financial information

Disagreements with management

Consultation with other accountants

Major issues discussed with management prior to retention

Difficulties encountered in performing the audit

Internal control deficiencies

Fraud and illegal acts

Independence

Other communications made to management

(AU 380)

Final Review

A final review of the audit involves several components. First, the auditor responsible for the engagement, typically the engagement partner, performs an overall review of the audit results. This review may identify audit procedures still needed for specific areas. In other words, as a result of the audit partner's final review, the audit team may need to conduct additional audit procedures. The auditor also performs or reviews overall analytical procedures related to the "big picture" of the final financial statements.

Analytical procedures are associated with various phases of the audit process. As a reminder, analytical procedures are required during planning. Substantive analytical procedures are used to provide audit evidence on specific account balances.

Overall analytical procedures are used in the wrap-up phase to assist the auditor in determining whether the evidence presents a consistent picture of the financial statements. If overall analytical procedures present any disconfirming evidence, the auditor investigates the source of the apparent inconsistencies.

AUDITING IN ACTION

Analytical Procedures in Final Review

The objective of analytical procedures used in the overall review stage of the audit is to assist the auditor in assessing the conclusions reached and in the evaluation of the overall financial statement presentation. A wide variety of analytical procedures may be useful for this purpose. The overall review would generally include reading the financial statements and notes and considering (a) the adequacy of evidence gathered in response to unusual or unexpected balances identified in planning the audit or in the course of the audit and (b) unusual or unexpected balances or relationships that were not previously identified. Results of an overall review may indicate that additional evidence may be needed.

(AU 329.23)

AUDITING IN ACTION

Examples of Wrap-Up Phase Analytical Procedures

The following can include statistical techniques such as trend analysis or regression analysis. Analytical procedures may be performed manually or with the use of computer-assisted techniques.

- Comparing current financial information with anticipated results, such as budgets or forecasts
- Comparing current financial information with relevant nonfinancial information
- Comparing ratios and indicators for the current period with expectations based on prior periods
   - Current ratio
   - Receivables turnover or days' sales outstanding
   - Inventory turnover
   - Depreciation to average fixed assets
   - Debt to equity
   - Gross profit percentage
   - Net income percentage
   - Plant operating ratios
- Comparing ratios and indicators for the current period with those of entities in the same industry
- Comparing relationships among elements in the current financial period with corresponding relationships in the financial information of prior periods
   - Expense by types as a percentage of sales
   - Assets by type as a percentage of total assets
   - Percentage of change in sales to percentage of change in receivables
- Comparing disaggregated data; financial statement items disaggregated
   - Into quarterly, monthly or weekly amounts
   - By product line or operating segment
   - By location, such as subsidiary, division or branch

(Adapted from AU 722.54)

AUDITING IN ACTION

Common Ratios

Profitability Ratios
- Net profit margin: Net income/Net sales
- Rate of return on assets: Net income + Interest expense/Average total assets
- Return on common equity:
  Net income-Preferred dividend/Average common stockholders' equity

Operations Ratios
- Gross profit margin: Gross profit/Net sales
- Receivables turnover: Net sales/Average accounts receivable
- Inventory turnover: Cost of goods sold/Average inventory
- Asset turnover: Net sales/Average total assets

Liquidity and Solvency Ratios
- Current ratio: Current assets/Current liabilities
- Quick ratio: Current monetary assets/Current monetary liabilities
- Debt to equity: Total liabilities/Total equity
- Operating cash flow to current debt:
  Cash provided by operating activities/Average current liabilities

Financial Distress Ratios (Altman)
  Working capital/total assets
  Retained earnings/total assets
  EBIT/total assets
  Market value of equity/total debt
  Net sales/total assets
  Discriminant Z score

Evaluating the misstatements that were identified during the financial statement audit and not proposed as adjusting journal entries is another step in the final review process. Typically, these are misstatements that were not deemed to be individually material. The auditor again considers these unadjusted misstatements, on both an individual and an aggregated basis. This review provides a final opportunity to assess whether the lack of adjustment for the identified misstatements makes the financial statements materially misstated.

AUDITING IN ACTION

Analysis of Unadjusted Differences

Identified misstatements not corrected by the client:

	Income Statement		Balance Sheet	
	Debit	Credit	Debit	Credit
Inventory shrinkage	74,000			74,000
Allowance for doubtful accounts	30,000			30,000
Unrecorded sales and receivables		120,000	120,000	
Revenue recognized from contract	130,000			130,000
Totals	234,000	120,000	120,000	234,000
Effect on net income	114,000			
Effect on total assets				114,000

After this step the auditor is satisfied that adjusting journal entries have been made as needed to prevent the financial statements from being materially misstated. The auditor must also trace the adjusting journal entries into the company's books to see that they are posted. In addition, the auditor reconciles the company's accounting records to the financial statements. These PCAOB requirements are the result of legal requirements based on SOX. PCAOB AU 326.19 states:

> [T]he auditor's substantive procedures must include reconciling the financial statements to the accounting records. The auditor's substantive procedures also should include examining material adjustments made during the course of preparing the financial statements.

The final aspects of the review during the wrap-up phase of the audit are:

1. Review of the documentation in the audit work papers to determine whether there is sufficient appropriate evidence to support the opinions being issued
2. Engagement quality review

Review of Audit Documentation

The final review of the audit documentation is intended to verify that the documentation of audit evidence supports the audit opinions. PCAOB AS 3, *Audit Documentation*, provides the guidance for audit documentation required in an audit performed for a public company.

AS 3 requires that the auditor prepare an **engagement completion document**. This document includes all the information needed for a reviewer to understand the significant findings or issues of the audit. An alternative format is for the engagement completion document to be indexed and cross referenced to the work papers that display that information. The engagement completion document must be as specific as necessary so that a reviewer can understand all the significant findings or issues of the engagement (AS 3.13). AS 3 clearly indicates that the engagement completion document is extremely important and will be critical to any subsequent PCAOB inspection of audit documentation. The auditor performing the final review of documentation pays close attention to the quality of this document.

Exhibit 11-11 lists examples of items provided in AS 3 as **significant findings or issues**. Significant findings or issues are "substantive matters that are important to the procedures performed, evidence obtained, or conclusions reached" (AS 3.12).

AS 3 also provides guidance regarding the completion date for audit documentation. All audit procedures must be complete, and necessary evidence must be obtained before the **audit report date**. However, the auditor has a limited additional period of time, 45 days, to finalize the audit documentation for retention. The end of the 45-day time period is called the **documentation completion date**.

AUDITING IN ACTION

Documentation

Documentation must:

- Show that the engagement complied with PCAOB standards
- Support the basis for audit conclusions for every relevant financial statement assertion
- Show that the underlying accounting records agreed or reconciled with the financial statements (AS 3.5)
- Show procedures performed, evidence obtained, and conclusions reached
- Permit an experienced auditor with no prior information on the engagement to:

    understand the procedures, evidence and conclusions

    determine who performed the work and when

    determine who reviewed the work and when (AS 3.6)

The auditor must document significant findings or issues, actions taken to address them...
and the basis for the conclusions reached in connection with each engagement. Significant
findings or issues... include, but are not limited to, the following:

a. Significant matters involving the selection, application, and consistency of accounting
principles, including related disclosures. Significant matters include, but are not limited to,
accounting for complex or unusual transactions, accounting estimates, and uncertainties as
well as related management assumptions.

b. Results of auditing procedures that indicate a need for significant modification of
planned auditing procedures, the existence of material misstatements, omissions in the
financial statements, the existence of significant deficiencies, or material weaknesses in
internal control over financial reporting.

c. Audit adjustments. For purposes of this standard, an audit adjustment is a correction of a
misstatement of the financial statements that was or should have been proposed by the auditor, whether or not recorded by management, that could, either individually or when aggregated with other misstatements, have a material effect on the company's financial statements.

d. Disagreements among members of the engagement team or with others consulted on the
engagement about final conclusions reached on significant accounting or auditing matters.

e. Circumstances that cause significant difficulty in applying auditing procedures.

f. Significant changes in the assessed level of audit risk for particular audit areas and the
auditor's response to those changes.

g. Any matters that could result in modification of the auditor's report.

(AS 3.12)

After the 45-day time period has passed, the auditor might determine that documentation was insufficient or incomplete. If this occurs, more documentation may be added,
along with information on the date the addition was made and by whom. No documentation can be removed after the documentation completion date. Electronic work papers document the date and time that work papers are accessed and changed. The use of electronic
work papers enhances the ability of both the audit firm and the PCAOB in monitoring compliance with documentation deadlines.

Engagement Quality Review

SOX Section 103 and AS 7 require that audits of public companies include a review by a
concurring or second partner who is not in charge of the audit engagement. This **independent review** is referred to as an **engagement quality review**. The review must result in the
reviewer's approval of the audit report.

Even though it is now required by law for audits of public companies, an independent
or engagement quality review is not new. Audit firms commonly required scrutiny of the work
papers by a second reviewer before it was legally mandated. A second review by someone who
is not involved with the audit engagement imposes the quality control that a qualified auditor who has not been involved in the engagement decisions evaluates all aspects of the audit
with "fresh eyes." Some firms add an additional internal requirement for audits of public companies that a review also be performed by the firm's SEC support group.

After completion of all the procedures involved in the wrap-up phase of the audit, the
auditor is ready to draft and issue the audit report.

REVIEW QUESTIONS

D.1 To what individuals does an auditor make communications? For an ICFR audit, briefly
explain how the communications required to go to the various individuals differ.

D.2 What authoritative bodies and sources require that the auditor make communications?

AUDITING IN ACTION

SOX Requirement for Concurring or Second Partner Review

Section. 103. Auditing, Quality Control, and Independence Standards and Rules

(a)(1)...The Board shall... establish... such auditing and related attestation standards... as required by this Act or the rules of the Commission, or as may be necessary or appropriate in the public interest or for the protection of investors.

(a)(2)...The Board

(A) shall include in the auditing standards that it adopts, requirements that each registered public accounting firm shall...

(ii) provide a concurring or second partner review and approval of such audit report (and other related information), and concurring approval in its issuance, by a qualified person... associated with the public accounting firm, other than the person in charge of the audit, or by an independent reviewer (as prescribed by the Board)...

D.3 What is a management letter?

D.4 What is an audit completion document? How is it useful?

D.5 Why does an auditor review audit documentation?

D.6 What is an engagement quality review of an audit, and why is it performed?

REPORTING [LO 2]

Audit reports are covered in both the PCAOB and AICPA auditing standards. AS 5 addresses audit reports for integrated audits. As a result, AS 5 includes guidelines on reporting for both financial statement and ICFR audits.

Audit reports often reflect differing situations, and the guidance needed to properly prepare these reports is extensive. Much of the guidance for the different situations relates to financial statement audits. A large amount of financial statement audit report guidance is specified in the AICPA auditing standards and has been adopted by the PCAOB in its interim standards and has not been changed to date.[2] AS 6, *Evaluating Consistency of Financial Statements*, is the PCAOB's most recent guidance affecting audit reports.[3]

When an auditor reports on the integrated audit of a public company, the report states that the audit has been performed based on "the standards of the Public Company Accounting Oversight Board (United States)" (PCAOB AS 1.3). When an auditor's report refers to an audit of a nonpublic company, the auditor references the "auditing standards generally accepted in the United States of America" (AU 508.08).

An auditor may report on an integrated audit using a combined report containing opinions on both the financial statements and ICFR. Alternatively, the auditor may use two separate reports, one for each opinion. The audit report is addressed to the company, or to the company's Board of Directors or stockholders.

Whenever an auditor is **associated with financial statements**, a report needs to be issued.

> An accountant is associated with financial statements when he has consented to the use of his name in a report, document, or written communication containing the statements. (AU 504.03)

Other types of reports, beyond audit reports, also describe the services provided by an accountant. For example, an accountant can perform an attest engagement and provide a report. An accountant can also perform a compilation or review engagement for a nonpublic company and provide a report. An auditor can perform a review of interim financial statements that are to be included in a form filed with the SEC. An auditor can

---

[2]See PCAOB Interim Standards, AU sections 500 and 600.

[3]PCAOB 6 supersedes AU 420 and parts of AU 508.

perform an engagement resulting in a letter to an underwriter. These engagements, which are other than financial statement and ICFR audits, are discussed in Chapter 16.

Auditors can also provide reports based on services that accompany or extend from the financial statement audit. As a result of a financial statement audit with extended procedures, an audit can provide an audit report on information accompanying the basic financial statements, such as additional details, consolidating information, statistical data, or historical summaries of extracted information (AU 551). The auditor can also audit a subset of financial information, called a specified element, account or item of the financial statements (AU 623.11). In certain circumstances, the audit guidance requires the auditor to issue an additional report. One such instance is when a company produces condensed financial statements and states that they are derived from the audited financial statements, without providing the full financial statements and audit report (AU 552).

Dating the Report

The audit report date is "no earlier than the date on which the auditor has obtained sufficient appropriate evidence to support the auditor's opinion" (AS 5.89). This date is consistent with the date on which the auditor completes all the audit work, including the wrap-up phase of the audit. The audit report date signifies the end of audit work. The auditor has a responsibility to know and understand subsequent events that may affect the financial statements, ICFR, and both audit opinions up through the date of the audit report.

Auditing standards indicate the auditor's responsibility through the date of the audit report by stating that the auditor cannot issue the report before sufficient appropriate evidence is obtained. Or, stated another way, the auditor *may* issue the report *only* when sufficient appropriate evidence is obtained. The auditor's level of responsibility for knowledge about the company drops after the report date.

Dating the Report with New Information after the Audit Report Date

Although the auditor does not have a responsibility to continue audit work after the audit report date, it is possible that the auditor becomes aware of new information between the audit report date and the time the client releases the financial statements. If this happens, the auditor investigates and assesses the new information. After investigating, if it is appropriate, the auditor takes steps consistent with the guidance on subsequent events. Remember that a recognized Type 1 subsequent event may mean that the client needs to reflect the event in the financial statements. A nonrecognized Type 2 subsequent event requires no more than financial statement disclosure. Deterioration in ICFR after the ICFR management report date, to a level where a material weakness exists, also requires disclosure. Even when this situation occurs after the audit is completed, the company and auditor can still take corrective action since the documents have not yet been released.

The financial statements and audit report may change because of new information that surfaces even after the audit is completed. The auditor has two options on dating the report when such a change occurs. The auditor may do more work on the overall audit in addition to the work done on the subsequent event. When this happens, the auditor changes the date of the whole report. Under this method the auditor continues all audit responsibilities through the new date. This requires obtaining management representations and attorney's letters with a later signature date, and extending the search for unrecorded liabilities and subsequent events review.

An alternative is that the auditor may use the earlier date for the entire audit report except as the report relates to the newly discovered information. The auditor uses a later date, concurrent with completion of the audit of the new information, only for that new information. This procedure is called **dual dating** the audit report. An example of dual dating is:

> ...for example, "February 16, 20__, except for Note __, as to which the date is March 1, 20__,"... (AU 530.05).

New Information after the Financial Statements Are Released

The audit procedures when new information is discovered *after* the release of the financial statements and audit report were discussed with "New Information after the Date of the Audit Report." These steps differ from the audit procedures that are appropriate when new information is discovered before the release of the financial statements.

When new information is learned *after* the financial statements are released, the auditor first considers whether the new information is important to anyone still using the financial statements and audit report. The auditor can still correct any problems with the audit report before the client has released the financial statements. However, the auditor has less control after the financial statements and audit report are released.

Even though the auditor has less control after the financial statements and audit report are released, the auditor advises the client to inform users and regulatory authorities, if appropriate, about the new information and that they should no longer rely on the audit report. If the client does not make the needed notifications, the auditor may need to communicate to users and regulators that the audit report is no longer to be used. Exhibit 11-12 displays a timeline reflecting information discovery after the audit is completed. Exhibit 11-13 displays the different possibilities resulting from the occurrence or discovery of important events after the financial statement date.

AUDITING IN ACTION

Auditing Guidance when the Audit Report Should No Longer Be Relied Upon

When the auditor has concluded… that action should be taken to prevent future reliance on his report, he should advise his client to make appropriate disclosure of the newly discovered facts and their impact on the financial statements to persons who are known to be currently relying or who are likely to rely on the financial statements and the related auditor's report. When the client undertakes to make appropriate disclosure, the method used and the disclosure made will depend on the circumstances.

a. If the effect on the financial statements or auditor's report of the subsequently discovered information can promptly be determined, disclosure should consist of issuing, as soon as practicable, revised financial statements and auditor's report. The reasons for the revision usually should be described in a note to the financial statements and referred to in the auditor's report. Generally, only the most recently issued audited financial statements would need to be revised, even though the revision resulted from events that had occurred in prior years.

b. When issuance of financial statements accompanied by the auditor's report for a subsequent period is imminent, so that disclosure is not delayed, appropriate disclosure of the revision can be made in such statements instead of reissuing the earlier statements. …

c. When the effect on the financial statements of the subsequently discovered information cannot be determined without a prolonged investigation, the issuance of revised financial statements and auditor's report would necessarily be delayed. In this circumstance, when it appears that the information will require a revision of the statements, appropriate disclosure would consist of notification by the client to persons who are known to be relying or who are likely to rely on the financial statements and the related report that they should not be relied upon, and that revised financial statements and auditor's report will be issued upon completion of an investigation. If applicable, the client should be advised to discuss with the Securities and Exchange Commission, stock exchanges, and appropriate regulatory agencies the disclosure to be made or other measures to be taken in the circumstances.

(AU 561.06)

Information Discovered between the Audit Completion and Financial Statement Release Dates

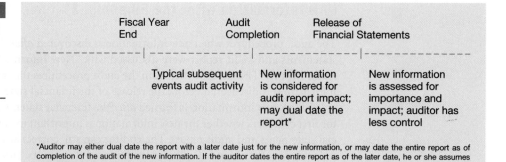

Fiscal Year End	Audit Completion	Release of Financial Statements
Typical subsequent events audit activity	New information is considered for audit report impact; may dual date the report*	New information is assessed for importance and impact; auditor has less control

*Auditor may either dual date the report with a later date just for the new information, or may date the entire report as of completion of the audit of the new information. If the auditor dates the entire report as of the later date, he or she assumes complete audit reponsibility until the later date. This includes extending the subsequent events review and extending the dates on the management representations and attorneys' letters.

Events and Information after the Fiscal Year End

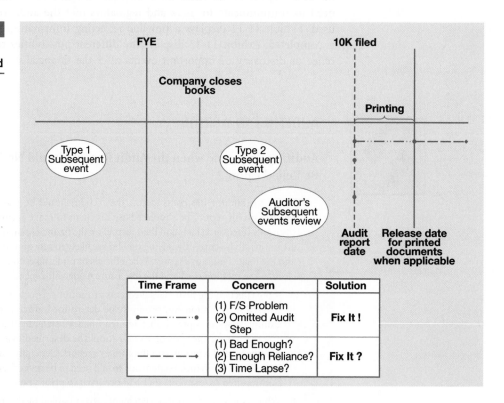

Time Frame	Concern	Solution
●—·—·—●	(1) F/S Problem (2) Omitted Audit Step	Fix It !
─ ─ ─ ─ →	(1) Bad Enough? (2) Enough Reliance? (3) Time Lapse?	Fix It ?

Integrated Audit Opinion Dates

ICFR and financial statement audit opinions resulting from an integrated audit can be presented in a single report or in separate reports. The report dates are the same for both the ICFR and financial statement audit opinions, even if the audit opinions are presented in separate reports. When separate reports are used for the ICFR and financial statement audits, each report includes a paragraph identifying the other report. The paragraph states the date of the other report and the opinion expressed. The financial statement audit opinion may address financial statements for multiple years, but the ICFR audit opinion addresses a single "as of" date. The "as of" date is the same as management's assessment of and report on the effectiveness of ICFR, which occurs as of the end of the most recent fiscal year.

Reissuing an Audit Report

A special reporting situation relates to an auditor **reissuing an audit report** on a prior year's financial statements. An auditor most often receives a request to reissue a report when the client has changed auditors and the successor auditor is auditing the current year. If the predecessor auditor does not reissue the audit report for the prior year's financial statements, a public company has no choice other than having the current auditor re-audit the prior year.[4]

Audit guidance addresses the steps an auditor must take to reissue a report. Depending on the circumstances, the auditor can reissue a report with the original date or dual date the report as a result of changes that have been made to the previously issued financial statements. The audit steps include reading and evaluating both the current and prior year's financial statements. The prior auditor also obtains representations letters from both management and the current auditor. This information helps the prior auditor decide whether more audit steps are needed. In addition, the prior auditor must decide whether the earlier audit report needs to be changed and whether any dual dating is appropriate. New information added to the prior financial statements may need to be labeled "unaudited" in the reissued audit report.

AUDITING IN ACTION:

Guidance on Reissuing an Audit Report

AU 530.06-.08
An independent auditor may reissue his report on financial statements contained in annual reports filed with the Securities and Exchange Commission or other regulatory agencies or in a document he submits to his client or to others that contains information in addition to the client's basic financial statements subsequent to the date of his original report on the basic financial statements. An independent auditor may also be requested by his client to furnish additional copies of a previously issued report. **Use of the original report date in a reissued report removes any implication that records, transactions, or events after that date have been examined or reviewed. In such cases, the independent auditor has no responsibility to make further investigation or inquiry as to events which may have occurred during the period between the original report date and the date of the release of additional reports...**

In some cases, it may not be desirable for the independent auditor to reissue his report...because he has become aware of an event that occurred subsequent to the date of his original report that requires adjustment or disclosure in the financial statements. In such cases, adjustment with disclosure or disclosure alone should be made as [required]. The independent auditor should consider the effect of these matters on his opinion and he should date his report in accordance with the procedures described [for dual dating].

However, if an event of the type requiring disclosure only...occurs between the date of the independent auditor's original report and the date of the reissuance of such report, and if the event comes to the attention of the independent auditor, the event may be disclosed in a separate note to the financial statements captioned somewhat as follows:

Event (Unaudited) Subsequent to the Date of the Independent Auditor's Report

Under these circumstances, the report of the independent auditor would carry the same date used in the original report.(emphasis added)

AU 508.70-73
A predecessor auditor ordinarily would be in a position to reissue his or her report on the financial statements of a prior period at the request of a former client if he or she is able to make satisfactory arrangements with the former client to perform this service and if he or she performs the procedures [that are required].

(continued)

---

[4]The SEC made an exception regarding the requirement to have the predecessor auditor reissue a prior audit report. This occurred when the SEC made the decision to refuse to accept audits of Arthur Andersen subsequent to the collapse of Enron.

Before reissuing (or consenting to the reuse of) a report previously issued on the financial statements of a prior period, when those financial statements are to be presented on a comparative basis with audited financial statements of a subsequent period, **a predecessor auditor should consider whether his or her previous report on those statements is still appropriate**. Either the current form or manner of presentation of the financial statements of the prior period or one or more subsequent events might make a predecessor auditor's previous report inappropriate. **Consequently, a predecessor auditor should**

a. **read the financial statements of the current period,**
b. **compare the prior-period financial statements that he or she reported on with the financial statements to be presented for comparative purposes, and**
c. **obtain representation letters from management of the former client and from the successor auditor.**

The representation letter from management of the former client should state

a. whether any information has come to management's attention that would cause them to believe that any of the previous representations should be modified, and
b. whether any events have occurred subsequent to the balance-sheet date of the latest prior-period financial statements reported on by the predecessor auditor that would require adjustment to or disclosure in those financial statements.

The representation letter from the successor auditor should state whether the successor's audit revealed any matters that, in the successor's opinion, might have a material effect on, or require disclosure in, the financial statements reported on by the predecessor auditor…

A predecessor auditor who has agreed to reissue his or her report may become aware of events or transactions occurring subsequent to the date of his or her previous report on the financial statements of a prior period that may affect his or her previous report (for example, the successor auditor might indicate in the response that certain matters have had a material effect on the prior-period financial statements reported on by the predecessor auditor). In such circumstances, **the predecessor auditor should make inquiries and perform other procedures that he or she considers necessary (for example, reviewing the working papers of the successor auditor as they relate to the matters affecting the prior-period financial statements).** The auditor should then decide, on the basis of the evidential matter obtained, whether to revise the report. If a predecessor auditor concludes that the report should be revised, he or she should follow the [audit standards] guidance…

A predecessor auditor's knowledge of the current affairs of his former client is obviously limited in the absence of a continuing relationship. Consequently, **when reissuing the report on prior-period financial statements, a predecessor auditor should use the date of his or her previous report to avoid any implication that he or she has examined any records, transactions, or events after that date. If the predecessor auditor revises the report or if the financial statements are restated, he or she should dual-date** the report. (emphasis added)

REPORTING ON THE AUDIT OF THE FINANCIAL STATEMENTS [LO 3]

An auditor's standard report on a financial statement audit is composed of certain required elements. Examples of the report are provided in the AICPA guidance (AU 508.08) as well as the PCAOB auditing standards (AS 5.87). The elements of a report expressing an opinion on the financial statements of a public company are:

a. A title that includes the word independent
b. A statement that the financial statements identified in the report were audited
c. A statement that the financial statements are the responsibility of the Company's management and that the auditor's responsibility is to express an opinion on the financial statements based on his or her audit

d. A statement that the audit was conducted in accordance with standards of the Public Company Accounting Oversight Board and an identification of the United States of America as the country of origin of those standards

e. A statement that those standards require that the auditor plan and perform the audit to obtain reasonable assurance about whether the financial statements are free of material misstatement

f. A statement that an audit includes

   a. Examining, on a test basis, evidence supporting the amounts and disclosures in the financial statements

   b. Assessing the accounting principles used and significant estimates made by management

   c. Evaluating the overall financial statement presentation

g. A statement that the auditor believes that his or her audit provides a reasonable basis for his or her opinion

h. An opinion as to whether the financial statements present fairly, in all material respects, the financial position of the Company as of the balance sheet date and the results of its operations and its cash flows for the period then ended in conformity with generally accepted accounting principles. The opinion should include an identification of the United States of America as the country of origin of those accounting principles

i. The manual or printed signature of the auditor's firm

j. The date of the audit report

(AS 5.85, AU 508.08)

An unqualified financial statement audit report is often referred to as a **standard report** or **clean opinion**. The term **unqualified opinion** reflects that the auditor is issuing an opinion that the financial statements are fair without the need to "qualify" or limit that opinion about fairness. In summary, an unqualified audit opinion states

> That the financial statements present fairly, in all material respects, the financial position, results of operations, and cash flows of the entity in conformity with generally accepted accounting principles. (AU 508.10)

The phrase "presents fairly" refers to the accounting standards applicable to the client's financial statements and whether the accounting representation of the financial statement is appropriate based on those standards. For public companies, SEC requirements prevail as the accounting standards. For nonpublic companies, generally accepted accounting principles apply. The country related to the standards must be identified.

The first three paragraphs of a standard, unqualified financial statement audit report are typically referred to as the introductory, scope, and opinion paragraphs. Sometimes audit firms modify the format of the standard audit report. This is acceptable if all the required elements are included. The description of the introductory, scope, and opinion paragraphs that follows is based on the most common format of a standard report.

Introductory Paragraph

The introductory paragraph identifies the entity that has been audited, the financial statements audited, and the time periods—typically years—that were audited. A declaration that the financial statements are management's responsibility is included. The auditor claims responsibility for auditing management's financial statements.

Scope Paragraph

The scope paragraph communicates to the reader what an audit consists of and the auditor's activities. It names the auditing standards under which the examination was conducted.

The scope paragraph language states that the auditor plans and performs steps that provide reasonable assurance. This highlights that the auditor has final responsibility for deciding what needs to be done on the audit. Also, the audit procedures do not result in an absolutely certain audit opinion.

The language indicates that when the auditor issues a clean opinion on the financial statements, the opinion incorporates a materiality threshold. The report accomplishes this by only extending an opinion regarding the absence of material misstatements. In describing the audit procedures, the language states that the examination does not investigate 100% of the items that make up the financial statements but instead uses a test-basis approach.

The scope paragraph communicates that management may have a choice of accounting principles and uses estimates in preparing the financial statements. This emphasizes that appropriate financial statements can be drafted in more than one way and that they lack exactness.

The auditor states an expectation that the audit provides a reasonable basis for the audit opinion. While the auditor is offering the opinion of an expert, it is still an opinion. Furthermore, the audit provides a reasonable basis for the opinion, rather than an infallible conclusion.

Opinion Paragraph

The most important language in this paragraph is that the statement being offered by the certified public accountant is an opinion. The opinion paragraph is straightforward in identifying the company audited, the financial statements, the years and the basis of accounting. The

AUDITING IN ACTION

Unqualified Report on the Audit of the Financial Statements of a Public Company

Report of Independent Registered Public Accounting Firm

We have audited the accompanying balance sheets of X Company as of December 31, 20X3 and 20X2, and the related statements of operations, stockholders' equity, and cash flows for each of the three years in the period ended December 31, 20X3. These financial statements are the responsibility of the Company's management. Our responsibility is to express an opinion on these financial statements based on our audits.

We conducted our audits in accordance with the standards of the Public Company Accounting Oversight Board (United States). Those standards require that we plan and perform the audit to obtain reasonable assurance about whether the financial statements are free of material misstatement. An audit includes examining, on a test basis, evidence supporting the amounts and disclosures in the financial statements. An audit also includes assessing the accounting principles used and significant estimates made by management, as well as evaluating the overall financial statement presentation. We believe that our audits provide a reasonable basis for our opinion.

In our opinion, the financial statements referred to above present fairly, in all material respects, the financial position of the Company as of [at] December 31, 20X3 and 20X2, and the results of its operations and its cash flows for each of the three years in the period ended December 31, 20X3, in conformity with U.S. generally accepted accounting principles.

We also have audited, in accordance with the standards of the Public Company Accounting Oversight Board (United States), X Company's internal control over financial reporting as of December 31, 20X3, based on [*identify control criteria*] and our report dated [*date of report, which should be the same as the date of the report on the financial statements*] expressed [*include nature of opinion*].

[*Signature*]
[City and State or Country]
[*Date*]
(Based on AS 5.88)

phrase "presents fairly in all material respects" includes several important constructs. The financial statements are prepared using a set of widely accepted standards. For a public company, this means that the accounting presentation reflects the SEC's requirements. Use of the words "all material respects" refers to financial statements that are not exact but are free of misstatements that would cause a reader to alter a judgment. When ICFR and the financial statements are not reported on together, the report includes a paragraph referring to the ICFR audit report.

FINANCIAL STATEMENT AUDIT REPORTS THAT DIFFER FROM UNQUALIFIED, STANDARD REPORTS

The audit report resulting from a company's financial statement audit may be changed or modified from the standard unqualified report for a variety of reasons.

1. The auditor may need to add **explanatory language** to the report. The report is changed with explanatory language or an additional explanatory paragraph when the audit opinion is "unqualified" but more information is needed. In other words, the auditor is still expressing an opinion that the financial statements are fairly presented but is adding to the standard report.

2. The audit report can also state a **qualified opinion**. A qualified opinion report is used when the financial statements are fair "except for" some matter that is specified in the report.

3. An audit report can express an **adverse opinion** on the financial statements. An adverse opinion report states that the financial statements "do not present fairly" the financial position, results of operations, or cash flows of the company.

4. An auditor can issue a report on the financial statements that disclaims an opinion. This type of report, sometimes called a **disclaimer**, states that the auditor is not expressing an opinion on the financial statements.

Although changes from a standard, unqualified report can be summarized as explanatory language, qualified opinion, adverse opinion, and disclaimer of opinion, the correct use of these options is very complex. For example, when a company changes accounting principles, an unqualified opinion with explanatory language may be appropriate unless the company's disclosure is inadequate. If the disclosure is inadequate, a qualified or an adverse opinion may be appropriate, even though the change in principle only required an explanatory paragraph.

When a change from one accepted accounting principle to another is handled through retrospective application, as called for by *Accounting Changes and Error Corrections* (FASB ASC 250-10), the explanatory paragraph is only included in the year of change. If the change is implemented in another way, the explanatory paragraph is included as long as an affected financial statement is presented.

If a company changes from one accepted accounting principle to another principle that, though accepted, is not preferred, the auditor may need to issue a qualified or adverse opinion based on the change in principle. This can happen even when the auditor expresses an opinion that use of the new standard creates a fair presentation. Further more, even though various reporting options may be available, generally speaking, the SEC will not accept financial statements with a qualified or an adverse audit opinion when the problem underlying the negative audit opinion can be remedied.

Explanatory Language

The addition of explanatory language is a change to an unqualified financial statement audit report. Reasons for explanatory language or an explanatory paragraph are as follows:

a. The auditor's opinion is based in part on the report of another auditor.
b. Substantial doubt exists about an entity's ability to continue as a going concern.

c. The accounting principles or the way they are applied has changed in a material way.

d. A previously issued financial statement contained a material misstatement that has been corrected.

e. Other circumstances, beyond a change in accounting principles, exist that affect the comparability of the financial statements.

f. Information required by the SEC as a part of the quarterly financial data has been omitted or has not been reviewed.

g. The company is required to provide supplementary information by a standard setting body (such as the FASB or GASB) and that information is either not provided, is not presented according to the guidelines, or the auditor has not been able to perform whatever procedures are required related to the information.

h. Other information in a document that includes the audited financial statements (such as when the audited financial statements are in the annual report) is materially inconsistent with information in the financial statements.

(AU 508.11)

The financial statement audit report includes an explanation if an adverse opinion on ICFR is issued. The auditor may choose to add language to the standard audit report to emphasize a matter included in the financial statements. Further explanation of some of these changes and sample reports are provided in the next section.

Opinion Based in Part on the Report of Another Auditor

Sometimes an auditor needs the assistance of another auditor to complete an audit. Guidance on this situation is provided in AU 543, *Part of Audit Performed by Other Independent Auditors*. One common reason for involvement of two audit firms is when a parent and subsidiary (or other investee) are audited by different auditors. Another common occurrence is that a company has multiple locations where it does business that are geographically dispersed.

One auditor, who is engaged by the client, does the majority of the work and is considered the **principal auditor.** The auditor assuming the role of **principal auditor** must evaluate whether it is appropriate to do so. The evaluation is based mainly on the volume, importance, and materiality of the work performed by each auditor.

The principal auditor plans and reviews the work of the assisting auditor and may take responsibility for the other auditor's work. In this situation the audit report does not change from the standard format and language. Another possibility is that the assisting auditor may perform such a significant amount of work that the initial auditor decides to refer to the report of the other auditor as a part of the basis for his or her opinion. When this is the situation, the change in the audit report indicates a division of responsibility between the auditors. The auditor modifies the audit report in both the introductory paragraph and the opinion paragraph.

AUDITING IN ACTION

Opinion Based in Part on Report of Another Auditor

We have audited the consolidated balance sheets of ABC Company and subsidiaries as of December 31, 20X2 and 20X1, and the related consolidated statements of income. ... We did not audit the financial statements of B Company, a wholly-owned subsidiary, which statements reflect total assets of $___ and $___ as of December 31, 20X2 and 20X1, respectively, and total revenues of $___ and $___ for the years then ended. Those statements were audited by other auditors whose report has been furnished to us, and our opinion, insofar as it relates to the amounts included for B Company, is based solely on the report of the other auditors. ...

In our opinion, based on our audits and the report of other auditors. ... (AU 508.13)

Substantial Doubt about an Entity's Ability to Continue as a Going Concern

When an auditor becomes aware that there may be significant doubt about an entity's ability to continue as a going concern, the auditor investigates the possibility. The investigation includes any plans management may have to deal with the situation. If, after performing the investigative audit procedures, the auditor concludes that there is substantial doubt about the entity's ability to continue as a going concern, and that the financial statement disclosure is appropriate, the audit report is modified with an explanatory paragraph. If the disclosure is not adequate, then the auditor should issue a qualified or an adverse opinion, depending on the severity of the disclosure problem.

AUDITING IN ACTION

Going Concern, Explanatory Paragraph

The accompanying financial statements have been prepared assuming that the company will continue as a going concern. As discussed in Note X to the financial statements, the company has suffered recurring losses from operations and has a net capital deficiency that raise substantial doubt about its ability to continue as a going concern. Management's plans in regard to these matters are also described in Note X. The financial statements do not include any adjustments that might result from the outcome of this uncertainty. (AU 341.13)

Changes Affecting Consistency within or between Periods

AS 6 (which superseded PCAOB Interim Standard AU 420) addresses the impact of consistency issues on the audit report for financial statements of a public company. Changes that affect consistency are grouped into two categories: changes in accounting principles and corrections of misstatements in financial statements of prior years.

> The auditor should recognize the following matters relating to the consistency of the company's financial statements in the auditor's report if those matters have a material effect on the financial statements:
>
> **a.** A change in accounting principle
>
> **b.** An adjustment to correct a misstatement in previously issued financial statements
>
> (AU 508.16 as amended to conform with AS 6)
>
> To determine whether the audit report needs an explanatory paragraph:
>
> … the auditor should evaluate whether the comparability of the financial statements between periods has been materially affected by changes in accounting principles or by material adjustments to previously issued financial statements for the relevant periods. (AS 6.02)

When a change has a material effect on the financial statements, the audit report includes an explanatory paragraph. If problems exist in addition to the impact on consistency, a qualified or an adverse opinion may be appropriate, along with the explanatory paragraph.[5]

---

[5]The guidance in AU 420, which is still in effect for nonpublic company audits at the time of this writing addresses consistency for the following situations:

Change in accounting principle (or how it is applied) that is not a violation of generally
    accepted accounting principles

Change in reporting entity

Correction of an error in principle

Change in principle inseparable from change in estimate

Change in accounting estimate

Change in classification and reclassifications

Changes expected to have a material future effect

Consistency: Change in Accounting Principle

An explanatory paragraph for a change in accounting principle is appropriate when the change in principle meets certain criteria:

1. The change must be to an accounting principle that is generally accepted.
2. The method of accounting for the effect of the change must be in conformity with generally accepted accounting principles. Since most new accounting standards have specific guidance for implementation, this usually means that the company has followed the guidance for adopting the particular standard.
3. The disclosure in the financial statement related to the change is adequate.
4. The company has justified that the change is to an accounting standard that is preferable over the standard currently adopted.

If any of these criteria are not met, then the change in accounting principle is a violation of generally accepted accounting principles and the auditor issues a report with a qualified or an adverse opinion.

Management is required to justify the new accounting principle as "preferable" to the prior principle. The requirement for justification of preferability is met if the new accounting principle or method is called for by a newly issued accounting standard. If the company initiates the decision to change, then it must justify preferability for the change to be acceptable.

AUDITING IN ACTION

Preferable Accounting Standards

PCAOB Interim Standards, AU 431.52. Based on conforming amendments for AS 6:

> The accounting standards indicate that a company may make a change in accounting principle only if it justifies that the allowable alternative accounting principle is preferable. If the company does not provide reasonable justification that the alternative accounting principle is preferable, the auditor should consider the accounting change to be a departure from generally accepted accounting principles and, if the effect of the change in accounting principle is material, should issue a qualified or adverse opinion.

PCAOB Interim Standards, AU 508.52:

Independent Auditor's Report

[Same first and second paragraphs as the standard report]

As disclosed in Note X to the financial statements, the Company adopted, in 20X2, the first-in, first-out method of accounting for its inventories, whereas it previously used the last-in, first-out method. Although use of the first-in, first-out method is in conformity with accounting principles generally accepted in the United States of America, in our opinion the Company has not provided reasonable justification that this accounting principle is preferable as required by those principles.

In our opinion, except for the change in accounting principle discussed in the preceding paragraph, the financial statements referred to above present fairly, in all material respects. ...

Consistency: Changes in the Method of Applying an Accounting Principle

A change in the way a company applies an accounting principle is considered to be a change in principle when analyzing consistency for the audit report. For example, the accounting standard on cash flows discusses the approach a company may take in determining its cash equivalents. Changes to that approach or policy are treated as changes to an accounting principle and require discussion in an explanatory paragraph of the audit report.

Consistency: Accounting Changes Expected to Have a Material Future Effect

AS 6 does not refer to changes that will not require mention in the audit report. An accounting change that does not have a current material effect but is expected to do so in the future fits this category. Accounting standards require this type of change to be disclosed in the financial statements. The change only requires modification of the audit report if it causes a violation of generally accepted accounting principles, for example, if disclosure is inadequate.

Exhibit 11-14 presents an auditor's report exemplifying the complexity that can result from various situations affecting a company. The report from the 10K of TOUSA, includes reference to the report of another auditor and is modified because of uncertainty about a company's going concern. The audit report includes an explanatory paragraph for adoption of a new accounting principle and a paragraph referring to a separate audit report on ICFR.

EXHIBIT 11-14

Audit Report: Reference to Another Auditor, Going Concern, New Accounting Principle, and Separate ICFR Audit Report

Report of Independent Registered Public Accounting Firm

The Board of Directors and Stockholders of TOUSA, Inc.

We have audited the accompanying consolidated statements of financial condition of TOUSA, Inc. and subsidiaries (the Company) as of December 31, 2007 and 2006, and the related consolidated statements of operations, stockholders' equity (deficit), and cash flows for each of the three years in the period ended December 31, 2007. These financial statements are the responsibility of the Company's management. Our responsibility is to express an opinion on these financial statements based on our audits. The consolidated financial statements of TE/Tousa, LLC and Subsidiaries (a corporation in which the Company, through July 31, 2007, had a 50% interest and which was accounted for under the equity method), as of and for the year ended December 31, 2006, have been audited by other auditors whose report, which has been furnished to us, included an explanatory paragraph that, as more fully described in Note 4, there is substantial doubt about TE/Tousa, LLC and Subsidiaries' ability to continue as a going concern. Our opinion on the consolidated financial statements, insofar as it relates to the amounts included for TE/Tousa, LLC and Subsidiaries as of and for the year ended December 31, 2006, is based solely on the report of the other auditors. In the consolidated financial statements, the Company's investment in TE/Tousa, LLC and Subsidiaries is stated at $0 at December 31, 2006, and the Company's equity in the net loss of TE/Tousa, LLC and Subsidiaries is stated at $145.1 million for the year then ended. On July 31, 2007, the Company consummated transactions to settle the disputes regarding the TE/Tousa, LLC and Subsidiaries which resulted in the TE/Tousa, LLC and Subsidiaries becoming a wholly-owned subsidiary of the Company by merger into one of its subsidiaries.

We conducted our audits in accordance with the standards of the Public Company Accounting Oversight Board (United States). Those standards require that we plan and perform the audit to obtain reasonable assurance about whether the financial statements are free of material misstatement. An audit includes examining, on a test basis, evidence supporting the amounts and disclosures in the financial statements. An audit also includes assessing the accounting principles used and significant estimates made by management, as well as evaluating the overall financial statement presentation. We believe that our audits and the report of other auditors provide a reasonable basis for our opinion.

In our opinion, based on our audits and the report of other auditors, the financial statements referred to above present fairly, in all material respects, the consolidated financial position of TOUSA, Inc. as of December 31, 2007 and 2006, and the consolidated results of

(continued)

their operations and their cash flows for each of the three years in the period ended December 31, 2007, in conformity with U.S. generally accepted accounting principles.

The accompanying financial statements have been prepared assuming that TOUSA, Inc. will continue as a going concern. As more fully described in Note 1, the Company filed a voluntary petition for reorganization under Chapter 11 of the United States Bankruptcy Code on January 29, 2008, which raises substantial doubt about the Company's ability to continue as a going concern. Management's plans in regard to this matter are also described in Note 1. The consolidated financial statements do not include any adjustments to reflect the possible future effects on the recoverability and classification of assets or the amounts and classification of liabilities that may result from the outcome of this uncertainty. Also, the consolidated financial statements of TE/Tousa, LLC and Subsidiaries, as of and for the year ended December 31, 2006, have been audited by other auditors whose report, which has been furnished to us, included an explanatory paragraph that, as more fully described in Note 4, there is substantial doubt about TE/Tousa, LLC and Subsidiaries' ability to continue as a going concern.

As discussed in Note 2 to the consolidated financial statements, effective January 1, 2006, the Company adopted Statement of Financial Accounting Standards No. 123(R), *Share-Based Payment*. In addition, as discussed in Note 9 to the consolidated financial statements, effective January 1, 2007, the Company adopted FASB Interpretation No. 48, *Accounting for Uncertainty in Income Taxes an interpretation of FASB Statement No. 109.*

We also have audited, in accordance with the standards of the Public Company Accounting Oversight Board (United States), TOUSA, Inc.'s internal control over financial reporting as of December 31, 2007, based on criteria established in Internal Control-Integrated Framework issued by the Committee of Sponsoring Organizations of the Treadway Commission and our report dated August 6, 2008 expressed an unqualified opinion thereon.

/s/ Ernst & Young LLP

Certified Public Accountants
West Palm Beach, Florida
August 6, 2008

Consistency: Correction of a Material Misstatement in Previously Issued Financial Statements

The second general category of change that requires explanatory language for consistency in an unqualified audit report is when previously issued financial statements are changed to correct a material misstatement. The auditor adds an explanatory paragraph after the opinion paragraph that includes:

- A statement that the previously issued financial statements have been restated for the correction of a misstatement in the respective period, and
- A reference to the company's disclosure of the correction of the misstatement. (AS 6.18A)

The language of the explanatory paragraph is relatively simple: "As discussed in Note X to the financial statements, the 20X2 financial statements have been restated to correct a misstatement."

Emphasis of a Matter

The auditor has the option of adding a paragraph to the audit report to emphasize a matter that is included in the financial statements. When the auditor adds a paragraph solely to emphasize something that is in the financial statements, it does not change the opinion paragraph. AU 508.19 suggests the following as topics that the auditor might include in an emphasis paragraph:

1. The entity is a component of a larger entity
2. Significant transactions have been conducted with related parties
3. Important subsequent events have occurred
4. Accounting matters other than a change in accounting principle have affected the financial statements' comparability with a prior period

Departure from a Promulgated Accounting Principle

A rare occurrence may affect the auditor's report for a *nonpublic* company's financial statements. Though unlikely, it is possible that the company and auditor may conclude that complying with an accounting standard set up by a standard-setting body such as the FASB or GASB causes the company's financial statements to be materially misstated. When this is the case, the auditor issues an unqualified opinion with explanatory language. The explanation describes the departure from the standards, the effects of the departure (if it is practical to determine and provide the information), and why following the accounting standard would make the financial statements misleading (ET 203.01).

The PCAOB did not adopt the AICPA ethics rule that permits this exception and does not provide for this explanatory paragraph in AS 6.

Qualified, Adverse, and Disclaimer Financial Statement Audit Reports

When the financial statements do not present the company's financial situation and events fairly, the audit report expresses either a qualified or an adverse opinion. This occurs when there is a departure from generally accepted accounting principles, including inadequate disclosures. A departure from generally accepted accounting principles may result from an accounting change that is not justified, to an accounting principle that is not accepted, or to an accounting principle that is implemented in a manner that is not according to the standards. Inadequate disclosure can apply to any aspect of the financial statements including management's estimates and uncertainties (such as contingent liabilities) that require disclosure.

Depending on the severity of the problem, the report will present either a qualified or an adverse opinion.

> A *qualified opinion* states that, *except for* the effects of the matter to which the qualification relates, the financial statements present fairly, in all material respects, financial position, results of operations, and cash flows in conformity with generally accepted accounting principles. (AU 508.20) (emphasis added)

When the financial statements, taken as a whole, are not in conformity with generally accepted accounting principles, the auditor issues an adverse opinion. Basically, the difference is that a qualified opinion is appropriate when the problem is limited to a specific issue. An adverse opinion is appropriate when the problem is so pervasive that it prevents the financial statements, as a whole, from being fairly stated.

Another possibility exists when the auditor does not have sufficient appropriate audit evidence or is unable to perform all the audit procedures needed to express an opinion on the financial statements. An inability to perform all the procedures necessary is called a *scope limitation*. The type of engagement and severity of insufficient evidence dictates the type of audit report that is appropriate.

For a financial statement audit, the auditor may either issue a qualified opinion or "disclaim" an opinion when a scope limitation occurs. When issuing a qualified opinion, the auditor states that, "except for the effects" of adjustments that might have occurred had additional evidence been examined, the financial statements are fair (AU 508.26). A "disclaimer of opinion" occurs when the auditor makes a statement that he or she does not express an opinion on the financial statements (508.61). AS 5 requires that when a scope limitation occurs on an ICFR audit the auditor must either disclaim an opinion or withdraw from the engagement (AS 5.C3). Whenever an independence violation occurs—in other words when an auditor is not independent of the client company—the only audit report that an auditor can issue is a disclaimer of opinion (AU 504.09).

The auditor issues a report containing an adverse audit opinion on the financial statements based on the conclusion that the financial statements "do not present fairly the financial position or the results of operations or cash flows in conformity with generally accepted accounting principles" (AU 508.58). When the auditor issues an adverse opinion, the report includes an explanatory paragraph stating the reasons for the opinion. If practical, the explanatory paragraph states the effects of whatever caused the adverse opinion on the financial position, results of operations, and cash flows. The auditor issues an adverse opinion on ICFR whenever the audit identifies a material weakness in ICFR.

The next section discusses in greater detail the qualified, adverse, and disclaimer opinions resulting from financial statement audits.

REVIEW QUESTIONS

E.1 What different forms of audit reports may be used as the result of a financial statement audit?

E.2 When are the different forms appropriate?

E.3 What specific words are characteristics of the different types of audit reports?

E.4 When is the audit report dated?

Qualified Opinion for a Departure from Generally Accepted Accounting Principles

If the auditor concludes that the financial statements include a material departure from generally accepted accounting principles, a qualified or an adverse opinion is issued. Whether the appropriate opinion is qualified or adverse depends on the materiality of the effects of the departure. Both quantitative and qualitative materiality effects are considered.

> The significance of an item to a particular entity (for example, inventories to a manufacturing company), the pervasiveness of the misstatement (such as whether it affects the amounts and presentation of numerous financial statement items), and the effect of the misstatement on the financial statements taken as a whole are all factors to be considered in making a judgment regarding materiality. (AU 508.36)

An auditor's report that is qualified for a violation of generally accepted accounting principles differs in several ways from an unqualified report. Prior to the opinion paragraph, the auditor includes an explanatory paragraph describing the generally accepted accounting principle departure. The explanatory paragraph can either include the information about the departure or refer the reader to the note to the financial statements that explains the violation. Then, the opinion paragraph expresses the qualification about the auditor's opinion of the fairness of the financial statements. The language used for the qualification is: "except for the effects" [of the departure from generally accepted accounting principles].

AUDITING IN ACTION

Qualified Opinion Because of a GAAP Departure

As more fully described in Note X to the financial statements, the Company has excluded certain lease obligations from property and debt in the accompanying balance sheets. In our opinion, accounting principles generally accepted in the United States of America require that such obligations be included in the balance sheets. (AU 508.40)

In our opinion, except for the effects of not capitalizing certain lease obligations as discussed in the preceding paragraph and Note X, the financial statements referred to above present fairly, in all material respects, the financial position of X Company as of December 31, 20X2 and 20X1, and the results of its operations and its cash flows for the years then ended in conformity with accounting principles generally accepted in the United States of America. (AU 508.39)

Another violation of generally accepted accounting principles may require a qualified or adverse opinion. This occurs when the financial statements do not include adequate disclosures. If it is practical to present the information that should be included in the disclosures, the auditor includes it in the audit report along with the modified opinion language. However, inadequate disclosure may result because management has not or cannot produce the information. When it is not practical to provide the required disclosure, the auditor uses the following language in the audit report:

> The Company's financial statements do not disclose [describe the nature of the omitted information and that it is not practicable to present it in the auditor's report]. In our opinion, disclosure of this information is required by accounting principles generally accepted in the United States of America. (AU 508.41-42)

If a qualified, rather than an adverse, opinion is appropriate as a result of the inadequate disclosure, the opinion paragraph states: "In our opinion, except for the omission of the information discussed in the preceding paragraph..." (AU 508.42).

Qualified Financial Statement Audit Opinion Because of a Scope Limitation

An auditor can only issue an unqualified opinion if he or she has performed all the procedures judged necessary. Sometimes, for various reasons, the auditor is not able to perform all of the financial statement audit procedures. As a result, the auditor must either issue a qualified opinion or disclaim an opinion.

Similar to the decision of whether a qualified or an adverse opinion is appropriate because of a departure from GAAP, whether a qualified opinion or disclaimer of opinion is appropriate depends on the cause and severity of the problem. The financial statement audit scope restriction may be limited and imposed by circumstances. An example is an inability to observe the client's physical count of inventories. In these situations, the auditor may judge a qualified opinion to be appropriate. In contrast, AU 508.24 states that when the restriction is imposed by the client, for example, the client will not permit the auditor to perform confirmations, the auditor will ordinarily disclaim an opinion.

A financial statement audit scope limitation or a lack of sufficient audit evidence can cause the auditor to issue a qualified opinion. When this occurs, the auditor changes the scope and opinion language of the audit report. The auditor describes the circumstances in

AUDITING IN ACTION

Qualified Opinion Because of a Scope Limitation

Except as discussed in the following paragraph, we conducted our audits in accordance with auditing standards generally accepted in the United States of America. ...

We were unable to obtain audited financial statements supporting the Company's investment in a foreign affiliate stated at $___ and $___ at December 31, 20X2 and 20X1, respectively, or its equity in earnings of that affiliate of $___ and $___, which is included in net income for the years then ended as described in Note X to the financial statements; nor were we able to satisfy ourselves as to the carrying value of the investments in the foreign affiliate or the equity in its earnings by other auditing procedures.

In our opinion, except for the effects of such adjustments, if any, as might have been determined to be necessary had we been able to examine evidence regarding the foreign affiliate investment and earnings. ... (AU 508.26)

an explanatory paragraph positioned before the opinion paragraph. The opinion paragraph states that the qualification relates to the possible effects on the financial statements.

When a scope limitation causes the auditor to disclaim an opinion on the financial statements, the audit report includes a paragraph describing the reasons for the disclaimer. If the auditor has any other concerns about the financial statements, the disclaimer communicates that information as well. The concerns are included with the disclaimer, even though the report does not state an opinion about the fairness of the financial statements.

The auditor may also need to issue a qualified opinion because of a scope limitation when sufficient evidence does not exist related to an uncertainty in the financial statements. An uncertainty is defined as a matter that will be resolved at a future date. Often management must make estimates when uncertainties exist. Sometimes the auditor can gather enough audit evidence to support management's estimates, and an unqualified opinion is appropriate.

A qualification or disclaimer for a scope limitation related to an uncertainty is only appropriate when the problem is simply a lack of evidence. If the auditor concludes that a management estimate is unreasonable, that generally accepted accounting principles have not been followed, or that disclosure is inadequate, the auditor will issue a qualified or an adverse opinion. Again, whether the opinion is qualified or adverse depends on the auditor's judgment regarding the severity of the problem.

Adverse Opinion

An adverse opinion resulting from a financial statement audit expresses the auditor's conclusion that the financial statements, taken as a whole, do not fairly present the company's financial position and the financial representation of its business activities. Adverse financial statement opinions are rarely actually issued. In practice, the company either corrects its problems, or the company or auditor severs the business relationship before the point of issuance of an adverse audit report.

An adverse opinion requires modification of the opinion paragraph and the addition of a paragraph preceding the opinion paragraph explaining the circumstances motivating the opinion. The explanatory paragraph includes all the important reasons for the adverse financial statement audit opinion. If it is practical to provide the information, the explanatory paragraph also states the impact of the underlying reasons on the financial position, results of operations, and cash flows.

AUDITING IN ACTION

Adverse Opinion

As discussed in Note X to the financial statements, the Company carries its property, plant and equipment accounts at appraisal values, and provides depreciation on the basis of such values. Further, the Company does not provide for income taxes with respect to differences between financial income and taxable income arising because of the use, for income tax purposes, of the installment method of reporting gross profit from certain types of sales. Accounting principles generally accepted in the United States of America require that property, plant and equipment be stated at an amount not in excess of cost, reduced by depreciation based on such amounts, and that deferred income taxes be provided.

Because of the departures from accounting principles generally accepted in the United States of America identified above, as of December 31, 20X2 and 20X1, inventories have been increased by \$___ and \$___ by inclusion in manufacturing overhead of depreciation in excess of that based on cost; property, plant and equipment, less accumulated depreciation, is carried at \$___ and \$___ in excess of an amount based on the cost to the Company. ...

In our opinion, because of the effects of the matters discussed in the preceding paragraphs, the financial statements referred to above do not present fairly, in conformity with accounting principles generally accepted in the United States of America, the financial position of X Company as of December 31, 20X2 and 20X1, or the results of its operations or its cash flows for the years then ended. (AU 508.60)

Disclaimer of Opinion

A disclaimer of opinion acknowledges that the auditor has been involved with the client. It also communicates that the auditor is not issuing an opinion regarding the fairness, or lack thereof, of the financial statements. A disclaimer is appropriate when an auditor is unable to provide an opinion (such as when the auditor is not independent) or when the auditor is unable to form an opinion. The auditor may be unable to form an opinion when a scope limitation exists, or for some other reason the auditor is unable to obtain sufficient appropriate audit evidence to come to a conclusion on the fairness of the financial statements.

An auditor's report disclaiming an opinion includes a paragraph stating the reasons for the disclaimer. Also, even though the auditor is not issuing an opinion, "the auditor should also disclose any other reservations… regarding fair presentation in conformity with generally accepted accounting principles" (AU 508.62).

AUDITING IN ACTION

Disclaimer of Opinion

We were engaged to audit. ... These financial statements are the responsibility of the Company's management.

The Company did not make a count of its physical inventory. ... The Company's records do not permit the application of other auditing procedures. ...

Since the Company did not take physical inventories and we were not able to apply other auditing procedures to satisfy ourselves as to inventory quantities and the cost of property and equipment, the scope of our work was not sufficient to enable us to express, and we do not express, an opinion on these financial statements.

(AU 508.63)

AUDITING IN ACTION

Disclaimer of Opinion, Independence Impairment

We are not independent with respect to XYZ Company, and the accompanying balance sheet as of December 31, 19X1, and the related statements of income, retained earnings, and cash flows for the year then ended were not audited by us and, accordingly, we do not express an opinion on them.

(AU 504.10)

REPORTING ON AN AUDIT OF INTERNAL CONTROL OVER FINANCIAL REPORTING

AS 5 covers reports on audits of internal control over financial reporting. Many of the elements of an audit report on ICFR are similar to those in an audit report on the financial statements. In addition to an introductory, scope, and opinion paragraph, an ICFR audit report also includes a definition and an inherent limitations paragraph. These additional paragraphs provide more information about the nature of internal control over financial reporting. Exhibit 11-15 presents the components of an audit report on ICFR.

EXHIBIT 11-15

Elements of an Audit Report on ICFR

The auditor's report on the audit of internal control over financial reporting must include the following elements—

a. A title that includes the word *independent*;

b. A statement that management is responsible for maintaining effective internal control over financial reporting and for assessing the effectiveness of internal control over financial reporting;

c. An identification of management's report on internal control;

d. A statement that the auditor's responsibility is to express an opinion on the company's internal control over financial reporting based on his or her audit;

e. A definition of internal control over financial reporting;

f. A statement that the audit was conducted in accordance with the standards of the Public Company Accounting Oversight Board (United States);

g. A statement that the standards of the Public Company Accounting Oversight Board require that the auditor plan and perform the audit to obtain reasonable assurance about whether effective internal control over financial reporting was maintained in all material respects;

h. A statement that an audit includes obtaining an understanding of internal control over financial reporting, assessing the risk that a material weakness exists, testing and evaluating the design and operating effectiveness of internal control based on the assessed risk, and performing such other procedures as the auditor considered necessary in the circumstances;

i. A statement that the auditor believes the audit provides a reasonable basis for his or her opinion;

j. A paragraph stating that, because of inherent limitations, internal control over financial reporting may not prevent or detect misstatements and that projections of any evaluation of effectiveness to future periods are subject to the risk that controls may become inadequate because of changes in conditions, or that the degree of compliance with the policies or procedures may deteriorate;

k. The auditor's opinion on whether the company maintained, in all material respects, effective internal control over financial reporting as of the specified date, based on the control criteria;

l. The manual or printed signature of the auditor's firm;

   m.   The city and state (or city and country, in the case of non-U.S. auditors) from
           which the auditor's report has been issued; and

   n.   The date of the audit report.
(AS 5.85)

AUDITING IN ACTION

Combined Audit Report: Financial Statements and ICFR Opinions

Report of Independent Registered Public Accounting Firm

[*Introductory paragraph*]

We have audited the accompanying balance sheets of W Company as of December 31,
20X8 and 20X7, and the related statements of income, stockholders' equity and comprehensive income, and cash flows for each of the years in the three-year period ended
December 31, 20X8. We also have audited W Company's internal control over financial reporting as of December 31, 20X8, based on [*Identify control criteria, for example, "criteria established in Internal Control—Integrated Framework issued by the
Committee of Sponsoring Organizations of the Treadway Commission (COSO)."*].
W Company's management is responsible for these financial statements, for maintaining effective internal control over financial reporting, and for its assessment of
the effectiveness of internal control over financial reporting, included in the accompanying [title of management's report]. Our responsibility is to express an opinion
on these financial statements and an opinion on the company's internal control over
financial reporting based on our audits.

[*Scope paragraph*]

We conducted our audits in accordance with the standards of the Public Company
Accounting Oversight Board (United States). Those standards require that we plan
and perform the audits to obtain reasonable assurance about whether the financial
statements are free of material misstatement and whether effective internal control
over financial reporting was maintained in all material respects. Our audits of the
financial statements included examining, on a test basis, evidence supporting the
amounts and disclosures in the financial statements, assessing the accounting principles used and significant estimates made by management, and evaluating the overall financial statement presentation. Our audit of internal control over financial
reporting included obtaining an understanding of internal control over financial
reporting, assessing the risk that a material weakness exists, and testing and evaluating the design and operating effectiveness of internal control based on the assessed
risk. Our audits also included performing such other procedures as we considered
necessary in the circumstances. We believe that our audits provide a reasonable basis
for our opinions.

[*Definition paragraph*]

A company's internal control over financial reporting is a process designed to provide reasonable assurance regarding the reliability of financial reporting and the
preparation of financial statements for external purposes in accordance with generally accepted accounting principles. A company's internal control over financial
reporting includes those policies and procedures that (1) pertain to the maintenance
of records that, in reasonable detail, accurately and fairly reflect the transactions and
dispositions of the assets of the company; (2) provide reasonable assurance that transactions are recorded as necessary to permit preparation of financial statements in
accordance with generally accepted accounting principles, and that receipts and
expenditures of the company are being made only in accordance with authorizations
of management and directors of the company; and (3) provide reasonable assurance

(continued)

regarding prevention or timely detection of unauthorized acquisition, use, or disposition of the company's assets that could have a material effect on the financial statements.

[Inherent limitations paragraph]

Because of its inherent limitations, internal control over financial reporting may not prevent or detect misstatements. Also, projections of any evaluation of effectiveness to future periods are subject to the risk that controls may become inadequate because of changes in conditions, or that the degree of compliance with the policies or procedures may deteriorate.

[Opinion paragraph]

In our opinion, the financial statements referred to above present fairly, in all material respects, the financial position of W Company as of December 31, 20X8 and 20X7, and the results of its operations and its cash flows for each of the years in the three-year period ended December 31, 20X8 in conformity with accounting principles generally accepted in the United States of America. Also in our opinion, W Company maintained, in all material respects, effective internal control over financial reporting as of December 31, 20X8, based on *[Identify control criteria, for example, "criteria established in Internal Control —Integrated Framework issued by the Committee of Sponsoring Organizations of the Treadway Commission (COSO)."]*.

[Signature]
[City and State or Country]
[Date]
(AS 5.87)

Audit Reports on ICFR that are not Unqualified

An auditor can make fewer language changes to an unqualified report for an ICFR audit than to an unqualified financial statement audit report. If the auditor determines that there is even one material weakness in ICFR, the auditor expresses an adverse opinion. If the audit is affected by a scope limitation, the auditor disclaims an opinion or withdraws from the engagement. Also, if management's assessment report on the effectiveness of ICFR includes additional information and users might conclude that the audit applies to that additional information, the auditor should disclaim an opinion.

An adverse opinion report on ICFR includes the following:

- The definition of a material weakness
- A statement that a material weakness has been identified
- Identification of the material weakness
- Either a statement that the material weakness is included in management's assessment, or that management's assessment does not include a description of the material weakness
- If the material weakness is not included in management's assessment, a description of the material weakness with specific information about its nature, and its actual and potential effect on the financial statements
- If the material weakness is included in management's assessment but is not fairly presented, a statement that this is the case and a description of the material weakness

While adverse opinions on financial statements are extremely rare, adverse ICFR opinions are not. Exhibit 11-16, from the 10K of Asyst Technologies, presents an example of

EXHIBIT 11-16

Adverse Opinion on
ICFR

Report of Independent Registered Public Accounting Firm

To the Board of Directors and Shareholders of Asyst Technologies, Inc.:

In our opinion, the accompanying consolidated balance sheets and the related consolidated statements of operations, of shareholders' equity and of cash flows present fairly, in all material respects, the financial position of Asyst Technologies, Inc. and its subsidiaries at March 31, 2008 and 2007, and the results of their operations and their cash flows for each of the three years in the period ended March 31, 2008 in conformity with accounting principles generally accepted in the United States of America. In addition, in our opinion, the financial statement schedule listed in the accompanying index presents fairly, in all material respects, the information set forth therein when read in conjunction with the related consolidated financial statements. Also in our opinion, the Company did not maintain, in all material respects, effective internal control over financial reporting as of March 31, 2008, based on criteria established in Internal Control—Integrated Framework issued by the Committee of Sponsoring Organizations of the Treadway Commission (COSO) because a material weakness in internal control over financial reporting related to maintaining a sufficient complement of personnel with an appropriate level of knowledge, experience and training in the application of generally accepted accounting principles commensurate with the Company's financial reporting requirements in the area of income taxes existed as of that date. A material weakness is a deficiency, or a combination of deficiencies, in internal control over financial reporting, such that there is a reasonable possibility that a material misstatement of the annual or interim financial statements will not be prevented or detected on a timely basis. The material weakness referred to above is described in Management's Report on Internal Control Over Financial Reporting appearing under Item 9A. We considered this material weakness in determining the nature, timing, and extent of audit tests applied in our audit of the 2008 consolidated financial statements, and our opinion regarding the effectiveness of the Company's internal control over financial reporting does not affect our opinion on those consolidated financial statements. The Company's management is responsible for these financial statements and financial statement schedule, for maintaining effective internal control over financial reporting and for its assessment of the effectiveness of internal control over financial reporting included in management's report referred to above. Our responsibility is to express opinions on these financial statements, on the financial statement schedule, and on the Company's internal control over financial reporting based on our integrated audits. We conducted our audits in accordance with the standards of the Public Company Accounting Oversight Board (United States). Those standards require that we plan and perform the audits to obtain reasonable assurance about whether the financial statements are free of material misstatement and whether effective internal control over financial reporting was maintained in all material respects. Our audits of the financial statements included examining, on a test basis, evidence supporting the amounts and disclosures in the financial statements, assessing the accounting principles used and significant estimates made by management, and evaluating the overall financial statement presentation. Our audit of internal control over financial reporting included obtaining an understanding of internal control over financial reporting, assessing the risk that a material weakness exists, and testing and evaluating the design and operating effectiveness of internal control based on the assessed risk. Our audits also included performing such other procedures as we considered necessary in the circumstances. We believe that our audits provide a reasonable basis for our opinions.

As discussed in Note 2 to the consolidated financial statements, the Company changed the manner in which it accounts for uncertain tax positions in fiscal 2008.

As discussed in Note 2 to the consolidated financial statements, the Company changed the manner in which it accounts for sabbatical leave in fiscal 2008.

As discussed in Note 2 to the consolidated financial statements, the Company changed the manner in which it accounts for share-based compensation in fiscal 2007.

As discussed in Note 9 to the consolidated financial statements, the Company changed the manner in which it accounts for defined benefit pension plans in fiscal 2007.

(continued)

A company's internal control over financial reporting is a process designed to provide reasonable assurance regarding the reliability of financial reporting and the preparation of financial statements for external purposes in accordance with generally accepted accounting principles. A company's internal control over financial reporting includes those policies and procedures that (i) pertain to the maintenance of records that, in reasonable detail, accurately and fairly reflect the transactions and dispositions of the assets of the company; (ii) provide reasonable assurance that transactions are recorded as necessary to permit preparation of financial statements in accordance with generally accepted accounting principles, and that receipts and expenditures of the company are being made only in accordance with authorizations of management and directors of the company; and (iii) provide reasonable assurance regarding prevention or timely detection of unauthorized acquisition, use, or disposition of the company's assets that could have a material effect on the financial statements.

Because of its inherent limitations, internal control over financial reporting may not prevent or detect misstatements. Also, projections of any evaluation of effectiveness to future periods are subject to the risk that controls may become inadequate because of changes in conditions, or that the degree of compliance with the policies or procedures may deteriorate.

/s/ PricewaterhouseCoopers LLP
San Jose, California
June 9, 2008

an adverse opinion report on ICFR. The exhibit also shows that the report can be structured differently from the model reports provided in the PCAOB standards as long as all of the required elements are included.

In addition to presenting an adverse opinion or disclaiming an opinion, the auditor may modify an unqualified opinion on ICFR to refer to the report of other auditors when it is used as part of the basis for the auditor's own report. Regarding subsequent events, assuming management modifies its report appropriately, the auditor adds only explanatory language to an unqualified ICFR audit report if a subsequent event occurs after the date of management's assessment causing ICFR to become ineffective.

REVIEW QUESTIONS

F.1   In what ways are the elements of an ICFR audit report different from the elements of a financial statement audit report?

F.2   Why is an adverse opinion issued for ICFR?

F.3   What type of ICFR audit opinion is appropriate when a scope limitation exists?

CONCLUSION

The final phase of an integrated audit includes procedures that will either support or disconfirm the earlier tests and procedures of the audit. Multiple steps are involved in the wrap-up phase, and many of them involve "big picture" issues. The review process is also critical to completing the audit. Assuming the final steps do not produce disconfirming information, the audit proceeds with a decision on the appropriate audit report. While general content and language of the audit report is straightforward, many different types of reports are available and may be necessary for different situations.

KEY TERMS

Adverse opinion. The audit opinion issued when the auditor concludes that the financial statements are not presented in accordance with GAAP or that a material weakness exists in ICFR.

Assessments. Obligations of an audit client for which an amount has already been set.

Associated with financial statements. Refers to the status of an auditor who has performed financial statement related work for a company; specifically, includes when the accountant has consented to the use of his or her name.

Audit report date. The date of the auditor's opinion; not to be before all the necessary audit procedures are completed and needed audit evidence is obtained.

Claims. In an audit context, refers to assertions made by an outside party regarding the obligations of an audit client.

Clean opinion. Unqualified opinion.

Commitment. An obligation to act in the future; has a set action and financial amount.

Contingent liabilities. Obligations that may exist but depend on events that have not yet occurred; may be uncertain in amount.

Disclaimer of opinion. Describes the audit report in which an auditor states that no opinion is given on the fairness of the financial statements or effectiveness of ICFR.

Documentation completion date. The deadline for finalizing the audit documentation for retention; after that date documentation may be added but may not be removed.

Dual dating. An auditor's use of one date for the overall audit report and a second later date for referring to a subsequent event.

Engagement completion document. Required documentation that summarizes significant findings and issues and aids a reviewer in understanding the audit and results.

Engagement quality review. Required by SOX as part of the audit of a public company; to be performed by a partner (or appropriately qualified person) other than the individual in charge of the engagement.

Explanatory language. Additional information, typically included in an extra paragraph, included in an auditor's report containing an unqualified opinion.

Going concern. Refers to whether a company can continue in business for a reasonable period of time after the financial statement date, not longer than one year.

Independent review. See Engagement quality review.

Inquiry of client's outside legal counsel. Letter returned from client's outside legal counsel to the auditor with information on litigation, claims, and commitments.

Management representations letter. Written documentation by management directed to the auditor confirming various statements or representations about the financial statements and information provided to the auditor.

Management's written representations. See *Management representations letter.*

Omitted audit procedure. Refers to the situation in which, after the audit report is released, the auditor determines that a necessary audit procedure was not performed.

Principal auditor. The audit firm that performs most of the work, or a significant enough part of the work, on an audit that it should author the audit report, either with or without mention of another auditor's work.

Qualified opinion. A financial statement audit opinion stating that the financial statements are fair except for the matter discussed in the opinion—including a scope limitation, uncertainty, or departure from generally accepted accounting principles.

Reissuing an audit report. A previously issued report of a prior year's audit is released again by the same auditor; the report may accompany the audit report from a different auditor for the current year.

Related party transactions. Business activities covered by accounting standards that set forth the definition of related parties and disclosures required; important to auditors because of the risk that the transcations may not be transparent and arms length.

Scope limitation. Refers to the situation in which the auditor is unable to complete all the procedures judged to be necessary for the audit.

Significant findings or issues. Results of audit procedures that are important to audit conclusions and must be included in the engagement completion document.

Standard report. Term used to refer to a report containing an unqualified audit opinion.

Subsequent events. Events that impact either the ICFR or financial statement audit and audit report that occur between the financial statement date and audit report date.

Unasserted claim. A company may have a contingent liability resulting from an event that has already occurred, but the injured party has not yet pursued the claim.

Unqualified opinion. An audit report stating the auditor's conclusion that the financial statements are fair, in all material respects, in accordance with GAAP, or that the company's ICFR is effective.

Unusual year-end transactions. Large or unusual transactions shortly before or after the fiscal year end, or those determined and entered outside the typical general ledger or closing processes.

Withdraw. Term that refers to the auditor's decision to no longer be a company's auditor.

MULTIPLE CHOICE[6]

11-1 **[LO 1]** Analytical procedures used during an audit's final review include

(a) identifying accounts that have not changed from the prior year and collecting evidence on them.

(b) retesting control procedures that were concluded to lack operating effectiveness during tests of controls.

(c) evaluating account balances that differ from expected amounts.

(d) performing additional substantive tests on quantitatively large financial statement amounts.

11-2 **[LO 1]** To be effective, analytical procedures in the overall review stage of an audit engagement should be performed by

(a) a staff-level member of the audit team.

(b) a staff-level member of another audit team.

(c) a manager or partner with knowledge and understanding of the client's business and industry.

(d) the individual who has responsibility for the firm's peer review program.

11-3 **[LO 1]** Which of the following procedures would an auditor perform during the completion phase of the audit to directly address the statement of cash flows?

(a) compare the cash balance amounts to similar accounts and balances in the prior year.

(b) reconcile the cutoff bank statements to year-end bank balances and recalculate a sample of client-prepared bank reconciliations.

(c) test the accuracy of the client's year-end inter-bank transfer schedule and trace the amounts to the related bank statements.

(d) reconcile the amounts included in the client's statement of cash flows to the other financial statements' balances and amounts, and to the audit work papers.

11-4 **[LO 1]** PCAOB AS 3, *Audit Documentation* establishes a cutoff after which nothing can be removed from the audit work papers. The cutoff is the

(a) company's fiscal year end.

(b) field work date.

(c) document completion date.

(d) SEC filing date.

11-5 **[LO 1]** Which of the following would *not* be included in management's written representations for either the ICFR or financial statement audits?

(a) description of a fraud that caused a material misstatement or any fraud involving senior management.

(b) information concerning subsequent events.

(c) management's knowledge of future plans that may eventually affect the price of the entity's stock.

(d) management's compliance with contractual agreements that may affect the financial statements.

11-6 **[LO 1]** When management provides written representations to the auditor, the concept of materiality applies to all of the following except

(a) guarantees that cause contingent liabilities.

(b) completeness and availability of all minutes of meetings of stockholders, directors, and committees of directors.

(c) financial statement misstatements identified by the auditor that management is not correcting.

(d) subsequent events.

11-7 **[LO 1]** Which of the following best describes the value of obtaining written representations from management when the auditor has difficulty obtaining sufficient appropriate evidence for a particular account balance assertion?

(a) Management's written assertions complement, but do not replace, substantive tests as evidence.

(b) Management's written assertions can constitute sufficient evidence to support the assertion for an account balance when considered in combination with reliance on internal control.

(c) Management's written assertions are not part of the evidential matter.

(d) Management's written assertions may replace reliance on internal control as evidence to support an account balance assertion.

(*Hint*: AU 333.03)

11-8 **[LO 2]** Which of the following is *not* true about a scope limitation?

(a) A scope limitation on an ICFR audit always results in a disclaimer of opinion or a withdrawal of the auditor from the engagement.

(b) A scope limitation imposed by management on a financial statement audit always results in a disclaimer of opinion or a withdrawal of the auditor from the engagement.

(c) A scope limitation imposed by management on a financial statement audit may result in either a qualified opinion or a disclaimer of opinion.

(d) A scope limitation exists when management will not provide a representation letter to the auditor.

11-9 **[LO 1]** If a client's attorney refuses to provide information requested in an inquiry letter, the

(a) auditor must issue an adverse opinion.

(b) refusal creates a scope limitation for the audit.

(c) auditor must withdraw from the engagement.

(d) lack of cooperation from the attorney is a material ICFR weakness.

11-10 **[LO 1]** All of the following are appropriate audit procedures for litigation, claims, and assessments except

(a) having management provide written representations that it has disclosed all unasserted claims that the lawyer has advised are probable of assertion and must be disclosed.

(b) asking the client's outside attorney to communicate directly with the auditor regarding whether all claims are recorded in the financial statements.

(c) during the ICFR audit, investigating the client's policies and procedures for identifying, evaluating, and accounting for litigation, claims, and assessments.

(d) obtaining from management a description and an evaluation of litigation, claims, and assessments existing at the balance sheet date.

11-11 **[LO 1]** Which of the following conditions or events is the *most important* to the auditor when assessing whether a client will likely continue as a going concern for a year from the financial statement date?

(a) The client has a number of related parties with which it conducts business transactions.

(b) For the first time many of the company's suppliers will not permit the company to purchase using its traditional credit arrangement.

(c) Preferred stock dividends were in arrears and have recently been paid.

(d) The Board of Directors has established restrictions preventing the company from disposing of certain principal assets.

11-12 **[LO 1]** An auditor's subsequent events review would include which of the following audit procedures?

(a) Investigate changes in employee pay rates that went into effect after year end to determine whether they were properly authorized.

(b) Investigate the sale of plant assets that were sold after year end to determine whether the company properly accounted for any gain or loss.

(c) Inquire about checks to suppliers that were cashed shortly after year end for purchases of inventory that were received prior to year end.

(d) Assess whether the company appropriately reclassified debt that became short term after year end.

11-13 **[LO 1]** Which of the following procedures is a part of the audit for subsequent events?

(a) Compare the most recent interim financial statements with the year-end financial statements being audited.

(b) Follow up with the client's customers who did not respond to initial accounts receivable confirmation requests.

(c) Make the mandatory communications to the Board of Directors and audit committee.

(d) Review the client's bank statements for several months after year end.

11-14 **[LO 1]** Six months after issuing an unqualified opinion on a company's financial statements, an audit partner was told by the audit manager working on the engagement that the audit team failed to confirm several of the client's material accounts receivable balances. The auditor should **first**

(a) ask the client for permission to confirm the accounts receivable balances.

(b) investigate whether the client's customers have paid off the accounts receivable that were due at the balance sheet date.

(c) assess whether having omitted the confirmations process on those particular accounts receivable impairs the ability to support the previously expressed audit opinion.

(d) ask the client whether anyone is currently relying on, or likely to rely on, the unqualified opinion.

11-15 **[LO 1]** Which of the following procedures occurs during the wrap-up stage of an integrated audit?

(a) Obtain a letter from the entity's attorney indicating that all material litigation has been disclosed in the financial statements.

(b) Recalculate the clerical accuracy of the entity's bank reconciliation and cutoff bank statement and trace final amounts into the general ledger.

(c) Follow up on a significant deficiency in ICFR regarding inadequate safeguarding of assets, to determine whether the problem has been corrected.

(d) Consider whether the risk of material misstatement due to fraud needs to be changed.

DISCUSSION QUESTIONS

11-16 **[LO 2]** What types of audit reports are issued for financial statement audits? Are all of those types of reports likely to be issued for audits of public companies? If not, which ones are not likely used and why?

11-17 **[LO 2]** Describe the different types of ICFR audit reports that can be issued and the circumstances justifying each type of report.

11-18 **[LO 2, 3]** How can the language of an *unqualified* ICFR audit report be modified and for what reasons?

11-19 **[LO 2, 3]** What are the reasons for explanatory language in an unqualified financial statement audit report?

11-20 **[LO 2]** When is the audit report dated? Why is the date of the audit report important?

11-21 **[LO 3]** What is added to both the ICFR audit report and financial statement audit report when separate reports (rather than a combined report) are issued? Provide a sample of the language.

11-22 **[LO 2, 3]** How is an unqualified ICFR audit report modified for a subsequent event indicating that ICFR is ineffective, when the subsequent event occurs after the balance sheet date?

11-23 **[LO 1, 2]** How is the financial statement *audit report* affected by a recognized, Type I subsequent event, assuming management adjusts the financial statements appropriately? A nonrecognized, Type II subsequent event, assuming management adjusts the financial statement disclosures appropriately?

11-24 **[LO 3]** What audit report language is used to describe the audit standards followed for a public company audit? A nonpublic company audit?

PROBLEMS

11-25 **[LO 2, 3]** Refer to the audit report for TOUSA Inc. in Exhibit 11-14 and answer the following questions:

(a) Why was another auditor involved in the audit? In what paragraphs of the report was the other auditor mentioned?

(b) Where is the going-concern problem discussed in the audit report? What language is used? Where is it discussed in the company's financial statements?

(c) What changes in accounting principles did the company adopt? When? Does the company describe the justification for the change in terms of preferability? If yes, how? If not, why?

(d) What can you find out about the audit of ICFR from this audit report on the financial statements?

11-26 **[LO 1, 3]** Refer to the audit report for Asyst Technologies in Exhibit 11-16. The report is presented as an example of an adverse opinion on ICFR. Answer the following questions regarding the other contents of the report.

(a) What is the auditor's opinion on the financial statements? To what financial statements and what years does the financial statement audit opinion apply?

(b) What ICFR framework did management and the auditor use?

(c) What was the material weakness in ICFR that caused the adverse opinion?

(d) To what is the audit report referring when it mentions Management's Report on Internal Control Over Financial Reporting appearing under Item 9A? What Section of SOX requires this particular management report? (*Hint:* If you need to, go to www.sec.gov and look up the company's 3/31/08 10K to reference Item 9A and the management report.)

(e) The audit report includes statements beginning with: As discussed in Note… Why are these statements included? Do they affect the auditor's opinion on the financial statements?

11-27 **[LO 1]** Triad, Inc. sells body armor to various governments around the world. One of its major customers was a country that was experiencing civil unrest throughout the past year. Triad, Inc. had a very material account receivable from this country's military government at its fiscal year end on December 31.

Although it was temporarily kept a secret from the press, the military government was overthrown in the last week of the calendar year and a new democratic government was set up with an interim president. When elections were held in January, one of the decisions made by the voters was to disavow any of the prior government's debts to any entities outside the country. Triad, Inc. management and the audit firm learn about these events from news reports in January while the integrated audit engagement is in process.

(a) How should these events affect Triad, Inc.'s financial statements? How should they affect the financial statement audit report? Does this scenario affect the auditor's report on ICFR?

(b) Assume that the military government was overthrown in early January and Triad and the auditor learned of it in February, when the audit was still in process. How does your answer change?

(c) Assume that the military government was overthrown in March and that Triad and the audit firm saw the news reports shortly after the 10K, including the audit report, was filed with the SEC. How does your answer change?

11-28 **[LO 1, 3]** Cohen and Single, LLP, are auditing the ICFR and financial statements of Copley and Sons, a public company that sells supplies to government agencies. Copley and Sons has a 12/31 fiscal year end. Cohen and Single conclude that the financial statements for the current and prior year are fairly stated. However, they found a material weakness in ICFR. There is a lack of separation of duties because the companys' CFO has the ability to change passwords on employee's computer identification numbers and has unlimited access to a computer terminal through which any journal entry can be entered without approval and review. Management's evaluation of ICFR is also as of 12/31, and management's report states that ICFR is not effective due to the computer security problem causing the lack of separation of duties. Draft Cohen and Single's combined audit report with opinions on the financial statements and ICFR as described.

11-29 **[LO 1]** Refer to Problem 11-28. Draft a management representations letter for Copley and Sons to submit to Cohen and Single LLP. The management representations letter should address all the points needed for both the financial statement and ICFR audits.

11-30 **[LO 1]** Assume you are a senior who has been assigned to the audit of Overkill Motor Yachts, when the senior previously assigned to the engagement left the firm for another position. Most of the audit planning has been completed, but the audit plan for the wrap-up phase is not finished.

Draft the audit plan for the wrap up, including all audit procedures and steps for the wrap up stage of the integrated audit of Overkill Motor Yachts.

11-31 **[LO 3]** Below is an audit report for an integrated audit combined to include the opinions on both ICFR and the financial statements. Phrases reflecting 20 items that are required to be in this report have been removed and are provided in the list after the report. Select the proper phrase for each missing item and place the letter of the phrase on the answer space provided. All phrases will be used, and none will be used twice.

Report of _1_ Registered Public Accounting Firm

We have audited the accompanying balance sheets of W Company as of December 31, 20X8 and 20X7, and the related statements of income, stockholders' equity and comprehensive income, and cash flows for each of the years in the three-year period ended December 31, 20X8. We also have audited W Company's internal control over financial reporting as of December 31, 20X8, based on [*Identify control criteria, for example, "criteria established in Internal Control—Integrated Framework issued by the Committee of Sponsoring Organizations of the Treadway Commission (COSO)."*]. W Company's management is responsible for these__2__, for maintaining __3__, and for__4__, included in the accompanying ___5__. Our responsibility is to __6__ and __7__.

__8__. Those __9__the audits to obtain reasonable assurance about whether the financial statements are free of material misstatement and whether effective internal control over financial reporting was maintained __10__. Our audits of the financial statements __11__ evidence supporting the amounts and disclosures in the financial statements, assessing the accounting principles used and significant estimates made by management, and __12__. Our audit of internal control over financial reporting included obtaining an understanding of internal control over financial reporting, assessing the risk that a material weakness exists, and testing __13__. Our audits also included performing such other procedures as we considered necessary in the circumstances. We believe that our audits provide a reasonable basis for our opinions.

A company's internal control over financial reporting is a process designed to provide reasonable assurance regarding __14__ and the preparation of financial statements for external purposes in accordance with generally accepted accounting principles. A company's internal control over financial reporting includes those policies and procedures that (1) pertain to the maintenance of records that, in reasonable detail, accurately and fairly reflect the transactions and dispositions of the assets of the company; (2) provide reasonable assurance that transactions are recorded as necessary to permit preparation of financial statements in accordance with generally accepted accounting principles, and that receipts and expenditures of the company are being made only in accordance with authorizations of management and directors of the company; and (3) provide reasonable assurance regarding prevention or timely detection of unauthorized acquisition, use, or disposition of the company's assets that could have a material effect on the financial statements.

__15__internal control over financial reporting may not prevent or detect misstatements. Also, projections of any evaluation of effectiveness to future periods __16__ may become inadequate __17__, or that the degree of compliance with the policies or procedures may deteriorate.

__18__, the financial statements referred to above present fairly, in all material respects, the financial position of W Company as of December 31, 20X8 and 20X7, and the results of its operations and its cash flows for each of the years in the three-year period ended December 31, 20X8 __19__. Also in our opinion, W Company maintained, in all material respects, effective internal control __20__as of December 31, 20X8, based on [*Identify control criteria, for example, "criteria established in Internal*

Control—Integrated Framework issued by the Committee of Sponsoring Organizations of the Treadway Commission (COSO)."].

[SIGNATURE]
[City and State or Country]
[Date]

Phrases to choose from:

a. express an opinion on these financial statements
b. because of its inherent limitations
c. standards require that we plan and perform
d. independent
e. included examining, on a test basis
f. because of changes in conditions
g. its assessment of the effectiveness of internal control over financial reporting
h. the reliability of financial reporting
i. over financial reporting
j. financial statements
k. we conducted our audits in accordance with the standards of the Public Company Accounting Oversight Board (United States)
l. in conformity with accounting principles generally accepted in the United States of America
m. effective internal control over financial reporting
n. in our opinion
o. and evaluating the design and operating effectiveness of internal control based on the assessed risk
p. [title of management's report]
q. evaluating the overall financial statement presentation
r. an opinion on the company's internal control over financial reporting based on our audits
s. in all material respects
t. are subject to the risk that controls

Place the letter of the correct phrase on the answer line.

1.____	11.____
2.____	12.____
3.____	13.____
4.____	14.____
5.____	15.____
6.____	16.____
7.____	17.____
8.____	18.____
9.____	19.____
10.____	20.____

11-32 **[LO 1, 2]** Hurwitch and Carson, CPAs, are auditing Company A. They decide that Company A's balance sheet will be materially misstated if assets are overstated by $1 million or more. To be sure that the financial statements are not materially affected by the aggregation of smaller misstatements, they decide to set tolerable misstatement for both the investment and accounts receivable accounts at $30,000 each. After performing substantive tests, Hurwitch and Carson concluded that the investment account is overstated by a likely error of $50,000. Because the conclusion was of likely rather than known error, Company A posted adjusting entries reducing investments by $20,000. The audit has also found a number of misstatements in other accounts, but they are all somewhat below the tolerable misstatement threshold set for each of the accounts in which the misstatements are found. Hurwitch and Carson have performed whatever additional steps are necessary to be confident in the audit results found.

(a) At the wrap-up stage of the audit, what step or steps are performed to determine whether more adjusting entries are needed?

(b) If the aggregated unadjusted misstatements are close to the $1million threshold, is there more work to be done on investments? If so, what?

(c) What impact does the investment account misstatement have on the ICFR opinion? What steps might the auditor perform on ICFR at the wrap-up stage to make a final ICFR opinion decision?

(d) What kind of audit opinions will Hurwitch and Carson issue? Justify your conclusions.

11-33 **[LO 1]** During the audit of Bryant Industries, Janet Smith, the auditor, reviewed matters with the company's president, Brock Morton, that were supposed to be included in a written client representation letter. Unfortunately, she received the letter below:

February 20, 2011

To Janet Smith, CPA:

Regarding your audit of the financial statements for Bryant Industries, as of December 31, 2010, for the purpose of expressing an opinion on the fair presentation of financial position, results of operations, and cash flows in conformity with generally accepted accounting principles, we confirm to the best of our knowledge and belief that the following representations were made to you during your examination. There were no:

a. Plans or intent to materially affect the carrying value or classification of either assets or liabilities.

b. Unasserted claims that our lawyer has determined are probable and must be disclosed according to GAAP.

c. Compensating balance or other restrictive arrangements on cash balances.

d. Agreements to repurchase previously sold assets.

e. Regulatory agency communications concerning noncompliance with financial reporting practices.

f. Violations of laws or regulations that should be disclosed in the financial statement or as a basis for loss contingencies.

g. Capital stock repurchases or options that are reserved for conversions, warrants, etc.

Regards,
Brock Morton, President
Bryant Industries

Required:

(a) Based on this letter, identify at least five other matters that Brock Morton's representation letter should specifically confirm.

(b) What other problems exist with the letter provided to Janet Smith?

11-34 **[LO 1]** In completing the Simpson Company audit for the fiscal year ended, December 31, 2010, the following events occurred after the close of the fiscal year but before all members of the audit team left the client headquarters.

1. On January 15, 2011, one of the company's four major plants was flooded, resulting in a loss of $20 million worth of inventory and equipment. Insurance will cover $15 million of the loss.

2. On February 14, 2011, the Board of Directors unanimously confirmed a resolution to issue $30 million of preferred stock.

Required:

State what disclosures, if any, would be made in each case in the Simpson Company notes to the financial statements.

11-35 **[LO 1, 2]** You have just completed the field work for Jameson Manufacturing Company and have noted the following issues:

1. The estimated useful life of the plant property was reduced due to obsolescence, even though it is only two years old.

2. After three years of computing depreciation under the declining balance method for income tax purposes and under the straight-line method for reporting purposes, the declining balance method was adopted for reporting purposes.

3. The company disposed of one of its four subsidiaries that had been included in its consolidated statements for prior years.

Required:

Indicate which issues, if any, require recognition in the auditor's opinion as to consistency and which issues require note disclosure in Jameson's financial statements.

11-36 **[LO 1]** You are the audit manager for the Johnson Company audit. In reading the minutes of the Board of Directors' meetings, you found that the following events or issues were discussed:

1. Approval of a major recapitalization plan

2. Decision to dispose of a segment

3. Approval of a bonus for officers applicable to the year under audit

In addition, you read the latest interim financial statements and found that there were:

4. major adjustments correcting for overstatement of earnings in prior years.

Required:

(a) Differentiate between recognized, Type I and nonrecognized, Type II subsequent events.

(b) Explain whether each subsequent event you uncovered is a Type 1 or Type 2 and why.

11-37 **[LO 2, 3]** Place the letter of the report type that best fits the language presented on the answer line. Each report type may be used more than once or not at all, but each item has only one best answer. If you think more than one answer may apply, choose the BEST answer.

a. Explanatory language

b. Unqualified opinion with qualification for GAAP departure

c. Qualified opinion

d. Qualified opinion because of a scope limitation

e. Qualified opinion because of an ICFR deficiency

f. Qualified opinion because of a GAAP departure

g. Qualified opinion because of a change in accounting standards

h. Qualified opinion because of lack of independence

i. Qualified opinion plus explanatory language

j. Qualified opinion for dual dating

k. Qualified opinion to reflect need to rely on another auditor

l. Disclaimer of opinion because of a scope limitation

m. Disclaimer of opinion because of lack of independence

n. Adverse opinion

o. Combined report with unqualified opinions on financial statements and ICFR

_____1. In our opinion, the Company did not maintain, in all material respects, effective internal control over financial reporting as of March 31, 2010, based on criteria established in Internal Control—Integrated Framework issued by the Committee of Sponsoring Organizations of the Treadway Commission (COSO)...

_____2. In addition, as discussed in Note 9 to the consolidated financial statements, effective January 1, 2007, the Company adopted *Accounting for Uncertainty in Income Taxes*, FASB ASC 740-10.

_____3. We are not independent with respect to XYZ Company, and the accompanying balance sheet as of December 31, 19X1, and the related statements of income, retained earnings, and cash flows for the year then ended. ...

_____4. ...because of the effects of the matters discussed in the preceding paragraphs, the financial statements referred to above do not present fairly. ...

_____5. We have also audited in accordance with the standards of the Public Company Accounting Oversight Board (United States) the company's internal control over financial reporting as of December 31, 2010, based on criteria established in Internal Control-Integrated Framework issued by the Committee of Sponsoring Organizations of the Treadway Commission and our report dated August 6, 2011 expressed an unqualified opinion thereon.

_____6. ... except for the effects of such adjustments, if any, as might have been determined to be necessary...

_____7. The accompanying financial statements have been prepared assuming that ABC, Inc. will continue as a going concern. As more fully described in Note 1, the Company filed a voluntary petition for reorganization under Chapter 11 of the United States Bankruptcy Code on January 29, 2010, which raises substantial doubt about the Company's ability to continue as a going concern. Management's plans in regard to this matter are also described in Note 1.

_____8. The Company did not make a count of its physical inventory...The Company's records do not permit the application of other auditing procedures. ...the scope of our work was not sufficient to enable us to express. ...

_____9. In our opinion, except for the omission of the information discussed in the preceding paragraph....

_____10. In our opinion, based on our audits and the report of other auditors, the financial statements referred to above present fairly, in all material respects...

_____11. In our opinion, the financial statements referred to above present fairly, in all material respects, the financial position of W Company as of December 31, 2010 and 2009.... Also in our opinion, W Company maintained, in all material respects, effective internal control over financial reporting as of December 31, 2010. ...

_____**12.** We did not audit the financial statements of B Company, a wholly-owned subsidiary, which statements reflect total assets and revenues constituting 20 percent and 22 percent, respectively of the related consolidated totals. ... In our opinion, based on our audit and the report of the other auditors, the consolidated financial statements referred to above present fairly. ...

_____**13.** In our opinion...the financial statements present fairly... Dated February 16, 2010, except for Note 16, as to which the date is March 1, 2010.

_____**14.** Except as discussed in the following paragraph, we conducted our audits in accordance with auditing standards.... In our opinion, except for the effects...the financial statements present fairly. ...

_____**15.** As discussed in Note X to the financial statements, the 20X2 financial statements have been restated to correct a misstatement.

11-38 [LO 3] The following two paragraphs are part of the audit report used to present the auditor's opinions of XYZ Company.

> In our opinion, the financial statements referred to above present fairly, in all material aspects, the financial position of XYZ company as of October 31, 2011 and 2010, and the changes in net assets and its cash flows for the years then ended in conformity with accounting principles generally accepted in the United States of America. ...
>
> Our audits were performed for the purpose of forming an opinion on the basic financial statements of XYZ Company taken as a whole. The accompanying Schedule of Expenditures of Federal Awards and State Projects is presented for purposes of additional analysis as required by the U.S. Office of Management and Budget Circular A-133, _Audits of States, Local Governments, and Non-Profit Organizations_, and Chapter 10.650, Rules of the Auditor General, and is not a required part of the basic financial statements. The Schedule of Explicit and Discrete Disclosure for Able County and the Schedule of Revenue and Expenses are presented for purposes of additional analysis and are not a required part of the basic financial statements. Such information has been subjected to the auditing procedures applied in the audit of the basic financial statements and, in our opinion, is fairly stated, in all material respects in relation to the basic financial statements taken as a whole.

Required:

Answer the following.

(a) What do you know about the nature of the XYZ Company based on the audit report?

(b) How are the deliverables in this audit engagement different from those of a "standard" integrated audit of a company that has to file with the SEC?

(c) Based on the information you can glean from the audit report paragraphs, how would the auditor change planning the scope, timing, and resources for the audit engagement from a typical financial statement audit of a nonpublic company?

ACTIVITY ASSIGNMENTS

11-39 Answer the following.

(a) Access AU 333.09 using either the AICPA Web site or PCAOB Web site Interim Standards. Who signs management's written representations?

(b) Access a 10K. Who signs the SOX Section 404 report? (You can find the answer to this question in authoritative guidance on the SEC Web site, but the source and language are difficult. Accessing a 10K is an easier way to answer the question.)

11-40 Look up the most recent 10K filing of a company of your choice by going to www.sec.gov. Find the notes to the financial statements that disclose commitments, contingencies, and litigation. Using information from the 10K and the financial statements, prepare a letter of inquiry from the company to its lawyer:

Christine Srygley Tuttle, Esq.

628 SW 25th Avenue

Anywhere, USA 90210

Because you are using the disclosed information you will not be able to list unasserted claims and assessments, so you may omit this from your letter. Print out the disclosure that you used when drafting the inquiry letter.

PROFESSIONAL SIMULATIONS

Go to the book's companion Web site at www.wiley.com/college/hooks to find simulations similar to those on the computerized CPA exam.

ADDITIONAL TRANSACTION CYCLES AND OTHER TOPICS

CHAPTER 12

Auditing Acquisitions and Payments Processes: Cash Disbursements and Related Activities in the Automotive Industries

LEARNING OBJECTIVES FOR THIS CHAPTER

1. Learn the activities, transactions, risks, and accounts associated with acquisition and payments in a variety of business environments.
2. Understand the significant characteristics of the automotive industry that affect acquisitions and payments.
3. Learn the common business processes, ICFR, and documents associated with acquisitions and payments.
4. Link management assertions, risks, procedures, and audit evidence, including the purposes and execution of tests of controls for acquisitions and payments and related accounts.

5. Describe the extension of control tests into dual purpose tests, and the financial statement audit purposes that the extension accomplishes for acquisition and payment and related accounts.

6. Link management assertions, risks, procedures, and audit evidence, including the purposes and execution of substantive analytical procedures and tests of details of balances for acquisitions and payments and related accounts.

7. Apply the assertions, controls, and audit tests for purchase and payment transactions to prepaid expenses, accrued liabilities, expenses, fixed assets, and intangible assets.

Chapter 12 Resources

AU 312, AICPA, PCAOB, *Audit Risk and Materiality in Conducting an Audit*

AU 314, AICPA, *Understanding the Entity and Its Environment and Assessing the Risks of Material Misstatement*

AU 316, AICPA, PCAOB, *Consideration of Fraud in a Financial Statement Audit*

AU 318, AICPA, *Performing Audit Procedures in Response to Assessed Risks and Evaluating the Audit Evidence Obtained*

AU 319, PCAOB, *Consideration of Internal Control in a Financial Statement Audit*

AU 322, AICPA, PCAOB, *The Auditor's Consideration of the Internal Audit Function in the Audit of Financial Statements*

AU 326, AICPA, *Audit Evidence*

AU 326, PCAOB, *Evidential Matter*

AU 329, AICPA, PCAOB, *Analytical Procedures*

AU 330, AICPA, PCAOB, *The Confirmation Process*

AU 342, AICPA, PCAOB, *Auditing Accounting Estimates*

AU 350, AICPA, PCAOB, *Audit Sampling*

FASB Codification 360-10-15, *Impairment or Disposal of Long Lived Assets*

FASB ASC 450-10, *Contingencies*

FASB ASC 460-10, *Guarantees*

FASB ASC 820-10, *Fair Value Measurements and Disclosures*

FASB ASC 825-10-45, *Financial Instruments, Fair Value Option*

FASB Concepts Statement No. 6 *Elements of Financial Statements*

PCAOB AS 3, *Audit Documentation*

PCAOB AS 5, *An Audit of Internal Control Over Financial Reporting That is Integrated with an Audit of Financial Statements*

SEC Staff Accounting Bulletin 108, *Considering the Effects of Prior Year Misstatements When Quantifying Misstatements in Current Year Financial Statements*

INTRODUCTION

The acquisitions and payments cycle includes the processes and transactions through which a company purchases and pays for goods and services. Purchases and payments for inventory, operating expenses and long-lived productive assets fall within this cycle. Purchase returns and purchase discounts are also included. Some cash disbursement transactions are not grouped with acquisitions and payments, but instead relate to other cycles that are presented in later chapters. The payments that fit into other cycles include those for payroll, investments, repayment of long-term debt, and other financing transactions.

The automotive industry is used in this chapter to illustrate the acquisitions and payments cycle. The chapter begins with an overview of acquisition and payment activities in retailing and manufacturing environments, both of which are found in the automotive industry. Characteristics of the automotive industry are then presented. The chapter discusses the foundation of important acquisitions and payments activities that are found in most businesses. After that, audit activities that are applied to acquisitions and payments are discussed. Finally, the chapter returns to auditing acquisitions and payments in the context of the automotive industry.

OVERVIEW

Buying goods and services is an activity that occurs in every type of industry and every business. The purpose of exploring the automotive industry is to show you how important it is for an auditor to understand the client business. The nature of the client business affects all aspects of the audit, including the focus here on acquisitions and cash disbursements. The automotive industry includes businesses involved in retail and wholesale trade and manufacturing. Consequently, the industry's acquisition and payment transactions cover items classified as product costs, period costs, and long-term assets. Thus, highlighting the automotive industry provides the opportunity to discuss a wide range of transactions, business functions, and audit activities.

Some cash disbursements fit more clearly into other cycles. However, they often interact with the **acquisitions and payments cycle**. For example, payroll is addressed as it relates to the human resources cycle in Chapter 13. Investments and debt are discussed in Chapter 15. Although repayment of debt associated with long-term assets is discussed in Chapter 15, other aspects of long-term assets are presented in this chapter. The acquisitions and payments cycle links with the manufacturing and inventory cycle when the items purchased are used to manufacture goods for sale or are purchased as finished goods to be resold. Manufacturing and inventory is the topic of Chapter 14. Since good ICFR calls for purchases to be paid in a manner that is documented, such as by check or electronic funds transfer, most acquisitions are recorded in some sort of payable account before they are paid. Thus, payables accounts are also considered a part of this cycle. Typical transaction activities in this cycle are:

Acquiring and paying for goods and services

Returning purchases and obtaining discounts

Accounts involved in this cycle are:

Cash   Accounts Payable

Prepaid Assets   Accrued Liabilities

Inventory   Expenses

Fixed Assets

Intangible Assets

ACQUISITION AND PAYMENT ASPECTS OF RETAILING [LO 1]

An introduction to the retailing environment was presented in Chapter 10, emphasizing sales and collection transactions. Here the emphasis is on purchasing goods and services. The main activity of a retail business is the purchase and resale of finished goods. What is described for retailers can also be applied to wholesalers because, in this regard, wholesale distributors and retailers do not differ substantially. The main difference is that wholesalers sell to retailers, and retailers typically sell to end consumers.

Retailers must decide what inventory to purchase for resale. Information that helps management make this decision comes from the inventory system. Therefore, inventory information, such as how many of a particular item was last purchased, the date the items were received, how many have since been sold, and the number now left in inventory, is important to the purchasing process. Regardless of the information basis for the decision, once the purchase decision is made the transaction is fairly straightforward.

For any business whose primary activity is the purchase of merchandise and resale of that merchandise to others, the inventory account is a major part of the company's balance sheet. For these companies, the purchasing process is a major activity. If a retailer purchases $100 worth of finished goods for resale to customers, the transaction is recorded as:

Inventory (or Purchases)   100

    Accounts Payable   100

When the items purchased arrive at the retailer's place of business, internal controls that are part of the receiving function include both physically safeguarding the inventory that is received and preparing documents to record the receipt and movement of the inventory.

The other purchase and payment transactions conducted by a retailer are representative of those conducted by most entities. For example, a retailer pays for the expenses related to the space the business occupies, such as rent and utilities. Retailers pay for other typical administrative costs such as insurance and supplies. Retailers also pay for selling expenses, such as advertising. A retailer who receives a $1,250 electric bill records it as:

| Utilities Expense | 1,250 | |
| Accounts Payable | | 1,250 |

As with most businesses, retailers purchase (or lease) long-term assets used in the business. Virtually all entities have productive fixed assets, although the type differs based on the activities of the business. For example, retailers are not as likely as **manufacturers** to own heavy equipment. In contrast, retailers' fixed assets often include major leasehold improvements that result from "**building out**" or customizing the space they lease and from which they sell their retail inventory.

Just as in all businesses, retailers pay for the goods and services purchased when the payment is due, using a **cash disbursements process**. The cash disbursement may result from physically preparing a **paper check** or initiating an electronic transfer. After the payment transaction is entered into the system, the **cash disbursements journal or report** and **accounts payable subsidiary ledger**, as well as the general ledger, are updated. When the retailer pays the electric bill, the transaction posted is:

| Accounts Payable | 1,250 | |
| Cash | | 1,250 |

The "mirror image" of the sales returns and allowances transaction discussed in Chapter 10 is the purchase returns and allowances transaction. Retail businesses may need to return inventory items they have purchased. Or they may receive refunds, called allowances, when the goods received are not what was ordered or are damaged. Other types of expenses may be refunded as well. For example, insurance that is prepaid and then canceled typically results in an allowance or a refund. An additional consideration in the acquisition and payments cycle is purchase discounts, which may result when a company pays for items it purchases within a shorter than required time frame.

REVIEW QUESTIONS

A.1 What kinds of transactions are included in the acquisition and payment cycle?

A.2 What is the main activity of a retail business?

A.3 Relating to inventory, once it has arrived at a retailer, what are some internal controls that should be implemented?

A.4 What types of fixed assets are common for retailers?

ACQUISITION AND PAYMENT ASPECTS OF MANUFACTURING

Manufacturing entities manufacture, create, build, assemble, or produce inventory to be sold to customers. The unique aspect of a **manufacturer** is that the business purchases raw materials inventory and adds labor and overhead to produce the finished goods. Thus, manufacturers purchase raw materials inventory rather than finished goods inventory.

The activities of purchasing, receiving, placing inventory into storage, and paying for the purchase are similar for a retailer and a manufacturer. Differences arise after that point because the manufacturer must track and control the inventory as it moves through the manufacturing process. This involves physical safeguards for the inventory, as well as maintaining whatever cost accounting records are needed. These activities are discussed in Chapter 14. Other expenditure activities for a manufacturer are similar to those for retailers. The purchase of a truckload of raw materials costing $2,000 is posted as follows:

Raw materials inventory (or Purchases)   2,000
    Accounts Payable   2000

ACQUISITION AND PAYMENT CONSIDERATIONS OF OTHER ENVIRONMENTS

Often the most significant "acquisition" and cash disbursements for an entity that provides services are for human resources. As mentioned earlier, human resources and payroll activities are addressed in Chapter 13. Even though payroll is a major cost for service entities, they also have occupancy and other day-to-day business expenses. These expenses are handled the same in a service industry environment as in retailing and manufacturing.

Acquisitions and disbursements by government entities differ significantly from for-profit businesses because they typically "encumber" the money for payment of a purchase either before or at the time of the purchase. The **encumbering process** effectively "sets aside" the amount that is committed from what is available to be spent, even before the invoice is received from the seller and the liability recorded. Governments operate using legally mandated budgets. The process of encumbering funds once the decision is made on how money is to be spent prevents the possibility that the government unit will commit to spending more cash than it has available. The accounting principles used by government entities is an important topic that is beyond the scope of this book. However, auditors who work on the audits of government clients need to understand how their accounting systems and processes differ. The acquisition and payments process is one example of differences in accounting by government units.

REVIEW QUESTIONS

B.1 What is the major business function of a manufacturing company?

B.2 How does encumbering funds help keep a government entity's spending within its budget?

THE AUTOMOTIVE INDUSTRY: AN OVERVIEW [LO 2]

A passenger vehicle dealership is often our first image when we think about the automotive industry, and with good reason. Passenger vehicles are a heavily marketed durable consumer good. Driving personal vehicles is often our primary form of transportation. We buy cars, trucks, and SUVs from retail showrooms. Passenger vehicles are part of our personal experience. Most people can rather easily consider the next level and acknowledge that the automotive industry includes the manufacture or assembly of those vehicles that are sold in dealer showrooms. The industry term for the large companies that we usually think of as the leaders in the industry is automotive **Original Equipment Manufacturers (OEM)**. Thus, people generally have a basic understanding that, in addition to retail sales, there are also manufacturing and wholesale components to the automotive industry. Accountants and auditors with automotive industry expertise understand that the industry is very complex.

AUDITING IN ACTION

What Is the Automotive Industry?

Edward is in his second year at a Big Four firm. He is excited because he has been assigned to the audit of a company in the automotive industry. He does not recognize the name of the company but has visions of all the new cars he will get to see before they even hit the retail market. He googles the client address and is a little confused because the location seems to be in the middle of a heavily industrial area of the city. His confusion turns to surprise when, during the audit planning meeting he learns that the company manufacturers a single part that is used in most of the fire trucks assembled in the United States.

A broader view of the automotive industry goes beyond personal passenger vehicles. Many vehicles are used for commercial purposes—for example, fire trucks, ambulances, and school busses. Commercial vehicles are typically purchased by private businesses, not-for-profit entities, and municipal governments. Commercial vehicles are sold either directly by the manufacturer or through a distributor. Other types of vehicles are purchased by governments for military purposes. In addition, the automotive industry extends beyond the vehicles and includes parts, accessories, and components. Sirius XM Radio is a company with a recognizable name for college students with sales in the automotive industry.

From "Sirius XM Radio, Inc." 10-K for the year ending 12/31/08:

Our primary means of distributing satellite radios is through the sale and lease of new vehicles. We have agreements with every major automaker—Acura/Honda, Aston Martin, Audi, Automobili Lamborghini, Bentley, BMW, Chrysler, Dodge, Ferrari, Ford, General Motors, Honda, Hyundai, Infiniti/Nissan, Jaguar, Jeep, Kia, Land Rover, Lincoln, Lexus/Toyota/Scion, Maybach, Mazda, Mercedes-Benz, Mercury, MINI, Mitsubishi, Porsche, Rolls-Royce, Volvo and Volkswagen—to offer either SIRIUS or XM satellite radios as factory or dealer-installed equipment in their vehicles. As of December 31, 2008, satellite radios were available as a factory or dealer-installed option in substantially all vehicle models sold in the United States.

Many automakers include a subscription to our radio service in the sale or lease price of their vehicles. In many cases, we receive subscription payments from automakers in advance of the activation of our service. We share with certain automakers a portion of the revenues we derive from subscribers using vehicles equipped to receive our service. We also reimburse various automakers for certain costs associated with the satellite radios installed in their vehicles, including in certain cases hardware costs, tooling expenses and promotional and advertising expenses.

AUDITING IN ACTION

Automotive SIC Codes[1]

3711	Motor Vehicles and Passenger Car Bodies
3713	Truck and Bus Bodies
3714	Motor Vehicle Parts and Accessories
3715	Truck Trailers
3716	Motor Homes

www.sec.gov/info/edgar/siccodes.htm

[1]**Standard Industrial Classification (SIC)** codes appear in the documents that a company files with the SEC and indicate the company's type of business.

If you explore the **EDGAR** database on the SEC Web site, and limit your search to the 3711 SIC code, you will find companies that are household names like Ford, General Motors, Honda, and Toyota. Smaller companies such as those that manufacture ambulances, small school busses, heavy-duty diesel trucks, and fire, emergency, and military vehicles fall within the 3711 SIC code as well. Numerous product and service lines are associated with nonpassenger vehicles in the automotive industry.

AUDITING IN ACTION

Nonpassenger Vehicle Product and Service Lines

Products

Fire and emergency equipment	Heavy and medium payload trucks
Tow trucks, wreckers, and recovery equipment	Armored vehicles
Ambulances	Concrete mixers
Snow removal vehicles	Tanker truckers
Mobile medical vehicles (e.g., mobile imaging services)	Vehicle adaptation kits
	After market parts
Broadcast and communication specialty vehicles	
Military all-wheel drive vehicles	

Services

Training	Test support
Field support	Repair services
Manual preparation	Parts delivery and related services
Financing	

Even though they are all public and under the jurisdiction of the SEC, the SIC 3711 companies vary greatly in size and capital structure. Some of the automotive companies are large as a result of growth over time; others have grown quickly by acquiring other companies. These companies often have purchased intangible assets either as individual purchases or as a result of mergers and acquisitions. Some of the intangible assets, such as patents, qualify as identifiable intangible assets. Goodwill is also common.

Some automotive businesses are in specialty markets with limited product lines, whereas others manufacture and sell multiple-product lines. The multiple-product lines range from personal and commercial vehicles and after-market parts to selling services such as training and financing. Activities related to the manufacturing process range from research and design of new products to fabrication of items for the company's own use or for sale to others and the assembly of parts into the final product.

Many different types of customers purchase vehicles and related products, and this also affects the selling company. For example, in its 2008 10K, Oshkosh Corporation discusses the impact of having the U.S. Department of Defense as one of its important customers.

> Approximately 29% of the Company's net sales for fiscal 2008 were made to the U.S. government, a substantial majority of which were under long-term contracts. … Accordingly, a significant portion of the Company's sales are subject to risks specific to doing business with the U.S. government, including uncertainty of economic conditions, changes in government policies and requirements that may reflect rapidly changing military and political developments, the availability of funds and the ability to meet specified performance thresholds. Long-term contracts may be conditioned upon continued availability of congressional appropriations, which could be impacted by a change in presidential

administrations in January 2009 and federal budget pressures arising from the federal bailout of financial institutions, insurance companies and others.

(10K, FYE 9/30/08)

Just as various types of business make up the automotive industry, so various types of customers purchase products and services from businesses in the automotive industry. An additional complexity is that these customers may be located in various countries throughout the world.

AUDITING IN ACTION

Customers of the Automotive Industry

Individuals	Universities
Passenger vehicle dealerships	Industrial companies
Municipal governments	Government defense departments
Airports	Mining companies
Construction companies	Transportation and delivery companies
Businesses of all types	

Business Risks Associated with Purchasing Activities

Although they are very diverse, all companies in the automotive industry share the common characteristic that they operate in a highly competitive industry. In their published documents the companies repeatedly state their need to retain or improve market share. They stress product quality, diversified and comprehensive product and service offerings, efficient manufacturing processes, design and engineering capabilities, and customer service and satisfaction as critical to their market positions.

Acquisition and payment activities may seem like routine "back-office" operations, but they are actually critical to the companies in the automotive sector as they strive to accomplish their market-related goals. Because of their comprehensive product and service lines, these companies generally purchase many goods and services from multiple vendors. For example, the automotive businesses that manufacture or assemble products usually purchase a variety of raw materials and component parts from different suppliers.

These companies must have sufficient purchasing process controls to be certain that they get needed raw materials in time for their scheduled manufacturing processes. Timely manufacturing is mandatory to meeting inventory needs to fulfill sales. In contrast, to achieve the lean manufacturing environment that allows them to be competitive, they also want to be certain that they only pay for what they receive.

Reliance on Vendors

The success of businesses in the automotive industry is often linked to the performance of the suppliers from which they purchase parts and components. Sometimes companies must or choose to rely on a single supplier for a particular part. Commitment to a single supplier exposes the business to greater potential problems if product quality or delivery performance is below expectations or if prices increase. Regardless of whether the company has one or multiple suppliers for a particular part, **just-in-time inventory** processes elevate the importance of reliable performance by suppliers. Even before experiencing its own major problems, General Motors was seriously impacted by a major supplier's bankruptcy.

ADDITIONAL TRANSACTION CYCLES AND OTHER TOPICS

From the 2006 SEC filings of General Motors:

On October 8, 2005, Delphi filed a petition for Chapter 11 proceedings under the United States Bankruptcy Code for itself and many of its U.S. subsidiaries. Delphi is GM's largest supplier of automotive systems, components and parts, and GM is Delphi's largest customer.

GM has worked and will continue to work constructively in the court proceedings with Delphi. … GM's goal is to achieve outcomes that are in the best interests of GM and its stockholders, and, to the extent conducive to those goals, that enable Delphi to continue as an important supplier to GM.

Delphi continues to assure GM that it expects no disruption in its ability to supply GM with the systems, components and parts it needs.

(10Q, 9/30/06, Note 8)

To manage these purchasing risks, automotive companies may investigate suppliers before committing to them and inspect suppliers' operations on an ongoing basis. Good controls over the purchasing and receiving processes help the company identify problems that arise on a timely basis. If problems develop with a supplier's product quality or delivery performance, the purchaser has to manage the resulting customer dissatisfaction and increased warranty costs.

Estimating the warranty liability accrual is an important process for automotive industry businesses. Increased warranty costs may not be an issue to the final retailer for some parts, for example, tires, for which the warranty may pass from the original producer to the customer. The company that sells the vehicle will likely still need to manage customer expectations and satisfaction, even when the warranty responsibility still rests with the initial supplier.

The National Highway Traffic Safety Administration (NHTSA) contacted Ford and Firestone in May, 2000 regarding tire failure. Significant failures had occurred with Firestone tires on Ford Explorers, Mercury Mountaineers, and Mazda Navajos. The ensuing investigation by Ford pinpointed high failure rates on several models of 15" Firestone tires. The particular models with the high failure rates were often manufactured at Firestone's Decatur, Illinois plant. The problem causing failures was tread separation from the underlying casings. Firestone announced a product recall, permitting owners of the potentially faulty tires to exchange them for other tires. At the time of the recall it was estimated that 6.5 million tires were in use.

(Information from http://money.cnn.com/2000/08/09/news/firestone_recall/, http://cbsnews.com/stories/2001/06/27/national/main298685.shtml)

The ultimate solution to a supplier's poor quality inventory or performance may be to change vendors. However, this is often not an easily executed option. The transition required when changing vendors takes time and can be expensive, especially if the component part is made to the purchasing company's specifications.

From Ford Motor Company's 12/31/08 10K:

Many components used in our vehicles [e.g., certain engines] are available from a single supplier and cannot be quickly or inexpensively re-sourced to another supplier due to long lead times and contractual commitments that might be required by another supplier.

Sometimes the ability of suppliers to deliver sufficient parts and components is limited simply because the quantity needed increases due to increased sales of final products. These market-driven shortages are difficult to guard against, regardless of the purchasing process controls in place. At the same time, the availability of supplies purchased on the international market may be affected by all of the typical risks of international trade.

AUDITING IN ACTION

Risks of International Trade

Political, religious, and economic instability
Local labor market conditions
Foreign tariffs and other trade barriers
Foreign government regulations
Effects of income and withholding taxes
Governmental expropriation
Differences in business practices

Toyota's 3/31/06 fiscal year-end information provides an example of the impact of operating in global markets in the following excerpt from a note to the financial statements:

> In September 2000, The European Union approved a directive that requires member states to promulgate regulation…: (i) manufacturers shall bear all or a significant part of the costs for taking back end-of-life vehicles put on the market after July 1, 2002 and dismantling and recycling those vehicles. … In addition, under this directive member states must take measures to ensure that car manufacturers … establish adequate used vehicle collection and treatment facilities and to ensure that hazardous materials and recyclable parts are removed from vehicles prior to shredding. This directive impacts Toyota's vehicles sold in the European Union and Toyota expects to introduce vehicles that are in compliance with … measures taken … pursuant to the directive.

Managing Acquisition-Related Costs

Generally, companies seek to mitigate the risk that their costs of manufacturing inputs and inventory will increase, and want to be certain they will have the required supply of inputs. To do this, automotive companies may enter into fixed price contracts with suppliers. Using fixed price contracts for the *purchase* of parts, components, and commodities is especially useful when a company has a fixed price contract to *sell* its product, as often happens, for example, with government entities. When an automotive company uses significant amounts of **commodities** such as steel, aluminum, and rubber, it is common to use financial instruments to hedge (or offset the risk of) commodity price changes. Investments used for hedging and the audit of these instruments are discussed in greater depth in Chapter 15.

A practice common in the automotive industry is to enter into purchase obligation arrangements or execute **blanket purchase orders** to suppliers, typically on an annual basis. Blanket purchase orders communicate expected needs to suppliers and become firm purchase obligations at some specified time prior to production. As part of their overall hedging and risk management strategy, automotive companies with significant reliance on international suppliers also hedge against price changes that may result from foreign currency exchange rate fluctuations.

Types of Acquisitions and Payments

Most businesses, including those in the automotive industry, purchase inventory, pay for operating expenses, and acquire long-lived productive assets. The notable exception is the business that only performs service activities. Service businesses typically do not purchase inventory or have product costs. While many exclusively service businesses exist in other industries, those classified as automotive typically have some type of inventory connected with their service activities. One such example is the sale of parts associated with providing repair services.

From Oshkosh Corporation, 10K:

Because the Company's vehicles must be ready to go to war, fight a fire, rescue, clean up, tow, broadcast, build and perform other critical missions, the Company has actively been expanding Company-owned service locations, encouraging dealers to expand service locations and add roving service vans to maintain high readiness levels of its installed fleets. ... The Company backs all products by same-day parts shipment, and its service technicians are available in person or by telephone to domestic customers 365 days a year.

(10K, FYE 9/30/08, Item 1)

Retailers purchase inventory in its finished form and sell it to the ultimate consumer. Wholesalers purchase inventory in its finished form and sell it to other businesses for resale. Manufacturers purchase materials that they process further into finished inventory.

Some companies participate very early in a chain of automotive manufacture and use raw metals or other commodities. Other companies purchase previously processed inputs for further manufacturing or processing. The processed inputs, which are the "raw" materials of the subsequent manufacturer, are typically finished goods of the company making the sale. An example is when an automotive parts fabricator purchases supplies, processes them into parts, and sells them to another company. The purchasing company then uses the parts in an assembly process with the output being either another component part or a completed product, such as a vehicle. The automotive industry uses an extremely large number of different parts, components, and end products, both purchased and sold, as well as multiple operating locations. Thus, companies in the automotive industry often utilize extensive IT systems to provide inventory information and support the purchasing process.

Beyond inventory, other acquisition and payment transactions involve operating expenses incurred and long lived assets. Long-lived assets acquired can be tangible or intangible. An example of tangible long-lived assets is property, plant, and equipment. Intangible asset examples are patents, customer lists, and goodwill. These transactions are similar across business types with no characteristics particularly unique to the automotive industry.

The varied activities of businesses in the automotive industry direct not only the items acquired, but also the categories of liabilities shown on the balance sheets. Most of the items addressed in this cycle are captured through a typical accounts payable account. But others are less common. For example, "floor plan notes payable" represents the liabilities of a car dealership to a manufacturer for unsold vehicles on the sales floor. These notes are generally non-interest-bearing for a period of time. Within the specified time frame the note is due (without interest) when the car is sold. If the dealership sells the inventory quickly enough, it can collect the proceeds and pay for the inventory purchase without incurring any financing costs. An important item captured in the liability section of virtually all automotive industry balance sheets is accrued warranty costs. Liabilities related to environmental remediation are common as well.

REVIEW QUESTIONS

C.1 Besides personal use vehicles, what are some other examples of products created in the automotive industry?

C.2 Why are acquisition and payment activities very important to the success of automotive industry companies (in contrast to being considered simply back-office functions?)

C.3 Why might automotive industry companies choose to investigate suppliers before entering into contracts with them?

C.4 How is the purchasing process complicated when a manufacturer sells products in various international markets?

C.5 How are fixed price contracts used to mitigate risk?

C.6 What does it mean when a financial instrument is used to hedge the cost of items that must be purchased for the manufacturing process?

C.7 Why do companies in the automotive industry need extensive IT systems linked to purchasing to manage their inventory?

BUSINESS PROCESSES, DOCUMENTS, AND INTERNAL CONTROL [LO 3]

Management has several important objectives related to acquisitions and payments. One objective is to limit items that are ordered and purchased to those the company legitimately needs for its use. For example, the business does not want to purchase and pay for items that are not needed for business activities or that an employee wants for personal use. To accomplish this, all requests for purchases and purchase transactions should be authorized.

Purchase authorization can occur in a variety of ways. Blanket purchase orders, previously mentioned related to the automotive industry, serve to inform the supplier of the expected need and to authorize the purchase of the input component as it is needed for production. Depending on the specifics of the contract, the purchase price may be initially agreed upon for the entire blanket purchase order or determined based on the market price at the time firm commitments for individual shipments are made.

In contrast to blanket purchase orders, transactions may also be authorized when they are consistent with a preapproved vendor and price list. This type of authorization may also require individual approval of the quantity being purchased as well as consistency with the approved list. Another approach is for a company's policy to require management approval of each individual order placed. IT systems are able to implement policy-based approvals by rejecting transactions inconsistent with parameters such as blanket purchase orders, approved vendor and price lists, and purchasing budgets.

A second management objective is to ensure that all cash disbursements are for goods and services that are actually received by the company and for correct amounts. This includes preventing duplicate payments. Proper payment is accomplished by having internal procedures that require appropriate documentation and authorization for any disbursement. Typically, this requires an **invoice** prepared by an outside entity, supported by internal evidence that the company authorized the purchase and received the item or the service ordered.

For the purchase of goods such as inventory, effective control is accomplished by matching the invoice to both purchasing and receiving documents before payment is authorized. For services such as electricity or insurance, internal documents in addition to the service provider's invoice may not be needed to support the payment. Management authorization at the time the contract was initially established with the service provider may be sufficient. When payment is made, the invoice and supporting documents are marked as paid, or "canceled" so that the bill will not be paid more than once.

A third management objective is to properly post transactions. An important financial statement outcome of proper posting is that accounts payable and other payables accounts are complete and shown appropriately. To accomplish this, transactions need to be posted accurately to the correct accounts and for the correct amounts. They also need to be posted in the correct period. In order to achieve proper matching, all expenses, asset purchases, cash disbursements, and liabilities must be included in the appropriate financial reporting period.

REVIEW QUESTIONS

D.1 What objectives does management have related to purchasing, and what controls help to accomplish these objectives?

D.2 What are management's objectives for cash disbursements, and what controls help to accomplish them?

D.3 What are business objectives for recording and reporting accounting information for acquisitions and payments?

Documents and Processes

Businesses purchase a wide variety of goods and services. Some, like telephone or electric service, are contracted with the service provider, and no repeated process for initiating the purchase is necessary. For example, once the telephone contract is established, the service provider simply sends a monthly invoice or statement that triggers the payment process.

Other types of purchases require that the purchase be actively initiated within the company. For example, if an office worker needs office supplies or a raw materials stores manager recognizes the need for more inventory, the transaction must be initiated. When the IT system for purchases is integrated with supplies or inventory records, the transaction may be triggered automatically.

The document used to initiate the purchase process is a **purchase requisition**. As was discussed in Chapter 10, documents may be in either electronic or paper form. A purchase requisition should be the responsibility of an individual (or computer application) with knowledge that an item needs to be purchased and with the authority to request the purchasing department to make the purchase. Regardless of the person's position, the important aspect of this function is that the request for the purchase should come from someone independent of the purchasing department—thus accomplishing segregation of duties—and with the authority to approve the need for the purchase. After the purchase requisition is produced, it goes to the purchasing department.

AUDITING IN ACTION

Purchase Requisition Document

Racy Car Parts Manufacturing Co.	
Purchase Requisition	98755623
Department: Raw Materials	**Date:** August 5, 2010 **Date Required:** September 3, 2010
Quantity: 11,000 caps	Description: 3 inch metal caps #456678
	Approved by: *M. Johnson*

The purchasing department receives the purchase requisition and arranges with a vendor to obtain the needed goods. The extent of autonomy and authority of the purchasing department varies among companies. Sometimes management contracts with certain vendors to purchase specific items at an agreed upon price. In this situation the purchasing department only has the authority to execute purchase transactions based on management's contracts, using approved vendor and price lists. In other businesses it may be the purchasing department's responsibility to shop for the best vendor to provide the item based on criteria such as price, quality, and ability to deliver within a specific time frame.

The purchasing department prepares a **purchase order** that documents the agreement and sends it to the vendor. Sometimes this purchase order document is in electronic form specifically to meet e-commerce protocols. The purchase order describes the item to be purchased, quantity, and price, and likely includes other information such as the delivery location and preferred delivery method or date.

AUDITING IN ACTION

Purchase Order Documents

PURCHASE ORDER   A06381039
Racy Car Parts Manufacturing Co.
410 El Camino
Santa Clara, CA 95050

TO: 123 Metals Fabrication Inc.   Date: August 7, 2010
     12109 Clinton St.   Ship via: Quick Delivery
     Portland, OR 97034

Enter our order for:

Qty.	Description	Price	Total
11,000 caps	3 inch metal caps # 456678	$4,00	$44,000

Racy Car Parts Manufacturing Co.
By: _T. McDonald_

PURCHASE ORDER

PO Number: 81357
Date: 1/15/2010

To:
Fancy Materials Supplies
620 Corporate Circle
Dalton, GA 30720

Ship to:
Expert Car Seats
444 El Camino
Santa Clara, CA 95050

SHIPPED VIA	F.O.B POINT	TERMS
Quick Delivery	Dalton	30 DAYS

ITEM NO	QTY	SIZE	DESCRIPTION	UNIT PRICE	TOTAL
V374	200	Yards	Black Vinyl, 60" W	12.00	2400.00
T674	600	Yards	Gray Vinyl Round Trim	3.00	1800.00
				TOTAL	**4200.00**

Authorized by: _Robert Zee_   Date: 1/15/2010

When goods that have been purchased are delivered to a business, they go through a "receiving" function. This means that someone at the purchasing company takes possession of the goods, counts and inspects the items, noting what was received and when, as well as the condition of the delivered goods. The receiving department prepares a **receiving report** documenting this information.

Receiving reports may also be used to create a **receiving log** that provides additional documentation and a way to cross reference information about what was received. This is useful if inventory receipt information is needed in other functional areas of the business. For example, the receiving log might be accessed by the individual investigating a discrepancy in documentation before approving an invoice for payment. Or it might be used by a warehousing supervisor checking to be sure that a needed shipment has arrived in the receiving department. In an automated IT environment, when a receiving department employee enters the information about items received, it may trigger automatic updates. For example, it can trigger updating a master document that has already captured purchasing activity, as well as generating a receiving report and receiving log.

AUDITING IN ACTION

Receiving Reports

Racy Car Parts Manufacturing Co.		
Receiving Report		503995443

Received From:	**Date:**	August 17, 2010
123 Metals Fabrication Inc.	**Order Number:**	A06381039
12109 Clinton St.	**Carrier:**	Quick Delivery
Portland, OR 97034		

Quantity:	Description: 3-inch metal caps
11,000 caps	#456678

Received by: _G. Chan_

RECEIVING REPORT

Expert Car Seats
444 El Camino
Santa Clara, CA 95050

No. 643

DATE		PURCHASE ORDER NO. OR RETURN REQUEST NO.
1/31/	2010	81357

RECEIVED FROM	PREPAID
FANCY MATERIALS SUPPLIERS	NO

ADDRESS	COLLECT
620 CORPORATE CIRCLE, DALTON GA, 30720	4200.00

FREIGHT CARRIER	FREIGHT BILL NO.
Quick Delivery	QD J10857344

	QUANTITY	ITEM NO.	DESCRIPTION
1.	200 Y	V 374	Black Vinyl, 60" W
2.	600 Y	T 674	Gray Vinyl Round Trim
3.			
4.			
5.			
6.			
7.			
8.			
9.			
10.			
11.			
12.			

REMARKS CONDITIONS , ETC. _NO DAMAGE, CORRECT MEASURE_

RECEIVED BY	DELIVERED TO
Karie Coburn	Raw Materials Stores, A Chea

AUDITING IN ACTION

Receiving Log

Expert Car Seats

	Date	PO Number	Received From	Qty	Item No.	Description
1	12/31/2009	639	XYZ	20	367	Black Paint
2	1/5/2010	642	ABC	100	1426	Black Thread
3	1/15/2010	640	NMO	1	1643	Fabric Liner
4	1/31/2010	643	Fancy Material Suppliers	200 yd	V374	Black Vinyl
5	1/31/2010	643	Fancy Material Suppliers	600 yd	T674	Gray Vinyl, Round Trim
6						

The documents prepared up to this point include the *purchase requisition, purchase order,* and *receiving report.* If the document is produced in electronic form, these three documents may actually be one record that is completed as it moves from department to department. Each department adds information to the relevant fields. For example, the requisitioning department may input information about the item and quantity needed. The purchasing department may add information on exactly what was ordered, the vendor with which the order was placed, and the agreed-upon price. The receiving department may then complete a field indicating the items and quantity actually received. The data input process of the receiving department may automatically add the information to the receiving log. The various departments will either receive copies of the paper document or have access to the electronic record. In the case of an electronic record, segregation of duties is achieved by granting access to different parts of the form based on functional needs and authority.

AUDITING IN ACTION

Multiuse Document

Racy Car Parts

Item No.	Description	Qty Requested		Qty Ordered		PO #	PO Date	Qty Received	
		#	Authorization Initials	#	Authorization Initials			#	Received by
WI20015	White Paint 5 gallons	10	KH	10	CW	A06382062	September 22, 2010	10	KD

The bill sent by the vendor to the company making the purchase may be in the form of an **invoice** or **monthly statement** provided in hard copy or electronically. An invoice usually covers only one transaction or shipment and includes itemized and detailed information. A monthly statement is more likely to simply list and summarize all of the transactions and amounts for the month. Some companies use both types of documents. An invoice may be sent along with the goods as a shipping document or may be provided separate from the shipment.

The accounts payable department compares the information on the invoice or statement to all the internal information that has been accumulated thus far regarding the purchase. In other words, the accounts payable department compares the purchase requisition, purchase order and receiving report information to the information on the seller's invoice or statement. If all the supporting information reconciles, then the accounts payable department posts the liability, which updates the *inventory or expense or other asset records, accounts payable subsidiary ledger,* and *general ledger.*

AUDITING IN ACTION

Vendor Invoice and Vendor Monthly Statement

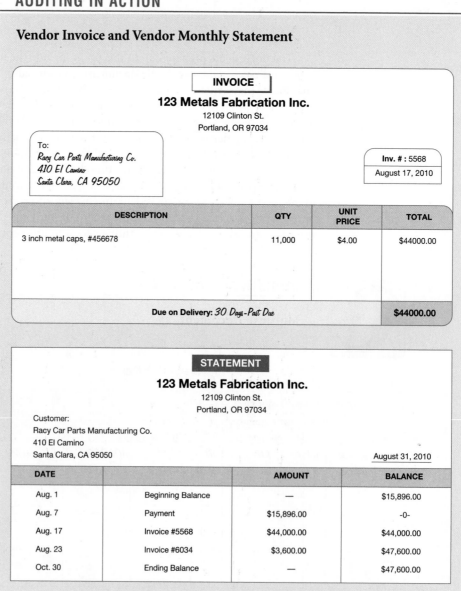

INVOICE

123 Metals Fabrication Inc.
12109 Clinton St.
Portland, OR 97034

To:
Racy Car Parts Manufacturing Co.
410 El Camino
Santa Clara, CA 95050

Inv. # : 5568
August 17, 2010

DESCRIPTION	QTY	UNIT PRICE	TOTAL
3 inch metal caps, #456678	11,000	$4.00	$44000.00

Due on Delivery: *30 Days-Past Due*	$44000.00

STATEMENT

123 Metals Fabrication Inc.
12109 Clinton St.
Portland, OR 97034

Customer:
Racy Car Parts Manufacturing Co.
410 El Camino
Santa Clara, CA 95050

August 31, 2010

DATE		AMOUNT	BALANCE
Aug. 1	Beginning Balance	—	$15,896.00
Aug. 7	Payment	$15,896.00	-0-
Aug. 17	Invoice #5568	$44,000.00	$44,000.00
Aug. 23	Invoice #6034	$3,600.00	$47,600.00
Oct. 30	Ending Balance	—	$47,600.00

Purchasers have a process to follow when a discrepancy is found among any of the documents, or noted on the receiving report. Typically, the process involves first investigating the issue internally. Then, if appropriate, the purchasing company notifies the vendor or shipper of any discrepancies, errors, or damage. The purchaser prepares a **debit memo** to document the amount that payment for a purchase should be reduced. If the purchaser has received agreement from the seller regarding the discrepancy, then the invoice or statement received may already reflect the corrected amount. The exact process for negotiating and documenting returns and allowances varies among businesses and may differ based on the circumstances of the individual transactions.

The purchase requisition, purchase order, receiving report, and vendor invoice or statement comprise a **payment support package**. The payment support packages goes through an approval process prior to the cash being disbursed. Different documents are required to complete the payment support package, depending on what was purchased.

Remember that in the earlier example of the purchase of telephone services, the trigger for payment was the monthly statement. Similarly, when a business purchases services—for example, the services of a lawyer or an accountant—the payment support package does not include a purchase requisition or receiving report. Alternatively, there may be a contract that was signed at the outset specifying the nature of the service and the way the fee is to be calculated. In an audit environment this contract is called an engagement letter, although the accounting firm will typically also create an invoice.

The payment support package is sometimes called a voucher package reflecting (somewhat outdated) terminology used when all the documents were in paper form and were collected and had a cover document called a voucher that was approved prior to payment. The term *voucher number* is also sometimes still used to refer to the identifying number associated with the payment support package.

After the payment support package is complete, the cash disbursement occurs. The cash disbursement is generally by paper check or electronic transfer. Final approval for the payment should be given by the "treasury" or cashier department of the business and should take place before the disbursement. The treasurer's department is independent of the purchasing and accounts payable departments, thus providing segregation of duties.

If the payment is by paper check, the check signer reviews the disbursement and supporting documents before signing the check. If check signing is done automatically using a signature plate, the responsible person reviews the supporting documents and then approves the list of checks to be produced and signed. If the disbursement is by electronic transfer, the responsible person reviews the supporting documents prior to authorizing transfer of the money. As mentioned earlier, supporting documents are canceled or marked that they have been paid so that they cannot be used to support a subsequent payment. The cash disbursement is recorded, updating the **cash disbursements journal or report**, accounts payable subsidiary ledger, and general ledger. Exhibit 12-1 shows the flow of purchase and payment transactions, and Exhibit 12-2 lists business activities in purchases and payments and the related documents.

REVIEW QUESTIONS

E.1 What is important regarding the organizational authority of the person who creates a purchase requisition?

E.2 Some businesses extend purchasing department employees the authority to perform a broader range of activities than do other businesses. What activities do all purchasing departments perform? What activities might be allowed in some businesses and not in others?

E.3 What function does a receiving department perform, and what are its activities?

E.4 What records does a receiving department prepare?

E.5 How is segregation of duties among the requisitioning, ordering, and receiving processes accomplished?

E.6 What should happen when discrepancies exist among supporting documents for a purchase or when the goods received are not what was ordered or arrive damaged?

E.7 What are the different ways cash disbursements can be reviewed and authorized before disbursement occurs?

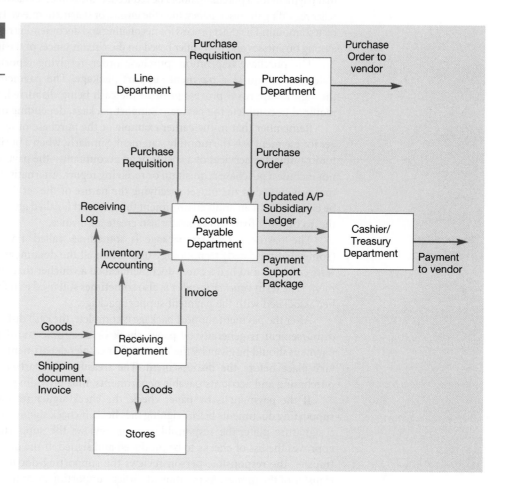

EXHIBIT 12-1

Purchase and Payment Activities

Potential Misstatements and Controls

Many of the potential misstatements associated with purchases and cash disbursements are prevented or detected by the following:

Segregation of duties

Authorized approval

Reliance on the documentation of the authorized approval

Safeguarding the assets

Controls over the process and outcomes of recording transactions

Segregation of Duties

The following functions should be conducted by individuals or within departments that are independent of each other:

- Approving the need for the purchase
- Executing the purchase

EXHIBIT 12-2

Business Activities and
Related Documents

Business Activity	Related Documents
Initiation of purchase process	Purchase requisition
Acquisition	Purchase order
Receiving goods	Receiving report
	Receiving log
Paying for purchase	Vendor's invoice
	Vendor's monthly statement
	Debit memo
	Payment support package
	Check or other payment authorization
Recording transactions	Accounts payable subsidiary ledger
	Cash disbursements journal
	Inventory, expense, and fixed asset files
	General ledger

- Receiving the shipment
- Recording the account payable
- Authorizing the cash disbursement

Segregation of these functions not only separates custody of the assets from the record-keeping function, but it also separates authorization of the transactions from execution. For example, the purchasing department cannot unilaterally initiate the order of goods that may turn out to be unneeded if the requisitioning department must initiate and authorize the request before the order is placed. If the purchasing department is only permitted to execute purchase transactions from a preapproved vendor and price list, the options for abuse are limited. No one in the purchasing department has the opportunity to collude with outsiders after the list is prepared to purchase goods at a price higher than market, with a side deal to receive kickbacks for the difference. Unordered or incorrect goods are not accepted by the receiving department if procedures require that all shipments received be supported by purchase requisitions and purchase orders that provide approval and documentation of what has been purchased. Finally, goods that were either not authorized purchases or not actually received by the company are not paid for if the check signer requires independent documented approval of each stage of the process.

Safeguarding Assets

Segregation of duties and required authorization for transactions must be supplemented by safeguarding of assets. For inventory purchases this safeguarding interrelates and even overlaps with activities of the inventory cycle. Once goods are received they are physically safeguarded, and appropriate documents are maintained to ensure that the goods are not lost or stolen. Physical safeguarding involves keeping goods in safe locations and storing them in locked facilities when appropriate. Documentary control assists the physical safeguarding if each person who takes responsibility for the goods signs for them, indicating the receipt and transfer of responsibility. Also, in the case of inventory, inventory records are reconciled with receiving documents to verify that goods received by the company were also received into inventory stores.

Accounting Processes

Proper posting of purchase and payment transactions prevents various financial statement misstatements. Controls emphasize posting the proper amount to the proper account and in the proper time period. Automated IT comparisons can be performed of control totals for invoices posted as accounts payables and checks prepared and posted as cash disbursements. These types of comparisons help verify that proper amounts are posted. Posting to the proper accounts is aided by review and approval of account classification. Additions to inventory accounts are also reconciled with payables records.

Automated IT controls are often used to verify the propriety of account classifications. Classification of disbursements as expenses also requires review and verification either through IT or human activities. Another possible control is reviewing postings to accounts used for nonroutine transactions, such as long-term assets. The potential impact of improper classification of the "debit side" of cash disbursement transactions is misstatement of net income. One of the strategies used in the fraud at WorldCom, which took place between 1999 and 2002, was misclassifying cash disbursements for expenses as long-term assets, thereby improperly increasing net income in the short run.

Cutoff

Proper matching and complete presentation of liabilities depends on proper **cutoff** and transactions being posted in the proper period. Cutoff refers to the company's procedures for identifying the economic transactions that are the last ones to occur in an accounting period. Cutoff procedures affect cash receipts and disbursements transactions as well as purchases and accruals. At the end of the fiscal time period transactions are reviewed carefully to ensure that "both halves" of the transaction, for example, the debit to an inventory asset account and related credit to an account payable, are posted in the same period. Invoices received around the end of the fiscal period are evaluated to determine in which period they should be recorded. Although not immediately related to cash disbursements, controls should also be in place for estimating the liabilities to accrue at period end, which provides for complete presentation of expenses and liabilities.

Cash Disbursement Procedures

Control activities over cash were discussed related to sales and collections but are also important to cash disbursements. Cash is also discussed in Chapters 13 and 15. All cash disbursements should be documented. Use of paper checks or authorized electronic funds transfers provides effective documentation.

Use of an *imprest petty cash fund* can provide an appropriate control for cash disbursements of small amounts. A petty cash fund should be the responsibility of one person. The custodian keeps the petty cash fund locked for safekeeping. Any disbursements from the petty cash fund must be documented, capturing information about the purpose, amount, and date of the disbursement. When the petty cash fund drops to a low enough level to be reimbursed—usually a predetermined amount—the custodian submits a request for reimbursement up to the full amount of the fund. The receipts submitted equal the amount of reimbursement required. Reimbursement of the fund is made through the company's standard mechanism of paper check or electronic funds transfer. Although disbursements from petty cash are usually for small amounts, some businesses require larger petty cash disbursements, such as when employees are required to travel on very short notice and need cash for the trip. Policies governing the amount in the petty cash fund, the purpose and amount of disbursements, and the dollar amount at which the fund should be reimbursed are designed to meet company needs while still providing documentary and physical control of the cash.

Other controls needed regarding cash disbursements include control over potentially valuable items such as stocks of blank checks, signature plates, and online banking authorization codes for electronic funds transfers. Cash records and bank statements should be reconciled on a timely basis by authorized personnel who are independent of the cash recordkeeping function—typically in the treasury department.

REVIEW QUESTIONS

F.1 What functions of acquisition and payment should be segregated from each other?

F.2 What steps can be taken to safeguard assets?

F.3 How can the improper posting of the debit side of a purchase transactions cause income to be misstated?

F.4 Why and how is cutoff important to acquisitions and payments?

F.5 What is an imprest petty cash fund, and how does it work?

AUDIT TESTS AND PROCEDURES

Management's financial statement assertions and the definitions of ICFR design and operating effectiveness were reviewed in Chapter 10, as were audit procedures to test ICFR and the financial statements. This chapter describes procedures used to audit purchase and expenditure transactions, cash disbursements, and related accounts. The discussion includes tests of controls, dual purpose tests, substantive analytical procedures, and tests of details of balances.

In an integrated audit, whenever possible the audit procedures should contribute evidence to both the ICFR and financial statement audits. Evidence collected in one part of the audit must be considered in other parts of the audit. For example, the auditor will consider ICFR and the expected quality of audit evidence available in planning the nature and timing of substantive audit procedures for the financial statement audit. Audit evidence consideration also flows in the reverse direction, from the financial statement audit to the ICFR audit. If the auditor finds a material error during the financial statement audit, he or she may reconsider ICFR. The auditor addresses whether ICFR functioned effectively, even though no material problems were found directly during the ICFR audit.

Since management as well as the auditor must test ICFR and conclude on effectiveness, both of them may use the same or similar procedures for testing controls. However, only the auditor typically performs procedures that investigate the appropriateness of account balances and disclosures. The exception is that this type of testing is also performed by internal auditors.

TESTS OF CONTROLS FOR PURCHASE AND EXPENDITURE TRANSACTIONS [LO 4]

The auditor first performs tests of ICFR design effectiveness and then examines ICFR operating effectiveness. Performing walkthroughs (or steps that accomplish the same objectives as walkthroughs) are important to the auditor. Walkthroughs help in planning, assessing risk, understanding the client's information system, and concluding on ICFR design effectiveness.

During a walkthrough the auditor may also gain evidence about the operating effectiveness of controls. This is especially true when the walkthrough includes reviewing client procedures and observing client personnel as they perform control steps. An example of this is when the auditor performs a walkthrough and observes employees as they execute authorization of purchase transactions and reconcile discrepancies in payment support packages.

Because not all of the steps of an audit progress sequentially, some of the steps described in this chapter will have been accomplished by the auditor during early phases of the audit. Also, some of the tests of controls presented in this chapter will be accomplished during testing the company's overall general IT controls (ITGC). ITCG is discussed in Appendix A of Chapter 7. As an example, audit tests to determine whether the general ledger is properly posted and reconciled with journals and subsidiary ledgers, though presented in this chapter, are likely performed for the entire system using computer-assisted audit techniques (CAATs).

Management's overall assertions continue to apply to all cycles of the business. As a reminder, they are:

1. Existence or occurrence
2. Completeness

3. Rights and obligations

4. Valuation or allocation

5. Presentation and disclosure

For convenience and ease of explanation *authorization* and *cutoff* assertions are also used in this discussion.

To audit the validity of management's financial statement assertions as they relate to purchase and acquisition transactions and cash disbursements, a lot of audit effort is directed toward making sure that (1) purchases are for goods and services actually needed by the company, (2) purchases are with vendors the company authorizes, and (3) the company actually receives the goods and services before any cash disbursements are made. Beyond those control concerns are the universal ones that all transactions are posted and that they are posted at the correct amounts, to the proper accounts and in the correct accounting period. Exhibit 12-3 presents tests of controls for purchase transactions. You should read and study this exhibit to understand the specific controls needed in the acquisition and payments cycle and how they are tested.

EXHIBIT 12-3

Examples of Tests of Controls for Purchase Transactions

If a company control (CC) is significant, both management and the auditor perform tests of controls (TofC). Management uses tests of controls to support its management report. The auditor uses tests of controls for the audit of ICFR and to confirm the planned reliance on controls in the financial statement audit. Related management assertions are displayed under the purpose of the controls. For ease of explanation, authorization and cutoff are used in addition to the five PCAOB management assertions.

Purpose of Controls	**Company Control and Tests of Controls**
To ensure that purchases and expenditures are consistent with company policies **(authorization)**	
	CC: *Purchase and expenditure transactions are authorized before they are executed, as evidenced by properly prepared and approved supporting documents*
	TofC: Examine a sample of document packages for inclusion of supporting documents appropriate for the specific transaction such as approved purchase requisitions and purchase orders
To ensure that purchase and expenditure transactions are approved by someone with appropriate authority before they are executed **(authorization, existence or occurrence)**	
	CC: *Authorizations are provided by individuals with institutional authority to authorize the specific transactions before the transactions are executed*
	TofC: Examine a sample of document packages for proper authorization by an appropriate individual and date of authorization preceding the order date
	CC: *When authorizations are computer-program-application based, the program uses the intended and approved parameters*
	TofC: Perform tests of the computer application for out-of-parameter conditions; for example, test whether the program executes the purchase of inventory transactions only when inventory counts fall to specified levels

CC: *All supporting documents, including purchase requisitions and purchase orders, are canceled at the time payment is made to prevent their reuse*

TofC: Examine a sample of document packages of paid invoices for cancellation on all documents within the sample; for documents in electronic form, examine for appropriate notation and test the program application for security of supporting document information

To ensure that purchase and expenditure transactions are conducted only with vendors and providers that are consistent with company policy
(authorization, existence or occurrence)

CC: *Purchase and expenditure transactions are initiated only with vendors and providers allowed by company policy, specified by (for example) authorized vendor list, blanket purchase order, contract, or the authority of the purchasing agent*

TofC: Examine a sample of document packages and trace the vendors and providers to preapproval or policy documents; when appropriate, examine purchasing agent documentation supporting vendor selection

TofC: Perform tests of the computer application to determine whether it will process purchase transactions with unapproved vendors and suppliers

CC: *Competitive bidding practices are used and followed when required by company policy*

TofC: Select a sample of purchase and expenditure transactions that are required to undergo competitive bidding and examine supporting documentation for evidence of the selection process; trace the vendor name used in the actual transaction to the vendor selected per the competitive bidding documents

To ensure that all purchase and expenditure transactions are recorded
(completeness)

CC: *Documents used to initiate and capture purchase activity are accounted for numerically*

TofC: Review established procedures for accounting for numerical sequence of supporting documents and observe employees performing the procedures

TofC: Account for a continuous numerical sequence of purchase transaction supporting documents; examine each document package for evidence of receipt of the good or service and the vendor's invoice and trace the amount to the expense or asset account and accounts payable subsidiary ledger

TofC: Select a sample from the file of receiving reports or the receiving log and trace the

(continued)

	transactions to vendor invoices, expense or asset accounts, and accounts payable subsidiary ledger; follow up on any open receiving reports when vendor invoices are received
To ensure that all purchase/expenditure transactions recorded as expenses or assets represent goods and services received by the company **(existence or occurrence, rights and obligations)**	
	CC: *Expense/asset and accounts payable transactions are recorded after: the goods are received as evidenced by an appropriate supporting document such as a receiving report, or for services based on a supporting document such as the vendor's invoice indicating an appropriate service period*
	TofC: Trace a sample of purchase/acquisition transactions from the general ledger, journals, and accounts payable subsidiary ledger to supporting documents, including the receiving report when appropriate
To ensure that all purchase/expenditure transactions are recorded at the proper amount for goods and services actually received **(rights and obligations, valuation or allocation)**	
	CC: *Quantities and prices on vendor's invoices are compared (either manually or electronically using IT) to purchase orders, receiving report, price lists, etc, before transactions are recorded; discrepancies are investigated and resolved*
	TofC: Ask employees about recent discrepancies identified from the comparison process and how they were handled; examine any available documentation
	TofC: Trace the amounts posted for a sample of recorded purchase/acquisition transactions to the supporting documents; recalculate vendor's invoice amounts using quantities indicated on receiving reports and prices on authorization documents (purchase orders, price lists, etc.)
To ensure that all recorded purchase/acquisition transactions are classified correctly and posted to the correct accounts **(existence or occurrence, presentation and disclosure)**	
	CC: *Transactions are recorded as inventory, expense or fixed assets in accordance with company policy and based on supporting documentation indicating the nature of the transaction*
	TofC: Select a sample of purchase/acquisitions transactions from the journals and ledgers including inventory files, fixed asset files, and expense accounts and examine the supporting documentation for evidence that the transaction was properly coded and posted to the correct asset or expense account

	CC: *Transactions are recorded to vendors' accounts payable records based on supporting documentation*
	TofC: Select document packages and trace purchase/acquisition transactions to the accounts payable subsidiary ledger agreeing specific transaction details and amounts
	TofC: Select transactions from the accounts payable subsidiary ledger and examine supporting document packages agreeing specific transaction details and amounts
To ensure that recorded purchase/acquisition transactions are recorded based on the correct dates **(cutoff)**	
	CC: *Purchase and expenditure transactions and related liabilities are posted in accordance with year-end cutoff procedures*
	TofC: Account for a continuous numerical sequence of supporting documents such as purchase orders, receiving reports (and voucher numbers, if used) shortly before and after year end and trace the related transactions to appropriate journals and subsidiary ledgers; examine for posting in the correct accounting period
	TofC: Examine unmatched receiving reports and unmatched vendor invoices at year end, and other related supporting documents and trace the transactions to appropriate journals and subsidiary ledgers; examine for posting in the correct accounting period
To ensure that purchase/acquisition transactions are properly included in the appropriate corresponding journals (such as expense, inventory, and fixed assets files), accounts payable subsidiary ledger, and general ledger **(existence or occurrence, presentation and disclosure)**	
	CC: *Inventory, fixed assets, accounts payable records, and the general ledger are reconciled*
	TofC: Examine evidence that postings to the expense, inventory, fixed assets and accounts payable records are reconciled, and totals are reconciled to the general ledger; use computer-assisted audit techniques as appropriate

REVIEW QUESTIONS

G.1 How do audit procedures in one part of an integrated audit (ICFR or financial statement audit) relate to conclusions in the other part of the audit?

G.2 How can walkthroughs provide evidence about the operating effectiveness of ICFR in the audit of acquisitions and payments?

G.3 Related to purchases, what are important concerns addressed by controls? What are the control concerns that are more universal in nature, but also apply to purchase activities?

TESTS OF CONTROLS FOR PURCHASE RETURNS AND DISCOUNTS

Purchase return transactions are typically few in number and of dollar amounts that are small relative to purchases and the overall financial statements. Company controls should require proper authorization of returns, production of documentation such as debit memos, and review by accounts payable personnel. Documentation and accounts payable review help ensure that when the liability is paid the disbursement is reduced by the cost of the return.

For the financial statement audit, purchase returns are likely to be tested primarily with analytical procedures. The analytical procedures are intended to identify any significant changes in the total amount of returns, or percentage changes that returns are as related to other accounts such as sales or purchases. Any major changes are investigated.

Purchase returns are tested in the ICFR audit if they are determined to be an important class of transactions. The auditor observes the receiving process. This allows an audit assessment of whether company employees examine the goods that are received to verify that they were intended purchases. The auditor tests the returns process by following goods that have been flagged for return through the system. In addition to observing employee activities, the auditor examines documentation of purchase returns to assess whether company controls are followed.

Companies typically have policies about whether payments are to be made within the discount window if purchase discounts are offered for paying bills quickly. From management's perspective, important control procedures include the processes intended to take advantage of discounts. Management also monitors when and why discounts are lost. From the auditor's perspective, even if the company does not take advantage of purchase discounts according to its policies, the actual cash disbursements need to be recorded properly and at the correct amounts. Therefore, audit procedures related to purchase discounts are subsumed into the audit of purchases and cash disbursements.

REVIEW QUESTIONS

H.1 How are purchase returns likely tested for the financial statement audit?

H.2 How can purchase returns be tested for the ICFR audit?

H.3 How do auditor's and management's concerns differ regarding purchase discounts?

TESTS OF CONTROLS FOR CASH DISBURSEMENTS

Specific controls for cash disbursements result from a company's mechanisms for approving disbursements and the way it makes payments. A small company may have only one authorized check signer. A larger company may permit several different people to individually sign checks for smaller amounts, but require two signatures or a higher ranking officer's signature on larger checks. A company may use paper checks that are electronically signed using signature plates, paper checks that are signed manually, or electronic funds transfers that require authorization codes instead of signatures. The digital signatures used in e-commerce basically rely on authorization codes, as well as electronic verification provided by an outside agency.

Regardless of the specific mechanism, an important component of preventive controls for cash disbursements is approval by an authorized person. Inherent in this control step is that the person providing the approval *actually reviews* the supporting documents prior to making the approval. When electronic funds transfers are used, important additional controls are to limit authorized access to and carefully safeguard authorization codes.

Appropriate segregation of duties is also critical for good internal control over cash disbursements. In contrast to the preventive control provided by authorization, reconciliations and monitoring procedures provide the detective controls that can catch inappropriate disbursements. Bank statements must be reconciled on a timely basis by someone who is independent of handling or recording cash receipts and disbursements.

AUDITING IN ACTION

The Bank Reconciliation Process in the Real World

Segregation of duties is often not ideal in the real world, even in large companies. A common organizational structure often places responsibility for authorizing disbursements in the hands of a top ranking financial officer such as the Chief Financial Officer (CFO) or treasurer. That person typically signs checks, authorizes check runs signed automatically with signature plates, or controls and authorizes the use of codes to initiate electronic funds transfers. This is not a problem from the purchasing perspective and actually provides good independent monitoring of the purchase function.

The real-world segregation of duties flaw exists because sometimes the person who reconciles the bank statement works in the CFO's or treasurer's department and consequently reports to that person. Assuming the CFO or treasurer has authority over the functions and people working in the department, the position may carry with it an ability to override issues raised in the bank reconciliation process—or even alter the reconciliation document after it is completed. To make the problem even worse, he or she probably has the authority to create and approve journal entries.

When one corporate officer has control over all of these activities, the auditor must look for other controls that compensate for the fact that too much authority resides in one individual. These compensating controls may come in the form of reviews by other officers or a strong internal audit department that reports to the audit committee of the Board of Directors. Other compensating controls may be second approvals required or electronic filters for certain types of journal entries, and additional controls over cash accounts. Another easy solution is to move the bank reconciliation function to another department.

As Exhibit 12-4 shows, the bank reconciliation process serves many purposes in the ICFR for cash disbursements. Another important detective control for cash disbursements is that vendor's invoices and statements are reconciled to accounts payable records by employees independent of ordering and recording transactions. You should read and study Exhibit 12-4 to understand the specific controls needed for cash disbursement activities and how they are tested.

EXHIBIT 12-4

Examples of Tests of Controls for Cash Disbursements

If a company control (CC) is significant, both management and the auditor perform tests of controls (TofC). Management uses tests of controls to support its management report. The auditor uses tests of controls for the audit of ICFR and to confirm the planned reliance on controls in the financial statement audit. Related management assertions are displayed under the purpose of the controls. For ease of explanation, authorization and cutoff are used in addition to the five PCAOB management assertions.

[Many of the controls and tests of controls for cash disbursements serve multiple purposes, and are coded with a matching letter when repeated in this exhibit.]

Purpose of Controls	Company Control and Tests of Controls
To ensure that cash disbursements are made only for goods and services received by the company and that the cash disbursements are for the authorized amount **(authorization, existence or occurrence)**	
	CC: *Checks and electronic funds transfers are executed only after approval by an independent and authorized person who has reviewed supporting documents to determine that the transaction was authorized, goods or services received, and the amount to be disbursed is correct*

(continued)

(Note: The authorization is often given by the check signer when paper checks are used or the person responsible for transfer code numbers when EFT is used. The institutional authority of this person is based on rank, proper segregation of duties, and the nature and size of the transaction.)

TofC: Obtain company policy regarding which individuals have authority to sign checks and approve EFT, including any limits on the individuals' authority; for a sample of disbursements, trace those names to evidence of their review of supporting documents and approval of the disbursements

TofC: Use computer-assisted audit techniques to scan the cash disbursements journal for unusual transactions and amounts, including such details as inappropriate times and unusual and unauthorized computer terminals; follow up on identified transactions by examining supporting documents for authorization, accuracy, and completeness

To ensure that all cash disbursements that:
1. occurred are recorded
2. are recorded actually occurred
(existence or occurrence, completeness, valuation or allocation)

CC: *Bank reconciliations are prepared regularly by an authorized and independent employee and, when appropriate a proof of cash is prepared (A)*

TofC: Observe the bank account reconciliation process, noting the authority and independence of the employee performing the work *(B)*

TofC: Review bank reconciliations (and proofs of cash when appropriate); note whether the reconciliations have been prepared, when, by whom, and the clerical accuracy of the reconciliation *(C)*

CC: *Vendor invoices and statements are reconciled to accounts payable subsidiary ledger records periodically (D)*

TofC: Review company procedures for the reconciliation, observe employees performing the reconciliation; inquire about discrepancies found and how they are resolved; review any available documentation *(E)*

To ensure that the amounts recorded as cash disbursements are the amounts actually disbursed
(existence or occurrence, completeness, valuation or allocation)

CC: *Each time disbursements are made resulting in the cash disbursements journal and accounts payable subsidiary ledger being updated, the summary report generated on checks disbursed or EFT executed is reconciled to the cash disbursements journal*

and accounts payable subsidiary ledger; this reconciliation may be performed manually or electronically; any errors and discrepancies are investigated and resolved

TofC: Review company procedures for the reconciliation, observe employees performing the reconciliation; inquire about discrepancies found and how they are resolved; review any available documentation *(E)*

To ensure that cash disbursements are recorded in the same accounting period in which they are made
(cutoff)

CC: *Bank reconciliations are prepared regularly by an authorized and independent employee and, when appropriate a proof of cash is prepared (A)*

TofC: Observe the bank account reconciliation process, noting the authority and independence of the employee performing the work *(B)*

TofC: Review bank reconciliations (and proofs of cash when appropriate); note whether the reconciliations have been prepared, when, by whom, and the clerical accuracy of the reconciliation *(C)*

To ensure that cash disbursements are properly posted to the correct cash account and correct vendor record in the accounts payable subsidiary ledger, and to the general ledger
(existence or occurrence, completeness, valuation or allocation, presentation and disclosure)

CC: *Vendor invoices and statements are reconciled to accounts payable subsidiary ledger records periodically (D)*

TofC: Review company procedures for the reconciliation, observe employees performing the reconciliation; inquire about discrepancies found and how they are resolved; review any available documentation *(E)*

CC: *Cash disbursements that were in payment for accounts payable are reconciled with postings to the accounts payable subsidiary ledger*

TofC: Review company procedures for the reconciliation, observe employees performing the reconciliation, inquire about any discrepancies found and how they are resolved; review any available documentation *(E)*

CC: *Bank reconciliations are prepared regularly by an authorized and independent employee and, when appropriate a proof of cash is prepared (A)*

TofC: Observe the bank account reconciliation process, noting the authority and independence of the employee performing the work *(B)*

(continued)

TofC: Review bank reconciliations (and proofs of cash when appropriate); note whether the reconciliations have been prepared, when, by whom, and the clerical accuracy of the reconciliation (C)

CC: *Journals, subsidiary ledgers, and the general ledger are reconciled*

TofC: Examine evidence that postings to the cash disbursements journal and subsidiary ledger are reconciled, are reconciled to the daily cash disbursements records, and totals are reconciled to the general ledger; use computer-assisted audit techniques to recalculate as appropriate

REVIEW QUESTIONS

I.1 What are the different ways that cash disbursements may be authorized in the current business environment? What important control step does the person providing the approval carry out?

I.2 When cash disbursements are made through electronic funds transfer, what is an important control?

I.3 What are important detective controls for cash disbursements?

I.4 What control purposes and management assertions are supported by bank reconciliations?

I.5 What control purposes and management assertions are supported by reconciling vendor invoices and statements to accounts payable subsidiary ledger records?

DUAL PURPOSE TESTS [LO 5]

Dual purpose tests provide the auditor with the opportunity to collect audit evidence about ICFR and the account balances in the financial statement using the same evidence items. AS 5 highlights the importance of planning the timing of audit steps so that dual purpose tests will provide the most useful information. Good planning can result in dual purpose tests being as useful as possible not only for the ICFR audit, but also for the financial statement audit.

In auditing acquisitions and payments, maximizing the usefulness of dual purpose tests usually means performing tests for cash disbursements as close to the end of the year as possible. End-of-the-year timing permits the information to be useful in determining whether the financial statement cash balance is presented fairly.

For dual purpose tests geared toward controls over acquisitions and other financial statement account balances, timing the tests close to year end may not be as critical. For example, examining the documents that directly support expense transactions can be performed at any time after the transactions have occurred. And, as will be discussed later in the chapter, auditing fixed assets calls for analyzing additions and deletions to the fixed asset accounts. Those transactions can also be examined at any point after they occur. When planning dual purpose tests, the auditor must consider both ICFR and financial statement audit objectives and select a large enough sample to accomplish the goals of both procedures.

Carefully read and study Exhibits 12-5 and 12-6 on dual purpose tests related to purchasing and cash disbursements. As you study these exhibits, compare them to the tests of controls already presented. Later, when you read about tests of details of balances, refer back to these exhibits. A major difference you should be able to identify is that each dual purpose procedure includes collecting evidence about ICFR and the account balance. For purposes of efficiency, whenever possible auditors modify tests of controls to also collect account balance evidence.

EXHIBIT 12-5

Examples of Dual
Purpose Tests for
Purchase Transactions

Purpose of Test	Dual Purpose Tests
To obtain audit evidence that: When purchase and acquisition transactions are posted, the asset or expense increase represents an economic benefit received by the company **(authorization, existence or occurrence)**	
	Select transactions that have been recorded in the expense, inventory, and fixed asset records; trace the entries to supporting documents such as purchase requisitions, purchase orders, and vendors' invoices; examine the underlying documents for proper approval, consistency with company policies and agree the amounts Using computer-assisted audit techniques, scan expense files, inventory files, and fixed asset files for unusual transactions and amounts, including such details as inappropriate times and unusual and unauthorized computer terminals; trace any that are identified to supporting documents; look for proper authorization and agree the amounts
All purchases and acquisitions are recorded **(completeness)**	
	Trace receiving reports and vendor invoices (for service acquisitions) to the accounts payable subsidiary ledger and other appropriate journals or ledgers; agree the amounts and other details of the purchase or acquisition transaction
Recorded purchases and acquisitions are for the amount of goods and services actually ordered and received, and the seller's invoice was correct and was correctly recorded **(existence or occurrence, rights and obligations, valuation or allocation, presentation and disclosure)**	
	Select transactions that have been recorded as expenses, inventory, and fixed assets and trace them to vendors' invoices or statements and agree the amounts; trace and agree transaction details other than amounts on vendors' invoices or statements to supporting documents such as purchase requisitions, purchase orders, receiving reports, and usage detail for services, noting proper approval on supporting documents Reperform calculations including dollar amounts on vendors' invoices or statements; use price lists, blanket purchase orders, contracts, etc. to verify approval of unit price
Transactions posted as expenses, inventory, and fixed asset purchases are properly classified **(existence or occurrence, rights and obligations, presentation and disclosure)**	
	Trace transactions from the purchases journal, inventory ledger, and fixed asset ledger to the related vendor invoices and other supporting documents and examine for proper classification, noting whether the amounts are posted to the correct accounts

(continued)

Expenses, inventory, and fixed asset purchases and the related liabilities are recorded in the correct accounting period **(cutoff)**

Select transactions from before and after year end from the purchases journal, inventory ledger, fixed assets ledger, and accounts payable subsidiary ledger; agree the date of posting to the appropriate date when the good or service was received and the liability existed, noting that the amounts are posted in the correct period

Recorded purchase and acquisition transactions are included in the accounts payable subsidiary ledger and general ledger **(completeness, presentation and disclosure)**

Select purchase and acquisition transactions from the purchases journal, inventory ledger, and fixed asset ledger and trace to the accounts payable subsidiary ledger; agree amounts, dates, and invoice, or other reference numbers

Use computer-assisted audit techniques to check the clerical accuracy of the accounts payable subsidiary ledger and agree the total amount to the general ledger

Amounts shown in journals and ledgers are clerically accurate summations of transactions **(presentation and disclosure)**

Use computer-assisted audit techniques to check the clerical accuracy of the supporting journals used such as a purchases journal, inventory ledger and fixed asset ledger, and trace amounts to the general ledger

---

EXHIBIT 12-6

Examples of Dual Purpose Tests for Cash Disbursements

Purpose of Test	Dual Purpose Tests
To obtain audit evidence that: Cash disbursements that are recorded are for purchases and expenditures of the company **(authorization, existence or occurrence)**	
	Using computer-assisted audit techniques, scan the cash disbursements journal for unusual transactions and amounts, including such details as inappropriate times, and unusual and unauthorized computer terminals; trace and agree any that are identified to supporting documents
	Examine document packages for proper authorization and consistency of transaction details, including vendor, item or service, and amount; trace the amount to the cash disbursements journal

All cash disbursement transactions recorded by the company occurred
(existence or occurrence)

Trace entries posted in the cash disbursements journal to bank statements, agreeing amounts

All cash disbursed by the company was recorded in the cash disbursements journal, and the amounts and details are shown correctly
(completeness, valuation or allocation, presentation and disclosure)

Trace disbursements shown on the bank statements to the cash disbursements journal and supporting document packages, agreeing amounts

Cash disbursements transactions are properly classified and recorded in the period the payment was made
(cutoff, presentation and disclosure)

Select transactions from the cash disbursements journal and examine bank statements and any other externally generated documents for evidence that the transactions are shown at the proper amounts, properly classified as cash, and that the cash was disbursed in the period shown

Select disbursements recorded in the cash disbursements journal shortly before year end and trace them to the bank statement agreeing the amount; investigate transactions for which time lags between the cash disbursements journal and bank statement are noted to determine if the disbursement occurred in the subsequent year

Postings of cash disbursements are correctly made to the accounts payable subsidiary ledger and general ledger
(completeness, presentation and disclosure)

Select transactions from the cash disbursements journal and trace to the accounts payable subsidiary ledger agreeing amounts, other account details, and dates

Select transactions from the accounts payable subsidiary ledger and trace to the cash disbursements journal agreeing amounts, other account details, and dates

Amounts shown in journals and ledgers are clerically accurate summations of transactions
(existence or occurrence, completeness, presentation and disclosure)

Use computer-assisted audit techniques to check the clerical accuracy of the cash disbursements journal and trace amounts to the general ledger

SUBSTANTIVE ANALYTICAL PROCEDURES [LO 6]

The auditor performs **substantive analytical procedures** to obtain audit evidence for the financial statement audit. Substantive analytical procedures augment the audit evidence collected through dual purpose tests and tests of details of balances. However, to rely on analytical procedures, the auditor must test ICFR and conclude that the accounting system produces results that reflect reasonable relationships among accounts. The underlying information tested through analytical procedures can only provide reliable results when it is materially complete and accurate.

Substantive analytical procedures alone do not provide sufficient evidence for the financial statement audit. Even though they are not sufficient on a stand-alone basis, analytical procedures are very important for auditing both balance sheet and income statement accounts. For acquisitions and payments, analytical procedures of accounts payable, expense accounts, and purchase returns can call the auditor's attention to unexpected relationships and trigger more tests of details of balances. Alternatively, analytical procedures can confirm the relationships the auditor expected to find based on work performed up to that point in the audit.

Substantive analytical procedures are particularly important for expense accounts. Typically, an auditor cannot examine the supporting documentation for enough transactions or dollars to be comfortable with the account balance. In this situation, the auditor relies heavily on tests of controls, dual purpose tests, and the relationship of expense account balances to various asset and liability accounts. These procedures support any direct testing conducted.

The auditor uses the aggregated findings of the various procedures to conclude on the fairness of income statement accounts. As is shown in Exhibit 12-7, the auditor performs analytical procedures on expense balances and on accounts such as purchases that relate to production and inventory. Purchase and production activities impact the amounts that are reported for inventory and cost of goods sold. Analytical procedures are very important for auditing these accounts.

Analytical procedures can involve comparing an account balance with prior years, a budget, or an industry benchmark. Analytical procedures also take the form of calculating a ratio or statistic and using the outcome of the calculation for comparison. The appropriate result of the comparison will not always be finding the numbers to be the same, or even similar.

For example, assume that a company started and ended the year with a small volume of completed inventory, made major changes to its production process that reduced the costs, and sold the same amount as in the prior year. The auditor would expect cost of sales to be much lower in the current than the prior year. At the same time, if the company did not pass on the cost savings through lower customer prices, the auditor would expect gross margin to increase. In contrast, if a company's business remained fairly stable from one year to the next, then the auditor might expect sales, cost of sales, and gross margin to remain fairly constant, perhaps only with changes that might be attributed to overall inflation.

In evaluating the results of analytical procedures for acquisition activities, the auditor considers levels of sales, production, and external economic influences. Important external influences are consumer demand and changing prices. Remember that the auditor uses analytical procedures to determine whether the observed relationships make sense in light of the business activities and economic environment. Exhibit 12-7 provides examples of analytical procedures for accounts payable, expenses, and purchase returns.

REVIEW QUESTIONS

J.1 What is the advantage of performing dual purpose tests?

J.2 How is underlying information tested, and why?

J.3 How are analytical procedures used for acquisitions and payments?

J.4 Why do analytical procedures help whether they confirm or dispute other findings?

J.5 What is involved in most common analytical procedures? What is compared?

EXHIBIT 12-7

Examples of
Substantive Analytical
Procedures for
Acquisition and
Payment Activities and
Related Accounts

To identify possible over- or understatement of accounts payable

Compare year-end accounts payable balance with previous years

Compare the composition of year-end balance with composition in previous years, noting and investigating as appropriate

> *Changes in major suppliers*

> *Changes in the number of overdue accounts*

> *Changes in the proportion of debit balances*

Calculate and compare accounts payable turnover rate with previous years

Calculate and compare accounts payable days outstanding with previous years

Calculate statistical relationship of accounts payable to purchase (or other volume-related production indicators) and compare to previous years

> *Consider price and volume issues when a change has occurred—should it have occurred?*

> *Consider price and volume issues when a change has not occurred—should a change have occurred?*

> *Relate to audit work on search for unrecorded liabilities*

To identify possible over- or understatement of various expenses

Compare year-end balances in individual acquisition-related expense accounts with previous years

To identify possible over- or understatement of purchase returns

Compare returns and allowances as a percent of sales or purchases to prior years

Compare returns and allowances as a percent of cost of sales to prior years

TESTS OF DETAILS OF BALANCES

Tests of details of balances contribute to audit evidence for financial statement account balances and disclosures. This section of the chapter continues the discussion about **accounts payable confirmations** that was introduced in Chapter 10. Next the discussion explores a set of audit procedures often called the search for unrecorded liabilities. These steps are used to examine the completeness assertion for liabilities. Tests of details of balances are then discussed for the remaining accounts affected by this cycle, including prepaid expenses, accrued liabilities, expenses, property, plant, and equipment, and intangible assets.

Accounts Payable Confirmations

Confirmations of accounts payable are not as uniformly used by auditors as confirmations of accounts receivable. Other reliable audit evidence supports accounts payable. For example, a vendor's invoice or statement and the audit client's subsequent cash disbursement in payment of the liability provide audit evidence. The billing documents coupled with cash disbursements support that the accounts payable shown on the balance sheet are real obligations of the company and amounts are appropriate.

The bigger audit concern for accounts payable is completeness. The auditor addresses the risk that some accounts payable are omitted or recorded at less than their full amounts. Confirmations help provide evidence that the accounts payable shown are complete by collecting information directly from the potential creditor about what is owed. Accounts payable confirmations are more likely to be used when the auditor has concerns about whether the accounting system properly captures and records all accounts payable.

Accounts payable confirmations are sent to vendors and providers with large balances. But, equally important, they are sent to a sample selected from the list of entities with which the company does business—regardless of the current account balance. A major audit goal is to identify any un- or underrecorded payables. Therefore, the population from which the sample is selected includes all the entities to which the company *may* have a liability. This includes any entity from which the company currently purchases goods and services, including those with zero or low accounts payable balances.

Auditors typically use positive confirmations for accounts payable. As a reminder, this means that the confirmation document requests the recipient to send a response to the auditor in all circumstances. Usually, the confirmation does not provide a balance to which the vendor can compare for agreement. Instead, the confirmation document asks for information about the amount the audit client owes to the vendor. In addition to information about accounts payable owed, the confirmation is likely to ask about any other form of liabilities, such as notes, and about consigned inventory.

Because of the blank format used to request information, the auditor almost always needs to reconcile the vendor response to the year-end balance listed on the company's books. Discrepancies are often due to timing differences. Items that cause timing differences are, for example, inventory in transit shipped since year end and payments made by the company not yet received by the vendor. If the client keeps records accessible in an electronic format that enables the auditor to "drill down" to the details underlying the balance, the reconciliation process is much easier.

AUDITING IN ACTION

Accounts Payable Confirmation

Audit Client Company
4 Yawkey Way
Boston, MA

January 19, 2011

Celtics Championship Inc.
23 Boston Gardens Way
Boston, MA 02217

Dear Mr. Williams:

Our auditors, Auditors & Co. LLP, are engaged in an audit of our financial statements. In connection therewith, please advise them in the space provided below whether or not there is a balance due you by this company as of December 31, 2010. If there is a balance due, please attach a statement of the items making up such balance.

After signing and dating your reply, please mail it directly to Auditors & Co. LLP , 2004 Patriot Way, Boston, MA 02218. A stamped, addressed envelope is enclosed for your convenience.

Kind regards,

Audrey Escobar

Audrey Escobar,

Controller, Audit Client Company

Auditors & Co. LLP:

Our records indicate that a balance of $ _____ was due from Audit Client Company at December 31, 2010 as itemized in the attached statements.

Date: _____   Signed: _____

REVIEW QUESTIONS

K.1 What other audit evidence besides confirmations are used to support the auditor's conclusions about accounts payable?

K.2 What is the important management assertion for accounts payable about which confirmations can provide audit evidence?

K.3 What is the purpose of sending confirmations to vendors with small or zero balances?

K.4 What is a "blank" confirmation? Why is this format often used for accounts payable?

K.5 What are common sources of discrepancies between responses on blank accounts payable confirmations and the audit client's accounts payable subsidiary ledger?

Search for Unrecorded Liabilities

A set of audit procedures focused on the completeness assertion is the search for **unrecorded liabilities**. This label is used for a group of audit procedures performed on every financial statement audit. Liabilities result when a company receives goods and services or borrows funds. An audit concern is that these transactions have occurred during the year under audit and the associated liability is not reflected in the financial statements.

An example of an unrecorded liability is an accrued expense that goes unrecorded because the service provider's invoice for utilities used during the year under audit was not received by year end. The invoice or statement is received in the subsequent year. The company records both the expense and liability in the subsequent year, even though both should be shown in the financial statements of the year being audited.

Another example is when inventory is received before year end, but the invoice is not received until the following fiscal year. In this situation, the goods are received and a receiving report is prepared, but the liability is not recorded because there is no invoice to indicate the amount that should be booked. Whether the item is included in the year-end inventory balance depends on the company's process of accounting for inventory and physically counting and calculating the inventory balance at year end. The correct accounting for this situation is for both the inventory and related liability to be included in the financial statements. The company's year-end cutoff procedures for inventory should coordinate with other accounting cutoff procedures to be sure all accounts payable are recorded. Similarly, audit procedures for inventory cutoff must coordinate with the search for unrecorded liabilities.

The following procedures are generally included in the search for unrecorded liabilities:

1. Ask the client what procedures it has established and followed to be sure that all liabilities are recorded.

2. Review cash disbursements and related supporting documents in the subsequent accounting period. All cash disbursements should relate and be traced to either a liability of the period under audit that is shown on the balance sheet, or an expense or asset purchase of the subsequent year. Supporting documents such as the vendor invoice indicating the date a service was provided or a receiving report indicating the date on which goods were received provide information on the accounting period in which the transaction should be included.

3. Review invoices and statements and relating supporting documents for liabilities not paid at the time the audit work at the client's location is completed. These unpaid bills should relate and be traced to either a liability of the period being audited that is shown on the balance sheet, or a payable that has been recorded in the subsequent accounting period.

4. Understand the client's year-end cutoff policies for inventory, and at year end identify the last receiving report used. Examine this last receiving report of the year and others shortly before and after year end. Examine the supporting documents for each receiving report. Trace the transactions to purchases/inventory and accounts payable accounts for inclusion in the proper accounting period. Identify any unmatched receiving reports (receiving reports for which a vendor's invoice has not yet been received) at year end and follow up when the invoice is received and posted in order to determine whether it is posted in the proper period.

5. Perform analytical procedures for the reasonableness of the accounts payable balance.

6. Read contracts that may indicate any purchase commitments that may need to be recorded or disclosed in the financial statements.

Tests of Details of Balances for Accounts Payable

The tests of details of balances are used to audit the liability accounts in the expenditures and payments cycle. The tests focus on:

Examining the supporting documents

Confirming accounts payable

Performing the search for unrecorded liabilities

Testing the clerical accuracy of the journals and ledgers

Examining the financial statement disclosures

Exhibit 12-8 provides examples of tests of details of balances for accounts payable and unrecorded liabilities in the acquisitions and payments cycle. You should read and study the exhibit. Also, compare the steps with those included in Exhibits 12-5 and 12-6 on dual purpose tests. Remember that tests of details of balances for the year-end cash account balance are discussed in detail in Chapter 10.

EXHIBIT 12-8

Examples of Tests of Details of Balances, Acquisitions and Payments Cycle, Accounts Payable, and Unrecorded Liabilities

Select a sample from the accounts payable listing and examine supporting documentation, including vendor statements

Develop and implement the confirmation plan for accounts payable

Use positive confirmation, blank or zero-balance format

With strong ICFR, confirm large balances

With auditor concern for payables not being recorded, include small or zero balance accounts and a sample of other accounts

Mail at year end

Perform follow-up and resolution procedures for nonresponse and discrepancies

Using computer-assisted audit techniques recalculate the clerical accuracy of the accounts payable subsidiary ledger

Trace the total of the accounts payable subsidiary ledger to the general ledger

Perform search for unrecorded liabilities; these steps should be coordinated with the inventory observation and inventory cutoff procedures

Ask client personnel about procedures for recording all liabilities

Examine cash disbursements after year end for recording in proper period

Examine unpaid liabilities at the end of the audit for recording in proper period

Examine receiving reports and other supporting documents before and after year end (including last one of the year and first of subsequent year) for posting of related transaction in proper period

Follow up on any receiving reports that are unmatched with vendor invoices at fiscal year end for eventual posting in the proper period

Read contracts to identify any commitments that must be recorded or disclosed

Review financial statements for proper disclosures including

Appropriate classification of any material debits of accounts payable

Separation of short- and long-term payables, nontrade payables, large individual amounts, as required

Balances of related parties

Long-term purchase contracts

Purchase commitments

AUDIT OF PREPAID EXPENSES AND ACCRUED LIABILITIES [LO 7]

Prepaid expenses are asset accounts representing economic value to be received by the company in the near future. In essence, they are bills that the company has paid in advance. Examples are prepaid rent, prepaid taxes, and prepaid insurance.

Accrued liabilities represent economic value that has already been received by the company but for which payment has not yet been made. Examples of accrued liabilities are accrued property taxes, accrued interest, and accrued warranty cost. Accruals may be for items with a fairly certain cost, like property taxes. They are recorded as accruals rather than payables simply because the payment is not yet due. Accrued warranty costs are an example of an *estimated* accrual. An accrual that must be estimated is a liability that is not yet due and for which the amount is uncertain. The company knows that there is warranty expense that must be matched against sales and paid at some unknown time in the future. However, the amount of the eventual liability is uncertain and must be estimated.

Tests of controls related to prepaid expenses and accrued liabilities are subsumed into tests of controls for acquisitions and payments of the related expenses. The amounts of prepaid expense and accrued liability accounts are typically not material to the financial statements and therefore do not require a significant amount of audit work. The auditor usually determines what is included in the account balance, examines documentation related to the underlying item, and performs analytical procedures. If the auditor chooses to examine a prepaid asset or accrued liabilities account more extensively the approach is to:

1. start with the beginning balance, which was audited in the prior year,
2. examine documents supporting additions to the account,
3. examine documents supporting decreases from the account, and
4. determine an audit conclusion about the fairness of the final balance.

For example, in a prepaid insurance account, the beginning balance is traced to the ending audited balance for the prior year. Additions to the balance are traced to the cash disbursements for insurance invoices paid. Decreases to the account are traced to the insurance expense account. The amount of expense is recalculated to be sure it is correct for the period of time that insurance coverage has been used. Based on these steps, the auditor can conclude on the fairness of the ending balance. Examples of analytical procedures for prepaid assets and accrued expenses are shown in Exhibit 12-9.

AUDITING IN ACTION

Sample Work Paper for Prepaid Insurance and Insurance Expense

Audit Client Company
Prepaid Expenses: Analysis of Prepaid Insurance and Expenses
December 31, 2010
Testing Performed by: JH, 1/22/11
Audit File:

Description	F-2 Balance 12/31/09	Current Premium	Amortization Expense	Prepaid Balance 12/31/10
Policy # WC 10394 for workman's compensation coverage of $300,000 from 1/1/10 to 12/31/10	✔ —	✔a 21,980	(21,980) Rx	—
Policy # FC 20498 for extended coverage on building and contents in the amount of $1,000,000 from 11/30/09 to 11/30/10	✔ 60,500	✔a —	(60,500) Rx	—
Policy # BC 8473 for fidelity bond coverage in the amount of $300,000 from 1/1/10 to 7/1/11	✔ —	✔a 50,400	(25,200) Rx	25,200
	60,500	72,380	(107,680)	25,200
	TB-1			TB-1

✔   Examined insurance policy noting provisions of the policy and annual premiums without exception.
a   Examined insurance company invoice and canceled check without exception.
Rx   Recalculated amortization expense without exception.

EXHIBIT 12-9

Examples of
Substantive Analytical
Procedures for Prepaid
Assets and Accrued
Liabilities

Compare year-end balances of assets and liability accounts and related expense accounts to prior-year balances

Compute the ratio of the prepaid assets or accrued liability to the related expense and compare the ratio to that of the prior year

Compare the composition of the account to its composition in the prior year and investigate changes (e.g., number of insurance policies, number of rental properties, months rent, etc.)

The SEC provides an important consideration for prepaid expenses and accrued liabilities in **Staff Accounting Bulletin (SAB) 108.** This SAB specifies that materiality must be considered from both a balance sheet and an income statement perspective. For example, assume the auditor examines supporting documentation and calculates that 12 months' worth of insurance costs are included in the insurance expense account. Furthermore, examination of the prepaid or accrued insurance account shows the change from the prior year to be immaterial. Based on only these steps the auditor might overlook the potential for balance sheet error. Even though the expense account on the income statement has been audited for fairness, the auditor must still address the question of whether the balance sheet amount in the prepaid or accrued account is what it should be. Just determining that the balance sheet amount is similar to that of the prior year is not sufficient. Although SAB 108 does not provide any guidance regarding the auditor's determination of how much is quantitatively material, it emphasizes that materiality judgments apply to both the balance sheet and the income statement.

Certain accounts audited with prepaid assets and accrued liabilities require auditor attention beyond the propriety of the financial statement amount. The potential impact on the company or disclosure requirements increases their importance. For example, auditors often review insurance expenses not only to see that they have been accounted for fairly, but also to consider whether insurance coverage is adequate. If insurance coverage is inadequate, the auditor may assist an unaware client by raising the issue. In addition, the underinsured or self-insured status resulting from the inadequate coverage may need to be disclosed as a risk in SEC filings.

AUDIT OF EXPENSES

The acquisitions and payments cycle includes many types of transactions for which an entity disburses money. Inventory purchases and payments were discussed in detail earlier. The operating expenses that companies incur and pay are also very important to their activities and financial statements. Auditors examine expenses largely with tests of controls, dual purpose tests, and analytical procedures that relate the expenses to asset and liability accounts. Analytical procedures usually involve comparing an expense account balance to that of the prior year and budget, and looking at the expense account balance in light of related asset and liability accounts. In addition, auditors perform tests of details of balances to directly analyze some expense accounts.

Account Analysis

One way that auditors analyze expenses is by identifying the transactions that make up the expense account balances and examining the supporting documents for those transactions. Auditors are more likely to perform account analysis for expenses with greater inherent risk because of their complexity or importance to material accounts.

For example, auditors analyze the transactions and examine underlying documents for repairs and maintenance expense because of the relationship of repairs and maintenance to

AUDITING IN ACTION

Example of an Expense Account Analysis Work Paper

Audit Client Company
Analysis of Legal Expenses
December 31, 2010
Testing Performed by: JH, 1/22/11
Audit File: K-2

Voucher #	Name	Amount		Description
2-124	Weiss & Lehman	23,500	✔	Retainer for Q1 2010
3-143	Roth & Levinson	18,200	✔	Outside legal work for an acquisition
2-395	Weiss & Lehman	24,250	✔	Representation for a liability complaint
		- 65,950	K-1	

✔   Examined properly approved voucher with supporting invoice from attorney and canceled check w/o/e.

a   Contingent liability. See letter from attorney evaluating the probability and estimation of the potential liability
Recalculated amortization expense without exception.

K-1 Tied to expense leadsheet in K-1 of current year audit file.

fixed assets. Companies usually have GAAP-based policies for what is to be expensed as repairs and maintenance and what is to be capitalized as fixed assets. One audit concern is that items that should have been capitalized are reported as repairs and maintenance expense. From a fraud risk perspective, a greater audit concern is that items that should be expensed are capitalized, thus deferring their total impact on net income. The WorldCom fraud was mentioned earlier. In that case, net income was fraudulently inflated by recording expenses as fixed assets and depreciating them over time.

The auditor may also analyze transactions classified as rent and lease expenses. In contrast to the repairs and maintenance account for which the auditor is primarily concerned that items may be capitalized when they should be expensed, for leases, the auditor is concerned that amounts are only shown as period expenses when appropriate. The concern is that a lease is shown as an operating lease, and therefore expensed, when it should be capitalized as an asset with a corresponding liability shown on the balance sheet. The potential management motivation for this situation is limiting the amount of debt that is shown on the balance sheet. Lease contracts and the analyses required to determine whether leases should be classified as operating or capital leases are complex. Therefore, the analysis may require significant audit effort. Capitalized lease obligations are discussed in Chapter 15.

Auditors also typically identify all the transactions and examine supporting documents for the legal expense account. Auditors do not usually perform this detailed analysis because the amount is quantitatively material. Instead, auditors examine legal expense accounts to be sure they are aware of the issues for which their audit clients need legal representation. Legal challenges and outcomes can have important financial statement impacts. They may give rise to contingent or certain liabilities that must be recorded. Even if they do not have to be recorded, contingent liabilities may need to be disclosed. FASB ASC 450-10 which includes, accounting for contingencies, provides guidance on recording contingent liabilities. Analyzing the transactions in the legal expense account provides the auditor with evidence regarding certain and potential liabilities.

Allocation Analysis

Another test of details of balances for expenses is analysis of allocation procedures and the resulting expenses. Allocation can spread the costs of a long-lived asset over time, such as depreciating fixed assets or amortizing intangibles. Specifics on auditing these expenses are discussed later with property, plant, and equipment and intangible assets.

Allocation procedures are also important when the cash disbursed must be divided between asset or liability and expense accounts. Payments allocated between prepaid assets and expense accounts are one example. Cash disbursements that reduce debt principal and pay interest expense are another. An important example is the allocation that occurs related to inventory. For instance, in a manufacturing company payroll costs often need to be allocated between expense accounts and inventory accounts. Overhead costs may need to be allocated among units of inventory. Allocations relating to inventory are discussed in Chapter 14.

REVIEW QUESTIONS

L.1 What audit procedures fall under the label Search for Unrecorded Liabilities? What management assertion do these audit procedures address?

L.2 What audit steps are typical for prepaid assets and accrued liabilities?

L.3 What are the steps to account analysis for a prepaid or accrual account?

L.4 What does SAB 108 say regarding the financial statements for which materiality must be considered?

L.5 What prepaid or accrued items might require additional auditor attention beyond the customary evaluation for appropriate financial reporting?

L.6 Which expense accounts is an auditor likely to specifically analyze and why?

AUDIT OF PROPERTY, PLANT AND EQUIPMENT

Two classes of long-term assets are often labeled (1) Property, Plant and Equipment or Fixed Assets, and (2) Intangible Assets. Depending on the nature of assets owned by a business, the title for property, plant and equipment may differ. For example, a retail establishment that leases its sales floor and offices may simply have Leasehold Improvements and Equipment. In contrast, businesses in the automotive industry likely own property (land), plant (buildings), and equipment.

ICFR related to the acquisition of property, plant and equipment differs from that for other purchase transactions mainly in the authorization that occurs. Fixed assets purchases are often high-dollar-amount transactions. The company may plan for fixed asset purchases using a capital budgeting process requiring specified internal rates of return or other performance thresholds. Sometimes fixed asset acquisitions are approved at the department or division level, while some approvals are by top management or the Board of Directors. For example, fixed assets that are self-constructed or that require new debt be incurred typically require the authorization of top management or the Board of Directors.

Tests of controls for purchases and payments of fixed assets may be included with other tests of controls for the acquisitions and payments cycle. The tests are modified to address the different authorization evidence examined. Beyond tests of controls the auditor uses dual purpose tests, substantive analytical procedures, and tests of details of balances to audit fixed assets.

Additions and Disposals

In auditing property, plant, and equipment, if the prior-year balance was audited, the auditor traces this year's beginning balance to last year's ending balance and analyzes additions and disposals. Additions and disposal are audited using dual purpose tests and tests of details of balances that provide audit evidence about authorization, existence, and proper recording. The auditor performs the steps shown in Exhibit 12-10 for fixed asset acquisitions. The audit procedures address either a sample or, if there were few fixed asset additions during the year, the entire population of additions.

The straightforward steps outlined in Exhibit 12-10 may lead you to believe that auditing fixed assets acquisitions is a simple process. Sometimes it is. However, under certain conditions, the accounting calculations required can make auditing the cost of acquisitions quite difficult. For example, sometimes the company constructs fixed assets for its own use—called self-constructed assets. For self-constructed assets the costs of resources used, including interest capitalized, must be captured, sometimes calculated, and recorded by the client. Analyzing the validity and accuracy of the items included and excluded from the cost of a self-constructed asset can be challenging. As another example, donated fixed assets often require appraisals or valuations to determine the cost to be recorded. Auditors must also determine that costs associated with making a fixed asset operational, such as freight-in, set up, and testing, are not omitted from the cost of the asset.

As was mentioned in the earlier discussion of repairs and maintenance expense, companies develop policies that are used to classify which transactions are fixed assets and which are expenses. The auditor evaluates the reasonableness of the company policies. If company policies are reasonable, the auditor relies on them in evaluating the appropriate classification of purchases as fixed asset acquisitions. During this process, the auditor is also aware of the possibility that expenses unrelated to fixed assets may be erroneously recorded as acquisitions in the property, plant, and equipment accounts.

Along with auditing additions, auditing the property, plant, and equipment account balance deals with disposals. The auditor examines supporting documents for disposal transactions, looking for authorization of the transactions. If cash or another asset was received in exchange for the disposed asset, the auditor may trace all aspects of the transaction to, for example, the cash receipts journal and fixed asset ledger. This step allows the auditor to determine whether the transaction was properly recorded. Sometimes disposals require

EXHIBIT 12-10

Auditing Fixed Asset
Additions

1. Recalculate the fixed asset ledger or schedule of fixed asset acquisitions for clerical accuracy, using computer-assisted audit techniques if appropriate, and trace amounts to the general ledger.

2. Select current-year fixed asset acquisition transactions and examine documentation associated with the acquisitions. The documentation to be examined includes evidence of whatever approval is required by company policies, receiving report or other evidence of receipt, vendor's invoice, deeds, titles, or other ownership documents. If the fixed asset is leased, evaluate the accounting for it as a capitalized lease and, when appropriate, trace the transaction to the related liability. Use the information on the supporting documents to agree the proper classification, timing, and amount of the posted transaction.

3. Physically inspect the asset. (Although auditors are not experts on fixed assets they can look for obvious differences between what was described in the documents and the asset and note the condition of the asset supporting consistency with the description in the documents. For example, the auditor can note whether the asset appears new or used and agree this to the supporting documents.)

minimal audit work because the amounts are small, especially if the assets disposed of are nearly or completely depreciated. Sometimes controls over recording disposals are poor because old equipment is "cannibalized" for parts or simply junked—typically referred to as abandoned. If the assets are fully depreciated, this poor recordkeeping has no net effect on the financial statements but increases the difficulty of keeping accurate fixed asset ledgers.

Most companies perform periodic counts or inventories of their fixed assets. In addition to analyzing any fixed asset acquisition and disposal transactions that occurred during the current year, the auditor may review the client documents prepared during a fixed asset count. The auditor may also choose to inspect a sample of the assets that were acquired in prior years to confirm their continued existence, particularly the newer fixed assets and those with large net book values.

Impaired Value

An additional complexity related to auditing the account balance for fixed assets is the ongoing value of the assets. *Accounting for the Impairment or Disposal of Long Lived Assets,* FASB Codification 360-10-05-4, requires that long-lived assets be written down if they are impaired. Impairment means that the carrying value of the asset (cost less accumulated depreciation) may not be recoverable. The language of the accounting standard states that impairment has occurred, and therefore the assets must be written down if the carrying value is greater than the aggregate of the asset's undiscounted estimated future cash flows. If impairment has occurred, another calculation of the difference between the asset's fair value and carrying value is required to determine the amount of the write down.

Fair Value Measurements is addressed in FASB ASC 820-10 and provides guidance that the auditor relies on to determine the sufficiency of disclosure about impaired and written down assets.

> For assets and liabilities that are measured at fair value on a nonrecurring basis in periods subsequent to initial recognition (for example, impaired assets), the reporting entity shall disclose information that enables users of its financial statements to assess the inputs used to develop those measurements. (FASB Codification 820-10-50-5)

The auditor addresses how a company handles possible impairment of long-lived assets long before the audit progresses to tests of details of balances. When gaining an understanding of the business and assessing entity-level controls for ICFR, the auditor inquires about the company's policies for determining whether impairment has occurred. The auditor may perform a walkthrough of the process called for by company policies. Accounting standards require that companies evaluate their fixed assets whenever an event has occurred or circumstances have changed that suggest possible impairment, although many companies also perform this evaluation at least once a year. When impairment is thought to have occurred, significant audit effort goes into reviewing the client's assumptions and analyzing the calculations and conclusions regarding the write-down of the asset.

AUDITING IN ACTION

The Real Purpose of Touring the Client's Facilities ....

At the beginning of any audit it is common for client personnel to take the audit team on a tour of the business. Although this is important for the auditor to evaluate the control environment, taking everyone on the tour helps the whole audit team feel familiar with the environment.

As a first year staff on her first manufacturing audit, Lee was just trying to make sure she paid attention when they told her where the bathroom was. The next thing she knew she was almost speechless as she and the rest of the team were led onto the manufacturing floor of the carpet plant. The number and size of the machines and the enormous rolls of carpet and thread, both on the machines and off, were like nothing she had seen before. She kept looking up because the equipment was so big. At the end of the tour the controller asked if anyone had any questions.

Lee felt a little stupid to be asking what she was sure was a silly question, but she had noticed that there was a very long piece of black plastic that was about three feet wide looped from hangers extending from the ceiling. She thought it looked a lot like the plastic that goes in a flower bed to prevent weeds. The continuous piece of black plastic started at the ceiling on one end of the room and traversed back and forth, particularly over the equipment and batches of inventory. It angled down as it made its way across the room. Close to where she and the rest of the team were standing the end of the plastic dropped from the ceiling and went into a trash can. Lee asked what the plastic was—if it had a purpose.

The controller grimaced and said that there had been a major wind and rain storm that had damaged the factory roof a month before. Until the roof could be repaired they were trying to keep the water off the machines and inventory—it ran down the plastic and into the trash can. Later the senior on the job pulled Lee off to the side and told her what a good job she had done by asking that question. The audit team was going to have to follow up to see if any of the long lived assets were impaired as a result of wind and water damage. The senior had been on that plant tour so many times that he had not even looked up, and hadn't noticed the plastic!

Depreciation

The next step for property, plant, and equipment is the audit of the depreciation expense and the resulting accumulated depreciation. Typically, companies maintain the fixed asset information in an electronic format, and this permits the auditor to use computer-assisted audit techniques to recalculate the depreciation expense and accumulated depreciation amounts. The auditor uses the company's chosen methods and parameters for useful life and residual value. In addition to checking the mathematical accuracy, the auditor evaluates whether the useful lives and residual values used by the client are reasonable. The amounts of depreciation expense and accumulated depreciation are traced to the fixed asset ledger and general ledger. If automated recalculation is not possible, the auditor manually performs recalculations on a sample of the fixed assets.

The remaining steps for the audit of fixed assets are substantive analytical procedures and review of financial statement disclosures. Exhibit 12-11 provides examples of analytical procedures for property, plant, and equipment. Disclosures for fixed assets include: whether fixed assets are stated at cost; the classes of fixed assets, such as land, buildings, equipment, and machinery; accumulated depreciation; methods of depreciation for tax and financial statement purposes; and useful lives. Information on capitalized leases related to fixed assets, capitalized interest on self-constructed assets, and liens and mortgages against fixed assets are also disclosed. If fixed assets are disposed of as part of the disposal or discontinuance of a line of business, that is also disclosed.

AUDITING IN ACTION

Sample Property, Plant and Equipment Work Paper

Audit Client Company
Property, Plant & Equipment and Accumulated Depreciation Lead Schedule
December 31, 2010
Testing Performed by: JH, 1/22/11
Audit File: P-1

Depr. Rate	Description	Property, Plant & Equipment					Allowance for Depreciation			
		Balance 12/31/09		Additions	Retirements	Balance 12/31/10	Balance 12/31/09	Additions	Retirements	Balance 12/31/10
–	Land	20,040		0	0	20,040	0	0	0	0
5%	Buildings	320,500	P-4	22,560	18,800	324,260	34,950	12,520	9,570	37,900
10%	Equipment	254,000	P-2	12,960	25,620	241,340	28,600	5,200	22,590	11,210
33%	Automobiles	48,900		0	0	48,900	15,700	4,200	0	19,900
		643,440		35,520	44,420	634,540	79,250	21,920	32,160	69,010
		TB-1			P-3	TB-1	TB-1		P-3	TB-1

TB-1   Tied to work paper TB-1
P-2   Tied to work paper P-2
P-3   Tied to work paper P-3
P-4   Tied to work paper P-4

Equipment Additions
Schedule
Audit File: P-2

Voucher #	Vendor	Amount		Description
1-40145	RLH Electric	9,450	✔	Electric Motor
3-49125	FHP Machinery	3,510	✔	Pressing Machinery
	Total Examined	12,960	P-1	

✔   Examined vendor invoice, receiving report, and canceled check and noted that
     the expenditure was a proper capital charge.
P-1 Tied to equipment balance on work paper P-1.

EXHIBIT 12-11

**Examples of
Substantive Analytical
Procedures for property,
Plant, and Equipment**

Compare year-end balances of Property, Plant and Equipment and Depreciation Expense
with prior-year balances; consider acquisitions and disposals in reconciling the
relationship

Compare the total Property, Plant and Equipment acquisitions recorded to the fixed asset
records to the amount provided for in the capital budget or approved in the Board of
Directors minutes

Compute the ratio of Depreciation Expense to the recorded Property, Plant and Equipment
account balance and compare the ratio to that of the prior year; consider changes in
depreciation methods, basis, or lives in reconciling the relationship

Compare repairs and maintenance expense with prior-year balances to investigate whether
there may be material items that should have been capitalized

AUDIT OF INTANGIBLE ASSETS [LO 7]

Intangible assets are very important in some industries, yet virtually nonexistent in others. For those businesses with immaterial balances in intangible assets, audit work may be limited to substantive analytical procedures. In contrast, for those industries in which they are important, intangible assets require significant financial statement audit work.

Recorded intangible assets are purchased. Therefore, many of these transactions fall within the tests of controls that apply to the overall acquisitions and payments cycle. The notable exception is intangible assets that a company acquires as a part of acquiring another company in its entirety. These merger and acquisition transactions are of such elevated importance that their ICFR procedures probably fall within the scope of the control environment and entity-level controls. Major investments in other companies, and mergers and acquisitions are discussed in Chapter 15.

Dual purpose tests, substantive analytical procedures, and tests of details of balances similar to those applied to property, plant, and equipment and depreciation are appropriate for identifiable intangible assets. Identifiable intangible assets—basically those that are not goodwill—may be purchased as investments or as productive assets. For example, large pharmaceutical companies often purchase patents that allow the company the right to manufacture and distribute the drugs the patent covers. Thus, the patents are related to the production process. Among other identifiable intangible assets are purchased franchise rights, customer lists, trademarks, and copyrights. The costs of purchased intangible assets are vouched by examining purchase documents and other legal documents indicating ownership rights. When research and development costs are capitalized rather than expensed, auditors perform extensive document examination to determine their validity as assets based on the guidance set forth in various accounting standards.

When identifiable intangible assets are received as part of the acquisition of another company, the purchase price is allocated to the various assets of the acquired company. The auditor performs procedures to understand the entire business merger or acquisition transaction. Through this process, the auditor is able to examine the cost of the identifiable intangible assets.

Some identifiable intangible assets are amortized based on the expected economic life of the asset. Other identifiable intangible assets fall into the category of those having indefinite useful economic life. Intangible assets with indefinite useful economic lives are analyzed for impairment rather than being amortized. Patents with clear legal lives present good examples of intangibles that are amortized. Generally, pharmaceutical companies estimate the useful life of patents based on the period of time they expect to have legal exclusivity for the drug to which the patent relates. Auditors recalculate amortization similarly to the steps followed in the audit of depreciation expense. Information from the company's legal counsel is also used by the auditor when the information indicates other impairment of an intangible asset's value.

REVIEW QUESTIONS

M.1 How does authorization for the purchase of property, plant, and equipment differ from authorization for other purchases?

M.2 What difficult analyses and calculations may be required in determining (and therefore auditing) the proper amounts to record for additions to fixed assets?

M.3 Why is the impact of poor ICFR related to the disposal of fixed assets not usually important to the financial statements?

M.4 Why is the auditor concerned about the impact of possible impairment of value on the fixed assets of audit clients? Summarize the accounting guidance regarding impairment. What are the related auditing procedures?

M.5 What is the main type of transaction that triggers an intangible asset being recorded?

M.6 What are identifiable intangible assets? Give examples. What audit procedures will the auditor likely apply to intangible assets?

AUDITING ACQUISITIONS AND PAYMENTS IN THE AUTOMOTIVE INDUSTRY

Auditing the acquisitions and payments cycle in the automotive industry begins with an understanding of the purchases made and the processes used for those purchase activities. Cash disbursements for inventory purchases and period costs such as operating expenses are the bulk of the cash disbursements in these types of businesses, with fixed assets and intangible assets being less frequent acquisitions.

ICFR

Businesses in the automotive industry usually have a high volume of inventory purchase transactions for many different items and from multiple vendors. This makes the ICFR for those transactions critical. The auditor needs to understand and test controls over the process for authorizing purchases, placing orders, receiving goods, and executing payment transactions.

Testing for adequate segregation of duties is a first step. Controls over the authorization process rely on requisition, ordering, receiving, and cash disbursements functions being independent of each other. This is accomplished when different people and departments perform the various functions.

Automated controls may be integrated into the processes. Controls and processes are often highly automated and linked to an electronic inventory data base. When this is the case, computer-assisted audit techniques are used to test for proper authorization and initiation of transactions, as well as to test application program controls. When sophisticated accounting and inventory management systems exist, the auditor needs strong IT skills to understand and test them.

Controls over the receiving function also receive significant auditor attention, especially because in the automotive industry goods may be received at multiple operating locations. Tests of controls over payments focus on determining whether only invoices for authorized and received goods are paid. In an environment with so much and such a varied amount of inventory, the receiving function links with the inventory processes. The auditor tests physical safekeeping and documentary tracking of goods as they move from receiving to the warehouse.

Inventory Costing and Period Expenses

The audit of the acquisition and payment cycle includes auditing expenses. SFAC 6, paragraph 80, defines expenses as

> outflows or using up of assets or incurrence of liabilities (or a combination of both) from delivering or producing goods, rendering services, or carrying out other activities that constitute the entity's ongoing major or central operations.

Related to inventory, audit tests deal with the accumulation and allocation of costs among inventory units. Audit tests distinguish between inventory that is still an asset and that which has been sold and is now included as an expense in costs of sales. Period expenses are also part of this cycle. The auditor includes cash outflows for period expenses as part of cash disbursement testing.

Estimated Accounts

Assuming an automotive industry client has good ICFR, the most challenging consideration for testing expenses or assets and related accounts payable and cash disbursements is the large volume of transactions. In contrast, the more technically difficult expense items to audit in the automotive industry are those that must be estimated and accrued rather than currently paid. Contingent liabilities are to be accrued if it is probable that a liability exists at the balance sheet date and the amount can be reasonably estimated. Accrued warranty liabilities fall into this category.

FASB Codification 460-10-20 defines a warranty as

> an obligation [that] may be incurred in connection with the sale of goods or services; if so, it may require further performance by the seller after the sale has taken place.

Some warranty costs are expected based on an automotive business's contractual commitments. These tend to be agreements to provide parts or service for a specified period of time after the sale. The expense is usually calculated based on past experiences. Current circumstances such as the roll-out of new products, inconsistent or different reliability of production inputs, and new regulations can affect the amount that is expensed and accrued as warranty liability.

To audit warranty expense and the related liability, auditors need to:

1. Understand management's estimation process
2. Evaluate the underlying assumptions for reasonableness
3. Examine documents supporting the inputs to the calculation
4. Reperform the calculation
5. Trace the results to the financial statements
6. Review the financial statement disclosure

A fair value accounting for a warranty obligation is permitted if the company is able to pay a third party to provide the goods and services (FASB Codification 825-10). Other complex expense amounts that require similar audit steps include any impairment of long-lived assets and new or changes to environmental remediation cost estimates.

Long-Term Assets

Fixed and intangible long-lived assets may be large dollar amounts on automotive company balance sheets. The auditor performs procedures to obtain audit evidence on the balance sheets amounts, related depreciation and amortization expense, and the possibility of impairment. Leases are often used in the automotive industry, and the auditor examines the underlying lease agreements for proper posting as either operating expenses or capitalized leases.

Accounts Payable and Accrued Liabilities

Accounts payable and accrued liabilities are likely to be significant dollar amounts and may be the largest current liabilities of some automotive industry businesses. The auditor is concerned with understatement—which theoretically can be as much as 100% if the liability is simply unrecorded. In addition, the auditor must remain aware that understatement can result from fraud as well as from error. Common audit steps for accounts payable and accrued liabilities include confirming accounts payable, reviewing cash disbursements in the subsequent period as part of the search for unrecorded liabilities, and performing analytical procedures.

Analytical procedures are effective for auditing accounts payable and expenses because automotive industry businesses often have well-designed budgets that link inventory purchases and cash needs to the manufacture and sale of goods. Statistical data about the company's operations, as well as industry benchmark data and competitor information, are often available. Data from all of these sources can be used for analytical procedures. Sometimes a business may have a limited number of either suppliers or customers. If this is the case, the auditor may be able to confirm a large percentage of sales or purchases transactions and use this information as part of analytical procedures to test relationships among a variety of account balances.

Disclosures

Understanding how transactions are supposed to be captured, calculated, and posted, and the disclosures required by GAAP and regulatory agencies, is necessary to audit disclosures. Financial statement disclosures for the expenditure and payments cycle reflect purchases, cash, inventory, long-lived assets, expenses, and liabilities. For automotive industry companies, many suppliers and distributors may be related parties. Therefore, the auditor particularly considers disclosures about related parties and intercompany transactions.

Many automotive companies engage in global purchase and sale activities. Consequently, the companies receive or extend payment for transactions using foreign currencies. This exposes the companies to foreign currency exchange risks. The companies probably engage in derivative financial instrument transactions to hedge this risk. These transactions necessitate disclosure. Given the large amount of commodities used in the manufacturing process, automotive manufacturers likely also enter into purchase commitments to control their risk of price increases, or futures contracts to hedge against commodities price increases. These transactions must be disclosed. Investments made to hedge risks are discussed with the financing cycle in Chapter 15. The list of disclosures shown here is not meant to cover all the possibilities, but represents the different disclosure possibilities the auditor must understand and consider.

REVIEW QUESTIONS

N.1 For what items are cash disbursements most frequent in the automotive industry?

N.2 What characteristics of the purchasing, receiving, and payment activities in the automotive industry make ICFR very important? What ICFR are important, and what does the auditor do to test them?

N.3 Why is the audit of warranties challenging?

N.4 Why are fixed assets likely to be important to the financial statements of a company in the automotive industry?

N.5 How does the auditor come to an audit conclusion regarding presentation and disclosure for acquisition and payment activities and related accounts?

CONCLUSION

The automotive industry includes elements of retail, wholesale, manufacturing, and service businesses, and therefore makes purchases, incurs accounts payable, and ultimately pays for inventory and operating expenses. Automotive businesses acquire tangible fixed assets that must be depreciated and identifiable intangible assets that may be amortized, both of which must be evaluated for impairment. The value of fixed assets may be acquired through leases, which may be either operating leases that must be expensed as the cash is disbursed or capitalized leases that are balance sheet assets and liabilities. Prepaid accounts and accrued liabilities common to most business operations also exist in the automotive industry. These companies must also estimate and record expenses and accrued liabilities for warranties. Environmental damage remediation often has to be estimated and accrued. Automotive businesses may purchase goods from many vendors or a single vendor. They may deal with related parties. They may hedge foreign currency and commodities risks.

Many industries do not deal with all of the different types of transactions discussed here. However, all businesses have an acquisition and payment function and deal with some subset of these processes and transactions. Consequently, an auditor must understand how to deal with all of them as they are addressed during an integrated audit.

KEY TERMS

Accounts payable confirmations. Requests sent to vendors of an audit client asking for direct communication to the auditor about amounts owed by the audit client to the vendor.

Accounts payable subsidiary ledger. A company's file containing all the individual records of payments owed; detail supporting the accounts payable "control account" in the general ledger.

Acquisition and payments cycle. The processes used by a business to make purchases, record payables, and make cash disbursements.

Blanket purchase order. Document used to authorize multiple purchases of an item from a vendor.

Building out. Process of a company customizing a leased space from which it operates.

Cash disbursements journal or report. A listing in either electronic or paper form of payments made by an entity.

Cash disbursements process. Process used by an entity to handle the transfer of funds held in a bank account to others for payments of liabilities.

Commodities. Term traditionally used to refer to physical items such as agricultural products and metals; raw materials classified as commodities may be important raw materials in the manufacturing process.

Cutoff. The management assertion that all transactions are recorded in the proper period.

Debit memo. Document of a purchaser used to communicate an amount of a payable that is not going to be paid; may be used after damaged or the wrong goods are received or an invoiced amount is reduced after negotiations with the vendor.

EDGAR. The acronym for the SEC's Electronic Data Gathering, Analysis, and Retrieval System found on the SEC Web site.

Encumbering process. Used in government and not-for-profit entities to set aside the amount that is committed to be paid from what is available to be spent at the time the decision to make the purchase is approved.

Invoice. Document provided by a vendor to a purchaser indicating the details about the item sold, amount of the sale and amount still owed on the sale; sometimes call a bill.

Just-in-time inventory. Describes the purchasing process used when vendors or suppliers ship inventory so that it is received by the purchaser only as it is needed to be included in the manufacturing process; may cause the manufacturer to place an increased dependence on its suppliers.

Manufacturer. Term applied to entities that produce, assemble, or build products for resale.

Monthly statement. Document provided by a vendor to a purchaser with information on beginning balance owed, purchase and payment activity during the month, and ending balanced owed; may be used instead of or in conjunction with invoices for individual purchases.

Original Equipment Manufacturers (OEM). Term used to indicate the company that manufactures goods; in the automotive industry, the company whose name is on the product sold to the end user.

Paper check. Commercial document in paper form used to authorize the removal of funds from a bank account and distribution of those funds to another party.

Payment support package. Set of documentation accumulated by a purchaser to support and authorize a payment to a vendor; may be in either paper or electronic form; may be referred to as a voucher package.

Purchase order. Document prepared by a purchasing department or purchasing agent that is sent to an outside vendor as a means of placing an order.

Purchase requisition. Document produced by a department or other business unit indicating a need for an item to be purchased.

Receiving log. Document that lists all of the shipments received by the shipping department; may include information included in the receiving report and other information such as time of arrival, and delivery company.

Receiving report. Document produced in the receiving department indicating what was received, vendor, number of items, and condition of items that arrive in a shipment.

Staff Accounting Bulletin (SAB) 108. Guidance by the SEC staff regarding the need to consider whether an amount is material to both the balance sheets and income statements, rather than addressing materiality for only one financial statement or the other.

Standard Industrial Classification (SIC). Codes identifying industry or line of business, used by the SEC for classification and identification purposes.

Substantive analytical procedures. Procedures that investigate relationships among and between financial and nonfinancial data, based on the assumption that expected relationships among information will exist and continue to do so unless there is a known reason for the change or a problem with the information.

Unrecorded liabilities. Amounts owed by an audit client that are not recorded on its financial statements at year end; specific audit procedures are directed to identifying any liabilities that are unrecorded at year end by examining payments made by the audit client at the beginning of the subsequent fiscal year.

MULTIPLE CHOICE

12-1 [LO 1] Which of the following sets of accounts is not affected by the acquisition and payment cycle?

(a) Cash, inventory, intangible assets

(b) Accounts payable, prepaid assets, accrued liabilities

(c) Accounts receivable, capital stock, retained earnings

(d) Cash, fixed assets, accounts payable

12-2 [LO 1] Information about inventory is extremely important for retailers and wholesalers to conduct business. Identify which of the following is not relevant information for retailers and wholesalers concerning their inventory.

(a) How many items were last purchased

(b) How many items remain in inventory

(c) The date the items were received

(d) All of the above are relevant.

12-3 [LO 3] Retail and wholesale businesses may need to return some of the inventory items that they purchase, or may receive a discount when items are paid for in a certain time frame. This process of purchase returns and allowances is the "mirror" image of

(a) the sales returns and allowances transaction.

(b) purchasing fixed assets from outside parties.

(c) the sale of inventory to the end user.

(d) financing a purchase by using a trade account.

12-4 [LO 2] When most people think about the automotive industry, they think of the cars sold to end users that they see each day on roadways. In addition to this aspect of the industry, the automotive industry includes

(a) repairs and maintenance.

(b) manufacturing and wholesale of parts.

(c) leasing and financing.

(d) all of the above.

12-5 [LO 2] Of the following, which is not an activity related to the manufacturing processes of an automotive business?

(a) Fabrication of items for the company's use or sale to outsiders

(b) Research and design of new products

(c) Financing of purchases sold to customers

(d) Assembly of parts into a final product

12-6 [LO 2] Which of the following is not typically identified as a risk of international trade?

(a) Foreign government regulations

(b) Foreign language barriers

(c) Local labor market conditions

(d) Political, religious, and economic instability

12-7 [LO 4] Which is an important objective of management relating to acquisitions and payments?

(a) All cash disbursements are for items that were actually received.

(b) Items purchased should always come from the same supplier.

(c) Sales employees approve items to be purchased for the manufacturing process.

(d) All purchased items are to be delivered to the company or employee's homes.

12-8 [LO 4] In order to ensure segregation of duties, a purchase requisition should come from

(a) the CEO.

(b) the head of the purchasing department.

(c) an employee with the authority to request that items be purchased.

(d) a member of the accounting department.

12-9 [LO 4] What should the procedure be if there are differences in the information included on various supporting documents for a purchase?

(a) Notify the vendor of the discrepancy.

(b) Investigate internally and communicate with the vendor as appropriate.

(c) Prepare a debit memo.

(d) Investigate the processes in the purchasing department.

12-10 [LO 4] To prevent potential financial statement misstatements, purchase and payment transactions should be

(a) properly approved before the purchase is initiated.

(b) posted in the right amount to the proper account.

(c) agreed to a receiving report before being approved for payment.

(d) all of the above.

12-11 [LO 4] Which of the following is not a control needed for cash disbursements?

(a) Control over blank checks

(b) Control over online authorization codes for fund transfers

(c) Prior approval by the employee who reconciles the bank statements

(d) Inspection of the supporting documents before disbursement is authorized

12-12 [LO 5] To increase the efficiency of the integrated audit, dual purpose tests for acquisitions and cash disbursements related to the year-end cash balances should be performed

(a) early in the fiscal year.

(b) late in the fiscal year.

(c) throughout the fiscal year.

(d) It does not matter when the steps are performed.

12-13 [LO 6] Which of the following tests would the auditor use to address concerns that some accounts payable accounts were omitted from the accounts payable subsidiary ledger at year end?

(a) Perform a search for unrecorded liabilities.

(b) Ask the CFO whether he or she has checked for any unposted invoices at year end.

(c) Send confirmations to the client's regular suppliers who have zero year-end balances at year end.

(d) All of the above.

12-14 [LO 6] If an auditor selects receiving reports and examines where they are posted to investigate whether they are posted at the correct amounts and in the correct periods, the receiving reports will be traced to

(a) sales and cash receipts.

(b) inventory and accounts payable.

(c) purchase returns and accounts payable.

(d) inventory and accounts receivable.

12-15 [LO 7] When an auditor analyzes additions to the fixed assets accounts,

(a) the main purpose is be sure depreciation expense is accurately calculated.

(b) he or she checks to be sure period expenses are not improperly classified as long-term assets.

(c) insurance coverage for the fixed assets is examined simultaneously.

(d) a main emphasis is evaluating going concern.

12-16 [LO 6] When confirming accounts payable to gain evidence on completeness, the auditor will select the accounts to be confirmed from

(a) all vendors with which the company has previously done business including those with current zero balances due.

(b) vendors to which the company owes large balances.

(c) only those vendors with whom the company has done business in the last month.

(d) vendors the company issues checks to in the first month of the next fiscal year.

12-17 [LO 6] Which of the following is not typically included in a document package supporting a cash disbursement?

(a) Invoice

(b) Purchase requisition

(c) Receiving report

(d) Credit approval

12-18 [LO 7] Regarding leases,

(a) the primary audit concern is to obtain evidence that they are not recorded as expenses when they should be recorded as fixed assets.

(b) the primary audit concern is to obtain evidence that they are not recorded as fixed assets when they should be recorded as expenses.

(c) the primary audit concern is to obtain evidence that the recorded amount is not over- or understated.

(d) The primary audit concern is to gain evidence that the recorded amount is not posted in the wrong period.

12-19 [LO 7] Regarding repairs and maintenance,

(a) the primary audit concern is to obtain evidence that they are not recorded as expenses when they should be recorded as fixed assets.

(b) the primary audit concern is to obtain evidence that they are not recorded as fixed assets when they should be recorded as expenses.

(c) the primary audit concern is to obtain evidence that the recorded amount is not over- or understated.

(d) the primary audit concern is to gain evidence that the recorded amount is not posted in the wrong period.

12-20 [LO 6] Auditors examine all the transactions that are posted to legal expenses

(a) because the amount is material.

(b) to determine whether the transactions are posted to the correct account.

(c) to identify issues for which the company needs legal representation.

(d) to audit completeness of legal expenses.

12-21 **[LO 7]** Fixed assets

(a) are always shown at historical cost.

(b) are always shown at historical cost less accumulated depreciation.

(c) must be evaluated when an event has occurred or circumstances have changed to suggest impairment.

(d) must be evaluated by management annually for possible impairment or the auditor cannot issue an unqualified audit report.

12-22 **[LO 7]** The audit of intangible assets

(a) is important in every industry.

(b) is important in industries with many self-constructed assets.

(c) is important in industries that rely on purchased patents for manufacture and sale of inventory.

(d) is important related to amortization expense when companies patent the outcomes of internal research activities.

DISCUSSION QUESTIONS

12-23 **[LO 2]** What are the most important risks for the audit of the acquisition and payments cycle in the automotive industry? Does this differ from the risks related to this cycle for other industries? If yes, how?

12-24 **[LO 4]** In an automated accounts payable system how does an auditor test and obtain audit evidence addressing the following questions? Discuss the appropriate audit steps likely to be applied in answering these questions.

(a) Can the receiving department record the receipt of goods without matching the receipt to a purchase order in the system?

(b) Can an invoice be paid without first matching the receipt and vendor invoice to an approved purchase order?

(c) Can an invoice be paid twice?

(d) Can an invoice be paid if the quantity, unit price, or total does not match the purchase order information?

(e) Will the system permit payment to a vendor who is not in the established vendor master file?

(AS 2, Example B-4)

12-25 **[LO 7]** Discuss what would be included in an audit program to test whether all additions to fixed assets for the year represent the purchase of real fixed assets. What overall audit procedures are required on the company's records and accounts so that the auditor can use the beginning general ledger balances for fixed assets as a starting point?

12-26 **[LO 4, 6]** From (1) an ICFR audit and (2) a financial audit perspective, identify and explain the most critical management assertion for the following:

(a) Cash disbursements

(b) Property, plant, and equipment

(c) Intangible assets

(d) Expenses

(e) Accounts payable

12-27 **[LO 4, 6]** For which accounts and management assertions does the search for unrecorded liabilities provide audit evidence? Related to these accounts and assertions, what procedures should the auditor perform for the ICFR audit? What substantive procedures will the auditor perform for the financial statement audit and why?

12-28 **[LO 3]** If an individual's job is purchasing agent, and that person is allowed to purchase from whatever vendor he or she chooses—in other words, the purchasing agent does not have to comply with an approved vendor and price list—how can that person steal from or perpetrate a fraud on his or her employer?

12-29 **[LO 3]** How are the auditor's concerns regarding purchase discounts different from those of management? Why?

PROBLEMS

Use the following information for Problems 12-30 and 12-31:

Your client, Raptor Manufacturing, is a large public company that manufactures afterburning turbofan engines for F-22 fighter jets. Many components that are used in the production process are purchased from nonrelated vendors. Since management can reasonably estimate how many engines will be produced per year, the company has drafted and preapproved a purchase budget based on their expectations. In addition, the company prepared an approved vendor list from which purchases should be made. All purchase requisition forms must be completed and signed by a production manager.

After conducting a walkthrough with management, you have identified the following processes related to purchases and cash disbursements:

- *Purchasing Department:* When the purchasing department receives a purchase requisition form, a purchasing agent conducts the following procedures. First, the purchasing agent looks for the proper signature on the purchase requisition. If properly approved, then the purchasing agent selects a vendor from the approved vendor list and contacts that vendor to check for availability and pricing. Once the vendor and price have been determined, it is time to place the order. Before the order can be placed, the purchasing agent must determine whether the purchase is part of the preapproved purchase budget. If the total purchase price is below $20,000 and the vendor is on the approved vendor list, then the purchasing agent can place the order. If the total purchase price is above $20,000 or the vendor is not on the approved vendor list, then the purchase must be approved by the department head. When an order is placed, a purchase order is prepared and sent to the receiving department, accounts payable, and purchasing department head, and is filed in the nonreceived orders file. When the receiving report is received, the purchase order is transferred to the received orders file. If a purchase order is in the nonreceived orders file for more than 45 days, the purchasing agent reviews and investigates the status of the order.

- *Receiving Department:* In advance of receiving an order, the receiving department is given a copy of the purchase order. When the order is received, a receiving clerk fills out a receiving report recording the date, the contents of the order, and any variance from the purchase order. A copy of the receiving report is then forwarded to the purchasing department, accounts payable, and receiving department head, and is filed in the received orders file.

- *Accounts Payable:* The purchase order and receiving report are kept in an unpaid file until the invoice is received. Upon receipt of the invoice, the accounts payable clerk matches the invoice with the receiving report and purchase order. Once the invoice amount is verified, the clerk records the transaction and files the invoice in the approved but unpaid file. Every Thursday, a different accounts payable clerk prepares checks for all the invoices in the approved but unpaid file and subsequently files the invoices in the paid invoices file. The checks are then sent to the treasurer for signature.

- *Treasurer:* Unsigned checks are received every Friday from accounts payable. For checks less than $20,000 and for a vendor on the approved vendor list, the cashier uses a signature plate to sign the checks. For checks greater than $20,000 or for a vendor not on the approved vendor list, the check is manually signed by the treasurer.

12-30 **[LO 1, 3, 4]** Identify and list the company controls in place related to purchase transactions and cash disbursements.

(a) For each control identified:

- state the purpose of the control.
- state which management assertion(s) are related to the control.
- list the procedures and documents needed to test the control.

(b) What are some additional controls that could be implemented to improve Raptor Manufacturing's control environment pertaining to its purchases and cash disbursements cycle?

12-31 **[LO 5]** Which of the controls identified in Problem 12-30 could be audited using a dual purpose test. How would this change the procedures and documents needed?

Use the following information for Problems 12-32 and 12-33:

J & J Auto Repair Service is a chain of automotive repair shops that performs various services for its customers. The company separates purchases into two categories, normal purchases and specialty purchases. Normal purchases include shop supplies (rags, cleaning products, etc.), general parts (oil, brake fluid, coolant, etc.), and high-demand specialty parts (car parts that are common to many vehicles). Specialty purchases include low-demand specialty parts (car parts that are specific to a vehicle) and equipment (tools, car lift, air compressor, etc). Normal purchases are estimated and made in advance of demand. Specialty purchases are only ordered upon demand for the specific part or equipment.

You are assigned to perform the audit procedures related to the accounts payable balance for the audit of the 2010 financial statements. After reviewing and testing internal controls for accounts payable, you determine that the control risk is fairly low. Below is the information that you have requested and received from the company.

Accounts Payable Subsidiary Ledger Balances (as of year end)

	2008	2009	2010
Best Price Automotive Parts	$16,000	$17,500	$16,400
Bob's Wholesaling	$5,200	$5,450	$0
That Tire Store	$5,600	$6,000	$3,100
Carson's Discount Auto Store	$20,000	$21,205	$28,700
Racer's Paradise	$9,600	$8,800	$4,000
Wholesale OEM Distributor	$19,200	$26,700	$46,000
King's Parts and Accessories	$0	$2,200	$0

Purchases Subsidiary Ledger Balances (as of year end)

	2008	2009	2010
Normal	$420,000	$424,500	$372,000
Specialty	$785,000	$845,000	$588,500

Cost of Goods Sold Ledger Balance (as of year end)

	2008	2009	2010
COGS	$932,000	$1,052,500	$876,000

Additional Information:

1. All purchases are made on credit.

2. The 2008 beginning balance for accounts payable was $79,500.

12-32 **[LO 2, 6]** Perform analytical procedures for accounts payable of J & J Auto Repair Service in the following manner:

(a) Calculate and list all necessary figures and comparisons.

(b) Explain what the result of each may indicate for the balance in accounts payable.

12-33 **[LO 6]** Using the information provided in the example and the results of analytical procedures performed in Problem 12-32, explain the substantive audit procedures, audit evidence, and related management assertions that you would need for the test of details of the accounts payable balance.

12-34 **[LO 7]** Your client, Brooks Manufacturing, Inc., is a large public company that produces small battery-powered cars for children. Three years ago, the company constructed an automated machine to produce the products more efficiently. During previous audits, the engagement team has performed impairment tests and found no impairment. After looking at the machine, you conclude there is no noticeable material physical damage to the machine.

Additional Information:

1. The machine was initially recorded at a cost of $3,482,550.

2. Accumulated depreciation on the machine to date is $969,765.

3. The machine has a salvage value of $250,000.

4. It is 2010 and the economy is in a major recession.

5. Due to the recession, management lowered its future sales expectation by 25%.

Following is the schedule of the machine's estimated future cash flows that was provided by management.

Schedule of Estimated Future Cash Flows—Automated Machinery (Prepared 01/08)

	2011	2012	2013	2014	2015	2016	2017
Cash Inflows	1,245,785	1,295,616	1,347,441	1,401,339	1,457,392	1,515,688	1,826,315
Cash Outflows	921,881	958,756	997,106	1,036,991	1,078,470	1,121,609	1,351,473

*Note: Salvage value of machine is included in the 2017 cash inflows.

Required:

Using FASB ASC 360-10 as guidance:

(a) Do you think the machine should be tested for impairment? Explain.

(b) If yes, perform an impairment test. (*Hint:* Remember the discussion in the chapter on carrying value vs. undiscounted cash flows.) Explain your decision and support your conclusion with your calculation.

12-35 **[LO 2, 3, 4]** Northwest Ford Distributors, Inc. (NFD) is a (fictional) large public company and the sole distributor of Ford vehicles for Washington State, Montana, Oregon, Idaho, and Wyoming. NFD purchases vehicles from Ford Motor Co. and distributes the vehicles to all the authorized Ford dealers in its area. In addition to its distribution duties, NFD reimburses the dealers for any official incentive amounts included in the sales price to the customers.

Based on a walkthrough of the Incentives Department of Northwest Ford Distributors, the auditors learn that the incentive process is conducted in the following steps:

1. At the beginning of every month, NFD releases an Incentive Summary that lists all the official incentives for every vehicle to each dealer. The Incentive Summary is approved by the CEO, CFO, Incentives Director, and VP of Sales.

2. If the dealer sold a vehicle and included an official incentive amount, the dealer applies for reimbursement from NFD through the NFD incentive Web site.

3. Every Monday, the payment process is initiated and completed by the end of the day. The process begins with the computer system conducting an audit of all incentives that were applied for and not yet paid. The computer system flags and rejects all units that have the following attributes:

    (a) The vehicle was rolled back (the vehicle was returned to the dealership).
    (b) The model is a nonapproved model.
    (c) The retail date is not within the approved time period.
    (d) Blank space exists in the application, including in the customer's name or the dealership's name.
    (e) A keyword included in the application suggests that a car dealer rather than an individual is the end customer.

4. Once the computer audit is completed, an Incentives Department clerk prints out a report of all computer-approved payments and conducts a brief scan of the report to look for errors that the computer may have missed. Once completed, the Incentives Department clerk approves the electronic transfer of payments to the dealerships.

5. For any units rejected by the computer or Incentives Department clerk, the dealer may submit a dispute packet. A dispute packet includes a copy of the sales receipt, a copy of the vehicle registration, and proof of payment by the customer.

6. Once the Incentives Department receives a dispute packet, a clerk reviews the documentation provided and decides whether the dealer is eligible for reimbursement by NFD.

Required:

Identify and list the company controls in place related to the incentives payment process. For each control identified:

(a) state the purpose of the control.

(b) state which management assertion(s) is (are) related to the control.

(c) list the procedures and documents needed to test the control.

12-36 **[LO 4]** The auditor determines that cash, accounts payable, and inventory are significant accounts for a company's ICFR. Through discussions with company personnel, the auditor learns that the company's computer system performs a three-way match of the receiving report, purchase order, and invoice. If there are any exceptions, the system produces a list of unmatched items that employees review and follow up on weekly.

Required:

(a) What are the assertions that the auditor needs to test?

(b) Does the above describe a preventive control or a detective control? (*Hint:* Preventive and detective controls are defined and discussed in Chapter 8.)

(c) What in the above description is an application control, and what is the audit step to test it? (*Hint:* Application controls are presented in Chapter 8.)

(AS 2, Example B-4)

12-37 **[LO 4]** Poiter & Cate, LLP, is the audit firm for Mueller Autohaus, a local dealership of luxury German automobiles located near St. Louis. Midwest Imports, Inc., a public company and the largest distributor of European automobiles in the midwestern region of the United States, is the parent company of Mueller Autohaus. Midwest Imports purchases vehicles from all of the major European auto manufacturers and distributes the vehicles to authorized dealerships in the region.

Despite an economic recession during 2010, Mueller Autohaus reported significant profitability and growth. During the same period, Midwest Imports, Inc. reported a significant net loss.

As part of its financial statement audit of Mueller Autohaus, Poiter & Cate targeted areas believed to have a high probability of risk of material misstatement, including the potential for understated liabilities. Upon inquiry of the client, the auditors were told that a year-end adjusting entry was made to record all bills that were received too late to be included in the purchases journal for the last month of the fiscal year. In addition, the auditors were told that Midwest's internal auditor had performed year-end tests in search of unrecorded liabilities. As a result, the client felt that it would not be worthwhile to examine the purchases journal in search of unrecorded liabilities.

Required:

(a) Should Poiter & Cate's audit procedures be affected by management's viewpoint regarding the search for unrecorded liabilities? Explain whether the comments regarding the adjusting journal entry and the tests performed by the internal auditor affect your response.

(b) What documents and records should Poiter & Cate examine in its search for unrecorded liabilities?

12-38 Elberon, Inc. provides procurement cards, or p-cards, to certain employees who travel for business or are authorized to make small purchases on behalf of the company. The company's policies pertaining to the issuance and use of the p-cards are documented in the company's code of conduct.

Required:

(a) What internal controls should be included in the code of conduct pertaining to the p-cards?

(b) For each internal control noted, describe a test of control that would be useful for testing the effectiveness of the control.

12-39 Maydenz, Inc. operates ten service centers that deliver parts and accessories used to service and repair all types of automobiles. The company uses three delivery trucks and ten service trucks for making service calls in the vicinity of its service center locations. At the beginning of 2010, Maydenz reported audited account balances totaling $304,000 for the three delivery trucks, with accumulated depreciation of $151,000, and $405,000 for the ten service trucks, with accumulated depreciation of $236,250. All of the trucks are depreciated on a straight-line basis using a six-year useful life and no salvage value. One half year's depreciation is applied in the year of acquisition and in the year of sale (if not fully depreciated at the sale date).

During 2010, Maydenz's accountant recorded the following journal entries for the various transactions affecting its trucks:

February 1:	Cash	5,000	
	Truck		5,000
	(Sold one delivery truck for $5,000.		
	The truck was purchased on 1/1/2001		
	for $100,000 and was fully depreciated.)		
March 1:	Truck	114,000	
	Cash		114,000
	(Bought one delivery truck for $114,000.)		

September 1:	Cash	17,000	
	Truck		17,000
	(Sold one service truck for $17,000.		
	The truck was purchased on 8/15/2006		
	for $40,500.)		
September 10:	Truck	41,016	
	Cash		41,016
	(Bought one service truck for $41,000.)		
December 31:	Depreciation Expense	94,750	
	Accumulated Depreciation—Trucks		94,750
	(Recorded depreciation for 2010 as follows:		
	Two delivery trucks @ $17,000 each;		
	Nine service trucks @ $6,750 each)		

Required:

(a) Prepare an audit work paper analyzing the accounts for Maydenz's Trucks, Accumulated Depreciation—Trucks, Depreciation Expense, and Gain or Loss on the Sale of Trucks. Start with beginning of year balances and reflect the transactions that occurred during the year as well as the end of year balances. It is not necessary to present audit procedures performed on this work paper.

(b) Prepare the adjusting journal entries the auditor is likely to propose.

(c) Describe appropriate audit procedures, beyond the tests of controls, to be applied to these accounts.

12-40 The following audit procedures were performed by Dale Hent, CPA, as part of his audit of the acquisition and payments cycle of Betsler Automotive, Inc. For each item, indicate whether the procedure represents a test of control, analytical procedure, dual purpose test, or test of details of account balances.

(a) Using computer assisted audit techniques, foot the purchases journal for a month; trace the totals to the general ledger.

(b) Review the purchases journal for large and unusual transactions.

(c) Send confirmation requests to several vendors, including some for which there is no balance at year end; ask them to inform the auditor of their balances due from Betsler at year end.

(d) Examine a sample of receiving reports and determine whether each one was properly recorded as an account payable.

(e) Observe the check signer's activities to determine whether he or she is marking "paid" on the supporting documentation before or after the checks are signed.

(f) Select a sample of canceled checks to trace to the cash disbursements journal, agreeing the payee, amount, and date.

(g) Recalculate the portion of prepaid rent and prepaid insurance that is applicable to future periods.

(h) Examine the file of unpaid invoices at year end to determine whether they were recorded in the proper period and for the proper amounts.

(i) Select a sample of fixed assets from the company's file of property, plant, and equipment, and inspect each item to determine its ongoing usefulness for the company.

(j) Calculate the ratio of repairs and maintenance expense to total equipment and compare with the prior year.

12-41 Ashlee Bracken is a CPA assigned to the audit of Rush Products, Inc. Internal controls were assessed to be effective, and no significant audit problems arose during the current or prior-year audit engagements. Although Rush has a small accounting department with only two full-time accountants, there is reasonable segregation of duties within the overall organization. There is a separate purchasing agent who is responsible for acquisitions of goods and a separate receiving clerk who prepares receiving reports upon determination of the quantity of goods received.

Acquisitions are handled by the first accountant, and the cash disbursements are handled by the second accountant. This is considered an enhancement to the control environment. The company's treasurer reviews all supporting documentation before signing checks, and he immediately mails the checks to the company's vendors. Check copies provide the basis for the second accountant to update the cash disbursements journal.

While performing the tests of controls for Rush Products, Ashlee noted the following auditing issues:

(a) Three invoices had not been initialed by the treasurer.

(b) Three receiving reports had not been recorded in the acquisitions journal until several weeks following their receipt.

(c) Four items in the acquisitions journal were recorded in the wrong accounts.

(d) One invoice was paid twice. A duplicate invoice was included in the accounting records, and both copies were marked "PAID."

(e) One check was written for an amount that was $10 less than the amount stated on the invoice.

(f) One voided check could not be located.

(g) Three receiving reports were missing from the payment support package.

Required:

Identify internal controls that could have prevented each of these issues.

ACTIVITY ASSIGNMENTS

12-42 Go to the SEC Web site, www.sec.gov. What industries are associated with the following SIC? List all the company names you recognize under each SIC.

2024	2711	3140	3651	8351
2080	2844	3571	6162	
2840	3021	3630	6324	

12-43 Find a manufacturing-related SIC not included in the list in Activity Assignment 12-42.

12-44 FASB's, *The Fair Value Option for Financial Assets and Liabilities* (FASB codification 825-10), was issued and allows companies to elect whether they want to present certain financial asset and/or financial liabilities at fair value on the balance sheet.

(a) Find an article from either a professional or an academic journal that discusses the flexibility inherent in management's elections related to using fair value for financial assets and liabilities. Prepare a one-page summary of the article and your opinion, specifically regarding the impact of this management flexibility on the audit, the difficulty it may create for an auditor, and the related ethical implications.

(b) Review FASB ASC 825-10 and summarize the contribution of this standard to the convergence of international accounting standards.

PROFESSIONAL SIMULATION

Go to the book's companion Web site at www.wiley.com/college/hooks to find simulations similar to those on the computerized CPA exam.

ACL

An exercise requiring the use of ACL software is available on the Auditing and Assurances Web site at www.wiley.com/college/hooks.

CHAPTER **13**

Auditing Human Resources Processes: Personnel and Payroll in Service Industries

LEARNING OBJECTIVES FOR THIS CHAPTER	1. Be familiar with the human resources activities in a public accounting firm.
	2. Learn the activities, transactions, risks, ICFR, and documents related to human resources. Recognize the impact of relevant accounting standards on the activities and transactions.
	3. Understand the general structure and activities of outsourcing the payroll function to an outside service provider.
	4. Understand the meaning and value of both types of service auditor (SAS 70) reports, how they may provide audit evidence, and under what circumstances more audit evidence is needed.
	5. Link the management assertions, purposes of specific controls, controls, and tests of controls for human resources.
	6. Describe the purposes and execution of related substantive audit procedures for human resources accounts and disclosures, including dual purpose tests, substantive analytical procedures, and details of balances.

Chapter 13 Resources

INTRODUCTION

The human resources cycle accounts for some very routine, yet specific, functions. Typically, the functions are divided into two categories. First is hiring workers, maintaining employment records, and terminating employment relationships. Second is paying employees for the work performed and other entities for related costs. These are often called personnel and payroll functions, respectively. The human resources cycle also houses the legally imposed tasks of accumulating and reporting information used by employees as the basis for calculating personal income taxes. In addition to being responsible for recordkeeping and reporting, businesses act as "quasi" collection agencies for taxing authorities by withholding money from payroll payments and remitting it to the government on each individual employee's behalf.

In this chapter two industry examples are used for the human resources cycle. A public accounting firm is used as an example of a services industry firm. The public accounting environment exemplifies a business for which people's time and knowledge are the primary input. Time spent by people at differing levels of experience and expertise is the basis for client billing—or at least, the basis for bidding on a job. In addition, the human resources cycle is discussed in relation to outsourcing. The discussion explains the responsibilities of the employer and the payroll-function service provider, and the interface between the two.

OVERVIEW

Virtually all businesses compensate people for their contributions as owners or employees. Therefore, all businesses have a human resources cycle. The number of people working for a business and the functions they perform can be almost infinitely varied. Manufacturers use human resources along with other inputs such as materials and capital to create products. However, in the United States, service industries that use people as the primary resource input for the business have taken the economic lead. Service industry examples are used in this chapter to exemplify the activities of the human resources cycle.

The *services industry* label actually overlaps with other industry labels that more specifically describe the services provided. For example, health care is primarily a service industry, as is education. Banking and related businesses such as investment, brokerage, and insurance firms are called financial services. Various professional and skilled workers associated with the manufacturing and building industries provide services, including architects, engineers, general contractors, mechanics, electronics specialists, computer and network specialists, plumbers, carpenters, and electricians. Personal services businesses such as hair styling, personal training, house cleaning, and a variety of others abound. Professionals such as lawyers and CPAs are in service industries.

Exhibit 13-1 provides a possible way to categorize businesses. The highlighted businesses in the exhibit are those most likely to include service rather than manufacturing or sales. Even so, whatever scheme is used for these groupings, it is never absolutely distinct. For example, as just mentioned, trade workers such as electricians and plumbers may be considered service providers, although they work in construction, which is not considered a service industry. Health-care and life sciences businesses, though considered service industries, may sell tangible goods as well as services.

In the case of a manufacturing entity, payroll accounting interacts with cost accounting. Human resources costs can be direct labor or manufacturing overhead that is part of the cost of inventory. In other environments, human resources costs are a period cost that is expensed when incurred.

In service environments that charge clients for services performed based on the input of human resources, a hybrid situation may exist. According to GAAP, unless they are to be capitalized as inventory, human resources costs are a period expense. However, for *internal* management and billing in services industries, human resources costs are often considered a part of work-in-process or unbilled labor until the task is completed and the client is billed. Consequently, in many services industries the human resources cycle interacts with the sales and collections cycle.

Regardless of the industry, **personnel functions** include maintaining personnel records and performing administrative responsibilities for benefit plans. In some environments personnel responsibilities extend to recruiting, hiring, and training employees. **Payroll functions** involve calculating, processing, and posting employee compensation and other related expenses and liabilities. As with other cash disbursements, paying employees is a treasury or cashier function.

In addition to paying employees, the human resources cycle involves recordkeeping, withholding and remitting taxes, and numerous other transactions. Beyond taxes, withholding and remittance transactions include health-care and other insurance programs, savings and retirement plans, court-ordered payments such as child support, and other payments

---

EXHIBIT 13-1

Service Industries within Business Categories

Energy and Natural Resources

Manufacturing, Industrial Products, and Chemicals

Consumer Business, Markets and Products: Retail, *Service Industries*

Transport Services, Automotive, Aviation

Health Care, Life Sciences, Pharmaceuticals

Financial and Legal Services

Banking, Capital Markets Services, Insurance

Hospitality, Entertainment, Media, Telecommunications

Real Estate, Construction

Public Sector and Not-for-Profit

Note: Highlighted businesses are those most likely to include service rather than manufacturing or sales.

such as parking fees and union dues. Typical human resources and payroll activities are as follows:

> Human Resources Department Activities
>> Hiring employees
>> Creating and updating personnel files
>> Terminating employment relationships
> Types of Payroll Transaction Activities
>> Preparing to pay and paying employees
>> Paying government and other entities

Accounts involved in this cycle are:

> Cash
> Liability accounts for amounts withheld
>> Taxes
>> Benefits
>> Other
> Accrued liability accounts
>> Compensation expense
>> Payroll taxes
>> Sick and vacation time
> Compensation and related expenses, including pension and postretirement benefits

Although the specifics vary, payroll processing is a routine activity. The transactions are standardized and repeated for each employee many times throughout the year, for all of the employees of the business. Payroll processing is routine, requires minimal judgment once the process is set up, and is performed frequently and repetitively. As a result, payroll calculation, recording, and payout is probably the most commonly outsourced business function that exists today.

Specifics on payroll outsourcing arrangements vary from company to company. The discussion in this chapter provides general information related to use of an outside service provider for payroll functions. Auditors of clients who use outside service providers for payroll often rely on the report of other auditors. Therefore, AU 324, *Service Organizations*, is also presented.[1]

The chapter begins with a discussion of public accounting as an example of a service firm. Then it presents aspects of the human resources cycle applicable to most businesses. Discussions of the use of an outside service provider for payroll and service auditor reports follow. Audit activities that apply to most human resources cycles are then described. Finally, the chapter ends by considering the audit of the human resources cycle for clients in the services industries.

REVIEW QUESTIONS

A.1 Give examples of industries for which a service is the primary productive output.

A.2 What activities make up personnel functions? Payroll functions?

A.3 For what reasons do businesses withhold funds from their employees' pay?

A.4 For sales and billing purposes of a company in the service industry, why is proper human resources accounting important?

---

[1]The common terms used in practice to identify auditor's engagements that report on the processing of transactions by service organizations are **SAS 70 engagement** and **SAS 70 report**.

HUMAN RESOURCES ASPECTS OF PUBLIC ACCOUNTING [LO 1]

Accountants who work for a public accounting firm are likely to be salaried employees.[2] They may or may not receive payment for overtime on an ongoing basis as it is worked. Sometimes when overtime is not directly compensated, it is considered in awarding year-end, performance-based bonuses.

AUDITING IN ACTION

A Public Accounting Time Report

Engagement - Individual Time Sheet

Name: Christine Walker   **Client:** Food & Wine   **Data Entry Period:** July 25, 2010
Personal Number : 06172   **Office:** JAX   August 7, 2010

AUDIT AREA	SAT 7/25	SUN 7/26	MON 7/27	TUE 7/28	WED 7/29	THU 7/30	FRI 7/31	SAT 8/1	SUN 8/2	MON 8/3	TUE 8/4	WED 8/5	THU 8/6	FRI 8/7
Cash										2				
Accounts Receivable										6	8			
Accounts Payable														
Expenses														
. . .														

Individual Summary Time Sheet

Name: Christine Walker   **Data Entry Period:** July 25, 2010
Personal Number : 06172   **Office:** JAX   August 7, 2010

Client Number:	Client Name	Work type Description	Total hours	SAT 7/25	SUN 7/26	MON 7/27	TUE 7/28	WED 7/29	THU 7/30	FRI 7/31	SAT 8/1	SUN 8/2	MON 8/3	TUE 8/4	WED 8/5	THU 8/6	FRI 8/7
38001	Food & Wine	2009 Audit	16										8	8			
12072	ABC Bank	2009 Audit	24												8	8	8
	VACATION	VACATION	40			8	8	8	8	8							
Total			80	0	0	8	8	8	8	8	0	0	8	8	8	8	8

Signature   Date

Approval   Date

---

[2]Partners, as owners, are compensated differently, and this discussion applies to them primarily regarding their role as engagement managers. Some public accounting firms also pay employees hourly.

Consistent with the definition of salaried payment, base compensation is not based on hours worked. Therefore submitting a time sheet is not necessary to calculate the proper amount of payment—unless overtime is paid on a current and ongoing basis. However, most public accounting firms require that their partners and employees submit time and expense reports. These reports permit firms to track time spent on each client, facilitate engagement management, and serve as input to the client billing process. Time sheet information also permits the firm to track sick leave and vacation time taken.

When a public accounting firm or any other entity hires a new employee, the process is similar. The human resources department collects information regarding tax status and the employee's decisions regarding participation in various benefit plans such as savings and health care. This information is collected in the employee's **personnel file**. An individual's personnel file may also include information from the hiring process such as verifications obtained about educational degrees received, state licenses held, and recommendation letters. The human resources department assigns the employee an identification number and authorizes that employee's information be input into the IT system.

The information added to the **payroll master file** includes the employee's name, contact information identification number, rank or staff classification, department, salary, and deduction information. With this information the **payroll processing system** is able to calculate and generate a salary payment for the employee, keep track of the employee's payroll information cumulatively for the tax year, and integrate with the **engagement management system**. The journal entry to record payroll is straightforward. For an employee with an annual salary of $75,000 who is paid every two weeks, the payroll entry might be as follows:

Salary Expense	2890	
FIT Withheld		500
Social Security Withheld		335
Medicare Withheld		85
Other Withholdings		300
Cash		1670

Employees working for a public accounting firm are likely paid via an **electronic funds transfer (EFT)** direct deposit and receive a "pay stub" or information document with details about gross pay, withholding, and net pay amounts. The firm aggregates these amounts for all employees and posts them to the general ledger. The firm also accumulates the information on a year-to-date basis by employee.

The payroll application program accumulates information about each employee's compensation payments and amounts withheld, and also aggregates amounts withheld for all employees. When the aggregated amount for all employees reaches certain levels—or when a specific period of time passes, whichever occurs first—it triggers the need to make payments to the government taxing authorities and other parties. At the end of the calendar year each individual employee's accumulated annual totals are provided to the employee on a **W-2 form** so that he or she is able to fill out tax returns. At the end of the public accounting firm's fiscal year, which may be different from the calendar year, the work time reported by the employee may be used as input for evaluation and bonus decisions.

In a typical accounting firm, employees are expected to periodically report their time, for example, every two weeks or monthly. Time worked is usually input via an electronic **time sheet** document. Employees input their employee ID number and report time spent on various clients by using the client billing code.

The billing code identifies the client and may specify the nature of the engagement or activities. Typical engagement or activities categories include financial statement audit, ICFR

EXHIBIT

A W-2 Tax Form

	a Employee's social security number		
		OMB No. 1545-0008	
b Employer identification number (EIN)		**1** Wages, tips, other compensation	**2** Federal income tax withheld
c Employer's name, address, and ZIP code		**3** Social security wages	**4** Social security tax withheld
		5 Medicare wages and tips	**6** Medicare tax withheld
		7 Social security tips	**8** Allocated tips
d Control number		**9** Advance EIC payment	**10** Dependent care benefits
e Employee's first name and initial　Last name　Suff.		**11** Nonqualified plans	**12a**
		13 Statutory employee　Retirement plan　Third-party sick pay	**12b**
		14 Other	**12c**
			12d
f Employee's address and ZIP code			

15 State　Employer's state ID number	**16** State wages, tips, etc.	**17** State income tax	**18** Local wages, tips, etc.	**19** Local income tax	**20** Locality name

Form **W-2** Wage and Tax Statement　　**2009**　　Department of the Treasury—Internal Revenue Service

Copy 2—To Be Filed With Employee's State, City, or Local Income Tax Return.

audit, quarterly financial statement review, or work on a securities offering. Some systems may collect more specific information on the type of work that is performed. The employee ID code not only functions to permit the IT system to process payroll information for each employee, but also enables the engagement management system to access and use appropriate rate-per-hour billing when employees post times worked for engagements. The engagement management system tracks items such as:

1. Hours worked on the engagement by each employee
2. The billable dollars correlated with hours worked based on billing rate-per-hour
3. Out-of-pocket expenses incurred by employees
4. Dollars calculated based on time worked that have not yet been billed
5. Dollar amounts billed to and receivable from the client
6. Dollar amounts collected

The time sheet information may also be used to trigger a compensation payment, particularly in the case of workers who are paid hourly or receive overtime payment as the overtime is worked.

Whether or not it is used for routine payroll processing, time sheet information is extremely important for engagement management in public accounting. The engagement management system automatically

1. Captures hours worked by employees that are input via time reports with a particular client's billing code
2. Assigns a dollar amount to those hours based on the various billing rates of the individual workers
3. Reports the resulting dollar amount as an addition to work-in-process or unbilled services for that client

When you hear someone in a public accounting firm comment about a person or dollar amount "hitting the 'wips,'" they are referring to hours worked that has resulted in a dollar amount being posted to work-in-process for that particular engagement. Engagement management programs often can calculate the dollar amount of time that has been charged to the billing code, not only using billing rates of individuals who have charged time to the job, but also incorporating any specific adjustments to standard billing rates designated for that engagement. Individuals responsible for managing the engagement are able to access the work-in-process information.

AUDITING IN ACTION

Public Accounting Firm Work-in-Process Record

PUBLIC ACCOUNTING FIRM WORK-IN-PROCESS REPORT

Client: PHONY COMPANY

ENGAGEMENT CODE:	ENGAGEMENT NAME:	HOURS WORKED	MARKET SCALE VALUE $	PLANNED RATE (%)	ENGAGEMENT VALUE $	AMOUNT BILLED $	AMOUNT COLLECTED $
632-001	2009 AUDIT						
STEVE	KERRY	14	13,868	80%	11,094		
PAUL	RORAN	44	18,049	80%	14,439		
CHRISTINE	MANNY	96	67,056	80%	53,645		
KAREN	CRAUTOR	4.5	3,200	80%	2,560		
BOBERT	BILLINGS	3.5	2,267	80%	1,814		
WILLIAM	RIB	6	4,191	80%	3,353		
JENNIFER	RUSSIE	19	5,526	80%	4,421		
632-002	Q1 2009 Review						
CHRISTINE	MANNY	43	30,100	45%	13,545		
PAUL	RORAN	31	12,710	45%	5,720		
JENNIFER	RUSSIE	106	30,740	45%	13,833		
632-002	Q2 2009 Review						
CHRISTINE	MANNY	14	9,800	90%	8,820		
PAUL	RORAN	96	34,360	90%	35,424		
JENNIFER	RUSSIE	161	46,690	90%	42,021		

Information about time worked on specific engagements is used by managers and partners who oversee client engagements. They use this information when they are making decisions on how much and when client billings are processed. Payments received from clients are also captured by the system, permitting those individuals managing engagements to monitor cash collected and bills still outstanding. Billing and collection information, along with information on employee time spent for which cash *is not* collected, is critical to managing an accounting practice. This information helps those who are managing the jobs, and their superiors determine whether the amount that was bid and collected for an engagement provides an appropriate return for the firm's resources.

Assume that an audit has many technical and difficult accounting issues that were unexpected by both the client and auditor during the proposal process. As a result, the engagement turns out to be unprofitable for the public accounting firm. This happens if—based on the contracted price, agreed to and documented in the engagement letter—the auditor is unable to collect for a large number of professional hours worked. In contrast, another possible outcome is that the information collected by the engagement management system justifies a departure from the original agreement. Information collected by the engagement management system might be used to support additional client billing related to the additional work performed on the unexpected accounting problems. The information can affect

EXHIBIT 13-2

Time and Expense
Report Input to payroll
Processing

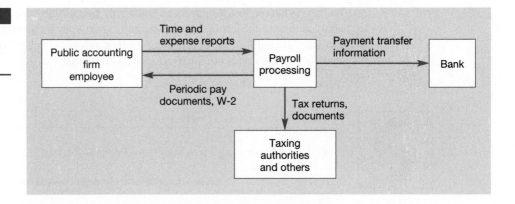

the firm's decision about whether to retain the client in future years and, if so, the contracted amount for future engagements.

On a geographical, line-of-service, or partnership-wide basis, information from the engagement management system can be used to assess how well a segment of the firm is doing. Engagement management information is also used to evaluate the performance of those partners responsible for bidding, managing, billing, and collecting fees for client engagements. Exhibit 13-2 shows a simple display of a public accounting firm employee's time and expense report interaction with payroll processing. Exhibit 13-3 shows the same input document affecting the engagement management process.

EXHIBIT 13-3

Time and Expense
Report Input to
Engagement
Management

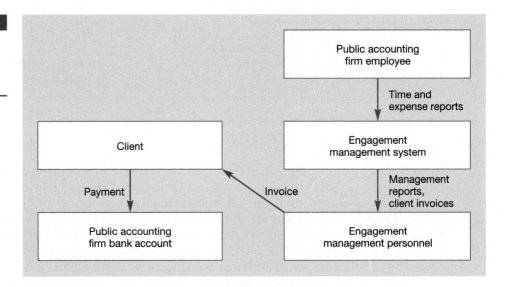

REVIEW QUESTIONS

B.1 Why do public accounting firms require their employees and partners to submit time sheets?

B.2 What functions does a human resources or personnel department perform when a new employee is hired?

B.3 When does an employer have to submit payroll tax payments?

B.4 What functions does an engagement management program perform? What information does it use and from what source is the information captured?

AUDITING IN ACTION

Treasury Advisory Committee

On October 6, 2008, the Treasury Advisory Committee on the Auditing Profession, led by former SEC Chairman Arthur Levitt, published its final report on the auditing profession. This was the first major study of the U.S. auditing profession since the enactment of the Sarbanes–Oxley Act of 2002. The report offiers 31 recomendations derived from deliberations of three of its subcommittees, each focused on one of three key areas. For the complete report, see http://www.treas.gov/offices/domestic-finance/acap/ocs/final-report.pdf.

The three key areas are: human capital, firm structure and finances, and concentration and competition within the profession. Basically, the Human Captial Subcommittee was charged with examining the auditing profession's ability to cultivate, attract, and retain the human capital necessary to meet developments in the business and financial reporting environment and ensure audit quality for investors. The Concentration and Competition Subcommittee was tasked with exploring audit market competition and concentration and the impact of the independence and other professional standards on the market and on investor confidence. Finally, the Firm Structure and Finance Subcommittee looked at the organizational structure, financial resources, and communication of the auditing profesion.

While all of the report is important to you as an accounting major or new graduate, the recommendations from the Human Capital Subcommittee will truly impact your engagement as a good auditior by first being a good accountant. The Human Capital Subcommittee focused on accounting education, minority representation, supply and experience of accounting faculty, adequate preparation of accounting students, updating of accounting certification examinations, accounting curricula, and teaching materials to reflect market changes.

BUSINESS PROCESSES, DOCUMENTS, AND INTERNAL CONTROLS [LO 2]

Management objectives related to payroll center around paying employees accurately, paying other entities for payroll-related liabilities as required, satisfying reporting obligations imposed by government, and accounting for the various transactions properly in the accounting records and financial statements. Human resources costs are significant dollar amounts and very important to most companies. Management needs to pay employees what they have earned and properly manage and account for payroll-related obligations in order to maintain a good relationship with its labor force. However, management also focuses on not paying any excess or inappropriate amounts for payroll. This means that management's objectives include:

Paying only real (*not fictitious*) and current (*not former*) employees for their work (*and not for any absences unless they are authorized vacation or sick time*) at the authorized rate (*and not at inflated or fictitious rates*).

Withholding the proper amounts from employee paychecks and paying the government and other entities the correct amounts at the correct times.

Creating and providing all the legally required tax forms and returns to the government and employees.

To accomplish management's goals, a company must have controls surrounding hiring, documenting workers' activity, processing payroll, and disbursing cash. Payroll costs can have major impacts on the income statement as part of operating expenses and cost of goods sold, and on the balance sheet as a part of inventory. Therefore, in addition to the goals of properly calculating, paying, and documenting payroll, management's objectives include properly reporting, in the proper periods, the balances of the financial statement accounts impacted by payroll costs.

Balance Sheet and Income Statement Effects

In many businesses, human resources costs significantly impact the income statement with limited balance sheet effects. For example, in service industries, human resources expenses may be the largest expense incurred. In manufacturing entities, direct labor and indirect labor via overhead flow from the balance sheet inventory accounts and ultimately have a significant impact on the income statement through cost of goods sold.

Period-end adjustments are important to the amounts reported on the income statement and balance sheets. Consequently, the end-of-period processes needed to calculate and control the adjustments are important. Adjustments include accruing payroll and labor expense and recording the liability for any unpaid amounts. SAB 108 highlights the requirement that both balance sheet and income statement amounts must be fairly presented.

Liabilities to taxing authorities, health-care, and other benefits providers must be properly accounted for. The liabilities include both unpaid employer expenses and liabilities that result from withholding money from employees' paychecks. Compensation expense for vacation and sick leave, and related liabilities, must be adjusted each year to reflect the appropriate balances at period end. The appropriate amount of expense and liability for these benefits depends on employee activities and the employer's policies. Important factors are how the benefits are earned and used, and what happens to unused benefits at period end.

For example, some companies permit employees to carry over unused vacation or sick time to the next year, whereas other companies state that if the time is not taken it is lost. Another commonly adopted policy is to permit carryover of time from one year to the next, up to a specified maximum. Management policy impacts calculation of the adjusting entry and proper financial statement reporting.

Government Required Records and Reports

Employers are responsible for maintaining records and preparing reports associated with taxes to be paid to various government agencies. Taxes can be owed to local, state, and federal governments. Federal government issues are discussed here because they apply to all U.S. businesses. Amounts due at other than the federal level include income taxes and items such as workers compensation insurance for workplace injuries and unemployment compensation taxes.

Employees document information regarding their identification and status for taxes on **W-4 forms**. Based on this information, employers withhold prescribed amounts from payroll payouts. The employer submits these withheld taxes to the federal government, along with the employer's payroll taxes. The manner and timing of payment of the taxes withheld depends on the aggregate amount of withholdings and taxes due. The dollar amount of the employer's compensation expense indirectly affects the procedures followed in submitting tax payments.

Employers must submit payroll tax forms on a quarterly basis as well. At the end of the calendar year, employers are required to prepare a W-2 form for each employee, describing information such as the gross amount earned and the amounts withheld for various taxes. These reporting requirements mean that employers must document and track personnel and payroll information on an individual employee level, as well as on an aggregate basis. The effort involved in this process has caused many businesses to outsource the payroll function.

Integration with Cost Accounting Records

In nonmanufacturing businesses payroll is a period expense. For these businesses, the only subsequent processing of payroll information is to meet management's needs as it runs the business. For example, management may want payroll expenses detailed by location or time period. Sales staff costs broken out from administrative costs might be useful for management decisions. In the earlier example of the public accounting firm, management needed payroll-related information detailed by client for billing purposes and profitability analysis. In contrast, in a manufacturing business, a significant part of human resources costs are likely product costs and according to GAAP must be included in the cost of inventory.

In a manufacturing company the cost accounting system integrates to at least some degree with the payroll system. The integration is required to record the appropriate amounts of human resources costs as an addition to inventory. In a manufacturing company some human resource costs are likely **period costs**, such as sales and nonmanufacturing administrative jobs. Other human resources costs are **product costs**. Product costs can be categorized as direct labor or overhead, depending on the way the company chooses to track and categorize them.

Typically, dollars are captured in the payroll system when employees are paid. The dollar amounts are then moved from payroll expense accounts to inventory cost records as a result of activities on the manufacturing floor and the records generated there. For example, **job time tickets** may be used to initiate a reclassifying entry to remove dollars from payroll expense and add them to work-in-process records for specific jobs.

In a manufacturing environment that uses process costing, all of the payroll costs related to employees working in the manufacturing process may be recorded as direct labor. The analysis that identifies work-in-process, finished goods, and cost of goods sold is then performed as a later step. The processes used by manufacturing businesses to track and record human resources costs are diverse. Regardless of the system used, proper categorization of the components of payroll payouts as either period or product costs is an important process.

In service industries a parallel exists to the manufacturing situation in which direct labor becomes part of the cost of inventory. Since service industries may charge customers for time worked, time records often provide input to the client billing process. It can therefore be important for service industry workers to track their time and link it to the jobs on which the time was spent. The tracking and linking is similar to how direct labor is linked to specific jobs or processes in a manufacturing environment. Especially when employees in a service business work on multiple jobs, accurate records are needed to justify the amount charged for the job. Lawyers, electricians, and personal trainers are easily recognizable examples of **service providers** who bill their customers based on time worked.

REVIEW QUESTIONS

C.1 What are management's objectives related to payroll?

C.2 For what functions should a human resources cycle have controls?

C.3 What types of period-end adjustments are made to payroll and related accounts?

C.4 When does payroll become part of inventory as a product cost?

Documents and Processes

The activities involved with human resources can usually be separated into authorizing transactions, processing them, and disbursing cash. Good segregation of duties calls for these activities to be separated. Segregation is often accomplished by separating the human resources department, which handles personnel functions, from the payroll department. The "line" departments, those involved in the main activity of the business, often have responsibility for approvals related to human resources. The treasury department is involved through its final approval of the cash disbursements.

When a new employee is hired, the decision to hire may be made by a management-level person in the line department or by someone in human resources. Regardless of where the approval to hire occurs, the human resources department documents the decision by preparing a variety of records that are kept in a file for that particular employee's information.

The documentation typically includes the *authorization to hire* the employee, *pay rate or salary* at which the employee is hired, *deductions* to be withheld from the employee's pay, and, if the payroll payment is to be made by EFT, information and authorization to pay by direct deposit. **Direct deposit** is the transfer of funds directly to the employee's bank account. Authorizations for deductions from the employee's pay are typically documented in hard copy using an original signature obtained from the employee. In some IT environments employees may input changes to certain types of information electronically.

AUDITING IN ACTION

A W-4 Tax Form

---------------- Cut here and give Form W-4 to your employer. Keep the top part for your records. ----------------

Form **W-4** Department of the Treasury Internal Revenue Service	**Employee's Withholding Allowance Certificate** ▶ Whether you are entitled to claim a certain number of allowances or exemption from withholding is subject to review by the IRS. Your employer may be required to send a copy of this form to the IRS.	OMB No. 1545-0074 20**09**

1	Type or print your first name and middle initial.	Last name		2	Your social security number

Home address (number and street or rural route)	**3** ☐ Single ☐ Married ☐ Married, but withhold at higher Single rate. **Note.** If married, but legally separated, or spouse is a nonresident alien, check the "Single" box.
City or town, state, and ZIP code	**4** If your last name differs from that shown on your social security card, check here. You must call 1-800-772-1213 for a replacement card. ▶ ☐

5	Total number of allowances you are claiming (from line **H** above **or** from the applicable worksheet on page 2)	**5**	
6	Additional amount, if any, you want withheld from each paycheck	**6**	$
7	I claim exemption from withholding for 2009, and I certify that I meet **both** of the following conditions for exemption.		

• Last year I had a right to a refund of **all** federal income tax withheld because I had **no** tax liability **and**
• This year I expect a refund of **all** federal income tax withheld because I expect to have **no** tax liability.
If you meet both conditions, write "Exempt" here . . . . ▶ | **7** |

Under penalties of perjury, I declare that I have examined this certificate and to the best of my knowledge and belief, it is true, correct, and complete.

Employee's signature
(Form is not valid unless you sign it.) ▶   **Date** ▶

8	Employer's name and address (Employer: Complete lines 8 and 10 only if sending to the IRS.)	**9** Office code (optional)	**10** Employer identification number (EIN)

For Privacy Act and Paperwork Reduction Act Notice, see page 2.	Cat. No. 10220Q	Form **W-4** (2009)

All information needed to process payroll and tax records on an ongoing basis is entered into the *payroll master file*. The payroll master file has a record for each employee and captures personal information, current payroll transactions, and year-to-date information. When an employee's information changes, such as from receiving a raise, changing deductions or EFT information, or separating from the company, human resources documents the change. The information in the employee's personnel file and payroll master file record is updated either by the human resources department or based on its authorization.

The capacity to authorize additions or changes to most fields and records in the payroll master file is limited to the human resources department. This allows the company to maintain segregation of duties between approval for changes to the information and processing the transactions based on the underlying data. The human resources department authorizes changes to the payroll master file that are input elsewhere in the organization, or by an outside service provider. Someone in human resources monitors that the authorized changes are input correctly and that no unauthorized changes are made. This monitoring is typically performed using a report itemizing payroll master file changes that is generated by the payroll application program. The monitoring report is produced after any processing run that updates the payroll master file.

An employee's work activity is documented before he or she is paid. This may mean *signing in and out* on a computer terminal in a service or retail establishment. In some nonautomated environments, it is accomplished by "punching in and out" on a timecard, using a time clock. Highly technology-based manufacturing environments may track employee activity on the manufacturing floor by the start and stop of machines and the use of ID codes. *Job time tickets* are often used to document when and on what jobs a manufacturing employee works. A salaried worker's compensation can be paid based solely on a contract or triggered by a **time sheet** that the worker fills out. The time sheet can be in either an electronic or a manual form. When time is not worked, but payment is based on *sick leave* or *vacation* used, this is also captured.

Once the data are captured, they are approved before being used by the system for payroll processing. Approval often is provided by a supervisor of a department or location. Data collected automatically through machines or terminals may be approved based on programmed criteria. For salaried workers who fill out time sheets, the approval may be technology based and linked to the time sheet submission or simply based on the preapproved contracted rate. Regardless of the methods, the data capture and approval processes are the first steps in paying a payroll.

AUDITING IN ACTION

A Job Time Ticket

Chief FORKS Company Employee Time Ticket	**Time Ticket No.** 4432 **Employee** Carlyle Collen	**Date.** 11/28 **Station** Location 10

Started	Ended	Time Completed	Rate	Amount	Job Number
8:30	12:30	4	$18	$45	11 - 16
1:30	5:00	3.5	18	18	11 - 4
5:00	5:30	0.5	18	9	Maintenance
Totals		8.0		$72	

Supervisor *Edward Swan*

Calculation of payroll payments is performed based on information stored in the payroll master file and, when appropriate, data captured on time worked. For each employee the calculations include gross wages, amounts withheld, and net payment. The amounts are posted to a payroll report for the current payout, sometimes called a **payroll register**. In addition, each employee's payroll master file record is updated with information related to the current earnings period and payment. The general ledger is also updated. Either a paper check is processed or an EFT is initiated to complete the transaction. Some employers may pay workers in cash. Usually, the employee receives detailed information regarding what was withheld from the payment. When compensation is paid using EFT, the detailed information also informs the employee of the net amount deposited to his or her account.

Employers withhold funds from employees for payment of taxes and various other purposes such as insurance and savings programs. The lag times before the employer makes payments are based on the nature of the liability and applicable laws and procedures. When a payment is due, the process is similar to what is used for other types of cash disbursements. For example, a disbursement of tax withholdings from wages is accompanied by a tax form. The form details employee information so that the payment can be appropriately applied. *Payroll tax returns* are also filed quarterly by employers. Exhibit 13-4 lists business activities and related documents for human resources and payroll.

AUDITING IN ACTION

A Sample Payroll Register

Chief Forks Company

Date	Employee ID	Name	Hourly Wage	Hours	Gross Pay	Federal Allow.	State Tax	Federal Income Tax	Social Security 6.2%	Medicare 1.45%	Total Tax Withheld	Insurance Deduction	Net Pay
1/2/2010	10-112	Charlie Clearwater	$13.25	36.00	$477.00	0	$34.33	$57.10	$29.57	$6.92	$127.92	$26.00	$323.08
1/2/2010	10-113	Renee Cullen	$25.00	40.00	$1,000.00	2	$74.86	$146.54	$62.00	$14.50	$297.90	$35.00	$667.10
1/2/2010	10-114	Carlisle Black	$31.00	39.00	$1,209.00	1	$96.49	$213.70	$74.96	$17.53	$402.68	$35.00	$771.32
1/2/2010	10-115	Alice Black	$13.00	20.00	$260.00	0	$17.73	$24.55	$16.12	$3.77	$62.17	$26.00	$171.83
1/2/2010	10-116	Isabella Newton	$7.50	30.00	$225.00	1	$13.03	$10.36	$13.95	$3.26	$40.60	$26.00	$158.40
1/2/2010	10-117	Emmet Black	$8.22	36.00	$295.92	0	$20.48	$29.94	$18.35	$4.29	$73.05	$26.00	$196.87
1/9/2010	10-112	Charlie Clearwater	$13.25	40.00	$530.00	0	$38.39	$65.05	$32.86	$7.69	$143.98	$26.00	$360.02
1/9/2010	10-113	Renee Cullen	$25.00	33.00	$825.00	2	$59.11	$102.79	$51.15	$11.96	$225.01	$35.00	$564.99
1/9/2010	10-114	Carlisle Black	$31.00	28.00	$868.00	1	$65.80	$128.45	$53.82	$12.59	$260.65	$35.00	$572.35
1/9/2010	10-115	Alice Black	$13.00	39.00	$507.00	0	$36.63	$61.60	$31.43	$7.35	$137.01	$26.00	$343.99
1/9/2010	10-116	Isabella Newton	$7.50	30.00	$225.00	1	$13.03	$10.36	$13.95	$3.26	$40.60	$26.00	$158.40
1/9/2010	10-117	Emmet Black	$8.22	36.00	$295.92	0	$20.48	$29.94	$18.35	$4.29	$73.05	$26.00	$196.87
1/16/2010	10-112	Charlie Clearwater	$13.25	33.00	$437.25	0	$31.29	$51.14	$27.11	$6.34	$115.88	$26.00	$295.37
1/16/2010	10-113	Renee Cullen	$25.00	40.00	$1,000.00	2	$74.86	$146.54	$62.00	$14.50	$297.90	$35.00	$667.10
1/16/2010	10-114	Carlisle Black	$31.00	39.00	$1,209.00	1	$96.49	$213.70	$74.96	$17.53	$402.68	$35.00	$771.32
1/16/2010	10-115	Alice Black	$13.00	20.00	$260.00	0	$17.73	$24.55	$16.12	$3.77	$62.17	$26.00	$171.83
1/16/2010	10-116	Isabella Newton	$7.50	28.00	$210.00	1	$11.88	$8.11	$13.02	$3.05	$36.06	$26.00	$147.94
1/16/2010	10-117	Emmet Black	$8.22	36.00	$295.92	0	$20.48	$29.94	$18.35	$4.29	$73.05	$26.00	$196.87
1/23/2010	10-112	Charlie Clearwater	$13.25	36.00	$477.00	0	$34.33	$57.10	$29.57	$6.92	$127.92	$26.00	$323.08
1/23/2010	10-113	Renee Cullen	$25.00	40.00	$1,000.00	2	$74.86	$146.54	$62.00	$14.50	$297.90	$35.00	$667.10

AUDITING IN ACTION

Electronic Funds Transfer Pay Stub Document

Employee: EDWARD SWAN

Pay Stub Summary   1/30/2010

Pay Stub Date: 1/30/2010

Gross Amount:	$1000.00	STATE TAX WITHHELD	74.86
Total Personal Deductions:	332.90	FIT WITHHELD	146.54
Net Amount:	$ 667.10	SOCIAL SECURITY WITHHELD	62.00
Total Employer Contributions:		MEDICARE WITHHELD	14.50
Insurance:	$70	Insurance Deduction	35.00
			332.90

Check or Credit Deposit

Number	Document Type	Bank Name	Account Type	Amount
639371	Direct Deposit	My Bank	Checking	$667.10

Earnings

Type	Hours	Rate	Amount
Regular Pay	40	$25.00	$1000.00

Employer Contribution: Insurance   70.00

Use of an Imprest Payroll Account

An **imprest payroll checking account** is similar to any other imprest account. The ultimate balance in the account is a specified amount. In the case of payroll, when an imprest account is used, the *net* amount of each payout is deposited in the payroll checking account before the payout is made. After all the electronic transfers out have been completed, the balance in the payroll checking account should be zero. Businesses sometimes maintain a minimum balance in the bank account rather than having it zero out. The same scenario occurs for a payroll system that distributes paper paychecks. The payroll checking account will have a zero or minimum balance after all the checks are cashed. Since the *net* amount of the payout is transferred to the payroll checking account, cash disbursements for withholdings, deductions, and any tax and benefits expenses of the employer are made from the general checking account.

The advantages of using an imprest payroll account are efficiency and control. When all pay distributions come from a separate payroll account, reconciling payroll records to the bank statement is much easier. From a controls perspective, a separate payroll account makes it easier to identify outstanding, uncashed checks, invalid receiving accounts for direct deposit payments, and any suspicious transactions.

REVIEW QUESTIONS

D.1 What information needs to be authorized or documented when a new person is hired?

D.2 What information is contained in the payroll master file? How and by whom is it updated when information changes?

D.3 How does an imprest payroll account work? What are the advantages of using an imprest account for payroll?

EXHIBIT 13-4

Business Activities and Related Documents

Business Activity	Related Documents
Produce personnel files for authorized new hires	Records, including: New hire authorization form, Pay rate or salary authorization form, Deduction authorization forms, Payroll master file
Produce and maintain EFT authorization files	EFT, direct deposit authorization documents
Change personnel information	Employee submission of new personal data, Pay rate or salary change authorization, Deduction change authorization, Termination, separation documentation, Payroll master file
Capture information and authorization to initiate payroll payment	Record of work "check-in," "check-out": Electronic record, Time card, Job time ticket, Sick leave record, Vacation leave record
Preparation and payroll payout	Authorized current data to initiate payment, Payroll master file, Paycheck or EFT direct deposit record, Payroll register
Pay governments and other entities	Payroll master file, Tax returns, Other disbursement documents
Provide annual reports to employees	Tax forms and other reports

Potential Misstatements and Controls

The major internal control concerns related to human resources and payroll are that payments are for valid transactions and are authorized. Payroll controls must be in place to verify that payments made are to real employees, who are currently employed—whose employment is not terminated—and who have worked the time commitment required.

To accomplish the payroll controls objectives, the company must have policies and procedures in place regarding human resources. The human resources department is the source of authorization for payroll master file changes for hiring, terminating and changing employee pay rates. In contrast, information and approval for time worked comes from the "line" department. Both of these authorizations are separate from the department that processes transactions to initiate payment to employees. This segregation prevents a person acting alone from being able to both (1) place a name on the payroll—a responsibility housed in the human resources department—for a person who does not exist and (2) also approve work information to be entered into the system—a responsibility housed in the line departments—to initiate a payroll payment for the nonexistent employee.

Check-in and check-out functions can be punching a time clock or logging in and out on a computer terminal. This activity is performed *only* by the individual employee, so that the employee must actually be present at the workplace or computer terminal. In addition, approval of a payroll before funds are paid out is given by an authorized supervisor who has personal knowledge of the employee and the work.

The IT system verifies that payroll information, such as ID numbers for the employees to be paid, matches information on the payroll master file. The verification is conducted before payment is executed. Automated procedures also verify that the rates at which employees are paid are the authorized rates. Similar types of automated controls verify that withholdings are authorized and at the proper amounts.

Other potential misstatements in the human resources accounts can be avoided with proper calculating and posting. For example, recalculation and redundancy checks ensure

> Employees are paid properly for hours worked
>
> Expenses and liabilities for unpaid work are properly recorded at the end of the accounting period
>
> Deductions and employer liabilities are properly calculated and recorded
>
> Postings are to the proper accounts

Proper accounting for amounts at period end includes controls to be sure that transactions are posted on a timely basis and in the proper period.

In most businesses, the human resources cycle has various monitoring controls that limit the magnitude of error or materiality of a fraud that may occur. One monitoring control is that employees pay attention to the amounts they are paid and amounts withheld. Any errors that inappropriately reduce gross or net pay or increase withholdings are likely to be caught by the affected employee. Another monitoring control is that in a business with, at a minimum, cost centers, managers who are held accountable for the costs of their unit pay attention to labor and compensation expense and will report any excess expense that they believe to be in error.

AUDITING IN ACTION

Employee Monitoring

Christie worked as a retail clerk at a national clothing store chain during her summer break between her sophomore and junior years of college. All of the company's payroll processes were automated and online. She "clocked in and out" on the cash terminal once she arrived at the store and her "paychecks" arrived via direct deposit to her checking account. Whenever she was paid, the floor manager for her shift handed her an envelope that held a statement with the breakdown of her gross pay, withholdings, and net deposit to her checking account. Christie quit at the end of summer to go back to school and was told that she would receive her W-2 form at her permanent address in the first couple of weeks of January. Christie had no idea that after she went back to the university, someone used her name to commit a payroll fraud.

The personnel files were kept in a locking file cabinet in the back office and were the responsibility of the store's general manager. But the general manager was careless and usually left the file cabinet unlocked. One of the floor managers, Liz, went into the file cabinet, accessed Christie's file, and copied down the information about Christie's bank account that was used when Christie was hired to set up her payroll direct deposit. All of the floor managers, including Liz, already knew Christie's job ID number and pass code—even though it was against company policy—it made it a lot easier to correct errors and follow up on problems if all the floor managers knew all the employee numbers. Liz logged on at the sales terminal, entered the employee human resources database, and used the information from Christie's personnel file to access her record. She changed Christie's direct deposit information so Christie's payments would go directly to a new checking account she had just set up. (She had to forge some documents with Christie's name and address to set up the bank account but that was pretty easy to do with a desktop publishing program she already had, especially since she had all the information from Christie's personnel file.) Liz held onto

(continued)

Christie's resignation information and didn't put it in for processing. Liz clocked Christie in and out at the cash terminal, "keeping her on a schedule" that was pretty typical for what Christie usually worked.

Everything was fine the first month. But the second month the general manager started asking to see the employee shift schedule. She said she had received a call from the company's regional office that it seemed like the store's payroll costs last month were pretty high. It didn't take much checking for the store manager to discover that an employee who no one had seen for a month was being clocked in and out and being paid. The first thing the general manager did was to lock the file cabinet that held the personnel files. Next, she processed Christie's resignation and then set about seeing who was behind the fraud. Liz didn't quit because she thought it would take a while for anyone to trace her to the bank account—if they ever could, since it was set up under Christie's name. Liz just made sure to go to the ATM and clean out all the cash that was in the account as soon as she heard what was going on. She never went into the bank and closed the account because she was worried about being identified from the bank's security cameras. (She didn't realize that the ATM had a security camera, too.) Since all the floor managers and a lot of the sales clerks know everyone else's numbers, she really didn't think the store could trace the fraud to her. She didn't think she would get caught. Anyone could have done it....

The general manager suspected that a floor manager was responsible because even though she thought some of the sales clerks knew each other's ID numbers and pass codes the sales clerks work part time and she couldn't find any one of the sales clerks who had been assigned the exact schedule the "fraudulent Christie" had worked. The person who executed the clock in and clock out activity had to be physically present with access to the sales terminal at the time of each one of those fraudulent log-ins. So, the general manager reasoned that it was likely one of the floor managers, who all work full time. Again, after a little more digging it was easy to see that Liz was the only person whose work hours overlapped the "fraudulent Christie" hours perfectly. The amount was not material to that particular store location, so definitely not to the region, and the regional VP decided the cheapest way to handle it was to simply fire Liz without pressing charges—with a clear message that it would be in her best interest never to ask for a referral from the company!

The fraud might not have been a material amount, but what a hassle! The regional controller immediately began a training program for all general mangers and floor managers emphasizing the importance of physical controls like locking up documents and security and confidentiality of ID numbers and pass codes. He had all personnel files transferred to the regional office. He came up with a rule that anyone who clocked in or out for someone else was subject to being fired. And he established a new procedure for store general managers. At the end of every week they now compare their weekly posted schedules that employees were supposed to work to the weekly report of who had actually worked and when, and investigate any differences.

THEN.... Christie received her W-2 form. She opened it and knew it was wrong because it showed earnings for about 5 months rather than the 4 she had worked. She had another job while she was at school and was going to have to pay some taxes anyway. She definitely did not want to have to pay taxes on money she didn't receive. Eventually she was able to get it worked out with her former employer and the company issued her an amended W-2 for the year.

REVIEW QUESTIONS

E.1 What segregation of duties is necessary and appropriate for payroll?

E.2 Who should perform employee check-in and check-out functions, and why?

E.3 What types of authorization and verification should occur before an employee is paid?

E.4 How does employee monitoring of personal records provide an additional control for payroll?

USING AN OUTSIDE SERVICE PROVIDER FOR PAYROLL: OVERVIEW [LO 3]

Many organizations use an outside **service provider** to perform the calculations and prepare the records associated with paying employees. Automatic Data Processing, Inc. (ADP) is one of the largest and most commonly known of these service providers. The following is an excerpt from the business description included in ADP's June 30, 2009 fiscal year end 10K.

> Automatic Data Processing, Inc., incorporated in Delaware in 1961…is one of the world's largest providers of business outsourcing solutions. Leveraging nearly 60 years of experience, ADP offers a wide range of human resource (HR), payroll, tax and benefits administration solutions from a single source…. Employers Services offers a comprehensive range of HR information, payroll processing, tax and benefits administration solutions and services, including traditional and Web-based outsourcing solutions, that assist approximately 540,000 employers in the United States, Canada, Europe, South America (primarily Brazil), Australia and Asia to staff, manage, pay and retain their employees.

The services typically provided by external payroll processing service organizations include:

Updating the payroll master file

Keeping track of current and year-to-date information by employee as well as for the company as a whole

Preparing documents and forms required for tax purposes such as W-2 forms and quarterly payroll tax returns

Submitting information for general ledger entries back to the organization

The **outsourcing** option is often more efficient and less expensive than having in-house accounting employees perform these tasks. Payroll processing outside the organization also contributes to segregation of duties. In many cases the organization contracts with the outside service provider to produce paychecks or process EFT transactions to pay employees. The following excerpt from ADP's June 30, 2009 10K lists some of the services it provides.

> ADP provides payroll services that include the preparation of client employee paychecks and electronic direct deposits and stored value payroll cards, along with supporting journals, summaries and management reports. ADP also supplies the quarterly and annual social security, medicare and federal, state and local income tax withholding reports required to be filed by employers…. Tax and Financial Services…processes and collects federal, state… and local payroll taxes on behalf of, and from, ADP clients and remit these taxes to the appropriate taxing authorities…. In fiscal 2009, Tax and Financial Services in the United States processed and delivered over 51 million year-end tax statements… to its clients' employees and over 39 million employer payroll tax returns and deposits, and moved over $1 trillion in client funds to taxing authorities and its clients' employees.

Outside service providers can also provide other services such as performing the tracking and calculations required for applying payroll costs to inventory, providing custom management reports on payroll expenses, and managing documents related to unemployment compensation. Although not addressed in this discussion, the services purchased from outside providers may be as limited as simply providing the computer programs, with associated support, to companies who then process their own payroll. In complete contrast to this minimal service, some companies may contract with outside payroll service providers to provide *all* human-resources-related services, including recruiting, payroll processing, cash disbursement, benefits management, and managing the company's employee cost effectiveness.

User Company Functions

Even when transaction processing and recordkeeping is outsourced, the company must perform a number of payroll-related functions. The exception to this may be when the company also outsources all of its human resources responsibilities. Initially, the company must determine how payroll is to be calculated, provide any company-specific information about amounts to be withheld, and communicate each employee's personal and specific information. Employee-specific information is required for payroll calculations. An example of company-specific information is the particular benefits offered by the company.

On an ongoing basis, the company's human resources department still maintains employee documents and authorizes any changes to the payroll master file records. Master file changes include adding new employees, dropping those employees who have separated from the company, changing pay rates, and updating employees' personal information. When compensation is based on variable inputs such as hours worked or commissions, the line departments must still provide and approve that information each pay period. Also, the company must establish various controls for the information that goes to and is received from the outside service provider, as well as for the cash disbursements.

The controls implemented by an outside payroll processor need to be designed and operate effectively to produce accurate information within the bounds of its activities. Even so, those controls are generally based on the assumption that the user company will also have effective controls.

REVIEW QUESTIONS

F.1 What payroll services are typically included in those outsourced to an outside service provider?

F.2 What functions does the user company need to perform when payroll processing is outsourced?

Inputs to the Outside Service Provider

An outside service provider needs company-level information from its client, typically called the **user organization**. The user organization information is required for the service provider to accurately process payroll and control the process. For example, whenever the user organization submits data, it identifies itself by company name and probably a company code. The user organization establishes and communicates how often it pays employees and whether and which employees are paid based on salary, commission, and hours worked. The distinction of how employees are paid can be made by name or based on department or rank. The user organization also communicates policies for paying for vacation and sick time.

Some withholdings are standard and calculated based on statutory information such as taxes. But, in addition to these, the company establishes and communicates any company-wide withholdings, such as for health and life insurance, and how the amounts are calculated. If the company provides benefits or reimbursements that are based on hours worked such as meal allowances, it informs the service provider of those policies. Based on that information, the service provider can perform calculations to support or generate those payments to employees. Companies that have the service provider apply payroll costs to inventory also establish the criteria used for that process.

Company-level information is initially provided to the outside service provider and updated when there are changes. The service provider is responsible for maintaining and using current information for externally determined criteria, such as tax-withholding rates, when it calculates payroll.

The company provides the payroll service provider with personal information about each employee, including: name, identification number, department (or other suborganization level) code, pay rate, number of exemptions for tax withholding, and deduction information. If the company pays employees via a direct deposit method, this process can also be managed by the service provider. In this situation, the company provides the outside service provider with information about the bank account to which each employee's payments are to be directed. All employee-specific information kept by the service provider as part of the company's payroll master file information is submitted once by the company. The user organization submits updates for any changes.

Changes to the payroll master file for new hires and separations, as well as updates to information on existing employees, are provided to the outside service provider each pay period. The service provider updates the master file before payroll for the current period is processed. The service provider retains the historical payroll master file information for some contracted period of time after it updates the payroll master file. The company also provides to the service provider current hours worked or other information about each employee's earnings for the current period.

Input to an outside service provider can be supplied through various mechanisms. While most companies provide input electronically, it can be provided orally by telephone or in written form by fax, mail, or courier. The service provider inputs the information when it is not provided electronically. When the input is captured automatically by the user company, it can be uploaded using an application program and transmitted to the service provider. For example, automatic capture occurs from the electronic time sheets in a public accounting firm or electronic sign in and sign out on a sales terminal for a retail business. If the information is entered manually, various tools such as input templates and data verification applications can assist in confirming the accuracy of the input. These tools are appropriate whether the user company or service provider performs the manual data input. When a user company manually inputs the payroll information, it can use a program in its own IT system or a Web-based application.

Accuracy and confidentiality are important considerations for input and transmission of payroll data between the company and the outside service provider. The company uses controls such as record counts and control totals to verify that the data sent to the outside processor were received accurately and completely. Web-based programs use login identification and pass codes, as well as encryption during transmission. Other transmissions between the company and the service provider use security measures such as encryption and passwords to authenticate the sender.

Processing by the Service Provider

Payroll processing by the outside service provider begins with payroll master file maintenance. The service provider uses the information on authorized changes it receives from the company to update the company's payroll master file. Next, the service provider processes the current payroll information. The processing calculates the current payroll. In addition, the program updates each employee's master file record so that the year-to-date totals include the current period transactions.

Typically, the service provider processes payroll based on a schedule. A tracking system is used that can determine at what point a particular company's files are in the process. Sometimes the service provider simply produces a printout of updated information for the company, such as the new payroll master file information. Other interface depends on the level of sophistication of the user company's IT and its contract with the service provider. The user company may be able to conduct online inquiry to determine where its payroll is in the process, as well as to query certain information, such as payroll master file data. The query capability allows the user company to determine whether the payroll master file has been updated properly with submitted changes.

During the processing run, edit checks verify employee numbers and various codes. The programmed checks used to address these potential errors are based on syntax and relational tests. Other programmed checks identify and flag transactions with processing or other errors and provide a message about the problem. Employees of the outside service provider will usually view, modify, and correct the errors if possible. When the service provider does not have enough information, the employees monitoring the process contact the user organization to get assistance in correcting the error.

Outputs of the Service Provider

The primary output from the service provider's processing run deals with the current payroll for the user company's employees. If the company pays its employees by issuing paper checks or stored value payroll cards, the initial output is checks or cards and earnings statements with current and year-to-date totals. For control purposes the service provider communicates the first and last check or card numbers in the run and the total dollar amount. The service provider communicates information about any breaks in the sequence that might have occurred from, for example, a printer jam. Service providers generally use up-to-date security features for the checks they produce, including using paper stock and ink that protect against being able to copy checks on color copiers or by using scanners.

When employees are paid by direct deposit, the service provider produces documents similar to those prepared when a company pays by check. The main difference is that the communication to each individual employee is in the form of a document marked "nonnegotiable" that provides compensation information. The information presents gross and net pay and specifics about amounts withheld on both a current and year-to-date basis. Although paying in cash is less common, for those companies that pay their employees in cash, the service provider produces a document for each employee to accompany the cash payment detailing employee's earnings, withholdings, and net cash being received.

Outputs can be communicated by the service provider in various combinations of hardcopy and electronic transmissions. For example, when direct deposit is used, directions for the transfer of funds can be transmitted electronically to banks. In addition, other outputs are transmitted electronically to the user organization. Another possible scenario is that all information is communicated electronically to the user company. The user company then prints checks or documents to accompany cash payrolls. Another option is for the outside service provider to print checks and all other documents and send them to the company via hired drivers, insured third-party couriers, or common mail carriers.

The service provider produces documents in addition to outputs directly relevant to paying employees for the current payroll. For example, other outputs from the outside service provider's processing run may include reports used for accounting and management purposes. Again, the output can be provided in either electronic or hard-copy form:

Updated payroll master file, listing the most currently used personal information for employees as well as their year-to-date information.

Payroll register or journal, listing all the detail related to each employee for the current payroll period payout.

Deduction exception report, detailing any exceptions from the expected deduction processing, such as when an employee's current period earnings amount is not large enough to cover the total planned deductions or the employee was not paid that pay period.

Management summary, providing company-wide information detail, based on management's preferences such as by department, location, product, or general ledger account; may include analyses such as percentages for comparison to budget.

Labor cost report, detailing the impact of this period's payroll expenses on inventory or jobs and may include cost by employee, cost by job, hours by job, and cumulative totals.

For all payroll processing runs, the service provider produces control reports and information. Examples of reports used for control purposes are a detailed listing of all employee master file *changes* processed and a count or distribution of the number of employee payments that fell within various dollar amount categories. In addition, the service provider may produce a report detailing unusual transactions.

The purpose of the unusual transactions report is to highlight items that may be legitimate but should be reviewed. For example, the unusual transaction report lists when any employee is paid an unusually high amount or an employee receives two paychecks. Although it could be a problem, a high dollar amount can result from payment of a bonus or commissions. Similarly, two paychecks might legitimately occur when an employee receives one paycheck for regular pay and a second paycheck for bonus pay.

The service provider produces a variety of control totals and statistics, such as the count of employees paid and totals for gross, net, and withheld amounts. A variety of hash totals, which are calculated by adding together numbers associated with a set of records and are meaningless for any purpose other than control, are also produced and reported. Exhibit 13-5 is a diagram of payroll outsourcing activities.

AUDITING IN ACTION

Payroll Processing Control and Hash Totals Produced

Current payroll gross, withholdings, and net amounts

Year-to-date payroll gross, withholdings, and net amounts

Hourly and salary rates used in current processing

Rate changes made during master file maintenance

Hours input and used in current processing

EXHIBIT 13-5

Payroll Outsourcing Activities

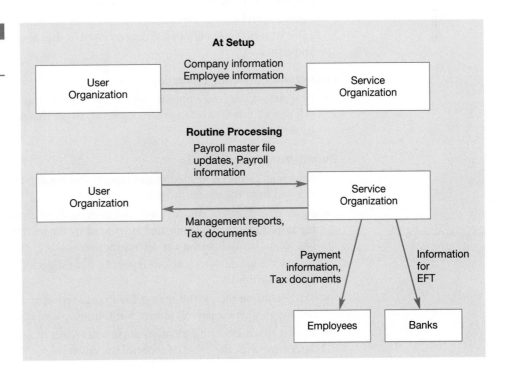

User Company Controls

A company that uses an outside service provider for payroll processing still needs numerous controls. The controls address both internal activities and those of the service provider. At the time that the service is originally established, the user company reviews the company-level information, payroll master file reports, and any direct deposit data to verify that the information being used to process payroll is accurate. If hard-copy paychecks are to be produced by the service provider, the user company inspects a prototype check for accuracy.

On an ongoing basis, the user company enforces controls around the payroll processing performed by the outside service provider. These controls around the service provider's activities can be grouped as controls over company employees, input and submission controls, controls for processing-error corrections, and output monitoring.

Employee-Related Controls:

- Train employees in the proper use of any activities and computer interface.
- Use passwords and IDs to authorize access for inputting and transmitting payroll information.
- Regularly review and update employee authorizations for payroll access.
- Establish, regularly review, and update a list of those who are authorized contacts for the outside service provider and keep the service provider informed.

Input and Submission Controls:

- Establish procedures to ensure payroll input data is submitted to the outside service provider as scheduled and on time.
- Establish verification and correction procedures to determine accuracy of data input. (Appropriate verification will differ for different methods of data input.)
- Create control and hash totals of all data submitted to the outside service provider.
- Use appropriate verification security measures for data submission (encryption, password authorization, etc.)
- Respond to and resolve any error reports received related to data submission.
- Review submission confirmation received from the outside service provider and agree control and hash totals of data received to data sent; resolve any discrepancies and errors.

Controls for Correcting Processing Errors:

- Designate authorized employees and establish procedures for responding to the outside service provider when processing errors occur that require company input for correction.

Output-Monitoring Controls:

- Review all control information and reports that result from processing when they are received from the service provider.
- Agree record counts, control totals and hash totals received after processing to the input data sent to and confirmed as received by the service provider before processing; follow up and resolve any discrepancies.
- Review the unusual transactions report and investigate the appropriateness of identified transactions.
- Trace items on the payroll master file change report to the input originally submitted and to the new payroll master file; follow up and resolve any discrepancies.
- Inspect paychecks or information documents when received for completeness and agreement with any counts or control information.

- Establish procedures for investigating and resolving any problems that employees report with payroll payments, including notifying the outside service provider.

The controls related to the use of a service provider are not the complete set of controls needed for the human resources cycle. The user company still needs all the controls appropriate for functions that occur in addition to payroll processing. For example, controls over the hiring process are needed. Controls are needed over cash activities, such as moving funds into a payroll bank account from which payments are disbursed and reconciling the payroll bank account. In addition, controls are needed over posting of payroll expense and related transactions to the records of the company.

REVIEW QUESTIONS

G.1 What information must the user organization submit to the service provider? By what means can the information be input and submitted?

G.2 What is payroll master file maintenance?

G.3 What outputs are produced by the service provider related to paying employees? Related to accounting and management?

G.4 What controls should a user organization have in place for the information and activities related to an outside service provider for payroll?

REPORTS ON THE PROCESSING OF TRANSACTIONS BY A SERVICE ORGANIZATION [LO 4]

Auditors of companies that use outside service providers must consider the impact of the outside service provider and its activities on the integrated audit. Although this chapter deals with payroll processing, the concepts apply regardless of the activity that is outsourced.

Outsourcing impacts the ICFR audit of an integrated audit. From an ICFR perspective the auditor must determine whether the activity outsourced is a significant process for the company. If the outsourced activity is a significant process, the auditor considers the controls for the process. Auditor consideration includes how the controls affect the significant accounts involved and the assertions for those accounts. Payroll is typically a significant process.

AS 5, Appendix B, and AU 324 state that if the outsourced activity is a significant process, then the service provider's services are part of the company's IT system. The auditing standards state that a service provider may need to be viewed as part of an entity's IT system. If the services affect any of the items in the following list, the service provider is considered a part of the entity's IT system.

Classes of transactions significant to the financial statements

Procedures of initiating, recording, processing and reporting transactions, from occurrence of the event through creation of the financial statements

Accounting records, supporting information and specific accounts related to the entity's transactions and financial statements

Method of capture of events and conditions significant to the entity's financial statements

The financial reporting process leading to preparation of financial statements, including estimates and disclosures

(Adapted from AU 324.03)

Again, if the service provider's activities are important and are part of the company's IT system, they must be addressed by the ICFR audit and considered when assessing risk for the financial statement audit. Outsourced payroll processing typically meets the criteria of being a part of the company's information system.[3]

In theory, the auditor can simply view the service organization as an extension of its audit client. The auditor then performs all the procedures deemed necessary relating to the design and operating effectiveness of ICFR, and to financial statement assertions at the outside service provider as well as at the audit client. However, this is an unlikely scenario.

More common is for the outside service provider to engage an auditor to perform an engagement resulting in a "Report on the Processing of Transactions by a Service Organization"—commonly called a **SAS 70 report**. This type of engagement results in a report that is made available to all of the service organization's clients and the clients' auditors. Details of this type of engagement, from the perspective of the auditor hired to do the work and create the report, are discussed in Appendix A to this chapter. A brief description is provided here.

An auditor hired to report on transaction processing at a service organization bases the work on a descriptive report prepared by the service organization. The service organization describes controls it believes are important to the audits of its clients and links the controls to the control objectives. The service organization auditor conducts the examination and assesses whether the description fits the actual situation, controls are in place, and controls are designed so that they satisfy the control objectives.

The engagement may be limited to this amount of work, with the auditor producing a report relating only to whether the controls are appropriately described, in place, and effectively designed to meet the described control objectives. This type of report is commonly referred to as a SAS 70, Type 1 report, "Report on Controls Placed in Operation." (See this chapter's appendix for a sample report.) While SAS 70, Type I reports occurred with some frequency prior to the PCAOB requirement for ICFR and integrated audits, they are no longer as common.

AS 5 requires the auditor to report not only on the design but also the operating effectiveness of controls. Therefore, the controls in a service organization affecting the significant transactions of a user organization, such as payroll, must be tested for operating effectiveness. The auditor who performs a **SAS 70 engagement** typically is engaged to continue the work beyond assessing design effectiveness, and also performs tests of operating effectiveness. The result is called a SAS 70, Type II report, "Report on Controls Placed in Operation and Tests of Operating Effectiveness." (See this chapter's Appendix for a sample report.)

If a SAS 70 report is not available, the auditor of the user organization may inquire about the possibility of the service provider contracting for a SAS 70 engagement. If a SAS 70, Type I report is available, it may provide the auditor of the user organization with enough information to plan the integrated audit and assess design effectiveness. If it is not sufficient for this purpose, the auditor may need to obtain more information from the service provider. Even if it is sufficient for planning the financial statement audit and assessing design effectiveness of controls, with only a SAS 70, Type I report available the auditor needs to perform tests of ICFR operating effectiveness.

If a SAS 70, Type II report is available, the auditor considers it, along with the rest of the ICFR audit work. These two sources of evidence *may* provide the auditor with enough information to express an opinion on ICFR and assess risk for the financial statement audit. However, the auditor may decide that the SAS 70, Type II report is not sufficient as the sole source of evidence on the operating effectiveness of the service provider's ICFR. When

---

[3]The outside service provider is also called a *service organization*. The client of the outside service provider is also called the *user organization*. The audit firm that performs an engagement and issues a report on the processing of transactions as discussed here is called the **service auditor**. The auditor of the user organization is called the **user auditor**. The *user auditor* may choose to accept the report issued by the *service auditor* as evidence in its integrated audit of the user organization.

deciding whether a SAS 70, Type II report provides sufficient evidence about the operating effectiveness of controls at the service organization, the auditor considers:

- Time period covered by the tests of controls
- Relationship of the time period tested to the date of management's assessment of ICFR
- Scope of the examination, applications covered, controls tested
- Relationship of the controls tested at the service organization to the controls of the user company
- Results of the tests of controls
- Service auditor's opinion (AS5.B21, 25)

The auditor may decide that additional audit evidence is needed despite the Type II report that is available. This is more likely if a long period of time has lapsed between the date of the service auditor's report and the date of management's report on its assessment of ICFR. Sometimes service organizations take this into consideration when planning the timing of their SAS 70 engagement. Some service providers have the test period end on September 30 to accommodate a large group of clients with December 31 fiscal year ends. As another example of a solution for the time lag problem, ADP has a six-month testing cycle twice a year. Presumably this frequency is intended to provide a current report to the auditors of its many user organizations with different fiscal year ends.

Assume that a SAS 70 report is available and it reports on tests that were performed in a time frame that makes them useful to the user auditor. The user auditor may still decide that more audit evidence is needed. This will likely occur if the SAS 70 report indicates problems with the service organization's controls or if the service organization changed its system after the tests were performed.

Even when none of these conditions exist, the auditor may decide to conduct more audit procedures on the outside service provider's activities. This is more probable if the auditor concludes that the service organization's activities are pervasive or very important to the company being audited. Regardless of the decisions the auditor makes about the sufficiency of the SAS 70 report, AU 324.14 states very clearly that the ultimate responsibility for assessing the impact of the outside service provider on the audit of the user company rests with the user company's auditor. As a consequence of this responsibility, the user auditor does not mention or refer to the service auditor's report when reporting on the user organization.

AUDITING IN ACTION

Assessing Control Operating Effectiveness at a Service Organization

If the user auditor decides to use a service auditor's report, the user auditor should consider the extent of the evidence provided by the report about the effectiveness of controls intended to prevent or detect material misstatements in the particular assertions. The user auditor remains responsible for evaluating the evidence presented by the service auditor for determining its effect on the assessment of control risk at the user organization. (AU324.14)

REVIEW QUESTIONS

H.1 Under what conditions does a company's auditor (the user auditor) have to consider the ICFR at the service organization?

H.2 What is a SAS 70 report? What is its purpose? Who has access to it?

H.3 What is the difference between a Type I and Type II report? What conditions might cause the auditor to decide that more evidence is needed beyond a Type II report?

AUDIT TESTS AND PROCEDURES

Definitions of management assertions were reviewed in Chapter 10. Procedures used to test these assertions and the general nature of the procedures were also reviewed. This chapter presents procedures used to audit human resources functions, payroll processing, and related accounts. The discussion includes tests of controls, dual purpose tests, substantive analytical procedures, and tests of details of balances.

In an integrated audit the procedures should, whenever possible, contribute evidence to both the ICFR audit and financial statement audit. Evidence collected in one part of the audit is considered in other parts of the audit. For example, the auditor considers ICFR and the resulting quality of available audit evidence when planning the nature, timing, and extent of substantive procedures for the financial statement audit.

Audit evidence consideration also flows from the financial statement audit to the ICFR audit. As an example, if the auditor finds a material error during the financial statement audit, the auditor will reassess whether ICFR functioned effectively. The auditor reassesses the preliminary ICFR audit conclusions even if no material problems were found directly during the ICFR audit.

TESTS OF CONTROLS FOR HUMAN RESOURCES TRANSACTIONS [LO 5]

After testing and concluding on the design effectiveness of ICFR, the auditor performs tests of controls that examine ICFR operating effectiveness. Performing walkthroughs, or procedures that are equivalent to walkthroughs, is an important step. The procedures allow the auditor to understand the client's information system and conclude on design effectiveness.

During walkthroughs the auditor also typically gains evidence about the operating effectiveness of controls. This is especially true for tests of controls that include reviewing client procedures and observing client personnel as they perform control steps. The auditor gains evidence about human resources while performing a walkthrough and observing employees documenting changes to employee personnel files. Similar evidence results from watching employees as they authorize or input changes to the payroll master file.

The different kinds of evidence gleaned from a walkthrough highlights the problems with describing audit evidence chronologically. In the "real world" some of the steps presented in this chapter will have been accomplished by the auditor during earlier phases of the audit. Also, some of the tests of controls presented in this chapter will be accomplished during testing the company's overall general IT controls (ITGC). For example, audit tests to determine whether the general ledger is properly posted and reconciled with the payroll register and payroll master file are performed while testing the entire system using computer-assisted audit techniques (CAATs), thus incorporating the various transaction processes.

Management's overall assertions continue to apply to all cycles of the business. As a reminder, they are:

1. Existence or occurrence
2. Completeness
3. Rights and obligations
4. Valuation or allocation
5. Presentation and disclosure

Auditors address the validity of these management assertions as they relate to human resources, payroll processing, and payroll cash disbursements. Significant audit effort goes into making sure that payments are to real employees based on authorized inputs, that all calculations on which withholdings and payments are based are accurate, and that payroll records on which government-required information documents and tax returns are based accurately reflect the activity. Beyond those control concerns are the universal ones that all transactions are posted, and are posted at the correct amounts, to the proper accounts and in the correct accounting period.

Exhibit 13-6 presents tests of controls for human resources cycle transactions. The exhibit includes the possibility of using a SAS 70 Type II report as a substitute for some of the controls tests. You should read and study this exhibit to understand the specific controls needed in the human resources cycle and how they are tested.

EXHIBIT 13-6 **Examples of Tests of Controls for Payroll Transactions**[4]	Note that either management or the auditor can perform tests of controls. Management uses tests of controls to support its management report. The auditor uses tests of controls for the audit of ICFR and to confirm the planned reliance on controls in the financial statement audit. Management assertions are presented parenthetically after the purpose of the control.

Purpose	Company Controls and Tests of Controls
To ensure that inputs to payroll calculations such as information on current employees to be paid, pay rates, and withholdings are accurate and authorized **(authorization, existence or occurrence)**	
	CC: *Company policy is followed for the hiring process including hiring only for authorized positions and investigating potential employees as appropriate for the position*
	TofC: Determine company policies for authorizing the HR department to hire; determine company policies for prehiring investigations for different positions; using this information, examine a sample of employee files for evidence of the authorized positions into which employees were hired and any prehiring investigations performed
	CC: *When a new hire occurs, appropriate documents (hard copy or electronic) are completed in and retained by the HR department according to company policy, including the hiring form that documents the authorization to add the employee to the payroll, pay rate form, withholding forms; any actual employee signatures required (legal documents, insurance documents, etc.) are obtained and retained; any authorization required by personnel outside the HR department is obtained*
	TofC: Examine a selection of employee files for the inclusion of all required documents, authorizations and approvals required, and employee signatures required
	CC: *Company policy is followed for the process when employees separate from the company such as the use of exit interviews, creation of appropriate documents and other departments advising the HR department of the separation on an immediate basis*
	TofC: Examine a selection of employee files for employees who have terminated their employment agreement, for the inclusion of all required documents, authorizations and approvals; note the date of the documents in the employee file and trace the date to the employee's

(continued)

CC: removal from active status on the payroll master file and the date of any documents related to the separation decision in the employee's line department

CC: *Inputs to the payroll master file are authorized or performed by employees in the HR department on a timely basis; controls specify and limit those in the HR department who may authorize or input initial or change information to the payroll master file on new hires, pay rates, withholdings, separations, etc.*

TofC: Review policies regarding who can authorize or make changes to personnel files and the payroll master file; discuss with employees in the department and observe employees as they work

TofC: Attempt to authorize or input changes to the payroll master file using false or unapproved data

TofC: Compare dates of changes recorded in employee files to the dates the changes are posted to the payroll master file

CC: *Programmed controls (IDs, passwords, limit checks, etc.) exist and are applied to inputs, including changes, to the payroll master files*

TofC: Test the various programmed controls over inputs to the payroll master files (or rely on SAS 70 Type II report)

CC: *Reports are prepared regularly specifying changes that have been made to the payroll master file; these reports are reviewed and reconciled to authorized input information and approved*

TofC: Review the file of reports generated on changes made to the payroll master file for completeness, inspecting whether all reports have been generated and are available

TofC: Review a sample of reports generated on changes made to the payroll master file for evidence of review, reconciliation to input, and approval; select items on a sample of the change reports and agree to the information used as the basis to input the change

To ensure that hours-worked information used to calculate pay reflects time actually worked. This applies when a performance measure such as hours worked is one criterion for amounts to be paid; would also apply to overtime, piece rate and commission situations. **(existence or occurrence)**

CC: *For employees whose pay depends on a variable input such as hours worked, productivity, or hours of overtime worked beyond a standard, these data are collected based on company policy*

(Note: Policy might be to punch a time clock, sign in on a computer terminal,

keep a time sheet, provide productive output for weighing or counting, etc.)

TofC: Examine a sample of input documents for evidence that the required data are collected

CC: *If company policy requires it, regular or OT hours (or if appropriate other productivity indicators) are approved before they can be entered as input to the payroll application process*

TofC: Examine a sample of processed payroll transactions that would require approval according to company policy and trace to approval in whatever form is appropriate; may likely be either electronic or manual evidence of approval

CC: *Time worked, etc. will not be accepted by the payroll application program for any employees not on the payroll master file*

TofC: Test the effectiveness of application controls by attempting to input time worked data for an employee not on the payroll master file (or rely on SAS 70 Type II report)

To ensure that payroll payments are made, and are made to individuals who are actual authorized employees of the company, for the correct amount using appropriate pay rate and withholding information, and using any required input about time worked or productivity **(authorization, existence or occurrence)**

CC: *Payroll is calculated only for employees existing on the updated payroll master file*

TofC: Test the effectiveness of application controls by attempting to input information on employees who are not on the payroll master file (or rely on a SAS 70 Type II report)

CC: *Payroll amounts for each employee are calculated using authorized and updated information on the payroll master file along with additional authorized input information (such as time worked)*

TofC: Select a sample of payroll payment documents and trace the amounts used to calculate the payment (such as rates, hours worked, commissions, and salary) to the underlying documents, examining the documents for proper authorization and agree the amounts of the input

TofC: Using computer-assisted audit techniques, recalculate a payroll using inputs that have been examined using audit procedures to test that they are authorized and updated (or rely on a SAS 70 Type II report)

TofC: Using computer-assisted audit techniques, scan the payroll register and master file for unusual transactions and amounts, including such details as

(continued)

inappropriate times and unusual and unauthorized computer terminals (or rely on a SAS 70 Type II report)

CC: *Employee EFT information is obtained, kept secure and updated only based on employee authorization*[4]

TofC: Obtain company policy on capture and maintenance of employee EFT information, scan employee files for proper documentation and discuss procedures with employees

TofC: Identify instances of employee EFT information changing and trace back to the point of change using historical payroll master file data; identify by whom and in what department the payroll master file record change was either authorized or input and examine supporting documentation of employee authorization

CC: *Checks or EFT transactions are approved based on review of the supporting documents before being issued or executed*

TofC: Obtain company policy regarding which individuals have authority to sign payroll checks and approve payroll EFT transactions; trace those names to evidence of their review of supporting documents and approval

CC: *Batch (control) totals of the input information are created and compared to batch (control) totals of summary reports of the payroll application run; discrepancies are followed up and resolved*

TofC: Review company procedures for the comparison of control totals and any follow-up and resolution procedures; observe employees performing the comparison and any resulting follow-up; inquire about discrepancies found and how they are resolved; review any available documentation (or perform this for inputs and outputs from an outside service provider and rely on a SAS 70 Type II report for other comparisons and reconciliations)

CC: *Payroll bank account is reconciled on a timely basis, including identifying and resolving any discrepancies by an authorized and independent employee*

TofC: Observe the bank account reconciliation process, noting the authority and independence of the employee performing the work

TofC: Review bank reconciliations; note whether the reconciliations have been prepared, when, by whom, and the clerical accuracy of the reconciliation

To ensure that all payroll transactions are recorded
(completeness)

CC: *Payroll transactions are recorded to the accounting records concurrently with the payout and to the general ledger on a timely basis*

TofC: Examine procedures manual or company policy regarding when recording should occur and examine general ledger for evidence of timely posting

CC: *Consecutive numbers of payroll checks or EFT transaction numbers are controlled, and used in the bank reconciliation process*

TofC: Review bank reconciliations; note whether the reconciliations have been prepared, when, by whom, and the clerical accuracy of the reconciliation; observe how accountability for consecutive numbers of payroll checks and EFT transaction number is handled

CC: *Compare payroll register totals to payroll master file update control totals; compare payroll master file totals to general ledger accounts*

TofC: Examine evidence that posting to the payroll register and payroll master file are reconciled; use computer-assisted audit techniques to recalculate as appropriate (or rely on SAS 70 Type II report)

TofC: Examine evidence that payroll register is reconciled to general ledger

To ensure that payroll transactions are recorded in the correct accounting period
(cutoff)

CC: *Payroll transactions are recorded based on company policy and any necessary adjusting entries are recorded at year end*

TofC: Examine procedures manual or company policy regarding when recording should occur on a routine basis and examine general ledger for evidence of timely posting and adjusting entries as appropriate for payroll payouts close to the end of the year

To ensure that payroll transactions are properly posted to the correct cash and other accounts in the general ledger (i.e., are properly classified) and to the appropriate employee records in the payroll master file
(presentation and disclosure)

CC: *Individual employee payroll master file records are verified using control or hash totals on a per-employee basis, and compared to payroll register (typically an IT application control)*

TofC: Examine evidence that control or hash totals for the payroll register and payroll master file are reconciled; use com-

(continued)

puter-assisted audit techniques to test IT application control as appropriate (or rely on SAS 70 Type II report)

CC: *Payroll master file totals are compared to general ledger totals*

TofC: Examine evidence that the payroll master file and general ledger are reconciled; use computer-assisted audit techniques to recalculate as appropriate

---

[4]For segregation of duties to serve as a *preventive* control, the best location for employee direct deposit instructions is the Treasury Department. However, in the "real world" this information is often collected and maintained in the human resources department. If the information is kept in the human resources department, the direct deposit instructions might be changed and funds diverted by keeping a terminated employee on the payroll. As a *detective* control, if the line departments are accountable for their expenses, the overpayment would likely be caught quickly. Another *detective* control is in place if the IT processing environment has good access controls, such as login IDs and passwords that will facilitate quick identification of anyone who makes unauthorized changes to direct deposit information.

TESTS OF CONTROLS FOR PAYROLL CASH DISBURSEMENTS

Tests of controls for payroll cash disbursements can fall within the auditor's overall payroll and general cash disbursements testing. When this is the case, additional focus addresses the specific manner in which payroll payouts are made. For example, a separate payroll bank account, often set up on an imprest basis, is typically used. Controls exist for the transfer of money from the general cash account into the payroll account. A transfer schedule is used to be sure the funds get into the payroll bank account at the proper time. Exhibit 13-6 includes a control step of reviewing supporting documents before EFT direct deposit or paycheck distribution occurs. Reconciliation of the payroll bank account is also included in Exhibit 13-6 in the controls to be tested. Bank account reconciliation is an important control over any cash disbursements.

When payroll payout is handled through direct deposit, an important issue is the custody of employee direct deposit information and authority for changes to that information. As the footnote in Exhibit 13-6 indicates, companies sometimes choose to house direct deposit information in the human resources department and rely on detective controls for any misuse of direct deposit instructions. Reliance on detective controls may be appropriate since there are other compensating controls and timely detection will limit to an immaterial amount the money that is at risk if a single employee's payroll payout is stolen for a small number of pay periods.

When direct deposit payout is used, controls exist for investigating and resolving any errors or discrepancies that occur from the electronic transfer of funds. These controls are tested as a part of the audit of the human resources cycle. If the direct deposit function is outsourced, the auditor may choose to rely on the description and test of controls reported in a SAS 70 Type II report.

Large companies rarely pay their employees in cash. However, if payroll is disbursed in cash, use of an imprest fund is even more important. Documentation is produced for each employee detailing the cash distributed. A receipt is obtained by the employer when cash is disbursed. Related tests of controls for cash payrolls include reading and evaluating company procedures and observing the payout process. The auditor tests a sample of pay periods, agreeing the amount of cash disbursed from the bank account with the net amount recorded in the payroll register and the total of signed receipts obtained.

DUAL PURPOSE TESTS [LO 6]

Dual purpose tests provide the auditor with audit evidence about ICFR and the account balances in the financial statement using the same items for evidence. AS 5 highlights the importance of planning the timing of audit steps so that dual purpose tests provide useful information not only for the ICFR audit, but also for the financial statement audit. Dual purpose tests that address both controls and proper balances of accruals should be performed close to or at year end so that they may support both ICFR conclusions and financial statement conclusions.

Since payroll processing is typically automated or outsourced, control tests that also support the payroll expense account balance may utilize computer-assisted audit techniques that start from authorized input and recalculate payroll transactions throughout or for the entire time period. When planning dual purpose tests that use a sample, the auditor must consider both ICFR and financial statement audit objectives and select a large enough sample to accomplish the goals of both audit procedures.

You should read and study Exhibit 13-7 on dual purpose tests for human resources. Compare the dual purpose tests to both tests of controls and tests of details of balances. A major difference is that each dual purpose test step includes collecting evidence about ICFR and the account balance. For purposes of audit efficiency, whenever possible auditors will modify tests of controls to also collect account balance evidence. When payroll is outsourced and the auditor relies on a SAS 70 Type II audit report, tests of controls for the payroll processing segment of the human resources cycle will not be performed again, so dual purpose tests are not relevant.

Dual purpose tests for payroll cash disbursements can be considered from the perspective of what you already know about accounts payable. Controls are intended to limit disbursements so that they are only for real obligations. Controls also focus on proper recording at the correct amount in the proper period and to the proper account. When disbursements

EXHIBIT 13-7

Examples of Dual Purpose Tests for Human Resources Transactions

Purpose of Test	Dual Purpose Tests
To obtain audit evidence that: Payroll transactions represent payments to legitimate employees that are appropriate for the services received by the company and consistent with terms of the employment contract such as hours worked and pay rate **(authorization, existence or occurrence)**	Select transactions that have been recorded to the payroll register, trace the entries to supporting documents such as the payroll master file, time cards, job time tickets, etc. and personnel records, agreeing underlying data (employee name, pay rate, hours worked); reperform calculation of amounts and agree to payroll register. Using computer-assisted audit techniques, scan payroll master file and payroll register or journal for unusual transactions and amounts including such details as inappropriate times and unusual and unauthorized computer terminals; trace any that are identified to supporting documents

(continued)

All payroll transactions are recorded (**completeness**)	
	Select inputs to the payroll process such as time cards, job time tickets, and lists of salaried employees and trace to transactions posted to the payroll register; reperform calculation of amounts based on inputs; agree amounts and other details of the payroll transaction
Transactions posted as payroll expenses and related liabilities are recorded in the correct accounting period (**cutoff**)	
	Select transactions from the payroll registers immediately before and after year end and agree the date of posting to the appropriate date when the payment was made; reperform the calculation of any related accrued liabilities, noting that the amounts are posted in the correct period
Transactions posted as payroll expenses and related liabilities are properly classified (**existence or occurrence, presentation and disclosure**)	
	Trace transactions from the payroll register to supporting documents and examine for proper classification, noting whether the amounts are posted to the correct accounts
	Trace transactions from the related liability accounts to supporting documents; examine for proper classification, noting whether the amounts are posted to the correct accounts
Recorded payroll transactions are included in the employee master file year-to-date records (**completeness, presentation and disclosure**)	
	Select payroll transactions from the payroll register and trace them to updates to the amounts in the payroll master file for the specific employee transactions selected; agree amounts, dates, and other reference information
Amounts shown in journals and ledgers are clerically accurate summations of transactions (**presentation and disclosure**)	
	Use computer-assisted audit techniques to check the clerical accuracy of the payroll records and agree the total amount to the general ledger

are for accounts payable, it is important that both the subsidiary ledger and general ledger are properly posted. The parallel for payroll disbursements is proper posting to the individual employee's payroll master file record and the general ledger. Since a separate payroll bank account is typically used, dual purpose tests for payroll cash disbursements address both the transfer of money from the general bank account to the payroll bank account and the cash disbursements from the payroll bank account to individual employees. Exhibit 13-8 presents dual purpose tests for payroll disbursements.

Purpose of Test	Dual Purpose Tests
To obtain audit evidence that: Cash disbursements that are recorded are for payroll costs of the company **(authorization, existence or occurrence)**	
	Using computer-assisted audit techniques, scan the payroll register for unusual transactions and amounts, including such details as inappropriate times, and unusual and unauthorized computer terminals; trace any that are identified to supporting documents
	Examine payroll registers and EFT documents for proper authorization for the payout to occur and trace the amount transferred to the payroll bank account to the cash disbursements journal
	Select transactions from the payroll register and trace related evidence of specific payroll cash disbursements (EFT transaction identification information, check number, date) to individual employee's records on payroll master files and agree amounts
All payroll cash disbursement transactions recorded by the company occurred **(existence or occurrence)**	
	Trace entries posted in the cash disbursements journal to the general account and payroll account bank statements, agree amounts
All cash disbursed by the company was properly recorded in the payroll register and cash disbursements journal, and the amounts and details are shown correctly **(completeness)**	
	Trace disbursements shown on the payroll bank statements to the related payroll register agreeing amounts; trace money transferred in on the payroll bank statement to a disbursement on the general bank statement agreeing dates and amounts
Cash disbursements transactions are properly classified and recorded in the period the payment was made **(existence or occurrence, cutoff, presentation and disclosure)**	
	Select transactions from the cash disbursements journal and examine general and payroll bank statements and any other externally generated documents for

(continued)

	evidence that the transactions are shown at the proper amounts, properly classified as cash, and that the cash, was disbursed in the period shown
	Select disbursements recorded in the cash disbursements journal shortly before year end and trace them to the general and payroll bank statements agreeing the amount; investigate transactions for which time lags between the cash disbursements journal and bank statements are noted to determine if the disbursement occurred in the subsequent year
Postings of cash disbursements correspond to the payroll register, appropriate employee records in the payroll master file, and general ledger **(presentation and disclosure)**	
	Select transactions from the cash disbursements journal and trace to the payroll register agreeing the total amount, other account details and dates
	Select individual employee transactions from the payroll master file and trace to the payroll register agreeing amounts, other account details and dates
Amounts shown in journals and ledgers are clerically accurate summations of transactions **(presentation and disclosure)**	
	Use computer-assisted audit techniques to check the clerical accuracy of the payroll register, payroll master file, cash disbursements journal, and trace amounts to the general ledger

SUBSTANTIVE ANALYTICAL PROCEDURES

Analytical procedures are an important part of the audit of the human resources cycle. Logical relationships exist not only among the accounts related to payroll, but also between payroll accounts and other accounts such as sales and inventory. Therefore, analytical procedures used as part of the planning process can highlight obvious inconsistencies. Analytical procedures can provide early indications of the areas that may require more audit effort.

Substantive analytical procedures also provide considerable audit evidence about the reasonableness of both payroll-related expenses and liability account balances. Current-year balances are compared to prior years, budget, and industry benchmarks. Estimates can be made of what the account balances should be. These estimates are calculated based on averages and aggregated inputs, such as average salary of a class of employees and the number of employees in the group. When comparing current-year account balances to those of prior years, the auditor is not necessarily expecting the dollar amounts to be the same. If inputs to the total amount have changed, for example, if pay rates have increased, the auditor tries to determine whether the overall balance has changed a reasonable amount given the pay rate change.

Payroll expense for the year is made up of many transactions. Consequently, it is not practical for the auditor to gather all of the audit evidence about the year-end account balance using the approach of examining underlying documents. Because of the number of transactions, the audit approach to payroll expense is similar to that for sales revenue in a business that has many small-dollar-amount sales transactions that occur throughout the year. The auditor examines other accounts and considers their relationships with payroll expense to assess whether the year-end payroll expense balance is fairly stated. Compensation-related expense accounts subjected to substantive analytical procedures include wages, commissions, bonuses, and officers' compensation. Payroll tax expenses are also addressed by these analytical procedures.

AUDITING IN ACTION

Example of Substantive Analytical Procedures for Payroll-Related Expenses

Compare compensation expense account balances with prior year and budget

Compare direct labor expanse as a percent of sales with prior year, budget, and industry benchmarks

Calculate commission expense as a percent of sales and compare to equivalent calculation for prior year and budget; consider reasonableness based on company policies on commissions

Calculate payroll tax expense as a percent of compensation expense and compare to equivalent calculation for prior year and budget; consider reasonableness based on company's payroll tax costs

Payroll-related liability accounts include:

- Compensation that has been earned by employees but not yet paid
- Amounts withheld from employee payments but not yet disbursed
- Accrued payroll taxes
- Accrued vacation and sick pay

When the fiscal year end does not coincide with the end of a pay period and pay date, accrual entries are needed. Accrued payroll, accrued payroll taxes, withheld payroll taxes, and other items are generally estimated. The estimate is based on the period of time for which employees have worked but not been paid at fiscal year end. Vacation and sick time liabilities are usually estimated based on company policies and information such as the number of employees and average tenure with the company. When comparing accrual balances with prior years, SAB 108 guidance indicates that that the accuracy of both the expense and liability accounts is important. Exhibit 13-9 provides examples of substantive analytical procedures for payroll-related liabilities.

EXHIBIT 13-9

Examples of Substantive Analytical Procedures for Payroll-Related Liabilities

Calculate estimated accrued payroll liability based on the time period or other data about unpaid work and pay rates; compare to recorded accrued payroll liability for reasonableness

Compare accrued payroll liability account balance to prior year

Compare account balances for withheld taxes and other items to prior year

Calculate estimated accrued payroll taxes based on accrued payroll liability; compare to recorded accrued payroll tax liability for reasonableness

Compare accrued payroll tax liability account balance to prior year

Calculate accrued vacation and sick time liability based on company policy and other relevant available inputs; compare to recorded accrued vacation and sick time liability for reasonableness

Compare accrued vacation and sick time liability account balance to prior year

TESTS OF DETAILS OF BALANCES

Tests of details of balances in the human resources cycle consist mainly of examining underlying documents related to specific transactions or account balances. As discussed in the section on substantive analytical procedures, examining underlying documents for specific payroll payments is not efficient given the number of transactions. However, a strong compensating control for this limitation regarding *individual payments* is that employees typically are very aware of what they are supposed to be paid and will report problems regarding individual payments.

To test aggregate amounts of recorded payroll expense, the auditor examines payroll tax returns. The limitation to this test is that payroll tax returns are often based on recorded amounts, so over- or understatement of payroll expense is unlikely to be identified with this procedure.

To test amounts of officers' salaries and bonuses, the auditor agrees amounts authorized in Board of Directors minutes to recorded amounts. Officer compensation is vulnerable to overpayment because management may be able to circumvent or override controls and authorize excess payments. Also, officer compensation is reported in SEC filings. For these reasons, officer compensation is often subjected to tests of details of balances. In addition, the auditor may be asked to perform special "agreed upon procedures" for officers' compensation to determine that the information provided to shareholders (in a proxy statement) represents the compensation package. Exhibit 13-10 presents examples of tests of details of balances for payroll-related expense accounts.

EXHIBIT 13-10

Examples of Tests of Details of Balances for Payroll-Related Expense Accounts

Reconcile total payroll expense to payroll tax returns and W-2 forms

Reconcile total payroll tax expense to payroll tax returns

Select large commission payments and agree to supporting documents

Agree individual elements of the officer salary and bonus expense accounts to amounts authorized in Board of Director meeting minutes

Tests of details of balances for payroll-related liability accounts involve document examination and recalculation. The main audit objectives are to determine that the amounts posted are accurate and that they are recorded in the correct period. Since the accrued liabilities are based on calculations, the auditor examines the client documents supporting the year-end adjusting entries and reperforms the client calculations.

Some liabilities such as payroll taxes withheld and accrued payroll taxes can be reconciled to subsequent period tax returns and payments. Liabilities for other withholdings can also be reconciled to subsequent payments and related documents. Client cash flow problems and previous payments for payroll-tax related penalties and interest are indicators to test more extensively for unrecorded or under-recorded payroll taxes. Examples of tests of details of balances for payroll-related liabilities are shown in Exhibit 13-11.

EXHIBIT 13-11

Examples of Tests of Details of Balances for Payroll-Related Liability Accounts

Examine client documentation supporting calculation of accrued compensation accounts; analyze calculation method for reasonableness and consistency with prior year; trace information used to perform calculation to relevant supporting documents; reperform calculation; agree calculation result to general ledger account balance

Examine client documentation supporting calculation of accrued payroll taxes; analyze calculation method for reasonableness and consistency with prior year; trace information used to perform calculation to relevant supporting documents; reperform calculation; agree calculation result to general ledger account balance; reconcile account balance to subsequent payroll tax return and cash disbursement

Examine client documentation supporting calculation of withholdings from employee payments; analyze calculation method for reasonableness and consistency with prior year; trace information used to perform calculation to relevant supporting documents; reperform calculation; agree calculation result to general ledger account balance; reconcile account balances to subsequent payroll tax return and other related documents and to cash disbursements

AUDITING IN ACTION

An Example of a Work Paper for Officer Salary and Bonus Expense

Audit		ACC Banking Corporation
Index:	E-2.1	Officer Compensation
		12/31/2010

Prepared by Client (PBC)
Reviewed by: JH (P&C LLP)

Executive Salary Expense

Position	Name	Compensation	F/N
CEO	Leilah Escalera	450,000	A
CFO	Thomas Cronwell	400,000	A
CIO	Eddard Stockton	350,000	A
COO	Audrey Chatman	350,000	A
		1,550,000	TB-1
		F	

Bonus Expense

Position	Name	Bonus	F/N
CEO	Leilah Escalera	250,000	B
CFO	Thomas Cronwell	250,000	B
CIO	Eddard Stockton	150,000	B
COO	Audrey Chatman	150,000	B
		800,000	TB-1
		F	

Tickmark Legend

F Footed without exception

TB-1 Traced and Agreed to the Trial Balance in w/p TB-1 of this year's audit index

A Traced and agreed without exception to the officers contracts examined by JH (P&C) in manual work paper E-2.5

B Traced and agreed without exception to Board of Directors minutes for 12/15/2010 in manual work paper E-2.6.

REVIEW QUESTIONS

I.1 What evidence about the human resources cycle can be obtained through substantive analytical procedures?

I.2 What liability accounts are related to payroll?

I.3 What tests of details can be applied to individual amounts and account balances?

HUMAN RESOURCES RELATED DISCLOSURES

Human resources controls rely heavily on ITGC, segregation of duties, authorization, and physical controls, and on the fact that the transactions are repetitive and routine. However, in addition, accounting for many human resources accounts must be controlled for compliance with specific accounting standards. Many of these accounting standards require specific disclosures. Pensions, postretirement benefits, and profit sharing are among the disclosures requiring careful auditor attention.

Pension and postretirement expenses are accrued based on the applicable accounting pronouncements. The standards call for a fair value measurement of the benefit obligation of pension plans and other postretirement benefit plans, such as health-care plans. The fair value is compared to the benefit obligation, and the overfunded or underfunded status of the plan is shown as an asset or liability on the balance sheet and the gain or loss resulting from this is posted to Other Comprehensive Income (FASB ASC 715-20-65-1). Auditors have to consider the estimation of fair value, proper posting, and disclosure for these assets and liabilities. **Share-based compensation**, discussed in the next section, is also important in the audit of the human resources cycle, including required disclosures.

AUDIT OF SHARE-BASED COMPENSATION

Share-based compensation refers to the situation in which a company pays employees with equity rather than cash. These types of payments are often used as a part of officer compensation packages and to reward employee and officer performance. Usually, the equity instruments cannot be converted into cash until some point in the future. Even so, the equity instruments used to pay officers and employees must have value. Otherwise, the individuals would not be willing to accept the equity instruments as a substitute for cash.

FASB ASC 718-10, *Stock Compensation*, provides the accounting and disclosure standards for share-based compensation. Important issues are the measurement of the fair value of the equity instruments, the calculation of compensation expense based on the fair value measurement, and the period of time over which the expense is recognized—typically, the period over which the options vest. The vesting period refers to the period of time the employee must remain with the company in order to be able to exercise the options. Other important issues are disclosure that must be provided and tax impacts. The fair value is estimated using an option pricing model; the Black-Scholes model is frequently used. Calculation of the compensation expense relies on the fair value that is estimated but also considers other future uncertainties. These uncertainties include the estimated quantity of stock options that employees will actually exercise in the future. The disclosure required is extensive and complicated. Finally, the accounting for stock-based compensation generally results in a timing difference that generates a deferred tax asset.

Auditing stock-based compensation can require vastly different amounts of audit effort for different companies. The audit effort required depends on the extent to which the companies use stock-based compensation and the complexity of the plans. For example, although a stock option is the equity instrument often mentioned, the standard also applies to restricted stock, restricted stock equivalents, and various types of stock rights such as stock appreciation rights and performance stock rights.

To audit stock-based compensation, the auditor must understand the required accounting and disclosure, as well as the company's use of stock-based compensation. The auditor reperforms the company's calculations leading up to and including the amount of compensation expense. Specialists are often used by both the company and the auditor in valuing the options. In addition, the auditor uses the calculation documentation to audit the appropriateness of the disclosure. Specialists are often hired by companies to perform the calculations. Specialists within the audit firm are likely to be used to audit the work of the client's contracted specialists. Audit work on stock-based compensation is part of the information used for auditing deferred taxes.

AUDITING HUMAN RESOURCES IN THE SERVICES INDUSTRIES

The process of auditing human resources for a service company is similar to what is required for most businesses. Direct and indirect labor, which becomes part of inventory in a manufacturing business, does not have to be considered in the service environment. However, the dollar amount of compensation expense is usually the largest expense on the income statement. The audit addresses the accuracy of the amount using some combination of analytical procedures, recalculation, and document examination.

The compensation expense account balance is made up of many transactions of relatively small amounts that occur throughout the year. Therefore, internal controls applied to functions of the human resources cycle are important. Controls over activities in the human resources department not directly related to payroll processing steps are important, as well as those addressing processing payroll and cash disbursements. In many companies an outside service provider is used, and a SAS 70 Type II report is provided. The auditor considers the contribution that the SAS 70 Type II report makes to audit evidence.

General risks related to human resources in a service business are that people who should not be paid may be paid, or they may be paid the wrong amounts. The primary management concern is overpayment. The monitoring of personal pay received that is performed by employees provides a detection control for the risk of underpayment. Management concerns also extend to proper capture of data on the use of employee time, especially if time is the basis for customer billings.

Fraud risks are related to potential frauds perpetrated by employees and management. Payroll fraud can result from inappropriate work hours reported, payments made to fictitious employees, and payments made to those who have separated from the company. These types of payroll frauds are generally not material to the company. In contrast, risk of fraud related to officer compensation is important. Not only may the amounts be quantitatively material, but fraud committed by management is material from a qualitative perspective.

Service industries often must follow regulations that affect human resources. This affects the integrated audit. Auditor responsibility for illegal acts that are not directly related to the financial statements arises only when the auditor becomes aware of the illegal acts. However, illegal acts may be uncovered during the audit of the human resources cycle.

In some service industries, for example the airline industry, employees are limited in the number of hours they may work without having time off. Other service industries, such as the fast-food industry, often employ minors whose total hours or work shift times are legally restricted. Companies that are highly vulnerable to the possibility of unintentionally employing undocumented immigrants provide another example. These companies may need more extensive controls over obtaining proper personnel documents to guard against illegal acts.

During the audit of human resources, the auditor may become aware of evidence indicating that the company appears to have violated laws related to human resources. As a result, the auditor needs to explore whether there exists the potential for material financial statement effects. Again, auditors are not qualified to decide whether an action is illegal, and therefore can only infer that client behavior appears to violate laws. The auditor then needs to consider the possibility of contingent liabilities or other resulting financial impacts.

CONCLUSION

All audits involve audit steps for the human resources cycle. Some businesses with few employees and a small dollar amount of compensation expense require less audit effort in this area. Audits of service industries typically require more human resources cycle effort because of the large dollar amounts involved. Audits of manufacturing entities require consideration of labor costs as a part of inventory.

Typical accounts involved are compensation expense, payroll tax expense, accrued liabilities, and liabilities for withheld amounts. Audit evidence for this cycle often includes the report of another auditor on the transaction processing performed by an outside service provider. Although much of the activity in this cycle is straightforward, it also involves extremely complex calculations such as those for stock-based compensation, and interaction with other complex accounting areas such as pensions.

KEY TERMS

Direct deposit. Payment of payroll via electronic funds transfer; an employee's pay is transferred into his or her designated bank account directly from the employer's bank account.

Electronic funds transfer. The movement of money from one bank account to another without the use of paper checks.

Engagement management system. In this chapter, refers to the IT system that captures information about particular client engagements in a public accounting firm, including hours worked, by whom, at what rates, on what kinds of activities, as well as billing and collections information.

Imprest payroll checking account. A bank account used exclusively for payroll transactions; the net amount of payroll payout is deposited into the account.

Job time ticket. A document of the cost accounting system that captures all the time worked on a particular job.

Outsourcing. The practice of contracting with an outside service provider to perform a particular task; for example, payroll, inventory count, and IT.

Payroll functions. Calculating, processing, and posting employee compensation and other related expenses and liabilities.

Payroll master file. A collection of documents, typically electronic, one for each employee that maintains all the payroll information about the employee on a pay period-by-pay period and year-to-date basis.

Payroll processing system. Usually automated, the combination of activities through which pay for employees is calculated, communicated, and disbursed.

Payroll register. A document that lists all the payments made to all employees (and owners) of a company during a specific payout.

Period cost. Costs that are expensed in the period they are incurred.

Personnel functions. Company activities of hiring, maintenance, and separating from employees.

Personnel file. Composed of a group of documents containing information about a specific employee, such as date of hire, pay rate, department, employee number, and withholding authorizations.

Product cost. Costs that are added to the cost of inventory and are expensed through cost of goods sold when the inventory item is sold.

SAS 70 engagement. A contracted engagement between a service organization and a service auditor; falls under the guidance of SAS 70.

SAS 70 report. A report of the service auditor about the service organization, intended for use by the user organization and user auditor; typically reports on the design of the service organization's ICFR (a Type I report), and may also report on tests of ICFR operating effectiveness (a Type II report).

Service auditor. The auditor who performs professional services such as a SAS 70 engagement for a service organization.

Service provider, service organization (outside service provider). A company or organization, external to its customers, that provides a service or activity on a contracted basis.

Share-based compensation. Payment to employees through equity instruments such as stock, options, and warrants.

Time sheet. A document, manual or electronic, on which the time an employee works is captured.

User auditor. Typically refers to the auditor of a company who uses a service organization.

User organization. A company that outsources an activity to a service organization.

W-2 form. A form provided by an employer to an employee indicating various payroll information for the year, including gross wages and amounts withheld.

W-4 form. A form completed by an employee to inform his or her employer about withholding status for taxes.

MULTIPLE CHOICE

13-1 **[LO 1]** In which type of organization would an auditor expend more audit effort addressing whether payroll costs were posted to the proper account?

(a) Not-for-profit

(b) Service

(c) Retail

(d) Manufacturing

13-2 **[LO 5]** If an auditor obtains the computer logs that record when employees check in through a computer terminal at a retail store and traces the names of employees who were paid to the computer check in log, the auditor is testing to determine

(a) whether all employees who worked were paid.

(b) whether all employees who paid actually worked.

(c) whether all employees were paid the proper amount.

(d) whether any unauthorized employees are able to use the terminal to log in.

13-3 [LO 2] Which department should control the information on employees' checking accounts when the employees have provided authorization to the employer to pay them by direct deposit?

(a) Personnel

(b) Treasurer or cashier

(c) Accounting and payroll

(d) Line department for each employee

13-4 [LO 2] Which of the following is not a service industry?

(a) Banking

(b) Health care

(c) Textbook publishing

(d) Public accounting

13-5 [LO 2] Which of the following human resources cycle activities includes direct, legally imposed responsibilities?

(a) Producing personnel documents for employee pay increases

(b) Withholding and remitting federal income taxes

(c) Proper calculation of gross amounts of employees pay

(d) Proper link between employee payroll calculations and the cost of inventory

13-6 [LO 3] Payroll is a commonly outsourced function because

(a) the process is routine and requires limited decisions requiring management judgment once it is set up.

(b) a large number of outside service providers are available to provide payroll processing.

(c) management prefers to delegate important hiring decisions to experts, even if they are outside the company.

(d) the transactions are so complex that an outside agency can typically perform the activity with higher quality than internal accountants.

13-7 [LO 2] Human resources can be a product cost within the company that incurs them if

(a) they are direct labor.

(b) they are manufacturing overhead.

(c) they are either direct labor or manufacturing overhead.

(d) the company is a wholesale business and the human resources costs are for selling activities related to inventory.

13-8 [LO 2] What information would not be included in an employee's personnel file?

(a) Tax-withholding information

(b) Current authorized pay rate

(c) Weekly time and expense reports

(d) Quarterly performance evaluations

13-9 [LO 2] Which department assigns a new employee a staff number and provides authorization to enter a new employee in the IT system?

(a) Payroll processing

(b) Personnel

(c) IT operations

(d) The department in which the employee will be working

13-10 [LO 5] Management's primary concern for payroll is

(a) paying employees appropriately to maintain a good labor relationship.

(b) not paying compensation expense in excess of what is contracted and due.

(c) withholding and remitting the right amount of taxes.

(d) all of the above are management objectives for payroll.

13-11 [LO 2] Payroll cost will affect a manufacturing company's

(a) income statement only.

(b) balance sheet only.

(c) balance sheet and income statement.

(d) income statement and disclosure only.

13-12 [LO 6] When evaluating the adjustments to payroll-related accounts that have been made at year end, SAB 108 guidance means the auditor should focus

(a) mainly on income statement amounts.

(b) on both material and immaterial income statement amounts.

(c) on amounts that are material to either the income statement or the balance sheet.

(d) mainly on balance sheet amounts.

13-13 [LO 5] Effective segregation of duties for payroll

(a) means that changes to the payroll master file can be made only by the human resources department.

(b) can be accomplished if the payroll processing department independently authorizes and inputs changes to the payroll master file.

(c) can be accomplished if the human resources department authorizes and monitors any changes to the payroll master file.

(d) is not necessary if payroll processing is outsourced.

13-14 [LO 5] An important control over payroll that may limit the magnitude of a fraud or misstatement is

(a) monitoring by employees receiving payroll payments and unit managers held accountable for performance.

(b) the requirement to pay payroll taxes and file payroll tax returns.

(c) outsourcing payroll to an outside service provider.

(d) a properly prepared personnel file for each employee with documentation of authorized pay rates and withholdings.

13-15 [LO 3] Using an outside service provider for payroll is not likely to provide

(a) efficiency of processing.

(b) some degree of separation of duties.

(c) a less costly way to process payroll than by having employees "in house."

(d) lower rates that must be paid to employees.

13-16 [LO 3] An outside service provider should not perform which of the following functions of payroll?

(a) Updating the payroll master file

(b) Updating year-to-date payroll records for each employee

(c) Approving pay rate changes

(d) Completing tax forms to distribute to individual employees

13-17 [LO 2] A user company is least likely to outsource which of the following tasks to a service provider?

(a) Initiate information about the company's payroll and information about specific individual employees

(b) Update the payroll master file

(c) Update the year-to-date payroll records for each employee

(d) Prepare and distribute year-end tax forms to employees

13-18 [LO 2] When a company outsources its payroll processing and EFT for payroll

(a) it does not need to establish any ICFR over human resources and payroll because it is now all housed at the service provider.

(b) it only needs to establish ICFR over personnel activities such as hiring and increasing pay rates because all ICFR for the actual payroll activities are housed at the outside service provider.

(c) it needs ICFR over personnel activities and the initial setup of payroll, and then ICFR over ongoing payroll processing are housed at the outside service provider.

(d) it needs ICFR over personnel activities, the initial setup of payroll, and ongoing payroll activities.

13-19 [LO 3] An auditor must consider the controls of an outside service provider

(a) never.

(b) always.

(c) when the activity outsourced is a significant process for the audit client.

(d) unless another auditor has issued a SAS 70, Type II report on them.

13-20 [LO 4] Which of the following is true when an audit client uses an outside service provider for payroll?

(a) The user auditor will be able to rely on a Type I and Type II report to the same extent for the user company's audit.

(b) A Type I report provides no value to a user company's auditor.

(c) A Type II report may, when combined with other ICFR audit work, provide the user auditor with enough audit evidence regarding human resources and payroll.

(d) A Type II report, on its own, will usually provide the user auditor with enough audit evidence regarding human resources and payroll.

13-21 [LO 6] In a large company total payroll expense can be audited by

(a) examining supporting documents for individual payroll transactions.

(b) confirming gross and net payroll payments with individual employees.

(c) confirming payroll taxes withheld and remitted with the IRS.

(d) substantive analytical procedures relating payroll tax expense to other accounts.

13-22 [LO 6] Which of the following is not true about share-based compensation?

(a) Equity instruments provided as compensation have no value, and therefore the auditor collects evidence to ensure that no expense is recorded.

(b) The equity instruments usually cannot be converted into cash until sometime in the future.

(c) The auditor will recalculate the fair value of the compensation calculated by the client.

(d) The company's calculation of fair value is used by the auditor in assessing the appropriateness of disclosure.

DISCUSSION QUESTIONS

13-23 [LO 1] Why do public accounting firms require their salaried employees to submit time and expense reports? Would these same reasons exist in a law firm? How would this differ from the situation for salaried nursing supervisors in a hospital?

13-24 [LO 1] How do management reports produced by a public accounting firm's engagement management system for the current year engagement assist them in bidding on the job in subsequent years? In justifying to the client human resources cost overruns in the current year?

13-25 [LO 4] Why would a service organization choose to hire an accountant to perform a SAS 70 engagement and issue a report? Would the clients of the service organization (in other words, the user organizations) want the service organization to provide a SAS 70 report? Why or why not? What might the service organization consider when it contracts for a SAS 70 engagement to make the resulting report the most useful for user organizations and their auditors?

13-26 [LO 1] Assume the role of a senior auditor on Genetech Corp, a large public corporation that performs evaluations of lab results submitted by physicians and hospitals. You have been assigned the task of planning and performing tests over the client's human resources cycle.

(a) What are the primary processes about which your work should be concerned?

(b) Discuss the types of activities and transactions significant to the human resources cycle.

(c) Which accounts might be significantly affected by this cycle?

13-27 [LO 2] Refer to 13-26 and once again, assume the role of senior auditor on the Genetech engagement assigned to perform tests over the human resources cycle. In designing tests, you are concerned with management's objectives and the associated risks with the payroll function.

(a) What are management's objectives related to the payroll function?

(b) What is the primary difference in the payroll function of a service company compared to that of a manufacturing company?

(c) What role does the government play in a company's payroll cycle?

(d) Why is the period-end so important to proper financial reporting, and what should you be concerned with as the auditor?

13-28 [LO 2] You are in an operations management class working on a team project. Your team is designing a new manufacturing floor for a cardboard processing company. The company uses large rolls of cardboard as raw materials and processes them into finished boxes and cartons used for product packaging by other manufacturing companies. Your task is to describe the way people and machinery can most efficiently interface, and how to control the processes. Your team knows you have just finished a cost accounting class and looks to you for "expert" input. They do not realize that your auditing class might also help you design data collection and control processes.

Describe some ways that the documentation of start and stop times on the machines can be accomplished through IT mechanisms. Give examples of ICFR that should exist for each IT mechanism to be effective and secure.

13-29 **[LO 2, 3]** Flat World Systems is a start-up company that develops computer games. As the company has grown, it has hired new programmers, and processing payroll has become a chore for the owners. Flat World Systems decides to utilize an outside service provider. The owners believe that using an outside service provider will eliminate the headache and probably cost less. They hope it will totally eliminate Flat World's risks over its payroll functions. Respond to the owners' expectations regarding risks over payroll after outsourcing the function. How does the extent of the activities outsourced affect the risks that Flat World retains?

13-30 A service provider has historically engaged a large CPA firm with significant experience in performing SAS 70 engagements to provide its Type II SAS 70 report. To reduce costs, in the current year it hires a small two-person CPA firm that has no SAS 70 experience to perform the engagement. Will this change affect the auditors of the user organizations? If so, what do you think the impact might be?

PROBLEMS

13-31 **[LO 5, 6]** Sam is a senior auditor on the integrated audit of the Patriots Dynasty Corporation and is in charge of designing tests for the ICFR and financial statement audits. You are the staff auditor on the engagement. Sam asks you to make a start on the audit program for the human resources and payroll tests.

Required: Create a chart with two columns. Column A (shown below) lists different types of tests the team can utilize for testing ICFR and financial statement audits. In Column B give one example for each type of test listed in Column (a).

Column A	**Column B**
Tests of controls for human resources transactions	
Tests of controls for payroll cash disbursements	
Dual purpose tests for human resources transactions	
Dual purpose tests for payroll disbursements	
Substantive analytical procedures for payroll-related expenses	
Substantive analytical procedures for payroll-related liabilities	
Tests of details of balances for payroll-related expenses	
Tests of details of balances for payroll-related liabilities	

13-32 **[LO 4]** John is about to start on the audit of Bourdain Restaurants, a local restaurant chain. In reviewing last year's work papers, John learns that Bourdain Restaurants uses an outside service provider for its payroll services. Last year the service organization was treated as a part of the Bourdain's information system, and the audit team relied on a Type II SAS 70 report. After carefully reviewing the work papers, John asks the senior for more information. What information will John receive from the senior on the following questions?

Required:

(a) What is a SAS 70 engagement? What is the difference between a Type 1 and Type II SAS 70 report?

(b) What characteristics should John look for this year to decide whether the outside service organization is still a part of Bourdain's information system?

(c) What must the audit team consider when deciding whether the SAS 70 audit report provides sufficient evidence about the operating effectiveness of controls?

(d) Assume that Bourdain Restaurants has made a change and for the current year obtains a Type I rather than a Type II SAS 70 report. List the audit procedures the senior will expect John and the audit team to perform.

13-33 **[LO 5]** For each item listed below identify:

(a) the answer to the question that establishes appropriate control,

(b) the problem or misstatement that exists if the control is missing,

(c) a test to see that the control is operating effectively, assuming it is effectively designed.

Set your answer up with the three columns shown.

(a) Appropriate control	(b) Potential problem or misstatement	(c) Test of control

1. What is proper segregation of duties between the line, human resources, and payroll processing departments for authorization to input changes to pay rates and payroll deductions?

2. What is proper segregation of duties for authorization to hire and fire employees?

3. What approvals are required on time worked by employees before payroll is processed?

4. What happens when an employee's bank information for EFT is improper and the transfer is not completed?

5. For hourly workers, what is required to verify check-in and check-out at the beginning and end of shifts?

6. How is the imprest payroll checking account funded and reconciled?

13-34 **[LO 6]** You have requested and received the following information from your audit client:

- Number of people employed at the beginning of each month throughout the current and prior year, and their positions in the company

- Pay rate range for each position for the current and prior year

- Budget information related to human resources for the current year

- Payroll tax returns filed, with documentation of the payments accompanying the returns

- Bank statements and bank reconciliations for the imprest payroll checking account

- Payroll registers for the year (payroll is processed and paid once monthly)

- Company policies on sick leave and vacation pay

- Board of Directors meeting minutes

You also have access to the general ledger.

Required:

(a) Design a list of analytical procedures for payroll and payroll-related accounts that you can perform with the above information.

(b) Design an audit program of substantive payroll tests using the above information. List any other documents you need to complete your substantive tests.

13-35 **[LO 5, 6]** For each of the following situations, draft an audit procedure appropriate to address the audit concern. Include any documents you need and describe the direction of the test.

1. You are auditing an agribusiness/farming company in California. You are aware that the company needs seasonal workers to harvest crops and are addressing the possibility of illegal acts related to employing undocumented workers.

2. You are auditing a nonpublic financial services company that compensates management with bonuses in addition to base salary. Bonuses are supposed to be determined and approved by the Board of Directors. Your audit concern is that management may have somehow authorized bonuses that were not approved by the Board of Directors.

3. You are auditing a company that awards employees three weeks of vacation per year and permits each employee to carry over two weeks of unused vacation at the end of each year. Your audit concern is that the vacation pay liability shown on the balance sheet may be too small because of increases in the average pay rate of the company's employees.

4. You are auditing a company that only needs to file payroll tax returns on a quarterly basis. You note that the company was late in filing its payroll tax returns. Your audit concern is whether the late filing reflects an ICFR problem or a cash flow problem.

13-36 **[LO 5, 6]** Tatum and Almer, Inc. is a fashion design firm specializing in the original sketches used by several major clothing manufacturers of women's business apparel. The company has a tangible product, clothing sketches, but the primary input into the product is labor. Only minimal materials are used because all of the sketches are simply drawn by the designers on art paper.

M&M LLP is auditing Tatum and Almer, Inc. Since M&M LLP is performing an integrated audit, it is testing the operating effectiveness of controls. Based on walkthrough procedures, M&M LLP has concluded that controls are effectively designed. M&M LLP wants to include as many dual purpose tests as possible relating to human resources and payroll, since it has to perform tests of operating effectiveness anyway.

Extend each of the following tests of controls for the Tatum and Almer, Inc. audit of human resources and payroll so that it becomes a dual purpose test. Indicate the financial statement audit evidence provided by the test.

Controls Test	Dual Purpose Test	F/S Evidence
1. Examine a selection of employee files for the inclusion of all required documents, authorizations and approvals required, and employee signatures required		
2. Review bank reconciliations; note whether the reconciliations have been prepared, when, by whom, and the clerical accuracy of the reconciliation; observe how accountability for consecutive numbers of payroll checks and EFT transaction number is handled		
3. Compare dates of changes recorded in employee files to the dates the changes are posted to the payroll master file		
4. Select a sample of payroll payment documents and trace the amounts used to calculate the payment (such as rates, hours worked, commissions, and salary) to the underlying documents, examining the documents for proper authorization and agreeing the amounts of the input		

Controls Test	Dual Purpose Test	F/S Evidence
5. Review the file of reports generated on changes made to the payroll master file for completeness, inspecting whether all reports have been generated and are available		
6. Examine evidence that the payroll master file and general ledger are reconciled; use computer-assisted audit techniques to recalculate as appropriate		

13-37 [LO 2] List appropriate steps and documents that an auditor could use in a walk-through of the following human resources processes:

- Hiring, authorizing input of a new employee to the payroll master file
- Change of pay rate, input of a change of pay rate to the payroll master file
- Obtaining employee authorization for voluntary withholdings from payroll pay-out such as medical and life insurance
- Separation of employees from the company, changes to the payroll master file following separation

13-38 [LO 3] Professional Payroll Plus: On a single day in May 2007 six businesses filed complaints against Professional Payroll Plus (PPP). The Florida-based payroll provider filed for bankruptcy. The IRS and the FBI initiated investigations.

When PPP processed payroll for its clients it withheld money for federal taxes. But at some point PPP stopped sending the withheld funds to the IRS and instead kept the money for itself. Clients of PPP discovered the problem when they received notices from the IRS regarding unpaid taxes. Many of PPP's clients had to lay off employees or make other cuts to keep their businesses afloat while paying the IRS.

Using an outside payroll service exposes a company to risk that must be considered by the auditor.

Required:

(a) List specific topics the auditor must address during the financial statement and ICFR audits when the audit client uses an outside service provider.

(b) List characteristics used to define the role a service organization plays in the user company's information system? For each characteristic, identify how it impacts whether the service provider is part of the company's information processing system.

(c) What factors influence an auditor's decision on whether a Type II audit report provides sufficient evidence about the effectiveness of controls at service organizations?

13-39 [LO 2, 6] Apple's Backdating Scandal: Backdating entails dating an employee stock option grant prior to the date the company actually granted the stock options. It was an action undertaken by some companies in an attempt to underreport compensation expense. In 2006, the SEC accused Apple of backdating, and Apple later settled a shareholder lawsuit for $14 million and several company executives paid fines without admitting guilt.

To audit stock-based compensation, auditors must ensure that they have complete information regarding the grants, as well as a level of knowledge and expertise suitable for this complex area of accounting.

Required:

(a) List important issues surrounding accounting and disclosure for share-based compensation.

(b) Develop five audit program steps for auditing share-based compensation, including related financial statement disclosures.

13-40 **[LO 5, 6]** Morrison Company is a manufacturing company. The senior auditor describes the essential characteristics of Morrison Company's internal control system for new staff auditors during a pre-audit conference. He notes that the payroll cycle controls have been deficient, although he has been satisfied with controls in the other cycles. He is concerned since material errors and fraud can occur readily within payroll departments. Some of the deficiencies he details are as follows.

- Supervisors do not review times cards prepared by employees.

- Pay rates, hours, extensions, and withholdings are not reviewed independently.

- After being signed, paychecks are returned to department supervisors for distribution.

- The company does not utilize direct deposits.

Required:

(a) Based on the information presented, what should the auditors do in response to these weak controls? What effects could these weak payroll controls have on the financial statements?

(b) What procedures might the auditors apply in testing the payroll controls?

13-41 **[LO 2]** Ryan Rogers is auditing the payroll of Shields Industries. A majority of Shields Industries' employees are Hispanic. Ryan sees that at the end of each pay period an employee gets two checks. One check covers all the hours worked up to 40 hours and has the proper deductions as mandated by the state and federal law. The second check is for hours in excess of a 40-hour work week and has no deductions.

Required:

(a) What do you think Ryan needs to discuss with management about these transactions?

(b) What audict concern does this raise?

13-42 **[LO 2, 5, 6]** You are beginning your first audit of Suncoast Network Systems, Inc., a company that develops network security software. During your investigation of internal controls you learn that the company's finance department has been instructed by the CFO to prepare a list of proposed stock option grant recipients multiple times each quarter. Also, during this investigation, you prepare a table of stock option grants and the dates that the Board of Directors compensation committee meets, as shown on the meeting minutes. Remarkably, there has been perfect correlation between the grant dates and the compensation committee meetings for the last three years. The CFO has signed Sarbanes-Oxley certifications for the last two years' fiscal reports, certifying that the company's financial reports contained no untrue statements and omitted no material facts and that the financial statements fairly presented in all material respects Suncoast's financial condition. You suspect the worst.

Required:

(a) What does the evidence point to? (You may need to research the rules for stock based compensation.)

(b) What additional information do you need to be secure in your suspicions?

(c) What are the implications for the CFO? (Hint: Is this an illegal act?)

13-43 **[LO 3, 4]** You are the independent auditor for Toson, Inc. Toson's CFO, Richard Moore, contacts you for information. Toson's audit committee has requested that he present a report on the benefits of obtaining a SAS 70 Type I report versus a SAS 70 Type II report. In preparing his report, Richard Moore has provided you with the following two questions.

Required:

(a) How can he best explain the two options to the audit committee?

(b) Moore has heard that the PCAOB has not established any "bright lines" around when a SAS 70 audit report is relevant or useful. Can you explain what this means?

13-44 **[LO 2, 5]** You are performing the audit of Erwin Corporation. Your audit team has begun to brainstorm about the fraud of claiming workers as independent contractors rather than as employees. In addition to knowledge of the employment laws in the state(s) the company operates, you use the session to generate questions related to whether Erwin Corporation keeps required payroll records.

Required:

(a) What are some of the important audit questions that might be generated during this brainstorming session, regarding payroll-related fraud? Regarding payroll-related ICFR?

(b) What audit procedures apply to those risks?

13-45 **[LO 2]** Your audit client, Techno Products, Inc., requests that you conduct a feasibility study that will be used to advise management on the best new system to install that will be used to handle the company's payroll and primary human resource activities. You are technically competent in this area and accept the engagement. Based on the completion of the study, the company adopts your recommendations and installs the system you recommended.

Required:

What are the ethical implications of this engagement and your independence in expressing an opinion on the financial statements of Techno Products, Inc.?

ACTIVITY ASSIGNMENTS

13-46 Go to the PCAOB Web site and access Interim Standards, AU 324, *Service Organizations*. The standard covers important aspects of when and how an auditor should consider the transactions by service organizations.

(a) According to AU 324.02, what is the difference between the user auditor and the service auditor?

(b) According to AU 324.03, what characteristics define a service organization's services as part of the user organization's information system?

(c) According to AU 324.14, what should the user auditor consider when deciding to use a service auditor's report?

(d) According to AU 324.14, who is ultimately responsible to the client for the content and reliance on a SAS 70 report?

(e) According to AU 324.24, what are the two types of engagements and reports?

13-47 Perform an Internet search and identify two payroll service providers. (*Hint:* ADP has already been identified in the chapter.) Research the two companies. Compare and contrast the types of services they provide. Include in your research any financial information, including what is provided on the SEC site. What are the primary sources of service revenue for the two companies? What do they describe about the controls they have in place to protect the user companies that are their customers?

13-48 Go to the SEC Web site and search for any company with which you are familiar that manufactures products. Read the company's financial statement note disclosure for inventory, both in note 1 and other notes. Do you see anything in the note that relates to payroll or the human resources cycle?

ACL

An exercise requiring the use of ACL software is available on the Auditing and Assurances Web site at www.wiley.com/college/hooks.

APPENDIX A: AN ENGAGEMENT TO ISSUE A REPORT ON THE PROCESSING OF TRANSACTIONS BY A SERVICE ORGANIZATION FOR USE BY OTHER AUDITORS

Entities that process certain transactions for other businesses may engage auditors to issue reports about the services they provide. The reports, often called SAS 70 reports, are intended for the use of other auditors. AU 324 addresses these engagements and reports as they relate to financial statement audits. AS 5 provides guidance for their use in an integrated audit.

Organizations and services that might utilize these auditor services include:

1. Bank trust departments that invest and service assets for employee benefit plans or for others
2. Mortgage bankers that service mortgages for others
3. Application service providers that provide packaged software applications and a technology environment that enables customers to process financial and operational transactions
4. Organizations that develop, provide, and maintain the software used by client organizations (AU 324.03)

Outside service providers that process payroll transactions are an example of entities that might engage an auditor for a SAS 70 engagement. The auditor reports produced by this type of engagement do not apply to

> situations in which the services provided are limited to executing client organization transactions that are specifically authorized by the client, such as the processing of checking account transactions by a bank or the execution of securities transactions by a broker…or to the audit of transactions rising from financial interests in partnerships, corporations, and joint ventures, such as working interests in oil and gas ventures, when proprietary interests are accounted for and reported to interest holders. (AU 324.03)

AUDITING IN ACTION

Terms Related to SAS 70 Engagements

User organization: The entity that has engaged a service organization and whose financial statements are being audited.

User auditor: The auditor who reports on the financial statements of the user organization.

Service organization: The entity (or segment of an entity) that provides services to a user organization that are part of the user organization's information system.

Service auditor: The auditor who reports on controls of a service organization that may be relevant to a user organization's internal control as it relates to an audit of the financial statements. (AU 324.02)

Types of Engagements

The service organization determines the type of service and report it wants from the service auditor. The user organizations may provide input regarding what they need or want from the engagement and service auditor report. The fundamental document used by the auditor in the engagement is a report about the controls at the service organization. The service organization prepares the report. The service auditor may actually be the author of the report, but even if this is the case the service organization is still responsible for the report.

In its report the service organization describes the controls and the specific control objectives that the controls are intended to achieve. The service auditor determines whether the controls are (1) appropriately described in the report, (2) designed so that they will accomplish the control objectives set forth, and (3) in place at the service organization as of a specific date. This type of engagement results in a report often called a SAS 70 Type I report. If desired, the service auditor can also test the controls to determine whether they are operating effectively. This type of engagement results in a report often called a SAS 70 Type II report.

AUDITING IN ACTION

Service Auditor Report Types

Reports on Controls Placed in Operation—A service auditor's report on a service organization's description of the controls that may be relevant to a user organization's internal control as it relates to an audit of financial statements, on whether such controls were suitably designed to achieve specified control objectives, and on whether they had been placed in operation as of a specific date. Such reports may be useful in providing a user auditor with an understanding of the controls necessary to plan the audit and to design effective tests of controls and substantive tests at the user organization, but they are not intended to provide the user auditor with a basis for reducing his or her assessments of control risk…

Reports on Controls Placed in Operation and Tests of Operating Effectiveness—A service auditor's report on a service organization's description of the controls that may be relevant to a user organization's internal control as it relates to an audit of financial statements, on whether such controls were suitably designed to achieve specified control objectives, on whether they had been placed in operation as of a specific date, and on whether the controls that were tested were operating with sufficient effectiveness to provide reasonable, but not absolute, assurance that the related control objectives were achieved during the period specified. Such reports may be useful in providing the user auditor with an understanding of the controls necessary to plan the audit and may also provide the user auditor with a basis for reducing his or her assessments of control risk…

(AU 324)

Responsibilities of the Service Auditor

An engagement to report on the processing of transactions by a service organization is not an audit prepared in conformance with generally accepted auditing standards. However, the auditor must follow the general standards and any field work and reporting standards that are relevant. The auditor has to be independent from the service organization but not from all the user organizations involved. The auditor is responsible for the representations in the report—in other words, for all that is stated in the audit report. The auditor must exercise due care in performing any of the procedures that support the representations in the report.

AU 324 provides guidance on what the service auditor should do if illegal acts, fraud, or uncorrected errors have occurred that affect any of the user organizations. Basically, this refers to the situation where, during the engagement, the auditor becomes aware that management or employees of the service organization are responsible for problems in the user organizations' transactions.

The auditor's first action is to go to the appropriate level of management within the service organization and determine whether any user organizations that were affected have been informed of the problem. The auditor must go further if affected user organizations have not been informed and management will not inform them. In this case the service auditor goes to the audit committee (or equivalent) of the service organization. After being informed of the illegal acts, fraud or uncorrected errors, and unwillingness of management to inform the affected user organizations, the audit committee should take appropriate action. If not, the service auditor should consult with an attorney and consider resigning from the engagement.

Performing the Engagement

The service auditor's work on an engagement to report on the processing of transactions begins with the service organization's description of controls and control objectives. The procedures performed by the auditor depend on the type of engagement and report to be prepared.

Service Organization's Report

The report on the service organization's controls addresses controls that affect the service provided to user organizations. Although the report does not have to follow a particular format, it includes the five control concepts that auditors use as the fundamentals of internal control:

Control environment

Risk assessment

Control activities

Information and communication

Monitoring

The description also states the control objectives. The controls are linked in the report to the control objectives they are intended to accomplish. The control objectives may be determined by the service organization, or they can be objectives set forth by others such as users or regulatory agencies. As stated earlier, it may actually be the service auditor rather than the service organization that writes the report—but even in this situation the report is the responsibility of the service organization.

AUDITING IN ACTION

Internal Control Concepts to be Included in a Service Organization's Controls Description

Control environment
   Hiring practices
   Key areas of authority and responsibility
Risk assessment
   Identifying risks associated with processing specific transactions
Control activities
   Policies and procedures over modifying computer programs
Information and communication
   Ways user transactions are initiated and processed
Monitoring
   Internal auditor involvement

(AU 324.26)

Service Auditor Activities for a Report on Controls in Place

When the service auditor is engaged to provide a report on controls placed in operation, the auditor begins with the service organization's report describing the controls and control objectives. If the control objectives are specified by the service organization rather than an outside third party, the auditor must assess the appropriateness of the control objectives. In this situation the auditor concludes whether the control objectives are reasonable given the service organization's contractual obligations to its clients, the user organizations.

For an engagement to report on controls that are in place, the auditor relies on inquiry, inspection, and observation of the service organization's activities. The auditor also utilizes any knowledge of the service organization based on past experience. These information sources allow the auditor to gain enough evidence to come to a conclusion on whether the controls are in place and their design is appropriate to accomplish the control objectives.

The inquiry activities are discussions with the service organization's personnel. Inspection activities consist of looking at the service organization's internal documents and records. The discussions with service organization personnel include addressing any changes that occurred within the past year. If any occurred that are judged to be important to user auditors, those changes should be included in the service organization's description of controls. Examples of changes that may have occurred that should be included in the service organization's controls description report are as follows.

- Procedural changes made to accommodate provisions of a new accounting pronouncement
- Major changes in an application to permit on-line processing
- Procedural changes to eliminate previously identified deficiencies
  (AU 324.28)

The service auditor considers any other information that becomes known if it may have an important effect on the user organizations, even it does not deal with the specified control objectives in the service organization's description. This means that any information that comes to the auditor's attention indicating the following is considered in the auditor's evaluation:

(a)...design deficiencies exist that could adversely affect the ability to initiate, record, process, or report financial data to user organizations without error, and (b)...user organizations would not generally be expected to have controls in place to mitigate such design deficiencies. (AU 324.47)

The fundamental goal of transaction processing is initiating, recording, processing, and reporting on financial data without error. Therefore, anything important that comes to the auditor's attention will likely be included in the specified control objectives.

An additional consideration for the service auditor is subsequent events.[5] The service auditor asks the service organization management if any subsequent events have occurred after the date covered by the examination but before the date of the service auditor's report. If any conditions (1) *occurred or existed* during the period the auditor is investigating, and (2) information about those conditions becomes available after the period under examination but before the date of the service auditor's report, this information is used by the service auditor in assessing the design of controls. If *events occur after* the period covered by the engagement but before the date of the service auditor's report that must be disclosed to keep users from being misled, the information is disclosed in the service organization's report. If this second type of subsequent event is not disclosed in the service organization's report, it should be disclosed in to the service auditor's report.

The service auditor obtains a representation letter from management that addresses the following issues.

1. Management is responsible for establishing and maintaining appropriate controls relating to the processing of transactions for user organizations.
2. The specified control objectives are appropriate.

---

[5]Subsequent events are presented in Chapter 11. One type of subsequent event is information becoming available after the end of the fiscal year but before the audit report date, which reflects on conditions that occurred or existed during the year that was audited. The second type of subsequent event is when something occurs after the end of the fiscal year but before the auditor report date that is sufficiently significant that it needs to be disclosed to keep the user from being misled.

3. The description of controls presents fairly, in all material respects, the aspects of the service organization's controls that may be relevant to a user organization's internal control.

4. The controls, as described, had been placed in operation as of a specific date.

5. Management believes its controls were suitably designed to achieve the specified control objectives.

6. Management has disclosed to the service auditor any significant changes in controls that have occurred since the service organization's last examination.

7. Management has disclosed to the service auditor any illegal acts, fraud, or uncorrected errors attributable to the service organization's management or employees that may affect one or more user organizations.

8. Management has disclosed to the service auditor all design deficiencies in controls of which it is aware, including those for which management believes the cost of corrective action may exceed the benefits.

9. Management has disclosed to the service auditor any subsequent events that would have a significant effect on user organizations.

The service auditor uses the accumulated evidence to evaluate the controls and control objectives. Based on the evaluation, the auditor concludes whether the controls were designed so that they will achieve the stated control objectives. The auditor's evaluation does not go beyond the design for the control objectives specifically stated in the service organization's report. The auditor must consider whether the service organization's report is accurate and the description of the controls that is included in the report is sufficient to be useful for user auditors. The service auditor also must consider whether, in designing its controls to accomplish the control objectives, the service organization assumes that the user organizations will also have controls in place. If the service organization assumes that users will also have controls, this is stated in the service organization's description.

Service Auditor Activities for a Report on Controls Placed in Operation and Tests of Operating Effectiveness

An engagement that results in a report that includes tests of operating effectiveness begins with the activities addressing whether controls are in place and designed to achieve control objectives, described above. The auditor also performs tests of the operating effectiveness of the controls. The service organization decides whether all, or if not all, which of the controls and control objectives, will be addressed by the service auditor's tests. Based on the service organization's decision of what is to be included, the service auditor determines the tests to be performed. This means that the service auditor makes the decisions about the nature, timing, and extent of the tests that are needed. The testing period should be at least six months because a shorter testing period is not likely to be helpful for user auditors.

For this type of engagement, the service auditor inquires about and considers subsequent events that may affect both design and operating effectiveness of controls. In addition, the written representations from management include the following statement: "Management has disclosed to the service auditor all instances, of which it is aware, when controls have not operated with sufficient effectiveness to achieve the specified control objectives."

The auditor concludes on whether there are deficiencies in the "design *or operation* of the service organization's controls that preclude . . . reasonable assurance that specified control objectives would be achieved" (AU 324.47). In other words, this engagement goes beyond assessing whether the design of controls is appropriate for the control objectives to be achieved. It also considers whether the operation of the controls is sufficiently effective to achieve the control objectives. The service auditor uses other guidance in the auditing standards in conducting the tests on the effectiveness of operations of the controls.

Service Auditor Reports

Service auditors' reports are generally referred to as Type I reports and Type II reports. Many components of the reports are fundamentally the same, with differences resulting from the additional scope and conclusions of a Type II report.

Type I Report

A service auditor's typical Type I report is accompanied by the service organization's descriptive report of controls discussed above. Auditors change the standard report for the following situations:

1. When the controls described are not actually in place or the description is inappropriate.
2. When deficiencies in the design of controls are identified.
3. When user organization controls are required for the control objectives to be accomplished.

Other changes are sometimes made in addition to these changes to the service auditor's typical Type I report. When there have been changes in the controls that the auditor concludes should be described that are not included in the service organization's report, the auditor includes them in the audit report. If important subsequent events disclosures are omitted from the service organization's descriptive report, this information is added to the service auditor's report. The service auditor's report includes a statement that the report is intended only for a specific group of users: management of the service organization, user organizations, and user auditors. The report states that controls are in place as of a specific date.

AUDITING IN ACTION

Service Auditor's Report on Controls in Place (Type I Report)

To the XYZ Service Organization:
We have examined the accompanying description of controls related to the application of XYZ Service Organization. Our examination included procedures to obtain reasonable assurance about whether (1) the accompanying description presents fairly, in all material respects, the aspects of XYZ Service Organization's controls that may be relevant to a user organization's internal control as it relates to an audit of the financial statements, (2) the controls included in the description were suitably designed to achieve the control objectives specified in the description, if those controls were complied with satisfactorily, and (3) such controls had been placed in operation as of (date). The control objectives were specified by (XYZ Organization or other third party). Our examination was performed in accordance with standards established by the American Institute of Certified Public Accountants and included those procedures we considered necessary in the circumstances to obtain a reasonable basis for rendering our opinion. We did not perform procedures to determine the operating effectiveness of controls for any period. Accordingly, we express no opinion on the operating effectiveness of any aspects of XYZ Service Organization's controls, individually or in the aggregate.

In our opinion, the accompanying description of the aforementioned application presents fairly, in all material respects, the relevant aspects of XYZ Service Organization's controls that had been placed in operation as of (date). Also, in our opinion, the controls, as described, are suitably designed to provide reasonable assurance that the specified control objectives would be achieved if the described controls were complied with satisfactorily.

The description of controls at XYZ Service Organization is as of (date) and any projection of such information to the future is subject to the risk that, because of change, the description may no longer portray the controls in existence. The potential effectiveness of specific controls at the Service Organization is subject to inherent limitations and, accordingly, errors or fraud may occur and not be detected. Furthermore, the projection of any conclusions, based on our findings, to future periods is subject to the risk that changes may alter the validity of such conclusions.

This report is intended solely for use by the management of XYZ Service Organization, its customers, and the independent auditors of its customers.

(AU 324.38)

AUDITING IN ACTION

Examples of Changes to the Type I Report

Description is inaccurate or incomplete:

The accompanying description states that XYZ Service Organization uses operator identification numbers and passwords to prevent unauthorized access to the system. Based on inquiries of staff personnel and inspections of activities, we determined that such procedures are employed in Applications A and B but are not required to access the system in Applications C and D.

In our opinion, *except for the matter referred to in the preceding paragraph*, the accompanying description of the aforementioned application presents fairly, in all material respects, the relevant aspects of XYZ Service Organization's controls that had been placed in operation as of (date).

(AU 324.39)

Design of controls is deficient:

As discussed in the accompanying description, from time to time the Service Organization makes changes in application programs to correct deficiencies or to enhance capabilities. The procedures followed in determining whether to make changes, in designing the changes, and in implementing them do not include review and approval by authorized individuals who are independent from those involved in making the changes. There are also no specified requirements to test such changes or provide test results to an authorized reviewer prior to implementing the changes.

In our opinion, *except for the deficiency referred to in the preceding paragraph*, the controls, as described, are suitably designed to provide reasonable assurance that the specified control objectives would be achieved if the described controls were complied with satisfactorily.

(AU 324.40)

User organization controls are needed:

We have examined the accompanying description of controls related to the application of XYZ Service Organization. Our examination included procedures to obtain reasonable assurance about whether (1) the accompanying description presents fairly, in all material respects, the aspects of XYZ Service Organization's controls that may be relevant to a user organization's internal control as it relates to an audit of the financial statements, (2) the controls included in the description were suitably designed to achieve the control objectives specified in the description, if those controls were complied with satisfactorily, *"and user organizations applied the controls contemplated in the design of the Service Organization's controls"* and (3) such controls had been placed in operation as of (date). The control objectives were specified by (XYZ Service Organization or other third party). Our examination was performed in accordance with standards established by the American Institute of Certified Public Accountants and included those procedures we considered necessary in the circumstances to obtain a reasonable basis for rendering our opinion. We did not perform procedures to determine the operating effectiveness of controls for any period. Accordingly, we express no opinion on the operating effectiveness of any aspects of XYZ Service Organization's controls, individually or in the aggregate.

In our opinion, the accompanying description of the aforementioned application presents fairly, in all material respects, the relevant aspects of XYZ Service Organization's controls that had been placed in operation as of (date). Also, in our opinion, the controls, as described, are suitably designed to provide reasonable assurance that the specified control objectives would be achieved if the described controls were complied with satisfactorily *"and user organizations applied the controls contemplated in the design of the Service Organization's controls."*

(AU 324, AU 324.31, AU 324[4])

Type II Report

The service auditor's Type II report adds to the content of a Type I report by referencing the tests of operating effectiveness of controls that were performed. A Type II report adds information about the period of time to which the control operating effectiveness conclusion applies, and the auditor's opinion about the operating effectiveness of the controls. If the service organization has excluded some of the control objectives from the testing process, the auditor's Type II report states that it only applies to the control objectives listed in the service organization's description. The service auditor's report addresses the interaction and interdependence of controls at the service organization with those at the user organization. The auditor's report states that no tests of effectiveness of controls have been conducted at user organizations. The service organization's report of its controls is attached to the Type II report just as it is to a Type I report. A Type II report also has attached a description of controls for which tests of operating effectiveness were performed, the control objectives the controls were intended to achieve, the tests applied, and the results of those tests. (AU 324)

AUDITING IN ACTION

Service Auditor's Report on Controls Placed in Operation and Tests of Operating Effectiveness (Type II Report)

Differences between a typical Type I and II report are presented in bold:

To the XYZ Service Organization:

We have examined the accompanying description of controls related to the application of XYZ Service Organization. Our examination included procedures to obtain reasonable assurance about whether (1) the accompanying description presents fairly, in all material respects, the aspects of XYZ Service Organization's controls that may be relevant to a user organization's internal control as it relates to an audit of the financial statements, (2) the controls included in the description were suitably designed to achieve the control objectives specified in the description, if those controls were complied with satisfactorily, and (3) such controls had been placed in operation as of (date). The control objectives were specified by (XYZ Service Organization or other third party). Our examination was performed in accordance with standards established by the American Institute of Certified Public Accountants and included those procedures we considered necessary in the circumstances to obtain a reasonable basis for rendering our opinion. *(Note—at this location in a Type I report is a statement that the auditor did not perform procedures on operating effectiveness of controls and does not express an opinion on them.)*

In our opinion, the accompanying description of the aforementioned application presents fairly, in all material respects, the relevant aspects of XYZ Service Organization's controls that had been placed in operation as of (date). Also, in our opinion, the controls, as described, are suitably designed to provide reasonable assurance that the specified control objectives would be achieved if the described controls were complied with satisfactorily. *In addition to the procedures we considered necessary to render our opinion as expressed in the previous paragraph, we applied tests to specific controls, listed in (attachment of service auditor's work), to obtain evidence about their effectiveness in meeting the control objectives, described in (attachment of service auditor's work), during the period from (date) to (date). The specific controls and the nature, timing, extent, and the results of the tests are listed in Schedule X. This information has been provided to user organizations of XYZ Service Organization and to their auditors to be taken into consideration, along with information about the internal control at user organizations, when making assessments of control risk for user organizations.*

In our opinion the controls that were tested, as described in Schedule X, were operating with sufficient effectiveness to provide reasonable, but not absolute, assurance that the control objectives specified in Schedule X were achieved during the period from (date) to (date). [However, the scope of our engagement did not include tests to determine whether control objectives not listed in Schedule X were achieved; accordingly, we express no opinion on the achievement of control objectives not included in Schedule X.] The relative effectiveness and significance of specific controls at XYZ Service Organization and their effect on assessments of control risk at user organization are dependent on their interactions with the controls and other factors present at individual user organizations. We have performed no procedures to evaluate the effectiveness of controls at individual user organizations.

(continued)

> The description of controls at XYZ Service Organization is as of (date) and ***information about tests of the operating effectiveness of specific controls cover the period from (date) to (date).*** *(A)*ny projection of such information to the future is subject to the risk that, because of change, the description may no longer portray the controls in existence. The potential effectiveness of specific controls at the Service Organization is subject to inherent limitations and, accordingly, errors or fraud may occur and not be detected. Furthermore, the projection of any conclusions, based on our findings, to future periods is subject to the risk that changes may alter the validity of such conclusions.
>
> This report is intended solely for use by the management of XYZ Service Organization, its customers, and the independent auditors of its customers.
> (AU 324.55)

Additional changes to a service auditor's Type II report are made if the description in the service organization's report is inaccurate or incomplete. The changes are the same as those made in a Type I report to reflect this situation. When a change in the service auditor's report is needed because the design or operations of controls is deficient, the change in a Type II report follows the general illustrative language provided above for a Type I report. However, when the deficiency is that the control does not operate effectively, the description discusses a deficiency in effectiveness of operations rather than design, and the opinion language states that except for the deficiency referred to. . .the controls that were tested. . .were operating with sufficient effectiveness (AU 324.39).

In contrast to a Type I report which can be changed to refer to the assumption of controls present at the user organization, the service auditor's Type II report always specifically refers to controls in place at the user organization. This is presented in the opinion paragraph on effectiveness of operations in a Type II report. The language used is:

> The relative effectiveness and significance of specific controls at XYZ Service Organization and their effect on assessments of control risk at user organization are dependent on their interactions with the controls and other factors present at individual user organizations. We have performed no procedures to evaluate the effectiveness of controls at individual user organizations. (AU 324.50)

Conclusion

SAS 70 engagements and reports have taken on added importance in the current environment of integrated audits for publicly traded companies. If a transaction processed by an outside service provider is significant to the company being audited, then the service organization becomes a part of the company for ICFR purposes. Since the ICFR audit requires an opinion on both the design and operating effectiveness of ICFR, the auditor must test the operations of ICFR. If auditors of numerous clients had to test the operating effectiveness of ICFR in a service provider company, it would cause major disruption to the service provider's operations. This potential disruption makes it a near necessity that a SAS 70 engagement is conducted for the service provider and that the engagement be one that produces a Type II report. Therefore, it is likely that more auditors than in the past are both performing SAS 70 engagements and using SAS 70 reports as a part of their audit procedures.

Auditing Inventory Processes: Tracking and Costing Products in the Land Development and Home Building Industry

LEARNING OBJECTIVES FOR THIS CHAPTER

1. Be familiar with inventory activities in the land development and home building industry, including important accounting standards.
2. Understand the activities, transactions, risks, ICFR, and documents related to inventory.
3. Understand the management assertions, purposes of specific controls, controls, and tests of controls for inventory.
4. Understand the purposes and execution of substantive audit procedures for inventory including dual purpose tests, substantive analytical procedures, and tests of details of balances, such as inventory counts and inventory observation.
5. Know processes and procedures performed by management and the auditor for estimates, and specifically for estimates related to inventory.

Chapter 14 Resources

AU 312, AICPA, PCAOB, *Audit Risk and Materiality in Conducting an Audit*

AU 314, AICPA, *Understanding the Entity and Its Environment and Assessing the Risks of Material Misstatement*

AU 316, AICPA, PCAOB, *Consideration of Fraud in a Financial Statement Audit*

AU 317, AICPA, PCAOB, *Illegal Acts by Clients*

AU 318, AICPA, *Performing Audit Procedures in Response to Assessed Risks and Evaluating the Audit Evidence Obtained*

AU 319, PCAOB, *Consideration of Internal Control in a Financial Statement Audit*

AU 326, AICPA, *Audit Evidence*

AU 326, PCAOB, *Evidential Matter*

AU 328, AICPA, PCAOB, *Auditing Fair Value Measurements and Disclosures*

AU 329, AICPA, PCAOB, *Analytical Procedures*

AU 331, AICPA, PCAOB, *Inventories*

AU 334, AICPA, PCAOB, *Related Parties*

AU 336, AICPA, PCAOB, *Using the Work of a Specialist*

AU 339, AICPA, *Audit Documentation*

AU 342, AICPA, PCAOB, *Auditing Accounting Estimates*

FASB ASC 330-10, Inventory

FASB ASC 360-10-05-4, Impairment or Disposal of Long-Lived Assets

FASB ASC 360-20, Real Estate Sales

FASB ASC 810-10-05-8, *Variable Interest Entities*

FASB ASC 835-20, Capitalization of Interest

FASB ASC 850-10, Related Party Disclosures

FASB ASC 970-10, Real Estate-General

PCAOB AS 3, *Audit Documentation*

PCAOB AS 5, *An Audit of Internal Control Over Financial Reporting That is Integrated with an Audit of Financial Statements*

INTRODUCTION

All businesses that sell products deal with managing inventory, both physically and through documents and records. Retailers and wholesalers purchase, manage, and sell finished goods. In contrast, the manufacturing process exists only in businesses that produce goods for sale from some type of input or raw materials. Production requires a greater inventory management effort than is required in companies that only purchase and sell finished goods because it requires processes of accounting for and controlling inventory as it is *transformed* from raw materials to finished goods.

The industry example presented in this cycle is the land development and home building industry. This industry provides the opportunity to discuss auditing management's decisions about which costs should be included in inventory, various methods of tracing and allocating costs to products, important estimations in determining the cost of inventory, and the process of assessing whether inventory has lost value and needs to be written down.

OVERVIEW

The **inventory cycle** interacts with other cycles of a business. In a retail or wholesale business, finished goods inventory is purchased as a function of the acquisitions and payments cycle and sold as a function of the revenue and collections cycle. In a manufacturing entity, the products purchased as a function of the acquisitions and payments cycle are raw materials or inputs to the manufacturing process.

When inputs to production are needed, they are physically moved from storage and into the manufacturing process. Labor and manufacturing overhead are added to the input materials until the manufacturing process is complete. At that point the work-in-process inventory becomes finished goods, is available for sale, and is ultimately sold as a function of the revenue and collections cycle. Documentation at each of these steps is required both to add to physical control and to trace and allocate the appropriate costs to the various items of finished goods inventory. The types of transaction activities affecting the inventory cycle follow.

Move materials from storage and into the production process

Process the goods

Move completed outputs from the production process to finished goods

Accounts involved in the cycle are:

Raw materials inventory   Direct labor

Work-in-process inventory   Manufacturing overhead

Finished goods inventory

This chapter introduces the land development and home building industry, followed by a general overview of the manufacturing environment. After this, the chapter presents aspects of the inventory cycle applicable to most manufacturing entities. Audit activities that apply to functions and accounts of most inventory cycles are discussed. The chapter ends with a discussion of auditing the inventory cycle for clients in the land development and home building industry.

LAND DEVELOPMENT AND HOME BUILDING INDUSTRY [LO 1]

Residential home building companies range in size from one-person entities to large publicly traded companies. The largest companies in this industry are associated with the process of turning large parcels of raw land into completed residential communities. Although what they do does not fit the typical definition of manufacturing, it does fit the concept of producing finished goods. The business consists of acquiring land; planning the community; preparing the land for building; constructing infrastructure (e.g., streets, homes, and amenities); and selling the units.

AUDITING IN ACTION

Land Development and Home Building Business Description

Our home building operations include the construction and sale of single-family attached and detached homes, and to a lesser extent multi-level buildings, as well as the purchase, development and sale of residential land directly and through unconsolidated entities in which we have investments…. Through our own efforts and unconsolidated entities in which we have investments, we are involved in all phases of planning and building in our residential communities including land acquisition, site planning, preparation and improvement of land and design, construction and marketing of homes.

(Lennar Corporation, November 30, 2008, 10 K)

Accounting for inventory in this industry is a complex process. The company accounts for costs related to all the activities that are part of the production process. Some costs can be traced to individual residential units, whereas others, such as the costs of large parcels of land, may be used for various projects in the community. One parcel of land can be used for homes, recreation facilities, and retail outlets. The cost of the parcel has to be allocated considering the types of projects as well as the number of units or size.

Some cash outlays, such as for legal costs and zoning applications, can occur even before the initial land purchase is completed. Other common costs, for example, capitalized interest, require complex calculations to determine the proper amount to include in inventory before beginning the process of allocating the cost across units. Toll Brothers, Inc., in its 10K for the fiscal year ended October 31 2009, describes interest capitalized as inventory as follows:

The Company capitalizes certain interest costs to qualified inventory during the development and construction period of its communities in accordance with ASC 835-20, "Capitalization of Interest" ("ASC 835-20"). Capitalized interest is charged to cost of revenues when the related inventory is delivered. Interest incurred on homebuilding indebtedness in excess of qualified inventory, as defined in ASC 835-20, is charged to selling, general and administrative expense ("SG&A") in the period incurred.

The financial statement note discloses the capitalized interest that reduced revenue as a cost of the sales of traditional homes and land, and related it to the recognition of revenue. The calculations and allocations involved are complex.

Costing Inventory

The land development and home building industry tracks and allocates costs to individual residential units. In typical manufacturing terms this is called **job order costing**. The specific identification method is generally used for costs that can be directly traced. The large home building companies engage subcontractors to perform the actual process of building residences, so tracking those costs to specific units is a straightforward process.

The dollar amounts paid to subcontractors for a unit are included in the unit's inventory cost. Often, the companies purchase large quantities of building materials and provide them to the subcontractors. Since houses are built to plan specifications, tracking the direct materials for each residence is also fairly straightforward. Materials are usually added to the inventory cost of a specific unit based on the actual purchase price of a standard quantity of materials. Multifamily residence buildings such as condominium towers have fewer costs that can be traced to individual units, with more common costs that must be allocated.

Allocation of Common Costs

FASB ASC 970-10, *Real Estate*, defines the proper accounting for inventory in the home building industry. The standard also provides additional guidance for methods of allocating common or shared costs. Common or shared costs can include the purchase price and improvement costs for a large tract of land on which many housing units are built. Other shared costs include preacquisition costs (for example, legal fees for zoning), taxes, insurance, amenities, and capitalized interest. Examples of common amenities are golf courses, clubhouses and fitness areas. FASB ASC 835-20, *Capitalization of Interest*, specifies that the amount of interest included in inventory and allocated among the various units is no greater than the company's actual interest cost. Interest included is based on a calculation of the company's cost of capital during the period of time while the inventory is under active development.

Common costs can be allocated based on the number of units relative to total project units, relative area of space of a parcel or unit compared to the total project's area, or relative sales value. The **relative area allocation method** is generally appropriate when all the parcels of land and residential units are relatively uniform. However, planned communities are often made up of a variety of units with different sales prices. Therefore, the area method may only be most effective for use within specific relatively homogeneous areas of a development project.

For many planned communities the **relative sales value allocation method** is the best allocation method because of the differing types of residential units offered. The inclusion of commercial buildings and recreational facilities in the community can also make the relative sales value method the best choice. When the relative sales value method is used, common costs are allocated to individual units based on the estimated relative sales value of each unit or parcel compared to the estimated sales value of the total project.

AUDITING IN ACTION

Inventory Costs at Comstock Homebuilding Companies, Inc.

Land, land development, and indirect land development costs are accumulated by specific area and allocated to various lots or housing units based upon the relative sales value, unit or area methods. Direct constructions costs are assigned to housing units based on specific identification. Construction costs primarily include direct construction costs and capitalized field overhead. Other costs are comprised of prepaid local government fees and capitalized interest and real estate taxes, and are assigned based upon the relative sales value, unit or area methods.

(Comstock Homebuilding Companies, Inc., 10K, December 31, 2008)

The importance and difficulty of estimating future amounts makes determining the cost of a home builder's inventory even more challenging. To allocate common costs using the relative sales value method, the company has to estimate sales prices that may not occur for years. If the company sells a home early in the life of the total project, before all the shared costs of the project have been incurred, the remaining shared costs must be estimated and allocated. Then, the cost of the unit that is being sold is increased by "its share" of the *estimated future* common costs.

AUDITING IN ACTION

Impact of Estimations on Inventory Amounts at Standard Pacific Corp.

The estimation process involved in determining relative sales or fair values is inherently uncertain because it involves estimating future sales values of homes before delivery. Additionally, in determining the allocation of costs to a particular land parcel or individual home, we rely on project budgets that are based on a variety of assumptions, including assumptions about construction schedules and future costs to be incurred. It is common that actual results differ from budgeted amounts for various reasons, including construction delays, increases in costs that have not been committed or unforeseen issues encountered during construction that fall outside the scope of existing contracts, or costs that come in less than originally anticipated.

While the actual results for a particular construction project are accurately reported over time, a variance between the budget and actual costs could result in the understatement or overstatement of costs and have a related impact on gross margins between reporting periods.

To reduce the potential for such variances, we have procedures that have been applied on a consistent basis, including assessing and revising project budgets on a periodic basis, obtaining commitments from subcontractors and vendors for future costs to be incurred, and utilizing the most recent information available to estimate costs. We believe that these policies and procedures provide for reasonably dependable estimates for purposes of calculating amounts to be relieved from inventories and expensed to cost of sales in connection with the sale of homes.

(Standard Pacific Corp., 10K, December 31, 2008)

Inventory Valuation

Just as with all other companies, the possibility of a decrease in the value of inventory below its cost must be addressed by land development and home building companies. The inventory in this industry is composed of long-lived assets. FASB ASC 360-10-05-4, *Impairment or Disposal of Long-lived Assets,* defines the method used to consider possible declines in value. Estimated future undiscounted cash flows of inventory assets are compared to the recorded costs of the assets. If impairment has occurred, an expense is recorded to write down the value of the inventory.

AUDITING IN ACTION

Inventory Impairment at Beazer Homes USA, Inc.

Our homebuilding inventories that are accounted for as held for development include land and home construction assets grouped together as communities. Homebuilding inventories held for development are stated at cost... unless facts and circumstances indicate that the carrying value of the assets may not be recoverable. We assess these assets no less than quarterly for recoverability in accordance with the provisions of Statement of Financial Accounting Standards (SFAS) 144, *Accounting for the Impairment or Disposal of Long-Lived Assets* (ASC 360). ... SFAS 144 requires that long-lived assets be reviewed for impairment whenever events or changes in circumstances indicate that the carrying amount of an asset may not be recoverable.

(Beazer Homes USA, Inc., 10K, September 20, 2009)

In addition to purchasing land, developers often acquire options to purchase land in the future. This allows the company to limit the current amount of capital it must invest in its inventory of land, while allowing it access to land on which it may choose to build at a later date. After a company acquires land options, conditions can change, causing an increase in cost or a decrease in the marketability of housing that the company initially planned to build on the land. For example, a downturn in the housing market increases the supply of housing already available. In this situation, newly constructed housing is expected to sell at lower prices producing a smaller gross profit. A change in regulations or the assessment of new fees on construction (for example, to build schools, streets, or parks) imposed by a local government, often called impact fees, can make building on certain parcels of land too costly. Consequently, the company may choose to forfeit its option to purchase the land. It then writes off the value previously recorded as inventory.

AUDITING IN ACTION

Termination and Write-offs of Land and Lot Option Contracts at WCI Communities

During 2006, due to the unfavorable residential real estate market, we entered into relatively few new land and lot contracts. In addition, we re-evaluated our land and lots under contract considering the significant changes in economic and market conditions. For the year ended December 31, 2006, we recorded write-offs of approximately $41.4 million in forfeited deposits, pre-development costs and estimated future payments associated with the termination or probable termination of land and lot option contracts. In addition we recorded real estate asset impairment losses of approximately $98.2 million.

During 2007, due to the unfavorable residential real estate market, we did not enter into any new land and lot contracts. In addition, we re-evaluated our land and lots under contract considering the significant changes in economic and market conditions. For the year ended December 31, 2007, we recorded write-offs of approximately $22.9 million in forfeited deposits, pre-development costs and estimated future payments associated with the termination or probable termination of land and lot option contracts.

(WCI Communities, 10K, December 31, 2007)

Variable Interest Entities

A complex accounting pronouncement, FASB ASC 810-10-05-8, *Variable Interest Entities* (VIE), can also impact the financial statements of a land development and home building company. The overall impact of the standard is on determining which investments a company consolidates in its financial statements. For companies in the home building industry, management and auditors must consider whether inventory transactions such as land purchase and option contracts, and joint ventures create a **variable interest entity** under the accounting rules. If so, this results in the need to consolidate the VIE, including land and lot options inventory. Although a complete discussion of the accounting for VIEs is beyond the scope of this book, a thorough understanding and ability to apply it are critical for any auditor of companies in this industry.

Revenue Recognition

Chapter 10, on the revenue and collection cycle, discusses issues of **revenue recognition.** In the land development and home building industry, the relationship between inventory and revenue recognition is direct, as a result of the use of the **percentage-of-completion method.** The appropriate timing of revenue recognition and the amount to recognize from the sale of inventory depend on the type of product and can be tied to actual and estimated inventory costs.

Revenue for single-family homes is recognized when the sale closes and the title transfers to the purchaser. The proper amount of revenue and timing of recognition can be objectively determined. For multifamily buildings such as condominiums, the percentage-of-completion method is typically used. Therefore, the cost of inventory and estimates about the total cost of the project affect revenue recognition.

When using the percentage-of-completion method, the company first estimates the proportion of actual costs incurred in the current period relative to the total expected cost of the product. Then, this percentage is applied to the sales price. The resulting amount of revenue is recognized in the current period. For multifamily buildings, the tracing and allocation of costs incurred to date, along with estimates of total inventory costs, directly impacts revenue recognition.

Inventory in the land development and home building industry presents complex accounting issues. The most important thing for you to understand from this example is that in any manufacturing or production company, inventory is a major focus of accounting and auditing effort. To effectively audit inventory the auditor must thoroughly understand the production processes and applicable accounting standards.

REVIEW QUESTIONS

A.1 Why is it fairly easy for large home building companies to use job order and specific identification costing methods?

A.2 What is the relative area method for allocating common costs in the home building industry, and when is it appropriate?

A.3 What is the appropriate way for inventory in the home building industry to be written down if its fair value permanently drops below cost? What is the applicable accounting standard?

A.4 When is the percentage of completion method used in the residential home building industry and why?

INVENTORY IN THE MANUFACTURING ENVIRONMENT: OVERVIEW [LO 2]

The unique aspect of the manufacturing industry is the process of producing finished goods from raw materials. Manufacturers experience the same types of business activities and transactions for the other cycles as other industries. However, major additional issues that manufacturers must manage include: physical security over inventory before, during, and after the production process; proper authorization for the movement of materials and finished goods; and effective cost accounting.

AUDITING IN ACTION

Toll Brothers, Percentage-of-Completion, and Completed Contract Methods

The following is from Note 1 of the October 31, 2006 and 2008 Toll Brothers financial statements describing the criteria and calculation for applying the percentage-of-completion method to high-rise/mid-rise multifamily residential projects.

2006 Disclosure

The Company is developing several high-rise/mid-rise projects that will take substantially more than one year to complete. Revenues are recognized in accordance with Statement of Financial Accounting Standards ("SFAS") No. 66, "*Accounting for Sales of Real Estate*" ("SFAS 66"). Under the provisions of SFAS 66, revenues and costs are to be recognized using the percentage of completion method of accounting when **construction is beyond the preliminary stage**, the buyer is committed to the extent of being unable to require a refund except for non-delivery of the unit, sufficient units in the project have been sold to ensure that the property will not be converted to rental property, the sales prices are collectible and the aggregate sales proceeds and the **total cost of the project can be reasonably estimated**. Revenues and costs of individual projects are recognized on an individual project's aggregate value of units for which home buyers have signed binding agreements of sale, less an allowance for cancellations, and are **based on the percentage of total estimated construction costs** that have been incurred. **Total estimated revenues and construction costs are reviewed periodically, and any changes are applied prospectively** (emphasis added).

2008 Disclosure

During the past two years, we completed construction on four projects for which we used the percentage of completion accounting method to recognize revenues and costs; the remaining units in these projects will be accounted for using the completed contract method of accounting. **Based upon the current accounting rules and interpretations, we do not believe that any of our current or future communities qualify for percentage of completion accounting.** Under the provisions of SFAS 66, revenues and costs are recognized using the percentage of completion method of accounting for those communities that qualify when construction is beyond the preliminary stage, the buyer is committed to the extent of being unable to require a refund except for non-delivery of the unit, sufficient units in the project have been sold to ensure that the property will not be converted to rental property, the sales proceeds are collectible and the aggregate sales proceeds and the total cost of the project can be reasonably estimated. Revenues and costs of individual projects are recognized on the individual project's aggregate value of units for which the home buyers have signed binding agreements of sale, less an allowance for cancellations, and are based on the percentage of total estimated construction costs that have been incurred. Total estimated revenues and costs are reviewed periodically, and any change is applied to current and future periods.

A strict definition of the term *raw materials* may include only goods that have not yet been processed. However, the term is often used to refer to whatever the input materials may be for the manufacturing process of the specific business being considered. Similarly, finished goods that are the outputs of a seller's manufacturing process may in turn be used as inputs for the purchaser's manufacturing process. As an example, one company's raw material may be wool and cotton that it uses to manufacture its finished good, which is thread. Another company may use thread as its raw material from which it manufactures fabric. Finally, another company may use fabric as its raw material to manufacture clothing.

The first step in the manufacturing process is to remove purchased raw materials from stores. This assumes that materials have already been requisitioned, purchased, and received through the purchasing function before they are needed for manufacturing. In some businesses the purchasing and manufacturing functions are so integrated and efficient that goods that are inputs to the manufacturing process are received only when they are needed for production. In industries that typically store a very small amount of inventory, an increase in raw materials, work-in-process, or finished goods inventories may indicate that something has changed or gone wrong in that particular company. If raw materials that cost $1,000 are put into the production process, a generalized form of the transaction is:

Work-in-process	1,000	
Raw Materials Inventory		1,000

The cost accounting records of the business accumulate the addition of inputs into work-in-process inventory. The source and form of information that goes into the cost accounting system varies widely among companies. The cost accounting system may account for the work-in-process based only on the quantity of units of inputs used or may have cost dollars included. The journal entry shown above is an example of a tracking system that includes dollar amount information. If just the quantity of inputs is tracked at this stage, then cost dollars are attached later. The movement of goods may be tracked using technology such as bar codes, weight measures, or even inventory locations. Alternatively, the tracking system may be as simple as recording the quantity of the inventory item removed from stores.

After entering the manufacturing function, input materials are processed. Typically, human labor is involved in the production process, along with machine time and supplies. Each company determines which costs to track individually, sometimes called **direct tracing**, and which to allocate. The costs that are tracked individually are called **direct costs** and those that are allocated are called **indirect costs** or overhead.

Direct costs are traced and added to work-in-process in the **cost accounting records**. For example, those human resources costs that are traced to inventory production are generally called direct labor and increase the work-in-process balance. The specific journal entry used to account for this transaction depends on the integration of the cost records with payroll records in the human resources cycle. One way to handle the transaction is to post a journal entry, increasing direct labor and decreasing compensation expense after the payroll cash disbursement. In some situations all of an employee's payroll costs are captured as direct labor at the time of the cash disbursement.

Overhead costs are usually posted to work-in-process when the manufacturing activities are completed. Overhead costs are also calculated and posted at the end of the fiscal period for any goods that are still in process at that time. A common method of accounting for overhead is to capture actual overhead expenses as they are incurred in a Manufacturing Overhead Control account. The entry that allocates overhead posts the allocated amount contra to the actual overhead expense. At the end of the year, the net difference between actual and allocated overhead expense is a variance called over- or underallocated overhead. The adjustment for the overhead variance is made according to the company's policy. If $500 of overhead is allocated to inventory when production is finished, just before the inventory is transferred to finished goods, the entry is:

Work-in-Process	500	
Manufacturing Overhead Allocated		500

When the manufacturing process is complete, the finished goods are moved from the production location to finished goods storage, or shipping, or they are otherwise made available for sale. For example, if the business has a physical facility for the sale of goods, the finished goods might be moved to a sales floor. An entry is recorded to reflect the completion of the manufacturing process and to indicate that the goods are available for sale. If manufacturing output with a cost of $2,000 is moved from work-in-process to finished goods, in a perpetual inventory system with cost accounting records that track dollars as well as units, the entry is:

Finished Goods Inventory	2,000	
Work-in-process		2,000

Methods for calculating overhead vary significantly. One consideration is the reasonableness and consistency of the calculation method. Beyond that, a primary concern is that all product costs are included in inventory either as direct or overhead and administrative costs. In addition, other period expenses are not to be included.

Companies must also consider any new accounting standards that may affect their method. For example, SFAS 151 (FASB ASC 330-10, *Inventory*) changed the accepted method of accounting for abnormal idle facility expense, excessive spoilage, double freight, and rehandling costs. The changed standard requires them to be expensed in the current period and also requires fixed production overhead allocation to be based on normal capacity of production facilities.

Regardless of the method for capturing and allocating overhead during the year, differences between actual and applied overhead are adjusted at period end. Again, various methods may be used. Typically, any under- or overapplied overhead is allocated among the inventory accounts and cost of goods sold, or simply posted to cost of goods sold.

REVIEW QUESTIONS

B.1 How does the inventory cycle interact with other business cycles?

B.2 What additional issues must manufacturers address regarding inventory that do not affect other types of businesses?

B.3 What is the purpose of a cost accounting system? What different types of information can be used in different businesses?

B.4 How does the human resources cycle and payroll affect the cost accounting records?

B.5 What should and should not be included in overhead?

B.6 What happens to variances known as over- and underapplied overhead?

BUSINESS PROCESSES, DOCUMENTS, AND INTERNAL CONTROLS

Management has several purposes in accounting for inventory in a manufacturing business. These purposes may be sufficiently different to require different tracking methods and the use of different kinds of information. For example, in order to manage the production process, a company needs to keep track of units of inputs on hand and units of inventory at various stages of completion. This permits the company to have an appropriate supply of inputs to run the manufacturing process efficiently, as well as to have sufficient finished goods to meet customer demand.

Managers may run the company, at least in the short run, using information on inventory units, and cost information only for those items they can control or change. In other words, they may focus on managing variable costs but not fixed costs. In contrast, the information needs are different to be able to produce financial statements according to GAAP for external use. The company needs to track and record the cost of direct materials, in-process inventory, and finished goods inventory in dollars, including any costs of manufacturing that must be allocated (usually called overhead or common costs). GAAP requires the use of full or **absorption costing**, which includes all costs in inventory.

Even within the boundaries of acceptable GAAP, a variety of different procedures can be used in accounting for inventory. Management of a manufacturing entity uses the financial and cost accounting systems that best meet the needs of the company. The choice of cost accounting system is based on characteristics such as the product being produced, volume, the inputs accounted for through tracing and allocation, and the level of IT sophistication. Auditors of manufacturing clients must know inventory accounting standards and thoroughly understand the processes, information system, and accounting methods used by their clients.

ACCOUNTING FOR INVENTORY

Accounting for inventory involves numerous accounting policy decisions. Although generally accepted accounting principles call for inventory to be based on absorption costing, meaning that direct (or traced) and indirect (or allocated) costs must be included, many options exist. For example, cost flows can be accounted for in various ways, such as LIFO, FIFO, weighted average, and specific identification.

Beyond the method of accounting for costs, businesses use cost accounting systems that fall somewhere along the continuum of job costing (or job order costing) to **process costing**. When job costing is used, work-in-process costs are aggregated for each individual inventory item or project. A job cost record is used to document total traced material costs. The job cost record also documents direct or traced labor costs and the allocated overhead or common costs. The file of all job cost records is the basis for the work-in-process inventory account. When process costing is used, work-in-process components are the same but are aggregated based on batches rather than specific inventory projects, and different supporting documents are appropriate.

Overhead or common cost allocations applied to inventory throughout the accounting period are based on estimates. Adjustments are made at the end of the period for any differences between actual costs and the estimates.

Some manufacturers also use estimates for assigning direct materials and labor costs to inventories throughout the accounting period. This approach is called **standard costing**. When standard costing is used, there will be differences between actual and estimated direct costs as well as actual and estimated overhead costs. These differences are called variances. Under standard costing, year-end adjustments must be made to appropriately account for all variances, and a variety of techniques may be used.

In addition to costing decisions, the timing of accounting for inventory transactions varies among manufacturers. For example, when inventory is accounted for using a **perpetual inventory** system, increases and reductions to the units and dollar amounts in the inventory accounts can be posted when the transaction occurs. Under a **periodic inventory** system, dollar amounts of inventory increases are captured through a purchases account. Reductions are posted only at the end of the period after inventory on hand is physically counted. Some companies track the quantity of their raw material, work-in-process, and finished goods inventory accounts on a perpetual basis, but only post dollar amounts at the end of the period.

Another posting method is a **backflush inventory** system used by companies whose inventory spends limited time in each stage. Inventory transactions are posted only at certain points called triggers. In a manufacturing environment using a backflush system, typical triggers for posting inventory transactions can be the purchase of raw materials, completion of production, sale of finished goods, or some combination of the three. Retail businesses sometimes use specific identification inventory systems made possible through scanning technology, or they may have inventory systems that differ from all those used by manufacturers.

All companies with inventory must periodically count the products on hand and adjust the records to agree to the physical count. Inventory is vulnerable to errors, loss, damage, and theft. All the sources of loss are sometimes lumped together under the term *shrinkage*.

Many procedures are acceptable as ways of counting inventory to identify shrinkage and adjust the inventory records. The method a company uses is influenced by the industry, products, and recordkeeping system.

Valuing Inventory

Regardless of the method and process of accounting for inventory, the amount initially recorded in the inventory accounts is based on cost. Whether a company's activities include manufacturing or are limited to distribution, when the balance sheet includes inventory the market value of the inventory must be considered and compared to the recorded cost. When the market value of inventory has permanently gone below its cost, the inventory must be written down. Various methods of determining the market value of inventory and checking for permanent decline below cost may be appropriate in different circumstances. For some industries, such as the land development and home building industry discussed in this chapter, the methods can be very complex and require significant estimates.

REVIEW QUESTIONS

C.1 In what ways might inventory recordkeeping differ when the purpose is for operating management versus the preparation of financial statements for external users?

C.2 How does job order costing differ from process costing?

C.3 When standard costing is used, multiple variances result. Why?

C.4 Why is market value important to the accounting for inventory?

Documents and Processes

Physical security, authorization for the movement of inventory before and during the manufacturing process and appropriate cost accounting are important components of the inventory cycle. Physical and documentary controls are synergistic in accomplishing these goals.

The receiving function that is a part of the purchasing process is the first point at which physical and documentary control over raw materials must occur. Shipments are typically received centrally, a receiving report is prepared, and the transfer of responsibility to the stores department is documented. The person in the stores department verifies that the materials being transferred into stores are consistent with what is documented on the receiving report. When materials are received into the stores department, the raw materials inventory records are adjusted to reflect the receipt. Vendors' invoices are matched to receiving reports and increases to raw materials inventory files before the related accounts payable are approved for payment.

When raw materials are needed for the manufacturing process, a **materials requisition** document is produced in the manufacturing department. This document authorizes the stores department to release the raw materials to the manufacturing floor. It also triggers the accounting entry to reduce raw materials inventory records and increase work-in-process.

The type of *raw materials inventory records* and *cost accounting records* that are used to track work-in-process depends on the nature of the cost accounting system. Whether the general ledger is updated at the time of the movement of raw materials to the manufacturing floor also depends on the methods and timing of the inventory accounting process. As the goods are processed, cost accounting records are used to capture the input of any other direct costs. Typically, these other direct costs are labor costs. However, depending on the cost system used, a company may choose to trace other costs as direct costs. Usually at the completion of the production process, overhead or common costs are added to work-in-process in the cost accounting records as the result of an allocation calculation. After all costs have been added, the finished goods are transferred to finished goods stores and the cost accounting records are updated to reflect the reduction in work-in-process inventory, and *finished goods inventory files*

AUDITING IN ACTION

Inventory Records

COST ACCOUNTING RECORD

Job Number _____10-6.387_____   Date Initiated _____6/15/10_____
                                        Date Completed _____
Department _____Painting_____   Units Completed _____
Item _____Bookcase Door_____
For Stock _____

Direct Materials		Direct Labor			Manufacturing Overhead		
Req. No.	Amount	Ticket	Hours	Amount	Hours	Rate	Amount
10-6.37	$160	17-B	8	$176			

Cost Summary			Units Shipped		
Direct Materials	$		Date	Number	Balance
Direct Labor	$				
Manufacturing Overhead	$				
Total Cost	$				
Unit Product Cost	$				

MATERIALS REQUISITION

Materials Requisition Number _10-6.37_   Date _6/15/10_
Job Number to be Charged _10-6.3 87_
Department _Painting_

Description	Quantity	Unit Cost	Total Cost
Black, Flat	16 gallons	$10	$160
			$160

Authorized Signature _Katherine Black_

are increased. Exhibit 14-1 presents the flow of materials and update of records. Exhibit 14-2 lists inventory activities and related documents.

Potential Misstatements and Controls

The primary control emphases in the inventory cycle are physical control over inventory items, authorization for movement of inventory, and proper accounting records, including proper costing. These controls prevent the loss of the assets, promote efficient and effective operations of the business, and enable the company to produce credible financial reports.

Physical control over raw materials and work-in-process is critical to the inventory cycle because of the significant exposure of the assets. The manufacturing environment differs from retail or wholesale businesses in that vulnerability to loss, theft, and damage is "in house" rather than from exposure to customers and the public. The dollar magnitude of inventory assets makes it important to design physical controls that are appropriate for the specific inventory and environment of the company. For example, small valuable items require more careful and extensive lock up protocols than large quantities of inexpensive raw materials. Everyone has seen a jewelry store's empty display windows after it has closed for the day and all the individual pieces of jewelry are locked in the store's vault.

EXHIBIT 14-1

Flow of Inventory through Production

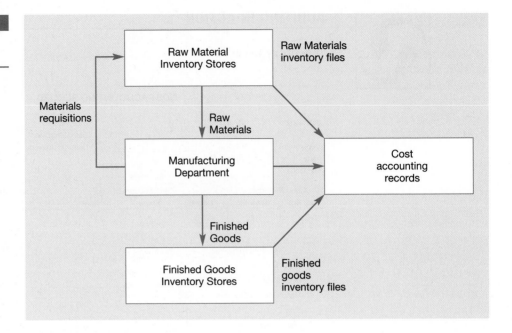

EXHIBIT 14-2

Activities and Related Documents

Business Activity	Related Documents
Put materials into production	Materials requisition
	Raw materials inventory files
	Cost accounting records
Process the goods	Cost accounting records
Make finished goods available for sale	Cost accounting records
	Finished goods inventory files
	General ledger

In contrast, a construction site leaves piles of inexpensive fill dirt and rocks unattended at the end of the day.

An important companion to physical controls is authorization for the movement of inventory, backed up by documentary support. An example is the documents that indicate approvals for raw materials to be moved from stores to the manufacturing process. Documentation supporting the accountability of each worker taking custody of goods provides control over movement.

Even with effective physical custody and documentary controls, businesses experience **inventory shrinkage**. The shrinkage results in discrepancies between accounting records and goods actually on hand. For this reason, companies must count their inventories periodically and adjust their accounting records to correctly reflect the physical count.

Effective cost accounting records and their integration with other aspects of the business is a major control emphasis. Job order systems are often used as examples in an academic environment because they are easy to explain. The classroom summation of a job order system is as follows:

1. Labor records capture the human input to inventory, which is posted to the applicable job's cost accounting record.

2. Materials requisitions capture the raw materials input to inventory which is posted to the applicable job's cost accounting record.

3. Overhead is calculated and posted to the applicable job's cost accounting record.
4. All the inputs on the job's cost accounting record are aggregated.
5. The summation of all the job cost records equals work-in-process.

Although this straightforward description is not a perfect fit for many manufacturing environments, it captures the essence of what is needed by cost accounting records. Cost accounting records show the inputs to work-in-process inventory, including the systematic method for allocating overhead or common costs. The records need to accurately capture the total costs of jobs or batches so that they can be matched against revenue at the time of sale. Updates to cost accounting records such as increases for direct labor and raw materials are reconciled with other records, such as payroll reports and raw materials inventory files. The specifics of the cost accounting documents and records must be tailored to fit the company's manufacturing process and level of technology. However, the types of information they capture and the controls they must provide are generally consistent, at least within industries.

REVIEW QUESTIONS

D.1 On what do controls in the inventory cycle focus?

D.2 What are the purposes of the controls? What do they try to accomplish?

D.3 What source is the biggest threat to inventory assets in a manufacturing business?

D.4 Why are physical controls over inventory assets important?

D.5 What controls are effective for the movement of inventory?

AUDIT TESTS AND PROCEDURES

Management's responsibility for testing and certification for the inventory cycle continues to relate only to ICFR. In contrast, the auditor's steps for inventory include few tests focused solely on controls. Most audit procedures that test inventory-related controls also enable the auditor to obtain evidence about the account balance. Therefore, inventory cycle audit steps are consistent with the cost-benefit goal in an integrated audit of contributing evidence to both the ICFR audit and financial statement audit.

As an example of the concept of procedures affecting both the ICFR and financial statement audits, ICFR for perpetual inventory records must be designed and operate effectively for the auditor to be able to rely on the client's **inventory count** if it is conducted at times other than year end. In addition, if the client counts inventory on a date other than at year end, the count information must be reconciled to the financial statement amounts. The inventory count information is *rolled forward* or *rolled back* to the financial statements based on recorded transactions between the date of the count and the fiscal year end. For this reconciliation to be reliable, the ICFR for inventory records must operate effectively. The ICFR and financial statement audit steps are interdependent.

Tests of Controls [LO 3]

Consistent with other cycles of the audit, the auditor performs tests of inventory controls that examine ICFR operating effectiveness. Operating effectiveness is tested after the auditor tests and concludes on the design effectiveness of ICFR.

Walkthroughs are one way for the auditor to understand the client's information system for inventory transactions and conclude on design effectiveness. During walkthroughs the auditor may also gain evidence about the operating effectiveness of controls, especially for tests of controls that include reviewing client procedures and observing client personnel as they perform control steps. In the inventory cycle the auditor can only use observation to test the operating effectiveness of many of the physical controls such as procedures for locking up inventory.

Some of the audit steps will have been accomplished during earlier phases of the audit, such as tests of controls performed during tests of the company's overall general IT controls (ITGC). For example, audit tests to determine whether the general ledger is properly posted and reconciled with journals and subsidiary ledgers, such as inventory and cost accounting records, are performed for the entire system using computer-assisted audit techniques. These tests include those that address whether inventory and cost accounting records reconcile to the general ledger.

Management's overall assertions continue to apply to all cycles of the business. As a reminder, they are:

1. Existence or occurrence
2. Completeness
3. Rights and obligations
4. Valuation or allocation
5. Presentation and disclosure

In the context of inventory, these assertions mean that all inventory shown on the financial statements exists, the company owns it, and the amounts shown represent cost or some fair or market value if inventory has been written down. In addition, all inventory is included in the amount shown on the financial statements, the methods used by management are in accordance with accepted accounting standards, the presentation is proper, and the disclosure is adequate.

Control concerns for inventory are:

Inventory is physically safeguarded through all stages of movement and the prodution process

Proper records are kept to support the units and costs of total inventory shown in the financial statements as well as to track and allocate costs to the proper jobs and batches

Inventory records are adjusted to reflect the inventory that has been verified through a physical count

Any decrement in inventory value is properly reflected in the amounts

The controls in the inventory cycle that support proper records of units and costs cannot be effective unless the documentation and controls for purchasing, payroll, and sales are also effective. The interaction of the transactions exist because purchasing, payroll, and sales are the functions through which transactions with parties outside the company are initially recorded. Purchases of input materials must be properly controlled and accounted for so that the additions to the cost of inventory are correct. Payment for labor that should be included in the cost of inventory must be properly captured so that it can be correctly added. And sales transactions that reduce finished goods inventory must be controlled and correctly recorded. To understand the importance to inventory of the controls in the other cycles it may be helpful for you to review ICFR for purchasing, payroll, and sales.

The significant audit steps used in the inventory cycle are observation, inspection, examining documents, and reperforming client steps such as counting inventory, calculating inventory quantities and costs, and estimating values. Other control concerns are that all transactions are posted and that they are posted at the correct amounts, to the proper accounts and in the correct accounting period. Exhibit 14-3 presents tests of controls for inventory activities. You should read and study this exhibit to understand the specific controls needed in the inventory cycle and how they are tested.

REVIEW QUESTIONS

E.1 What is accomplished through a walkthrough?

E.2 What are the five management assertions?

E.3 How and why are controls in the other cycles important to the inventory cycle?

EXHIBIT 14-3

Examples of Tests of Controls for Inventory

Note that either management or the auditor can perform tests of controls. Management uses tests of controls to support its management report. The auditor uses tests of controls for the audit of ICFR and to confirm the planned reliance on controls in the financial statement audit. In the audit of inventory, the auditor will extend many of the steps in this exhibit to include examination of the related amounts making them dual purpose tests. The associated management assertion is shown in parentheses under the purpose of the controls.

Purpose of Controls	Company Control and Tests of Controls
To ensure that raw materials, in process inventories, and finished goods inventories are physically protected from theft or damage. **(existence or occurrence)**	
	CC: *Raw materials and finished goods are locked up or otherwise physically secured, consistent with company policies (determined based on vulnerability of the inventory to theft or damage)*
	CC: *Inventory in the production process (WIP) is physically controlled and safeguarded consistent with company policies (determined based on vulnerability of the WIP and security of the production location)*
	TofC: Tour the storage and production facilities and observe the physical security procedures being used for inventory
To ensure that inventory recorded as raw materials, WIP, and finished goods exists. **(existence or occurrence)**	
	CC: *Entries to post raw materials, WIP, and finished goods inventories are based on documentation supporting the transfer of custody of inventory from one accountable party to another, such as receiving reports, requisitions and completed WIP inventory records*
	TofC: Select a sample from raw materials, WIP, and finished goods inventory records and inspect the physical goods for existence and consistency with the category of inventory records
To ensure that inventory in the production process is properly recorded in WIP inventory records. **(existence or occurrence, completeness, valuation or allocation)**	

(continued)

CC: *Documents supporting raw materials received into production and payroll information on direct labor are used to update WIP inventory records*

TofC: Select a sample of in-process inventory and trace to the WIP inventory records and supporting documents from purchasing and payroll

To ensure that all completed inventory is physically moved to finished goods and made available for sale, and that WIP and finished goods inventory records are updated concurrent with physical movement.

(authorization, existence or occurrence, completeness, valuation or allocation)

CC: *When production of inventory is complete, overhead is recorded to WIP based on company procedures; WIP and finished goods inventory files are updated; inventory is physically relocated as appropriate*

TofC: Scan production records and WIP inventory files; select a sample of inventory for which production is complete and examine physical and documentary evidence available showing that the inventory was physically transferred

TofC: Select a sample of finished goods inventory and trace to finish goods inventory records; agree increase in finished goods inventory records with decrease in WIP inventory records including descriptions and dates

To ensure that procedures for cost accounting and other inventory records are appropriate to produce accurate results and that procedures are followed.

(authorization, completeness, valuation or allocation)

CC: *Information from the human resources and acquisitions cycles is used correctly in increasing the costs of WIP, including proper costing of jobs or batches*

TofC: Select additions of raw materials and direct labor made to cost accounting and other inventory records; trace units and costs to supporting acquisition and payroll records (*Note:* The auditor may conduct this step during the audit of the other relevant cycles)

TofC: Select a sample of overhead additions made to cost accounting records; reperform calculation for accuracy and consistency with company methods

CC: *The inventory method used is in accordance with GAAP and is applied appropriately, according to company policy*

TofC: Review company inventory policy for adherence to GAAP; reperform critical calculations for accuracy and appropriate application of policy

CC: *Company policy for making accounting estimates related to inventory, such as estimates of overhead and percent of inventory completion (and standard costs if applicable), is designed to produce reasonable results and is properly implemented*

TofC: Review management policies for making estimates for reasonableness of underlying assumptions, relevant factors, and process

TofC: Review inventory documents and assess whether all estimates needed have been made by management; select a sample of estimates and review to determine whether the established processes have been followed; reperform calculations

To ensure that the process for the physical count of inventory includes proper procedures and procedures are followed.

(authorization)

CC: *The physical count of inventory is made according to management's designated processes and following management instructions*

TofC: Evaluate whether management's inventory count controls and procedures are appropriate and observe inventory count to assess whether they are followed

To ensure that the correct result of the physical count, in conjunction with cost information is used to update the accounting records.

(authorization, completeness, valuation or allocation)

CC: *The results of the physical count (either based on quantities or quantities multiplied by unit costs) are compared to the raw materials, WIP and finished goods inventory records, and the records are updated as appropriate*

TofC: Test the mathematical accuracy of any calculations performed on the results of the inventory count

TofC: Inspect inventory records for evidence that they have been adjusted based on results of the inventory count

To ensure that policies for assessing inventory valuation are appropriate and that they are followed.

(authorization, valuation or allocation)

CC: *Inventory is evaluated for reduction in value at regular intervals and whenever an event occurs suggesting the need for evaluation using established company procedures that are appropriate for the specific inventory*

TofC: Inspect documentation of the evaluations of inventory performed to identify declines in value; reperform any calculations of inventory value for accuracy and compliance with company procedures

Dual Purpose Tests [LO 4]

The discussion of tests of controls for inventory states that most of the auditor's controls tests include investigation of the unit and dollar amounts for those items included in the sample. Therefore, these are dual purpose tests. The following tests from Exhibit 14-3 are likely performed as dual purpose tests. To obtain audit evidence about account balances for the financial statement audit, the steps presented in Exhibit 14-3 are modified with the following added activity:

> **Trace the amount(s) tested [in the sample] to the final compilation of inventory and agree the total of the inventory compilation to the amount(s) shown in the general ledger.**

1. Select a sample from raw materials, WIP, and finished goods inventory records and inspect the physical goods for existence and consistency with the category of inventory records; **trace the amounts in the sample to the final compilation of inventory and agree the total of the inventory compilation to the amount shown in the general ledger.**

2. Select a sample of in-process inventory and trace to the WIP inventory records and supporting documents from purchasing and payroll; **trace the WIP inventory records to the final compilation of inventory and agree the total of the inventory compilation to the amounts shown in the general ledger.**

3. Scan production records and WIP inventory files; select a sample of inventory for which production is complete and examine physical and documentary evidence available showing that the inventory was physically transferred; **trace the amounts to the final compilation of inventory and agree the total of the inventory compilation to the amount shown in the general ledger.**

4. Select a sample of finished goods inventory and trace to finish goods inventory records; agree increase in finished goods; **trace the amounts to the final compilation of inventory and agree the total of the inventory compilation to the amount shown in the general ledger.**

5. Select additions of raw materials and direct labor made to cost accounting and other inventory records; trace units and costs to supporting acquisition and payroll records; **trace the amounts to the final compilation of inventory and agree the total of the inventory compilation to the amount shown in the general ledger.**

6. Select a sample of overhead additions made to cost accounting records; reperform calculation for accuracy and consistency with company methods; **trace the amounts to the final compilation of inventory and agree the total of the inventory compilation to the amount shown in the general ledger.**

7. Test the mathematical accuracy of any calculations performed on the results of the inventory count; **trace the amounts to the final compilation of inventory and agree the total of the inventory compilation to the amount shown in the general ledger.**

8. Inspect inventory records for evidence that they have been adjusted based on results of the inventory count; **trace the amounts to the final compilation of inventory and agree the total of the inventory compilation to the amount shown in the general ledger.**

9. Inspect documentation of the evaluations of inventory performed to identify declines in value; reperform any calculations of inventory value for accuracy and compliance with company procedures; **trace the amounts to the final compilation of inventory and agree the total of the inventory compilation to the amount shown in the general ledger.**

Dual purpose tests provide evidence about ICFR operation and the fairness of the inventory amounts on the general ledger and in the financial statements. As was mentioned in Exhibit 14-3, a number of audit steps are conducted when the company's count of inventory is observed. Many audit steps are applied to estimates made by management that affect inventory. When dual purpose tests are conducted for all of these inventory activities, the auditor is able to efficiently gather a significant amount of audit evidence for the integrated audit.

Substantive Analytical Procedures

Analytical procedures performed in the planning stages of the audit inform the auditor regarding changes in inventory that may affect the way the audit is conducted. Large quantity increases or changes in the composition of various inventory components influence the amount of audit effort required by this cycle. Substantive analytical procedures are also important in testing the account balances.

The auditor performs tests of controls, dual purpose tests, and tests of details of balances. In addition to these procedures, analytical procedures provide a "big picture" view of the reasonableness of the inventory balances that is more difficult to obtain through other procedures. For example, auditors use analytical procedures to address whether the inventory balance makes sense related to purchases and cost of goods sold. The relationship among accounts can suggest whether inventory includes operating costs that should be expensed rather than being capitalized as a part of inventory. Changes such as an increase in the inventory balance, a decrease in cost of goods sold, or an increase in purchase discounts or purchase returns can signal that the auditor needs to dig deeper into the audit of transactions affecting inventory. Substantive analytical procedures can also suggest slow-moving inventory and the need to further examine the value of inventory or possibility of obsolescence.

Inventory amounts are vulnerable to manipulation and fraud. Although good ICFR always makes manipulation and fraud more difficult, internal control is subject to management override. Segregation of duties can be ineffective when perpetrators collaborate to avoid or circumvent controls. The auditor needs to understand the overall role of inventory and verify the logic of relationships amount accounts. In the past, inventory has frequently been tied to frauds, elevating the need for critical and objective auditor evaluation.

Exhibit 14-4 provides examples of substantive analytical procedures for inventory.

| **EXHIBIT 14-4**

Examples of Substantive Analytical Procedures for Inventory Activities and Related Accounts | Compare total inventory amounts with budgets and prior years

Compare gross profit margin ratio to prior years and budgeted amount to deal with over- and understatement of CGS and inventory:
    If the ending inventory balance is overstated, cost of goods sold is likely understated, resulting in an increase in the gross profit margin ratio

Calculate inventory turnover ratio (cgs/average inventory) and compare to prior years:
    If the ending balance is overstated, inventory turnover ratio goes down

    If average inventory goes up, this causes inventory turnover ratio to decrease and might be because of obsolescence (average inventory is increasing because it is obsolete and not turning)

Calculate number of days sales in inventory (number of days in a period/inventory turnover ratio) and compare to prior years:
    If the ending inventory balance is overstated, inventory turnover ratio goes down and the number of days sales in inventory increases

Compare per unit costs of inventory to standards or budget and to prior years |

AUDITING IN ACTION

Examples When Inventory Was Used in a Fraud

Crazy Eddie, Inc.: included fictitious inventory in inventory balances
Health Management, Inc.: overstated year-end inventory using inventory in transit
Leslie Fay Companies: overstated units produced, included phantom inventory
MiniScribe: overstated inventory, misstated inventory in transit
Phar-Mor, Inc.: overstated inventory, included inventory multiple times
Rite Aid Corporation: failed to write down inventory

TESTS OF DETAILS OF BALANCES

Auditors' tests of details of balances for inventory are intended to provide evidence that the inventory-related amounts and disclosures included in the financial statements fairly represent the events and position of the company. Although inventory transactions affect both the income statement and balance sheet, tests of account balances in this cycle primarily address the ending balance sheet amounts. Inventory activities integrate with sales, purchases, and human resources cycles. Therefore, the detailed tests described here not only provide evidence about inventory assets, but also can support or contradict evidence accumulated for other areas of the audit. Many of the tests of details of balances are integrated with tests of operating effectiveness of ICFR, producing dual purpose tests.

The company's physical inventory count and auditor's observation and tests of that process and its result are central to the auditor's assessment of inventory. The count of inventory is a relatively "stand-alone" process performed by the company for the purpose of maintaining the accuracy of the inventory records. The audit process for "observing inventory" provides evidence on ICFR and inventory amounts and disclosures in the financial statements.

In addition to properly recording inventory transactions and adjusting inventory based on the physical count, management typically must make a number of estimates to properly account for inventory. Estimates are also important for other cycles, for example, related to the allowance for uncollectible accounts receivable and warranty expenses. Inventory count and observation are discussed next. The critical aspects of management's estimation process and audit steps related to accounting estimates are discussed after inventory observation.

Inventory Observation

One of the early well-known financial statement frauds, known as the McKesson and Robbins case, involved fraudulent inventory that management included on the balance sheet even though it did not exist. Since that time, various frauds have been identified that involved the manipulation of inventory. Not surprisingly, as a consequence of the early known frauds, one of the long-standing audit requirements is for **inventory observation** whereby the auditor directly and personally obtains evidence about the existence of inventory through observing the company's physical verification or count of inventory.

> When inventory quantities are determined solely by means of a physical count, and all counts are made as of the balance-sheet date, it is ordinarily necessary for the independent auditor to be present at the time of count, and, by suitable observation, tests, and inquiries, satisfy himself respecting the effectiveness of the methods of inventory-taking and the measure of reliance which may be placed upon the client's representations about the quantities and physical condition of the inventories. (AU 331.09)

Management of the company sets up the procedures and is responsible for the inventory count. The auditor evaluates the process, observes, and assesses the reliability of the inventory information based on the process and count.

In the current business environment in which inventory may be tracked using technology, companies often keep perpetual inventory records. These records are used for business decisions, rather than relying on a periodic inventory count at the balance sheet date to determine ending inventory and cost of goods sold. However, even with perpetual records and solid internal controls over inventory, companies must perform physical counts to adjust their records for shrinkage that results from events such as errors, theft, and damage. These counts may be performed at year end or at other times, and often are performed at regular intervals. The counts may include all the inventory at one time, or parts of it. Some companies perform counts on a test basis and adjust their records based on the tests.

As methods for inventory counts have changed, so have audit procedures. For a client with perpetual records and a counting process that differs from a complete year-end count, the auditor observes whatever procedures the client uses and considers that evidence, along with evidence about the records to determine the fairness of the inventory amounts.

> When the well-kept perpetual inventory records are checked by the client periodically by comparisons with physical counts, the auditor's observation procedures usually can be performed either during or after the end of the period under audit. (AU 331.10)

When ICFR and the quality of perpetual inventory records justify relying on an inventory count by the company at other than fiscal year end, the auditor tests transactions that occur between the time of the count and year end. The auditor also reconciles the count result to the final inventory-related amounts in the financial statements. These steps are presented in Exhibit 14-5. The audit standards are very direct in stating that relying on records alone for audit evidence is not sufficient. The auditor must gather direct evidence supporting the existence of inventory.

> When the independent auditor has not satisfied himself as to inventories in the possession of the client through [observation, whether 100 percent at year end or samples at other times when appropriate], tests of the accounting records alone will not be sufficient for him to become satisfied as to quantities; it will always be necessary for the auditor to make, or observe, some physical counts of the inventory and apply appropriate tests of intervening transactions. This should be coupled with inspection of the records of any client's counts and procedures relating to the physical inventory on which the balance-sheet inventory is based. (AU 331.12)

Sometimes an auditor is hired for an audit engagement that covers several years—for example, the current year and several years prior—and the auditor did not observe the inventory in the prior years. This is a relatively common occurrence when a company changes auditors. It is still possible to complete the engagement and issue an opinion on the multiple years as long as the auditor performs the steps needed for physically observing the inventory count related to the current year. The auditing standards suggest tests of prior transactions, reviews of the records of prior counts, and gross profit tests to tie the current-year inventory, for which the count has been observed by the auditor, to inventory balances reported in prior years (AU 331.13). Auditing standards also provide guidance regarding any client's inventory that is stored in a "public warehouse." When this situation occurs, the auditor may use confirmation processes with the custodian of the inventory to gather evidence on the inventory's existence. The auditor still has to test other assertions related to the warehoused inventory, such as ownership and valuation.

Some procedures for the auditor's observation of the client's inventory account were presented earlier in the tests of controls shown in Exhibit 14-3. In addition to providing evidence about ICFR, the inventory observation is also a source of evidence leading to conclusions about the inventory-related amounts included in the financial statements. In observing the client's inventory count, the auditor is accumulating evidence regarding whether the inventory amounts on the balance sheet represent actual inventory and are complete. Exhibit 14-5 lists audit steps commonly used for the observation of a client's inventory count. Many tests of details of balances include and rely on steps for observing inventory.

EXHIBIT 14-5

Audit Steps for
Observing the Client's
Inventory Count

At the time of the count:

Inquire of client and understand the locations where client inventory is kept.

Inquire of client and understand the major types and items of inventory.

Inquire of client and understand whether any inventory owned by others is held on consignment.

Inquire of client and understand processes for cutoff of shipping and receiving during the count process.

Obtain client's instructions for counting inventory. Assess whether there is appropriate verification of counts through the process.

Observe sufficient and proper supervision of inventory count teams.

Walk through inventory storage, observing whether all inventory is tagged or otherwise marked for counting.

Observe that client employees (or others if count is outsourced) performing the count are following instructions. (If the auditor observes that count teams are not following instructions, notify a supervisor immediately.)

Understand the method used for detailing the count, such as sequential inventory tags, detailed inventory listings or handheld computers. Check for the sequential numbering of tags used in different departments and obtain copies of count sheets or other documentation appropriate for the counting method used and any control files including inventory totals and details.

Perform test counts and create documentation of the test counts and results.

- Sample from the tag numbers or inventory lists and re-perform physical count to assess existence of recorded inventory; include items that are large dollar amounts, items with large fluctuations in units or dollars, representative sample of other items.
- Sample from physical inventory, re-perform physical count and trace to tag numbers or inventory lists to assess completeness of recorded inventory.
- Agree description of item on count documentation to physical appearance.
- Open boxes and other containers to determine actual physical existence.

At the beginning and end of the count collect numbering information on all tags or count sheets used and unused.

Obtain the number of the receiving report for the last shipment received and check to see that the inventory was included in the count.

Obtain the number of the shipping document for the last shipment made and check to see that the inventory was not included in the count.

Observe shipping and receiving areas for any inventory items set aside and excluded from the count.

Observe for any movement of inventory during the count.

Inquire of employees about old inventory. Observe condition of inventory for any indications of damage or obsolescence. Look for inventory stored in out of the way places.

After the count is complete:

Trace totals used for the physical count on the count documentation into client inventory records, including classification as raw materials, WIP, and finished goods.

Trace items selected and included in audit test recounts into client inventory records.

REVIEW QUESTIONS

F.1 What kinds of information about inventory can be obtained through substantive analytical procedures?

F.2 How has inventory fraud been used to misstate financial statements?

F.3 What aspect of the inventory audit is mandatory?

F.4 At what times during the financial accounting cycle do companies perform physical counts of inventory, and why might it be different for different companies?

Auditing Estimates [LO 5]

The importance of estimates in accounting for inventory was highlighted in the discussion of the land development and home building industry. Estimates play an important role in accounting for many items in the financial statements. Inventory provides a useful example to present the activities of management and the auditor related to estimates. Estimates included in the inventory process include the percent to which in-process inventory has been completed, the **allocation** of overhead or common cost, and any reduction in value below recorded cost. Standard cost systems are, by definition, based on estimates. Accounting estimates are explained in the auditing standards:

> Accounting estimates in historical financial statements measure the effects of past business transactions or events, or the present status of an asset or liability. Examples of accounting estimates include net realizable values of inventory and accounts receivable, property and casualty insurance loss reserves, revenues from contracts accounted for by the percentage-of-completion method, and warranty expenses. (AU 342.02)

Estimates are unavoidable because:

a. The measurement of some amounts or the valuation of some accounts is uncertain, pending the outcome of future events.

b. Relevant data concerning events that have already occurred cannot be accumulated on a timely, cost effective basis. (AU 342.01)

The importance of estimates has perhaps increased as a result of more financial statement amounts being presented on a fair-value basis. Exhibit 14-6 lists the steps management follows in making accounting estimates.

The quality of accounting estimates made by management is affected by the internal control of the process. In other words, if management has implemented good internal controls for the process of making accounting estimates, it is less likely that the estimates will be materially misstated.

Good internal controls begin with management understanding and setting policies for making proper estimates. Internal controls should also be in place to ensure that data collected are relevant, sufficient, and reliable for making the estimates. Only those company personnel qualified to make estimates should do so. Sources of relevant factors used, the development and reasonableness of assumptions, and resulting estimates should be reviewed and approved by a qualified person within the company. The internal controls should address whether the assistance of specialists is needed. Methods that have been used for estimating

EXHIBIT 14-6 Management Process for Financial Statement Estimates	Identify situations for which accounting estimates are required. Identify relevant factors that may affect accounting estimates. Accumulate relevant, sufficient, and reliable data on which to base estimates. Develop assumptions of the most likely circumstances and events with respect to the relevant factors. Determine estimated amounts based on assumptions and other relevant factors. Determine that estimates are presented in conformity with accounting standards and disclosure is adequate. (AU 342.05)

in the past should be reviewed to determine whether they continue to be appropriate. The results of prior estimates should be compared to subsequent outcomes to assess whether the estimating methods are reliable. Finally, management should consider whether the estimates that are made are consistent with the company's operational plans.

The auditor assesses whether all the estimates needed have been made by management, are reasonable, are in conformity with accounting standards, and are properly disclosed in the financial statements. Estimates are, by definition, related to amounts that are not known with certainty. Typically, they are for items that *cannot* be known with certainty. No single estimate can be determined to be the best. Consequently, if the auditor's best estimate differs from the client's best estimate, this does not mean that the client's number is wrong. The auditor generally concludes that the client estimate is appropriate if it is within a range of accepted amounts that can be considered reasonable.

To determine whether the estimates are reasonable, the auditor considers whether the underlying **assumptions** are: (1) the important factors affecting the estimate, (2) sensitive enough to produce a good estimate when underlying factors change, and (3) consistent or different from the company's experiences. The auditor also assesses the subjectivity of the assumptions and whether they are likely to be biased.

For example, in a company that manufactures computer parts, management estimates the market value of inventory using assumptions. The assumptions might be that the need for the parts, and therefore sales, will continue until the computer they are designed for is replaced by the next generation. This assumption (1) is relevant, (2) will predict obsolete inventory when the next generation of computers is released, (3) can be compared to the company's past experiences, and (4) is objective.

In addition to assessing the reasonableness of the underlying assumptions, the auditor obtains audit evidence about the resulting estimate. This can be accomplished by understanding the process used to make the estimate and testing it. Alternatively, the auditor can develop an estimate independent of management's estimate for comparison. The auditor can also compare subsequent outcomes to the estimate to determine that the amount is not materially misstated. Exhibit 14-7 summarizes common audit steps used for accounting estimates. The audit evidence used to assess whether the accounting estimates in the financial statements are reasonable depends on the nature of the specific items and the evidence available at the time of the audit.

A standard cost system for inventory is a good example of an important inventory process that relies on estimates. When management uses standard costing, estimates are prepared in advance of production for the expected cost of materials, labor, and overhead for each unit of inventory or "run" of the production process. Management may base estimates on engineering specifications, past experience updated for changes in prices, or some combination of specifications and experience.

The auditor evaluates the reasonableness of management's assumptions and the relevant factors used to estimate the standard costs. Variance reports are produced and used in

EXHIBIT 14-7

Common Audit Steps for Accounting Estimates

Review estimates to assess whether all estimates needed have been made.
Review management estimation process and assess assumptions used:

> Are underlying assumptions appropriate?
>
> Are underlying assumptions sufficiently sensitive?
>
> Are underlying assumptions consistent with prior periods and if not are the changes appropriate?
>
> Are underlying assumptions subjective and if so will their use bias the resulting estimates?

Recalculate accounting estimates using management's process.
Independently prepare accounting estimates and compare to the amounts calculated using management's process.
Compare subsequent actual amounts to the accounting estimates.

standard cost environments to control business operations and to adjust financial statement amounts at the end of the financial period. The auditor can test actual cost performance against standard costs, using variance reports and other evidence, to determine the validity of the estimates used for the standard cost system. During the audit of the financial statements, the auditor also investigates how the variances are used to adjust the cost of inventory at year end. The audit question is whether, whenever possible, all actual costs, rather than estimates, are presented on the financial statements.

REVIEW QUESTIONS

G.1 What items related to inventory may need to be estimated?

G.2 What internal controls and other policies should management implement and follow relating to estimates?

G.3 What does the auditor need to consider in assessing accounting estimates?

G.4 What does the auditor consider in concluding on whether management's underlying assumptions for estimates are appropriate?

Tests of Account Balances

Tests of account balances are intended to obtain audit evidence about the fairness of the inventory accounts or, alternatively, identify material misstatements in the amounts presented. Exhibit 14-8 provides examples of tests of details of balances for the inventory cycle. These tests complete the audit work on the inventory balances that are started in dual purpose tests, inventory observations, and the audit of estimates. You should study Exhibit 14-8 and relate the steps to those discussed earlier in the chapter.

EXHIBIT 14-8

Examples of Tests of Details of Balances for the Inventory Cycle

Obtain a copy of fiscal year-end raw materials, WIP, and finished goods inventory files **(existence or occurrence, completeness)**

Using computer-assisted auditing techniques, reperform calculations testing mathematical accuracy including totals, extensions of price and quantity, and unit or batch aggregations; recalculation is based on appropriate application of client costing method (FIFO, LIFO, weighted average, specific identification, etc.); identify any changes in applying the method from prior years

Trace totals of inventory files to the general ledger, including proper classification as raw materials, WIP, finished goods

For raw materials inventory or finished goods inventory that is purchased in final form, select a sample of inventory items from inventory files and examine underlying supporting documents from the purchasing process agreeing amounts (or cross reference inventory work papers to purchases work papers where this step was performed)

For WIP and produced finished goods inventory, select a sample of inventory items or batches from the inventory files or cost accounting records; examine product or engineering specifications if applicable; examine supporting documents for raw materials used agreeing unit costs and number of units; examine supporting documents for direct labor included in WIP, agreeing hourly costs and number of hours included; recalculate overhead using company methods and agree the amounts

Select a sample of inventory items from inventory files and recalculate cost amounts for proper inclusion of components based on the costing method used and client policy such as freight, storage, discounts, and interest

(continued)

Obtain a copy of documentation used for the client inventory count; documentation will vary based on timing of the count, whether it is a sample or complete count, whether different segments of inventory are counted on a rotating basis or all counts are performed at the same time, whether count is in-house or outsourced and manual or automated
(existence or occurrence, completeness)

Using computer-assisted auditing techniques, reperform calculations testing mathematical accuracy including total extensions of price and quantity and unit or batch aggregations; recalculation is based on appropriate application of client costing method (FIFO, LIFO, weighted average, specific identification, etc.)

Agree documentation to audit work papers at date of inventory observation

Review differences identified by the count between physical and recorded inventory

Review and recalculate client analysis supporting adjusting entries resulting from the inventory count, trace components of the analysis to the inventory count documentation, trace adjusting entries to the general ledger

If the inventory count was performed at a date other than fiscal year end, perform roll-back or roll-forward procedures
(existence or occurrence, completeness, presentation and disclosure)

Test additions to inventory by selecting a sample of recorded purchases from the inventory records and examining supporting documents (this may be performed with audit of purchases)

Test reductions of inventory by selecting a sample of sales transactions from the inventory records and examining supporting documents (this may be performed with audit of sales)

Test movements between raw materials, WIP, and finished goods by selecting transactions from the recorded inventory, and examining supporting documents agreeing amounts and classification

Calculate fiscal year-end inventory balances using count date information, inventory purchases, changes to WIP, and sales; compare calculated amounts to inventory records and general ledger for reasonableness, including classification as raw materials, WIP and finished goods

Test cutoff and in-transit inventory
(cutoff)

Examine contracts or other information about transfer of ownership of goods purchased and sold regarding fob shipping point and fob destination

Examine shipping documents for a few days before and after fiscal year end and trace to inventory records agreeing for proper inclusion and exclusion; consider fob contracts (primary concern is for exclusion of inventory for sales of goods still in transit that may be refused by the purchaser at the time of receipt); consider detail about last shipment of the year obtained at inventory observation (if the count was performed at year end)

Examine company documentation of calculations of accruals of inventory costs incurred but not yet paid at year end; trace adjusting entries for accruals to the general ledger

If standard costs are used, calculate estimated ending inventory using quantity and standards data, and variance information from variance reports; compare to amounts in general ledger for reasonableness and see that variances are properly included in year-end balances
(valuation and allocation)

Test ownership
(rights and obligations)

Review consignment contracts and scan inventory records for inclusion of amounts for any consigned items not owned

Review sales contracts for bill-and-hold agreements; determine proper accounting based on terms of the agreements and accounting standards; trace amounts of bill-and-hold contracts to inventory records for proper inclusion or exclusion

Review loan agreements for any inventory that has been pledged or assigned and examine inventory records for proper treatments (this may be performed with audit of debt)

Test valuation
(valuation or allocation)

Review company policies for writing inventory down as a result of impaired value; evaluate compliance with GAAP (for example, use of replacement cost, net realizable value or other value), any year-to-year changes that have been made to the policy, and reasonableness based on any engineering and production information or underlying assumptions

Inspect client documentation of its formal review for overstated inventory value, obsolescence, and slow-moving inventory

Reperform calculations supporting decisions about write-downs or write-offs of inventory and trace any adjustment amounts to the inventory records

Auditing Inventory Disclosures

All cycles of a company's business have different disclosures based on the requirements set forth by applicable accounting standards. In the case of inventory, the auditor needs to analyze whether disclosures are complete and consistent with what was determined as a result of other audit steps. One "big picture" example is the required disclosure for any transactions with related parties. The primary audit emphasis regarding related party transactions is that they are adequately disclosed. These transactions are important to the audit of inventory because suppliers may be related to their major customers through ownership or management.

More specific to inventory disclosures, the auditor will have already assessed whether the costing method used by the client meets GAAP requirements and is consistent with prior years. In auditing disclosures the auditor considers whether the method is properly described, and any changes in the method or the way it is applied are adequately explained. If the company uses LIFO, this includes disclosure of any LIFO liquidations. The auditor will have tested the breakdown of inventory classification among raw materials, work-in-process, and finished goods and will need to determine that the classification of amounts is shown properly in the financial statements, along with information of any valuation adjustments made.

In some cases inventory disclosures are related to other parts of the financial statements. Examples are required disclosures for: inventory that is pledged, warranty obligations, and significant commitments made to purchase or sell inventory.

An example of product warranty disclosure from the Lennar Corporation's financial statement for November 30, 2008 follows:

Warranty and similar reserves for homes are established at an amount estimated to be adequate to cover potential costs for materials and labor with regard to warranty-type claims expected to be incurred subsequent to the delivery of a home. Reserves are determined based on historical data and trends with respect to similar product types and geographical areas. The Company constantly monitors the warranty reserve and makes adjustments to its pre-existing warranties in order to reflect changes in trends and historical data as information becomes available. Warranty reserves are included in other liabilities in the consolidated balance sheets.

An example of excerpts of purchase commitments from the Toll Brothers, Inc., October 31, 2009 financial statements follows:

> Generally, the Company's option and purchase agreements to acquire land parcels do not require the Company to purchase those land parcels, although the Company may, in some cases, forfeit any deposit balance outstanding if and when it terminates an option and purchase agreement. If market conditions are weak…the Company may not expect to acquire the land. Whether an option and purchase agreement is legally terminated or not, the Company reviews the amount recorded for the land parcel subject to the option and purchase agreement to determine if the amount is recoverable. … At October 31, 2009, the aggregate purchase price of land parcels under options and purchase agreements, excluding parcels… that the Company does not expect to acquire was approximately $568.5 million… Of the $568.5 million… at October 31, 2009, it had deposited $78.7 million… was entitled to receive a credit for prior investments in unconsolidated entities of approximately $36.7 million, and, if the Company acquired all of these land parcels, would be required to pay an additional $453.1 million. …

AUDITING IN ACTION

Trade-Ins

In an attempt to increase home sales during a slumping market, some homebuilders took a page from auto dealerships and accepted trade-ins. Trading in an old house for a new one eliminates a burden on the homeowner to service two mortgages and removes one of the biggest obstacles to purchasing a new home.

For builders, the marginal costs to refurbish and sell the trade-in may be minimal, particularly if there is an in-house sales staff.

However, financial statement readers may not expect a homebuilder's inventory to include trade-in models, which may be of a lesser quality or in a less-desirable location.

Homebuilders who run substantial trade-in programs may need to consider providing detailed disclosures.

AUDITING INVENTORY IN THE LAND DEVELOPMENT AND HOME BUILDING INDUSTRY

The land development and home building industry involves a variety of activities, many of which are accounted for using complex methods. Auditors of these clients need a thorough understanding of the activities in the industry, businesses of their specific clients and applicable accounting standards. The audit processes applied to inventory of a land development and home building client are the typical ones of observing, examining documents, and reperforming calculations. Understanding the complex accounting involved and assessing the validity of important estimates requires a extensive accounting knowledge.

Specific Identification of Costs of Inventory

Preliminary activities in auditing land and home building inventory involve understanding and testing the basics of the accounting system for direct, traceable costs. The auditor selects from expenditures and tests whether the direct costs are recorded correctly as inventory costs for individual units. Specific identification inventory methods allow this precise audit testing. Another concern regarding direct costs is whether these direct, specifically identified costs are properly estimated and accrued at the end of the quarter or year.

A home building company may have six to ten houses, or more, under construction at a time. When the sales process works as the company hopes it will, contracts-to-sell the houses under construction have already been executed with prospective buyers before the houses are completed. This means that when the construction process is completed, the transaction to sell a house is executed quickly. In contrast to the quick execution of the sale, there is typically a time lag between when the house is finished and all the bills are received. The company estimates the costs for which bills have not yet been received at the time of the sale to match the cost of sales to revenue.

Estimating and accruing costs appropriately is most important when a sale takes place just before the period end, and bills for the direct costs are not received until the following accounting period. The auditor reviews estimates of costs of sales for the individual units sold just before year end for completeness. Audit tests include examining invoices received in the following period and tracing them to the costs for the units sold. These steps are similar to those for other accrued expenses.

Estimates and Allocations

A striking characteristic of the inventory in the land development and home building industry with which auditors must deal is the uncertainty of many amounts that are included in both total costs and costs of individual units. Auditing estimates is crucial to the audit of inventory in this industry.

The only component of the cost of an individual residential unit that is based on known amounts is the traceable cost specifically identified with that unit. Although the total amounts of common costs already incurred are known, they are often allocated (or divided up among individual houses) using a relative sales value method. This means there must be an estimate of future amounts for which the houses are expected to be sold even in allocating the common costs that have already been paid. And, as was mentioned in the industry discussion early in this chapter, future common costs that have not yet been incurred sometimes have to be estimated first and then allocated to an individual unit in order to match the costs of a unit against sales revenue.

Audit steps to evaluate the company's cost allocations first require audit steps on estimates. Audit steps for estimates of future sales values and costs include obtaining the company's methods for making the estimates, assumptions underlying the estimates, and documentation supporting the calculations. The auditor evaluates the method and assumptions for reasonableness and recalculates the estimates. These estimates are traced into the company's allocation calculations for common costs. In addition to supporting documents for estimates of future sales value and costs, the auditor examines supporting documents for the purchase of common costs already incurred. The types of documents that support incurred common costs include contracts, closing statements, invoices, checks supporting cash disbursements, debt instruments with interest information, and the company's calculations of its costs of capital.

Once the auditor has investigated the estimates going into the allocations and the resulting allocation amounts, the amounts are traced into inventory records for individual units. Just like any other business with job order work-in-process records, the totals of the costs on the work-in-process records are aggregated to make up total work-in-process. Following is a summary of the items likely to be included in the estimating and allocating processes:

Estimates	Allocations
Future sales values of individual homes	Preacquisition costs
Expected cancellations of binding sale agreements	Land acquisition and improvement
Future sales value of a total project	Taxes and interest
Common costs yet to be incurred	Amenities
Total cost of a project	Capitalized interest
Percent of total construction costs incurred	Indirect project costs
Future undiscounted cash flows	

Valuation

The auditor assesses management estimates for calculations related to inventory valuation. Management must estimate future undiscounted cash flows expected from inventory and compare that amount to recorded cost as required by accounting standards. Audit steps for these estimates and calculations follow the same general procedures used for estimates and allocations of common costs.

For units already under construction, the auditor examines sales contracts that have been executed, providing some fairly firm information for making estimates of future cash flows. However, since prospective buyers can cancel these contracts, the company must estimate expected cancellations using current economic information and integrate that information into the estimate of future cash flows. Again, the auditor assesses the company's process and underlying assumptions as well as the quality of the resulting estimate. More uncertainty exists regarding estimates of future cash flows when development and construction are still in the early stages.

AUDITING IN ACTION

KB Home and Countrywide

In May 2009, KB Home was sued by home buyers in a class-action lawsuit claiming KB Home conspired with Countrywide (later owned by Bank of America) to inflate appraisals. The alleged inflated appraisals allowed KB Home to overstate revenues during a period of falling home prices.

The lawsuit alleged that KB Home steered buyers to Countrywide and that Countrywide in turn steered buyers to an appraisal service that was wholly owned by Countrywide. These appraisers would then allegedly submit an appraisal at whatever value was necessary to close the deal at the inflated price.

At one time, Countrywide was the biggest mortgage lender in the United States. In late 2008, it settled a multistate lawsuit alleging deceptive practices in its mortgage-lending business.

Homebuilders need to estimate and consider the future sales values of homes as well as expected cancellations of sales contracts. Auditors of homebuilders then test the reasonableness of these estimates.

Risks of Construction Defects and Long-term Product Problems

Land development and home building companies provide warranties for defects. Just as with the automobile industry discussed in Chapter 12, some of the warranties are passed through to the original manufacturers, such as the maker of the kitchen appliances or roofing tiles included in a residence. Other defects may be associated with the building process.

For example, the worker who installs a window may not seal it properly and water may leak into the building. In this type of situation, the seller warranties correction of the problem. The cost may be absorbed by the builder or ultimately be passed on to the subcontractor responsible for the work. For these types of defects, home builders may have "insurance policies" with outside third parties. Expenses and liabilities for these construction defects are accounted for in a manner consistent with warranties in other industries. The amounts are accrued based on current activity and historical information. The auditor examines the supporting evidence and assesses whether the amounts shown in the financial statements are reasonable.

Another type of construction defect might be called a **latent defect**. These problems are not likely to show up right away. For example, if a builder in Florida did not install enough screws in the roofs in a community of homes, the problem might not be identified until a major hurricane has a direct hit on the community. When the hurricane hits and a high percentage of homes in the community suffer roof, water, and wind damage, the builder may be the target of a class-action suit. When the homebuilder is sued, the concern is not only for the **asserted claim** (the lawsuit already filed) but for the **unasserted claims** (those that have not been filed but might be in the future) that might come from other communities in which the builder also constructed roofs without enough screws.

These types of potential liabilities are certainly related to inventory, but searching for them is not part of the standard inventory audit process. Instead, the auditor investigates claims filed against the company as part of its investigation of legal expenses and evidence collected from the company's outside lawyers. Similar to the concept that construction defects might not become apparent until long after the construction process is complete, in its October 31, 2008 10K, Toll Brothers, Inc. discloses a request for information from the EPA about storm water runoff in its projects.

> In January 2006, the Company received a request for information pursuant to Section 308 of the Clean Water Act from Region 3 of the Environmental Protection Agency (the "EPA") requesting information about storm water discharge practices in connection with our homebuilding projects in the states that comprise EPA Region 3. The U.S. Department of Justice ("DOJ") has now assumed responsibility for the oversight of this matter. To the extent the DOJ's review were to lead it to assert violations of state and/or federal regulatory requirements and request injunctive relief and/or civil penalties, the Company would defend and attempt to resolve any such asserted violations.

Inventory is central to the activities of companies that develop land and build homes. Consequently, the inventory audit activities and findings often relate to balances and disclosures throughout the financial statements.

AUDITING IN ACTION

Chinese Drywall

In early 2009, a number of homebuilders received complaints from homeowners regarding odors and safety concerns related to drywall used to build the interior walls. At issue is drywall imported from China during the height of the housing boom. Drywall is manufactured in the United States, but due to material shortages some builders imported drywall from China. The defective drywall emits a sulfur-like gas that is corroding copper piping, causing respiratory problems and causing homeowners to worry about their ability to resell their homes. Homebuilders need to address these complaints, possibly resulting in an accrual for remediation costs.

REVIEW QUESTIONS

H.1 What are the important aspects of disclosure for inventory that need to be assessed by the auditor?

H.2 "Specific identification of direct, traceable cost is used for inventory costs in residential homebuilding." What does this statement mean?

H.3 Why is the auditor concerned about proper matching of revenues and costs of sales for houses that are sold shortly before the fiscal year end?

H.4 What steps does the auditor follow for estimates of future sales values and costs?

H.5 What documents can the auditor examine to obtain evidence about common costs already incurred?

CONCLUSION

The inventory cycle is unique in its integration with other cycles of a company's business. Revenue and collections, acquisitions and payments, and human resources are all critical to effective accounting for a production business. Even for companies whose activities are limited to buying and selling finished goods, the inventory cycle is tied to purchases and sales. ICFR for all the related cycles must be designed and operate effectively if inventory ICFR is to be effective.

Most of the audit activities for the inventory cycle produce audit evidence about final account balances, even if they also address ICFR. The breadth of product variations and acceptable ways to account for inventory make it almost impossible to discuss accounting for inventory in a way that is relevant to all companies. To plan and conduct an audit of the inventory cycle, the auditor must understand the industry, the audit client's business and accounting system, and the relevant accounting standards.

KEY TERMS

Absorption costing. Required by GAAP and refers to the costing approach that includes all direct and indirect costs in the cost of inventory.

Allocation. For inventory, refers to a systematic method of dividing costs amount the items, batches, or processes that are benefited.

Asserted claims. Generally legal complaints, claims, or charges that have been formally filed or processed.

Assumptions (underlying estimates). Management must make explicit assumptions in creating estimates, and the auditor must evaluate the reasonableness of those assumptions in coming to a conclusion about the quality of management's estimates.

Backflush inventory. System in which transactions are posted to cost accounting records only when certain trigger points are reached.

Cost accounting records. Records that are used to keep track of the inputs added to inventory during the manufacturing and production process and that provide a source of total costs when production is complete.

Direct costs. Any inventory costs that are traced rather than allocated.

Direct tracing. Term used to describe costs that are identified with the individual units, batches, or processes on which they are used, in contrast to indirect costs which are allocated.

Indirect costs. Any inventory costs that are allocated.

Inventory count. A process conducted under the direction of management of a company to physically count the units of inventory on hand.

Inventory cycle. The set of business processes and accounting activities that begins when raw materials are requisitioned from storage and ends when finished goods are ready for sale.

Inventory observation. Describes an audit procedure; the auditor observes the client's inventory count, performs test counts, and reconciles the records used on the count day to the client's books and records as a means of obtaining audit evidence about inventory.

Inventory shrinkage. The loss of inventory that results from a variety of factors such as waste, damage, and theft; because of shrinkage, physical inventory must actually be counted so that the inventory records can be adjusted to reflect the actual amount on hand.

Job order costing. A costing approach in which the costs of an individual item of inventory are traced or allocated to that item.

Latent defects. Quality problems in inventory that may not be discovered until a much later date, usually as the result of some event.

Materials requisition. A document used to request materials from stores to be used in the production process.

Overhead costs. Another term for indirect costs; refers to costs that are not directly traced to inventory; typically includes the cost of the building, equipment, supervisory labor, and other costs directly related to the manufacture or production of the inventory.

Percentage-of-completion method. For long-term projects, revenue is recognized and matched by a proportionate amount of inventory costs in a period before the project is complete; the amount recognized is based on the estimate of the percent of project completion that occurred during the period.

Periodic inventory. Reductions of inventory are not posted during the year; the only way to determine inventory on hand and cost of goods sold is to count inventory and back into the amount of cost of goods sold.

Perpetual inventory. Inventory records are kept current and are posted for both additions and reductions.

Process costing. A costing approach in which the costs of a batch of inventory are traced or allocated to the batch; the cost of an individual item is usually based on its percentage of the batch costs.

Relative area allocation method. A method of costing inventory in the land development and home building inventory; the costs of units of inventory are estimated by dividing the cost of a complete parcel among its subparts based on the area of each subpart relative to the area of the entire parcel.

Relative sales value allocation method. A method of costing inventory in the land development and home building inventory; the costs of units of inventory are estimated by allocating the cost of a complete parcel of land to the subparts based on the estimated sales value of each inventory item relative to the estimated sales value of the entire parcel.

Revenue recognition. Booking revenue; should occur when performance is complete and collection is reasonably certain.

Standard costing. When an estimate is used to add costs to inventory for direct as well as overhead costs during the year while the inventory is being produced; results in variances for direct costs as well as overhead that must be handled at the end of the year.

Unasserted claims. Potential complaints, claims, or charges of which the defending party is aware but that have not been formally filed or processed.

Variable interest entities. Entities set up for a particular purpose that must be consolidated into the financial statements of an entity that is a primary beneficiary, whether or not that entity owns a majority.

Walkthrough. An audit procedure in which the auditor follows a transaction from inception through to the financial statements; involves observation, inquiry, and reperformance; useful for understanding the client's transactions, accounting system, and ICFR and for assessing design effectiveness.

MULTIPLE CHOICE

14-1 [LO 2] Cost accounting records can keep track of

(a) only unit counts of inventory.

(b) only dollar amounts of inventory.

(c) units and/or dollars of inventory.

(d) none of the above.

14-2 [LO 2] When auditing overhead for inventory in a manufacturing environment, the auditor's primary concern is:

(a) All appropriate costs are included in overhead.

(b) Period expenses are not included in overhead.

(c) Overhead is captured and calculated properly according to GAAP, is consistent with prior years, and is reasonable.

(d) All of the above.

14-3 [LO 2] Which of the following is true about inventory?

(a) When a company uses a perpetual inventory system, it does not have to perform a periodic inventory count.

(b) When a company uses a backflush inventory system, it does not have to perform a period inventory count.

(c) When a company uses a pure job order cost system, it does not have to perform a periodic inventory count.

(d) All companies with inventory have to conduct a period inventory count.

14-4 [LO 3] Which of the following is not an important control of the inventory cycle?

(a) Proper documentary support for cash disbursements

(b) Physical security

(c) Authorization for movement

(d) Appropriate cost accounting records

14-5 [LO 2] The document used to authorize the release of raw materials to the manufacturing floor is

(a) materials order.

(b) materials requisition.

(c) manufacturing order.

(d) inventory authorization.

14-6 [LO 3] Appropriate and effective physical control over raw materials and work-in-process inventory in a manufacturing environment

(a) must protect against threats from customers and public as well as those "in house."

(b) is important regardless of the value of the item.

(c) may differ significantly based on the value and physical characteristics of the item.

(d) is less important than in a retail environment.

14-7 **[LO 4]** When an audit client counts inventory at a time other than year end,

(a) periodic inventory records must be effective.

(b) ICFR for inventory can be less than effective in design as long as it operates effectively.

(c) the count must be rolled back or rolled forward to the fiscal year end.

(d) year-end inventory must be estimated since it cannot be reconciled to the records.

14-8 **[LO 3]** The operating effectiveness of which of the following controls must be tested by observation?

(a) Physically locking up inventory

(b) Properly posting cost accounting records based on source documents

(c) Allocating of overhead to inventory using an appropriate method

(d) Writing down inventory from cost to market as appropriate

14-9 **[LO 4]** Which of the following are audited by recalculation?

(a) Count of physical inventory

(b) Adjustment of records based on inventory count

(c) Company policy for accounting estimates

(d) Calculations of costs based on results of the inventory count

14-10 **[LO 3]** _____ sets up the procedures and is responsible for the inventory count.

(a) The audit team

(b) Management

(c) The audit team supervised by management

(d) Management supervised by the audit team

14-11 **[LO 4]** When a client has a perpetual inventory system with effective ICFR, the auditor

(a) still must make or observe some physical counts of inventory.

(b) can rely on records alone.

(c) can rely on records in combination with the client's physical count and does not need to observe the count.

(d) must confirm the inventory quantity with the warehouse custodian.

14-12 **[LO 4]** The auditor's observation of the client's inventory

(a) is limited to watching client employees count.

(b) involves only recounting a selection of items on a test basis.

(c) includes understanding and observing the count, and recounts of samples only.

(d) includes understanding and observing the count, recounts of samples, and tracing count results into records after the count is completed.

14-13 **[LO 5]** When the auditor considers estimates included in the financial statements,

(a) management assumptions are accepted.

(b) management's assumptions are evaluated for reasonableness.

(c) the auditor's assumptions are the starting point for considering appropriateness of estimated amounts.

(d) assumptions of outside experts are the basis for determining reasonableness of estimated amounts.

14-14 **[LO 5]** When auditing estimates, a guiding consideration is:

(a) If the auditor's best estimate differs from the client's best estimate, this does not mean that the client's number is wrong.

(b) There is always a single amount that can be determined to be the best estimate.

(c) There is usually no objective, verifiable information about the estimate available to the auditor.

(d) Methods that have been used in the past are considered acceptable for the current year.

14-15 **[LO 2]** For retail and wholesale businesses, the most important inventory account is

(a) finished goods merchandise.

(b) work-in-process inventory.

(c) raw materials.

(d) All are important.

14-16 **[LO 2]** In a manufacturing company that produces identical batches of goods for distribution to various discount stores, the inventory and warehousing cycle begins with

(a) the receipt of the customer's order.

(b) the completion of production of a customer's order.

(c) the initiation of production of a customer's order.

(d) the acquisition of raw materials for production of an order.

14-17 **[LO 3]** Companies need physical controls over their inventory assets. Which of the following is NOT a physical control?

(a) Perpetual inventory master files

(b) Segregated, limited-access storage areas

(c) Custody of assets assigned to specific responsible individuals

(d) Approved prenumbered documents for authorizing movement of inventory

14-18 **[LO 4]** The audit of disclosure for inventory includes examining

(a) whether the use of a master list of vendors is disclosed.

(b) the explanation in the notes to the financial statement of the volume of inventory held compared to the volume of inventory held by competitors.

(c) whether the GAAP cost method used is properly described and any changes in the method of using it are explained.

(d) only inventory information presented on a "stand-alone" basis since the disclosure cannot be evaluated in relationship to other financial statement disclosures.

DISCUSSION QUESTIONS

14-19 **[LO 1]** Briefly explain why an auditor of clients in the land development and home building industry needs a thorough understanding of the following accounting standards and methods. How do they impact the audit of inventory in the land development and home building industry?

(a) Allocation methods

(b) Asset impairment

(c) Variable interest entities

(d) Percentage of completion revenue recognition

14-20 **[LO 2]** Why are controls in the purchasing, payroll, and sales cycles important to the audit of inventory?

14-21 **[LO 4]** The chapter presents various ways inventory accounts have been used to perpetrate financial statement fraud. Explain how the following inventory misstatements would cause the financial statements to also be misstated, and what audit procedures might be used to catch these misstatements.

(a) Overstate ending inventory.

(b) Overstate inventory in transit.

(c) Fail to write inventory down from cost to market.

14-22 **[LO 5]** Explain how auditing inventory of a company with a standard cost system requires an audit of estimates. What are the estimates? What procedures would the auditor perform related to variances produced by the system at year end? Why?

14-23 **[LO 1]** What estimates are included in the cost of inventory in the land development and home building industry? Specifically, what past costs are allocated? What future amounts must be predicted? What future amounts must be predicted and allocated? Distinguish between revenue amounts and costs.

14-24 **[LO 5]** What are the steps an auditor follows for estimates such as those described in Question 14-23?

14-25 **[LO 1]** How does the auditor investigate the client's application of the accounting standard on asset impairment to inventory in the land development and home building industry? Would the audit procedures be different for auditing impairment issues related to a company's fixed assets?

14-26 **[LO 3,4]** The following audit procedures relate to tests of details of balances for inventory:

For raw materials inventory or finished goods inventory that is purchased in final form, select a sample of inventory items from inventory files and examine underlying supporting documents from the purchasing process, agreeing amounts (or cross reference inventory work papers to purchases work papers where this step was performed).

Required:

For these procedures, explain how the steps might be extended so that the evidence contributes to the:

(a) ICFR audited related to purchasing.

(b) ICFR audit related to inventory.

(c) ICFR audit related to sales.

(d) auditor's inventory observation.

14-27 **[LO 3, 4]** The following audit steps test ownership of inventory.

> Review consignment contracts and scan inventory records for inclusion of amounts for any consigned items not owned.
>
> Review sales contracts for bill-and-hold agreements; determine proper accounting based on terms of the agreements and accounting standards; trace amounts of bill-and-hold contracts to inventory records for proper inclusion or exclusion.
>
> Review loan agreements for any inventory that has been pledged or assigned and examine inventory records for proper treatments (this may be performed with audit of debt).

Required:

What information might these procedures provide the auditor regarding:

(a) management integrity?

(b) going concern?

(c) fraud risk?

(d) quality of choice of accounting principals used?

(e) quality of financial statement disclosure?

PROBLEMS

14-28 **[LO 2]** Golden Manufacturing, Inc. is a large public company that manufactures and distributes a variety of handheld electronic devices. The company purchases a large quantity of raw materials in advance because it receives substantial volume discounts from its suppliers. Upon delivery of the raw materials, the storage warehouse manager fills out a receiving report and sends a copy to the accounting department. The raw materials are kept in the storage warehouse until the storage warehouse manager approves the release of raw materials after receiving a materials requisition form. During the manufacturing process, all documents that support the use of raw materials and direct labor that go into the products are forwarded to the accounting department for entry into the accounting system. After the product is completed, the finished good is transferred to the finished goods warehouse. The finished goods warehouse is locked up at the end of every day.

Required:

Fill out the columns below. Identify the specific company controls in the example above. For each control, state the purpose(s) of the control and the related management assertion(s).

Control	Control's Purpose	Management Assertions

14-29 **[LO 4]** Your client, Carson Electronics, Inc., is a wholesaler that distributes computer chips to major retailers around the world. Since the gross profit margin is normally low in this industry, the company makes large discounted purchases of every item in its inventory. In addition, it is normal for items in its inventory to become outdated with the release of new technology. Selected financial statement information for Carson Electronics, Inc. for the last three years is as follows:

(in millions)	2008	2009	2010
Sales	148.8	160.7	136.2
COGS	137.1	147.8	114.5
Beginning Inventory	522.0	545.3	586.3
Ending Inventory	545.3	586.3	558.4
Purchases	160.4	188.8	58.5
Operating Expenses	2.5	2.7	1.1

Additional Information:

1. The number of units sold for 2008, 2009, and 2010 are 457,000, 492,667, and 392,000, respectively.
2. The number of units from the inventory count at year end for 2008, 2009, and 2010 are 2,519,000, 2,655,666, and 2,495,000, respectively.
3. The company did not write off any inventory during the three years.

Required:

(a) Explain the possible misstatement that is being tested by each of the following analytical procedures. Compare:
   1. gross margin percentage with previous years.
   2. the per unit cost of inventory with previous years.
   3. the number of days sales in inventory with previous years.
   4. the current year manufacturing costs with previous years.
   5. the inventory turnover ratio with previous years.

(b) Perform the analytical procedures in (a) for the inventory activities of the company for the years provided.

(c) Explain what the results of the analytical procedures could indicate with regard to the balances of inventory and cost of goods sold.

14-30 **[LO 4]** Ballpark Distributors, Inc. is a large public company with a calendar year end that distributes sports memorabilia to various retailers. Ballpark conducted an inventory count on November 30 of the year being audited. Instead of conducting another inventory count at year end, the company decided to estimate the year-end inventory using a sample of the year-end inventory on hand. The company uses a perpetual inventory system and feels that sampling to estimate the year-end inventory will produce a reliable financial statement amount.

Required:

Assume that the auditor observed and tested Ballpark's physical inventory count on November 30, and was satisfied that the count and resulting adjustments produced an appropriate inventory account balance on November 30.

(a) What roll-forward procedures between the inventory count date and year end might the auditor perform?

(b) What additional tests of details of balances can the auditor perform?

14-31 **[LO 2, 3, 4]** Tests of account balances are intended to obtain audit evidence about the fairness of the inventory accounts or, alternatively, identify material misstatements in the amounts presented. Audit procedures can only be selected after the auditor determines specific audit objectives related to management assertions.

Management Assertions

1. Existence or occurrence
2. Completeness
3. Rights and obligations
4. Valuation or allocation
5. Presentation and disclosure

Required:

For each audit procedure below, identify the related management assertion(s) that the audit procedure tests and explain the audit objective of the procedure.

(a) Trace totals of inventory files to the general ledger, including proper classification as raw materials, WIP, or finished goods.

(b) Test additions to inventory by selecting a sample of recorded purchases from the inventory records and examining supporting documents.

(c) Review consignment contracts and scan inventory records for inclusion of amounts for any consigned items not owned.

(d) Reperform calculations supporting decisions about write-downs or write-offs of inventory and trace any adjustment amounts to the inventory records.

(e) Using computer-assisted auditing techniques reperform calculations testing mathematical accuracy, including totals extensions of price and quantity and unit or batch aggregations; recalculation is based on appropriate application of the client costing method (FIFO, LIFO, weighted average, specific identification, etc.).

14-32 **[LO 5]** Your client, Cardinal Homes Corp., is a large residential real estate developer that currently has over 100 projects in process across the Southeast of the United States. Similar to most companies in the land development and home building industry, the company must make many estimates in preparation of its financial statements. Below is an excerpt from Cardinal Homes's 2009 annual report (10-K):

> These estimates include, but are not limited to, those related to the recognition of income and expenses; impairment of assets; estimates of future improvement and amenity costs; estimates of sales levels and sales prices; capitalization of costs to inventory; provisions for litigation, insurance and warranty costs; cost of complying with government regulations; and income taxes.

You are a senior associate and this is your third year on the Cardinal Homes engagement. You have never performed the audit steps for the estimations, but this year you were assigned these steps. The manager of the Cardinal Homes engagement team has performed these audit steps during the last two years' audit engagements without identifying any misstatements. Management of the company has informed the audit team during the planning stage that no "major" changes were made to the assumptions or method of calculation for all estimates.

Required:

(a) Do you still have to perform any audit steps for these estimations? Explain.

(b) If so, what audit steps would you perform?

14-33 **[LO 2, 3]** Each of the following audit procedures is being used in the audit of Morgan Fabricated Homes, Inc. to test production activities.

Required:

For each of these procedures: identify (a) the strength of the internal control procedure being tested and (b) the internal accounting objectives being addressed.

Audit Procedure	(a) Strength	(b) Objective
1. Scan job cost sheets for missing numbers in the sequence.		
2. Locate the materials requisitions forms and see if they are prenumbered, stored in a secure location, and accessible by authorized personnel only.		
3. Use inquiry and inspection to determine if cost clerks review dates on the job cost sheets for units completed in the accounting period.		

14-34 **[LO 2, 3]** Each of the following audit procedures is being used in the audit of Newport Homebuilders, Inc. to test the production control activities.

Required:

For each of these procedures identify (a) the strength of the internal control procedure being tested and (b) the internal accounting objectives being addressed.

Audit Procedure	(a) Strength	(b) Objective
1. Select several journal entries for work-in-process inventory. For these vouch to weekly labor reports, weekly material reports, and job cost sheets.		
2. Balance and reconcile detailed job cost sheets to the work-in-process inventory control account.		
3. Vouch a sample of open and completed job cost sheet entries to labor reports and material usage reports.		

14-35 **[LO 2, 3]** Each of the following audit procedures is being used in the audit of Rockport Homes, Inc., to test the production control activities.

Required:

For each of these procedures identify (a) the strength of the internal control procedure being tested and (b) the internal accounting objectives being addressed.

Audit Procedure	(a) Strength	(b) Objective
1. Select a sample of the documents prepared when raw materials are released from stores. Examine and tie the job number to the cost accounting records.		
2. Select a sample of the materials release documents in the production department file. Examine for foreman's signature or initials.		
3. Select a sample of the materials release documents in the production department file. Examine for issue date/material usage report date.		
4. Select a sample of the materials release documents in the production department file. Examine for name and item number of the material.		
5. Select a sample of the materials release documents in production department file. Examine for the clerk's signature or initials who issued the raw materials.		
6. Select a sample of the materials release documents in the production department file. Examine for matching material requisition in raw materials stores file, noting the date of requisition.		

14-36 [LO 2, 3] Coral Springs Foods, Inc. is diversifying its operations through the sale of snack vending equipment. The plans call for the purchase of 350 machines, which will be located at 70 different sites within the regional area, and one warehouse to store snack inventory.

Management has hired an inventory clerk to oversee the warehouse. Two drivers will periodically fill the machines with product and deposit the cash collected at a designated bank. Drivers report to the warehouse on a daily basis.

Required:

Based on this scenario, what controls might Coral Springs Foods initiate that would provide assurance about the integrity of the cash receipts and warehouse process?

14-37 [LO 2] Dayton Publishers performs services on a job-cost basis. Most jobs take a week or less to complete. These typically involve at least two of Dayton's five departments. Actual costs are accumulated by job, but the company prepares sales invoices based on cost estimates in order to assure timely billing.

Unfortunately, several recent jobs have resulted in losses, and management has decided to refocus efforts on cost control at the departmental level. Dayton's processes are highly labor intensive, so management has proposed the development of a departmental labor cost report. The report will originate in the payroll department as part of the biweekly payroll. From there it will go to an accounting clerk for comparison to total labor cost estimates by department. In the event that actual total departmental labor costs in payroll are not much more than the estimated total department labor cost during the period, the accounting clerk will send the report to the departmental foreman. On the other hand, significant variance differences require the accounting clerk to send the report to the assistant controller, who will investigate the cause (if time is available) and recommend corrective action to the production manager.

Required:

Discuss at least three common aspects of control with which the departmental labor cost report proposal complies, giving examples about Dayton to support each.

14-38 [LO 2] Use the information given in the Dayton Publishers scenario from Problem 14-37 to answer the following.

Required:

Discuss at least three common aspects of control with which the departmental labor cost report proposal *does not comply*, giving examples from Dayton to support each.

14-39 [LO 4] Don Martin, the in-charge auditor, is observing the year-end inventory procedures for Haverson Fabricated Buildings, Inc. Donn notes the following issues when observing Haverson employees involved in this process:

1. Inventory tags are prenumbered and show the description and quantity of inventory. These tags are attached upon counting and only removed when authorized by the independent auditor. The tags are issued to two-person count teams, and each number series issued is recorded by the plant supervisor on a control sheet.

2. All inventory, except work-in-process (considered minor), is housed in the central warehouse.

3. The client makes no provision for double-checking the original inventory count.

4. Martin did not test-count one of the six finished goods bays but did a walk-through with the supervisor and saw all goods tagged.

5. There were no auditor copies of the inventory tags, so Martin recorded all the test counts on inventory count sheets as part of the audit work papers.

6. At the end of the observation, Martin did not consider it realistic to account for all of the issued and unissued inventory tags, so he had the client furnish him with a copy of the control sheet maintained by the plant supervisor.

Required:

How effective were Martin's inventory-count observation procedures? What specific warning signs in this scenario could result in possible overstatement of inventory?

14-40 [LO 4] Review the Problem 14-39 scenario, regarding the inventory-taking observation by Don Martin in the course of an audit of Haverson Fabricated Buildings to answer the following question.

Required:

What additional substantive audit procedures would you recommend to test Haverson's inventories?

14-41 [LO 4] Jackson Brown, CPA, has two clients, Tarpan Financial, Inc. and Oscar Industries. During his most recent audit of Oscar, Brown discovered a potential overstatement of inventories because customer returns and scrap were often counted as being in good condition. Because the plant supervisor assured Jackson that an extensive new rework policy was in place to ensure the usefulness of this inventory within three months, he did not adjust the inventories downward.

Now, Tarpan is considering buying out Oscar Industries, using the information generated from Brown's audit report and accompanying financial statements. While it is not public knowledge, Jackson knows that some financial dealings at Oscar have deteriorated since his audit. In driving home one day after the news of the possible buy-out, he notices that the scrap lot has filled up significantly since his last walkthrough inspection.

At that point, Jackson thinks that the deal may be great news for Oscar but will involve many risks for Tarpan and wonders whether he should provide Tarpan with information about the potential danger.

Required:

Identify the ethical considerations in the scenario. Should Brown reconsider the audit steps performed on the Oscar Industries inventory? Is the full scrap lot important new information?

ACTIVITY ASSIGNMENTS

14-42 During the economic downturn beginning around 2006, many companies concluded that their inventory was overvalued. The same thing occurred in 2001, after the *technology bubble* burst and many technology companies made huge write-offs in inventory. Find two companies (from either time frame) and compare their disclosures related to the write-off of obsolete inventory. Briefly describe the write-offs and explain similarities and differences in the disclosures. Find the audit report and note whether the inventory write-off was mentioned in the report.

14-43 Perform an Internet search to identify a company that has recently been reported to have improper accounting for its inventory. Go to the SEC Web site and find the company's filings for years surrounding the time of the improperly reported financial information. Write a one-page summary of the improper financial reporting of the company. Were financial statements restated as a result of the impropriety?

14-44 Refer to the Auditing in Action feature that lists companies that committed fraud related to inventories. Select one of the companies from the list and research how the fraud was committed. Prepare a memo summarizing the fraud committed related to inventories.

14-45 Using EDGAR on the SEC's Web site, search for Concord Camera Corp.'s 2008 annual report (10-K). Read the 10-K and find the disclosures related to its going concern issue. Explain your findings. Follow up to see what the outcome was in subsequent years.

PROFESSIONAL SIMULATIONS

Go to the Book's Web site at www.wiley.com/college/hooks to find simulations similar to those on the computerized CPA exam.

ACL

An exercise requiring the use of ACL software is available on the Auditing and Assurances Web site at www.wiley.com/college/hooks.

Auditing Assets, Liabilities, and Equity Related to the Financing Cycle

1. Describe the activities, controls, accounting standards, and audit steps for cash, near cash, and cash equivalents.
2. Describe the activities, transactions, controls, accounting standards, and audit steps for investments.
3. Explain the audit processes for other comprehensive income and the consolidation process.
4. Recognize important issues for auditing disclosures of assets in the financing cycle.
5. Describe the activities, transactions, controls, accounting standards, and audit steps for long-term debt and other long-term accounts.
6. Explain the audit processes for auditing pensions and postretirement benefits and taxes.
7. Recognize important issues for auditing disclosures of liabilities in the financing cycle.
8. Describe the activities, transactions, controls, accounting standards, and audit steps for equity accounts.

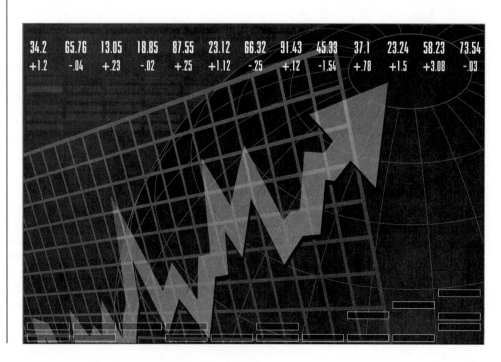

9. Explain the audit processes for mergers and acquisitions, and retained earnings.

10. Recognize important issues for auditing disclosures of equity in the financing cycle.

11. Discuss the risks, accounting standards, and audit procedures for related parties and related party transactions in the financing cycle.

Chapter 15 Resources

AU 312, AICPA, PCAOB, *Audit Risk and Materiality in Conducting an Audit*

AU 314, AICPA, *Understanding the Entity and Its Environment and Assessing the Risks of Material Misstatement*

AU 316, AICPA, PCAOB, *Consideration of Fraud in a Financial Statement Audit*

AU 317, AICPA, PCAOB, *Illegal Acts by Clients*

AU 318, AICPA, *Performing Audit Procedures in Response to Assessed Risks and Evaluating the Audit Evidence Obtained*

AU 319, PCAOB, *Consideration of Internal Control in a Financial Statement Audit*

AU 326, AICPA, *Audit Evidence*

AU 326, PCAOB, *Evidential Matter*

AU 328, AICPA, PCAOB, *Auditing Fair Value Measurements and Disclosures*

AU 329, AICPA, PCAOB, *Analytical Procedures*

AU 332, AICPA, PCAOB, *Auditing Derivative Instruments, Hedging Activities, and Investments in Securities*

AU 334, AICPA, PCAOB, *Related Parties*

AU 336, AICPA, PCAOB, *Using the Work of a Specialist*

AU 339, AICPA, *Audit Documentation*

AU 341, AICPA, PCAOB, *The Auditor's Consideration of an Entity's Ability to Continue as a Going Concern*

AU 342, AICPA, PCAOB, *Auditing Accounting Estimates*

FASB ASC 220-10, *Comprehensive Income*

FASB ASC 320-10, *Investments—Debt and Equity Structures*

FASB ASC 505-10-50, *Equity Disclosure*

FASB ASC 715, *Compensation—Retirement Benefits*

FASB ASC 718-10, *Compensation—Stock Compensation*

FASB ASC 740-10, *Income Taxes*

FASB ASC 810-10-5, *Consolidation, Variable Interest Entities*

FASB ASC 820-10, *Fair Value Measurements and Disclosures*

FASB ASC 825-10, *Financial Instruments*

FASB ASC 850-10, *Related Party Disclosures*

FASB Concepts Statement No. 6, *Elements of Financial Statements*

PCAOB AS 3, *Audit Documentation*

PCAOB AS 5, *An Audit of Internal Control Over Financial Reporting That is Integrated with an Audit of Financial Statements*

INTRODUCTION

The financing cycle deals with the capital of a business. Businesses raise capital using both debt and equity. When additional resources are available, businesses invest those resources to earn a return. This chapter focuses on auditing investment assets, debt, other long-term accounts, and equity. Year-end audit activities for cash and cash equivalents are also included in this chapter.

OVERVIEW

Investments, long-term liabilities, and equity activities have in common that they likely have fewer transactions than other cycles and the amounts of the transactions may be large. The accounting methods, as well as the transactions may be complex. Valuation may be challenging and disclosures extensive. In addition, these transactions likely involve legal relationships and contracts with parties outside the company. Liabilities involve a legal obligation of the company to pay an outsider. Equity transactions involve ownership rights. When the company is an investor, these same legal relationships exist, but the company is in the position of being the creditor or owner. Although companies can enter into any kind of transaction with related parties, the auditor is particularly aware of the possibility of related parties being involved in investment, debt, and equity transactions.

Some level of investment, debt, and equity activities are likely in all businesses. The frequency and type of investment activities depend on the needs of the company. Most businesses obtain capital through some combination of debt and equity. Because investments, debt, and equity are common to most entities, this chapter does not highlight a specific industry, but instead uses examples from a variety of companies. The chapter first addresses cash and investments, and then moves on to debt, other long-term accounts, and equity.

ASSETS AND THE FINANCING CYCLE

Businesses need funds to operate. This fundamental certainty underpins a company's transactions related to the assets a company holds as cash, near cash, and investments. The other motivation for many investment transactions is to manage risk. Understanding cash and investment-related transactions and the proper accounting for them is far more difficult than learning the audit procedures that apply.

Various audit procedures provide evidence that the amounts are stated and disclosed properly. Collecting the evidence is not the auditor's biggest challenge. Rather, the most difficult challenge is assessing whether the account amounts and disclosures are prepared and presented according to the applicable accounting standards. A complete discussion of the accounting standards related to assets and the financing cycle is beyond the scope of this book, but a brief introduction to some of the standards is provided to help you better understand the auditor's objectives and procedures.

Cash and Near Cash [LO 1]

Most of the audit procedures related to cash are discussed in Chapters 10 and 12 in the context of cash receipts and cash disbursements. Cash movement between bank accounts and disbursements are discussed in Chapter 13 as they relate to payroll. Cash and near cash also relate to investments and the financing cycle because when a company needs funds in the very near future the assets will be kept in bank accounts or short-term investments designated as near cash and cash equivalents. Common items considered near cash or cash equivalents are certificates of deposit, United States Treasury bills, and commercial paper. **Commercial paper** is the term used for the short-term debt of corporations. These investment instruments are considered "equivalent" to cash because the amount of cash that will be received for them is known. The risk that the value will change before they are converted back into cash is not significant.

What Is a Cash Equivalent?

Currently, there is no clear guidance regarding the definition of **cash equivalent** and the types of disclosures required for these investments. The Financial Accounting Standards Board (FASB) is working with the International Accounting Standards Board to clarify these issues and to harmonize accounting standards.

In 2007, the FASB approved a staff recommendation that the term *cash equivalents* be eliminated from financial statements. Staff recommended that items currently classified as cash equivalents would be classified in the same manner as short-term investments, supported by footnote disclosures. This move was in response to criticism that the old definition of "cash equivalents" was outdated.

The market events of 2008 also impacted the accounting for cash equivalents. For example, some money market funds and other types of short-term investments restrict the ability of the owner to make withdrawals of cash. The example cited in an AICPA response to a technical inquiry was a withdrawal restriction of 20% of the balance, with the remaining balance spread over six months to two years. In this type of situation, the client and the auditor need to address not only the ability of the investment to meet the definition of cash equivalent, but might also need to address whether the investment is a current asset.

Auditors must carefully consider how cash and near-cash items are reported and disclosed.

Auditing Cash and Near Cash

Beyond the controls discussed in earlier chapters, the overall audit goal for cash and near cash is to determine whether the amount is fairly presented in the financial statements and the disclosure is adequate. The auditor counts cash on hand and inspects near cash items at year end. This audit step is performed concurrently with examining the existence of the company's other highly liquid investments. Concurrent examination is needed since the funds can easily be converted from one form to the other. The auditor confirms cash accounts and near cash with the depository institutions. The bank confirmation process is discussed in Chapter 10. The confirmation request includes information on the cash balance, restrictions on the cash balance, loans, collateral and unused lines of credit. The auditor reviews and recalculates the client's bank reconciliations and examines underlying documents, including the bank statements and support for reconciling items.

Just as the audit must examine the existence of cash and very liquid investments concurrently, an important part of the audit of cash is to simultaneously consider all bank accounts. This simultaneous examination is needed because of the risk that funds transferred between bank accounts might be counted twice. Duplicate inclusion resulting in a cash overstatement might be the result of an error. However, it can also be intended to cover up a theft. The term **kiting** is used to refer to an act of intentional duplication to cover a theft or misrepresent the actual cash balance. An **interbank transfer schedule** may be used to trace transfers between accounts for a few days before and after year end to identify any duplicate inclusion of cash. A **proof of cash** may also be performed to reconcile the cash balance with cash receipts and cash disbursements. The nature of a company's cash transactions affects whether an interbank transfer schedule and proof of cash are needed. If these reconciliations are needed as part of the company's ICFR, they are prepared by the client and the audit steps will be similar to those for auditing a bank reconciliation.

AUDITING IN ACTION

Interbank Transfer Schedule

Maggie Manley Corporation
Interbank Transfer Schedule
For the Period 12-20-10 to 1-12-11
Prepared by JH, 1/13/11

Check #	Description	Deposits		Withdrawals		Bank A	Bank B
		Per Books	Per Bank	Per Books	Per Bank		
4201	Transfer from B to A	12/29/10 ✔	12/29/10 C	12/29/10 ✔	12/30/10 C	2,000	(2,000)
1230	Transfer from A to B	12/31/10 ✔	1/2/11 C	12/31/10 ✔	1/3/11 C	(4,500)	4,500

✔ Traced to cash book
C Traced to bank statement

(Based on Taylor and Glezen, p.478.)

AUDITING IN ACTION

Proof of Cash

Maggie Manley Corporation

Interim Proof of Cash, 3/31/10

Prepared by: JH 4/14/10

Account: 10001 General Cash

	t/m	2/28/10	Receipts	Disbursements	3/31/10
Balance per Bank	1	205,300	1,034,500	1,026,500	213,300
Deposits in transit					
2/28/10	2	15,700	(15,700)		
3/31/10	2		18,200		18,200
Outstanding Checks					
2/28/10	3	(22,400)		(22,400)	
3/31/10	3			14,200	(14,200)
NSF Checks	4		(2,400)	(2,400)	
Balance per bank, adjusted		198,600	1,034,600	1,015,900	217,300
Balance per books, unadjusted		198,600	1,034,600	1,016,080	217,120
Bank debit memos	5			180	(180)
Balance per books, adjusted		198,600	1,034,600	1,015,900	217,300

1	Per 3/31/10 bank statement
2	Traced to subsequent bank statements
3	Examined cancelled checks
4	All NSF checks were redeposited in March and cleared as of 3/31/10
5	Account maintenance fees; traced to journal entry

Disclosure

Proper financial statement presentation and disclosure of cash items requires more than disclosing a correct account balance, particularly to comply with SEC rules. For example, the company must disclose its accounting policy for cash and near cash. Another example is disclosure when a bank requires a company to maintain a **compensating balance**. A compensating balance is a minimum deposit amount or a minimum average deposit amount required by the bank. Compensating balances must be disclosed.

Companies often maintain their cash bank accounts in an "overdraft" position. In other words, they write checks or disburse funds via electronic funds transfer (EFT). However, the company keeps the funds in a short-term investment and transfers them to the checking account only when the checks or EFT actually start to clear the bank. A company's banking relationship often permits overdrafts to be offset against other accounts. Overdrafts that are not offset by other cash accounts are classified as accounts payable or accrued liabilities.

Proper presentation also requires use of the appropriate exchange rate for cash that is foreign currency. Another required disclosure includes restrictions on cash.

AUDITING IN ACTION

Cash, Cash Equivalents, and Restricted Cash
Host Hotels and Resorts,
Inc., December 31, 2008

Cash and Cash Equivalents

We consider all highly liquid investments with a maturity of 90 days or less at the date of purchase to be cash equivalents.

Restricted Cash

Restricted cash includes reserves for debt service, real estate taxes, insurance, furniture and fixtures, as well as cash collateral and excess cash flow deposits due to mortgage debt agreement restrictions and provisions. For purposes of the statement of cash flows, changes in restricted cash that are used for furniture, fixture, and equipment reserves controlled by our lenders are shown as investing activities. The remaining changes in restricted cash are the direct result of restrictions under our loan agreements, and, as such, are reflected in cash from financing activities.

The following table represents our restricted cash balances as of December 31, 2008 and 2007, which are restricted as a result of lender requirements (in millions):

	2008	2007
Debt service	$ 11	$ 10
Real estate taxes	7	7
Cash collateral	8	7
Excess cash flow requirements	3	5
Furniture, fixtures and equipment reserves controlled by lenders	8	14
Special projects reserve	4	20
Other	3	2
Total	$ 44	$ 65

All of this financial statement information that affects proper cash presentation and disclosure is inspected by the auditor while performing audit steps that utilize confirmations, reconciliations, and underlying documents. Therefore, the auditor assesses financial statement presentation and disclosure by reviewing the financial statements and considering evidence collected as part of the overall audit of cash.

REVIEW QUESTIONS

A1. Why is it important to thoroughly understand the accounting standards when auditing investments?

A2. How important is the valuation assertion for cash equivalents? Why?

A3. Why does the auditor examine cash, near cash, and highly liquid investments simultaneously?

A4. What is an interbank transfer schedule, and why is it needed?

Investments [LO 2]

A company keeps funds that will be needed in the very near term in the form of cash or cash equivalents. When the period of time before the funds need to be disbursed is longer, a company typically puts the funds in a different kind of investment with a greater earnings return or yield. Companies also make investments to offset, or **hedge**, business risks.

For example, a company might hedge against a possible future change in the price of raw materials, interest rates, or foreign currency exchange rates. Companies can manage specific risks using investments because there are now many types of investment instruments designed specifically for that purpose.

As a result of the increased availability of tailored investment instruments, auditors of even smaller and less complex companies are often confronted with auditing complex investments. Auditors may have to spend more time on the audit of investments than they did before the financial markets provided these risk management opportunities. Consequently, auditors need extensive knowledge about investment transactions and instruments.

Derivatives is a term used to describe certain types of investments. The term is used to refer to a financial instrument that contains some part of the contract that is "derived" based on something else. Derivatives are often the type of financial instruments used as investments to hedge against business risks. An example is *interest rate swaps*, which are derivative financial instruments that a company can purchase to hedge against the risk that interest rates will change and negatively affect its financial position. An example of investments to hedge interest rate risk is shown in the following December 31, 2008 notes to the financial statements of Merck & Co., Inc.:

Interest Rate Risk Management:

The Company may use interest rate swap contracts on certain investing and borrowing transactions to manage its net exposure to interest rate changes and to reduce its overall cost of borrowing. The Company does not use leveraged swaps and, in general, does not leverage any of its investment activities that would put principal capital at risk.

At December 31, 2008, the Company was a party to two pay-floating, receive-fixed interest rate swap contracts maturing in 2011 with notional amounts of $125 million each designated as fair value hedges of fixed-rate notes in which the notional amounts match the amount of the hedged fixed-rate notes. The swaps effectively convert the fixed-rate obligations to floating-rate instruments. The fair value changes in the notes are offset in interest expense by the fair value changes in the swap contracts. The fair values of these contracts are reported in Accounts receivable, Other assets, Accrued and other current liabilities, or Deferred income taxes and noncurrent liabilities. During 2008, the company terminated four interest rate swap contracts with notional amounts of $250 million each, and terminated one interest rate swap contract with a notional amount of $500 million. These swaps had effectively converted its $1.0 billion, 4.75% fixed-rate notes dues 2015 and its $500 million, 4.375% fixed-rate notes due 2013 to variable rate debt. As a result of the swap terminations, the Company received $128.3 million in cash, excluding accrued interest which was not material. The corresponding gains related to the basis adjustment of the debt associated with the terminated swap contracts was deferred and are being amortized as a reduction of interest expense over the remaining term of the notes. The cash flows from these contracts are reported as operating activities in the Consolidated Statement of Cash Flows.

Hedging the cost of fuel affects airline profitability, as displayed in the following quotes excerpted from the financial statement notes of Southwest Airlines, December 31, 2008 and December 31, 2006. As the change in disclosure from 2006 to 2008 displays, these transactions are complex and affected by changes in the overall economy. The Southwest disclosures for the two years also highlights that many types of investments to hedge risks are available and that the structure of the transactions and accounting for them is typically complex.

Southwest Airlines and Fuel, 2008:

Airline operators are inherently dependent upon energy to operate and, therefore, are impacted by changes in jet fuel prices. Jet fuel and oil consumed during 2008, 2007, and 2006 represented approximately 35.1 percent, 29.7 percent, and 28.0 percent of the Company's operating expenses, respectively. The primary reason that fuel and oil has become an increasingly large portion of the Company's operating expenses has been due to the dramatic increase in all energy prices in recent years. The Company endeavors to acquire jet fuel at the lowest possible cost. Because jet fuel is not traded on an organized futures exchange, there are limited opportunities to hedge directly in jet fuel. However, the Company has found that financial derivative instruments in other commodities, such as crude oil, and refined products such as heating oil and unleaded gasoline, can be useful in decreasing its exposure to jet fuel price increases. The Company does not purchase or hold any derivative financial instruments for trading purposes.

The Company has utilized financial derivative instruments for both short-term and long-term time frames, and typically utilizes a mixture of purchased call options, collar structures, and fixed price swap agreements in its portfolio. In recent years, as fuel prices have risen, the Company has held fuel derivative positions that have resulted in significant gains recognized in earnings. However, as of December 31, 2008, the Company held a net position of fuel derivative instruments that effectively represented a hedge of approximately 10 percent of its anticipated jet fuel purchases for the years from 2009 through 2013. Prior to fourth quarter 2008, the company had fuel derivative instruments for a much larger portion of its anticipated fuel purchases for these years; however, due to recent precipitous decline in fuel prices, the company significantly reduced its hedge in order to minimize fuel hedging losses related to further oil price declines and to minimize the potential for the Company to provide additional cash collateral deposits to counterparties. The company accomplished this reduced hedge by entering into additional derivative contracts—basically by selling zero-cost collars and fixed-price swap derivatives. This strategy enables the Company to participate in further price declines via the sold derivatives, which should materially offset further declines in value of the Company's previously purchased derivatives. If prices rise, the Company no longer has the protection it had in place prior to reducing its hedge.

Southwest Airlines and Fuel, 2006:

… In addition to the significant protective fuel derivative positions the Company had in place during 2006, the Company also has significant future positions. The Company currently has a mixture of purchased call options, collar structures, and fixed price swap agreements in place to protect against nearly 95 percent of its 2007 total anticipated jet fuel requirements at average crude oil equivalent prices of approximately $50 per barrel, and has also added refinery margins on most of those positions. Based on current growth plans, the Company also has fuel derivative contracts in place for 65 percent of its expected fuel consumption for 2008 at approximately $49 per barrel, over 50 percent for 2009 at approximately $51 per barrel, over 25 percent for 2010 at $63 per barrel, approximately 15 percent in 2011 at $64 per barrel, and 15 percent in 2012 at $63 per barrel.

Investment Transactions

The terms **financial instruments**, **marketable securities**, and **commodities** are often used when referring to short-term investments. The terms are not easily defined because they can be overlapping and are often used in an imprecise manner. **Financial assets** and **financial liabilities**, defined in FASB codification 825-10 *Financial Instruments*, include financial instruments.

Equity security investments that represent a company's ownership interest in another business, or its rights related to an ownership interest, can be marketable securities if they are traded on a stock exchange. In addition to shares of stock, warrants, rights, and call options are equity investments that represent the right to acquire an equity interest. Put options represent the right to dispose of an equity interest. Equity instruments such as stock options are a part of employee compensation. A **debt security** investment represents an obligation on the part of the debtor to repay a principal amount plus a specified rate of interest and can be a marketable security if it is traded on an exchange. Some investments are called hybrid securities because they have characteristics of both debt and equity, such as convertible or redeemable features.

The key to equity and debt investments being considered "marketable" is being traded in the securities markets. Commodities markets traditionally handled transactions related to physical items such as agricultural products and metals, as well as contracts to buy or sell those items. As reported on the television show *60 Minutes,* contracts to buy and sell oil traded on the commodities markets are believed to have been a major contributor to the spike in gasoline prices during the summer of 2008. The contracts to buy or sell commodities fall within the definition of financial assets or liabilities.

Accounting for Investments

Most securities that are marketable are classified as short-term investments. They may be classified as long term if the company intends, and has the ability, to hold them for a longer period of time. Proper classification as short or long term must be addressed for both equity and debt investments. Equity investments can range from a small percentage of the ownership of a company to a controlling or complete ownership interest. When a company owns an influencing or controlling interest in another entity, the proper method of accounting for the investment is consolidating it into the owner's financial statements, and thus, differs from when the investment is a smaller number of shares.

Various accounting standards determine how a company records, presents, and discloses investments, and therefore the audit procedures necessary also vary. Accounting standards establish the financial assets and financial liabilities that a company can elect to account for using **fair value** and include many types of investments. FASB ASC 820-10, *Fair Value Measurements and Disclosures,* sets forth the ways to determine fair value and amends many previous standards. The investments that cannot be carried at fair value or that the client company chooses to show at other than fair value are reported based on the accounting standards applicable to that particular type of investment.

Accounting standards determine both the value and proper account classification for different investments. For example, if a company does not elect the fair value option, FASB ASC 320-10, *Investments–Debt and Equity Securities,* specifies amortized cost for debt securities that the company plans to hold to maturity. If an equity investment is not accounted for using fair value, the **equity method** or consolidation in the financial statements may be appropriate. Some **variable interest entities** (VIEs) must be consolidated. This is covered in the FASB ASC 810-10 *Consolidation.*

Even with this limited introduction, it is clear that the accounting standards for investments are extensive and complex. Audit procedures address whether the proper accounting standards have been applied to investments and the methods used to apply the standards produce a fair presentation in the financial statements. Therefore, as stated

AUDITING IN ACTION

FASB ASC 810-10-05, Consolidation-Overall-Overview and Background Consolidation of VIEs

05-8 The Variable Interest Entities Subsections clarify the application of the General Subsections to certain legal entities in which equity investors do not have the characteristics of a controlling financial interest or do not have sufficient equity at risk for the legal entity to finance its activities without additional subordinated financial support. Paragraph 810-10-10-1 states that consolidated financial statements are usually necessary for a fair presentation if one of the entities in the consolidated group directly or indirectly has a controlling financial interest in the other entities. Paragraph 810-10-15-8 states that the usual condition for a controlling financial interest is ownership of a majority voting interest. However, application of the majority voting interest requirement in the General Subsections of this Subtopic to certain types of entities may not identify the party with a controlling financial interest because the controlling financial interest may be achieved through arrangements that do not involve voting interests.

05-9 The Variable Interest Entities Subsections explain how to identify variable interest entities (VIEs) and how to determine when a reporting entity should include the assets, liabilities, noncontrolling interests, and results of activities of a VIE in its consolidated financial statements. Transactions involving VIEs have become increasingly common. Some reporting entities have entered into arrangements using VIEs that appear to be designed to avoid reporting assets and liabilities for which they are responsible, to delay reporting losses that have already been incurred, or to report gains that are illusory. At the same time, many reporting entities have used VIEs for valid business purposes and have properly accounted for those VIEs based on guidance and accepted practice.

EXHIBIT 15-1

Key Terms for Fair Value

Fair value: The price that would be received to sell an asset or paid to transfer a liability in an orderly transaction between market participants at the measurement date.

Financial asset: Cash, evidence of an ownership interest in an entity, or a contract that conveys to one entity a right to do either of the following:

a. Receive cash or another financial instrument from a second entity

b. Exchange other financial instruments on potentially favorable terms with a second entity

Financial liability: A contract that imposes on one entity an obligation to do either of the following:

a. Deliver cash or another financial instrument to a second entity

b. Exchange other financial instruments on potentially unfavorable terms with the second entity

Firm commitment: An agreement with an unrelated party, binding on both parties and usually legally enforceable, with the following characteristics:

a. The agreement specifies all significant terms, including the quantity to be exchanged, the fixed price, and the timing of the transaction. The fixed price may be expressed as a specified amount of an entity's functional currency or of a foreign currency. It may also be expressed as a specified interest rate or specified effective yield.

b. The agreement includes a disincentive for nonperformance that is sufficiently large to make performance probable.

(FASB ASC 825-10-20)

earlier, the auditor must know the accounting standards for investments. Exhibit 15-1 provides definitions related to fair value. Exhibit 15-2 presents a simplified list of financial assets and financial liabilities that a company may elect to present at fair value.

Financial assets and financial liabilities except:

Subsidiaries or variable interest entities that must be consolidated

Obligations for pensions, postretirement benefits and post-employment benefits

Employee stock option and stock purchase plans and other deferred compensation

Capitalized leases

Certain liabilities of banks and similar financial institutions

Financial instruments that are classified as equity

Firm commitments that would not otherwise be recorded that involve only financial instruments

Written loan commitments

Certain insurance contracts, warranties and other financial instruments

(FASB ASC 825-10-15-4, 5)

Valuing Investments

The simplest investment entries result when companies enter into transactions to purchase and sell investments. However, when required by the accounting standards, companies must also record entries to value investments before producing financial statements. For instance, entries are required when fair value is used or the value of an investment has permanently declined. Companies must also record the receipt of investment income. The auditor must gather evidence on these transactions, related ICFR, and the resulting financial statement amounts and disclosures. The auditor must understand the company's business purpose for each type of investment, as well as the nature of the investment and its liquidity. The most complex aspects of auditing investments are assessing the amounts recorded at purchase, sale, and any valuation dates in between, and determining whether disclosures are adequate.

The auditor may choose to enlist the help of a valuation specialist when investments, particularly financial instruments, are extremely complex. These inputs are audited along with the valuation process to assess the appropriateness of the financial statement amounts and disclosures. Use of a specialist in an audit engagement is covered in AU 336. The auditor's use of a specialist is discussed later in this chapter related to valuations for pension and postretirement benefit obligations. For investments, the auditor must go beyond valuation and disclosure, and also address management assertions of existence, ownership, and completeness. Exhibit 15-3 summarizes audit procedures for auditing fair value measurements and disclosures that are covered in AU 328. Think about the audit of fair value as a subset of the audit of estimates—the guidance has many similarities.

REVIEW QUESTIONS

B1. Why do investments generally require more audit time and effort than they did in the past?

B2. Based on the accounting standards, what are the different methods an audit client might possibly use to account for investments?

B3. What are the types of transactions that an auditor must consider when auditing investments?

B4. Besides the auditing standards, what must an auditor understand about the audit client's investments to be able to audit valuation and disclosure of the investments?

EXHIBIT 15-3

Auditing Fair Value Measurements and Disclosures

Obtain sufficient competent audit evidence to provide reasonable assurance that fair value measurements and disclosure are in conformity with GAAP.

Obtain an understanding of the entity's process for determining fair value measurements and disclosures and of the relevant controls sufficient to develop an effective audit approach.

Evaluate whether the fair value measurements and disclosures in the financial statements are in conformity with GAAP.

Consider whether to engage a specialist and use the work of that specialist as audit evidence in performing substantive tests to evaluate material financial statement assertions.

Test the entity's fair value measurements and disclosures. This may involve

    a. testing management's significant assumptions, the valuation model, and the underlying data,

    b. developing independent fair value estimates for corroborative purposes, or

    c. reviewing subsequent events and transactions.

Evaluate whether the disclosures about fair values made by the entity are in conformity with GAAP.

Evaluate the sufficiency and competence of the audit evidence obtained from auditing fair value measurements and disclosures as well as the consistency of that evidence with other audit evidence obtained and evaluated during the audit.

Obtain written representations from management regarding the reasonableness of significant assumptions, including whether they appropriately reflect management's intent and ability to carry out specific courses of action on behalf of the entity where relevant to the use of fair value measurements or disclosures.

Determine that the audit committee is informed about the process used by management in formulating particularly sensitive accounting estimates, including fair value estimates, and about the basis for the auditor's conclusions regarding the reasonableness of those estimates.

(AU Section 328)

AUDITING IN ACTION

Information Used to Determine Fair Value

Inputs refer broadly to the assumptions that market participants would use in pricing the asset or liability.... Inputs may be observable or unobservable.

> Observable inputs are inputs that reflect the assumptions market participants would use in pricing the asset or liability developed based on market data obtained from sources independent of the reporting entity.
>
> Unobservable inputs are inputs that reflect the reporting entity's own assumptions about the assumptions market participants would use in pricing the asset or liability developed based on the best information available in the circumstances.

(FASB ASC, Glossary)

Valuation techniques used to measure fair value shall maximize the use of observable inputs and minimize the use of unobservable inputs. (FASB ASC 820-10-35-.35, .36)

Tests of Controls and Dual Purpose Tests

Controls needed for investments vary based on the nature, frequency, dollar amounts, and complexity of the company's investing activity. Purchase and sale transactions and the receipt of income from investments have the same types of controls over cash receipts and disbursements that are discussed in Chapters 10 and 12. If a company has limited investment activity, the procedures and ICFR surrounding them may be relatively simple. Some companies, for example, banks, insurance companies, investment companies, and broker-dealers, hold large and complex investment portfolios. In these companies, the investment processes and related controls are extensive. Exhibit 15-4 lists examples of company controls and audit tests for investments.

EXHIBIT 15-4

Examples of Controls and Related Tests for Investments

Note that either management or the auditor can perform tests of controls. Management uses tests of controls to support its management report. The auditor uses tests of controls for the audit of ICFR and to confirm the planned reliance on controls in the financial statement audit. Many of these tests of controls may be extended by the auditor to include a component providing evidence for the financial statement audit. Examples of these extensions are indicated in **bold,** and the procedures can be characterized as dual purpose tests.

Purpose of Controls	Company Control and Audit Tests
To ensure that investments that are acquired and disposed of are consistent with the intent of the Board of Directors **(authorization)**	
	CC: *Policies exist for selecting investments (at a minimum directing the level of risk to be assumed), and providing for general or specific authorization by the Board of Directors*
	CC: *Policies exist for assessing and monitoring risks when the investment portfolio contains complex financial instruments*

TofC: Inspect policy documents and review for continued appropriateness for the current investment environment and activities

CC: *Management reviews and approves investment decisions before they are executed*

TofC: Select acquisition and disposal transactions from the investments ledger and review supporting documents for management approval

CC: *If purchase and sale transactions are handled by an outside party (for example, a financial institution), appropriate guidance for transaction parameters, such as an approved acquisition list, is provided, monitored, and updated*

TofC: Inspect guidance documents and review for continued appropriateness

CC: *Investments that are unique events (such as the acquisition of a large ownership share in a company) are individually approved by management or the Board of Directors*

TofC: Scan investment ledger and general ledger for major investment acquisitions and review Board of Directors minutes for approvals

To ensure that all investment transactions are recorded (all investments owned are recorded, all recorded investments are owned, at the date shown)

(completeness, rights and obligations, cutoff)

CC: *An investment ledger is maintained with an account for each investment including (as appropriate) full description, number of shares, certificate numbers, interest or dividend rate, any notable features (conversion, call, etc.), amortization of any premium or discount, and location where the security is held if applicable*

TofC: Scan the investment ledger for completeness and for inclusion of recent transactions; test for mathematical accuracy; **trace total to the general ledger**

TofC: Examine internal authorizations and broker's advices for transactions and trace to the investments ledger, **agreeing all information and amounts and that all transactions are recorded in the proper period (as of the trade date)**

To ensure that investment documents that are negotiable or that provide evidence of legal ownership are physically secured

(existence, rights and obligations)

CC: *Securities are kept in a vault or safe deposit box, or an outside financial institution is engaged to provide safekeeping; securities maintained internally are periodically counted and compared to detailed records*

(continued)

TofC: Observe the count of securities; **follow necessary audit procedures to determine the existence of securities at the time of the physical count and to trace into investment ledger (similar to inventory observation)**

CC: *Employees who have access to securities do not authorize investment transactions, record transactions, or handle cash; two people are present when securities are handled*

TofC: Observe employee activities related to handling securities for proper segregation of duties

CC: *Securities held by an outside financial institution are recorded in detailed company records and these are compared to documents issued by the financial institution*

TofC: Select investments from the investments ledger that are identified as being located with an outside custodian and trace to the supporting documents, **agreeing amounts and details;** (Auditor will consider any **SAS 70** report that is available)

To ensure that investments are valued according to the applicable accounting standards
(valuation)

CC: *Valuation policy is in place and followed appropriate for the company's investment activities*

TofC: Inspect valuation policy document and evidence of valuation procedures executed for investments; **compare inputs used in the valuation process to underlying documents, evaluate valuation process for correspondence with applicable accounting standards, recalculate amounts and trace to accounting records, general ledger and financial statements**

To ensure that income from investments and related receivables are recorded at the proper amount and in the correct accounts and time period
(existence or occurrence, cutoff)

CC: *Receipts from investments are subject to the same ICFR as other cash receipts*

TofC: Tests of the cash receipts cycle

CC: *For marketable securities, published records of dividends and interest are compared to recorded income by an employee independent of recording investment acquisitions and investment earnings, to determine whether cash was received and income posted; any discrepancies are investigated*

TofC: Review documentation of comparison performed by company employees; check for accuracy of amounts in comparison documents using dates of purchase and disposal, interest rates and published dividend records; **trace amounts in comparison to cash receipts journal**

CC: *For equity investments accounted for by the equity method, copies of financial statements of the investee are obtained and used to calculate the appropriate amount of earnings or losses to record*

TofC: Review documentation of calculation and recalculate; **trace entries based on calculation into detailed investment records or general ledger**

Substantive Analytical Procedures

Many of the audit procedures conducted to gain evidence on year-end financial statement investment amounts and disclosures are performed along with tests of controls making them dual purpose tests as shown in Exhibit 15-4. Others are performed as separate tests of details of balances and are discussed in the next section. However, analytical procedures may also be used. Examples of analytical procedures are:

> *Calculate interest income and interest receivable based on principal amounts and rates*
> *Review fluctuation in investment income*
> *Compare investment income with budget and prior-year amounts*
> *Review investment balances for reasonableness*
> *Review current-period activity for large or unusual journal entries*

Tests of Details of Balances

The tests of details of balances used for investments depend on the investments held by the company and on the audit procedures already performed. As with other accounts, the intent is to gain audit evidence corresponding with management's assertions and what is shown in the financial statements. Management's assertions applied to investments are as follows.

1. The items shown as investments are real. (existence)
2. All investments have been recorded and are shown in the financial statements. (completeness)
3. The company owns or has rights to all the investments shown in the financial statements. (rights and obligations)
4. The amounts shown in the financial statements are appropriate and reflect any valuation adjustments. (valuation and allocation)
5. Investments are properly classified and disclosed in the financial statements based on the requirements of the applicable accounting standards. (presentation and disclosure)

Examples of specific tests of details of balances that were not presented as dual purpose tests are:

> *Inspect investment documents; agree information on individual investments to the investment ledger for existence and ownership of all securities (existence or occurrence, rights and obligations)*
> *Confirm any securities that are not held by the audit client with the financial institution or outside custodian holding the securities; agree information on individual*

investments to the investment ledger for existence and ownership of all securities (existence or occurrence, rights and obligations)

Examine documentation of management's intent with respect to securities (available for sale, held to maturity) and agree to the financial statement classification; evaluate company investment activities for consistency with stated intent; obtain representations letter from management regarding intent (authorization, existence or occurrence, valuation)

Analyze the recorded amount of investments evaluating the choice and application of accounting standards (fair value, cost, equity method, and considering any impairment) and trace to the financial statements evaluating the account classification (existence or occurrence, valuation)

The audit of investments is challenging as a result of the complexity of the underlying investments. The possibilities for protecting against various business risks have increased with the development of different types of financial instruments. As a result, more companies are taking advantage of these risk management opportunities and investing in complex financial instruments. Consequently, the expertise required of auditors and the audit effort required for investments has increased even for companies with a primary business completely separate from investing activities. Exhibit 15-5 summarizes a general list of audit steps that apply to financial instruments and other types of investments.

EXHIBIT 15-5

Summary of Tests Related to Sophisticated Financial Instruments and Other Investments

1. Review the records for transactions involving purchases and sales of financial instruments of all types and other investments.

2. Develop an understanding of the nature of each financial instrument and other investment the entity has acquired, including the terms of individual transactions.

3. For each type of financial instrument and other investment, determine the appropriate accounting measurement and recognition principles. Review management's documentation describing the methodology, underlying assumptions, and calculations that support the valuation of each type of financial instrument and other investment. Determine whether the valuation principles, assumptions, and methods are appropriate.

4. Identify the risks associated with each financial instrument and other investment and evaluate how those risks affect the realizability of the investment.

   a. the risk that the issuer of the instrument or the outside party involved in the investment transaction will be unable to make payment or otherwise complete the transaction at the scheduled time of maturity

   b. the risk that fluctuations in interest rates, foreign exchange rates, or commodity prices may change the underlying value of the investment.

5. Count or confirm securities delivered to the investor or its agent, as appropriate.

6. Confirm transaction details with relevant outside parties.

7. Determine where securities are held and, when appropriate, confirm their existence and the custodian's legal obligation to the investor. Consider

   a. obtaining a report from the custodian's auditor on the custodian's internal control with respect to securities held in safekeeping, for example, a SAS 70 report,

   b. requesting that specific tests be performed by that auditor, or

   c. personally performing such tests.

8. Evaluate the appropriateness of the financial statement classification and disclosure of investment transactions and the degree of risk involved in them.

(Adapted from Montgomery's *Auditing* 12th edition, pp. 21–17, 21–18.)

Auditing Other Comprehensive Income [LO 3]

Comprehensive income is defined in FASB codification 220-10, *Comprehensive Income.* It is also defined in FASB Concepts Statement No. 6. Both describe it as a business enterprise's change in equity resulting from transactions and other events from nonowner sources. When net income is considered separately, the term used to refer to all nonowner-related changes in equity *except* net income is **other comprehensive income**. Other comprehensive income is often shortened to OCI. Even though the change in the fair value of investments is only one of the components of OCI, it is a common one that is easily understood. Therefore, the audit of OCI is discussed here.

The auditor obtains information about OCI as a result of auditing the changes in the related balance sheet accounts that make up its components, for example, financial assets and financial liabilities. After verifying the accuracy of the underlying balance sheet-related amounts that make up its components, the OCI audit procedures are straightforward. The auditor traces the components to the OCI account balance and determines whether the presentation and disclosure is accurate and consistent with the requirements of the accounting standards.

Auditing the Consolidation Process

Auditing the inputs to the process of consolidating the financial statements occurs throughout the audit as various accounts are audited. Auditing the final financial statement presentation is accomplished by tracing, evaluating, and recalculating the consolidating process. Again, investment accounts are not the only ones affected by the consolidation process. But auditing the consolidation process is presented here because investment accounts are important to the consolidation and require auditor attention in several areas.

The magnitude of ownership interest and the level of control a company has over its investees affect the proper accounting for the investment. Wholly owned subsidiaries for which there is no question about control are obviously at the extreme end of the ownership continuum. For other ownership interests, the company and consequently the auditor, must address how to properly account for an investment. The accounting may be based on fair value, cost, or the equity method, or the ownership interest may be consolidated into the company's financial statements. Variable interest entities require special consideration in this evaluation. As stated earlier, the accounting rules may require an investee to be consolidated even with a small percentage ownership interest if the owner meets the criteria for being the primary beneficiary. In summary, auditing a consolidated entity calls for procedures addressing:

- The choice of entities to be included
- Accounts of the consolidated entities
- Process of consolidation
- Final presentation and disclosures

REVIEW QUESTIONS

C1. How are investments related to changes in OCI?

C2. What procedures does the auditor perform to audit the consolidation process? When do these audit procedures occur?

C3. Why does the auditor have to be concerned about variable interest annuities when auditing the consolidation process?

AUDITING IN ACTION

Ford Motor Company and Subsidiaries, December 31, 2008
NOTES TO THE FINANCIAL STATEMENTS

NOTE 11. VARIABLE INTEREST ENTITIES

We consolidate VIEs of which we are the primary beneficiary. The liabilities recognized as a result of consolidating these VIEs do not necessarily represent additional claims on our general assets; rather, they represent claims against the specific assets of the consolidated VIEs. Conversely, assets recognized as a result of consolidating these VIEs do not represent additional assets that could be used to satisfy claims against our general assets.

Automotive Sector

VIEs of which we are the primary beneficiary:

Activities with the joint ventures described below include purchasing substantially all of the joint ventures' output under a cost-plus-margin arrangement and/or volume dependent pricing. These contractual arrangements may require us to absorb joint venture losses when production volume targets are not met or allow us, in some cases, to receive bonuses when production volume targets are exceeded. Described below are the significant VIEs that were consolidated.

AutoAlliance International, Inc. ("AAI") is a 50/50 joint venture with Mazda in North America. AAI is engaged in the manufacture of automobiles on behalf of Ford and Mazda, primarily for sale in North America.

Ford Otomotiv Sanayi Anonim Sirketi ("Ford Otosan") is a 41/41/18 joint venture in Turkey with the Koc Group of Turkey and public investors. Ford Otosan is the single-source supplier of the Ford Transit Connect model, and an assembly supplier of the Ford Transit van model, both of which we sell primarily in Europe.

Getrag Ford Transmissions GmbH ("GFT") is a 50/50 joint venture with Getrag Deutsche Venture GmbH and Co. KG. GFT is the primary supplier of manual transmissions for use in our European vehicles.

Getrag All Wheel Drive AB is a 40/60 joint venture between Volvo Cars and Getrag Dana Holding GmbH. The joint venture produces all-wheel-drive components.

Tekfor Cologne GmbH ("Tekfor") is a 50/50 joint venture with Neumayer Tekfor GmbH. Tekfor produces transmission and chassis components for use in our vehicles.

Pininfarina Sverige, AB is a 40/60 joint venture between Volvo Cars and Pininfarina, S.p.A. The joint venture was established to engineer and manufacture niche vehicles.

We also hold interests in certain Ford and/or Lincoln Mercury dealerships. At December 31, 2008, we consolidated a portfolio of approximately 67 dealerships that are part of our Dealer Development program. We supply and finance the majority of vehicles and parts to these dealerships, and the operators have a contract to buy our equity interest over a period of time.

Auditing Disclosures [LO 4]

Required disclosures for investments are influenced by the nature of the investment and the applicable accounting standards. To determine whether disclosures are adequate, the auditor must understand the company's investments and the disclosure requirements of the applicable standards. Then, the auditor reviews the financial statements to determine whether the disclosures effectively communicate the required information. The stated intent of the FASB fair value disclosure requirements portrays the challenges related to providing adequate disclosure of investments.

> The principal objectives of the disclosures required… are to **facilitate** both of the following comparisons:
>
> a. **Comparisons between entities** that choose **different measurement attributes** for **similar assets and liabilities**
> b. Comparisons between assets and liabilities in the financial statements **of an entity** that selects **different measurement attributes** for **similar assets and liabilities.**

Those disclosure requirements are expected to result in the following:

a. Information to enable users of its financial statements to understand management's reasons for electing or partially electing the fair value option
b. Information to enable users to understand how changes in fair values affect earnings for the period
c. The same information about certain items (such as equity investments and nonperforming loans) that would have been disclosed if the fair value option had not been elected
d. Information to enable users to understand the differences between fair values and contractual cash flows for certain items.

(FASB codification 825-10-50-24, 25)

In summary, the auditor must determine whether the applicable accounting standard is followed and whether the financial statements disclosure:

1. Represents the transactions and events
2. Is complete, appropriately and clearly described
3. Presents the amounts fairly for the investments

LIABILITIES AND THE FINANCING CYCLE

The next part of the financing cycle is debt, long-term liabilities, and other long-term accounts. Long-term liabilities can take many forms, such as notes, contracts, and mortgages. However, not all activities and transactions associated with long-term liabilities fit the definition of debt. Other long-term accounts discussed in the following section are pensions, postretirement benefits, and taxes. Although these accounts often represent liabilities, they can also represent asset balances.

Long-Term Debt [LO 5]

Most companies have long-term debt as a part of their capital structures. The debt represents a legal obligation on the part of the company to pay some amount to the other party. Prior to the requirement for an ICFR audit, debt was commonly audited without testing controls. Even now, the auditor may test related ICFR only at year end and may rely on substantive tests for the financial statement audit.

The auditor can rather easily determine the proper year end balance of the debt principal and interest expense and any related account balances. Relatively few transactions affect the debt principal, and a direct relationship exists between debt and interest expense. Determining proper amounts can be straightforward. An equally important characteristic causing the auditor to rely on substantive tests is that even though there may be relatively few transactions outside of paying interest, each may be material and therefore require the auditor's specific attention.

Undertaking new debt occurs with less frequency than a company's routine transactions. New debt obligations are approved by the Board of Directors or are authorized by the Board and approved by an upper level member of management. These approvals are documented and provide the auditor with evidence. Important aspects of accounting for debt are:

Including all debt at the proper amounts

Classifying debt appropriately as long or short term

Providing the required presentation and disclosure

Debt can be structured in various forms and can include notes, loans, contracts, bonds, and mortgages payable. Debt transactions can also be structured as leases. As was discussed in the earlier part of the chapter on investments, debt can have features such as being convertible into stock; combined with stock warrants, options, or rights; and being callable by the creditor. Debt can be secured or unsecured. The auditor has to know the accounting standards and understand the nature of the debt transaction to determine whether it is accounted for properly.

Determining the proper amount to record for most debt is straightforward. The amount is generally based on the contract underlying the transaction. However, several situations require different measurement and presentation.

When debt is issued at a discount or premium, the financial statements reflect the contract amount net of any unamortized discount or premium. The amortization of discount or premium at the effective interest rate means that interest expense is not necessarily the same as the cash disbursement. In addition to examining the cash disbursement transaction, the auditor also recalculates interest considering the effects of discount and premium. When a company enters a lease that is actually a financing arrangement, the financial statements reflect the debt and interest. Auditors also recalculate these amounts.

Proper classification of debt as long or short term is fairly straightforward unless currently maturing long-term debt is to be refinanced or the company is in violation of debt covenants. Currently maturing long-term debt may be properly *excluded from short-term liabilities* when the company has the intent and can demonstrate the ability to refinance the debt for a long-term period. In this situation the auditor investigates the client's evidence of its intent and ability to refinance.

Violation of **debt covenants** can also affect the proper classification of debt. Debt may have to be *shown as short term*, if, as a result of the debt covenant violation, the lender can change the terms of the debt so that the entire principal amount becomes currently due. When debt covenant violations exist or have occurred during the year, the auditor considers whether the debt is properly classified and the disclosure adequate.

Audit guidelines require disclosure of covenant violations; therefore, auditors must be aware of a client's compliance with covenants to ensure that the financial statements disclosures are adequate and that the appropriate audit opinion is issued.

AUDITING IN ACTION

Waivers on Debt Covenants

During the economic crisis of 2008–2009, numerous companies, including MGM and Pilgrim's Pride, received debt covenant waivers from their lenders. In the case of Pilgrim's Pride, two waivers were issued in late 2008, the last of which expired on November 26, 2008. On December 11, 2008 the company entered Chapter 11 bankruptcy protection. MGM received a three-month waiver in March 2009 and subsequently was able to issue $2.5 billion in stock and bonds to buy itself some time.

Other Long-Term Accounts

FASB codification section 715 addresses retirement benefits, and governs accounting for deferred compensation vehicles. The accounting standards require that, in addition to the current calculation of pension expense and any related liability, a company with a defined benefit pension plan or a plan of postretirement benefits show the funded status of the plan in its balance sheet. The company must measure the fair value of the plan assets at its financial statement date and compare that amount to the projected pension benefit obligation to determine the plan's funded status. Entries to record changes in the funded status are posted to other comprehensive income. The audit considers the company's transactions and expert's valuations that go into calculating the plan's status.

The funded status of a pension or postretirement plan can result in an asset if it is overfunded or a liability if it is underfunded. Similarly, deferred taxes can be an asset or a liability. Many estimates are made in determining the amount of taxes to record. The amounts calculated and posted by the company reflect a tax liability or refund for the current year as well as a deferred tax liability or asset for estimated future tax effects.

Tests of Controls and Dual Purpose Tests

The auditor tests debt-related activities to ascertain that processes are in place that permit all debt and interest to be properly authorized and recorded. In addition, the audit of debt addresses the company's timely payments of principal and interest due, and ability to service or pay back its debt and any interest that is due within the next year.

If a company cannot service its debt either through current operations or by obtaining new financing, the auditor will analyze whether the company can continue as a "going concern." When a company's continued existence is in doubt because it may not have the resources to satisfy its obligations, the auditor modifies the audit opinion on the financial statements to reflect the uncertainty related to the company's ability to continue. Going concern audit opinions are discussed in Chapter 11.

Consistent with audit steps that were discussed for investments earlier in the chapter, many of the audit procedures to test controls over debt transactions are combined with steps to gather evidence on the account balance, and thus are dual purpose tests. Examples of company controls and tests for debt activities and accounts are shown in Exhibit 15-6.

EXHIBIT 15-6

Examples of Controls and Related Tests for Debt

Note that either management or the auditor can perform tests of controls. Management uses tests of controls to support its management report. The auditor uses tests of controls for the audit of ICFR and to confirm the planned reliance on controls in the financial statement audit. Many of these tests of controls may be extended by the auditor to include a component providing evidence for the financial statement audit. Examples of these extensions are indicated in **bold**, and the audit procedures can be characterized as dual purpose tests.

Purpose of Controls	Company Control and Tests
To ensure that debt incurred is authorized and approved **(authorization)**	
	CC: *Policies exist and are followed for authorization and approval of new debt by the Board of Directors and specified members of management*
	TofC: Examine policies for authorization and approval of new debt
	TofC: Examine copies of agreements, supporting documents and minutes of Board of Directors meetings for approval of new debt incurred
To ensure that cash received from debt is physically controlled and properly documented **(existence or occurrence, completeness)**	
	CC: *Receipts from debt are subject to the same ICFR as other cash receipts*
	TofC: Tests of the cash receipts cycle

(continued)

To ensure that all debt is recorded
(**completeness**)

CC: *A detailed subsidiary ledger is maintained for all debt and the total is periodically reconciled to the general ledger*

TofC: Check the subsidiary ledger of notes and bonds payable for mathematical accuracy and **trace the total to the general ledger**

To ensure that all debt and related interest and other amounts are shown at the proper value
(**valuation**)

CC: *Debt is recorded at face value with a separate account (to net plus or minus) for any discount or premium*

CC: *Amortization of premiums and discounts are calculated using the effective interest method and posted to the debt and interest expense accounts*

TofC: **Recalculate the amortization of premium or discount and use the amount to recalculate the current amount of debt; trace the debt to the general ledger; trace the amortization to interest expense**

CC: *Underwriter, legal, and accounting fees are recorded in a separate account and amortized over the life of the related debt*

TofC: **Recalculate the amortization of fees and trace to the general ledger**

To ensure that required interest payments are made and properly recorded
(**existence or occurrence, completeness**)

CC: *Payments for interest expense are subject to the same ICFR as other cash disbursements*

TofC: Tests of the cash disbursements cycle

TofC: **Select interest payments, agree to underlying documents, and recalculate amount; select debt instruments, recalculate interest amount based on information specified in the debt instrument, and trace to cash disbursements**

To ensure that the company stays in compliance with debt covenants
(**existence or occurrence, valuation, presentation and disclosure**)

CC: *Policies exist and are followed for monitoring compliance with debt covenants*

TofC: Obtain and read policies for monitoring compliance with debt covenants; test whether company activities that are specified in the policies are followed, for example, review documentation created as a result of the monitoring process

Substantive Analytical Procedures

The relationship between debt and interest expense means that substantive analytical procedures can provide the auditor with "big picture" evidence regarding the reasonableness of both interest-related accounts and debt principal. Similarly, a relationship exists between compensation expense, pension contributions, and a part of the pension obligation. Taxable income, the effective tax rate, tax payments, and the current tax obligation also have an expected relationship. Unexpected outcomes in analytical procedures suggest that either the auditor does not understand this part of the client activities or the amounts are misstated. Examples of substantive analytical procedures for debt follow:

Compare total balances of debt and interest accounts to prior year and budget.

Compare the composition of items that make up the total balances in the accounts to the prior year.

Recalculate interest expense based on overall terms of the debt.
If recorded interest expense is too low, the company may have failed to record or pay interest. If recorded interest expense is too high, the company may have failed to record all the debt.

Calculate ratios and compare to prior year and industry as appropriate.

AUDITING IN ACTION

Common Financial Ratios Applicable to Debt

- Interest-bearing debt/Total assets

    Compare to prior years or industry; reasonableness of debt amount

- (Current portion of debt + Dividends)/Cash flow from operations

    An indicator of liquidity status; less than 1.0 indicates problems

- "Times interest earned"

    Income before interest and taxes/(Interest expense + Capitalized interest)

    An indicator of ability to cover cost of debt service; less than 1.0 indicates problems

- (Interest expense + Capitalized interest)/Average interest-bearing debt

    Reasonableness test for recorded interest

Tests of Details of Balances

The auditor's primary concerns regarding debt are that all debt is recorded and that the amount of each component—including interest—is proper and recorded in the correct account. This means:

All debt is shown.

When appropriate, balances are shown as debt rather than a component of equity.

When applicable, payments affect debt and interest rather than being shown as lease expense.

Another concern regarding debt is that classification as long or short term is consistent with the accounting standards. Investigating debt covenants generally is directed toward the audit of disclosure. But if the company has violated a debt covenant, the audit procedures can also provide evidence on how the amounts should be shown in the financial statements. For example, as mentioned earlier, a debt covenant violation may mean a debt must be classified as short term rather than long term.

To perform tests of controls, dual purpose tests, and substantive analytical procedures, the auditor obtains a detailed schedule of debt from the company that reflects principal, interest expense, and interest payable. If the schedule provided by the company only includes debt still outstanding at year end, the auditor or client must add the following information:

- Debt that existed at the end of the prior year that has been retired
- Debt that was incurred and completely paid off during the year

Some of the tests of details of balances that provide information for the audit of debt are likely performed using computer auditing programs. An example is scanning files for cash activity. A list of tests of details of balances for debt is shown in Exhibit 15-7.

EXHIBIT 15-7

Examples of Tests of Details of Balances for Debt

Obtain a copy of the company's detailed schedule of debt; verify mathematical accuracy and trace the total of year end debt to the general ledger (existence and occurrence, completeness)

Read long-term debt contracts and agreements, including lease contracts

    Trace amounts in the contracts to the detailed schedule agreeing principal amount, classification as long term or short term; analyze that principal amount posted is proper, with special attention to new debt (existence or occurrence, completeness, cutoff)

    Consider any debt being refinanced and excluded from short term for propriety of the presentation based on GAAP (existence or occurrence, rights and obligations, presentation and disclosure)

    Assess whether leases should be shown as capital leases; trace any capital leases to debt schedule and general ledger (completeness)

    Identify debt covenants specified in the agreements such as restrictions on payment of dividends, restrictions on issuing additional debt, required debt and equity ratios, required financial performance and ratios; evaluate whether the company was in compliance at the end of the fiscal year (and, for SEC disclosure requirements, at any time during the year) (rights and obligations, presentation and disclosure)

Read Board of Directors minutes for approval of new long-term debt and trace into detailed schedule (authorization)

Review schedule for any new debt not approved by Board of Directors (authorization)

Trace cash receipts from any new debt to the cash receipts journal and agree the amount to the debt schedule and general ledger (existence or occurrence, cutoff)

Scan interest expense accounts for payments; trace amounts to the debt analysis schedule agreeing timing and amount as appropriate for terms of the debt; note any interest paid for debt not listed on the debt analysis schedule and follow up to determine whether debt has been inappropriately omitted from the schedule (existence or occurrence, rights and obligation, completeness, cutoff)

Independently recalculate interest expense and agree to interest expense account in general ledger (existence or occurrence, completeness)

Independently recalculate accrued interest payable and trace to general ledger (existence or occurrence, completeness)

Scan the cash receipts journal for agreement to recorded debt and any deposits or payments indicating debt not on the debt schedule (completeness)

Perform search of cash activity after year end for payments of interest that are related to debt that was not recorded or cash receipts indicating major debt taken on after the end of the year that would need to be disclosed (completeness, presentation and disclosure)

Confirm long-term debt (existence or occurrence, completeness, rights or obligations)

    Send confirmations to creditors and any guarantors (could be banks, insurance companies, and trustees representing creditors); Use standard bank confirmations for any debt with banks

Confirm amount (principal, accrued interest), terms, including any assets pledged as security for the debt

Evaluate whether debt is properly classified as long or short term based on confirmation information, particularly as related to any debt refinancing

Inquire of management regarding the existence of any "off-balance sheet" activities (authorization, presentation, and disclosure)

Read the Board of Directors minutes specifically for any indications of off-balance sheet debt (authorization, presentation, and disclosure)

AUDITING IN ACTION

Example of a Work Paper for the Audit of Debt

Maggie Manley Company
Long-Term Debt Lead Schedule
Fiscal year-end
12/31/10
Prepared by: JH
1/14/11

	Debt			
	Balance			Balance
Description	12/31/09	Additions	Retirements	12/31/10
8% note payable to a bank, due $50,000 per year. Secured by land and building.	350,000 PY	-	(50,000) a	300,000 c

	TB			TB
		Interest Payable		
	Balance			Balance
Description	12/31/09	Provision	Payments	12/31/10
8% Interest on note payable	2,333 PY	27,665 (1)	(27,998) b	2,000 (2)

Test of Accrued Interest:

Note balance	300,000
Interest rate	0.08
	24,000
Accrual Period	
12–1 to 12–31	x 1/12
	2000 (2)

Test of Accrued Expense

350,000 x .08 x 11/12 =	25,665
300,000 x .08 x 1/12 =	2,000
	27,665 (1)

Tickmarks:

PY	Traced to prior year working paper
TB	Traced to trial balance
C	Confirmed by bank
a	Examined cancelled check
b	Examined cancelled checks for February and November payments

(*Source:* Based on Taylor and Glezen, p. 561.)

Debt Covenants

The general nature of debt covenants must be disclosed, along with any violation of debt covenants at year end. SEC rules require disclosure of debt covenant violations that occurred during the year even if the problem has since been corrected. Typical debt covenants require the debtor to maintain financial ratios within a specified range, or restrict dividends or additional borrowings. Debt covenants are important because, in some cases, if they are violated the creditor can demand that the entire amount of the debt be paid immediately. Even though this is possible, it is not the common outcome. If a company is in violation of a debt covenant for any reason other than carelessness, the company is likely having financial or cash flow problems. In that situation, the debtor company probably could not pay the debt even if the creditor declared the debt to be due immediately.

Debt covenants and any violations are important to the auditor for several reasons. First, the auditor must consider whether the debt covenants and violations are properly disclosed in the financial statements. Second, if debt covenants have been violated, the auditor has to consider the impact on the company's financial viability and whether the company has **going concern risk**.

If a company violates its debt covenants, it may be able to obtain a waiver from the lender. A waiver is a commitment in writing that the lender is not going to make the debt immediately payable as a result of the debt covenant violation. This waiver may provide the auditor with sufficient evidence to conclude that the company does not have a going concern problem.

Whenever a company is having financial or cash flow problems, the auditor must carefully consider the fraud risk. Financial difficulties increase the risk that account balances may have been manipulated or misstated by management. A motivation for manipulating financial records might be to hide information about loan covenant violations.

REVIEW QUESTIONS

D1. What information does the auditor obtain by using substantive analytical procedures on account balances related to debt?

D2. What are the primary audit concerns for debt and debt-related account balances and disclosures?

D3. Why does the auditor undertake procedures to identify any debt covenant violations that occurred throughout the year and at year end?

D4. What is a waiver related to debt covenants, and how does it affect the auditor's work?

D5. How does the going concern status of a company relate to the violation of debt covenants?

Auditing Pensions and Postretirement Benefits Accounts [LO 6]

Company financial statements report expenses and liabilities related to pensions, **postretirement benefits**, and **postemployment benefits**. Generally, pensions can be **defined benefit** or **defined contribution plans**. Defined benefit describes those plans in which the amount the employee will receive is a contractual amount. Defined benefit plans are less common now than in the past. They have often been noncontributory, meaning that the employee does not contribute to the plan. Defined contribution plans are those in which the contracted amount is the amount the employer contributes to the plan. Defined contribution plans are typically contributory, meaning that the employee may also contribute to the fund.

Defined benefit pension plans can be funded or unfunded. In a funded defined benefit pension plan, the employer contributes cash to cover the pension obligation when the pension obligation is created. The other option is for the employer to provide funding when the pension benefit is due to be paid to the retiree. In other words, in a funded pension plan the assets from which the retirement benefits will be paid are "set aside" by the company while the employee is still working. Funded pension plans are often managed by a trust. The trust itself is a separate entity from the company with its own financial statements that must be audited.

The term *postretirement benefits* usually refers to health benefits provided to retired employees. Postemployment benefits, which are benefits paid to former employees who are not retired, are not addressed in this discussion.

Prior to the Employee Retirement Income Security Act of 1974 (ERISA), little guidance existed for accounting for pension plans. Now, numerous laws, regulations, and accounting standards apply to pensions and postretirement benefits. Pension and postretirement benefits are a form of deferred compensation. Therefore, the costs are a part of the company's compensation expenses during the years that employees are earning the deferred compensation.

The audit investigates funding and disclosure adequacy. The auditor also addresses whether the current portion of the expense and any liability related to that current expense are calculated properly and properly recorded. Determination of the amount of pension expense relies heavily on calculations performed by actuaries, who are specialists. In addition, the accounting standards require that the financial statements show whether a pension plan and postretirement benefits are overfunded or underfunded, based on the difference between the fair value of plan assets at the financial statement date and the obligation to retired employees. As with the amount of pension expense, the determination of the funded status relies heavily on actuarial calculations.

A description of the impact of SFAS No. 158 (later codified as section 715) on pensions as a new accounting standard on Delta's December 31, 2006 financial statements follows. The disclosure provides an example of the complexity of the disclosures required for other long-term accounts. The actual pension disclosure, Note 10 to the Delta financial statements, which presents all of the specific documentation on pensions, is 10 pages long. Similar to the audit of investments, auditing pensions can require an extensive amount of knowledge, experience, and effort.

> In September 2006, the Financial Accounting Standards Board ("FASB") issued SFAS No. 158, "Employers Accounting for Defined Benefit Pension and Other Postretirement Plans, an amendment of SFAS Nos. 87, 88, 106 and 132(R)" ("SFAS 158"). This statement, among other things, requires that we recognize the funded status of our defined benefit pension and other postretirement plans in our Consolidated Balance Sheet as of December 31, 2006, with changes in the funded status recognized through comprehensive loss in the year in which such changes occur. Application of this standard resulted in (1) a $685 million net decrease in accrued pension and other postretirement and postemployment liabilities, (2) a $248 million decrease in the intangible pension asset in other noncurrent assets and (3) a $437 million decrease in shareowners' deficit. The adoption of SFAS 158 had no effect on our Consolidated Statement of Operations for any period presented. For additional information regarding the impact of SFAS 158 on our Consolidated Financial Statements, see Note 10.

Exhibit 15-8 lists steps for auditing pensions.

EXHIBIT 15-8 Examples of Steps in Auditing Pension Costs	Identify and gain an understanding of the plans Compare current-year amounts and disclosures to prior years Test the accuracy of data provided by the company to the specialist and trace it into the work of the specialist Trace costs and other amounts to the specialist's report and any related client documents and audit work papers Examine specialist's report for inclusion of all plans Evaluate costs related to ERISA compliance Determine whether the basis of the computation is consistent with prior years and in compliance with GAAP Recalculate overfunded or underfunded status based on supporting documents and trace transactions and balances to general ledger accounts

Using the Work of a Specialist

When auditing pension and postretirement benefits, some of the steps are expected and fairly typical audit procedures. Among these are determining the mathematical accuracy of the calculated amounts based on the supporting documentation and tracing them into the general ledger. In addition, the auditor also considers the work of the specialist, in this case an actuary. AU 336, *Using the Work of a Specialist,* requires the auditor to assess the reasonableness of the assumptions made by the company and methods used by the specialist. The auditor considers whether the amounts calculated conform with the accounting standards.

Whenever a specialist is used, the auditing standard calls for an understanding among the auditor, company, and specialist on the following:

Objectives and scope of the specialist's work

The specialist's representations of his or her relationship with the company

Methods and assumptions to be used

How the methods and assumptions compare to those used in the prior period

Whether the specialist's findings corroborate the financial statement presentations

The form and content of the specialist's report to be provided to the auditor

The auditor evaluates the specialist's qualifications, reputation, and experience. The auditor also tests the information provided to the specialist by the company for the specialist to use in making the calculations. In the case of pension and postretirement benefits, this includes information about the company's employees who are earning benefits. The auditor addresses any unusual or unexpected changes from the prior period in either the inputs provided by the company or outputs derived by the specialist.

REVIEW QUESTIONS

E1. What is the difference between a defined benefit and a defined contribution pension plan? What does it mean when a plan is "funded"?

E2. What are postretirement benefits?

E3. During what period of time are pension and other postretirement benefits expensed?

E4. What is the auditor supposed to understand when a specialist is involved with an audit? What other audit steps are appropriate related to the specialist?

Auditing Taxes

Taxes and the audit of taxes are included here, even though taxes impact more than long-term liability accounts. When auditing income taxes, the auditor addresses all tax liabilities and refunds receivable, tax provisions, and deferred tax accounts. The objectives are to obtain reasonable assurance that the amounts are properly measured, classified, and disclosed in the financial statements. FASB ASC 740, *Income Taxes,* provide guidance for the proper accounting treatment.

The audit of taxes is important because the amounts are typically material to the financial statements. The auditor will understand, test, and conclude on ICFR, usually over the areas of tax planning, compliance with laws, and recording tax transactions. Good ICFR over these functional areas requires the company to

- have competent people responsible for management of the tax area—including any branches or subsidiaries, maintaining sufficiently detailed records,
- reconcile the ledger balances to the supporting detail, and
- use outside advisors when appropriate.

AUDITING IN ACTION

Basic Principles of Accounting for Income Tax

A current tax liability or asset is recognized for estimated taxes payable or refundable on the current year's tax returns.

A deferred tax liability or asset is recognized for the estimated future tax effects attributable to temporary differences and carryforwards, including operating loss carryforwards.

All measurements are based on regular tax rates and provisions of the enacted tax law; the effects of anticipated changes in tax laws or rates are not considered.

The amount of deferred tax assets is reduced, if applicable, by any tax benefits that, based on available evidence, are not expected to be realized.

Source: Montgomery's *Auditing,* 12th edition, p. 24-2.

Substantive audit procedures include obtaining an analysis of the accounts, testing tax payments by examining supporting documents, and recalculating the tax provision. The auditor considers management's estimates when evaluating deferred taxes and contingent liabilities related to taxes. As a reminder, auditing estimates is discussed in Chapter 14 in relation to inventory.

Auditing Disclosures [LO 7]

Disclosures for debt, pension and postretirement benefits, and taxes are extensive and specified by the accounting standards applicable to the accounts. Typical debt disclosures include future cash payments, including the amount of both maturities and sinking fund requirements for all long-term borrowings for each of the five years following the date of the latest balance sheet. The auditor obtains evidence about this information during the audit of debt and equity. Therefore, to audit the disclosure, the auditor reads the information on the face of the financial statements and in the notes. Then the auditor assesses whether the disclosure describes the company's debt information, includes all the information required, is appropriately presented and clearly expressed, and includes amounts that are accurate.

REVIEW QUESTIONS

F1. What are the objectives related to the audit of taxes?

F2. What are important ICFR for taxes?

F3. What substantive audit procedures apply to taxes?

F4. How does the auditor investigate disclosures for debt, pension and postretirement benefits, and taxes?

EQUITY AND THE FINANCING CYCLE

The complexity of equity accounts varies dramatically among companies based on the number and nature of transactions. Recording net income to retained earnings, issuing common stock for cash, and paying cash dividends are all relatively straightforward, typically infrequent transactions. Consequently, the audit of these transactions is also straightforward.

In contrast, transactions involving preferred classes of stock, stock dividends and splits, share-based payments, treasury stock, and mergers and acquisitions can be very complex. As with debt transactions, the audit of these accounts has traditionally been based mainly on substantive procedures. Now, controls testing is included as part of the ICFR audit.

AUDITING IN ACTION

Equity and Related Accounts Addressed in the Audit

Capital Stock, Common	Dividends declared
(can have multiple classes)	Dividends payable
Capital Stock, Preferred	Treasury Stock
(can have multiple classes)	Retained Earnings
Paid in capital	Appropriated Retained Earnings
(for each stock account)	

Equity Transactions and Activities [LO 8]

Publicly traded companies issue stock relatively infrequently compared to the other business transactions in which they participate. The importance of a stock issue, involvement of the Board of Directors, and oversight by regulators all contribute to the high level of control exercised over these transactions. Stock offerings and other equity transactions are authorized and reviewed both internally and external to the company.

Execution and recordkeeping for equity transactions are often outsourced. In placing a stock offering with investors, companies work with a variety of outsiders, such as investment banks and stock brokerage firms. In publicly traded companies, an outside **registrar** determines that all stock a company issues complies with its corporate charter. Even after a company has issued shares, it needs to track current owners to provide them with information and distribute dividends. To maintain a record of current stock owners, most publicly traded companies contract with an outside **stock transfer agent**. Aso, companies often use a **dividend disbursing agent** who has the responsibility for sending dividend payments to stockholders of record.

Proper accounting for certain equity transactions can be complex. For example, the proper posting of preferred stock that has characteristics of debt requires careful consideration. The SEC requires that stock that has mandatory redemption requirements or has redemption considerations that are out of the issuer's control be shown outside of the stockholders' equity section. In addition, when stock or stock instruments, such as options and warrants, are issued for reasons other than raising cash, determining the proper value to record can be complex. This situation occurs when, for example, stock is issued as part of a merger or an acquisition, a stock split, or a dividend. Valuation is also necessary when stock is issued to pay for goods or services, as in the case of share-based compensation. Valuation methods must be based on the underlying accounting standards for the particular type of transaction.

FASB ASC 718-10, *Compensation–Stock Compensation,* is an example of an accounting standard that calls for transactions using fair value. The movement toward accounting standards using fair value is intended to increase the comparability among financial statements, as well as increase the convergence of United States and international accounting standards. As with fair value of investments that was discussed earlier in the chapter, fair values of share-based payments rely on estimates. A company must have an appropriate method for making these accounting estimates. Often a specialist is involved in valuing the transaction.

Tests of Controls and Dual Purpose Tests

The main control concerns for equity transactions are that they are properly authorized, correctly recorded, and properly presented and disclosed. Board of Directors authorization is generally required for issuing capital stock, repurchasing capital stock (treasury stock), and declaring dividends. Correctly recording equity transactions means that the company properly records transactions with a cash or financial statement effect. In addition, the company or outside agents must also maintain records on the identity of actual current share owners and on the amounts of dividends paid to stockholders as of the date of record.

Controls over the payment of cash dividends are the same as for the payment of other cash disbursements discussed in earlier chapters. If the payment is handled internally rather than through an outside agent, controls must exist to ensure that payments are made to the correct individuals and for the correct amounts. Sometimes an imprest account is used to add to the control over cash disbursements for dividends. Tests of controls and dual purpose tests (in bold) follow:

> *Identify and read policies for authorizing stock and dividend transactions and determining that they are in compliance with corporate charter.*
>
> **Read minutes for evidence of Board of Directors or shareholders vote approving stock and dividend transactions, including amounts authorized.**
>
> *Examine documents supporting recorded stock and dividend transactions for consistency with corporate charter, proper authorization and oversight.*
>
> *Confirm engagement and activities of outside registrar, stock transfer agent and dividend disbursing agent, **including agreeing amounts of recorded transactions with those confirmed by outside parties.** (If no outside agents are used, a program auditing the company's ICFR for these transactions is needed.)*

Substantive Analytical Procedures

Although most capital stock and equity transactions are examined by the auditor in detail, analytical procedures can provide big picture evidence regarding the appropriateness of the balances and whether the balances are consistent with known underlying information. Some common ratios calculated on equity accounts provide information to the auditor.

AUDITING IN ACTION

Ratios Related to Equity Accounts

Return on common stockholders' equity:
Net income—preferred dividends/average common stockholders' equity
  Can indicate to the auditor when the rate of return is different from industry expectations or company trends

Equity to total Liabilities and equity:
Stockholders' equity/stockholders' equity + total liabilities
  Provides an indicator of equity to debt financing sources

Dividend payout rate:
Cash dividends/net income
  Can indicate to the auditor the reasonableness of dividends based on historical trends and industry average; expected dividend payout rate may relate to whether the company is considered "high growth"

Earnings per share:
Net income/weighted average common shares outstanding

Tests of Details of Balances

Transactions affecting stockholders equity accounts are generally examined carefully by auditors. In addition to the professional care required for all parts of an audit, one reason for this careful consideration is that changes in stockholders' equity accounts appear

EXHIBIT 15-9

Examples of Tests of
Details of Balances for
Equity Accounts

Trace additions and reductions of the capital stock records (or analysis prepared by client or outside agent) to the general ledger

Identify outside transfer agents and dividend disbursing agents used and confirm transactions with these outside parties

Examine the corporate charter for the authorized amount of par value and trace to the recorded capital stock transactions; after the first year of audit this information may be included in the permanent file and those work papers may be used as the source of information

Recompute the recorded amounts of stock and dividend transactions for conformity with GAAP and agree to the amounts recorded and disclosed.

Trace any cash disbursed for the purchase of treasury stock and payment of cash dividends to the cash disbursements journal and appropriate general ledger equity accounts

Examine the contracts related to employee stock compensation plans and agree to terms of transactions; recalculate amounts recorded as compensation expense and additional paid in capital, using specialists to recalculate valuation as appropriate

Recalculate components and transactions affecting the Statement of Stockholders' Equity and trace underlying numbers and results to company books and records and financial statements

in the financial statements in the Statement of Stockholders' Equity. These changes are often subjected to critique by stock analysts. The intensity of audit work depends on the nature of the transactions and can range from tracing and balancing retained earnings to other financial statements to examining underlying documents and recalculating specific amounts for transactions such as share-based employee compensation. Examples of tests of details of balances for equity accounts are shown in Exhibit 15-9.

Auditing Mergers and Acquisitions [LO 9]

Among the most complicated transactions affecting equity accounts are mergers and acquisitions that involve stock. These transactions require the auditor to understand the transaction and address valuation and classification issues. The capital stock portion of the transaction is typically straightforward and based on the terms of the contract. Alternatively, the proper valuation and classification of the assets and liabilities affected usually requires analysis of the proper accounting treatment and may require the involvement of a valuation specialist.

The audit procedures for any merger or acquisition transaction begin with carefully reading the underlying agreement. The audit procedures needed to determine the appropriateness of the amounts and classifications used to record the transaction depend on the specifics of the transaction activities.

Auditing Retained Earnings

The most common transactions affecting retained earnings record net earnings and dividends declared. Net earnings is the mathematical result of combining other accounts. Therefore, auditing net earnings is based mainly on the result of other audit procedures. In this regard, auditing retained earnings is similar to what was discussed earlier in the chapter relating to comprehensive income and other comprehensive income, and is mainly based on the result of other audit procedures. After audits of the other accounts have been completed, the auditor traces the resulting net earnings to retained earnings. Dividends declared are traced to retained earnings as part of the audit of dividends. Only a limited number of other entries, such as an appropriation of retained earnings or stock dividends, are posted to retained earnings. For these transactions the auditor examines the supporting documents to determine that the amount is correct and the transaction is properly posted to retained earnings.

AUDITING IN ACTION

Merrill Lynch Acquisition by Bank of America

Bank of America Financial Statements Disclosure (partial), December 31, 2008

Note 2—Merger and Restructuring Activity

Merrill Lynch

On January 1, 2009, the Corporation acquired Merrill Lynch through its merger with a subsidiary of the Corporation in exchange for common and preferred stock with a value of $29.1 billion, creating a premier financial services franchise with significantly enhanced wealth management, investment banking and international capabilities. Under the terms of the merger agreement, Merrill Lynch common shareholders received 0.8595 of a share of Bank of America Corporation common stock in exchange for each share of Merrill Lynch common stock. In addition, Merrill Lynch non-convertible preferred shareholders received Bank of America Corporation preferred stock having substantially identical terms. Merrill Lynch convertible preferred stock remains outstanding and is convertible into Bank of America common stock at an equivalent exchange ratio. With the acquisition, the Corporation has one of the largest wealth management businesses in the world with more than 18,000 financial advisors and more than $1.8 trillion in client assets. Global investment management capabilities will include an economic ownership of approximately 50 percent (primarily preferred stock) in BlackRock, Inc., a publicly traded investment management company. In addition, the acquisition adds strengths in debt and equity underwriting, sales and trading, and merger and acquisition advice, creating significant opportunities to deepen relationships with corporate and institutional clients around the globe. Merrill Lynch's results of operations will be included in the Corporation's results beginning January 1, 2009.

The Merrill Lynch merger is being accounted for under the acquisition method of accounting in accordance with SFAS 141R. Accordingly, the purchase price was preliminarily allocated to the acquired assets and liabilities based on their estimated fair values at the Merrill Lynch acquisition date as summarized in the following table. Preliminary goodwill of $5.4 billion is calculated as the purchase premium after adjusting for the fair value of net assets acquired and represents the value expected from the synergies created from combining the Merrill Lynch wealth management and corporate and investment banking businesses with the Corporation's capabilities in consumer and commercial banking as well as the economies of scale expected from combining the operations of the two companies. The allocation of the purchase price will be finalized upon completion of the analysis of the fair values of Merrill Lynch's assets and liabilities.

(Retrieved from *http://idea.sec.gov/Archives/edgar/data/70858/000119312509041126/d10k1.pdf*; p. 125)

Auditing Disclosures [LO 10]

Disclosures for equity transactions are extensive but straightforward. The financial statements must disclose the number of shares authorized, issued, and outstanding for each class of stock. FASB ASC 505-10-50, *Equity Disclosure*, requires entities to disclose a summary of the pertinent rights and privileges of outstanding securities. Examples are dividend and liquidation preferences, participation rights, call prices and dates, conversion or exercise prices or rates and pertinent dates, and sinking-fund requirements. Information on stock option plans and stock purchase plans are disclosed. Disclosure also includes any restrictions on retained earnings and dividends, and pending transactions such as stock splits and dividends.

As with debt, the approach and amount of audit effort required for equity disclosures depends largely on the complexity of the company's information and transactions. The auditor knows about the underlying accounts and transactions as a result of the audit of the debt and equity areas. Using knowledge of the disclosures required, the auditor reads the disclosures to determine whether they are appropriate, accurate, complete, and understandable.

REVIEW QUESTIONS

G1. Which equity transactions tend to be more complicated? Less complicated?

G2. What stock-related activities do many public companies outsource and to whom?

G3. What are the primary control concerns regarding equity transactions?

G4. What information can an auditor obtain about equity accounts and transactions from substantive analytical procedures?

G5. What aspects of merger and acquisition transactions involving stock are highly complicated? How are merger and acquisition transactions audited?

G6. Why is auditing retained earnings a relatively simple audit procedure?

AUDITING RELATED PARTY TRANSACTIONS [LO 11]

Auditors scrutinize investment, debt, and equity transactions and accounts in the financing cycle for information on related parties. Audit steps dealing with related parties are mentioned in various chapters and discussed in Chapter 9. Related party transactions are highlighted here because of their importance related to the financing cycle. Any information on related parties identified from financing cycle transactions provides important information if the audit client also conducts business transactions with those related parties. Related parties and transactions with related parties are addressed in both accounting and auditing standards. Accounting standards define related parties. Auditing standards stress the importance of identifying related parties with which the audit client does business, understanding the transactions, and focusing on the adequacy of disclosure.

AU 334.02 explains the reason for the auditor's need to identify and understand transactions with related parties, as follows:

> the auditor should be aware that the substance of a particular transaction could be significantly different from its form and that financial statements should recognize the substance of particular transactions rather than merely their legal form. (AU 334.02)

AUDITING IN ACTION

Definition of Related Parties

a. *Affiliates of the enterprise*

b. *Entities for which investments in their equity securities would be required... to be accounted for by the equity method by the investing entity*

c. *Trusts for the benefit of employees, such as pension and profit-sharing trusts that are managed by or under the trusteeship of management*

d. *Principal owners of the entity and members of their immediate families*

e. *Management of the entity and members of their immediate families*

f. *Other parties with which the entity may deal if one party controls or can significantly influence the management or operating policies of the other to an extent that one of the transacting parties might be prevented from fully pursuing its own separate interests.*

g. *Other parties that can significantly influence the management or operating policies of the transacting parties or that have an ownership interest in one of the transacting parties and can significantly influence the other to an extent that one or more of the transacting parties might be prevented from fully pursuing its own separate interests*

(FASB ASC, Glossary)

The audit issue for these types of transactions is the possibility that they may have been transacted under special terms or constructed by the related parties to create a particular financial result. If either of these conditions exists, the transactions, as posted, may be different from what would have occurred if the parties were not related and did not have a mutual business goal.

The audit challenge is that, particularly with financing cycle transactions, it is usually not possible to determine whether transactions were conducted as they would have been with nonrelated parties. Another way to say this is that the auditor cannot really tell if the transactions were conducted at "arms length." AU 334 specifically addresses this audit challenge:

> Except for routine transactions, it will generally not be possible to determine whether a particular transaction would have taken place if the parties had not been related, or assuming it would have taken place, what the terms and manner of settlement would have been. Accordingly, it is difficult to substantiate representations that a transaction was consummated on terms equivalent to those that prevail in arm's-length transactions. (AU 334.12)

FASB codification 850-10, *Related Party Disclosures,* defines related parties. Generally, it includes entities in which a company has a major investment, owners and managers of the company and their families, pension and profit-sharing trusts (that are managed "by or under the trusteeship of management"), and other entities and people who have significant influence on the company's actions.

Just as an audit may not always uncover fraud, even a properly conducted audit may not identify all related party transactions. The auditor is supposed to be aware of the "possible existence of material related party transactions that could affect the financial statements and of common ownership or management control relationships" (AU334.04). According to the accounting standards, the common ownership or management control relationships must be disclosed even when there have been no transactions between the audit client and that entity. Even though an audit might not uncover all material related party transactions, the following types of transactions should alert the auditor to the possibility of the existence of related parties:

1. Borrowing or lending on an interest-free basis or at a rate of interest significantly above or below market rates prevailing at the time of the transaction.
2. Selling real estate at a price that differs significantly from its appraised value.
3. Exchanging property for similar property in a nonmonetary transaction.
4. Making loans with no scheduled terms for when or how the funds will be repaid.
(AU 334.03)

Some obvious and disclosed related party situations are parent–subsidiary and other investment relationships. The auditor performs specific procedures intended to identify other related parties that may not be as obvious. The following procedures are based on the guidance for identifying related parties that is provided in AU 334.07.

1. Identify the company's procedures for related parties. Assess whether the company's processes are appropriate for identifying related parties and accounting for any transactions with those parties.
2. Ask management to provide the names of any related parties and state whether there have been any transactions with those parties.
3. Review the company's filings with the SEC (and any other regulatory agencies, if there are any) for any information on related parties that has been reported in the filings.

4. Identify any pension or other trusts that are set up for the benefit of employees and determine whether any of the officers and trustees are related to the company.

5. Review stockholder listings (when there may be principal stockholders) and prior year audit work papers.

6. Ask prior auditors or other auditors performing work for the audit client of any information they may have about related parties.

7. Review material investment transactions to determine whether any of these transactions have created new related parties.

After performing procedures to identify related parties, the auditor investigates whether there are any material transactions with those entities. In addition, the auditor performs steps that may highlight any material transactions with related parties that have not yet been identified. Procedures used to identify material related party transactions are shown in Exhibit 15-10.

First, the auditor identifies related parties with which the company has conducted material transactions. The next steps are to understand the transactions and determine whether financial statement disclosure is appropriate and sufficient. The auditor investigates the transactions to understand the underlying business purpose and examines supporting documentation such as invoices, contracts, and receiving reports.

If a transaction is complex, the auditor may need a specialist to assist in understanding the transaction. If the transaction is one that should have been approved by the Board of Directors, the auditor inspects documentation for evidence of the approval. The auditor investigates the calculation of amounts included in financial statement disclosures, exam-

---

EXHIBIT 15-10

Identifying Transactions with Related Parties

a. Provide audit personnel performing segments of the audit or auditing and reporting separately on the accounts of related components of the reporting entity with the names of known related parties so that they may become aware of transactions with such parties during their audits.

b. Review the minutes of meetings of the Board of Directors and executive or operating committees for information about material transactions authorized or discussed at their meetings.

c. Review proxy and other material filed with the SEC and comparable data filed with other regulatory agencies for information about material transactions with related parties.

d. Review conflict-of-interest statements obtained by the company from its management.

e. Review the extent and nature of business transacted with major customers, suppliers, borrowers, and lenders for indications of previously undisclosed relationships.

f. Consider whether transactions are occurring, but are not being given accounting recognition, such as receiving or providing accounting, management, or other services at no charge or a major stockholder absorbing corporate expenses.

g. Review accounting records for large, unusual, or nonrecurring transactions or balances, paying particular attention to transactions recognized at or near the end of the reporting period.

h. Review confirmations of compensating balance arrangements for indications that balances are or were maintained for or by related parties.

i. Review invoices from law firms that have performed regular or special services for the company for indications of the existence of related parties or related party transactions.

j. Review confirmations of loans receivable and payable for indications of guarantees. When guarantees are indicated, determine their nature and the relationships, if any, of the guarantors to the reporting entity.

(AU 334.08)

EXHIBIT 15-11

Red Flags for Related
Party Transactions

a. Lack of sufficient working capital or credit to continue the business

b. An urgent desire for a continued favorable earnings record in the hope of supporting the price of the company's stock

c. An overly optimistic earnings forecast

d. Dependence on a single or relatively few products, customers, or transactions for the continuing success of the venture

e. A declining industry characterized by a large number of business failures

f. Excess capacity

g. Significant litigation, especially litigation between stockholders and management

h. Significant obsolescence dangers because the company is in a high-technology industry

(AU 334.06)

ines any intercompany amounts for proper accounting, shares and receives information with other auditors of related parties when appropriate, and investigates or confirms the value of any assets that are used as collateral for financing. If necessary the auditor confirms information with various entities, such as the related party involved in the transaction, banks, or attorneys. The auditor may examine documentation that is not usually a part of the audit such as documents held by the related party, externally produced financial publications or trade journals, and information about the related party obtained from its financial statements and tax returns.

In the audit of related party transactions, the auditor is trying to substantiate the business purpose and nature of the transactions. Again, this is because the substance of the transaction may differ from its form. Exhibit 15-11 lists red flags identified in AU 334 that, when they exist, should be considered by the auditor as possible motivators for the related party transactions. When these conditions exist, the auditor must carefully consider whether the form in which the transaction is presented represents its actual substance.

The ultimate purpose of investigating these related party transactions is to be able to conclude whether financial statement disclosure is adequate. As stated in AU 334.12, unless it is a common and routine transaction, the auditor will probably not be able to determine whether the company would have entered into the same transactions with nonrelated parties. However, by understanding the relationship of the involved parties and the business purpose of the transaction, the auditor should be able to understand the impact of the related party transaction on the financial statements. With this understanding the auditor can judge whether financial statement disclosure is adequate.

REVIEW QUESTIONS

H1. Why does the auditor need to identify and understand related party transactions?

H2. What standards define related parties, and what is the definition?

H3. What steps does the auditor conduct to identify related parties?

H4. What steps does the auditor conduct to identify material related party transactions?

H5. Once material related party transactions have been identified, what steps does the auditor perform on those transactions? What is the purpose of performing those steps?

H6. What is the auditor ultimately trying to determine regarding material related party transactions and the financial statements?

CONCLUSION

Investments, debt, and equity are three areas of activity that, for most companies, are not the primary focus of business activities. Even so, they are critical to supporting the entity's ongoing operations. Before the mandate for ICFR audits, these accounts were typically audited using a substantive approach. Since ICFR considerations must now be addressed, controls as well as financial statement amounts and disclosures are included in the audit of the financing cycle. Auditors may still choose to focus on substantive procedures for financial statement audit evidence.

Investments have always been important as a means of enhancing a company's earnings from resources not currently being put to use in operations. However, in recent years investments have become an increasingly important and valuable tool for businesses in managing risks related to inventories, interest rates, and foreign currency rate shifts. Because more businesses now use investments to manage their risks, auditors invest significant time and effort in auditing investments. The complexity of investment instruments and accounting standards, as well as the measurement and valuation challenges associated with investments, makes auditing investments an important part of the audit effort.

The audit of debt, long-term accounts, and equity is also a significant part of the audit effort. The composition and activity of these accounts vary significantly among companies. Consequently, the necessary audit procedures also vary. While some companies have straightforward debt and equity accounts, others have equity that behaves like debt, defined benefit pension and postretirement benefit plans that require analysis of funding status, and stock options awards as a method of employee compensation. Like investments, auditing debt and equity requires a thorough knowledge of the accounting standards as well as auditing skills.

KEY TERMS

Cash equivalent. A very short term investment; the name shows that there is no uncertainty regarding the cash to be received for the investment.

Commercial paper. Short-term promissory notes issued primarily by corporations.

Commodities. Term traditionally used to refer to unprocessed or partially processed goods such as agricultural and mining products; now also includes financial instruments linked to those products.

Compensating balance. A minimum balance required by a depository institution.

Comprehensive income. Changes in equity from nonowner sources.

Debt covenants. Agreements between a debtor and creditor that are part of the financing arrangement.

Debt securities. The instruments and contracts associated with borrowing funds.

Defined benefit pensions. Plans that are structured so that retirees receive a specified amount per period in retirement.

Defined contribution pensions. Plans structured so that the amounts added to the fund are specified, but the amount to be received by the retiree is not; the periodic receipts are based on contributions and earnings.

Derivatives. Financial instruments with terms that depend on, or are derived from, other events, assets, or liabilities.

Dividend disbursing agent. An entity external to a company to which the company outsources the task of distributing dividends.

Equity method. A method used to account for investments; typically appropriate when the investor owns between 20 and 50% of the investee.

Equity securities. The instruments associated with an ownership investment.

Fair value. Defined as the price that would be received to sell an asset or paid to transfer a liability in an orderly transaction between market participants at the measurement date.

Financial assets. Cash, evidence of an ownership interest in an entity, or a contract that conveys to one entity a right (1) to receive cash or another financial instrument from a second entity or (2) to exchange other financial instruments on potentially favorable terms with a second entity.

Financial instrument. A real or virtual document representing a legal agreement involving some sort of monetary value.

Financial liabilities. A contract that imposes on one entity an obligation (1) to deliver cash or another financial instrument to a second entity or (2) to exchange other financial instruments on potentially unfavorable terms with the second entity.

Funded status, over/under. Refers to whether a company's assets set aside for pension and other postretirement benefits are sufficient for the future obligation.

Going concern risk. Describes the risk that a company will not be able to meet its commitments that are required within the next fiscal year to stay in business as a going concern.

Hedge investment. Describes an investment made to offset a known risk.

Interbank transfer schedule. An analysis that tracks the movement of cash between bank accounts of a company for a specific period of time, usually shortly before and after the end of the financial period.

Kiting. A fraud scheme in which funds are reported in more than one account to cover a theft.

Marketable securities. Financial instruments representing debt or equity that are traded on a market.

Other comprehensive income. Changes in equity, other than from net income, from nonowner sources.

Postemployment benefits. Funds or other benefits received after a person separates from a company for reasons other than retirement.

Postretirement benefits. Usually refers to health insurance or similar plans provided to individuals after they retire from employment.

Proof of cash. Sometimes called a four-column proof of cash; provides a bank reconciliation for the beginning and ending of a time period and an analysis of increases and decreases to the cash account during the time period covered.

Registrar. An outside entity that may be hired to perform the function of determining that all stock a company issues complies with its corporate charter.

SAS 70. An engagement to issue a report on controls of a service company directed to the user companies and user company auditors. See Chapter 13 Appendix A.

Stock transfer agent. An outside entity that may be hired by a public company to keep a record of the current owners of the company's stock.

Variable interest entities. Equity investments that have multiple equity investors in which ownership interest may not be indicative of control or benefits received.

MULTIPLE CHOICE

15-1 **[LO 11]** After identifying related party transactions,

(a) the auditor assumes that the transactions were arms length business transactions unless the audit client provides evidence to the contrary.

(b) the auditor assumes that the transactions were outside of the ordinary course of business.

(c) the auditor must obtain evidence that the transactions were on the same terms that arms length transactions would be.

(d) the auditor must obtain evidence that the transactions would have occurred at the same amounts even if the parties were not related.

15-2 **[LO 6]** When using the work of a specialist,

(a) the auditor is not responsible for anything the specialist does.

(b) the auditor should understand the methods and assumptions the specialist uses.

(c) the client must select the specialist or the auditor is responsible for the work.

(d) the auditor may only select a specialist who is certified.

15-3 **[LO 5]** When an auditor performs analytical procedures and determines that interest expense is large in relation to long-term debt, the auditor may perform additional audit procedures to explore whether

(a) the principal is understated.

(b) the principal is overstated.

(c) the discount is understated.

(d) the premium is overstated.

15-4 **[LO 1, 8]** As a result of scanning cash disbursements for large and unusual transactions, the auditor identifies a payment for the purchase of the company's own stock. The auditor will then

(a) confirm the sale to the company with the former stockholders.

(b) trace the cash disbursement to the bank statement.

(c) recalculate the discount or premium on the stock transaction.

(d) examine the Board of Directors minutes for authorization of the purchase.

15-5   **[LO 2]** To obtain audit evidence about the existence of an investment in shares of stock of a company that is actively traded on the stock exchange, the auditor should inspect and count the securities documents at the fiscal year end, simultaneously with the inspection and count of cash, near cash, and other marketable securities. If unable to inspect the stock documents at the balance sheet date because they are held by a custodian, the auditor should

(a) inspect them at the soonest possible date.

(b) confirm the shares owned by the company and held by the custodian at the fiscal year end.

(c) recalculate the amount at which the value of the shares is recorded.

(d) request verification of ownership from the company's whose stocks the audit client owns.

15-6   **[LO 5, 6]** Which of the following statements is correct?

(a) A primary audit concern related to debt is existence.

(b) Pensions and postretirement transactions deal mainly with the cash disbursed to retirees.

(c) Transactions in the financing cycle tend to occur less frequently and to be larger dollar amounts than transactions in other cycles.

(d) Substantive analytical procedures are not useful in the audit of the financing cycle due to the limited ability to predict relationships among accounts.

15-7   **[LO 5, 8]** Which of the following is not a characteristic of accounts and transactions in the financing cycle?

(a) There may be a legal relationship between the audit client and the holder of the equity securities.

(b) There is a direct relationship between interest and dividend accounts and the underlying debt and equity accounts.

(c) Major transactions such as issuing securities and borrowing funds are subject to significant external rather than internal scrutiny and authorization.

(d) Major transactions will often be authorized by the Board of Directors and documented in the minutes of Board of Directors meetings.

15-8   **[LO 8]** Which of the following transactions are documented in records outside of the audit client's accounting information system?

(a) Cash payments for dividends

(b) Original issue of and cash collection for preferred stock

(c) Cash outflow for the purchase of stock as an investment

(d) Sales transactions of audit company stock to subsequent owners after the stock is originally issued

15-9   **[LO 8]** Which of the following owners' equity transactions does not usually require specific authorization from a company's Board of Directors?

(a) Cash payment for dividends after the dividends payable have been authorized and posted

(b) Repurchasing common stock as treasury stock

(c) Issuing an offering of stock

(d) Deciding to pay a dividend

15-10   **[LO 1]** Which of the following is not true about the audit of cash and near cash?

(a) The auditor does not focus on the valuation assertions.

(b) The auditor simultaneously investigates highly liquid, marketable securities.

(c) An interbank transfer schedule is always required.

(d) The time and effort needed to audit disclosure may vary dramatically because of client circumstances.

15-11   **[LO 2, 5]** For which of the following management assertions about investments is the auditor most likely to use a specialist?

(a) Existence

(b) Ownership

(c) Completeness

(d) Valuation

15-12   **[LO 2]** Why is the audit of variable interest entities different from that of other equity investments?

(a) Criteria for whether it is proper to consolidate are based on benefit rather than ownership percentage or control.

(b) The auditor assesses the appropriateness of the amount recorded, which must be determined using a fair value approach.

(c) The transactions must be recorded using the same amounts for all investors, so the auditor must investigate other investors also.

(d) The auditor spends significant time assessing the amount recorded, and disclosure is straightforward.

15-13   **[LO 2]** Auditors investigate whether investment transactions are properly authorized using which of the following procedures?

(a) Agreeing cash received from dividends to the amount posted for investment income

(b) Reviewing policies, agreeing them to Board of Directors minutes, and inspecting investment purchases for correspondence with the policies

(c) Recalculating the total amounts of investments recorded and agreeing the amount to the general ledger

(d) Physically inspecting all investments held in the custody of others

15-14 **[LO 3]** The audit of which of the following is almost completely finished based on completing the audit of all other areas?

(a) Other comprehensive income

(b) Consolidation of the financial statements

(c) Equity accounts

(d) Debt transactions

15-15 **[LO 5]** Auditors include debt covenants in their audit procedures because

(a) when debt covenants have been violated, the company may be having cash flow problems.

(b) when debt covenants have been violated, the status of debt may change, such as from long term to short term.

(c) debt covenants may affect the disclosure required in a company's financial statements.

(d) All of the above.

15-16 **[LO 8]** Which receives the most attention during the audit of the stockholder's equity section?

(a) Stock dividends are capitalized at par or stated value on the dividend declaration date.

(b) Changes in the capital stock account are verified by an independent stock transfer agent.

(c) Cash dividends during the year under audit are approved by stockholders.

(d) Entries in the capital stock account can be traced to the minutes of a Board of Directors' meeting.

15-17 **[LO 5]** An auditor reviews the renewal of a long-term note payable that occurs shortly after the balance sheet date to obtain evidence concerning management's assertion about

(a) existence or occurrence.

(b) presentation and disclosure.

(c) valuation or allocation.

(d) completeness.

15-18 **[LO 5]** How does the auditor verify interest expense on bonds payable?

(a) Recomputing interest expense

(b) Examining the canceled checks and other disbursement documents supporting payments of interest

(c) Tracing interest declarations to an independent record book

(d) Confirming interest rate with the holder of the bond

15-19 **[LO 9]** An audit program for the audit of retained earnings should include a step that requires verification of

(a) authorization for both cash and stock dividends.

(b) gain or loss resulting from disposition of treasury stock.

(c) market value used to charge retained earnings to account for a 2-for-1 stock split.

(d) approval of the adjustment to the beginning balance as a result of a write-down of an account receivable.

15-20 **[LO 2]** When evaluating the appropriateness of nonconsolidation of a variable interest entity (VIE), the auditor should seek guidance from

(a) FASB Accounting Standards Codification.

(b) AICPA SAS.

(c) PCAOB AS.

(d) SEC Regulations.

DISCUSSION QUESTIONS

15-21 **[LO 5]** In an integrated audit the auditor must issue an opinion on ICFR effectiveness only at management's report date, which is typically at year end. Yet if ICFR is to be relied upon for the financial statement audit, the ICFR effectiveness must be tested for the entire year. Is long-term debt an area for which the auditor of a public company might not rely on ICFR for the financial statement audit? Why or why not? How would the audit procedures be different under the different approaches to the audit?

15-22 **[LO 6]** Discuss an auditor's objectives in the audit of long-term liabilities. Describe appropriate analytical procedures an auditor may apply to long-term liabilities.

15-23 **[LO 8]** Discuss an auditor's objectives in the audit of equity accounts. Describe appropriate analytical procedures an auditor may apply to equity accounts.

15-24 **[LO 5]** Why is it more important for an auditor to perform a search for unrecorded notes payable than for unrecorded notes receivable? Discuss some audit procedures the auditor may use to uncover any unrecorded notes payable.

15-25 **[LO 8]** What are the major controls over owner's equity? What are management's key assertions over the equity accounts?

15-26 **[LO 5]** It is common practice to audit the balance in notes payable in conjunction with the audit of interest expense and interest payable. Why? What are the advantages of this strategy?

15-27 **[LO 3]** Variable interest entities were discussed in the chapter, including an Auditing in Action about Ford Motor Company. Why does consolidating the VIEs for which Ford Motor Company owns or controls less than a 50% interest seem to be an accounting treatment that differs from the typical treatment for consolidations? What would the audit procedures be for the consolidation of these VIEs? About which assertions would the auditor be concerned in addition to the proper accounting of the VIEs selected by management for consolidation?

PROBLEMS

15-28 **[LO 1]** Kyle is a staff auditor on the annual audit of Goodhue & Company, a major electronics retailer. In examining Goodhue & Company's accounts, he found an account entitled "Restricted Cash."

Required:

(a) What is included in Restricted Cash?

(b) How can Kyle audit Restricted Cash? List the audit steps.

(c) Besides the account on the balance sheet, what else should Kyle be concerned about in the financial statements that the Restricted Cash account and transactions affect?

15-29 **[LO 2, 5]** Assume the role of a staff auditor assigned to audit the financing cycle for Pear Computer's annual audit. During the course of the audit, you discover a footnote revealing that "for many assets and liabilities, we have adopted the Fair Value Option in accordance with FASB ASC 825-10-05.

Required:

(a) What is the definition of fair value under the FASB ASC?

(b) Define a financial asset.

(c) Define a financial liability.

(d) List some of the additional audit steps required when fair value is used.

15-30 **[LO 5, 8]** In performing tests for the appropriateness of the FASB ASC 825-10-05 fair value option for the financial assets and liabilities introduced in Problem 15-29, you ask Pear Computer's accountant for a detailed list of the items that the company decided to carry at fair value. When you received the list, you found that Pear utilized the fair value option for all derivatives, firm commitments, and employee stock options.

Required:

(a) Did Pear Computer appropriately apply the fair value option in accordance with FASB accounting standards? Why or why not? (You may need to do some additional reading in the FASB ASC to answer this.)

(b) Assume that upon examining the list you conclude that Pear Computer used fair value for certain assets when not permitted. Prepare a list of the audit steps that you carry out subsequent to this discovery.

15-31 **[LO 2]** Andrew is in charge of auditing internal controls over the investments section on the year-end Big City Defense Company audit. In the course of his testing, Andrew comes across an internal control that requires securities to be kept in a vault or safe deposit box or with an outside financial institution engaged to provide safekeeping. The purpose of the control is *to ensure that investment documents that are negotiable or that provide evidence of legal ownership are physically secure.*

Required:

(a) To which assertion does the control concerning the investments account relate?

(b) What is an appropriate test of the control? How can Andrew determine whether the control exists and is effectively designed?

(c) Assume that the control you described in (b) exists and is effectively designed. Can Andrew use a dual purpose test that tests the operating effectiveness of the control and also provides evidence for the financial statement audit of the investments account? If yes, what test will Andrew use? What evidence does the dual purpose test provide for the financial statement audit?

15-32 **[LO 2]** Jillian is on the Big City Defense Company's audit with Andrew (described in 15-31) but has been assigned the task of performing tests of details of balances for the investment account. She has never audited investments before and asks Andrew for some advice. Andrew tells her that she needs to review which management assertions are relevant for the investment account. Then she needs to understand appropriate tests that will provide evidence on these assertions.

Required:

(a) What are management's key assertions for the investment accounts?

(b) How can Jillian utilize inspection in the tests of details of balances for investments? How can she utilize confirmations? What evidence will these audit procedures provide for the financial statement audit?

15-33 **[LO 6]** Assume you are the senior auditor in a large public accounting firm in charge of auditing the pension account of a large multinational corporation based in the United States. You ask the company for support regarding its pension expense for its defined benefit pension plan. The company gives you a multitude of very detailed, complicated support. You are pretty good at math, but this is out of your league.

Required:

(a) What kind of specialist would you consider bringing in to assist you in testing the reasonableness of the pension account transactions and balance?

(b) If you decide to use a specialist, what must you, as the auditor, along with the client and the specialist, understand according to AU 336?

(c) What evidence can the specialist provide for the ICFR audit? For the financial statement audit?

(d) List the audit steps you perform related to the specialist. List the audit steps you perform related to the specialist's work.

15-34 **[LO 8]** Veronica is an experienced staff auditor in charge of performing tests over equity accounts. According to the audit program, Veronica is supposed to utilize analytical procedures over the equity balances using various financial ratios.

Required:

(a) Which equity and related accounts should Veronica test?

(b) List four ratios relating to equity accounts that Veronica can use in her analytical procedures. Describe the information that each ratio provides and how this is useful evidence for the financial statement audit.

15-35 [LO 1] Near cash is a term used to identify very liquid items that a company uses to hold cash that will be needed in the very short term.

Required: Construct and fill in a chart, such as the one shown below, with relevant management assertions for near cash as Column 1. Column 2 is documentation that can provide the auditor evidence related to the management assertion. Column 3 is the auditor activity applied to the document (include what the auditor will look at or do).

	Near Cash	
Relevant Management Assertions	Useful Client Documentation for the Assertion	Auditor Activity
1.	1.	1.
2.	2.	2.

15-36 [LO 5] First Issue of Long-term Debt: In early May 2009, the 34-year-old Microsoft Corp. issued its first ever long-term debt. The company took advantage of its AAA rating and low rates to issue $3.75 billion of 5-year, 10-year, and 30-year bonds. Now, for the first time ever, auditors of Microsoft Corp. must consider long-term debt during the engagement.

Required:

(a) List some of the issues the auditors should have addressed during the 2009 audit of Microsoft Corp., considering particularly that this is such a recent issue of debt and the company has no history with debt. In subsequent years, what are some of the audit issues?

(b) When performing their analytical procedures on long-term debt, what are some of the common financial ratios that auditors will likely use? Since this is Microsoft's first debt issue, what can auditors use for comparative purposes?

(c) What impact is the issuance of long-term debt likely to have on Microsoft's audit fees and duration of the audit?

15-37 [LO 5,7] Find the Auditing in Action in the chapter that presents the cases of debt covenant waivers at MGM and Pilgrim's Pride.

Required:

(a) State why debt covenant violations are important to auditors. If the violation is "cured" so that the company is no longer in violation at the financial statement date, is there an audit issue?

(b) What client or lender information will an auditor review to identify any debt covenant violations?

(c) If a company has a debt covenant violation and a waiver is required, who initiates the process to obtain the waiver? What is the implication for the financial statement audit and audit report of a waiver obtained for a period of less than one year from the balance sheet date?

15-38 [LO 5] Jon Hampton, president and CEO of Plasticks, Inc. is living a life-style beyond his means. He has several short positions to cover with his stock brokers. His creditors are becoming especially aggressive in collecting his debts. Unable to cut back his spending, he borrowed the needed funds from Plasticks, Inc. In order to make the transactions as complex as possible for any auditor, he used a wholly owned subsidiary and several banks as tools to move the funds. The usual procedure was to have Plasticks issue a note to his subsidiary, Extrusions, Inc. Extrusions discounts the note at one of the banks and transfers the money to Plasticks. Plasticks then loans the funds to Extrusions, which loans them to Jon Hampton. Although Hampton pledges his stock to Plasticks as collateral, the stock's true value rests on Hampton's ability to repay the loans. In this case the loans receivable make up 40% of Plasticks's total assets. Hampton becomes insolvent due to his bad investing decisions in the stock market.

Required:

What audit procedures would have alerted the auditor to the risk in this situation and identification of the fraud?

15-39 **[LO 3]** Winton Marx, a producer of motorcycle parts, has experienced poor income, due to foreign competition. In a move to try to undercut a possible proxy fight with dissident stockholders, Geoff Daniels, the company's CEO, formed a shell company known as Turbo Repair Shops, Inc. The company was supposedly a regional chain of motorcycle repair shops, and fictitious documents were created showing fabricated parts purchased from Winton Marx. As a result of the fraudulent documents, Winton Marx sales appeared significantly increased over the preceding year, and as compared to other industry competitors, who showed declines and losses.

Required:

What audit procedures would have alerted the auditor to the risk in this situation and identification of the fraud?

15-40 **[LO 2]** For the year ended 2010, Jocelyn Morris, CPA, has been engaged to audit Rogers, Inc., which is a continuing client. Jocelyn has assessed the control risk for the company at the maximum for all financial statement assertions involving investments. Consequently, the ICFR audit report will indicate material weaknesses and rather than relying on ICFR during the financial statement audit, all audit evidence will come from substantive procedures. Jocelyn determines that Rogers is unable to exercise significant influence over any investee and there are no related parties.

Morris receives an investment analysis from Rogers's management revealing the following:

- There is a notation indicating that all securities either are in the treasurer's safe or held by an independent bank custodian.
- Investments are classified as current or noncurrent.
- The beginning and ending balances are shown at cost and market.
- Unamortized premiums or discounts are associated with bonds.
- The face amount of bonds or number of shares of stock are given for the beginning and ending of the year.
- Accrued investment income for each investment at the beginning and ending of the year is presented.
- Investment income earned and collected is presented.
- Valuation allowances at the beginning and ending of the year are shown.
- Any sales or additions to portfolios for the year include date, number of shares, face amount of bonds, proceeds, cost, and realized gain/loss.

Required: Explain the audit objective for each of the listed management financial statement assertions relative to investments.

<u>Assertion</u>	<u>Audit Objective</u>
Existence	
Completeness	
Rights	
Valuation/allocation	
Presentation and Disclosure	

15-41 **[LO 2, 4]** *Required:* Using the information given in Problem 15-40, identify several additional substantive auditing procedures that Jocelyn Morris should consider applying in her audit of Rogers, Inc. investments.

15-42 **[LO 5, 7]** Glenda's Exercise Equipment, Inc. leases its warehouse from Country Leasing Company. The terms of the lease provide for minimum lease payments of $390,000 every six months payable at the beginning of each biannual period. The initial lease term runs for 16 years with no renewal or purchase options. Glenda is responsible for paying property taxes and also for any needed repairs to the warehouse. The cost of the warehouse to Country was $3.6 million, and the market value at the date of completion was $5.2 million. The explicit interest rate stated in the lease is 10%. The lease was signed and occupation occurred on January 3, 2010.

Whitehall & Associates, CPAs have audited Glenda's accounts for four years. The company has a December 31 year end. Melinda Halsey is in charge of the 2010 audit, and she has asked you to audit the Country warehouse lease.

Required:

What are the general objectives in the audit of the Country warehouse lease?

15-43 **[LO 5, 7]** You have been engaged to audit the financial statements of Quinn Corporation for the year ended December 31, 2010. During the year Quinn obtained a long-term loan from a local bank. The finance terms are as follows:

1. The loan is secured by inventory and accounts receivable of the company.

2. The company's debt-to-equity ratio should not exceed 2:1.

3. Monthly installment payments will begin July 1, 2010.

4. The company must get permission from the bank before paying dividends.

In addition to this loan, you learn that the company borrowed short-term funds from the company president. The loan is material and the transaction occurred just prior to year end.

Required:

(a) What procedures (other than internal control tests) should you use when auditing the described loans?

(b) What issues do you believe should be addressed by the financial statement disclosures with respect to the president's loan?

15-44 **[LO 5, 7]** Atkin and James formed a corporation called Financial Magic Services, Inc. In the corporation, Stan Atkin is a CPA (audits and tax services) and Morgan James is a casualty insurance underwriter. Atkin accepted an audit engagement with Ralston Company. Ralston had total assets of $750,000 and total liabilities of $275,000. During the audit, Atkin found that Ralston's building with a book value of $300,000 was pledged as collateral for a 10-year note amounting to $225,000. The client did not mention the lien, but Atkin found that all of the other financial statement amounts were satisfactory, so he issued an unqualified opinion. About 60 days after the audit, Atkin learned that an insurance company, which was unaware of the lien, was planning to loan $175,000 in the form of a first mortgage on the building. Atkin talked to James, a CPCU (Chartered Property Casualty Underwriter), who agreed to notify the insurance company.

Required:

What does this situation suggest about important ethical and professional issues that may relate to auditing client debt?

ACTIVITY ASSIGNMENTS

15-45 Find the financial statement note for cash for the most recent financial statements of American Eagle Outfitters and compare it to the cash note disclosure for Host Hotels and Resorts shown in the chapter. How do the two note disclosures compare? Why do you think Host Hotels and Resorts needs to provide so much more disclosure on cash?

15-46 Go to the 10K for Tiffany and Co. and find information related to hedging for foreign currency. What audit steps would be performed on these accounts and disclosures?

15-47 Find the debt description in the financial statement notes and management discussion and analysis (MD&A) in the 10K of The Boeing Corporation. How many paragraphs or pages comprise the debt-related disclosure in the MD&A? In the financial statements? List the types of information included in the two disclosure sources noting when they are the same and different.

15-48 Continuing with The Boeing Corporation's 10K, look for disclosure on leases. Does Boeing have operating leases? Capital leases? For what?

CHAPTER 16

Topics Beyond the Integrated Audit

1. Describe forensic accounting and contrast it with ICFR and financial statement audits.
2. Understand internal audit activities and the role of the internal audit function within organizations.
3. Learn the extension of typical audit activities required when auditing state and local government entities.
4. Explain the purposes and activities of compilation and review engagements, applicable standards, and accountants' reports.
5. Discuss the types of information for which accountants can issue attest reports, list the requirements for an attest service to be possible, and distinguish attest engagements from other services.
6. Identify other auditors' services provided for public companies, explain the auditors' work activities, and describe the resulting report.

Chapter 16 Resources

AU 634, AICPA, PCAOB, *Letters for Underwriters and Certain Other Requesting Parties*

AU 722, AICPA, PCAOB, *Interim Financial Information*

AU 801, AICPA, PCAOB, *Compliance Auditing Considerations in Audits of Governmental Entities and Recipients of Governmental Financial Assistance*

Committee of Sponsoring Organizations of the Treadway Commission, *Internal Control–Integrated Framework*

Government Auditing Standards

Institute of Internal Auditors, *Code of Ethics*

Institute of Internal Auditors, *The International Standards for the Professional Practice of Internal Auditing*

Office of Management and Budget, Circular A-133, *Audits of States, Local Governments, and Non-Profit Organizations and Supplement*

Single Audit Act of 1984

Single Audit Act Amendments of 1996

Statements on Standards of Attestation Engagements

Statements on Standards for Accounting and Review Services

Sarbanes-Oxley Act of 2002

Securities Act of 1933

INTRODUCTION

Those qualified as CPAs provide services beyond rendering opinions on internal control over financial reporting (ICFR) and the financial statements. Auditing and accounting professionals are involved in a variety of other activities. Some of the other activities are performed by auditors and accountants employed by public accounting firms. Others are conducted by auditors and accountants within corporations and government units. This chapter looks at some of these other activities, including:

Forensic accounting

Internal auditing

State and local government audits

General Accountability Office (GAO) activities

Review and compilation engagements

Attest engagements

SEC-related engagements

FORENSIC ACCOUNTING [LO 1]

The term **forensic accounting** most commonly refers to fraud investigations and accounting work to support legal actions. Auditors were playing important roles in fraud investigation long before Enron and WorldCom brought financial statement fraud to the front pages of local newspapers. But just as television shows such as *CSI* have made forensic science exciting, well-publicized financial reporting failures have put forensic accounting in the spotlight.

The **Association of Certified Fraud Examiners (ACFE)** is one of the premier organizations for forensic accountants. The ACFE provides training and education in fraud detection and investigation, and it oversees all aspects of the **Certified Fraud Examiner (CFE)** certification process. In a study published in 2008, the ACFE reported that U.S. organizations lose 7% of their annual revenues to fraud.[1] The study found that accounting department employees perpetrated 29% of the frauds examined. Nearly 18% of the fraud cases involved executives or members of upper management.

---

[1] *2006 Report to the Nation on Occupational Fraud and Abuse.* 2008. Association of Certified Fraud Examiners, Inc.

Although audit work is important for discovering fraud, the ACFE reported that frauds are also detected as a result of tips from whistleblowers. Frauds involving losses of $1 million or more were detected by tips in 46% of the cases examined. Detection rates of occupational frauds for internal audits, external audits, and internal controls were only 19, 9, and 2%, respectively. The ACFE study makes it easy to see that fraud detection work is very different from rendering an audit opinion based on a traditional audit.

A forensic accountant is often likened to Sherlock Holmes, a sleuth out to solve a crime. Like Sherlock Holmes, forensic accountants are investigators. However, forensic accountants perform more than just an investigative role. The AICPA Forensic and Litigation Services Committee notes that forensic accounting encompasses two major components: **investigative forensic services** and **litigation support**.[2] Litigation support generally involves the forensic accountant serving as an expert witness in a court case. Investigative services typically focus on investigations of accounting records and transactions or suspected frauds and may or may not involve testifying in court.

To perform investigative services and litigation support, forensic accountants need broad knowledge and an extensive skill set. Forensic accountants need knowledge of financial transactions and internal control systems, and an understanding of criminology, fraud investigation, legal systems, and legal elements of fraud. They also rely on psychology and theories of human behavior as they develop their work plans. Forensic accountants must understand common fraud schemes and how frauds are perpetrated. They need strong interpersonal and excellent quantitative skills to effectively collect, analyze, and evaluate evidence.

Differences between Audits and Forensic Accounting

In an integrated audit the financial statements and ICFR define the scope of an auditor's work. In contrast, the scope of a forensic accountant's work is not limited to financial statement issues and financial statement fraud. Forensic accountants investigate many situations and suspected illegal acts including:

Employee theft

Vendor fraud

Customer fraud

Tax evasion

Conflicts in divorce and bankruptcy proceedings

Insurance claim filings

Identity theft

Organized crime

Many people misunderstand forensic accounting and believe it is limited to fraud investigations. The potential investigative and litigation support roles on the broad range of subjects show that forensic accounting is much more comprehensive than just fraud auditing. However, fraud audits are an important part of forensic work.

Under PCAOB and AICPA audit standards, audits must be planned and designed to provide reasonable assurance that financial statements are free of material misstatements from any source. As a reminder, providing only reasonable assurance and avoiding only misstatements that are material to the overall financial statements are important boundaries on the purposes of an integrated audit. In contrast, fraud investigations are intended to detect and provide concrete evidence on specific alleged fraudulent behavior and often result in criminal and civil actions against the wrongdoers.

A forensic accountant performs a fraud investigation with a different mind-set than an accountant working on an audit. While auditors are expected to maintain professional

---

[2]*Discussion Memorandum: Forensic Services, Audits, and Corporate Governance: Bridging the Gap.* 2004. American Institute of Certified Public Accountants.

skepticism, the forensic accountant's mind-set is that all cases may involve illegal acts and result in litigation. Because of the expectation of possible litigation, the forensic accountant is likely to have an adversarial relationship with the entity under examination and its personnel. Also, forensic accountants usually have much lower materiality thresholds than traditional auditors.

Forensic accountants use investigative methods that are similar to audit procedures. A forensic investigation of financial statements or other accounting records typically begins with analytical procedures. Other forensic procedures include client interviews, document inspection, physical examination, and inspection of tangible assets, and analysis of financial transactions. However, differences exist in the ways forensic accountants and auditors carry out these tasks. As one example, when examining documents, a forensic accountant might *begin* by using sophisticated techniques to uncover alterations to electronic and paper records—activities that are beyond the scope of a traditional audit unless audit evidence first points out a potential problem.

Forensic accountants and auditors approach client interviews differently. Fraud detection often relies on the ability to notice small discrepancies and oddities in physical evidence and human behavior. Consequently, interviews conducted by a forensic accountant can be more extensive and probing than a traditional auditor's inquiries of a client. During an interview, the forensic accountant may focus on a range of issues, including:

The tone set by top management toward ethical behavior

Management's values and beliefs

Reward systems

The potential for management override of internal controls

These issues listed above are certainly within the scope of an auditor's client interviews. But a forensic accountant, searching for illegal acts and fraud, likely investigates them with greater intensity. Similar to law enforcement personnel, forensic accountants pay close attention to verbal and nonverbal cues to assess whether an interviewee is responding truthfully or evasively. An interview may become confrontational as the forensic accountant pushes the interviewee to reveal critical information or explain inconsistencies.

Fraud Triangle

Forensic accountants rely on the **fraud triangle** theory. Recall that auditors also use the fraud triangle concept. A fraud-conducive environment exists in the presence of pressure, opportunity, and rationalization. Pressure refers to incentives to commit fraudulent acts and is different for each person. For example, one individual may have personal financial problems and seek ways to use company resources to solve them. Another individual may suffer from a substance abuse addiction or an addiction to gambling, and feel pressure to commit fraud to support the addiction. The forensic auditor looks for evidence of these types of situations.

In addition to feeling pressure, the individual who commits fraud must have the opportunity. In other words, the environment must allow the person to perpetrate fraud. Even in an environment with good internal controls there can be problems. For example, an environment may foster collusion and therefore allow fraud, even though an individual cannot carry out a fraud alone. The forensic auditor has to consider the atmosphere of the company and attitudes of employees, as well as internal controls.

The last component of the fraud triangle is that the person must be capable of rationalizing or personally justifying his or her illegal behavior. Again, this component differs among individuals. One person may rationalize illegal behavior as a result of feeling that it is the only way to provide for family needs. Another may feel angry at his or her employer and rationalize illegal behavior such as theft as a way to "get even." Interviews of company personnel serve as a major information source for forensic accountants to assess whether the three factors of the fraud triangle are present.

Evidence

In the course of an investigation, forensic accountants may look at evidence from a different perspective than traditional auditors. For example, information supplied by whistleblowers or through fraud hotlines may be the *starting point* for a forensic investigative path. In this example, the difference in evidence evaluation between a forensic investigation and an audit is that although traditional auditors investigate whistleblower reports, these reports are not the primary trigger for conducting a traditional audit. Auditors investigate whistleblower reports as part of an audit. In contrast, the company may choose to initiate a forensic investigation *because* of a whistleblower report.

Evidence outside the company's financial records can be helpful in identifying events that motivate fraud. Forensic accountants may rely on evidence obtained from real estate records, court records, corporate and partnership records, and other public records to uncover potential fraud motives. Employees living beyond their means or with substantial debt from family medical costs leave behind a trail of public records that provide evidence. When legal authorization gives them appropriate access, forensic accountants also find valuable information in restricted databases. An example of a restricted source of information is the **Financial Crimes Enforcement Network** (FinCen). This database tracks data such as:

Deposits of more than $10,000 in currency in customer accounts at financial institutions

Shipments of more than $10,000 in currency or monetary instruments into or out of the United States

Business receipts of more than $10,000

Other forensic evidence comes from physical and electronic surveillance, laboratory analysis of physical and electronic evidence, and confidential disclosures.

Career Paths

Forensic accounting's unique aspects allow it to stand apart from other career tracks available to accounting and auditing professionals. Increasingly, students are interested in pursuing careers in forensic accounting, and many universities now offer forensic accounting courses. The AICPA devotes a significant portion of its student-centered *Start Here Go Places* Web site[3] to forensic accounting. To help students experience forensic accounting, *Start Here Go Places* includes an interactive game called *Catch Me If You Can*. Participants in the game collect, classify, and evaluate evidence and ultimately try to solve the game by identifying the crime that has occurred and the perpetrator of the crime. Based on the current enthusiasm, forensic accounting will likely remain a hot career for years to come.

REVIEW QUESTIONS

A.1 What is ACFE?

A.2 What are investigative services? Litigation support?

A.3 In what way does a forensic accountant approach an engagement differently from an auditor?

A.4 What is the fraud triangle, and how is the theory useful to a forensic accountant?

A.5 What types of evidence might a forensic accountant use that are typically beyond the scope of an audit?

---

[3]You can access the site at startheregoplaces.com.

INTERNAL AUDITING [LO 2]

This book focuses on the activities of accountants who work for public accounting firms and perform audits of public companies. Accountants who work within entities as internal auditors also perform important functions for companies, not-for-profit organizations, and government units. A complete discussion of the internal auditing profession is beyond the scope of this book, but a brief summary is presented here.

The **Institute of Internal Auditors** (IIA) is the most notable professional organization for internal auditors. The IIA defines **internal auditing** as follows:

> Internal Auditing is an independent, objective assurance and consulting activity designed to add value and improve an organization's operations. It helps an organization accomplish its objectives by bringing a systematic, disciplined approach to evaluate and improve the effectiveness of risk management, control, and governance processes.
> (www.theiia.org/guidance/standards-and-guidance/ippf/definition-of-internal-auditing/)

This definition of internal auditing highlights some important distinctions between the internal audit function and audits performed by CPAs who are external to the company being audited. When the IIA definition states that internal auditing is an independent activity, the concept of independence is different from its meaning in the context of an AICPA or PCAOB audit. External auditors are organizationally independent because they work for a different entity. Internal auditors are independent because they are objective in performing their tasks and reporting results, even though they are employed by the company being audited. Internal auditors also enhance their independence by avoiding conflicts of interest. The formal-upward-reporting hierarchy within an entity greatly impacts whether an internal audit department can function with professional independence.

The internal auditor's goal is to help improve the organization's operations, risk management, internal controls, and governance. An entity's internal audit function may coordinate with activities of the external auditor, and thus help make the external auditor more efficient. But in contrast to the objective of an AICPA or PCAOB audit, internal audit activities are primarily intended to benefit the organization, management, and Board of Directors.

A common title for the head of the internal audit function is the **Chief Audit Executive (CAE)**. Because of the need for objectivity in internal audit activities and for as much independence as organizationally possible, the IIA recommends that the CAE report directly to the audit committee of the organization's Board of Directors. For administrative matters and day-to-day concerns, the CAE may report to the organization's management. But it is vital that the CAE have access to and regular and direct communication with the audit committee. The IIA also recommends that the audit committee appoint and evaluate the CAE, determine the CAE's compensation, and have the power to remove the CAE.

Code of Ethics

Internal auditors follow a code of ethics. The principles of the IIA Code of Ethics are integrity, objectivity, confidentiality, and competency. These are similar to the concepts communicated through PCAOB and AICPA guidance and standards, with the exception of the external audit requirement for independence. Although an internal auditor cannot be independent of the entity he or she is auditing due to the employment relationship, the code requires that internal audit activities be performed objectively. This means that the activities are conducted professionally, without bias, and that the internal auditor avoids any conflicts of interest. The principles and rules of conduct of the IIA's Code of Ethics are presented in Appendix A of this chapter.

Professional Standards

Internal auditors are guided by professional standards known as **The International Standards for the Professional Practice of Internal Auditing** (Standards). The Standards are established by the IIA and include **attribute standards** and **performance standards**. Attribute standards outline the characteristics and qualities expected of internal audit departments and individuals who work as internal auditors. Performance standards guide the work performed by internal auditors and provide criteria for assessing the quality of internal audits. The Standards are supplemented by practice advisories that provide implementation guidance. The Standards can be found on the IIA Web site and are presented in Appendix B of this chapter.

SOX Compliance

As companies work to comply with the Sarbanes-Oxley Act of 2002 (SOX) and particularly to provide the management certifications required by Sections 302 and 404, they often turn to their internal auditors. As a reminder, **SOX Section 302** requires company management to acknowledge its responsibility for the contents of the company's financial reports and internal control, as well as communications to the audit committee and auditor. **SOX Section 404** requires management to assess and report on the effectiveness of the company's ICFR.

What role should internal auditors play in SOX compliance? In 2004, the IIA released a position paper, *Internal Auditing's Role in Sections 302 and 404 of the U.S. Sarbanes-Oxley Act of 2002*. The paper cautions that internal auditors must not jeopardize their independence and objectivity in any activities related to Section 404 compliance. The recommended role of the internal auditor includes project oversight, consulting, project support, ongoing monitoring and testing, and project audit. The position paper states that internal auditors should not make decisions on behalf of management or become key decision makers during this process because that would impair the auditor's objectivity.

The IIA position paper discusses broad roles played by internal audit, management, and the audit committee in complying with Sections 302 and 404 of SOX. But the IIA does not clearly identify specific activities that may be conducted by internal auditors without jeopardizing their independence and objectivity. Deloitte & Touche gathered together a group of leading practitioners and developed a consensus list of appropriate and inappropriate SOX-related activities for internal auditors.[4] Activities believed to be appropriate include:

- Consulting on internal control
- Assisting the organization in identifying, evaluating, and implementing risk and control assessment methodologies
- Assisting with designing internal controls
- Conducting effectiveness testing on behalf of management
- Aiding management in design of tests for control effectiveness

Activities thought to be inappropriate include:

- Concluding on the effectiveness of internal controls on behalf of management
- Making or directing key management decisions regarding internal controls, remediation activities, and SOX compliance
- Implementing internal controls
- Performing control activities

---

[4]*Optimizing the Role of Internal Audit in the Sarbanes-Oxley Era, Second Edition.* 2006. Deloitte Development LLC.

AUDITING IN ACTION

Sarbanes-Oxley Act, Sections 302 and 404

SEC. 302. CORPORATE RESPONSIBILITY FOR FINANCIAL REPORTS.

(a) REGULATIONS REQUIRED.—The Commission shall, by rule, require, for each company filing periodic reports under section 13(a) or 15(d) of the Securities Exchange Act of 1934 (15 U.S.C. 78m, 78o(d)), that the principal executive officer or officers and the principal financial officer or officers, or persons performing similar functions, certify in each annual or quarterly report filed or submitted under either such section of such Act that—

(1) the signing officer has reviewed the report;

(2) based on the officer's knowledge, the report does not contain any untrue statement of a material fact or omit to state a material fact necessary in order to make the statements made, in light of the circumstances under which such statements were made, not misleading;

(3) based on such officer's knowledge, the financial statements, and other financial information included in the report, fairly present in all material respects the financial condition and results of operations of the issuer as of, and for, the periods presented in the report;

(4) the signing officers—

   (A) are responsible for establishing and maintaining internal controls;

   (B) have designed such internal controls to ensure that material information relating to the issuer and its consolidated subsidiaries is made known to such officers by others within those entities, particularly during the period in which the periodic reports are being prepared;

   (C) have evaluated the effectiveness of the issuer's internal controls as of a date within 90 days prior to the report; and

   (D) have presented in the report their conclusions about the effectiveness of their internal controls based on their evaluation as of that date;

(5) the signing officers have disclosed to the issuer's auditors and the audit committee of the board of directors (or persons fulfilling the equivalent function)—

   (A) all significant deficiencies in the design or operation of internal controls which could adversely affect the issuer's ability to record, process, summarize, and report financial data and have identified for the issuer's auditors any material weaknesses in internal controls; and

   (B) any fraud, whether or not material, that involves management or other employees who have a significant role in the issuer's internal controls; and

(6) the signing officers have indicated in the report whether or not there were significant changes in internal controls or in other factors that could significantly affect internal controls subsequent to the date of their evaluation, including any corrective actions with regard to significant deficiencies and material weaknesses.

SEC. 404. MANAGEMENT ASSESSMENT OF INTERNAL CONTROLS.

(a) RULES REQUIRED.—The Commission shall prescribe rules requiring each annual report required by section 13(a) or 15(d) of the Securities Exchange Act of 1934 (15 U.S.C. 78m or 78o(d)) to contain an internal control report, which shall—

(1) state the responsibility of management for establishing and maintaining an adequate internal control structure and procedures for financial reporting; and

(2) contain an assessment, as of the end of the most recent fiscal year of the issuer, of the effectiveness of the internal control structure and procedures of the issuer for financial reporting.

(b) INTERNAL CONTROL EVALUATION AND REPORTING.—With respect to the internal control assessment required by subsection (a), each registered public accounting firm that prepares or issues the audit report for the issuer shall attest to, and report on, the assessment made by the management of the issuer. An attestation made under this subsection shall be made in accordance with standards for attestation engagements issued or adopted by the Board. Any such attestation shall not be the subject of a separate engagement.

The bottom line is that to maintain their objective stance, internal auditors cannot expand their role to include decision making or assuming responsibility for internal controls. SOX specifies these responsibilities as resting with management.

Internal Audit Careers

SOX has spurred a shift in the workload of internal auditors. Internal auditors have less time for traditional internal audit activities such as operational and **performance audits**, systems work, and fraud investigations. Changes to the internal audit function are expected to continue. In 2007 PricewaterhouseCoopers issued a report on trends for the internal audit function.[5] The study's findings are based on surveys of Fortune 250 CAEs, in-depth interviews with a small cross section of CAEs, and surveys of 25 academics and other "thought leaders." The major trends identified in the study are as follows.

Globalization

Outsourcing and off-shoring internal audit functions

Organizing global internal audit operations

Additional demands for compliance work, including compliance with the Foreign Corrupt Practices Act

Understanding political risks and their effects on global markets

Considering cultural differences in the ways in which people think and act

Increased Internal Audit Responsibilities

Enterprise risk management

Antifraud measures

Technology and IT security audits

Globalization (e.g., auditing off-shore operations)

Changes in Risk Management

Focus on continuous auditing

Real-time risk assessments and risk monitoring

Audits on an as-needed basis based on key risk indicators

Knowledge and Skills Needed by Internal Auditors

Data mining

Risk assessment and risk management

Fraud detection and investigation

Information technology

Information security

Technological Advancement

Strengthens the internal audit function

Poses a higher risk to the organization

These trends suggest that the internal audit function will play an even more vital role within organizations in the years ahead. Internal auditors will have significant opportunities to add value and improve the operations of their organizations.

---

[5]*Internal Audit 2012.* 2007. PricewaterhouseCoopers.

REVIEW QUESTIONS

B.1 Based on the IIA definition, what are the components of internal auditing?

B.2 How can an internal auditor be independent while being an employee of the entity?

B.3 What is the name of the professional standards that apply to internal auditors, and what two types of standards are included?

B.4 How do management and internal audit activities differ in evaluating and assessing ICFR to comply with Sections 302 and 404 of SOX?

STATE AND LOCAL GOVERNMENT AUDITS [LO 3]

Financial statement audits of state and local governments are performed by external auditors who work either for public accounting firms or separate government-related units.

Whether conducted by public accounting firms or accountants working within special state offices, audits of state and local governments involve some activities not required in the financial statement audits of the majority of for-profit corporations. The most significant of these activities is the compliance work associated with federal grants and contracts.

When state and local governments receive funds from the United States government, they are held accountable for the expenditures they make using those funds. This accountability also extends to entities other than governments that receive federal money. Federal money is often distributed by entities other than the federal government. The money is passed from the federal government through state and local governments or other not-for-profits to the ultimate receiving organization. **Compliance audit** work may also be required when companies have contracts to sell goods or services to government entities.

As a result of the requirement for accountability, auditors must determine whether government units are "in compliance" with the provisions of any federal awards received. In

AUDITING IN ACTION

Example of Government Auditor Unit: Florida Auditor General's Office

In Florida, the Auditor General is a constitutional officer appointed by the Joint Legislative Auditing Committee. His appointment is confirmed by both houses of the Legislature.

Mission: As the State's independent auditor, the Auditor General provides unbiased, timely, and relevant information which can be used by the Legislature, Florida's citizens, public entity management, and other stakeholders to promote government accountability and stewardship and improve government operations.

The Auditor General:

- Conducts financial audits of the accounts and records of State agencies; State universities; district school boards; community colleges; and, as directed by the Legislative Auditing Committee, of local governments.
- Conducts operational and performance audits of public records and information technology systems and performs related duties as prescribed by law or concurrent resolution of the Legislature.
- Adopts rules for financial audits performed by independent certified public accountants of local governmental entities, charter schools, district school boards, and Florida Single Audit Act nonprofit and for-profit organizations.
- Reviews all audit reports of local governmental entities, charter schools, charter technical career centers, and district school boards submitted pursuant to Section 218.39, Florida Statutes.

(www.myflorida.com/audgen)

other words, in addition to auditing the financial statements, auditors must evaluate whether the government entity spent the federal money it received as it was supposed to.

Single Audit Act

The Single Audit Act of 1984 and the Single Audit Act Amendments of 1996 reduced the audit burdens on state and local governments. This legislation called for audits to be conducted on an entity-wide basis replacing requirements for multiple audits of one entity on a grant-by-grant basis. The Office of Management and Budget (OMB) **Circular A-133**, *Audits of States, Local Governments, and Non-Profit Organizations,* outlines the provisions of the Single Audit Act. The Act applies when a nonfederal entity expends $500,000 or more in federal awards in one year.

When a governmental entity meets the $500,000 expenditure threshold, it is subject to a **single audit** of both its financial statements and its compliance with the provisions of any federal awards it received. The governmental entity is required to prepare financial statements that reflect its financial position, results of operations or changes in net assets, and, where appropriate, cash flows for the fiscal year audited. The entity also must prepare a schedule of expenditures of federal awards for the same period covered by the financial statements.[6] The auditor is required to perform an audit of the financial statements, review and test internal controls, follow up on prior audit findings, and perform compliance testing. Compliance testing utilizes many procedures used on financial statement audits such as examining documents, tracing information, and performing recalculations.

The *Circular A-133 Compliance Supplement*[7] details the auditor's required compliance work. *Part 3* of the *Compliance Supplement* identifies 14 types of compliance requirements and the related audit objectives for every audit conducted under *Circular A-133*. For example, auditors must address whether the entity receiving the funds is eligible for program participation and which activities of the entity are allowed and disallowed under the federal award.

After the audit is completed, the auditor's report includes the following in either one combined report or in separate reports[8]:

- An opinion as to whether the financial statements are presented fairly in all material respects in conformity with generally accepted accounting principles
- An opinion as to whether the schedule of expenditures of Federal awards is presented fairly in all material respects in relation to the financial statements taken as a whole
- A report on internal control related to the financial statements and major programs
- A report on compliance with laws, regulations, and the provisions of contracts or grant agreements, and any noncompliance that could have material effects on the financial statements
- An opinion on compliance matters related to major programs
- A schedule of findings and questioned costs

The schedule of audit findings summarizes the results of the audit. The types of opinions rendered on the financial statements and on compliance with major program requirements are listed. Explanations are given for opinions other than unqualified opinions. For internal controls, the auditor must identify reportable conditions. **Reportable conditions**

---

[6]*OMB Circular No. A-133, Audits of States, Local Governments, and Non-Profit Organizations.* 2007. Office of Management and Budget. § ____.310.

[7]*OMB Circular No. A-133, Audits of States, Local Governments, and Non-Profit Organizations Compliance Supplement.* 2007. Office of Management and Budget.

[8]*OMB Circular No. A-133, Audits of States, Local Governments, and Non-Profit Organizations.* 2007. Office of Management and Budget. § ____.505.

are deficiencies in internal controls that individually or cumulatively constitute a material weakness. The findings also include noncompliance with the requirements of Federal programs, which result in questioned costs greater than $10,000. Finally, the findings must include any known fraud affecting a Federal award.[9]

GOVERNMENT AUDITING STANDARDS AND THE YELLOW BOOK

Audits of government entities, including those under *OMB Circular A-133*, are conducted according to **generally accepted government auditing standards (GAGAS)** issued by the **Government Accountability Office (GAO)** under the direction of the Comptroller General of the United States. GAGAS are published in **Government Auditing Standards**, commonly called the **Yellow Book**, a term that derives from the color of its cover. The latest revision of the Yellow Book was released in July 2007 and can be found on the GAO Web site, *www.gao.gov/govaud/ybk01.htm*.

The Yellow Book contains standards covering financial statement audits, attestation engagements, and performance audits. Financial statement audits are conducted for the purpose of expressing an opinion on an entity's financial statements. Attestation engagements provide varying levels of assurance on assertions about subject matter of a financial or nonfinancial nature. Attestation engagements under government standards are similar to those conducted under the AICPA standards. Performance audits assess the performance or management of the entity, program, or service against objective criteria.

Parallel to the standards applying to public accountants and internal auditors, the Yellow Book identifies ethical principles for government auditors. The principles are:

The public interest

Integrity

Objectivity

Proper use of government information, resources, and position

Professional behavior

For the most part, these concepts are similar to those described for accountants in other professional careers. Yellow Book ethical principles are presented in Appendix C of this chapter.

In addition to ethical guidance, the Yellow Book contains general, field work, and reporting standards. For financial statement audits, GAGAS incorporate the AICPA field work and reporting standards as well as related Statements on Auditing Standards (SAS) unless specifically excluded or modified. GAGAS include additional field work and reporting standards to address the unique aspects of government audits. Many of these standards are related to required compliance procedures.

GOVERNMENT ACCOUNTABILITY OFFICE (GAO) ACTIVITIES

The Government Accountability Office (GAO) does much more than issue GAGAS. The GAO's primary role is to support congressional oversight of the executive branch of the U.S. government. Its mission is to "help improve the performance and accountability of the federal government for the benefit of the American people."[10] To carry out this mission, the GAO audits federal government expenditures, evaluates whether federal government programs are meeting objectives, investigates alleged illegal and improper acts, and issues legal opinions in various areas of federal law.

---

[9]*OMB Circular No. A-133, Audits of States, Local Governments, and Non-Profit Organizations.* 2007. Office of Management and Budget. § ____.510.
[10]http://www.gao.gov/about/history/gaohistory_present.html.

A specific example of the GAO's important contribution is its assigned work related to the American Recovery and Reinvestment Act. This $787 billion spending bill was passed in 2009 with the purpose of promoting economic recovery in the United States. The unprecedented size of the amount of spending that was authorized motivated legislators to build reporting responsibilities and monitoring into the law. As part of the bill, the GAO is charged with a significant oversight role to enhance accountability for the funds that are spent.

Among other responsibilities, the GAO conducts and reports on reviews every two months of how the stimulus funds are used by states and localities. The GAO is responsible for reviewing and reporting on the impact of funds in the specific areas of: trade, education, small business, and health care. The GAO must also review reports required to be filed by fund recipients. The reports include estimates of the jobs created and retained as a result of the projects on which the American Recovery and Reinvestment Act funds are spent. Working with the Congressional Budget Office, the GAO evaluates and reports on the reported estimates.

AUDITING IN ACTION

Work of the GAO

Our Work is done at the request of congressional committees or subcommittees or is mandated by public laws or committee reports. We also undertake research under the authority of the Comptroller General. We support congressional oversight by

auditing agency operations to determine whether federal funds are being spent efficiently and effectively;

investigating allegations of illegal and improper activities;

reporting on how well government programs and policies are meeting their objectives;

performing policy analyses and outlining options for congressional consideration; and

issuing legal decisions and opinions, such as bid protest rulings and reports on agency rules.

We advise Congress and the heads of executive agencies about ways to make government more efficient, effective, ethical, equitable and responsive.

(www.gao.gov/about/index.html)

GAO Careers

The GAO operates as an independent, nonpartisan body and is headed by the Comptroller General. The Comptroller General is appointed by the president and confirmed by the Senate for a term of 15 years. GAO staff members are hired out of many academic disciplines, including accounting, law, public administration, business administration, economics, engineering, social sciences, and physical sciences. Staff members are career employees rather than political appointees. GAO staff are expected to uphold the GAO's core values of accountability, integrity, and reliability.

Currently, the GAO workforce consists of approximately 3,300 employees. The GAO Web site states that two-thirds of its employees work at its headquarters in Washington, D.C. The GAO is currently organized into 13 teams, one for each of the following issues and functions:

- Acquisition and Sourcing Management
- Applied Research and Methods
- Defense Capabilities and Management
- Education, Workforce, and Income Security

- Financial Management and Assurance
- Financial Markets and Community Investment
- Health Care
- Homeland Security and Justice
- Information Technology
- International Affairs and Trade
- Natural Resources and Environment
- Physical Infrastructure
- Strategic Issues

Information about each team and its work, recent accomplishments, and ongoing projects is available on the GAO Web site (*www.gao.gov*). The GAO issues an annual Performance and Accountability Report that summarizes the results of its work and provides audited financial statements.

REVIEW QUESTIONS

C.1 What is the difference between financial statement and compliance audit work? Why do government units and other entities need compliance audits?

C.2 What is the benefit of the Single Audit Act?

C.3 What is included in the Yellow Book, and who publishes it?

C.4 What does GAGAS stand for?

C.5 What is the primary purpose of the Government Accountability Office (GAO)? What activities does it carry out to accomplish its purpose?

COMPILATION AND REVIEW ENGAGEMENTS [LO 4]

Entities often hire public accounting firms to provide financial statement services other than audits. **Compilations** and **reviews** are two types of engagements commonly desired by non-public companies. Audits, reviews, and compilations provide a spectrum of assurance on financial statement assertions, respectively, from most to none. Exhibit 16-1 describes the three different types of engagements with their respective degrees of assurance, from the highest level of assurance to none.

EXHIBIT 16-1
Hierarchy of Financial Statement Assurance Activities

Audits
In a financial statement audit, the auditor examines the financial statements and issues an opinion. An unqualified opinion provides assurance that the financial statements are presented fairly in all material respects in conformity with GAAP or whatever basis of accounting is used. An audit provides the highest level of assurance. When appropriate, the auditor's report includes a qualified or adverse opinion, or a disclaimer.

Reviews
A review engagement has a more limited scope and provides a lower level of assurance than a financial statement audit. Review engagement procedures consist of inquiry, analytical procedures and obtaining written management representations. After conducting a review, the accountant can state that he or she is not aware of any material modifications that would be needed to present the financial statements in conformity with GAAP, or whatever basis of accounting is used.

Compilations
In a compilation engagement, the accountant uses information provided by management to draft financial statements. Because no examination or review procedures are conducted, a compilation provides no assurance regarding the fairness of the financial statements.

Certified public accountants follow the AICPA **Statements on Standards for Accounting and Review Services (SSARS)** when performing reviews and compilations. SSARS are codified in the "AR" section of the AICPA Professional Standards. This distinguishes them from auditing standards, which are codified using an "AU" label. Rather than referring to the professional performing the engagement as "the auditor," the standards refer to the person performing the engagement as "the accountant."

Compilations

In a compilation engagement, an accountant drafts financial statements of an entity based on information provided by the management or owners. A compilation engagement does not have to include any steps or procedures verifying the accuracy or integrity of the information provided by the entity as the basis for the financial statements. A compilation engagement is defined in the AICPA standards.

> A compilation is a service, the objective of which is to assist management in presenting financial information in the form of financial statements without undertaking to provide any assurance that there are no material modifications that should be made to the financial statements in order for the statements to be in conformity with the applicable financial reporting framework.
>
> (SSARS 19, 1.5)

Before compiling financial statements, an accountant must be knowledgeable about the accounting principles and practices of the industry in which the entity operates. This enables the accountant to draft financial statements that are appropriate for that industry. If he or she does not already have the industry knowledge, the accountant may obtain it from a variety of sources including AICPA guides, industry publications, financial statements of other entities, and knowledgeable individuals.

In addition to industry knowledge, the accountant must have knowledge about the specific client. Client knowledge required includes a general understanding of the client's:

Organization

Operating characteristics

Nature of its assets, liabilities, revenues and expenses

Accounting principles and practices

Changes in accounting principles and practices

Business model as compared to normal practices within the industry

The accountant needs to establish an understanding with the client about the terms of the engagement, any limitations on the use of the financial statements, and must document the understanding through a written communication with management. The typical way to establish this understanding is through an engagement letter that documents the information. Achieving this understanding between the accountant and client is especially important for compilation engagements to establish that the company understands what service the accountant is providing and the limits of the accountant's activities. The engagement letter clearly distinguishes a compilation as an engagement that provides no assurance on the financial statements. Exhibit 16-2 presents a sample engagement letter for a compilation.

The financial statements prepared in a compilation engagement may be for management use only or management and third-party use. If the statements are for management use only, the financial statements include a reference such as "Restricted for Management's Use Only." When the financial statements are for management use only, the accountant is not required to submit a compilation report. In this situation, the engagement letter states that the financial statements are only for the client's internal use and that a report will not be issued. If the financial statements can reasonably be expected to be used by third parties, they must be accompanied by a compilation report.

EXHIBIT 16-2

Illustrative Compilation Engagement Letter

[*Appropriate Salutation*]

To: XYZ Company

This letter is to confirm our understanding of the terms and objectives of our engagement and the nature and limitations of the services we will provide.

We will perform the following services:

[*If an accountants compilation report is to be issued:*]

We will compile, from information you provide, the annual [*and interim, if applicable*] financial statements of XYZ Company as of December 31, 20XX, and issue an accountant's report thereon in accordance with Statements on Standards for Accounting and Review Services issued by the American Institute of Certified Public Accountants.

[*If the compilation is of financial statements not intended for third party use:*]

We will compile, from information you provide, the [*monthly, quarterly, or other frequency*] financial statements of XYZ Company for the year 20XX.

The objective of a compilation is to assist you in presenting financial information in the form of financial statements. We will utilize information that is your representation without undertaking to obtain or provide any assurance that there are no material modifications that should be made to the financial statements in order for the statements to be in conformity with [*the applicable financial reporting framework (for example accounting principles generally accepted in the United States)*].

You are responsible for

a. the preparation and fair presentation of the financial statements in accordance with [*the applicable financial reporting framework (for example, accounting principles generally accepted in the United States)*].

b. designing, implementing, and maintaining internal control relevant to the preparation and fair presentation of the financial statements.

c. preventing and detecting fraud.

d. identifying and ensuring that the entity complies with the laws and regulations applicable to its activities.

e. making all financial records and related information available to us.

We are responsible for conducting the engagement in accordance with Statements on Standards for Accounting and Review Services issued by the American Institute of Certified Public Accountants.

A compilation differs significantly from a review or an audit of financial statements. A compilation does not contemplate performing inquiry, analytical procedures, or other procedures performed in a review. Additionally, a compilation does not contemplate obtaining an understanding of the entity's internal control; assessing fraud risk; testing accounting records by obtaining sufficient appropriate audit evidence through inspection, observation, confirmation, or the examination of source documents (for example, cancelled checks or bank images); or other procedures ordinarily performed in an audit. Accordingly, we will not express an opinion or provide any assurance regarding the financial statements being compiled.

Our engagement cannot be relied upon to disclose errors, fraud, or illegal acts. However, we will inform the appropriate level of management of any material errors, and of any evidence or information that comes to our attention during the performance of our compilation procedures that fraud may have occurred. In addition, we will report to you any evidence or information that comes to our attention during the performance of our compilation procedures regarding illegal acts that may have occurred, unless they are clearly inconsequential.

[*If the compilation is of financial statements not intended for third party use:*]

The financial statements will not be accompanied by a report and are for management's use only and are not to be used by a third party.

[*If, during the period covered by the engagement letter, the accountant's independence is or will be impaired, insert the following:*]

(continued)

> *We are not independent with respect to XYZ Company. We will disclose that we are not independent in our compilation report.*
>
> If, for any reason, we are unable to complete the compilation of your financial statements, we will not issue a report on such statements as a result of this engagement.
>
> Our fees for these services:
>
> We will be pleased to discuss this letter with you at any time. If the foregoing is in accordance with your understanding, please sign the copy of this letter in the space provided and return it to us.
>
> Sincerely yours,
>
> _____
>
> [*Signature of accountant*]
>
> Acknowledged:
>
> XYZ Company
>
> _____
>
> President
>
> _____
>
> Date
>
> (SSARS 19, 2.63)

The accountant does not have to perform steps to verify the accuracy or integrity of the information provided by management for a compilation engagement. But the accountant must read the financial statements and consider whether the information seems appropriate and is free of obvious errors. The accountant's work papers must include:

a. The engagement letter documenting the understanding with the client

b. Any findings or issues that, in the accountant's judgment, are significant (for example, the results of compilation procedures that indicate that the financial statements could be materially misstated, including actions taken to address such findings and, to the extent that the accountant had any questions or concerns as a result of his or her compilation procedures, how those issues were resolved)

c. Communications, whether oral or written, to the appropriate level of management regarding fraud or illegal acts that come to the accountant's attention

(SSARS 19, 2.15)

The standards do not require that the accountant perform procedures to verify, corroborate, or review the information that management provides. However, through any procedures the accountant performs, or other sources of information, he or she may gain knowledge about problems. For example, the accountant may learn that:

> The information supplied by the entity is incorrect, incomplete, or otherwise unsatisfactory.
>
> Fraud or an illegal act may have occurred.
>
> (SSARS 19, 2.13)

In this situation, the accountant asks management to consider the effect of the information, and communicate back to the accountant with the results of its analysis. If the accountant concludes that the problem causes the financial statements to be materially misstated he or she must obtain additional or revised information from the client. If the client refuses to provide the needed additional or revised information, the accountant must withdraw from the engagement.

AUDITING IN ACTION

Accountant's Compilation Steps

Before submission [of the financial statements and accountant's compilation report], the accountant should read the financial statements and consider whether such financial statements appear to be appropriate in form and free from obvious material errors. In this context, the term *error* refers to mistakes in the preparation of financial statements, including arithmetical or clerical mistakes, and mistakes in the application of accounting principles, including inadequate disclosure.

(SSARS 19, 2.13)

Each page of compiled financial statements includes a reference such as "See Accountant's Compilation Report." Accountants need not be independent in order to perform a compilation, but the compilation report must disclose any lack of independence. The accountant may elect to provide a description of the reason why he or she is not independent, as long as the description is complete. One other special circumstance for compilation engagements covered by the SSARS is when the financial statements lack substantially all disclosures. These financial statements are sometimes called *plain paper* statements. An accountant can compile financial statements that omit substantially all disclosures, provided there is no apparent intent by management to mislead and the accountant's compilation report discloses the omission.

AUDITING IN ACTION

Standard Compilation Report on Financial Statements Prepared in Accordance with Accounting Principles Generally Accepted in the United States

Accountant's Compilation Report

[*Appropriate Salutation*]

I (we) have compiled the accompanying balance sheet of XYZ Company as of December 31, 20XX, and the related statements of income, retained earnings, and cash flows for the year then ended. I (we) have not audited or reviewed the accompanying financial statements and, accordingly, do not express an opinion or provide any assurance about whether the financial statements are in accordance with accounting principles generally accepted in the United States.

Management (owners) is (are) responsible for the preparation and fair presentation of the financial statements in accordance with accounting principles generally accepted in the United States and for designing, implementing, and maintaining internal control relevant to the preparation and fair presentation of the financial statements.

My (our) responsibility is to conduct the compilation in accordance with Statements on Standards for Accounting and Review Services issued by the American Institute of Certified Public Accountants. The objective of a compilation is to assist management in presenting financial information in the form of financial statements without undertaking to obtain or provide any assurance that there are no material modifications that should be made to the financial statements.

[Signature of accounting firm or accountant, as appropriate]

[Date]

(SSARS 19, 2.64)

AUDITING IN ACTION

Additional Compilation Paragraph Report When the Financial Statements Omit Substantially All Disclosures

Management has elected to omit substantially all of the disclosures required by accounting principles generally accepted in the United States. If the omitted disclosures were included in the financial statements, they might influence the user's conclusions about the company's financial position, results of operations, and cash flows. Accordingly, the financial statements are not designed for those who are not informed about such matters.

(SSARS 19, 2.64)

Reviews

An engagement to review a nonpublic company's financial statements provides some assurance regarding the fairness of the financial statements. Consequently, the level of assurance provided by the accountant's report falls between an audit and a compilation. The accountant's report states that the financial statements do not need any material modifications to be in conformity with GAAP. The objective of a review engagement as stated in the SSARS is as follows:

> The objective of a review engagement is to express **limited assurance** that there are no material modifications that should be made to the financial statements in order for the statements to be in conformity with the applicable reporting framework.
>
> (SSARS 19, 3.4)

The review of a nonpublic company's financial statements covered by SSARS differs from an engagement to review interim financial statements of a public company. Standards for an auditor's review of interim financial statements of a public company are presented in PCAOB AU 722. The AICPA AU 722 also provides guidance to an auditor if a nonpublic company hires its auditor to perform a review of interim financial statements.

The procedures performed in a review are more limited than those of a financial statement audit. A review does not include understanding internal control, assessing fraud risks, and testing accounting records. Reviews generally are limited to inquiry, analytical procedures, and obtaining written representations from management. The results of these procedures form the basis for the accountant's determination of whether material modifications are needed for the statements to be in conformity with GAAP.

Just as was described for a compilation, the accountant must establish a written understanding with the client regarding the services to be performed in the review engagement Again, this is accomplished using an engagement letter. The elements included in a review engagement letter provide an effective description of a review engagement. One of the important differences between a review and compilation, reflected in the different engagement letters, is that the accountant must be independent to perform a review.

An accountant performing a review must possess industry knowledge as well as an understanding of the entity's organization, its operating characteristics, and the nature of its assets, liabilities, revenues, and expenses. The accountant uses that knowledge and applies professional judgment to plan appropriate inquiry and analytical procedures. These procedures allow the accountant to accumulate review evidence. General areas of inquiry are presented in Exhibit 16-3. An illustrative list of specific questions that might be asked during a review is displayed in Appendix D. If other accountants have reviewed or audited any components of the entity, its subsidiaries or investees, the accountant obtains and considers those reports in addition to the other procedures of a review. If the inquiry and analytical procedures are not sufficient for the accountant to obtain the limited assurance needed, more procedures must be performed.

AUDITING IN ACTION

Elements of an Engagement Letter for a SSARS Financial Statement Review Engagement

The objective of a review is to obtain limited assurance that there are no material modifications that should be made to the financial statements in order for the statements to be in conformity with the applicable financial reporting framework.

Management is responsible for the preparation and fair presentation of the financial statements in accordance with the applicable financial reporting framework.

Management is responsible for designing, implementing, and maintaining internal control relevant to the preparation and fair presentation of the financial statements.

Management is responsible to prevent and detect fraud.

Management is responsible for identifying and ensuring that the entity complies with the laws and regulations applicable to its activities.

Management is responsible for making all financial records and related information available to the accountant.

Management will provide the accountant, at the conclusion of the engagement, with a letter that confirms certain representations made during the review.

The accountant is responsible for conducting the engagement in accordance with SSARS issued by the AICPA.

A review includes primarily applying analytical procedures to management's financial data and making inquiries of company management.

A review is substantially less in scope than an audit, the objective of which is the expression of an opinion regarding the financial statements as a whole. A review does not contemplate obtaining an understanding of the entity's internal control; assessing fraud risk; testing accounting records by obtaining sufficient appropriate audit evidence through inspection, observation, confirmation, or the examination of source documents (for example, cancelled checks or bank images); or other procedures ordinarily performed in an audit. Accordingly, the accountant will not express an opinion regarding the financial statements as a whole.

The engagement cannot be relied upon to disclose errors, fraud, or illegal acts.

The accountant will inform the appropriate level of management of any material errors and of any evidence or information that comes to the accountant's attention during the performance of review procedures that fraud or an illegal act may have occurred. The accountant need not report any matters regarding illegal acts that may have occurred that are clearly inconsequential and may reach agreement in advance with the entity on the nature of any such matters to be communicated.

(SSARS 19, 3.4)

As part of the review, the accountant is required to obtain written representations from management. The representations relate to the following:

  acknowledgement of management's responsibility for the preparation and fair presentation of the financial statements in conformity with the applicable financial reporting framework

  management's belief that the financial statements are fairly presented in accordance with the applicable financial reporting framework

  acknowledgement of management's responsibility for designing, implementing, and maintaining internal control relevant to the preparation and fair presentation of the financial statements

  acknowledgement of management's responsibility to prevent and detect fraud

  knowledge of any fraud or suspected fraud affecting the entity involving management or others where the fraud could have a material effect on the financial statements, including any communications received from employees, former employees, or others

EXHIBIT 16-3

Inquiries Made during a Review

Areas of inquiry to members of management who have responsibility for financial and accounting matters:

Whether the financial statements have been prepared in conformity with the applicable financial reporting framework

The entity's accounting principles and practices and the methods followed in applying them and the entity's procedures for recording, classifying, and summarizing transactions, and accumulating information for disclosure in the financial statements

Unusual or complex situations that may have an effect on the financial statements

Significant transactions occurring or recognized near the end of the reporting period

The status of uncorrected misstatements identified during the previous engagement

Questions that have arisen in the course of applying the review procedures

Events subsequent to the date of the financial statements that could have a material effect on the financial statements

Their knowledge of any fraud or suspected fraud affecting the entity involving management or others where the fraud could have a material effect on the financial statements (for example, communications received from employees, former employees, or others)

Significant journal entries and other adjustments

Communications from regulatory agencies

Actions taken at meetings of stockholders, board of directors, committees of the board of directors, or comparable meetings that may affect the financial statements

(SSARS 19, 3.19)

management's full and truthful response to all inquiries

completeness of information

information concerning subsequent events (SSARS 19, 3.22)

The representation letter is addressed to the accountant and signed by the chief executive officer and chief financial officer or other member of management who is knowledgeable about the matters discussed in the representation letter.

The accountant's work paper documentation of the review engagement is tailored to the circumstances of the work performed. The engagement letter is included the work papers. The documentation indicates the review procedures performed—such as matters covered through inquiry and analytical procedures, conclusions reached, and the basis for the conclusions. Any review findings or issues that are significant are documented, along with actions addressing the findings. Documentation also includes factors considered in developing expectations for analytical procedures, additional procedures performed to respond to unexpected results, unusual matters considered, and the disposition of the unusual matters. The work paper files also document any communications by the accountant to management regarding fraud or illegal acts, and the representations letter.

A standard review report contains specific components, including a description of the service provided and identification of the financial statements reviewed. If the accountant becomes aware of any material departures from the applicable financial reporting framework and those departures are not corrected by management, the report should disclose the departure in a separate paragraph of the report. A number of other changes can also be made to a review report, for example, restricting the use of the review report or providing emphasis of a matter.

REVIEW QUESTIONS

D.1 What are the different levels of financial statement assurance provided by audits, reviews, and compilations?

AUDITING IN ACTION

Independent Accountant's Review Report on Financial Statements Prepared in Accordance with Accounting Principles Generally Accepted in the United States

[*Appropriate Salutation*]

I (We) have reviewed the accompanying balance sheet of XYZ Company as of December 31, 20XX, and the related statements of income, retained earnings, and cash flows for the year then ended. A review includes primarily applying analytical procedures to management's (owner's) financial data and making inquiries of company management (owners). A review is substantially less in scope than an audit, the objective of which is the expression of an opinion regarding the financial statements as a whole. Accordingly, I (we) do not express such an opinion.

Management (owners) is (are) responsible for the preparation and fair presentation of the financial statements in accordance with accounting principles generally accepted in the United States and for designing, implementing, and maintaining internal control relevant to the preparation and fair presentation of the financial statements.

My (our) responsibility is to conduct the review in accordance with Statements on Standards for Accounting and Review Services issued by the American Institute of Certified Public Accountants. Those standards require me (us) to perform procedures to obtain limited assurance that there are no material modifications that should be made to the financial statements. I (We) believe that the results of my (our) procedures provide a reasonable basis for my (our) report.

Based on my (our) review, I am (we are) not aware of any material modifications that should be made to the accompanying financial statements in order for them to be in conformity with accounting principles generally accepted in the United States.

[Signature of accounting firm or accountant, as appropriate]

[Date]

(SSARS 19, 3.73)

D.2 What is required of an accountant to perform a compilation? Do any procedures have to be conducted to verify the accuracy or integrity of information received from the entity and used as the basis for the financial statements?

D.3 Why is it particularly important to establish an understanding with the client about the terms and limitations of a compilation engagement?

D.4 What level of assurance is provided by an accountant resulting from a review engagement and what does this mean?

D.5 What procedures are performed in a review engagement? What additional procedures are performed if another accountant has performed a review or an audit related to the entity?

ATTEST ENGAGEMENTS [LO 5]

The subject matter of **attest engagements** broadens the auditing and accounting practitioner's work from the financial statement arena to a wide array of financial and nonfinancial subjects. Targets of attest engagements include financial forecasts and projections, compliance with laws and regulations, effectiveness of internal controls for nonpublic companies, the accuracy and reliability of reported performance measures, and the compliance with SEC regulations of a company's **management discussion and analysis**. Other subject matter that is of particular interest to the involved parties can also be the target of an attest engagement.

AUDITING IN ACTION

Examples of Attest Engagements

Internal Controls:

Beginning in 1993, aspects of the Federal Deposit Insurance Corporation Improvement Act (FDICIA) have required attest services from accountants. Depository institutions insured by the Federal Deposit Insurance Corporation are required to prepare annual financial statements that are audited by an independent public accountant. Additionally, management of these institutions reports on its responsibilities for establishing and maintaining an adequate internal control structure and procedures for financial reporting. Management's report on internal control and procedures for financial reporting must be accompanied by an attest report prepared as the result of an attestation engagement performed in accordance with generally accepted standards for attestation engagements. SSAE 15, *An Examination of an Entity's Internal Control Over Financial Reporting that is Integrated with an Audit of its Financial Statements* is the authoritative standard covering these required engagements.

(FDIC 2000 Rules and Regulations §363.2-.3)

Laws and Regulations:

The Federal Reserve initiated the Term Asset-Backed Securities Loan Facility (TALF) in 2009 to assist in enhancing the secondary markets and flow of credit backed by auto loans, student loans and credit card loans. Before lending funds to be used by the debtor to purchase asset-backed securities, the Federal Reserve Bank of New York requires an accountant's report attesting that the loan collateral (the asset-backed security) meets the requirements of the TALF program. The attestation report relates to credit rating, type of loan related to the security and date at which the loan was made. The attestation report is a limited distribution report.

(*http://www.newyorkfed.org/markets/Form_Certification_TALF_Eligibility.pdf*, retrieved April 7, 2009)

In an attest engagement, the accountant usually provides either positive or limited assurance. When the service is a compilation of a forecast or projection, the accountant provides no assurance. The subject matter on which the accountant provides the assurance is the responsibility of another party. The accountant's written report on the subject matter may be for sole use of the client or for the client and third parties interested in the subject matter.

Two key elements in an attest engagement are:

1. An **assertion** about the subject matter
2. **Suitable criteria** against which the accuracy of the assertion can be compared

During an attest engagement, the accountant generally obtains a written assertion from the responsible party that declares something about the subject matter. The responsible party may be the entity to which the subject matter relates, or a third party. For example, the assertion may be that the company maintained an effective internal control system over financial reporting based on the Committee of Sponsoring Organizations (COSO) Internal Control (IC) Framework. Items in the COSO IC Framework then become the criteria for the accountant to use in judging the accuracy of the assertion. Another example is an assertion that real property, such as a warehouse, is actually the size that is described in a contract. The criterion in this case is the size measurement description in the contract. The accountant examines the property to see whether the assertion about size is consistent with actual size measurements.

The assertion and suitable criteria concepts in attest engagements have parallel concepts in financial statement audits. The assertions for financial statements are the management assertions of existence or occurrence, completeness, rights and obligations, valuation or allocation, and presentation and disclosure. The suitable criteria are all the requirements of GAAP. In performing a financial statement audit, the auditor evaluates the financial statements in light of GAAP requirements to judge whether management's assertions are appropriate and thus the financial statements are fair. In an attest engagement the accountant evaluates the subject matter using the criteria suitable for that particular engagement to determine whether the responsible party's assertions about the subject matter are reasonable or accurate.

The conduct of attest engagements is guided by the AICPA **Statements on Standards of Attestation Engagements (SSAE),** which are codified in the AT section of the AICPA Professional Standards. The third general standard emphasizes the importance of evaluative criteria in an attest engagement. The standard is as follows.

> The practitioner shall perform the engagement only if he or she has reason to believe that the subject matter is capable of evaluation against criteria that are suitable and available to users. (AT 101.23)

For criteria to be "suitable" according to the standards, they must have each of the following attributes:

- *Objectivity—freedom from bias*
- *Measurability—permit reasonably consistent qualitative or quantitative measurements of the subject matter*
- *Completeness—relevant factors that would alter a conclusion about subject matter are not omitted*
- *Relevance—be pertinent to the subject matter* (AT 101.24)

The client or responsible party selects the criteria and is responsible for determining that the criteria are appropriate. The criteria must be available to users in one or more ways. If the criteria are only available to a limited group of users, then the accountant's attest report should be restricted to that group. Exhibit 16-4 presents the different possible ways that criteria may be made available to user groups.

Attestation risk is the risk that an accountant will fail to appropriately modify his or her attest report on subject matter or an assertion that is materially misstated. This risk description is worded consistently with the definition used for audit risk. Similar to audit requirements, to minimize attestation risk the second standard of field work for an attest engagement requires that the accountant obtain sufficient evidence to provide a reasonable basis for the conclusion expressed in the report (AT 101.51). Again, like the audit standards, evidence from independent sources outside the entity is expected to provide more assurance than evidence secured from within the entity. Direct personal knowledge is more persuasive than indirect evidence.

EXHIBIT 16-4	The criteria should be available to users in one or more of the following ways:
Availability of Criteria	**a.** Available publicly
	b. Available to all users through inclusion in a clear manner in the presentation of the subject matter or in the assertion
	c. Available to all users through inclusion in a clear manner in the practitioner's report
	d. Well understood by most users, although not formally available (for example, "The distance between points A and B is twenty feet;" the criterion of distance measured in feet is considered to be well understood)
	e. Available only to specified parties; for example, terms of a contract or criteria issued by an industry association that are available only to those in the industry
	If criteria are only available to specified parties, the practitioner's report should be restricted to those parties who have access to the criteria.
	(AT 101.33-34)

EXHIBIT 16-5

**Types of Attest
Engagements and
Reports**

Examination		Positive Assurance
Review		Moderate/Limited/Negative Assurance
Agreed Upon Procedures		Statement of procedures and findings

Attest engagements may consist of examinations, reviews, or agreed-upon procedures. In addition, compilations can be performed for **forecasts** and **projections**. Examinations are designed to provide **positive assurance**, which is the highest level of assurance. In examinations, practitioners should use search, verification, inquiry, and analytical procedures to accumulate sufficient evidence to restrict attestation risk to a low level. Reviews provide a moderate level of assurance. Therefore, practitioners generally limit attest procedures in a review to inquiries and analytical procedures, similar to the types of procedures used in a financial statement review. These procedures are planned and conducted to accumulate sufficient evidence to restrict attestation risk to a moderate level. An agreed-upon procedures report states what was done and the results of the procedures. Exhibit 16-5 summarizes the types of engagements and level of assurance provided in the related accountants' attest reports.

An attest report states a conclusion about the subject matter or assertion based on the selected criteria. The report identifies the subject matter or assertion being reported on and states the character of the engagement (AT 101.63). The character of the engagement includes the nature and scope of the work performed—examination, review, or agreed upon procedures—and the standards governing the engagement. The term *examination* or *review* should be used to describe an engagement designed to provide a high level and moderate level of assurance, respectively (AT 101.65). In an examination, the conclusion should be expressed in the form of an opinion, while the conclusion for a review is communicated in the form of negative assurance.

AUDITING IN ACTION

Independent Accountant's Attest Examination-Level Report

We have examined the [*identify the subject matter—for example, the accompanying schedule of investment returns of XYZ Company for the year ended December 31, 20XX*]. XYZ Company's management is responsible for the schedule of investment returns. Our responsibility is to express an opinion based on our examination.

Our examination was conducted in accordance with the attestation standards established by the American Institute of Certified Public Accountants and, accordingly, included examining, on a test basis, evidence supporting [*identify the subject matter—for example, XYZ Company's schedule of investment returns*] and performing such other procedures as we considered necessary in the circumstances. We believe our examination provides a reasonable basis for our opinion.

[*Additional paragraph(s) may be added to emphasize certain matters relating to the attest engagement or the subject matter.*]

In our opinion, the schedule referred to above presents, in all material respects, [*identify the subject matter—for example, the accompanying schedule of investment returns of XYZ Company for the year ended December 31, 20XX*] based on [*identify criteria—for example, the ABC criteria set forth in Note 1*].

[Signature]
[Date]

(AT101.114, Example 1)

In some situations an attestation report for either an examination or a review engagement can be issued for general use. The term *general use* means that the report does not have a restricted distribution. However, when the following conditions exist, an examination or review attest engagement report may only be distributed to and used by specific parties:

1. the criteria used to evaluate the subject matter are appropriate only for a limited number of parties who participated in their establishment or have an adequate understanding of the criteria
2. the criteria used to evaluate the subject matter are available only to specified parties
3. a written assertion has not been provided by the responsible party (AT 101.78)

Basically, these restrictions mean that a general use attest report can only be prepared for an examination or review engagement when (1) a written assertion exists, and (2) the assertion and criteria used to evaluate the assertion are widely understood and publicly available. The restriction is logical because if the assertion or criteria are either private or not widely understood, then only those people with knowledge of the assertion and criteria should use the accountant's report.

Attest engagements can also consist of the accountant performing agreed-upon procedures. In an agreed upon procedures attest engagement, the accountant performs the specific procedures that the other party desires. Similar to when the *criteria* used are specified by the parties to the engagement, when the *procedures performed* by the accountant are specified and agreed upon, the attest report has a limited distribution. For an agreed upon procedures attest engagement, only specific parties—presumably those who understand the agreed upon procedures and why they were used—can receive the accountant's report. Restricted-use reports should include a paragraph such as:

This report is intended solely for the information and use of [the specified parties] and is not intended to be and should not be used by anyone other than these specified parties. (AT 101.80)

REVIEW QUESTIONS

E.1 What subjects are common targets of attest engagements?

E.2 What levels of assurance can an accountant provide as the result of an attest engagement, and what are the respective engagements called?

E.3 What is the meaning of the term assertion as it relates to an attest engagement? Who makes the assertion?

E.4 What are the characteristics of suitable criteria? Why are they needed for an attest engagement to be possible? What are the objective criteria for financial statements?

E.5 Under what circumstances do attest reports have limited distribution?

SEC-RELATED ENGAGEMENTS [LO 6]

CPAs perform many services in connection with SEC filings such as issuing comfort letters to underwriters, performing interim reviews, and conducting activities related to **registration statements** for **public offerings** of securities.

Letters for Underwriters

Letters for **underwriters** are commonly called **comfort letters** because of the concept that they provide "comfort" on specific issues in a company's financial information. They do not offer the positive level of assurance that results from an audit. Comfort letters report to the underwriter the specific procedures performed by the auditor and the results of those procedures.

Comfort letters are commonly issued to underwriters in connection with public offerings. When a company, the **issuer**, sells stock or offers debt that is to be publicly traded, it files a registration statement with the SEC. The registration statement filing is required by the Securities Act of 1933 (the Act). The company's financial statements and financial statement schedules are part of the registration statement. Under the Act, underwriters can be held liable if any part of the registration statement contains material omissions or misstatements.

If anything goes wrong with a public offering leading to litigation, an affirmative defense for an underwriter is to demonstrate that it has conducted **due diligence** procedures. The due diligence results are used to establish that the underwriter has reasonable grounds to believe there are no material omissions or misstatements in the registration statement. As part of the due diligence process, underwriters request comfort letters from the issuer's accountants.

Comfort letters focus on financial data and financial information that have not been audited. Nonaudited information is the target of a comfort letter since underwriters, like everyone else, rely on the audit report for assurance on audited information. The subjects typically covered in a comfort letter are:

- the independence of the accountants
- whether the audited financial statements and financial statement schedules included in the registration statement conform as to form in all material respects with the applicable accounting requirements of the Act and the related rules and regulations adopted by the SEC
- unaudited financial statements
- condensed interim financial information
- capsule financial information
- pro forma financial information
- financial forecasts
- management's discussion and analysis
- changes in selected financial statement items during a period subsequent to the date and period of the latest financial statement included in the registration statement
- tables, statistics, and other financial information included in the registration statement
- negative assurance as to whether certain non-financial statement information, included in the registration statement complies as to form in all material respects with Regulation S-K (AU 634.22)

The letter is dated on or shortly before the **effective date** of the registration statement and is addressed to the client and the named underwriters. The effective date is the date the issuer can sell the securities in a public market.

Interim Financial Information

The procedures in a review of interim financial information of a public company are similar to those in a SSARS review of financial statements for a nonpublic company. The objective of a review of a public company's interim financial information is to provide the auditor with a basis for communicating whether he or she is aware of any material modifications that should be made to the interim financial information for it to conform with generally accepted accounting principles. Auditors' activities related to reviews of public companies (those defined by the SEC as issuers) are governed by the PCAOB's standards. Auditors' activities related to reviews for companies with private placements (under SEC Rule 144A) are governed by the AICPA's AU 722. For nonpublic companies, the SSARS apply. Interim financial information most often refers to a company's quarterly financial statements filed with the SEC in a Form 10Q.

Just as with an AICPA SSARS review of a nonpublic company, a review of a public company consists primarily of inquiry and analytical procedures and is limited in scope compared to an audit. The auditor should establish an understanding with the client about the nature of the services to be performed and should document that understanding. The understanding should cover matters such as:

- the objective of the review
- management's responsibility for the entity's financial information
- management's responsibility for establishing and maintaining effective internal control over financial reporting
- management's responsibility for ensuring the entity complies with laws and regulations
- responsibility to make all financial records and related information available to the accountant
- management's responsibility to provide a representation letter at the end of the engagement
- management's responsibility to adjust the interim financial information to correct material misstatements
- the accountant is responsible for conducting the review in accordance with standards
- a review includes obtaining sufficient knowledge of the entity's business and its internal control as it relates to the preparation of annual and interim financial information to identify types of potential material misstatements and to select the inquiries and analytical procedures that will be performed
- a review is not designed to provide assurance on internal control (AU 722.09)

The auditor should perform analytical procedures to identify individual items and relationships that appear to be unusual and that may be materially misstated. The procedures should include

1. Comparing quarterly and year-to-date information with comparable information for the corresponding periods in the previous year
2. Comparing recorded amounts or ratios of recorded amounts with expectations
3. Comparing disaggregated revenue during the current period with that of comparable prior periods

The auditor should recognize that expectations will be less precise for reviews of interim information than those developed in an audit of annual financial statements.

The auditor should develop inquiries based on the results of the analytical procedures. Inquiries also result from other sources such as:

Knowledge of the entity's business and internal controls

Documentation from the preceding year's audit and prior interim periods' reviews

Other documents including minutes of board meetings

This provides a very substantial base on which to develop inquiries because, except in a first-year engagement, the auditor has significant knowledge about the client from performing the audit in the prior year. The auditor is not required to use other evidence to corroborate management's responses. Even so, the auditor should consider the reasonableness and consistency of management's responses in light of the results of other procedures, knowledge about the entity, and knowledge about the entity's internal controls (AU 722.17).

Companies are required to have an auditor complete a review of interim financial information before filing a 10Q with the SEC. The SEC does not require that the auditor issue a written review report unless the client makes some reference to the review in one of its SEC filings.

Although in most circumstances it is not required, in some cases the auditor issues a report to accompany the reviewed interim financial information. The report is similar to the report prepared for a review of a nonpublic company's financial statements. The report can provide only negative assurance because the review procedures do not provide the auditor with a basis for expressing an opinion on the interim financial information. The report states whether the auditor is aware of any material modifications that would need to be made to the interim financial information for the information to conform with GAAP.

AUDITING IN ACTION

Auditor's Review Report on Interim Financial Statements

REPORT OF INDEPENDENT REGISTERED PUBLIC ACCOUNTING FIRM

To the Board of Directors and Stockholders
of Stratus Properties Inc.:

We have reviewed the accompanying consolidated balance sheet of Stratus Properties Inc. and its subsidiaries as of June 30, 2008 and the related consolidated statements of operations for each of the three-month and six-month periods ended June 30, 2008 and 2007 and the consolidated statements of cash flows for the six-month periods ended June 30, 2008 and 2007. These interim financial statements are the responsibility of the Company's management.

We conducted our review in accordance with the standards of the Public Company Accounting Oversight Board (United States). A review of interim financial information consists principally of applying analytical procedures and making inquiries of persons responsible for financial and accounting matters. It is substantially less in scope than an audit conducted in accordance with the standards of the Public Company Accounting Oversight Board (United States), the objective of which is the expression of an opinion regarding the financial statements taken as a whole. Accordingly, we do not express such an opinion.

Based on our review, we are not aware of any material modifications that should be made to the accompanying consolidated interim financial statements for them to be in conformity with accounting principles generally accepted in the United States of America.

We previously audited in accordance with the standards of the Public Company Accounting Oversight Board (United States), the consolidated balance sheet as of December 31, 2007, and the related consolidated statements of income, of changes in stockholders' equity and of cash flows for the year then ended (not presented herein), and in our report dated March 14, 2008, we expressed an unqualified opinion on those consolidated financial statements with an explanatory paragraph for the Company's change in accounting for stock-based compensation. In our opinion, the information set forth in the accompanying consolidated balance sheet information as of December 31, 2007, is fairly stated in all material respects in relation to the consolidated balance sheet from which it has been derived.

/s/ PricewaterhouseCoopers LLP

Dallas, Texas
August 11, 2008
(From the 10Q of Stratus Properties Inc.)

Activities Related to Registration Statements

When issuers file registration statements with the SEC for public offerings of securities, they include financial statements and other financial information. Under the provisions of Section 7 of the Securities Act of 1933, the registration statement must include the written consent of the accountants who were involved in preparing or certifying any part of the registration statement. This means that the auditors who rendered an opinion on the annual financial statements that are incorporated in the registration statement have to consent to their opinion being used. The audit firm must also provide a consent if it performed a review of the quarter prior to the effective date. Because the effective date of the registration statement will likely never coincide with the company's fiscal year or quarter end, the auditor performs a subsequent events review between the end of the most recent quarter and the effective date of the registration statement before providing the required consent.

REVIEW QUESTIONS

F.1 Why do underwriters require comfort letters?

F.2 What procedures are performed in a review of interim financial information of a public company?

F.3 Are public companies required to have their interim financial information reviewed? When are reviews performed?

F.4 In what circumstances does the auditor performing a review of a public company's interim financial information have to issue a review report?

F.5 What is required of the auditor when a company offers securities for sale in a public market?

CONCLUSION

Accounting professionals who work for public accounting firms and their counterparts within other types of entities perform a wide range of activities in addition to audits. While the activities are diverse, they share a common thread through the accounting professionals who provide unbiased insights into the organizations. Through this work, auditing and accounting professionals add significant value to client entities and to the financial reporting they provide. These other services provide for many accounting career paths outside of public accounting.

KEY TERMS

Assertions. In an attest engagement, statements made about the subject matter by a responsible party.

Association of Certified Fraud Examiners (ACFE). The major organization associated with fraud professionals.

Attest engagement. An engagement in which the accountant evaluates an assertion made about a subject matter by comparison against objective criteria and issues a report.

Attribute standards. A section of the *International Standards for the Professional Practice of Internal Auditing* that describes the characteristics expected of internal auditors and internal audit departments.

Certified Fraud Examiner (CFE). A credential awarded by the ACFE as a result of education, experience, and passing an examination.

Chief Audit Executive (CAE). Title of the head of the internal audit function.

Circular A-133. Government document stating the provisions and requirements of the *Single Audit Act of 1984* and *Single Audit Act Amendments of 1996.*

Comfort letter. A report issued by an auditor, for the specific use of an underwriter, identifying specific procedures performed and the outcomes.

Compilation. An engagement that provides no assurance in which the accountant uses information provided by the entity to prepare financial statements.

Compliance audit. Most often refers to an engagement performed by an accountant to determine whether an entity met the requirements associated with a grant or contract.

Due diligence. Activities performed by those associated with registration statements to show that they have sufficient cause to believe the information is truthful and accurate.

Effective date. The date at which a company offering securities is allowed to sell them in a public market.

Financial Crimes Enforcement Network. A restricted database that tracks information about currency and cash transactions over specified thresholds.

Forecast. A forward-looking set of financial statements based on the set of assumptions believed to be most likely.

Forensic accounting. Accounting work that is likely to be associated with legal actions; often refers to fraud audits.

Forensic accounting, investigative. Accounting work focusing on transactions, accounting records, and suspected fraud.

Fraud triangle. Components of a situation that makes it conducive to fraud: pressure, opportunity, and rationalization.

GAGAS Generally accepted government audit standards.

Government Accountability Office (GAO). A federal government entity with the mission of assisting Congress in its oversight of the executive branch.

Government Auditing Standards. Standards published by the GAO in the Yellow Book covering financial audits, performance audits, and attest engagements; also called generally accepted government audit standards (GAGAS).

Institute of Internal Auditors (IIA). The major organization associated with internal auditors.

Internal auditing. Assurance and consulting activities performed by employees that are designed to add value to an organization.

International Standards for the Professional Practice of Internal Auditing. Professional standards of the IIA that guide the practice of internal auditing.

Issuer. Term for a company selling or "issuing" securities to the public in a public market.

Limited assurance. The level of assurance that results from a review of financial statements of a nonpublic company.

Litigation support. One function of forensic accounting that typically involves providing expert testimony in court cases.

Management discussion and analysis. Additional required disclosure in SEC filings that include financial statements expressing management's views on additional information that affects a company's financial health and outlook, including trends.

Performance audit. An engagement assessing the performance or management of an entity, program, or service against objective criteria; typically performed under GAGAS but may also be performed by internal auditors.

Performance standards. A section of the *International Standards for the Professional Practice of Internal Auditing* that relates to the work performed by internal auditors and provides criteria to evaluate the quality of internal audits.

Positive assurance. The highest level of assurance; expressed in an audit or examination-level attest engagement.

Projection. A forward-looking set of financial statements based on a stated set of assumptions.

Public offering. Sale by a company of its own equity or debt securities in a public market.

Registration statement. Document filed with the SEC associated with a public offering; assigned an effective date by the SEC, at which time the company can sell the securities.

Reportable conditions. Under *Circular A-133*, deficiencies in internal control that individually or cumulatively constitute a material weakness.

Review. A type of financial statement or attest engagement provided by accountants that results in moderate or limited assurance.

Single Audit. An entity-wide rather than grant-by-grant audit for an entity that receives federal grants in excess of a specified dollar threshold; covers both financial statements and compliance.

Statements on Standards for Accounting and Review Services (SSARS). AICPA standards covering compilation and review engagements.

Statements on Standards for Attestation Engagements (SSAEs). AICPA standards covering attest engagements.

SOX Section 302. Applies to interim and annual financial statement filings with the SEC and requires management to acknowledge responsibility for the financial statements, internal control, and various required communications.

SOX Section 404. Applies to annual financial statement filings with the SEC and requires management to assess and report on the effectiveness of the company's ICFR; also requires an ICFR audit and audit report.

Suitable criteria. Standards against which assertions can be compared that are objective, measurable, complete, and relevant.

Underwriter. An entity that provides the service of offering a company's securities for sale in a public market.

Yellow Book. Published by the GAO and includes government auditing standards for financial statement audits, performance audits, and attestation engagements.

MULTIPLE CHOICE

16-1 **[LO 1]** Forensic accounting

 (a) is best described by the term *fraud audit*.

 (b) includes investigative services and litigation support.

 (c) can only be carried out by CPAs.

 (d) follows the same approach as traditional auditing except that materiality thresholds are lower.

16-2 **[LO 1]** Because of the possibility that a forensic accounting engagement may result in litigation,

 (a) forensic accountants must be law enforcement officers, lawyers, or officers of the court.

 (b) forensic accountants must be certified by the ACFE.

 (c) forensic accountants do not rely on interviews as a source of evidence.

 (d) forensic accountants are likely to have an adversarial relationship with the employees of their clients.

16-3 **[LO 2]** The Institute of Internal Auditors (IIA) states that internal auditors

 (a) conduct an independent objective assurance and consulting activity.

 (b) cannot be independent because they have an employment relationship with the target of their activities.

(c) add value by enhancing management's efficiency.

(d) are an integral part of management's decision-making team in assessing the effectiveness of ICFR.

16-4 **[LO 2]** The independence of internal auditors and the internal audit function is enhanced by

(a) avoiding conflicts of interest.

(b) being placed high in the organizational hierarchy and having access to the audit committee.

(c) conducting their tasks in an objective manner.

(d) all of the above.

16-5 **[LO 2]** Internal auditors

(a) must follow all AICPA professional guidance in their work.

(b) are guided by the International Standards for the Professional Practice of Internal Auditing.

(c) may be guided by AICPA or IIA standards, but neither is preferred over the other.

(d) none of the above.

16-6 **[LO 2]** SOX Section 302 places requirements on management

(a) for quarterly filings only.

(b) for an audit of ICFR.

(c) for annual and quarterly reports.

(d) for the auditor to assume responsibility for assessing and reporting on the effectiveness of ICFR.

16-7 **[LO 1]** Compliance auditing

(a) involves assessing whether the entity being audited complies with stipulations such as laws, regulations, and the terms of a contract, for example, the requirements of a Federal grant.

(b) deals with assessing whether management complies with all the expectations of the auditor as the financial statement and ICFR audit progresses.

(c) is the same as operational auditing.

(d) must be performed for all departments of the federal government.

16-8 **[LO 3]** OMB *Circular A-133, Audits of States, Local Governments, and Non-Profit Organizations,*

(a) is the Yellow Book.

(b) outlines the provisions of the Single Audit Act.

(c) must be followed on the audit of every entity that receives federal funds.

(d) all of the above.

16-9 **[LO 3]** Which of the following is an ethical concept that is included in both the IIA and the Yellow Book ethics?

(a) Integrity

(b) Objectivity

(c) Proper use of information, resources, and position

(d) All of the above are in both the IIA Code and the Yellow Book.

16-10 **[LO 3]** The head of the General Accountability Office is the

(a) Auditor General.

(b) Secretary of the Treasury.

(c) Director of the OMB.

(d) Comptroller General.

16-11 **[LO 4]** A service provided under the AICPA guidance that provides no assurance about the financial statements that are the target of the engagement is a(n)

(a) operational audit.

(b) review.

(c) attestation.

(d) compilation.

16-12 **[LO 4]** The abbreviation used by the AICPA in codifying guidance that deals with compilations and reviews is

(a) AR.

(b) AU.

(c) AT.

(d) ET.

16-13 **[LO 4]** Under which of the following circumstances is the accounting practitioner required to issue a compilation report to accompany financial statements?

(a) The financial statements are for management use only, and a written engagement letter was executed.

(b) The financial statements are for management use only, and a written engagement letter was not executed.

(c) The financial statements are for management use only, substantially all disclosures were omitted, and a written engagement letter was executed.

(d) A compilation report must be issued in all the circumstances above.

16-14 [LO 4] Which of the following is not true?

(a) An accountant does not have to be independent to perform a compilation.

(b) The standards that apply to a review of interim financial information of a public company are different from those that apply to a review of financial statements of a nonpublic company.

(c) Because the engagement provides no assurance on the financial statements, no professional requirements exist for qualifications or procedures on a compilation engagement.

(d) The procedures on both a review of interim financial information of a public company and a review of financial statements of a nonpublic company consist mainly of inquiry and analytical procedures.

16-15 [LO 5] An examination attest engagement provides

(a) positive assurance.

(b) moderate or limited assurance.

(c) no assurance.

(d) agreed upon procedures assurance.

16-16 [LO 5] For which of the following attest engagements can the report be for general distribution?

(a) An examination engagement when the assertion is agreed upon

(b) An agreed-upon procedures engagement when the criteria are publicly known and widely understood

(c) An examination engagement when the criteria are publicly known and widely understood

(d) A review engagement when the criteria are agreed upon

16-17 [LO 6] "Comfort letters" are requested by underwriters because

(a) the SEC requires underwriters to obtain them.

(b) they are a required part of the public disclosure included in a registration statement.

(c) the issuer must provide one to the underwriter.

(d) they can contribute to an underwriter's due diligence defense.

16-18 [LO 6] The engagement to provide a "comfort letter" is most like which of the following?

(a) An agreed-upon procedures engagement

(b) An examination

(c) A review

(d) A legal services engagement

16-19 [LO 6] A review of a public company's interim financial information

(a) always results in a review report that becomes part of the SEC filing.

(b) can be performed at any time before the end of the fiscal year.

(c) provides a basis for the auditor to state whether he or she is aware of any material modifications that need to be made to the financial statements.

(d) involves obtaining an understanding of internal control in addition to inquiry and analytical procedures.

16-20 [LO 6] In order for audited annual financial statements or reviewed quarterly financial statements to be included in a registration statement,

(a) the effective date must coincide with the auditor's report date.

(b) the auditor must give consent.

(c) the subsequent events review report must be included in the registration statement.

(d) the company must correct any problems that caused the auditor's report to be other than unqualified.

DISCUSSION QUESTIONS

16-21 [LO 1] Minutes after your college graduation, your family is gathered around discussing your achievements and future plans. Your uncle asks what exactly you plan to do with your degree in accounting. While there are many career opportunities, you explain, you are going to become a CPA and gain experience as an auditor. "You're going to work for the IRS!" your uncle exclaims. "No," you clarify, "I'm going to audit companies, not individuals' taxes." Your uncle replies, "Great, we need more people out there to catch those corporate crooks. You're going to make a great financial detective."

What type of accountant is your uncle really thinking of? What other designations are beneficial to such an accountant? What are the job responsibilities and activities performed by an accountant who is a "financial detective"?

16-22 **[LO 2]** Gene is a new staff-level auditor on the audit of CalPower, a publicly traded energy and utility company. On his first day, his senior informs him that the engagement team is scheduled to have lunch with the internal auditor to discuss ways to improve this year's audit. While Gene has heard a lot about internal auditing in school and has some friends who recently began working as internal auditors, he is unfamiliar with exactly what internal auditors do and how internal and external auditors can work together to improve the audit process. Gene decides to take a look at last year's internal audit report prepared by CalPower's internal auditors. He notices that the report includes a sentence that reads, "CalPower's Internal Audit group maintains a high level of independence from management." Because Gene is intimately familiar with the extensive independence requirements of his own firm, he cannot figure out how CalPower's internal audit group can possibly assert their own independence.

Ethics

What is meant by independence from management for internal auditors?

16-23 **[LO 2]** During the meeting with CalPower's internal audit group (introduced in Problem 16-22), Gene learns that the internal audit group's focus has shifted significantly from operational audits to Sarbanes-Oxley Section 302 and 404 compliance. Section 302 deals with management's responsibility over financial reports, and Section 404 deals with management's assessment of internal control. Once again, Gene asks himself, "How can the internal audit department assist in Section 302 and 404 compliance and still claim independence from management?"

Ethics

According to the IIA's position paper entitled *Internal Auditing's Role in Section 302 and 404 of the U.S. Sarbanes-Oxley Act of 2002*, which SOX-related activities are appropriate and which are inappropriate for the internal audit group to perform?

How do these activities fit within the concept of objectivity, which is the hallmark of an internal auditor's independence?

16-24 **[LO 3]** During her studies at Florida Keys University, a public university that is part of Florida's state university system, Amanda took a work-study position in the university's financial reporting and accounting department. She figured it would be a great opportunity to gain some experience because she plans to become an auditor once she graduates. One day, Amanda's supervisor informs her that she will be assisting the "independent auditors" as they audit the university over the next several weeks. As she knows many classmates who have graduated and have begun careers in public auditing firms, she is curious to find out who will perform Florida Keys University's audit. However, when she asks around, she finds that none of her friends' firms are engaged to audit her university.

If there are no public accounting firms engaged on the audit, who is most likely performing the audit of the state agency? Do you think the audit fits the description of an independent audit? Why or why not?

16-25 **[LO 3]** Annie's audit firm has recently won the bidding for the audit of Big Spending, an organization supported by public funds provided from the federal government. Annie has never been involved in an audit of a government organization and is unfamiliar with the standards governing an audit of a government-related entity. The night before she is scheduled to begin the engagement, Annie decides to do her homework. First, she goes to the PCAOB Web site and searches for any relevant information. Since the PCAOB governs audits of publicly traded companies, she finds no guidance from the ASs and the AUs. Next, she searches on the AICPA Web site, but once again finds no guidance from the SASs. Since she has exhausted all of the resources she is aware of, she gives up.

Where can Annie find guidance on standards affecting the Big Spending audit? What are governmental auditing standards called? How do audits of government entities vary from those of for-profit entities? How do entities that receive funds from government grants fit in?

16-26 **[LO 6]** Your firm has recently been engaged as the auditor for Samwiches, a publicly traded restaurant holding company with yearly revenues of $15 billion. You are assigned to the quarterly review engagement in the first quarter after your firm picks up the client. Planning is being conducted for the quarterly review engagement and the first-year audit. In the planning stages of the review, you must determine the materiality threshold for the service revenue account. You begin by discussing materiality with the manager who is planning the audit. She plans a materiality threshold for revenue of $200 million.

Do you think your materiality threshold for revenue for Samwiches quarterly review should be higher or lower than the $200 million threshold used in the audit? Why?

16-27 **[LO 4]** After completing your quarterly review of Samwiches (Problem 16-26), you are assigned to perform a SSARS review of the annual financial statements of Soops & Sal-lids—a nonpublic company.

How will your review of Soops & Sal-lids (nonpublic) annual financial statements differ from your quarterly review of Samwiches? Include in your discussion applicability of the different professional standards.

16-28 **[LO 4, 5]** Compare and contrast the differences between the following services that an auditor may provide—audit, attest, review, and compilation. Comment on the scope, work performed, level of assurance provided, extent of work performed, and underlying information used when forming the auditor's opinion.

16-29 **[LO 2]** By now, you should be thoroughly familiar with the roles, responsibilities, duties, and so on, of an external auditor. Compare and contrast the work of an external auditor to that of an internal auditor. Similarly, compare and contrast the work of an external auditor to that of a forensic accountant. Comment on the roles, goals, relationship with management, testing performed, duty to independence, and to whom they are ultimately responsible.

16-30 **[LO 1]** Some universities now offer degrees in forensic accounting. Based on what you read about the activities of a forensic accountant, what are your thoughts about someone starting out fresh with an accounting degree going directly into forensic accounting? Is entering forensic accounting first a good option rather than starting out in auditing, corporate accounting, or consulting? Do you think your accounting training to date is a good background for forensic accounting activities?

PROBLEMS

16-31 **[LO 4]** The firm of Kay and Cee, CPAs, was engaged to perform a compilation of TCV Corporation, a private company, for the year ended 2010. The owner of TCV Corporation signed the engagement letter provided by Kay and Cee and then provided all the underlying data needed for the financial statements. Kay and Cee knew the industry and was acquainted with TCV Corporation because it had prepared the corporate tax return the prior year.

(a) TCV Corporation requests that Kay and Cee compile the financial statements in accordance with generally accepted accounting principles and include all the appropriate disclosures. Kay and Cee determine that they are independent of TCV Corporation and at the end of their work conclude that, on the face, there are no problems with the financial statements as they are compiled. The financial statements are for management use only, and even though TCV Corporation management signed the written engagement letter, Kay and Cee choose to issue a compilation report to accompany the financial statements.

Prepare the compilation report that Kay and Cee, CPAs, submit with the compiled financial statements.

(b) Instead of engaging them to compile the financial statements, TCV Corporation hires Kay and Cee to review its financial statements for the year ended 2010.

What steps do Kay and Cee have to carry out as part of the review?

(c) At the end of the review, Kay and Cee conclude that nothing has come to their attention causing the need for any modification of the financial statements for them to be in accordance with GAAP. Draft the review report that Kay and Cee issue for TCV Corporation.

16-32 **[LO 5]** Yacht Crew Training, Inc. is a privately owned corporation that has been in business for 15 years. The company specializes in training individuals who work on private yachts. Its promotion materials state that in 2009 the company trained 600 deckhands and 900 stewards and that the two mock-up yacht environments on the property used for training replicate a 120' and 180' yacht, respectively. Yacht Crew Training, Inc. is a legitimate training company with a sound reputation among everyone who has personal knowledge of the business. The environment usually "sells itself" when anyone personally visits the site. However, the company encounters difficulty when potential customers are not local and want some means to establish that it is a legitimate business. Up to this point, Yacht Crew Training has provided references and has referred potential customers to the local Better Business Bureau. The manager is wondering about the possibility of having an accountant's report as a way to respond to potential customers' inquiries.

(a) Given that there is no organization that sets standards for yacht crew training, and there is no certification regarding the skills, can management state any assertions about the quality or effectiveness of its training *process* that an accountant can attest to for a general use report? Why or why not?

(b) Write a management assertion for attestation purposes on: (1) the years Yacht Crew Training has been in business; (2) the number of individuals trained in 2009; (3) the size of its mock-up environments.

Can the auditor provide a general distribution attest report on these assertions?

(c) Yacht Crew Training states that it teaches basic seamanship, docking procedures, ropes and knots, bartending, and flower arranging.

Write management assertions and agreed-upon procedures that would provide useful information to someone who lives a distance from Yacht Crew Training and wants to know that these subjects are actually covered in the training materials.

Is there any way that an attestation report addressing these assertions could have general distribution?

Would your answer be different if the Coast Guard wrote standards on training for seamanship, docking, and ropes and knots, and the American Hotel and Restaurant Association wrote standards for training on bartending and flower arranging? Write the attest report assuming the standards exist.

16-33 **[LO 2]** Brad Jolie is a CPA who has worked for a very large public accounting firm for 12 years. He is being considered for the partnership but will likely have to move to another city if he is elected and accepts the position. He really does not want to move so he started looking around to see what job prospects may exist in his city of Po-Dunck, California. A headhunter recently contacted him about the top position in the internal audit department of a large, publicly traded company that is headquartered in Po-Dunck. He researched the company, and what he found was encouraging enough that he told the headhunter to schedule an interview.

Draft a list of questions that Brad should ask. What responses might cause him concern or motivate him to follow up with more questions?

16-34 **[LO 1-6]** Place letters of an accountant's career position in front of each description of services that fit. You may use any number of letters on each line and use the letters as many times as they fit.

(a) An accountant working for a public accounting firm performing audits and quarterly reviews of public companies

(b) An accountant working for a public accounting firm providing audits and reviews of nonpublic companies

(c) An accountant working for the GAO

(d) An internal auditor working for a public company

(e) An accountant working for a consulting firm that specializes in forensics

_____1. Audit activities focusing on efficiency

_____2. Specialists in physical evidence indicating fraud

_____3. Independence from the organization receiving the service is required

_____4. May be involved with accomplishing a company's SOX requirements

_____5. May be involved with assessing whether ICFR operates effectively

_____6. Service is based on inquiry and analytical procedures

_____7. Findings from activities are expected to be used as evidence in court

_____8. Uses procedures such as inquiry, document inspection, reperformance

16-35 **[LO 1-6]** Match the accountants with the services provided

_____1. Attest	**a.** Independent auditors
_____2. Financial statement review	**b.** Forensic accountants
_____3. Financial statement compilation	**c.** Auditors employed by governments
_____4. Agreed-upon procedures	**d.** GAO employees
_____5. Comfort letters for underwriters	
_____6. Special projects for those in governance	

16-36 **[LO 1, 4, 5, 6]** Kate and Sawyer, CPAs, have been hired by Kate's mother in relation to the financial statements of her company, a local diner that she owns 100%. Although she is 35 and can support herself, Kate still lives in her mother's home.

(a) Fill out the chart below. List the engagements Kate and Sawyer, CPAs, can provide to nonpublic companies. Identify those they can provide to Kate's mother on the financial statements of her diner. For the services they cannot provide, state why.

Service	Available to Kate's mother?	Reason
1.		
2.		
3.		
4.		
5.		

(b) Jack, a friend of Kate and Sawyer (of Kate and Sawyer, CPAs), is a spinal surgeon who provides medical services to people in remote locations of the world. His company is so successful that he plans to have a public offering. What services can Kate and Sawyer, CPAs, provide to Jack's company while it is going public and after? Briefly summarize what is involved in the services.

Service	Activities
1.	
2.	
3.	
4.	
5.	

16-37 **[LO 5]** You have been engaged by Markus Industries to examine its projected financial statements for 2011.

Required:

For each of the following, state the evidence sources and procedures you would use to evaluate the reasonableness of the assumption.

(a) The Molding Division's sales forecast assumes that the Orlando facility will be completed and operating at 42% of capacity on February 2, 2011. It is highly improbable that the facility will be operational before December 31, 2010. For every month's delay in opening the facility, the sales of the Molding Division are reduced by $82,000 and operating earnings are reduced by $32,000.

(b) Markus intends to sell certain real estate and facilities held by the Assembly Division at an after-tax profit of $625,000. The proceeds of this sale will be used to retire outstanding debt (described in c).

(c) Markus will call and retire all outstanding 8% subordinated debentures (callable at 107). Given the present interest rate of 7% on similar debt, it is expected that the debentures will require the full call premium. A rise in market interest rates to 8% would reduce the loss on bond retirement from the projected $195,000 to $185,000.

16-38 **[LO 5]** Magnolia Snook and Associates, CPAs, has been engaged by the Dobson Fabrication Company to apply agreed upon procedures to forecast assumptions with respect to a new labor contract for 2011. The current labor contract at Dobson will expire on August 31, 2011, and the new contract is expected to result in a 3.5% wage increase. As a result of forecasting production and sales levels, after-tax earnings is expected to be reduced by about $75,000 for each percentage point in wage increase concessions in excess of the expected contract.

Required:

What evidence sources and agreed-upon procedures might Magnolia Snook & Associates and Dobson Fabrication Company specify as appropriate if the company's intent is to investigate the reasonableness of the assumptions upon which forecasted information is derived?

16-39 **[LO 5]** Upton Industries, a public company, prepared a comprehensive interim financial report covering the first two quarters of their fiscal year 2011, which ends December 31. Upton management engaged Jamison, CPAs, to perform a review, and the following review report was published with the interim financial statements:

To the Board of Directors of Upton Industries:

In accordance with generally accepted auditing standards, we have made a review of the interim balance sheet of Upton Industries as of June 30, 2011, and of the interim statements of operations and changes in financial position for the three month and six month periods then ended.

Based on this review, we are not aware of any material modifications that should be made to the accompanying interim financial statements for them to be in conformity with GAAP.

Signed,

Jamison CPAs
July 14, 2011

Required:

Based on this information and without rewriting the report, identify the deficiencies in the report and how they should be corrected.

16-40 **[LO 4]** Hobson Brothers, Inc., engaged Young, Simpson, and Norris, CPAs, to compile their financial statements from books and records maintained by Jim Hobson, one of the principals in the business. The Hobsons own and operate three air-conditioning businesses in Kansas City. Although the business is growing, they have not employed a full-time bookkeeper. Jim indicates that he wants a balance sheet, a statement of operations, and a statement of cash flows. He is unable to provide footnotes to accompany the statement because he is too busy in the operation of the business.

Jim directed the physical count of inventory on March 31, 2011, and then adjusted and closed the books on that date. The auditors find that Jim is a pretty good accountant and has taken a few university accounting courses. The records appear to have been maintained in accordance with GAAP and they find no obvious errors.

Required:

Prepare a compilation services report that Young, Simpson, and Norris, CPAs, might issue.

16-41 **[LO 4]** Smothers & Nelson, CPAs, have previously been engaged by Garrison Corporation to perform compilations and tax returns. Henry Garrison, the company's president, indicated to the accountants that he needed "something more" than they previously provided. Mr. Garrison told Jose Vegas, the partner in-charge of the engagement, that the resulting financial statements from this proposed engagement would be used primarily for management's purposes internally, as well as short-term bank loans. Vegas recommended that a review of the financial statements be performed, and work commenced without an engagement letter.

As Vegas proceeded with the work, he indicated an uneasiness about certain figures and conclusions but said he would take the client's word about the validity of some entries, since the review was primarily for internal use and was not an audit.

If Vegas had not relied on the representations of management, he would have detected a material act of fraud committed by management.

Required:

(a) Explain the role that an engagement letter could have played in this scenario and indicate what should have been covered in the letter.

(b) What was Vegas's duty in this review? What is the potential liability faced by Smothers & Nelson, CPAs? Who may assert claims against the firm?

16-42 **[LO 4]** You are performing a review for a company with a plant that uses many different types of metals, including steel, aluminum, and copper. As part of your inquiry, you ask about the inventory and control of scrap. The plant manager says: "We don't inventory scrap, but I know where it is. We accumulate it in separate bins for each type of metal. When the bins are full, I call the scrap dealer and he gives me cash for what it is worth and a journal entry is made when the cash is deposited." You feel uneasy, but another person working on the engagement, Vince Easton, suggests that scrap is less than 0.5% of inventories and that your inquiry about scrap has achieved the limited assurance level that there are not material modifications that should be made to the financial statements to be in conformity with GAAP.

Requirement:

(a) If you accept Vince's premise and also know that the internal controls for the company are good overall, what procedures, at a minimum, should you consider to validate your questions?

(b) If you feel that the company may have no basis to know the true total value of the scrap, and without that knowledge, cannot conclude about the magnitude of any potential modifications to the financial statements, what are some of the questions you should ask as part of your additional inquiry?

ACTIVITY ASSIGNMENTS

16-43 Go to the AICPA Web site and find AU 801, titled *Compliance Auditing Considerations in Audits of Governmental Entities and Recipients of Governmental Financial Assistance.* Read AU 801. Based on the information provided in Chapter 16 on GAS, how does AU 801 seem to coordinate with and overlap the government-issued standards?

16-44 Find and examine a 10Q of five different public companies. Do any of the 10Q's include auditor's review reports? If yes, what was the circumstance that caused the accountant to issue the report? Go to Exhibit 16-15 and read the review report provided. Can you tell whether any circumstance caused an auditor's review report to be issued with this 10Q?

16-45 Go to the GAO Web site at *www.gao.gov.* Under the "Reports and Testimonials" tab, click on the most recent report and read the Summary. What was the report and what did the GAO find? Under the "Legal Decisions and Opinions" tab, click on the most recent report. What issue was considered, and what was the result?

16-46 Go to the Auditor General (or comparable) Web site for your state. Find the list of reports issued in the last year. Was your university examined? What type of engagement was performed? What was the outcome of the engagement?

16-47 If information in a registration statement is not true, professionals associated with the public offering may be sued by those who suffer a loss. However, they may offer as a defense that they did not know that the information was untrue and they had reasonable grounds for their belief.

Go to the AICPA Web site, to AU 634 *Letters for Underwriters and Certain Other Requesting Parties.* Note that in paragraph 1 (AU 634.01) the standard states that it gives guidance to accountants who are providing reports to underwriters and others who have a "due diligence defense" under Section 11 of the Securities Act of 1933.

Next go to the SEC Web site and click through the following menu choices: About the SEC, What We Do, The Laws that Govern the Securities Industry. Then click on the link to the Securities Act of 1933. (If you want to go directly to the law, go to: *www.sec.gov/about/laws/sa33.pdf*)

(a) Find and read Section 11(b)3: What is the language in this section of the law that indicates that a valid defense is that a person had reason to believe that the information in the registration statement is true?

(b) Find and read Section 11 (c): What is the standard that is appropriate to be used for "reasonable investigation and reasonable ground for belief?"

16-48 Go to the AICPA Web site and find AU 622 describing the withdrawal of the auditing standard on "Agreed Upon Procedures." Why do you think "Agreed Upon Procedures" was originally included as an audit standard when those activities did not culminate in an audit opinion or audit report? Why was the standard withdrawn?

PROFESSIONAL SIMULATIONS

Go to the book's companion Web site at www.wiley.com/college/hooks to find simulations similar to those on the computerized CPA exam.

APPENDIX A: THE INSTITUTE OF INTERNAL AUDITORS

Code of Ethics

Principles
Internal auditors are expected to apply and uphold the following principles:

1. Integrity
The integrity of internal auditors establishes trust and thus provides the basis for reliance on their judgment.

2. Objectivity
Internal auditors exhibit the highest level of professional objectivity in gathering, evaluating, and communicating information about the activity or process being examined. Internal auditors make a balanced assessment of all the relevant circumstances and are not unduly influenced by their own interests or by others in forming judgments.

3. Confidentiality
Internal auditors respect the value and ownership of information they receive and do not disclose information without appropriate authority unless there is a legal or professional obligation to do so.

4. Competency
Internal auditors apply the knowledge, skills, and experience needed in the performance of internal audit services.

Rules of Conduct
1. Integrity
Internal auditors:

1.1. Shall perform their work with honesty, diligence, and responsibility.
1.2. Shall observe the law and make disclosures expected by the law and the profession.
1.3. Shall not knowingly be a party to any illegal activity, or engage in acts that are discreditable to the profession of internal auditing or to the organization.
1.4. Shall respect and contribute to the legitimate and ethical objectives of the organization.

2. Objectivity
Internal auditors:

2.1. Shall not participate in any activity or relationship that may impair or be presumed to impair their unbiased assessment. This participation includes those activities or relationships that may be in conflict with the interests of the organization.
2.2. Shall not accept anything that may impair or be presumed to impair their professional judgment.
2.3. Shall disclose all material facts known to them that, if not disclosed, may distort the reporting of activities under review.

3. Confidentiality
Internal auditors:

3.1. Shall be prudent in the use and protection of information acquired in the course of their duties.
3.2. Shall not use information for any personal gain or in any manner that would be contrary to the law or detrimental to the legitimate and ethical objectives of the organization.

4. Competency

Internal auditors:

4.1. Shall engage only in those services for which they have the necessary knowledge, skills, and experience.

4.2. Shall perform internal audit services in accordance with the *International Standards for the Professional Practice of Internal Auditing.*

4.3. Shall continually improve their proficiency and the effectiveness and quality of their services.

APPENDIX B: THE INSTITUTE OF INTERNAL AUDITORS

International Standards for the Professional Practice of Internal Auditing

Introduction to the International Standards

Internal auditing is conducted in diverse legal and cultural environments; within organizations that vary in purpose, size, complexity, and structure; and by persons within or outside the organization. While differences may affect the practice of internal auditing in each environment, conformance with The IIA's *International Standards for the Professional Practice of Internal Auditing (Standards)* is essential in meeting the responsibilities of internal auditors and the internal audit activity.

If internal auditors or the internal audit activity is prohibited by law or regulation from conformance with certain parts of the *Standards,* conformance with all other parts of the *Standards* and appropriate disclosures are needed.

If the *Standards* are used in conjunction with standards issued by other authoritative bodies, internal audit communications may also cite the use of other standards, as appropriate. In such a case, if inconsistencies exist between the *Standards* and other standards, internal auditors and the internal audit activity must conform with the *Standards,* and may conform with the other standards if they are more restrictive.

The purpose of the *Standards* is to:

1. Delineate basic principles that represent the practice of internal auditing.
2. Provide a framework for performing and promoting a broad range of value-added internal auditing.
3. Establish the basis for the evaluation of internal audit performance.
4. Foster improved organizational processes and operations.

The *Standards* are principles-focused, mandatory requirements consisting of:

- Statements of basic requirements for the professional practice of internal auditing and for evaluating the effectiveness of performance, which are internationally applicable at organizational and individual levels.
- Interpretations, which clarify terms or concepts within the Statements.

The *Standards* employ terms that have been given specific meanings that are included in the Glossary. Specifically, the *Standards* use the word "must" to specify an unconditional requirement and the word "should" where conformance is expected unless, when applying professional judgment, circumstances justify deviation.

It is necessary to consider the Statements and their Interpretations as well as the specific meanings from the Glossary to understand and apply the *Standards* correctly.

The structure of the *Standards* is divided between Attribute and Performance Standards. Attribute Standards address the attributes of organizations and individuals performing internal auditing. The Performance Standards describe the nature of internal auditing and provide quality criteria against which the performance of these services can be measured. The Attribute and Performance Standards are also provided to apply to all internal audit services.

Implementation Standards are also provided to expand upon the Attribute and Performance standards, by providing the requirements applicable to assurance (A) or consulting (C) activities.

Assurance services involve the internal auditor's objective assessment of evidence to provide an independent opinion or conclusions regarding an entity, operation, function, process, system, or other subject matter. The nature and scope of the assurance engagement are determined by the internal auditor. There are generally three parties involved in assurance services: (1) the person or group directly involved with the entity, operation, function, process, system, or other subject matter—the process owner, (2) the person or group making the assessment—the internal auditor, and (3) the person or group using the assessment—the user.

Consulting services are advisory in nature, and are generally performed at the specific request of an engagement client. The nature and scope of the consulting engagement are subject to agreement with the engagement client. Consulting services generally involve two parties: (1) the person or group offering the advice—the internal auditor, and (2) the person or group seeking and receiving the advice—the engagement client. When performing consulting services the internal auditor should maintain objectivity and not assume management responsibility.

The review and development of the *Standards* is an ongoing process. The Internal Audit Standards Board engages in extensive consultation and discussion prior to issuing the *Standards*. This includes worldwide solicitation for public comment through the exposure draft process. All exposure drafts are posted on The IIA's Web site as well as being distributed to all IIA institutes.

Suggestions and comments regarding the *Standards* can be sent to:

The Institute of Internal Auditors
Standards and Guidance
247 Maitland Avenue
Altamonte Springs, FL 32701-4201, USA
E-mail: guidance@theiia.org

Attribute Standards

1000 – Purpose, Authority, and Responsibility

The purpose, authority, and responsibility of the internal audit activity must be formally defined in an internal audit charter, consistent with the Definition of Internal Auditing, the Code of Ethics, and the *Standards*. The chief audit executive must periodically review the internal audit charter and present it to senior management and the board for approval.

Interpretation:
The internal audit charter is a formal document that defines the internal audit activity's purpose, authority, and responsibility. The internal audit charter establishes the internal audit activity's position within the organization; authorizes access to records, personnel, and physical properties relevant to the performance of engagements; and defines the scope of internal audit activities. Final approval of the internal audit charter resides with the board.

1000.A1 – The nature of assurance services provided to the organization must be defined in the internal audit charter. If assurances are to be provided to parties outside the organization, the nature of these assurances must also be defined in the internal audit charter.

1000.C1 – The nature of consulting services must be defined in the internal audit charter.

1010 – Recognition of the Definition of Internal Auditing, the Code of Ethics, and the *Standards* in the Internal Audit Charter

The mandatory nature of the Definition of Internal Auditing, the Code of Ethics, and the *Standards* must be recognized in the internal audit charter. The chief audit executive should discuss the Definition of Internal Auditing, the Code of Ethics, and the *Standards* with senior management and the board.

1100 – Independence and Objectivity

The internal audit activity must be independent, and internal auditors must be objective in performing their work.

Interpretation:

Independence is the freedom from conditions that threaten the ability of the internal audit activity or the chief audit executive to carry out internal audit responsibilities in an unbiased manner. To achieve the degree of independence necessary to effectively carry out the responsibilities of the internal audit activity, the chief audit executive has direct and unrestricted access to senior management and the board. This can be achieved through a dual-reporting relationship. Threats to independence must be managed at the individual auditor, engagement, functional, and organizational levels.

Objectivity is an unbiased mental attitude that allows internal auditors to perform engagements in such a manner that they believe in their work product and that no quality compromises are made. Objectivity requires that internal auditors do not subordinate their judgment on audit matters to others. Threats to objectivity must be managed at the individual auditor, engagement, functional, and organizational levels.

1110 – Organizational Independence

The chief audit executive must report to a level within the organization that allows the internal audit activity to fulfill its responsibilities. The chief audit executive must confirm to the board, at least annually, the organizational independence of the internal audit activity.

1110.A1 – The internal audit activity must be free from interference in determining the scope of internal auditing, performing work, and communicating results.

1111 – Direct Interaction with the Board

The chief audit executive must communicate and interact directly with the board.

1120 – Individual Objectivity

Internal auditors must have an impartial, unbiased attitude and avoid any conflict of interest.

Interpretation:

Conflict of interest is a situation in which an internal auditor, who is in a position of trust, has a competing professional or personal interest. Such competing interests can make it difficult to fulfill his or her duties impartially. A conflict of interest exists even if no unethical or improper act results. A conflict of interest can create an appearance of impropriety that can undermine confidence in the internal auditor, the internal audit activity, and the profession. A conflict of interest could impair an individual's ability to perform his or her duties and responsibilities objectively.

1130 – Impairment to Independence or Objectivity

If independence or objectivity is impaired in fact or appearance, the details of the impairment must be disclosed to appropriate parties. The nature of the disclosure will depend upon the impairment.

Interpretation:

Impairment to organizational independence and individual objectivity may include, but is not limited to, personal conflict of interest, scope limitations, restrictions on access to records, personnel, and properties, and resource limitations, such as funding.

The determination of appropriate parties to which the details of an impairment to independence or objectivity must be disclosed is dependent upon the expectations of the internal audit activity's and the chief audit executive's responsibilities to senior management and the board as described in the internal audit charter, as well as the nature of the impairment.

1130.A1 – Internal auditors must refrain from assessing specific operations for which they were previously responsible. Objectivity is presumed to be impaired if an internal auditor provides assurance services for an activity for which the internal auditor had responsibility within the previous year.

1130.A2 – Assurance engagements for functions over which the chief audit executive has responsibility must be overseen by a party outside the internal audit activity.

1130.C1 – Internal auditors may provide consulting services relating to operations for which they had previous responsibilities.

1130.C2 – If internal auditors have potential impairments to independence or objectivity relating to proposed consulting services, disclosure must be made to the engagement client prior to accepting the engagement.

1200 – Proficiency and Due Professional Care

Engagements must be performed with proficiency and due professional care.

1210 – Proficiency

Internal auditors must possess the knowledge, skills, and other competencies needed to perform their individual responsibilities. The internal audit activity collectively must possess or obtain the knowledge, skills, and other competencies needed to perform its responsibilities.

Interpretation:

Knowledge, skills, and other competencies is a collective term that refers to the professional proficiency required of internal auditors to effectively carry out their professional responsibilities. Internal auditors are encouraged to demonstrate their proficiency by obtaining appropriate professional certifications and qualifications, such as the Certified Internal Auditor designation and other designations offered by The Institute of Internal Auditors and other appropriate professional organizations.

1210.A1 – The chief audit executive must obtain competent advice and assistance if the internal auditors lack the knowledge, skills, or other competencies needed to perform all or part of the engagement.

1210.A2 – Internal auditors must have sufficient knowledge to evaluate the risk of fraud and the manner in which it is managed by the organization, but are not expected to have the expertise of a person whose primary responsibility is detecting and investigating fraud.

1210.A3 – Internal auditors must have sufficient knowledge of key information technology risks and controls and available technology-based audit techniques to perform their assigned work. However, not all internal auditors are expected to have the expertise of an internal auditor whose primary responsibility is information technology auditing.

1210.C1 – The chief audit executive must decline the consulting engagement or obtain competent advice and assistance if the internal auditors lack the knowledge, skills, or other competencies needed to perform all or part of the engagement.

1220 – Due Professional Care

Internal auditors must apply the care and skill expected of a reasonably prudent and competent internal auditor. Due professional care does not imply infallibility.

> **1220.A1** – Internal auditors must exercise due professional care by considering the:
>
> - Extent of work needed to achieve the engagement's objectives;
> - Relative complexity, materiality, or significance of matters to which assurance procedures are applied;
> - Adequacy and effectiveness of governance, risk management, and control processes;
> - Probability of significant errors, fraud, or noncompliance; and
> - Cost of assurance in relation to potential benefits.
>
> **1220.A2** – In exercising due professional care internal auditors must consider the use of technology-based audit and other data analysis techniques.
>
> **1220.A3** – Internal auditors must be alert to the significant risks that might affect objectives, operations, or resources. However, assurance procedures alone, even when performed with due professional care, do not guarantee that all significant risks will be identified.
>
> **1220.C1** – Internal auditors must exercise due professional care during a consulting engagement by considering the:
>
> - Needs and expectations of clients, including the nature, timing, and communication of engagement results;
> - Relative complexity and extent of work needed to achieve the engagement's objectives; and
> - Cost of the consulting engagement in relation to potential benefits.

1230 – Continuing Professional Development

Internal auditors must enhance their knowledge, skills, and other competencies through continuing professional development.

1300 – Quality Assurance and Improvement Program

The chief audit executive must develop and maintain a quality assurance and improvement program that covers all aspects of the internal audit activity.

Interpretation:

A quality assurance and improvement program is designed to enable an evaluation of the internal audit activity's conformance with the Definition of Internal Auditing and the Standards and an evaluation of whether internal auditors apply the Code of Ethics. The program also assesses the efficiency and effectiveness of the internal audit activity and identifies opportunities for improvement.

1310 – Requirements of the Quality Assurance and Improvement Program

The quality assurance and improvement program must include both internal and external assessments.

1311 – Internal Assessments

Internal assessments must include:

- Ongoing monitoring of the performance of the internal audit activity; and
- Periodic reviews performed through self-assessment or by other persons within the organization with sufficient knowledge of internal audit practices.

Interpretation:

Ongoing monitoring is an integral part of the day-to-day supervision, review, and measurement of the internal audit activity. Ongoing monitoring is incorporated into the routine policies and practices used to manage the internal audit activity and uses processes, tools, and information considered necessary to evaluate conformance with the Definition of Internal Auditing, the Code of Ethics, and the Standards.

Periodic reviews are assessments conducted to evaluate conformance with the Definition of Internal Auditing, the Code of Ethics, and the Standards.

Sufficient knowledge of internal audit practices requires at least an understanding of all elements of the International Professional Practices Framework.

1312 – External Assessments

External assessments must be conducted at least once every five years by a qualified, independent reviewer or review team from outside the organization. The chief audit executive must discuss with the board:

- The need for more frequent external assessments; and
- The qualifications and independence of the external reviewer or review team, including any potential conflict of interest.

Interpretation:

A qualified reviewer or review team consists of individuals who are competent in the professional practice of internal auditing and the external assessment process. The evaluation of the competency of the reviewer and review team is a judgment that considers the professional internal audit experience and professional credentials of the individuals selected to perform the review. The evaluation of qualifications also considers the size and complexity of the organizations that the reviewers have been associated with in relation to the organization for which the internal audit activity is being assessed, as well as the need for particular sector, industry, or technical knowledge.

An independent reviewer or review team means not having either a real or an apparent conflict of interest and not being a part of, or under the control of, the organization to which the internal audit activity belongs.

1320 – Reporting on the Quality Assurance and Improvement Program

The chief audit executive must communicate the results of the quality assurance and improvement program to senior management and the board.

Interpretation:

The form, content, and frequency of communicating the results of the quality assurance and improvement program is established through discussions with senior management and the board and considers the responsibilities of the internal audit activity and chief audit executive as contained in the internal audit charter. To demonstrate conformance with the Definition of Internal Auditing, the Code of Ethics, and the Standards, the results of external and periodic internal assessments are communicated upon completion of such assessments and the results of ongoing monitoring are communicated at least annually. The results include the reviewer's or review team's assessment with respect to the degree of conformance.

1321 – Use of "Conforms with the *International Standards for the Professional Practice of Internal Auditing*"

The chief audit executive may state that the internal audit activity conforms with the *International Standards for the Professional Practice of Internal Auditing* only if the results of the quality assurance and improvement program support this statement.

1322 – Disclosure of Nonconformance
When nonconformance with the Definition of Internal Auditing, the Code of Ethics, or the *Standards* impacts the overall scope or operation of the internal audit activity, the chief audit executive must disclose the nonconformance and the impact to senior management and the board.

Performance Standards

2000 – Managing the Internal Audit Activity
The chief audit executive must effectively manage the internal audit activity to ensure it adds value to the organization.

Interpretation:
The internal audit activity is effectively managed when:

- *The results of the internal audit activity's work achieve the purpose and responsibility included in the internal audit charter;*
- *The internal audit activity conforms with the Definition of Internal Auditing and the Standards; and*
- *The individuals who are part of the internal audit activity demonstrate conformance with the Code of Ethics and the Standards.*

2010 – Planning
The chief audit executive must establish risk-based plans to determine the priorities of the internal audit activity, consistent with the organization's goals.

Interpretation:
The chief audit executive is responsible for developing a risk-based plan. The chief audit executive takes into account the organization's risk management framework, including using risk appetite levels set by management for the different activities or parts of the organization. If a framework does not exist, the chief audit executive uses his/her own judgment of risks after consultation with senior management and the board.

> **2010.A1 –** The internal audit activity's plan of engagements must be based on a documented risk assessment, undertaken at least annually. The input of senior management and the board must be considered in this process.
> **2010.C1 –** The chief audit executive should consider accepting proposed consulting engagements based on the engagement's potential to improve management of risks, add value, and improve the organization's operations. Accepted engagements must be included in the plan.

2020 – Communication and Approval
The chief audit executive must communicate the internal audit activity's plans and resource requirements, including significant interim changes, to senior management and the board for review and approval. The chief audit executive must also communicate the impact of resource limitations.

2030 – Resource Management
The chief audit executive must ensure that internal audit resources are appropriate, sufficient, and effectively deployed to achieve the approved plan.

Interpretation:
Appropriate refers to the mix of knowledge, skills, and other competencies needed to perform the plan. Sufficient refers to the quantity of resources needed to accomplish the plan. Resources

are effectively deployed when they are used in a way that optimizes the achievement of the approved plan.

2040 – Policies and Procedures

The chief audit executive must establish policies and procedures to guide the internal audit activity.

Interpretation:

The form and content of policies and procedures are dependent upon the size and structure of the internal audit activity and the complexity of its work.

2050 – Coordination

The chief audit executive should share information and coordinate activities with other internal and external providers of assurance and consulting services to ensure proper coverage and minimize duplication of efforts.

2060 – Reporting to Senior Management and the Board

The chief audit executive must report periodically to senior management and the board on the internal audit activity's purpose, authority, responsibility, and performance relative to its plan. Reporting must also include significant risk exposures and control issues, including fraud risks, governance issues, and other matters needed or requested by senior management and the board.

Interpretation:

The frequency and content of reporting are determined in discussion with senior management and the board and depend on the importance of the information to be communicated and the urgency of the related actions to be taken by senior management or the board.

2100 – Nature of Work

The internal audit activity must evaluate and contribute to the improvement of governance, risk management, and control processes using a systematic and disciplined approach.

2110 – Governance

The internal audit activity must assess and make appropriate recommendations for improving the governance process in its accomplishment of the following objectives:

- Promoting appropriate ethics and values within the organization;
- Ensuring effective organizational performance management and accountability;
- Communicating risk and control information to appropriate areas of the organization; and
- Coordinating the activities of and communicating information among the board, external and internal auditors, and management.

  2110.A1 – The internal audit activity must evaluate the design, implementation, and effectiveness of the organization's ethics-related objectives, programs, and activities.

  2110.A2 – The internal audit activity must assess whether the information technology governance of the organization sustains and supports the organization's strategies and objectives.

  2110.C1 – Consulting engagement objectives must be consistent with the overall values and goals of the organization.

2120 – Risk Management

The internal audit activity must evaluate the effectiveness and contribute to the improvement of risk management processes.

Interpretation:

Determining whether risk management processes are effective is a judgment resulting from the internal auditor's assessment that:

- *Organizational objectives support and align with the organization's mission;*
- *Significant risks are identified and assessed;*
- *Appropriate risk responses are selected that align risks with the organization's risk appetite; and*
- *Relevant risk information is captured and communicated in a timely manner across the organization, enabling staff, management, and the board to carry out their responsibilities.*

Risk management processes are monitored through ongoing management activities, separate evaluations, or both.

> **2120.A1 –** The internal audit activity must evaluate risk exposures relating to the organization's governance, operations, and information systems regarding the:
> - Reliability and integrity of financial and operational information.
> - Effectiveness and efficiency of operations.
> - Safeguarding of assets; and
> - Compliance with laws, regulations, and contracts.
>
> **2120.A2 –** The internal audit activity must evaluate the potential for the occurrence of fraud and how the organization manages fraud risk.
>
> **2120.C1 –** During consulting engagements, internal auditors must address risk consistent with the engagement's objectives and be alert to the existence of other significant risks.
>
> **2120.C2 –** Internal auditors must incorporate knowledge of risks gained from consulting engagements into their evaluation of the organization's risk management processes.
>
> **2120.C3 –** When assisting management in establishing or improving risk management processes, internal auditors must refrain from assuming any management responsibility by actually managing risks.

2130 – Control

The internal audit activity must assist the organization in maintaining effective controls by evaluating their effectiveness and efficiency and by promoting continuous improvement.

> **2130.A1 –** he internal audit activity must evaluate the adequacy and effectiveness of controls in responding to risks within the organization's governance, operations, and information systems regarding the:
> - Reliability and integrity of financial and operational information;
> - Effectiveness and efficiency of operations;
> - Safeguarding of assets; and
> - Compliance with laws, regulations, and contracts.
>
> **2130.A2 –** Internal auditors should ascertain the extent to which operating and program goals and objectives have been established and conform to those of the organization.
>
> **2130.A3 –** Internal auditors should review operations and programs to ascertain the extent to which results are consistent with established goals and objectives to determine whether operations and programs are being implemented or performed as intended.
>
> **2130.C1 –** During consulting engagements, internal auditors must address controls consistent with the engagement's objectives and be alert to significant control issues.

2130.C2 – Internal auditors must incorporate knowledge of controls gained from consulting engagements into evaluation of the organization's control processes.

2200 – Engagement Planning

Internal auditors must develop and document a plan for each engagement, including the engagement's objectives, scope, timing, and resource allocations.

2201 – Planning Considerations

In planning the engagement, internal auditors must consider:

- The objectives of the activity being reviewed and the means by which the activity controls its performance;
- The significant risks to the activity, its objectives, resources, and operations and the means by which the potential impact of risk is kept to an acceptable level;
- The adequacy and effectiveness of the activity's risk management and control processes compared to a relevant control framework or model; and
- The opportunities for making significant improvements to the activity's risk management and control processes.

2201.A1 – When planning an engagement for parties outside the organization, internal auditors must establish a written understanding with them about objectives, scope, respective responsibilities, and other expectations, including restrictions on distribution of the results of the engagement and access to engagement records.

2201.C1 – Internal auditors must establish an understanding with consulting engagement clients about objectives, scope, respective responsibilities, and other client expectations. For significant engagements, this understanding must be documented.

2210 – Engagement Objectives

Objectives must be established for each engagement.

2210.A1 – Internal auditors must conduct a preliminary assessment of the risks relevant to the activity under review. Engagement objectives must reflect the results of this assessment.

2210.A2 – Internal auditors must consider the probability of significant errors, fraud, noncompliance, and other exposures when developing the engagement objectives.

2210.A3 – Adequate criteria are needed to evaluate controls. Internal auditors must ascertain the extent to which management has established adequate criteria to determine whether objectives and goals have been accomplished. If adequate, internal auditors must use such criteria in their evaluation. If inadequate, internal auditors must work with management to develop appropriate evaluation criteria.

2210.C1 – Consulting engagement objectives must address governance, risk management, and control processes to the extent agreed upon with the client.

2220 – Engagement Scope

The established scope must be sufficient to satisfy the objectives of the engagement.

2220.A1 – The scope of the engagement must include consideration of relevant systems, records, personnel, and physical properties, including those under the control of third parties.

2220.A2 – If significant consulting opportunities arise during an assurance engagement, a specific written understanding as to the objectives, scope, respective responsibilities, and other expectations should be reached and the results of the consulting engagement communicated in accordance with consulting standards.

2220.C1 – In performing consulting engagements, internal auditors must ensure that the scope of the engagement is sufficient to address the agreed-upon objectives. If internal auditors develop reservations about the scope during the engagement, these reservations must be discussed with the client to determine whether to continue with the engagement.

2230 – Engagement Resource Allocation

Internal auditors must determine appropriate and sufficient resources to achieve engagement objectives based on an evaluation of the nature and complexity of each engagement, time constraints, and available resources.

2240 – Engagement Work Program

Internal auditors must develop and document work programs that achieve the engagement objectives.

2240.A1 – Work programs must include the procedures for identifying, analyzing, evaluating, and documenting information during the engagement. The work program must be approved prior to its implementation, and any adjustments approved promptly.

2240.C1 – Work programs for consulting engagements may vary in form and content depending upon the nature of the engagement.

2300 – Performing the Engagement

Internal auditors must identify, analyze, evaluate, and document sufficient information to achieve the engagement's objectives.

2310 – Identifying Information

Internal auditors must identify sufficient, reliable, relevant, and useful information to achieve the engagement's objectives.

Interpretation:

Sufficient information is factual, adequate, and convincing so that a prudent, informed person would reach the same conclusions as the auditor. Reliable information is the best attainable information through the use of appropriate engagement techniques. Relevant information supports engagement observations and recommendations and is consistent with the objectives for the engagement. Useful information helps the organization meet its goals.

2320 – Analysis and Evaluation

Internal auditors must base conclusions and engagement results on appropriate analyses and evaluations.

2330 – Documenting Information

Internal auditors must document relevant information to support the conclusions and engagement results.

2330.A1 – The chief audit executive must control access to engagement records. The chief audit executive must obtain the approval of senior management and/or legal counsel prior to releasing such records to external parties, as appropriate.

2330.A2 – The chief audit executive must develop retention requirements for engagement records, regardless of the medium in which each record is stored. These retention requirements must be consistent with the organization's guidelines and any pertinent regulatory or other requirements.

2330.C1 – The chief audit executive must develop policies governing the custody and retention of consulting engagement records, as well as their release to internal and external parties. These policies must be consistent with the organization's guidelines and any pertinent regulatory or other requirements.

2340 – Engagement Supervision

Engagements must be properly supervised to ensure objectives are achieved, quality is assured, and staff is developed.

Interpretation:

The extent of supervision required will depend on the proficiency and experience of internal auditors and the complexity of the engagement. The chief audit executive has overall responsibility for supervising the engagement, whether performed by or for the internal audit activity, but may designate appropriately experienced members of the internal audit activity to perform the review. Appropriate evidence of supervision is documented and retained.

2400 – Communicating Results

Internal auditors must communicate the engagement results.

2410 – Criteria for Communicating

Communications must include the engagement's objectives and scope as well as applicable conclusions, recommendations, and action plans.

> **2410.A1** – Final communication of engagement results must, where appropriate, contain internal auditors' overall opinion and/or conclusions.
>
> **2410.A2** – Internal auditors are encouraged to acknowledge satisfactory performance in engagement communications.
>
> **2410.A3** – When releasing engagement results to parties outside the organization, the communication must include limitations on distribution and use of the results.
>
> **2410.C1** – Communication of the progress and results of consulting engagements will vary in form and content depending upon the nature of the engagement and the needs of the client.

2420 – Quality of Communications

Communications must be accurate, objective, clear, concise, constructive, complete, and timely.

Interpretation:

Accurate communications are free from errors and distortions and are faithful to the underlying facts. Objective communications are fair, impartial, and unbiased and are the result of a fair-minded and balanced assessment of all relevant facts and circumstances. Clear communications are easily understood and logical, avoiding unnecessary technical language and providing all significant and relevant information. Concise communications are to the point and avoid unnecessary elaboration, superfluous detail, redundancy, and wordiness. Constructive communications are helpful to the engagement client and the organization and lead to improvements where needed. Complete communications lack nothing that is essential to the target audience and include all significant and relevant information and observations to support recommendations and conclusions. Timely communications are opportune and expedient, depending on the significance of the issue, allowing management to take appropriate corrective action.

2421 – Errors and Omissions

If a final communication contains a significant error or omission, the chief audit executive must communicate corrected information to all parties who received the original communication.

2430 – Use of "Conducted in Conformance with the *International Standards for the Professional Practice of Internal Auditing*"

Internal auditors may report that their engagements are "conducted in conformance with the *International Standards for the Professional Practice of Internal Auditing*," only if the results of the quality assurance and improvement program support the statement.

2431 – Engagement Disclosure of Nonconformance

When nonconformance with the Definition of Internal Auditing, the Code of Ethics or the *Standards* impacts a specific engagement, communication of the results must disclose the:

- Principle or rule of conduct of the Code of Ethics or *Standard(s)* with which full conformance was not achieved;
- Reason(s) for nonconformance; and
- Impact of nonconformance on the engagement and the communicated engagement results.

2440 – Disseminating Results

The chief audit executive must communicate results to the appropriate parties.

Interpretation:

The chief audit executive or designee reviews and approves the final engagement communication before issuance and decides to whom and how it will be disseminated.

2440.A1 – The chief audit executive is responsible for communicating the final results to parties who can ensure that the results are given due consideration.

2440.A2 – If not otherwise mandated by legal, statutory, or regulatory requirements, prior to releasing results to parties outside the organization the chief audit executive must:

- Assess the potential risk to the organization;
- Consult with senior management and/or legal counsel as appropriate; and
- Control dissemination by restricting the use of the results.

2440.C1 – The chief audit executive is responsible for communicating the final results of consulting engagements to clients.

2440.C2 – During consulting engagements, governance, risk management, and control issues may be identified. Whenever these issues are significant to the organization, they must be communicated to senior management and the board.

2500 – Monitoring Progress

The chief audit executive must establish and maintain a system to monitor the disposition of results communicated to management.

2500.A1 – The chief audit executive must establish a follow-up process to monitor and ensure that management actions have been effectively implemented or that senior management has accepted the risk of not taking action.

2500.C1 – The internal audit activity must monitor the disposition of results of consulting engagements to the extent agreed upon with the client.

2600 – Resolution of Senior Management's Acceptance of Risks

When the chief audit executive believes that senior management has accepted a level of residual risk that may be unacceptable to the organization, the chief audit executive must discuss the matter with senior management. If the decision regarding residual risk is not resolved, the chief audit executive must report the matter to the board for resolution.

APPENDIX C: YELLOW BOOK ETHICAL PRINCIPLES

Principle	Explanation
The public interest	2.06 The public interest is defined as the collective well-being of the community of people and entities the auditors serve. Observing integrity, objectivity, and independence in discharging their professional responsibilities assists auditors in meeting the principle of serving the public interest and honoring the public trust. These principles are fundamental to the responsibilities of auditors and critical in the government environment. 2.07 A distinguishing mark of an auditor is acceptance of responsibility to serve the public interest. This responsibility is critical when auditing in the government environment. GAGAS embody the concept of accountability for public resources, which is fundamental to serving the public interest.
Integrity	2.08 Public confidence in government is maintained and strengthened by auditors performing their professional responsibilities with integrity. Integrity includes auditors' conducting their work with an attitude that is objective, fact-based, nonpartisan, and nonideological with regard to audited entities and users of the auditors' reports. Within the constraints of applicable confidentiality laws, rules, or policies, communications with the audited entity, those charged with governance, and the individuals contracting for or requesting the audit are expected to be honest, candid, and constructive. 2.09 Making decisions consistent with the public interest of the program or activity under audit is an important part of the principle of integrity. In discharging their professional responsibilities, auditors may encounter conflicting pressures from management of the audited entity, various levels of government, and other likely users. Auditors may also encounter pressures to violate ethical principles to inappropriately achieve personal or organizational gain. In resolving those conflicts and pressures, acting with integrity means that auditors place priority on their responsibilities to the public interest.
Objectivity	2.10 The credibility of auditing in the government sector is based on auditors' objectivity in discharging their professional responsibilities. Objectivity includes being independent in fact and appearance when providing audit and attestation engagements, maintaining an attitude of impartiality, having intellectual honesty, and being free of conflicts of interest. Avoiding conflicts that may, in fact or appearance, impair auditors' objectivity in performing the audit or attestation engagement is essential to retaining credibility. Maintaining objectivity includes a continuing assessment of relationships with audited entities and other stakeholders in the context of the auditors' responsibility to the public.

Proper use of governmental information, resources, and position	2.11 Government information, resources, or positions are to be used for official purposes and not inappropriately for the auditor's personal gain or in a manner contrary to law or detrimental to the legitimate interests of the audited entity or the audit organization. This concept includes the proper handling of sensitive or classified information or resources.

2.12 In the government environment, the public's right to the transparency of government information has to be balanced with the proper use of that information. In addition, many government programs are subject to laws and regulations dealing with the disclosure of information. To accomplish this balance, exercising discretion in the use of information acquired in the course of auditors' duties is an important part in achieving this goal. Improperly disclosing any such information to third parties is not an acceptable practice.

2.13 As accountability professionals, accountability to the public for the proper use and prudent management of government resources is an essential part of auditors' responsibilities. Protecting and conserving government resources and using them appropriately for authorized activities is an important element in the public's expectations for auditors.

2.14 Misusing the position of an auditor for personal gain violates an auditor's fundamental responsibilities. An auditor's credibility can be damaged by actions that could be perceived by an objective third party with knowledge of the relevant information as improperly benefiting an auditor's personal financial interests or those of an immediate or close family member; a general partner; an organization for which the auditor serves as an officer, director, trustee, or employee; or an organization with which the auditor is negotiating concerning future employment. |
| Professional behavior | 2.15 High expectations for the auditing profession include compliance with laws and regulations and avoidance of any conduct that might bring discredit to auditors' work, including actions that would cause an objective third party with knowledge of the relevant information to conclude that the auditors' work was professionally deficient. Professional behavior includes auditors putting forth an honest effort in performance of their duties and professional services in accordance with the relevant technical and professional standards. |

Source: *Government Auditing Standards*. 2007. General Accountability Office.

APPENDIX D: ILLUSTRATIVE INQUIRIES FOR A SSARS REVIEW ENGAGEMENT

1. **General**

   a. Have there been any changes in the entity's business activities?

   b. Are there any unusual or complex situations that may have an effect on the financial statements (for example, business combinations, restructuring plans, or litigation)?

   c. What procedures are in place related to recording, classifying, and summarizing transactions and accumulating information related to financial statement disclosures?

   d. Have the financial statements been prepared in conformity with generally accepted accounting principles or, if appropriate, a comprehensive basis of accounting other than generally accepted accounting principles? Have there been any changes in accounting principles and methods of applying those principles? Have voluntary changes in accounting principles been reflected in the financial statements through retrospective application of the new principle in comparative financial statements?

   e. Have there been any instances of fraud or illegal acts within the entity?

   f. Have there been any allegations or suspicions that fraud or illegal acts might have occurred or might be occurring within the entity? If so, where and how?

   g. Are any entities, other than the reporting entity, commonly controlled by the owners? If so, has an evaluation been performed to determine whether those other entities should be consolidated into the financial statements of the reporting entity?

   h. Are there any entities other than the reporting entity in which the owners have significant investments (for example, variable interest entities)? If so, has an evaluation been performed to determine whether the reporting entity is the primary beneficiary related to the activities of these other entities?

   i. Is the reporting entity a general partner in a limited partnership arrangement? If so, has an evaluation been performed to determine whether the limited partnership should be consolidated into the financial statements of the reporting entity?

   j. Is the reporting entity a controlling partner in a general partnership arrangement? If so, has an evaluation been performed to determine whether the partnership should be consolidated into the financial statements of the controlling partner?

   k. Have any significant transactions occurred or been recognized near the end of the reporting period?

2. **Cash and Cash Equivalents**

   a. Is the entity's policy regarding the composition of cash and cash equivalents in accordance with Financial Accounting Standards Board (FASB) Statement of Financial Accounting Standards No. 95, Statement of Cash Flows (paragraphs 7–10)? Has the policy been applied on a consistent basis?

   b. Are all cash and cash equivalent accounts reconciled on a timely basis?

   c. Have old or unusual reconciling items between bank balances and book balances been reviewed and adjustments made where necessary?

   d. Has there been a proper cutoff of cash receipts and disbursements?

   e. Has a reconciliation of intercompany transfers been prepared?

   f. Have checks written but not mailed as of the financial statement date been properly reclassified into the liability section of the balance sheet?

   g. Have material bank overdrafts been properly reclassified into the liability section of the balance sheet?

   h. Are there compensating balances or other restrictions on the availability of cash and cash equivalents balances? If so, has consideration been given to reclassifying these amounts as noncurrent assets?

   i. Have cash funds been counted and reconciled with control accounts?

3. Receivables

a. Has an adequate allowance for doubtful accounts been properly reflected in the financial statements?

b. Have uncollectible receivables been written off through a charge against the allowance account or earnings?

c. Has interest earned on receivables been properly reflected in the financial statements?

d. Has there been a proper cutoff of sales transactions?

e. Are there receivables from employees or other related parties? Have receivables from owners been evaluated to determine if they should be reflected in the equity section (rather than the asset section) of the balance sheet?

f. Are any receivables pledged, discounted, or factored? Are recourse provisions properly reflected in the financial statements?

g. Have receivables been properly classified between current and noncurrent?

h. Have there been significant numbers of sales returns or credit memoranda issued subsequent to the balance sheet date?

i. Is the accounts receivable subsidiary ledger reconciled to the general ledger account balance on a regular basis?

4. Inventory

a. Are physical inventory counts performed on a regular basis, including at the end of the reporting period? Are the count procedures adequate to ensure an appropriate count? If not, how have amounts related to inventories been determined for purposes of financial statement presentation? If so, what procedures were used to take the latest physical inventory, and what date was that inventory taken?

b. Have general ledger control accounts been adjusted to agree with the physical inventory count? If so, were the adjustments significant?

c. If the physical inventory counts were taken at a date other than the balance sheet date, what procedures were used to determine changes in inventory between the date of the physical inventory counts and the balance sheet date?

d. Were consignments in or out considered in taking physical inventories?

e. What is the basis of valuing inventory for purposes of financial statement presentation?

f. Does inventory cost include material, labor, and overhead where applicable?

g. Has inventory been reviewed for obsolescence or cost in excess of net realizable value? If so, how are these costs reflected in the financial statements?

h. Have proper cutoffs of purchases, goods in transit, and returned goods been made?

i. Are there any inventory encumbrances?

j. Is scrap inventoried and controlled?

k. Have abnormal costs related to inventory been expensed as incurred?

5. Prepaid Expenses

a. What is the nature of the amounts included in prepaid expenses?

b. How are these amounts being amortized?

6. Investments

a. What is the basis of accounting for investments reported in the financial statements (for example, securities, joint ventures, or closelyheld businesses)?

b. Are derivative instruments properly measured and disclosed in the financial statements? If those derivatives are utilized in hedge transactions, have the documentation or assessment requirements related to hedge accounting been met?

c. Are investments in marketable debt and equity securities properly classified as trading, available-for-sale, and held-to-maturity?

d. How were fair values of the reported investments determined? Have unrealized gains and losses been properly reported in the financial statements?

e. If the fair values of marketable debt and equity securities are less than cost, have the declines in value been evaluated to determine whether the declines are other-than-temporary?

f. For any debt securities classified as held-to-maturity, does management have the positive ability and intent to hold the securities until they mature? If so, have those debt securities been properly measured?

g. Have gains and losses related to disposal of investments been properly reflected in the financial statements?

h. How was investment income determined? Is investment income properly reflected in the financial statements?

i. Has appropriate consideration been given to the classification of investments between current and noncurrent?

j. For investments made by the reporting entity, have consolidation, equity, or cost method accounting requirements been considered?

k. Are any investments encumbered?

7. Property and Equipment

a. Are property and equipment items properly stated at depreciated cost or other proper value?

b. When was the last time a physical inventory of property and equipment was taken?

c. Are all items reflected in property and equipment held for use? If not, have items that are held for sale been properly reclassified from property and equipment?

d. Have gains or losses on disposal of property and equipment been properly reflected in the financial statements?

e. What are the criteria for capitalization of property and equipment? Have the criteria been consistently and appropriately applied?

f. Are repairs and maintenance costs properly reflected as an expense in the income statement?

g. What depreciation methods and rates are utilized in the financial statements? Are these methods and rates appropriate and applied on a consistent basis?

h. Are there any unrecorded additions, retirements, abandonments, sales, or trade-ins?

i. Does the entity have any material lease agreements? If so, have those agreements been properly evaluated for financial statement presentation purposes?

j. Are there any asset retirement obligations associated with tangible long-lived assets? If so, has the recorded amount of the related asset been increased because of the obligation and is the liability properly reflected in the liability section of the balance sheet?

k. Has the entity constructed any of its property and equipment items? If so, have all components of cost been reflected in measuring these items for purposes of financial statement presentation, including, but not limited to, capitalized interest?

l. Has there been any significant impairment in value of property and equipment items? If so, has any impairment loss been properly reflected in the financial statements?

m. Are any property and equipment items mortgaged or otherwise encumbered? If so, are these mortgages and encumbrances properly reflected in the financial statements?

8. Intangibles and Other Assets

a. What is the nature of the amounts included in other assets?

b. Do these assets represent costs that will benefit future periods? What is the amortization policy related to these assets? Is this policy appropriate?

c. Have other assets been properly classified between current and noncurrent?

d. Are intangible assets with finite lives being appropriately amortized?

e. Are the costs associated with computer software properly reflected as intangible assets (rather than property and equipment) in the financial statements?

f. Are the costs associated with goodwill (and other intangible assets with indefinite lives) properly reflected as intangible assets in the financial statements? Has amortization ceased related to these assets?

g. Has there been any significant impairment in value of these assets? If so, has any impairment loss been properly reflected in the financial statements?

h. Are any of these assets mortgaged or otherwise encumbered?

9. Accounts and Short-Term Notes Payable and Accrued Liabilities

a. Have significant payables been reflected in the financial statements?

b. Are loans from financial institutions and other short-term liabilities properly classified in the financial statements?

c. Have there been any changes in major contracts with suppliers that may impact classification or valuation of payables?

d. Have significant accruals (for example, payroll, interest, provisions for pension and profit-sharing plans, or other postretirement benefit obligations) been properly reflected in the financial statements?

e. Has a liability for employees' compensation for future absences been properly accrued and disclosed in the financial statements?

f. Are any liabilities collateralized or subordinated? If so, are those liabilities disclosed in the financial statements?

g. Are there any payables to employees and related parties?

10. Long-Term Liabilities

a. Are the terms and other provisions of long-term liability agreements properly disclosed in the financial statements?

b. Have liabilities been properly classified between current and noncurrent?

c. Has interest expense been properly accrued and reflected in the financial statements?

d. Is the company in compliance with loan covenants and agreements? If not, is the noncompliance properly disclosed in the financial statements?

e. Are any long-term liabilities collateralized or subordinated? If so, are these facts disclosed in the financial statements?

f. Are there any obligations that, by their terms, are due on demand within one year from the balance sheet date? If so, have these obligations been properly reclassified into the current liability section of the balance sheet?

11. Income and Other Taxes

a. Do the financial statements reflect an appropriate provision for current and prior-year income taxes payable?

b. Have any assessments or reassessments been received? Are there tax authority examinations in process?

c. Are there any temporary differences between book and tax amounts? If so, have deferred taxes on these differences been properly reflected in the financial statements?

d. Do the financial statements reflect an appropriate provision for taxes other than income taxes (for example, franchise, sales)?

e. Have all required tax payments been made on a timely basis?

f. Has the entity assessed uncertain tax positions and related disclosures in accordance with FASB Interpretation No. 48, Accounting for Uncertainty in Income Taxes?

12. Other Liabilities, Contingencies, and Commitments

a. What is the nature of the amounts included in other liabilities?

b. Have other liabilities been properly classified between current and noncurrent?

c. Are there any guarantees, whether written or verbal, whereby the entity must stand ready to perform or is contingently liable related to the guarantee? If so, are these guarantees properly reflected in the financial statements?

d. Are there any contingent liabilities (for example, discounted notes, drafts, endorsements, warranties, litigation, and unsettled asserted claims)? Are there any potential unasserted claims? Are these contingent liabilities, claims, and assessments properly measured and disclosed in the financial statements?

e. Are there any material contractual obligations for construction or purchase of property and equipment or any commitments or options to purchase or sell company securities? If so, are these facts clearly disclosed in the financial statements?

f. Is the entity responsible for any environmental remediation liability? If so, is this liability properly measured and disclosed in the financial statements?

g. Does the entity have any agreement to repurchase items that previously were sold? If so, have the repurchase agreements been taken into account in determining the appropriate measurements and disclosures in the financial statements?

h. Does the entity have any sales commitments at prices expected to result in a loss at the consummation of the sale? If so, are these commitments properly reflected in the financial statements?

i. Are there any violations, or possible violations, of laws or regulations the effects of which should be considered for financial statement accrual or disclosure?

13. Equity

a. What is the nature of any changes in equity accounts during each reporting period?

b. What classes of stock (other ownership interests) have been authorized?

c. What is the par or stated value of the various classes of stock (other ownership interests)?

d. Do amounts of outstanding shares of stock (other ownership interests) agree with subsidiary records?

e. Have pertinent rights and privileges of ownership interests been properly disclosed in the financial statements?

f. Does the entity have any mandatorily redeemable ownership interests? If so, have these ownership interests been evaluated so that a proper determination has been made related to whether these ownership interests should be measured and reclassified to the liability section of the balance sheet? Are redemption features associated with ownership interests clearly disclosed in the financial statements?

g. Have dividend (distribution) and liquidation preferences related to ownership interests been properly disclosed in the financial statements?

h. Do disclosures related to ownership interests include any applicable call provisions (prices and dates), conversion provisions (prices and rates), unusual voting rights, significant terms of contracts to issue additional ownership interests, or any other unusual features associated with the ownership interests?

i. Are syndication fees properly reflected in the financial statements as a reduction of equity (rather than an asset)?

j. Have any stock options or other stock compensation awards been granted to employees or others? If so, are these options or awards properly measured and disclosed in the financial statements?

k. Has the entity made any acquisitions of its own stock? If so, are the amounts associated with these reacquired shares properly reflected in the financial statements as a reduction in equity? Is the presentation in accordance with applicable state laws?

l. Are there any restrictions or appropriations on retained earnings or other capital accounts? If so, are these restrictions or appropriations properly reflected in the financial statements?

14. **Revenue and Expenses**

a. What is the entity's revenue recognition policy? Is the policy appropriate? Has the policy been consistently applied and appropriately disclosed?

b. Are revenues from sales of products and rendering of services recognized in the appropriate reporting period (that is, when the products have been delivered and when the services have been performed)?

c. Were any sales recorded under a "bill-and-hold" arrangement? If yes, have the criteria been met to record the transaction as a sale?

d. Are purchases and expenses recognized in the appropriate reporting period (that is, matched against revenue) and properly classified in the financial statements?

e. Do the financial statements include discontinued operations, items that might be considered extraordinary, or both? If so, are amounts associated with discontinued operations, extraordinary items, or both properly displayed in the income statement?

f. Does the entity have any gains or losses that would necessitate the display of comprehensive income (for example, gains/losses on available-for-sale securities or cash flow hedge derivatives)? If so, have these items been properly displayed within comprehensive income (rather than included in the determination of net income)?

15. **Other**

a. Have events occurred subsequent to the balance sheet date that would require adjustment to, or disclosure in, the financial statements?

b. Has the entity considered whether declines in market values subsequent to the balance sheet date may be permanent and/or caused the entity to no longer be in compliance with its loan covenants?

c. Have actions taken at stockholders, directors, committees of directors, or comparable meetings that affect the financial statements been reflected in the financial statements?

d. Are significant estimates and material concentrations (for example, customers or suppliers) properly disclosed in the financial statements?

e. Are there plans or intentions that may materially affect the carrying amounts or classification of assets and liabilities reflected in the financial statements?

f. Have there been any material transactions between or among related parties (for example, sales, purchases, loans, or leasing arrangements)? If so, are these transactions properly disclosed in the financial statements?

g. Are there uncertainties that could have a material impact on the financial statements? Is there any change in the status of previously disclosed material uncertainties? Are all uncertainties, including going-concern matters, that could have a material impact on the financial statements properly disclosed in the financial statements?

h. Are barter or other nonmonetary transactions properly recorded and disclosed? Have nonmonetary asset exchanges involving commercial substance been reflected in the financial statements at fair value? Have nonmonetary asset exchanges not involving commercial substance been reflected in the financial statements at carrying value?

(*Source*: AR 100.98.)

Index

Text Credits

Chapter 1

Auditing in Action, p. 6, from AICPA, *Reports on Audited Financial Statements*, AU 508.08, p. 814. Copyright 2009 by the American Institute of Certified Public Accountants, Inc. All rights reserved. Adapted with permission.

Auditing in Action, p. 33, "Top Fives" Definitions of the CPA Vision Project. http://www.cpavision.org/final_report/page08.htm. Copyright 2009 by the American Institute of Certified Public Accountants, Inc. All rights reserved. Adapted with permission.

Chapter 2

Exhibit 2-2, p. 44, from AICPA, *Evidential Matter*, AU 326.15, pp. 448–449. Copyright 2009 by the American Institute of Certified Public Accountants, Inc. All rights reserved. Adapted with permission.

Auditing in Action, p. 61, from AICPA, *Reports on Audited Financial Statements*, AU 508.08, p. 814. Copyright 2009 by the American Institute of Certified Public Accountants, Inc. All rights reserved. Adapted with permission.

Appendix A, pp. 74–75, from AICPA, *Generally Accepted Auditing Standards*, AU 150.02, pp. 81–82. Copyright 2009 by the American Institute of Certified Public Accountants, Inc. All rights reserved. Adapted with permission.

Chapter 3

Exhibit 3-3, pp. 95–98, from AICPA, *Code of Professional Conduct*, Section 92. http://www.aicpa.org/about/code/et_92.html. Copyright 2009 by the American Institute of Certified Public Accountants, Inc. All rights reserved. Adapted with permission.

Exhibit 3-5, pp. 100–102, from AICPA, *Code of Professional Conduct*, Sections 100 through 500. Copyright 2009 by the American Institute of Certified Public Accountants, Inc. All rights reserved. Adapted with permission.

Exhibit 3-7, pp. 109–111, from http://www.aicpa.org/about/code/et_101.html#et_101_interpretations. Copyright 2009 by the American Institute of Certified Public Accountants, Inc. All rights reserved. Adapted with permission.

Chapter 5

Text, pp 197–198, from PCAOB, AICPA, *Appointment of the Independent Auditor*, AU 310.06, 310.07. Copyright 2009 by the American Institute of Certified Public Accountants, Inc. All rights reserved. Adapted with permission.

Chapter 6

Auditing in Action, pp. 245–246, from PCAOB, AICPA, *Consideration of Fraud in a Financial Statement Audit*, AU 316.85, Appendix A.2. Copyright 2009 by the American Institute of Certified Public Accountants, Inc. All rights reserved. Adapted with permission.

Auditing in Action, p. 247, from AICPA, *Consideration of Fraud in a Financial Statement Audit*, AU 316.85, Appendix A.3. Copyright 2009 by the American Institute of Certified Public Accountants, Inc. All rights reserved. Adapted with permission.

Chapter 7

Excerpts, pp. 288, 289, and 291, from COSO, *Internal Control Framework*. Copyright 1992 by the Committee of Sponsoring Organizations of the Treadway Commission (COSO). All rights reserved. Used with permission.

Auditing in Action, p. 292, from COSO, *Internal Control Framework*, Chapter 3, p. 6. Copyright 1992 by the Committee of Sponsoring Organizations of the Treadway Commission (COSO). All rights reserved. Used with permission.

Auditing in Action, p. 295, from COSO, *Internal Control Framework*, Chapter 5, p. 3. Copyright 1992 by the Committee of Sponsoring Organizations of the Treadway Commission (COSO). All rights reserved. Used with permission.

Auditing in Action, p. 296, adapted from COSO, *Internal Control Framework*, Chapter 6, p. 7. Copyright 1992 by the Committee of Sponsoring Organizations of the Treadway Commission (COSO). All rights reserved. Used with permission.

List of monitoring procedures, p. 297, from COSO, *Internal Control—Integrated Framework: Guidance on Monitoring Internal Control Systems*, January 2009, p. 3. Copyright 2009 by the Committee of Sponsoring Organizations of the Treadway Commission (COSO). All rights reserved. Used with permission.

Exhibit 7-6, p. 313, adapted from Donald H. Taylor and G. William Glezen, *Auditing: An Assertions Approach*, 7th ed. (New York: Wiley, 1997), Figure 9.4, p. 254. Reprinted with permission of John Wiley & Sons, Inc.

Exhibit 7-7, p. 319, from PCAOB, *Consideration of Internal Control in a Financial Statement Audit*, AU 319; and AICPA, *Understanding the Entity and Its Environment and Assessing the Risks of Material Misstatement*, AU 314.59–60. Copyright 2009 by the American Institute of Certified Public Accountants, Inc. All rights reserved. Adapted with permission.

List of likely sources of misstatement, pp. 322–323, from PCAOB, *Consideration of Internal Control in a Financial*

Statement Audit, AU 319.17; and AICPA, *Understanding the Entity and Its Environment and Assessing the Risks of Material Misstatement*, AU 314.58. Copyright 2009 by the American Institute of Certified Public Accountants, Inc. All rights reserved. Adapted with permission.

Bulleted list, p. 324, from PCAOB, *Consideration of Internal Control in a Financial Statement Audit*, AU 319.31; and AICPA, *Planning and Supervision*, AU 311.23. Copyright 2009 by the American Institute of Certified Public Accountants, Inc. All rights reserved. Adapted with permission.

Exhibit B7-1, pp. 350–351, from COSO *Enterprise Risk Management—Integrated Framework*, September 2004, p. 22. Copyright 2004 by the Committee of Sponsoring Organizations of the Treadway Commission (COSO). All rights reserved. Used with permission.

Chapter 8

Auditing in Action, p. 380 (top), from PCAOB, AICPA, *Considerations of Fraud in a Financial Statement Audit*, AU 316.68. Copyright 2009 by the American Institute of Certified Public Accountants, Inc. All rights reserved. Adapted with permission.

Auditing in Action, p. 380 (bottom), from PCAOB, AICPA, *Illegal Acts by Clients*, AU 317.09. Copyright 2009 by the American Institute of Certified Public Accountants, Inc. All rights reserved. Adapted with permission.

List of related parties, p. 381: Portions of various FASB documents, copyright © by the Financial Accounting Foundation (FAF), 401 Merritt 7, PO Box 5116, Norwalk, CT 06856-5116, USA, are reproduced with permission. Complete copies of the documents are available from the FAF.

Bulleted lists, pp. 400, 401, from PCAOB, AICPA, *Service Organizations*, AU 324.03. Copyright 2009 by the American Institute of Certified Public Accountants, Inc. All rights reserved. Adapted with permission.

Exhibit B8-1, p. 424, from AICPA, *Audit Sampling: AICPA Audit Guide* (AICPA, January 2008), Table A.1, p. 112. Copyright 2008 by the American Institute of Certified Public Accountants, Inc. All rights reserved. Adapted with permission.

Exhibit B8-2, p. 425, from AICPA, *Audit Sampling: AICPA Audit Guide* (AICPA, January 2008), Table A.3, p. 114. Copyright 2008 by the American Institute of Certified Public Accountants, Inc. All rights reserved. Adapted with permission.

Chapter 9

Exhibit 9-6, p. 455, adapted from Donald H. Taylor and G. William Glezen, *Auditing: An Assertions Approach*, 7th ed. (New York: Wiley, 1997), p. 473. Reprinted with permission of John Wiley & Sons, Inc.

Auditing in Action, p. 456, adapted from Donald H. Taylor and G. William Glezen, *Auditing: An Assertions Approach*, 7th ed. (New York: Wiley, 1997), pp. 474, 476. Reprinted with permission of John Wiley & Sons, Inc.

Exhibit 9-7, p. 457, adapted from Donald H. Taylor and G. William Glezen, *Auditing: An Assertions Approach*, 7th ed. (New York: Wiley, 1997), p. 482. Reprinted with permission of John Wiley & Sons, Inc.

Auditing in Action, p. 457, adapted from Donald H. Taylor and G. William Glezen, *Auditing: An Assertions Approach*, 7th ed. (New York: Wiley, 1997), p. 483. Reprinted with permission of John Wiley & Sons, Inc.

Exhibit 9-8, p. 458, adapted from Donald H. Taylor and G. William Glezen, *Auditing: An Assertions Approach*, 7th ed. (New York: Wiley, 1997), p. 510. Reprinted with permission of John Wiley & Sons, Inc.

Auditing in Action, p. 459 (top), adapted from Donald H. Taylor and G. William Glezen, *Auditing: An Assertions Approach*, 7th ed. (New York: Wiley, 1997), p. 511. Reprinted with permission of John Wiley & Sons, Inc.

Exhibit 9-9, p. 459, adapted from Donald H. Taylor and G. William Glezen, *Auditing: An Assertions Approach*, 7th ed. (New York: Wiley, 1997), pp. 554–555. Reprinted with permission of John Wiley & Sons, Inc.

Auditing in Action, p. 459 (bottom), adapted from Donald H. Taylor and G. William Glezen, *Auditing: An Assertions Approach*, 7th ed. (New York: Wiley, 1997), p. 556. Reprinted with permission of John Wiley & Sons, Inc.

Exhibit 9-10, p. 461, adapted from Donald H. Taylor and G. William Glezen, *Auditing: An Assertions Approach*, 7th ed. (New York: Wiley, 1997), p. 524. Reprinted with permission of John Wiley & Sons, Inc.

Exhibit 9-11, p. 462, adapted from Donald H. Taylor and G. William Glezen, *Auditing: An Assertions Approach*, 7th ed. (New York: Wiley, 1997), pp. 559–560. Reprinted with permission of John Wiley & Sons, Inc.

Auditing in Action, p. 462, adapted from Donald H. Taylor and G. William Glezen, *Auditing: An Assertions Approach*, 7th ed. (New York: Wiley, 1997), p. 560. Reprinted with permission of John Wiley & Sons, Inc.

Auditing in Action, p. 464, from PCAOB, AICPA, *Analytical Procedures*, AU 329.22 (Documentation of Substantive Analytical Procedures). Copyright 2009 by the American Institute of Certified Public Accountants, Inc. All rights reserved. Adapted with permission.

Text section, pp. 481–482, adapted from Donald H. Taylor and G. William Glezen, *Auditing: An Assertions Approach*, 7th ed. (New York: Wiley, 1997), pp. 441–449. Reprinted with permission of John Wiley & Sons, Inc.

Exhibit A9-4, p. 484, from AICPA, *Audit Sampling: AICPA Audit Guide* (AICPA, January 2008), Table C.3, p. 126, and Table C.4, p. 127. Copyright 2008 by the American Institute of Certified Public Accountants, Inc. All rights reserved. Adapted with permission.

Text section, pp. 486–489, adapted from Donald H. Taylor and G. William Glezen, *Auditing: An Assertions Approach*, 7th ed. (New York: Wiley, 1997), pp. 453–459. Reprinted with permission of John Wiley & Sons, Inc.

Chapter 10

Auditing in Action, p. 500, from PCAOB, AICPA, *Consideration of Fraud in a Financial Statement Audit*, AU 316.54. Copyright 2009 by the American Institute of Certified Public Accountants, Inc. All rights reserved. Adapted with permission.

Quotation, p. 527, from PCAOB, AICPA, *Audit Sampling*, AU 350.44. Copyright 2009 by the American Institute of Certified

Public Accountants, Inc. All rights reserved. Adapted with permission.
Quotation, p. 530, from PCAOB, AICPA, *Analytical Procedures*, AU 329.02. Copyright 2009 by the American Institute of Certified Public Accountants, Inc. All rights reserved. Adapted with permission.
Quotations, p. 532, from AICPA, *Performing Audit Procedures in Response to Assessed Risks and Evaluating the Audit Evidence Obtained*, AU 318.57 and AU 318.14. Copyright 2009 by the American Institute of Certified Public Accountants, Inc. All rights reserved. Adapted with permission.

Chapter 11
Exhibit 11-2, p. 565, from PCAOB, AICPA, *Inquiry of a Client's Lawyer Concerning Litigation, Claims and Assessments*, AU 337.05–06. Copyright 2009 by the American Institute of Certified Public Accountants, Inc. All rights reserved. Adapted with permission.
Exhibit 11-3, p. 565, from PCAOB, AICPA, *Inquiry of a Client's Lawyer Concerning Litigation, Claims and Assessments*, AU 337.09. Copyright 2009 by the American Institute of Certified Public Accountants, Inc. All rights reserved. Adapted with permission.
Auditing in Action, p. 566, from PCAOB, AICPA, *Inquiry of a Client's Lawyer Concerning Litigation, Claims and Assessments*, AU 337A. Copyright 2009 by the American Institute of Certified Public Accountants, Inc. All rights reserved. Adapted with permission.
Exhibit 11-5, pp. 570–571, from PCAOB, AICPA, *Management Representations*, AU 333.06. Copyright 2009 by the American Institute of Certified Public Accountants, Inc. All rights reserved. Adapted with permission.
Exhibit 11-8, p. 574, from PCAOB, AICPA, *Subsequent Events*, AU 560.12. Copyright 2009 by the American Institute of Certified Public Accountants, Inc. All rights reserved. Adapted with permission.
Auditing in Action, p. 585, from PCAOB, AICPA, *Analytical Procedures*, AU 329.23. Copyright 2009 by the American Institute of Certified Public Accountants, Inc. All rights reserved. Adapted with permission.
Auditing in Action, p. 585, from PCAOB, AICPA, *Interim Financial Information*, AU 722.54. Copyright 2009 by the American Institute of Certified Public Accountants, Inc. All rights reserved. Adapted with permission.
Auditing in Action, p. 591, from PCAOB, AICPA, *Subsequent Discovery of Facts Existing at the Date of the Auditor's Report*, AU 561.06. Copyright 2009 by the American Institute of Certified Public Accountants, Inc. All rights reserved. Adapted with permission.
Auditing in Action, pp. 593–594, from PCAOB, AICPA, *Dating of the Independent Auditor's Report*, AU 530.06–.08; PCAOB, AICPA, *Reports on Audited Financial Statements*, AU 508.70–73. Copyright 2009 by the American Institute of Certified Public Accountants, Inc. All rights reserved. Adapted with permission.
Auditing in Action, p. 598, from PCAOB, AICPA, *Reports on Audited Financial Statements*, AU 508.13. Copyright 2009 by the American Institute of Certified Public Accountants, Inc. All rights reserved. Adapted with permission.

Auditing in Action, p. 599, from PCAOB, AICPA, *The Auditor's Consideration of an Entity's Ability to Continue as a Going Concern*, AU 341.13. Copyright 2009 by the American Institute of Certified Public Accountants, Inc. All rights reserved. Adapted with permission.
Auditing in Action, p. 605, from PCAOB, AICPA, *Reports on Audited Financial Statements*, AU 508.39. Copyright 2009 by the American Institute of Certified Public Accountants, Inc. All rights reserved. Adapted with permission.
Auditing in Action, p. 606, from PCAOB, AICPA, *Reports on Audited Financial Statements*, AU 508.26. Copyright 2009 by the American Institute of Certified Public Accountants, Inc. All rights reserved. Adapted with permission.
Auditing in Action, p. 607, from PCAOB, AICPA, *Reports on Audited Financial Statements*, AU 508.60. Copyright 2009 by the American Institute of Certified Public Accountants, Inc. All rights reserved. Adapted with permission.

Chapter 13
Auditing in Action, p. 715, from AICPA, *Service Organizations*, AU 324.14. Copyright 2009 by the American Institute of Certified Public Accountants, Inc. All rights reserved. Adapted with permission.
Auditing in Action, p. 742, from PCAOB, AICPA, *Service Organizations*, AU 324.02. Copyright 2009 by the American Institute of Certified Public Accountants, Inc. All rights reserved. Adapted with permission.
Auditing in Action, p. 743, from PCAOB, AICPA, *Service Organizations*, AU 324.24. Copyright 2009 by the American Institute of Certified Public Accountants, Inc. All rights reserved. Adapted with permission.
Auditing in Action, p. 744, from PCAOB, AICPA, *Service Organizations*, AU 324.26. Copyright 2009 by the American Institute of Certified Public Accountants, Inc. All rights reserved. Adapted with permission.
Auditing in Action, p. 747, from PCAOB, AICPA, *Service Organizations*, AU 324.38. Copyright 2009 by the American Institute of Certified Public Accountants, Inc. All rights reserved. Adapted with permission.
Auditing in Action, p. 748, from PCAOB, AICPA, *Service Organizations*, AU 324.39, 324.40. Copyright 2009 by the American Institute of Certified Public Accountants, Inc. All rights reserved. Adapted with permission.

Chapter 14
Quotations, pp. 772, 773, from PCAOB, AICPA, *Inventories*, AU 331.09, 331.10, 331.12. Copyright 2009 by the American Institute of Certified Public Accountants, Inc. All rights reserved. Adapted with permission.
Exhibit 14-6, p. 775, from PCAOB, AICPA, *Auditing Accounting Estimates*, AU 342.05. Copyright 2009 by the American Institute of Certified Public Accountants, Inc. All rights reserved. Adapted with permission.

Chapter 15
Auditing in Action, p. 803, excerpted from the Summary of FIN 46R, http://www.fasb.org/st/summary/finsum46r.shtml. Portions of various FASB documents, copyright © by the

AICPA Statements on Standards for Attestation Engagements

AT 20   Defining Professional Requirements in Statements on Standards for Attestation Engagements

AT 50   Statements on Standards for Attestation Engagements Hierarchy

AT 101   Attest Engagements

AT 201   Agreed-Upon Procedures Engagements

AT 301   Financial Forecasts and Projections

AT 401   Reporting on Pro Forma Financial Information

AT 501   An Examination of an Entity's Internal Control Over Financial Reporting That Is Integrated With an Audit of Its Financial Statements

AT 601   Compliance Attestation

AT 701   Management's Discussion and Analysis

Financial Statement Assertions – PCAOB

Existence or occurrence
Completeness
Rights and obligations
Valuation or allocation
Presentation and disclosure

Financial Statement Assertions – AICPA

Assertions about classes of transactions and events for the period under audit:

Occurrence
Completeness
Accuracy
Cutoff
Classification

Assertions about account balances at the period end:

Existence
Rights and obligations
Completeness

Assertions about presentation and disclosure:

Occurrence and rights and obligations
Completeness
Classification and understandability
Accuracy and valuation

Auditing and Regulatory Organizations

Securities and Exchange Commission, *www.SEC.gov*

Public Companies Accounting Oversight Board, *www.pcaobus.org*

American Institute of Certified Public Accountants, *www.aicpa.org*

Government Accountability Office, *www.gao.gov*

International Auditing and Assurance Standards Board, *www.ifac.org/iaasb*

The Institute of Internal Auditors, *www.theiia.org*

Association of Certified Fraud Examiners, *www.acfe.com*

Information Systems Audit and Control Association, *www.isaca.org*